W9-BXD-823

A Dictionary of American History

To Lisa Marie Purvis Kidd,
whom I was privileged
to give away in marriage

A Dictionary of AMERICAN HISTORY

THOMAS L. PURVIS

First published 1995
First published in paperback 1997

Blackwell Publishers Inc.
238 Main Street
Cambridge, Massachusetts 02142, USA

Blackwell Publishers Ltd
108 Cowley Road
Oxford OX4 1JF, UK

Library of Congress Cataloging in Publication Data
Purvis, Thomas L., 1949–
A dictionary of American history / Thomas L. Purvis
p. cm. — (Blackwell reference)
ISBN 1–55786–398–9 (hbk) — ISBN 1–55786–099–2 (pbk)
1. United States—History—Dictionaries. I. Title.
E174.P87 1995 95–9717
973'.003 CIP

British Library Cataloguing in Publication Data
A CIP catalogue record for this book is available from the British Library

Typeset in 9 on 10pt Times
by Graphicraft Typesetters Limited, Hong Kong
Printed and bound in Great Britain by T. J. Press Ltd, Padstow, Cornwall

This book is printed on acid-free paper

Contents

Preface vii
Abbreviations viii
Dictionary 1

Preface

Two trends have characterized historical scholarship since 1950. The first is the ever-increasing rate at which new monographs and articles appear. It now requires heroic efforts just to keep abreast of every publication in topical fields like religious or political history, much less of every significant book and article across the broad spectrum of the American past. This explosion of new literature has produced the second trend: increasing specialization among scholars. Few academics define themselves so specifically as the newly minted Ph.D., whose résumé I once read, who described himself as an historian of the Michigan frontier from 1820 to 1840, but all scholars have been forced to sacrifice breadth of knowledge for depth in order to keep up to date with their primary research and teaching areas.

This *Dictionary of American History* has accordingly been conceived as a reference tool for college professors or secondary-school teachers investigating topics outside their individual specializations, students pursuing history degrees, participants in high-school advanced placement programs, and members of the general public needing a convenient, easy-to-use, and up-to-date compendium of historical facts. Such a single-volume work has particular usefulness at a time when professional and amateur historians find themselves in a state of information-overload. It provides essential facts, chronology, definitions, and explanations in their most abbreviated form across the broadest range of subjects.

This book is intended to resemble a dictionary rather than an encyclopedia. Like a portable dictionary, it can only include several thousand entries if their average length is brief. Unlike an encyclopedia, it cannot provide extended essays with an interpretative theme, but must limit its coverage to the essentials of each subject. Of necessity, it emphasizes the who, what, when, and where of its topics, but has skimped on the why, except when that factor can be simply stated.

The Dictionary deliberately emphasizes facts, events, and data over interpretation. One reason for doing this was to insulate the entries, as far as possible, from the biases every author possesses. A more important reason was the author's conviction that a general de-emphasis upon factual knowledge in history has led to a growing lack of perspective about the past. When one generation's exciting scholarship is judged insignificant by the next, it is often because this scholarship rests on insufficient evidence due to a lack of knowledge-in-depth on the part of its authors. The only way to avoid reading the concerns or attitudes of the present into the past – which is the great sin of so much contemporary scholarship – is to know precisely what the past was like, and this knowledge is achieved through intensive mastery of its distinguishing characteristics. Likewise, the only means of determining an event's true significance is to find out as much about that event as possible, and not to rely on current interpretations, which are so often transitory. While I sympathize with the reviewer of this manuscript who scribbled next to the paragraph recounting World War II's military mobilization and casualties, "useless list of numbers," I insist that he missed the point: such data is vital to the comprehension of the nature and extent of that conflict.

A cross-reference to an associated entry is indicated by capitalizing its name, for example CASABLANCA CONFERENCE within World War II. Cross-references are not always indicated for commonly known events or organizations, such as World War II or the Democratic party, if they do not directly relate to the understanding of the entry in which they appear.

I wish to express my appreciation to Professor Robert Middlekauff of Berkeley and Dr John W. Tyler of Groton Academy, for their encouraging and helpful comments on the manuscript. Professor Colin G. Calloway of the University of Wyoming deserves commendation for his many suggestions regarding Native Americans. My gratitude goes out to Michael Averdick and the Kenton County, Ky., Library for their consideration in allowing me to use several important non-circulating books. A bravo is extended to John A. Kerley, Jr., of Newport, Ky., for his delightful and insightful entry on ee cummings. I finally wish to thank editorial director John Davey for his confidence and patience while this project extended longer than we had originally planned.

Thomas L. Purvis
Associate Editor
American National Biography

Abbreviations

Ala.	Alabama
Ariz.	Arizona
Ark.	Arkansas
b.	born
ca.	circa (Latin, about)
Calif.	California
Colo.	Colorado
Conn.	Connecticut
d.	died
D.C.	District of Columbia
Del.	Delaware
Fla.	Florida
Fr	Father
Ga.	Georgia
Ill.	Illinois
Ind.	Indiana
Kans.	Kansas
Ky.	Kentucky
La.	Louisiana
Mass.	Massachusetts
Md.	Maryland
Mich.	Michigan
Minn.	Minnesota
Miss.	Mississippi
Mo.	Missouri
Mont.	Montana
N.C.	North Carolina
N.Dak.	North Dakota
Nebr.	Nebraska
Nev.	Nevada
N.H.	New Hampshire
N.J.	New Jersey
N.Mex.	New Mexico
N.Y.	New York
Okla.	Oklahoma
Oreg.	Oregon
Pa.	Pennsylvania
R.I.	Rhode Island
S.C.	South Carolina
S.Dak.	South Dakota
Tenn.	Tennessee
Tex.	Texas
US	United States, American
v.	versus (Latin, against)
Va.	Virginia
Vt.	Vermont
Wash.	Washington
Wis.	Wisconsin
W.Va.	West Virginia
Wyo.	Wyoming

A

AAA *see* AGRICULTURAL ADJUSTMENT ADMINISTRATION

Abbate* v. *US *see* *UNITED STATES* v. *LANZA*

Abelman* v. *Booth On 7 March 1859, the Supreme Court unanimously ruled that the Constitution's supremacy over state law preempts state courts from serving writs of HABEAS CORPUS on federal courts and their officials, or from otherwise interfering with the enforcement of US laws. The ruling blocked northern abolitionists from using state courts or PERSONAL LIBERTY LAWS to nullify the FUGITIVE SLAVE LAW (1850), whose constitutionality was also (improperly) affirmed.

Abernathy, Ralph David (b. Linden, Ala., 11 March 1926; d. Atlanta, Ga., 17 April 1990) A Baptist minister, Rev. Abernathy helped organize the MONTGOMERY BUS BOYCOTT, was arrested with the first FREEDOM RIDERS, and helped found the SOUTHERN CHRISTIAN LEADERSHIP CONFERENCE (SCLC), of which he was the first secretary-treasurer and second president. White supremacists once dynamited his home. He led the Poor People's campaign of May–June 1968, during which demonstrators camped out in a hut village called Resurrection City in Washington, D.C., until the police dispersed them and jailed him for 20 days. After directing OPERATION BREADBASKET in Atlanta, he headed the SCLC (1968–77).

Abington Township* v. *Schempp On 17 June 1963, the Supreme Court (8–1) extended *ENGEL* v. *VITALE* by overturning a Pa. law mandating that school days start with the Lord's Prayer and a Bible reading.

ABM Treaty *See* ANTIBALLISTIC MISSILE TREATY

Abnaki Indians Speakers of one of the ALGONQUIAN LANGUAGES, perhaps 2,000 Abnakis occupied Maine, Vermont, and N.H. in 1600. They traded furs with both English and French (but preferred dealing with the latter), accepted Jesuit missionaries, and were French allies in the colonial wars. In 1722 they raided settlements on the Kennebec River, but in the resulting DUMMER'S WAR, Mass. and N.H. militia dispersed them along the Kennebec River, and drove many as far north as Canada. During the SEVEN YEARS' WAR, ROGERS' RANGERS destroyed their main town at Ste Françoise, Quebec. After 1763 Abnakis drifted back and forth across the US–Canadian border, but most relocated in Canada; by 1800, probably less than 300 remained in Maine and Vt.

abolitionism The earliest proponents of the abolition of SLAVERY were QUAKERS, starting with William Edmundson's denunciation at Newport, R.I., in 1676 and an antislavery declaration written in April 1688 by the Germantown, Pa., Monthly Meeting. Every yearly meeting of the Quakers, or Society of Friends, between 1770 and 1776, forbade slaveowning. By 1779 over 80 percent of Quaker slaves were free, but not until 1796 were the last released from bondage.

The American Revolution led to the abolition of slavery in Vt. (1777), Pa. (1780), Mass. (1783), Conn. (1784), R.I. (1784), N.Y. (1799), and N.J. (1804). In 1787 Congress excluded slavery from the NORTHWEST TERRITORY. Every southern state but N.C. passed laws making it easier for masters to free their own slaves. The AMERICAN COLONIZATION SOCIETY also originated as a means of encouraging voluntary emancipation by masters. The proportion of blacks who were free rose from about 2 percent in 1770 to 11 percent by 1810.

Although northern whites held strong convictions about keeping slavery out of unsettled territories, they demonstrated little interest in abolitionism after 1800. It would again become politically influential after William Lloyd GARRISON founded the LIBERATOR in 1831 and the AMERICAN ANTISLAVERY SOCIETY was formed in 1833. Abolitionism was a major cause of southern alienation from the Union, because its fanatical wing advocated the disregard of slavery's constitutional protections and routinely disparaged southern society in a highly insulting fashion.

In the CIVIL WAR, Congress's first Confiscation Act (6 August 1861) allowed the military to free any slaves seized while being used for Confederate military purposes, and a second Confiscation Act (17 July 1862) permitted the army to liberate all slaves owned by active rebels. On 16 April 1862, Lincoln signed a law to free slaves in the DISTRICT OF COLUMBIA and compensate their owners. A proposal made in March 1862 to pay federal subsidies for reimbursing owners if any legislature adopted gradual emancipation failed because of opposition by the BORDER STATES. After Lincoln's EMANCIPATION PROCLAMATION, Md., W.Va., Mo., and Tenn. voluntarily abolished human bondage, and the THIRTEENTH AMENDMENT finally ended the institution in Del. and Ky.

abortion In 1973 the Supreme Court invalidated abortion laws in 46 states in *ROE v. WADE*. In 1972, when N.Y. was the only state with a liberal abortion law, there had been 586,000 legal abortions and perhaps 200,000 illegally-terminated pregnancies. Abortions doubled from 744,000 in 1973 to 1,550,000 in 1980, when they stabilized at around 40 percent of live births. Many states enacted laws discouraging abortions, and Congress passed the HYDE AMENDMENT to halt federal financing of them. The Senate demonstrated that it was unwilling to confirm anti-abortion nominees to the Supreme Court with Robert BORK's defeat in 1987.

On 29 January 1988, Ronald REAGAN forbade federally-funded health clinics to advise women on abortion, and in 1989, George BUSH banned the use of fetal tissue in medical experiments. William CLINTON reversed these policies by executive order on 22 January 1992 and committed his administration to appointing judges who were pro-abortion.

Anti-abortion protests turned increasingly confrontational and violent after 1992, when massive pro-life demonstrations led to thousands of arrests in Wichita, Kans., where a family-planning center physician was later wounded on 19 August 1993. At a Pensacola, Fla., abortion clinic, pro-life activists killed one doctor on 10 March 1993; on 29 July 1994, they killed another doctor and wounded two helpers at the clinic. Congress responded with legislation in 1993 that made intimidation or use of force against abortion clinic personnel a federal offense.

Abraham Lincoln battalion This battalion was the best known unit of US citizens who fought with the Republican forces in the Spanish civil war. The earliest US volunteers arrived in Spain on 6 January 1937. Most Americans were assigned to the Abraham Lincoln and George Washington battalions, which were consolidated in July 1937 as the 58th Battalion, 15th International Brigade, while others formed the John Brown Artillery Battery and the First Transport Regiment. Of the 3,200 US soldiers who joined in the conflict, perhaps 1,600 were killed.

Abrams, Creighton (b. Springfield, Mass., 16 September 1914; d. Washington, D.C., 4 September 1974) In 1936 Abrams graduated from West Point and he commanded armored troops in World War II. He assumed command of US forces in the VIETNAM WAR in July 1968, and carried out the gradual US withdrawal in that conflict until August 1972, when only advisors and support troops remained. He then became army chief of staff and held that post until he died.

Abrams* v. *United States In 1919 the Supreme Court upheld the SEDITION ACT's (1918) constitutionality by ruling that the FIRST AMENDMENT did not protect harmful speech, such as encouraging interference with military operations during a declared war.

Acadians Following the defeat of French forces at Nova Scotia in 1755 during the SEVEN YEARS' WAR, French Canadians there and in modern New Brunswick refused to swear to cease resistance against British forces. British authorities then ordered all enemy civilians to be forcibly deported, beginning on 8 October, to the THIRTEEN COLONIES. Over 6,000 persons were exiled until the war's end, at which time many hundreds refused to go back to Canada, which had come under British jurisdiction, and resettled in Spanish LOUISIANA, where they and their descendants became known as "Cajuns."

Acheson, Dean Gooderham (b. Middletown, Conn., 11 April 1893; d. Sandy Spring, Md., 12 October 1971) After serving as private secretary for Louis BRANDEIS (1918–21), Acheson practiced law in Washington until 1941, when he entered the State Department. He was secretary of state during the KOREAN WAR. He became foreign policy advisor to John F. KENNEDY and Lyndon JOHNSON, and was influential in persuading Johnson to seek a negotiated settlement for ending the VIETNAM WAR.

ACLU *see* AMERICAN CIVIL LIBERTIES UNION

ACTION This independent federal agency was established on 1 July 1971 to administer the PEACE CORPS, VISTA, Retired Senior Volunteers, Foster Grandparent Program, Active Corps of Executives, and SCORE. (The last two programs have been abandoned, and the Peace Corps became independent in 1981.) By 1974 it included the ACTION Cooperative Volunteers program, which helped finance one-year volunteer projects with matching funds to community groups, and the Senior Companion Program, which paid retirees to assist needy adults. It grew from 23,000 volunteers in 1971 to 127,000 in 1974. It was later responsible for the Demonstration Grant, Mini-Grant, and Student Community Service Projects.

Adair* v. *United States On 27 January 1908, the Supreme Court ruled (6–2) that the ERDMAN ACT (1898) was unconstitutional for forbidding railroads to require that their employees sign YELLOW-DOG CONTRACTS. The Court held that the FIFTH AMENDMENT gave businesses the widest range of latitude to protect their property rights in contract negotiations, and that federal regulation of interstate commerce did not properly concern the organization of unions.

Adams, Charles Francis (b. Boston, Mass., 18 August 1807; d. Boston, Mass., 21 November 1886) Son of John Q. ADAMS, he opened a law office at Boston in 1829. He strongly supported ABOLITIONISM, was the nominee of the FREE-SOIL PARTY for vice-president in 1848, and sat in Congress as a Republican (1859–61). As ambassador to Britain (1861–8), he performed valuable services by placating British anger over the *TRENT* AFFAIR, blocking the shipment of IRONCLAD rams for the CSA navy, and countering the efforts of CSA envoys for British aid or recognition for the Confederacy.

Adams, John (b. Quincy, Mass., 19 October 1735; d. Quincy, Mass., 4 July 1826) In 1768 Adams opened a law office in Boston, where he was the political lieutenant of his second cousin, Samuel ADAMS. He successfully defended the British troops tried for the BOSTON MASSACRE. At the first and second CONTINENTAL CONGRESSES, he molded support for the DECLARATION OF INDEPENDENCE. He was the principal author of the Massachusetts Constitution (1780), which influenced the federal CONSTITUTION's structure. He helped negotiate the treaty of PARIS (1783), was minister to Britain (1785–8), and as first vice-president, decided the fate of legislation in 20 tie-votes during his term. His term as president, representing the FEDERALIST PARTY (1797–1801) was dominated by extremists from that party who controlled Congress, and after Adams broke with them in 1800, he lacked sufficient support for reelection. He then left politics.

Adams, John Quincy (b. Quincy, Mass., 11 July 1767; d. Washington, D.C., 23 February 1848) Son of John ADAMS, he was envoy to the Netherlands (1794–6) and Prussia (1797–1801). Elected to the Senate in 1803, he resigned in 1808 under pressure from his Mass. constituents for having supported the embargo (*see* EMBARGO ACT). He headed the US delegation at the negotiations for the treaty of GHENT and was ambassador to Britain (1815–17). He negotiated the ADAMS–ONIS TREATY. Running for president in 1824 as a Democrat, he gained just 30.5 percent of the ballots but won through the "CORRUPT BARGAIN."

His domestic agenda was the boldest yet proposed by a president, and included federal funding of INTERNAL IMPROVEMENTS, scientific explorations, an astronomical observatory, a national university, and an Interior Department, but Congress enacted little of his program. Adams suffered another major defeat when Ga. forced him to accept the treaty of Indian Springs. It was Adams and Henry Clay around whom the National Republicans formed. In part because he refused on principle to use patronage to build a political machine, he took only 44.0 percent of the popular vote against Jackson in 1828. While in Congress (1831–48), he opposed the annexation of Texas and the extension of slavery to the territories. He was known as "Old Man Eloquent" for his efforts to overturn the Gag Rule.

Adams, Samuel (b. Boston, Mass., 27 September 1722; d. Boston, Mass., 2 October 1803) By 1764, Adams had become the dominant influence over Boston's town meeting. By his shrewd use of demonstrations and written propaganda, he made Boston the principal center of resistance to unconstitutional parliamentary measures. He helped found the Sons of Liberty, created the committees of correspondence and published the inflammatory account of Boston's occupation by British troops, *A Journal of the Times*. Recognizing before any other major colonial leader that American rights would never be assured under British rule, he pressed resolutely for the Declaration of Independence at the first and second Continental Congresses. He was governor of Mass. (1794–7).

Adams–Onis Treaty To end tensions caused by the first Seminole War and establish the Louisiana Purchase's precise southern line, John Q. Adams negotiated this treaty with Luis de Onis, Spain's ambassador at Washington. Spain agreed to cede both East and West Florida to the US. The US gave up its claim to much of east and central Tex. under the Louisiana Purchase, and accepted the Sabine River as La.'s border. Spain and the US fixed their western boundary as the Red and Arkansas rivers, north along the Rockies' eastern slope, and then west along the 42nd parallel to the Pacific. The US gained 72,000 square miles, including Fla. and most of the Santa Fe Trail; it also reinforced the US claim to Oregon. Adams and Onis signed the agreement on 22 February 1819. The Senate ratified it on 19 February 1821, and the treaty went into effect three days later.

Adamson [Eight-hour] Act (3 September 1916) In 1916 the largest railway unions threatened to strike on 4 September unless an eight-hour workday was instituted. Urged by Woodrow Wilson to avoid nationwide transportation disruption, a day before the strike date Congress set an eight-hour work day, plus time-and-a-half pay after that, for interstate railroad workers. *Wilson* v. *New* upheld the law.

Addams, Jane Laura (b. Cedarville, Ill., 6 September 1860; d. Chicago, Ill., 21 May 1935) She became one of the Progressive Era's most important reformers by pioneering techniques of fighting urban poverty. At Chicago in 1889, she founded Hull House, a community center for improving neighborhood life, educational opportunities, and civil values among the poor. Hull House's success stimulated a widespread settlement house movement among social workers. She also supported Prohibition, women's suffrage, stricter child labor laws, and pacifism. She was president of the Women's International League for Peace and Freedom in 1919, and co-recipient of the Nobel peace prize with Nicholas Murray in 1931.

Addyston Pipe and Steel Company* v. *United States In 1899 the Supreme Court held that collusion by businesses to split markets among themselves fell within federal regulation of interstate commerce and violated the Sherman Antitrust Act. The decision partly offset the restrictive interpretation of that act in *United States* v. *E. C. Knight Company*.

Adelman, Kenneth *see* Strategic Arms Reduction Talks

Adena Culture This culture flourished from 700 BC to AD 200 in the eastern Ohio River valley and was centered in southern Ohio. The Adena was the first Indian society east of the Mississippi to settle in sedentary villages, establish widespread trade networks, and construct large earthworks for burial sites. The Adena coexisted with, and was succeeded by, the Hopewell Culture.

Adjusted Compensation Acts (1924–36) *see* Bonus Bill (1924)

Adkins* v. *Children's Hospital On 9 April 1923, the Supreme Court struck down (5–3) a 1918 US law allowing the District of Columbia Wage Board to set minimum salaries for women and children, as a price-fixing measure violating the FIFTH and FOURTEENTH AMENDMENTS' guarantee to negotiate free contracts. On 1 June 1936, in *Morehead* v. *New York ex rel. Tipaldo*, the Court ruled (5–4) that all minimum wage laws violated DUE PROCESS. *WEST COAST HOTEL COMPANY* v. *PARRISH* overruled these decisions.

Adler* v. *Board of Education *see* *GERENDE* v. *BOARD OF SUPERVISORS OF ELECTIONS*

Administration of Justice Act (20 May 1774) Parliament passed this law in the aftermath of the BOSTON TEA PARTY. In cases where a royal soldier or civil officer was accused of a crime punishable by death in Mass., the trial could be transferred to Britain or another colony if the governor believed public prejudices would not permit a fair trial in Mass. It was dubbed the "Murder Act" in the colonies and considered one of the INTOLERABLE ACTS.

Administration on Aging *see* OLDER AMERICANS ACT

Administrative Reorganization Act (1939) *see* BUDGET AND ACCOUNTING ACT

Admiralty courts Under British law, the High Court of Admiralty had jurisdiction over criminal and civil cases concerning foreign trade and the merchant marine. Beyond London, Vice-admiralty courts heard maritime cases. All verdicts were given by a judge sitting without a jury. Vice-admiralty courts were established in the THIRTEEN COLONIES after 1696; although they had jurisdiction over the NAVIGATION ACTS, they did not try smuggling cases – which were heard in common law courts with juries – until the SUGAR ACT.

AEC *see* ATOMIC ENERGY COMMISSION

AEF *see* ALLIED EXPEDITIONARY FORCE

affirmative action This concept originated as a means of eliminating racial prejudice in hiring to comply with Title VII of the CIVIL RIGHTS ACT (1964) either voluntarily or in consequence of a lawsuit. By providing compensatory advantages to disadvantaged minorities or fixing specific goals to hire nonwhites, affirmative action plans sparked complaints that they inflicted reverse discrimination upon whites by hiring according to racial quotas regardless of personal merit. The Supreme Court ruled on this issue in *REGENTS OF UNIVERSITY OF CALIFORNIA* v. *BAKKE*, *UNITED STEELWORKERS OF AMERICA ET AL.* v. *WEBER*, and *WYGANT* v. *JACKSON BOARD OF EDUCATION*.

Affluent Society, The In 1958 John K. Galbraith published this study, which confirmed that Americans enjoyed the world's highest standard of living, but argued that their quality of life suffered from inadequately financed government services. The book became exceptionally influential among political leaders, especially in the Kennedy and Johnson administrations, which accepted its premise that the country could afford a significant expansion of government to improve education, transportation, health care, and other services.

AFL-CIO *see* AMERICAN FEDERATION OF LABOR-CONGRESS OF INDUSTRIAL ORGANIZATIONS

African Methodist Episcopal church This denomination originated in a dispute over segregated seating arrangements at Philadelphia's St George METHODIST CHURCH. Richard Allen led his fellow blacks out of the congregation in protest and formed the Free African Society. Allen founded the Bethel church and was ordained the first black Methodist deacon in 1793. In 1816 the Bethel church called a general conference of black Methodists, which founded the African Methodist Episcopal church, with Allen as bishop. By 1865, the church included 53,670 members and 2,613 clergy. In 1990 it had 6,200 churches and 2,210,000 members (1.5 percent of all churchgoers).

African Methodist Episcopal Zion church This denomination originated in 1796 when James Varick led black members of New York's John Street METHODIST CHURCH to withdraw in protest at discriminatory treatment. In 1821 a conference representing six churches, 19 preachers, and 1,426 members organized the African Methodist Episcopal Zion church. Varick became the first bishop in 1822. By 1865 it had 30,600 members and 661 clergy. In 1990 it had 6,060 congregations and 1,220,260 members.

Agee, James *see* *LET US NOW PRAISE FAMOUS MEN*

Agency for International Development (AID) The Foreign Assistance Act (4 September 1961) established AID to supervise US foreign assistance programs for economic development, FOOD FOR PEACE, and direct relief for famines or other disasters. It has four divisions, for Latin America, the Far East, the Near East and South Asia, and Africa and Europe. It was part of the State Department until 1979, when it was transferred to the US International Development Cooperation Agency.

agent orange The US Air Force used this herbicide to defoliate jungles and deny cover to Communist forces in the VIETNAM WAR. In 1962–9, the defoliation program sprayed almost half (7,800 square miles) of the country's rain forest and contaminated 800 square miles of farmland. US veterans alleged that agent orange, which contained dioxin, caused many service-connected disabilities; they filed a class-action suit in 1979, and in 1984 accepted an out-of-court settlement creating a court-administered fund of $180,000,000 to pay $3,200 to each veteran injured by exposure to the chemical.

Agnew, Spiro Theodore (b. Baltimore, Md., 9 November 1918) In 1947 Agnew began practicing law at Baltimore. He became active in Republican politics, and was elected Md. governor in 1966. He became vice-president under Richard NIXON in 1969 and emerged as a caustic, cruel critic of libelous, leftist liberals who not only negatived Nixon and vexed Vietnam victory, but also failed to appreciate his genius for alliteration. Agnew's political career ended in disgrace on 10 October 1973, when he resigned as vice-president after being accused of bribe-taking, criminal conspiracy, and income tax fraud.

Agricultural Adjustment Act, first (12 May 1933) This law created the AGRICULTURAL ADJUSTMENT ADMINISTRATION (AAA) to stabilize farm income by setting price supports and capping crop acreage. Its provisions were eventually extended to cotton, tobacco, beef, pork, wheat, corn, barley, rye, potatoes, grain sorghum, flax, peanuts, sugar beets, and sugar cane. It was supplemented by the JONES–CONNALLY FARM RELIEF ACT, JONES–COSTIGAN SUGAR ACT, BANKHEAD COTTON CONTROL ACT, KERR–SMITH TOBACCO CONTROL ACT, and WARREN POTATO CONTROL ACT. The AAA operated the COMMODITY CREDIT CORPORATION. By spring 1934, 3,000,000 farmers had joined 4,000 local AAA marketing associations to set limits on output. The law inadvertently led to large-scale dispossession of tenants, especially cotton sharecroppers, who were evicted so that landlords could receive AAA stipends for taking land out of production; it consequently stimulated the migration of southern blacks to northern cities. The law was held unconstitutional on 6 January 1936 in *UNITED STATES* v. *BUTLER*. Congress satisfied the Court's objections by passing the SOIL CONSERVATION AND DOMESTIC ALLOTMENT ACT (1936) and another AGRICULTURAL ADJUSTMENT ACT in 1938.

Agricultural Adjustment Act, second (16 February 1938) Congress revived the 1933 AGRICULTURAL ADJUSTMENT ADMINISTRATION (AAA) because the SOIL CONSERVATION AND DOMESTIC ALLOTMENT ACT failed to keep an imbalance of supply over demand from depressing farm prices in 1937–8. To satisfy constitutional objections raised in *UNITED STATES* v. *BUTLER*, Congress financed its operations from general revenues instead of taxes on food-processing companies; it also required compulsory crop-limitation programs to win two-thirds approval from affected farmers in special elections. The law used subsidies, loans, and soil conservation stipends as incentives for farmers to accept government limits on acreage in production; it established a permanent federal storage program to take surplus commodities off the market; it authorized the COMMODITY CREDIT CORPORATION to value surplus crops used as collateral on loans to farmers at PARITY; and it created the Federal Crop Insurance Corporation to insure wheat crops, and capitalized it at $100,000,000. It was held constitutional in *Mulford* v. *Smith* (1939).

Agricultural Adjustment Administration (AAA) This agency supervised marketing agreements between farmers and local associations that attempted to raise commodity prices by restricting crop acreage and livestock production. To compensate farmers who agreed to limit output, the AAA paid them a fixed price for their reduced output until their commodities attained PARITY. The AAA also managed the COMMODITY CREDIT CORPORATION. After the

AGRICULTURAL ADJUSTMENT ACT (1933) was ruled unconstitutional, the AAA was continued under the SOIL CONSERVATION AND DOMESTIC ALLOTMENT ACT and the second AGRICULTURAL ADJUSTMENT ACT (1938).

Agricultural Credits Act (4 March 1923) Because falling commodity prices cut farm income sharply, Congress funded relief through short-term credit for crop financing. This law created 12 federal intermediate credit banks, capitalized with $60,000,000, to lend to farm cooperatives, which would reloan the money to farmers.

agricultural depression of the 1920s *see* RECESSION OF THE 1920S

Agricultural Marketing Act (15 June 1929) This law created an eight-member federal farm board. The board promoted organization of agricultural cooperatives that could stabilize farm prices. The cooperatives could win voluntary agreement from farmers to reduce commodity surpluses by reducing land under cultivation, or they could purchase large amounts of commodities and hold them from sale until market prices rose. The sum of $500,000,000 was appropriated to loan to cooperatives for such purposes. In 1930 the Federal Farm Board set up its own marketing cooperatives to buy and hold cotton, grains, and wool. By 1931 the US was holding large amounts of these commodities, which could not be sold without large losses, but had failed to halt the steady decline in crop prices because it could not prevent overproduction by the majority of farmers, since the act's crop-limitation programs were entirely voluntary.

Agricultural Trade and Development Act (10 July 1954) To reduce the cost of US storage programs for surplus farm crops, this law gave the president authority for three years to exchange $1 billion in surplus food stocks for foreign currency, and use the money to promote US trade, buy strategic materials, or assist friendly nations. The law also allowed up to $300 million in surplus food to be donated as emergency famine relief overseas. It was renewed several times until replaced by the FOOD FOR PEACE Act.

Agriculture, Department of Congress established this department on 15 May 1862 out of the agricultural division of the Patent Office and gave it a budget of $64,000. It was raised to cabinet status on 11 February 1889 and funded at over $1,000,000. It took charge of food inspections under the PURE FOOD AND DRUG ACT. The AGRICULTURAL ADJUSTMENT ADMINISTRATION (AAA) acts gave it enormous authority to set production limits, make farm loans, and store surplus commodities. In 1989 its budget was $21,700,000,000.

Aguinaldo, Emilio *see* PHILIPPINE INSURRECTION

AID *see* AGENCY FOR INTERNATIONAL DEVELOPMENT

Aid to Families with Dependent Children (AFDC) (1962) Congress separated funding for dependent children from the SOCIAL SECURITY ADMINISTRATION and created this independent program, which is state-administered but operates mainly with federal funds. It grew into the second-largest public assistance program (after FOOD STAMPS), and by 1993 covered 5,000,000 households with 9,600,000 children, one in eight children. Fewer than 1 percent of AFDC parents were required to work, and half of AFDC families remained dependent on welfare for over 10 years.

Air America This organization was a front for operations by the CENTRAL INTELLIGENCE AGENCY during the VIETNAM WAR. The airline operated as a regular commercial business carrying freight and passengers in southeast Asia. Only about a quarter of its missions concerned intelligence gathering or military activities in Vietnam, Cambodia, or Laos.

Air Force On 1 August 1907, the Air Force originated as the Aeronautical Division of the US Army Signal Corps, with a strength of one officer and two enlisted men. It became the Aviation Service and included 65 officers (35 pilots) and 55 planes when the US entered WORLD WAR I. Renamed the Army Air Corps in June 1941, it grew from 10,329 planes (including 2,846 combat aircraft) in December 1941 to 79,908 planes (including 43,248 combat aircraft) in WORLD WAR II, when its strength peaked at 2,411,294 personnel in 1944. By April 1946, it had been reduced to 485,000 personnel. It separated from the army on 26 July 1947. It is divided into an Aerospace Defense Command, a

Military Airlift Command, and a Strategic Air Command.

Air Mail Act (1925) *see* KELLY AIR MAIL ACT

Air Mail Act (12 June 1934) Congress forbade several abusive practices that had developed under the KELLY AIR MAIL ACT by denying air mail contracts to monopolies or holding companies, requiring competitive bids for all air mail contracts, setting maximum rates and mail loads, and directing the Interstate Commerce Commission to set "fair and reasonable" air mail rates.

Air Pollution Control Act (1955) *see* ENVIRONMENTAL LEGISLATION

air traffic controllers' strike On 29 July 1981, the largest strike by federal employees began when 95 percent of the Professional Air Traffic Controllers' Organization (PATCO) walked out in violation of their employment oath. After failing to heed Ronald REAGAN's demand to return to their terminals, 11,000 were fired on 5 August and PATCO ceased to exist. The system was rebuilt without any air disasters, using 521 military controllers to supplement the nonstrikers. In 1993, William CLINTON gave fired PATCO strikers the right to apply for vacancies as air traffic controllers.

Airline Deregulation Act *see* DEREGULATION

Aix-La-Chapelle, treaty of (18 October 1748) This treaty ended KING GEORGE'S WAR. Britain returned LOUISBOURG to France in exchange for certain concessions in Europe, but otherwise the situation in North America remained the same as in 1744. An Anglo-French boundary commission was established to determine the Nova Scotia–Acadian boundary, but it had reached no agreement by 1754.

Alabama In 1702, at Mobile Bay, France built Fort St Louis, the first white settlement in Ala. and capital of its La. colony until 1722. Anglo-American settlement began in 1805 at Huntsville, but proceeded slowly until after the CREEK WAR. After becoming a territory on 3 March 1817, it grew rapidly (especially in the BLACK BELT region) and became the 22nd state on 14 December 1819. The CREEK INDIANS were relocated west in 1834–5. Cotton-growing dominated its economy. By 1860 Ala. ranked 12th among states, with 964,201 inhabitants, of whom 45 percent were slaves and 1 percent were foreign-born; it stood 11th in the value of its farmland and livestock and 25th in manufactures.

Ala. became the third CSA state on 11 January 1861. In the CIVIL WAR, it furnished 75,000 CSA troops and 7,545 USA soldiers (2,576 white and 4,969 black). Ala. was the site of 336 military engagements.

In June 1865, Andrew JOHNSON instituted a provisional civilian government, which ended slavery in September. White supremacists took over the legislature and passed a black code (*see* BLACK CODES). Congress imposed military rule on 2 March 1867, but restored self-government and congressional representation on 25 June 1868. Republican control of Ala. ended six-and-a-half years later, on 14 November 1874. Ala. disfranchised most blacks in 1901 and then legislated SEGREGATION.

In 1900 it was the 18th state in size and had 1,828,697 people, who were 83 percent rural, 45 percent black, and 1 percent foreign-born; it ranked 19th in the value of its agricultural goods and 30th in manufactures. From 1920 to 1970, it lost 1,258,500 residents, mostly blacks moving to northern cities, and its racial composition shifted greatly. Ala. was a prominent battleground of the CIVIL RIGHTS MOVEMENT and site of the MONTGOMERY BUS BOYCOTT, the BIRMINGHAM DESEGREGATION VIOLENCE, SELMA FREEDOM MARCH, and Governor George WALLACE's defiance of federal court orders to integrate the University of Alabama in 1963. By 1990 Ala. ranked as the 22nd state, with 4,040,587 residents (73 percent white, 25 percent black, 1 percent Hispanic, 1 percent Asian), of whom 67 percent were urban and 1.1 percent were foreign-born. Manufacturing employed 23 percent of the work force and mining 8 percent.

***Alabama*, CSS** This cruiser was the Confederacy's most successful raider of Union commerce. Under Captain Raphael Semmes, she captured, burned, or sank 69 USA ships, valued at $6,547,609, from September 1862 to 19 June 1864, when Captain John Winslow's USS *Kearsage* sank her off Cherbourg, France.

***Alabama* claims** The USA lodged demands

that Britain pay $19,021,000 for 100,000 tons of cargo destroyed by 11 CSA cruisers built at British shipyards in the CIVIL WAR. Known as the *Alabama* claims, after the rebel ship that did the most damage to USA shipping, these grievances were submitted to international arbitration by the treaty of Washington (8 May 1871). Britain was obliged to reimburse the US $15,500,000 for direct damages, but exempted from paying for indirect losses or collateral damage.

Alamance Creek, battle of (N.C.) On 16 May 1771, Governor William Tryon's 1,300 militia (mostly from eastern N.C.) defeated 2,500 regulators (*see* REGULATOR), mostly from western N.C., near Hillsborough. Tryon's losses: 9 killed and 61 wounded. Regulators' losses: about 20 killed and 100 wounded. The regulator uprising then ended.

Alamo, battle of the On 24 February 1836, President Antonio Lopez de Santa Anna's 5,500 Mexicans began artillery bombardment of Colonel James Bowie and Lieutenant Colonel William Travis's garrison of 183 Texans at San Antonio's Alamo mission. On 6 March 1,100 attackers took the fortifications by storm. Texas losses: 175 killed, 8 captured (of whom 7 were murdered after surrendering and 1 Hispanic survived by claiming he had been a prisoner). Mexican losses: 1,600 killed, 500 wounded.

Alaska In 1741 Vitus Bering mapped the Aleutian Islands and nearby Alaskan coastline. On 22 September 1784, Russia founded its first permanent settlement at Three Saints Bay, Kodiak Island, and first occupied the Alaska panhandle near Sitka in 1799. The Russians used Alaska primarily as a source of sea otters and other furs, which were obtained by subjecting ESKIMOS and Aleuts to a brutal system of labor exploitation. The TLINGIT INDIANS kept up a fierce resistance against Russian efforts to control them through the 1760s. Wishing to escape the cost of defending the colony from Tlingits and avoid its possible annexation to Canada, the Czar sold SEWARD'S FOLLY to the US on 18 October 1867 for $7,200,000.

Washington did not appoint a governor until 1884, when Alaska contained about 33,000 natives and 430 whites, and did not make Alaska a territory until 24 August 1912. Commercial fishing and canning then became the biggest industry. After 1896, the main route for 50,000 miners who went to Canada's Klondike gold rush was via Alaska, where more gold was found at Nome in 1899 and Fairbanks in 1902. In 1900 Alaska had 63,592 inhabitants (approx. 48 percent white, 46 percent Indian, 5 percent Chinese), of whom 76 percent were rural and 20 percent were foreign-born; it ranked 49th in population, 51st in farm goods and 48th in manufactures. Few of the miners remained permanently, but development expanded by military facilities at Dutch Harbor, which were threatened in WORLD WAR II by the ALEUTIAN ISLANDS CAMPAIGN. The ALASKAN HIGHWAY, first land route to the territory, opened in 1942. The expansion of defense installations led the white population to double in both the 1940s and 1950s.

It became the 49th state on 3 January 1959, when it had 43,000 natives and 150,400 nonnatives. In January 1968, the largest US oil field was discovered on the North Slope near Prudhoe Bay and began flowing in 1977 via the ALASKA PIPELINE. Alaska ranked as the 49th state in 1990 with 550,043 residents (74 percent white, 15 percent Indian, 4 percent black, 3 percent Hispanic, 3 percent Asian), of whom 41 percent were urban and 4.5 percent were foreign-born. Manufacturing and mining employed 16 percent of workers.

Alaska Native Claims Settlement Act (18 December 1971) This law extinguished the land and royalty claims of the state's 55,000 native people, who received title to 62,500 square miles, payment of $462,500,000, and royalties not to exceed $500,000,000. It was the largest award for Indian claims ever granted.

Alaska pipeline In January 1968, the largest oil field yet found in the US was discovered on the North Slope of Prudhoe Bay, Alaska. Proposals to tap this energy source were blocked by environmental suits in federal court until the OIL EMBARGO, when Congress passed the Alaska Pipeline Act (16 November 1973), which forbade further court review of the project's environmental impact. In June 1977, oil began to flow 799 miles to Valdez via a 48-inch pipeline built at a cost of $4.5 billion.

Alaskan highway After the ALEUTIAN ISLANDS CAMPAIGN showed the need for a land route for military supplies to Alaska, army forces (mostly African Americans) began building a road on 12 March 1942 from Canada's Yukon Territory. On 1 December, the 1,523-mile route was completed at Fairbanks. It was opened to non-commercial travelers in mid-1948.

Albany Congress On 18 September 1753, Britain's BOARD OF TRADE directed N.Y. Lieutenant Governor, James De Lancey, to invite representatives from nearby provinces to meet with the IROQUOIS CONFEDERACY, who gave signs of seeking closer relations with the French. Between 19 June and 10 July 1754, delegates from New England, N.Y., Pa., and Md. prevented an open break with the Iroquois by presenting them with gifts, but failed to gain their active support. The congress then debated the ALBANY PLAN OF UNION.

Albany Plan of Union As delegates to the ALBANY CONGRESS, Benjamin FRANKLIN and Thomas HUTCHINSON offered a proposal to unite the THIRTEEN COLONIES on 19 June 1754. Their plan would have established a grand council composed of members elected by their legislatures in proportion to tax collections in each province, plus a president general named by the king to perform executive duties between council sessions. The government would have authority over Indian affairs and military defense, and could require the colonies to provide funds (in emergencies) according to a prearranged formula. Approved at Albany on 10 July, this plan of union was rejected (or ignored) by all the colonies. Despite the imminence of a war with the French, no assembly was willing to surrender any of its local autonomy – especially over taxes – to an outside legislative body.

Albany Regency This was a political organization that evolved around Martin VAN BUREN and kept the N.Y. state government Democratic for most of 1820–50. By perfecting the method of winning votes with contracts and patronage, the Regency served as a model for later government machines managed by political bosses. The HUNKERS and BARNBURNERS fought over the Regency's control after 1844.

Albertson* v. *Subversive Activities Control Board *see* MCCARRAN ACT.

Alcatraz Prison Seizure *see* AMERICAN INDIAN MOVEMENT

Aldrich, Nelson Wilmarth (b. Foster, R.I., 6 November 1841; d. New York, N.Y., 16 April 1915) He entered politics as a Republican, was elected R.I. congressman in 1878, and in 1880 was chosen for the Senate, where he remained until retiring in 1911. He emerged as an expert on government finance, an opponent of government regulation of business, and a firm advocate of high tariffs. He successfully attached amendments weakening the INTERSTATE COMMERCE COMMISSION, SHERMAN ANTITRUST, and HEPBURN ACTS, and supervised passage of the MCKINLEY TARIFF. By 1890, he ranked among the inner circle of Republican leaders who dominated Senate proceedings. He sponsored the Aldrich–Vreeland Act during the PANIC OF 1907 and chaired the National Monetary Commission, whose Aldrich Plan formed the basis of the FEDERAL RESERVE SYSTEM.

Aldrich Plan *see* FEDERAL RESERVE SYSTEM

Aldrich–Vreeland Act *see* PANIC OF 1907

Aldrin, Edwin E. *see* APOLLO PROJECT

Aleutian Islands campaign Having bombed Dutch Harbor and Fort Mears, Alaska, since 3 June 1942, Japanese forces seized Attu and Kiska in the Aleutian Islands on 12–21 June. Rear Admiral Francis W. Rockwell's US task force recaptured Attu between 11 May and 3 June 1943. Japanese forces evacuated Kiska before US–Canadian troops landed on 15 August. US losses: 1,000 killed and wounded. Japanese losses: 2,500 dead.

Aleuts *see* ESKIMOS

Alger, Horatio, Jr (b. Chelsea, Mass., 13 January 1832; d. Natick, Mass., 18 July 1899) A former Unitarian minister and bohemian expatriate in Paris, Alger authored nearly a hundred books for boys that sold 800,000 copies from 1866 to his death. His characters and plots popularized the American myth that perseverance, dedication, and thrift will inevitably overcome poverty and lead to success.

Algonkin Indians Speakers of one of the ALGONQUIAN LANGUAGES. They lived along the eastern Great Lakes. They traded furs with the French and were their allies against the English. They now live in Ontario.

Algonquian languages The largest family of INDIAN LANGUAGES north of Mexico, Algonquian was spoken over much of eastern Canada, New England, the Atlantic coast north of S.C., the Ohio valley–Great Lakes region, and isolated parts of the Great Plains. Its major subdivisions are the languages of the ABNAKI-Penobscot, Passamaquoddy, Micmac, Cree-Montagnais, ALGONKIN, MASSACHUSETT, NARRAGANSETT, WAMPANOAG, MAHICAN-PEQUOT, DELAWARE (Lenni Lenape), POWHATAN, SHAWNEE, MIAMI, KICKAPOO-FOX-SAUK, POTAWATOMI, ILLINOIS, CHIPPEWA, OJIBWA-OTTAWA, MENOMINEE, ARAPAHO, CHEYENNE, BLACKFOOT-PIEGAN, and GROS VENTRE INDIANS.

Alien and Sedition acts With the US then engaged in an undeclared naval war with FRANCE, and French agents and spies known to be operating in the country, Congress declared that national security required passage of the ALIEN [FRIENDS] ACT, ALIEN ENEMIES ACT, NATURALIZATION ACT (1798), and SEDITION ACT. Although enacted at a time when war with France seemed imminent, most of the laws were drafted so that they could also be used to muzzle DEMOCRATIC PARTY criticism of the FEDERALIST PARTY in the 1800 election.

Alien Enemies Act (6 July 1798) This law authorized the US to compel foreign citizens of an enemy power to register with the US in wartime, and provided further powers to detain or banish any aliens deemed dangerous. It went into effect in the WAR OF 1812.

Alien [Friends] Act (25 June 1798) This law authorized the president to deport foreign citizens in peacetime if he believed them to be engaged in espionage or sowing treason among US citizens. Neither legal hearings nor proof of guilt was required. It was applied against several immigrant editors of newspapers supporting the DEMOCRATIC PARTY before it expired on 25 June 1800.

Alien Property Custodian scandal The Alien Property Custodian's office was caretaker for enemy-owned businesses under the TRADING WITH THE ENEMY ACT and had responsibility for transferring them to private ownership after WORLD WAR I. In 1921 the custodian took a $274,000 bribe to transfer the American Metal Co. to Richard Merton and associates, and shared $50,000 with Attorney General Harry DAUGHERTY. The episode became one of the worst scandals tarnishing Warren HARDING's administration.

Alien Registration Act (1940) *see* SMITH ACT

Allen, Ethan (b. Litchfield, Conn., 10 January 1738; d. Burlington, Vt., 12 February 1789) After moving to VERMONT in 1772, Allen organized the Onion River Land Co. to speculate in land grants issued there by N.H. To protect his claims from rival speculators holding N.Y. titles, he organized the GREEN MOUNTAIN BOYS. Allen became a major leader in the Vt. statehood movement. In the REVOLUTIONARY WAR, he took FORT TICONDEROGA in 1775, was captured at MONTREAL on 25 September 1775, and exchanged on 6 May 1778. After the war, he continued working to make Vt. independent of N.Y.

Allen, Richard *see* AFRICAN METHODIST EPISCOPAL CHURCH

Allgeyer* v. *Louisiana On 1 March 1897, the Supreme Court ruled without dissent that the FOURTEENTH AMENDMENT protected the right to make contracts free of state interference as a guarantee of DUE PROCESS; it invalidated a law barring out-of-state companies from selling insurance in La. The Court extended *Allgeyer*'s logic to cases involving business regulation in *HOLDEN* v. *HARDY*, *LOCHNER* v. *NEW YORK*, and *ADKINS* v. *CHILDREN'S HOSPITAL*.

Alliance for Progress In 1961 John F. KENNEDY appointed Adolph BERLE to chair the Latin-American Task Force, which recommended a new initiative in US–Latin-American relations. The alliance charter was signed at the Punta del Este Conference in Uruguay on 17 August 1961. The alliance was less an organization than a series of bilateral agreements that promised $10 billion in US foreign aid and private banking capital over 10 years to nations that would adopt social and economic reforms such as land redistribution. By 1969, Latin-American nations had received about

$18 billion in loans and grants – much of it for refinancing national debts – of which just under half came from the private sector.

Allied Expeditionary Force (AEF) This term referred to the US ground forces (DOUGHBOYS) fighting in France in WORLD WAR I under General John J. PERSHING.

Altgeld, John Peter (b. Nieder Selters, Germany, 30 December 1847; d. Chicago, Ill., 12 March 1902) He matured in Richland County, Ohio, served in the Union army, became a self-taught lawyer in Mo. and moved to Chicago in 1875. He became Ill.'s first foreign-born governor in 1893 and the first Democrat elected since the Civil War. He was a model governor of the PROGRESSIVE ERA, who fought successfully for improving workplace conditions, increased funding for colleges, prison reform, and a trade school for the blind. He stirred controversy by pardoning three anarchists convicted for murder in the HAYMARKET RIOT, by protesting the use of federal troops to break the PULLMAN STRIKE, and supporting William Jennings BRYAN over Grover CLEVELAND at the 1896 Democratic convention. He was voted out of office in 1897.

Altman, Roger *see* RESOLUTION TRUST CORPORATION

American Antislavery Society On 4 December 1833, William Lloyd GARRISON, James BIRNEY, Robert PURVIS, Arthur Tappan, Theodore Weld, Wendell Phillips, and 55 others founded this organization to campaign for ABOLITIONISM. It publicized its views through the *LIBERATOR*. The society split between followers of Garrison, who advocated the immediate end of SLAVERY and denied that it deserved any constitutional protections, and supporters of Birney, who favored gradual abolition legally accomplished by political means. Most of its members belonged to the Garrison camp.

American Board of Customs Act (29 June 1767) Charles TOWNSHEND proposed this law to end jurisdiction by London's Customs Board over the colonies and to establish a separate American Customs Board, with headquarters at Boston. Utilizing ambiguous or ill-considered provisions of trade statutes like the SUGAR ACT, the board's agents often broke the spirit of the law to press smuggling charges based on innocent, technical mistakes made by merchants or ship captains in loading cargoes. Abuses of authority by the American Customs Board officials became a serious cause of alienation from parliamentary authority in seafaring towns. Resentment against this body turned violent in the LIBERTY RIOT and HMS *GASPEE* INCIDENT. The service was reformed by Britain in the early 1770s.

American Booksellers Association* v. *Hudnut On 24 February 1986, the Supreme Court declined an appeal from Indianapolis to overturn a federal circuit court's decision to declare its anti-obscenity ordinance unconstitutional. Indianapolis had attempted to eliminate pornography by defining it as a violation of women's collective civil rights and allowing women to sue for damages. The Court upheld the lower court's position that characterizing pornography as discrimination entailed censorship of ideas that went beyond the high court's definition of obscenity in *MILLER* v. *CALIFORNIA*.

American Civil Liberties Union (ACLU) In 1917 Norman THOMAS and Roger Baldwin organized the American Civil Liberties Bureau to assist persons charged with opposing US policy in WORLD WAR I. It was renamed as the ACLU in 1920 while aiding defendants of the RED SCARE. By accepting, on a pro bono basis, cases concerning infringements of constitutional rights, it has represented more clients before the Supreme Court than any other private group.

American Colonization Society In 1816 this organization was founded to raise funds for financing the settlement of free blacks in Africa. Its first president was Supreme Court Justice Bushrod Washington (nephew of the president), and members included Henry CLAY and John RANDOLPH of Roanoke. The society's ultimate aim was to encourage more masters to emancipate their bondsmen, by ending white fears that, once released from the controls of slavery, blacks would be unable to support themselves and would either become financial wards of local government or criminals. It reasoned that if masters expected that free blacks would leave the US, they would manumit more of them. The legislatures of Va., Md., Ky., N.C., and Miss. endorsed the society's mission.

Through 1831, the society helped 1,420 blacks reach Liberia, whose governing elite was descended from US slaves until a military coup in 1980.

American Communications Association, CIO, et al.* v. *Douds On 8 May 1950, the Supreme Court rejected arguments (5–1) that the TAFT–HARTLEY ACT's Section 9 – which compelled labor union officers to swear they were not Communists – constituted a BILL OF ATTAINDER, an EX POST FACTO LAW, and a violation of the FIRST AMENDMENT.

American Dilemma, An In 1944 Swedish economist Gunnar Myrdal and a team of researchers published this two-volume study of the status of blacks in the US. Myrdal not only documented the social and legal barriers that kept blacks in second-class citizenship, but also highlighted the contradiction between the injustice of US race relations and the ideals it professed during WORLD WAR II. The study became highly influential among academics and government officials, and played a major role in sensitizing influential whites to the problems of SEGREGATION and black DISFRANCHISEMENT.

American Federation of Labor (AFL) In May 1881, the Federation of Organized Trade and Labor Unions of the US and Canada was founded at Pittsburgh; its 13 CRAFT UNIONS were reorganized at Columbus, Ohio, on 8 December 1886 as the American Federation of Labor, with Samuel GOMPERS as the first president. It limited its membership to skilled workers and allowed each craft union to be self-governing within the federation; it pursued a nonpolitical agenda of higher wages, shorter work hours, and better workplace conditions. The PANIC OF 1893 stimulated its growth, and by 1904 it contained 1,676,200 members. It then grew to 2,020,670 by 1914 and 3,260,000 by 1920, at which size it stabilized until the GREAT DEPRESSION, during which it lost 2,000,000 members.

The NEW DEAL's pro-labor laws enabled it to rebound to 3,045,350 in 1935 and 9,000,000 in 1943. The AFL was the dominant force in American unionism and usually accounted for 70–80 percent of all non-company union members during 1904–35. In 1935 it allowed the newly-formed Committee of Industrial Organization to organize INDUSTRIAL UNIONS, but expelled these unions in May 1938. On 5 December 1955, it merged with the CIO as the AFL-CIO.

American Federation of Labor-Congress of Industrial Organizations (AFL-CIO) The traditional hostility between these groups subsided after George MEANEY took over the AFL and Walter REUTHER took over the CIO. Both unions perceived a need to combat an anti-labor political atmosphere symbolized by the TAFT–HARTLEY ACT. On 5 December 1955, the AFL's 109 unions (10,900,000 members) merged with the CIO's 32 unions (5,200,000 members). Meaney became president and Reuther vice-president. The AFL-CIO included 90 percent of US unionized workers and 33.6 percent of nonagricultural laborers. It expelled the Teamsters, Laundry and Dry-cleaning Workers, and Bakery Workers in December 1957 for violating anti-racketeering standards. Reuther's disagreements with Meaney over strategy resulted in his leading the 1,339,000 United Auto Workers out of the AFL-CIO in 1968. After replacing Meaney as president in 1979, Lane KIRKLAND engineered a reconciliation with the Auto Workers in July 1981, and readmitted the 1,100,000 Teamsters in October 1987. AFL-CIO membership declined from 16,100,000 in 1955 to 13,933,000 in 1991, about 15 percent of nonagricultural workers.

American Friends Service Committee *see* QUAKERS

American Independent party This party was organized to nominate George WALLACE for president in 1968, with Curtis Le May, a former air force general, as vice-president. Wallace campaigned against social welfare programs and liberal politics in general; he supported law and order, lower taxes, and victory in the VIETNAM WAR. The party carried five southern states and won 13.5 percent of the ballots, the fourth-best showing for a third party to that date. It was renamed the American party in 1969. When Wallace declined to run as its candidate in 1972, it nominated John G. Schmitz and Thomas J. Anderson, who won 1.4 percent of the ballots, but carried no states. In 1976 it nominated Lester Maddox, who received just 168,724 votes (0.2 percent). It ran no candidates in 1980.

American Indian Movement Founded in 1968 at Minneapolis by Dennis Banks, Clyde Bellecourt, and George Mitchell, this group became the most militant Indian organization. Its members occupied the abandoned Alcatraz prison in 1969–71 and organized the WOUNDED KNEE RESERVATION SEIZURE and TRAIL OF BROKEN TREATIES CARAVAN. Abetted by Calif. Governor Jerry Brown and N.Y. Governor Mario Cuomo, Banks was a fugitive from justice from 1975 to his surrender in 1984, when he began a 3-y.ear sentence for rioting.

American Indian Religious Freedom Act (1978) This statute required federal agencies to adopt policies that respected the legitimate exercise of traditional Native American and Hawaiian religions, and also protected their access (within reasonable bounds) to sacred sites and objects. The law spawned many cases concerning the degree to which Indians are exempt from environmental protection regulations and other laws in order to conduct ancient ceremonies.

American Insurance Company* v. *Canter *see* LOUISIANA PURCHASE

American Liberty League This organization was the NEW DEAL's most vocal critic. Founded in 1934, it was a nonpartisan body whose president, Jouett Shouse, had chaired the Democratic National Committee, and whose directors included former presidential nominees Alfred SMITH and John DAVIS. The league raised $1,200,000 to denounce the New Deal as a threat to democracy and free enterprise; it collected almost as much money to defeat Franklin D. ROOSEVELT in 1936 as the Democratic party spent to reelect him. The league withdrew from politics as the New Deal waned, and finally disbanded in 1940.

American Party *see* KNOW-NOTHING PARTY *and* AMERICAN INDEPENDENT PARTY

American Plan Between 1919 and 1929, the NATIONAL ASSOCIATION OF MANUFACTURERS led the US business community in a major offensive against labor unions under this name (it was also termed welfare capitalism). To lessen the appeal of unionization, it promoted voluntary wage hikes, workweek reductions, and improved workplace conditions. It fought to replace UNION SHOPS with "open shops," in which workers were free not to join a union. It also encouraged businesses to organize their own COMPANY UNIONS. The plan helped set back labor, and membership in non-company unions fell from 5,034,000 in 1920 to 3,567,000 in 1928.

American school of painting This was a circle of Anglo-American expatriate artists who studied or convened at Benjamin WEST's studio in London from about 1770 to 1795; it included John S. COPLEY, Charles W. PEALE, Gilbert STUART, and John TRUMBULL. The sculptress Patience WRIGHT was also acquainted with its members. The American school marked the first instance when American artists achieved international recognition for their work.

American System Henry CLAY's program to stimulate national economic development was known by this term. Under Clay's system, Congress would foster manufacturing by protective tariffs, ensure the stable currency necessary for interstate business transactions through a national bank, and link farmers to urban and overseas markets by funding INTERNAL IMPROVEMENTS from western land sales. Clay's goal was to have each region of the US serve as an ever-expanding domestic market for the others' goods, so that northern industrial centers might buy foodstuffs and cotton from westerners and southerners, who in turn would buy northern manufactures.

American Temperance Society *see* PROHIBITION

Americans for Democratic Action This public-interest lobby was organized in 1947 to promote policies to continue the NEW DEAL's social welfare legislation and to oppose isolationism in foreign policy. Its founders included Eleanor ROOSEVELT, Hubert HUMPHREY, Reinhold NIEBUHR, and Walter REUTHER. It advocated an active role for government in promoting prosperity and solving social problems, but rejected socialism or pervasive government intrusion upon private enterprise (very similar to the FAIR DEAL). Its influence upon the Democratic party waned in the 1970s, as its positions veered increasingly left of the

American mainstream. In 1991 it had about 85,000 members.

Americans with Disabilities Act (13 July 1990) This measure enabled the disabled to sue for damages in federal court for job discrimination. It also set deadlines (from 26 January 1992 to 26 July 1996) for public walkways, buildings, mass transit systems, and telephone services to be made accessible to the handicapped. Of 35,000 allegations of discrimination received by the Equal Employment Opportunity Commission from 1992 to mid-1994, most concerned persons with work-related injuries or emotional problems rather than those born with serious impairments (40 percent concerned back pain, wrist problems, or depression, while just 6 percent involved the blind or deaf). By November 1994, two-thirds of all severely disabled adults remained unemployed.

Amherst, Jeffery (b. Riverhead, Kent, England, 29 January 1717; d. Montreal, Kent, England, 3 August 1797) In 1731 Amherst entered the army. When the SEVEN YEARS' WAR began, he was sent to the colonies in command of the 15th Foot. In 1758 he was appointed commander in chief of British forces in North America. He was the architect of victory over France and won the second siege of LOUISBOURG, second campaign against FORT TICONDEROGA, CROWN POINT, and first battle of MONTREAL. He returned to England in 1763 and served as the British army's commander in chief (1772–95).

Amnesty Act (22 May 1872) Motivated in part by fears that the LIBERAL REPUBLICAN PARTY's call for reconciliation with the South would hurt their chances in the coming presidential election, Republicans in Congress restored the rights of voting and holding office to about 150,000 ex-Confederate military and government officers, and left just 500 of the highest-ranking CSA leaders excluded from political activity.

AMTRAK The Rail Passenger Service Act (1970) established the National Railroad Passenger Corporation to assume operation of most intercity passenger services from private railroads. Its service was originally termed Railpax, but went into operation on 1 May 1970 as AMTRAK. It immediately cut the number of passenger trains by 50 percent to 184 serving 319 communities along 21 basic routes over 20,000 miles of track. In 1991 it carried 22,000,000 people on an average of 210 trains daily, serving 500 station locations over 24,000 route miles; it owned 2,611 miles of right-of-way in the northeastern US. It has required federal subsidies each year since 1970, but they have fallen from 52 percent of costs in 1981 to 21 percent in 1991.

Anaconda Plan In April 1861, General Winfield SCOTT prepared the Union's first strategic plan for defeating the Confederacy. By blockading the rebels' salt-water ports and closing the Mississippi to southern commerce, Scott hoped to avoid invading the South, but still force its leaders into negotiating reunion by strangling the economy and encouraging peace sentiment among southerners. Abraham LINCOLN rejected this policy because it might take years to work, and insisted that Union armies advance on a broad front to find weak points that could be exploited to reclaim enemy territory.

Anasazi Culture This culture (*Anasazi* means "Ancient Ones") began emerging about 100 BC around the modern juncture of Ariz., N.Mex., Colo., and Utah. It paralleled the MOGOLLON CULTURE in creating sedentary agricultural villages and developing handcrafts. The Anasazi were the most advanced Indian basket-makers to AD 750, and were the first Indians to build PUEBLOS from stone or adobe, instead of pit-houses, after 750. Between 1276 and 1299, an extended drought led to the abandonment of mesa-top pueblos like Mesa Verde, Colo., and the people's resettlement along the Rio Grande in N.Mex.

Anderson, John Bayard (b. Rockford, Ill., 15 February 1922) In 1952 Anderson entered the diplomatic corps, and he went into state politics, as a Republican, in 1956. He sat in Congress (1961–79) and chaired the House Republican Conference (1969–79). In 1980 he campaigned for president as a moderate, independent alternative to the major parties, with ex-Governor Patrick J. Lucey (Democrat, Wis.) as running mate. He carried no states, but took 6.6 percent of ballots.

Anderson, Marian (b. Philadelphia, Pa., 17 February 1902; d. Portland, Oreg., 8 April

1993) She became recognized as a leading contralto in opera while performing in Europe during the 1930s. In 1939 she became the center of controversy when the Daughters of the American Revolution (DAR) withdrew permission for her to give a concert in their hall upon learning that she was black. Eleanor ROOSEVELT then resigned from the DAR and arranged for Anderson to perform for 75,000 fans at the Lincoln Memorial. The incident was a powerful symbolic gesture signifying the NEW DEAL's willingness to accept blacks as part of the ROOSEVELT COALITION. Anderson was the first black to sing at New York's Metropolitan Opera in 1955. She later served as a US delegate to the UN. On 7 December 1973, she received the highest US civilian decoration, the Medal of Freedom.

Anderson, Robert, Major *see* FORT SUMTER, BATTLES OF

Anderson, Sherwood (b. Camden, Ohio, 13 September 1876; d. Cristobal, Panama Canal Zone, 8 March 1941) He received little formal education, served in the SPANISH-AMERICAN WAR, and became a successful paint manufacturer in Elyria, Ohio. He abandoned business for writing and went to Chicago, where he was encouraged by Theodore DREISER. His literary reputation rests on his skill as an author of short stories. He won widespread acclaim for his *Winesburg, Ohio* collection (1919), in which he drew an unflattering portrait of small-town life. *Winesburg, Ohio*, like *Main Street* by Sinclair LEWIS, was in the vanguard of a new literary theme – the "revolt from the village" of the 1920s – that expressed an urban society's alienation from rural America's traditional values.

Andersonville Prison (Ga.) This was the most infamous of prisoner of war camps during the CIVIL WAR. While operational from February 1864 to April 1865, it confined only enlisted men. In mid-1864, its 26 acres held 32,899 Union prisoners. Malnourishment, contaminated water, inadequate medical care, and insufficient housing led to monthly death rates that peaked at 3,000 in August 1864. The US later identified a minimum of 12,912 soldiers who died there. Hanged on 10 November 1865 for abetting these deaths, commandant Henry Wirz was the only person executed by the US for serving the Confederacy.

Anglican church This church was the colonial extension of the Church of England; it never had a resident bishop and was under the archbishop of Canterbury's supervision. Its first parish was founded at Jamestown, Va., in 1607. The number of parishes grew from 41 in 1660 to 111 in 1700, and 246 in 1740, but many were always vacant. It became the established church in every southern colony and four N.Y. counties. The GREAT AWAKENING influenced many of its communicants to join the PRESBYTERIAN or BAPTIST CHURCHES. In 1776 there were 383 Anglican parishes with 500,000 members (25 percent of all whites); 54 percent of its parishes were in the South, 25 percent in the middle colonies, and 21 percent in New England. Because most Anglican clergy were TORIES who left the country during the Revolution, the church declined greatly after the war. Va. and Md. disestablished it in 1776, N.C., Ga., and N.Y. in 1777, and S.C. in 1778. It was revived as the PROTESTANT EPISCOPAL CHURCH.

Anglican Church of North America *see* PROTESTANT EPISCOPAL CHURCH

Anglo-Dutch War, first In July 1652, England declared war on the Netherlands. In June 1653, Mass. vetoed a planned attack upon NEW NETHERLAND by the UNITED COLONIES OF NEW ENGLAND, which required unanimous consent for war. Conn. agents failed to incite English towns on Long Island to rebel against Dutch rule, but seized the DUTCH WEST INDIA COMPANY's trading post of Fort Good Hope (near Hartford) on 5 July 1653 and refused to return it at the end of the war. An English fleet sent to capture NEW AMSTERDAM was recalled at Boston with news that hostilities had ended in April 1654.

Anglo-Dutch War, second In December 1664, the Netherlands and England went to war. On 7 September 1664, Peter STUYVESANT had surrendered NEW NETHERLAND without resistance to a task force of four frigates, 300 redcoats, and 2,000 Yankee militia at NEW AMSTERDAM. English forces peacefully occupied Fort Orange (Albany) on 20 September and took Fort Casimir, Del., by storm on 10 October. In

June 1667, a Dutch warship captured 19 merchant vessels and a Royal Navy frigate in Va.'s James River. On 21 July 1667, the peace of Breda ended the war and awarded New Netherland to England.

Anglo-Dutch War, third In March 1672, the Netherlands and England went to war. In July 1673, eight Dutch men-of-war under Cornelius Evertsen and Jacob Binkes raided Chesapeake Bay and captured or burned 11 English ships in the James River. After a brief bombardment on 8 August, they captured New York City's British garrison and appointed their marines' captain, Anthony Colve, governor of "New Orange" (former New Netherland). Suffolk County's English towns on east Long Island annexed themselves to Conn., but N.Y. and N.J. accepted Dutch rule. On 19 February 1674, the treaty of Westminster returned N.Y. and N.J. to England, which did not reinstall its own government until 10 November.

Anglo-Spanish War (1727–8) After Spain declared war on Britain in February 1727, YAMASEE INDIANS from Fla. killed five S.C. fur traders. On 9 March 1728, Colonel John Palmer's 100 S.C. militia and 100 CREEK INDIANS burned the Yamasees' fortified village beneath the guns of ST AUGUSTINE. S.C. losses: few. Yamasee losses: 30 killed, 15 prisoners. The victory greatly raised British prestige among the southeastern Indians. Spain made peace with Britain in March 1728.

Annapolis convention Following the successful MOUNT VERNON CONFERENCE, Va. called for a convention at Annapolis to discuss solutions to commercial problems among the states. Of nine states that accepted the invitation, only the delegations of Va., Pa., Del., N.J., and N.Y. arrived in time to participate during 11–14 September. The delegates elected John DICKINSON chair, turned their attention from commerce to politics, and endorsed an address by Alexander HAMILTON proposing that a convention meet in May 1787 to discuss strengthening the ARTICLES OF CONFEDERATION. Congress endorsed the idea on 21 February 1787 and recommended that the states send delegates to the CONSTITUTIONAL CONVENTION.

Anne (b. St James's Palace, Middlesex, England, 6 February 1665; d. Kensington Palace, Middlesex, England, 1 August 1714) Most of Anne's reign was dominated by fighting against the French, which spilled over to the colonies and was known as QUEEN ANNE'S WAR.

Anthony, Susan Brownell (b. Adams, Mass., 15 February 1820; d. Rochester, N.Y., 13 March 1906) Her career as a reformer began in the temperance movement, in which she was active from 1859 to 1869. She helped found the first all-female society to combat alcoholism in the US. After being elected president of the National Woman Suffrage Association in 1869, she devoted the rest of her life to obtaining the vote for women. She was one of the women who filed *MINOR V. HAPPERSETT*. She chaired the National American Woman Suffrage Association from 1892 to 1900.

anthracite coal strike of 1902 *see* COAL STRIKE OF 1902

Anti-Masonic party After William Morgan, a Batavia, N.Y., bricklayer, disappeared in September 1826, it was widely believed that Masons murdered him for betraying the order's secrets. Widespread publicity concerning the case, which revealed that large numbers of high government officials were Masons, led to the creation of the Anti-Masonic party in N.Y. during 1830. This organization influenced politics in three ways: (1) as the first "third party" to run a candidate for president; (2) as the first party to hold a national nominating convention; and (3) as the first party to announce a platform. In the 1832 election, it ran William Wirt (Md.) for president, with Amos Ellmaker (Pa.) as running mate. This ticket carried Vt. and received 8.0 percent of the ballots. Its last presidential contest was in 1836, when it backed Whig candidate William H. HARRISON, with Francis Granger (N.Y.) as running mate.

Antiballistic Missile Treaty (ABM Treaty) (26 March 1972) The US and USSR signed this agreement at the Strategic Arms Limitation talks (*see* STRATEGIC ARMS LIMITATION TREATY). It restricted each country to building no more than two ABM sites, each with 100 launchers, to defend itself against nuclear ICBMs. The Senate ratified it on 3 August 1972. A protocol of 3 July 1974 restricted each side to a single ABM system around its capital. The USSR built an ABM system, but the US did not.

Antietam, battle of (Md.) On 17 September 1862, Major General George B. McClellan's 75,316 Federals inflicted heavy casualties on General Robert E. Lee's 51,844 Confederates, but were unable to break the Southern lines. USA losses: 2,108 killed, 9,549 wounded, 753 missing. CSA losses: 2,700 killed, 9,024 wounded, 2,000 missing. Interpreted as a Union victory because Lee retreated from Md. the next day, Antietam created the position of military strength needed for Abraham Lincoln to issue the Emancipation Proclamation.

Antifederalists This name was applied to opponents of the federal Constitution during the ratification process. Among the leading Antifederalists were Patrick Henry and George Mason of Va., George Clinton of N.Y., and Elbridge Gerry of Mass. They were strongest in N.H., R.I., Mass., N.Y., Va., and N.C. The Antifederalists' most important contribution was to orchestrate a surge of public opinion demanding adoption of the Bill of Rights.

antimiscegenation laws *see* miscegenation

Antinomian controversy In 1636 the New England clergy came under strong criticism from Rev. John Wheelwright and his sister-in-law Anne Hutchinson, who insinuated that most ministers had not received saving grace and had no right to exercise authority over church members that had been born again. John winthrop and other critics likened these views to the heresy of Antinomianism (against the rule of order), which asserted that saving grace freed the elect to judge morality for themselves. After being convicted of contempt and sedition on 20 January 1637, Wheelwright left Mass. Hutchinson was banished on 17 November after discrediting herself with claims that she and God communicated directly with one another.

Antirent War This was the only significant tenant uprising in the US after the 1766 outbreak on the New York manors. It began in 1839 when leaseholders opposed efforts to collect $400,000 in unpaid rents due to the Rennselaerwyck manor near Albany, N.Y. After being suppressed by militia, tenants opposed efforts to seize their property for rent or evict them, by secret societies that harassed landlords and their loyal tenants. The disturbances spread through much of the Hudson valley and ended in 1846 with legislation granting tenants more legal rights.

Antisaloon League of America In 1893 Rev. Howard H. Russell of Oberlin, Ohio, founded the first local chapter of this interdenominational (but primarily Protestant) body to press for Prohibition. It was organized on a national basis in 1895 at Washington, D.C. By 1900 the league had become a major political lobbying group because of its $2,000,000 budget and publications. It played the most influential role in eliminating alcoholic consumption through state laws and the Eighteenth Amendment. It remained active in the 1920s, when it opposed the "wet" candidacy of Alfred Smith and pressured Congress for the Jones Act (1929). It declined after ratification of the Twenty-first Amendment.

antitrust laws *see* trusts

antiwar movement *see* Vietnam antiwar movement

Anzio, battle of (Italy) On 22 January 1944, Major General John P. Lucas's US VI Corps (50,000 men) landed behind German lines at Anzio, 30 miles south of Rome. The enemy bottled up the US beachhead by 30 January, inflicted heavy losses during 16 February–2 March, and kept the US perimeter besieged until May, when Allied forces resumed their drive on Rome.

Anzus Treaty On 4 August 1951, Australia, New Zealand, and the US created a mutual security pact as an anti-Communist measure during the cold war. Australia and New Zealand contributed combat troops to the Vietnam War. New Zealand's refusal to let US ships carrying nuclear weapons use its harbors in 1985 led both nations to abrogate their mutual defense responsibilities in 1986.

Apache campaigns (1) In February 1862, fighting broke out with the Chiricahuas after the army wrongfully accused them of kidnaping a boy, and then killed five Apache hostages; under Cochise, they raided whites until late 1872. From 1862 to 1865, Major

General James Carleton's Calif. and N.Mex. volunteers forced 500 Mescaleros onto a reservation, which they fled in December 1865 to raid the southwest. Between 1866 and 1870, the army fought 170 skirmishes against Apaches; it claimed to have killed 741 Indians at a loss of 26 dead and 58 wounded.

(2) On 4 September 1879, Victorio's Apaches (up to 150 warriors) began raiding N.Mex., Tex., and Mexico; they were wiped out by Mexican troops on 15 October 1880. On 30 September 1881, GERONIMO and Chato led 74 Chiricahuas off their reservation to raid Ariz. and Mexico, but they surrendered and returned to their reservation in July 1883. In November Geronimo and 133 followers ran for Mexico, from which they killed 38 US settlers. After being pursued for 2,000 miles through Mexico, Geronimo surrendered to General Nelson Miles on 4 September 1886. On 8 September Miles serenaded Geronimo's Apaches with "Auld Lang Syne" as he put them on trains to prison in Fla.

Apache Indians The Zuni word *apachu*, meaning "enemy," has been used since the 17th century in reference to several bands of speakers of ATHAPASKAN LANGUAGES in N.Mex. and Ariz.: the Lipan, Western Apache, Mescalero, Chiricahua, Jicarilla, and Kiowa-Apache. The earliest estimate of their population was 6,500 about 1680. By the 19th century they had engaged in frequent conflict with Mexicans and mission Indians, who later retaliated with the CAMP GRANT MASSACRE. The US Army's APACHE CAMPAIGNS began in 1862 and ended in 1886. The Lipans merged with other bands. The Western Apache were settled at Fort Apache (White Mountains) and San Carlos reservations in Ariz. Most Chiricahua now live at their Fort Sill, Okla., reservation or at the Mescalero reservation in Otero County, N.Mex. The Jicarilla were put on a reservation in Sandoval and Rio Arriba counties, N.Mex. The Kiowa-Apache lived on the southern plains and most settled on a reservation in Caddo County, Okla., headquartered at Anadarko.

Apollo Project On 25 May 1961, after the USSR orbited the first man of the SPACE RACE, John F. KENNEDY declared the US intention of landing on the moon before 1970. On 20 February 1962, John Glenn became the first US astronaut to orbit the earth. In 1964 unmanned Ranger missions circled the moon for photographic reconnaissance. Lunar Orbiter missions began in August 1966 and eventually photographed the moon's entire surface. The first US unmanned lunar landing was Surveyor I in June 1966. Following NASA's Mercury Program to gain experience in weightless flight by single astronauts, the Gemini Program began sending two-man crews into outer space in March 1963, to perfect techniques of docking and extra-vehicular activities.

The Apollo Project, which would conduct the moon landings, was set back on 27 January 1967 when faulty wiring caused a fire that left Virgil Grissom, Edward White, and Roger Chafee dead in a simulated launch at Cape Canaveral, Fla. From 21 to 27 December 1968, Apollo 8 carried the first three men to leave the earth's gravitational pull and orbit the moon. Apollo missions 9 and 10 conducted manned lunar orbits in 1969. On 16 July 1969, Apollo 11 left Cape Canaveral for the moon. On 20 July, with Michael Collins hovering in Apollo 11, Neil Armstrong (first) and Edwin Aldrin became the first men to walk on the moon; they returned to earth on 24 July. Five more lunar landings were conducted (another was aborted), with the last such mission from 7 to 19 December 1972. Apollo's final exercise was a joint docking with USSR cosmonauts orbiting the earth from 26 July to 7 August 1975. Putting an American on the moon required efforts by 420,000 NASA employees or contractors in 1969, when the project absorbed almost 1 percent of US GNP, and ultimately cost $25 billion.

Appalachian Regional Development Act (6 March 1965) Congress appropriated $1.1 billion for the Appalachian Regional Commission to finance a broad range of economic development programs which would benefit the 13-state Appalachian region, such as highway building, flood control, agricultural improvement, soil reclamation, and vocational training centers. Highway construction was its most successful program, and led to long-term employment gains of 10 percent for counties bordering new roads.

Appomattox Court House, surrender at (Va.) On 9 April 1865 (Palm Sunday), outnumbered by Union forces by over four to one, General Robert E. LEE surrendered his Army of NORTHERN VIRGINIA's 26,765 men to Lieutenant General Ulysses S. GRANT's Army of the POTOMAC. The surrender made further CSA resistance futile and effectively ended the CIVIL WAR.

Aptheker* v. *Secretary of State *see* MCCARRAN ACT

***Arabic* pledge** *see LUSITANIA*, HMS

Arapaho Indians Speakers of one of the ALGONQUIAN LANGUAGES, the Arapahos numbered about 3,000 in 1780 and were closely allied with the CHEYENNE INDIANS. Under attack by the SIOUX, they migrated from Minn. to Nebr.-Wyo. in the early 1800s, and split into northern and southern bands. After fighting against the US in the CHEYENNE CAMPAIGNS, RED RIVER WAR, and third SIOUX WAR, they accepted reservation status along the Canadian River in Okla. (headquartered at Concho) and on the Wind River Reservation in Wyo. with the Northern SHOSHONIS, who were once their enemies. Wind River now contains 5,124 Indians.

Ardennes Forest, battle of *see* BULGE, BATTLE OF THE

Argersinger* v. *Hamlin *see GIDEON* V. *WAINWRIGHT*

Arikara Indians This CADDOAN LANGUAGE group migrated from the lower Great Plains to the Missouri Riv. in S.Dak., where they established contact with French fur traders about 1770. They allied with the HIDATSA and MANDAN, as the "three affiliated tribes." They defeated a party of William ASHLEY's fur traders in 1823, and then briefly engaged in small-scale hostilities against the US before a lasting peace was made. Smallpox and other epidemics cut their numbers from around 3,000 in 1780, to 1,650 in 1871, to 500 in 1888, and 380 in 1904. The survivors merged with Mandans and Hidatsa at the Fort Berthold Reservation, N.Dak.

Arizona On 28 April 1700, Fr Eusebio KINO dedicated the first mission in Ariz. with a resident priest at San Javier del Bac near Tucson. The area contained fewer than 2,000 Spanish-speaking people when acquired by the treaty of GUADALUPE HIDALGO. The GADSDEN PURCHASE added its southern border. Anglo-American settlement was stimulated when silver mines were opened at Tubac in 1856. In the CIVIL WAR, CSA troops briefly occupied Ariz. in 1862 on an invitation from pro-CSA citizens at Tucson and Mesilla. Washington detached Ariz. from N.Mex. as a separate territory on 24 February 1863, when it had about 4,200 whites. APACHE CAMPAIGNS were waged in 1862–86. Mining for silver and copper, cattle ranching, and sheep grazing dominated the economy.

In 1900 Ariz. was 48th in population with 122,931 residents (approx. 40 percent white, 35 percent Hispanic, 1 percent black, 22 percent Indian, and 1 percent Chinese), of whom 84 percent were rural, 11 percent Mexican-born, and 9 percent other foreign-born; it ranked 47th in farm produce and 41st in manufactures. It became the 48th state on 14 February 1912. Rapid urbanization doubled the population and diversified the economy from 1950 to 1970. In 1990 Ariz. was the 25th state in size and had 3,665,228 inhabitants (72 percent white, 3 percent black, 19 percent Hispanic, 5 percent Indian, and 1 percent Asian), of whom 79 percent were urban and 7.6 percent foreign-born. Manufacturing employed 13 percent of workers and mining 8 percent.

Arkansas In 1686, near the mouth of the Arkansas River, the French built Fort Arkansas, the first permanent white settlement. It became part of the US by the LOUISIANA PURCHASE, a territory on 2 March 1819, and the 25th state on 15 June 1836. Cotton dominated its economy and by 1860 Ark. had 435,450 inhabitants, of whom 26 percent were slaves and under 1 percent were foreign-born; it ranked 23rd among the states in the value of its farmland and livestock and 33rd in manufactures.

It became the eighth CSA state on 6 May 1861. In the CIVIL WAR, it furnished 60,000 CSA troops and 13,815 USA soldiers (8,289 white and 5,526 black). Ark. was the site of 336 military engagements. Union forces won control over much of the state after the battle of PEA RIDGE.

By March 1864, a tenth of voters had sworn Union allegiance and Abraham LIN-

COLN instituted a provisional civilian government, which abolished slavery. White supremacists took over the legislature in 1866 and passed a black code (*see* BLACK CODES). Congress imposed military rule on 2 March 1867, then restored congressional representation and self-government on 22 June 1868. Republican control of Ark. ended six-and-a-half years later, on 10 November 1874. The state disfranchised most blacks by POLL TAX and legislated racial SEGREGATION after 1900.

In 1900 it was the 25th state in size and had 1,311,564 inhabitants, of whom 92 percent were rural, 28 percent were black, and 1 percent were foreign-born; it ranked 22nd among states in the value of its agricultural goods and 38th in manufactures. From 1920 to 1970, it lost 1,239,100 residents, mostly blacks moving to northern cities, and its racial composition shifted significantly. During the CIVIL RIGHTS MOVEMENT, it actively resisted integration under Governor Orval Faubus and US troops were dispatched in the LITTLE ROCK DESEGREGATION VIOLENCE. Statewide school desegregation was not achieved until the late 1960s. Ark. ranked 33rd among states by 1990, when its population was 2,350,725 (82 percent white, 16 percent black, 1 percent Hispanic, and 1 percent Asian), of whom 40 percent were urban and 1.1 percent were foreign-born. Manufacturing and mining employed 29 percent of workers.

Armed Forces Reserve Act *see* ARMY RESERVES

Armed Ship Bill On 26 February 1917, Woodrow WILSON asked Congress to approve arming the US MERCHANT MARINE against German submarines. The House passed this bill on 1 March, but Robert LA FOLLETTE led a filibuster from 28 February to 4 March that killed it. Wilson then ordered merchantmen armed by his own authority on 12 March.

Armistice Combat in WORLD WAR I was ended by an armistice signed at 5 a.m. 11 November, and designed to end fighting at the symbolic moment of 11 a.m.: the 11th hour of the 11th day of the 11th month. Its terms stipulated: (1) German withdrawal from France, Belgium, and the west bank of the Rhine; (2) German surrender of Rhine crossings at Cologne, Koblenz, and Mainz; (3) destruction of German planes, tanks, and heavy artillery; (4) surrender of German submarines and internment of surface warships; (5) continued blockade of German ports until a formal peace; (6) exchange of prisoners of war and civilian deportees; (7) transfer of 150,000 rail cars, 5,000 locomotives, and 5,000 trucks to the Allies; (8) German renunciation of treaties with its military allies; (9) recognition of Allied rights to demand war reparations.

arms control *see* NUCLEAR ARMS CONTROL

Armstrong, Neil A. *see* APOLLO PROJECT

Army Appropriations Act (2 March 1867) Congress added a rider to this law (which Andrew JOHNSON vetoed) intended to forestall the president from hindering its policies on RECONSTRUCTION by forbidding him to issue any orders for military forces in the field except through the army's commander in chief. (This rider was an unconstitutional infringement of presidential powers.) Two of the 11 charges in Johnson's impeachment trial alleged that he violated this law by giving direct orders to General William Emory.

Army of Northern Virginia *see* NORTHERN VIRGINIA, ARMY OF

Army of the Potomac *see* POTOMAC, ARMY OF THE

Army of the Tennessee (CSA) *see* TENNESSEE, CSA ARMY OF THE

Army of the Tennessee (US) *see* TENNESSEE, USA ARMY OF THE

Army of Virginia *see* VIRGINIA, ARMY OF

Army Reserves These are stand-by military units trained and equipped by the US Army rather than the states; they are specialty and support units (the NATIONAL GUARD provides combat forces). The NATIONAL DEFENSE ACT (1916) created the Reserves as a manpower pool, and its members were not organized into units until the Armed Forces Reserve Act (9 July 1952). This Reserve Act created a Ready Reserve of units that could be ordered into active federal service for up to two years if the president declared a national emergency; it also created a manpower reserve of ex-soldiers, the Standby Reserve, who were not organized into units and could not be individually recalled to active duty unless Congress declared a national emergency.

Arnold, Benedict (b. Norwich, Conn., 14 January 1741; d. London, England, 14 June 1801) He served as a private in the SEVEN YEARS' WAR. He was co-commander at FORT TICONDEROGA's capture (1775), wounded at the second battle of QUEBEC, and made brigadier general in January 1776. He won important victories at VALCOUR ISLAND and BEMIS HEIGHTS, at which he was seriously wounded. Although a major general with a distinguished war record, Arnold was not rewarded with a major command, but stationed in Philadelphia (where he married a girl with Tory connections, *see* TORIES) and then assigned to a fortress at West Point, N.Y. Frustrated by lack of US recognition, Arnold schemed to surrender West Point to the British, but fled to enemy lines when his plot was discovered on 25 September 1780. Arnold was made a British brigadier general and led Tory raids on Conn. and Va. He became a merchant in Canada after the war, then moved to England in 1791.

Aroostook War Because Britain and the US had never agreed on Maine's boundary with Canada, title to the Aroostook valley was in doubt in the 1830s. During the winter of 1838–9, Canadian loggers began cutting trees there and sparked conflict with Yankees holding land claims to the valley. Violence remained bloodless and small-scale, but Maine and New Brunswick called out their militia, Congress voted $10,000,000 in contingency funds, and General Winfield SCOTT was sent there with troops. Tensions eased when Scott negotiated a truce in March 1839. The WEBSTER–ASHBURTON TREATY ended the dispute.

Arthur, Chester Alan (b. Fairfield, Vt., 5 October 1830; d. New York, N.Y., 18 November 1886) In 1853 Arthur opened a law office at New York City. An abolitionist and early Republican, he was N.Y.'s quartermaster general in the CIVIL WAR. Arthur was deeply enmeshed in patronage politics and became a leading STALWART in N.Y.'s Republican party machine. Although not personally corrupt, he was removed from the N.Y. Customs Collectorship in 1878 by Rutherford HAYES for ignoring an executive order forbidding presidential appointees to engage in partisan politics. Placed on the Republican ticket in 1880 to help James GARFIELD carry N.Y., Arthur became president on 19 September 1881 upon Garfield's death. He shocked the Republican party bosses by signing the PENDLETON ACT, vetoing wasteful pork-barrel appropriations, and prosecuting corrupt Republicans for graft. He also opened diplomatic relations with Korea and began the navy's modernization. He lost the bosses' support and was not renominated.

Article X (of the LEAGUE OF NATIONS) The tenth article of the League of Nations Treaty obliged each member nation to defend all other nations from armed aggression or other threats to its independence. The Senate made it legally unenforceable by adopting Henry Cabot LODGE's reservation that the US would not uphold its provisions unless Congress specifically approved US involvement. Because Woodrow WILSON viewed it as "the heart of the Covenant," its evisceration was the most important consideration which led him to order Senate Democrats to vote against the treaty if Lodge's reservations were attached, even at the cost of the treaty's defeat.

Articles of Confederation On 12 June 1776 Congress named John DICKINSON to chair a committee for drafting a plan of national union. On 12 July, Dickinson transmitted the first US constitution, the Articles of Confederation and Perpetual Union. Congress sent them to the states for ratification on 17 November 1777, but official adoption did not come until 1 March 1781, due to efforts by small states to force the cession of land claims north of the Ohio River.

The articles established a government in which the states kept their sovereignty. National government consisted of a unicameral Congress, but no chief executive and no judicial system. Diplomacy, warfare, and finance were supervised by congressional committees. Major issues required the approval of nine states in Congress, and no tax could be levied without unanimous consent. The ORDINANCE OF 1785 and NORTHWEST ORDINANCE were the articles' most important accomplishments. The articles functioned poorly after peace came in 1783, and their weaknesses – especially in financial affairs – led to the CONSTITUTIONAL CONVENTION's calling.

Arver* v. *United States On 7 January 1918, the Supreme Court upheld the SELECTIVE SERVICE ACT (1917) as a constitutional exercise of federal sovereignty and a legitimate power under Article I, Section 8's authority for Congress "to declare war . . . to raise and support armies" and under Article I, Section 8's authority to "make all Laws which shall be necessary and proper." The Court denied that a military DRAFT was involuntary servitude as understood by the THIRTEENTH AMENDMENT. *Arver* was later clarified by *Rostker* v. *Goldberg*.

Asbury, Francis *see* METHODIST CHURCH

Ashley, William Henry (b. Powhatan County, Va., ca. 1778; d. Cooper County, Mo., 26 March 1838) He was a St Louis fur merchant who had suffered heavy casualties from Indian ambushes in expeditions sent by boat up the Missouri River in 1822 and 1823. He revolutionized the fur trade in 1824 by sending small parties of trappers overland on horseback instead of by water. In the spring of 1825, he held the first rendezvous to exchange skins for money and trade goods on the Green River. Ashley's system of having mounted trappers live off the land in small groups, range over a wide area, and then carry their catches to a central rendezvous proved to be the most profitable manner of large-scale organization for the beaver trade; it also accelerated the discovery of the best overland routes to reach Oreg. and Calif., most of which were found by Ashley's men.

Ashwander* v. *Tennessee Valley Authority On 17 February 1936, the Supreme Court ruled (5–4) that the US could legally build dams under the Tennessee Valley Authority (TVA) law by its authority to control navigable waterways and provide for national defense. It denied a motion to prevent the sale of surplus electricity generated from TVA dams by declaring that the US had unrestricted authority to dispose of government property.

Asian immigration The largest sources of the Asian population in the US have come from CHINESE and JAPANESE IMMIGRATION, and the BOAT PEOPLE. By 1991 legal immigration from other Asian countries totaled 1,095,403 Philippinos and 667,678 Koreans, most of whom have arrived since 1970.

Assiniboine Indians Speakers of one of the SIOUAN LANGUAGES, the Assiniboines were possibly the most numerous Great Plains Indians, numbering perhaps 20,000 about 1780. They divided between a Canadian band and groups inhabiting the Missouri River basin in Mont. Their early involvement in the fur trade made them among the earliest Plains Indians to acquire guns. They fought with neighboring SIOUX INDIANS, but had peaceful relations with whites. Smallpox epidemics in 1837–8 cut their population to just 4,000, and they had declined further by 1885, when they settled on the Fort Belknap and Fort Peck reservations in Mont.

associationism *see* TRADE ASSOCIATIONS

assumption of state debts *see* REPORT ON THE PUBLIC CREDIT

Astor, John Jacob (b. Waldorf, Germany, 17 July 1763; d. New York, N.Y., 29 March 1848) He immigrated to the US in 1784 and entered the fur trade in 1796. In 1808 he founded the American Fur Co., which became the largest US fur organization by 1830 and controlled 75 percent of US fur exports by 1834. Foreseeing the trade's impending decline, Astor sold out in 1834 and used his profits to become New York's greatest real estate speculator. When he died, he was the richest man in the US and left an estate of $20,000,000.

Athapaskan languages This family of INDIAN LANGUAGES includes over 50 languages, spoken in central Canada and Alaska, the Pacific northwest coast, and Ariz. and N.Mex. Its subdivisions include the languages of the NAVAHO and APACHE INDIANS. From the group's homeland in northern Calif. and southwestern Oreg., groups began breaking up and migrating south and east between 200 BC and AD 200.

Atlanta, battles for (Ga.) On 4 May 1864, Major General William T. SHERMAN's 105,000 Federals left Chattanooga for Atlanta, defended by General Joseph E. JOHNSTON's 62,000 Confederates. On 13–16 May, Sherman forced Johnston to withdraw from Resaca, Ga.; on 27 June, he suffered 2,000 casualties (against 270 Southern losses) at Kennesaw Mountain; on 4–9 July, he drove Johnston from defensive positions on the Chattahoochee River near

Roswell. On 18 July, General John B. Hood assumed command from Johnston; he unsuccessfully attacked Federal forces on 20 July at Peachtree Creek, on 22 July before Atlanta, and on 28 July at Ezra Chapel. With 42,000 troops, Hood blocked Sherman's 85,000 men until 1 September, when he evacuated Atlanta, which Federals occupied the next day. During the 120 days of fighting, USA losses were 26,000 killed and wounded, compared to 23,000 Southern casualties.

Atlantic, battle of the The submarine offensive by the AXIS against Allied shipping in the Atlantic began on 12 January 1942, when a British ship was torpedoed 300 miles east of Cape Cod. U-boats had sunk 1,027 Allied and neutral ships (5,700,204 gross tons) in the Atlantic–Arctic theater by 31 December 1942, at a loss of 106 of their own number. In 1942, the Axis had destroyed Allied tonnage at a rate 15 percent higher than replacements came out of shipyards, but had built over twice as many U-boats as they lost. The tide turned during January–May 1943, when Allied losses of 259 ships (1,549,891 gross tons) were a third less than the previous year's rate, and Allied ship production began to exceed the tonnage sunk. Axis fortunes were also reversed in the same five months, as the loss of 104 U-boats neutralized the construction of 105 new submarines. The offensive then shifted to the Allies.

Atlantic Charter On 14 August 1941, Franklin D. ROOSEVELT and Winston Churchill met at sea off Newfoundland and issued this statement of principles for international relations. It endorsed: respect for political self-determination, the ending of armed aggression, disarmament of aggressor states, free trade, freedom of the seas, and international efforts to establish the FOUR FREEDOMS.

atomic bomb *see* MANHATTAN PROJECT

Atomic Energy Act (1 August 1946) Congress gave complete control over research and development of fissionable materials to a five-man, civilian ATOMIC ENERGY COMMISSION (AEC) that was linked to the Pentagon by a Military Liaison Committee. David Lilienthal became the first chairman on 28 October. The AEC was charged with promoting peaceful uses for nuclear power, but spent at least 90 percent of its budget on arms development. The law was amended on 30 August 1954 to allow private utility companies to own reactors and fissionable material for generating electricity, and to file patents for nuclear technology.

Atomic Energy Commission (AEC) Created by the ATOMIC ENERGY ACT (1946), the AEC had the mission of regulating and licensing nuclear power technology, and of protecting public health and the environment by publishing safety standards and conducting inspections. The Energy Reorganization Act (1974) reconstituted the AEC as the Nuclear Regulatory Commission (NRC) as of 19 January 1975. The NRC has responsibility over both civilian and military uses of nuclear energy.

Atsina Indians *see* GROS VENTRE INDIANS

attorney general The office of attorney general (chief legal officer for the president) was established with a seat in the CABINET by the JUDICIARY ACT (1789). The task of arguing cases before the Supreme Court has been assigned to the solicitor general. The attorney general received control over the Department of JUSTICE in 1870. Charges of misconduct tainted the careers of Edmund RANDOLPH and Harry DAUGHERTY. Richard KLEINDIENST and John MITCHELL were convicted of criminal offenses.

Auden, W(ystan) H(ugh) (b. York, England, 21 February 1907; d. Vienna, Austria, 28 September 1973) Educated at Oxford, Auden was a Fabian socialist who published his first book, *Poems*, in 1930. After driving an ambulance in the Spanish Civil War, he received the King George Medal for poetry in 1937. He emigrated to the US in 1940, took US citizenship in 1946, and won the Pulitzer prize for *The Age of Anxiety* (1947). He held a chair in poetry at Oxford (1956–61), and later divided his year between New York and Italy. Upon his death, he was generally ranked the most important author writing verse in English.

Audubon, John James (b. Les Cayes, Santo Domingo, 26 April 1785; d. New York, N.Y., 27 January 1851) A refugee from Haiti's slave revolt, Audubon was educated in France and came to Pa. in 1803. He became obsessed with studying and painting wild birds, and consequently spent much of his life in penury. He did most of his fieldwork on trips from his homes in Louisville, Henderson, Ky., and Cincinnati. He won renown as the foremost US ornithologist for *The Birds of America* (1827–38), which included over 1,000 lifesize pictures of some 500 species. After 1827, he primarily resided in Edinburgh, Scotland, and produced an *Ornithological Biography* (5 vols., 1831–9) and *Synopsis of the Birds of North America* (1839).

Austin, Stephen Fuller (b. Wythe County, Va., 3 November 1793; d. Austin, Tex., 27 December 1836) A Mo. resident from 1798, Austin was the earliest promoter of Anglo-American migration to Tex. In 1821 he organized a colony on the lower Brazos River out of a 200,000-acre Spanish grant given to his father, Moses, and by 1832 he had drawn over 8,000 pioneers from the US to his lands. Austin was a leading political figure who hoped to win an autonomous status for Tex. within the Mexican republic, but emerged as a leader in the TEXAS REVOLT after being briefly imprisoned in Mexico in 1835 on suspicion of sedition. He was the first envoy to the US, lost election as president to Samuel HOUSTON, and was first Tex. secretary of state.

Australian ballot This term refers to the secret ballot, which was first popularized in Australia. Until its adoption, US citizens voted by depositing one of their party's preprinted ballots, which listed only its own nominees, at the polling place. Since each party's tickets were specially printed, it was impractical to keep one's preferences hidden. The first use of a general ballot listing both parties' candidates was at the 1888 Louisville, Ky., municipal elections. The practice was nearly universal by 1900 and was an important reform of the PROGRESSIVE ERA.

automobile Charles E. Duryea received the first US patent for an automobile on 11 June 1895, based on a prototype he perfected and operated between April 1892 and September 1893. Henry FORD pioneered manufacturing and retailing innovations that made cars affordable to ordinary workers. The FEDERAL AID ROAD ACT (1916) initiated a major effort to improve highways for private motor travel. New car sales rose from 1,951,000 in 1920 to 4,500,000 by 1929, while registered automobiles tripled from 9,200,000 to 26,700,000 in the same period. By 1929 the number of operational cars averaged nearly one per family, and almost 3,000,000 jobs – 10 percent of all nonagricultural employees – depended (directly or indirectly) on the auto industry.

In the 1920s, General Motors developed annual model changes as a marketing strategy to encourage customers to buy new cars at shorter intervals than necessity would ordinarily require. During the 1950s, Americans bought 58,000,000 cars, and by 1960, 75 percent of all families owned one. Widespread car ownership enabled metropolitan areas to suburbanize in the 1950s. By 1992 there was one car for every 1.8 US residents. By 1993 the motor vehicle industry employed about 1,600,000 persons in over 4,000 car, truck, or parts factories; it accounted for 4.5 percent ($250 billion) of GDP.

Axis The Fascist and imperialist powers in WORLD WAR II were known as the Axis. Allied with the principal Axis nations of Germany, Italy, and Japan were Romania, Bulgaria, Hungary, Finland, and the Croatian Ustashi government.

Ayers* v. *Fordice *see* MISSISSIPPI

Ayonhwathah *see* HIAWATHA

B

Baby and Child Care *see* Spock, Benjamin M.

baby boom This term refers to the generation born in the period 1946–65, which followed a period of delayed marriages for young adults and suppressed normal population growth due to World War II. Almost 74,000,000 babies arrived in that period, which peaked between 1 April 1959 and 2 April 1960, when the US recorded its greatest number of births. Fertility declined steadily from then until 1972, when the birth rate barely sufficed to replace losses from death. As the baby boom ended, immigration contributed a greater share to population growth, including 32.8 percent of total growth in the 1980s.

Bacon's Rebellion Panicked by hostilities with Susquehannock Indians from September 1675 to January 1676, settlers from northern Va. joined forces under Nathaniel Bacon to retaliate for 36 whites killed in raids. In May 1676, Bacon began attacking all Indians within reach, including the Occaneeches, who had just attacked three Susquehannock towns. Governor William Berkeley, who had forbidden any Indian campaigns, declared Bacon a traitor on 10 May and had him arrested on 7 June, but pardoned him five days later when Bacon's supporters seemed likely to rescue him. Berkeley approved another Indian offensive, but called back Bacon and his 1,300 men when they advanced on peaceful Pamunkeys.

After killing and capturing many Pamunkeys in August, Bacon drove Berkeley and his 300 followers from Jamestown, which he entered on 19 September, and burned that night. Widespread lawlessness ensued as 1,600 Baconians plundered the plantations of the governor and his followers. The rebellion soon collapsed after Bacon died on 26 October of chronic diarrhea. Berkeley hanged 14 rebels under martial law before Bacon's death, and nine later. Fighting between the rebels and loyalists took about 25 lives, besides hundreds of Indians enslaved or killed by rebels.

Baghdad Pact *see* Central Treaty Organization

Bailey* v. *Drexel Furniture Company On 15 May 1922, in a case related to *Hammer* v. *Dagenhart*, the Supreme Court struck down (8–1) the Child Labor Act's (1919) 10 percent tax on profits of companies using child labor to make goods for interstate sale (*see* child labor laws), because the tax was neither a proper use of federal police power nor a legitimate means of raising revenue, but rather a selective penalty. The Court reversed *Bailey* in *United States* v. *Darby Lumber Company*.

Baker* v. *Carr On 26 March 1962, the Supreme Court ruled (6–2) that federal courts had jurisdiction over challenges to how state legislatures were apportioned, to protect the constitutional rights of voters. *Baker* overturned *Colegrove* v. *Green* (10 June 1946), which declared (4–3) that redistricting disputes were political issues over which the courts had no authority. This ruling laid the basis for increasing federal involvement with apportionment controversies. *See Wesberry* v. *Sanders and Reynolds* v. *Sims*.

Ballew* v. *Georgia *see Burch* v. *Louisiana*

Ballinger–Pinchot controversy On 7 January 1910, William Taft fired Gifford Pinchot as chief US forester for accusing Interior Secretary Richard Ballinger of subordinating the conservation of natural resources to the benefiting of business interests. A congressional committee found the charges unwarranted, but Ballinger was discredited and resigned on 6 March 1911. The episode alienated many Progressive Republicans from Taft, and helped push Theodore ROOSEVELT into challenging him for the 1912 presidential nomination and later running against him on the PROGRESSIVE PARTY ticket.

Baltimore, Lord *see* PROPRIETORS OF MARYLAND

Bancroft, George (b. Worcester, Mass., 3 October 1800; d. Washington, D.C., 17 January 1891) After graduating from Harvard in 1817, and receiving a Ph.D. from the University of Göttingen in 1820, Bancroft became active in the politics of JACKSONIAN DEMOCRACY. He unsuccessfully ran for governor of Mass. in 1844, was secretary of the US Navy (1845–6), established the US Naval Academy at Annapolis, and was ambassador to Britain (1846–9) and to Germany (1867–74). In 1831 he began research for his 10-volume *History of the United States* (1834–76), which he based on a relentless search through public and private archives for documentary evidence. Bancroft's *History* reflected the filiopietistic spirit of a young nation, but its careful attention to accuracy set new standards for historical writing and earned Bancroft his reputation as the first truly great American historian.

bank holiday On 5 March 1933, facing the BANK PANIC OF 1933, Franklin D. ROOSEVELT ordered all 12,756 solvent banks to close until 12 March. A bank would only reopen when federal examiners guaranteed its financial soundness. The EMERGENCY BANKING RELIEF ACT legalized the holiday. On the first day banks reopened, deposits exceeded withdrawals by $10,000,000 in spite of the pent-up need for cash created by the holiday. On 12 March, Roosevelt gave his first FIRESIDE CHAT to explain procedures for certifying banks and to guarantee that no institution had been allowed to reopen unless it was entirely sound. From 12 to 15 March, 4,507 national banks and 567 state-chartered banks (74 percent of banks in the FEDERAL RESERVE SYSTEM) resumed business, and another 1,419 were operational by 15 April with loans from the RECONSTRUCTION FINANCE CORPORATION (RFC).

The bank holiday broke the panic's hold on the public, and stimulated an influx of $1 billion in hoarded currency back to the banks by May. Of the remaining 4,215 banks, a quarter had reopened by 31 December with RFC loans, half reopened in early 1934, and a quarter had to be liquidated. The holiday took nearly all unsafe banks out of business, and the BANKING ACT (1933) ended fears about the financial system's soundness with the Federal Deposit Insurance Corporation (FDIC).

Bank of Augusta* [Ga.] v. *Earle In 1839 the Supreme Court ruled that state-chartered corporations did not have all the rights guaranteed to "legal persons" by the Constitution. States might consequently limit or exclude other states' corporations from doing business within their own borders, although the Court recognized the general right of corporations to conduct business anywhere under the principle of "interstate comity." The opinion that corporations were not legal persons with full constitutional rights was overturned in *SANTA CLARA COUNTY* V. *SOUTHERN PACIFIC RAILROAD COMPANY*.

Bank of the United States, first On 13 December 1790, Alexander HAMILTON issued his Report on a National Bank, in which he proposed that Congress charter a bank. Modeled upon the Bank of England, Hamilton's bank would serve the Treasury as a depository for its surplus funds, a source of short-term credit, and a supplemental source of currency through its issue of bank notes; it would also serve the private sector by providing capital for commercial and industrial loans. The bank would be a semi-public entity, in which the US government subscribed 20 percent of its initial stock and named 20 percent of its directors. The bank stimulated the first debate over LOOSE CONSTRUCTIONISM, and received a 20-year charter 25 February 1791. In 1811, despite support by Albert GALLATIN, a bill extending the bank's charter was defeated by the House (24 January) and Senate (20 February), in part because two-thirds of its stock was then held by British investors. The bank was then liquidated among the shareholders.

Bank of the United States, second On 10 April 1816, a second Bank of the United States received a national charter. The US government subscribed $7,000,000 of its $35,000,000 capitalization and named a fifth of its 25 directors. In return for safeguarding Treasury surpluses without having to give government interest, the bank paid the US a bonus of $1,500,000, which funded the BONUS BILL. The 1816 charter otherwise resembled the first bank's charter of 1791. The PANIC OF 1819 left widespread resentment against the bank in the south and west, where the panic was blamed on its hard money policies. Nicholas BIDDLE was its president (1823–36). On 10 July 1832, Andrew JACKSON vetoed an extension of its charter as unconstitutional; on 10 September 1833, he ordered all Treasury funds in the bank to be withdrawn and placed in PET BANKS. On 23 September he dismissed Treasury Secretary William Duane for refusing to do so, and replaced him with Roger TANEY, whom the Senate refused to confirm on 24 June 1834, due to Henry CLAY's opposition. Before the bank's federal charter expired on 1 March 1836, it received a state charter in February as the Bank of the United States of Pennsylvania, which failed in 1841 but paid off all its debts. It was eventually replaced by the INDEPENDENT TREASURY.

Bank of the United States* v. *Deveaux In 1809 the Supreme Court set a rigorous test for federal jurisdiction over cases concerning state-chartered corporations: unless all the company's owners lived in different states than their legal adversaries, then federal courts must refer the case to a state venue. The ruling greatly limited the number of issues concerning corporations resolved by federal judges, until its reversal by *LOUISVILLE RAILROAD COMPANY* v. *LETSON*.

bank panic of 1933 The CRASH OF 1929 precipitated a spiraling number of bank failures resulting from uncollectable loans and depreciated mortgage collateral. Attempts to break this cycle with loans from the RECONSTRUCTION FINANCE CORPORATION (RFC) failed because the RFC lacked sufficient capital to offset bank losses. From 1930 to March 1932, 5,504 banks had closed with deposits of $3.4 billion. In late 1933, a financial panic swept the US as depositors demanded their savings and forced banks to close. Between 4 February and 3 March, almost every state closed its banks, or left them open subject to severe restrictions. On 5 March, a day after taking office, Franklin D. ROOSEVELT declared a BANK HOLIDAY to halt the panic.

Bankhead Cotton Control Act (21 April 1934) This law acted to reduce the chronic overproduction of cotton, which partly stemmed from the reluctance of many producers to join voluntary agreements to either restrict output under the AGRICULTURAL ADJUSTMENT ADMINISTRATION (AAA) or harvest more than their allotment. To reduce the surpluses, the Bankhead Act taxed all cotton ginned in excess of individual quotas, at the prohibitive rate of 5 cents per pound. Any farmers who failed to enroll in an AAA crop-limitation agreement would be taxed on their entire output. It successfully cut production and raised taxes, but became moot when the AAA was declared unconstitutional in 1936.

Bankhead–Jones Farm Tenancy Act (22 July 1937) This law funded low-interest, 40-year mortgages to tenants so that they could become landowners, and created the FARM SECURITY ADMINISTRATION to make these loans. It also established the RURAL REHABILITATION PROGRAM and RESETTLEMENT ADMINISTRATION.

Banking Act (16 June 1933) This first Glass-Steagall act created the FEDERAL DEPOSIT INSURANCE CORPORATION to restore faith in the banking system by insuring deposits up to $2,500 (raised to $5,000 in 1934). It forbade banks to underwrite investment loans or stock issues for corporations (this line of business was thereafter limited to brokerage firms) and restricted banks to sponsoring bond issues of states or their localities. It also strengthened the FEDERAL RESERVE SYSTEM's regulatory powers and opened membership to more banks.

Banking Act (23 August 1935) This law redesignated the Federal Reserve Board as the Board of Governors and increased its members to 7 from 6. It reconstituted the Federal Reserve Open Market Committee – formerly composed of all governors of the 12 federal reserve banks – to consist of all seven of the Board of Governors and five heads of federal reserve banks. These changes stripped the 12 federal reserve banks of their former power to set interest rates and reserve requirements for bank assets, and they centralized authority over these open market transactions with the Board of Governors in Washington. The law completed the establishment of a truly national banking system that centralized control in Washington over interest rates, expansion of credit, the money supply, and all other aspects of monetary policy.

Bankruptcy Act, first (4 April 1800) The first federal Bankruptcy Act applied only to merchants and traders, and was motivated to permit the release of Robert MORRIS, superintendent of finance during the Revolution, from debtors' prison. It was repealed 19 December 1803.

Bankruptcy Act, second (19 August 1841) The second US Bankruptcy Act provided universal access to voluntary bankruptcy for citizens regardless of occupation, but allowed creditors to attach assets of merchants. It was repealed in 1846.

Banks, Dennis *see* AMERICAN INDIAN MOVEMENT *and* WOUNDED KNEE RESERVATION SEIZURE

Bannock Indians Speakers of one of the UTO-AZTECAN LANGUAGES, the Bannocks are a subgroup of the Northern PAIUTE INDIANS, but developed their own tribal identity. Their homeland was southeastern Idaho and they incorporated horses into their culture in the 1700s. They might have numbered 2,000 before smallpox sharply decreased their population in 1853. For harassing emigrants on the OREGON and CALIFORNIA TRAILS, they were settled on the Fort Hall reservation by 1869. Large-scale violence erupted a decade later in the BANNOCK–PAIUTE CAMPAIGN. They now share the Fort Hall reservation with the SHOSHONI.

Bannock–Paiute campaign Suffering from hunger because hunting and other sources of food had declined due to increased settlement in Idaho, a Bannock wounded two whites grazing hogs on Indian prairie on 30 May 1878. About 900 Bannocks and PAIUTES (including 500 warriors) left their reservations for an 800-mile trek through Oreg. and Wyo. under pursuit by Brigadier General Oliver Howard's 1,000 troops. By the last skirmish on 12 September, the army held 600 Paiute and 131 Bannock prisoners. US losses: 9 soldiers killed and 15 wounded, 31 settlers murdered. Indian losses: 78 dead.

Baptist church The American Baptist tradition derived from English dissenters who adopted teachings of central Europe's 16th-century Anabaptists (re-baptizers). The Puritan Roger WILLIAMS founded the first Baptist church at Providence, R.I., in 1639. There were four Baptist congregations in 1660, 33 in 1700, and 96 in 1740. The GREAT AWAKENING began a period of rapid growth for the denomination, which won many converts through its lay preachers who used revival techniques. In 1776 there were 415 Baptist churches and just 25,000 members (1 percent of all whites); by 1791 there were 60,970 Baptist laymen, 564 clergy, and 748 congregations.

In 1845 a schism split the largest Baptist association (the "Regular" Baptists) over SLAVERY when the Southern Baptist convention was founded. Northern "Regulars" became the Northern Baptist convention in 1907, and changed their name to the American Baptist convention in 1950. So many ex-slaves joined the fellowship that 40 percent of all Baptists were African-American by 1910; in 1880 they formed the National Baptist convention of the US, from which a large body seceded to organize the National Baptist convention of America in 1915.

The Baptists numbered 100,000 by 1800, and increased at a rate of 66 percent per decade over the next thirty years. The number of all Baptist pulpits rose from 2,700 in 1820, to 12,150 in 1860, and 49,905 in 1900. Membership grew from almost 1,000,000 in 1860 to over 4,000,000 in 1900. During the 20th century, the Baptists surpassed the Methodists as the largest Protestant faith, and experienced the largest growth of any mainline Protestant church. Membership in all Baptist conventions or associations was 28,464,000 (19 percent of all churchgoers) in 1990, when there were 97,994 congregations. Over half of these totals belonged to the Southern Baptist convention (14,907,800 members in 37,739 churches), and 29 percent belonged to the two largest black conventions (8,168,800 members in 37,398 churches).

Barbary pirates, wars with By 1801, the US had sent $2,000,000 to ransom seamen imprisoned on Africa's Barbary Coast – plus annual tribute paid to Algiers, Morocco, Tripoli, and Tunis to keep their pirates from plundering American commerce. Between 2 April 1801 and mid-1802, the Navy Department deployed ten warships in the Mediterranean to prevent piracy. On 14 May 1801, Tripoli declared war on the US for not increasing the annual tribute paid as protection money to prevent raids on its ships.

On 7 August, in the war's first engagement, the USS *Enterprize* captured the pirate *Tripoli.* In June 1802 a naval blockade of Tripoli commenced. On 31 October 1803, the USS *Philadelphia* fell into enemy hands while aground in shallow water, but Lieutenant Stephen Decatur burned it on 16 February 1804. The Navy severely bombarded Tripoli harbor (3 August–4 September). On 27 April 1805, the Tripolitan seaport Derna surrendered to a navy cannonade and land attack by William Eaton, US consul at Tunis, and Lieutenant Presley O'Bannon, US Marines. Tripoli made peace on terms favorable to the US on 4 June 1805.

Tunis withdrew a threat to make war on the US in July 1805 when nine US warships threatened immediate retaliation. Algiers declared war on the US during the War of 1812 and its pirates began seizing American ships. On 10 May 1815, Decatur took ten ships to the Mediterranean and defeated two armed Algerian vessels. Algiers agreed to release American captives, pay restitution for hijacked American cargoes, and end its policy of demanding annual tribute to restrain pirates from attacking US commerce, by a treaty signed on 30 June. Decatur ended Barbary piracy by negotiating similar agreements with Tunis (26 July), and Tripoli (5 August).

barbed wire On 27 October 1873, Joseph F. Glidden of De Kalb, Ill., patented a barbed wire whose spurs remained firmly in place and that could be machine-twisted. The Washburn and Moen Co. bought his patent for $60,000 and began mass production at Worcester, Mass., in 1876. By 1880 its output had risen from 2,800,000 lb. to 80,500,000 lb. By providing inexpensive fencing, barbed wire stimulated large-scale homesteading on the Great Plains; it also ended the era of open grazing range and long-distance cattle drives.

Barenblatt* v. *United States On 8 June 1959, the Supreme Court modified (5–4) *WATKINS* v. *UNITED STATES* by extending the scope of questions that a congressional committee might force an unwilling witness to answer. The Court upheld the contempt conviction of a witness for refusing to give evidence about subversive activity to the HOUSE COMMITTEE ON UN-AMERICAN ACTIVITIES, because conflicts between government and private interests may be decided in the public's favor concerning vital matters such as preventing the overthrow of the Constitution.

Barkley, Alben William (b. Graves County, Ky., 24 November 1877; d. Paducah, Ky., 30 April 1956) He served as Ky. congressman (1913–27), and entered the Senate in 1926, where he was one of the NEW DEAL's strongest and most effective supporters. To ensure his reelection in a hard-fought challenge by Albert Chandler in 1938, the Democratic party politicized PUBLIC WORKS ADMINISTRATION and WORKS PROGRESS ADMINISTRATION workers in Ky. to such a degree that the resulting scandal was a major factor in the HATCH ACT's passage (1939–40). He was US vice-president (1949–53).

Barlow, Joel (b. Redding, Conn., 24 March 1754; d. near Cracow, Poland, 24 December 1812) In 1778 Barlow graduated from Yale as "class poet." He was a chaplain in the Revolution, and later opened a law office at Hartford. He spent several years overseas as a land agent for US speculators, consul in Algiers, and ambassador to France. He answered critics of the French Revolution in prose with *Advice to the Privileged Orders* (1791) and in verse with *The Conspiracy of Kings* (1792). In 1807 he published a revision of his *The Vision of Columbus* (1787), as *The Columbiad*, an epic poem tracing the history of the New World.

barnburners These were Martin VAN BUREN's faction of N.Y. Democrats who supported democratic reforms and ABOLITIONISM against the entrenched ALBANY REGENCY. (They were so called for refusing to compromise on principle. Their enemies, the HUNKERS, compared them to a farmer who would burn his barn to kill rats.) In 1848 the barnburners quit the Democrats for not endorsing the WILMOT PROVISO, and helped found the FREE-SOIL PARTY, which ran Van Buren for president. The Free-Soil vote was blamed for Whig victory that year.

Barnum, Phineas Taylor (b. Bethel, Conn., 5 July 1810; d. Bridgeport, Conn., 7 April 1891) After going bankrupt manufacturing clocks, Barnum became an entertainer. He developed shows with surefire potential for luring customers to see freaks, frauds, and curiosities, ranging from the midget Tom Thumb to singer Jenny Lind. He dominated the circus industry, initially with his Greatest Show on Earth, and then with the Barnum and Bailey Circus. As his age's most spectacular showman, who toured successfully in Europe, Barnum prefigured the later emergence of the US as the foremost center of the global entertainment industry.

Barron* v. *Baltimore In 1833 the Supreme Court unanimously held that the BILL OF RIGHTS was intended only to prevent abuses by the US government, and was not obligatory upon state courts; it denied a claim under the FIFTH AMENDMENT that Baltimore pay restitution for a city policy that reduced a wharf's value. The Court reversed this ruling in *CHICAGO, BURLINGTON AND QUINCY RAILROAD* v. *CHICAGO*, which also concerned EMINENT DOMAIN; it later extended the entire Bill of Rights piecemeal, starting with *GITLOW* v. *NEW YORK*.

Bartkis* v. *Illinois *see UNITED STATES* v. *LANZA*

Barton, Bruce *see MAN NOBODY KNOWS, THE*

Barton, Clara Harlowe (b. Oxford, Mass., 25 December 1821; d. Glen Echo, Md., 12 April 1912) Born Clarissa, Barton became a US nurse during the CIVIL WAR who was known as the "angel of the battlefield." She demonstrated exceptional organizational skill in the war, and then headed a bureau to compile records on missing and dead soldiers until 1869. She assisted the Red Cross in the Franco–Prussian War; upon returning to the US, she led the campaign that established the National Society of the Red Cross in 1881, and was its president until 1904.

Baruch, Bernard Mannes (b. Camden, S.C., 19 August 1870; d. New York, N.Y., 20 June 1965) He entered Wall Street as an office boy for a brokerage firm, transformed a small investment into a fortune, and was renowned as the "wizard of Wall Street" for his uncanny knack at investing money. He took over the badly mismanaged WAR INDUSTRIES BOARD in 1918, reformed it, and oversaw US industrial production for WORLD WAR I. He was US economic advisor for the negotiations for the treaty of VERSAILLES. His views on economic policy were highly influential in the Democratic Party during the 1920s, but he lacked enthusiasm for the NEW DEAL. He served as special advisor for every president from Wilson to Kennedy.

Bataan, battle of Heavy Japanese air attacks hit the Philippines on 8 December 1941. General Douglas MACARTHUR's 65,000 Philippino and 16,000 US troops began retreating to Bataan Peninsula on 23 December. By 28 January 1942, Allied forces had lost half the peninsula to General Masaharu Homma's 100,000 Japanese; they held a perimeter 10 miles square until their surrender by Major General Edward King on 9 April.

Bataan death march Following the surrender of BATAAN, Japanese troops forced 55,000 Philippino and 11,500 US troops (all of them malnourished and a third disease-ridden) to endure a 60-mile forced march, marked by beatings and other physical abuse, without water or food, to prison camps. Just 45,000 Philippino and 9,300 US troops arrived at the camps. Of the US survivors, 1,500 died from Japanese mistreatment before the war ended.

Bay of Pigs invasion On 17 April 1961, the US allowed 1,400 anti-Communist Cubans, whom it had trained and supplied, to launch an invasion of Cuba to spark a popular revolt against Fidel Castro. When Cubans failed to arise, and Communist forces trapped their opponents on the beachhead, John F. KENNEDY refused to support them with combat missions by US aircraft. Castro's forces wiped out the beachhead in two days, and left Kennedy's administration humiliated in its first months. The fiasco encouraged the Soviet Union to order the BERLIN WALL built in August and to precipitate the CUBAN MISSILE CRISIS by shipping nuclear weapons to Cuba. On 23–4 December 1962, 1,113 Cuban prisoners of war were flown to the US in exchange for $53,000,000 in medical equipment for Cuba.

Bayonne Decree On 17 April 1800, Napoleon reacted to the EMBARGO ACT by ordering the confiscation of all US ships in ports under French control; he justified the seizures by claiming that since the embargo ordered the US MERCHANT MARINE to remain at home, any vessels flying the US flag in Europe must be British ships with falsified US papers. American merchants suffered over $10,000,000 in losses of shipping and cargoes.

Bear Flag Revolt Tensions created by the impending MEXICAN WAR led US citizens to attack Mexican authorities they believed were preparing to arrest them on 10 June 1846 near John SUTTER's fort in Calif. On 14 June US insurgents occupied Sonoma, where they soon declared Calif. a republic and designed a flag with a grizzly bear facing a red star, from which the rebellion took its name. Army explorer John FRÉMONT took command of the rebels on 25 June and occupied San Francisco on 1 July, but the Bear Flag Republic lost its legitimacy on 7 July when US Commander John Sloat occupied Monterey and declared Calif. to be under US control. Military activities then merged into the Mexican War.

Beard, Charles Austin (b. Knightstown, Ind., 27 November 1874; d. New Haven, Conn., 1 September 1948) After earning his Ph.D. in history from Columbia (1904), Beard taught there and then helped found the New School for Social Research in 1919. Beard's *An Economic Interpretation of the Constitution* (1913) profoundly influenced his generation's scholarship. By arguing that issues of financial self-interest shaped the CONSTITUTION's structure, Beard emerged as the historian most responsible for popularizing economic determinism and social conflict as the perspectives that would dominate his discipline until after 1945. By appropriating the techniques of Marxist analysis, without endorsing the Communist ideology behind them, Beard made it possible for the mainstream of US scholars to investigate class conflict without subscribing to Marxism itself. Other major works included *Economic Origins of Jeffersonian Democracy* (1915), *The Economic Basis of Politics* (1919), *The Republic* (1943), and – with wife Mary Ritter Beard – *The Rise of American Civilization* (1927).

beat generation This was a social and literary movement that reacted against conformism and materialism in US life during the 1950s. Beat generation (or beatnik) subculture idealized individuality and sought to attain self-knowledge through a constant succession of intellectual challenges and physical experiences. Significant beatnik communities emerged in Greenwich Village and San Francisco. The leading beat spokesmen were Jack KEROUAC, who coined the term, and Allen GINSBERG. The beats lost their identity during the 1960s, but had a major influence on the generation of the WOODSTOCK ROCK FESTIVAL.

Beaver Dam, battle of (Ontario) On 24 June 1813, Captain Dominique Ducharme's 500 Iroquois, 200 Canadians, and Lieutenant James FitzGibbon's 80 redcoats, defeated Lieutenant Colonel Charles Broerstler's 14th US Infantry and forced its surrender. British losses: 15 killed, 25 wounded. US losses: 600 men and 2 cannon captured. The defeat led to Henry Dearborn's removal from command of US forces on the Niagara River.

beaver trade *see* FUR TRADE

beaver wars The IROQUOIS CONFEDERACY waged five campaigns against rivals for the FUR TRADE. (1) Iroquois robbed HURON INDIAN fur convoys along the St Lawrence valley and Great Lakes, August 1642 to 14 July 1645, when they agreed to a truce. Warfare resumed in October 1646. In March 1649, 1,000 Iroquois raided Hurons in Ontario, killed 300 warriors, and drove their enemies into the wilderness, where 10,000 may have starved; in December Iroquois devastated the Petuns, who sheltered many Huron refugees. In 1651 the Iroquois dispersed the Neutrals of Ontario. Having set three tribes toward extinction, the Iroquois made peace with the French on 5 November 1653. (2) From mid-1654 to 1656, Iroquois dispersed the Eries of Ohio, who soon disappeared. (3) In 1656 the Iroquois attacked various ALGONQUIAN INDIANS along Lake Huron and French on the St Lawrence. French armies ravaged Iroquois towns in 1666 and forced peace on them in June 1667. (4) From April 1663 to 1675, Iroquois fought the SUSQUEHANNOCK INDIANS of Pa., who fled south and dispersed in the late 1670s. (5) In September 1680, Iroquois attacked the ILLINOIS INDIANS, took several hundred captives, and plundered two MIAMI

INDIAN towns. In 1683 they raided the OTTAWA INDIANS near Mackinac, Mich. Iroquois unsuccessfully besieged the French at Fort St Louis on the Illinois River (21–7 March 1684), and attacked the Illinois nation.

Beecher's bibles Because Rev. Henry Ward Beecher and his Congregational church in Brooklyn, N.Y., held such fanatical antislavery views, the Sharp's rifles sent to ABOLITIONIST settlers in BLEEDING KANSAS by several groups of northern Protestants (including Beecher's parishioners) were termed "Beecher's bibles."

Beer-Wine Revenue Act (22 March 1933) Congress passed this law to implement the TWENTY-FIRST AMENDMENT. It redefined spirituous liquors as containing over 3.2 percent alcohol and transferred any responsibility for regulating them to the states.

Beirut bombing *see* LEBANON, US INTERVENTION IN

Belknap, William Worth (b. Newburgh, N.Y., 22 September 1829; d. Washington, D.C., 13 October 1890) On 2 March 1876, after the House of Representatives impeached him for taking bribes from Indian traders on western reservations, Secretary of War Belknap resigned. On 1 August the Senate voted not to try him, for lack of jurisdiction over a cabinet member no longer in office. The scandal added to the Ulysses S. GRANT administration's reputation for corruption.

Bell, Alexander Graham (b. Edinburgh, Scotland, 3 March 1847; d. Cape Breton Island, Nova Scotia, 2 August 1922) He immigrated to Canada with his parents, joined the faculty of Boston University in 1873, and became a citizen in 1882. He invented the telephone in 1876, but his patent rights had to be confirmed by the Supreme Court in 1893. He connected New York and Chicago by phone in 1892. He was the National Geographic Society's president (1898–1904).

Bell, John (b. near Nashville, Tenn., 15 February 1797; d. Stewart County, Tenn., 10 September 1869) He entered politics as a Jacksonian Democrat, but joined the WHIG PARTY in 1836. He served in Congress (1827–41), and was elected speaker in 1834. He was secretary of war in 1841 and senator (1847–59). Bell was the CONSTITUTIONAL UNION PARTY's presidential candidate in 1860. He ran last in the race with just 12.6 percent of votes cast, but by carrying Va., Ky., and Tenn., he was placed third in electoral votes with 39. He supported SECESSION for Tenn. when he realized the North would invade the Confederacy.

Bellamy, Edward (b. Chicopee Falls, Mass., 26 March 1850; d. Chicopee Falls, Mass., 22 May 1898) He was a journalist who wrote *Looking Backward: 2000–1887* (1888), which sold over 500,000 copes in its first two years and was the most influential utopian novel ever printed in the US. Bellamy's futuristic social order contained collective ownership of industry, no labor strife, free education, high cultural attainment, equal opportunity for women, no pollution, enlightened programs to rehabilitate criminals, and credit cards instead of money. Bellamy's ideas affected the way that virtually every intellectual, author, and social critic of the PROGRESSIVE ERA viewed American society. His greatest legacy was to provide American thinkers with an indigenous alternative to Marxism for use in critiquing urban-industrial society.

Belleau Wood, battle of (France) *see* WORLD WAR I

Bemis Heights, battle of (N.Y.) On 7 October 1777, two brigades of Continental infantry (about 2,500) under Brigadier General Benedict ARNOLD repulsed an assault by 2,000 of Major General John Burgoyne's troops on Major General Horatio Gates's army. US losses: 30 killed, 100 wounded. Estimated British losses: 600. Burgoyne's defeat forced his surrender at nearby SARATOGA on 17 October.

Benét, Stephen Vincent (b. Bethlehem, Pa., 22 July 1898; d. New York, N.Y., 13 March 1943) When Benét entered Yale in 1915, he had already published a poem in a national magazine, the *New Republic*. He became a poet known for his epic treatment of US historical themes. He won Pulitzer prizes for *John Brown's Body* (1928) and *Western Star* (1943).

Bennett, James Gordon (b. Newmills, Scotland, 1795; d. New York, N.Y., 1 June 1872) In 1819 Bennett emigrated to Nova Scotia and soon after went to New York, where he bought the *Sunday Courier* in 1825. In 1835 he founded the New York *Herald*, through which he launched many of the innovations that would transform journalism in the next decade. To increase circulation – and remain competitive with the first "penny paper," the New York *Sun* – he cut each issue's price to one cent. To expand the reading public, he increased the volume of news printed, provided a steady stream of human-interest stories – from crime to sensational scandals or tragedies – and encouraged his writers to narrate events like an interesting story, rather than a dry series of facts. He hired a large stable of correspondents to conduct investigative reporting, and was among the first editors to exploit the telegraph for relaying fast-breaking events. These tactics raised the *Herald*'s circulation from less than 15,000 in 1835 to 100,000 in 1864.

Bennington, battle of (Vt.) On 17 August 1777 Brigadier General John Stark's 2,600 N.H. militia destroyed Lieutenant Colonel Friedrich Baum's foraging party of 800 HESSIANS, and then defeated Lieutenant Colonel Francis Breymann's relief force of 600 Hessians. US losses: 30 killed, 50 wounded. Hessian losses: 200 killed, 696 captured (including wounded). The defeat cost Major General John Burgoyne a tenth of his expeditionary force invading N.Y.

Benton, Thomas Hart (b. near Hillsboro, N.C., 14 March 1782; d. Washington, D.C., 10 April 1858) He settled in Tenn., where he opened a law practice in 1806, but left for Mo. after a bar room brawl in which he shot Andrew JACKSON and was stabbed five times by Jackson's friends. He was the first US senator to serve thirty consecutive years (1821–51). The antebellum era's fourth-greatest orator (behind Henry CLAY, Daniel WEBSTER, and John CALHOUN), Benton was the voice of the west. He anticipated the first HOMESTEAD ACT by proposing annual reductions in the price of public land to 25 cents per acre, until the national domain could be given away free. He was an expansionist who wanted to build national highways and railroads for moving American pioneers west, but opposed taking new territories by war. He became reconciled with Jackson, whom he supported on the Second BANK OF THE UNITED STATES and INDIAN REMOVAL. Benton owned slaves, but his failure to defend slavery vigorously was unpopular in Mo. and he lost his Senate seat in 1851.

Benton, Thomas Hart (b. Neosho, Mo., 15 April 1889; d. Kansas City, Mo., 19 January 1975) He was the most important regional painter of the period after 1920. He chose subjects and themes of the Mississippi valley for his settings, and portrayed them with a bold, sweeping realism. Most of his characters represented the region's working class, such as struggling white farmers, black sharecroppers, or industrial labor. He ranks as the foremost US painter of murals, of which his most powerful group were completed for the Mo. State Capitol (1936).

Benton* v. *Maryland On 23 June 1969, the Supreme Court extended (6–2) the FIFTH AMENDMENT's guarantee against double jeopardy to state courts through the DUE PROCESS clause of the FOURTEENTH AMENDMENT; it reversed *Palko* v. *Connecticut* (6 December 1937), in which the justices held (8–1) that states might try persons twice.

Bentsen, Lloyd Millard (b. Mission, Tex., 11 February 1921) Son of a wealthy Tex. rancher, Bentsen was a Democratic congressman (1949–54), senator (1971–92), and chair of the Senate Finance Committee. He was running mate of Michael DUKAKIS in 1988 and treasury secretary under William CLINTON.

Berger, Victor Louis (b. Nieder-Rehbach, Austria, 28 February 1860; d. Milwaukee, Wis., 7 August 1929) In 1878 Berger emigrated to the US and came to Milwaukee, where he became a journalist. He helped found the SOCIALIST PARTY OF AMERICA in 1901, and in 1911 became the first Socialist congressman. After being convicted under the ESPIONAGE ACT, he was twice denied a seat in Congress, but later served six years after the Supreme Court reversed his conviction.

Berkeley, John Lord *see* WEST JERSEY *and* PROPRIETORS OF WEST JERSEY

Berkeley free-speech movement After police arrested a student for defying a Berkeley University ban on recruitment for political causes on 1 October 1964, Mario Savio formed the free-speech movement. By protest rallies, demonstrations, a boycott of classes, and a sit-in occupying the main administration building that led to 800 arrests, Savio's movement forced the university to permit unrestricted political activity on campus in early 1965. The movement was the first large-scale episode of college activism in the 1960s. Because it was widely publicized, it served as both inspiration and a primer on campus rebellion for radical students; its tactics were widely imitated, especially by the VIETNAM ANTIWAR MOVEMENT.

Berle, Adolph Augustus (b. Boston, Mass., 29 January 1895; d. New York, N.Y., 17 February 1971) He was an original member of the BRAINS TRUST. He influenced the FIRST NEW DEAL by arguing that antitrust laws were an outdated approach to preventing abuses of corporate power and that federal programs were needed to institute a managed national economy. Berle resisted joining Roosevelt in Washington, except for a short stint at the RECONSTRUCTION FINANCE CORPORATION, but remained influential through his writings and finally served as assistant secretary of state (1938–44). In 1961 he chaired the commission that proposed the ALLIANCE FOR PROGRESS.

Berlin, Irving (b. Temun, Russia, 11 May 1888; d. New York, N.Y., 22 September 1989) Born Isidore Baline, Berlin emigrated to New York in 1893. His first commercially successful song, "Dorando" (1909), was followed in 1911 by his first major hit, "Alexander's Ragtime Band." Despite his lack of any musical training, he became the most successful US songwriter, and composed the best-selling song ever written, "White Christmas."

Berlin, treaty of After rejecting the treaty of VERSAILLES, Congress passed a joint resolution on 2 July 1921 ending the state of hostilities with Germany. On 25 August 1921, the US and Germany signed a treaty that formally reestablished peace and agreed that German property confiscated by the US would count toward reducing Germany's reparations debt. The Senate ratified it on 18 October.

Berlin airlift On 24 June 1949, as tensions grew over the imminent establishment of a constitutional government in West Germany, the Soviet Union closed its German occupation zone to US, British, and French ground travel. The western allies refused to abandon West Berlin to the Soviets and initiated an airlift to supply their sectors' 2,100,000 residents with food, fuel, and other essential materials. At its height in September 1949, it was transporting 4,000 tons of cargo daily, and had created a 300-day reserve of food. After 321 days, the Soviets ended the blockade and allowed land transport to West Berlin on 5 May 1949.

Berlin conference of 1889 *see* SAMOA

Berlin Wall crisis At midnight, 12–13 August 1961, the Soviet Union staged an international crisis by refusing US troops access to East Berlin and beginning the construction of a fortified wall to prevent East Germans from defecting to the West. The West's inability to enforce its rights of free access in Berlin encouraged the USSR to send nuclear weapons systems to Cuba in the CUBAN MISSILE CRISIS. Berliners destroyed the wall on 9 November 1989.

Bernstein, Leonard (b. Lawrence, Mass., 25 August 1918; d. New York, N.Y., 14 October 1990) A graduate of Harvard (1939) and the Curtis Institute of Music (1941), Bernstein catapulted to fame in 1943 after conducting the New York Philharmonic as a short-notice replacement for Bruno Walter. After assuming the Philharmonic's music directorship in 1958, he became the first native American to be recognized internationally as a conductor of the first rank. He was also a significant composer, whose works included *Symphony No. 1 "Jeremiah"* (1942), *Symphony No. 2 "The Age of Anxiety"* (1949), *Clarinet Sonata* (1942), and scores for the Broadway musicals *On the Town* (1944), *Candide* (1956), and *West Side Story* (1957).

Bessemer process *see* KELLY, WILLIAM

Bethune, Mary McLeod (b. Mayesville, S.C., 10 July 1875; d. Daytona Beach, Fla., 18 May 1955) She graduated from Scotia College and Moody Bible Institute. In 1904 she founded a female teaching academy at Daytona Beach, Fla., that became Bethune-Cookman College in 1923. She was college president until 1947, besides heading the National Association of Colored Women's Clubs (1924–8), the National Association of Colored Women (1926), and the National

Council of Negro Women (1935–49). In 1935 she became the first black woman to supervise a federal agency, the NATIONAL YOUTH ADMINISTRATION's Division of Negro Affairs. She was a confidante of Eleanor ROOSEVELT and one of the BLACK CABINET.

Betts* v. *Brady *see GIDEON* v. *WAINWRIGHT*

BIA Bureau of Indian Affairs *see* INDIAN AFFAIRS, BUREAU OF

bicameral legislatures Like the HOUSE OF BURGESSES and Mass. GENERAL COURT, most of the THIRTEEN COLONIES' assemblies began as unicameral bodies and did not divide into two houses until a decade or more had passed. All colonies but Pa. had bicameral assemblies. Every state established a bicameral legislature but Nebr.

Biddle, Nicholas (b. Philadelphia, Pa., 8 January 1766; d. near Philadelphia, Pa., 27 February 1844) He was a publisher, diplomat, Pa. legislator, congressman, and a federal director of the second BANK OF THE UNITED STATES, before becoming bank president (1823–36). In the struggle over renewing the bank's charter, Biddle tried compromising with Andrew JACKSON and appointed some of the president's supporters to head the bank's branches, but to no avail. When Biddle sought renewal of the bank's charter before the 1832 election, Democrats demonized him as a symbol of monopoly, special privilege, and corrupt influence during the campaign, which demonstrated widespread antipathy toward the bank and doomed its chances for a new US charter. Biddle operated the bank under a Pa. charter from 1836 to 1841.

Big Four This term applied to the four leading Allied statesmen who conducted negotiations for the treaty of VERSAILLES: Georges Clemenceau (France), David Lloyd George (Britain), Vittorio Orlando (Italy), and Woodrow WILSON (US).

big stick diplomacy During Theodore ROOSEVELT's administration, the US adopted a greater willingness to threaten (and in extreme cases employ) armed force to win foreign policy goals, such as in the ROOSEVELT COROLLARY. The policy's title came from an African saying paraphrased by Roosevelt in 1900: "Speak softly and carry a big stick, you will go far."

Big Three This term referred to the principal Allied leaders in WORLD WAR II: Franklin D. ROOSEVELT, Winston Churchill, and Joseph Stalin. Not included in summits to coordinate overall strategy against the AXIS were Charles De Gaulle and Chiang Kai-shek.

bill of attainder The CONSTITUTION (Article I, Section 9) forbids Congress from enacting bills of attainder (laws declaring persons guilty of treason or other offenses and imposing punishment without any trial or conviction). The Supreme Court ruled on this issue in *GARNER* v. *BOARD OF PUBLIC WORKS*.

Bill of Rights In the Revolutionary era, a bill of rights was any statement of principles, appended to a constitution, which set apart fundamental liberties that could never be violated by law or executive action. Influenced by the British Parliament's Bill of Rights (1689), George MASON authored America's first such document, Virginia's Declaration of Rights, adopted with that state's constitution on 12 June 1776. By 1784, seven states had attached similar documents to their constitutions, and the rest had written guarantees of basic freedoms into the text of their constitutions.

Representative James MADISON narrowed 210 constitutional amendments suggested by the states to twelve, which Congress submitted to the legislatures on 25 September 1789. Ten were ratified by 15 December 1791 and became known as the federal Bill of Rights. *BARRON* v. *BALTIMORE* exempted state courts from the US Bill of Rights' provisions. *Barron* was first selectively overturned by *CHICAGO, BURLINGTON AND QUINCY RAILROAD* v. *CHICAGO*. The Court later made all the Bill of Rights obligatory upon state judges in a series of separate rulings following *GITLOW* v. *NEW YORK*, most of which were issued under Earl WARREN's chief justiceship. PUBLIC LAW 284 extended the Bill of Rights to RESERVATION courts. (*See* FIRST *through* TENTH AMENDMENTS)

Billings, William (b. Boston, Mass., 7 October 1746; d. Boston, Mass., 26 September 1800) He was the first important American composer. A tanner who taught himself the essentials of music, Billings was just 24 when he published his first collection of hymns,

The New-England Psalm-Singer (1770). He later published *The Singing Master's Assistant* (1778), *Music in Miniature* (1779), and *The Psalm-Singer's Amusement* (1781). Of 264 religious songs known to be written in New England by 1782, Billings authored 226. His hymns became a key component in the American folk tradition of shape-note singing that flowered after his death. As New England's foremost choir director, Billings led the way in setting polished standards for choral performances, especially by the introduction of synchronized gospel singing.

bimetallism *see* SILVER COINAGE CONTROVERSY *and* GOLD STANDARD

Birmingham desegregation violence (Ala.) In the spring of 1963, the SOUTHERN CHRISTIAN LEADERSHIP CONFERENCE (SCLC) launched a major desegregation and anti-discrimination drive, which encountered the most prolonged and intense violence directed at the CIVIL RIGHTS MOVEMENT, and was prominently reported by the news media. SCLC protesters earned widespread sympathy nationwide for their forbearance under police intimidation, water cannons, and attack dogs directed by Police Chief Eugene "Bull" Connor, who became a symbol of racial bigotry at its ugliest. Connor made about 3,000 arrests, including Martin Luther KING, but only produced a backlash of sympathy for the demonstrators after King published his "Letter from a Birmingham Jail" of 23 April 1963. After bombs exploded on 11 May at an SCLC meeting hall and at Rev. King's brother's home, several thousand blacks rioted. On 15 September a bomb killed four black Sunday school students and injured 14 persons at a church. The city then agreed to desegregate public facilities, hire more blacks, and create a fair employment committee.

Birney, James Gillespie (b. Danville, Ky., 4 February 1792; d. Eagleswood, N.J., 25 November 1857) He was a slaveowning planter and lawyer, who moved from Ky. to Ala. in 1818. He sat in each state's legislature. He joined the AMERICAN COLONIZATION SOCIETY and AMERICAN ANTISLAVERY SOCIETY, freed his own slaves in 1834, and resettled in 1836 at New Richmond, Ohio, to edit a paper espousing ABOLITIONISM by gradual means. As presidential candidate for the LIBERTY PARTY, he won 7,059 votes in 1840 and 62,300 votes (2.3 percent) in 1844. He left public life after being crippled by a fall from a horse in 1845.

birth control *see* SANGER, MARGARET

Bismarck Sea, battle of On 2–3 March 1943 US and Australian aircraft sank five destroyers and 12 transports bound for NEW GUINEA with Japan's 51st Division, which lost 3,500 men. The Allies owed success to the substitution of low-level flight tactics in place of inaccurate high-altitude bombing.

Bituminous Coal Stabilization Act *see* GUFFEY–SNYDER . . . ACT

bituminous coal strike of 1943 *see* COAL STRIKE OF 1943

bituminous coal strike of 1946 *see* COAL STRIKE OF 1946

Black, Hugo La Fayette (b. Harlan, Ala., 27 February 1886; d. Washington, D.C., 25 September 1971) After graduating from the University of Alabama law school in 1906, Black entered politics; he was elected Ala. senator in 1927, and co-sponsored the BLACK–CONNERY BILL. To reward his loyalty to NEW DEAL measures, he was appointed to the Supreme Court in 1937. Although later criticized for having belonged to the KU KLUX KLAN (1923–5), he was a progressive justice and voted for *BROWN V. BOARD OF EDUCATION OF TOPEKA* (1954) and civil-rights cases. He was the leading justice to argue that the FOURTEENTH AMENDMENT made the entire BILL OF RIGHTS obligatory upon state courts, and by 1969 the Court had esssentially vindicated his position. He was famous for always having a copy of the Constitution in his pocket available for reference.

Black Belt This term refers to a crescent-shaped area of 6,250 square miles in southern Ala. and northeastern Miss. drained by the Alabama, Tombigbee, and Black Warrior rivers. The region's name came from the deep, black soils that yielded bumper crops, rather than from the fact that its population was predominantly slave. Its rich earth, level terrain, and relatively unforested condition attracted rapid settlement after 1820. The area became the antebellum South's most concentrated center of cotton production and slave ownership.

black cabinet This term refers to a group of black public figures, both in and outside the federal government, who advised Franklin D. and Eleanor ROOSEVELT on issues concerning minority problems during the NEW DEAL. The black cabinet's main accomplishment was to press the administration into ordering federal agencies and defense contractors to eliminate job discrimination; its most prominent members were Mary McLeod BETHUNE and Robert WEAVER.

black codes These were state laws passed by former Confederate states in 1865–6 to control the behavior of ex-slaves. Most codes restricted the ability of freedmen to travel at large, bargain for wages, and own firearms for self-defense. The codes outraged northerners, who viewed them as attempts to reinstate the conditions of SLAVERY, and they influenced Congress to adopt a radical program for RECONSTRUCTION, especially passage of the CIVIL RIGHTS ACT (1866) and the FOURTEENTH AMENDMENT. The US Army nullified them before they could take effect.

Black–Connery Bill In December 1932, Senator Hugo BLACK (Democrat, Ala.) introduced a bill to reduce unemployment in the GREAT DEPRESSION by setting a 30-hour maximum workweek and outlawing interstate shipment of goods made by factories with longer hours. The AFL strongly backed the bill, which passed the Senate on 6 April 1933. As representative William Connery (Democrat, Mass.) began hearings on his version of the bill in the House Labor Committee, Franklin D. ROOSEVELT mobilized his BRAINS TRUST to formulate an alternative, which emerged as the NATIONAL INDUSTRIAL RECOVERY ACT (NIRA). The administration blocked the Black-Connery Bill by substituting the NIRA.

black disfranchisement *see* DISFRANCHISEMENT, BLACK

Black Friday In June 1869, New York financiers Jay Gould and James Fisk devised a scheme to drive up the price of gold by convincing speculators that the US Treasury was withholding gold from sale. Ulysses S. GRANT, although unaware of these intentions, badly compromised himself by meeting with the conspirators, who were partners with his brother-in-law. By manipulating gold from $132 to $163 per ounce within three months, Gould and Fisk aroused the suspicion of Grant, who ordered large sales of US gold on 24 September 1869 ("Black Friday"). The price of gold immediately plummeted, bankrupted many brokers, and caused a minor panic, although Gould had prior warning and saved himself by selling out (without warning his partner Fisk). The episode, along with several other scandals, tainted Grant's administration with the stigma of corruption.

Black Hawk War Large numbers of SAUK and FOX INDIANS repudiated an 1804 treaty ceding their lands east of the Mississippi to the US and continued living in northeastern Ill. and southeastern Wis. In 1831 Sauk leader Black Hawk tried to unite local Indians to fight further white settlement, but fled to Iowa with 1,000 followers when US troops arrived. When Black Hawk's band returned to Ill. after a hungry winter on 5 April 1832 to plant crops, panic convulsed Ill. The 1,000 Sauk soon faced 7,790 Ill. militia and 1,500 US regulars, plus perhaps 2,700 Mich. militia and hostile DAKOTA INDIANS under General Henry Atkinson. Atkinson's force chased the Sauk for fifteen weeks; they finally killed perhaps a third of Black Hawk's people at Bad Axe River on 2 August, after which Dakota warriors ran down the survivors and took 68 more scalps at the Red Cedar River. US losses: 72 troops and civilians killed. Sauk losses: 442–592 killed, 200 captured (including Black Hawk). To make peace, Black Hawk's Sauk gave up their lands fifty miles west of the Mississippi for $40,000 and a $20,000 annuity paid over thirty years.

Black Monday (1929) After two days of heavy-volume trading begun on BLACK THURSDAY, the New York Stock Exchange sustained heavy losses on 28 October 1929, when the Dow Jones Industrial Average fell 12.8 percent. It was followed by the unrestrained panic of BLACK TUESDAY.

Black Monday (1935) On 27 May 1935, the Supreme Court struck down the NATIONAL INDUSTRIAL RECOVERY ACT and the FRAZIER–LEMKE FARM BANKRUPTCY ACT. Coupled with the invalidation of the RAILROAD RETIREMENT ACT (1934) on 6 May, the Court's verdicts invalidated critical NEW DEAL measures, and questioned whether the Roosevelt administration's program to end the depression was constitutional.

Black Monday (1987) After experiencing its first daily decline exceeding a hundred points (down 108.36 to 2304.34) the previous Friday, on Monday 19 October 1987, the Dow Jones Industrial Average sustained its greatest one-day loss in New York Stock Exchange history by falling 508 points (22.6 percent). The plunge resulted from waves of computer-generated sell orders triggered by a price imbalance between New York stocks and options on the Chicago Board of Options Exchange. Stocks rebounded 102 points on 20 October, a record one-day rise, and regained most of their losses within six months. Black Monday led the SECURITIES AND EXCHANGE COMMISSION to impose regulations to limit market volatility by halting the execution of orders when the Dow Jones Industrial Index rose or fell by over 50 points in a day.

Black Muslims This is the popular term by which the World Community of Islam in the West (The Lost-found Nation of Islam, prior to a name change in 1976) is known. The church began at Detroit in 1930 under self-proclaimed prophet Wallace D. Fard. Fard had won 8,000 converts by June 1934, when he disappeared and was succeeded by Elijah (Poole) Muhammad. Muhammad mixed the church's message of African pride with hostility toward whites and advocated separatism rather than integration.

During Muhammad's imprisonment for encouraging draft resistance in World War II, membership dropped to about 1,000, but later rose sharply under charismatic leaders like Malcolm X, and reached 100,000 by 1960. Upon Elijah Muhammad's death in 1975, his son Warith Deen Muhammad ended many practices contrary to traditional Islamic theology and made the sect conform to Sunni orthodoxy; he also called on Muslims to demonstrate a sense of US patriotism. These changes led to a schism that formed the NATION OF ISLAM.

Black Panther party A radical wing of the BLACK POWER MOVEMENT, it was organized in October 1966 at Oakland, Calif., by Bobby SEALE and Huey NEWTON. The Panthers defined their mission as protecting the black community by monitoring – with guns and cameras – the police, whom they viewed as the main instrument of white oppression. They also established neighborhood centers and gave out charitable relief. By brandishing guns, demanding financial reparations from whites, and running Eldridge CLEAVER, a former convict, for president in 1968, they played a major role in provoking a white backlash against the CIVIL RIGHTS MOVEMENT. The Panthers' violent rhetoric attracted heavy police surveillance, which resulted in so many violent clashes that they reported 28 members dead in shootouts during 1968–9. Although high-profile indictments kept public attention focused on the party – including an alleged conspiracy to bomb New York City police stations and murder charges against Seale and Newton – Panthers had great success in winning acquittals or having their convictions overturned on appeal. The party endorsed Shirley CHISHOLM for president in 1972. It disintegrated due to quarrels among its leaders and disenchantment with radicalism among blacks. By the late 1970s, Newton, Seale, and Cleaver had all renounced violence.

black power movement In the summer of 1966, Stokely CARMICHAEL advocated that the CIVIL RIGHTS MOVEMENT redefine itself by the concept "black power," by which he meant that blacks should create their own base of political, economic, and social power independent of – and separate from – whites. Black power advocates argued that white involvement in the civil rights struggle constituted racial domination under another guise and had to be eliminated before true black liberation could be attained. They denied that blacks could be fully autonomous in an integrated society, and contended that only by separatism could blacks protect their own culture and fend off white attempts to manipulate them. The emphasis upon black autonomy was accompanied by militant, even violent, rhetoric that helped trigger a backlash against the civil rights movement among whites. The STUDENT NONVIOLENT COORDINATING COMMITTEE, the CONGRESS OF RACIAL EQUALITY, and the BLACK PANTHER PARTY were most closely identified with black power, while it was opposed by mainstream civil rights leaders like Roy

WILKINS, Whitney Young (*see* URBAN LEAGUE, NATIONAL), and Martin Luther KING. Black power rapidly fell out of favor after 1970.

black Republicans Southern Democrats used this phrase as an insult when referring to white Republicans who won elections through the votes of FREEDMEN during RECONSTRUCTION.

Black Thursday On 24 October 1929, trading on the stock market rose to a record 12,894,650 shares. Only aggressive buying by a consortium led by J. P. Morgan & Co. enabled the market to stabilize. Although the New York *Times* stock index closed just 3.1 percent lower, the unprecedented volume was an indication of the stock market's underlying instability that would trigger heavy losses on BLACK MONDAY (1929) and BLACK TUESDAY.

Black Tuesday Following several days of exceptionally heavy trading volume from BLACK THURSDAY to BLACK MONDAY (1929), panic selling swept the stock market on 29 October 1929. A record 16,000,000 shares were traded and the Dow Jones Industrial Average fell 11.7 percent. The day marked the true beginning of the CRASH OF 1929. Within two weeks, the value of listed stocks had fallen by about $30 billion, and before the slide stopped in July 1932, over $75 billion of capital would be wiped out. The crash inaugurated the GREAT DEPRESSION.

Blackfoot Indians Speakers of one of the ALGONQUIAN LANGUAGES, the Blackfeet included the Bloods, Piegans, and Northern (Canadian) Blackfeet. About 1780, they numbered perhaps 15,000 and inhabited northeastern Mont. and Saskatchewan. Various epidemics reduced their numbers to about 9,000 in 1837, when 6,000 of these perished in a smallpox outbreak. Although involved in many small hostilities with Mountain Men and miners, they never fought a full-scale war with the US Army. In 1877 most of them permanently moved to Canada. About 2,000 US Blackfeet settled on a reservation headquartered at Browning, Mont. In 1984 its population was 7,193 Blackfeet.

Bladensburg, battle of (Md.) On 24 August 1814, Major General Robert Ross's 4,500 British troops routed Brigadier General William Winder's 6,000 US militia. US losses: 71 killed, 100 captured. British losses: 64 killed, 185 wounded. Ross's victory allowed him to capture Washington, D.C. (*see* DISTRICT OF COLUMBIA), without opposition that day.

Blaine, James Gillespie (b. West Brownsville, Pa., 30 January 1830; d. Washington, D.C., 27 January 1893) He sat for Maine in Congress (1862–76, speaker of the House, 1869–76), was senator (1877–81), and was secretary of state (1881). As leader of the HALF-BREEDS, he unsuccessfully sought the Republican presidential nomination in 1876 and 1880. Burdened by corruption charges dating from the MULLIGAN LETTERS, and lampooned in rhyme as “Blaine, Blaine, James G. Blaine – The Continental liar from the state of Maine,” he became one of only two Republicans from 1860 to 1908 defeated as president, when he lost in 1884 because Grover CLEVELAND carried N.Y. by 600 votes. While secretary of state (1889–92), he pursued policies intended to open commercial markets for US business in Latin America, such as convening the first Pan-American Conference (*see* PAN-AMERICAN UNION) on 2 October 1889.

Bland–Allison Act (28 February 1878) Acting to reverse the CRIME OF ’73, Congress reestablished silver coins as part of the US currency (at a ratio to gold of 16 to 1). Representative Richard P. Bland (Democrat, Mo.) had demanded that the Treasury mint silver in unlimited quantities, but an amendment by Senator William B. Allison (Republican, Iowa) prescribed that the Treasury have discretion to purchase no less than $2,000,000 and no more than $4,000,000 per month. The act did not inflate the money supply to the degree intended because the Treasury kept silver purchases at the legal minimum. Congress next tried to expand silver coinage by the SHERMAN SILVER PURCHASE ACT.

Bleeding Kansas This expression referred to the struggle between free-soil and proslavery settlers to control that territory after the KANSAS–NEBRASKA ACT's passage in 1854. Major violence first occurred on 22 May 1856, when BORDER RUFFIANS looted Lawrence and wounded a citizen. On 24–5 May, abolitionists under John BROWN murdered five unarmed men at Pottawatomie. Before US troops restored order in late 1856, about 200 men had been killed and $2,000,000 in property destroyed. Bloodletting subsided after 1856, but revived on a smaller scale in 1858 with the MARAIS DES CYGNES MASSACRE. Conflict gradually ended in 1859.

block grants Block grants are disbursements of US funds in lump sums to state governments, which then have wide discretion on how to use this money. Lyndon JOHNSON issued the first two block grants at the urging of governors, who sought less federal control over their expenditures, and Richard NIXON's administration added three more. Because combining federal programs into block grants made it easier to slow US budgetary growth, Ronald REAGAN's administration folded 77 programs into 9 block grants. In 1993, the federal budget included 15 block grants valued at about $20 billion, or about a tenth of all US money distributed to the states. After the 1994 mid-term elections, a major Republican party goal was to restrain the US budget's rate of increase by collapsing hundreds of Federal programs into a handful of block grants.

Blood Indians *see* BLACKFOOT INDIANS

bloody shirt The expression "waving the bloody shirt" described Republican demagoguery against Democrats that pandered to anti-Confederate hatreds after the CIVIL WAR. Its name came from an episode when General Benjamin BUTLER exhibited before Congress the blood-stained shirt of a Republican killed by the KU KLUX KLAN.

Bloody Swamp, battle of (Ga.) On 5 July 1742 Fla. Governor Manuel de Montiano landed 1,800 Spanish troops on St Simon's Island, Ga., where Governor James OGLETHORPE commanded 900 Ga. militia and Scottish Highlanders. After minor skirmishing, Oglethorpe's troops routed 500 Spaniards marching to assault Fort Fredericka. Spanish losses: 19 killed, 21 wounded, and 12 captured. British losses: negligible. Demoralized by defeat and worried that British reinforcements would arrive, Montiano retreated to Fla. on 14 July. This campaign marked the last Spanish invasion of British colonies.

blue eagle This was the symbol of the NATIONAL RECOVERY ADMINISTRATION and was displayed by all firms that had adopted its industry-wide codes. Member businesses were obliged to limit their dealings to firms displaying the symbol.

Board of Education of Oklahoma City* v. *Dowell On 15 January 1991, the Supreme Court ruled (5–4) that court-imposed orders to desegregate schools by busing could end once a school district had taken all feasible steps to integrate the schools, if failure to achieve full integration did not stem from any deliberate efforts to frustrate desegregation.

Board of Trade In 1660 CHARLES II appointed a Council of Trade (7 November) and a Council for Foreign Plantations (1 December) to advise his PRIVY COUNCIL on overseas affairs. After the councils became defunct in 1665, they were succeeded by several temporary committees until 1675, when the Committee on Trade and Plantations (known as the Lords of Trade) was formed as a component of the Privy Council. Under William Blathwayt, the Lords became the first effective agency for gathering information on American affairs and enforcing English policies overseas, but then lost much of their authority and effectiveness to ad hoc committees added to the Privy Council under JAMES II and WILLIAM III.

On 15 May 1696, the Lords were replaced by a new institution, the Lords Commissioners of Trade and Plantations, known as the Board of Trade. The board was charged with monitoring trade and the fisheries, nominating appointees for governor and other high offices, advising the Privy Council on American events, and making recommendations on which acts passed by provincial legislatures should receive royal assent. The board pursued its work vigorously at first, but steadily declined under the Hanoverian dynasty and lost control of colonial patronage to the secretary of state for the Southern Department in the 1720s. The board sank into a long period of lethargy – benign neglect – after 1720, except for a brief resurgence of activity and influence under the Earl of Halifax after 1748. Of 8,563 colonial laws reviewed, it allowed all but 469 (5 percent) to receive the royal signature.

boat people Perhaps 1,500,000 refugees from communism left Vietnam and Laos after

1975; they became known as boat people, because most fled across the South China Sea to foreign countries. The US began allowing large numbers of boat people to immigrate in 1978; from then through mid-1984, it admitted 443,000 Vietnamese, 137,000 Laotians, and 98,000 Cambodians. The influx of Indochinese refugees slowed to about 30,000 yearly in the late 1980s. The 1990 census counted 535,825 Vietnamese, 231,753 Laotians, and 137,934 Cambodians, including US-born children of immigrants.

Boland amendments To end US intervention in NICARAGUA, Representative Edward Boland (Democrat, Mo.) amended the Defense Appropriations Act (21 December 1982) to forbid the CIA or Defense Department from using any funds "for the purpose of overthrowing the Government of Nicaragua or provoking a military exchange between Nicaragua and Honduras." (The amendment allowed the US to provide nonmilitary aid for the anti-Communist, Contra guerrillas, who were reported to have committed human-rights abuses; it was only in effect for a year.)

After it was revealed that the CIA had mined harbors in Nicaragua in January 1984, Boland amended the Defense Appropriations Act (12 October 1984) to forbid any direct or indirect financial aid to the Contras by the CIA, Defense Department, or any agency involved in "intelligence activities" through 19 December 1985. The IRAN-CONTRA SCANDAL arose from attempts by NATIONAL SECURITY COUNCIL officials to circumvent these measures by funneling arms to the Contras.

boll weevils This sobriquet referred to supporters of Ronald REAGAN's fiscal and economic policies in Congress who were conservative southern Democrats, especially a bloc of two dozen in the House led by Charles Stenholm of Tex. Their votes were critical in halting the rise in federal domestic spending, enacting tax cuts, and undertaking a sharp military build-up.

bonus army During May–June 1932, a "bonus army" of 17,000 unemployed veterans built a shanty-town at Washington, D.C. and lobbied for immediate payment of BONUS BILL benefits. The Senate killed such legislation on 17 June and voted money to send the army home. When police tried to evict 2,000 veterans who refused to disband and continued pressing their demands, a riot ensued that left two police and two bonus marchers dead. On 29 July General Douglas MACARTHUR removed the bonus army violently with truncheons, tear gas, and tanks. The episode reinforced the common view that Herbert HOOVER lacked compassion for the victims of the GREAT DEPRESSION.

Bonus Bill (1817) On 4 February 1817, John CALHOUN introduced a bill to create a permanent federal fund for INTERNAL IMPROVEMENTS with the $1,500,000 bonus paid by the second BANK OF THE UNITED STATES and all future dividends earned on the government's share of bank stock. Arguing from a position of LOOSE CONSTRUCTIONISM, Calhoun argued that the Constitution authorized Congress to finance transportation systems under its power to build post roads and promote the general welfare. James MADISON vetoed the measure on grounds of STRICT CONSTRUCTIONISM, arguing that the Constitution did not authorize subsidies for internal improvements (as opposed to reserving proceeds from sales of the PUBLIC DOMAIN to finance transportation improvements, as in the NATIONAL ROAD). The MAYSVILLE ROAD VETO upheld Madison's general position.

Bonus Bill (1924) On 15 May 1924, Congress passed the Adjusted Compensation Act, which created an endowed account for each WORLD WAR I veteran calculated at $1.00 for each day of honorable service ($1.25 for each day overseas). In 1945 veterans would receive triple the base amount in cash, and until then they could borrow as much as 25 percent of its worth. On 27 February 1931, Congress raised the borrowing limit to 50 percent, because of the GREAT DEPRESSION. Demands for immediate payment of the $2.4 billion accrued in the accounts led to the BONUS ARMY. Congress passed a bonus bill distributing $2.2 billion to three million veterans in 1935, but Franklin D. ROOSEVELT vetoed it on 22 May. Congress enacted a bonus bill to issue $1.5 billion of interest-bearing, nine-year bonds to veterans, by overriding a presidential veto of 24 January 1936.

Boone, Daniel (b. near Reading, Pa., 2 November 1734; d. near St Charles, Mo., 26

September 1820) In 1751 Boone settled in the N.C. backcountry. While a teamster en route to BRADDOCK'S DEFEAT, he first learned of KENTUCKY. As a LONG HUNTER, he explored Ky. (May 1769–March 1771), and became the foremost authority on its resources. He abandoned an attempt to settle Ky. in 1773 when Indians scalped one of his sons. (Boone later lost another son, a brother, and two brothers-in-law during the Indian wars, in which he was wounded twice and captured twice.) He helped the TRANSYLVANIA COLONY buy Ky. at the treaty of SYCAMORE SHOALS, blazed the WILDERNESS ROAD and founded Boonesborough, which he held with just 60 men against a siege by 400 Indians and Canadian militia in September 1778. He achieved renown as a militia colonel and legislator, but was nearly ruined by land speculation, in which he lost 12,000 acres. Disgusted by the legal chaos surrounding land titles in Ky., he moved to Mo. in 1799.

Booth, John Wilkes (b. near Bel Air, Md., 10 May 1838; d. near Bowling Green, Va., 26 April 1865) A Shakespearean actor, Booth served in the Va. militia unit that captured John BROWN at Harper's Ferry. In late 1864, he began conspiring with eight others to abduct Abraham LINCOLN, but when the war ended he decided to assassinate the president, Andrew JOHNSON, Ulysses S. GRANT, and William SEWARD. On 14 April, Booth shot Lincoln as he watched *Our American Cousin* at Ford's Theater shortly after 10 p.m., and co-conspirator Lewis Paine stabbed Seward. Booth was hunted down and shot on 26 April.

Borah, William Edgar (b. Jasper Township, Ill., 29 June 1865; d. Washington, D.C., 19 January 1940) In 1890 Borah opened a law office at Boise, Idaho, and entered Republican politics. As a senator (1906–40), he sponsored the SIXTEENTH and SEVENTEENTH AMENDMENTS and the bill creating the Department of LABOR. He fought the LEAGUE OF NATIONS, WOMEN'S SUFFRAGE, the HAWLEY–SMOOT TARIFF, and the COURT-PACKING BILL. He was a leading isolationist and opposed US efforts to support Britain's stand against Nazi aggression.

border ruffians Proslavery Missourians who terrorized free-soil settlers during BLEEDING KANSAS were given this name. So many border ruffians voted illegally in the March 1855 election that a pro-slavery majority was elected to the territorial legislature.

border states During the CIVIL WAR, the four slave states remaining in the Union – Del., Md., Ky., Mo. – were called by this term. W.Va. and Okla. are often considered border states because their popular culture and political sentiments have southern roots.

Bork, Robert H. (b. Pittsburgh, Pa., 1 March 1927) He served as US solicitor general (1973–7). As acting attorney general, he fired Archibald Cox in the SATURDAY NIGHT MASSACRE. He was appointed federal appeals court judge for the District of Columbia in 1982. On 23 October 1987, he became the first Supreme Court nominee rejected, for having criticized ABORTION as a constitutional right.

Boston, siege of Following the battles of LEXINGTON and CONCORD, New England militia besieged Boston. By June, 15,000 Yankees under General Artemus Ward encircled the city, held by 6,500 redcoats under General Thomas Gage. Defeat at BUNKER HILL left the British too weak to break the siege. George WASHINGTON assumed the American command on 2 July. On 25 January 1777, Colonel Henry KNOX arrived from FORT TICONDEROGA with 52 cannon and nine mortars, which were mounted on Dorchester Heights and made Gage's position untenable. Gage evacuated the city on 17 March. The Yankees lost about 20 killed in the siege. With Boston's capture, the focus of the war shifted to New York, never again to return to New England.

Boston massacre On 5 March 1770, at 9:00 p.m., a crowd began harassing a British soldier on guard at the customs service's headquarters. After a captain and seven redcoats arrived, the soldiers became targets for snowballs, and then chunks of ice and staves. After one redcoat was knocked down by a block of ice, he fired his musket without orders and the other soldiers discharged theirs. The volley killed five and wounded six townspeople. The "massacre" revived opposition to British policies and led to the removal of British troops from Boston. On 30 October, John ADAMS convinced a Boston jury to acquit the soldiers of murder charges.

Boston police strike This strike was the first major labor dispute in a US city. On 9 September 1919, the police walked out over several grievances, including their demand to form a union under the AFL. After Governor Calvin COOLIDGE sent the National Guard to keep order and applauded the police commissioner's insistence that none of the strikers be rehired, the strike failed. The strike contributed to labor's poor public image in the 1920s, and induced Warren HARDING to pick Coolidge as his running mate in 1920.

Boston Port Bill (31 March 1774) Reacting.to the BOSTON TEA PARTY, Parliament gave the Boston town meeting until 1 June 1774 to make satisfaction for the Boston Tea Party by voting to reimburse the East India Company £9,000 for damages suffered. If restitution was not voted, the port would be closed to all traffic except cargoes of food necessary to prevent starvation. The ministry refused an offer by British merchants to post bond for the sum required and closed the harbor on 1 June when the town meeting refused to act. This law was one of the INTOLERABLE ACTS.

Boston Tea Party When three ships carrying East India Company tea docked at Boston on 27 November 1773, Samuel ADAMS' town officials tried peacefully to have the cargo sent back to England so that no taxes would be collected under Parliament's TEA ACT, but Governor Thomas HUTCHINSON insisted on enforcing customs rules requiring the tea to be landed and taxed. On the last night before the tea would be unloaded, 80 men disguised as Indians boarded the ships (without violence) and heaved overboard 342 chests valued at £9,000. Parliament responded by passing the INTOLERABLE ACTS.

bourbons During the era of POPULISM, this term referred to the same political leaders formerly called REDEEMERS. Their enemies borrowed the characterization of the Bourbon royalists restored after the French Revolution, whom Napoleon III had described as having forgotten nothing and learned nothing. Bourbons attracted widespread criticism for mobilizing black voters against Populists and other agrarian reformers.

Boxer Rebellion In the spring of 1900, a secret society known as the Boxers began widespread violence against European imperialism in China. In May an international military force of 337 men (including 57 US marines and sailors) arrived to protect 3,500 foreigners and Chinese Christians at Beijing's embassies, which the Boxers began besieging on 31 May. A relief expedition of 19,000 troops (including 2,500 US soldiers and marines under Major General Adna Chaffee) assembled at US bases at Manila and relieved the Beijing embassies on 15 August. US forces suffered 200 casualties. The Boxer Protocol of 7 September 1901 forced the Chinese to pay $333,000,000 for the expedition's expenses, including $24,500,000 to the US. By declining to accept more than $12,000,000 and forgiving the unpaid balance in 1924, the US allowed China to spend $18,000,000 of the indemnity to send its students to US colleges.

Boynton* v. *Virginia In 1960 the Supreme Court expanded the scope of *MORGAN* v. *VIRGINIA* by ruling that a bus terminal doing business as part of an interstate transportation system could not segregate passengers traveling across state lines, even if the terminal's operations primarily involved intrastate commerce.

Bozeman Trail Pioneered by John Bozeman in 1863–5, this route linked Fort Laramie, Wyo., with the Virginia City, Mont., gold fields; it was the scene of the second SIOUX WAR. After 1877 it became an important route for bringing Texan cattle north.

Bracero Program In July 1942 the US and Mexico agreed on conditions for hiring Mexican seasonal laborers (braceros) on US farms in the southwest. The program was extended in 1947 and 1951. Despite provisions for decent wages, working conditions, and living accommodations, the program degenerated into legalized exploitation of cheap foreign labor. When Congress repealed it in December 1964, 4,800,000 Mexicans had entered the US under the program and many had remained as illegal immigrants.

Braddock's Defeat, battle of On 9 July 1755, Captain Daniel de Beaujeu's 108 French regulars, 146 Canadian militia, and 650 Indians routed Major General Edward Braddock's 1,400 British and colonials (600 troops in reserve never engaged the enemy). British losses: 456 regulars killed (including

Braddock) and 421 wounded, 60 colonials killed and 58 wounded, 13 cannon. French losses: 23 killed (including Beaujeu and 15 Indians), 16 wounded. The British retreated to Philadelphia and Indian attacks engulfed the frontier.

Bradford, William (b. Austerfield, Yorkshire, England, 1590; d. Plymouth Colony, 19 May 1657) A SEPARATING PURITAN who moved to Amsterdam in 1609, Bradford was one of the PILGRIMS who founded PLYMOUTH in 1620. The next year he was elected the colony's second governor, and was reelected every year until 1656, except for 1633, 1634, 1636, 1638, and 1644. Bradford bore most of the responsibility for establishing policies that ensured Plymouth's political, economic, and military security. From about 1630 to 1651, he composed a *History of Plimmoth Plantation*, a comprehensive – and often eloquent – account of the colony's development.

Bradley* v. *Fisher In 1872 the Supreme Court propounded (7–2) the doctrine of judicial immunity, which holds that in order to insulate court proceedings from any fear of later retribution, judges must be exempt from prosecution for all actions taken while performing their official duties – even if they misinterpret the law or cause injurious consequences.

Bradstreet, Anne (b. Northamptonshire, England, ca. 1612; d. Boston, Mass., 16 September 1672) In 1630 Bradstreet came to Mass. with her husband Simon. While raising eight children, she composed poems on religious, political, and household topics. Her *The Tenth Muse Lately Sprung Up in America* (London, 1650) was the first book of verse published by an American woman. Published posthumously in London was a second edition, with new works, titled *Several Poems Compiled with Great Variety of Wit and Learning, Full of Delight* (1678).

Brady Bill (24 November 1994) The passage of this law, after a five-year struggle, marked the National Rifle Association's first major failure to prevent gun-control legislation. Congress required anyone buying a handgun to wait five days for police to verify that he/she was not ineligible as a felon, fugitive, substance addict, or illegal alien. It also appropriated $200,000,000 to improve computerization of crime records, required police notification of multiple handgun sales, and made weapons-theft from arms dealers a federal crime.

brains trust This team of advisors was formed by Franklin D. ROOSEVELT in his final year as N.Y. governor, and initially included Raymond MOLEY, Rexford TUGWELL, and Adolph BERLE. They played a major role in his 1932 campaign for president through speech-writing, clarifying policy questions, and preparing legislation to be introduced in the HUNDRED DAYS. Its membership expanded to many others, most notably Donald RICHBERG and Hugh JOHNSON.

Branch* v. *Texas *see FURMAN* v. *GEORGIA*

Brandeis, Louis Dembitz (b. Louisville, Ky., 13 November 1856; d. Washington, D.C., 5 October 1941) At the age of 21, Brandeis received his law degree with the highest academic average ever earned at Harvard law school. Nicknamed the "people's attorney," he was reviled in business circles for defending legislation in the PROGRESSIVE ERA to improve working conditions and break up concentrations of economic power like the MONEY TRUST. He pioneered the use of statistical, economic, and sociological evidence in court with his "Brandeis brief" that won *MULLER* v. *OREGON*. When nominated to the Supreme Court, he met strong resistance from big business for his political views and also found many in the American Bar Association opposing him because of anti-Semitism. His confirmation was delayed five months, but on 1 June 1916 he became the Court's first Jewish justice. Long in the minority in a conservative court, he often joined in dissent with Oliver W. HOLMES and Harlan STONE. He retired at 82 and devoted himself to philanthropic work.

Brandywine Creek, battle of (Pa.) On 11 September 1777, General William HOWE's 12,500 British troops defeated General George WASHINGTON's 11,000 Continentals. US losses: about 300 killed, about 300 wounded, 315 captured, and 11 cannon lost. British losses: 90 killed, 448 wounded, and 6 missing. Howe's victory prompted Congress to evacuate Philadelphia.

Brant, Joseph (b. N.Y., 1742; d. Grand River, Ontario, 24 November 1807) A

MOHAWK INDIAN leader, Brant was brother-in-law to Sir William JOHNSON. He fought with the British in PONTIAC'S WAR. In the REVOLUTIONARY WAR, he was the principal IROQUOIS CONFEDERACY war leader under the British; he led the raid on CHERRY VALLEY, was defeated in SULLIVAN'S CAMPAIGN, and then raided the Ohio valley settlements. He relocated in Canada after N.Y. confiscated his plantation. He established the first Episcopal church in Upper Canada.

Breckinridge, John Cabell (b. Lexington, Ky., 15 January 1821; d. Lexington, Ky., 17 May 1875) After fighting with the Third Kentucky Volunteers in the MEXICAN WAR, Breckinridge sat in Congress and was James BUCHANAN's vice-president. As Democratic nominee for president in 1860, he ran behind Abraham LINCOLN in electoral votes (72), won 11 slave states, and received 18.1 percent of the popular vote. He resigned as US senator from Ky. to become CSA brigadier general in November 1861 (to major general, April 1862), won the battle of New Market, Va., on 15 May 1864, and was made CSA secretary of war in February 1865. After exile in Cuba, Europe, and Canada, he resumed his Ky. law practice.

Breedlove* v. *Suttles On 6 December 1937, the Supreme Court upheld unanimously a Ga. law that disfranchised any adult who did not pay a $1.00 POLL TAX; it held that the tax violated neither the equal protection guaranteed by the FOURTEENTH AMENDMENT nor the FIFTEENTH AMENDMENT's protection of black voters. The Court held poll taxes unconstitutional in *HARPER* v. *VIRGINIA STATE BOARD OF ELECTIONS*.

Breeds Hill, battle of *see* BUNKER HILL

Bretton Woods conference (N.H.) During 1–22 July 1944, the US and 43 other countries met to establish a framework for world trade and economic development that would avoid a repetition of the GREAT DEPRESSION. Its goals were to avoid competitive devaluations among nations, stabilize price levels, and encourage the flow of investment capital needed by international business. Its main feature was a fixed-rate exchange system based on gold to stabilize world currencies and to provide for any revaluations required by balance-of-payments adjustments or changes in national reserves of gold or foreign currencies.

All nations agreed to keep their currencies pegged at certain rates to gold, and the US dollar unofficially replaced the British pound sterling as the world's reserve currency for trade and international credit (at $35 per ounce of gold). The conference founded the International Monetary Fund (capitalized at $8,800,000,000, of which the US donated 25 percent) and International Bank for Reconstruction and Development (capitalized at $9,100,000,000, of which the US donated 35 percent).

The Bretton Woods system was fatally undermined on 15 August 1971, when Richard NIXON suspended the dollar's convertibility into gold to end a run on US gold reserves. At Washington on 17–18 December 1971, international finance ministers created a new system of fixed exchange rates for their currencies and raised the value of gold to $38 per ounce, but the US refused to resume the convertibility of dollars into gold. At Basel, Switzerland, on 12 November 1973, US and European central bank governors terminated the Bretton Woods gold agreement by allowing the US dollar and European currencies to float against one another based on exchange rates set by the market place. The US FEDERAL RESERVE SYSTEM thereafter acted alone to control the dollar's foreign exchange rates. The European monetary system was established on 13 March 1979 to maintain an appropriate relationship between western Europe's major currencies.

Bricker amendment On 7 January 1953, Senator John Bricker (Republican, Ohio) proposed a constitutional amendment that would prevent any treaty from taking effect as US internal law unless authorized by special congressional legislation. (Bricker feared that UN treaties might entail provisions infringing US sovereignty or compromising the free-market economic system.) Dwight D. EISENHOWER's opposition stopped the amendment, which failed (50–42) on 25 February 1954. On 26 February, the Senate considered an alternative offered by Walter George (Democrat, Ga.), which would have invalidated any treaty whose provisions violated the Constitution; it killed George's version by one vote short of the two-thirds majority required (60–31). Defeat of the Bricker amendment left it possible for treaties to take effect even when their terms conflicted with the Constitution, as under *MISSOURI* V. *HOLLAND*.

Bridger, James (b. Richmond, Va., 17 March 1804; d. Kansas City, Mo., 17 July 1881) He grew up near St Louis and was orphaned at 14. He joined William ASHLEY's first fur trapping expedition to the Rockies at 18. He then became a mountain man and in late 1824 was the first Anglo-American to reach the Great Salt Lake. In 1843 he founded Fort Bridger, an important way station on the OREGON TRAIL. After 21 years as a fur trader, he emerged as the foremost expert on the northern Rockies and was eagerly sought as a guide by the army's topographical engineers.

brinkmanship This term refers to the diplomacy during the COLD WAR of John DULLES, who portrayed the US as prepared to go beyond the brink of war and use MASSIVE RETALIATION to contain communism.

Briscoe* v. *Bank of Kentucky In 1837 the Supreme Court (6–1) gave states authority to regulate banks and their paper money by ruling that legislatures could charter banks empowered to issue notes for general circulation, if those notes did not have legal tender status but rather were private obligations voluntarily accepted from a corporation that could sue and be sued in court over contracts concerning the notes' value. It further stipulated that even if all of a bank's stock were owned by the state that issued its charter, it might still issue notes.

British immigration Prior to 1775, the THIRTEEN COLONIES were settled by ENGLISH, SCOTTISH, SCOTCH-IRISH, and WELSH IMMIGRATION, about 337,000 people altogether. By 1820 their descendants numbered about 6,250,000, or about 80 percent of all whites. From 1820 to 1991, 5,135,918 immigrants arrived from Great Britain and Northern Ireland – plus 784,796 British Canadians – a number exceeded only by arrivals from Germany. The 1990 census counted 31,421,362 persons who described their primary ethnic identity as British (16 percent of all whites), but this figure failed to take into account that the great majority of the 18 percent of whites who failed to identify their European origins were "old stock" Anglo-Saxons who had long lost any sense of kinship with Europe. The British stock probably included 25–34 percent of whites, and was the largest US ethnic group.

broad constructionism *see* LOOSE CONSTRUCTIONISM

Brodhead's campaign During 11 August–14 September 1779, Colonel Daniel Brodhead's 600 troops marched 400 miles along the Allegheny River and burned 10 Seneca villages (*see* SULLIVAN'S CAMPAIGN).

broken voyage This was a subterfuge by the US merchant marine to evade the RULE OF 1756. Because France and Spain had forbidden US ships to carry cargoes directly between their ports in peacetime, they could not, by the Rule, allow such trade in the Napoleonic wars. US shippers nevertheless began carrying much of the exports from French and Spanish colonies to their home countries by taking these cargoes to a US port and obtaining a customs clearance for France or Spain. British courts ruled this stratagem illegal in the ESSEX CASE.

Brook Farm This utopian community, organized on the principles of TRANSCENDENTALISM was founded by George Ripley in 1841 near Boston, and reorganized as a phalanx of FOURIERISM in 1845. Nathaniel HAWTHORNE was a temporary resident, and Ralph W. EMERSON visited there. It disbanded after a fire in 1846.

Brooks, Preston *see* "CRIME AGAINST KANSAS" SPEECH

Browder, Earl *see* COMMUNIST PARTY

Brown, Charles Brockden (b. Philadelphia, Pa., 17 January 1771; d. Philadelphia, Pa., 22 February 1810) He ranks as the most talented American author of the Revolutionary era, and could arguably be called the father of the American novel. He abandoned a legal career to write Gothic romances and described himself as a "story-telling moralist." He was a lifelong Philadelphian, except for a New York sojourn (1798–1801), when he authored his best novels: *Wieland* (1798), *Edgar Huntly* (1799), *Ormond* (1799), *Arthur Mervyn* (1800), and *Clara Howard* (1801).

Brown, H(ugo Gold) "Rap" (b. Baton Rouge, La., 4 October 1943) He was a student volunteer in the CIVIL RIGHTS MOVEMENT to register voters in Miss.; he succeeded Stokely CARMICHAEL as STUDENT NONVIOLENT COORDINATING COMMITTEE president in 1967. He became a symbol of the militant BLACK POWER MOVEMENT because of his extremist rhetoric and a mounting police record, including a conviction (22 May 1968) for illegally taking firearms across state lines, violating bail, and inciting riots. In March 1970, after a mysterious explosion killed two of his associates near Bel Air, Md., and a second bomb damaged the Cambridge, Md., courthouse where he was facing trial for inciting a riot on 24–5 July 1967, Brown went underground. He stayed on the FBI's most-wanted list from May 1970 to 16 October 1971, when he was captured with three accomplices in a shootout during the robbery of a N.Y. bar. He was sentenced to prison in 1973. He converted to Islam in prison, took the name Jamil Abdullah Al-Amin, and opened a grocery store in Atlanta after parole.

Brown, John (b. Torrington, Conn., 9 May 1800; d. Charleston, W.Va., 2 December 1859) He was born into a family with a pronounced history of mental disease, experienced several episodes of emotional disorder in his own life, and failed at every occupation he tried. In 1855 he left Ohio to join the free-soil migration to stop SLAVERY's expansion during BLEEDING KANSAS. After he and four sons murdered five men in cold blood at Pottawatomie on 24 May 1856, a $3,000 reward was placed on his head. Aiming to spark a slave insurrection, he captured the US Arsenal at Harper's Ferry, Va., on 16 October 1859, helped by 16 whites and five blacks. Va. militia and US marines under Robert E. LEE retook it on 18 October. Brown's men killed 3 militia and 1 marine, but lost 10 killed and 7 captured (including Brown himself).

The US allowed Va. to try Brown, who was found guilty on 31 October, and hanged on 2 December. Brown became a martyr to many northerners out of concern that his trial was rigged and because he died with resolution and dignity. The north's eulogizing of Brown shocked white southerners and sparked wild rumors of abolitionist conspiracies. These rumors engulfed the election of 1860 in an atmosphere of hysteria. Brown's raid was the decisive event that convinced the South that, if Abraham LINCOLN became president, only SECESSION could save it from future SLAVE REVOLTS.

Brown* v. *Board of Education of Topeka (1954) On 17 May 1954, the Supreme Court unanimously reversed *PLESSY* v. *FERGUSON* and *CUMMING* v. *COUNTY BOARD OF EDUCATION* by declaring that segregated public schools violated the FOURTEENTH AMENDMENT's guarantee of equal protection under the law. *BROWN* v. *BOARD OF EDUCATION OF TOPEKA* (1955) and *COOPER* v. *AARON* reaffirmed this ruling.

Brown* v. *Board of Education of Topeka (1955) On 31 May 1955, the Supreme Court issued unanimous guidelines for desegregating schools. It vested federal district courts with jurisdiction to supervise this process, but gave the task of implementation to school boards. These received flexibility to end SEGREGATION according to timetables based on local circumstances, but that moved ahead "with all deliberate speed." Federal district courts would supervise this process, and could extend deadlines for desegregation, but only if school boards showed good faith. Local resistance led the Supreme Court to rule on federal desegregation orders in *GREEN* v. *COUNTY SCHOOL BOARD OF NEW KENT COUNTY*, *SWANN* v. *CHARLOTTE-MECKLENBERG COUNTY BOARD OF EDUCATION*, *KEYES* v. *DENVER SCHOOL DISTRICT NUMBER 1*, *MILLIKEN* v. *BRADLEY*, *PASADENA CITY BOARD OF EDUCATION* v. *SPANGLER*, and *BOARD OF EDUCATION OF OKLAHOMA CITY* v. *DOWELL*. By 1968, 76 percent of black children attended mostly minority schools, and 66 percent still did in 1994. Over 450 school districts remained under federal court supervision to ensure desegregation as late as May 1994.

Brown* v. *Maryland In 1827 the Supreme Court (6–1) limited the states' legislative powers over foreign trade through the "original package" doctrine. This declared that, so long as imports remained in the containers or wrapping delivered to the importer, they were interstate commerce subject only to congressional regulation. Only when such items became "mixed up with the mass of property in the country," could the states tax or pass other laws concerning them. *Brown* formed an important precedent for expanding federal authority over interstate commerce. (*See also* COOLEY v. *BOARD OF WARDENS and* PASSENGER CASES) In *Woodruff* v. *Parham* (1869), the Court affirmed a state's right to tax "imports" manufactured in another state, once the goods have ceased to be part of interstate commerce, even if they are in their original packages, because the Constitution (Article I, Section 10) only prohibits state duties on foreign imports.

Brown* v. *Mississippi On 17 February 1936, the Supreme Court ruled unanimously that state courts violated DUE PROCESS if they allowed testimony extorted under extreme police duress to be used in convicting a person who confessed or otherwise spoke unwillingly.

Brownsville incident (Tex.) On 13 August 1906, shooting erupted between white citizens of Brownsville, Tex., and about 12 black troops of the 25th Infantry at Fort Brown. One townsman was killed and another wounded. When the fort's garrison refused to identify the dozen involved, Theodore ROOSEVELT ordered all 167 black soldiers dishonorably discharged and declared them ineligible for civil service employment. Criticism by Roosevelt's political enemies led Congress to order a formal investigation of his actions, but the court of inquiry's establishment was delayed indefinitely. The dismissals cost Roosevelt the black vote in 1912. In 1972 the army changed the men's discharges from dishonorable to honorable.

Bruce, Blanche Kelso (b. Prince Edward County, Va., 1 March 1841; d. Washington, D.C., 17 March 1898) Born a slave, Bruce left his master in the CIVIL WAR to build schools for blacks in Kans. and Mo. In 1869 he went to Miss., which elected him as the second black US senator (1874–80), and the only black to serve a full term before 1966. He then became registrar of the US Treasury.

Brushaber* v. *Union Pacific Railroad Company *see* SIXTEENTH AMENDMENT

Bryan, William Jennings (b. Salem, Ill., 19 March 1860; d. Dayton, Tenn., 26 July 1925) In 1887 Bryan opened a law office in Lincoln, Nebr. As a Democratic congressman (1891–4), he became a leading pro-silver advocate in the SILVER COINAGE CONTROVERSY, but was defeated for the Senate in 1895 for opposing the SHERMAN SILVER PURCHASE ACT's repeal. By the 1896 Democratic convention, Bryan was the party's leading exponent of inflating the currency with silver, and his gripping CROSS OF GOLD SPEECH won him nomination as president. Also endorsed by the Populist party (*see* POPULISM), Bryan stumped 18,000 miles and gave 600 speeches. He carried the South and West, but could not win over northeastern laborers or midwestern farmers; he lost by 95 electoral votes to William MCKINLEY, but received 47.7 percent of the ballots. In 1900 he lost badly to McKinley by 137 electoral votes (with just 45.5 percent of the ballots); in 1908 he lagged William TAFT by 321 to 162 in the electoral college, and won only 43.1 percent of the popular vote. Bryan was influential in making Woodrow WILSON the 1912 Democratic nominee and became his secretary of state, but left the cabinet when Wilson's policy on the HMS *LUSITANIA*'s sinking clashed with his own preferences for strict neutrality. He died after helping prosecute the SCOPES TRIAL.

Bryant, William Cullen (b. Cummington, Mass., 3 November 1794; d. New York, N.Y., 12 June 1878) He published his first poem, a political satire called "The Embargo" (*see* EMBARGO ACT), at the age of 14. After attending Williams College, he abandoned a brief law practice for journalism and literary pursuits. He ranked as the leading American poet from the publication of his first volume of *Poems* (1821) until the prime of Henry Wadsworth LONGFELLOW. Bryant moved to New York in 1825 and joined the staff of the *Evening Post*. During his editorship (1829–78), this newspaper became the leading national advocate for progressive change in US society. His works included *Poems* (1832), *The Fountain, and Other Poems* (1842), and *The White-Footed Doe, and Other Poems* (1844).

Buchanan, James (b. near Mercersburg, Pa., 23 April 1791; d. Lancaster, Pa., 1 June 1868) In 1812 Buchanan opened a law office at Lancaster. He entered national politics as a Whig congressman (1820–31) and then was envoy to Russia (1832–3), Democratic senator (1835–45), secretary of state (1845–9), and ambassador to Britain (1853–6). While ambassador, he co-authored the OSTEND MANIFESTO. As Democratic nominee for president, he carried 45.3 percent of the popular vote to defeat John FRÉMONT and Millard FILLMORE. He alienated free-soil northerners with partiality toward pro-slavery settlers in BLEEDING KANSAS. He declined to seek a second term and endorsed his vice-president, John BRECKINRIDGE. As a lame-duck president, he declared SECESSION illegal, but took no action, hoping the Union might reunite under terms like the CRITTENDEN COMPROMISE. He nevertheless rejected S.C. demands to evacuate FORT SUMTER and ordered it held.

Buchanan* v. *Warley On 5 November 1917, the Supreme Court unanimously ruled that a Louisville, Ky., ordinance segregating neighborhoods by race violated the FOURTEENTH AMENDMENT. Attempts to evade the ruling resulted in white homeowners organizing private, community-wide covenants that forbade selling or renting homes to blacks. The Court addressed these schemes in *CORRIGAN* V. *BUCKLEY*.

Buckner, Simon Bolivar (b. near Munfordville, Ky., 1 April 1823; d. Hart County, Ky., 8 January 1914) Buckner graduated from West Point in 1844, retired from the army in 1855, and became commander of the Ky. militia. Offered the rank of general by both sides in the CIVIL WAR, he led the Ky. militia into CSA service. He commanded at FORT HENRY. He edited the Louisville *Courier* in 1868, was Ky. governor (1887–92), and the NATIONAL DEMOCRATS' vice-presidential nominee in 1896.

Budget, Bureau of the *see* BUDGET AND ACCOUNTING ACT

Budget and Accounting Act (10 June 1921) In the first major reform of federal finances, as recommended by the COMMISSION ON EFFICIENCY AND ECONOMY, Congress created the Bureau of the Budget and General Accounting Office (GAO). The president was responsible for having the Budget Bureau provide each session of Congress with a complete statement of government financial accounts. The GAO would independently audit US finances. The Administrative Reorganization Act (3 April 1939) transferred the Budget Bureau from the Treasury to the White House staff. In 1970 the Budget Bureau was renamed the Office of Management and Budget (OMB). (*See also* CONGRESSIONAL BUDGET AND IMPOUNDMENT CONTROL ACT, 1974)

Buena Vista, battle of (Mexico) On 22–3 February 1847, Brigadier General Zachary TAYLOR's 667 US regulars (with 18 cannon) and 4,217 volunteers defeated President Antonio Lopez de Santa Anna's 15,000 Mexicans. US losses: 267 killed, 456 wounded, 23 missing. Mexican losses: 1,800 killed and wounded, 300 captured. Santa Anna retired to his capital, but Taylor's army did not pursue and did no more campaigning. Taylor's victory made him a national hero.

buffalo At the onset of European colonization, buffalo herds ranged as far east as the Carolinas. Westward expansion eliminated them east of the Mississippi River during the early 19th century. By the 1860s, approximately 15,000,000 bison grazed on the Great Plains, where they were central to the Indians' economy and culture. Following the development of a commercial process for treating buffalo hides in 1871, large-scale hunting killed 9,000,000 bison by 1875. After the last large kill in 1883, the species was almost extinct from the US, although a wild herd survived in northern Alberta. By 1990 buffalo had revived and numbered about 130,000 head.

Buffalo Bill *see* CODY, WILLIAM

buffalo soldiers This term referred to black soldiers who fought Indians on the Great Plains in four segregated army regiments: 9th Cavalry, 10th Cavalry, 24th Infantry, and 25th Infantry. Between 1870 and 1890, these units participated in nearly 200 engagements and 14 of their troops won the Medal of Honor.

Bulge, battle of the Intending to isolate, and then destroy, Bernard Montgomery's British forces from US support by driving to Antwerp, 25 German divisions, backed by 2,000 artillery pieces, 600 tanks and 1,000 planes, attacked Lieutenant General Courtney Hodges's First US Army (75,000 men) in Belgium's Ardennes Forest (16 December 1944). Hodges's withdrawal left a 45-mile bulge in US lines, but resistance at St Vith and Bastogne upset enemy timetables and enabled Allied troops to maneuver against the penetration, which was eliminated by 7 February 1945. The Bulge was the final German offensive and set back Allied operations by six weeks. US losses: 19,000 killed, 47,000 wounded, and 15,000 captured. German losses: 100,000 casualties.

Bull Moose party This catchphrase was a jocular expression for the list of candidates for the PROGRESSIVE PARTY headed by Theodore ROOSEVELT. It derived from his acceptance speech at the Chicago convention on 5 August 1912, when he said he felt "as strong as a bull moose."

Bull Run, first battle of (Va.) On 21 July 1861, Brigadier General Pierre G. T. Beauregard's 32,200 Confederates defeated Brigadier General Irwin A. McDowell's 30,600 Federals. USA losses: 418 killed, 1,011 wounded, 1,216 missing. CSA losses: 387 killed, 1,582 wounded, 12 missing. The defeat caused McDowell to be replaced by George B. MCCLELLAN, ended hopes of early Federal victory, and led Congress to authorize the enlistment of 500,000 additional US volunteers.

Bull Run, second battle of (Va.) Between 28 August and 1 September 1862, General Robert E. LEE's 48,500 Confederates engaged Major General John Pope's 75,700-man Army of VIRGINIA. On 28 August, Stonewall JACKSON's corps kept US forces from taking Centreville. On 29–30 August, Lee's troops defeated Pope's men at Bull Run Creek. On 1 September, Jackson's corps attacked and defeated retreating Federal forces at Chantilly. Total USA losses: 1,724 killed, 8,372 wounded, 5,958 missing. Total CSA losses: 1,481 killed, 7,627 wounded, 89 missing. Second Bull Run forced the complete evacuation of USA troops from northern Va. and emboldened Lee to invade Md. in the campaign for ANTIETAM.

Bullfinch, Charles (b. Boston, Mass., 8 August 1763; d. Boston, Mass., 4 April 1844) A Harvard man (1781), Bullfinch toured Europe (1785–6) and returned with the inspiration to design city buildings that were not merely functional – as were most urban structures – but also expressed a sense of symmetry, elegance, and sophistication. Bullfinch was primarily responsible for introducing Americans to the ornamental style and proportioned lines of Robert and James Adam that he had seen in Edinburgh. Bullfinch ranked as the most influential US architect; he designed the state capitols of Mass., Conn., and Maine, and was architect of the US Capitol Building from 1817 to 1830.

Bunche, Ralph Johnson (b. Detroit, Mich., 7 August 1903; d. New York, N.Y., 9 December 1971) He joined the UNITED NATIONS shortly after its founding. Between 1947 and 1949, he mediated an armistice to end the Israeli–Arab war in Palestine. Upon receiving the Nobel peace prize in 1950, he attempted to decline the honor because "peacemaking at the UN was not done for prizes," but was persuaded by his superiors to accept. In 1951 he was appointed UN under-secretary for special political affairs, that organization's highest ranking American. He was the principal architect of UN peace-keeping operations from the KOREAN WAR to his retirement in September 1971. He was also a dignified civil-rights advocate for his fellow African Americans. On 7 December 1963, he received the highest US civilian decoration, the Medal of Freedom.

Bunker Hill, battle of (Mass.) On 17 June 1775 Colonel William Prescott's 1,200 Mass. militia repulsed two assaults by Major General Thomas GAGE's 2,500 British troops before shortage of ammunition forced their withdrawal during a third attack. US losses: 140 killed, 271 wounded, 30 captured. British losses: 226 killed, 828 wounded. Heavy British casualties reinforced American determination to resist British authority and ended any hope that Britain's government would compromise with the rebels.

Bunting* v. *Oregon *see* *MULLER* V. *OREGON*

Burch* v. *Louisiana On 17 April 1979, the Supreme Court ruled unanimously that the SIXTH AMENDMENT's guarantee of jury trials is violated when juries of just six persons convict defendants without a unanimous vote. In *Ballew* v. *Georgia* (21 March 1978), the Court declared that state juries must have at least six persons.

Bureau of Indian Affairs *see* INDIAN AFFAIRS, BUREAU OF

Burford, Anne *see* ENVIRONMENTAL PROTECTION AGENCY

Burger, Warren Earl (b. St Paul, Minn., 17 September 1907) He was US assistant attorney general (1953–6), active in Republican party politics, and judge on the US court of appeals for Washington, D.C. (1956–69), before being confirmed as chief justice on 9 June 1969. Burger led the Court in modifying the judicial activism that characterized its decisions under Earl WARREN, but upheld most of Warren's landmark decisions, if rather modified in scope. The Burger court was often deeply divided over ABORTION and the rights of criminal defendants. Burger announced his retirement on 17 June 1986. His major opinions include *GRIGGS* v. *DUKE POWER COMPANY*, *SWANN* v. *CHARLOTTE-MECKLENBERG COUNTY BOARD OF EDUCATION*, *LEMON* v. *KURTZMAN*, *MILLER* v. *CALIFORNIA*, *MILLIKEN* v. *BRADLEY*, and *FULLILOVE* v. *KLUTZNIK*.

Burgoyne, Major General John *see* FREEMAN'S FARM *and* BEMIS HEIGHTS, battles of, *and* SARATOGA, SURRENDER AT

Burke Act (1906) This act nullified *In Re Heff* (1905), a Supreme Court ruling that clarified the DAWES SEVERALTY ACT by declaring that Indians granted land under its terms were US citizens and not wards of the government. Since *Heff* blocked the Bureau of Indian Affairs from enforcing many paternalistic restrictions on RESERVATIONS (chiefly its ban on whiskey sales), Congress amended the Dawes Severalty Act to delay Indian citizenship during the 25 years while the US held their land grants in trust (i.e. at least through 1912).

Burke–Wadsworth Bill *see* SELECTIVE TRAINING AND SERVICE ACT

Burma campaigns *see* MERRILL'S MARAUDERS

burned-over district In the early 19th century, upstate N.Y., from Buffalo to the Adirondacks, was given this name for the frequent revivals that stoked religious enthusiasm like raging fires. The region produced Charles Grandison FINNEY and Joseph SMITH.

Burns, Lucy *see* NATIONAL WOMAN'S PARTY

Burr, Aaron (b. Newark N.J., 6 February 1756; d. Port Richmond, N.Y., 14 September 1836) In June 1778, Burr organized the earliest US espionage agency, the Headquarters Secret Service on Washington's staff. He was N.Y. attorney general (1789–91), US senator (1791–7), and N.Y. legislator (1797–9). He won 30 electoral votes for president in 1796. His mobilization of the Friendly Sons of St Tammany in 1800 was critical in the DEMOCRATIC PARTY's electoral college victory, which gave equal votes to Burr and Thomas JEFFERSON. After deadlocking for 35 ballots, the House relegated Burr to vice-president. In 1804, he courted the ESSEX JUNTO during an unsuccessful race for N.Y. governor. Having ruined his political career by killing Alexander HAMILTON in a duel, Burr embarked in 1806 on a scheme to conquer Spanish colonies – and perhaps lead the western states to secede – for which he was arrested in Ala., on 19 February 1807 and charged with treason. He was acquitted on 1 September 1807 as a result of John MARSHALL's narrow (and partisan) interpretation of proving guilt for that crime. He went into exile until 1812 and then practiced law in New York City.

Bus Deregulatory Reform Act *see* DEREGULATION

Bush, George Herbert Walker (b. Milton, Mass., 12 June 1924) He saw combat as a navy pilot in WORLD WAR II and then moved to Tex., where he entered the oil leasing and drilling business. He ran unsuccessfully as a Republican for the Senate in 1964 and 1970, sat in Congress (1967–70), was US ambassador to the UN (1971–2), chaired the Republican National Committee (1972–4), served as ambassador to China (1974–5), was CIA director (1976), ran a losing race to be Republican nominee for president in 1980, served as vice-president (1981–9), and was elected president in 1988 by winning 54 percent of the ballots and taking all but 10 states. He directed the 1989 US intervention in PANAMA. He organized the allied coalition that fought the PERSIAN GULF WAR, but ordered combat operations ended before Iraq was decisively defeated. His reelection prospects were crippled by his cynical repudiation of a campaign pledge not to raise taxes and by his failure to confront a lingering recession. He was defeated in 1992, when he polled just 38 percent of the vote – the worst showing by a Republican nominee since Barry GOLDWATER. Before leaving office, he initiated the US intervention in SOMALIA.

Bushy Run, battle of (Pa.) On 5–6 August 1763, Colonel Henry Bouquet's 460 Highlanders and Royal Americans routed 600 Indians under the Seneca Guyasuta and the Delaware Custaloga 26 miles from FORT PITT. British losses: 55 killed, 60 wounded. Indian losses: about 120 killed, wounded. The Indians then abandoned their siege of Fort Pitt.

Butler, Benjamin Franklin (b. Deerfield, N.H., 5 November 1818; d. Washington, D.C., 11 January 1993) A "political general" during the CIVIL WAR, Butler became a US major general in May 1861 because he was a prominent Democrat. An incompetent who repeatedly embarrassed his superiors, Butler's popularity among Democrats kept him from being relieved from active command until 1865. He switched parties, served as a Republican congressman (1866–79), and was prominent in Andrew JOHNSON's impeachment. He became Mass. governor in 1883, and won 1.8 percent of votes as GREENBACK PARTY presidential nominee in 1884.

Byrd, Harry Flood (b. Martinsburg, W.Va., 10 June 1887; d. Berryville, Va., 20 October 1966) Brother of Richard BYRD, he was a journalist, Va. state senator (1915–25), governor (1926–30), and US senator (1933–65). His political machine dominated Va. politics until the 1960s. He was a critic of the NEW DEAL and a leading Senate conservative, especially while chair of the Finance Committee (1955–65). Although not a candidate for president in 1960, he received 15 electoral votes from Miss., Ala., and Okla.

Byrd, Richard Evelyn (b. Winchester, Va., 25 October 1888; d. Boston, Mass., 11 March 1957) In 1912 Byrd graduated from Annapolis and became a naval aviator. In 1925 he headed the aviation team of a naval expedition mapping the North Pole, and he piloted the first plane over the Pole on 9 May 1926. During his first Antarctic expedition (1928–30), he made the earliest flight over the South Pole on 29 November 1929. On subsequent expeditions (1933–5, 1939, and 1946–7), he made significant scientific observations and performed pioneering geographic and geological surveys that placed the US at the forefront of Antarctic exploration.

Byrd, William (b. Henrico County, Va., 28 March 1674; d. Charles City County, Va., 26 August 1744) After spending most years from 1681 to 1700 in England, Byrd inherited a large landed estate, emerged as one of Virginia's most influential politicians, and built a library of 3,600 titles. The colonial South's most important man of letters, he recorded one of the richest descriptions of the Va. gentry's life in his encoded diaries (1709–12, 1717–19, 1739–41). He also described backcountry life in his *History of the Dividing Line Run in the Year 1728*, written in parallel with a secret manuscript lampooning the Va.–N.C. border region as a "lubberland" populated by yokels, outcasts, and social misfits.

C

cabinet The president's cabinet consists of the heads of executive departments. The original cabinet consisted of the Departments of STATE, the TREASURY, and WAR, plus the ATTORNEY GENERAL, but not the postmaster general. The KITCHEN CABINET emerged in the 1830s. An informal BLACK CABINET evolved in the 1930s. The "inner cabinet" includes the four most influential department heads (of the Treasury, State, JUSTICE, and DEFENSE), who work most closely with the president. By 1993, the cabinet had grown to 14 departments.

Cabot, John (b. Genoa[?], Italy, ca. 1455; d. in the north Atlantic, 1498) Born Giovanni Caboto, Cabot established himself as a merchant-mariner in Bristol, England, about 1490. Commissioned by Henry VII to make a voyage of discovery for England, he left Bristol on 2 May 1497 and commanded the first European ship to reach the North American mainland. After sighting Newfoundland or Cape Breton Island on 24 June, he sailed to New England. England's territorial claims to North America derived from his discovery. In 1498 he was lost at sea on another transatlantic voyage.

Cabot, Sebastian (b. Venice, Italy, ca. 1483; d. London, England, 1557) Son of John CABOT, Sebastian may have joined his father's first voyage of 1497. In 1508–9, he made the earliest English voyage searching for the NORTHWEST PASSAGE. He entered Spain's service in 1512, but returned to England in 1548. He was Muscovy Company president (1553–7).

Cabrillo's explorations On 27 June 1542, Juan Rodriguez Cabrillo began the first Spanish voyage along the Calif. coast and claimed the region for Spain. Cabrillo died on 3 January 1543, and Bartolomé Ferrelo continued exploring until March 1543, when he turned back near southern Oreg.

Caddoan languages This family of INDIAN LANGUAGES was spoken by groups west of the Mississippi River from La. to Nebr. Its major subdivisions included the languages of the PAWNEE-ARIKARA INDIANS, the Caddo, and WICHITA Indians.

Cahuenga, treaty of (Calif.) On 13 January 1847, John FRÉMONT and Andres Pico signed a truce between US forces and Mexican loyalists. Frémont granted pardons to those fighting the US, promised to protect their property, and gave them the rights of US citizens. The treaty ended pro-Mexican resistance to US authority in Calif.

Cairo conference, first From 22 to 26 November 1943, Winston Churchill, Chiang Kai-shek, and Franklin D. ROOSEVELT planned a strategy to defeat Japan. On 1 December, in the Cairo Declaration, they announced a policy of fighting until unconditional surrender, stripping Japan of all its Pacific island territories and Chinese conquests, and restoring Korean independence.

Cairo conference, second From 4 to 6 December 1943, Winston Churchill and Franklin D. ROOSEVELT negotiated arrangements to maintain Turkey's status as a non-belligerent with friendly ties to the Allies; they also named Dwight D. EISENHOWER supreme Allied commander in Europe.

Cajuns *see* ACADIANS

Calder* v. *Bull In 1798 the Supreme Court ruled that the Constitution's prohibition against EX POST FACTO LAWS (Article I, Section 10) extended only to criminal statutes, and that states could enact civil statutes with retroactive provisions affecting property.

Calhoun, John Caldwell (b. Abbeville District, S.C., 18 March 1782; d. Washington, D.C., 30 March 1850) Educated at Yale, Calhoun entered Congress from S.C. as a nationalistic Democrat and WAR HAWK. Only Henry CLAY and Daniel WEBSTER surpassed Calhoun as an orator. He served as secretary of war (1817–25), and vice-president (1825–32). The TARIFF OF ABOMINATIONS led him to abandon his former support for protective trade duties and to espouse NULLIFICATION through his anonymous SOUTH CAROLINA EXPOSITION AND PROTEST. Returning to the Senate in 1832, he became the foremost exponent of STATES RIGHTS and defender of SLAVERY. He accomplished the annexation of TEXAS as secretary of state (1844–5). Back in the Senate, he introduced the CALHOUN RESOLUTIONS and tried to block Calif.'s admission as a free state, but as his health failed, he reluctantly acceded to the COMPROMISE OF 1850. His theories on CONCURRENT MAJORITY were published posthumously.

Calhoun Resolutions Attacking the WILMOT PROVISO, Senator John CALHOUN introduced resolutions on 19 February 1847 to demand that territories be opened to SLAVERY. He stated that as territories were the common property of all states, Congress must organize the west to give equal access to all citizens, including slaveowners who wished to move there with their bondsmen. To force masters moving west to abandon their slaves would violate FIFTH AMENDMENT guarantees against taking property without DUE PROCESS. To deny a territory's people the right to adopt slavery violated their right to self-determination; it also exceeded Congress's authority over the PUBLIC DOMAIN, since the Constitution placed no condition for admitting states except that they have republican governments. Calhoun's position defined the South's argument on slavery in the territories until the DAVIS RESOLUTIONS.

California Calif. had perhaps 150,000 Indians in 1500. In 1769 European settlement began with the first of 21 CALIFORNIA MISSIONS. Mexicans founded Los Angeles in 1781. By 1800, the Spanish-speaking population numbered about 4,000 in three towns and four garrisons. Russians from ALASKA placed a temporary colony at FORT ROSS in 1812. When it passed to the US by the treaty of GUADALUPE HIDALGO, the Spanish-speaking population was about 8,000. By 1850, the CALIFORNIA GOLD RUSH had increased its non-Indian population to over 100,000. It entered the Union on 9 September 1850 by the COMPROMISE OF 1850. In 1860 it ranked 26th among states, with 379,994 people, of whom 1 percent were black and 38 percent were foreign-born; it stood 26th in the value of its farmland and livestock and 7th in manufacturing and mining. Calif. furnished 15,725 USA troops in the CIVIL WAR.

In-migration remained heavy over the CALIFORNIA TRAIL until 1869, when the first TRANSCONTINENTAL RAILROAD was completed. The only significant Indian disturbance was the MARIPOSA WAR. Miners disrupted land resources needed by Indians for food, and infected remote groups with lethal diseases. Indians declined from 100,000 in 1845 to 15,377 in 1900. In 1900 Calif. was the 21st state in size, with 1,485,053 residents (91 percent white, 3 percent Hispanic, 1 percent Indian, 1 percent black, 3 percent Chinese, and 1 percent Japanese), of whom 48 percent were rural and 25 percent foreign-born; it ranked 14th in agricultural goods and 12th in products manufactured or mined.

Heavy CHINESE and JAPANESE IMMIGRATION produced resentment among whites, who demanded federal reaction by the CHINESE EXCLUSION ACT, the Gentlemen's Agreements (*see* JAPANESE IMMIGRATION), and (in WORLD WAR II), JAPANESE RELOCATION. In 1911 decades of political domination by railroad interests were swept aside by PROGRESSIVE ERA reformers led by Hiram JOHNSON, who left Republicans so politically dominant that no Democrat was elected governor until 1938. The GREAT DEPRESSION added perhaps 400,000 OKIES to the state's population. Under the BRACERO PROGRAM, large agriculturalists stimulated the beginning of a large MEXICAN IMMIGRATION. About half of all BOAT PEOPLE eventually came to Calif. The oil, aerospace, and entertainment industries fanned rapid population growth after 1900, and Calif. became the most populous state in 1964. In 1990 Calif. had

29,760,021 residents (57 percent white, 26 percent Hispanic, 7 percent black, 9 percent Asian, 1 percent Indian) of whom 96 percent were urban and 21.7 percent were foreign-born. Manufacturing and mining employed 24 percent of workers.

California gold rush On 24 January 1848, James Marshall found gold nuggets at Sutter's Fort on the American River. When James K. POLK mentioned the discovery in his farewell address in January 1849, he set off a stampede of FORTY-NINERS. The gold country stretched 150 miles along the Sierra Nevada's western slope due east of San Francisco. Since so much gold lay as surface ore, rather than in underground veins, it was well suited for recovery by amateurs with no mining experience and limited capital. By 1855, when perhaps $200,000,000 in gold had been sifted, the rush had peaked. In the late 1850s, smaller gold deposits were found in northern Calif. and southwestern Oreg., and underground mining commenced.

California missions On 16 July 1769, European settlement of Calif. began with San Diego de Alcala's founding by Fr Junipero SERRA. Spanish missionaries thereafter established San Carlos Boromeo on 3 June 1771, San Antonio de Padua on 14 July 1771, San Gabriel Arcangel (near Los Angeles) on 8 September 1771, San Luis Obispo de Tolosa on 1 September 1772, San Francis de Asis on 9 October 1776, San Juan Capistrano on 1 November 1776, Santa Clara de Asis on 12 January 1777, San Buenaventura on 31 March 1782, Santa Barbara on 4 December 1786, Purisma Concepcion on 8 December 1787, Santa Cruz on 28 August 1791, Nuestra Señora de la Soledad on 9 October 1791, San José de Guadaloupe on 11 June 1797, San Juan Bautista on 24 June 1797, San Miguel Arcangel on 25 July 1797, San Fernando Rey de Espana on 8 September 1797, San Luis Rey de Francia on 13 June 1798, Santa Inés, Virgin y Martyr on 17 September 1804, San Rafael Arcangel on 14 December 1817, and San Francisco Solano on 4 July 1823. The 21 missions converted 54,000 Indians (about 40 percent of all), but many epidemics resulted from European diseases and kept the mission population low. In 1834, when the missions contained 17,000 Indians, they were secularized by Mexico and became parish churches.

California Trail This trail departed from the OREGON TRAIL along the Snake River in southern Idaho near Fort Hall, followed the Humboldt River to its sink, and crossed the Sierras by the Truckee River. John Bartleson and John Bidwell's party blazed it in 1841. The first wagons reached Calif. via the trail in 1844. Large-scale migration began in 1846, when 200 wagons crossed to Calif. The trail was the site of the DONNER PARTY disaster.

California* v. *Southern Pacific Company On 18 March 1895, the Supreme Court ruled (7–2) that original jurisdiction over suits brought by a state against its own residents belongs to that state's courts, and lies outside the federal judiciary's scope. The decision increased the difficulty of regulating TRUSTS involved in interstate commerce.

Calley, William L. *see* MY LAI MASSACRE

Calvert family of Maryland *see* PROPRIETORS OF MARYLAND

Cambodia, invasion of On 30 April 1970, US and South Vietnamese forces crossed the Cambodian border to destroy North Vietnamese bases in Operation Binh Tay. The invasion sparked militant protests on US college campuses and fanned support for the VIETNAM ANTIWAR MOVEMENT. On 16 May, US troops began withdrawing from Cambodia, but South Vietnamese forces remained until June. On 22 December 1970, Congress forbade US ground forces from entering Cambodia or Laos.

Cambodian immigration *see* BOAT PEOPLE

Cambridge agreement (England) On 26 August 1629, the shareholders of the MASSACHUSETTS BAY COMPANY voted to be ready to emigrate to Mass. by the following March, provided that the company officers would agree to relocate the charter and corporate headquarters there. Anyone unwilling to emigrate would sell his shares. The company assented to the agreement on 29 August to make it more difficult for royal courts to revoke the charter by quo warranto proceedings.

Cambridge Platform of Church Discipline (Mass.) From 1646 to 1648, a synod of ministers led by John COTTON drafted this document as an ecclesiastical constitution outlining the basic elements and beliefs of PURITANISM in Mass. It limited the autonomy of congregations by authorizing both state officials and religious synods to discipline wayward ministers and churches, but while civil officers might maintain proper religious order, only the church could pronounce on questions of doctrine. It continued the requirement for a profession of saving grace for full church membership (*see* HALF-WAY COVENANT). It provides the best example of Puritan orthodoxy among New England's first generation.

Camden, battle of (S.C.) On 16 August 1780, Lieutenant General Charles CORNWALLIS's 2,100 troops routed Major General Horatio Gates's 1,000 Continentals and 1,100 militia. US losses: 250 killed, 800 wounded, 800 captured. British losses: 68 killed, 256 wounded. Camden was the most complete US defeat in the REVOLUTIONARY WAR.

Cameron, Simon (b. Lancaster, County, Pa., 8 March 1799; d. Donegal Springs, Pa., 26 June 1889) He sat in the Senate (1845–9), for the WHIG PARTY, but joined the REPUBLICAN PARTY in 1856. He quickly emerged as Pa.'s most powerful Republican by organizing a party machine that lasted until 1921. Cameron delivered Pa.'s votes to Abraham LINCOLN at the 1860 Republican convention after Lincoln's managers promised him a CABINET post without Lincoln's knowledge. Lincoln reluctantly honored this promise and made him secretary of war. Cameron was a divisive element in the cabinet, and a poor administrator whom Congress censured for mismanaging the army. In January 1862, he resigned to become acting minister to Russia. He was again senator (1867–77).

Camp Charlotte, treaty of (Ohio) On 30 August 1774, the SHAWNEE INDIANS ended DUNMORE'S WAR by agreeing to give up their claims to KENTUCKY – in which they only hunted and did not live – to cease hunting there, and to allow whites to travel the Ohio River unmolested. Along with the treaty of SYCAMORE SHOALS, the agreement enabled Anglo-Americans to establish the first settlements beyond the Appalachians.

Camp David accords (Md.) From 6 to 17 September 1978, Jimmy CARTER hosted a summit between Israeli and Egyptian leaders at which peace accords were negotiated that resulted in a formal peace treaty in March 1979. The summit was a giant step toward peace for the Middle East, and was largely due to Carter's personal diplomacy. Informed public opinion was shocked when the Nobel Prize Committee failed to recognize Carter with its peace prize.

Camp Grant massacre (Ariz.) On 30 April 1871, six Anglo-Americans from Tucson joined 48 Mexicans and 94 Papago Indians in a daylight raid on 500 Apaches suspected of raids in the US and Mexico. The attack left 100 APACHE INDIANS dead and 27 enslaved by the Papagos, but no casualties on the other side. Many of the attackers were tried for murder at Tucson in December, but all were acquitted.

Campbellites *see* DISCIPLES OF CHRIST

Canadian immigration From 1820 to 1900, 1,051,275 Canadians officially entered the US, although this figure is less than the 1,179,922 Canadians (784,796 British and 395,126 French) listed by the 1900 census. British Canadians comprised about 70 percent of all arrivals. Canadian immigration was heaviest from 1911 to 1930, when 1,666,700 came. From 1820 to 1991, 4,315,516 Canadians immigrated to the US, the seventh greatest number of arrivals from any country.

Canadian Reciprocity Treaty Because the exclusion of its goods from US markets had spawned sentiment in Canada that union with the US would have economic benefits, Britain moved to end incentives for US annexation by opening up Yankee markets to Canadian exports. On 5 June 1854, the US and Britain resolved disputes over fishing privileges left unspecified by the CONVENTION OF 1818, and exchanged reciprocal fishing rights for each other's citizens. US fishermen received access to the inlets south of the St Lawrence River, and Canadians could use US waters down to the 36th parallel. The treaty also placed many trade items, chiefly farm goods, on duty-free status. It was to remain valid for a decade, and was abrogated on 17 March 1866.

canal boom Canal building began on a small scale during 1789–1800, when 61 corporations were chartered. In 1825, the ERIE CANAL's completion stimulated a major boom. Private investment (and to a lesser extent government subsidies) financed the highpoint of canal construction in the 1830s. By 1850, the US had 3,698 miles of canals, including 1,757 in N.Y. and Pa., 792 in Ohio, 214 in Ind., and 100 in Ill. The canal system's main corridor connected Hudson River with the Great Lakes, and the commerce along its axis made that region into the country's most populous section. Competition from railroads led to a steady decline in canal traffic from 1846 to 1860. The last great domestic canal endeavor was the St Lawrence Seaway.

Cane Ridge camp meeting (Ky.) During August 1801, the greatest revival in US history occurred when Barton Stone and 17 other Presbyterian and Methodist clergymen held a camp meeting in Bourbon County. The ministers preached in seven-man shifts from wagon beds or tree stumps to crowds estimated at 10,000–20,000 (5–11 percent of the state's free population). The listeners demonstrated a wide range of emotional responses, including trances, trembling, uncontrolled jerking of limbs, weeping, the "holy laugh," talking in tongues, barking, and an exercise known as "treeing the devil."

Cannon, Joseph Gurney (b. New Garden, N.C., 7 May 1836; d. Danville, Ill., 12 November 1926) He first entered Congress as an Ill. Republican in 1872 and became speaker of the House in 1901. Through his power over committee assignments and ability to name his backers to the Rules Committee, which set limits on debate, he blocked much PROGRESSIVE ERA legislation. CANNONISM ended in 1910 when progressive Republicans under George NORRIS and liberal Democrats under Champ CLARK voted to make the Rules Committee electable by the entire House and deny the speaker membership on it. Cannon's defeat eliminated a major barrier to enacting reform legislation.

Cannonism This term was coined to characterize the arbitrary and partisan control of parliamentary procedures and committee rules by congressional leaders, in the manner of Joseph CANNON.

Cantigny, battle of (France) *see* WORLD WAR I

Cantwell* v. *Connecticut On 20 May 1940, the Supreme Court unanimously ruled that the FOURTEENTH AMENDMENT'S DUE PROCESS clause obliged state courts to uphold the FIRST AMENDMENT's guarantees of free exercise of religion. In a case involving the Jehovah's Witnesses, the Court denied states the authority to outlaw street preaching as a disturbance of the peace, so long as there was no "clear and present menace" to public order. It also struck down a state statute that forbade street preaching without a permit, because it gave the government arbitrary power to discriminate against unpopular religious groups.

CAP *see* COMMUNITY ACTION PROGRAMS

Cape Esperance, battle of On 11–12 October 1942, Rear Admiral Norman Scott's 4 US cruisers and 5 destroyers defeated Rear Admiral Aritomo Goto's cruiser squadron (2 carriers, 3 cruisers, and 8 destroyers) carrying troops to GUADALCANAL. US losses: 1 destroyer. Japanese losses: 1 cruiser, 3 destroyers.

capital punishment *see* *FURMAN* v. *GEORGIA*

Capper–Tincher Act (24 August 1921) This law was passed to prevent unwarranted profits from speculation in farm commodities at a time of falling farm income. It defined certain types of contract trading as speculative and placed a prohibitive tax on them. The Supreme Court struck down the law in 1922, but its objections were remedied in the Grain Futures Trading Act (21 September 1922).

Capper–Volstead Act (18 February 1922) This law was a Republican attempt to halt a steep slide in agricultural prices without resorting to direct government intervention in the marketplace. It exempted farm cooperatives from the antitrust laws so that they could buy large volumes of commodities and withhold them from the market until prices improved. It was also hoped that the cooperatives' overheads would be lower than private businesses', and that consequently they could charge farmers less to haul and warehouse their commodities. Continuing price declines led to demands for the MCNARY–HAUGEN BILL and enactment of the AGRICULTURAL MARKETING ACT.

Carey Act (18 August 1894) This law was one of the first federal conservation measures. It authorized federal grants of up to

1,000,000 acres if the states would finance projects to reclaim arid soil by irrigation projects. Any profits from selling tillable acreage were to be used for further land reclamation. The law produced few conservation projects, in part because irrigation problems often required interstate solutions, but state cooperation was rare.

Carlisle Peace Commission On 16 March 1778, to induce the US to end its rebellion and return to the British empire, the House of Commons established a peace commission. The commissioners were empowered to promise repeal of the INTOLERABLE ACTS, the TEA ACT, and any other objectionable laws passed since 1763; they might also promise America future exemption from parliamentary taxation. On 17 June, the CONTINENTAL CONGRESS refused to negotiate upon any terms but withdrawal of British troops, and US independence.

Carmichael, Stokely (b. Port-of-Spain, Trinidad, 29 June 1941) He grew up in Harlem and became a FREEDOM RIDER while attending Howard University. In 1964 he joined a voter registration project in Miss. with the STUDENT NONVIOLENT COORDINATING COMMITTEE (SNCC). After being elected president of SNCC in 1966, he was the first to argue that the CIVIL RIGHTS MOVEMENT should evolve into a BLACK POWER MOVEMENT. He was arrested for inciting the Atlanta riots of 6–12 September 1966. Influenced by the Pan-Africanism of Marcus GARVEY, he moved his family to Uganda and became a citizen of that country in 1973.

Carnegie, Andrew (b. Dunfermline, Scotland, 25 November 1835; d. Lenox, Mass., 11 August 1919) He emigrated to the US in 1848 and served in the US War Department's transportation division in the CIVIL WAR. He abandoned his early career in railroading and devoted himself solely to the steel business from 1873 at Pittsburgh. Carnegie was the dominant force in the rising US steel industry, which surpassed British output by 1890; he was among the first industrialists to organize a business by VERTICAL INTEGRATION. By 1900, the Carnegie Steel Co. controlled the bulk of US steel manufacturing and was the first US corporation to be valued at $1 billion. It was sold to J. Pierpont MORGAN and Henry FRICK, who reorganized it as the US Steel Co. in 1901. He then devoted himself to philanthropic causes, to which he donated $350,000,000, and built 1,408 libraries.

Carolina On 3 April 1663, CHARLES II established Carolina as a PROPRIETARY COLONY. The PROPRIETORS OF CAROLINA hoped to organize its society and politics according to the FUNDAMENTAL CONSTITUTIONS OF CAROLINA, but were unable to win approval from the settlers. In 1665 the proprietors established separate assemblies for the Cape Fear and Albemarle Sound regions, from which the colony of N.C. evolved. In 1671 the first assembly met in S.C. The proprietors never enlisted the settlers' political cooperation. S.C. became a ROYAL COLONY on 29 May 1721 and N.C. on 25 July 1729.

***Caroline*, USS, affair** In 1837 US citizens actively supported Canadian rebels against British authority. On 29 December, under orders from British authorities, Canadian militia crossed the Niagara River and burned the steamboat USS *Caroline*, which had been supplying the rebels, and killed Amos Durfee, a US citizen. A brief military crisis ensued as militia mobilized on both sides of the border. On 29 May 1838, US citizens retaliated by burning the Canadian steamer *Sir Robert Peel* in the St Lawrence River. US citizens tried to instigate further insurrections in Canada long after the original rebellion had collapsed, and despite Martin VAN BUREN's efforts to maintain US neutrality. The affair finally ended on 12 October 1841 when a Canadian deputy sheriff, Alexander McLeod, was acquitted at Utica, N.Y., of Durfee's murder in the *Caroline* affair.

Caroline Islands *see* MICRONESIA, US TRUST TERRITORY OF

carpetbaggers Republican politicians in the South during RECONSTRUCTION received this derogatory title from Democrats who lampooned them as opportunists who left their northern homes with all their possessions in a carpetbag, in order to win, and profit from, government offices denied to ex-Confederates.

Carroll, John (b. Annapolis, Md., 19 September 1737; d. Baltimore, Md., 14 November 1832) Educated abroad in France and London's Inns of Court, Carroll was a wealthy planter whose Catholicism made him ineligible for public office in Md. He emerged as an influential Whig (*see* Whigs [Revolutionary]) leader after writing anonymous essays defending the colonists' claim to the rights of Englishmen. He sat in the extra-legal Md. Convention (1774–6), which sent him to both Continental Congresses. He became a national hero when signing the Declaration of Independence because when it was jokingly remarked that his name was so common in Md. that the British could never identify him for arrest, he appended "of Carrollton" after his signature. His national service largely ceased after the war, except as US senator (1789–91). As the Declaration's longest-surviving signer, he was acclaimed as the nation's senior statesman in his final years.

Carroll, John (b. Upper Marlboro, Md., 8 January 1735; d. Baltimore, Md., 3 December 1815) In 1769 Carroll was ordained as a Jesuit priest in France, and he returned to Md. in 1774. In 1776 he joined a delegation sent by the Continental Congress to encourage Canadians to declare independence with the US. He became superior of US missions in 1784, and in 1789 was appointed the Catholic church's first bishop for the US, with Baltimore as his diocese. He founded the first US Catholic college (Georgetown) in 1789, established the first US seminary for training priests in 1791, and began construction of the Baltimore Cathedral in 1806. He became archbishop of Baltimore in 1808.

Carson, "Kit" (Christopher Houston) (b. Madison County, Ky., 24 December 1809; d. Fort Lyon, Colo., 23 May 1868) At the age of 14, Carson ran away from a Mo. saddler to whom he was apprenticed and went to Taos, N.Mex., where he became a mountain man. During 1842–8, he was a civilian guide on John Frémont's explorations and participated in the Bear Flag Revolt. He became a N.Mex. rancher in 1849 and agent to the Navaho Indians in 1853. A US brigadier general in the Civil War, he fought both Confederates and Apache Indians, and won the second Navaho campaign.

Carson, Rachel *see Silent Spring*

Carter, Jimmy (James Earl) (b. Plains, Ga., 1 October 1924) In 1946 Carter graduated from Annapolis as a nuclear engineer. As Democratic Ga. governor (1971–4), he reconciled racial tensions. He won over Gerald Ford in 1976 with 50.1 percent of the popular vote. His major initiatives were the Camp David accords, ceding control of the Panama Canal, the Carter Doctrine, and the National Energy Act (1978). Soaring inflation (*see* Humphrey-Hawkins Bill) and the Iran hostage crisis discredited his leadership. In 1980 he took only five states and won just 41.0 percent of popular votes in a massive defeat by Ronald Reagan.

Carter raised $150 million in contributions to fund his Presidential Library and Carter Center, which promoted peaceful solutions for international conflicts. As envoy extraordinary in 1994, he was instrumental in defusing a military crisis with North Korea over its compliance with the Nuclear Non-Proliferation Treaty. His personal diplomacy averted an armed invasion of Haiti in 1994 and persuaded its junta to accept a peaceful US occupation at the last minute. "Quite often," Carter explained his rapport with military dictators, "these little guys, who might be making atomic weapons or who might be guilty of some human-rights violations or whatever, are looking for someone to listen to their problems and to help them communicate."

Carter Doctrine On 23 January 1980, Jimmy Carter declared that the Persian Gulf's oil reserves were of vital interest to the US, and claimed that the US would be justified in preventing outside domination of the region by military intervention. George Bush claimed the doctrine as authority for US leadership in the Persian Gulf War.

Carter* v. *Carter Coal Company On 18 May 1936, the Supreme Court (6–3) declared unconstitutional the Guffey–Snyder Bituminous Coal Stabilization Act. The Court held that it impermissibly delegated legislative powers to private citizens by authorizing the coal industry to regulate its own wages and working hours; it also held that federal jurisdiction could not be extended over intrastate commerce by granting collective bargaining rights to miners.

Carteret, Sir George *see* EAST JERSEY *and* PROPRIETORS OF EAST JERSEY

Cartier's explorations Commissioned by Francis I of France to explore North America, Jacques Cartier reconnoitered the Canadian coast from Newfoundland to the Gulf of St Lawrence during June–July 1534. During May–August 1535, he explored the St Lawrence River as far as the Montreal rapids, wintered at modern Quebec, and left for France in May 1536. In August 1541, he established a temporary trading post near Quebec. Cartier's voyages were the earliest French efforts to exploit Canada.

Carver, George Washington (b. near Diamond Grove, Mo., ca. 1864; d. Tuskegee, Ala., 5 January 1943) Born into slavery, Carver earned a college degree in 1891 at Iowa State College and joined Tuskegee Institute's faculty in 1896 as the agriculture department's chair. He excelled as an experimental chemist and discovered 300 byproducts or new uses for familiar crops (including over 100 from the peanut and sweet potato), which collectively helped diversify southern farming away from an overdependence on cotton. He used his life savings to found Tuskegee's Carver Research Foundation in 1940.

Casablanca conference, (Morocco) Between 14 and 24 January 1943, Winston Churchill discussed strategy for WORLD WAR II with Franklin D. ROOSEVELT and Charles De Gaulle. The Allies agreed to demand unconditional surrender from the AXIS and to invade Italy.

Casey, Albert *see* RESOLUTION TRUST CORPORATION

Cass, Lewis (b. Exeter, N.H., 9 October 1782; d. Detroit, Mich., 17 June 1866) In 1799 Cass moved to Ohio; he opened a law office in 1802, entered the legislature in 1806, fought in the WAR OF 1812, and was Michigan Territory's governor (1813–31). He became one of the Democrats' leading exponents of MANIFEST DESTINY while secretary of war (1831–6), and promoted a stridently anti-British foreign policy while ambassador to France (1836–42). While US senator (1845–57), he supported the annexation of TEXAS and demanded British recognition of US claims that OREGON extended to 54°40′. After failing to win the Democratic presidential nomination in 1844, he headed the Democratic ticket in 1848 but lost to Zachary TAYLOR because the FREE-SOIL PARTY kept him from polling more than 42.5 percent of the ballots. He opposed the WILMOT PROVISO and supported the COMPROMISE OF 1850. In 1857 Cass became secretary of war, but resigned in 1860 to protest James BUCHANAN's refusal to reinforce FORT SUMTER.

Cassat, Mary (b. Allegheny City, Pa., 22 May 1847; d. Mesnil-Théribus, Oise, France, 14 June 1926) Trained in painting at the Pa. Academy of Fine Arts (1861–5) and Academy of Parma in Italy (1872), she established a studio at Paris in 1872. She primarily painted the human figure, most commonly on the subject of mother and child (Cassat was single). She was the only American invited to exhibit with the French Impressionists, and did all her work abroad. Cataracts in both eyes rapidly ended her career after 1912.

Castillo de San Marcos (Fla) *see* ST AUGUSTINE

Castro, Fidel (b. Mayari, Oriente, Cuba, 13 August 1926) Son of a wealthy sugar planter, Castro initiated revolutionary action on 26 July 1953 against the Batista regime, which he overthrew on 1 January 1959. On 20 August 1960, the US embargoed exports to Cuba in protest against Castro's nationalization of 26 US firms with $1 billion in assets. Castro proclaimed Cuba a Communist-bloc nation and suspended all further elections on 1 May 1961. US efforts to depose him failed at the BAY OF PIGS INVASION. Soviet efforts to emplace ICBMs failed in the CUBAN MISSILE CRISIS. Cuban efforts to export its revolution led to sanctions by the ORGANIZATION OF AMERICAN STATES (OAS) from 1964 to 1975. He sent Cuban troops to assist Marxist regimes in Angola, Ethiopia, and GRENADA. In 1979 he was elected chair of the Nonaligned Nations Movement. He stimulated a large CUBAN IMMIGRATION of political refugees to the US. Castro faced increasing difficulty in governing Cuba after 1991, when the economic collapse of the USSR led to an end of the $5 billion in subsidies it had provided him.

Catawba Indians Speakers of one of the SIOUAN LANGUAGES, the Catawba occupied the S.C. PIEDMONT and may have numbered about 1,500 (570 warriors) in 1715. They assisted whites in the TUSCARORA WAR, briefly warred against whites in the YAMASEE WAR, and adopted a pro-English stance after dispersing the Waxhaws for S.C. in 1716. After 1720 they absorbed numerous Siouan bands and remained the only significant Indian group in central S.C. During 1722–51, they withstood many IROQUOIS CONFEDERACY raiding parties. After smallpox devastated the nation in 1759, it numbered about 500 and voluntarily sought reservation status on 225 square miles in 1760. By the treaty of Nation Ford (1840), Catawbas agreed to join the CHEROKEE INDIAN remnant in N.C., but could not get along with their former enemies and stayed in S.C. at a reservation near Rock Hill, where most still remain. They were the only southeastern Indians to avoid wholesale removal to the west.

Cather, Willa (b. near Winchester, Va., 7 December 1876; d. New York, N.Y., 24 April 1947) Taken by her family to Red Cloud, Nebr., in 1884, she graduated from the University of Nebraska in 1895. After publishing a book of poetry, *April Twilights* (1903), and of stories, *The Troll Garden* (1905), she was editor of *McClure's Magazine* from 1907 to 1912, when she resigned to write full-time. Although the west (particularly Nebr.) was the preferred setting for her novels, Cather was no mere regional author; she was not only a graceful stylist, but also infused her fiction with broad issues concerning the conflict between enduring moral traditions and materialism. She won the Pulitzer prize for *One of Ours* (1927). Her other works included *O Pioneers!* (1913), *The Song of the Lark* (1915), *My Antonia* (1918), *A Lost Lady* (1923), *Death Comes to the Archbishop* (1927), and *Shadows of the Rock* (1931).

Catholic church The first Catholic church was founded in 1634 at St Mary's, Md. MARYLAND originated as a refuge for English Catholics, but relatively few came and Protestants dominated the colony. Because Catholicism was popularly associated with Britain's longstanding enemies, France and Spain, public opinion and government policy discouraged open Catholic worship before the Revolution. In 1785 there were approximately 25,000 practicing Catholics (less than 1 percent of the population) and 30 priests in the US. Under its first American bishop John CARROLL, the church progressed rapidly and may have numbered 50,000 members by 1800.

In the 19th century, the church made few domestic converts, but gained millions of foreign immigrants. It was the chief target of the KNOW-NOTHING PARTY. The number of parishes rose from 124 in 1820 to 2,250 in 1860, and 10,339 in 1900, when the US contained 12,000,000 Catholics (15.7 percent of its population). In 1908 the Vatican declared that the US was no longer a mission field. By 1921, it had 20,000,000 members (18.7 percent of the population). Its only major, enduring schism occurred in 1907 with the forming of the Polish National Catholic church (282,400 members in 1990). Membership rose from 45,640,600 in 1965 to 57,019,900 (23 percent of all Americans, but 38.6 percent of all churchgoers) in 1990, when there were 23,500 parishes.

Catt, Carrie Chapman (b. Ripon, Wis., 9 January 1859; d. New Rochelle, N.Y., 9 March 1947) In the 1890s Catt joined the WOMEN'S SUFFRAGE movement, and helped found the National American Woman Suffrage Association in 1900. She founded the Women's Peace party in 1915, but supported the war effort after US entry into WORLD WAR I. She was the League of Women Voters' first president in 1920, and chaired the Commission on the Cause and Cure of War (1925–32). She moderated her pacifism as German anti-Semitism rose in the 1930s.

cattle kingdom Extensive cattle grazing had developed by 1800 in the Carolinas and then spread west to TEXAS, where cattlemen adopted many practices from Hispanic herdsmen. The cattle kingdom's heart lay in the area bounded by Corpus Christi, Laredo, and San Antonio, a grassy region of mild winters and abundant water. When the CIVIL WAR disrupted a small-scale trade in range cattle between Tex. and New Orleans, cattle multiplied until they numbered 5,000,000 head by 1866. To dispose of the surplus, then worth just $6 per head in Tex., ex-rebels began making long drives over routes like the thousand-mile CHISHOLM and

GOODNIGHT–LOVING TRAILS to railroad depots like Abilene, Wichita, Dodge City, and Denver, where cows might fetch five times their original price. From 1866 to 1890, perhaps 10,000,000 cattle were driven out of Tex.

Ranchers brought herds from overstocked Tex. pastures to replace BUFFALO being exterminated on the Great Plains; they usually grazed livestock free on open range, and by 1880 there were 4,500,000 cattle north of Tex. An influx of farmers and sheepherders, along with widespread use of BARBED WIRE, steadily closed the open ranges in the 1880s, but a rising tide of eastern and British investment capital expanded herds to the point of overgrazing. Disaster came in the winter of 1885–6, when blizzards wiped out over 80 percent of the western herds. Enclosed pastures and the use of hay as winter fodder replaced open-range grazing, and long drives disappeared.

Cayuga Indians One of the FIVE NATIONS, the Cayugas occupied lands east of Cayuga Lake, N.Y., between the ONONDAGA and SENECA INDIANS. In 1771 they numbered 1,040, about 10 percent of all the IROQUOIS CONFEDERACY. As British allies in the American Revolution (*see* REVOLUTIONARY WAR), they fled from their villages in SULLIVAN'S CAMPAIGN, suffered a 15 percent population decline, and lost a third of their number who migrated to Canada. By 1795, they had sold all their N.Y. lands but 4 square miles. Many went to Ohio with Senecas and then moved to Okla. Cayugas now have reservations at Miami, Okla., and Oshweken, Ontario.

Cayuse Indians Of Penutian language stock, the Cayuse occupied northeast Oreg., where they acquired horses in the 1720s and raised large herds. They may have numbered 500 about 1800. Because they sold so much stock to pioneers on the OREGON TRAIL, "cayuse" was used as slang for a wild range horse. Contact with whites brought a high deathrate from disease and contributed to the CAYUSE WAR. The Cayuse declined in numbers and most moved to reservations set up for the Nez Perce or Umatillas. Most now live on the Umatilla reservation near Pendleton, Oreg.

Cayuse War During the winter of 1846–7, numerous CAYUSE INDIANS caught white diseases and died under the care of Presbyterian missionaries led by Rev. Marcus Whitman. The Cayuse assumed Whitman's group was murdering them, and on 29 November 1847, they massacred 14 missionaries near Walla Walla, Wash., and captured 53 women and children. Oregon Territory volunteers harassed both Cayuse and innocent tribes until 1850, when six Cayuse surrendered, confessed, and were hanged.

CCC *see* CIVILIAN CONSERVATION CORPS

CENTO *see* CENTRAL TREATY ORGANIZATION

Central Intelligence Agency (CIA) On 13 June 1942, Executive Order 13 established the Office of Strategic Services (OSS), under the joint chiefs of staff, to collect and analyze intelligence under the direction of Major General William J. Donovan. In 1945 the OSS was reorganized as the Central Intelligence Group, which formed the nucleus of the CIA when the NATIONAL SECURITY ACT established it to modernize and coordinate intelligence and espionage operations.

The CIA attracted criticism for poor intelligence during the BAY OF PIGS INVASION, for plotting to assassinate Fidel CASTRO, for involvement in the domestic political affairs of Chile and other nations, and unwittingly supplying equipment used in the WATERGATE SCANDAL. In 1974 amendments to the Foreign Assistance Act restricted the CIA's freedom of action. In response to the Nelson ROCKEFELLER Commission report, both houses of Congress formed permanent oversight committees for monitoring CIA operations, and director William Colby was replaced by George BUSH.

CIA operatives stirred controversy in April 1984 upon being exposed for sowing harbors in NICARAGUA with mines that had damaged a Soviet tanker and seven other ships from six nations. In October 1984, Congress discovered that the CIA had provided guidance on assassinating government officials in a manual for Nicaraguan anti-Communist guerrillas. Evidence from the IRAN-CONTRA SCANDAL later revealed that the CIA had cooperated in violations by the National Security Council of the BOLAND AMENDMENTS.

Central Pacific Railroad *see* TRANSCONTINENTAL RAILROADS

Central Treaty Organization (CENTO) This organization grew out of the Baghdad Pact, which was a mutual defense alliance signed by Turkey and Iraq in February 1955, and expanded to include Pakistan, Iran, and Britain in November. The US declined an offer to join, but it sent observers to the first meeting in November 1955 and supported the organization as a vehicle for its CONTAINMENT POLICY. US representatives sat with the pact's committees on military, counterespionage, and economic affairs, beginning in 1957. The alliance became known as the Central Treaty Organization in August 1959, after Iraq withdrew following a coup in the previous year. When Pakistan and Iran withdrew in early 1979, Britain and Turkey dissolved CENTO.

Cerro Gordo, battle of (Mexico) On 17–18 April 1847, Major General Winfield SCOTT's 8,500 US troops routed President Antonio Lopez de Santa Anna's 12,000 Mexicans. US losses: 64 killed, 353 wounded. Mexican losses: 1,200 killed and wounded, 3,041 captured, 43 cannon. Having taken more prisoners than he could feed, Scott released them on parole.

CETA *see* COMPREHENSIVE EMPLOYMENT AND TRAINING ACT

Chae Chan Ping* v. *United States *see* CHINESE EXCLUSION RULING

Chafin, Eugene Wilder (b. East Troy, Wis., 1 November 1852; d. Long Beach, Calif., 30 November 1920) In 1875 Chafin opened a law office at Waukesha, Wis., but moved to Chicago in 1901. He began to work for PROHIBITION at an early age, leaving the Republicans and joining the PROHIBITION PARTY in 1881. Chafin unsuccessfully sought election to Congress in 1882 and 1902, for Wis. governor in 1898, and as Ill. attorney general in 1904. He spent most of his life after 1904 lecturing for prohibition. As Prohibition Party nominee for president, he polled 1.7 percent of the vote in 1904 and 1.4 percent in 1908.

***Challenger*, USS** *see* NATIONAL AERONAUTICS AND SPACE ADMINISTRATION

Champion* v. *Ames In 1903 the Supreme Court affirmed (5–4) a US law forbidding lottery tickets to be sent via mail; it ruled that federal authority to regulate interstate commerce implicitly included the right of prohibiting access to the postal service for activities deemed injurious to public morals, and that this right did not encroach on state police powers. The decision established a concept later termed federal police power, which allowed Congress to bar offensive or harmful materials from the mails.

Champlain, Samuel de (b. Brouage, Saintonge, France, ca. 1570; d. Quebec, Canada, 25 December 1635) He was the individual most responsible for founding French Canada. After exploring the St Lawrence River during 1603 and 1604–6, he founded France's first permanent settlement at Quebec on 8 July 1608. He established a strong basis for friendly relations with the local tribes speaking ALGONQUIAN LANGUAGES, based on the FUR TRADE. In 1616 his journeys with HURON INDIAN war parties raiding central N.Y. resulted in the earliest armed conflict between the French and IROQUOIS CONFEDERACY.

Chancellorsville, battle of (Va.) On 27 April 1863, attempting to envelop General Robert E. LEE's 61,000 Confederates, Major General Joseph Hooker divided his 134,000 Federals to attack Lee's lines at FREDERICKSBURG, Va. On 1–3 May, 26,000 Confederates under Stonewall JACKSON and J. E. B. STUART routed 75,000 men under Hooker at Chancellorsville. On 4 May, Lee led 20,000 men to recapture Fredericksburg from Major General John Sedgwick's 40,000 Federals, who had taken the town on 3 May. On 6 May, Hooker ordered a retreat. USA losses: 1,575 killed, 9,594 wounded, 5,676 missing. CSA losses: 1,665 killed, 9,081 wounded, 2,018 missing. Stonewall Jackson, Lee's best subordinate, died in the battle. Encouraged by Lee's victory, the CSA government ordered him to invade the North (*see* GETTYSBURG).

Channing, William Ellery (b. Newport, R.I., 7 April 1780; d. Bennington, Vt., 2 October 1842) In 1798 Channing graduated from Harvard and was installed in 1803 as a Congregationalist minister at Boston's Federal Street church, his lifelong pastorate. His humane critique of orthodox Calvinism formed the core of UNITARIAN theology, which Channing first propounded in an ordination sermon at Baltimore in 1819. In 1820 he organized his supporters into the Berry Street conference, the precursor of the American Unitarian Association (1825). Channing's scholarship included *Remarks on American Literature* (1830), *Slavery* (1835), *The Abolitionist* (1836), and *Duty of the Free States* (1842); his writings were a major influence on TRANSCENDENTALISM.

Chaos, Operation *see* OPERATION CHAOS

Chapin, Dwight Lee (b. Wichita, Kans., 2 December 1940) He held several jobs for Richard NIXON and H. R. HALDEMAN after 1962 and was Nixon's appointments secretary (1969–73). He helped coordinate the "dirty-tricks" strategy against George MCGOVERN's campaign during the WATERGATE SCANDAL, was indicted on perjury charges for lying to Congress, and resigned on 28 February 1973.

Chaplin, Charlie (b. London, England, 16 April 1889; d. Vevey, Switzerland, 25 December 1977) Born Charles Spencer Chaplin, he came to the US in 1913 and stayed in Hollywood to become a world-renowned master of comedy by virtue of his tragicomic character, the "little tramp." As an actor, writer, and director, Chaplin played a major role in transforming film comedy from slapstick to an art capable of eliciting pathos and satirizing society. He never renounced his British citizenship. He became a victim of MCCARTHYISM in 1953, when he was accused of Communist sympathies and denied reentry to the country from abroad. He then made Switzerland his home. The US motion picture industry honored him with several tributes in the 1970s, and he was knighted in 1975.

Chaplinsky* v. *New Hampshire On 9 March 1942, the Supreme Court unanimously declared that the FIRST AMENDMENT was intended to protect speech of potential benefit to society, but not to sanction "fighting words" that arouse anger that could lead to violence, libelous statements, or obscene material. States may prohibit such expressions so long as they do so in language crafted precisely to protect the community from public nuisances.

Chapultepec, battle of (Mexico) On 8–13 September 1847, Major General Winfield SCOTT's 8,000 US army troops and marines captured Mexico City's main fortress. The capital surrendered on 14 August. US losses: 262 killed, 1,255 wounded. Mexican losses: 3,800 killed, captured, and wounded. The victory ended fighting in the MEXICAN WAR.

Charles I (b. Dunfermline, Scotland, 19 November 1600; beheaded outside Whitehall Palace, Middlesex, England, 30 January 1649) In 1625 Charles proclaimed VIRGINIA the first ROYAL COLONY, and he gave MARYLAND to Lord BALTIMORE as the first PROPRIETARY COLONY. His support for high-church Anglicanism was a major factor driving PURITANS to settle New England. He patented the MASSACHUSETTS BAY COMPANY and then tried to revoke its charter, but could not compel its appearance in court before the English Civil War overtook him.

Charles II (b. St James's Palace, Middlesex, England, 29 May 1630; d. Whitehall Palace, Middlesex, England, 6 February 1685) In exile since the end of the English Civil War, Charles II was not crowned until 23 April 1661. He made CHARTER COLONIES of CONNECTICUT and RHODE ISLAND, conquered NEW NETHERLAND, fought the second and third ANGLO-DUTCH WARS, and made ROYAL COLONIES of NEW HAMPSHIRE and MASSACHUSETTS. He patented the PROPRIETARY COLONIES of CAROLINA, NEW YORK, EAST JERSEY, WEST JERSEY, and PENNSYLVANIA. He aroused much unrest in the colonies by naming Catholics to high office and establishing the DOMINION OF NEW ENGLAND.

Charles River Bridge* v. *Warren Bridge In 1837 the Supreme Court modified *DARTMOUTH COLLEGE* v. *WOODWARD* in deciding whether Mass. violated a 1785 charter allowing the Charles River Bridge Co. to operate a toll bridge, by subsequently chartering the Warren Bridge Co. to build a competing structure nearby. In ruling against Charles River Bridge, the Court noted (4–3) that because its charter had not granted exclusive rights to monopolize local traffic, a second bridge might be erected without transgressing the constitutional prohibition against laws impairing contractual obligations, even though erecting the second bridge would reduce Charles River Bridge's value. The

Court then elaborated an expansive rule for determining the extent of vested rights protected by a business charter: corporations retained no more privileges than were specified by the obvious meaning of their charter's specific terms, and governments might interpret ambiguous clauses against the corporation in order to promote the public interest. The decision provided a legal basis for closer state regulation of corporations.

Charles Town, battles of (S.C.) (1) On 27 August 1706, five French and Spanish privateers anchored off Charles Town harbor. On 27 and 29 October and in November, S.C. militia defeated two landing parties and captured one of the privateers. French and Spanish losses: 30 killed, 320 captured. S.C. losses: 1 killed.

(2) On 28 June 1776, Major General Charles Lee's 435-man garrison on Sullivan Island repulsed an attack by eight British warships and forced Lieutenant General Henry CLINTON to abandon plans to seize Charles Town with 3,000 troops. US losses: 10 killed, 22 wounded. British losses: 64 killed, 141 wounded.

(3) From 1 April to 12 May 1780, Clinton besieged and captured Charles Town with 10 warships (530 guns), 90 transports, 5,000 sailors and marines, and 8,700 soldiers. US losses: 89 killed, 138 wounded, 2,571 Continentals and 800 S.C. militia captured. British losses: 76 killed, 189 wounded. The British occupied Charles Town until 27 October 1782.

charter colonies These were colonies established by a royal patent granting them exclusive control over their own internal governance, free from involvement by the Crown. Va. was a charter colony until 1624, Mass. until 1684, and Ga. from 1732 to 1752. By 1776, only Conn. and R.I. retained charter status.

Chase, Salmon Portland (b. Cornish, N.H., 13 January 1808; d. New York, N.Y., 7 May 1873) A Cincinnati lawyer who defended runaway slaves several times, Chase emerged as a towering antislavery spokesman. He ran unsuccessfully for the Republican presidential nomination in 1860, and became secretary of the Treasury in 1861. Abraham LINCOLN found Chase's extreme views on SLAVERY increasingly divisive within his cabinet; he accepted Chase's resignation in 1864 and appointed him chief justice of the Supreme Court. Chase presided over Andrew JOHNSON's impeachment trial, which proceeded according to strict judicial rules – much to Johnson's advantage – rather than as an investigative hearing. He dissented from the second LEGAL TENDER CASE and the SLAUGHTERHOUSE CASES.

Chase, Samuel (b. Somerset County, Md., 17 April 1741; d. Baltimore, Md., 19 June 1811) As one of the SONS OF LIBERTY, Chase opposed the STAMP ACT in 1764. He signed the DECLARATION OF INDEPENDENCE, and was one of the ANTIFEDERALISTS in 1788. He became associate justice on the Supreme Court on 27 January 1796. Unable to exercise his judicial responsibilities impartially because of his strong prejudices toward the FEDERALIST PARTY, he presided at trials under the SEDITION ACT (1798) with extreme partisan vindictiveness and was impeached in 1804. His acquittal by the Senate, due to an incompetent prosecution by John RANDOLPH, ended the inclination of Thomas JEFFERSON and other Democrats to purge the federal bench of Federalists.

Château-Thierry, battle of (France) *see* WORLD WAR I

Chateaugay River, battle of the On 25–6 October 1813, Brigadier General Wade Hampton's 4,500 US troops made futile attacks on Lieutenant Colonel Charles De Salaberry's 1,400 Canadians and British, and withdrew to winter quarters at Plattsburg, N.Y. US losses: 50 killed, wounded, missing. British losses: 5 killed, 20 wounded, missing. Hampton's withdrawal forced Major General James Wilkinson to abandon his campaign against Montreal.

Chattahoochee River, battle of the (Ga.) *see* ATLANTA, BATTLES FOR

Chattanooga, battles for (Tenn.) On 23 November 1863, Major General Ulysses S. GRANT's 56,400 Federals began assaulting General Braxton Bragg's 64,200 Confederates, who besieged them at Chattanooga. Union forces took Lookout Mountain on 24 November and Missionary Ridge on 25 November. USA losses: 753 killed, 4,722 wounded, 349 missing. CSA losses: 361 killed, 2,160 wounded, 4,146 missing.

Missionary Ridge's loss broke Bragg's siege and allowed William T. SHERMAN to use Chattanooga as a logistical base in the battles for ATLANTA.

Chautauqua movement This was a program for bringing cultural enrichment to rural Americans through speakers who lectured in small towns. The movement was inspired by a fortnight's training session for Methodist Sunday-school teachers held in August 1874 at Lake Chautauqua, N.Y. By 1900, about 200 assembly centers had been founded to feature speakers on religious or educational subjects in the northeast and midwest. In 1904 traveling Chautauquas began making circuits to lecture at numerous isolated communities; they visited 12,000 localities and addressed perhaps a third of the US population at the movement's peak in 1924. As movies and radio ended rural isolation, and rural inhabitants gained access to a wider range of recreational and cultural activities, Chautauqua's appeal declined. The program ceased in 1932.

Chavez, Cesar (b. Yuma, Ariz., 31 March 1927; d. San Luis, Ariz., 23 April 1993) He became a migrant laborer at the age of 10 when his family lost their small farm in Ariz. In 1952 he joined the Community Services Organization as an organizer, but left in 1962 when it rejected his ideas for mobilizing itinerant farm workers. He founded the National Farm Workers Association for this purpose in September 1962, and this became the National Farm Workers' Organizing Committee in 1966. Chavez attained national prominence by calling a strike against grape growers around Delano, Calif., in September 1965. In the spring of 1968, Chavez escalated the labor dispute with a national boycott of non-union grapes from Calif. By July 1970, his union had forced growers to negotiate contracts covering two-thirds of the Calif. grape crop. His success in organizing a rootless work force, demanding equal treatment for Hispanics, and adhering to nonviolent principles made Chavez the most respected Chicano leader of his generation.

Chavis, Benjamin Franklin, Jr. (b. Oxford, N.C., 22 January 1948) At the age of 14, he successfully demanded the desegregation of his hometown library after being denied a lending card. Chavis was a field worker for the United Church of Christ's Commission for Racial Justice while organizing protests against school SEGREGATION in Wilmington, N.C. In 1971, when extensive violence led to two deaths, Chavis and nine others (the Wilmington Ten) were charged and convicted of firebombing a white-owned store. Before the conviction was overturned, Chavis was in prison from 1976 to 1980, during which time he earned a graduate divinity degree from Duke. He became a United Church of Christ minister in 1980, and later earned a Ph.D. in theology from Howard. He was executive director of the Commission for Racial Justice (1986–93) and of the NATIONAL ASSOCIATION FOR THE ADVANCEMENT OF COLORED PEOPLE (NAACP) (1993–4). The NAACP fired him on 20 August 1994 for secretly using $332,400 of its funds for an out-of-court settlement with a woman acusing him of sexual harassment.

Cherokee Indians One of the FIVE CIVILIZED TRIBES, Cherokees speak one of the IROQUOIAN LANGUAGES. In 1650, 22,000 Cherokees may have occupied the eastern slopes of the Appalachians in N.C., S.C., and Ga. They participated in the S.C. deerskin trade and suffered heavy losses from smallpox in the 1730s, but avoided war until the indecisive CHEROKEE WAR. In the American Revolution (*see* REVOLUTIONARY WAR), they attacked the frontier as British allies in 1776, but were driven back and forced to abandon most of their Carolina lands. They raided Tenn. incessantly until deprived of Spanish supplies by the treaty of SAN LORENZO. In the period 1776–96, their population probably declined from 16,000 to 10,000. Some Cherokees fought with US forces in the CREEK WAR, but most were neutral in the WAR OF 1812. By the 1820s, they were concentrated in northern Ga.; they won legal battles before the Supreme Court in *CHEROKEE NATION* v. *GEORGIA* and *WORCESTER* v. *GEORGIA*, but found the victories to be hollow. They exchanged their Ga. lands for a reservation in Indian Territory (*see* OKLAHOMA) by the treaty of NEW ECHOTA, but under great duress, and most had to be forced west on the TRAIL OF TEARS. A few hundred hid out in the Smoky Mountains to become the Eastern Band. The nation had many slaves in Okla. and most were pro-Confederate in the CIVIL WAR. The Western Band's reservation is at Tahlequah, Okla., where 58,232 live, and the Eastern Band's reservation is at Cherokee, N.C.

Cherokee Nation* v. *Georgia When the CHEROKEE INDIANS applied to the Supreme Court to forbid Ga. to extend its laws over their reservation, the Court declared in March 1831 that it lacked jurisdiction to intervene because the Cherokee were not a foreign state under the Constitution, but it nevertheless stated that the Indians – as "domestic dependent nations" – could not be deprived of their lands until they sold them. The Court again denied state jurisdiction over the Cherokees in *WORCESTER* V. *GEORGIA*.

Cherokee Strip This strip was an area of 1,920,000 acres in northwestern Okla., between its panhandle and the Arkansas River, that was reserved for the CHEROKEE INDIANS in case their own reservation became inadequate to support them. They forfeited title to the strip for having supported the Confederacy in the CIVIL WAR. In 1889 Congress declared the strip PUBLIC DOMAIN and opened it to settlement. It was the site of the OKLAHOMA LAND RUSH and the main area designated as Oklahoma Territory before the Indian Territory's dissolution.

Cherokee War In the winter of 1760, CHEROKEE INDIANS killed 23 S.C. settlers. In May–June, Colonel Archibald's 1,300 Highlanders burned several Cherokee towns, suffered 50 wounded in an ambush near Echoee Pass, N.C., and inflicted about 80 Indian casualties, but failed to reach 150 British troops at Fort Loudoun, Tenn., which surrendered on 7 August and whose men were massacred on 9 August. Lieutenant Colonel James Grant's 2,500 redcoats and militia survived ambush at Echoee Pass, N.C., on 7 June 1761 and burned the Cherokee towns. Hostilities then ended and a peace treaty was signed on 17 December 1761.

Cherry Valley, raid on (N.Y.) On 11 November 1778, Major John Butler's 700 Tories and Iroquois attacked Fort Alden, which did not fall, and burned the community of Cherry Valley, N.Y. US losses: 39 killed, 71 captured (mostly civilians). British losses: minimal. American outrage over raids on Cherry Valley and WYOMING VALLEY, Pa., resulted in SULLIVAN'S and BRODHEAD'S CAMPAIGNS.

***Chesapeake*, USS–HMS *Leopard* incident** On 22 June 1807, off Norfolk, Va., Captain S. P. Humphreys of the HMS *Leopard* demanded that Captain James Barron permit a search of the USS *Chesapeake* for British deserters, and opened fire when Barron refused. After killing three Americans and wounding 18, Humphreys' men seized four ex-British sailors. The attack stirred strong anti-British passions, and influenced Congress to enact an embargo (*see* EMBARGO ACT) on US commerce in December.

Chesapeake*, *USS* v. *HMS Shannon On 1 June 1813, off Boston, Captain Philip Broke's *Shannon* (38 guns, 330 seamen) defeated Captain James Lawrence's *Chesapeake* (38 guns, 379 seamen) in 15 minutes. US losses: 70 killed (including Lawrence), 309 captured (among them 100 wounded). British losses: 24 killed, 59 wounded (among them Broke). Lawrence became a national hero because of his dying words: "Don't give up the ship."

Chesapeake Capes, battle of On 5 September 1781, Admiral François de Grasse's 24 ships (1,788 guns, 19,000 seamen) drove off Admiral Thomas Graves's 19 ships (1,402 guns, 13,000 seamen) from the mouth of Chesapeake Bay. French losses: 220 killed and wounded. British losses: 90 killed, 246 wounded, the 64-gun *Terrible* damaged beyond repair and scuttled. De Grasse prevented Graves from intercepting a supply convoy under Admiral de Barras destined for Washington's army, and trapped Cornwallis's army at YORKTOWN, Va.

Cheyenne campaigns (1) In the spring of 1864, Colo. volunteers wrongly accused CHEYENNE INDIANS of horse stealing and attacked them. After the SAND CREEK MASSACRE, the treaties of the Little Arkansas River ended hostilities in October 1865.

(2) In 1867–8, Cheyennes harassed US forts on the BOZEMAN TRAIL until US troops withdrew by the treaty of FORT LARAMIE. Southern Cheyennes raided Kans., but ceased after US cavalry destroyed large camps at Washita Creek, Okla., on 27 November 1868 and at Summit Springs, Colo., on 11 July 1869.

(3) The army fought 2,000 southern Cheyennes in the RED RIVER WAR until most surrendered in March 1875 and returned to the Indian Territory.

(4) Northern Cheyennes comprised a fifth of Sitting Bull's force in the third SIOUX WAR; they returned to reservations in mid-1876.

Cheyenne Indians Speakers of one of the ALGONQUIAN LANGUAGES, the Cheyennes numbered about 3,500 in 1780 and were closely allied with the ARAPAHO INDIANS. Hard pressed by war with the SIOUX, they migrated from northwestern Minn. to Nebr.–Wyo. in the early 19th century. They split into northern and southern bands on the plains. After fighting in the CHEYENNE CAMPAIGNS and the RED RIVER WAR, they accepted RESERVATION status along the Canadian River in Okla. (headquartered at Concho) and in Mont. within Big Horn and Rosebud counties.

Chicago, Burlington and Quincy Railroad* v. *Chicago On 1 March 1897, the Supreme Court (7–1) overturned *BARRON* v. *BALTIMORE* by ruling that the DUE PROCESS clause of the FOURTEENTH AMENDMENT required state courts to uphold FIFTH AMENDMENT guarantees of providing fair compensation for property taken in cases of EMINENT DOMAIN. This case was the earliest instance when the federal BILL OF RIGHTS was extended to proceedings in state trials; it undermined the Court's ruling in the GRANGER CASES and made it difficult for states to regulate corporations.

Chicago Democratic convention riot (Ill.) While the Democratic party prepared to nominate Hubert HUMPHREY, many groups in the VIETNAM ANTIWAR MOVEMENT demonstrated outside the convention hall and YIPPIES conducted disruptive tactics. On 28 August 1968, massive and violent riots ensued when police charged demonstrators, who fought back and engaged in widespread vandalism. Because the news coverage raised public anxiety that the US was becoming anarchic, Richard NIXON's law-and-order campaign gained support. Since Humphrey was strongly backed by Chicago's mayor, who had directed police security for the convention, the riots also alienated many antiwar Democrats from Humphrey. The CHICAGO EIGHT were tried for inciting the riots.

Chicago Eight On 24 September 1969, the Chicago Eight were tried for conspiracy to incite the CHICAGO DEMOCRATIC CONVENTION RIOT. They included three members of the National Mobilization to End the War in Vietnam (David Dellinger, Thomas Hayden, and Rennie Davis), two YIPPIES (Abbie Hoffman and Jerry Rubin), a BLACK PANTHER (Bobby SEALE), a graduate student (Lee Weiner), and a college teacher (John Froines). Seale was later remanded for separate trial. Judge Julius J. Hoffman issued 175 contempt citations during the trial, and allowed his impartiality to be discredited by overreacting to the defendants' disruptive tactics. WEATHERMEN rioted outside the court on 11 October. On 18 February 1970, all remaining defendants were found innocent of conspiracy, but Davis, Dellinger, Hoffman, Hayden, and Rubin were found guilty of crossing a state line to incite a riot. The five convictions were overturned on appeal in 1973, and Seale was never tried for conspiracy.

Chicago, Milwaukee and Saint Paul Railroad Company* v. *Minnesota In 1890 the Supreme Court struck down an 1887 Minn. law that empowered a state regulatory board to set railroad rates and barred railroads from appealing those rates in court. Elaborating upon *SANTA CLARA COUNTY* v. *SOUTHERN PACIFIC RAILROAD COMPANY*, the Court ruled that by denying corporations access to the courts, Minn. had violated the FIFTH AMENDMENT's guarantee that no property be taken for public use without DUE PROCESS. By allowing corporations to appeal decisions by state regulatory agencies in US courts (which often ruled for big business), the decision undermined the powers acquired by states through the GRANGER CASES. The Court extended this ruling in *SMYTH* v. *AMES* and *REAGAN* v. *FARMERS' LOAN AND TRUST COMPANY*.

Chicago race riot (Ill.) In July 1919, a black teenager was killed, while police watched, for swimming at a white beach on Lake Michigan. Whites then invaded black neighborhoods and attacked inhabitants over a period of three days. Twenty blacks and 14 whites died.

Chickamauga, battle of (Ga.) On 19–20 September 1863, General Braxton Bragg's 66,300 Confederates routed Major General William Rosecrans's 58,200 Federals. USA losses: 1,657 killed, 9,756 wounded, 4,757 missing. CSA losses: 2,312 killed, 14,674 wounded, 1,468 missing. The Federals retreated to CHATTANOOGA.

Chickasaw Indians These Indians were speakers of one of the MUSKOGEAN LANGUAGES and occupied lands southwest of the Tennessee River in Tenn. and northern Miss. They may have numbered 8,000 by 1720, when they came under attack for rejecting a French ultimatum to expel S.C. deerskin traders from their towns. During the periods 1720–4, 1729–36, and 1752, they repelled invasions by French forces and their CHOCTAW INDIAN allies. In the American Revolution (*see* REVOLUTIONARY WAR), they attacked US settlements in Tenn. and Ky. as British allies. In 1786 they accepted white settlement of central Tenn. in return for peace and US recognition of their land claims. They helped the US fight Indians north of the Ohio River and raided the CREEK INDIANS in the 1790s. After selling their lands west of the Tennessee River in 1818, they won reasonable terms for removal to Okla. with the other FIVE CIVILIZED TRIBES; they moved in 1837–8 with little hardship or unnecessary loss of life. In 1987, 11,780 Chickasaws lived at their Ardmore, Okla., reservation.

Chief Joseph (b. Wallawalla Valley, Oreg., 1840; d. Colville Reservation, Wash., 21 September 1904) Joseph was a leader of the NEZ PERCE INDIANS who advocated nonviolence toward white squatters on his nation's lands and peaceful resistance to the Oreg. government's efforts to move his people from the Grande Ronde valley to a 1,000 square-mile reservation in Idaho. Although he believed that opposing the US Army was futile, he joined the resistance of other Nez Perce who fought rather than accept forcible resettlement in 1877. Joseph initially ranked as a minor figure in the NEZ PERCE CAMPAIGN, but was the only major leader left when the nation's survivors capitulated to the army in October 1877. "I am tired of fighting," Joseph lamented in an eloquent surrender speech that has long troubled US consciences. "Our chiefs are killed. . . . The old men are all dead. . . . The little children are freezing to death. . . . I am tired. My heart is sick and sad. From where the sun now stands, I will fight no more forever."

child labor laws Child labor was first recognized as a problem as the US industrialized. By 1842, Mass. and Conn. had set 10 hours as a child's maximum workday, and in 1848 Pa. made 12 the minimum age for performing factory work. Other states passed similar laws, but none enforced them by inspections until the 1870s. In 1904 the National Child Labor Commission was founded to press for a federal law to end child labor. The Keating-Owen Act (1 September 1916) forbade the interstate shipment of products made by child labor, but was struck down by *HAMMER* v. *DAGENHART*. The federal Child Labor Act (1919) put a prohibitive (10 percent) tax on such items sold across state lines, but was struck down by *BAILEY* v. *DREXEL FURNITURE COMPANY*. A constitutional amendment forbidding child labor passed Congress on 2 June 1924, but by 1950 only 26 states had ratified it. The NEW DEAL outlawed child labor by the FAIR LABOR STANDARDS ACT.

Chimel* v. *California On 23 June 1969, the Supreme Court defined (6–2) a reasonable search made during a proper arrest without a warrant. The FOURTH AMENDMENT permitted police to examine only the immediate area around the suspect to confiscate weapons or prevent destruction of evidence; it did not sanction searching a suspect's entire residence if the arrest occurred there.

China, US intervention in (1) *see* BOXER REBELLION

(2) During 1912–38, the US stationed 1,000 troops of the 15th Army Infantry at Tientsin, patrolled the Yangtze River with seven navy gunboats (1912–41), and garrisoned Shanghai with the Fourth USMC Regiment (1927–41). US military forces peaked at 4,000 marines, 1,000 soldiers, and 50 naval vessels after the Nanking incident of May 1927, when Chiang Kai-shek's troops sacked foreign embassies and killed an American and five other diplomats. After China ignored US military threats and demands for reparations, the US abandoned its saber-rattling.

Chinese Exclusion Act (6 May 1882) Congress excluded all CHINESE IMMIGRATION for 10 years. The Supreme Court upheld this law in its CHINESE EXCLUSION RULING. The Geary Law reenacted this measure in 1892 and Chinese were indefinitely excluded in 1902.

Chinese Exclusion Ruling (*Chae Chan Ping* v. *United States*) On 13 May 1889, the Supreme Court unanimously upheld the CHINESE EXCLUSION ACT. The Court ruled that Congress must have absolute and exclusive authority over admitting foreigners to domestic residence, in order to safeguard national sovereignty.

Chinese immigration Chinese first arrived during the CALIFORNIA GOLD RUSH and large numbers helped build the TRANSCONTINENTAL RAILROAD. The Burlingame Treaty (1868) officially authorized Chinese immigration (which primarily consisted of male laborers who did not intend to remain permanently in the US), but on 17 November 1880, China agreed to revise this treaty by allowing the US to restrict or temporarily suspend entry of its citizens. In 1880, 105,000 Chinese (all but 5,000 were male) lived in the West, and by 1882, 5 percent of all US immigrants were from China. The CHINESE EXCLUSION ACT ended this migration. The US annexation of Hawaii ended Chinese immigration there in 1898, when those islands contained 25,800 Chinese.

The US Chinese population peaked at 107,488 in 1890 and fell to 74,954 by 1930. On 17 December 1943, Congress readmitted Chinese with an annual quota of 105. The COLD WAR enabled many ostensibly anti-Communist Chinese to immigrate, and 237,293 Chinese resided in the US by 1960 (with 40 percent in Calif. and 16 percent each in Hawaii and N.Y.). Many Indochinese BOAT PEOPLE were overseas Chinese. By 1991, 938,371 immigrants had entered from China and 318,125 from Hong Kong. In 1990 Chinese Americans numbered 1,648,000 and were 0.7 percent of the US population.

Chippewa Indians *Chippewa* is the common name used in the US for a group speaking one of the ALGONQUIAN LANGUAGES; it is a corrupt derivation of OJIBWA, by which name they are known in Canada. They may have numbered 35,000 about 1650, when they became linked to the FUR TRADE by the French. From an initial base around Sault Sainte Marie, they expanded throughout the northern Great Lakes into lands formerly used by the HURON, FOX, and SIOUX INDIANS. They fought in PONTIAC'S WAR and were British allies in the WAR OF 1812, but relations with the US were peaceful after 1815. Except for two small bands that went to Kans. in 1839, they escaped relocation to the Indian Territory. They now have seven reservations in Minn., six in Wis., three in Mich., and one in Mont.

Chippewa River, battle of (Ontario) On 5 July 1814, Brigadier General Winfield SCOTT's 1,300 US regulars, 200 Pa. militia, and 400 Indians defeated Major General Phineas Riall's 1,500 British regulars, 300 Canadians, and 300 Indians. US losses: 60 killed, 235 wounded. British losses: 148 killed, 321 wounded. Chippewa River marked the first time in the WAR OF 1812 that US troops bested an equal force of British regulars in open combat.

Chisholm, Shirley Anita (b. Brooklyn, N.Y., 30 November 1924) She was a teacher and administrator in New York City's Child Welfare Bureau before 1964, when she won election to the state legislature from Bedford-Stuyvesant in Brooklyn, as a Democrat. She became the first black congresswoman in 1968. In 1972 she was the first woman to seek the presidential nomination of a major party, and was also endorsed by the BLACK PANTHER PARTY, but won few delegates. She retired in 1983 after seven terms in Congress.

Chisholm Trail Blazed by Indian trader Jesse Chisholm, this trail connected San Antonio, Tex., with Abilene, Kans. From 1867–1871, it was the most important route for driving cattle northward to market and handled 300,000 cattle annually.

Chisholm* v. *Georgia In 1793 the Supreme Court affirmed the federal courts' jurisdiction to try suits brought by a citizen in one state against the government of another state, when the S.C. executors of a British subject sued Ga. for wrongfully confiscating a Tory's estate (*see* TORIES) during the Revolution. The Court ruled (4–1) that Ga. could not excuse itself from the suit under SOVEREIGN IMMUNITY, because Article III, Section

2 of the Constitution expressly allowed federal courts to hear "controversies between a state and citizens of another state." Outrage against this decision resulted in the ELEVENTH AMENDMENT's ratification, to protect states with sovereign immunity so that federal courts could not appropriate a state's treasury funds and transfer them to citizens in other states.

Choctaw Indians Speakers of one of the MUSKOGEAN LANGUAGES, about 14,000 Choctaws lived in western Ala. and southern Miss. about 1780. They fought for the French in the NATCHEZ WAR, fought CHICKASAW INDIANS continuously after 1720, harassed Spanish troops and commerce as British allies in the American Revolution (*see* REVOLUTIONARY WAR), and helped crush the CREEK INDIANS at the battle of HORSESHOE BEND. In 1830 the US forced the nation to exchange its remaining lands (about a quarter of Miss.) for land in Okla. and $5,000,000 paid over 20 years by the treaty of Dancing Rabbit Creek. During 1831–4, they moved to a reservation now headquartered at Durant, Okla., where 21,858 lived in 1987.

Christian Church *see* DISCIPLES OF CHRIST

Christian Churches *see* DISCIPLES OF CHRIST

Christiansen, Parley P. *see* FARMER-LABOR PARTY

Chrysler's Farm, battle of (Canada) On 11 November 1811, Colonel J. W. Morrison's 800 British regulars repulsed Brigadier General John Boyd's 2,000 US regulars about 70 miles from Montreal. US losses: 102 killed, 237 wounded, 100 captured. British losses: 22 killed, 48 wounded, 12 missing. This defeat, coupled with US failure at the battle of the CHATEAUGAY RIVER, forced US troops to retreat from a planned attack on Montreal.

Church of Christ, Scientist *see* EDDY, MARY BAKER

Church of England *see* ANGLICAN CHURCH

Church of Jesus Christ of Latter-day Saints *see* MORMONS

Churches of Christ *see* DISCIPLES OF CHRIST

Churubusco, battle of (Mexico) *see* CONTRERAS-CHURUBUSCO

Chy Lung* v. *Freeman *see* IMMIGRATION CASES

CIA *see* CENTRAL INTELLIGENCE AGENCY

Cincinnati, Society of the Named after the Roman citizen-soldier hero, Cincinnatus, this society was formed on 13 May 1783 as a fraternal organization of Continental Army officers. Naval officers later became eligible to join. George WASHINGTON became its first president on 19 June 1783, and was succeeded in 1799 by Alexander HAMILTON. Its members disproportionately supported the FEDERALIST PARTY. The society was criticized as an embryonic order of nobility because it was a hereditary organization open to each officer's descendants in the line of first sons. After nearing extinction, it was revived in 1902 and new state chapters formed.

CIO *see* CONGRESS OF INDUSTRIAL ORGANIZATIONS

city commission government This reform of the PROGRESSIVE ERA replaced the traditional municipal governments, divided between a mayor's executive duties and a council's legislative powers, with a unitary commission empowered to oversee city administration and pass local laws. Galveston, Tex., pioneered this system in 1900 with its five-man commission. About 500 cities had adopted the system by 1917.

city manager government This reform of the PROGRESSIVE ERA made city governments more efficient by assigning daily operations and routine financial responsibilities to an appointive, professional public administrator, who was responsible to the city council. This arrangement freed the councilors to frame long-range plans and left supervision of daily affairs to a specialist in urban administration, who was often an engineer or lawyer. In 1913 Dayton, Ohio, became the first large city to institute this governing structure, which originated in Staunton, Va. A City Managers' Association was founded in 1914. City manager governments existed in about 150 cities by 1920 and in over 270 by 1923.

Civil Rights Act (9 April 1866) To override the BLACK CODES and nullify the decision in *DRED SCOTT* v. *SANDFORD*, Congress passed this measure over Andrew

JOHNSON's veto (the first major law passed over a president's veto). It declared that all persons born in the US, except tribal Indians, were US citizens entitled to "full and equal benefit of laws," and foreshadowed the FOURTEENTH AMENDMENT. The CIVIL RIGHTS CASES (1883) reduced this act to impotency in fighting private discrimination. *JONES V. ALFRED H. MAYER COMPANY* (1968) revived its provisions by interpreting the THIRTEENTH AMENDMENT's purpose of eliminating "the badges of slavery" as authority to move against private acts of racial discrimination.

Civil Rights Act (1 March 1875) This measure forbade the exclusion of blacks from juries, from public accommodations like licensed taverns or theaters, or from common carriers like trolley cars or trains; it extended federal jurisdiction to such crimes, which would be subject to Supreme Court review in every case. While under consideration, its unpopularity led to Republican losses during the 1874 elections. The Supreme Court struck down its provisions outlawing private discrimination in the CIVIL RIGHTS CASES.

Civil Rights Act (9 September 1957) This law created the Commission on Civil Rights to investigate violations in this area and suggest remedies; it established the Civil Rights Division within the Justice Department; and it authorized federal judges to use injunctions for protecting black voting rights, and to enforce them with criminal contempt proceedings that could be tried without juries.

Civil Rights Act (6 May 1960) This law authorized criminal proceedings against racially-motivated violence and obstruction of federal court orders, required desegregated education for children of military personnel, and strengthened the power of courts to prevent obstruction of voting rights by nonwhites.

Civil Rights Act (2 July 1964) This law restored the federal government's power to bar racial discrimination for the first time since the CIVIL RIGHTS CASES. It contains 11 titles, of which II, VI, and VII are the most important. Title II requires open access for nonwhites to public accommodations serving interstate commerce (gas stations, restaurants, lodging houses having over five rooms, and all places of entertainment or exhibition). Title VI forbids any form of discrimination in programs that accept federal funds. Title VII outlaws employment discrimination; it created the Equal Employment Opportunity Commission, whose five members need Senate approval, to end unfair job practices through litigation and voluntary programs.

Title II was upheld in *HEART OF ATLANTA MOTEL V. UNITED STATES*. Title VI was the subject of *REGENTS OF UNIVERSITY OF CALIFORNIA V. BAKKE*. Cases involving Title VII were *GRIGGS V. DUKE POWER COMPANY*, *WASHINGTON V. DAVIS*, *UNITED STEELWORKERS OF AMERICA V. WEBER*, and *FIREFIGHTERS LOCAL UNION NUMBER 1784 V. STOTTS*. Sexual discrimination cases under Title VII were *COUNTY OF WASHINGTON V. GUNTHER* and *MERITOR SAVINGS BANK V. VINSON*.

Civil Rights Act (1965) *see* VOTING RIGHTS ACT

Civil Rights Act (11 April 1968) This law had been held up in Congress for two years, and was enacted in response to Martin Luther KING's assassination. It outlawed racial discrimination in the sale or rental of 90 percent of the nation's housing. It also made it a federal crime to harm civil rights workers, to cross a state line to incite a riot, or to teach the use of incendiary devices for riots.

Civil Rights Act (22 June 1970) This law amended and extended for five years the VOTING RIGHTS ACT. It increased its scope to northern cities or counties that used LITERACY TESTS, and established uniform residence requirements to vote in presidential elections. It lowered the voting age from 21 to 18 in federal, state, and local elections, but this last provision was held unconstitutional regarding states in *OREGON V. MITCHELL*.

Civil Rights Act (21 November 1991) This law reversed several Supreme Court decisions that held plaintiffs to a high standard of proof in winning job discrimination cases, in particular *WASHINGTON V. DAVIS*. Previously vetoed by George BUSH as a "quotas bill," and not a legitimate AFFIRMATIVE ACTION measure, it allowed class-action suits against employers if statistical evidence showed that their hiring or personnel standards had a "disparate impact" on minorities or women, even if there was no proof of discriminatory intent. It included a clause disavowing racial hiring quotas, but indicated that if the racial composition of an employer's work force diverged from that of the local labor market, he could be sued. The act increased employers' liability, by allowing plaintiffs to sue for damages, besides back pay and lost benefits. In 1994, ruling upon *Landgraf* v. *USI Film Products* and *Rivers* v. *Roadway Express, Incorporated*, the Supreme Court held (8–1) that the statute could not be applied retroactively to bias that allegedly occurred before the law's enactment; the Court's action denied federal jurisdiction to an estimated 8,000 cases pending suit.

civil rights cases On 15 October 1883, the Supreme Court decided whether the CIVIL RIGHTS ACT (1875) prohibited private discrimination against blacks regarding equal accommodations or privileges. It ruled (8–1) that the FOURTEENTH AMENDMENT forbade only states from violating civil rights, and did not pertain to behavior by persons who acted on their own. The Court held that neither the THIRTEENTH nor FOURTEENTH AMENDMENT gave the US any power to outlaw racial discrimination by employers, railroads, hotels, and any private citizens. By striking down such provisions of the Civil Rights Act (1875), this ruling ended federal efforts to ensure that blacks could exercise their full rights as citizens until passage of the CIVIL RIGHTS ACT (1964). The Court then reversed its 1883 ruling in *HEART OF ATLANTA MOTEL* V. *UNITED STATES*.

civil rights movement World War II made many whites aware of the fact that SEGREGATION undermined American claims to exert moral leadership worldwide (*see AMERICAN DILEMMA, AN*), and informed public opinion became hostile to JIM CROW LAWS. The civil rights movement is customarily dated as starting with *BROWN* V. *BOARD OF EDUCATION OF TOPEKA* (1954), which encouraged the filing of more lawsuits to challenge segregation and demand equal rights. This ruling sparked massive resistance among southern whites, primarily via WHITE CITIZENS COUNCILS, and led to the LITTLE ROCK DESEGREGATION VIOLENCE. The NATIONAL ASSOCIATION FOR THE ADVANCEMENT OF COLORED PEOPLE (NAACP) and National URBAN LEAGUE, which emphasized court actions, led the movement in the 1950s, but after 1960 the most influential organizations were the SOUTHERN CHRISTIAN LEADERSHIP CONFERENCE (SCLC), STUDENT NONVIOLENT COORDINATING COMMITTEE (SNCC), and CONGRESS OF RACIAL EQUALITY (CORE), whose tactics emphasized nonviolent civil disobedience.

The MONTGOMERY BUS BOYCOTT (1956) was the first success in a campaign of public demonstrations and protests to integrate US society for African Americans and demand passage of federal civil rights laws. FREEDOM RIDERS and the SIT-IN MOVEMENT helped galvanize black organizations to focus national attention on segregated public facilities through well-publicized incidents of peaceful civil disobedience, which often ended in law officials reacting with excessive force. Major conflicts erupted during the James MEREDITH riots at the University of Mississippi, the BIRMINGHAM DESEGREGATION VIOLENCE, and the SELMA FREEDOM MARCH.

The movement's major goal was for federal action to outlaw racial discrimination. After enactment of the limited CIVIL RIGHTS ACTS (1957 and 1960), Congress failed to pass stronger measures until Martin Luther KING organized the MARCH ON WASHINGTON (1963), which was critical in obtaining the CIVIL RIGHTS ACT (1964). After gaining the VOTING RIGHTS ACT (1965), the movement began to fragment among BLACK POWER MOVEMENT advocates, leaders seeking to redress economic inequality between the races, and more conservative groups like the NAACP and Urban League. White support ebbed after large-scale rioting became an annual ritual in urban ghettos from 1964 to 1968. Passage of the CIVIL RIGHTS ACT (1968), which had been sparked by King's assassination, was the movement's last great achievement. Progress on racial injustice thereafter largely came through court cases brought under various civil rights statutes.

civil service reform This became a major issue after a deranged office-seeker killed James GARFIELD. Its leading advocate was George Curtis, who founded the National Civil Service Reform League in 1881 and chaired it until 1892. Curtis wished to end the SPOILS SYSTEM by basing federal hiring and promotion on merit, preferably through competitive examinations, and protect officeholders from dismissal for political reasons. Reform began with the PENDLETON ACT (1883). The number of competitive civil service employees grew slowly, from 13,700 out of 100,000 in 1884, to 33,873 out of 157,442 by 1891, 106,205 out of 239,476 by 1901, and 222,278 out of 388,708 by 1910. By 1957, 86 percent of all federal workers occupied competitive civil service positions. To prevent political abuse of the civil service, the HATCH ACT was passed in 1939.

Civil War On 12 April 1861, Confederate bombardment of FORT SUMTER, S.C., began hostilities. By 20 May, 11 states had left the Union; the Confederacy later recognized Ky. and Mo. as states, but neither seceded (*see* SECESSION). Jefferson DAVIS's CSA government moved to Richmond, Va., from Montgomery, Ala., in June. The USA retained 23 states, and had admitted W.Va. and Nev. by 1864.

The Union's population was 21,930,000 (including 429,000 slaves), compared to 8,970,000 in the South (including 3,520,000 slaves). The USA war effort was served by 2,190,000 men (including 220,000 blacks), but no more than 900,000 men fought in CSA forces. The USA military's strength stood at 1,000,962 soldiers and 58,296 sailors in 1865, while the CSA army's maximum strength peaked at 481,000 in 1864. Half of all males aged 18–45 entered military service in the North, while two-thirds did so in the South.

The North produced 93 percent of American manufactures – including 97 percent of firearms, 94 percent of iron, and 96 percent of railroad materials – and held 71 percent of railroad mileage. The North built over 95 percent of American ships and expanded its navy from 90 vessels (21 unserviceable) to 641. The CSA navy commissioned just 108 warships.

Confederate victory at first BULL RUN in July 1861 ended Union attempts to take Richmond for nine months. Federal troops, meanwhile, established military superiority over W.Va. at RICH MOUNTAIN (July 1861), over central Mo. at WILSON'S CREEK (August 1861) and PEA RIDGE (March 1862), over central Ky. at MILL SPRINGS (January 1862), and over west Tenn. and west Ky. at FORTS HENRY and DONNELSON (February 1862). CSA forces failed to regain control of either west Tenn. at SHILOH (April 1862) or of Ky. at PERRYVILLE (October 1862), but they blocked a USA advance into east Tenn. at MURFREESBORO (December 1862).

By capturing ISLAND NUMBER 10 and NEW MADRID, Mo. (April 1862), US Navy amphibious operations allowed the army to start advancing down the Mississippi. After the duel of IRONCLADS USS *MONITOR* v. CSS "*MERRIMACK*," the USA navy took Norfolk (May 1862), NEW ORLEANS (May 1862), and MOBILE BAY (August 1864); it intercepted 10 percent of CSA blockade-runners in 1861, 33 percent in 1864, and 50 percent in 1865, for a total of 1,149 ships captured and 351 destroyed. CSA cruisers captured 260 USA merchant vessels worth over $20,000,000.

In the spring of 1862, Major General George MCCLELLAN's PENINSULAR CAMPAIGN failed after Stonewall JACKSON bottled up his reinforcements in the first SHENANDOAH VALLEY CAMPAIGN. After routing the USA Army of VIRGINIA at second BULL RUN, General Robert E. LEE invaded Md., but was beaten at ANTIETAM. President Abraham LINCOLN then issued his EMANCIPATION PROCLAMATION. After repulsing USA attacks at FREDERICKSBURG (December 1862) and CHANCELLORSVILLE (April 1863), Lee invaded the North.

July 1863 marked the war's turning point. Driven from Pa. at GETTYSBURG, Lee was never again able to resume the offensive. Union victories at VICKSBURG and PORT HUDSON established Federal control over the Mississippi River and split the Confederacy.

A Union offensive into Ga. was crushed at CHICKAMAUGA (September 1863), the last instance when CSA troops routed a major USA force. Federal forces broke the CSA siege of CHATTANOOGA in November, but not until May 1864 did they begin advancing on ATLANTA, which fell in September. The Federals crippled the CSA's main western army at FRANKLIN, Tenn. (November 1864), and then destroyed it at NASHVILLE

(December 1864). Major General William T. SHERMAN meanwhile completed his MARCH TO THE SEA and drove CSA troops in the Carolinas northward to Va.

Ulysses S. GRANT's Army of the POTOMAC inflicted heavy losses on Lee's Army of NORTHERN VIRGINIA at the WILDERNESS and SPOTSYLVANIA COURT HOUSE, but took extremely heavy casualties itself at COLD HARBOR (May–June 1864). Major General Philip SHERIDAN eliminated CSA resistance in the SHENANDOAH VALLEY (November 1864). Lee delayed Grant at PETERSBURG until April 1865, when the loss of FIVE FORKS-WHITE OAK ROAD compelled his retreat and allowed USA occupation of Richmond. Lee capitulated on 9 April at APPOMATTOX COURT HOUSE. The remaining CSA armies were surrendered by Joseph JOHNSTON at Durham Station, N.C. (26 April), Richard Taylor at Citronelle, Ala. (4 May), and Kirby Smith at New Orleans (26 May).

USA military spending equaled $6,157,691,000 and raised the national debt from $64,844,000 to $2,755,764,000. USA losses: 100,070 battle deaths, 30,218 deaths in CSA prison camps, 219,240 other deaths, 275,175 nonfatal wounds, and 194,743 captured. CSA losses: about 94,000 battle deaths, 25,976 deaths in USA prison camps, 138,000 other deaths, over 100,000 nonfatal wounds, and 214,865 captured.

Civil Works Administration (CWA) Because the PUBLIC WORKS ADMINISTRATION (PWA) created jobs too slowly to combat the GREAT DEPRESSION, Franklin D. ROOSEVELT created the CWA by executive order on 9 November 1933 with funds from the PWA budget. Within three months, the CWA had provided 4,200,000 jobs building 40,000 schools, 469 airports, and 255,000 miles of streets or highways. It was terminated by the summer of 1934, but reincarnated in 1935 as the WORKS PROGRESS ADMINISTRATION (WPA).

Civilian Conservation Corps (CCC) On 31 March 1933, Congress passed the Civilian Conservation Corps Reforestation Relief Act to fund federal hiring of 250,000 males aged 18–25 at $30 a month (of which $25 went directly to their families) plus subsistence at work camps. The Department of LABOR enrolled men by state quotas based on population and the Department of WAR ran the camps, while the Departments of AGRICULTURE and INTERIOR planned the projects. The program was later expanded to hire 500,000 annually. By 1935, over 2,650 CCC camps operated in the US. The CCC completed tree-planting and other conservation programs worth $1,500,000,000, culled dead timber, built fire-lookout stations, fought forest fires, laid telephone lines, and stocked 2,000,000,000 fish. Three million men had worked for the CCC before its disbanding in July 1942, second only to the WORKS PROGRESS ADMINISTRATION (WPA).

Clark, (James Beau) Champ (b. Anderson Co., Ky., 7 March 1850; d. Washington, D.C., 2 March 1921) "Champ" Clark was a lawyer and newspaper editor who settled in Bowling Green, Mo., in 1880. He sat in Congress as a Democrat (1893–1921, except 1895–7) and was House speaker (1911–19). He was the leading candidate for the 1912 Democratic presidential nomination, and had 440.5 votes on the first ballot to 324 for Woodrow WILSON. Unable to reach the 60 percent needed for nomination, he was unable to attract a large southern bloc which held firm for Oscar Underwood (Ala.), and steadily lost support after William Jennings BRYAN backed Wilson. By the 14th ballot, Clark had lost the lead and finished with only 84 delegates when Wilson was nominated. Wilson called for his defeat after he opposed the LEAGUE OF NATIONS, and he lost his seat in 1920.

Clark, George Rogers (b. Albemarle County, Va., 19 November 1752; d. Louisville, Ky., 13 February 1818) Before turning 21, Clark had explored Ky. and served in Lord DUNMORE'S WAR. As lieutenant colonel of Ky. militia (1778–9), he extinguished British authority south of Detroit by taking Kaskaskia, Ill., and VINCENNES, Ind. He defended Ky. with aggressive raids north of the Ohio that destroyed numerous Indian towns in 1779, 1780 and 1782. His exploits in the REVOLUTIONARY WAR established the US claim to retain the territory below the Great Lakes in the treaty of PARIS (1783).

Clark, William (b. Caroline County, Va., 1 August 1770; d. St Louis, Mo., 1 September

1838) Brother of George Rogers CLARK, he came to Ky. in 1784, was commissioned a regular army officer in 1792, and fought at the battle of FALLEN TIMBERS. As captain, he shared command of the LEWIS AND CLARK EXPEDITION. He became principal Indian agent for Louisiana Territory in 1807, governor of Missouri Territory in 1813, and superintendant of Indian affairs for the west (1822–38).

Clay, Cassius Marcellus (b. Madison County, Ky., 19 October 1810; d. Madison County, Ky., 22 July 1903) Henry CLAY's cousin, he fought in the MEXICAN WAR, freed his slaves, and was mobbed while editing an ABOLITIONIST paper in Lexington, Ky. He reached the rank of USA major general in the CIVIL WAR, and during 1863–9 he was minister to Russia, where he helped coordinate the US purchase of ALASKA. He was a prominent supporter of the LIBERAL REPUBLICAN PARTY.

Clay, Henry (b. Hanover County, Va., 12 April 1777; d. Washington, D.C., 29 June 1852) In 1799 Clay moved to Lexington, Ky., and began to practice law. He represented 300 criminal defendants and won every case. He was speaker of the Ky. legislature (1807–9) and the House of Representatives (1811–20, 1823–5), a leading WAR HAWK, and peace commissioner for the treaty of GHENT. The foremost orator of antebellum America, he won a reputation as the "great compromiser," by influencing the MISSOURI COMPROMISE, devising the compromise TARIFF OF 1833, and proposing the COMPROMISE OF 1850. Clay's AMERICAN SYSTEM became the WHIG PARTY's central program. He ran unsuccessfully for president in 1824 (during which election he engineered the "CORRUPT BARGAIN"), 1832, and 1844. After his last defeat, which was due to his opposing the annexation of TEXAS, he remarked that he "would rather be right than president."

Clayton Antitrust Act (15 October 1914) To correct weaknesses in the SHERMAN ANTITRUST ACT, Congress outlawed several business schemes used to build monopolies: discriminatory pricing designed to drive competitors out of business, wholesale contracts requiring purchasers not to do business with the seller's competitors ("tying contracts"), interlocking boards of directors that controlled competing corporations capitalized at over $1,000,000, and gaining control of competitors through buying their stock. Congress also exempted union and farmers' associations from antitrust statutes; it reversed IN RE DEBS by exempting strikes and SECONDARY BOYCOTTS from court injunctions (except to prevent irreparable property losses); and it provided that union officers could only be jailed for contempt of court injunctions by a jury trial, and not upon a ruling by the judge who issued the injunction as before. Federal courts later weakened its labor provisions. *DUPLEX PRINTING PRESS COMPANY* v. *DEERING* invalidated its prohibition of injunctions against SECONDARY BOYCOTTS. *TRUAX* v. *CORRIGAN* circumvented the act by permitting state courts to issue injunctions in labor disputes.

Clayton–Bulwer Treaty When boundary disputes between Nicaragua and British Honduras threatened to frustrate US ambitions to build an Atlantic–Pacific canal across Nicaragua, the US and Britain negotiated this agreement (ratified 19 April 1850). It specified that any canal would be a joint Anglo-American venture, have neutral status, and be equally open to each nation's shipping; it also pledged each nation not to establish any new colonies in central America. It was nullified by the first HAY–PAUNCEFOTE TREATY.

Clean Air Act (1963) This law defined national criteria for clean air and established guidelines for reducing atmospheric pollutants, especially those created by cars and coal-burning power plants. It was amended in 1970 to set standards and deadlines for minimizing automobile emissions, and in 1977 to set tougher rules on car pollutants and air quality.

Clean Water Act (18 October 1972) Technically an amendment to the Water Pollution Control Act (1948) (*see* WATER QUALITY ACT (1965)), this law required permits to release waste into natural waterways; it also demanded that all pipelines discharging sewage or industrial refuse meet clean-up standards set by the best available technology. It mandated an end to all discharge of water pollutants by 1985, but failed to accomplish this goal, which had still not been met by

1995. By stimulating a great increase in sewage-treatment plant construction, the law reduced the proportion of US citizens discharging human waste directly into watercourses, from a large majority in 1972 to a steadily declining minority by 1994.

Clean Water Restoration Act (3 November 1966) This law appropriated $4 billion for antipollution control projects, primarily grants to pay 30–55 percent of the cost of building local sewage-treatment plants.

Cleaver, (Leroy) Eldridge (b. near Little Rock, Ark., 31 August 1935) In 1968 Cleaver became a minor literary celebrity after publishing *Soul On Ice*, a collection of essays concerning race and American life written while a prisoner at Folsom Prison in Calif. He joined the BLACK PANTHER PARTY, which nominated him for president in 1968 while he was on parole. He fled overseas later in 1968 to avoid charges for parole violation and murder in a shootout between the Panthers and police. After an exile in Cuba, Guinea, Algeria, North Korea, and France, Cleaver returned to the US on 17 November 1975 and surrendered to the authorities. He renounced violence as a means of political change and announced a conversion to Christianity.

Clemens, Samuel Langhorne *see* TWAIN, MARK

Cleveland, (Stephen) Grover (b. Caldwell, N.J., 18 March 1837; d. Princeton, N.J., 24 June 1908) In 1859 Cleveland began practicing law at Buffalo, N.Y. He paid a substitute to take his place when drafted in the CIVIL WAR. He was mayor of Buffalo (1881–2), and governor of N.Y. (1882–4) before becoming the only Democrat to win the presidency between 1860 and 1908; he took 48.5 percent of the popular vote in 1884 on a platform that promised conciliation to the South and tariff reform. During his first administration, he vetoed two-thirds of Congress's bills (which were mainly private measures for veterans' relief) – more than any other president. He outpolled Benjamin HARRISON in 1888 by 60,728 ballots, but did not win enough states for an electoral majority. He won the election of 1892 with 46.1 percent of the vote to Harrison's 43.0 percent. In his second term, he used the army against labor in the PULLMAN STRIKE, blocked the annexation of HAWAII in 1893, threatened war with Britain in the VENEZUELA BOUNDARY DISPUTE, and won repeal of the SHERMAN SILVER PURCHASE ACT, which led rank-and-file Democrats to repudiate his leadership.

Clifford, Clark McAdams (b. Fort Scott, Kans., 25 December 1906) After practicing law in St Louis, and navy duty in World War II, Clifford was Harry S. TRUMAN's special advisor (1946–50), during which time he influenced US policy on the COLD WAR and Israel. He emerged as Washington's best-connected Democratic lawyer in the 1950s, and became the Foreign Intelligence Advisory Board's chair in 1963. He became a major figure during the VIETNAM WAR after being named secretary of defense in 1968. He turned skeptical about US chances for victory after the TET OFFENSIVE, and concluded that military victory was unattainable when General William WESTMORELAND requested 206,000 additional troops for Vietnam on 27 February. On 25 March, he led other senior advisors in advising Lyndon JOHNSON to end the war by a negotiated settlement, not military victory. After leaving office in 1969, he sharply criticized Richard NIXON's Vietnam policies and urged an accelerated end to US involvement.

Clinton, De Witt (b. Little Britain, N.Y., 2 March 1769; d. Albany, N.Y., 11 February 1828) He learned politics as secretary to his uncle, Governor George CLINTON. He served as US senator, New York mayor, and candidate for the FEDERALIST PARTY for president in 1812, when he carried seven states. Elected N.Y. governor in 1817, 1820, and 1825, he was the primary advocate of the ERIE CANAL (an idea first proposed by George Clinton in 1783), and opened that waterway in 1825.

Clinton, George (b. Little Britain, N.Y., 26 July 1739; d. Washington, D.C., 20 April 1812) A lawyer who attended the second CONTINENTAL CONGRESS, Clinton led N.Y. militia in the REVOLUTIONARY WAR, and served as N.Y. governor for seven terms (1777–95 and 1801–4). He led the ANTIFEDERALISTS in N.Y., who nearly rejected the CONSTITUTION under his influence. He ran second to John ADAMS for vice-president in 1792 and received six N.Y.

votes for president in 1808. Having hoped to be president in 1808, he was openly hostile to James MADISON. As vice-president (1805–13), he was a poor presiding officer of the Senate, and cast the deciding vote against rechartering the first BANK OF THE UNITED STATES.

Clinton, Henry (b. Newfoundland, ca. 1738; d. Gibraltar, 23 December 1795) The son of a British army officer, Clinton grew up in N.Y. and became a grenadier officer in 1751. As major general, he served at the siege of BOSTON and battle of BUNKER HILL in 1775, was repulsed at the first battle of CHARLES TOWN, S.C., in June 1776, and performed occupation duty at New York in 1777. In March 1778, Clinton replaced William HOWE as commander in chief and fought at MONMOUTH COURT HOUSE that July. Upon winning the second battle of CHARLES TOWN, which enabled British forces to occupy the LOWER SOUTH, Clinton returned to his New York City headquarters. He failed to anticipate Washington's YORKTOWN campaign, and was replaced as commander in chief by Guy Carleton in May 1782.

Clinton, Hillary Rodham *see* RODHAM CLINTON, HILLARY

Clinton, William ("Bill") Jefferson (b. Hope, Ark., 3 November 1942) Born William J. Blythe, Clinton rose above economic deprivation through academic excellence, was a Rhodes scholar, earned a Yale law degree in 1973, and taught at the University of Arkansas law school. He ran for Congress unsuccessfully at 32, was elected Ark. attorney general in 1976, and became the youngest governor ever chosen in Ark. in 1978. Although defeated in 1980, he won reelection in 1982, 1984, and 1986. As Democratic candidate for president, he defeated George BUSH with 43 percent of the vote (the first minority president since 1968).

As president, he proposed a budget package in 1993 that – as amended – cut the deficit from $255 billion in 1993 (4 percent of GDP) to an estimated $167 billion in 1995 (2.4 percent of GDP). He prevailed over heavy odds to win ratification for the NORTH AMERICAN FREE TRADE AGREEMENT, was instrumental in achieving success for the Uruguay round of GATT, and fought the National Rifle Association's lobbying to influence passage of the BRADY BILL and a $30 billion Omnibus Crime Bill (13 September 1994). His most ambitious initiative, a program of comprehensive health care reform developed in partnership with Hillary RODHAM CLINTON, was blocked in 1994. He ended US involvement in SOMALIA and occupied HAITI. The WHITEWATER SCANDAL slowly tarnished his reputation and crippled his leadership.

closed shop This term refers to a union contract that forbids the employment of any persons who are not already members of the union that negotiated it, before being hired. (*See also* UNION SHOP) The TAFT–HARTLEY ACT outlawed closed shops.

coal strike of 1902 Having won a small pay raise in a brief strike in 1900, 140,000 members of the United Mine Workers (UMW) struck again on 12 May 1902 when management rejected demands for a 20 percent pay hike, an eight-hour workday (down from ten), and recognition of the UMW. When the strike threatened a winter shortage of anthracite coal, Theodore ROOSEVELT intervened with binding arbitration by a presidential commission to end the strike, which was halted on 21 October. On 22 March 1903, the commission awarded the miners a 10 percent raise and cut their workday by an hour, but denied the UMW union recognition. The compromise settlement exemplified Roosevelt's SQUARE DEAL for labor and big business.

coal strike of 1943 When John L. LEWIS called a strike by 450,000 bituminous and 80,000 anthracite miners during WORLD WAR II, Franklin D. ROOSEVELT seized the eastern US coal fields on 1 May 1943 and forced Lewis to cancel the stoppage on 2 May. The event led Congress to pass the SMITH–CONNALLY ANTI-STRIKE ACT.

coal strike of 1946 On 1 April 1946, John L. LEWIS called 400,000 bituminous coal miners out on strike for improved wages, health benefits, and safety regulations. By mid-May, the strike was crippling industrial production and threatened to end the economy's postwar recovery. When Lewis rejected Harry S. TRUMAN's efforts to find a compromise, the president seized the mines and ordered the strikers back to work. When the companies refused a settlement negotiated between the workers and government, Lewis took his men out of the pits on 21 November. Upon refusing an injunction to resume work, a US judge found Lewis in contempt of court and fined the United Mine Workers (UMW) $3,500,000 – later reduced to $700,000 – before Lewis ended the strike on 7 December. The government acceded to most UMW demands while operating the mines, and the coal companies agreed to the bulk of Lewis's terms in 1947 to regain their property.

Coast Guard This service originated on 4 August 1790, when Congress established the Revenue Marine (later Revenue Cutter Service) consisting of 10 vessels to enforce customs laws. In 1799 the service's ships were assigned to cooperate with the navy, which has jurisdiction over the service in wartime. On 28 January 1915, the Revenue Cutter and Life-saving Services merged into the modern Coast Guard. The guard took over the Light House Service in 1939 and it received control of the Bureau of Navigation and Steamboat Inspection in 1942. It helped escort merchant convoys in WORLD WAR I and lost 574 killed and 432 wounded. The Department of the TREASURY financed the Coast Guard until 1967, when it was assigned to the Department of TRANSPORTATION.

In WORLD WAR II, Coast Guard cutters protected convoys during the battle of the ATLANTIC, and the service lost 1,919 men dead. By 1967, the Coast Guard had sent two squadrons (52 ships) for the VIETNAM WAR. The guard performed over 6,000 missions and boarded 250,000 small craft before turning over their cutters to Vietnamese crews in 1972. Besides protecting coastal and inland waterways, the Coast Guard interdicts smugglers, oversees harbor construction, certifies ships for launching, performs ice-breaking missions, enforces pollution and maritime-conservation laws; in peace, it maintains about 38,000 military and 6,000 civilian personnel.

Cochise (b. Ariz., ca. 1824; d. Chiricahua Reservation, Ariz., 7 June 1874) A leader of the Chiricahua APACHE INDIANS, Cochise raided Mexico but maintained friendly relations with Anglo-Americans until 1861. In this year a US Army officer wrongly accused his band of kidnaping a Hispanic farm boy, and killed five Chiricahuas being held as hostages for the boy's return. Cochise wreaked vengeance until 1872, when he voluntarily made peace in return for a US executive order creating a large Chiricahua reservation in southeastern Ariz.

Cody, William Frederick (b. LeClaire, Iowa, 26 February 1846; d. near Golden, Colo., 10 January 1917) He served as a rider for the PONY EXPRESS, a teamster in the Civil War, a scout for the US Cavalry, and a BUFFALO hunter (for which he was known as "Buffalo Bill"). He entered show business by starring as himself in Ned Buntline's Chicago drama *The Scout of the Prairie*, and became the hero in an endless stream of dime novels. His paramount contribution to American culture was his spectacular Wild West Show, organized at Omaha in 1883. Cody created an image of the plains frontier that was so compelling that it has passed into folklore as the classic image of how gunslingers, cowboys, cavalry, and Indians acted and looked in the late 19th century. Cody (with Buntline) was the leading mythologizer of the wild west.

Coelho, Anthony *see* WRIGHT, JAMES C.

Coercive Acts *see* INTOLERABLE ACTS

Coeur d'Alene War This term is a synonym for the YAKIMA WARS' culminating phase, which occurred in 1858.

Cohens* v. *Virginia In 1821 the Supreme Court, returning to an issue first addressed in *MARTIN* v. *HUNTER'S LESSEE*, unanimously affirmed the constitutionality of Section 25 of the JUDICIARY ACT (1789), which allowed federal courts to review any case from a state's highest tribunal if one party claimed rights under the US Constitution, federal laws, or treaties. The Court denied Virginia's assertion that if the US government were the final judge of its own powers through its own court system, then the states lacked the sovereignty fundamental to a federal system of government; it also denied Virginia's argument that the ELEVENTH AMENDMENT preempted federal courts from accepting appeals from state courts when the state government was a litigant. The Court declared that the states were no longer fully sovereign, because they had accepted the supremacy of US law in ratifying the Constitution, and could not claim that their supreme courts were exempt from review by the federal judiciary.

Coker* v. *Georgia *see* *Gregg* v. *Georgia*

Colby, William *see* Central Intelligence Agency

Cold Harbor, battle of (Va.) On 1 June 1864, General Robert E. Lee's 59,000 entrenched Confederates repulsed assaults by Lieutenant General Ulysses S. Grant's 108,000 Federals at Cold Harbor, Va. USA losses: 2,200 killed, wounded. On 3 June, Grant lost 7,000 killed and wounded assaulting the Confederates, whose casualties were about 1,500. Grant then withdrew and attacked Petersburg.

cold war This term described the armed hostility accompanying the rivalry for world leadership between the US and the Soviet Union after 1945. It was first used in testimony by Bernard Baruch on 24 October 1948 to the Senate War Investigating Committee. The US reacted with efforts to stimulate overseas economic development like the Marshall Plan, a containment policy, and calculated use of brinkmanship by John Dulles. The cold war ended in the late 1980s when the Soviet economy and political structure collapsed.

Cole, Thomas (b. Bolton-le-Moors, England, 1 February 1801; d. Catskill, N.Y., 11 February 1848) After emigrating in 1819 to Philadelphia, where he studied at the Pa. Academy of Fine Arts (1823–5), Cole became an itinerant portrait painter in Ohio. His wilderness travels stirred a passion to paint landscapes of North America in an original and accurate style. He discovered the ideal setting for this endeavor in the Hudson River valley, where he emerged as the Hudson River school's guiding spirit and his generation's most important landscape painter. His works include *View Near Ticonderoga* (1826), the allegorical series *The Course of Empire* (1836), and *The Voyage of Life* (1840).

Colegrove* v. *Green *see* *Baker* v. *Carr*

Coleman* v. *Miller On 5 June 1939, the Supreme Court held (7–2) that the courts lack jurisdiction to rule on what constitutes a "reasonable" period to set for ratifying a constitutional amendment and on whether a state might retract a vote for ratification, since both issues are political matters within Congress's discretion.

Colfax, Schuyler (b. New York, N.Y., 23 March 1823; d. Mankato, Minn., 13 January 1885) He began his career as an antislavery and Whig journalist in South Bend, Ind. He entered Congress as a Know-Nothing in 1854, became a Republican, and was speaker (1863–9), during which time he opposed Andrew Johnson's policies. He became vice-president under Ulysses S. Grant in 1868, but was not renominated in 1872. The Credit Mobilier scandal ruined his reputation and career.

Colfax massacre On Easter Sunday, 13 April 1873, the Republican sheriff of Grant Parish, La., placed armed black militia at the Colfax courthouse to bar its occupation by a rival politician, who then drove out the defenders with 200 armed whites and a cannon. Killed in the battle were two whites and 59 blacks, including several shot down in cold blood. The Supreme Court dismissed murder indictments against the whites in *United States* v. *Cruikshank*.

Collector* v. *Day In 1871 the Supreme Court (8–1) applied *Dobbins* v. *Erie County* to the question of subjecting a state officer's salary to federal income tax, and denied the US could do so. This case led to a multiplicity of disputes over the extent of state exemption from federal taxes (and vice versa) until *Graves* v. *New York ex rel. O'Keefe* settled matters.

Collier, John (b. Atlanta, Ga., 4 May 1884; d. Taos, N. Mex., 8 May 1968) He began his career as a settlement worker among immigrants in urban ghettos, but became disillusioned with his co-workers' paternalistic approach toward helping the poor and left that field. After living among Pueblo Indians near Taos, in 1922 he founded the American Indian Defense Association, which soon emerged as the most vocal critic of US Indian policy. While serving as US Commissioner of Indian Affairs (1932–45), he fashioned an "Indian New Deal" designed to lessen federal interference with reservation governments, to end the policy of eradicating native customs and traditional beliefs, to build economic self-sufficiency, and to curtail the sale of Indian lands to whites. His most important achievement was the

WHEELER–HOWARD ACT. By advocating a tribunal for rectifying past treaty violations, he built a base of political support for the eventual formation of the INDIAN CLAIMS COMMISSION.

Collins, Michael *see* APOLLO PROJECT

Colombia, US intervention in *see* PANAMA REVOLT

Colorado The US acquired Colo. by the LOUISIANA PURCHASE and treaty of GUADALUPE HIDALGO. Permanent white settlement began in 1851 when Hispanic farmers from N.Mex. settled by the San Luis River. In July 1858, gold was discovered near Pike's Peak and after two years the population stood at 34,277, of which 88 percent were male, 8 percent foreign-born, and just 46 were black. On 28 February 1861, Colorado Territory was formed from Kans. In the CIVIL WAR, Colo. sent the USA army 4,903 troops, who helped drive CSA forces from NEW MEXICO. Colo. grew rapidly after 1870, due primarily to railroad construction, and became the 38th state on 1 August 1876. The CHEYENNE CAMPAIGNS (1864–5) largely ended Indian hostilities on the eastern slope and the first UTE CAMPAIGN relocated the western slope's Indians to Utah. Ranching, farming, and mining dominated the state's economy.

In 1900 Colo. ranked 31st among states with 539,700 residents, (95 percent white, 3 percent Hispanic, 2 percent black) of whom 52 percent were rural and 17 percent foreign-born; it stood 36th in the value of its farm products and 27th in products mined or manufactured. DUST BOWL conditions devastated its agriculture. Urbanization diversified the economy and rapidly increased population after 1945. In 1990 Colo. ranked 26th among states, with 3,294,394 residents (81 percent white, 4 percent black, 13 percent Hispanic, 2 percent Asian) of whom 82 percent were urban and 4.3 percent foreign-born. Manufacturing employed 17 percent of workers and mining 7 percent.

Colson, Charles Wendell (b. Boston, Mass., 16 October 1931) He was a lawyer, former US Senate aide (1945–67), and was named special counsel to Richard NIXON in 1969. He helped coordinate the "dirty-tricks" campaign against George MCGOVERN in 1972, took the FIFTH AMENDMENT to avoid self-incrimination during the WATERGATE SCANDAL hearings on 19 September 1973, and served seven months in prison after pleading guilty to obstruction of justice in 1974.

Columbus, Christopher (b. Genoa, Italy, ca. September 1451; d. Valladolid, Spain, 20 May 1506) Properly termed Cristoforo Colombo in Italian or Cristóbal Colón in Spanish, he went to sea early and moved to Portugal in 1476. Unable to win Portuguese funding for a voyage of exploration across the Atlantic, he obtained money and the title "Admiral of the Ocean Sea" from Isabella of Aragon on 30 April 1492. He made four transatlantic expeditions: (1) 3 August 1492–15 March 1493, when he reached the Bahamas on 12 October; (2) 25 September 1493–11 June 1496, when he founded a permanent settlement on Hispaniola and explored the Caribbean; (3) 30 May–25 November 1500, when he was brought back to Spain under arrest; and (4) 11 May 1502–7 November 1504, when he was shipwrecked on Jamaica.

Columbus, raid on (N.Mex.) On 8 March 1916, Francisco "Pancho" Villa's 700 Mexican insurgents raided Columbus, N.Mex., and engaged the US 13th Cavalry. Fourteen US soldiers and 10 civilians were casualties, of whom 17 died. The raid provoked the MEXICAN BORDER INVASION.

Comanche campaigns In 1858–9, expeditions by Tex. Rangers and the Second US Cavalry pursued COMANCHE INDIANS that had been raiding Tex. US losses: 9 dead, 23 wounded. Comanche losses: 206 warriors dead. Continuing Comanche raids led to an army incursion in 1868–9 and the RED RIVER WAR (1874–5), which ended Comanche hostilities.

Comanche Indians Speakers of one of the UTO-AZTECAN LANGUAGES, Comanches were closely related to the SHOSHONI INDIANS and migrated to the southern plains from their Mont. homeland in the 1600s. By 1690, when they numbered 7,000, they had acquired horses and had become nomadic hunters on the southern plains. Unusually warlike toward both Indians and whites, they were raiding Tex. and Mexico by the 1720s. Between 1837 and 1849, smallpox and cholera reduced their numbers by half. They finally accepted reservation status in Okla. after defeat in the COMANCHE CAMPAIGNS and RED RIVER WAR.

comity cases *see BANK OF AUGUSTA* v. *EARLE*

Commerce, Department of On 14 February 1903, Congress created a Department of Commerce and Labor to monitor the activities of businesses engaged in interstate commerce. On 4 March 1913, Congress divided it into separate departments for Commerce and Labor. Commerce has the mission of collecting economic statistics, promoting business expansion, and encouraging technological development.

Commission on Civil Rights *see* CIVIL RIGHTS ACT (1957)

Commission on Efficiency and Economy In March 1911, William TAFT appointed a three-member task force to evaluate federal administrative efficiency. The commission identified numerous outdated practices, but their primary recommendation was the establishment of a centralized, detailed accounting system for the US budget. Partisan politics kept this reform from being immediately adopted, but the report ultimately spawned the BUDGET AND ACCOUNTING ACT.

Commission on Law Observance and Enforcement *see* PROHIBITION

Commissioners of Immigration* v. *The North German Lloyd *see* IMMIGRATION CASES

Committee for Industrial Organization *see* CIO

Committee on Public Information During WORLD WAR I, this agency was created to build support for the war effort. Its head, George Creel, printed 75,000,000 pamphlets, issued press releases at the rate of almost 10 per day, and mobilized 75,000 "four-minute men" to give short, patriotic speeches to neighbors. By creating an atmosphere of anxiety over domestic subversion, it stimulated ethnic prejudice against Germans, persecution of socialists, and general intolerance of free speech concerning the US war effort. A sense of national insecurity lingered after the war and contributed to the RED SCARE.

Committee to Reelect the President Known as CREEP, this was Richard NIXON's reelection organization for the 1972 campaign. Headed by John MITCHELL, it planned the "dirty-tricks" tactics against George McGOVERN that led to the WATERGATE SCANDAL.

committees of correspondence On 2 November 1772, Samuel ADAMS led the Boston town meeting to form a committee of correspondence and ask other Mass. towns to do likewise, for the purpose of exchanging information. On 12 March 1773, the Va. assembly formed a committee of correspondence to communicate with other colonies, and by February 1774, every province but N.C. and Pa. had created such a body. This system established the first ongoing network for coordinating resistance to British policies, and was critical in enabling Americans to formulate a united response to the INTOLERABLE ACTS.

Commodity Credit Corporation Franklin D. ROOSEVELT created this NEW DEAL agency by Executive Order 6340 on 18 October 1933 to make farm loans under the AGRICULTURAL ADJUSTMENT ADMINISTRATION. It succeeded the Federal Intermediate Credit Banks established by the AGRICULTURAL CREDITS ACT (1923) and operated under the RECONSTRUCTION FINANCE CORPORATION to 1939, when it became an independent agency. Initially funded at $3,000,000, it was capitalized at $100,000,000 in 1936 and authorized to lend another $900,000,000 by 1939. It primarily operated by having banks make loans to farmers and buying the loans from the banks. Farmers used the credit to withhold crops from the market until they could be sold at reasonable prices. By mid-1940, it had loaned $1,571,000,000: $46,000,000 on 253,249,000 pounds of tobacco, $889,000,000 on 16,674,000 bales of cotton, $470,000,000 on 897,776,000 bushels of corn, and $166,000,000 on 253,391,000 bushels of wheat.

common law Developed over centuries in England, common law is a body of doctrines and rules that became recognized as legally valid precedents, despite not having originated as Parliamentary laws, based on longstanding custom and usage by the courts. Before 1776, colonial courts freely relied on common law; afterwards, US courts continued to respect the common law's authority regarding DUE PROCESS, but did so with increasing selectivity. In 1816, in *UNITED*

States v. *Hudson*, the Supreme Court ruled that the US had not inherited that part of English common law concerned with criminal behavior.

Common Sense In January 1776, Thomas Paine published this pamphlet in Philadelphia. *Common Sense* attacked George III and monarchy in plain, direct language any literate adult could understand. It may have sold 100,000 copies in both English and German by July. Prior to *Common Sense*, most Americans did not favor independence, but Paine revolutionized public opinion by dissolving the loyalty most colonists felt to George III and creating a climate ready to accept independence by July 1776.

Communications Act (1934) *see* Federal Communications Commission

Communist Control Act (24 August 1954) This law strengthened the McCarran Act's restrictions on employing Communists for defense-related work and denied Communist-infiltrated unions any rights under the National Labor Relations Act.

Communist Party In 1919 two rival Communist organizations were founded in the US – the Communist Labor Party and the Communist Party of America – and in 1922 they merged as the United Communist Party, which was renamed the Communist Party of the United States in 1924. Members ran for public office not as Communists, but as candidates of the Workers Party of America, founded in 1924. The Communists initially attacked the New Deal as a program to save capitalism, but softened their criticism under orders from Moscow to seek accommodation with mainstream liberals. The party lost all credibility in 1939 for reversing itself and appeasing Nazism after the German–Soviet Non-aggression Pact. Its presidential vote peaked in 1932 at 102,785 ballots for William Foster, then declined to 80,869 for Earl Browder in 1936 and 46,251 for Browder in 1940. Its members were subject to many legal restrictions after 1940, especially the Smith Act, McCarran Act, Taft–Hartley Act, and Communist Control Act, which eventually won them much unwarranted sympathy as victims of political prejudice. The party's popular appeal plummeted in the cold war after Communist sympathizers like the Rosenbergs and Alger Hiss were convicted on espionage charges.

community action programs (CAPs) The Economic Opportunity Act (1964) financed these local organizations, which provided special programs to alleviate poverty but were operated by community agencies exempt from political control or review by states or localities. By 1967, 1,000 CAPs were operating as nonprofit organizations. The Nixon administration gradually withdrew funding from them.

company union After 1919, the US business community (and especially the National Association of Manufacturers) encouraged their workers to form unions independent of national organizations like the AFL. Company union membership expanded from 1,369,000 members (in 400 unions) in 1926 to 2,500,000 members in 1935. Company unions declined sharply during the New Deal because of laws like the Railway Labor Act (1934) and the National Labor Relations Act, which allowed federal regulatory agencies to decertify them as bargaining agents when they did not represent workers' true choice.

comparable worth In the 1970s, feminist lawyers argued that sex discrimination explained why men earned higher average salaries than women; they held that women could sue for equitable wages under the theory of comparable worth, which alleged that the Civil Rights Act (1964) required salary scales to be adjusted so that women were not paid less than men working at different tasks, if the men possessed similar skills and did labor of comparable value for their employers. The federal courts rejected the theory in *County of Washington* v. *Gunther*, but many local governments and businesses raised female wages to avoid appearing sexist.

Comprehensive Employment and Training Act (CETA) (20 December 1973) This act took over the Job Corps and other manpower training programs of the Great Society. It allocated federal funds for public-service employment programs run by cities and counties with populations over 100,000. It subsidized 750,000 jobs at its height. It was renewed for four years on

November 1978, but another extension was blocked in 1982 by Ronald REAGAN, who criticized it as pork-barrel legislation continually abused by local governments.

Comprehensive Environmental Response, Compensation and Liability Act (1980) This law required polluters to pay for detoxifying or closing hazardous waste sites through a "superfund," which was financed by a tax on chemical companies. Of 1,200 hazardous sites identified by the ENVIRONMENTAL PROTECTION AGENCY, only 150 had been sanitized by June 1994.

Compromise of 1850 Faced with the problem of establishing governments in territories acquired in the MEXICAN WAR, Zachary TAYLOR recommended on 4 December 1849 that CALIFORNIA be admitted to the Union under its free-state constitution, and that Congress accept the territorial constitutions adopted in NEW MEXICO and UTAH, which excluded SLAVERY. Led by John CALHOUN, southerners objected that Calif. statehood would create a free-state majority in the Senate, argued that N.Mex. and Utah should be opened to slavery, and renewed demands for strengthening the FUGITIVE SLAVE LAW (1793). Abolitionists then fulminated against slavery in the District of Columbia, and Texans claimed to own all of N.Mex. east of the Rio Grande.

Based on his resolutions of 29 January 1850, Henry CLAY fashioned a compromise measure termed the Omnibus Bill. Daniel WEBSTER supported Clay on 7 March. Calhoun opposed Clay until he died on 31 March, then Jefferson DAVIS led southern opposition to the Omnibus Bill. Stephen DOUGLAS devised the stratagem of separating the compromise into five separate acts, each of which commanded majority support from different coalitions. When the necessary votes for each measure were assured, the package passed during 9–20 September.

The Compromise of 1850 provided for: (1) admitting Calif. as a free state; (2) giving N.Mex. and Utah the option to authorize slavery by territorial law; (3) fixing the Tex.–N.Mex. border at its present line and compensating Tex. with $10,000,000 for giving up its claims west to the Rio Grande; (4) passing a more stringent FUGITIVE SLAVE ACT; and (5) abolishing the slave trade within the District of Columbia (without ending slavery itself). Southern reaction to the compromise was expressed by the GEORGIA PLATFORM and NASHVILLE CONVENTION. The problem of slavery in the territories then receded until the KANSAS–NEBRASKA ACT's passage.

Compromise of 1877 Meeting in Washington on 26 February 1877, southern Democrats informally agreed not to prevent Congress from deciding the disputed presidential election of 1876 in favor of Rutherford HAYES. This was in return for Republican assurances to withdraw the last US troops occupying the South and to give a southern Democrat control of most patronage as postmaster general. The deal greatly increased the prospect of a Hayes victory, ended northern commitment to RECONSTRUCTION, and enabled white Democrats to complete the South's political REDEMPTION.

Comstock lode In January 1859, James Finney discovered the largest silver lode in the US. Virginia City, Nev., rose at the location and had 11,000 inhabitants at its peak in 1870, after which the city slowly declined as the veins were tapped.

Concord, battle of (Mass.) On 19 April 1775, Colonel James Barrett's 400 MINUTEMEN evacuated Concord after a brief exchange of fire with Lieutenant Colonel Francis Smith's 800 redcoats at a bridge. Mass. losses: 2 killed, 2 wounded. British losses: 3 killed, 8 or 10 wounded. While Smith's men destroyed military supplies at Concord, almost 4,000 Minutemen gathered to harass the redcoats on their return to Boston. Smith suffered heavy casualties before linking up with Lord Percy's relief column of 1,400 troops. Mass. losses: 39 killed, 27 wounded, 5 missing. British losses: 70 killed, 182 wounded, 22 captured. The siege of BOSTON then commenced.

concurrent majority In his "Disquisition on Government" (1843), John CALHOUN argued that a historical weakness of democracies was their tendency to degenerate into the oppression of regional or class interests by numerical majorities. To prevent the popular will of a northern majority turning despotic against the southern minority, he advocated a constitutional amendment to create a dual executive, with one president elected by the free states and another by the slave states, and to require that no bill become federal law without the signature of both.

Conestoga Indians *see* SUSQUEHANNOCK INDIANS

Conestoga massacre *see* PAXTON MASSACRE

Confederacy Following the first SECESSION of seven states after Abraham LINCOLN's election, a provisional constitution was adopted for the Confederate States of America on 8 February 1861 at Montgomery, Ala., and Jefferson DAVIS was elected president for six years on 9 February. Between FORT SUMTER's fall and 20 May, when Richmond, Va., was made capital, four more states seceded. Mo. was admitted as the 12th state on 31 October 1861 and Ky. as the 13th state on 10 December; both had dual status as USA and CSA states. The Confederacy never won foreign diplomatic recognition during the CIVIL WAR. Union forces captured Richmond on 3 April 1865. Military resistance collapsed after the Army of NORTHERN VIRGINIA surrendered at APPOMATTOX COURT HOUSE, and the last CSA army capitulated on 26 May.

Confederation of New England *see* UNITED COLONIES OF NEW ENGLAND

Confiscation Acts *see* ABOLITIONISM

Congregational Christian Churches *see* CONGREGATIONAL CHURCH

Congregational church American Congregationalism evolved from PURITANISM. The first Congregational church was founded at PLYMOUTH Colony in 1620. Congregationalism became the established church in all of New England but R.I. In the 17th century, it surmounted major challenges over ANTINOMIANISM and the HALF-WAY COVENANT. Few Congregational churches existed outside New England before 1776, except for N.Y. There were 75 Congregational pulpits in 1660, 146 in 1700, and 423 in 1740. The denomination grew more slowly after the GREAT AWAKENING, which badly split its members. In 1776 there were 668 Congregational churches with 575,000 members (29 percent of the white population).

Because Congregational ministers were strongly Whig in the Revolution (*see* WHIGS [REVOLUTIONARY]), the church kept its established status for another generation (until 1818 in Conn., 1819 in N.H., 1820 in Maine, and 1833 in Mass.). The church expanded into N.Y. and the NORTHWEST TERRITORY, but 90 percent of its pulpits were still in New England by 1830. As late as 1906, a third of all its congregations were in New England and another third in the five "Old Northwest" states. The number of churches grew from 1,100 in 1820 to 2,234 in 1860, and 5,604 in 1900, but membership increased at a far slower rate. By 1930, Congregationalists numbered only 1,000,000, less than 1 percent of all whites. In 1931 they merged with the General Convention of the Christian church (100,000 members) to become the Congregational Christian Churches. In 1957 this body merged with the Evangelical and Reformed Church to form the UNITED CHURCH OF CHRIST.

Congress of Industrial Organizations (CIO) On 9 November 1935, a Committee for Industrial Organization was formed within the AMERICAN FEDERATION OF LABOR by John L. LEWIS (Mine Workers), David Dubinsky (International Ladies Garment Workers), Sidney HILLMAN (Amalgamated Clothing Workers), Thomas McMahon (Textile Workers), and Charles Howard (Typographers). The committee's goal was to charter new INDUSTRIAL UNIONS in the unorganized, mass-production corporations. In May 1938, the CRAFT UNION-dominated AFL suspended the committee, which was reconstituted as the rival Congress of Industrial Organizations (CIO) in 1938.

The CIO used aggressive organizing tactics such as the sit-down strike (ruled unconstitutional in 1939) and encountered much violence, culminating in the MEMORIAL DAY MASSACRE. Strengthened greatly by the NATIONAL LABOR RELATIONS ACT, it soon unionized the automobile, steel, rubber, and mining industries. By 1940, the CIO included 41 unions with 2,654,000 workers, and its membership grew to 5,285,000 by 1943. By 1945, CIO affiliates had won 40 percent of their NATIONAL LABOR RELATIONS BOARD (NLRB) elections, more than any other group of unions. In 1943 the CIO was the first major union organization to form a committee for political mobilization of labor voters. The CIO ended its problem with subversive penetration by expelling 11 Communist-dominated unions during 1949–50. It severed ties in 1953 with the International Longshoremen's Association, Dry-cleaning Workers, and Bakery Workers, which were riddled with racketeering and corruption. Under Walter REUTHER, it merged with the AFL to form the AFL-CIO in 1955.

Congress of Racial Equality (CORE) James Farmer founded CORE in June 1942 at the University of Chicago. CORE became nationally prominent in the CIVIL RIGHTS MOVEMENT by pioneering important tactics of nonviolent civil disobedience, especially the SIT-IN MOVEMENT and FREEDOM RIDERS. After its Baltimore convention of 1–4 July 1966 endorsed the BLACK POWER MOVEMENT, CORE lost much of the financial support from whites on which it depended, and by 1979 was bankrupt.

Congress of the Confederation The second CONTINENTAL CONGRESS ceased its existence and became this body on 2 March 1781 after the ARTICLES OF CONFEDERATION were ratified. No special elections were held to choose new representatives, however, and each state filled vacancies as individual members resigned or died. The Congress of the Confederation sat until 1789.

Congressional Budget and Impoundment Control Act (1974) Congress created the Congressional Budget Office (as its own counterpart to the Office of Management and Budget, *see* BUDGET AND ACCOUNTING ACT) and special House and Senate budget committees. It redesignated its fiscal year as 1 October to 30 September, obliged Congress to set a maximum limit on expenditures that could not be exceeded by budget subcommittees, and forced the president to obtain congressional approval before impounding or deferring any appropriations.

Congressional Budget Office *see* CONGRESSIONAL BUDGET AND IMPOUNDMENT CONTROL ACT

Congressional Reconstruction *see* RECONSTRUCTION

Congressional Union *see* NATIONAL WOMAN'S PARTY

Conkling, Roscoe *see* STALWARTS

Connally Act (22 February 1935) This statute of the LITTLE NIRA reversed *Panama Refining Company* v. *Ryan*, which declared unconstitutional the president's power to regulate interstate petroleum shipments under Title I, Section 9(c) of the NIRA, because the law granted the executive department excessive discretionary power. The Connally Act eliminated that legal problem by giving the executive department specific authority to set state quotas for crude oil production (as a means of raising oil prices) and forbidding interstate delivery of excess amounts.

Connecticut European settlement began in 1633, when Dutch from NEW NETHERLAND placed a trading post at modern Hartford in June and English PURITANS founded towns at Windsor and Wethersfield in September. In 1637 Thomas Hooker settled Hartford, which the Dutch then left. In 1636–7 the PEQUOT WAR ended Indian resistance to settlement. In 1639 these three river towns agreed to govern themselves under the FUNDAMENTAL ORDERS OF CONNECTICUT. By 1662, 15 towns later founded in the Connecticut valley had adopted the Fundamental Orders, which were never confirmed by a royal charter.

In 1638 Puritans under John DAVENPORT founded New Haven. In 1643 Davenport's followers in eight towns established the colony of NEW HAVEN in southwestern Conn., but never obtained a royal charter. After the Stuart Restoration, John Winthrop, Jr., won legal standing from Charles II for Conn. as a CHARTER COLONY on 3 May 1662. The charter gave Conn. jurisdiction over New Haven, which was then annexed. Conn. was under the DOMINION OF NEW ENGLAND's authority (1687–9). In 1700 it had 26,000 colonists, of whom 450 were slaves.

Conn. was the sixth largest state in 1775 and provided eight of 80 Continental regiments. No major campaigns occurred there in the Revolution, but 39 military actions took place. It abolished slavery in 1784. It was the fifth state to ratify the CONSTITUTION, on 9 January 1788. In 1800 it was the eighth largest state with 251,002 inhabitants, of whom 97 percent were white and 90 percent of English-Welsh stock. It disestablished the CONGREGATIONAL CHURCH in 1818.

Conn. emerged as an early center for manufacturing after 1800, especially for textiles and firearms, but from 1800 to 1860, its population grew only 83 percent to 460,147. In 1860 it had 460,147 inhabitants, of whom 98 percent were white and 17 percent were foreign-born; it ranked 24th among the states in population, 24th in the value of farmland and livestock, and fifth in manufactures. In the CIVIL WAR, it furnished 55,864 USA troops (including 1,764 blacks).

Its population doubled from 1860 to 1900, when it ranked as the 29th state in size. In 1900 it was 30 percent rural and had 908,420 residents, of whom 98 percent were white and 26 percent were foreign-born; it ranked 38th among the states in the value of its agricultural goods and 11th in manufactures. The state's economy grew strongly during 1950–70, when it gained 448,000 residents through in-migration that was stimulated by its concentration of defense industries. By 1990, Conn. ranked 28th among states, with 3,287,116 people (84 percent white, 8 percent black, 7 percent Hispanic, 1 percent Asian), of whom 92 percent were urban and 8.5 percent were foreign-born; manufacturing or mining employed 27 percent of the work force.

Connecticut Compromise On 12 July 1787, the CONSTITUTIONAL CONVENTION voted on whether legislative representation should be based on population or on an equal vote among the states. The members agreed to give each state equal representation in the upper house and apportion the lower house by population, based on the total of all free persons and 3/5 of all slaves. This solution, primarily devised by the Conn. delegation, was the convention's turning point and enabled the small states to support the CONSTITUTION.

Connor, Eugene "Bull" *see* BIRMINGHAM DESEGREGATION VIOLENCE

conquistador This word referred to a military participant in an expedition of conquest in one of Spain's American colonies.

Conscription Act (1863) *see* DRAFT

Constitution The CONSTITUTIONAL CONVENTION proposed this document to replace the ARTICLES OF CONFEDERATION on 17 September 1787. On 28 September, Congress submitted the Constitution for the necessary ratification by nine states. N.H. became the ninth state to ratify on 21 June, but not until its approval by Va. on 25 June and N.Y. on 26 July was it certain that the Constitution would be established with sufficient national support to be workable. N.C. refused to join the Union until 21 November 1789 and R.I. did not join until 29 May 1790. The BILL OF RIGHTS was ratified in 1791, and by 1994, a total of 27 amendments had been added to the Constitution. (*See amendments under* FIRST AMENDMENT, SECOND AMENDMENT, *etc.*)

***Constitution*, USS** *see* "OLD IRONSIDES"

Constitutional Convention Called upon recommendation of the ANNAPOLIS CONVENTION, this body convened with a quorum of seven states on 25 May 1787; it was attended by 55 delegates from every state but R.I. On 30 May, it adopted the VIRGINIA PLAN (favored by large states) as the basis for debating the national government's structure. After hearing and rejecting the NEW JERSEY PLAN (favored by small states), it resolved the problem of legislative representation by the CONNECTICUT COMPROMISE. Rejecting the Virginia Plan's proposal for a consolidated national government empowered to veto state laws, it created FEDERALISM, but defined Congress's statutes and foreign treaties as the supreme law of the land. The members sent the CONSTITUTION to Congress and adjourned on 17 September.

Constitutional Union party On 9 May 1860, at Baltimore, WHIG and KNOW-NOTHING PARTY representatives formed this party whose platform denounced sectional politics. It had strong backing in the BORDER STATES, which would be the main battleground in any civil war. Its nominees, John BELL of Tenn. and Edward Everett of Mass. carried Va., Ky., and Tenn., and polled 12.6 percent of the popular vote.

containment policy Containment was the central concept defining US foreign policy in the COLD WAR. First articulated by State Department official George F. Kennan in a 1947 *Foreign Affairs* article, containment committed the US to block expansion by the Soviet Union beyond those areas occupied by its troops in 1945. Containment began as a nonmilitary strategy for frustrating Communist political agitation and was exemplified by the MARSHALL PLAN. To counter

Communist guerrilla movements and offset the large Soviet military presence in eastern Europe, containment became explicitly military through the TRUMAN DOCTRINE, BERLIN AIRLIFT, and EISENHOWER DOCTRINE. US policymakers encouraged three major mutual defense treaties to restrain Soviet aggression: NATO, SEATO, and CENTO.

After China became Communist in 1949, Asia replaced Europe as the focus of containment. The KOREAN WAR confirmed US fears of a Communist threat in Asia. The cynosure of containment then shifted to Indochina. Influenced by the DOMINO THEORY, the US became deeply involved in assisting the South Vietnamese and Laotian governments to suppress Communist insurgencies based in North Vietnam. The VIETNAM WAR – which failed to prevent Communist takeovers of South Vietnam, Laos, and Cambodia – discredited containment among a large body of the US public and resulted in the policy's severe modification in the NIXON DOCTRINE. Under Ronald REAGAN, containment remained a foreign policy goal, and justified US intervention in NICARAGUA and GRENADA. Containment's era ceased during 1989–90, when most of eastern Europe's Communist regimes collapsed.

Continental Association On 18 October 1774, the CONTINENTAL CONGRESS adopted procedures for a trade boycott. Unless the INTOLERABLE ACTS were repealed, this Continental Association dictated that Americans would stop importing goods from Britain and interrupt the slave trade on 1 December 1774, cease purchasing British goods and specific luxury items on 1 March 1775, and halt all exports to the British Isles and the British Caribbean on 1 September 1775. To enforce the Association, Congress established Committees of Observation and Safety, which marked Congress's first effort to create governmental machinery to enforce its policies.

Continental Congress, first On 5 September 1774, 54 delegates from every colony but Ga. met in Philadelphia to formulate policies to press for repeal of the INTOLERABLE ACTS. On 17 September, Congress endorsed the SUFFOLK RESOLVES. On 28 September, it rejected the GALLOWAY PLAN OF UNION. On 14 October, it adopted the "Declaration and Resolves," which denounced 13 Parliamentary laws for violating the RIGHTS OF ENGLISHMEN in America. On 18 October, it approved the CONTINENTAL ASSOCIATION. Its first session adjourned on 26 October.

The second session convened on 10 May 1775. This session created the Continental Army and POST OFFICE, approved an invasion of Canada, and appointed commissioners to negotiate with Indians. On 5 July, it approved the "Declaration of the Causes and Necessities of Taking Up Arms," and adopted the OLIVE BRANCH PETITION on 6 July. On 31 July, it rejected a plan of conciliation from Lord NORTH. It adjourned on 2 August 1775.

Continental Congress, second This body's first session convened on 12 September 1775 and admitted the first Ga. delegation to Congress. It authorized the Continental navy (*see* NAVY, US) on 13 October and appointed members to contact foreign nations on 29 November. It approved the DECLARATION OF INDEPENDENCE in July 1776 and voted to adopt the ARTICLES OF CONFEDERATION in November 1777. The second Continental Congress sat until 2 March 1781, when the Articles went into effect and it became the CONGRESS OF THE CONFEDERATION.

continentals This term refers to paper money printed by the CONTINENTAL CONGRESS to finance the REVOLUTIONARY WAR. Congress first authorized paper money on 22 June 1775 and declared its dollar equal to a Spanish dollar's silver content (4 shillings, 6 pence in sterling). When Congress ceased printing paper money in 1778, it had issued $241,500,000. By December 1780 the currency had lost 99 percent of its value. The US offered to redeem any outstanding continentals in 1790 for a half-cent on the dollar.

Contract Labor Act (26 February 1885) Passed after lobbying by unions like the KNIGHTS OF LABOR, who wished to decrease the competition domestic workers faced from foreign immigrants, this statute outlawed the importation of contract laborers, with the exception of domestics and those with certain professional skills. Congress amended it in 1891, 1907, and 1917.

Contract with America During the 1994 mid-term elections, Newton GINGRICH won an endorsement from almost every Republican candidate for the House of Representatives behind a ten-point legislative agenda that would be voted on during the upcoming Congress's first hundred days. This Contract with America promised votes on a balanced-budget amendment, harsher punishments for criminals, tightening of eligibility for welfare, stiffer penalties on child pornography, a $500-per-child tax credit, stronger national defense, a 50 percent reduction in capital gains taxes, reform of punitive-damage awards in product liability lawsuits, and an amendment limiting terms served in Congress. The contract played a prominent role in giving Republicans control over both houses of Congress in the election.

Contreras-Churubusco, battle of On 18–19 August 1847, Major General Winfield SCOTT's 8,497 US troops defeated President Antonio Lopez de Santa Anna's 20,000 Mexicans, who lost 700 dead and 813 prisoners. On 20 August they routed the 18,500 Mexican survivors, who lost 4,297 killed and wounded, and 2,637 captured (including eight generals). US losses: 131 killed, 865 wounded, 40 missing. Defeat induced Santa Anna to accept an armistice, which lasted from 24 August to 7 September.

Convention of 1800 (30 September 1800) US negotiators William Vans Murray, Oliver ELLSWORTH, and William Davie negotiated this treaty (also known as the treaty of Morfontaine). It ended the undeclared naval war with FRANCE and released the US from its mutual-defense obligations toward France under the FRANCO-AMERICAN ALLIANCE (1778). The Senate ratification was conditional on complete abrogation of the 1778 treaty. The convention became effective on 21 December 1800.

Convention of 1815 (3 July 1815) This commercial agreement restored trade between the US and Britain after the WAR OF 1812. It eliminated discriminatory duties imposed against both nations and opened India to US shipping, but ignored markets in the British West Indies, from which US vessels were excluded until the 1820s.

Convention of 1818 (20 October 1818) This treaty with Britain recognized the 49th parallel, west to the crest of the Rockies, as the LOUISIANA PURCHASE's northern boundary. OREGON Territory was to be jointly occupied for 10 years (later renewed), without prejudicing either country's claims there. The CONVENTION OF 1815 was extended, and the Newfoundland and Labrador fisheries were opened to US citizens. Later disputes over US fishing rights off Canadian shores were settled by the CANADIAN RECIPROCITY TREATY.

convict servants In 1718 Parliament passed the Transportation Act, which subsidized merchants who agreed to handle the selling of convicts or vagabonds sentenced to work as INDENTURED SERVANTS for terms of 7–14 years in the THIRTEEN COLONIES. From then until 1775, approximately 36,000 English, 13,000 Irish, and 700 Scots were sent to North America as convict laborers, mostly to Va. or Md. An attempt to revive the trade failed in 1784.

Conway Cabal In the fall of 1777, Brigadier General Thomas Conway, a foreign mercenary, began consulting with several continental congressmen about replacing George WASHINGTON as commander in chief with Major General Horatio Gates and promoting himself to major general. After it was leaked in October that Conway had attempted to discredit Washington in a letter to Gates, the army's officers and most congressmen not only rallied to Washington's support, but also pressured Conway to resign a promotion as major general obtained from his political allies in December. After being wounded in a duel with another officer, Conway resigned in April and returned to France. The cabal's failure ended all serious challenges to Washington's leadership from Congress.

Coode's Revolt On 25 July 1689, John Coode, Henry Jowles, Kenelm Cheseldyne, and Nehemiah Blakiston formed a Protestant association to usurp the Md. government from Governor William Joseph, who had refused to recognize WILLIAM III as England's monarch in place of Catholic JAMES II. Coode and several hundred men forced Joseph to resign on 1 August. Called into session by Coode on 22 August, the assembly petitioned the Crown to end Lord Baltimore's political authority, which was done in 1691.

Cooley* v. *Board of Wardens In 1851 the Supreme Court upheld *WILLSON* v. *BLACKBIRD CREEK MARSH COMPANY* and affirmed a Pa. statute governing the operation of Philadelphia's harbor by ruling (7–2) that although Congress enjoyed unrestricted power over interstate commerce, states enjoyed a concurrent power to regulate local commerce in the absence of federal action (a distinction termed "selective exclusiveness").

Coolidge, Calvin (b. Plymouth, Vt., 4 July 1872; d. Northampton, Mass., 5 January 1933) In 1897 Coolidge opened a law practice at Northampton, Mass. He held no federal offices, but came to national prominence for vigorously suppressing the BOSTON POLICE STRIKE as Mass. governor. Despite Henry Cabot LODGE's vow that no man who lived in a two-family house would be US vice-president, he became Warren HARDING's running mate and assumed the presidency in 1923. He won election in 1924 with 54.0 percent of the popular vote. A strong believer in laissez-faire principles, he retained Andrew MELLON as treasury secretary and vetoed the MCNARY–HAUGEN BILL as price-fixing. Through his personal rectitude and strong cabinet appointments, especially of Harlan F. STONE as attorney general, he restored Americans' faith in honest government after the Harding scandals.

Cooper, James Fenimore (b. Burlington, N.J., 15 September 1789; d. Cooperstown, N.Y., 14 September 1851) He was raised on his father's large estate at Cooperstown, N.Y., an area that served as the setting for many of his historical novels. After being expelled from Yale for a student prank, he served as a navy midshipman (1808–10), and then became a gentleman farmer. After writing his first novel, *Precaution*, in 1820, he produced his first commercial success, *The Spy* (1821). In 1823 he authored *The Pioneers*, first of his "Leatherstocking" series about Natty Bumppo ("Hawkeye"), who later appeared in *The Last of the Mohicans* (1826), *The Prairie* (1827), *The Pathfinder* (1840), and *The Deerslayer* (1841). Cooper was the first American who succeeded in making a living primarily as a novelist.

Cooper, Peter (b. New York, N.Y., 12 February 1791; d. New York, N.Y., 4 April 1883) He began life as a coachmaker's apprentice, but developed a strong aptitude for the steel business. In 1828 he co-founded an ironworks at Baltimore, and in 1830 he designed and manufactured the earliest locomotive built in the US (the Tom Thumb). In 1854 one of his N.J. mills produced the first structural iron for fireproof structures, and in 1856 he refined the first US steel according to the Bessemer process. He was the TRANSATLANTIC CABLE's primary financial sponsor, and his philanthropy founded Cooper Union in New York. He was nominated by the GREENBACK PARTY for president in 1876, but won less than 1 percent of the vote.

Cooper* v. *Aaron On 12 September 1958, the Supreme Court unanimously reaffirmed *BROWN* v. *BOARD OF EDUCATION OF TOPEKA* by ruling that the FOURTEENTH AMENDMENT forbade any type of racial discrimination by school systems wherein "there is state participation through any arrangement, management, funds or property." The Court precluded state attempts to maintain racially separate schools by "evasive schemes" and ordered immediate desegregation in Little Rock, Ark.

Copland, Aaron (b. Brooklyn, N.Y., 14 November 1900; d. North Tarrytown, N.Y., 2 December 1990) From 1921 to 1924 Copland studied composition at Paris. In 1925 his *Symphony for Organ and Orchestra* had its US debut at New York and Boston. Jazz and folk music increasingly influenced his music. His most frequently performed compositions have been his *Clarinet Concerto* (for Benny Goodman, 1948), the orchestral score for *El Salon Mexico* (1936), opera suite for *The Tender Land* (1954), and dance suites for the ballets *Billy the Kid* (1938), *Rodeo* (1942), and *Appalachian Spring* (1944), which received the Pulitzer prize. Considered the mid-20th century's most prominent US composer, he received the US Medal of Freedom in 1964.

Copley, John Singleton (b. in Boston, Mass., 1738; d. London, England, 9 September 1815) A self-taught Mass. portrait-maker, Copley startled London's artistic circles in 1766 by exhibiting his *Boy With Squirrel*, the first American painting to win international recognition. England's Society of Artists elected him a member the next year. Copley left Boston for London in 1774, joined the AMERICAN SCHOOL, and gained admission to the Royal Academy [of Art] in 1777. The premier of his *Death of Chatham* (1780) drew 20,000 paying visitors in six weeks. His *Death of Major Pierson* (1784) brought Copley to the zenith of his reputation and resulted in commissions to paint GEORGE III's daughters. He never returned to America.

Copperheads In the CIVIL WAR, residents of free-soil states who favored allowing the Confederacy to leave the Union were termed Copperheads, because they used copper pennies as a silent, secret recognition symbol. Copperhead societies included the Knights of the Golden Circle, Sons of Liberty, and the Order of American Knights. Their center of strength lay in Ill., Ind., and Ohio.

Coral Sea, battle of the On 4–8 May 1942, Rear Admiral Frank Fletcher's US task force (2 carriers, 8 cruisers, 12 destroyers) intercepted an invasion force under Rear Admiral Aritomo Goto and Vice Admiral Takeo Takagi (3 carriers, 4 heavy cruisers, 1 destroyer) steaming to capture Port Moresby, NEW GUINEA. Tactically a draw, the battle checked Japan from advancing beyond northern New Guinea, gave the US its first naval success in the Pacific, and was the first classic carrier battle, in which enemy fleets never saw each other. US losses: 1 carrier sunk, 1 destroyer sunk. Japanese losses: 1 carrier sunk, 1 carrier disabled.

CORE *see* CONGRESS OF RACIAL EQUALITY

Cornwallis, Charles (second Earl) (b. London, England, 31 December 1738; d. Ghazipore, India, 5 October 1805) Cornwallis entered the army in 1756 and the House of Lords in 1762. He came to America as major general in 1776, and fought at LONG ISLAND, KIP'S BAY, and FORT LEE. After returning twice to England, he became lieutenant general and deputy commander in chief in April 1778. He commanded British forces in the South after the second battle of CHARLES TOWN and won victories at CAMDEN and GUILFORD COURTHOUSE. By disobeying Henry CLINTON's orders not to invade Va., he led his army to capture at YORKTOWN. Cornwallis was one of the war's best battlefield commanders, but lost his army for lack of overall strategic vision.

Coronado, Francisco Vasquez de (b. Salamanca, Spain, 1510; d. Mexico City, November 1554) On 23 February 1540, Coronado left Mexico City with 300 Spaniards and 800 Indians to search for gold. After crossing into Ariz., he marched east to the Arkansas River in Kans., then passed through the Tex. panhandle to N.Mex. He returned to Mexico City in October 1542. Scouting parties sent out by Coronado reached the Grand Canyon and probably Calif., and his expedition was the first major exploration of the southwest.

Corporate Bankruptcy Act (7 June 1934) This law eased the requirements for firms seeking reorganization through bankruptcy; it ended the power of small minorities of shareholders to block settlements that resulted in assets being reduced or debt payments prolonged. Federal courts could accept bankruptcy petitions if just 25 percent of stockowners consented to restructuring, and could approve plans that were accepted by creditors holding 67 percent of total debt. The measure was a significant step enabling businesses to devise plans for returning to profitability in the GREAT DEPRESSION.

Corregidor Island, battle of After BATAAN's fall, Lieutenant General Jonathan Wainwright's 8,700 US and 3,000 Philippino troops resisted the Japanese for 27 days. After enduring an artillery barrage of 16,000 shells on 4 May, virtually out of supplies, Corregidor surrendered on 6 May. Its fall ended the first PHILIPPINE CAMPAIGN.

Corrigan* v. *Buckley Having ruled in *BUCHANAN* v. *WARLEY* that city ordinances establishing racially segregated neighborhoods were unconstitutional, on 24 May 1926, the Supreme Court unanimously ruled that since neither the FIFTH, FOURTEENTH, nor FIFTEENTH AMENDMENTS forbid discriminatory behavior by private individuals, a neighborhood's homeowners may form a restrictive covenant in which they agree not to sell or rent their houses to blacks. On 3 May 1948, the Court modified (6–0) *Corrigan* in *Shelley* v. *Kraemer* by reaffirming the legality of private covenants but holding that the Fourteenth Amendment forbade state courts to enforce them. *Jones* v. *Alfred H. Mayer Company* reversed *Corrigan.*

"corrupt bargain" of 1824 When the election of 1824 failed to produce an electoral majority, the president had to be elected by Congress (with votes cast by states) among Andrew Jackson (99 electoral votes), John Q. Adams (84), and William Crawford (41). Speaker of the House Henry Clay, who had run last with 37 electoral votes from Ky., Mo., and Ohio, could decide the election by swinging those delegations to his choice. Because Clay frustrated the public will by securing Adams's election over Jackson, who had run first, and because Adams named Clay his secretary of state, the House election became known as the "corrupt bargain."

Cotton, John (b. Derby, Derbyshire, England, 4 December 1584; d. Boston, Mass., 23 December 1652) In 1610 Cotton was ordained a priest and became a follower of Puritanism shortly afterward. He emigrated to Mass. in 1633. He emerged as New England's most influential cleric and chief architect of the Cambridge Platform, which codified the Mass. ecclesiastical structure. Each congregation was to have autonomous power over its own affairs (including the power to call and dismiss ministers), yet belong to an established church protected by the state.

cotton gin In October 1793, Eli Whitney perfected a gin to perform the labor-intensive task of removing seeds from cotton lint. By enabling one person to clean 50 pounds of fiber per day, his invention made cotton a profitable staple for the first time, produced a rapid expansion of its cultivation in the lower south, and stimulated increased demand for slave labor.

Coughlin, Charles Edward, Fr (b. Hamilton, Ontario, 25 October 1891; d. Bloomfield Hills, Mich., 27 October 1979) A Catholic priest who broadcast "The Golden Hour of the Little Flower" by radio from his church at Royal Oaks, Mich., Coughlin reached 45,000,000 listeners nationwide about 1932. He was an early supporter of the New Deal, but became a severe critic of Franklin D. Roosevelt in 1934 and formed the National Union for Social Justice, which attracted 500,000 members. Coughlin advocated inflation through a massive coinage of silver to end the Great Depression, and in 1936 helped create the Union party. His popularity waned as his message became progressively more conspiratorial, anti-Semitic, and pro-Fascist. Catholic authorities condemned his views in 1937 and suppressed his broadcast in 1942 after he denounced US entry into World War II.

Council for New England *see* Plymouth Company

Council of Economic Advisors The Employment Act (20 February 1946) established this agency to advise the White House staff on economic issues and make recommendations to promote economic stability and full employment. The president appoints its chair, who requires Senate confirmation. On 17 July 1949, Senator Harry Byrd described its members as "a strange group of men" whose "fanciful ideas should be investigated." Congress initially seems to have assumed that its members would come from the business community, but the council is now staffed by professional economists who are generally chosen because they reflect the president's views.

Counselman* v. *Hitchcock On 11 January 1892, the Supreme Court declared unconstitutional a law that allowed the US government to compel testimoney about illegal activities, if the information could not be used directly as evidence against the witness in a later trial, but might be used indirectly to discover new facts that would prove his/her guilt. The Court held that nothing less than absolute immunity from prosecution for any crimes revealed during compelled testimony warranted a waiver of the Fifth Amendment's protection against involuntary self-incrimination. *Counselman* was precedent for *Ullmann* v. *United States.*

County of Washington* v. *Gunther In 1981 the Supreme Court issued its only opinion on comparable worth, while declining to review an appeals court decision. The Court indicated that if allegations of sex discrimination were made against an employer, more evidence was required to prove deliberate intent than statistics that showed women in certain job classifications earning less than men in other job categories – even if the work done by both was comparable in skills and value to their employer. The Court affirmed Title VII of the Civil Rights Act (1964) as a means of ending sex discrimination, but discredited comparable worth as a legal remedy for salary inequities between men and women.

coureurs de bois French Canadians gave their fur traders this name, which meant "runners of the forest." The coureurs lived among Indians and created a personal link between them and Montreal's fur merchants. Their half-Indian offspring formed a mixed race known as Metis. The coureurs performed much of the initial exploration or the area north of the Ohio and Arkansas rivers.

Court-packing bill After the Supreme Court struck down the Agricultural Adjustment Administration, National Recovery Administration, and other measures of the New Deal, Franklin D. Roosevelt sent Congress a Judiciary Reorganization Bill on 5 February 1937 to authorize an extra justice for each member aged over 70, of whom there were six. On 22 July, the Senate withdrew the bill from consideration because public opinion and leading Democrats feared it would destroy the judiciary's independence. The issue split Democrats badly and led many to begin voting with Republicans against Roosevelt. The Court moderated its anti-New Deal stance by affirming the social security Administration and National Labor Relations Act. Resignations and death also enabled Roosevelt to name four new justices by 1939, and by 1941 he had placed seven appointees on the bench.

Cowan* v. *Montana On 28 March 1994, the Supreme Court, without comment, let stand a 1979 Mont. law abolishing insanity as an affirmative defense in criminal cases. The decision followed past rulings that states were not obliged to use any particular insanity test, and left other states free to follow the example of Mont. (as Idaho and Utah had already done).

Cowpens, battle of (S.C.) On 17 January 1781, Brigadier General Daniel Morgan's 600 Continentals and 400 militia routed Lieutenant Colonel Banastre Tarleton's 1,100 Tories and Highlanders. US losses: 12 killed, 60 wounded. British losses: 110 killed, 527 captured (including 229 wounded), 2 cannon captured. As the worst British defeat since Saratoga, Cowpens raised morale among dispirited southern Whigs and cost the British their best corps of light, mounted infantry.

Cox, Archibald (b. Plainfield, N.J., 17 May 1912) Cox served as a solicitor for the Justice and Labor departments (1941–5), and then became a Harvard law school professor. On 18 May 1973, he was appointed special prosecutor to investigate the Watergate scandal by his ex-law student Elliot Richardson. When Cox insisted on subpoenaing White House tapes linking Richard Nixon to illegal activities he was fired in the Saturday night massacre. His dismissal was critical in leading the House to begin hearings on whether to impeach Nixon. He was replaced by Leon Jaworski.

Cox, James Middleton (b. Jacksonburg, Ohio, 31 March 1870; d. Dayton, Ohio, 15 July 1957) He was a journalist who built the Cox newspaper syndicate, Democratic congressman (1909–13) and Ohio governor (1913–14 and 1917–21). As the 1920 Democratic presidential candidate, Cox advocated continuing Woodrow Wilson's domestic policies and US entry to the League of Nations. He won just 34.2 percent of the popular vote and carried only 11 southern states in a crushing defeat that ended his national political career.

Cox* v. *New Hampshire On 31 March 1941, the Supreme Court ruled unanimously that the First Amendment does not preclude ordinances that regulate parades or mass assemblies on public streets, so long as their regulations are carefully drafted to prevent such gatherings from becoming a nuisance and do not discriminate against any group of citizens.

Coxey's Army After the panic of 1893 forced him to lay off 40 of his quarry workers at Masillon, Ohio, Jacob S. Coxey (1854–1951) called upon all unemployed men to march on Washington and demand that the government provide jobs by undertaking a $500,000,000 public works program. Seventeen other groups of protesters began tramping toward the capital about 25 March, but only about 500 arrived there under Coxey's leadership on 30 April. This "army" disintegrated when Washington police arrested Coxey and two lieutenants for trespass. Coxey spent 20 days in jail, then joined the Populist party (*see* POPULISM). The march drew widespread sympathy for victims of the panic, generated favorable publicity for parties like the Populists who championed their cause, and increased President Grover CLEVELAND's unpopularity.

craft union This type of labor union organized workers who shared a common trade or line of work, and excluded unskilled workers. The AMERICAN FEDERATION OF LABOR originated to represent craft unions rather than their opposite, the INDUSTRIAL UNION.

Craig* v. *Boren On 20 December 1976, the Supreme Court ruled (7–2) that states may not establish gender-based classifications unless they serve a compelling need for some public policy. In *Rostker* v. *Goldberg*, the Court ruled that exempting women from the DRAFT was a legitimate legal distinction between women and men.

Craig* v. *Missouri In 1830 the Supreme Court (4–3) refused to exempt states from a strict interpretation of the Constitution's prohibition against their issuing bills of credit or other types of fiat money. The Court disallowed a Mo. law that authorized the emission of loan certificates that were not legal tender, but which the state pledged to accept at face value for payment of taxes or any other obligations due to it. The Court later gave states more flexibility, in *BRISCOE* v. *BANK OF KENTUCKY*, to legislate on regulations concerning notes issued by local banks.

Crane, Stephen (b. Newark, N.J., 1 November 1871; d. Badenweiler, Germany, 5 June 1900) After studies at Syracuse University, Crane became a reporter in New York for the *Tribune* and *Herald*; he served as a war correspondent in the SPANISH-AMERICAN WAR. His first novel, *Maggie: A Girl of the Streets*, appeared in 1892, and he won national acclaim for *The Red Badge of Courage* (1895). Crane became a leading figure in the creation of American literature that portrayed the struggle of life in realistic terms. His other works include *The Little Regiment and Other Episodes of the Civil War* (1896), *The Third Violet* (1897), *Active Service* (1899), *Wounds in the Rain* (1900), *The Monster* (1899), *Whilomville Stories* (1900), and *The O'Ruddy* (1903). He lived his last two years in England and died of tuberculosis.

crash of 1929 This term refers to the 1929 stock market plunge, which precipitated the GREAT DEPRESSION. The New York *Times* stock index peaked at 449 on 31 August, but faltered on BLACK THURSDAY and plunged on BLACK TUESDAY. The index had fallen 50 percent from its peak by November. The decline reached its trough of 58, an 87 percent loss, in July 1932, when $75,000,000,000 of equity capital had been wiped out.

crater, battle of the *see* PETERSBURG, BATTLES OF

Crawford, William Harris (b. Amherst County, Va., 24 February 1772; d. Lexington, Ga., 15 September 1834) He moved to Lexington, Ga., in the 1790s, and entered the Senate in 1807. He became leader of a Democratic faction that criticized the nationalistic policies of John Q. ADAMS and supported STRICT CONSTRUCTIONISM and STATES RIGHTS. In 1824 he became the last presidential candidate nominated by the Democratic congressional caucus, but soon suffered a stroke that left him half-paralyzed and partially blind. He ran last in the popular vote, with 13.1 percent of the ballots, and carried Ga., Va., and Del.

Credit Mobilier scandal On 4 September 1872, newspapers accused prominent Republicans of corrupt involvement with the Credit Mobilier Co., a shell corporation controlled by the Union Pacific Railroad Co. Union Pacific directors had siphoned off large amounts of money, including federal subsidies, by awarding fraudulent construction contracts to Credit Mobilier, and they tried to prevent a congressional investigation by bribing influential politicians, including Vice-President Schuyler COLFAX and James GARFIELD, with sales of discounted stock. On 27 February 1873, Congress censured two of its thirteen members involved. The scandal added to the Ulysses S. GRANT administration's reputation for corruption.

Creek Indians Known to themselves as the Muskogees, the Creeks speak one of the

MUSKOGEAN LANGUAGES and numbered over 20,000 in the area between the Savannah and Alabama rivers in 1790. They were deeply involved in the deerskin trade, had good relations with the English, and fought against US forces in the American Revolution (*see* REVOLUTIONARY WAR). Under Alexander MCGILLIVRAY, through war and diplomacy, they enjoyed much success in halting whites from encroaching on their lands. In 1811 a pro-war faction initiated the CREEK WAR, which crushed the nation's military power to resist US expansion. When pressed by the US, they agreed to sell their homeland. A badly organized relocation of 15,000 Creeks in 1834–5 resulted in over 3,000 deaths, and the army had to mobilize for a second Creek War in July 1837 and force the remaining members to migrate at gunpoint. Their reservation at Okmulgee, Okla. contained 54,606 Creeks in 1987.

Creek War About 1810, the Red Stick movement emerged among the CREEK INDIANS to curtail white settlement on the Alabama River and rid their culture of white influence. Starting with an ambush on whites on 26 March 1812, at Catoma Creek, Ala., Red Stick attacks grew in number until 27 July 1813, when 100 Creeks bringing ammunition from Spanish Pensacola defeated an ambush by Colonel James Caller's 180 Mississippi militia at Burnt Corn Creek, Ala. Miss. losses: 2 killed, 15 wounded. Creek losses: 2 killed, 5 wounded. A month later, full-scale war began with the destruction of FORT MIMS, Ala.

On 29 November 1813, John Floyd's Ga. militia burned Autosse fort and two towns (losses: 11 Georgians killed, 54 wounded; 200 Red Sticks killed). On 24–5 December, William Claiborne's Third US Infantry and Miss. militia stormed Holy Ground stockade and burned 260 cabins (losses: 1 US killed, 20 wounded; 33 Creeks killed). On 27 January 1814, Paddy Welsh's Creeks badly mauled Floyd's men (losses: 21 Georgians killed, 128 wounded; 5 Ga. Indians killed, 15 wounded; 49 Red Sticks killed).

On 3 November 1813, John Coffee's Tenn. militia annihilated the Tallushatchee Creeks (losses: 5 Tennesseeans killed, 41 wounded; 200 Creek men killed, 84 women and children taken). On 9 November, Andrew JACKSON's Tenn. militia destroyed Talledega (losses: 14 Tennesseeans killed, 81 wounded; 299 Creek warriors killed). On 11–18 November, John Cocke's Tenn. militia and Cherokees burned Little Oakfusky, Genalga, and Hillabee (losses: 64 Creek men killed, 34 men and 237 women and children captured). On 22–4 January 1814, Jackson raided Emuckfau and Enitachopco (losses: 20 Tenn. militia killed, 75 wounded; 189 Creeks dead).

On 27 March 1814, Jackson crushed Creek resistance by destroying their last major stronghold at HORSESHOE BEND. Mass surrenders of Red Sticks then ensued. On 9 August, most Creeks ended hostilities by the treaty of FORT JACKSON, but Indian raids continued to 1818. The war established US military superiority on the southwestern frontier and ended all realistic prospects of armed resistance by the FIVE CIVILIZED TRIBES to Indian removal (*see* INDIAN REMOVAL ACT).

Creel, George *see* COMMITTEE ON PUBLIC INFORMATION

CREEP *see* COMMITTEE TO REELECT THE PRESIDENT

***Creole*, USS, incident** After embarking from Hampton Roads, Va., for New Orleans on 27 October 1841, this slave ship was seized in a slave mutiny – which took the life of a crewman – and forced to sail for the Bahamas. Authorities at Nassau freed the slaves according to British law and refused US demands for their return. The episode poisoned Anglo–US relations until 1855, when Britain awarded the US $110,330 as compensation for the slaveowners.

Crèvecoeur, Michel-Guillaume Jean de (b. Caen, France, 31 January 1735; d. Sarcelles, France, 12 November 1813) A French officer who settled in Orange County, N.Y., after the Seven Years' War, he assumed the pseudonym J. Hector St Jean de Crèvecoeur in order to write *Letters from an American Farmer* (London, 1782). This book influenced generations of historians to romanticize Anglo-American society as a utopia of economic prosperity and a melting pot of relatively harmonious relations among different ethnic stocks. The Revolution nevertheless devastated Crèvecoeur's life, and by 1783 (when he became France's consul at New York), his wife was dead, his house had burned, and his three children lived in foster homes.

"crime against Kansas" speech On 19 May 1856, in a speech condemning the proslavery party in Kans., Senator Charles SUMNER made insulting remarks about Senator Andrew Pickens (S.C.), including sexual innuendos and mocking references to a stroke-related speech impairment. On 22 May, after Sumner had failed to apologize for his behavior and the Senate had taken no action to censure him, Congressman Preston Brooks, Pickens's nephew, assaulted him on the Senate floor with a cane and caused severe brain damage, which kept Sumner's seat vacant until December 1859. Brooks resigned from the House, but was returned by his constituents. The episode further polarized southerners, who applauded Brooks, from northerners, who condemned southerners as fanatics capable of any violence.

Crime of '73 The SILVER COINAGE CONTROVERSY began because a surplus of silver made it uneconomical for the Treasury to buy the metal at the official ratio of 16 ounces of silver to 1 ounce of gold, since the government would be paying more than silver's market value. On 12 February 1873, Congress directed the US Mint to stop coining silver dollars. The measure unofficially put the US on the GOLD STANDARD. The act was branded a crime by those who believed it would hurt farmers and debtors by making money more scarce.

Crittenden Compromise On 18 December 1860, Senator John J. Crittenden (Democrat, Ky.) attempted to preserve the Union with a resolution that would have permitted SLAVERY in territories south of the line set by the MISSOURI COMPROMISE and established guarantees that slavery would be left undisturbed in states where it already existed. A Senate panel named to consider the compromise could not agree to recommend its passage. Abraham LINCOLN opposed the measure as a violation of free-soil principles. Its failure demonstrated that the US was too polarized to avoid CIVIL WAR through compromise.

Crockett, David (b. Greene County, Tenn., 17 August 1786; d. San Antonio, Tex., 6 March 1836) "Davy" Crockett served in the CREEK WAR as a militia sergeant. He entered the Tenn. legislature in 1820, became a political enemy of Andrew JACKSON, and was elected to Congress for the WHIG PARTY in 1827, 1831, and 1833. Upon his final political defeat in 1835, he reportedly told his constituents, "You can go to Hell, I'm going to Texas," and joined the TEXAS REVOLT. He was among seven Americans murdered in cold blood after surrendering at the ALAMO.

Croly, Herbert D. *see PROMISE OF AMERICAN LIFE, THE*

Crop Loan Act (23 February 1934) This law funded $40,000,000 for the FARM CREDIT ADMINISTRATION to extend credit for planting and harvesting. Farmers used about 95 percent of the money for the 1934 crop.

cross of gold speech On 8 July 1896, William Jennings BRYAN won the Democratic nomination for president at the Chicago convention with this superlative speech. After recounting the grievances of farmers and workers, he ended his oration with the ringing words: "You shall not press down upon the brow of labor this crown of thorns. You shall not crucify mankind upon a cross of gold."

Crow Indians Speakers of one of the SIOUAN LANGUAGES, the Crows were a nomadic branch of the sedentary HIDATSA INDIANS; they numbered about 4,000 in 1780 and occupied the Yellowstone and upper Missouri rivers. They never warred against the US and furnished many army scouts in the SIOUX and NEZ PERCE WARS. By an 1868 treaty, they received title to a large hunting reserve in south-central Mont., now the Crow Agency.

Crown Point (N.Y.) In 1731 the French built Fort St Frederic on Lake Champlain, 10 miles from FORT TICONDEROGA, inside N.Y.'s borders. Colonel William JOHNSON's colonials abandoned plans to besiege the fort after the battle of LAKE GEORGE in 1755. Facing imminent capture by Major General Jeffery AMHERST, in July 1759 the French blew up the post, which Amherst rebuilt as Crown Point. A token garrison of nine redcoats capitulated to US forces on 10 May 1775. British troops reclaimed the post on 14 July 1777 and held it until 1783.

CSA Confederate States of America (*see* CONFEDERACY)

Cuba, US intervention in (*See also* SPANISH-AMERICAN WAR, BAY OF PIGS INVASION, *and* CUBAN MISSILE CRISIS) By treaty in 1903, the US leased Guantanamo Bay as a military base for 99 years. In September 1906, 2,900 marines landed at Havana to impose a ceasefire on a civil war; the US added 5,000 soldiers and occupied the island with an Army of Cuban Pacification until 1909. In 1912 a USMC brigade landed to protect American sugar interests from rebels. In 1917 a USMC brigade landed to guard US plantations and railroads from rebels, and was not fully withdrawn until 1922.

Cuban immigration Prior to 1959, 40,000 Cubans lived in the US. Between 1959 and August 1965, about 50,000 persons fled Fidel CASTRO's Communist regime. During December 1965–16 August 1971, Castro allowed an airlift to fly 246,000 Cubans to Miami. During 1973–9, about 38,000 escaped to Fla. In 1980 Castro allowed the MARIEL BOATLIFT. During 1983–93, 9,513 Cubans fled to the US by sea; by 1991, 758,184 Cubans had immigrated. The 1990 census reported that 805,204 persons (0.3 percent) described their *primary* ethnic background as Cuban. Since 1965, $1.66 billion in federal funds have been spent to resettle Cuban refugees.

The refugee flow resumed en masse during August–September 1994, when 30,000 were rescued at sea from makeshift rafts as Castro threatened to allow unlimited embarkation if the US trade embargo continued. William CLINTON rescinded the legal right of Cuban refugees to US residency on 19 August 1994 and ordered all escapees to be intercepted at sea and held at Guantanamo Bay. On 9 September, Castro promised to halt further departures from Cuba, and the US agreed to issue 20,000 visas per year for Cuban immigrants.

Cuban missile crisis During July–August 1962, 30 Soviet ships landed 2,000 Russian military personnel and much equipment in Cuba. On 14 October, intelligence sources confirmed that missile sites were being prepared that threatened the US nuclear deterrent. On 22 October, John F. KENNEDY announced that the USSR was preparing offensive missile bases in Cuba, and warned that the island would be quarantined if assurance of their removal was not given. On 24 October, he initiated the quarantine with eight aircraft carriers and 170 other vessels to keep 25 Soviet ships from landing there. One US plane was shot down by 26 October, when Premier Nikita Khrushchev secretly indicated a willingness to pull out the missiles if the US agreed not to invade Cuba. When Kennedy accepted this offer, Khrushchev agreed on 28 October to dismantle the bases, and abandoned his public position that the US should also remove its own missiles in Turkey that threatened the USSR. The US quarantine was ended on 20 November with the assurance that all USSR bombers would be evacuated in 30 days.

Culpeper's Rebellion After arriving in the Albemarle district as customs agent and acting governor for the PROPRIETORS OF CAROLINA, Thomas Miller aroused intense resentment for arresting a political opponent, George Durant, for violating the NAVIGATION LAWS. John Culpeper then organized a coup and arrested Miller on 3 December 1677. After traveling to England to justify his actions, Culpeper was tried for treason in 1680, but acquitted with assistance from the proprietors, who viewed him as a useful ally in winning political support for themselves in N.C. Miller was dismissed.

Cumberland Gap (Ky.) On 13 April 1750, while exploring the west for the Ohio Land Co., Dr Thomas Walker discovered this natural passageway (initially called Cave Gap) through the Cumberland Mountains, named after the Duke of Cumberland. Daniel BOONE routed the WILDERNESS ROAD via this pass in 1775. It was the southern alternative to moving west via the Ohio River and 100,000 pioneers may have crossed it by 1800.

Cumberland Road *see* NATIONAL ROAD

Cumming* v. *County Board of Education In 1899 the Supreme Court applied *PLESSY* V. *FERGUSON* to education by holding that separate schools for blacks and whites were constitutional if they provided both races with equal facilities. *Cumming* was reversed by *BROWN* V. *BOARD OF EDUCATION OF TOPEKA* (1954).

cummings, ee

edward estlin cummings poet
(14 Oct) 1894 born cambridgemass

received harvard m.a. 1916 and
when of the ambulance corps
in France was wrongfully
[imprisoned]
owing to an overzeal
ous
CENSOR
helping create a
life long
aversion to
and attacks upon
the solemn the
impersonal the established the mech
ani
cal the abstract and his
joyous dancing
celebration
of freedom the individual
instinct spont(yes)eity a
,beautiful always,
love
then left the world a drier place who
churchbells in conway, newhamp
in (3 Sep) 19and62 good
bye
(hello)

Cummings* v. *Missouri *see* Test Oath Cases

Currency Act (1751) *see* Currency Act (1764)

Currency Act (19 April 1764) After being lobbied by British merchants, Parliament extended the Currency Act (1751), which forbade the New England colonies to issue legal-tender paper money, to all the colonies after 1 September 1764 and threatened any governor who signed such a law with a £1,000 fine and lifetime exclusion from any Crown office. The law denied the colonies a highly useful tool for dealing with their perennial shortage of hard money and would have caused great disaffection had many colonies not succeeded in winning exemptions to issue paper currency.

Curtis, Charles (b. North Topeka, Kans., 25 January 1860; d. Washington, D.C., 8 February 1936) Of mixed British-Osage ancestry, Curtis was the only person registered as an Indian tribal member to become vice-president. He began practicing law in 1881, sat in Congress as a Republican from Kans. (1893–1907), was senator (1907–29, except 1913), and was Senate majority leader (1924–9). He was Herbert Hoover's running mate.

Curtis, George *see* Civil Service Reform

Custer, George Armstrong (b. New Rumley, Ohio, 5 December 1839; d. Little Big Horn Creek, Wyo., 25 June 1876) Upon graduating last in his class at West Point, Custer entered the US cavalry. He rose from lieutenant to brigadier general by the age of 23, and then reverted to captain when the Civil War ended. Named lieutenant colonel of the Seventh Cavalry in 1867, he fought in the Red River War and perished in the third Sioux War at the battle of the Little Big Horn.

CWA *see* Civil Works Administration

D

D-Day This was a WORLD WAR II term for the launch date of an amphibious or airborne assault upon territory controlled by the AXIS. It is often used as a synonym for the invasion of NORMANDY.

Dakota Indians This name is the preferred title used by the group commonly called SIOUX INDIANS.

Dallas, George Mifflin (b. Philadelphia, Pa., 10 July 1792; d. Philadelphia, Pa., 31 December 1864) A Princeton man (1810) and lawyer, Dallas was US senator (Democrat, Pa., 1831–3), Pa. attorney general (1833–5), ambassador to Russia (1837–9), US vice-president (1845–9), and ambassador to Britain (1856–61). Although a protectionist, he cast the deciding Senate vote for the WALKER TARIFF.

Danbury–Hatters case *see LOEWE* v. *LAWLER*

"**Danger of an Unconverted Ministry, The**" *see* TENNENT, GILBERT

Danish West Indies *see* VIRGIN ISLANDS

Darrow, Clarence (b. Kinsman, Ohio, 18 April 1857; d. Chicago, Ill., 13 March 1938) After a year's study at the University of Michigan law school, Darrow was admitted to the Ohio bar in 1878 and joined the Chicago law office of John P. ALTGELD in 1887. He won renown as the greatest defense lawyer of his generation by his handling of many sensational trials. He defended Eugene DEBS against charges of conspiracy in the PULLMAN STRIKE, represented William HAYWOOD against the charge of assassinating the governor of Idaho, was defense counsel at the SCOPES TRIAL, and represented the defendants in the notorious Leopold and Loeb murder case so skillfully that they received life imprisonment rather than death.

Dartmouth College [Trustees of]* v. *Woodward On 2 February 1819, the Supreme Court overruled (5–1) a N.H. law revoking Dartmouth's 1769 charter to transform the school from a private to a public college. The Court held that corporation charters were contracts enjoying constitutional protection and thus were inviolable. The decision forbade state interference with charters of existing corporations, but most states countered by granting subsequent charters that could be selectively amended by their legislatures in special cases. The Supreme Court further addressed this issue in *CHARLES RIVER BRIDGE* v. *WARREN BRIDGE*.

Daugherty, Harry Micajah (b. Washington Court House, Ohio, 26 January 1860; d. Columbus, Ohio, 12 October 1941) One of the OHIO GANG's most influential members, Daugherty became attorney general in 1921. When evidence surfaced that he failed to pursue charges of corruption in the Veterans Bureau and had taken kickbacks in connection with bootleggers and the ALIEN PROPERTY CUSTODIAN SCANDAL, Harding forced him to resign in May 1924. He was the first US ATTORNEY GENERAL tried for high crimes committed while in office. Although undeniably guilty, he was acquitted of bribery and criminal conspiracy on 4 March 1927.

Davenport, John (b. Coventry, England, 1597; d. Boston, Mass., March 1670) When Davenport emigrated to Boston in 1637, he was esteemed one of New England's most learned Puritan ministers. He founded Quinnipiac in 1638 and was the principal organizer of NEW HAVEN Colony. Under his influence, New Haven based its legal code on Mosaic Law, which did not recognize inconveniences to righteous justice like jury trials.

Davis, Jefferson (b. Todd County, Ky., 3 June 1808; d. New Orleans, La., 6 December

1889) Raised in Miss., Davis graduated from West Point in 1828, served in the BLACK HAWK WAR, was wounded at BUENA VISTA in the MEXICAN WAR, and was offered the rank of brigadier general, but returned to his Miss. plantation. As Miss. senator, he opposed the COMPROMISE OF 1850. He was secretary of war (1853–7); then again as senator he offered the DAVIS RESOLUTIONS. He left Congress after the SECESSION of Miss. on 21 January 1861. He was inaugurated as the Confederacy's president on 18 February 1861. His administration was crippled by a lack of cooperation from state governors and squabbling within Congress, neither of which Davis had the political skills to solve nor the executive authority to surmount. He convened his last cabinet session on 24 April 1865, was captured at Irwinville, Ga., on 10 May, indicted for treason in 1867, and released from Fort Monroe, Va., in 1867 without being tried. He spent his last years writing *The Rise and Fall of the Confederate Government*. Davis has been criticized unduly for the Confederacy's defeat, which largely stemmed from its decentralized structure, its parochial governors, and the north's numerical advantage.

Davis, John William (b. Clarksburg, W.Va., 13 April 1873; d. Charleston, W.Va., 24 March 1955). He was congressman from W.Va. (1911–13), US solicitor general (1913–18), and ambassador to Britain (1918–21). He was fiscally conservative and attracted to internationalism, but was considered a moderate Democrat. On the 103rd ballot of the 1924 Democratic convention, after the delegates deadlocked between William MCADOO and Alfred SMITH, be became the compromise candidate for president. He polled just 28.8 percent of the ballots, the worst defeat ever by a Democrat running for president. After returning to his law practice, he fiercely assailed the NEW DEAL, and opposed Franklin D. ROOSEVELT's reelection in 1940.

Davis Resolutions On 2 February 1860, Jefferson DAVIS introduced resolutions into the Senate for congressional action to protect SLAVERY. To implement *ABLEMAN* v. *BOOTH*, Congress would forbid legislatures from frustrating enforcement of the FUGITIVE SLAVE LAW (1850). To prevent the FREEPORT DOCTRINE from undermining *DRED SCOTT* v. *SANDFORD*, Congress would forbid territorial citizens from outlawing slavery before ratifying a state constitution, and also would enact a federal SLAVE CODE for all territories. To protect slavery from ABOLITIONISM, Congress would declare interference with state laws protecting slavery to be unconstitutional. Adopted by the Senate on 24 May, but not the House, these positions split the northern and southern wings of the Democratic party. When the 1860 Democratic convention would not endorse the resolutions, southern delegates left and nominated John BRECKINRIDGE as their candidate.

Davyes' Uprising On 3 September 1676, in Calvert County, Md., about 60 men met under William Davyes and John Pate to criticize taxes owed to the proprietary government, voting qualifications, and a loyalty oath owed to Lord Baltimore. Although little more than an emotional venting of political anger, the government tried Davyes and Pate for inciting rebellion, and hanged them.

Dawes, Charles Gates (b. Marietta, Ohio, 27 August 1865; d. Evanston, Ill., 23 April 1951) He was a lawyer, businessman, and banker, who became US comptroller of the currency (1898–1901) and US vice-president (1925–9). He shared the Nobel peace prize (1925) for formulating the Dawes Plan, which attempted to settle the problem of how Germany would pay reparations from WORLD WAR I.

Dawes Plan *see* DAWES, CHARLES GATES

Dawes Severalty Act (8 February 1887) This law's purpose was to break up the RESERVATION system into private holdings, integrate Indians into Anglo-American culture, and make them citizens. The law authorized the US to survey reservations into plots for farming (160 acres for a family, 80 acres for single adults over 18, and 40 acres for dependent minors – to be doubled for grazing land). An Indian became a citizen upon accepting land. To prevent exploitation by unscrupulous whites, Indians could not sell or rent their grants for 25 years. Because whites could buy excess reservation lands, Indian landholdings declined from 138,000,000 to 47,000,000 acres between 1887 and 1934.

(*See changes under* BURKE ACT *and* WHEELER–HOWARD ACT)

daylight saving time By a law of 30 March 1918, Congress mandated that the day begin one hour earlier on the last Sunday of March and have that hour restored on the last Sunday in October, but popular opposition led to its repeal on 20 August 1919. Daylight saving time was left to state option until WORLD WAR II, and then Congress reimposed it from 6 February 1942 to 30 September 1945, when it again became subject to state option. The Uniform Time Act (1966) instituted daylight saving time from the last Sunday in April to the last Sunday in October, but allowed states to exempt themselves. This exemption was eliminated on 15 December 1973 during the OIL EMBARGO, but restored a year later. In 1987 Congress shifted the start of daylight saving time to the first Sunday in April.

de facto segregation This refers to racial SEGREGATION that has not resulted from compliance with laws requiring racial separation in housing or education, as opposed to DE JURE SEGREGATION.

De Jonge* v. *Oregon On 4 January 1937, the Supreme Court (8–0) ruled that the DUE PROCESS clause of the FOURTEENTH AMENDMENT obliged state courts to uphold FIRST AMENDMENT protections of free assembly and petition. The Court threw out a conviction for organizing and speaking at the meeting of an organization that advocated the US government's violent overthrow. The Court ruled that the BILL OF RIGHTS protected gatherings at which no unlawful activities were discussed, and required that prosecutions be based on evidence that a "clear and present danger" of public harm might ensue from the speaker's words.

de jure segregation This refers to legally enforced racial SEGREGATION that set apart whites from minorities in housing, education, or public accommodations, as opposed to DE FACTO SEGREGATION.

De Leon, Daniel (b. Curaçao, 14 December 1852; d. New York, N.Y., 11 May 1914) In 1874 De Leon emigrated to the US. He joined the Socialist Labor Party in 1890 and became its dominant leader, but his dogmatic Marxism led to a schism that produced the rival SOCIALIST PARTY OF AMERICA in 1901. He tried to convert the AFL's politically conservative CRAFT UNIONS to socialism, but found them entirely unreceptive. In 1905 he helped found the INDUSTRIAL WORKERS OF THE WORLD, but his doctrinaire attitudes proved so disruptive that he was later expelled. De Leon's career showed that even among socialists and labor radicals, an uncompromising adherence to Marxist ideology had limited attraction in the US.

De Lima* v. *Bidwell On 27 May 1901, the Supreme Court ruled (5–4) that PUERTO RICO's status as a foreign nation ceased with the end of the SPANISH-AMERICAN WAR; it consequently held that customs could not be collected on the island's imports unless Congress approved them. On the same day, the Court ruled that US merchandise shipped to the island was duty-free, in *Dooley* v. *United States*. The Court further clarified Puerto Rico's constitutional status in *DOWNES* v. *BIDWELL* and *DORR* v. *UNITED STATES*.

De Sapio, Carmine *see* TAMMANY HALL

De Soto, Hernán *see* SOTO, HERNÁN DE

Dean, John Wesley III (b. Akron, Ohio, 14 October 1938) He was a former associate deputy attorney general when he became counsel to Richard NIXON in 1970. He assisted the attempted cover-up of the WATERGATE SCANDAL, but became the first White House insider to reveal details of the conspiracy on 27 April 1973, when he accused H. R. HALDEMAN and John EHRLICHMAN of illegal activities. He resigned from the White House on 30 April, cooperated with Senate investigators of the scandal, pleaded guilty to conspiracy to obstruct justice, and served four months' imprisonment in 1974.

Dearborn, Henry *see* BEAVER DAM *and* FORT GEORGE, BATTLES OF

death penalty *see FURMAN* v. *GEORGIA*

Debs, Eugene Victor (b. Terre Haute, Ind., 5 November 1855; d. Elmhurst, Ill., 20 October 1926) After serving as a Democratic legislator in Ind. (1884–6), Debs devoted himself to the labor movement. He was first president of the American Railway Union in 1893. Convicted for his role in the PULLMAN STRIKE, he spent six months in prison after IN RE DEBS affirmed his conviction for conspiracy to obstruct the mails. He helped organize the Social Democratic Party in 1897 and the INDUSTRIAL WORKERS OF THE WORLD in 1905. Debs endorsed William Jennings BRYAN for president in 1896, but ran as Socialist candidate in 1900 and polled 0.7 percent of the ballots. As nominee of the SOCIALIST PARTY OF AMERICA, he won 3.0 percent of the vote in 1904, 2.8 percent in 1908, 6.0 percent in 1912, and 3.4 percent in 1920. He was imprisoned for agitating against the ESPIONAGE ACT (1918–21). Stripped of his citizenship, he ended his days editing socialist newspapers.

Declaration of Independence On 12 April 1776, N.C. became the first state to authorize its congressmen to vote for independence. On 7 June, Richard Henry LEE resolved that the THIRTEEN COLONIES declare independence. The second CONTINENTAL CONGRESS debated Lee's resolves until 2 July, when 12 delegations voted for independence and N.Y. abstained. On 4 July, a preamble written by Thomas JEFFERSON was approved as a statement of principles, but without any legal force in US law.

Declaratory Act (18 March 1766) Parliament passed this law simultaneously with its repeal of the STAMP ACT. Modeled after a Declaratory Act for Ireland (1719), it proclaimed Parliament's authority to legislate for the colonies "in all cases whatsoever." Although a denial of American claims to be exempt from taxes passed in Britain, it was ignored in the THIRTEEN COLONIES, and so did not emerge as a major issue contributing to the DECLARATION OF INDEPENDENCE.

Deerfield, raids on (Mass.) In 1676 Indians almost wiped out Deerfield and the survivors abandoned the settlement. In 1694 the town repulsed a French and Indian raiding party. On 29 February 1704, Hertel de Rouville's 50 French and 200 Indians captured half the townspeople and burned 17 of the 41 houses, but failed to take 140 people who held out in fortified houses. English losses: 48 killed, 112 captured (of whom 16 were killed and 2 starved en route to Canada). French losses: 3 French and 8 Indians killed in the attack, and 30 casualties under pursuit by Mass. militia. The captives returned after their relatives paid ransom. Deerfield was the worst civilian massacre of QUEEN ANNE'S WAR, and its loss of civilian lives was exceeded only by the SCHENECTADY RAID during the French and Indian Wars.

Defense, Department of On 26 July 1947, Congress appointed a secretary of defense, with cabinet status, to oversee the affairs of all the military services. On 10 August 1949, the National Security Act created the Department of Defense to replace the WAR and NAVY DEPARTMENTS; under the secretary of defense were separate (civilian) secretaries for the army, navy, and air force, and the (military) chairman of the joint chiefs of staff.

Delaney clause In 1958 Representative James J. Delaney (Democrat, N.Y.) amended the FOOD, DRUG, AND COSMETIC ACT to forbid the sale of any additive found to cause cancer in laboratory animals, even if the experiments used doses far in excess of any rate that would be consumed by a human. The clause has been the FOOD AND DRUG ADMINISTRATION'S major weapon in preventing distribution of products deemed carcinogenic, but has been criticized as imposing an unnecessarily restrictive standard.

Delaware In April 1631, the Dutch made the first European settlement in Del. (near Lewes) at Swanendael, which was destroyed by Indians a year later. In March 1638, the first Swedes landed near Lewes and claimed the area as NEW SWEDEN; they placed their capital at Fort Christina (near Wilmington). They competed for control of the local FUR TRADE with NEW NETHERLAND, which annexed the colony (then about 350 persons) on 26 September 1655. England acquired Del. by its conquest of New Netherland in 1664. In 1681 William PENN was awarded Del. as part of PENNSYLVANIA. In 1701 Del. resumed its standing as a separate colony when Penn agreed to let it elect its own legislature, which first met on 22 November 1704. The governor of Pa. also sat as chief executive of Del., which was properly termed the Three Lower Counties on the Delaware.

Del. was the smallest colony in 1775 and provided just one of the Continental army's 80 regiments. It was the site of 20 land and 17 sea engagements during the REVOLUTIONARY WAR. It was the first state to ratify the Constitution, on 7 December 1787. In 1800 it was the smallest state and had 64,273 inhabitants, of which 78 percent were white (of these 69 percent were English or Welsh) and 22 percent were black.

Del. had poor soil for grains, but it emerged as an early center for manufacturing after 1800, with flour milling and the Du Pont family's gunpowder factories. It was the only state north of Md. that preserved slavery after 1820. In 1860 2 percent of its 112,216 residents were slaves, 18 percent were free blacks, and 8 percent were foreign-born; it ranked 34th among the states in size, 28th in the value of farmland and livestock, and 28th in manufactures.

In the CIVIL WAR, Del. furnished 12,284 USA troops (including 954 blacks). It refused to either free its slaves by state law or to ratify the THIRTEENTH, FOURTEENTH, or FIFTEENTH AMENDMENTS. The state deliberately made it hard for blacks to vote and exercise their civil rights, and did not appropriate money for black education until 1875. The Democratic Party remained dominant until 1897, when a new constitution reapportioned a fair share of legislative seats to the Republican districts of Wilmington and its suburbs.

In 1900 Del. was 54 percent rural and had 184,735 inhabitants, of whom 83 percent were white and 8 percent were foreign-born; it ranked 45th among states in size, 47th in the value of its agricultural goods, and 36th in manufactures. The state's economy grew moderately until the period from 1950 to 1970, when it gained 101,000 new residents by in-migration. In 1990 Del. was 66 percent urban and had 666,168 people (approx. 79 percent white, 17 percent black, 2 percent Hispanic, 1 percent Asian), of whom 3.3 percent were foreign-born. Manufacturing or mining employed 27 percent of workers.

Delaware Indians Speakers of one of the ALGONQUIAN LANGUAGES, the Delawares may have numbered 8,000 in N.J., northern Del., and eastern Pa. in 1600. They enjoyed peace with the Quaker settlers there (*see* QUAKERS), but sold large quantities of land and declined in population due to European diseases. They became badly alienated from Anglo-Americans in 1737, when they were tricked into selling 1,200 square miles of their best Pa. lands by the Walking Purchase. They drifted west toward the Ohio valley, raided English settlements in the SEVEN YEARS' WAR and PONTIAC'S WAR, and relocated in Ohio during the 1760s. As British allies in the REVOLUTIONARY WAR, they raided Pa., Va., and Ky., and continued fighting Anglo-American expansion until 1794. They ceded most of their Ohio lands by the first TREATY OF GREENVILLE. They were British allies in the WAR OF 1812. They accepted relocation to Kans. in 1835, and went to Okla. in 1867. Delaware reservations now exist at Bowler, Wis., Andarko, Okla. Bothwell and Muncey, Ontario.

Democratic Party The Democrats are the oldest, continuously active political party in the world. They began as a coalition organized by Thomas JEFFERSON, James MADISON, and George CLINTON in 1791 to oppose the policies of Alexander HAMILTON and the emerging FEDERALIST PARTY. They called themselves Republicans, while Federalists called them Democratics. Initially a minority party (except for controlling the House of Representatives, 1793–6), they took over both houses of Congress and the presidency in 1800.

The party's ideology evolved from JEFFERSONIAN DEMOCRACY, STRICT CONSTRUCTIONISM, and Albert GALLATIN's fiscal policies. The early party included a broad spectrum of opinion ranging from the QUIDS to NATIONAL REPUBLICANS. In Andrew JACKSON's administration, the party split into the WHIG PARTY and Democrats, as orthodox party members were thereafter known. Democrats strongly supported free trade, the INDEPENDENT TREASURY, and MANIFEST DESTINY. From 1800 to 1860, the party controlled the presidency every year except during 1841 and 1849–52, the Senate every year except during 1841–4, and the House every year except 1841–2, 1847–8, and 1855–60.

Tarnished with a reputation for disloyalty during the CIVIL WAR, Democrats entered a long period as a minority party based primarily in the SOLID SOUTH and northern urban machines. From 1860 to 1928, they elected only two presidents (Grover CLEVELAND and Woodrow WILSON), held the Senate only in 1879–80, 1893–4, and 1913–18, and controlled the House only during 1875–80, 1883–8, 1891–4, 1911–18, and 1931–2. During the NEW DEAL, they created the

ROOSEVELT COALITION, which gave them control of Congress until 1947 and the White House until 1953. They regained control of Congress in 1949 and thereafter held both houses, except for the Senate during 1981–6. From 1952 to 1992, they won only four of 11 presidential contests (John KENNEDY, Lyndon JOHNSON, Jimmy CARTER, and William CLINTON), because they lost support among the SOLID SOUTH's white voters and the SILENT MAJORITY. In 1994 they lost control of both houses of Congress and half the governorships.

Demonstration Cities and Metropolitan Development Act (3 November 1966) This program of the GREAT SOCIETY appropriated funds for transportation projects and rehabilitating ghettos, and it also coordinated federal programs for new housing, parks, and urban landscaping. It initially targeted only a dozen cities for special development, but it eventually awarded grants to over 150. It expired in June 1974 after spending $2,000,000.

Denmark Vesey *see* VESEY'S CONSPIRACY

Dennis et al.* v. *United States On 4 June 1951, the Supreme Court affirmed (6–2) the SMITH ACT, which made it a crime to advocate the forceful overthrow of the US government. The ruling followed the logic of *ABRAMS* V. *UNITED STATES*, which stated that the FIRST AMENDMENT did not protect speech intended to have a "bad tendency," even if it presented no "clear and present danger." The Court later modified the Smith Act's scope in *YATES* V. *UNITED STATES*.

Dependent Pension Act (27 June 1890) Until this measure, the US had only awarded pensions after the CIVIL WAR for disabilities arising from military service. Lobbied hard by the GRAND ARMY OF THE REPUBLIC, Congress passed this measure to pension any Union veteran who perfomed 90 days' duty and was honorably discharged, if he was too disabled to support himself by his own labor. Grover CLEVELAND vetoed it on 11 February 1887, but Benjamin HARRISON signed it in 1890. From 1891 to 1895, the number of pensioners rose by 43 percent, to 970,000, and appropriations increased by 67 percent to $135,000,000.

Deposit Act (1836) *see* DISTRIBUTION ACT

Depository Institution Deregulation and Monetary Control Act *see* DEREGULATION

depression of 1837 *see* PANIC OF 1837

depression of 1857 *see* PANIC OF 1857

depression of 1873 *see* PANIC OF 1873

depression of 1893 *see* PANIC OF 1893

depression of 1929 *see* GREAT DEPRESSION

deregulation In the 1970s, a significant loosening of federal regulations was begun under Jimmy CARTER through the leadership of of Civil Aeronautics Board chair Alfred Kahn, and continued under Ronald REAGAN. The major deregulation statutes were: the Railroad Revitalization and Regulatory Reform Act (1976) and Staggers Rail Act (1980), which both allowed railways greater freedom in setting rates; the Airline Deregulation Act (1978), which phased out the Civil Aeronautics Board through 1985 and gave airlines control over fares and mergers; the Motor Carrier Act (1980), which reduced trucking regulations; the Depository Institution Deregulation and Monetary Control Act (1980), which gave mutual savings banks greater freedom to compete for customers through interest rates; the Bus Deregulatory Reform Act (1982), which let companies enter busing independently of the Interstate Commerce Commission; and the Thrift Institutions Restructuring Act (1982), which allowed savings and loan (mortgage) institutions to write commercial loans and invest money outside of real estate. In the air industry, fierce competition reduced fares but also led to major bankruptcies by overextended or poorly run companies. Once deregulated, the mortgage industry burdened itself with bad investments and brought on the SAVINGS AND LOAN CRISIS.

desegregation *see* SEGREGATION

Deseret This was a proposed Mormon state (see MORMONS) encompassing UTAH, most of Ariz. and Nev., and parts of Colo., N.Mex., Calif., Wyo., Idaho, and Oreg., with seaports at San Diego and the mouth of the Colorado River. Congress denied it statehood in 1851, and created Utah Territory with reduced boundaries. Deseret supporters organized a shadow government as a standby alternative to that of Utah (1862–70).

détente This was a policy of reducing tensions with the USSR and Communist China engineered by Richard NIXON. Nixon initiated this shift in foreign relations during 20–5 February 1972 at a summit meeting in Beijing, where he ended the US policy of isolating China and blocking its admission to the UN. (Full diplomatic relations were not established until January 1979.) During 22–9 May 1972, at a summit meeting in Moscow, Nixon signed the STRATEGIC ARMS LIMITATION and ANTIBALLISTIC MISSILE TREATIES, several accords for scientific exchanges, and a declaration pledging the US and USSR to peaceful coexistence and further progress on NUCLEAR ARMS CONTROL. Relations with the USSR gradually improved until January 1980, when the USSR invaded Afghanistan.

Detroit race riot (Mich.) On 20 June 1943, fighting erupted among an interracial crowd at a large park and quickly spread over much of the city as crowds of whites assaulted individual blacks on the streets and began rampaging through black neighborhoods. Order was not restored until the National Guard arrived on 21 June. The riots left 25 blacks and 9 whites dead, 700 injured, and $2,000,000 of property destroyed.

Dewey, George (b. Montpelier, Vt., 26 December 1837; d. Washington, D.C., 16 January 1917) In 1858 Dewey graduated from the Naval Academy, and fought in the CIVIL WAR. Although trained on wooden sailing vessels, he achieved full tactical mastery over steam-powered, armored warships. He assumed command of the Pacific squadron just before the SPANISH-AMERICAN WAR. When told of the war's commencement, Dewey left Hong Kong on 26 April and steamed 600 miles to MANILA BAY in six days; he destroyed Spain's fleet on 1 May and directed amphibious operations in the Philippines. Dewey became a national hero, but spurned offers to seek high political office.

Dewey, John (b. Burlington, Vt., 20 October 1859; d. New York, N.Y., 1 June 1952) After studying pedagogy and philosophy at Johns Hopkins (Ph.D., 1884), Dewey emerged as a prominent educational theorist at the University of Chicago and Columbia. He hoped that a modernized school system would liberate society to make reforms like those espoused by Edward BELLAMY. By arguing that teachers must develop children's full range of artistic and creative abilities, rather than focus on rote memorizing, he became the leading proponent of progressive educational change.

Dewey, Thomas Edmund (b. Owosso, Mich., 24 March 1902; d. Miami Beach, Fla., 16 March 1971) He first became prominent when he was made special prosecuting attorney investigating organized crime in 1935. He was defeated for N.Y. governor in 1938, but won in 1942, 1946, and 1950. He represented the internationalist wing of the Republican Party and accepted the need for social-welfare legislation. Nominated for president in 1944, with Governor John Bricker for vice-president, he carried 12 states and won 46.0 percent of ballots against Franklin D. ROOSEVELT. Renominated in 1948 with Earl WARREN for vice-president, he expected an easy victory based on the public opinion polls and waged a lackadaisical campaign, but lost with just 45.1 percent of the popular vote to Harry S. TRUMAN in the greatest presidential upset ever recorded. He was instrumental in obtaining the 1952 Republican nomination for vice-president for Richard NIXON.

Dickinson, Emily Elizabeth (b. Amherst, Mass., 10 December 1830; d. Amherst, Mass., 15 May 1886) She had little formal education, and lived a life of seclusion in Amherst, where she ultimately wrote 1,775 poems, of which just two were published in her lifetime. The first significant publication of her verse came posthumously in 1890, when she gained recognition as a major talent. She was the late 19th century's most gifted poet.

Dickinson, John (b. Talbot County, Md., 8 November 1732; d. Wilmington, Del., 14 February 1808) He attended the STAMP ACT CONGRESS and helped draft its resolutions. His *LETTERS FROM A FARMER IN PENNSYLVANIA* (1767) made him a major spokesman for the WHIGS. At the first and second CONTINENTAL CONGRESSES, he drafted the OLIVE BRANCH PETITION and co-authored the "Declaration of the Causes of Taking up Arms," but opposed the DECLARATION OF INDEPENDENCE and declined to sign it. He chaired the committee that drafted the ARTICLES OF CONFEDERATION, served with the Del. militia in the war, attended the CONSTITUTIONAL CONVENTION, and authored essays for the FEDERALISTS under the pseudonym Fabius. He helped found Dickinson College.

Dies Committee *see* HOUSE COMMITTEE ON UN-AMERICAN ACTIVITIES

Dingley Tariff (7 July 1897) This tariff replaced the WILSON–GORMAN TARIFF after the 1896 elections gave the Republicans control of Congress. It raised import duties to their highest average in history: 57 percent. It was succeeded by the PAYNE–ALDRICH TARIFF.

direct primary A reform of the PROGRESSIVE ERA designed to reduce the power of party bosses by selecting statewide political candidates through direct elections rather than at state conventions, this reform was pioneered by southern states, beginning with S.C. in 1896, and spread northward with its adoption by Wis. in 1903.

Disaster Loan Corporation *see* RECONSTRUCTION FINANCE CORPORATION

Disciples of Christ This denomination is rooted in the non-denominational, western revival that began with the CANE RIDGE CAMP MEETING. Its origins lay in theological declarations by Presbyterians Barton Stone of Ky. (1804) and Thomas Campbell of Pa. (1809), in which both ministers argued for the freedom to admit all Christians to their services – even to the extent of offering the Lord's Supper to members of other denominations. Stone's followers and the Campbellites merged in 1832 as the Christian Church. By 1850 the church had over 500,000 members. By 1906 the fellowship had split between the "progressive" Disciples of Christ (just under 1,000,000 members in 8,000 churches) and the "fundamentalist" Churches of Christ (160,000 members in 2,649 churches). In 1990 there were 23,067 congregations in all the organized Churches of Christ, which included 3,748,900 members (2.5 percent of all churchgoers), of whom 43 percent were affiliated with the Churches of Christ, 28 percent with the Christian Church (Disciples), and 29 percent with the Christian Churches and Churches of Christ.

disestablishment of state churches *see* ANGLICAN CHURCH *and* CONGREGATIONAL CHURCH

disfranchisement, black All THIRTEEN COLONIES limited voting to whites, but upon adopting state constitutions in the Revolution, all either gave free blacks the vote – or did not specifically exclude them – except three: Va., S.C., and Ga. The new states of Vt., Ky., and Tenn. also enfranchised free blacks. Between 1792 and 1807, Del., Ky., Md., and N.J. disfranchised free blacks. No free blacks voted in the South after disfranchisement by Tenn. (1834) and N.C. (1835). By 1860, only Mass., N.H., Vt., and Maine allowed free blacks to vote on equal terms with whites; Conn., N.J., and Pa. had disfranchised them, and all others discouraged black voting by discriminatory property or residency requirements. Even after the CIVIL WAR, from 1865 to 1868, Conn., N.J., Pa., Ohio, Mich., Wis., and Minn. rejected bills allowing blacks to vote.

The first RECONSTRUCTION ACT forced the ex-CONFEDERACY to enfranchise FREEDMEN. The FIFTEENTH AMENDMENT was seriously weakened as a means of protecting black voting rights by *UNITED STATES* v. *REESE* (1876). White supremacists devised LITERACY TESTS and POLL TAXes, to deny suffrage to most blacks without violating the Fifteenth Amendment, in Miss. (1890), S.C. (1895), La. (1898), N.C. (1900), Ala. (1901), Va. (1902), Ga. (1908), and Okla. (1910). (GRANDFATHER CLAUSES were used to ensure that whites would remain voters.) Poll taxes eliminated most blacks from the voting rolls in Fla., Tenn., Ark., and Tex. The WHITE PRIMARY was also used by Democrats to minimize black political influence.

In 1964 a majority of blacks were excluded from the voting rolls in every ex-CSA state but Tenn. and Fla. The CIVIL RIGHTS MOVEMENT won ratification of the TWENTY-FOURTH AMENDMENT (1964) and passage of the VOTING RIGHTS ACT (1965). These measures tripled the number of black voters in the South from under 1,000,000 in 1964 to 3,100,000 by 1971, and enabled a majority of blacks to register in every state but two by 1971. Blacks then resumed playing a major role in southern politics.

Disney, Walter Elias (b. Chicago, Ill., 5 December 1901; d. Los Angeles, Calif., 15 December 1966) After maturing in

Marceline, Mo., Disney established an animation studio at Hollywood in 1923, and produced his first Mickey Mouse cartoon, "Steamboat Willie," in 1928. He became the largest producer of animated cartoons (including full-length features), built the first large-scale theme park at Disneyland, and started producing movies and television shows in the 1950s. His film innovations contributed significantly to Hollywood's rapid emergence as the world's largest center for film-making. He won a record 30 Academy awards.

Displaced Persons acts *see* IMMIGRATION

Distribution Act (23 June 1836) After the second BANK OF THE UNITED STATES's federal charter expired, this law directed the treasury Secretary to specify at least one bank in every state and territory as a depository or pet bank (*see* PET BANKS) for surplus federal funds. The law directed the Treasury to apportion $5,000,000 among the states as a loan, which would be distributed from federal funds in pet banks beginning 1 January 1837. Although the loan was subject to recall, it was the intention of the law's sponsor, Henry CLAY, that it not be repaid, and it was not. (The US lost $9 million due to the failure of pet banks in the PANIC OF 1837.) Distribution was abandoned after the protectionist TARIFF OF 1842 slashed customs duties by setting rates higher than could be paid on most manufactured goods.

District of Columbia On 23 December 1788, Md. ceded 10 square miles as the site of a federal capital on the Potomac, and on 10 July 1790, Congress voted to establish the capital there. It officially replaced Philadelphia as capital on 17 November 1800. Washington was incorporated as a city on 3 May 1802, but its mayor was appointed by the president rather than elected. In the WAR OF 1812, every government building but the Patent Office was burned by the British (24–5 August 1814). The slave trade was outlawed by the COMPROMISE OF 1850 and slavery itself was abolished on 16 April 1862. Congress took over direct administration of the district in 1874. It was allowed to cast three electoral votes for president in 1964. On 24 December 1973, Washington received the right to elect a mayor and city council. On 22 August 1978, Congress sent an amendment to the states giving Washington congressional representation, but this was not ratified by its deadline of 22 August 1985.

Dix, Dorothea Lynde (b. Hampden, Maine, 4 April 1802; d. Trenton, N.J., 17 July 1887) In 1838 Dix put aside a career as a Boston teacher to promote reform of prisons, poorhouses, and mental asylums. From 1841 to 1844, she inspected 18 penitentiaries, over 300 jails, and about 500 almshouses. Largely because of her published reports on the appalling conditions in these institutions, 20 states had begun reforming their penal and mental health systems by 1860. She supervised the Union army's female nurses in the CIVIL WAR and organized the bureaucracy charged with accounting for Union war dead and notifying next-of-kin.

Dixie This was a popular name for the antebellum South which became the title for a popular minstrel tune, adopted as the unofficial anthem of the Confederacy. It may have derived from an abbreviated pronunciation of MASON–DIXON LINE.

Dixiecrats *see* STATES' RIGHTS PARTY

Dobbins* v. *Erie County In 1842 the Supreme Court held without dissent that states could not tax the salaries of US employees, because – as it stated in *MCCULLOCH* V. *MARYLAND* – the power to tax entailed the power to destroy. This ruling was applied to state salaries in *COLLECTOR* V. *DAY*, and spawned numerous disputes over the extent of exemption from intergovernmental taxation, until *GRAVES* V. *NEW YORK EX REL. O'KEEFE*.

Dodge* v. *Woolsey *see* SUPREME COURT

Dole, Robert Joseph (b. Russell, Kans., 22 July 1923) While an infantry officer in WORLD WAR II, Dole was severely wounded in Italy. After a long recuperation, he entered politics as a Republican and served in the Kans. legislature (1951–3). He was elected to Congress in 1960 and has served continuously in the Senate since 1968. He became Senate majority leader in 1984, reverted to minority leader in 1987, and became majority leader again in 1995. He ran for vice-president under Gerald FORD. He unsuccessfully campaigned for the Republican presidential nomination in 1980 and 1988.

Dole, Sanford Ballard (b. Honolulu, Hawaii, 23 April 1844; d. Honolulu, Hawaii, 9 June

1926) Son of a Yankee missionary, Dole was educated in the US and opened a law office in Hawaii. He participated in the 1887 revolution that instituted a constitutional monarchy, and headed the rebel government that overthrew Queen Liliuolalani in 1893. Named president of the Republic of Hawaii in 1894, he negotiated its annexation by the US and was first governor of the territory.

dollar diplomacy This policy advocated using diplomacy to promote US business interests overseas; it significantly influenced foreign affairs after 1900, especially under William TAFT, and motivated armed intervention in Latin America under the ROOSEVELT COROLLARY. The GOOD NEIGHBOR POLICY largely replaced it in 1933.

Dominican Republic, US intervention in (1) From 1905 to 1924, the Dominican Republic placed its customs duties in US receivership to settle its foreign debts.

(2) In 1914 US marines landed to protect US interests during civil strife.

(3) Marines occupied the country to enforce the US customs receivership from 26 May 1916, and on 29 November 1916 the US displaced Dominican authorities and named Rear Admiral Harry Knapp as military governor. The occupation ended on 16 September 1924, by which time marines had sustained 133 casualties, including 17 killed in action.

(4) On 28 April 1965, Lyndon JOHNSON ordered a USMC reinforced battalion to secure the US embassy at Santo Domingo, where troops loyal to ousted President Juan Bosch fought to topple General Elias Wessin y Wessin's military junto. On 29 April, the US 82nd Airborne Division began landing. Fearing that Bosch's forces posed a Communist threat, the US sent 12,000 soldiers and 8,000 marines to enforce a ceasefire that enabled the military to block Bosch's return. US forces peaked at 30,000 before the ORGANIZATION OF AMERICAN STATES took over their mission with an Inter-American Peace Force of 6,500 men (including 5,000 from the US). Elective government resumed on 1 July 1966, and the final US peacekeeping troops left on 20 September.

Dominion of New England In September 1685, JAMES II consolidated Mass. and N.H. under Acting Governor Joseph Dudley. When Sir Edmund Andros replaced Dudley on 20 December 1686, Plymouth came under his administration. The dominion annexed R.I. on 30 December, Conn. on 1 November 1687, and N.Y., East Jersey, and West Jersey on 7 April 1688. The dominion alienated New Englanders by ending legislative government; it was overthrown in consequence of the REVOLUTION OF 1688 on 18 April 1689, when the Boston militia arrested Andros and disarmed his troops in a bloodless coup. Its authority in N.Y. and N.J. ended with LEISLER'S REBELLION.

domino theory Harry S. TRUMAN first used this metaphor in 1946 to argue that unless Communist subversion were defeated in Greece and Turkey, their neighboring states would also fall like a line of dominos. After 1954, the concept largely defined US foreign policy toward Indochina, where it was believed that if North Vietnam extended control over South Vietnam and Laos, Communist insurgencies would inevitably topple nearby countries in a piecemeal fashion, perhaps as far as Burma. The theory influenced John F. KENNEDY to initiate US involvement in the VIETNAM WAR.

Donnelly, Ignatius (b. Philadelphia, Pa., 3 November 1831; d. Minneapolis, Minn., 1 January 1901) In 1852 Donnelly opened a law office in Minn. He was lieutenant governor (1859–63), and US congressman (1863–9). He reacted to the painful dislocations in US agriculture after 1870 by affiliating himself with the LIBERAL REPUBLICANS, the GRANGE, and the GREENBACK PARTY, before helping found the Populist Party (*see* POPULISM), which nominated him as vice-president in 1900.

Donner party In the spring of 1846, Jacob and George Donner organized an 89-person party to travel the CALIFORNIA TRAIL by a shortcut south of the Great Salt Lake and through the Sierra Nevada Range via the Truckee River. The route proved difficult and left them 22 days behind schedule when they reached the Sierras. On 28 October, a winter storm struck a month early and stranded them in Donner Pass. On 16 December, 15 volunteers left to secure help in Calif., and arrived there on 10 January 1847 after eight had died. The main party was rescued on 19 February.

Only 49 persons lived through the ordeal. All the survivors resorted to cannibalism except for one family's members.

Donovan, William J. *see* CENTRAL INTELLIGENCE AGENCY

Dooley* v. *United States *see DE LIMA* v. *BIDWELL*

Doolittle Raid On 18 April 1942, Lieutenant Colonel James H. Doolittle's 16 US army B-25 bombers made the first Allied air attack on Tokyo, Yokohama, Yokosuka, and Nagoya after flying 600 miles from the carrier *Hornet*. One crew landed at Vladivostok and 15 crash-landed in or near China, where 69 airmen reached safety. US losses: 3 killed, 8 captured, and 3 prisoners executed by the Japanese. To prevent further US air raids from offshore Midway Island, Japan's navy approved the operation that resulted in the battle of MIDWAY.

Dorr Rebellion By 1841, R.I. was still governed by its Royal Charter of 1663, which limited the electorate to less than half of adult males. In October 1841, an extra-legal convention drafted a constitution allowing white manhood suffrage. A majority of adult males voted in December to adopt the document, but the legislature rejected its legitimacy. In the spring of 1842, after dual elections were held under both constitutions, rival governments existed under Governor Thomas Dorr (a reformer) and Governor Samuel King (a conservative). When King began arresting reformers, Dorr led an abortive attack on the state arsenal in May and was charged with treason. The revolt discredited the Charter of 1663 and forced ratification in April 1843 of a constitution providing for a wide suffrage. The Supreme Court ruled on the revolt in *LUTHER* v. *BORDEN*.

Dorr* v. *United States In 1904 the Supreme Court clarified the relation of overseas territories to the Constitution by enunciating the incorporation theory, which declared that territories remained beyond the Constitution's protection until Congress incorporated them into the United States by either ratifying a treaty with such provisions or enacting appropriate legislation. The case clarified rulings on PUERTO RICO's status given in *DE LIMA* v. *BIDWELL* and *DOWNES* v. *BIDWELL*.

Dos Passos, John (Roderigo) (b. Chicago, Ill., 14 January 1896; d. Baltimore, Md., 28 September 1970) A Harvard graduate (1916), Dos Passos was an ambulance driver in World War I, which inspired his earliest novels, *One Man's Initiation – 1917* (1920) and *Three Soldiers* (1921). Dos Passos became one of the LOST GENERATION's most prominent writers; he was best known for his trilogy *U.S.A.*: *The 42nd Parallel* (1930), *Nineteen-Nineteen* (1932), and *The Big Money* (1936), which portrayed American society from 1900 to 1930 from a profoundly pessimistic and anticapitalist perspective like that of the GREAT DEPRESSION's alienated intellectuals. His ideology later shifted from radical left to extreme conservatism.

double jeopardy The FIFTH AMENDMENT prohibits double jeopardy, which is the retrial of a defendant on criminal charges of which he has been found innocent. This protection was extended to state court proceedings by *BENTON* v. *MARYLAND*. *UNITED STATES* v. *LANZA* ruled that because of FEDERALISM, indictments for the same crime can be filed in both federal and state courts without violating double jeopardy.

doughboy This was slang during WORLD WAR I for a US soldier in France.

doughface This term referred to northern politicians who supported southern positions on SLAVERY, US annexation of Caribbean islands, or the tariff. John Randolph coined it in 1820 to refer to northern congressmen who voted to admit Mo. as a slave state, but evidently intended it as "doe-face." Among those so ridiculed were Millard FILLMORE, Franklin PIERCE, and James BUCHANAN.

Douglas, Stephen A. (b. Brandon, Vt., 23 April 1813; d. Chicago, Ill., 3 June 1861) In 1833 Douglas settled in Jacksonville, Ill., where he practiced law. As a Democratic congressman (1843–7), he supported MANIFEST DESTINY and the MEXICAN WAR, and thereafter served continuously in the Senate, where his political skills were crucial in passing the COMPROMISE OF 1850. Nicknamed the "Little Giant," he introduced POPULAR SOVEREIGNTY by his KANSAS–NEBRASKA ACT. While seeking reelection against Abraham LINCOLN (1858), he alienated southern voters by his FREEPORT DOCTRINE in the LINCOLN–DOUGLAS

DEBATES. The Democrats ran Douglas as president (1860), but the party's southern wing left it in favor of John BRECKINRIDGE. Douglas ran second to Lincoln in popular votes, with 29.5 percent, but won only Mo. and three of N.J.'s electoral votes. He died soon after.

Douglass, Frederick (b. near Easton, Md., ca. February 1817; d. Washington, D.C., 20 February 1895) Born Frederick Augustus Washington Bailey and sired by his own master, he escaped from slavery in Baltimore in 1838 and took the name Douglass in New Bedford, Mass. He gave his first antislavery speech at Nantucket in 1841, emerged as the best-known black abolitionist after writing a brief account of his slavery years in 1845, and edited the Rochester, N.Y., *North Star* (1847–63). He used his influence to recruit Negro troops in the CIVIL WAR. He held several senior posts in Washington, D.C., before becoming US consul general to Haiti (1889–91).

doves This term originated in the mid-1960s to describe persons who opposed continued US involvement in the VIETNAM WAR – most notably Clark CLIFFORD and Secretary of Defense Robert McNamara – and was later indiscriminately applied to the VIETNAM ANTIWAR MOVEMENT.

Downes* v. *Bidwell In 1901 the Supreme Court declared that the annexation or purchase of foreign territories did not by itself extend the US Constitution or US citizenship to residents of such areas. Congress had the option of extending any constitutional privileges that it saw fit. The Court ruled further on this issue in *DORR* V. *UNITED STATES*.

draft This term refers to the compulsory induction of soldiers in wartime to serve outside their home communities, as opposed to the enrollment of MILITIA for local defense. The first Anglo-American draft occurred in the SEVEN YEARS' WAR, when seven of the THIRTEEN COLONIES (New England, N.Y., Va., S.C.) passed laws to impress men out of the militia for offensive operations. In the Revolution, drafting was universally employed to fill the Continental army's ranks. The WAR OF 1812 and MEXICAN WAR were too brief to require conscription.

The CSA Congress passed the first national draft law on 16 April 1862. The US later adopted the Conscription Act (3 March 1863), which made all men of 20–45 years liable for military duty, but allowed inductees to furnish a substitute or pay $300 for the army to use as bounties to attract enlistees. The US law provoked the New York City Civil War DRAFT RIOTS; this draft raised 46,347 conscripts and 200,921 substitutes, 25 percent of Union soldiers raised after its inception.

The SELECTIVE SERVICE ACT (1917) was ruled constitutional in *ARVER* V. *UNITED STATES*. The law registered 23,900,000 men for WORLD WAR I. It inducted 2,800,000, of whom 16 percent did not report for duty or immediately deserted. The draft provided 53 percent of the army's troops and 45 percent of all military personnel.

The SELECTIVE TRAINING AND SERVICE ACT (1940) instituted the first peacetime draft. In WORLD WAR II, it registered 49,000,000 men and inducted 10,002,000. It provided 80 percent of the army (including the air corps), and 61 percent of all personnel. The courts imprisoned 11,879 men for draft evasion during the war.

The selective service system expired on 31 March 1947. It was restored by law on 24 June 1948 (to expire on 9 July 1950), and 30,000 men were inducted before the draft was suspended in January 1949. Congress extended conscription for two years when the KOREAN WAR began in June 1950. The war's 1,560,000 draftees constituted 55 percent of the army and 27 percent of all the armed forces. The government prosecuted 15,590 men for draft evasion.

Selective service continued without interruption in the 1950s. During 1954–61, 1,530,000 men were drafted for the army, 41 percent of all incoming soldiers. Over 2,000,000 men were conscripted in the VIETNAM WAR era, 23 percent of all military personnel and 45 percent of the army, of whom 136,900 refused to report for duty. The Defense Department stopped the draft on 27 January 1973, and the selective service law expired on 30 June 1973. Draft registration continued until it was ended by executive order in 1975. Jimmy CARTER pardoned all Vietnam draft evaders on 21 January 1977. Following the Soviet invasion of Afghanistan, a law imposing draft registration was signed on 27 June 1980, but without Carter's proposal that women be eligible. The Supreme Court upheld exclusion of women in *Rostker* v. *Goldberg*. Ronald REAGAN again ended draft registration by executive order.

draft riots, Civil War On 13 July 1863, in New York, several thousand working-class, Irish immigrants began attacking officials drafting men for the US army. Mobs lynched a half-dozen blacks, burned the Negro orphanage, looted pro-Republican and pro-abolitionist newspapers, and destroyed federal offices. US troops sent from GETTYSBURG suppressed the disorders by firing into the crowds on 15–16 July. Two policemen, 8 soldiers, 11 blacks, and 84 rioters died. Enforced by 20,000 troops, conscription resumed peacefully on 19 August, but New York's city council paid to hire substitutes for all men drafted, in order to avoid further violence. The draft riots claimed more deaths than any other US civil disturbance

Dred Scott* v. *Sandford On 6 March 1857, the Supreme Court acted on the claim of Dred Scott, a Mo. slave, that he had become free because he had resided from 1834 to 1838 with his master in Ill. and Wisconsin Territory, where the ORDINANCE OF 1787 and MISSOURI COMPROMISE had forbidden SLAVERY. The Court ruled (7–2) that Scott had no standing to sue before the federal bench, not only because slaves had no right to claim the Constitution's protection – which was correct – but also because no free black person might legally claim US citizenship – which was false. The Court ordered Scott's status to be determined according to *STRADER* V. *GRAHAM*. The Court then declared the Missouri Compromise an unconstitutional infringement of the FIFTH AMENDMENT's guarantee that no person be deprived of property without DUE PROCESS of law. The decision produced furor in the North by denying that Congress could bar slavery from any territory. The FREEPORT DOCTRINE was a reaction to it. *Dred Scott* marked only the second instance of the Supreme Court declaring a federal statute unconstitutional. The FOURTEENTH AMENDMENT nullified the decision's ruling that blacks lacked US citizenship.

Dreiser, Theodore (b. Terre Haute, Ind., 27 August 1871; d. Hollywood, Calif., 28 December 1945) Rising above his childhood poverty, Dreiser attended college and became a journalist. He emerged as one of the PROGRESSIVE ERA's most effective social critics after publishing his first book, *Sister Carrie*, in 1900. Dreiser wrote realistic novels describing ordinary Americans trapped by forces beyond their control in tragic lives; he also portrayed America's business leadership as morally corrupt and insensitive toward human suffering. His most notable works were *Jennie Gerhardt* (1911), *The Financier* (1912), *The Titan* (1914), *The "Genius"*(1915), and *An American Tragedy* (1925). He wrote and lectured enthusiastically about socialism, pacifism, and the Soviet Union.

Du Bois, W. E. B. (b. Great Barrington, Mass., 23 February 1868; d. Accra, Ghana, 27 August 1963) Born William Edward Burghardt, Du Bois was the first black to earn a Ph.D. at Harvard (1895) before doing postgraduate work at the University of Berlin. He emerged as the leading opponent of Booker T. WASHINGTON's conservative policy on race relations, and advocated that blacks exert greater pressure to end racial discrimination. He helped found the NIAGARA MOVEMENT (1905) and the NATIONAL ASSOCIATION FOR THE ADVANCEMENT OF COLORED PEOPLE (NAACP, 1909). He directed the NAACP's research and publicity (1910–34 and 1944–48), and edited its magazine, *Crisis*, then the foremost civil rights publication. Du Bois turned more radical out of frustration with the CIVIL RIGHTS MOVEMENT's slow pace, was investigated for subversive beliefs by Senator Joseph MCCARTHY, and finally joined the Communist Party in 1957. He renounced his US citizenship in 1960 and moved to Ghana.

dual executive *see* CONCURRENT MAJORITY

due process The FIFTH and FOURTEENTH AMENDMENTS guarantee citizens due process, or the operation of courts by impartial and regular procedures that ensure protection for life, liberty, and property. The Supreme Court first defined the scope of due process under the Fifth Amendment in *MURRAY'S LESSEE* V. *HOBOKEN LAND AND IMPROVEMENT COUPANY*. In 1925 the Court issued *GITLOW* V. *NEW YORK*, the first major decision extending the BILL OF RIGHTS to state actions through the Fourteenth Amendment's due process clause.

Dukakis, Michael Stanley (b. Brookline, Mass., 3 November 1933) He was elected Mass. governor in 1974, 1982, and 1986 (he declined to run in 1978). He won nomination for president representing his party's moderate wing in 1988, but was successfully portrayed as a liberal by Republicans. He carried only 10 states and lost the election with only 46 percent of the popular vote. He retired as governor in 1990 under heavy criticism for permitting a budgetary crisis to develop.

Dulany, Daniel (b. Annapolis, Md., 28 June 1722; d. near Baltimore, Md., 17 March 1797) He was educated and trained as an attorney in England before becoming a Md. lawyer in 1747. His pamphlet, *Considerations on the Propriety of Imposing Taxes in the British Colonies, for the Purpose of Raising a Revenue* (1765), was the most effective rebuttal of VIRTUAL REPRESENTATION, and made him the leading American opponent of Parliamentary taxation during the STAMP ACT crisis. He nevertheless opposed independence and became a Tory (*see* TORIES), for which Md. confiscated much of his property.

Dulles, John Foster (b. Washington, D.C., 25 February 1888; d. Washington, D.C., 24 May 1959) A career foreign service officer, Dulles was named secretary of state in 1953. To achieve the containment of Soviet expansion (*see* CONTAINMENT POLICY), he used BRINKMANSHIP and the threat of MASSIVE RETALIATION, backed up by an enormous nuclear arsenal and a huge peacetime army committed to defending NATO. In 1954 he advised sending US troops to prevent Communist victory in French Indochina, but Dwight D. EISENHOWER overruled him. By insisting that southeast Asia was vital to US foreign security, Dulles laid the foundation for the VIETNAM WAR. More than any other official, he defined the COLD WAR as an uncompromising crusade against atheistic, international communism. He resigned from the cabinet in April 1959 and died of abdominal cancer a month later.

Dumbarton Oaks conference From 21 August to 7 October 1944, US, British, Russian, and Chinese diplomats met near Washington and drafted the Dumbarton Oaks Plan, which became the foundation for the UNITED NATIONS charter.

Dummer's War In 1724 fighting commenced in the Kennebec River valley over conflicting land claims between Maine settlers and the ABNAKI INDIANS, whose belligerency was encouraged by a French priest among them. Local militia won a decisive victory on 23 August 1724 by destroying the stockaded mission village of Norridgewock, where they killed over 80 Indians while losing just two English wounded and one Mohawk auxiliary killed. The conflict, which continued through May 1725, opened much of south-central Maine for settlement.

Duncan, Isadora (b. San Francisco, Calif., 27 May 1878; d. Nice, France, 14 September 1927) At the age of 10, Duncan resolved to devote her life to interpretive dance, an endeavor in which her sister Elizabeth collaborated. She joined a New York dance troupe in 1895, but was frustrated by America's unimaginative approach toward this art and became an expatriate in Europe. By flouting convention with daring, sensuous, and often self-indulgent performances, she achieved success as a touring artiste in Europe. Her career inspired successors like Martha GRAHAM to develop the image, vocabulary, and substance of dance into a mature art form.

Duncan* v. *Louisiana On 20 May 1968, the Supreme Court ruled (8–1) that the FOURTEENTH AMENDMENT'S DUE PROCESS clause obliged state courts to uphold the SIXTH AMENDMENT'S guarantee that all defendants charged with felonies receive a jury trial.

Dunmore's War Following the murder of a white trader on 16 April 1774 by unknown Indians, whites under Michael Cresap killed three SHAWNEE INDIANS on 27–8 April, and settlers near Wheeling, W.Va., treacherously murdered six MINGO INDIANS on 30 April. After Mingos under Logan killed 13 whites in revenge and Shawnees attacked settlers in Va., Governor Dunmore (John Murray, 4th Earl of) ordered Va. militia against them. In August, Major Angus McDonald raided Shawnee villages on Ohio's

Muskingum River. In October, Colonel Andrew Lewis defeated their warriors at the battle of POINT PLEASANT, W.Va. Facing 2,500 militia ready to burn their villages and winter food caches, the Shawnee made peace through the treaty of CAMP CHARLOTTE.

Duplex Printing Press Company* v. *Deering On 3 January 1921, the Supreme Court examined the CLAYTON ANTITRUST ACT's labor provisions and reaffirmed (6–3) *LOEWE* v. *LAWLER*'s ruling that a SECONDARY BOYCOTT illegally restrained trade. The decision authorized courts to issue injunctions to block this practice, and any other tactics used by labor unions that were deemed unlawful restraints of trade.

Duryea, Charles E. *see* AUTOMOBILE

dust bowl In 1935 an Associated Press journalist coined this term for parts of Okla., Kans., Colo., N.Mex., and the Tex. panhandle devastated by drought and huge dust storms since 1933. The disaster forced perhaps 400,000 OKIES to relocate in Calif. as migrant workers and inspired the New Deal's SHELTERBELT PROGRAM.

Dustin, Hannah (b. 23 December 1657; d. 1736?) Captured on 15 March 1697 at Haverhill, Mass., with a woman and a boy, she led the prisoners in finding hatchets, killing their sleeping captors, and taking ten scalps to earn the Mass. bounty for dead enemy Indians.

Dutch immigration The DUTCH WEST INDIA COMPANY recruited a wide variety of immigrants to colonize NEW NETHERLAND. The majority of the first settlers sent out by the company in 1624 were French-speaking Walloons (from modern Belgium). Of the 2,500 Europeans who colonized New Netherland prior to 1664, half were Dutch, a quarter were German, a seventh were Walloons or HUGUENOTS, one in fourteen were Scandinavians, and many of the rest were English. The minorities adopted the language and religion of the Dutch. In 1790, 3 percent of all whites in the US were "Dutch," and by 1820 the Dutch stock probably numbered 235,000. From 1820 to 1991, 375,535 immigrants came to the US from the Netherlands. The 1990 census counted 3,475,400 persons who described their primary ethnic identity as Dutch, mostly in Mich., N.Y., N.J., and Pa.

Dutch West India Company On 3 June 1621, the company was chartered as a trading monopoly with colonization rights in the Americas. Its founders primarily hoped to profit by promoting piracy against Spain. The company established NEW NETHERLAND, which was intended as a base for the FUR TRADE and a source of agricultural provisions for other Dutch colonies in the Caribbean.

Dwight, Timothy (b. Northampton, Mass., 14 May 1752; d. New Haven, Conn., 11 January 1817) Grandson of Jonathan EDWARDS, Dwight was a chaplain in the Revolution, ordained a Congregational minister (1783), and president of Yale (1795–1817). His crusade against religious indifference and deism among his Yale students was the primary event that stimulated the SECOND GREAT AWAKENING in New England. He was a leading figure in the movement to shift the focus of Calvinist theology from predestination to the responsibility of individuals for cultivating godliness in their spiritual lives.

Dyer, Mary Barrett (b. England, ca. 1610; d. Boston, Mass., 1 June 1660) In 1633 Dyer married at London, and she emigrated with her husband to Boston in 1635. She supported Anne HUTCHINSON in the ANTINOMIAN CONTROVERSY and moved to R.I. with her. She returned to England in 1650 and joined the QUAKERS. To protest a 1659 Mass. law prescribing death for Quakers who reentered the colony after being expelled – as she had already been – she went back to Boston in 1659 and was sentenced to hang, but was reprieved on the scaffold. She again came back in 1660 to challenge the ban on Quakers, was again condemned to hang, and was executed.

E

Eagleton, Thomas Francis (b. St Louis, Mo., 24 September 1929) He served as US senator (Democrat, Mo., 1969–86). Chosen as vice-presidential candidate with George McGOVERN, he resigned on 31 July 1972 after the press reported he had suffered from severe depression and received electric-shock therapy during 1960–6. Sargent SHRIVER replaced him.

Eakins, Thomas (b. Philadelphia, Pa., 25 July 1844; d. Philadelphia, Pa., 25 June 1916) After studying painting at the Pa. Academy of Fine Arts, Eakins attended the École des Beaux Arts in Paris and traveled in Europe (1866–70). He joined the faculty of the Pa. Academy of Fine Arts in 1873, and was later a dean. His sophisticated compositions infused his oil canvases with a rich mood of drama and a heightened sense of realism. His intimate knowledge of anatomy, which he studied at Jefferson Medical College, made him a complete master of the human form. Eakins was the greatest American artist who ever painted, and *The Gross Clinic* is his masterpiece. Other major works include *Max Schmitt in a Single Scull, The Agnew Clinic, The Swimming Hole, The Thinker, The Concert Singer, The Writing Master, The Chess Players, Between Rounds, Katherine, Edith Mahon*, and *Whistling for Plover.*

Earhart, Amelia Mary (b. Atchison, Kans., 24 July 1898; d. ca. 2 July 1937) After learning to fly in 1921, Earhart became the country's most prominent female aviator. She became the first woman passenger to fly across the Atlantic in 1928, and piloted a solo flight in 1932 that set a new time record. She continued setting speed and altitude records, and in 1935 completed the first solo flight from Honolulu to Calif. She became *Cosmopolitan*'s aviation editor and vice-president of Luddington Airlines. While attempting to fly around the world with copilot Frederick Noonan in 1937, she disappeared while flying between New Guinea and Howland Island.

East and West Texas Railway Company* v. *United States *see* SHREVEPORT RATE CASES

East Florida Acquired by Britain by the SEVEN YEARS' WAR, East Florida became a ROYAL COLONY, bounded by Ga. and the Apalachicola River. From 1763 to 1771, it received 300 American or British settlers. Another 1,300 immigrants from Greece or Italy founded New Smyrna in 1768, most of whom died of swamp fevers. Spain regained it by the Treaty of PARIS (1783), and redesignated its western border as the Perdido River. It was the site of the first SEMINOLE WAR, which led to its cession by the ADAMS–ONIS TREATY.

East Jersey On 4 July 1664, anticipating the conquest of NEW NETHERLAND, CHARLES II granted modern N.J. to John Lord Berkeley and Sir George Carteret. After Berkeley sold his proprietary rights in 1674, Carteret received title to East Jersey. Frustrated by problems of governing and collecting quitrents from the settlers, Carteret's heirs sold his title to the PROPRIETORS OF EAST JERSEY on 1 February 1681. The proprietors stirred widespread resentment by challenging the validity of the settlers' land titles, and their authority crumbled when rioting convulsed the colony in 1698–1701. They surrendered East Jersey to the Crown on 15 April 1702.

Eastern Solomons, battle of the On 24–5 August 1942, Vice Admiral Frank Fletcher's task force (2 battleships, 5 cruisers, 8 destroyers) intercepted Admiral Chuichi Nagumo's convoy (3 carriers, 2 battleships, 1 cruiser, 7 destroyers) ferrying Japanese troops to GUADALCANAL. The battle gave the US daytime control of local sealanes, but left the Japanese dominant in night operations. US losses: 20 planes. Japanese losses: 1 carrier, 1 cruiser, 1 destroyer, 1 troop transport, 60 planes.

Eastman, George (b. Waterville, N.Y., 12 July 1854; d. Rochester, N.Y., 14 March 1932) He matured in Rochester, where he began experimenting with photography in the 1870s. In 1884, he revolutionized photography, which still depended on making prints from hard plates, by patenting a flexible film that could be loaded as a roll inside a camera, which he called a Kodak. In 1891 he discovered how to shield film with black paper so that a camera could be loaded during daylight, and the next year he renamed his firm the Eastman Kodak Co. Eastman's innovations enabled the US to dominate the industry, and his ongoing program of advanced research allowed Americans to set international standards for technical excellence. He adopted enlightened labor policies and gave away $100,000,000 to worthy causes, especially higher education.

Eaton [,Peggy,] Affair In 1829 Andrew JACKSON's administration became polarized when the wives of his CABINET, led by Mrs John CALHOUN, snubbed Peggy O'Neale Eaton, wife of Secretary of War John Eaton. Peggy was considered unfit company because of rumors that her previous husband had committed suicide on account of an adulterous affair between her and Eaton. Jackson sympathized with Peggy and took her side, and so this minor disagreement played a major role in alienating him from Calhoun and improving his relationship with Secretary of State Martin VAN BUREN, who was a bachelor and showed much solicitude toward Mrs Eaton. Jackson reorganized his cabinet in April 1831.

Economic Opportunity Act (30 August 1964) An omnibus measure of the GREAT SOCIETY's WAR ON POVERTY, this law created the Office of Economic Opportunity to administer youth training, community action programs, and volunteer agencies. It appropriated $947,500,000 for 1965 ($1.8 billion in 1966) to finance VOLUNTEERS IN SERVICE TO AMERICA, HEAD START, the JOB CORPS, and COMMUNITY ACTION PROGRAMS. Most of its programs were taken over by ACTION in 1971, and the Office of Economic Opportunity was terminated on 4 January 1975.

Economic Recovery Tax Act (13 August 1981) This law reversed a long upward drift in INCOME TAXes and marked the first major cut enacted since John F. KENNEDY's administration. Proposed by Ronald REAGAN, it was the largest tax cut in US history ($750 billion through 1987) and lowered individual rates by 25 percent over three years. It reduced the top marginal rate from 70 percent to 50 percent and cut the long-term capital gains levy from 28 percent to 20 percent. Largely due to efforts by Senator Robert DOLE, the law required tax brackets to be indexed by the inflation rate so that taxpayers would not be subjected to higher rates while their real incomes remained constant. (Indexing became effective in 1985, and saved taxpayers approximately $100 billion in its first decade.) Further tax reductions came under the TAX REFORM ACT (1986).

Economy Act (20 March 1933) This law was designed to fulfill Franklin D. ROOSEVELT's campaign pledge to eliminate wasteful federal expenditures. It was projected to cut $500,000,000 from the budget by salary reductions (including 15 percent from congressmen, senators, the vice-president, and president), eliminating various veterans' allowances, and reorganizing the bureaucracy, but the actual amount saved was only $243,000,000. The savings were eliminated in 1934 by the INDEPENDENT OFFICES APPROPRIATIONS ACT.

Eddy, Mary Baker (b. Bow, N.H., 16 July 1821; d. Newton, Mass., 3 December 1910) Following a history of ill health and the death of her first husband by a fever, she experienced relief from a serious injury in 1866 after seeking cure through prayer. This experience led her to the doctrines of spiritual self-healing that became the Christian Scientists' Association, which was organized in 1876 and chartered as the Church of Christ, Scientist in 1879 at Boston. She established the Mass. Medical College in 1881, opened the first Christian Science reading room in 1888, and first published the *Christian Science Monitor* in 1908.

Edison, Thomas Alva (b. Milan, Ohio, 11 February 1847; d. West Orange, N.J., 18 October 1931) Despite having just three months' formal education, Edison became the foremost US research scientist after an itinerant existence as a telegrapher. In 1870 he reaped a windfall profit when he and a partner sold an electric stock-ticker, and then opened a laboratory at Newark, N.J. In 1876 he built a major research facility at Menlo Park (moved in 1887 to larger quarters at Orange); in 1878 he formed the Edison Electric Light Co., which evolved into the General Electric Co. Edison filed over 1,000 patents, including the phonograph, the first incandescent lamp to be commercially viable, the vitaphone moving-picture projector, alkaline storage batteries, dictaphone, mimeograph, and an electric railroad train. He was the key scientist to pioneer the use of electricity as the basic source of illumination. His laboratories made the US the leading center for electronics research. Edison's success revolutionized business attitudes toward research, and produced near universal recognition that any major manufacturer must build a laboratory to remain technologically competitive.

Education, Department of On 17 October 1979, Congress created this department by separating educational agencies from the HEALTH, EDUCATION, AND WELFARE DEPARTMENT. Ronald REAGAN favored its elimination, but found no support for the proposal. The department's budget grew from $14.7 billion in 1981 to $21.5 billion in 1989.

education, public Beginning with the OLD DELUDER ACT, New England created the first compulsory system of primary education. Only eight of the first 16 states included provisions concerning schools in their constitutions. The NORTHWEST ORDINANCE promoted the expansion of public schools by reserving one section of each township for their support.

The struggle for free public schools with mandatory attendance laws and professional teachers was pioneered by Mass. after 1827 under Horace MANN's leadership. Boston established the first high school in 1821, and in 1827 Mass. required every town of 500 families to maintain a high school. Free public education did not become universal until well after 1871. Kindergartens first appeared between 1855 and 1860. John DEWEY was most influential in stimulating the movement for progressive educational reform.

Higher education began with the founding of Harvard (1636) and continued with William and Mary (1693); by 1776 nine colleges were founded in the colonies. Ga. chartered the first state university (1785), and five state universities existed by 1819. By 1860 there were just 17 state universities, compared with 229 private colleges. The MORRILL ACT helped expand higher education by awarding land grants for state universities. The federal government later made major contributions to collegiate education through the GI BILL OF RIGHTS, NATIONAL DEFENSE EDUCATION ACT, second GI BILL, the HIGHER EDUCATION ACTS (1965 and 1967), and Department of EDUCATION.

Edwards, Jonathan (b. East Windsor, Conn., 5 October 1703; d. Princeton, N.J., 22 March 1758) In 1720 Edwards graduated from Yale. He ministered to a Presbyterian congregation at New York (1722–3), and preached at the Northampton, Mass., Congregational church after 1727. In 1735 he cultivated a revival at Northampton foreshadowing the GREAT AWAKENING. In 1741 he delivered the most famous sermon ever preached in America: "Sinners in the Hands of an Angry God." Edwards was early America's most profound theologian, and examined from a Calvinist perspective fundamental questions about the nature of spiritual development, the will's moral autonomy, God's omnipotence, and the relationship between reason and religious experience in spiritual rebirth. His writings are notable for the metaphysical dimension added by his understanding of ENLIGHTENMENT concepts and Newtonian physics. His most important work was *Of Freedom of the Will* (1754). He became missionary to the Stockbridge MAHICAN INDIANS after 1750 and president of Princeton in 1757.

Edwards* v. *Arizona On 18 May 1981, the Supreme Court extended *MIRANDA* V. *ARIZONA* by unanimously ruling that a suspect under arrest, after being told of his "*Miranda* rights," may demand that all interrogation cease until his lawyer arrives, and the police must honor his request.

Edwards* v. *California On 24 November 1941, the Supreme Court judged a law intended to hinder migration by OKIES from the DUST BOWL by penalties on persons bringing indigent persons to live in Calif.; it unanimously ruled that the law obstructed interstate commerce. The Court later extended *Edwards*'s right to travel via interstate commerce in *SHAPIRO* v. *THOMPSON*.

Ehrlichman, John Daniel (b. Tacoma, Wash., 20 March 1925) He was a longtime associate of H. R. HALDEMAN and was the second most powerful insider on Richard NIXON's staff, as assistant for domestic affairs. He coordinated campaign tours with CREEP in the 1972 election and participated in covering up the "dirty tricks" against George MCGOVERN that led to the WATERGATE SCANDAL. He was implicated in the conspiracy by John DEAN's testimony and was forced to resign on 30 April 1973. On 12 July 1974, he was found guilty of conspiracy to commit burglary and of three counts of perjury, for which he was later sentenced to 20 months in prison. On 1 January 1975, he was found guilty of two counts of perjury before Congress, conspiracy to obstruct justice, and obstruction of justice, and later sentenced to 30 months in prison.

1877 railroad strike *see* RAILROAD STRIKE OF 1877

Eighteenth Amendment Submitted to the states on 18 December 1917, last ratified on 16 January 1919, and officially proclaimed on 29 January 1919, it imposed a PROHIBITION on the sale or transportation of spirituous liquors a year after its ratification. When ratified, 26 states had imposed prohibition, 19 permitted prohibition by local option, and only three had no anti-liquor laws. The VOLSTEAD and JONES ACTS enforced it. The TWENTY-FIRST AMENDMENT repealed it.

Eighth Amendment Submitted to the states on 25 September 1789, last ratified on 15 December 1791 by Va., and officially proclaimed on 30 December 1791, it prohibited excessive bail and it forbade judges from imposing excessive fines and cruel or unusual punishments. Its protections were extended to state court proceedings by *ROBINSON* v. *CALIFORNIA*. The Supreme Court's first major ruling on the death penalty was *FURMAN* v. *GEORGIA*.

Einstein, Albert (b. Ulm am Donau, Germany, 14 March 1879; d. Princeton, N.J., 18 April 1955) Shortly after earning a Ph.D. from the University of Zurich (1905), Einstein propounded the theory of relativity and the equation $E = mc^2$. In 1921 he won the Nobel prize for research on the photoelectric effect of light. After most of his important work was done, he emigrated from a university post at Berlin in 1932 and joined the Princeton faculty. On 2 August 1939, he strongly urged Franklin D. ROOSEVELT that the US develop an atomic bomb, in a critical letter that marked the first step in the MANHATTAN PROJECT.

Eisenhower, Dwight David (b. Denison, Tex., 14 October 1890; d. Washington, D.C., 28 March 1969) In 1915 Eisenhower graduated from West Point into the infantry. After spending WORLD WAR I in the US, he remained a major for 16 years, but after reaching lieutenant colonel in March 1941, he rose to full general by February 1943. In WORLD WAR II, he commanded US forces in the Mediterranean theater, and was named supreme commander of the Allied Expeditionary Force in Western Europe on 31 December 1943 as general of the army. On 7 May 1945, he accepted Germany's surrender and returned to the US as army chief of staff. He was president of Columbia University (1948–53), but took leave of absence to organize NATO forces in Europe as supreme commander (December 1950–June 1952). He was elected Republican president in 1952 (taking 55.1 percent of the vote and 39 states) and 1956 (taking 57.6 percent of the vote and 41 states). His implied threat to use nuclear weapons hastened the end of the KOREAN WAR. His foreign policy was shaped by John F. DULLES. The LEBANON intervention implemented his EISENHOWER DOCTRINE. In September 1957, he sent US troops to quell the LITTLE ROCK DESEGREGATION VIOLENCE. The U-2 AFFAIR ended his hopes for a US–Soviet summit meeting in 1960. He retired to Gettysburg, Pa.

Eisenhower Doctrine On 5 January 1957, Dwight D. EISENHOWER pledged US military assistance to any Middle East nation that was invaded and incapable of repelling aggression with its own forces. On 7 March, Congress voted $200,000,000 for economic and military aid to the Middle East. In 1958, when Syria and Egypt menaced Lebanon, US intervention was taken under this doctrine.

Eisenhower's farewell address *see* MILITARY-INDUSTRIAL COMPLEX

El Brazito, battle of (Tex.) On 25 December 1846, Colonel Alexander W. Doniphan's First Missouri Regiment (850 men) defeated Colonel Ponce de Leon's 1,200 Mexicans. US losses: 7 wounded. Mexican losses: 43 killed, 60 wounded. Victory enabled Doniphan to occupy El Paso on 27 December.

El Caney, battle of (Cuba) On 1 July 1898, Brigadier General Henry Lawton's 5,400 troops captured the town overlooking Santiago from 520 Spaniards. US losses: 81 killed, 360 wounded. Spanish losses: 235 killed and wounded, 120 captured. Combined with SAN JUAN HILL's capture, El Caney allowed US artillery to shell the enemy fleet, which was then forced into the battle of SANTIAGO BAY.

elastic clause The CONSTITUTION's "elastic clause" (Article I, Section 8) grants Congress the power to "make all Laws which shall be necessary and proper for carrying into Execution the foregoing Powers and all other Powers vested by this Constitution in the Government of the United States, or in any other Department or Officer thereof." This clause is the principal foundation for the theory of LOOSE CONSTRUCTIONISM.

electoral college The CONSTITUTION (Article II, Section 1) directed that the president and vice-president be chosen by a "number of electors" from each state equal to its representatives and senators in Congress. Since no party system then existed, it was assumed that few individuals (after George WASHINGTON) would receive a majority because the electors would divide among too many favorite sons. The college was accordingly expected to serve as a de facto nominating caucus that would winnow the number of potential candidates to three, from whom the House of Representatives would make the final choice. The TWELTH AMENDMENT modified the college's balloting system.

The electoral college evolved to reflect public opinion without other amendments because it was organized under state law. By 1800, five of the 15 states chose electors by popular balloting rather than by the state legislature, and by 1828 all did so except Del. and S.C. Legislatures also mandated that all electors be awarded to whomever won a majority or plurality of ballots. This innovation ended the need for Congress to choose presidents after John Q. ADAMS, by enabling candidates with a plurality of the popular vote to win a majority of electoral ballots in 1844, 1848, 1856, 1860, 1880, 1884, 1892, 1912, 1916, 1948, 1960, 1968, and 1992, but allowed candidates with less than a plurality to win in 1876 (*see* ELECTORAL COUNT ACT) and 1888. The DISTRICT OF COLUMBIA was allowed to cast three electoral ballots in 1964. The Supreme Court has ruled that electors may vote contrary to a state's popular returns, as has been done in 1948 and all elections from 1956 to 1976 except for 1964.

Electoral Count Act (3 February 1887) To avoid future repetition of the partisan methods used by Congress to deny Samuel TILDEN a fair determination of electoral votes in 1876, this law gave each state sole authority to certify which presidential candidate took its electoral votes, according to the state's election statutes. If a state cannot certify a victor, or has done so improperly, both houses of Congress must agree on who has carried the state. If neither the state government nor Congress can agree on who won, then the governor shall decide who should receive the electors.

Electric Home and Farm Authority *see* RECONSTRUCTION FINANCE CORPORATION

Elementary and Secondary Education Act (11 April 1965) This law marked the first instance of Congress appropriating money to aid elementary and secondary schools; it was the most far-reaching federal education law in US history. (The first bill for federal funding of general education was submitted to Congress in 1881.) This innovation of the GREAT SOCIETY provided $1,300,000,000 to aid schools in low-income school districts (including parochial schools), to improve libraries, to establish community education centers, and to fund programs by state education departments.

Eleventh Amendment Drafted to reverse *Chisholm* v. *Georgia*, submitted to the states on 5 March 1794, adopted after ratification of Ky. was certified on 4 December 1797, and officially proclaimed on 8 January 1798, it exempted state governments from being sued, without their consent, in federal courts by citizens of other states or of foreign countries. The Supreme Court clarified its scope in *Osborn* v. *Bank of the United States* and *United States* v. *Texas*.

Elgin Treaty *see* Canadian Reciprocity Treaty

Eliot, John (b. Widford, England, ca. 5 August 1604; d. Roxbury, Mass., 21 May 1690) The most successful Puritan missionary, Eliot began preaching to Indians in 1646. He translated the Bible into the local Algonquian language (1653–63) and was responsible for the establishment of most praying towns.

Eliot, T(homas) S(tearns) (b. St Louis, Mo., 26 September 1888; d. London, England, 4 January 1965) In 1914 Eliot graduated from Harvard, and then studied abroad at Oxford and the Sorbonne. He moved to London in 1914, and became a British subject in 1927. A poet, dramatist, critic, and editor, he was the 20th century's premier American man of letters, and authored its most compelling verse and most influential criticism. His poetry expressed a scholarly mourning that an increasingly secular and materialistic culture was extinguishing the life of the spirit. His style succeeded in expressing his deep literary erudition in a contemporary voice. He received the Nobel prize for literature (1948), the British Order of Merit (1948), and the American Medal of Freedom (1964). Among his major works were "The Love Song of J. Alfred Prufrock" (1911), "Portrait of a Lady" (1915), *The Waste Land* (1922), *Murder in the Cathedral* (1935), and *Four Quartets* (1943).

Elizabeth I (b. Westminster Palace, Middlesex, 11 February 1533; d. Richmond Palace, Surrey, 24 March 1603) Her reign saw the first efforts to promote English colonization by Richard Hakluyt. She commissioned the voyages of Humphrey Gilbert and granted Sir Walter Raleigh lands for a colony, which he named Virginia after her nickname, the "virgin queen."

Elkins Act (19 February 1903) Congress made it illegal for railroads to give rebates to customers who shipped large volumes of goods on their lines. Although the law satisfied complaints by small users that they were being treated unfairly, the railroads favored the measure because their biggest customers had been forcing them to give large discounts by threatening to take their business to rival lines. The law enabled the carriers to enforce their published rate schedules and make greater profits on high-volume orders.

Ellis Island On 1 January 1892, Ellis Island, an Immigration Service facility of 27.5 acres, became the primary processing station for Europeans entering the US. Until its closure in 1954, the center approved 17,000,000 persons for admission to the country and rejected 300,000 who failed to meet physical and mental standards.

Ellsberg, Daniel *see* Pentagon papers

Ellsworth, Oliver (b. Windsor, Conn., 29 April 1745; d. Windsor, Conn., 26 November 1807) In 1777 Ellsworth opened a law office. He represented Conn. in the Continental Congress and at the Constitutional Convention (1787), where he helped devise the Connecticut Compromise but was not present at the Constitution's signing. As one of Conn.'s first senators, he chaired the committee to draft the Judiciary Act (1789) and voted with the Federalist party. He was confirmed as the Supreme Court's second chief justice on 15 December 1795, but resigned on 30 September 1800.

Elrod* v. *Burns On 28 June 1976, the Supreme Court ruled (5–3) that the First Amendment protects freedom of political association, and prohibits state officials from firing employees of a different political party for partisan, patronage reasons.

Emancipation Proclamation On 22 July 1862, Abraham Lincoln presented to his cabinet a draft of an executive order freeing slaves in CSA areas under Union control, which might cause the south to reconsider secession and deter foreign recognition of the Confederacy. Waiting for a Union victory to make the declaration credible, on 22 September, soon after Antietam, he threatened to free all slaves in areas not under USA control. On 1 January 1863, Lincoln issued his Emancipation Proclamation, as a "fit and necessary war measure," declared free all slaves in areas yet in rebellion, and authorized the military to enroll them, but enjoined slaves to wait peacefully for liberation. The proclamation left unfree 800,000 slaves in Del., Md., Ky., Mo., Tenn., and parts of Va. and La.

Embargo Act (22 December 1807) Unable to prevent Great Britain or France from seizing US merchant shipping during the Napoleonic wars, Thomas JEFFERSON proposed an embargo to end the danger of a war being sparked by either nation violating American neutrality. The embargo outlawed all export of US goods and forbade US ships to sail outside the nation's territorial waters. About 800 ships nevertheless exploited the law's loopholes and engaged in overseas trade, while many goods were sent across the Canadian border to be exported via the St Lawrence River. Napoleon used the embargo as a pretext for seizing even more ships under the BAYONNE DECREE. The embargo created a recession in the seaports, caused commodity prices to drop, and revived the FEDERALIST PARTY's popularity in New England; it was replaced by the NONINTERCOURSE ACT (1809).

Emergency Banking Relief Act (9 March 1933) This law was introduced, passed, and signed in eight hours to counteract the BANK PANIC OF 1933. It legalized Franklin D. ROOSEVELT's emergency actions in declaring the BANK HOLIDAY, set procedures for the Treasury to certify banks as safe to reopen, empowered the Comptroller of the Currency to place unsound banks in receivership, enabled the RECONSTRUCTION FINANCE CORPORATION to invest in banks with low assets if they needed additional capital to resume operations, authorized the FEDERAL RESERVE to issue more currency if the money supply contracted from hoarding, and forbade hoarding or export of gold. Permanent reforms were instituted by the BANKING ACT (1933).

Emergency Quota Act (19 May 1921) First passed in 1920 and pocket-vetoed by Woodrow WILSON, it was reenacted and signed by Warren HARDING. It capped immigration from Europe at 357,000 per year, but put no limits on Latin America or Canada. It marked the first time Congress set a ceiling on annual immigration; it also created the first quota system by restricting entrants from any country to 3 percent of persons born there as counted by the 1910 census. The NATIONAL ORIGINS ACT (1924) modified it.

Emergency Railroad Transportation Act (16 June 1933) This law created a Federal Coordinator of Transportation to oversee joint ventures by the railroads in order to end wasteful duplication of services and find other ways to return the railroads to profitability. The act waived antitrust laws to allow cooperation among railroads to cut unnecessary costs and gave the coordinator authority to compel participation by all carriers. The railroads resisted federal efforts to eliminate overhead expenses by consolidating routes or services, and the coordinator had little impact on returning the lines to profitability before his office lapsed in 1936.

Emergency Relief and Construction Act (21 July 1932) This law expanded the RECONSTRUCTION FINANCE CORPORATION'S (RFC) funding and responsibilities. It gave the RFC authority to loan an additional $500 million, of which $300 million was reserved to fund state relief agencies aiding the poor. It also appropriated $1,500,000,000 in loans for states and localities to build sewage works, roads, bridges, and hydroelectric dams.

Emergency Relief Appropriation Act (8 April 1935) This act implemented a policy decision to replace FEDERAL EMERGENCY RELIEF ADMINISTRATION funding for local poor relief with massive employment programs. It authorized the spending of $4.8 billion, the largest single appropriation ever voted by Congress, of which the largest share (30 percent) went to the newly established WORKS PROGRESS ADMINISTRATION.

Emergency Tariff Act (27 May 1921) This law began the process of reversing the Woodrow WILSON administration's tariff reductions. To counteract declining US farm prices, which fell after the ending of WORLD WAR I allowed European harvests to increase, it set rates on 28 commodities at exclusionary levels. The tariff did not increase prices (except for wool and sugar), because US overproduction left supply exceeding demand. The Fordney–McCumber Tariff replaced it.

Emerson, Ralph Waldo (b. Boston, Mass., 25 May 1803; d. Concord, Mass., 27 April 1882) He gave up his career as a Unitarian minister to become a professional essayist and lecturer. He settled at Concord, where he became the center of New England's most vibrant intellectual circle. The concepts of transcendentalism were principally publicized by his writings, especially *Nature* (1836), *Essays* (1841), and *Addresses and Lectures* (1849).

eminent domain Eminent domain is the authority of the government to take private property for the public good. The elastic clause of the Constitution confers this power. The Fifth Amendment requires fair compensation for any property so appropriated.

Employee Retirement Income Security Act (1974) (ERISA) To ensure that workers in employer-financed retirement programs would not lose their pensions, this law obligated the federal government to refund pension funds left insolvent by corporate bankruptcy. It also set national fiduciary standards for pension fund managers, who were required to discharge their duties "solely in the interest of the [employee] participants and beneficiaries." By 1994, its provisions regulated $3.6 trillion in private pension plans.

Employment Act (20 February 1946) This measure of the Fair Deal declared for the first time an official federal policy for the government "to promote maximum employment, production, and purchasing power." To recommend policies for doing so, it created the Council of Economic Advisors. A later attempt to rededicate the government to this goal was the Humphrey–Hawkins Act.

Endangered Species Preservation Act (1969) This law outlawed importation to the US of any species (or products made from such a species) threatened with extinction, unless importation would help in its preservation. (Exceptions were made for limited scientific and educational purposes.) When it became effective in June 1970, the number of endangered species worldwide totaled 118 birds, 98 mammals, 22 reptiles or amphibians, and 1 mollusk.

Endangered Species Preservation Act (2[illegible] December 1973) This law protected the vital habitats of all domestic species (flora and fauna) threatened with extinction. When the law was passed, the US contained 10[illegible] endangered species (53 birds, 31 fish, 1[illegible] mammals, and 8 reptiles or amphibians), but over 700 (including vegetation) were so classified by 1993. Between 1973 and 1990, 3[illegible] US species of animals or plants became extinct.

Energy, Department of On 2 August 1977 Congress created this department to oversee the Federal Energy Administration, Federal Power Commission, Energy Research and Development Administration, and various energy-related agencies from other departments.

energy crisis *see* Oil embargo

Energy Reorganization Act (1974) *see* Atomic Energy Commission

Enforcement Acts, first and second *see* Force Act, first *and* second

Enforcement Act, third *see* Ku Klux Klan Act

Engel* v. *Vitale On 25 June 1962, the Supreme Court ruled (6–1) that public school officials cannot lead students in repeating a state-authored prayer, even one that is nondenominational and from which students may excuse themselves. Such a ceremony violates the First Amendment's prohibition against established religions. The Court reaffirmed *Engel* in *Abington Township* v. *Schempp*.

English immigration In the vanguard of English immigration were 8,000 colonists who settled Va. and Mass. before 1630. Large-scale immigration then commenced with the Great Migration, and by 170[illegible] about 163,000 English had arrived. Perhaps 125,000 came from 1700 to 1820. By 1820 the English stock had multiplied to an estimated 4,700,000 persons, or 60 percent of all whites, and was doubling through natural increase about every 30 years.

The 1850 census counted 278,675 persons born in England, 12.4 percent of all the foreign-born. Between 1820 and 1900, at least 1,824,054 English arrived (plus perhaps 250,000 of the 793,681 identified simply as "British"), of which two-thirds came after 1870. After 1900, Canada and Australia became the favored destinations for Englis[illegible] emigrants, and only 929,389 came to the US through 1950 (including 100,000 "war brides" in the 1940s). From 1950 to 1990, the US received about 556,000 English immigrants, including the highest ratio of physicians and engineers among any foreign group. The 1990 census counted 21,834,160 persons who described their primary ethnic identity as English; since most of the 17 percent of whites who failed to identify their European origins were probably "old stock" Anglo-Saxons descended from the Great Migration, it is likely that at least 20 percent of whites were of direct English extraction. (*See* WELSH *and* BRITISH IMMIGRATION)

Eniwetok, battle of *see* MARSHALL ISLANDS CAMPAIGN

Enlightenment This was a broad intellectual and cultural movement that dominated western Europe and Anglo-America in the 18th century. It encouraged skepticism toward inherited beliefs and institutions, and also affirmed a belief in social progress through education, science, and disinterested political reform. Enlightenment ideas were most influential among southerners and much less so among New Englanders. This liberal spirit underlay the disestablishment of state religions, ABOLITIONISM, and numerous constitutional reforms in the Revolutionary era.

entail This was a provision of Anglo-American inheritance law allowing wills to be written that made it illegal for the heirs – and any of their descendants – to sell the land they received. Since it was relatively easy to break these "absolute inheritances" by laws passed for that purpose, they had little impact on how wealth was distributed. N.Y., Pa., N.J., Va., N.C., S.C., and Ga. allowed entails in 1770, but by 1786, entails were legal in only two states.

enumerated commodities These goods were articles that could only be exported to world markets from the British colonies after first being landed at a British port. The earliest such items were defined by the NAVIGATION ACT (1660). On the enumerated list were tobacco, rice (with numerous exemptions), indigo, furs, masts, tar, turpentine, hemp, sugar, copper, dyewoods, and ginger. Left unenumerated were provisions, lumber, fish, and rum.

environmental legislation Few major environmental laws passed Congress before 1970, except the Refuse Act (1899), which restricted hazardous waste dumping, the Water Pollution Control Act (1948), which gave federal aid to state water quality programs, the Air Pollution Control Act (1955), which gave federal aid to state air quality programs), the CLEAN AIR ACT (1963, amended 1970, 1977), the WILDERNESS AREAS ACT (1964), the WATER QUALITY ACT (1965), and the CLEAN WATER RESTORATION ACT (1966). Major federal laws to combat pollution, toxic emissions, and hazardous waste since then are: the ENDANGERED SPECIES PRESERVATION ACTS (1969 and 1973); the National Environmental Protection Act (1970), which created the ENVIRONMENTAL PROTECTION AGENCY and required environmental impact statements for major federal projects; the Water Quality Improvement Act (1970), which held oil firms responsible for damage from oil spills; the CLEAN WATER ACT (1972); the Safe Drinking Water Act (1974), which set standards for potable water; the Toxic Substances Control Act (1976), which banned PCBs – polychlorinated biphenyls – and ordered testing of toxic materials; the 1977 amendments to the Water Pollution Control Act (1948), which required industry to eliminate pollutants by the best available technology; the FEDERAL STRIP MINE ACT (1977); and the COMPREHENSIVE ENVIRONMENTAL RESPONSE, COMPENSATION AND LIABILITY ACT (1980). By November 1992, there were 16 volumes of federal environmental regulations.

Environmental Protection Agency (EPA) Congress established the EPA on 2 December 1970. Its mission is to monitor pollution levels, fund research on solving environmental problems, set pollution-control standards for toxic emissions, and offer solutions for eliminating environmental hazards. The agency has administered the "superfund" used to clean up hazardous waste sites since 1980. A major scandal tarnished the EPA when Anne Burford resigned on 9 March 1983 after being accused of mismanaging the superfund and showing favoritism toward certain corporations for political reasons. On 1 December 1983, Rita Lavelle was convicted on four counts of perjury for denying at congressional hearings that political considerations had influenced her decisions while administering the EPA toxic waste program.

Episcopal Church *see* Protestant Episcopal Church

Equal Employment Opportunity Commission *see* Civil Rights Act (1964)

Equal Pay Act (11 June 1963) This law amended the Fair Labor Standards Act to forbid sex discrimination in employment by requiring, as of 11 June 1964, equal pay and benefits for men and women working at the same skill level. It was supplemented by the stronger Title VII of the Civil Rights Act (1964), under which nearly all litigation alleging sex discrimination has been argued.

Equal Rights amendment (ERA) From 1923 to 1972, support for an amendment outlawing sex discrimination emerged in every Congress. On 22 March 1972, Congress passed an ERA that provided that: (1) equality of rights under the law shall not be denied or abridged in the US on account of sex; (2) legal implementation would be delayed two years after ratification. Widespread resistance to the measure led Congress to extend its deadline by three years, but on 30 July 1982 the amendment failed. It had received 30 of the 38 states needed for ratification, excluding five that had rescinded their ratifications.

ERA *see* Equal Rights amendment

Era of Good Feelings This phrase is used to describe James Monroe's presidency, when the Federalist Party's disintegration left no formal opposition to the president and overt factionalism within the Democratic party was muted. Boston's *Columbian Sentinel* coined the phrase on 12 July 1817, during a visit by Monroe, to characterize the political atmosphere after the War of 1812.

Erdman Act (1 June 1898) This law provided for mediation of railroad strikes by the Interstate Commerce Commission's Chairman (*see* Interstate Commerce Commission Act) and the Bureau of Labor's commissioner (until it was superseded by the Newlands Act, 1913); it was invoked 26 times from 1906 to 1913 to settle labor disputes by voluntary arbitration. It outlawed yellow-dog contracts by railroads involved in interstate commerce, until the Supreme Court struck down this provision in *Adair v. United States*.

Eric the Red A Viking exile from Iceland, Eric explored Greenland from 982 to 985 and there founded the western hemisphere's first European settlement in 986. Greenland was the base for Vinland's exploration by Leif Ericson, and remained an outpost for Europeans until its settlements were abandoned about 1420.

Ericson, Leif Son of Eric the Red, Leif discovered Vinland, made the first extensive exploration of the North American coast and reconnoitered the coastline perhaps to Cape Cod, about 1000.

Ericsson, John (b. Langbanshyttan, Sweden, 31 July 1803; d. New York, N.Y., 8 March 1889) After service as a military engineer in the Swedish army, and residence as a maritime inventor in London, he immigrated to the US in 1839. In 1840 he designed the first naval ship (USS *Princeton*) maneuvered by a screw propeller placed under water to shield it from enemy fire. In 1861 he produced plans for monitor-type ironclads, which ensured the USA navy would remain technologically superior to the CSA fleet.

Erie Canal In 1817 Governor De Witt Clinton persuaded N.Y. to fund construction of a waterway linking Hudson River, near Albany, with Buffalo. In October 1825 Clinton formally opened the waterway, which traveled 363 miles through 83 locks and 18 aqueducts. This event marked the start of the canal boom. By rerouting the flow of western foodstuffs to market from New Orleans to New York, the Erie Canal transformed N.Y. into the fastest growing state and cemented the economies (and politics) of the Midwest and Northeast.

ERISA *see* Employee Retirement Income Security Act

Ervin, Sam James, Jr (b. Morganton, N.C., 27 September 1896; d. Winston-Salem, N.C., 23 April 1985) After entering the US Senate in 1954, Ervin (Democrat, N.C.) earned a reputation as a constitutional scholar. He sponsored Public Law 284. On 7 February 1973, he was named chair of the Senate Select Committee on Presidential Elections to investigate the Watergate scandal. His stewardship was crucial in forcing testimony by White House aides and eliciting evidence that implicated Richard NIXON and forced his resignation. He retired from the Senate in 1974.

Esch–Cummins Act (28 February 1920) Congress ended wartime controls over the railroads as of 1 March 1920 and increased the Interstate Commerce Commission's (ICC) powers (*see* INTERSTATE COMMERCE COMMISSION ACT) to set rates and block anticompetitive practices. The law's purpose was to increase the ICC's flexibility to ensure fair, competitive practices while allowing railroads the chance to make a fair profit. It also replaced the NEWLANDS ACT'S (1913) provisions for settling labor disputes with a nine-man Railroad Labor Board – equally divided between management, labor, and public members – with authority just short of compulsory arbitration. The mediation panel failed to prevent or solve a major strike in 1922 and was replaced under the RAILWAY LABOR ACT (1926).

Escobedo* v. *Illinois On 22 June 1964, the Supreme Court ruled (5–4) that police violated the SIXTH AMENDMENT by interrogating a suspect without telling him of his right to legal advice (or denying him counsel). Any confessions so given cannot be used as evidence against him. On 12 June 1967, in *United States* v. *Wade*, it expanded *Escobedo* by declaring unanimously that unless a suspect's lawyer attends a police line-up, any identification by a witness cannot be admitted as evidence in court. *Escobedo* was further expanded by *MIRANDA* v. *ARIZONA*.

Eskimo-Aleut languages This family of INDIAN LANGUAGES was spoken below the Arctic Circle from Greenland to Siberia. Eskimo and Aleut were a common tongue until they began separating about 4,000 years ago. The family's major subdivisions are Transarctic (Central-Greenlandic) Eskimo, Kuskokwim (Alaskan) Eskimo, Eastern Aleut (Unalaskan), and Western Aleut (Attuan and Atkan).

Eskimos This people crossed the Bering Strait from Siberia about 3,000–1,000 BC in boats, and eventually spread 5,000 miles across the arctic and subarctic regions from Alaska to Greenland. The term Eskimo is a corruption of an Algonquian word meaning "eaters of raw meat," and the group calls itself the Inuit ("the people"); those living on the Aleutian Islands are often called Aleuts. Their culture was centered around maritime hunting of seal, walrus, and whales. Russian fur traders made contact with Aleuts in the 1740s and introduced epidemic diseases, exploitative labor conditions, and the Eastern Orthodox Church. The 1990 census counted 42,024 Alaskans with some Eskimo blood and 10,244 with some Aleut ancestry (including many of mixed descent).

Esopus wars (1) On 20 September 1659, settlers at Esopus (Wiltwyck), N.Y., killed a drunken Indian. On 21 September, 500 warriors killed or captured five Dutch, began a 23-day siege of Esopus, burned outlying homes, and slaughtered all livestock. The Dutch burned several Indian towns in March–April 1660, and in July sold 11 Indians to the Caribbean colony of Curaçao as slaves. Peter STUYVESANT concluded a peace treaty on 15 July 1660.

(2) On 7 June 1663, Indians besieged Wiltwyck, burned a nearby settlement, killed about 20 Dutch, and captured about 45. On 29–31 July 1663, the Dutch destroyed abandoned Indian camps, along with cornfields and winter food supplies. On 5 September, 55 Dutch stormed an enemy fort (near Bloomingburg), killed or captured 30 Indians, and freed 23 captives, at a cost of 3 dead and 6 wounded. The Indians slowly released Dutch captives, and on 16 May 1664 ceded much of the central Hudson valley in a peace treaty.

Espionage Act (15 June 1917) Congress set fines of up to $10,000 and prison terms of up to 20 years for obstructing the US war effort in WORLD WAR I by spying, sabotage, interfering with recruiting, fomenting insubordination among the military, and refusing to perform armed service. Using the mails to ship treasonous materials was punishable by a $5,000 fine, and the postmaster general was authorized to deny delivery to any publications deemed seditious or dangerous. The SEDITION ACT (1918) amended it. It was ruled constitutional in *SCHENCK* v. *UNITED STATES* and expired in 1921.

Essex case On 23 July 1805, a British ADMIRALTY COURT ruled that the RULE OF 1756 was violated by US shippers who used BROKEN VOYAGES to carry cargoes from

French or Spanish colonies to their home ports in Europe. The Essex case declared that US merchant ships could not claim protection under neutral rights when they took French or Spanish goods via American ports to a final destination, because they were merely rerouting a continuous voyage that had been illegal in peacetime. The decision led to a sharp rise in seizures of American ships by the British navy, which was trying to choke off the flow of enemy military goods in the Napoleonic wars.

Essex junto This term refers to a clique of leaders of the FEDERALIST PARTY, primarily from Essex County, Mass., that formed about 1803 under Timothy Pickering's influence. Appalled that their party seemed unlikely to regain control of Congress or the presidency, and that New England's political influence was diminishing as the west was settled, they formed highly speculative plans for New England to leave the Union. They took Aaron BURR into their confidence and hoped that if he became governor of N.Y. in 1804, they might engineer the northeast's secession as a separate nation. When Burr was defeated as governor, the project was given up as impractical, but secessionist sentiment resurfaced at the HARTFORD CONVENTION.

Eutaw Springs, battle of (S.C.) On 8 September 1781, Lieutenant Colonel Alexander Stewart's 1,800 British and TORIES repulsed 2,200 of Major General Nathanael GREENE's army after its attack disintegrated into uncontrolled looting of the Royal army's liquor supplies. US losses: 138 killed, 375 wounded, 41 missing. British losses: 85 killed, 351 wounded, and 257 missing.

Evangelical and Reformed Church *see* UNITED CHURCH OF CHRIST

Evangelical United Brethren Church *see* METHODIST CHURCH

Everson* v. *Board of Education of Ewing Township On 10 February 1947, the Supreme Court ruled (5–4) that the FIRST AMENDMENT obliged state courts to enforce the prohibition against any government establishment of religion. It then authorized state expenses incurred while transporting children to parochial schools as a subsidy to their parents, not to church-affiliated education.

Ex Parte Crow Dog *see* *UNITED STATES* v. *KAGAMA*

Ex Parte Garland *see* TEST-OATH CASES

Ex Parte McCardle On 12 April 1869, the Supreme Court ruled unanimously that Congress could rescind its jurisdiction over certain types of cases, even if a decision from the Court was pending when Congress acted. Congress had threatened to curtail the Court's jurisdiction because it feared the justices would hold that various RECONSTRUCTION measures were unconstitutional. On the same day, the Court issued *TEXAS* v. *WHITE*, which ended the struggle for power between the legislative and judicial branches by sustaining congressional policies to reconstruct the South.

Ex Parte Merryman In 1861, while acting in his capacity as a circuit judge, Chief Justice Roger TANEY issued a writ of HABEAS CORPUS for John Merryman, who was imprisoned in Md. by military authorities as an active rebel. When the army refused to release Merryman, Taney filed this opinion declaring that only Congress, and not the Executive Department, could suspend habeas corpus, and castigating the suppression of civil rights by military force. US authorities continued to refuse the writ of habeas corpus to rebel sympathizers arrested throughout the Civil War. The full Supreme Court declined to rule on this issue, or rejected cases as in *EX PARTE VALLANDIGHAM*, until after the war, when it issued *EX PARTE MILLIGAN*.

Ex Parte Milligan On 3 April 1866, the Supreme Court heard an appeal from civilians tried by a military tribunal at Indianapolis; it ruled unanimously that it was unconstitutional to try civilians by martial law in areas where civil courts might conveniently hear such cases. Five justices held that civilians could never be subjected to martial law outside immediate war zones, even under the joint authority of Congress and the president. The decision denied the US the option of maintaining order in the South through martial law during RECONSTRUCTION.

Ex Parte Quirin On 31 July 1942, the Supreme Court ruled (8–0) that the SIXTH AMENDMENT's guarantee of jury trials concerns only civilian hearings and not military tribunals.

Ex Parte Siebold In 1880 the Supreme Court upheld (7–2) the federal government's right to enact laws making state officials liable for prosecution if they permitted fraud in congressional elections by negligence or fraud. (*See also* *Ex Parte Yarbrough*)

Ex Parte Vallandigham In 1864 the Supreme Court heard the petition, for a writ of HABEAS CORPUS, of Clement Vallandigham, who had been arrested for activities in support of the COPPERHEADS and tried by a military commission. The Court declined to hear his case by saying that military tribunals were outside its jurisdiction.

Ex Parte Yarbrough In 1884, in an issue similar to *Ex Parte Siebold*, the Supreme Court affirmed Congress's right to pass the FORCE ACT (1870) forbidding private individuals from hindering citizens from voting in federal elections. It distinguished between the federal and state franchise as decided in *United States* v. *Reese*. This ruling was reaffirmed by *United States* v. *Mosley* in 1915.

ex post facto laws The Constitution (Article I, Section 9) forbids laws that punish behavior committed before their own enactment. The Supreme Court ruled on this subject in *Calder* v. *Bull*, the TEST-OATH CASES, and *Garner* v. *Board of Public Works*.

Exclusion Act (1882) *see* IMMIGRATION

Exclusionary Rule *see* *Weeks* v. *United States*

Executive Order 8802 *see* MARCH ON WASHINGTON (1941)

Executive Order 9981 On 26 July 1948, Harry S. TRUMAN directed the armed forces to desegregate all military units. Integration lagged until the KOREAN WAR, when it was implemented vigorously.

executive privilege This is the prerogative of US presidents to keep their official documents confidential and decline to give testimony. George WASHINGTON first claimed this right when turning down a request by the House of Representatives (24 March 1794) to see papers relating to JAY'S TREATY. Thomas JEFFERSON cited the principle in 1807 when refusing a subpoena from John MARSHALL to appear as a witness and furnish certain papers at Aaron BURR's treason trial. In *United States* v. *Nixon* (24 July 1974), the Supreme Court ruled that executive privilege could not be invoked to avoid complying with subpoenas for evidence needed in criminal trials.

Explorer I *see* SPACE RACE

Export-Debenture Plan During 1926 and 1928, Congress debated a GRANGE-endorsed plan to subsidize exports of farm commodities. The proposal would have entitled farmers to receive certificates (debentures) equaling the value of any loss they sustained selling crops overseas. Foreign companies needing to buy dollars to pay import fees on goods sent to the US would instead buy the farmers' debentures, which the Treasury would cancel when their goods passed through customs. Farmers endorsed the plan because it reduced the domestic surplus of agricultural produce through overseas exports. It also had the advantage of not spending any money, since the debentures would be issued as non-negotiable credits and canceled by bookkeeping entries, while foreign firms paid US farmers cash for their debentures. In April–May 1929, the Senate approved the proposal, but the House rejected it three times. It died when Herbert HOOVER promised to veto any version enacted.

external taxation During the Revolutionary era, external taxes were defined as revenues raised on overseas trade by Parliament, such as by the SUGAR ACT's duty on molasses or the TOWNSHEND REVENUE ACT's duties on imports from Britain.

Exxon *Valdez* oil spill On 24 March 1989, Captain Joseph Hazelwood's 987-foot Exxon Corporation tanker, the *Valdez*, hit a reef about 25 miles from Valdez, Alaska. Approximately 240,000 barrels of oil flowed into the sea, where winds up to 73 mph dispersed them over 45 miles of coastline. The spill was the greatest (manmade) environmental disaster in US history, and led to an estimated 580,000 seabird deaths. Exxon spent $2.2 billion cleaning up the coastline through May 1991, and in 1994 was fined another $2 billion for negligently discharging pollutants.

F

Fair Deal Beginning in September 1945, Harry S. TRUMAN had recommended that Congress enact numerous laws concerning employment conditions and social problems, to which he gave the name Fair Deal on 5 January 1949. This agenda was intended as a second-generation NEW DEAL, and included a higher minimum wage, broader coverage for Social Security (*see* SOCIAL SECURITY ADMINISTRATION), pro-labor legislation, federal subsidies for public housing, sponsorship of scientific research, a system of national health care, civil rights legislation, expanded soil conservation programs, agricultural subsidies, federal grants to education, and renewed spending on dams, power-generating stations, and other public works. Republicans took over both houses of Congress in 1946, and so much of the Fair Deal languished until Truman's election triumph in 1948, when Democrats regained Congress. Congress then provided money for the HOUSING ACT (1949), hydroelectric power stations, western land reclamation, farm subsidies, and it created the National Science Foundation. Truman failed to win aid for national health insurance, education, civil rights legislation, and either a fair employment commission or repeal of the TAFT–HARTLEY ACT.

Fair Employment Practices Committee This agency was created on 25 June 1941 by Executive Order 8802 to carry out presidential directives against job discrimination in the civil service and war production industries, including a decree of 27 May 1943 requiring nondiscrimination clauses in war contracts. The committee's achievements were limited, however. A bill to establish it as a permanent federal agency was defeated by a filibuster in February 1946, but by that time Wash., Mass., Conn., N.Y., and N.J. had established similar bodies. The committee was a precursor of the CIVIL RIGHTS ACT's (1964) Equal Employment Opportunity Commission.

Fair Housing Act *see* CIVIL RIGHTS ACT (1968)

Fair Labor Standards Act (25 June 1938) Congress set the MINIMUM WAGE at $0.40 an hour, established the 40-hour workweek with wages of 150 percent for overtime, outlawed gainful employment for children under 16, and excluded anyone under 18 from dangerous work. It affected 63,000,000 full-time and part-time workers, of whom 750,000 received immediate raises. (Domestic help, farm laborers, and certain small businesses were exempted.) The Supreme Court upheld it in *UNITED STATES* v. *DARBY LUMBER COMPANY*. It was amended to forbid sex discrimination by the EQUAL PAY ACT (1963).

Fair Oaks, battle of (Va.) *see* PENINSULAR CAMPAIGN

fair trade laws *see* MILLER–TYDINGS ACT

Fairbanks, Charles Warren (b. Unionville Center, Ohio, 11 May 1852; d. Indianapolis, Ind., 4 June 1918) A newspaperman and railroad lawyer, Fairbanks was a US senator (Republican, Ind., 1897–1905). He was Theodore ROOSEVELT's vice-president (1905–9), although they represented opposite wings of their party.

Fall, Albert B. *see* TEAPOT DOME SCANDAL

Fallen Timbers, battle of (Ohio) On 20 August 1794, Major General Anthony WAYNE's 1,000 regulars and 1,400 Ky. militia defeated 1,500 Indians and 60 Canadians two miles from the British FORT MIAMIS. US losses: 33 killed, 100 wounded. Indian and Canadian losses: 19 killed. Wayne's victory, along with his occupation of Forts Defiance and Recovery in the heart of hostile territory cowed the Indians into signing the first treaty of Greenville and induced the British to surrender all military posts on US soil by Jay's Treaty.

Falwell, Rev. Jerry *see* Moral Majority

Farley, James Aloysius (b. Grassy Point, N.Y., 30 May 1888; d. New York, N.Y., 9 June 1976) He helped to manage Franklin D. Roosevelt's campaigns for N.Y. governor in 1928 and president in 1932. In 1933 he became US postmaster general and chair of the Democratic National Committee. His shrewd use of patronage was a major factor in maintaining party discipline in Congress in behalf of legislation for the New Deal, but he was never among Roosevelt's closest advisors. He ran Roosevelt's 1936 campaign, but opposed his plan to seek a third term because he wished to run himself, and he resigned from the cabinet in 1941 to chair Coca-Cola's overseas division.

Farm Credit Act (16 June 1933) This law consolidated the Federal Intermediate Credit Bank (*see* Agricultural Credits Act), Federal Farm Board, Federal Farm Loan Board, and other credit agencies for agricultural production and marketing, into a network of local lending institutions. Its operations were managed by the Farm Credit Administration.

Farm Credit Administration (FCA) Created by executive order on 27 March 1933, this agency assumed control of federal programs under the Farm Credit Act and the Farm Mortgage Foreclosure Act. By June 1934, the FCA had refinanced over 20 percent of all farm mortgages. By 31 December 1940, it had lent a total of $6.87 billion, of which over half had been repaid. In 1939 the FCA ceased to have independent status and became a branch of the Department of Agriculture.

Farm depression of the 1920s *see* Recession of the 1920s

Farm Mortgage Foreclosure Act (12 June 1934) This law allowed the Farm Credit Administration to make loans so that farmers could regain title to property they had lost by foreclosure. It was an interim measure until the Frazier–Lemke Farm Bankruptcy Act.

Farm Mortgage Moratorium Act (29 August 1935) After the Frazier–Lemke Farm Bankruptcy Act was declared unconstitutional, Congress passed this measure permitting courts to grant insolvent farmers a three-year moratorium against dispossession if they paid a fair rent. It was held constitutional by the Supreme Court in *Wright* v. *Vinton Branch* on 29 March 1937.

Farm Mortgage Refinancing Act (31 January 1934) This law created the Federal Farm Mortgage Corporation to refinance $2 billion of farm debts. It was operated by the Farm Credit Administration.

Farm Security Administration (FSA) The Bankhead–Jones Farm Tenancy Act created this agency to give low-interest mortgages so that tenants could become landowners. Between 1937 and 1947, it gave 47,104 mortgages worth $293,000,000. It also operated the Rural Rehabilitation Program. Congress cut the FSA's budget sharply in World War II and replaced it with the Farmers' Home Administration in 1946.

Farmer, James *see* Congress of Racial Equality

Farmer-Labor Party In 1919 the Labor party was founded as a vehicle for uniting socialistic union members. It was renamed the Farmer-Labor party in 1920 to be competitive in rural states, and ran a presidential ticket with Parley Christiansen for president and Max Hayes for vice-president. Its platform supported a $1.00-an-hour minimum wage, unemployment insurance, business regulation, the end of child labor, tariff reduction, pro-labor legislation, the repeal of the Owen–Glass Act (*see* Federal Reserve system), and independence for the Philippines. The ticket received 1.0 percent of the vote. After the party fell under the control of the Communist party, an exodus of moderate members led to its demise everywhere but Minn., where it allied with the Democratic party after 1933 and has managed to survive to the present.

Farmers' Alliance and Industrial Union *see* Populism

Farrakhan, Louis *see* Nation of Islam

Faulkner, William (b. New Albany, Miss., 25 September 1897; d. Byhalia, Miss., 6 July 1962) After brief service in the Canadian air force in World War I, Faulkner attended the University of Mississippi (1919–21), but did not earn a degree. He first achieved commercial success with *Sanctuary* (1931), a gothic novel laced with prurient elements. He lived in Oxford, Miss., wrote nineteen novels and seven volumes of short stories, and became the leading figure in the "southern renaissance" of literature. Although he set his fiction in the South – especially his mythical "Yoknapatawpha County, Miss." – Faulkner examined questions about human character, destiny, and psychology in such depth that he elevated the South's regional culture to a level of profound universal relevance. He won Pulitzer prizes for *A Fable* (1954) and *The Reivers* (1962), and received the Nobel prize for literature in 1949. Other major works include *The Sound and the Fury* (1929), *Light in August* (1932), *Absolom, Absolom* (1936), *Go Down, Moses, and Other Stories* (1942), and *Intruder in the Dust* (1948).

FBI *see* FEDERAL BUREAU OF INVESTIGATION

FCA *see* FARM CREDIT ADMINISTRATION

FCC *see* FEDERAL COMMUNICATIONS COMMISSION

FDA *see* FOOD AND DRUG ADMINISTRATION

FDIC *see* FEDERAL DEPOSIT INSURANCE CORPORATION

Federal Aid Highway Act *see* INTERSTATE HIGHWAY SYSTEM

Federal Aid Road Act (1916) This law provided the first significant federal appropriation for highway construction to accommodate the needs of transportation by AUTOMOBILE. It allocated $75,000,000 in matching funds for state road construction, but required states to establish highway departments to be eligible. It was succeeded by the FEDERAL HIGHWAY ACT (1922).

Federal Anti-Price Discrimination Act *see* ROBINSON–PATMAN ACT

Federal Aviation Agency Congress passed the Federal Aviation Act (1958) to merge the Air Navigation Development Board, the Air Coordinating Committee, the Defense Landing Area Program, the Civilian Pilot Training Program, and the Civil Aeronautics Authority into the Federal Aviation Agency of the Department of COMMERCE.

Federal Bureau of Investigation (FBI) The Department of JUSTICE's chief investigative section began in 1907 as the Bureau of Investigation. It was extensively used in the Palmer raids (*see* RED SCARE). Appointed as director in 1924, J. Edgar HOOVER significantly raised its professionalism and prominence as a crime-fighting and counter-espionage force; but he also ignored the rise of national crime syndicates, reluctantly enforced civil rights laws, and sanctioned violations of the FBI charter by wiretaps or other domestic surveillance of citizens with unpopular political views. L. Patrick GRAY was acting director upon Hoover's death in 1972, but because of the WATERGATE SCANDAL, was never confirmed. William Webster then took over, and strove to restore a spirit of nonpartisanship. William Sessions succeeded him in 1987, but was dismissed in July 1993 after allegations were made that he took financial advantage of his position's perquisites. Louis Freeh replaced him.

Federal Communications Commission (FCC) The proliferation of radio stations from the first in 1921 to 681 in 1927, led to passage of the Radio Act (1927), which established the Federal Radio Commission to license stations and regulate their operations. On 19 June 1934, the Communications Act replaced the Radio Commission with the Federal Communications Commission and broadened its regulatory powers.

Federal Crop Insurance corporation *see* AGRICULTURAL ADJUSTMENT ACT, SECOND

Federal Deposit Insurance Corporation (FDIC) Congress created the FDIC, by the BANKING ACT (1933), to restore public faith in the banking system, which had suffered over 5,500 bank failures since 1930. Modeled after the Federal Home Loan Bank Act (*see* FEDERAL HOME LOAN BANK BOARD), it wrote insurance coverage for savings or checking accounts and other instruments of deposit to give the confidence needed to avoid runs on banks during financial panics. It became effective on 1 January 1934 and covered deposits up to $2,500, a figure raised to $5,000 later that year. Over 14,400 banks and thrift institutions had FDIC protection by 1935. A requirement that state banks subscribing to the FDIC become Federal Reserve members ended in 1939. Since then, the only bank panics have occurred within the state-insured systems of Ohio and Md. in the 1980s. In the SAVINGS AND LOAN CRISIS, the RESOLUTION TRUST CORPORATION saved the FDIC from insolvency. In 1994 the FDIC insured deposits up to $100,000 at 7,200 banks and thrifts.

Federal Elections Campaign Act (7 February 1972) This law (as amended in 1974, 1976, and 1979) regulates all federal elections and provides public financing for presidential candidates through the Federal Election Commission. Campaign contributions by individuals are limited to $1,000 per candidate per election, and no individual can make total donations exceeding $25,000 in one year. Political action committees (PACs) cannot give over $5,000 to one candidate per election, but have no limit on their total donations. No spending limit exists on candidates for Congress, but presidential candidates cannot spend more than $20,200,000 on primaries and their parties may not spend more than two cents per voter in their behalf (about the total spent in the primaries). Independent or third-party candidates can receive federal matching funds for primaries once they raise over $100,000 in voluntary contributions; they can be reimbursed for general election costs if they win at least 5 percent of the vote.

Federal Emergency Relief Administration (FERA) On 12 May 1933 the Federal Emergency Relief Act established this agency to operate under the RECONSTRUCTION FINANCE CORPORATION. It broke with previous practice by funding direct relief to the states (as opposed to loans); it also subsidized state and municipal construction projects by paying 25 percent of their costs. Under Harry HOPKINS, it resettled farmers from lands that were hopelessly infertile, developed programs to employ migrant workers, and spent $2 billion putting 2,500,000 men to work on 235,000 projects. Because it became embroiled in acrimonious disputes over the political use of federal funds, FERA was replaced with the WORKS PROGRESS ADMINISTRATION in 1935.

Federal Farm Bankruptcy Act *see* FRAZIER–LEMKE FARM BANKRUPTCY ACT

Federal Farm Board *see* AGRICULTURAL MARKETING ACT

Federal Farm Loan Act (17 July 1916) This law created a Federal Farm Loan Board (chaired by the secretary of the Treasury) to oversee farm loan banks in 12 districts. Each district bank was capitalized at $750,000 and offered long-term, low interest loans or mortgages (at lower rates than commercial banks) to members of national farm loan cooperatives enrolled with the district banks. Woodrow WILSON opposed the bill, but signed it to win the farm vote in 1916.

Federal Highway Act (1922) This law succeeded the FEDERAL AID ROAD ACT and established a significant federal commitment to funding highway improvements. By appropriating grants for state projects to improve road systems, it quadrupled federal highway spending from $19,500,000 in 1920 to $88,000,000 in 1923.

Federal Home Loan Bank Board This agency was founded on 22 July 1932 by the Federal Home Loan Bank Act, which was recommended by Herbert HOOVER to supervise building and loan banks (the primary source of home mortgages) and to discount their home mortgages. The NATIONAL HOUSING ACT (1934) authorized the board to operate the Federal Savings and Loan Insurance Corporation (FSLIC) to insure savings accounts so that depositors could be assured their money was safe during financial panics or depressions. Losses in the SAVINGS AND LOAN CRISIS exceeded the FSLIC's assets and bankruptcy was only avoided by funding provided by the RESOLUTION TRUST CORPORATION.

Federal Housing Administration *see* NATIONAL HOUSING ACT (1934)

Federal Intermediate Credit Bank *see* AGRICULTURAL CREDITS ACT

Federal Maritime Board and Administration *see* MERCHANT MARINE ACT (1936)

Federal Power Commission This commission was created on 10 June 1920 by the Water Power Act to place electric utilities under federal regulation; it licensed and set rates for power stations and transmission lines built on the PUBLIC DOMAIN or any navigable waterway. The PUBLIC UTILITY HOLDING COMPANY ACT gave it authority over all interstate transmission of electric power.

Federal Radio Commission *see* FEDERAL COMMUNICATIONS COMMISSION

Federal Reserve system The immediate origins of the Federal Reserve system lay in the PANIC OF 1907, which revealed the inadequacy of the US banking system to prevent a credit crisis from spiraling into a recession. On 30 May 1908, Congress created the National Monetary Commission, chaired by Senator Nelson ALDRICH, to suggest reform and reorganization of the banking system. On 17 January 1911, the commission reported its Aldrich Plan, which formed the basis for the Federal Reserve system, except that it recommended the central bank be a private corporation and not a government institution. The PUJO HEARINGS on the MONEY TRUST, and Woodrow WILSON's opposition, blocked Aldrich's plan for the financial community to control the central bank. On 23 December 1913, the Owen-Glass Act established the Federal Reserve system to oversee all credit and monetary affairs. A six-member Federal Reserve Board (named by the president and confirmed by the Senate) would direct the system through 12 regional Federal Reserve banks, whose capital came from a 6 percent levy on the assets of all national banks and any state banks that voluntarily joined.

The Federal Reserve system provided credit and other banking services to member banks; it also issued a new paper currency, Federal Reserve notes, as part of the circulating money supply. The 12 regional banks were each empowered within their region to: (1) expand or contract the money supply by buying or selling US bonds from member banks; (2) raise or lower interest rates; and (3) expand or contract credit by changing the level of reserves that member banks must maintain as security on their deposits. By 1929, about 80 percent of banks were members. The system's modern structure and centralized authority was established by the BANKING ACT (1935).

Federal Savings and Loan Insurance Corporation *see* FEDERAL HOME LOAN BANK BOARD

Federal Securities Act (27 May 1933) This law required full disclosure of material facts concerning any initial public offering of corporate stock by the issuing company and its underwriters. (Not covered were government and railroad bonds.) Any false or misleading information could be punished by imprisonment and fines. All reports had to be made available in writing to prospective purchasers 20 days ahead of the sale date. The FEDERAL TRADE COMMISSION enforced these regulations until the SECURITIES EXCHANGE ACT.

Federal Strip Mine Act (3 August 1977) Mining interests blocked passage of this measure for a decade before 1977. It was the first US statute to regulate strip mining, and required owners to restore land to its approximate original contour and to prevent pollution or siltation of streams.

Federal Surplus Commodity Corporation *see* FEDERAL SURPLUS RELIEF CORPORATION

Federal Surplus Relief Corporation Following criticism of destruction by the AGRICULTURAL ADJUSTMENT ADMINISTRATION (AAA) of farm commodities while hunger was widespread in the GREAT DEPRESSION, the AAA established this agency in October 1933 to buy agricultural surpluses for distribution to the needy. The corporation coordinated the transfer of excess foodstuffs from the Agriculture Department to the FEDERAL EMERGENCY RELIEF ADMINISTRATION, and then to state relief agencies. The program was dismantled in November 1935, but revived as the Federal Surplus Commodities Corporation, which launched the first program for FOOD STAMPS. It served as the earliest precedent for direct federal involvement in maintaining healthy diets among the poor and schoolchildren.

Federal Trade Commission (FTC) (26 September 1914) Congress established this five-member body to investigate complaints that TRUSTS were violating the SHERMAN ANTITRUST ACT or CLAYTON ANTITRUST ACT. The commission could demand that corporations provide reports on their financial operations, and then either publish their findings or issue a cease-and-desist order halting any unfair trade practices. Objections to cease-and-desist orders could be appealed in federal court, where a judge would decide their validity. Courts may punish violations of cease-and-desist orders with fines for each offense. The ROBINSON-

PATMAN ACT authorized it to abolish unreasonably low price discounting (primarily by chain retailers), intended to destroy competition. The FOOD, DRUG, AND COSMETIC ACT (1938) empowered it to forbid misleading advertising that harmed consumers or competitors.

Federal Works Agency (FWA) The Administrative Reorganization Act (3 April 1939) consolidated the WORKS PROGRESS ADMINISTRATION, PUBLIC WORKS ADMINISTRATION, Bureau of Public Roads, and US Housing Agency into the FWA under John Carmody. It established the Public Buildings Administration. On 1 July 1949, it was disbanded and the GENERAL SERVICES ADMINISTRATION assumed its duties.

federalism This is the CONSTITUTION's system of sharing authority between the national and state governments. Although the Constitution, congressional statutes, and foreign treaties are the supreme law of the land, states enjoy full latitude to legislate on local issues or criminal behavior, so long as no conflict exists with federal law or the BILL OF RIGHTS. The national government likewise is forbidden to encroach on essential elements of each state's sovereignty, such as the right to keep a MILITIA, the right to be exempt from civil suits filed by citizens of other states in federal court, and the right to issue state bonds or other financial instruments exempt from federal taxation.

Federalist Papers During the ratification struggle over the federal CONSTITUTION, James MADISON, Alexander HAMILTON, and John JAY wrote 85 essays (175,000 words) between 27 October 1787 and 28 May 1788 in order to swing public opinion in N.Y. toward the new government. Hamilton authored 51, Madison 26, and Jay 5, while 3 were co-authored by Hamilton and Madison. Copies of the first collected edition were sent to Va. and were used at that state's ratifying convention. The *Papers* are the classic exposition of the political theories that underlay the Constitution's creation.

Federalist party This party coalesced around those members of George WASHINGTON's administration who favored a pro-British foreign policy, especially Alexander HAMILTON and John ADAMS. Federalists dominated New England and were very strong in N.Y., N.J., Del., and eastern Pa. In domestic politics, they generally supported LOOSE CONSTRUCTIONISM and a strong national government vis-à-vis the states. Federalists controlled the presidency under Adams, the Senate (1791–1800), and the House (1791–2, 1797–1800). After being decisively defeated in 1800, the Federalists never again challenged the DEMOCRATIC PARTY for the national government's control. The embargo (*see* EMBARGO ACT) revived their popularity, but Federalists essentially remained a N.Y.–New England party to 1816, the last year they nominated a candidate for president.

Federalists Supporters of the federal CONSTITUTION were called by this name during the ratification struggle. They were strongest in small states, which ratified quickly. The *FEDERALIST PAPERS* provide the most sophisticated summary of Federalist philosophy.

Federated States of Micronesia *see* MICRONESIA, US TRUST TERRITORY OF

Federation of Organized Trade and Labor Unions of the US and Canada *see* AMERICAN FEDERATION OF LABOR

Feminine Mystique, The In 1963 Betty Friedan published this best-selling book, which argued that women experienced a profound malaise because of a lack of opportunities to develop their talents and make social contributions outside the family environment. By creating an awareness that American culture limited options for women by overt discrimination and subtle barriers, Friedan was instrumental in sparking the FEMINIST MOVEMENT against sexist attitudes and unequal treatment of women.

feminist movement Public discussion of the cultural and social barriers blocking women's aspirations suddenly became widespread after *The FEMININE MYSTIQUE*'s publication and founding of the NATIONAL ORGANIZATION OF WOMEN. On 26 August 1970, feminism held its first major event, the Women's Strike for Equality, which issued three demands: equal opportunity in jobs and education, 24-hour child care centers, and ABORTION on demand. Dissatisfied with the protection offered by the CIVIL RIGHTS ACT (1964), feminists revived calls for an EQUAL RIGHTS AMENDMENT, but failed to achieve its ratification.

The movement persuaded the Supreme Court to expand opportunity by declaring gender-based laws to be inherently suspect (in *Craig* v. *Boren*), but its argument that all sex-related legal distinctions were illegal was rejected by the Court in regard to the DRAFT and COMPARABLE WORTH. Its efforts to end sexual harassment in the workplace were vindicated by *Meritor Savings Bank* v. *Vinson*, but its efforts to have pornography recognized as an illegal way of victimizing women failed in *American Booksellers Association* v. *Hudnut*. Feminism influenced politics by forcing major political parties to confront issues of sexual discrimination and become more open to women officeholders.

Fendall's revolts (1) In March 1660, the Md. assembly, with Governor Josias Fendall's encouragement, resolved to deny Lord Baltimore's authority to veto its laws or dissolve a session without the speaker's agreement to end its deliberations. Fendall's "pigmie Rebellion" fizzled out when CHARLES II fully recognized Lord Baltimore's right to govern. Fendall was dismissed, but pardoned for rebellion.

(2) In April 1681, Fendall and John Coode attempted to instigate an uprising in Charles County against proprietary authority, but were arrested, fined, and banished in November.

Fenian invasions On 31 May 1866, several hundred Fenians (members of an Irish revolutionary society) invaded Canada near Buffalo, N.Y., engaged Canadian forces at Limestone Ridge, and retreated to N.Y. The US Army broke up attacks in 1866 from Campo Bello Island and other locations, before they were launched. On 25 May 1870, Fenians invaded Canada from Franklin, Vt. US marshals then arrested their leaders and the army dispersed their bands.

FERA *see* FEDERAL EMERGENCY RELIEF ADMINISTRATION

Fermi, Enrico *see* MANHATTAN PROJECT

Ferraro, Geraldine Anne (b. Newburgh, N.Y., 26 August 1935) In 1974 Ferraro opened a law practice in New York City, and later entered politics as a Democrat. After serving in Congress (1979–84), she became the first woman nominated for vice-president, in 1984. Her ticket lost in a landslide, and even failed to win a majority of women's votes. She was defeated in a bid for the Senate in 1992.

Fetterman massacre On 21 December 1866, near Fort Phil Kearney, Wyo., Red Cloud and Crazy Horse's 1,500 Sioux annihilated 78 soldiers and two civilians under Captain William Fetterman in an ambush.

FHA Federal Housing Association (*see* NATIONAL HOUSING ACT, 1934).

Field, Cyrus West *see* TRANSATLANTIC CABLE

Fifteenth Amendment Submitted to the states on 26 February 1869, last ratified on 3 February 1870, and officially proclaimed on 30 March 1870, it gave every US citizen the right to vote, regardless of his race or former status as a slave. Congress then passed three FORCE ACTS to prevent it from being subverted. *United States* v. *Reese* interpreted the amendment so narrowly that it failed to stop most southern states from disfranchising nonwhites. *Breedlove* v *Suttles* and *Lassiter* v. *Northampton County Board of Elections* further weakened the amendment's ability to prevent voting discrimination. The amendment nevertheless gave some protection for minority voting rights (usually in federal elections) in *Ex Parte Yarbrough*, *United States* v *Mosley*, *Guinn* v. *United States*, *Smith* v. *Allwright*, and *Terry* v. *Adams*. It upheld the VOTING RIGHTS ACT (1965) in *South Carolina* v. *Katzenbach*.

Fifth Amendment Submitted to the states on 25 September 1789, last ratified by Va. on 15 December 1791, and officially proclaimed on 30 December 1791, it provided that civilians only be tried for a felony after a grand jury's indictment, that no one be subject to DOUBLE JEOPARDY or involuntary self-incrimination, that courts adhere to DUE PROCESS, and that just compensation be paid for property taken under EMINENT DOMAIN. Its protections were extended to state court proceedings by *Chicago, Burlington and Quincy Railroad* v *Chicago* (eminent domain), *Malloy* v *Hogan* (compulsory self-incrimination), and *Benton* v. *Maryland* (double jeopardy). Other significant cases involving the Fifth are *Murray's Lessee* v. *Hoboken Land and Improvement Company*, *United*

States v. *Lanza*, *Counselman* v. *Hitchcock*, *Ullmann* v. *United States*, *Miranda* v. *Arizona*, and *Murphy* v. *Waterfront Commission of New York*.

Fifty-Four, Forty, or Fight This phrase was the slogan of US expansionists who insisted that the US claim to OREGON included British Columbia to 54°40′. The US claim derived from Robert GRAY's discovery of the Columbia River, the ADAMS–ONIS TREATY, and an 1824 treaty with Russia that specified 54°40′ as the US boundary with ALASKA. Britain claimed all land north of the Columbia. The CONVENTION OF 1818 established a joint occupation (later extended) leaving Oreg. open to settlers of both nations, but on 2 December 1845, James POLK demanded British recognition of the entire US claim. On 15 June 1846, the Senate ratified a hastily-drafted compromise treaty that divided the territory in half by extending the US–Canadian boundary due west at 49° to the Pacific.

filibustering This term referred to efforts by filibusterers (i.e. freebooters who invaded nations with which their own country was at peace) aimed at forcibly annexing Latin-American countries as slave states to the US. In May 1850 Narcisco Lopez led an abortive invasion of Cuba from New Orleans that included about 200 southern volunteers, many of whom were captured and executed. In 1855 William WALKER seized Nicaragua. George Bickley laid plans in the late 1850s to carve 25 slave states from a conquered Mexico.

Fillmore, Millard (b. Locke, N.Y., 7 January 1800; d. Buffalo, N.Y., 8 March 1874) In 1823 Fillmore opened a law office. He entered politics in the ANTI-MASONIC PARTY, but joined the WHIG PARTY in 1834. He supported Henry CLAY while in Congress (1833–43), and drafted the TARIFF OF 1842. He lost a race for N.Y. governor in 1844, then ran as Zachary TAYLOR's vice-president in 1848. Taylor's death made Fillmore president on 9 July 1850. He backed Clay's COMPROMISE OF 1850, tried to enforce the unpopular FUGITIVE SLAVE ACT (1850), and sent Matthew PERRY to open trade with Japan. Denied renomination in 1852, Fillmore ran as president with the KNOW-NOTHING PARTY in 1856, when he polled 21.6 percent of the popular vote but carried only Md.

Finney, Charles Grandison (b. Warren, Conn., 29 August 1792; d. Oberlin, Ohio, 16 August 1875) In 1821, while a lawyer at Adams, N.Y. (in the BURNED-OVER DISTRICT), Finney had a spiritual reawakening that led him to become a licensed Presbyterian preacher in 1823. He emerged as his era's most innovative, successful, and famous revivalist by preaching along the ERIE CANAL (1826–31), but he also pioneered the use of camp meeting techniques in urban settings. He took the lead in modifying American Calvinism by discrediting predestination and arguing for universal salvation. In 1835 he became professor of theology at Oberlin College.

fire-eaters These were southern politicians like Edmund Ruffin of Va., Robert Rhett of S.C., and William Yancey of Ala., who helped panic the South into SECESSION by their fanaticism and rabid demagoguery. Their extremist rhetoric made them appear too unstable for office after the Confederacy was formed, and few held important positions during the CIVIL WAR.

Firefighters Local Union Number 1784* v. *Stotts On 12 June 1984, the Supreme Court ruled (5–4) that a seniority system calling for involuntary layoffs under the principle of "last hired, first fired," does not violate Title VII of the CIVIL RIGHTS ACT (1964), even if it has a disproportionate impact on minorities, so long as it was not adopted for discriminatory reasons.

fireside chats On 12 March 1933, Franklin D. ROOSEVELT spoke to an estimated 60,000,000 Americans about his BANK HOLIDAY in the first of 28 informal radio messages known as fireside chats. Roosevelt's gift for explaining his policies in everyday terms, and his engaging personality, made the chats exceptionally effective in winning public support for his policies. Polling surveys indicated that 25–40 percent of the public regularly heard his chats.

First Amendment Submitted to the states on 25 September 1789, last ratified by Va. on 15 December 1791, and officially proclaimed on 30 December 1791, it prohibited the federal government from preferring one church over another or interfering with the free exercise of religious beliefs. Freedom of speech, of assembly, of the press, and of petitioning were also protected. Its provisions were extended to state court proceedings by *GITLOW* v. *NEW YORK* (freedom of speech and press), *DE JONGE* v. *OREGON* (freedom of assembly and petition), *CANTWELL* v. *CONNECTICUT* (freedom of religion), and *EVERSON* v. *BOARD OF EDUCATION OF EWING TOWNSHIP* (separation of church and state).

The Supreme Court interpreted rights of assembly or association in *AMERICAN COMMUNICATIONS ASSN., CIO ET AL.* v. *DOUDS*, *NATIONAL ASSOCIATION FOR THE ADVANCEMENT OF COLORED PEOPLE* v. *ALABAMA EX REL. PATTERSON*, *SCALES* v. *UNITED STATES*, and *ELROD* v. *BURNS*. It ruled on freedom of press or speech in *SCHENCK* v. *UNITED STATES*, *LOVELL* v. *GRIFFIN*, *CHAPLINSKY* v. *NEW HAMPSHIRE*, *DENNIS ET AL.* v. *UNITED STATES*, *YATES* v. *UNITED STATES*, *NEW YORK TIMES* v. *SULLIVAN*, and *AMERICAN BOOKSELLERS ASSOCIATION* v. *HUDNUT*. It decided issues of religious liberty in *WEST VIRGINIA STATE BOARD OF EDUCATION* v. *BARNETTE*, *ENGEL* v. *VITALE*, and *LEMON* v. *KURTZMAN*.

first families of Virginia Custom defines this term as those families whose ancestors emerged as the wealthiest planters after 1650, and dominated Va. politics by 1725. These individuals formed an interrelated oligarchy that led the state in the Revolution and Civil War. Among the most prominent of these lineages are those of the Bland, Braxton, Byrd, Carter, Corbin, Fitzhugh, Harrison, Lee, Ludwell, Nelson, Randolph, Washington, and Wormley families.

First New Deal The NEW DEAL's first phase began with the HUNDRED DAYS and lasted through 1934's legislation. Its short-term goal was to provide relief and temporary work for the jobless while the GREAT DEPRESSION lasted. Its long-term objective was to restore prosperity by creating federal agencies to establish a proper balance among supply, demand, prices, and investment. The First New Deal attempted to replace unrestricted competition with a planned economy managed through voluntary cooperation by representatives from labor, business, and government. Its prototypical agencies were the AGRICULTURAL ADJUSTMENT ADMINISTRATION (AAA) and NATIONAL RECOVERY ADMINISTRATION (NRA), which used production quotas and industry-wide regulatory codes to set business standards, govern competition in each economic sector, and cap output to match supply with demand.

first party system This term refers to the emergence of the DEMOCRATIC and FEDERALIST PARTIES in the 1790s and their ensuing competition. This period ended in 1820, when the Federalists failed to nominate a candidate. After a period when the US had just one major political party, a SECOND PARTY SYSTEM evolved in the 1830s.

Fish, Hamilton (b. New York, N.Y., 3 August 1808; d. Garrison, N.Y., 6 September 1893) A lawyer who was elected N.Y. lieutenant governor in 1842, Fish was elected to the US Senate as a Whig in 1851. He became a Republican and left politics after 1860 until serving as secretary of state (1869–77) for Ulysses S. GRANT. His diplomatic accomplishments rank as that administration's only major achievements. Fish oversaw a resolution of the *ALABAMA* CLAIMS favorable to the US. He dissuaded Grant from a scheme to annex the Dominican Republic. During the Cuban Revolution, he resisted pressure from the press, Congress, and Grant that the US adopt unwise measures that could have led to an unnecessary war with Spain. He was also Grant's most honest and statesmanlike advisor on domestic questions, and helped persuade the president to dismiss several corrupt associates.

Fisk, Clinton Bowen (b. New York, N.Y., 8 December 1828; d. New York, N.Y., 9 July 1890) Bankrupted by the PANIC OF 1857, Fisk left Mich. for St Louis. Previously acquainted with Abraham LINCOLN and Ulysses S. GRANT, he rose to major general in the CIVIL WAR. Appointed to the FREEDMEN'S BUREAU, he commandeered a deserted military barrack in 1866 and created Fisk University within a year. He chaired the Board of Indian Commissioners (1881–90). In 1888 he received 2.2 percent of the popular vote as the PROHIBITION PARTY's presidential nominee.

Fisk, James, Jr. *see* BLACK FRIDAY

Fiske* v. *Kansas *see* *GITLOW* v. *NEW YORK*

Fitch, John (b. Windsor, Conn., 21 January 1743; d. Bardstown, Ky., 2 July 1798) An inventor who demonstrated the first successful steamboat, the *Perseverance*, at Philadelphia on 22 August 1787, he operated the vessel commercially on the Delaware River, but his venture went bankrupt. After a series of business failures and personal frustrations, he killed himself by an opium overdose.

Fitzgerald, Francis Scott (Key) (b. St Paul, Minn., 24 September 1896; d. Hollywood, Calif., 21 December 1940) A Princeton man (1917) who performed army duty in World War I, Fitzgerald published his first novel, *This Side of Paradise*, in 1920 and won critical acclaim. He became one of the most prominent authors of the LOST GENERATION. His dysfunctional marriage to Zelda Sayre steadily degenerated from glamor and mirthmaking to alcoholism and mental despair. His other major books were *The Beautiful and the Damned* (1922), *The Great Gatsby* (1925), *Tender is the Night* (1933), and *The Crack-Up* (1936). He ended his career as a film writer.

five civilized tribes This term refers to the CHEROKEE, CHOCTAW, CHICKASAW, CREEK, and SEMINOLE INDIANS of the southeast, who were less nomadic than most Indians, often lived in large towns, and incorporated black SLAVERY into their society.

Five Forks-White Oak Road, battle of (Va.) On 30 March–1 April 1865, Major General Philip SHERIDAN's 26,000 Federals defeated Major General George Pickett's 11,000 Confederates near Dinwiddie Court House. CSA losses: 5,200 captured. The victory broke CSA railroad connections between Richmond and General Robert E. LEE, who was forced to retreat from PETERSBURG to APPOMATTOX COURT HOUSE.

Five Nations This term was a synonym for the IROQUOIS CONFEDERACY before it incorporated the TUSCARORA INDIANS.

Flathead Indians Speakers of one of the SALISH LANGUAGES, the Flatheads lived in the Bitterroot Mountains of Idaho and Mont. Extensive contact with whites began with the LEWIS AND CLARK EXPEDITION. The Flatheads never warred against the US, welcomed missionaries, and settled on a reservation at Dixon, Mont., by the 1880s.

Fletcher–Rayburn Act *see* FEDERAL SECURITIES ACT (1933)

Fletcher* v. *Peck In 1810 the Supreme Court unanimously ruled that in 1796 the Ga. legislature had improperly repealed a 1795 law vesting vacant lands in the Yazoo Land Co. (*see* YAZOO LAND CLAIMS). Although the Court knew that the Yazoo Land Co. had used bribery and corruption to obtain the land, it held that a land grant was a contract, and that Ga.'s nullification violated the Constitution, which forbade states from impairing the obligation of contracts (Article I, Section 10). This decision marked the first time that the Court struck down a state law as inconsistent with the Constitution itself, rather than for being incompatible with a federal treaty or statute. By clarifying that Article I, Section 10 protected not only private contracts, but also public contracts such as land grants and acts of incorporation, this ruling (along with *DARTMOUTH COLLEGE* v. *WOODWARD*) made it more difficult for states to regulate businesses with state charters.

flexible response *see* MASSIVE RETALIATION

Florida Spaniards founded ST AUGUSTINE, the first white settlement in the US, and established the FLORIDA MISSIONS. Fla. was a battleground in QUEEN ANNE'S WAR, the ANGLO-SPANISH WAR of 1727–8, and the war of JENKINS' EAR. Britain acquired it by the treaty of PARIS (1763) and organized the colonies of EAST and WEST FLORIDA, but returned them to Spain after the REVOLUTIONARY WAR, in which Fla. was the site of 21 military actions on land and five at sea. The US annexed West Florida in the WAR OF 1812, invaded East Florida in the first SEMINOLE WAR, and acquired the territory by the ADAMS–ONIS TREATY. It was the site of the second and third SEMINOLE WARS.

It grew slowly and did not enter the Union until 3 March 1845. By 1860, it was the 30th state in size and had 140,424 people, of whom 44 percent were slaves and 2 percent were foreign-born; it ranked 31st in the value of its farmland and livestock and 34th in manufactures. Fla. became the third CSA state on 10 January 1861. In the CIVIL WAR, it furnished 10 CSA regiments of infantry, 2 of cavalry, and 6 artillery batteries. It also provided 2,334 USA soldiers (1,290 white and 1,044 black). It was the site of 168 military actions.

In July 1865, Andrew JOHNSON instituted

a provisional civilian government, which abolished slavery, but refused to let FREEDMEN vote, enacted a strict black code (*see* BLACK CODES), and rejected the FOURTEENTH AMENDMENT. Washington imposed military rule on 2 March 1867, but restored self-government and congressional representation on 25 June 1868. Republican control ended eight-and-a-half years later on 2 January 1877. Fla. disfranchised most blacks by POLL TAX, and then legislated racial SEGREGATION.

In 1900 it had 528,542 residents, of whom 80 percent were rural, 44 percent were black, and 4 percent were foreign-born. It then ranked 32nd among the states in population, 42nd in the value of its agricultural goods, and 39th in manufactures.

Fla. development accelerated rapidly in the early 1920s. Growth was heavy around Miami, St Petersburg, Tampa, Sarasota, and Coral Gables. Out-of-state investors created an overextended real-estate boom by bidding up land prices to unrealistic levels. The bubble burst on 18 September 1926 when a hurricane killed 400 people, left 50,000 homeless, precipitated a tidal wave of bankruptcies and municipal-bond defaults, and deflated the state economy.

It grew rapidly from 1950 to 1970 and gained 3,520,000 in-migrants. It maintained separate-but-equal schools until 1964, when federal judges began forcing compliance with court-ordered integration, and all county education systems had instituted desegregation plans – half of them voluntarily – by 1970. Fla. was the major destination for CUBAN and HAITIAN IMMIGRATION. It was the fourth-largest state in 1990, with 12,937,926 people (approx. 73 percent white, 13 percent black, 12 percent Hispanic, 1 percent Asian), of whom 91 percent were urban and 12.8 percent foreign-born. Manufacturing employed 19 percent of workers.

Florida missions Catholic missionary efforts began in Spanish Fla. under Fr Alonso de Reynoso in 1577, but made little progress until Fr Juan de Silva assumed direction in 1595. A chain of missions was established north of ST AUGUSTINE into southeastern Ga., but all were eventually abandoned except for two south of the St Mary's River. A second center of activity lay around, and east of, Apalachee Bay, where nine missions were founded from 1606 to 1655. Missionaries had their greatest success along the Apalachicola River, where they founded 38 missions (many staffed by itinerant priests) and won 26,000 converts by 1655. The missions were plundered and most of their inhabitants enslaved by English–CREEK INDIAN forces in QUEEN ANNE'S WAR.

flower power *see* HIPPIES

Floyd, John (b. Floyd Station, Ky., 24 April 1783; d. Christianburg, Va., 16 August 1837) Born two weeks after his father was killed by Indians, Floyd served in the WAR OF 1812 and established a medical practice in Montgomery County, Va. While in Congress as a Democrat (1817–28), he repeatedly sponsored legislation for the US to occupy and organize the OREGON Territory. He served as Va. governor (1831–4). Because neither major candidate for president in 1832 – Andrew JACKSON or Henry CLAY – was acceptable to S.C., its legislature cast its 11 electoral votes for Floyd.

Flying Tigers Organized in December 1940 as a unit of 100 civilian pilots under Claire Chennault (the American Volunteer Group–Chinese Air Force), the "Flying Tigers" supported Chiang Kai-shek's forces against the Japanese. They received credit for shooting down 297 enemy planes and 150 probable kills, at a loss of 14 planes in combat until 4 July 1942, when the unit was expanded to become the 24th Control Unit, 14th Army Air Force. The Flying Tigers destroyed 2,303 Japanese planes and claimed another 772 probable kills.

Food and Drug Administration (FDA) To enforce the MEAT INSPECTION ACT and the PURE FOOD AND DRUG ACT, the Food, Drug, and Insecticide Administration was established on 18 January 1927 under the Department of AGRICULTURE. It was renamed the Food and Drug Administration on 27 May 1930. It came under the Federal Security Agency on 30 June 1940, and under the Department of HEALTH, EDUCATION, AND WELFARE on 11 April 1953.

Food, Drug, and Cosmetic Act (24 June 1938) Following the death of over 100 persons in October 1937 from internal damage caused by sulfanilamide, a Massengill Co.

drug, Congress replaced the PURE FOOD AND DRUG ACT (1906) with this law. It demanded strictly accurate labeling of ingredients in processed foods and drugs. It forbade false or misleading advertising about the effectiveness of drugs, and required that a product's effectiveness be demonstrated before it could be sold. It allowed the FOOD AND DRUG ADMINISTRATION (FDA) to set legally enforceable nutritional and sanitary standards for food. The FDA assumed responsibility for ensuring drug effectiveness and content labeling, while the FEDERAL TRADE COMMISSION enforced provisions concerning unfair trade practices and false advertising. Its provisions still form the core of federal policy to safeguard consumers from dangerous products. It was amended by the DELANEY CLAUSE.

Food for Peace The AGRICULTURAL TRADE AND DEVELOPMENT ACT was the forerunner of this program, which made surplus commodities available to foreign nations on easy terms or gratis for three years. It was repeatedly extended, placed under the AGENCY FOR INTERNATIONAL DEVELOPMENT in 1961, and revised by the Food for Peace Act (11 November 1966). During its initial two decades, most shipments went to South Korea, South Vietnam, Egypt, India, Pakistan, Turkey, Israel, Indonesia, and Brazil. In 1974, when 70 percent of all commodities went to South Vietnam and Cambodia, Congress required that 75 percent of all aid go to nations with per capita incomes under $300. Through 1990, it has sent $43 billion of food abroad.

food stamps The earliest food stamp plan was adopted in the NEW DEAL and first tried at Rochester, N.Y., on 16 May 1939; it allowed the stamps' purchasers to receive surplus agricultural stocks worth 150 percent of their stamp purchases from the Federal Surplus Commodities Corporation. The plan operated in over 100 cities by late 1940, but ended with WORLD WAR II rationing. After the GREAT SOCIETY enacted the Food Stamp Act (1964), food stamps became the most widely used federal welfare program and reached $10.2 billion by 1982. By 1994, 26,000,000 Americans in 11,000,000 households (10 percent of the population) received $24 billion in food stamps, of which the SECRET SERVICE estimated $2 billion were obtained fraudulently.

Foraker Act *see* PUERTO RICO

Force Act (1833) *see* NULLIFICATION CRISIS

Force Act, first (31 May 1870) To enforce the FIFTEENTH AMENDMENT, Congress provided stiff punishments for interfering with the right of FREEDMEN to vote, outlawed conspiracies to intimidate voters, and authorized the army to enforce these measures. *EX PARTE YARBROUGH* and *UNITED STATES* v. *MOSLEY* upheld the statute, but *UNITED STATES* v. *REESE* limited its provisions to federal elections. After the Democrats won control of Congress in 1879, they attempted to nullify this law by a rider to the Army Appropriations Act (1880), but Rutherford HAYES's veto of 29 April killed the rider.

Force Act, second (28 February 1871) Congress augmented the first FORCE ACT by authorizing federal supervision of congressional elections in cities with populations exceeding 20,000. The Supreme Court declared parts of it unconstitutional in *UNITED STATES* v. *HARRIS* (1883). After the Democrats won control of Congress in 1879, they tried to nullify this law by a rider to the Army Appropriations Act (1880), but Rutherford HAYES's veto of 29 April killed the rider.

Force Act, third (1871) *see* KU KLUX KLAN ACT

Force Bill On 2 July 1890, the House of Representatives passed this measure authorizing federal officials to oversee national elections to protect the right of blacks to vote, but it was never adopted by the Senate, in which Democrats were just two votes short of a majority.

Ford, Gerald Rudolph (b. Omaha, Nebr., 14 July 1913) Born Leslie King and then adopted by his stepfather, Ford was raised in Grand Rapids, Mich. He opened a law practice at Grand Rapids in 1941, served in the navy (1941–6) as lieutenant commander, and in 1948 became a Republican congressman. He was elected Republican minority leader in the House (1965–73), and took Spiro AGNEW's place as vice-president on 6 December 1973. He became president on 9 August 1974 when Richard NIXON resigned.

He nominated Nelson ROCKEFELLER as his own vice-president. Ford ordered a major show of US military force in the *MAYAGUEZ* INCIDENT. His popularity never recovered from pardoning Nixon (8 September 1974), which prevented any prosecutions for his WATERGATE SCANDAL actions, and he lost the 1976 election to Jimmy CARTER, who outpolled him by 50.1 percent to 48.0 percent, and won by 57 electoral votes in a close race.

Ford, Henry (b. near Dearborn, Mich., 30 July 1863; d. Dearborn, Mich., 7 April 1947) His classroom education ended when he was 15, and he was apprenticed to a machine shop. By 1893, he had assembled an operational two-cylinder, four-horsepower gasoline-fueled car. Unlike other automobile manufacturers, who did low-volume business making custom-crafted cars, Ford saw the possibility of mass-producing a standard vehicle for middle-class consumers. In 1903 he founded the Ford Motor Co., and in 1909 he introduced the first large-scale application of assembly-line operations to put out his Model-T. Besides sparking a revolution in factory efficiency with the assembly line and making the AUTOMOBILE affordable to average workers, Ford adopted the eight-hour workday and paid higher wages than the industry average. He turned the company over to his son Edsel in 1919, a year after he introduced installment buying, which made the auto affordable to most Americans.

Fordney–McCumber Tariff (21 September 1922) This law continued the Republican program of protectionism. It raised rates on industrial goods 26 percent above those of the PAYNE–ALDRICH TARIFF and set higher levies on farm goods than those of the EMERGENCY TARIFF ACT (1921). It allowed the president to approve recommendations by the Tariff Commission for rate changes up to 50 percent of congressional duties. By excluding large quantities of European farm, chemical, and manufactured items, it raised domestic prices and provoked about 60 nations to retaliate with higher tariffs on US goods through 1928.

Forrest, Edwin (b. Philadelphia, Pa., 9 March 1806; d. Philadelphia, Pa., 12 December 1872) In 1820 Forrest played his first professional role in Philadelphia. After six years of acting on the road, he premiered in New York as Othello, a role that started his rapid rise as the foremost American interpreter of Shakespearean tragedy. When Forrest first toured Europe in 1834, he became the first native of America to receive international renown as a great actor.

Forrest, Nathan Bedford (b. Chapel Hill, Tenn., 13 July 1821; d. Memphis, Tenn., 29 October 1877) He was a self-made man who rose to prominence in Memphis, raised a Confederate cavalry battalion at his own expense, and rose to major general. A self-taught strategist and the South's best guerrilla fighter, he nearly forced William T. SHERMAN to withdraw from Atlanta by disrupting Union supply lines. He had 30 mounts shot from under him and personally killed 31 enemy soldiers. After the war, he was the imperial wizard of the KU KLUX KLAN.

Forrestal, James Vincent (b. Beacon, N.Y., 15 February 1892; d. Bethesda, Md., 22 May 1949) A Princeton man (1915) who served in the navy during World War I, Forrestal became president of a Wall Street brokerage firm by 1937. He became under secretary of the navy in 1940, and was promoted to secretary in 1944. He was the earliest cabinet officer to recognize the danger of postwar Soviet expansion, and influenced CONTAINMENT POLICY and the MARSHALL PLAN. He opposed merging all armed forces under one military command, because he believed it would create a huge bureaucracy unresponsive to civilian control, and would be dominated by the army and air force to the detriment of the navy and marines, but was appointed first secretary of the Department of DEFENSE in September 1947. Intra-service rivalries, which sometimes verged on insubordination, undermined his attempts to bring order to the Department of Defense, and resulted in merciless criticism of Forrestal from prominent journalists. Suffering from nervous exhaustion and deep depression, he was fired in March 1949 and committed suicide that October while hospitalized.

Fort Dearborn, massacre at (Ill.) Under orders to withdraw to FORT DETROIT, Captain Nathan Heald evacuated his 57 troops at Chicago on 15 August 1812. Five hundred POTAWATOMI INDIANS, who had promised Heald safe conduct, attacked his force on Lake Michigan, accepted their surrender, and then treacherously killed most of them, including 29 soldiers, 11 adult civilians, and 12 children.

Fort Detroit, battles of (1) On 7 May 1763, Pontiac's 1,600 Indians began besieging Major Henry Gladwin's 145 redcoats at Fort Detroit. By 29 July, Gladwin received 315 reinforcements. Pontiac ended the siege on 12 October. British losses: about 73 killed, 42 wounded. Indian losses: about 80–90 killed. Detroit was the only post beyond FORT PITT not taken by Pontiac; its resistance sapped the Indians' will to keep fighting and denied them victory in PONTIAC'S WAR.

(2) On 16 August 1812, without having fired a shot in defense, Brigadier General William Hull surrendered the fort, 300 US regulars, and 1,500 Ohio militia to Major General Isaac Brock's 300 regulars, 400 Canadian militia, and 600 Indians. The British held the post until 18 September 1813. Hull was sentenced to death for cowardice by court-martial in 1814, but was pardoned.

Fort Donnelson, battle of (Tenn.) On 6 February 1862, Brigadier General Ulysses S. GRANT's 15,000 Federals (supported by four navy gunboats) took Brigadier General Lloyd Tilghman's garrison, most of which had gone to FORT HENRY to avoid capture. USA losses: none. CSA losses: 5 killed, 11 wounded, 63 captured. The victory opened the Tennessee River to US naval operations and forced the retreat of General Albert JOHNSTON's 26,000 Confederate troops from Ky.

Fort Duquesne (Pa.) In March 1754, 40 Virginians began erecting Trent's Fort at the forks of the Ohio, but withdrew on 16 April with the arrival of 600 French, who then built Fort Duquesne. Britain's first effort to take Duquesne failed at BRADDOCK'S DEFEAT. Facing certain capture by approaching British forces, Duquesne's 200 French defenders blew up the fort on 24 November 1758, and Brigadier General John Forbes occupied it the next day with 2,500 redcoats and colonials. The British rebuilt the post as FORT PITT.

Fort Erie, battles of (Ontario) (1) On 28 November 1812, 400 US forces failed to take Fort Erie, whose artillery barred Brigadier General Alexander Symth's 3,000 US forces from invading Canada by the Niagara River near Buffalo. On 1 December Smyth canceled the attack and called off the invasion. British losses: 17 killed, 57 wounded, 56 missing.

(2) The US capture of FORT GEORGE forced British troops to evacuate Fort Erie on 27 May 1813; US troops held the post until Britain's victory at STONY CREEK dictated its abandonment on 9 June.

(3) On 3 July 1814, Major General Jacob Brown's 3,500 US regulars and militia took the garrison and 165 prisoners without loss of life. After LUNDY'S LANE, Brown retreated to Fort Erie and held it with 2,125 troops. Lieutenant General George Drummond began besieging the post on 2 August, and made a vain frontal assault on 15 August in which he lost 57 killed, 307 wounded, and 538 missing, while US losses were 26 killed, 92 wounded, and 11 missing. On 17 September, a sortie by 1,600 US troops destroyed two-thirds of Drummond's artillery and inflicted 609 British casualties at a loss of 511 killed or wounded. On 21 September, Drummond withdrew. On 5 November, US forces evacuated the post and left Canadian soil.

Fort Frontenac, battle of (Ontario) On 27 August 1758, Lieutenant Colonel John Bradstreet's 3,765 colonials captured France's main logistical base for its forts on the Great Lakes (now Kingston, Ontario). British losses: 14 wounded. French losses: 110 prisoners, 60 cannon, 16 mortars, 8 ships (of 8 to 18 guns), and supplies worth £70,000.

Fort George, battles of (Ontario) On 27 May 1813, Major General Henry Dearborn's 4,000 US troops invaded Canada From FORT NIAGARA, N.Y., and captured Fort George (under US artillery fire since 24 May) from Brigadier General John Vincent's 1,900 troops, who escaped capture. US losses: 40 killed, 100 wounded. British losses: 50 killed, 500 wounded, 200 missing. The fort's fall allowed five warships trapped in the Niagara River to reinforce Oliver H. PERRY at the battle of LAKE ERIE. On 10 December, Vincent retook the post from Brigadier General Samuel McClure's N.Y. militia.

Fort Henry, battle of (Tenn.) On 12 February 1862, Brigadier General Simon BUCKNER surrendered his garrison to Ulysses S. GRANT's 27,000 Federals. USA losses: 500 killed, 2,108 wounded, 224 missing. CSA losses: 2,000 killed or wounded, 14,623 captured. The siege was Grant's first major victory; it forced the Confederates to abandon Nashville and give up much of central Tenn.

Fort Jackson, treaty of To end the CREEK WAR, that tribe agreed, on 9 August 1814, to give up its lands west of the Coosa and north of the Alabama rivers, about 34,375 square miles opened to white settlement. The treaty punished all Creeks, including many who had fought as US allies. Had the Creeks held out until December, the treaty of GHENT would have required the US to refrain from using armed force to demand any territory from them.

Fort Laramie, 1st treaty of (Wyo.) On 17 September 1851 the United States agreed to pay $50,000 in trade goods for 50 years to all Plains nations that permitted white people to travel along the OREGON TRAIL. To establish accountability for any attacks on whites, the treaty required all Indian signatories to declare the boundaries of their territory and stay within them. The treaty ended US policy of seeing the Great Plains as an all-inclusive RESERVATION, over which its original tribes would have unrestricted freedom to roam. Congress refused to give compensation for more than 15 years.

Fort Laramie, 2nd treaty of (Wyo.) On 6 November 1868, the second SIOUX WAR ended when Red Cloud signed this treaty, by which the US agreed to evacuate army forts on the BOZEMAN TRAIL. The treaty recognized specific Sioux land rights in Wyo., Mont., Nebr., and the Dakotas.

Fort Lee, battle of (N.J.) Following the fall of FORT WASHINGTON, Major General Charles CORNWALLIS moved to seize Fort Lee, which sat on the opposite bank of the Hudson River, but he could not advance quickly enough to keep Brigadier General Nathanael GREENE's garrison of 2,000 from evacuating the post before he arrived. On 18 November 1776, the British took 300 tents, 1,000 barrels of flour, 50 cannon, and 160 US stragglers.

Fort McHenry, battle of (Md.) On 13–14 September 1814, Major George Armistead's 1,000 troops at Fort McHenry withstood a 10-hour bombardment of 1,500 artillery rounds (of which 400 hit the fort) by Admiral Alexander Cochrane's British fleet. US losses: 4 killed, 24 wounded. Armistead's defense prevented Cochrane from providing the naval support needed by the British army to capture Baltimore, and inspired Francis Scott Key to compose "The Star-spangled Banner."

Fort Meigs, battle of (Ohio) On 1 May 1813, Brigadier General Henry Proctor's 450 British and 475 Canadians, with TECUMSEH's 1,200 Indians, began besieging Major General William H. HARRISON's garrison of 550 troops. On 5 May a relief force of 1,200 Ky. militia attacked the British batteries and suffered two-thirds casualties; just 400 reached Harrison's lines. On 9 May, Proctor raised the siege. US losses: 108 killed, 25 wounded, 700 captured (including 250 wounded). British losses: 15 killed, 47 wounded, 47 captured. On 20 July Proctor's 2,500 regulars and Tecumseh's 2,000 Indians resumed the siege of the post, held by Brigadier General Green Clay's 400 Ky. militia, but withdrew on 28 July. Proctor's failure at Fort Meigs, after his defeat at FORT STEPHENSON, ended his offensive against US forces in Ohio and Indiana.

Fort Miamis (Ohio) In 1785 British forces rebuilt a former French trading post on the Maumee River on US soil (near Toledo) as a base for encouraging Indian resistance to American settlers. Two miles from the site of the battle of FALLEN TIMBERS, its garrison coexisted in uneasy tension with US troops at nearby Fort Defiance from August 1794 until 11 July 1796, when US troops took peaceful possession. The British returned to Canada to comply with JAY'S TREATY.

Fort Mims, battle of (Ala.) On 30 August 1813, William Weatherford's 750 CREEK INDIANS destroyed the post held by Major Daniel Beasley's 170 Mississippi Territory militia and 250 civilians. US losses: 247 bodies of men, women, children found on battlefield, and about 150 captured. Creek losses: 100 killed, many wounded. The battle outraged Americans and inaugurated the CREEK WAR.

Fort Necessity, battle of (Pa.) On 3 July 1754, 900 French and Indians under Coulon de Villiers besieged Colonel George WASHINGTON's 300 Virginians and 100 redcoats at Fort Necessity, 65 miles from FORT DUQUESNE. Washington surrendered on 4 July and was allowed to march back to Va. under arms. British losses: 30 killed, 70 wounded. The battle inaugurated the SEVEN YEARS' WAR.

Fort Niagara, battles of (N.Y.) (1) On 7 July 1759, Brigadier General John Prideaux's 2,200 British and colonials commenced besieging Fort Niagara, under Captain François Pouchot. Prideaux was killed and Sir William JOHNSON assumed command. On 25 July 1759, a relief force of 700 French and 900 Indians under François de Ligneris was almost annihilated. Pouchot surrendered Fort Niagara that night. Pouchot's losses: 109 killed and wounded, 486 captured. De Ligneris's losses: 250 killed, 220 captured. British losses: 60 killed, 118 wounded.

(2) On 18 December 1813, Lieutenant Colonel Christopher Hamilton's 560 British regulars stormed the fort, then under Captain Nathaniel Leonard. US losses: 67 killed, 356 captured (including 12 wounded). British losses: 6 killed, 5 wounded. The British held Fort Niagara to the end of the war.

Fort Ontario, treaty of *see* OSWEGO, TREATY OF

Fort Pitt (Pa.) After French evacuation of FORT DUQUESNE, colonial troops built Mercer's Fort at Pittsburgh between December 1758 and July 1759. British engineers replaced this wooden stockade with Fort Pitt, a stone fortification enclosed by a moat. During PONTIAC'S WAR, Captain Simeon Ecuyer's redcoats and militia held off 900 Indians for 19 days after 22 June. The Indians then fled after the battle of BUSHY RUN. The British army abandoned Fort Pitt in 1772.

Fort Recovery, battle of (Ohio) On 29 June 1794, Little Turtle and Blue Jacket's 2,000 Indians attacked a supply convoy leaving the post and besieged Captain Alexander Gibson's 150 men, but took heavy casualties and retreated a day later. US losses: 22 killed, 30 wounded. Fort Recovery was the first significant US victory after ST CLAIR'S DEFEAT; it demoralized the Indians threatening Anthony WAYNE and led many to desert before the battle of FALLEN TIMBERS.

Fort Ross (Calif.) In 1812 the Russian-American Co. founded Fort Ross (Fort Russia) about 60 miles north of San Francisco. The post's purpose was to grow food for Russia's ALASKA colony, and serve as a base for hunting local sea otter. After the sea otters were overhunted and relations worsened with Mexican authorities, the Russians sold the post to John SUTTER in 1841 and left.

Fort San Fernando de Barrancas (Tenn.) In the spring of 1795, Spanish troops under Don Manuel Gayoso de Lemos occupied US territory and fortified modern Memphis. In 1797, to comply with the treaty of SAN LORENZO, Spanish troops burned the fort and departed to Fort Esperanza, Ark., immediately across the Mississippi River. US troops occupied the site on 20 July and built Fort Adams.

Fort St Frederic (N.Y.) *see* CROWN POINT

Fort Stanwix, battle of (N.Y.) On 2 August 1777, Lieutenant Colonel Barry St Leger's 2,000 British, Tories, and Iroquois placed Colonel Peter Gansevoort's 750 Continentals under siege. After being deserted by his Indians, who were discouraged by heavy battle casualties at ORISKANY, St Leger retreated to Fort Oswego on 23 August. US losses: 3 killed, 9 wounded. By holding Stanwix, Gansevoort prevented St Leger from reinforcing Major General John Burgoyne's army and contributed to Burgoyne's surrender at SARATOGA.

Fort Stanwix, first treaty of (N.Y.) On 5 November 1768, the IROQUOIS CONFEDERACY and their dependent tribes (DELAWARE and eastern SHAWNEE INDIANS) sold their claims to all lands south of the Ohio River as far west as the Tennessee River for trade goods worth £10,460.7.3 sterling. The Iroquois were hoping to deflect white settlement from their own lands and into this territory, where no Indians then lived.

Fort Stanwix, second treaty of (N.Y.) On 23 October 1784, in order to end the state of war which had continued since the REVOLUTIONARY WAR, the IROQUOIS CONFEDERACY ceded their claims to all their lands in Pa. (about 18,000 square miles) to that state.

Fort Stephenson, battle of (Ohio) On 1 August 1813, Major George Croghan's 160 Ky. militia and one cannon repulsed attacks by Brigadier General Henry Proctor's 385 British regulars, supported by 3 cannon, several gunboats on the Maumee River, and several hundred Indians under TECUMSEH. US losses: minor. British losses: 150 killed and wounded. Croghan's victory led numerous Indians to desert Proctor and compelled British forces to withdraw from Ohio.

Fort Sumter, battles of (S.C.) The Civil War began at 4:30 a.m., 12 April 1861, when Brigadier General Pierre Beauregard's CSA artillery began bombarding Major Robert Anderson's garrison. After 34 hours, Anderson surrendered. USA losses: 2 killed, 1 wounded, 76 captured. CSA losses: none. The loss galvanized northern support for the war. USA attacks on the fort were repulsed on 7 April and 8 September 1863.

Fort Ticonderoga, battles of (N.Y.) (1) On 6–8 July 1758, General Montcalm's 3,500 French repulsed an assault by Major General James Abercrombie's 6,300 redcoats and 5,900 colonials. British losses: 464 redcoats and 87 colonials killed, 1,117 redcoats and 240 colonials wounded; 29 redcoats and 8 colonials captured. French losses: 106 killed and 266 wounded.

(2) On 10 May 1775, 83 Yankees under Ethan ALLEN and Benedict ARNOLD scaled Fort Ticonderoga's walls at night and forced Captain William Delaplace to surrender. US losses: 1 wounded. British losses: 48 men captured, plus 78 serviceable cannon, 6 mortars, 3 howitzers, 30,000 musket flints, and miscellaneous ammunition. In January, Colonel Henry KNOX transported the artillery to Boston, where its firepower enabled Washington to drive British troops from the city.

(3) On 5 July 1777, after three days under attack, Major General Arthur St Clair's 2,500 Americans abandoned the fort to Major General John Burgoyne's 9,500 troops. Ticonderoga's loss raised British morale, but the escape of a large garrison and its artillery helped lead to Burgoyne's surrender at SARATOGA.

Fort Toronto, battle of (Canada) On 27 April 1813, Brigadier General Zebulon Pike's 1,700 US troops forced Major General Roger Sheaffe's 800 British defenders to retreat from Fort Toronto, whose powder magazine exploded, killing Pike and many US troops. US losses: 52 killed, 180 wounded. British losses: 62 killed, 34 wounded, 50 missing. By looting homes in York (modern Toronto) and burning two parliament houses and the governor's mansion on 30 April, US troops inspired the British to take revenge by burning Washington, D.C. (*see* DISTRICT OF COLUMBIA), in 1814. US forces abandoned York on 8 May.

Fort Washington, battle of (N.Y.) On 16 November 1776, General William HOWE's 8,000 redcoats and HESSIANS captured the last important US fortification east of Hudson River. US losses: 54 killed, 2,858 captured (including 100 wounded), 146 cannon, 2,800 muskets, 12,000 shot and shell, and 400,000 cartridges. British losses: 67 killed, 335 wounded, 6 missing. The garrison's loss forced Washington to abandon FORT LEE., N.J. (opposite Fort Washington), on 20 November. The loss of these posts compelled Washington to abandon efforts to recapture New York City and begin retreating across N.J.

Fort William Henry, battle of (N.Y.) On 3 August 1757, the Marquis de Montcalm's 6,200 French and 1,800 Indians commenced besieging Lieutenant Colonel George Monro's 970 redcoats and 1,400 provincials, who surrendered on 9 August. British losses: 60 killed, 2,308 captured (including 60 wounded). French losses: 5 killed, 18 wounded. Montcalm paroled the British on promise that they not fight for 18 months, but on 10 August Indians attacked them as they marched home; they seized 129 redcoats and 400 colonials, of whom 69–185 were either killed that day or died as prisoners. The French ransomed the rest. Arguing that the massacre nullified the terms of the capitulation, the paroled British units returned to combat.

Fortas, Abe (b. Memphis, Tenn., 19 June 1910; d. Washington, D.C., 5 April 1982) He worked in agencies of the NEW DEAL as a lawyer and became under secretary of the interior. He defeated a legal challenge to Lyndon JOHNSON's 1948 Senate victory. Johnson named Fortas to the Supreme Court in 1965, and nominated him as chief justice in 1968. Johnson had to withdraw his name when the press revealed that Fortas had improperly augmented his judicial income by teaching law courses and had accepted – and already returned – funds from a charitable foundation controlled by individuals under indictment for securities fraud. Amid partisan calls for his impeachment, Fortas resigned from the Supreme Court in May.

forty acres and a mule In 1865 Senator Charles SUMNER and Representative George Julian of the RADICAL REPUBLICANS recommended granting FREEDMEN 40-acre farms from lands taken from rebels under the Confiscation Act (1862) (*see* ABOLITIONISM). The proposal fanned a rumor among ex-slaves that they would receive "40 acres and a mule," and this rumor soon swept the South, although it had little support in Congress or from any president. The FREEDMEN'S BUREAU auctioned off much acreage acquired by military confiscation, however, and from 1866 to 1872, Congress extended the first HOMESTEAD ACT to the PUBLIC DOMAIN in former CSA states so that blacks could claim land at minimal expense.

Forty-eighters This term described Germans dissatisfied with the political repression that followed the abortive Revolution of 1848, who emigrated to the US. Carl SCHURZ exemplified the liberal, idealistic, public-spirited character of this group.

Forty-niners This term described the prospectors who flocked to the CALIFORNIA GOLD RUSH in its first year. About 55,000 came via the CALIFORNIA TRAIL or the southern route from Tex. About 25,000 arrived by ship from the east or Europe. Some 8,000 Mexicans and 5,000 South Americans also came. Over half the adult males in Oreg. went to Calif. Perhaps 250,000 miners had reached the gold fields by 1855.

Foster, Stephen Collins (b. Allegheny City, Pa., 4 July 1826; d. New York, N.Y., 13 January 1864) He briefly attended Jefferson College. His first songs were published in Cincinnati as part of *Songs of the Sable Harmonists* (1848). He then began composing full-time, and became the first American to make a living entirely by writing music. Although originally intended for performance in minstrel shows, his ballads and songs possessed such charming harmony and melody that they have endeared themselves to succeeding generations. Foster's most popular songs included "O Susanna" (1848), "De Camptown Races" (1850), "Swanee River" (1851), "Massa's in de Cold, Cold Ground" (1852), "My Old Kentucky Home" (1853), "Jeannie With the Light Brown Hair" (1854), and "Old Black Joe" (1860).

Foster* v. *Neilson In 1829 the Supreme Court refused, without dissent, jurisdiction over a boundary dispute concerning territory claimed by both the US and Spain; the Court held that it was prevented from becoming involved in essentially political questions by the Constitution's separation of powers. (*see* *RHODE ISLAND* v. *MASSACHUSETTS* on the Court's authority over interstate boundaries)

four freedoms On 6 January 1941, Franklin D. ROOSEVELT justified Lend Lease (*see* LEND LEASE ACT) as a program intended to provide international support for the "four freedoms": freedom of worship and speech, and freedom from fear and want. The ATLANTIC CHARTER committed Anglo-American foreign policy to this goal.

Four-Minute Men *see* COMMITTEE ON PUBLIC INFORMATION

Four Power Treaty Signed on 13 December 1921 at the WASHINGTON NAVAL CONFERENCE, this pact obligated the US, Britain, France, and Germany to honor each other's Pacific island possessions and submit any disputes to negotiation. In 1935 Japan renounced the treaty, and US bases on GUAM, WAKE ISLAND, the PHILIPPINES, and PEARL HARBOR could no longer assume that they were exempt from Japanese attack.

Fourierism Frenchman Charles Fourier (1772–1837) outlined this utopian theory of cooperative living, which was popularized in the US by Albert Brisbane's *Social Destiny of Man* (1840). Fourierists divided themselves into phalanxes, self-supporting communities of 1,500. All crops and handicrafts produced became the phalanx's collective property, but private property and inheritance were retained. Over 40 phalanxes were founded, with at least one in every northern state, but few in the South. The most famous phalanx was BROOK FARM.

Fourteen Points On 8 January 1918, Woodrow WILSON made these proposals as the basis for restoring peace after WORLD WAR I: (1) a treaty consisting of "open covenants of peace, openly arrived at"; (2)

freedom of the seas; (3) free trade; (4) disarmament by victors and vanquished; (5) impartial adjustment of disputed claims concerning European colonies; (6) withdrawal of foreign armies from Russia; (7) restoration of Belgian sovereignty; (8) restoration of Alsace-Lorraine to France; (9) redrawing Italy's borders to include all Italians; (10) self-determination for ethnic minorities within Austria-Hungary; (11) foreign evacuation from Montenegro, Romania, and Serbia, plus Serbian access to seaports; (12) self-determination for the Ottoman empire's ethnic minorities; (13) Polish independence; and (14) formation of a "LEAGUE OF NATIONS."

Fourteenth Amendment Submitted to the states on 13 June 1866, last ratified on 9 July 1868, and officially proclaimed on 18 July 1868, it overturned *DRED SCOTT* v. *SANDFORD*'s ruling that blacks were not US citizens, guaranteed them rights of DUE PROCESS and equal protection under the law, and forbade states to violate any of their privileges as citizens. It also disqualified from federal office any former state or federal official who violated his oath to uphold the Constitution by engaging in rebellion, and it forbade ex-CSA states from honoring their war debts. The Supreme Court made the provisions to protect black civil rights ineffective in the SLAUGHTERHOUSE CASES, *UNITED STATES* v. *CRUIKSHANK*, CIVIL RIGHTS CASES, and *PLESSY* v. *FERGUSON*. After *SANTA CLARA COUNTY* v. *SOUTHERN PACIFIC RAILROAD COMPANY* interpreted its due process clause to include corporations as legal persons, TRUSTS exploited the amendment to frustrate state efforts to end anticompetitive practices (*see SMYTH* v. *AMES*) and improve workplace conditions (*see ALLGEYER* v. *LOUISIANA*).

Beginning with *CHICAGO, BURLINGTON AND QUINCY RAILROAD* v. *CHICAGO*, the Fourteenth Amendment's due process clause extended the BILL OF RIGHTS to state court proceedings. It conferred rights of due process and equal protection under the laws to resident aliens in *YICK WO* v. *HOPKINS*. It accorded constitutional protection to sexual autonomy and marriage in *SKINNER* v. *OKLAHOMA* and *LOVING* v. *VIRGINIA*. It required state legislatures to redistrict according to "one man, one vote" in *REYNOLDS* v. *SIMS*. It directed that legal classifications based on gender be justified as furthering a significant government purpose in *CRAIG* v. *BOREN*.

Fourth Amendment Submitted to the states on 25 September 1789, last ratified by Va. on 15 Dec. 1791, and officially proclaimed on 30 December 1791, it prohibited unreasonable searches and seizures, and it required that warrants be issued only upon probable cause and for specific purposes. Its provisions were extended to state court proceedings by *MAPP* v. *OHIO*. Other major rulings include *WEEKS* v. *UNITED STATES* and *KATZ* v. *UNITED STATES*.

Fox, George *see* QUAKERS

Fox Indians Speakers of one of the ALGONQUIAN LANGUAGES, the Mesquakies were misnamed Foxes by French explorers who mistook a clan name for the group's full title. They may have numbered 3,000 about 1650, when they lived east of the Mississippi around Lake Michigan. The Foxes cooperated closely with the SAUK INDIANS, but the two never merged. In April 1712, Foxes and Sauks went to war with the French by attacking Fort Ponchartrain (Detroit), but were defeated and resettled in Iowa. About 2,000 Foxes lived in eastern Iowa about 1800. Because a small Fox faction joined in the BLACK HAWK WAR, they ceded all their lands 50 miles west of the Mississippi in 1832. They eventually sold all their lands in Iowa and moved to Kans. in 1845. They now have reservation headquarters at Horton, Kans., and Shawnee, Okla.

France, undeclared war with JAY'S TREATY severely strained US relations with France. France refused to accept Ambassador Charles C. PINCKNEY's credentials in December 1797, and demanded a forced loan from US diplomats in the XYZ AFFAIR. From May 1796 to March 1797, French seamen captured 316 US merchant ships, and took 134 more by February 1799, for a total of $12,000,000 in seizures. On 16 July 1798, Congress authorized the army's expansion from 4,101 to 12,660 (its strength totaled only 7,600 by January 1800). On 3 May 1798, it established the Department of the NAVY, which had outfitted 14 men-of-war (484 guns) and commissioned 200 PRIVATEERS by January 1799 to carry out armed neutrality against French aggression. While

Britain's navy convoyed American ships to Europe, the US Navy protected shipping in the Caribbean. From 7 July 1798 to 1 October 1800, the US Navy captured 94 privateers (10 in 1798, 26 in 1799, 58 in 1800), and lost only one ship (14 guns). The CONVENTION OF 1800 ended this "quasi-war."

Franco-American Alliance (6 February 1778) The British surrender at SARATOGA, N.Y., convinced Louis XVI to sign two treaties with the US. The first treaty recognized US independence and provided for commercial relations. The second treaty was a secret agreement to be made public if war erupted between France and Britain; it provided for military cooperation against Britain and created a perpetual defensive alliance between the US and France. The secret treaty went into effect after an engagement between British and French ships on 17 June 1778. (France never made a formal declaration of war.) The CONVENTION OF 1800 abrogated the treaty of alliance.

Frank* v. *Mangum *see MOORE* v. *DEMPSEY*

Frankfurter, Felix (b. Vienna, Austria, 15 November 1882; d. Washington, D.C., 22 February 1962) In 1894 Frankfurter emigrated to the US, and in 1906 earned a law degree from Harvard, where he taught (1914–39). He declined appointment to the Mass. Supreme Court in 1932, and to be US solicitor general in 1933, but accepted a seat on the US Supreme Court in 1939. To remove any doubts of his own impartiality, he then resigned from the AMERICAN CIVIL LIBERTIES UNION (although a founding member) and the NATIONAL ASSOCIATION FOR THE ADVANCEMENT OF COLORED PEOPLE. Although long a defender of individual rights, Frankfurter argued – in such cases as *WEST VIRGINIA STATE BOARD OF EDUCATION* v. *BARNETTE* and *DENNIS ET AL.* v. *UNITED STATES* – that the exercise of personal freedom was not absolute, but must be balanced against the state's legitimate right to protect society and to demand that all persons fulfill the legal obligations of their citizenship when required for the public good.

Franklin In August 1784, a convention at Jonesboro voted to seek recognition as a state for the east Tennessee area, which it named in honor of Benjamin FRANKLIN. Congress rejected the proposal on 24 August. Despite opposition from N.C., which had title to the area, efforts to establish Franklin continued until 1790, when the US placed the area under the Southwest Territory's jurisdiction.

Franklin, Benjamin (b. Boston, Mass., 17 January 1706; d. Philadelphia, Pa., 17 April 1790) He began life as a printer's apprentice in Boston and in 1723 relocated to Philadelphia, where he became wealthy publishing the *Pennsylvania Gazette*, *Poor Richard's Almanac*, and government documents. He helped found numerous civic improvements (like the American Philosophical Society), emerged as a leader of the Pa. assembly, and shared a joint commission as colonial postmaster general (1753–74). He co-authored the ALBANY PLAN OF UNION. While residing in England (1757–74), he represented Pa., Ga., and Mass. as a lobbyist, was the most notable colonist to explain American opposition to the STAMP ACT before Parliament, and exposed the HUTCHINSON LETTERS. He signed the DECLARATION OF INDEPENDENCE, was first US postmaster general, and ambassador to France. His greatest achievement was negotiating the FRANCO-AMERICAN ALLIANCE. His final public service was at the CONSTITUTIONAL CONVENTION.

Franklin, battle of (Tenn.) On 30 November 1864, Major General John Schofield's 27,900 Federals repulsed six charges by Brigadier General John Hood's 26,900 Confederates. USA losses: 189 killed, 1,033 wounded, 1,104 missing. CSA losses: 1,750 killed (including 5 generals), 3,800 wounded, 702 missing. Defeat left Hood too weak to retake NASHVILLE, where his army was shattered on 16 December.

Frazier–Lemke Farm Bankruptcy Act (28 June 1934) This law amended the Bankruptcy Act by delaying foreclosure on insolvent farmers for five years, during which they might either agree to buy back the property at its currently appraised value over six years at 1 percent interest, or remain in possession as a paying tenant if the mortgagor did not agree to sell. The law was struck down as violating the FIFTH AMENDMENT in *Louisville Joint Stock Land Bank* v. *Radford* (May 1935). In its place, Congress passed the FARM MORTGAGE MORATORIUM ACT.

Fredericksburg, battle of (Va.) On 11–13 December 1862, General Robert E. LEE's 72,500 Confederates repulsed six charges by Major General Ambrose Burnside's 114,000 Federals. USA losses: 1,284 killed, 9,600 wounded, 1,769 missing. CSA losses: 595 killed, 4,061 wounded, 653 missing.

free silver controversy *see* SILVER COINAGE CONTROVERSY

Free-Soil party This party was formed in the aftermath of the WILMOT PROVISO by northern Democrats and Whigs to protest the refusal of the major parties to take positions on SLAVERY in the territories; it was not organized to promote ABOLITIONISM. In 1848 its ticket was Martin VAN BUREN and Henry Dodge (Wis.), who carried no states, but won 10.1 percent of ballots, and it siphoned enough votes from Democrat Lewis CASS to throw the election to Zachary TAYLOR. In 1852 Free-Soil nominees John P. HALE (N.H.) and George W. Julian (Ind.) attracted just 5 percent of the vote. Most Free-Soilers supported the Republicans in 1856.

free-speech movement *see* BERKELEY FREE-SPEECH MOVEMENT

freedmen This word became a synonym for ex-slaves after 1863.

Freedmen's Bureau Officially named the Bureau of Refugees, FREEDMEN, and Abandoned Lands (of the War Department), Congress established this agency on 3 March 1865. Andrew JOHNSON vetoed an act to give the bureau jurisdiction to try cases in which blacks were denied equal protection under the law, but on 16 July 1866, Congress enacted the measure over a second Johnson veto. The agency mainly provided humanitarian aid, legal protection for labor contracts, and education. Under Major General Oliver Howard, the bureau issued 21,000,000 rations (5,000,000 to whites) during 1865–9, spent $2,000,000 to operate 46 hospitals and treat 450,000 patients, and built 4,329 schools at which 247,333 pupils were enrolled in 1870. The agency was phased out from 1869 to 1872.

Freedom of Information Act (July 1966) This law required that federal agencies make their records publicly available for citizen requests (except materials concerning national security, law enforcement investigations, trade secrets, and confidential business reports filed with regulators). Because bureaucrats devised stratagems to frustrate the implementation of the law, Congress strengthened it in November 1974 by setting penalties for unjustifiable refusal to provide materials, by forcing officials to justify withholding documents from public access, and by allowing federal judges to declassify files. The law was supplemented by the Privacy Act (1974), which obliged US agencies to provide individuals with any information collected on them and to amend incorrect data.

freedom riders A nonviolent, civil disobedience tactic used to protest SEGREGATION of public accommodations, freedom riding was initiated by the CONGRESS OF RACIAL EQUALITY (CORE) during the CIVIL RIGHTS MOVEMENT. (In 1960 *BOYNTON* V. *VIRGINIA* had ruled that bus facilities for interstate travelers could not be segregated.) The first freedom ride began on 4 May 1961, when CORE sent seven blacks and six whites by bus to test equal access to services at bus terminals from Washington, D.C., to New Orleans. The CORE riders were beaten by Ala. mobs in Anniston and Birmingham and then reinforced by volunteers from the STUDENT NONVIOLENT COORDINATING COMMITTEE; both groups were attacked in Montgomery and then arrested, along with Ralph ABERNATHY. On 22 September 1961, the Interstate Commerce Commission banned interstate buses from using segregated terminals. News coverage of the first, and subsequent, freedom rides, which encountered ugly hostility from whites, was a major factor in creating a national consensus to pass the CIVIL RIGHTS ACT (1964), which outlawed segregation in public facilities.

freeman In the Tudor-Stuart period, this term referred to a stockholder in a business venture (i.e. one who was "free of the corporation" and could vote in its affairs). In colonial New England, *freeman* was a synonym for an adult male qualified to vote.

Freeman's Farm, first battle of On 19 September 1777, Major General John Burgoyne's 4,400 troops failed to dislodge Major General Horatio Gates's 7,000 Continentals from fortified positions on Bemis Heights. US losses: 65 killed, 218 wounded, 36 missing. British losses: 556 killed, wounded, captured.

Freeman's Farm, second battle of *see* BEMIS HEIGHTS, BATTLE OF

Freeport Doctrine On 27 August 1858, at Freeport, Ill., during the LINCOLN–DOUGLAS DEBATES, Stephen DOUGLAS stated that although *DRED SCOTT* V. *SANDFORD* extended SLAVERY to the territories, free-soil settlers might prevent its establishment by refusing to enact a territorial SLAVE CODE to protect masters from lawsuits for assault and manslaughter. The proposition reassured northerners but outraged southerners, who demanded it be nullified by the DAVIS RESOLUTIONS. The doctrine ruined Douglas's chances of winning southern support for his presidential candidacy in 1860.

Frémont, John Charles (b. Savannah, Ga., 31 January 1813; d. New York, N.Y., 13 July 1890) After becoming a second Lieutenant of army engineers in 1838, Frémont earned a reputation as "the Pathfinder" by mapping routes across the Rocky Mountains. In 1846 he arrived in Calif., where he played a leading role in establishing US authority during the MEXICAN WAR. He resigned from the army in 1848 and served as senator from Calif. (1853–4). As the REPUBLICAN PARTY's first presidential candidate in 1856, he received 33.1 percent of the popular vote. In the CIVIL WAR, as a major general with orders to hold Mo. for the Union, he attempted to free the slaves by proclamation under martial law, but was countermanded from Washington and finally relieved on 2 November 1861 for lack of military success. Reassigned to command USA forces in W.Va., he was defeated in the first of the SHENANDOAH VALLEY CAMPAIGNS and again relieved on 28 June 1862. He never again held a command. He declined an offer from RADICAL REPUBLICANS to run for president in 1864. He became a western railroad entrepreneur after the war and governor of Ariz. (1878–81).

French and Indian War *see* SEVEN YEARS' WAR

French immigration From 1820 to 1991, just 791,565 French came to the US. Most Americans of French descent are derived from HUGUENOTS, ACADIANS and other colonists of French LOUISIANA, or the approximately 1,300,000 French-speaking Canadians who entered the US after 1820. The 1990 census reported 6,194,501 persons who described their primary ethnic identity as French, 3 percent of all whites.

Frenchtown, battle of (Mich.) *see* RIVER RAISIN, BATTLE OF

Freneau, Philip Morin (b. New York, N.Y., 2 January 1752; d. near Middletown Point, N.J., 18 December 1832) The Revolutionary era's major poet, Freneau's work included "The Beauties of Santa Cruz" (1776), "The House of Night" (1779), "Eutaw Springs" (1781), "The British Prison Ship" (1781), "To a Wild Honeysuckle" (1786), and "The Indian Burying Ground" (1788). His poetry expressed 18th-century concepts of the ENLIGHTENMENT and JEFFERSONIAN DEMOCRACY. He edited the first post-Revolutionary political newspaper, the *National Gazette* (1791–3) for Thomas JEFFERSON and James MADISON.

Freylinghausen, Rev. Theodore *see* REFRESHINGS

Frick, Henry Clay (b. West Overton, Pa., 19 December 1849; d. New York, N.Y., 2 December 1919) An entrepreneur who rose to be a millionaire through the coal business by 1880, Frick then became a steel executive and rose to be chairman of Carnegie Steel Co. While directing its response to the HOMESTEAD STRIKE, in which there were 10 deaths, Frick himself was shot. In 1901 he and J. P. MORGAN bought out Andrew CARNEGIE and organized the United States Steel Corp., the country's largest holding company, and Frick became president.

Friedan, Betty *see FEMININE MYSTIQUE, THE*

Fries' Rebellion While collecting a federal property tax passed on 14 July 1798 to raise money for expanding the army, US marshals sparked widespread resistance in northeast Pa. The main leader was John Fries, a minor militia officer who released several prisoners jailed for nonpayment of taxes at Bethlehem in 1799. The protests dissolved peacefully when US dragoons arrested Fries, who was sentenced to death for treason, but pardoned by John ADAMS.

Frost, Robert (b. San Francisco, Calif., 26 March 1875; d. Boston, Mass., 29 January 1963) He spent his early life in San Francisco, matured in Lawrence, Mass., and briefly studied at Dartmouth and Harvard. In

1912, he decided to move to England and write full-time. His *A Boy's Will* (1913) brought him critical acclaim, as did *North of Boston* (1914). He returned to New England in 1915. Beginning with *New Hampshire: A Poem with Notes and Grace Notes* (1923), he won four Pulitzer prizes (also *Collected Poems*, 1931, *A Further Range*, 1937, and *A Witness Tree*, 1943). Over forty universities, including Oxford and Cambridge, awarded him honorary degrees for his verse, which is marked by simplicity of expression and subtlety of meanings.

Frothingham* v. *Mellon *see* *Massachusetts* v. *Mellon*

FSA *see* Farm Security Administration

FSLIC Federal Savings and Loan Insurance Corporation (*see* Federal Home Loan Bank Board).

FTC *see* Federal Trade Commission

Fugitive Slave Act, first (12 February 1793) This law allowed slaveowners, or their agents, to demand warrants from federal or state magistrates to return alleged runaways to their home state. Although slaves were not entitled to protection under the Bill of Rights, the law failed to guarantee rights under the Fifth and Sixth Amendments to free blacks wrongly arrested as slaves. Despite this fundamental denial of rights to black citizens, the Supreme Court upheld the law in *Prigg* v. *Pennsylvania*.

Fugitive Slave Act, second (18 September 1850) Passed as part of the Compromise of 1850, this law provided such ironclad guarantees for slaveowners to reclaim their property, that it eliminated any protection under the Bill of Rights for free blacks wrongly brought before US commissioners as slaves. No more proof of ownership was required at a hearing than the alleged owner's affidavit, and the accused had no right to testify or produce witnesses in his behalf. US commissioners gave summary verdicts without juries and received a fee of $10 for upholding the master's claim, but only $5 if the accused were declared a free person. Law officers who refused to serve warrants on suspected slaves, or who allowed arrestees to escape by negligence, could be fined up to $1,000. Citizens who helped arrestees escape faced $1,000 fines and six months in jail. *Abelman* v. *Booth* upheld the law and struck down personal liberty laws intended to frustrate its operation.

Fuller, Melville Weston (b. Augusta, Maine, 11 February 1833; d. Sorrento, Maine, 4 July 1910) He opened a law office in Chicago, managed Stephen Douglas's 1858 Senate campaign, and sat in the Ill. legislature (1863–4). He became enormously rich and built close ties with big business as an attorney for large corporations. He had never held federal office when nominated as seventh chief justice, and was described as the most obscure man named to that office. Confirmed on 20 July 1888, Fuller later helped arbitrate the British Guiana–Venezuela border dispute and sat on the Permanent Court of Arbitration at The Hague. His most important opinions were *United States* v. *E. C. Knight Company*, *California* v. *Southern Pacific company*, *Pollock* v. *Farmer's Loan and Trust company*, and *Loewe* v. *Lawler*.

Fuller, (Sarah) Margaret (b. Cambridgeport, Mass., 23 May 1810; d. off Fire Island, N.Y., 19 July 1850) She was the early 19th century's most influential female intellectual, co-editing the *Dial*, Transcendentalism's leading journal (1840–2). Although she declined Horace Greeley's offer to join his staff at the New York *Tribune*, she wrote as its literary critic (1844–6) during which time she wrote *Woman in the Nineteenth Century* (1845) and *Literature and Art* (1846). While traveling in Italy, she wed Marquis Angelo Ossoli (becoming Marchioness Ossoli) and participated in Mazzini's Roman Revolution. She and her family drowned in a shipwreck on their return to the US.

Fullilove* v. *Klutznik On 2 July 1980, the Supreme Court ruled (6–3) that Congress could enact limited, affirmative-action racial quotas in a 1977 law that reserved 10 percent of public works funds for minority contractors in order to redress past discrimination. It held that the Fourteenth Amendment's equal protection clause would allow special treatment to compensate for extreme denial of rights.

Fulton, Robert (b. Fulton, Pa., 14 November 1765; d. New York, N.Y., 24 February 1815) From 1786 to 1805, Fulton pursued a career as a civil engineer and inventor in France and England, where he designed improved canal locks, aqueducts, bridge trestles, and a torpedo-carrying submarine. He built the *Clermont*, a boat with two paddle wheels powered by a steam engine, and sailed it from New York to Albany during 17–21 August 1807. Although John FITCH had already demonstrated the first operational steamboat, Fulton was the earliest entrepreneur to produce commercially successful, steam-propelled vessels and organize profitable steamboat enterprises.

Fundamental Constitutions of Carolina On 11 March 1669, the PROPRIETORS OF CAROLINA issued this document, drafted by John Locke and Anthony Ashley Cooper, as a plan for establishing the colony's social and political order. It envisioned dividing the land into counties of 480,000 acres, of which each proprietor would hold 12,000 acres as a seigniory, two caciques would each receive 24,000 acres as a barony, four landgraves would each receive 12,000 acres as a barony, and 60 percent (288,000 acres) would be organized as colonies, in which most land would be held by small freeholders, but manors of 3,000–12,000 acres could also be established. Each seigniory, barony, and manor would have its own court with the owner as judge. The oldest resident proprietor would be governor. Other proprietors would form a Palatine Court, held in England or Carolina, that would appoint officials, approve or disallow laws, and hear appeals from the colonists. The resident proprietors and deputies of absentee proprietors would form a Grand Council that would recommend all bills considered by the assembly. The assembly would consist of all resident proprietors, deputies appointed by absentee proprietors, all caciques and landgraves, and a freeholder elected for each of a colony's four precincts. Voters were required to own 50 acres and assemblymen had to own 500 acres. Freedom of religion was guaranteed and officeholders faced no religious tests, but a revision of 1670 would have established the Church of England. The Carolina legislatures refused to enact the Constitutions.

Fundamental Orders of Connecticut On 24 January 1639, the towns of Hartford, Windsor, and Wethersfield united to organize the colony of Conn. by establishing a legislature and court system by this frame of government. It remained in effect until Conn. became a CHARTER COLONY in 1662.

fur trade This trade dominated the economies of early NEW NETHERLAND and NEW SWEDEN, and to a lesser extent PLYMOUTH. It also served as the major motivation for exploring the American interior. The greatest demand was for beaver, which made highly durable and water-resistant hats. By the 1660s, few beaver remained within the THIRTEEN COLONIES, and the best trapping grounds lay near the Great Lakes. French COUREURS DE BOIS ensured that the greatest volume of furs would be sold at Montreal, but only after a failed IROQUOIS CONFEDERACY attempt to dominate the trade in the BEAVER WARS. Albany, N.Y., was the capital of the Dutch-English fur trade, and furs composed about 20 percent of N.Y.'s exports in the period 1700–55. The deerskin trade grew steadily in S.C., and by 1770 the value of this export from the thirteen colonies exceeded that of beaver pelts.

Fur exports from the thirteen colonies fell sharply after the SEVEN YEARS' WAR, except for deerskins. The US fur trade did not revive until the 1820s under John Jacob ASTOR and William ASHLEY. Ashley revolutionized the industry by organizing it around brigades of "mountain men" who wintered in the Rockies and rendezvoused at a central location with their caches. This period was the only phase of the fur trade in which trapping was primarily done by whites rather than Indians. Furs accounted for about 1 percent of US exports about 1830. The substitution of silk for beaver in hats destroyed the trade after 1835, and the last rendezvous was held in 1840. The last phase of the skin trade involved the BUFFALO.

Furman* v. *Georgia (decided with *Jackson* v. *Georgia* and *Branch* v. *Texas*) On 29 June 1972, the Supreme Court voted (5–4) to nullify all state death penalties; it ruled that the wide range of discretion given to judges and juries made capital punishment a capricious sentence that violated DUE PROCESS. The Court clarified *Furman* in *GREGG* v. *GEORGIA*.

FWA *see* FEDERAL WORKS AGENCY

G

Gabriel's Conspiracy *see* PROSSER'S CONSPIRACY

Gadsden Purchase On 30 December 1853, James Gadsden obtained Mexican assent for the sale to the US of 29,640 square miles south of the Gila River in Ariz. and N.Mex., at a price of $15,000,000. The US wanted the area as a route for a TRANSCONTINENTAL RAILROAD, but northern opposition to this southern route blocked ratification by the Senate until 29 June 1854. The US reduced the price to $10,000,000, which Mexico accepted because its treasury was bankrupt.

Gag Rule On 26 May 1836, the House of Representatives resolved (117–68) to table all petitions concerning ABOLITIONISM without entering them in its journal or referring them to any committee. It also resolved that Congress had no power to interfere with SLAVERY where it was lawful (182–9) and that it would be inappropriate to interfere with slavery in the DISTRICT OF COLUMBIA (132–45). (The Senate simultaneously adopted this practice, but without a formal vote.) Despite its infringement of FIRST AMENDMENT rights, the Gag Rule was renewed at every session until rescinded on 3 December 1844.

Gage, Thomas (b. Firle, Sussex, England, ca. 1721; d. Portland, England, 2 April 1787) In 1740 Gage entered the Royal Army. In the SEVEN YEARS' WAR, he was wounded at BRADDOCK'S DEFEAT and FORT TICONDEROGA (1758). He raised a royal regiment of American colonists (the 80th), married a N.J. girl in 1758, and was noted for his pro-American sympathies throughout his career. He directed operations in PONTIAC'S WAR and was commander in chief of British forces in North America after 1763, with headquarters at New York City, before returning to England in 1773. He was reappointed commander in chief in America, and made Mass. governor in April 1774. He showed little vigor in suppressing rebellion after LEXINGTON and CONCORD, was replaced by William HOWE in October 1775, and saw no more action.

Gaines's Mill, battle of *see* PENINSULAR CAMPAIGN

Galbraith, John K. *see* *AFFLUENT SOCIETY, THE*

Gallatin, (Abraham Alfonse) Albert (b. Geneva, Switzerland, 29 January 1761; d. Astoria, N.Y., 12 August 1849) In 1780 Gallatin immigrated to the US, settled in western Pa., and became active in the DEMOCRATIC PARTY. He was elected to the US Senate in 1793, but was declared ineligible to serve for having been a US citizen less than nine years. While in Congress (1795–1801), he became minority leader of the Democratic Party and its chief expert on finance. As treasury secretary (1801–14), Gallatin laid down the fiscal policies associated with JEFFERSONIAN DEMOCRACY: eliminating waste from the domestic budget, financing the government by excise taxes and customs duties rather than internal taxes, and steady reductions in the NATIONAL DEBT by sales of the PUBLIC DOMAIN. Gallatin cut the national debt from $83,000,000 in 1801 to $57,000,000 by 1809, despite financing the cost of the war with the BARBARY PIRATES and the LOUISIANA PURCHASE. He helped negotiate the treaty of GHENT and served as ambassador to France (1816–23) and Britain (1826–7).

Galloway, Joseph (b. Anne Arundel County, Md., ca. 1731; d. Watford, England, 29 August 1803) He was a Philadelphia lawyer who sat in the Pa. assembly (1756–76, except for 1764–6), allied with Benjamin FRANKLIN to change Pa. from a

PROPRIETARY to a ROYAL COLONY, and was speaker of the Pa. assembly (1766–76). One of the few colonials to support the STAMP ACT and American representation in Parliament, he proposed the GALLOWAY PLAN OF UNION. He became a Tory in the Revolution (*see* TORIES), was British administrator of Philadelphia (1777–8), and in 1779 went into lifetime exile.

Galloway Plan of Union At the first CONTINENTAL CONGRESS, Joseph GALLOWAY drafted this constitutional compromise to protect the political rights of the THIRTEEN COLONIES in the British Empire. He proposed the creation of a Grand Council, to which all colonies would elect delegates every three years, and a governor general, who would be appointed by the crown as its executive representative. The Grand Council could legislate on matters concerning more than one colony, but its ordinances would require Parliament's approval to be lawful (save in wartime); it would likewise possess a veto over any parliamentary statutes concerning North America. Congress rejected the plan of union on 28 September 1774 by a vote of 6–5.

Galveston Plan *see* CITY COMMISSION GOVERNMENT

GAR *see* GRAND ARMY OF THE REPUBLIC

Garfield, James Abram (b. Cuyahoga County, Ohio, 19 November 1831; d. Elberon, N.J., 19 September 1881) He rose from humble origins to become a lawyer, college president, and Ohio state senator. In the CIVIL WAR, he rose to USA major general before becoming a Republican congressman in 1863. Although tarnished by the CREDIT MOBILIER SCANDAL, he displaced James G. BLAINE as the leading Republican contender for president in 1880. He won the presidency with 48.5 percent of the popular vote, a margin of just 39,213 ballots. His assassination by Charles J. Guiteau, who was embittered at not having received a political patronage job, sparked the PENDLETON ACT's passage.

Garland, Hamlin (b. West Salem, Wis., 14 September 1860; d. Los Angeles, Calif., 4 March 1940) He matured on farms in Wis. and Iowa, and briefly farmed in N.Dak. before becoming a professional writer in 1884. He authored the best accounts of agricultural life in the midwest during the era of POPULISM. His best known works are *Main-Traveled Roads* (1887), *Son of the Middle Border* (1917), and *Daughter of the Middle Border* (1917), which won the Pulitzer prize. He was a director of the American Academy of Arts and Letters.

Garner, John Nance (b. Red River County, Tex., 22 November 1868; d. Ulvade, Tex., 7 November 1967) A Tex. lawyer, Garner entered Congress in 1902, became Democratic minority leader in 1920, and speaker of the House in 1931. His support was critical in Franklin D. ROOSEVELT's presidential nomination in 1932 and he was made vice-presidential candidate. He was renominated as vice-president in 1936, but broke with Roosevelt, unsuccessfully sought the Democratic nomination for president in 1940, and was replaced by Henry WALLACE. He then retired to Tex.

Garner et al.* v. *Louisiana *see* SIT-IN MOVEMENT

Garner* v. *Board of Public Works On 4 June 1951, the Supreme Court ruled (5–4) that civil servants can be made to take loyalty oaths as a condition of employment without violating DUE PROCESS or enacting an EX POST FACTO LAW or BILL OF ATTAINDER.

Garnett's Farm, battle of *see* PENINSULAR CAMPAIGN

Garrison, William Lloyd (b. Newburyport, Mass., 10 December 1805; d. New York, N.Y., 24 May 1879) Apprenticed at the age of 13 to the Newburyport *Herald*'s editor, Garrison founded his own paper in 1826 and moved to Boston in 1828 when it failed. On 1 January 1831, he founded the *LIBERATOR* and began his crusade for ABOLITIONISM. He helped found the New England Antislavery Society in 1831 and the American Antislavery Society in 1835. On 21 October 1835, a proslavery mob attacked and beat him severely. He advocated that northern states leave the Union rather than have any complicity in SLAVERY's preservation, and in 1854 he burned a copy of the Constitution on Independence Day. He only gave wholehearted support to the Union war effort after the EMANCIPATION PROCLAMATION. His fanatical antislavery beliefs coexisted with a condescending attitude toward African-Americans, and he closed the *Liberator* upon the THIRTEENTH AMENDMENT's ratification in 1865 rather than continue the struggle for racial justice by fighting to win full civil rights for blacks.

Garvey, Marcus Mosiah (b. St Anne's Bay, Jamaica, 17 August 1887; d. London, England, 10 June 1940) In 1914 Garvey founded the Universal Negro Improvement Association (UNIA) as an international organization to foster self-help and racial pride among blacks. He hoped to lead blacks from the Americas to Africa and expel European colonial powers forcibly with a Universal African Legion. In 1916 he came to the US on a speaking tour and by 1919 had at least 500,000 followers in 700 chapters of the UNIA. Garvey disdained leaders of the NATIONAL ASSOCIATION FOR THE ADVANCEMENT OF COLORED PEOPLE (NAACP) like W. E. B. DU BOIS, who were equally contemptuous of him. Between 1919 and 1921, Garvey collected $10,000,000 from his followers, but was convicted in 1923 of fraudulently diverting $1,000,000 to his steamship company. He ran his movement from prison during 1925–7 and was then deported. His "back to Africa" movement soon died out.

***Gaspee*, HMS, incident** Operating under the AMERICAN BOARD OF CUSTOMS ACT, Lieutenant William Dudingston's revenue schooner *Gaspee* had aroused widespread hatred in Narragansett Bay by improperly seizing cargoes for technical violations of the NAVIGATION ACTS and the SUGAR ACT, abusive behavior toward mariners, and various trespasses and thefts on land. After the ship ran aground near Providence on 9 June 1772, eight boatloads of local men boarded it, wounded Dudingston, removed the crew, and burned it to the waterline. Efforts by the British government to identify the perpetrators were futile.

GATT *see* GENERAL AGREEMENT ON TARIFFS AND TRADE

GDP *see* GROSS DOMESTIC PRODUCT.

Gemini Space Program *see* APOLLO PROGRAM

General Accounting Office *see* BUDGET AND ACCOUNTING ACT

General Agreement on Tariffs and Trade (GATT) On 30 October 1947, at Geneva, 28 countries negotiated the GATT Treaty (effective from 1 June 1948) to stimulate the postwar economy by reviving international trade. By 1951, GATT had sponsored three rounds of tariff reductions that cut average US import duties from over 50 percent to about 15 percent. The KENNEDY ROUND (1962–7) accomplished especially steep cuts. Since then, four additional rounds of tariff reductions have been made, concluding with the URUGUAY ROUND, in which the 111 member nations replaced GATT with the World Trade Organization.

General Convention of the Christian Church *see* CONGREGATIONAL CHURCH

General Court The MASSACHUSETTS BAY COMPANY charter allowed its overseas FREEMEN to govern themselves by an elective assembly termed the General Court. The first General Court met in 1630. In 1634 every town received the option of electing two delegates, provided they paid for their expenses. In 1644 the General Court became a BICAMERAL LEGISLATURE, divided between a House of Representatives (lower chamber) and Court of Assistants (upper chamber). The term General Court was no longer used after the 1780 Massachusetts Constitution.

General Services Administration (GSA) This agency was established on 1 July 1949 to oversee the financial and administrative services necessary for the US government's operation.

General Treaty of Peace and Amity Negotiated at the second Central American Peace Conference (4 December 1922–7 February 1923) to restore good relations between Nicaragua and Honduras, this treaty declared that diplomatic recognition should be denied to any Central American government that took power by revolution. It also established a regional court of justice and limited military forces.

Genêt, Citizen Edmond Charles (b. Versailles, France, 8 July 1763; d. Rensselaer County, N.Y., 15 July 1834) On 8 April 1793, Citizen Genêt, ambassador of France's revolutionary republic, landed at Charleston S.C., where he began outfitting privateers against British commerce. Despite the NEUTRALITY PROCLAMATION, Genêt continued enlisting Americans as privateers commissioned George Rogers CLARK to launch a land attack on New Orleans, tried to instigate an invasion of Fla., and became actively involved in US politics by encouraging partisan opposition to the Washington administration's policy of maintaining neutrality between France and Britain. (In retaliation for attacks by Genêt's privateers, Britain seized over 250 US ships trading with the French West Indies in early 1794.) On 2 August 1793, Washington's cabinet agreed to demand Genêt's recall, but France ordered him home in 1794 to answer charges after his political enemies came to power. Genêt received asylum in the US and became George CLINTON's son-in-law.

Gentlemen's Agreements *see* JAPANESE IMMIGRATION

Geofroy* v. *Riggs On 3 February 1890, the Supreme Court declared unanimously that the US could negotiate a treaty interfering with the property rights of aliens who stood to inherit land or other possessions; it held that the government's power to ratify treaties was limited by no constraints other than those mentioned explicitly in the Constitution. The Court extended this ruling's scope even further in *MISSOURI* v. *HOLLAND*.

George I (b. Osnabrück, Hanover, 28 March 1660; d. Osnabrück, Hanover, 11 June 1727) He ascended the throne in 1714, established the Hanover dynasty, and secured a Protestant succession for the Crown. He took little interest in his American colonies.

George II (b. Herrenhausen Castle, Hanover, 10 November 1683; d. Kensington Palace, Middlesex, England, 25 October 1760) He ascended the throne on 11 June 1727. During his reign were fought the wars of JENKINS' EAR and of the Austrian Succession (known in the colonies as KING GEORGE'S WAR). GEORGIA was named after him. He showed little interest in policies concerning the THIRTEEN COLONIES.

George III (b. Norfolk House, Westminster, England, 4 June 1738; d. Windsor Castle, England, 29 January 1820) He ascended the throne on 25 October 1760. Because his position as a constitutional monarch masked his support for Parliamentary taxation of the colonies, George III remained popular there until he began taking concrete actions such as refusing to accept the OLIVE BRANCH PETITION and proclaiming on 23 August 1775 that New England was in a state of rebellion. Not until Thomas PAINE's *COMMON SENSE* swayed most Americans to view him as a "royal brute," however, were the last ties of loyalty to the Crown dissolved and the final emotional barrier to independence removed.

George, Henry (b. Philadelphia, Pa., 2 September 1839; d. New York, N.Y., 29 October 1897) He ran away to sea at 13, mined for gold in the west, and became a journalist. In 1879 he published *Progress and Poverty*, which appeared in over 100 editions and may have been read by 6,000,000 persons worldwide through 1906. George blamed poverty on uneven division of land in the US. He proposed redressing the maldistribution of wealth by levying a single tax on land to offset the historic rise in real estate prices. He believed this solution would not only prevent wealth from being concentrated among a small elite, but also would promote upward mobility among the poor, who would not see their incomes siphoned off by excise, poll, or income taxes. George's book spawned a wave of single-tax societies throughout the US, but its most lasting impact was to persuade the PROGRESSIVE ERA's intellectuals that government action was needed to keep the rich from getting richer.

Georges Banks These banks are a submerged shelf several hundred feet deep east of Cape Cod, through which the Gulf Stream passes. Since the 1630s, the area has been a major mainstay of New England's fishing industry. By 1977, it had become so overfished that quotas on catches were adopted until 1982. On 26 October 1994, the New England Fishing Management Council recommended that fishing for cod, haddock, and yellowtail flounder be halted to allow the fish population to recover.

Georgia On 20 June 1732, GEORGE II issued a charter to 21 trustees, who were responsible for overseeing the colony of Ga. for 21 years. On 12 February 1733, James OGLETHORPE founded Savannah. The trustees planned to populate Ga. with parolees from British debtors' prisons and Protestant refugees from continental Europe, and also to create a large silk industry (without SLAVERY), but the colony languished under their direction. Ga. was a major battleground in the war of JENKINS' EAR. It became a ROYAL COLONY on 4 July 1752, when it had about 5,500 residents. Initially limited to 1,800 square miles bought from the CREEK INDIANS between 1733 and 1743, the area open to settlement grew by another 8,700 square miles during 1763–73 to include about 18 percent of modern Ga. After the legalization of slavery in 1750, Ga. became a major center of rice production and by 1775 its population was 33,000, including 15,000 slaves.

In the REVOLUTIONARY WAR, it was badly divided between WHIGS and TORIES. It furnished one of the 80 Continental regiments and was the site of 60 military actions. The British captured SAVANNAH in 1778 and occupied much of the state until 1782. Frontier expansion was slow because of opposition by the Creeks, especially under Alexander MCGILLIVRAY, but accelerated after 1800, when Creeks and CHEROKEE INDIANS sold large tracts. The final removal of Cherokees came in 1838–9. After the COTTON GIN's invention, cotton quickly displaced rice as the main export staple.

It was the 11th largest state in 1860 and had 1,057,286 people, of whom 44 percent were slaves and less than 1 percent were foreign-born; it ranked 13th among states in the value of its farmland and livestock and 20th in manufactures. Ga. became the fifth CSA state on 19 January 1861. In the CIVIL WAR, it furnished 120,000 CSA troops and 3,486 USA soldiers (all black). It was the site of 549 military actions. After the battles for ATLANTA, the MARCH TO THE SEA devastated Ga.

In July 1865, Andrew JOHNSON instituted a provisional civilian government, which abolished slavery, but denied FREEDMEN political rights and enacted a black code (*see* BLACK CODES). Washington imposed military rule on 2 March 1867, but restored congressional representation and self-government on 15 July 1870. Republican control ended a year later on 1 November 1871. Ga. disfranchised most blacks in 1908, and legislated a thorough system of racial SEGREGATION.

In 1900 it was the 11th largest state and had 2,216,331 people, of whom 84 percent were rural, 47 percent were black, and 1 percent were foreign-born; it ranked 17th among states in the value of its agricultural goods and 26th in manufactures. From 1920 to 1970, it lost 1,102,000 residents, mostly blacks moving to northern cities, and its racial composition shifted greatly. Despite widespread opposition to the CIVIL RIGHTS MOVEMENT, especially during the administration of Governor Lester Maddox (1967–71), it was the first deep-south state to integrate its schools peacefully, and made important progress in improving race relations after 1971 under Governor Jimmy CARTER. Ga. ranked as the 11th largest state in 1990, when its population was 6,478,216 (70 percent white, 27 percent black, 2 percent Hispanic, 1 percent Asian), of whom 65 percent were urban and 2.7 percent were foreign-born. Manufacturing and mining employed 26 percent of the work force.

Georgia Platform On 10 December 1850, at Milledgeville, a Ga. convention passed resolutions criticizing the COMPROMISE OF 1850, and hinting that secession would be justified if Congress ever weakened the second FUGITIVE SLAVE ACT, abolished SLAVERY in the DISTRICT OF COLUMBIA, or interfered with the interstate slave trade.

Gerende* v. *Board of Supervisors of Elections In 1951 the Supreme Court unanimously upheld a Md. statute making anyone ineligible for public employment who belonged to a "subversive" organization, which the Court defined as any group actively engaged in trying to overthrow the government forcefully or violently.

Georgia* v. *Stanton *see MISSISSIPPI v. JOHNSON*

German immigration The arrival of 84,500 PENNSYLVANIA DUTCH by 1775 marked the beginning of German immigration. By 1790, 9 percent of all whites were German in background, and by 1820 the German stock probably numbered 700,000 persons. German immigration became heavy in the 1850s, when 976,072 came. Of the 5,010,248 Germans who immigrated by 1900, 78 percent came during the four decades after 1850. Germany provided 26 percent of all immigrants from 1820 to 1900, but only 4.0 percent of alien arrivals were German in the period 1900–19 and just 2.7 percent in

1910–19. Over 2,000,000 Germans nevertheless came to the US after 1900, of whom a quarter arrived in the 1950s. By 1991, 7,094,352 Germans had immigrated to the US, more than any other nation, and 12.1 percent of all legal arrivals. The 1990 census reported 45,555,748 persons who described their primary ethnic identity as German, more than any other group, and 23 percent of all whites.

Germantown, battle of (Pa.) On 4 October 1777, General William HOWE's 9,000 troops repulsed attacks by Washington's 8,000 Continentals and 3,000 militia. US losses: 152 killed, 500 wounded, 438 captured. British losses: 537 killed and wounded, 14 captured. The defeat left Philadelphia firmly in British control, and the Continental army went into winter quarters at VALLEY FORGE.

Geronimo (b. along the upper Gila River, Ariz., June 1829; d. Fort Sill, Okla., 17 February 1909) After Mexican soldiers killed his mother, wife, and children, Geronimo ruthlessly raided south of the Rio Grande border. In 1877 the US arrested him and resettled his band on the San Carlos, Ariz., reservation, from which they escaped in 1881 and began raiding the US and Mexico. With his band of 50 warriors and their families, Geronimo eluded 5,000 US and 4,000 Mexican troops until 1886, when he ended the APACHE CAMPAIGNS by becoming the last Indian leader to surrender formally to the US. He was barred from returning to Ariz. and technically remained a prisoner of war until his death, but became a celebrity touring large eastern exhibitions and drew large crowds who bought his pictures and souvenirs.

Gerry, Elbridge (b. Marblehead, Mass., 17 July 1749; d. Washington, D.C., 23 November 1814) A Harvard man (1762), Gerry signed the DECLARATION OF INDEPENDENCE, served in Congress (1776–85), and sat in Congress (1789–93). He was a merchant who became Democratic governor of Mass. (1810–12) and US vice-president (1813–14). He is chiefly remembered for the GERRYMANDER.

Gerrymander In 1811 Mass. governor Elbridge GERRY signed the first redistricting law that deliberately redrew boundaries to one party's advantage, rather than establishing boundaries that were compact and followed natural borders. Because the most unusually shaped of Gerry's new districts resembled a salamander, this scheme was lampooned as a gerrymander. Gerrymandering (in various degrees) was a common tactic used to give all major parties an electoral advantage, but was increasingly curbed by the Supreme Court in the 20th century. Under the VOTING RIGHTS ACT, congressional districts have been Gerrymandered to enhance the chances of minority candidates being elected to Congress.

Gershwin, George (b. Brooklyn, N.Y., 26 September 1898; d. Hollywood, Calif., 11 July 1937) In 1916 Gershwin published his first song, "When You Want 'Em You Can't Get 'Em," and composed his first orchestral score in 1919 for the musical comedy *La, La, Lucille*. Much of his originality flowed from an ability to blend jazz themes into traditional classical structures. He achieved both critical acclaim and commerical success for his symphonic works and stage productions. He won the Pulitzer prize for the musical comedy *Of Thee I Sing* (1931). His works included *Rhapsody in Blue* (1924), *Concerto in F* (1925), *An American in Paris* (1928), and the opera *Porgy and Bess* (1935).

Gettysburg, battle of (Pa.) On 1 July 1863, General Robert E. LEE's 75,000 Confederates attacked Major General George MEADE's 88,300 Federals. After repeated repulses, climaxing on 3 July in 10,000 CSA casualties among 15,000 men of Pickett's Charge, Lee retreated on 4 July. USA losses: 3,155 killed, 14,529 wounded, 5,365 missing. CSA losses: 3,903 killed, 18,735 wounded, 5,425 missing. Gettysburg was the bloodiest battle fought on US soil. Defeat forced Lee to abandon his invasion of the North, but Meade failed to pursue him and crush the Army of NORTHERN VIRGINIA.

Gettysburg Address On 19 November 1863, Abraham LINCOLN followed Edward Everett's two-hour oration with a five-minute dedication of the GETTYSBURG, Pa., army cemetery. He modeled his address on Pericles' eulogy for Athenians who died in the Peloponnesian War, but infused it with his own moral vision of the CIVIL WAR's meaning for American democracy. Although slightly applauded then, the 286-word speech now stands as a masterpiece of simple eloquence and commands near universal recognition for describing the US as a "government of the people, by the people, and for the people."

Ghent, treaty of (Belgium) On 15 January 1814, the US accepted a British offer for direct negotiations to end the WAR OF 1812. US mediators included Henry CLAY, Albert GALLATIN, and John Q. ADAMS, who met with Admiral James Gambier, Henry Goulbourn, and William Adams. US victories along the Great Lakes prevented Britain from pressing for territorial concessions, while America's military weakness kept it from winning a British repudiation of IMPRESSMENT or compensation for ships seized by the Royal Navy. The negotiators signed a treaty exacting no significant concessions from either side on 24 December 1814, too late to prevent the first battle of NEW ORLEANS. Formal US ratification came on 17 February 1815.

Ghost Dance religion In 1879 Wovoka, a PAIUTE shaman, began popularizing a religious revival that promised reunion with the dead, eternal life, peace, and a world free from whites. Ghost Dance beliefs spread rapidly on the Great Plains. Many SIOUX INDIANS added apocalyptic, militantly anti-white teachings that prophesied war. Attempts to suppress the religion led to SITTING BULL's death on 15 December 1890 and the WOUNDED KNEE massacre.

GI Bill of Rights, first (31 March 1944) This law paid tuition fees, cost of classroom supplies, and a living stipend for veterans of WORLD WAR II and the KOREAN WAR, through 25 July 1956. It financed 2,200,000 bachelor and graduate degrees, 3,500,000 lesser degrees, occupational training for 1,400,000 vets, and agricultural training for 700,000 others.

GI Bill of Rights, second (3 March 1966) This law paid for educational costs of veterans who served after 31 January 1955. Benefits fell far short of the first GI BILL OF RIGHTS, despite Lyndon JOHNSON's call on 31 January 1967 for Congress to equalize allowances for veterans of the VIETNAM WAR.

Gibbons* v. *Ogden In 1824 the Supreme Court considered whether N.Y. could grant a monopoly to a steamboat company for carrying passengers between N.Y. and N.J. The Court ruled without dissent that the US government's power to regulate commerce comprehended "every species of commercial intercourse," including both trade and navigation; it then invalidated the monopoly as an infringement of federal powers. By asserting the federal government's right to regulate navigation through a broad interpretation of the commerce clause, the decision prevented states from stifling the growth of internal transportation through monopolies or excessive regulation.

Giddings Resolutions Inspired partly by the *CREOLE* INCIDENT, Representative Joshua Giddings (Whig, Ohio) offered resolutions on 21–2 March 1842 condemning the coastal slave trade between US ports. When the House censured him on 23 March for ignoring SLAVERY's constitutional protections, Giddings resigned his seat, but was reelected that April. Like the GAG RULE, these resolutions showed that ABOLITIONISM had extremely weak support in Congress and that little likelihood existed of the federal government posing a threat to slavery.

Gideon* v. *Wainwright On 18 March 1963 the Supreme Court ruled unanimously that the FOURTEENTH AMENDMENT'S DUE PROCESS clause obliged state courts to uphold the SIXTH AMENDMENT's requirement that counsel must be provided for indigent persons charged with felonies. (It reversed *Betts* v. *Brady*, 1 June 1942, which had ruled that defendants unable to afford a lawyer could not require the states to provide them counsel.) In *Argersinger* v. *Hamlin* (12 June 1972), the Court unanimously extended *Gideon* by ruling that the right to counsel applies to all federal and state hearings that might impose a jail sentence.

Gilbert, Sir Humphrey (b. near Dartmouth, Devon, England, ca. 1539; d. at sea near Newfoundland, 9 September 1583) He fought in Ireland in the 1560s and was involved in establishing English PLANTATIONS there. Authorized by a royal patent of 11 June 1578, he led the first English colonizing venture to North America late that year, but merely established a temporary base to raid the Spanish. He led five ships and 260 men across the Atlantic again in 1583, but the expedition broke up after his own ship sank in a gale.

Gilbert, Raleigh *see* PLYMOUTH COMPANY *and* SAGADAHOC

Gilbert Islands campaign During 20–3 November 1943, marines of Admiral Charles Pownall's task force quickly overran Makin Atoll, but took heavy casualties on TARAWA ATOLL, while a Japanese submarine sank one of Pownall's carriers. The Gilberts provided a base for the MARSHALL ISLANDS CAMPAIGN.

Gilded Age Historians apply this term to the interval from RECONSTRUCTION to the PROGRESSIVE ERA (1870–1900). It comes from *The Gilded Age* (1873), a novel by Mark TWAIN and Charles D. Warner satirizing the greed, shallowness, materialism, and corruption then prevalent in US society.

Gilman, Daniel Coit (b. Norwich, Conn., 6 July 1831; d. Norwich, Conn., 13 October 1908) A Yale man (1852), Gilman served as a US diplomat at St Petersburg and planned the Sheffield Scientific School at Yale. After serving as president of the University of California (1872–5), he became president of the Johns Hopkins University (1876–1901). Gilman modeled Hopkins after German, rather than English, collegiate education, by establishing the seminar as the core of instruction and emphasizing graduate study for the Ph.D. Hopkins was the first major US university to establish a formal Ph.D. program (but not the first to award a Ph.D.). Gilman helped advance US medical training by founding the Johns Hopkins Hospital (1889) and the Johns Hopkins Medical School (1893).

Gingrich, Newton Leroy (b. Harrisburg, Pa., 17 June 1943) Born Newton McPherson, Gingrich grew up the adopted son of a career army officer. After earning a Ph.D. in history at Tulane and teaching college, he became active in Ga. politics and entered Congress in 1978. He led the fight to force House Speaker James WRIGHT's resignation. As author of the CONTRACT WITH AMERICA, he was the foremost strategist behind the Republican takeover of Congress in 1994. He became speaker of the House in 1995.

Ginsberg, Allen (b. Newark, N.J., 3 June 1926) He grew up in Paterson, N.J., and graduated from Columbia (1948). He led an itinerant life and held a wide variety of jobs. In 1956, he published *Howl and Other Poems*, in which he vividly expressed the BEAT GENERATION's alienation from and frustration with the conformism and materialism then evident in US society. *Howl* also became a cult classic among the Woodstock generation (*see* WOODSTOCK ROCK FESTIVAL). Ginsberg became a prominent advocate of experimenting with drugs or hallucinogens, was a highly visible participant in the VIETNAM ANTIWAR MOVEMENT, and received the National Book Award in 1974 for *The Fall of America*. His other works included *Kaddish* (1961), *Reality Sandwiches* (1963), *Jukebox All'idrogeno* (1965), and *Planet News* (1969).

Gist exploration On 31 October 1750, Christopher Gist left the vicinity of Cumberland, Md., crossed the mountains, and descended the Ohio until just east of its falls (Louisville). He became the first English explorer to traverse central Ky. before ending his journey on 18 May 1751 in Yadkin Valley, N.C.

Gitlow* v. *New York On 8 June 1925, the Supreme Court stated (7–2) that the FOURTEENTH AMENDMENT obliged states to uphold FIRST AMENDMENT protections of freedom of speech and of the press. The Court first enforced the guarantee of free speech in *Fiske* v. *Kansas* (1927) and of a free press in *Near* v. *Minnesota* (1931). *Gitlow* marked the start of the systematic extension of the BILL OF RIGHTS to the states under the Fourteenth Amendment's DUE PROCESS clause.

Glass–Steagall Act, first (27 February 1932) In the GREAT DEPRESSION, a major reason why the economy would not revive was a 33 percent drop in outstanding bank loans from 1929 to 1932. To enable banks to extend more credit to business, Congress passed this law, which relaxed Federal Reserve standards (*see* FEDERAL RESERVE SYSTEM) for lending money to member banks. By liberalizing the requirements for the amount of gold and the types of securities required for issuing currency to banks, the law allowed the Federal Reserve to make available $750 million to its member banks for credit expansion. By May, when this money began flowing to banks, total US loan volume had declined by $13 billion, which was far too great for the law's limited means to counteract.

Glass–Steagall Act, second *see* Banking Act (1933)

Glenn, John *see* Apollo Project *and* Space Race

Glorious Revolution *see* Revolution of 1688

Gnadenhuetten massacre (Ohio) On 7 March 1782, Colonel David Williamson's Pa. militia killed 96 Christian Delaware and Mahican Indians whom they believed had helped other Indians kill their neighbors.

GNP gross national product.

Goddard, Robert Hutchings (b. Worcester, Mass., 5 October 1882; d. Baltimore, Md., 10 August 1945) Goddard was the foremost US pioneer of missile propulsion. This Clark University (Mass.) physics professor launched the world's first liquid-fuel rocket on 16 March 1926 near Auburn, Mass. He ignited the first missile to break the sound barrier in 1935. Beginning in 1914, he received numerous patents for rocket technology, including the first automatic steering device. In World War II, he supervised the navy's jet propulsion research.

Goethals, George W *see* Panama Canal

Gold Democrats *see* National Democrats

gold standard The US maintained a bimetallic monetary standard by minting both silver and gold dollars until 1873, when the Crime of '73 dropped the silver dollar and the silver coinage controversy began. Silver dollars were reintroduced as a supplement to gold by the Bland–Allison Act, and paper money was made redeemable for silver by the Sherman Silver Purchase Act. On 14 March 1900, the US joined the major European nations in placing all its currency on par with gold (at 25.8 grains, nine-tenths fine per dollar); it also set apart a gold reserve of $150,000,000 to back the dollar.

During the Great Depression, the Emergency Banking Relief Act (9 March 1933) stopped the use of gold to pay US debts abroad. The Congressional Joint Resolution (5 June 1933) officially took the US off the gold standard by rescinding the legal right of vendors and creditors to demand gold for government obligations. On 18 February 1935, the Supreme Court (5–4) ruled – in *United States* v. *Bankers Trust Company, Norman* v. *Baltimore and Ohio Railroad Company,* and *Nortz* v. *United States*; in *Perry* v. *United States* – that while the Joint Resolution abrogated the government's obligation to redeem its bonds in gold, bondholders lacked standing to sue in federal court because their losses were negligible.

By the Bretton Woods agreement (*see* Bretton Woods conference), the US resumed convertibility of dollars and gold in 1944 at $35 per ounce. On 15 August 1971, the US went off the gold standard by refusing to redeem dollars with gold. As of May 1994, the US Treasury maintained $11.05 billion of gold bullion as reserve assets for the currency.

Golding's Farm, battle of *see* Peninsular campaign

Goldwater, Barry Morris (b. Phoenix, Ariz. 1 January 1909) He served an an army air corps pilot in World War II. He entered the Senate as a Republican in 1952, became a leading spokesman against the liberal consensus when he published *The Conscience of a Conservative* (1960), and was Republican nominee for president in 1964. In an election dominated by hysteria that Goldwater would escalate the Vietnam War or provoke a nuclear war, he took only six states and just 38.3 percent of the ballots. Goldwater's landslide defeat was blamed for massive Republican losses, totaling 1 senator, 37 congressmen, and over 500 state legislators.

Goliad massacre (Tex.) On 27 March 1836 (Palm Sunday), General Jose Urrea's Mexican troops murdered 390 unarmed prisoners of war in the Texas Revolt on orders from General Antonio Lopez de Santa Anna. Only 27 Americans managed to escape.

Gompers, Samuel (b. London, England, 27 January 1850; d. San Antonio, Tex., 13 December 1924) He was apprenticed as a cigarmaker at the age of 12 and came to the US in 1863. In 1877 he became president of the Cigarmakers' Union. He helped found the parent organization of the American Federation of Labor (AFL) in 1881 and served as AFL president from 1886 to his death (except for 1894–5). Under Gompers, the AFL became the largest US labor union. He was a conservative leader who eschewed partisan politics, opposed socialism, and dedicated himself to achieving gains in wages and working conditions.

good neighbor policy On 4 March 1933, President Franklin D. ROOSEVELT broke with the ROOSEVELT COROLLARY by endorsing "the policy of the good neighbor – the neighbor who . . . respects the rights of others." On 26 December 1933, US Secretary of State Cordell HULL signed the Montevideo, Uruguay, conference's resolution that "No state has the right to intervene in the internal or external affairs of another." On 28 December, Roosevelt declared that US policy in Latin America would be "one opposed to armed intervention."

Goodnight–Loving Trail In 1866 Charles Goodnight and Oliver Loving blazed the 700-mile Goodnight Trail from Fort Belknap, Tex., to Fort Sumner, N.Mex., and then on to Denver. The route became one of the most heavily used cattle trails in the southwest.

Goodyear, Charles (b. New Haven, Conn., 29 December 1800; d. New York, N.Y., 1 July 1860) After working as a hardware retailer in Conn. and Pa., Goodyear went bankrupt at the age of 29. For five years after 1834, he experimented with improving the commercial applications of rubber. In 1839 he discovered how to eliminate rubber's plasticity and strengthen it through vulcanization. Goodyear laid the scientific foundation for the US rubber industry, but made little money from his research because he was forced to sell the rights over most of his royalties to settle debts.

GOP Grand Old Party (Republican party).

Gore, Albert, Jr (b. Carthage, Tenn., 31 March 1948) Gore served with the army in the VIETNAM WAR (1969–71). After sitting in Congress (1977–84), he entered the Senate in 1985, where he emerged as a leading expert on military, foreign, and environmental affairs. He broke with his party to support George BUSH on the PERSIAN GULF WAR. He unsuccessfully sought the Democratic nomination for president in 1988. He became US vice-president in 1993.

Gorgas, William Crawford *see* PANAMA CANAL

Gorges, Sir Fernando *see* PLYMOUTH COMPANY

Gottschalk, Louis Moreau (b. New Orleans, La., 8 May 1829; d. Rio de Janeiro, Brazil, 18 December 1869) After studying music at Paris for six years, Gottschalk made his debut as a concert pianist in 1849. He became the first American musician to establish a major international reputation as a touring artist. He gave his premier performance in the US at New York in 1853. Gottschalk authored many compositions, of which some seem to reflect his mother's Creole and African-American heritage. Gottschalk's orchestra had much financial success touring the US, the Caribbean islands, and Latin America until he died of yellow fever in Brazil.

Gould, Jay *see* BLACK FRIDAY

Graduation Act (3 August 1854) This law was successor to the PREEMPTION ACT. It established a scale of selling prices for all lands in the PUBLIC DOMAIN left unsold for specific periods. Land would be sold (by the acre) at $1.00 after 10 years, $0.75 after 15 years, $0.25 after 20 years, and $0.12½ after 30 years. It allowed preemption claims on graduated acreage, but not on lands with mineral deposits or granted for INTERNAL IMPROVEMENTS. By offering marginal lands at reasonable prices, it resulted in the sale of over 30,000,000 acres within a year. The HOMESTEAD ACTS succeeded it.

Grafton, third Duke of (b. Suffolk, England, 1 October 1735; d. Euston Hall, Suffolk, England, 14 March 1811) Augustus Henry Fitzroy, third Duke of Grafton, assumed leadership of William PITT's ministry after Pitt's health failed and Charles TOWNSHEND died. In October 1768, he succeeded Pitt as prime minister. Largely due to Lord NORTH's influence, the Grafton ministry resisted repealing the TOWNSHEND REVENUE ACT. Grafton resigned as prime minister in January 1770 and was succeeded by Lord North.

Graham, Billy (William Franklin) (b. near Charlotte, N.C., 7 November 1918) Ordained a Southern Baptist minister in 1939, Graham earned a B.A. from Wheaton College in 1943. He launched his first national evangelistic campaign in 1949 by preaching to 350,000 persons in Los Angeles over eight weeks. Between 1949 and 1950, his preaching inspired 28,000 persons to make declarations of faith. A four-month revival at New York's Madison Square Garden attracted 2,000,000 attendees and achieved 80,000 conversions (including 30,000 who watched on TV). In 1954 his campaign first went global with a tour of Britain. Graham is the late 20th century's foremost evangelist, and deserves to be ranked with John Wesley, George WHITEFIELD, Dwight MOODY, and Billy SUNDAY.

Graham, Martha (b. Allegheny, Pa., 11 May 1894; d. New York, N.Y., 1 April 1991) Graham toured with a dancing troupe from 1919 to 1923. In 1927 she established a studio in New York, where she became the foremost US innovator in modern dance. Her company gave its first performance, *Primitive Mysteries*, in 1931, and commissioned Aaron COPLAND's Pulitzer prize-winning *Appalachian Spring* (1944). She remained active in dance to her death.

Graham* v. *Richardson In a ruling akin to *SHAPIRO* V. *THOMPSON*, on 14 June 1971, the Supreme Court ruled unanimously that states could not declare resident aliens and illegal aliens ineligible for welfare. It declared that classifying this group by alien status served no compelling need and violated the aliens' right to equal protection under the FOURTEENTH AMENDMENT. (*See YICK WO* V. *HOPKINS*)

Grain Futures Trading Act *see* CAPPER–TINCHER ACT

Gramm, Phil (b. Fort Benning, Ga., 8 July 1942) He earned a Ph.D. from the University of Georgia and taught college. In 1979 he won election to Congress from Tex. as a Democrat. He co-authored the Gramm-Latta legislation enacting Ronald REAGAN's budget proposals. He found his views on balancing the budget incompatible with the Democratic Party's position and ran successfully as a Republican in 1983. In 1984 he won election to the Senate, where he was the moving force behind the GRAMM–RUDMAN–HOLLINGS ACT. He played a leading role in defeating William CLINTON's health-care proposals in 1994.

Gramm–Rudman–Hollings Act (12 December 1985) This law set a timetable for eliminating the federal budget deficit by 1991. It would force reductions in the deficit by equal amounts every year until the budget was balanced. If Congress and the president could not agree on spending cuts or tax increases to meet the ceilings, then the president could impose an automatic, across-the-board sequestration in all areas but entitlement programs. (On 7 July 1987, the Supreme Court ruled that one aspect of the deficit reduction procedures violated the separation of executive and legislative powers, but because the law included alternative procedures for making spending cuts, it continued in operation.) The law nevertheless failed to close the deficit because it was riddled with loopholes allowing leaders to avoid the automatic spending cuts. The budget was not balanced in fiscal year 1991, but rather ran a deficit of $268 billion. The law's failure led President William CLINTON to propose a heavy tax increase when he took office.

Grand Army of the Republic (GAR) Dr Benjamin Stephenson founded this association of Union veterans of the CIVIL WAR in 1866. Formed for social and philanthropic purposes, it soon became one of the nation's most powerful lobbying groups (primarily to win liberal pension laws for its members such as the DEPENDENT PENSION ACT) and the Republican Party's most reliable body of voters. GAR membership peaked at over 400,000 about 1890. Six members attended its last encampment at Cincinnati in 1949.

Grand Banks This is a submerged plateau, about 240 feet deep, stretching 500 miles southeast from Newfoundland to the latitude of Boston, in the locale where the Gulf Stream meets the Arctic Current. This shoal has supported New England's fishing industry since the 1630s. Its annual catch was two billion tons of cod in the 1960s, but overfishing has since reduced amounts caught.

grandfather clause After RECONSTRUCTION, southern states tried to prevent blacks from registering to vote by devices like LITERACY TESTS and POLL TAXES. To keep such stratagems from disfranchising whites, clauses were added granting suffrage to adults whose grandfather could vote or was a CSA soldier. The Supreme Court first ruled on such devices in *GUINN* V. *UNITED STATES*.

Grange Officially titled the Order of the Patrons of Husbandry, the Grange was founded on 4 December 1867 at Washington, D.C., by Oliver H. Kelley and six associates. It began as an organization to relieve the social and cultural isolation of many rural areas, and also heal the Civil War's divisions through mutual cooperation between northern and southern farmers. By 1874 there were 20,000 lodges with 800,000 members, mostly in 14 states of the midwest and Great Plains. The movement quickly became politically active. It endorsed candidates, elected many supporters to state legislatures, won passage of the GRANGER LAWS, and strongly supported POPULISM and antitrust laws (*see* TRUSTS). By 1917 its membership had fallen to 297,000. The Grange endorsed the MCNARY–HAUGEN BILL in the 1920s and supported NEW DEAL programs for crop reduction, rural development, and soil conservation. In 1990 it had 365,000 members.

Granger cases These cases heard challenges by corporations to the GRANGER LAWS. The first of these rulings, *Munn* v. *Illinois* (1877), elaborated the basic legal principles for the rest. In *Munn*, the Court affirmed an 1873 Ill. law setting a cap on charges for storing crops; it held that the law did not interfere with Congress's authority over interstate commerce, because the states might regulate commerce in the absence of federal legislation for the sake of protecting the public interest from harmful business practices. The Court also denied that Ill. had confiscated any corporate property in violation of the FOURTEENTH AMENDMENT'S DUE PROCESS clause. It averred that the issue was one of public policy, over which the courts were obliged to defer to the voters' elected representatives. It added that the due process clause was not intended to restrict the states' police powers.

The wide scope afforded state regulation of business was later rescinded by *SANTA CLARA COUNTY* V. *SOUTHERN PACIFIC RAILROAD COMPANY*, *WABASH, ST LOUIS AND PACIFIC RAILROAD COMPANY* V. *ILLINOIS*, *CHICAGO, MILWAUKEE AND ST PAUL RAILROAD COMPANY* V. *MINNESOTA*, *CHICAGO, BURLINGTON AND QUINCY RAILROAD* V. *CHICAGO*, and *REAGAN* V. *FARMERS' LOAN AND TRUST COMPANY*. The Court finally reversed itself and authorized broad authority for states to regulate business activity in *NEBBIA* V. *NEW YORK*.

Granger laws During the 1870s, the GRANGE pressed for laws to establish state commissions for regulating the rates and business practices of railroads, warehouses, and elevator silos. Iowa, Ill., Minn., Mo., and Wis. passed model legislation known as Granger laws. These measures set maximum rates for railroad freight, required rates to be charged on a uniform and nondiscriminatory basis, outlawed merging of parallel rail lines to eliminate competition, prohibited companies from giving bribes or special favors to government officials, and formed railway and warehouse commissions to implement these regulations. (*See* GRANGER CASES)

Grant, Madison (b. New York, N.Y., 18 November 1865; d. New York, N.Y., 30 May 1937) He was an active member of the Immigration Restriction League. In 1916 he published *The Passing of the Great Race*, which argued that US society and culture were being debased by heavy immigration from eastern and southern Europe. His book was widely read and helped influence enactment of the EMERGENCY QUOTA ACT (1921) and the NATIONAL ORIGINS ACT (1924).

Grant, Ulysses S. (b. Point Pleasant, Ohio, 27 April 1822; d. Mount McGregor, N.Y., 23 July 1885) Originally named Hiram Ulysses, he adopted Ulysses Simpson due to a clerical error at West Point, from which he graduated in 1843. Given the brevet rank of captain for bravery at CHAPULTEPEC in the MEXICAN WAR, Grant left the army in 1854. He reentered as colonel of 21st Illinois Infantry in the CIVIL WAR and was brigadier general at the end of 1861.

In 1862 he took FORT DONNELSON and FORT HENRY, and won at SHILOH. In 1863 he took VICKSBURG and ended the siege of CHATTANOOGA. On 9 March 1864, he became commander in chief of all USA armies and the first soldier to hold rank as lieutenant general since George WASHINGTON. Grant made his headquarters with the Army of the POTOMAC, over which he exercised strategic control. During 1864–5, he steadily bled the Army of NORTHERN VIRGINIA at the WILDERNESS, SPOTSYLVANIA COURT HOUSE, COLD HARBOR, and PETERSBURG, and ended the war by forcing its surrender at APPOMATTOX COURT HOUSE. Grant captured three enemy armies, more than any other USA general.

As a Republican, he defeated Horatio SEYMOUR for president with 52.7 percent of the popular vote in 1868, and won over Horace GREELEY in 1872 with 55.6 percent. Grant deferred to Congress and showed little executive initiative. The BLACK FRIDAY, CREDIT MOBILIER, and WHISKEY RING SCANDALS tarnished his administration, most of whose achievements were due to Hamilton FISH. Business failure left him bankrupt in 1884, but he reimbursed his creditors from royalties of his *Personal Memoirs* (1885).

Graves* v. *New York ex rel. O'Keefe On 27 March 1939, the Supreme Court settled the general issue of intergovernmental tax immunities raised in *DOBBINS* v. *ERIE COUNTY* and *COLLECTOR* v. *DAY* by declaring (7–2) that a state tax on federal workers placed no unconstitutional burden on the US government, and that both national and state governments could tax each other's employees.

Gray, L(ouis) Patrick III (b. St Louis, Mo., 18 July 1916) Gray graduated from Annapolis in 1940, received a law degree in 1949, and assisted Richard NIXON in the campaigns of 1960 and 1968. He joined Nixon's administration in 1969, rose to deputy attorney general, became acting FBI director in May 1972, and was nominated as director in February 1973. At his confirmation hearings, he admitted having given the White House staff secret FBI files on the WATERGATE SCANDAL and having destroyed others at the request of John EHRLICHMAN and John DEAN. Richard Nixon withdrew his nomination on 5 April and Gray resigned as acting director on 27 April. He was not charged with any Watergate-related crimes.

Gray, Robert (b. Tiverton, R.I., 10 May 1755; d. at sea, en route to Charleston, S.C., summer 1806) Gray fought on privateers in the REVOLUTIONARY WAR. In September 1787, he sailed from Boston to obtain furs in the Pacific northwest for trade in China and was the second US mariner to sell a cargo there. Upon returning to Boston on 17 April 1790, he became the first American ship captain to navigate around the world. On 11 May 1792, while on a return voyage he discovered the Columbia River, which he named for his ship.

Great Awakening, first This was America's first large-scale revival. It was anticipated by the REFRESHINGS and a well-publicized revival led by Jonathan EDWARDS at Northampton, Mass., in 1735. The Awakening was sparked in 1739 by George WHITEFIELD's itinerant preaching, which introduced Americans to the Methodist style of evangelization. Every major denomination split between pro-revivalists ("New Lights") and antirevivalists ("Old Lights"). Edwards and Gilbert TENNENT were the most prominent New Lights. The Awakening climaxed in the CONGREGATIONAL and PRESBYTERIAN CHURCHES in the northern colonies about 1742, but spread slowly southward by the efforts of exhorters in the BAPTIST and METHODIST CHURCHES. The Awakening began the process by which the established ANGLICAN CHURCH and Congregational Church, whose clergy were mainly Old Lights lost their religious influence to New Light Presbyterians, Baptists, and Methodists.

Great Awakening, Second *see* SECOND GREAT AWAKENING

Great Crash *see* CRASH OF 1929

Great Depression The CRASH OF 1929 precipitated the worst business contraction in US history, which was rooted in widespread undercapitalization within the banking system, chronic agricultural overproduction, and a shrinkage in world trade stemming from the FORDNEY–MCCUMBER and HAWLEY–SMOOT TARIFFS. The crash wiped out $7[illegible] billion in equity capital on the stock market by mid-1932. By 1933, 10,797 bank failures or mergers had resulted in a 29 percent reduction in bank assets (from $72.3 billion in 1929 to $51.3 billion in 1933). Commercial bank loans dropped from $38 billion in 1930 to $20 billion in 1935. Gross national product plunged from $104.4 billion in 1929 to $74.2 billion in 1933. US exports fell 6[illegible] percent, from $5.4 billion in 1929 to $2.[illegible] billion in 1933. Unemployment rose from 3.2 percent in 1929 to a peak of 24.9 percent in 1933, and never fell below 14.3 percent (1937) during the 1930s.

Efforts during the NEW DEAL to revive the economy provided relief, but not recovery, because the loss of $96 billion in equity and banking capital could not be offset by a federal budget that never exceeded $8.4 billion (in 1936) during the 1930s. Economic recovery was interrupted by the RECESSION OF 1937–8. GNP did not regain its level of 1929 until 1939, when unemployment still remained at 17.2 percent. Military rearmament cut unemployment to 9.9 percent in 1941 and entry into WORLD WAR II ended the depression.

Great Migration Between 1630 and 1660, England, whose population was about 5,500,000, lost at least 214,000 emigrants, including 25,000 to New England, 50,000 to Va. and Md., 110,000 to the West Indies, 4,000 to Bermuda, and 25,000 to Ireland. The Great Migration constituted nearly all IMMIGRATION to 17th-century New England and over 40 percent of emigrants to the Chesapeake before 1700; it raised the number of English colonists on the North American mainland from under 5,000 in 1630 to over 70,000 in 1660. (*See* ENGLISH IMMIGRATION)

Great Society This catchphrase was used by Lyndon JOHNSON to symbolize his administration's domestic agenda. He first used the term at a rally of 31 October 1964 and called on Congress to enact his program on 4 January 1965. Johnson proposed to create a network of social welfare assistance through an ambitious WAR ON POVERTY and attempted to outlaw racial discrimination. His antipoverty programs fell short of their promise, in part because attempts to fund them simultaneously with the VIETNAM WAR created large budget deficits and fanned inflation, but also because few were later subjected to the critical analysis that might identify and correct deficiencies. During the five-year Johnson administration, federal spending on education rose from $2.3 billion to $10.8 billion, spending on health rose from $4.1 billion to $13.9 billion, and spending for the disadvantaged rose from $12.5 billion to $24.6 billion.

The CIVIL RIGHTS ACT (1964) and the VOTING RIGHTS ACT (1965) were its most important civil rights laws. MEDICARE, MEDICAID, and the OLDER AMERICANS ACT were its most important health legislation. The OMNIBUS HOUSING ACT, DEMONSTRATION CITIES AND METROPOLITAN DEVELOPMENT ACT, HOUSING AND URBAN DEVELOPMENT ACT, and MASS TRANSIT ACT were its most important housing and urban-renewal measures. FOOD STAMPS, the broadly-conceived ECONOMIC OPPORTUNITY ACT, and APPALACHIAN REGIONAL DEVELOPMENT ACT were its main antipoverty initiatives. The HEAD START PROGRAM and HIGHER EDUCATION ACTS (1965 and 1967) were its most important educational initiatives. Its most important ENVIRONMENTAL LEGISLATION was the CLEAN WATER RESTORATION ACT and WILDERNESS AREAS ACT.

Great Wagon Road After 1730, the Great Wagon Road was extended 800 miles from Philadelphia to Augusta, Ga., via Hagerstown, Md., the Shenandoah Valley, Salisbury, Salem, and Charlotte in N.C., and Chester and Newberry in S.C. The WILDERNESS ROAD met it at Roanoke, Va. It was the principal highway for southern frontier expansion.

Great White Fleet From 16 December 1907 to 22 February 1909, Theodore ROOSEVELT sent US battleships on a world tour to demonstrate US sea power (the US Navy ranked as the world's second-largest). The fleet served as part of his BIG STICK DIPLOMACY, with a major purpose of deterring any challenges to US spheres of influence by Japan, which had just won the Russo-Japanese War.

Greeley, Horace (b. Amherst, N.H., 3 February 1811; d. New York, N.Y., 29 November 1872) He moved to New York City and in 1841 founded the New York *Tribune*, which became one of the country's most influential papers. He was an ABOLITIONIST, supporter of most social reforms, and an idealist who coined the saying, "Go West, young man." He helped found the REPUBLICAN PARTY and advocated freeing the slaves at the earliest moment in the CIVIL WAR, but after peace arrived he became less sympathetic toward the FREEDMEN's problems and took a moderate position on RECONSTRUCTION. Nominated in 1872 for president by both the Liberal Republican and Democratic parties, he lost badly to Ulysses S. Grant. He buried his wife during that campaign, and since he died before the electoral college met, no electoral votes were ever officially recorded in his name.

Green Mountain Boys During the conflict in Vermont between speculators holding land titles from N.H. and N.Y., Ira, Levi, and Ethan Allen formed this group in 1772 to harass settlers defending N.Y. titles. N.Y. title-holders who ignored the Boys' warnings were beaten, dispossessed from their farms, or otherwise terrorized out of Vt. Ethan Allen and some of the Boys captured Fort Ticonderoga (1775).

Green* v. *Biddle In 1823 the Supreme Court ruled that the protection given to contracts in Article I, Section 10 extended to contracts between states, when it struck down a Ky. law that reneged on a settlement over land titles reached with Va. in 1791.

Green* v. *County School Board of New Kent County On 27 May 1968, the Supreme Court elaborated on *Brown* v. *Board of Education of Topeka* (1955), and ruled unanimously that local school boards are obliged to take realistic steps to end classroom segregation. The Court invalidated a "freedom-of-choice" plan as a subterfuge for continued segregation and said such programs could only be used if they were effective in ending racial separation among pupils. The decision demonstrated the Court's growing impatience with the slow pace of school desegregation.

Greenback Party This party was formed after the panic of 1873, when members of the Indiana Grange demanded political action to keep greenbacks from being withdrawn from circulation in November 1874. In 1876 the party nominated Peter Cooper (N.Y.) for president, and Samuel Carey (Ohio) for vice-president, but attracted only 83,000 votes. Reorganized as the Greenback-Labor party, it polled 1,000,000 votes and elected 14 congressmen in 1878. This success influenced Congress to pass the Bland–Allison Act. It ran James Weaver for president, with B. J. Chambers (Tex.), in 1880 and received 3.4 percent of the popular vote. Although it joined with the Anti-Monopoly party in 1884, its presidential nominee, Benjamin Butler, with A M. West (Miss.) won just 1.8 percent of ballots. Its supporters drifted to the Populist party (*see* populism).

Greenback-Labor party *see* Greenback party

greenbacks The Legal Tender acts (1862 and 1863) authorized printing $450,000,000 in paper money, nicknamed greenbacks for their color, which all creditors and vendors were required to accept as payment for debts, goods, and services. The Supreme Court affirmed their constitutionality in the legal tender cases. The Treasury contracted the supply of greenbacks from $433,000,000 in August 1865 to $399,000,000 in October 1866. By 1869 when $356,000,000 remained in circulation a deflationary spiral in the money supply stirred public opposition to the Republican policy of redeeming the outstanding notes In response to the panic of 1873, the Treasury released $26,000,000 between September 1873 and January 1874. On 22 April 1874, Ulysses S. Grant vetoed an act raising the supply of paper money to $400,000,000, and then signed an act (20 June) to limit greenbacks outstanding at $382,000,000; on 14 January 1875, he signed the Specie Resumption Act requiring the US government to make all payments in gold by 1 January 1879. By 17 December 1878 the $346,680,000 greenbacks outstanding stood at par to gold for the first time since 1862.

Greene, Nathanael (b. Warwick, R.I., 7 August 1742; d. near Savannah, Ga., 19 June 1786) Despite his Quaker upbringing (*see* Quakers), Greene was appointed brigadier general in the Continental Army in June 1775. His superior administrative abilities led to appointment as quartermaster general in February 1778. In October 1780, he assumed command of US forces in the Carolinas, then under British occupation. He waged a brilliant campaign at the battles of Guilford Courthouse, Eutaw Springs, and Hobkirk's Hill, which proved such costly victories for the British that they lost control of the Carolina hinterland and Charles Cornwallis advanced toward Yorktown. Only George Washington contributed more to US victory in the Revolution than Greene.

Greenland, US occupation of On 9 April 1941, Denmark agreed to allow US air, naval, and radio bases on Greenland in return for the island's defense against a Nazi invasion. US forces occupied Greenland during WORLD WAR II while Germans controlled Denmark.

Greenville, first treaty of (Ohio) On 3 August 1795, General Anthony WAYNE concluded a peace with the NORTHWEST TERRITORY's Indians, who agreed to surrender about two-thirds of Ohio and small tracts in Ind. totaling about 28,000 square miles. The treaty ended warfare in the Ohio valley until the battle of TIPPECANOE CREEK and stimulated about 150,000 easterners to settle there over the next five years.

Greenville, second treaty of (Ohio) On 22 July 1814, the US made peace with the northwestern Indians by requiring SHAWNEE, MIAMI, DELAWARE, WYANDOT, and MINGO INDIANS to repudiate their alliance with the British and assist the US in the WAR OF 1812.

Gregg* v. *Georgia (decided with *Proffitt* v. *Florida* and *Jurek* v. *Texas*) On 2 July 1976, the Supreme Court clarified *FURMAN* v. *GEORGIA* by ruling (7–2) that death for first degree murder was not a cruel or unusual punishment under the EIGHTH AMENDMENT, but that DUE PROCESS required judge and jury to consider both the offender's individual character and the crime's unique circumstances before imposing death. On 29 June 1977, the Court held (7–2) in *Coker* v. *Georgia* that death was an excessive punishment for rape. (*See TISON AND TISON* v. *ARIZONA and McCLESKEY* v. *KEMP*) Numerous difficulties continued to frustrate the imposition of death sentences after *Gregg*, and by 16 September 1994 – when 37 states authorized capital punishment – just 251 executions had taken place in the US, of which over half occurred in Tex., Fla., and Va.

Grenada, US intervention in After Maurice Bishop's New Jewel Movement overthrew Grenada's government in March 1979, Bishop turned bitterly anti-US, formed close ties with Communist Cuba, invited Cuban soldiers to garrison Grenada, and encouraged political unrest on nearby British Commonwealth islands. Four days after rival Marxists killed Bishop on 19 October 1983, the Organization of Eastern Caribbean States suggested joint action with the US to restore order. Citing a danger to 700 US students at the country's medical school, Ronald REAGAN sent 1,900 US troops, assisted by 300 troops from six West Indian nations, into Grenada on 25 October. Leftist resistance crumbled in five days. US forces suffered 18 dead, 115 wounded, and 36 other injuries; they killed 45 Grenadians and 24 Cubans, and captured 638 Cubans. US troop strength peaked at 7,355 on 31 October, but all except 300 noncombat personnel withdrew by 15 December. Grenada held free elections in December 1984.

Grenville, George (b. Wotton Hall, Buckinghamshire, England, 14 October 1712; d. London, England, 13 November 1770) In 1741 Grenville entered Parliament, and he became prime minister in April 1763. He was brother-in-law to William PITT. It was during his ministry that the CURRENCY ACT, SUGAR ACT, QUARTERING ACT (1765), and STAMP ACT were passed. He was dismissed from office in July 1765 by GEORGE III and replaced by the Marquis of ROCKINGHAM.

Griffith, David Lewelyn Wark (b. Oldham County, Ky., 22 January 1875; d. Hollywood, Calif., 23 July 1948) Originally a Louisville *Courier Journal* reporter and actor, Griffith moved to Los Angeles where the climate favored outdoor movie production. He directed almost 500 films (1908–13), and then made the first epic film, *The Birth of a Nation* (1915). He then completed a series of commercial successes that pioneered new approaches to the cinema. Griffith was the first giant of the US motion picture industry and established Hollywood's dominance.

Griggs* v. *Duke Power Company On 8 March 1971, the Supreme Court upheld the constitutionality of the CIVIL RIGHTS ACT's (1964) ban on racial discrimination in hiring; it declared that the act might properly forbid employers from hiring or promoting individuals on the basis of their level of education or scores on standardized tests, provided that such criteria had no relation to actual job skills and tended to favor whites over minorities. The Court clarified *Griggs* in *Washington* v. *Davis*.

Griswold* v. *Connecticut On 7 June 1965, the Supreme Court ruled (7–2) that the Constitution implicitly protects a right to personal privacy, which is transgressed by state laws forbidding the sale of birth control devices, but the justices disagreed on the precise origin of the privilege.

Gros Ventres Indians Two groups received this name. The first were the Siouan Hidatsa Indians. The second were an Algonquian language group, the Atsina, whom the French nicknamed the "Big Bellies of the Prairie." The Atsina were closely related to the Arapaho and Blackfoot Indians and left Minn. for the northern plains under Dakota Indian pressure. By 1780 they had incorporated the horse into their culture and were selling skins of buffalo and big cats to the British. They numbered only 2,500 after heavy losses to smallpox in the 1780s, 1829, and 1837–8, and after several hundred were killed fighting Crow and Assiniboine Indians in the 1830s. They relentlessly harassed Anglo-American fur trappers, but fought no wars against the US Army. An 1855 treaty established a common hunting reserve for them in northern Mont., where Fort Belknap Reservation was established for the Atsina and Blackfoot in 1873, by which time they numbered about 1,000.

gross domestic product (GDP) This is the total value of GNP minus the retained earnings from overseas operations of US corporations.

gross national product (GNP) This is the total value of domestic economic production, plus retained earnings from overseas operations of US corporations. (*See* Gross Domestic Product)

Grovey* v. *Townsend On 1 April 1935, the Supreme Court unanimously reversed *Nixon* v. *Herndon*'s ban on the white primary; it ruled that the Tex. Democratic Party could exclude blacks from membership, because the Fourteenth Amendment did not extend to acts by private organizations like political parties. *Smith* v. *Allwright* and *Terry* v. *Adams* overturned this decision.

GSA *see* General Services Administration

Guadalcanal, naval battle of On 12–15 November 1942, while escorting 13,000 Japanese reinforcements to Guadalcanal, Vice Admiral Hiroake Abe's task force (2 battleships, 1 cruiser, 6 destroyers) engaged Rear Admiral Daniel Callaghan's 7 destroyers and 5 cuisers. Abe withdrew without landing the reinforcements. Japanese losses: 1 battleship, 2 cruisers. US losses: 2 cruisers, 4 destroyers.

Guadalcanal campaign On 7 August 1942, the First USMC Division (19,000 men) landed and seized an airfield held by 2,200 Japanese menacing US sealanes in the Solomon Islands. US naval forces defended the island in six major battles: Savo Island, Eastern Solomons, Cape Esperance, Santa Cruz, Guadalcanal, and Tassafaronga. Japan landed 35,000 troops to retake "Henderson Field," while the US ultimately sent 45,000 reinforcements (one USMC and two army divisions). US forces repulsed major Japanese assaults on 20 August, 12 September, and 21–8 October 1942. The Japanese withdrew their final 9,000 troops in February 1943. Guadalcanal blocked the Japanese from advancing toward Australia and cost the Imperial Army unacceptably high casualties. US losses: 5,000 sailors dead, 1,700 USMC-army killed, 5,000 USMC-army wounded, 25 warships sunk, 4 transports sunk, 260 planes lost. Japanese losses: 3,000 sailors dead, 25,000 land forces killed, 24 warships sunk, 14 transports sunk, 450 planes destroyed.

Guadalupe Hidalgo, treaty of On 2 February 1848, Nicholas Trist concluded unauthorized negotiations to end the Mexican War by this agreement. Mexico accepted the Rio Grande as the boundary of Tex.; it ceded 529,200 square miles (Calif., N.Mex., and parts of Ariz., Utah, Nev., and Colo.) in return for $15,000,000 cash and the assumption of $3,250,000 in claims by US citizens against Mexico. The Senate ratified it on 10 March 1848. (*See also* Gadsden Purchase)

Guam On 10 December 1898, the US acquired Guam by the treaty ending the Spanish-American War. It was administered by the navy, which maintained a large military base. In World War II, it was the site of the battles of Guam. On 1 August 1950, Guam became a self-governing territory and its residents were granted US citizenship. In 1970 the island elected its first governor, and in 1972, it was allowed to elect a nonvoting delegate to Congress.

Guam, battles of On 10 December 1941, 5,500 Japanese captured Guam's garrison of 200 US marines and 300 Guamanian police. US losses: 4 marines and 15 police killed. On 21 July 1944, the Third USMC and 77th Army Divisions landed on Guam. Organized resistance ended by 10 August, but 8,000 poorly armed Japanese undertook ineffective guerrilla harassment from jungles. US losses: 1,400 killed, 6,500 wounded. Japanese losses: 10,000 killed or captured.

Guatemala, US intervention in Under president Jacobo Arbénz Guzman, Guatemala expropriated 1,000,000 acres of corporate land, most of which was owned by the US Fruit Co. After a Soviet-bloc ship brought military supplies to Puerto Barrios on 15 May 1954, the US grew alarmed and the ORGANIZATION OF AMERICAN STATES (OAS) passed a resolution of concern. The CIA helped organize rightist exiles under Carlos Castillo Armas, who invaded via Honduras on 18 June. On 29 June, Arbénz resigned. The US offered Guatemala $6,425,000 in economic aid on 30 October and establisheed a military assistance program on 18 June 1955.

Guffey–Snyder Bituminous Coal Stabilization Act (30 August 1935) After the NATIONAL INDUSTRIAL RECOVERY ACT (NIRA) was ruled unconstitutional, this measure, part of the LITTLE NIRA, created the National Bituminous Coal Commission, which was authorized to establish industry-wide regulations for coal prices, production levels, mine closures, wages, hours, and collective bargaining. To force independent operators to subscribe to its codes, the commission could levy a nationwide coal tax, which would be rebated to member firms. The law was invalidated by *CARTER* v. *CARTER COAL COMPANY* in 1936, but much of it was reenacted as the *GUFFEY–VINSON BITUMINOUS COAL ACT*.

Guffey–Vinson Bituminous Coal Act (26 April 1937) This law revived all the major features of the GUFFEY–SNYDER BITUMINOUS COAL STABILIZATION ACT except for its wages and hours specifications, which had been held unconstitutional in a new national code for the soft-coal industry that was made exempt from antitrust legislation. This measure helped unions organize miners, but left the coal industry's economic problems unresolved until WORLD WAR II drove up demand for coal.

Guilford Courthouse, battle of (N.C.) On 15 March 1781, Lieutenant General Charles CORNWALLIS's 2,000 redcoats drove Major General Nathanael GREENE's 1,700 Continentals and 2,600 militia from Guilford Courthouse. US losses: 78 killed, 183 wounded. British losses: 143 killed, 389 wounded. Greene saved his poorly trained army by an orderly retreat; by inflicting serious British losses, which could not be replaced as easily as his own, he also crippled Cornwallis's fighting ability.

Guinn* v. *United States On 21 June 1915, the Supreme Court ruled (8–0) that an Okla. voting law violated the FIFTEENTH AMENDMENT with a GRANDFATHER CLAUSE enfranchising anyone who failed a literacy test (*see* LITERACY TESTS) if any of their forebears could vote by 1866. Okla. circumvented *Guinn* by discriminatory legislation that effectively extended the old grandfather clause, which was again held unconstitutional on 22 May 1939 in *Lane* v. *Wilson*.

Guiteau, Charles J. *see* GARFIELD, JAMES ABRAM

Gulf of Tonkin Resolution On 2 August 1964, after requesting help against an attack by three North Vietnamese patrol boats, the destroyer USS *Maddox* opened fire (with assistance from USS *C. Turner Joy*) and reported one boat sunk and two damaged. On 4 August, the *C. Turner Joy* radioed that it was under attack by five patrol boats, but the *Maddox*'s radar did not confirm hostile action. On 7 August, Congress gave the president authority to "take all necessary measures to repel any armed attack against the forces of the United States and to prevent further aggression," and to give South Vietnam military aid. The resolution became the main statutory basis for US involvement in the VIETNAM WAR until its repeal after the invasion of CAMBODIA.

Gurney, Joseph John *see* QUAKERS

H

habeas corpus The writ of habeas corpus (i.e. "you have the body") orders law officers to release a detainee from custody unless they can justify his arrest. The Constitution protects it under Article I, Section 9. Union authorities denied habeas corpus to over 14,000 persons arrested in the CIVIL WAR in actions judged illegal by *EX PARTE MERRYMAN* and *EX PARTE MILLIGAN*. The KU KLUX KLAN ACT suspended habeas corpus in nine S.C. counties in 1871.

Haiti, US intervention in From 1900 to 1912, the US sent armed military parties for brief periods on 13 occasions, and in 1913 the marines landed three times. Between 28 July and 15 August 1915, a marine brigade landed to keep order following a coup. On 16 September Haiti signed a treaty that gave the US control of its finances and police force. Haiti remained a protectorate under armed occupation until 15 August 1934, during which time marines sustained 172 casualties, including 10 killed in action.

On 11 October 1993, Haitian demonstrators kept the USS *Harlan County* from disembarking 600 US troops assigned as UN peacekeepers to permit the return of President Jean Bertrand Aristide, who had been deposed by a military coup in September 1991. US warships blockaded the country on 18 October. By early November, UN health officials estimated that the blockade may have indirectly raised infant mortality by an extra 1,000 deaths per month. By July 1994, Haiti's economy had collapsed under the strain of the blockade, annual per capita income had dropped from $350 to $200, commodity shortages burdened the poor with heavy price increases for basic necessities, and 25 percent of Haitians depended on food distributed by relief organizations.

On 31 July, the UN Security Council authorized the US to restore Aristide's presidency by armed invasion. After 11 US warships carrying marines and soldiers took station off Port-au-Prince in September, envoy Jimmy CARTER persuaded the Haitian military to relinquish power. On 19 September, the US began landing an occupation force of 20,000 troops.

Haitian immigration Sizeable Haitian immigration first gained attention in 1957, and from then to 1977, the Immigration Service apprehended about 7,000 Haitians illegally entering the US. Arrests rose to 3,900 in 1978, 4,450 in 1979, 25,000 in 1980, and 15,000 through June 1981. Most Haitians settled in New York City or southern Fla. Political unrest in Haiti led the US to deploy the Coast Guard and Navy to prevent a mass exodus to Fla. in 1991–3. An estimated 281,803 Haitians entered the US through 1991. The 1990 census counted 290,000 persons (0.1 percent of the US population) who reported themselves of Haitian birth or background.

Hakluyt, Richard (b. near London, England, ca. 1552; d. Westminster, Middlesex, England, 23 November 1616) He was an Oxford professor who became the leading visionary for English exploration and colonization across the Atlantic. In 1582 he published *Divers Voyages Touching the Discoverie of America* (an account of other nations' explorations) and in 1584 he drafted the manuscript "A Discourse of Western Planting" for ELIZABETH I at Sir Walter RALEIGH's suggestion. In 1588 he published *The Principall Navigations, Voiages, and Discoveries of the English Nation.*

Haldeman, Harry Robbins (b. Los Angeles, Calif., 27 October 1926; d. Santa Barbara, Calif., 12 November 1993) "H. R." Haldeman entered Republican politics as a campaign worker for Richard NIXON in 1956. After holding important positions in Nixon's 1960 and 1968 campaigns, he was made chief of the White House staff in 1969. He controlled a $350,000 slush fund tapped by the WATERGATE SCANDAL's participants. His involvement in the scandal led to his resignation on 30 April 1973 and a 30-month prison sentence on 21 February 1975 for conspiracy to obstruct justice, obstruction of justice, and lying to the FBI.

Hale, John Parker (b. Rochester, N.H., 31 March 1806; d. Dover, N.H., 19 November 1873) In 1827 Hale opened a law practice at Dover, N.H. He sat in Congress as a Democrat (1843–4), but was read out of the party for opposing the annexation of TEXAS and served in the Senate for the WHIG PARTY (1847–52). Nominated for president by the LIBERTY PARTY in 1848, he withdrew his candidacy to strengthen the FREE-SOIL ticket headed by Martin VAN BUREN. He ran as Free-Soil nominee for president in 1852 and polled 5.0 percent of the ballots. After joining the Republicans, he returned to the Senate (1855–64). He bore principal responsibility for the abolition of flogging in the navy. His career ended as ambassador to Spain (1865–9).

half-breeds This name refers to a political faction during the GILDED AGE, that struggled with the STALWARTS to control the Republican Party. Their acknowledged leader was James BLAINE. The chief issue dividing the two factions was CIVIL SERVICE REFORM, which stalwarts opposed and half-breeds grudgingly supported as means of weakening their opponents. Both groups were opposed by the MUGWUMPS.

Half-way Covenant After 1650, a large – and growing – proportion of New England's young adults failed to meet full standards for membership in Congregational churches because they had not been born again, although they had been baptized. A synod met in 1662 to clarify the status of these individuals and their families. The synod abandoned the long-standing Puritan practice of restricting infant baptism to children of full members (i.e. those who could testify to having received saving grace); it instead permitted any child to be baptized so long as one of its parents had been baptized, even if neither parent was saved. This compromise ended the danger of Congregationalism becoming a minority church in New England.

Halleck, Henry W. (b. Westernville, N.Y., 16 January 1815; d. Louisville, Ky., 9 January 1872) He graduated third in his West Point class and was known as "Old Brains" for his books on military science. He served in California during the MEXICAN WAR and resigned his commission in 1854. He reentered the army as major general in 1861, and was recommended by Winfield SCOTT to command the Army of the POTOMAC, but was instead given command of all western forces. Named "general in chief" of all Federal armies on 11 July 1862, he served primarily as Abraham LINCOLN's chief military advisor and exercised no significant control over the field armies. When Ulysses S. GRANT assumed his position on 9 March 1864, Halleck functioned as a chief of staff by coordinating communications with the army's seventeen different commands and acting as liaison between Grant and Lincoln. Although reportedly the most unpopular man in Washington, Halleck played a major – and unappreciated – role in eventual Union victory.

Hamilton, Alexander (b. Nevis Island, 11 January 1755; d. New York, N.Y., 11 July 1804) He came to the US as a student to attend King's College (Columbia). He entered the Continental army as an artillery officer in March 1776 and was promoted to George WASHINGTON's staff (as lieutenant colonel) in March 1777. He left the army in December 1783 and became a lawyer in New York City. He attended the CONSTITUTIONAL CONVENTION and co-authored the *FEDERALIST PAPERS*. As first secretary of the treasury, he established national finances on a sound basis by his REPORT ON THE PUBLIC CREDIT and Report on a National Bank (*see* BANK OF THE UNITED STATES, FIRST). Congress ignored his REPORT ON MANUFACTURES' call for a protective tariff. After resigning from the treasury in 1795, he was a leading figure in the FEDERALIST PARTY. His rival for control of N.Y. politics, Aaron BURR, killed him in a duel.

Hamlin, Hannibal (b. Paris Hill, Maine, 27 August 1809; d. Hampden, Maine, 4 July 1891) He entered politics as a Democrat, but his ABOLITIONISM led him to join the REPUBLICAN PARTY in 1856, when he entered the Senate. He rapidly rose in national prominence and became Abraham LINCOLN's running mate in 1860, only to be replaced in 1864 by Andrew JOHNSON. He was again senator (1869–81), and then became ambassador to Spain.

Hammer* v. *Dagenhart On 3 June 1918, the Supreme Court struck down (5–4) the Keating–Owen CHILD LABOR ACT's clauses that outlawed interstate transportation of goods made by child labor. It ruled these provisions unconstitutional in accordance with *UNITED STATES* v. *E. C. KNIGHT COMPANY*, because they concerned intrastate manufacturing rather than interstate commerce; it also held that Congress had no power to prohibit shipments of products unless they were harmful, and goods made by children were not inherently dangerous. The Court reaffirmed *Hammer* in *BAILEY* v. *DREXEL FURNITURE COMPANY* before reversing it in *UNITED STATES* v. *DARBY LUMBER COMPANY*.

Hammerstein, Oscar *see* RODGERS AND HAMMERSTEIN

Hancock, John (b. North Braintree, Mass., 12 January 1737; d. Quincy, Mass., 8 October 1793) He inherited a fortune (including a mercantile firm) from a bachelor uncle at the age of 27 and was soon considered New England's wealthiest man. After Samuel ADAMS and James OTIS, he was the third most important Bostonian involved in the protests against unconstitutional Parliamentary measures. The LIBERTY RIOT concerned one of his sloops and he chaired the town committee investigating the BOSTON MASSACRE. He became president of the Massachusetts provincial congress created by the SUFFOLK RESOLVES in 1774, and president of the second CONTINENTAL CONGRESS in 1775. He served as Massachusetts governor (1780–5 and 1787–93).

Hancock, Winfield Scott (b. Montgomery Square, Pa., 14 February 1824; d. Governors Island, N.Y., 9 February 1886) In 1840 Hancock graduated 18th of 25 cadets from West Point. He served in the SEMINOLE WAR, MEXICAN WAR, and BLEEDING KANSAS. He commanded a corps in the Army of the POTOMAC, rose to major general and was cited for gallantry at GETTYSBURG (where he was badly wounded) and SPOTSYLVANIA COURT HOUSE. As Democratic candidate for president in 1880, he polled just 39,213 ballots less than Republican James GARFIELD.

Handsome Lake (b. N.Y. ca. 1749; d. Onondaga, N.Y., 10 August 1815) A SENECA warrior, tribal leader, and shaman, Handsome Lake experienced a vision while recovering from a bout of heavy drinking on 15 June 1799. This vision and other revelations formed the basis for the LONGHOUSE RELIGION, for which Handsome Lake became the principal prophet and apostle, spreading its beliefs among the IROQUOIS.

Hanna, Marcus Alonzo (b. New Lisbon, Ohio, 24 September 1837; d. Washington, D.C., 15 February 1904) He was a Cleveland industrialist who became active in Republican politics in 1880 to support James GARFIELD. Hanna emerged as Ohio's most powerful and knowledgable political boss. Hanna managed William MCKINLEY's race for Ohio governor in 1892 and maneuvered his first-ballot victory for president in 1896 at the Republican convention. As Republican national committee chair, he shrewdly orchestrated McKinley's victory over William Jennings BRYAN; he financed electioneering in swing districts by raising an unprecedented $3,500,000 from businessmen who feared Bryan's radical rhetoric, and then organized a sophisticated front-porch campaign that offset Bryan's oratorical advantages with effective publicity for the quiescent McKinley. Hanna enabled McKinley to win by 95 electoral votes, despite outpolling Bryan by just 610,000 votes out of 13,500,000 ballots. While yet governor, McKinley appointed Hanna senator from Ohio, and as president relied heavily for his advice on patronage and policies. To reformers of the PROGRESSIVE ERA, Hanna symbolized the antidemocratic underbelly of machine politics.

Hard Labor, treaty of (S.C.) The first instance of adjusting the PROCLAMATION LINE west occurred on 18 October 1768, when the CHEROKEE INDIANS sold 2,700 square miles in southwestern Va., including an area along the New River that had been settled since the 1750s.

Harding, Warren Gamaliel (b. Corsica, Ohio, 2 November 1865; d. San Francisco, Calif., 2 August 1923) He was a Marion, Ohio, newspaper editor who entered Republican politics. He was state senator (1900–4), lieutenant governor (1904–6), losing candidate for governor (1910), and US senator (1915–21). An excellent orator and keynote speaker at the 1916 Republican convention, he was a dark horse candidate for president in 1920, when the Republicans chose him after deadlocking between Leonard WOOD and Frank Lowden. He pledged a "return to normalcy" (and virtually nothing else) and won in a landslide with 60.4 percent of the ballots. Credit for his administration's major accomplishment, the WASHINGTON NAVAL CONFERENCE, was due to Charles Evans HUGHES, and Andrew MELLON directed his fiscal policy. He was personally honest, but surrounded himself with the OHIO GANG, whose corruption was exposed in the ALIEN PROPERTY CUSTODIAN SCANDAL, the TEAPOT DOME SCANDAL, and Harry DAUGHERTY's malfeasance. He died of ptomaine poisoning contracted from tainted Japanese crabmeat.

Harlan, John Marshall (b. Boyle County, Ky., 1 June 1833; d. Washington, D.C., 14 October 1911) Although a slaveowner, Harlan commanded the Union 10th Ky. Infantry. At the 1876 Republican presidential convention, he was critical in swinging victory toward Rutherford HAYES, who put him on the Supreme Court in 1877. Nicknamed "the last of the tobacco-spitting judges," he wrote 380 dissents in 33 years, more than any other justice. History has vindicated his firm opposition to his fellow justices' narrow interpretation of the FOURTEENTH AMENDMENT, especially his lone dissent from *PLESSY* v. *FERGUSON* that declared "our Constitution is color-blind."

Harlem Heights, battle of (N.Y.) On 16 September 1776, three British regiments (later reinforced to 5,000 men) patrolling Washington's front lines retreated with heavy casualties under US attack. US losses: 20 killed, 40 wounded. British losses: 14 killed, 154 wounded. The action marked the first US victory in the fight for New York, raised American morale, and relieved enemy pressure on Washington by delaying the next major British assault for a month.

Harlem Renaissance This term encompasses a period of literary and artistic creativity that made Harlem the cultural center of African-American life. It flourished about 1919–29, and marked the first major flowering of black literature, theater, and the visual arts. Its most prominent authors included Langston Hughes, James Weldon Johnson, Claude McKay, Jean Toomer, Countee Cullen, and Walter White. Noted artists included Aaron Douglas, Laura Wheeling Waring, Edward A. Harleston, and Wingold Reiss.

Harmar's Defeat Between 30 September and 3 November 1790, Brigadier General Josiah Harmar led 320 regulars, 1,133 militia, and a pack train of 578 horses against Little Turtle's Indian confederacy. After two of his patrols took heavy losses on 20–1 October near modern Fort Wayne, Ind., he returned to Fort Washington, Ohio, without having fought a major battle. US losses: 75 regulars and 108 militia killed, 3 regulars and 28 militia wounded. Indian losses: minor casualties, 5 villages (184 cabins) burned, 20,000 bushels of corn plundered.

Harper, William Rainey (b. New Concord, Ohio, 24 July 1856; d. Chicago, Ill., 10 January 1906) A graduate of Muskingum (Ohio) College, Harper received a Ph.D. from Yale at the age of 18 and became a professor of Semitic languages. As president of the University of Chicago (1891–1906), he emerged as a leading educational reformer. He pioneered innovations like the academic year's division into quarters, the summer quarter, university extension centers, and the university-sponsored press.

Harper* v. *Virginia State Board of Elections On 24 March 1966, the Supreme Court decided that the FOURTEENTH AMENDMENT's equal protection clause prohibited states from imposing POLL TAXes or otherwise using taxes to discourage citizens from voting.

Harper's Ferry Raid (Va.) *see* BROWN, JOHN

Harrington, Michael *see* *OTHER AMERICA, THE*

Harris, Joel Chandler (b. near Eatonton, Ga., 9 December 1848; d. Atlanta, Ga., 3 July 1908) He was one of the most talented regional humorists in the late 19th century. Writing in the Atlanta *Constitution*, he won national fame with his "Uncle Remus Stories," such as the "Tar-Baby" tale. His first collection, *Uncle Remus, His Songs and His Sayings* (1880), achieved widespread commercial success, and new volumes appeared regularly until 1918. Along with Mark TWAIN, Harris was one of the two authors most responsible for pioneering the realistic use of folk dialects in US literature.

Harris, Townsend (b. Sandy Hill, N.Y., 3 October 1804; d. New York, N.Y., 25 February 1873) He was a self-made retailer who was instrumental in building a coalition to found the City College of New York. On 4 August 1855, he became the first US diplomat to enter Japan (as consul general). On 18 June 1857, he negotiated the opening of Nagasaki to US commerce; on 29 July 1858, he concluded the Harris Convention granting trading rights at five additional Japanese ports, authorizing US merchants to reside in Japan, and arranging a three-month visit to Washington in 1860 by imperial diplomats (Japan's first such mission to any western country).

Harris* v. *Forklift Systems, Incorporated *see* *MERITOR SAVINGS BANK* v. *VINSON*

Harris* v. *McRae On 30 June 1980, the Supreme Court ruled (5–4) that the HYDE AMENDMENT neither exceeded Congress's powers nor transgressed on DUE PROCESS, equal protection of the laws, or free exercise of religion; it also held that the Social Security Act (*see* SOCIAL SECURITY ADMINISTRATION did not make states responsible for financing abortions essential for maternal health in the absence of federal funding.

Harris* v. *New York On 24 February 1971, the Supreme Court modified *MIRANDA* v. *ARIZONA* by ruling (5–4) that if police failed to warn a person in custody that he could remain silent and have a lawyer, and the suspect made statements contradicting testimony later given by him in court, then his earlier words could be used to discredit his trial testimony, even though he was not properly apprised of his legal rights when he gave them.

Harrison, Benjamin (b. North Bend, Ohio, 20 August 1833; d. Indianapolis, Ind., 20 August 1901) Grandson of William Henry HARRISON, he moved to Ind. to practice law in 1854 and rose to brigadier general in the CIVIL WAR. As Republican senator from Ind. (1881–7), he supported higher veterans' pensions and CIVIL SERVICE REFORM. He became president by defeating Grover CLEVELAND in 1888, despite polling 60,728 votes less than the Democrat. He signed the MCKINLEY TARIFF and SHERMAN SILVER PURCHASE ACT, liberalized pension laws, and backed US expansion into the Pacific. He lost reelection to Cleveland, who outpolled him 46.1 percent to 43.0 percent, and retired to practicing law.

Harrison, William Henry (b. Charles City County, Va., 9 February 1773; d. Washington, D.C., 4 April 1841) He served in the army (1791–8), during which time he fought at FALLEN TIMBERS. He became the NORTHWEST TERRITORY's first delegate to Congress in 1799 and was governor of Ind. Territory (1801–12), during which time he won the battle of TIPPECANOE CREEK. He was the most successful US general in the WAR OF 1812. He established an estate near Cincinnati, sat in Congress (1817–18) and the Senate (1826–8). He won 36.5 percent of the ballots for president in 1836 and carried seven states for the WHIG PARTY. He died soon after his election as president in the LOG CABIN CAMPAIGN with 53.1 percent of the ballots and all but seven states.

Hartford convention (Conn.) Between 15 December 1814 and 5 January 1815, delegates from every New England state held a convention to propose constitutional amendments. The convention passed resolutions to reduce federal control over state militias in wartime, to cease counting slaves for congressional representation, to prohibit any EMBARGO ACT exceeding 60 days, to forbid naturalized citizens from holding high federal office, to limit presidents to one term, and to require a two-thirds vote by Congress for restricting overseas commerce, declaring war, and admitting new states. The convention's report declared that INTERPOSITION might be necessary to protect the sovereignty of New England's states. Because the convention deliberated in secrecy, and New England had opposed entry into the WAR OF 1812, false rumors circulated that the members were plotting secession or disloyal actions. These unfounded charges were widely believed and badly discredited the FEDERALIST PARTY, to which most delegates belonged, and hastened its disintegration.

Hat Act (1 June 1732) Parliament amended the WOOLEN ACT by forbidding the export of hats made in one colony, either overseas or to another colony. It required American hatters to have served a seven-year apprenticeship before setting up shop and prohibited them from using more than two apprentices or slaves.

Hatch Act (2 March 1887) This law appropriated federal funds to finance state-operated experimental stations for agriculture to promote and publicize scientific advances in farming. It was Congress's only major farm legislation between the second HOMESTEAD ACT and the CAREY ACT.

Hatch Act (1939–40) The provisions of two federal statutes forbidding political activities by government workers were collectively referred to as the Hatch Act. The first law (2 August 1939) was a reaction to the use of political pressure upon WORKS PROGRESS ADMINISTRATION (WPA) workers during the 1938 elections to reelect candidates favorable to the NEW DEAL in Ky., Md., and Tenn. The law was intended to prevent the rise of a national political machine. A second statute (19 July 1940) applied the 1939 act's restrictions to state and local employees in positions that were subsidized by federal funds. The Hatch Act excluded political appointees and elected officials, but it forbade all other employees from seeking elective office, speaking at political rallies, leading political meetings, seeking contributions or votes in an election, serving as an officer for a political organization, and acting as a delegate to a party nominating convention.

The Supreme Court held it constitutional (4–3) on 10 February 1947 in *United Public Workers* v. *Mitchell*. The initial statutes required that violators be fired, but amendments allowed transgressions to be punished by suspensions without pay. Labor unions lobbied repeatedly, and unsuccessfully, for its repeal until 6 October 1993, when President William CLINTON signed legislation ending most political restrictions on all federal employees except the most senior 85,000 positions in law enforcement and national security. Federal workers could then endorse candidates for office, distribute campaign literature, and engage in most volunteer partisan activity, but still could not run for office.

Havana, battle of (Cuba) On 12 October 1762, 14,000 British and Yankee troops (including regiments from Conn., R.I., N.Y., and N. J.) captured Havana after a two-months' siege. To regain Cuba, Spain gave FLORIDA to Britain in the treaty of PARIS (1763).

Hawaii On 18 January 1778, Captain James Cook of England made the first European contact with Hawaii. The onslaught of European diseases unknown to the Hawaiians probably reduced their population from 300,000 in 1778 to 135,000 in 1819. The islands became a way station for Yankee ships en route to China. US missionaries arrived in 1820 and stimulated interest by American investors in developing the islands. US sugar plantations came to dominate the islands' economy after 1854. The continuing decline in the Hawaiian population (to 40,000 by 1890), led US businessmen to seek field laborers through JAPANESE and CHINESE IMMIGRATION.

On 30 January 1875, Hawaii negotiated a treaty that allowed its sugar to enter the US duty-free and obliged it to refrain from giving territorial or economic concessions to foreign powers. The US became the best market for Hawaiian sugar until the MCKINLEY TARIFF imposed heavy duties, which led American sugar planters to favor US annexation. On 20 January 1887, the US obtained the exclusive right to build a navy base at Pearl Harbor. In 1887, US expatriates helped engineer a revolt that instituted a constitutional monarchy. Queen Liliuokalani rescinded the constitution in 1891 and assumed autocratic powers. US citizens overthrew the monarchy on 16 January 1894, with assistance from US marines, and proclaimed a republic, which the US recognized on 7 August 1894 and annexed on 7 July 1898.

When the islands were made a territory on 14 June 1900, they had 154,001 inhabitants (26 percent Hawaiian, 17 percent white, 40 percent Japanese, 17 percent Chinese), of whom 75 percent were rural and 59 percent foreign-born. They ranked 47th in population, 40th in the value of agricultural goods, and 40th in manufactures. Pineapple cultivation started in 1903.

Hawaii became the navy's Pacific headquarters, where WORLD WAR II began at PEARL HARBOR. Hawaii became the 50th state on 21 August 1959. Tourism emerged as its major industry. The population doubled from 1950 to 1990, when it ranked 39th among states, with 1,108,229 people (approx. 58 percent Asian, 32 percent white, 7 percent Hispanic, 2 percent black), of whom 76 percent were urban and 14.7 percent were foreign-born. Manufacturing and mining employed 14 percent of workers.

hawks This term originated in the mid-1960s to describe US policy makers who advocated prosecuting the VIETNAM WAR to a full victory, or negotiating a peace from a position of military strength. The most consistent hawk was Dean RUSK.

Hawley–Smoot Tariff (17 June 1930) Against the near unanimous opposition of professional economists, Congress passed the highest import duties since the DINGLEY TARIFF. It raised duties on 75 farm products and 925 industrial items, and increased average ad valorem rates to 40 percent from the FORDNEY–MCCUMBER TARIFF's average of 26 percent. By excluding a large volume of European exports from the US market, it led to retaliatory tariffs against US exports and was a major factor in stifling world trade; it also stimulated a cycle of currency devaluations overseas that helped trigger a European monetary crisis in 1931. The TRADE AGREEMENTS ACT replaced it.

Hawthorne, Nathaniel (b. Salem, Mass., 4 July 1804; d. Plymouth, N.H., 19 May 1864) An orphan since the age of four who became friends with William Wadsworth LONGFELLOW and Franklin PIERCE at Bowdoin College, Hawthorne anonymously published his first novel, *Fanshawe*, in 1828. He emerged as a leading novelist and short-story author in the Romantic era. His writings explored dark themes involving corruption, hypocrisy, or evil, and were often set in his native New England. His major works include *Twice-Told Tales* (1837), *Mosses from an Old Manse* (1846), *The Scarlet Letter* (1850), *The House of the Seven Gables* (1851), *The Life of Franklin Pierce* (1852) – which won him appointment as US consul at Liverpool, England (1853–60) – *The Marble Faun* (1860), and *The Ancestral Footstep* (1883).

Hay, John Milton (b. Salem, Ind., 12 October 1838; d. Lake Sunapee, N.H., 1 July 1905) He opened a law office at Springfield, Ill., where he became acquainted with Abraham LINCOLN, who hired Hay as a private secretary while president. Hay then served in the diplomatic corps (1865–70) at Paris, Madrid, and Vienna. After working as a journalist, he became assistant secretary of state (1879–81) and ambassador to Britain (1897–8). As secretary of state (1898–1905), he inaugurated the OPEN DOOR POLICY, and negotiated the HAY–BUNAU–VARILLA and HAY–PAUNCEFOTE TREATIES and the HAY–HERRÁN CONVENTION.

Hay–Bunau–Varilla Treaty In a treaty signed on 18 November 1903 and ratified on 23 February 1904, the US received perpetual control over a 10-mile-wide zone across the Isthmus of Panama, for building and fortifying a PANAMA CANAL, in return for $10,000,000 compensation, annual fees of $250,000 starting nine years after the canal's opening (*see* HAY–HERRÁN CONVENTION), and US promises to protect Panama from Colombian reconquest. On 18 April 1978, the US ratified a treaty transferring canal operations in stages to Panama and handing over the canal zone by 31 December 1999.

Hay–Herrán Convention On 28 June 1902, Congress appropriated $40,000,000 to purchase existing rights to build a canal across Central America from the New Panama Canal Co., but left Colombia's payment for a lease to be settled by diplomacy. US–Colombian negotiations produced the Hay–Herrán Convention, which promised Colombia $10,000,000 and annual royalties of $250,000 for a 99-year lease on a canal zone across modern Panama. The Senate ratified the agreement on 22 January 1903, but Colombia rejected it because it wished at least $25,000,000 for right-of-way. The convention's failure led to US military intervention in the PANAMA REVOLT.

Hay–Pauncefote treaties On 20 December 1900, the Senate ratified the first Hay–Pauncefote Treaty, which abrogated certain clauses of the CLAYTON–BULWER

TREATY by giving the US sole rights to build and operate an Atlantic–Pacific canal across Central America. A second Hay–Pauncefote Treaty (ratified 16 December 1901) nullified most of the 1850 treaty's other clauses and reaffirmed the canal's neutrality, but failed to concede the US any right to fortify it. Britain recognized US rights of fortification in a memorandum of 3 August.

Hayden, Thomas *see* CHICAGO EIGHT

Hayes, Rutherford Birchard (b. Delaware, Ohio, 4 October 1822; d. Fremont, Ohio, 17 January 1893) He practiced law in Cincinnati and entered politics in the WHIG PARTY. Although not an abolitionist, he joined the REPUBLICAN PARTY to oppose the extension of slavery to the western territories. In the CIVIL WAR, he rose to US brigadier general and was twice cited for gallantry. He served three terms as Ohio governor and was the Republican presidential nominee against Samuel TILDEN in the disputed election of 1876, in which he polled 48.0 percent of the popular vote and won by a single electoral vote. As president, Hayes ended RECONSTRUCTION by withdrawing US occupation troops according to the COMPROMISE OF 1877. He deployed federal troops to break the RAILROAD STRIKE OF 1877 and vetoed the BLAND–ALLISON ACT.

Haymarket riot On 3 May 1886, Chicago police killed four workers striking at the McCormick Harvester Co. On 4 May, at a protest rally at Haymarket Square, a riot started when an unknown assailant threw a bomb and police fired on the crowd. The violence left 11 dead (including 7 police) and 67 injured. On 20 August 1886, after a trial dominated by public hysteria, an anarchist was sentenced to 15 years' confinement and seven others to death, of whom one committed suicide and two had their executions commuted to life imprisonment. The episode turned public opinion strongly against labor unions.

Haywood, William Dudley (b. Salt Lake City, Utah, 4 February 1869; d. Moscow, Russia, 18 May 1928) "Big Bill" Haywood was a labor officer tried in 1905 as an accomplice in the assassination of Idaho governor Frank Steunenberg, who took management's side during a violent mining strike. Although acquitted, Haywood became renowned as the country's most radical union leader, especially after becoming an organizer for the INDUSTRIAL WORKERS OF THE WORLD (IWW), which he helped found in 1905. Long a socialist, he was convicted of Sedition (*see* SEDITION ACT, 1918) in 1918 with several other IWW officers. In 1921, he sought political asylum in Soviet Russia, where he helped expand coal output.

Head Start Program The ECONOMIC OPPORTUNITY ACT (1964) created this program as part of the GREAT SOCIETY to prepare handicapped and culturally deprived children for elementary school. It started in 1965 as a summer enrichment program for 550,000 pre-school children at 3,300 centers. In 1982, Head Start expanded into a nine-month program offering educational, recreational, motivational, nutritional, and health-related services. About 597,000 children participated in Head Start during 1991.

headright In 1618, the VIRGINIA COMPANY OF LONDON offered a headright, or land grant, of 50 acres to anyone who financed the passage of a new settler, INDENTURED SERVANT or slave to Va. Md. gave more generous headrights in 1633, limited them to 50 acres per head in 1658, and ended the system in 1681. Neither colony awarded land to anyone transported at another's expense, although in 1640 Md. entitled ex-servants to claim 50 acres – provided they found an unpatented tract and paid the surveyor's and clerk's fees themselves. By 1700, Va. had issued headrights for 86,000 persons and Md. did so for over 30,000. S.C. issued headrights from 1664 until the 1750s.

Health, Education, and Welfare, Department of On 1 April 1953, Congress abolished the Federal Security Agency and established this department to consolidate a wide variety of social welfare programs enacted since the NEW DEAL. In 1979 it was split into the Departments of EDUCATION and HEALTH AND HUMAN SERVICES.

Health and Human Services, Department of On 17 October 1979, Congress created this department by reorganizing the Department of HEALTH, EDUCATION, AND WELFARE, placing all education agencies under a separate cabinet-level secretary. It oversees Social Security (*see* SOCIAL SECURITY

ADMINISTRATION) and other programs involving public assistance and health problems.

Hearst, William Randolph (b. San Francisco, Calif., 29 April 1863; d. Beverly Hills, Calif., 14 August 1951) In 1885 Hearst entered journalism and used his father's fortune to build the greatest media empire of his day. While editing the New York *Journal*, he pioneered YELLOW JOURNALISM. By stridently espousing US intervention in Cuba's revolt against Spain, he helped create the war fever that led to the SPANISH-AMERICAN WAR. After founding the Hearst News Service in 1900, he bought 23 papers in 18 cities, became the country's leading magazine publisher, and acquired radio stations and movie studios. He made a strong bid to be Democratic nominee for president in 1904, but lost on the first ballot to Alton PARKER.

Heart of Atlanta Motel* v. *United States On 14 December 1964, the Supreme Court unanimously upheld Title II of the CIVIL RIGHTS ACT (1964), which outlawed racial discrimination in all public accommodations. Its power to regulate interstate commerce authorized Congress to forbid privately-owned establishments that provided any services for interstate travelers to refuse service to nonwhites. The ruling reversed the CIVIL RIGHTS CASES of 1883.

Helper, Hinton Rowan *see* *IMPENDING CRISIS OF THE SOUTH*

Helvering* v. *Davis *see* SOCIAL SECURITY ADMINISTRATION

Hemingway, Ernest (b. Oak Park, Ill., 21 July 1898; d. Ketchum, Idaho, 2 July 1961) He served as both a volunteer ambulance driver and an enlistee in the Italian army in World War I, during which he was wounded badly and twice decorated. He then became a foreign correspondent, and covered the Spanish civil war. Hemingway spent most of his life abroad in Europe or Cuba. He published his first book of stories, *In Our Time*, in 1924, and became one of the most prominent authors of the LOST GENERATION. His fiction portrayed men of action, resembling himself, as they confront challenges to their physical and moral courage. His other major works include *The Sun Also Rises* (1926), *A Farewell to Arms* (1929), *To Have and Have Not* (1937), *For Whom the Bell Tolls* (1940), *Across the River and Into the Trees* (1940), and *The Old Man and the Sea* (1952). He won the Nobel prize for literature in 1954.

Henderson, Richard *see* TRANSYLVANIA COLONY

Henderson* v. *Wickham *see* IMMIGRATION CASES

Hendricks, Thomas Andrews (b. Zanesville, Ohio, 7 September 1819; d. Indianapolis, Ind., 25 November 1885) A lawyer, Hendricks was US congressman (Democrat, Ind., 1851–5), US senator (1863–9), Samuel TILDEN's running mate in 1876, and Ind. governor (1883–7). He died eight months after taking office as vice-president.

Hennepin, Fr Louis (b. Ath, Hainaut, Belgium, 7 April 1640; d. after 1701) In December 1678, Hennepin wrote the first description of Niagara Falls while accompanying the Sieur de LA SALLE across the Great Lakes. Hennepin explored the northern Mississippi and discovered its falls at modern St Paul in 1680.

Henry, Patrick (b. Hanover County, Va., 29 May 1736; d. Charlotte County, Va., 6 June 1799) He first came to prominence in the PARSONS CAUSE and entered the HOUSE OF BURGESSES in 1765, when he introduced the earliest – and most sweeping – resolutions against the STAMP ACT. Henry's resolutions inspired other colonies to follow suit and marked the beginning of united opposition to taxation without representation. As the most effective orator in Va., he led resistance to unconstitutional Parliamentary measures. He played a principal role in drafting the first Va. constitution, was its first governor, directed the ANTIFEDERALISTS in Va., and was a leading advocate for a federal BILL OF RIGHTS. He declined offers to be secretary of state and US chief justice.

Hepburn Act (29 June 1906) This law empowered the INTERSTATE COMMERCE COMMISSION (ICC) to set maximum railroad rates and establish uniform bookkeeping procedures for determining the profitability of carrier services. Railroads could appeal its decisions to the courts, but had to show their rates were reasonable. The law gave the ICC jurisdiction over express, sleeping-car, and oil pipeline companies.

ferries, bridges, and terminal facilities. It forbade carriers to issue free passes or to carry freight for subsidiaries not engaged in the railroad business. The law marked the start of effective railway regulation. The MANN–ELKINS ACT strengthened it.

Hepburn v. Griswold *see* LEGAL TENDER CASES

Hessians These were German mercenaries hired from the rulers of Anhalt-Zerbst, Anspach-Bayreuth, Brunswick, Hesse-Cassel, Hesse-Hanau, and Waldeck during the REVOLUTIONARY WAR. They were termed Hessians because out of the 29,875 recruited, 16,992 came from Hesse-Cassel and 2,422 from Hesse-Hanau. They gained an unsavory reputation as looters early in the war. In the only battles when they engaged US forces by themselves, at TRENTON and BENNINGTON, they suffered heavy defeats. A quarter of them (7,754) died in service, and over 5,000 deserted and remained in the US.

Hiawatha (fl. 16th century) Properly called Ayonhwathah, Hiawatha was an ONONDAGA INDIAN who was inspired to work toward peace among all the IROQUOIS CONFEDERACY after listening to the HURON INDIAN visionary Deganawida. Legend credits Hiawatha with primary credit for ending internecine feuding and establishing the league of the FIVE NATIONS about 1520–40.

Hicksites *see* QUAKERS

Hidatsa Indians This group, speakers of one of the SIOUAN LANGUAGES, was also known as the Gros Ventres ("Big Bellies") of the Missouri River. In 1760, they occupied the Dakotas and had but recently adopted horses into their culture and entered the FUR TRADE. Smallpox cut their population from 3,500 to 2,100 in the 1770s; the great epidemic of 1837–8 may have killed half of them. They fought no wars with the US, but came under heavy attacks from the SIOUX INDIANS. In 1880, they settled at the Fort Berthold, N.Dak., Reservation with the MANDAN and ARIKARA Indians.

Higher Education Act (8 November 1965) This measure, part of the GREAT SOCIETY, marked the first major expansion of federal aid to higher education since the NATIONAL DEFENSE EDUCATION ACT. It authorized $803,350,000 in 1966, including $42,000,000 for interest subsidies on student loans and $219,000,000 for college work-study programs (59 percent), scholarships (32 percent), and university extension or continuing education (9 percent). It furnished money to small colleges and created a Teacher Corps to work among economically disadvantaged students. This law, as supplemented by the HIGHER EDUCATION ACT (1967) was instrumental in raising college enrollment from 6,000,000 in 1965 to 7,600,000 in 1968, and 9,100,000 in 1973.

Higher Education Act (29 June 1967) This measure, part of the GREAT SOCIETY, significantly expanded federal aid to colleges by appropriating $547,200,000 in low-interest loans and scholarships for disadvantaged students, grants for state education programs, funds for improving libraries and laboratories, and an extension of the Teacher Corps.

Hill, James Jerome (b. near Rockwood, Ontario, 16 September 1838; d. St Paul, Minn., 29 May 1916) He began working as a store clerk at 14 and settled in St Paul in 1856. Having accumulated capital as a merchant and transportation agent, in 1879 he led a partnership in reorganizing a bankrupt railroad (renamed the Great Northern in 1890), which Hill pushed from St Paul to Seattle by 1893. He accomplished this feat without the federal land grants showered on other TRANSCONTINENTAL RAILROADS. His line was one of the few major railways to avoid bankruptcy in the PANIC OF 1893. In 1901, Hill formed his empire into a trust (*see* TRUSTS), which was ordered dissolved in *NORTHERN SECURITIES COMPANY* V. *UNITED STATES*. Known as the "Empire Builder," Hill did much to stimulate the Pacific northwest economy.

Hillman, Sidney (b. Zagare, Lithuania, 23 March 1887; d. Point Lookout, N.Y., 10 July 1946) In 1907 Hillman came to the US and became a clothing cutter in Chicago. Elected first president of the Amalgamated Clothing Workers of America in 1914, he led its rise to become one of the largest INDUSTRIAL UNIONS and was a founder of the CIO. He influenced the NATIONAL INDUSTRIAL RECOVERY ACT (NIRA) and acquired much political influence by pioneering techniques to organize the labor vote for the Democratic Party as part of the ROOSEVELT COALITION. He became the Democratic Party's most legendary power-broker. (Before Henry WALLACE was willing to settle on a prospective running mate at the 1948 Democratic convention, he told an aide, "Check it with Sidney.")

Hillsborough Circular Letter Learning of the MASSACHUSETTS CIRCULAR LETTER, Lord Hillsborough (Wills Hill, secretary of state responsible for colonial affairs) attacked it in a letter of his own (21 April 1768) sent to every colonial assembly. Hill forbade any legislature to endorse the Mass. Letter and ordered Mass. to repudiate it; he also directed every royal governor to dissolve any legislature disobeying his instructions. Hill's heavy-handed tactics backfired and led many legislatures previously apathetic about the Mass. statement to approve its denunciation of the TOWNSHEND REVENUE ACT. On 1 July, Governor Bernard dissolved the Mass. assembly for voting to stand by its original principles. The Hillsborough Letter helped mobilize opposition to the Townshend taxes and build support for the second NONIMPORTATION AGREEMENT.

hippie During the 1960s, the term hippie was applied to college students or associated dropouts who were alienated from US society and created a counterculture involving drug use, rejection of materialism, free love, support for the VIETNAM ANTIWAR MOVEMENT, and "flower power" (a vague faith that enough good will could resolve any conflict peacefully and fairly). The WOODSTOCK ROCK FESTIVAL exemplified hippie behavior and attitudes. YIPPIES were the hippies' radical left wing.

Hirabayashi* v. *United States On 21 June 1943, the Supreme Court ruled unanimously that a wartime curfew imposed during the JAPANESE RELOCATION was constitutional, even though only persons of Japanese background were restricted; it held that national security justified imposing a curfew on one race in wartime when enemies of the same nationality might commit sabotage or espionage.

Hiroshima, bombing of (Japan) At 8:16 a.m., 6 August 1945, Colonel Paul Tibbets's B-29 *Enola Gay* detonated the first atomic bomb used in warfare. The explosion equaled 20,000 tons of TNT, destroyed four square miles, killed 66,000–78,000, injured at least 80,000, and exposed 300,000 people to radiation.

Hispanic immigration The largest source of the US Hispanic population has come from MEXICAN and CUBAN IMMIGRATION. By 1991 legal immigration from other Hispanic countries totaled 551,558 Dominicans, 321,590 Salvadorans, 608,858 other Central Americans, 314,625 Colombians, and 1,015,986 other South Americans.

Hiss, Alger (b. Baltimore, Md., 11 November 1904) A Harvard-trained lawyer, Hiss entered federal service in the NEW DEAL, rose to be an influential State Department official, and became president of the Carnegie Endowment for World Peace. In 1948 Whitaker Chambers identified him as a member of the COMMUNIST PARTY who sent classified documents to Moscow in the 1930s, and Hiss became the object of a major investigation by the HOUSE COMMITTEE ON UN-AMERICAN ACTIVITIES, during which Richard NIXON gained national prominence for pressing the case against him. On 8 July 1949, a jury failed to reach a verdict on charges stemming from this case, but on 21 January 1950 he was convicted on two counts of perjury and given five years in prison. Despite repeated efforts to prove his innocence, no conclusive evidence has surfaced to win a reversal of his conviction.

Hobart, Garret Augustus (b. Long Branch, N.J., 3 June 1844; d. Paterson, N.J., 21 November 1899) A lawyer, businessman, and banker, Hobart served in the N.J. legislature (Republican, 1876–82) and was US vice-president (1897–9). He presided ably over the Senate and cast the deciding vote against independence for the PHILIPPINES.

Hobkirk's Hill, battle of (S.C.) On 25 April 1781, Lord Rawdon's 900 redcoats and TORIES defeated Major General Nathanael GREENE's 1,200 Continentals and 400 militia near Camden. US losses: 18 killed, 108 wounded, 138 missing. British losses: 38 killed, 220 wounded. By saving his supplies and artillery, Greene frustrated Rawdon's main objective but left the British weaker by inflicting casualties they would find more difficult to replace than the Americans would

Hodgson* v. *Minnesota On 25 June 1990, the Supreme Court modified *Roe* v. *Wade* by ruling (5–4) that states may set a 48-hour waiting period for abortions (*see* ABORTION) and may require underage girls either to notify both parents before pursuing this option or to request permission from a judge for terminating a pregnancy.

Hoe, Richard March (b. New York, N.Y., 12 September 1812; d. Florence, Italy, 7 June 1886) He learned the printer's trade from his father. Beginning in 1837, he invented – and then improved – a series of cylindrical presses that increased a printer's hourly output ten times over the production rate of traditional flatbed hand presses. His rotary presses allowed printers to run off 8,000 sheets per hour by 1847. In 1871, he and Stephen D. Tucker developed the web press, which simultaneously printed both sides of sheets fed into it from large rollers, and could print 18,000 sheets per hour. By reducing the cost of producing books and newspapers, Hoe's inventions encouraged an expansion of the reading public. His presses also enabled journalists to print longer and more comprehensive newspapers at greatly reduced costs.

Hoffa, Jimmy (James Riddle) (b. Brazil, Ind., 14 February 1913; d. ca. 30 July 1975) He began working full-time at 14 in Detroit, and by the age of 18 had organized his fellow warehouse workers and received a union charter from the AFL. He affiliated with the International Brotherhood of Teamsters in 1932, and became president of Detroit Local 299 in 1935. He was elected international vice-president in 1952, and became president in 1957, the same year as the AFL-CIO ousted the Teamsters for corruption. Hoffa rapidly expanded Teamster membership, negotiated a comprehensive contract for all long-distance truckers in 1964, and planned to attract railway, airline, and maritime unions into a massive federation of US transport workers. Robert KENNEDY directed a massive federal effort to investigate Hoffa's illegal activities, which eventually led to his entering prison in March 1967 under sentences totaling 13 years for jury-tampering, mail fraud, and embezzlement of union funds. Hoping to win the Teamsters' political support, Richard NIXON commuted Hoffa's remaining sentence in December 1971, on condition that he abstain from union affairs until 1980. Hoffa was indicating that he intended to reassert control over the Teamsters when he disappeared in Bloomfield Township, Mich., and was presumably murdered.

Hoffman, Abbie *see* CHICAGO EIGHT *and* YIPPIES

Hohokam Culture This culture developed along the Gila and Salt rivers of Ariz. after 100 BC. Its evolution paralleled the MOGOLLON CULTURE, but was distinctive in engineering huge canal systems to irrigate the desert at modern Phoenix and other sites. The Hohokam communities were abandoned for unknown reasons by 1500.

HOLC Home Owners' Loan Corporation (*see* HOME OWNERS REFINANCING ACT).

Holden* v. *Hardy In 1898 the Supreme Court affirmed (7–2) an 1896 Utah law regulating the length of miners' workdays, as a proper application of the state's police powers; it also declared that in cases where one side bargains at a distinct disadvantage to the other, a state might intrude upon the usual right of parties to make contracts free from government interference. The Court reversed this general position in *Lochner* v. *New York*.

holding company *see* TRUSTS

Holmes, Oliver Wendell, Jr (b. Boston, Mass., 8 March 1841; d. Washington, D.C., 6 March 1935) A thrice-wounded veteran of the Union 20th Massachusetts Infantry, Holmes wrote over 1,000 opinions while on the Mass. supreme court (1882–1902). He joined the US SUPREME COURT in 1902. Famed as the "Great Dissenter," he issued 173 contrary opinions, a tenth of which influenced later courts to reverse his colleagues' majority rulings. Holmes's decisions include *Swift and Company* v. *United States*, *United States* v. *Mosley*, *Schenck* v. *United States*, *Missouri* v. *Holland*, *Moore* v. *Dempsey*, *Nixon* v. *Herndon*. Holmes resigned at the age of 90 in 1932.

Holmes* v. *Jennison In January 1840, a divided Supreme Court enunciated the principle that the Constitution gives state officers no power to take any independent actions concerned with foreign governments.

Although the justices split evenly (4–4) and declined jurisdiction over the case, later courts accepted as precedent its restrictive view of the states' authority over foreign affairs.

Home Owners' Loan Corporation (HOLC) *see* HOME OWNERS REFINANCING ACT

Home Owners Refinancing Act (13 June 1933) This law created the Home Owners' Loan Corporation, with capitalization of $200 million from the RECONSTRUCTION FINANCE CORPORATION and authority to issue $2 billion in bonds (raised to $4.75 billion by 1935). The HOLC could take over first mortgages up to $14,000 and loan up to half a home's value for taxes or repairs. When the HOLC began operations, 40 percent of the $20 billion market in home mortgages were not making payments; it extended $3 billion for 992,531 loans and refinanced a fifth of all urban mortgages (at 5 percent for 15 years) by June 1936, when it ceased making loans.

home rule During the PROGRESSIVE ERA, home rule was a reform that transferred authority to amend municipal charters, set local taxes, issue bonds, and appoint all city officials from state legislatures to city governments. Home rule was inaugurated in Mo. and was adopted by most states for their largest cities by 1930.

Homer, Winslow (b. Boston, Mass., 24 February 1836; d. Scarboro, Maine, 29 September 1910) In 1857 Homer began his career as a magazine illustrator; he sketched battlefield scenes during the Civil War, and also produced such excellent war paintings as *Prisoners from the Front*, *Sunday Morning in Virginia*, *Sharpshooter on Picket Duty*, and *Rainy Day in Camp*. He abandoned commercial artwork about 1882 to pursue serious painting full-time on the Maine coast, which provided the setting for many of his best canvases. He rejected European influences and was defiantly American in his choice of subjects. Homer produced vivid scenes of vigorous people grown rugged from their struggle with nature. Among his works are *The Fallen Deer, Northeaster, The Life Line, Cannon Rock, Eight Bells, The Wreck, Rowing Home, Winter Coast*, and *All's Well*.

Homestead Act, first (20 May 1862) Congress allowed any citizen or resident alien to claim 160 acres of his choosing from any surveyed, but unpatented, range of PUBLIC DOMAIN, provided he live on it for five years, improve it for agriculture, and pay modest registration fees. Later amendments permitted Union veterans to subtract their military service from the five years. Homesteaders could also claim another 160 acres free under the TIMBER CULTURE ACT and could buy an additional 160 acres at $1.25 an acre under the PREEMPTION ACT. In all, a settler might acquire 480 acres for just $200. Lax administration allowed large ranchers and corporations to acquire vast tracts by fraud. In 1935 public lands were closed to homesteaders for purposes of conservation following passage of the TAYLOR GRAZING ACT. Under the Homestead Act, 1,623,691 land entries were filed.

Homestead Act, second (21 June 1866) Congress extended the first HOMESTEAD ACT to public lands in Ala., Miss., Ark., La., and Fla. by offering to sell 80 acres for $5 to FREEDMEN or others who could swear they had not been rebels. The act stimulated little settlement, because little good land remained in the southern PUBLIC DOMAIN and ex-slaves lacked capital to develop farms; it was repealed in 1876.

Homestead strike On 30 June 1892, the Carnegie Steel Co. locked out 3,800 workers from its Homestead, Pa., works after they refused to accept wage cuts of 18–26 percent. On 6 July, strikers fought with 300 armed Pinkerton detectives hired by the company; three detectives and seven strikers died. On 12 July, 8,000 militia arrived to keep peace, and on 23 July an immigrant anarchist shot plant manager Henry FRICK. By hiring scabs, evicting strikers from company-owned housing, and filing legal charges against many workers, the Carnegie Co. broke the Amalgamated Association of Iron and Steel Workers by November. This victory enabled the firm (and its successor, US Steel) to prevent its workers from forming an effective union until the 1930s.

Honduras, US intervention in By 1910 US firms owned 80 percent of all bananalands in Honduras. To protect their interests or shore up the ruling elite during armed unrest, US marines landed for short periods in 1903, 1907, 1911, and 1913.

honest graft This term characterized the actions of 19th-century political machine members, who used advance knowledge of government projects to win contracts for their own businesses or buy real estate that would quickly appreciate in value. The practice was closely associated with TAMMANY HALL and was eventually outlawed in the PROGRESSIVE ERA.

Hoover, Herbert Clark (b. West Branch, Iowa, 10 August 1874; d. New York, N.Y., 20 October 1964) He was born in Iowa, raised in Oreg., first came to national prominence as director of relief operations for Belgium during WORLD WAR I and then for the Soviet Union during the Russian civil war. He served as secretary of commerce (1921–8), and headed relief operations for the MISSISSIPPI FLOOD OF 1927. He was elected president in 1928 with 58.2 percent of the ballots and carried all but six states in the SOLID SOUTH. He was the first president born west of the Mississippi and who was a millionaire. His laissez-faire philosophy kept him from combating the GREAT DEPRESSION with measures more imaginative than the AGRICULTURAL MARKETING ACT or RECONSTRUCTION FINANCE CORPORATION. He won just 39.7 percent of the ballots and carried just five states in the 1932 election.

Hoover, J(ohn) Edgar (b. Washington, D.C., 1 January 1895; d. Washington, D.C., 2 May 1972) In 1917 Hoover entered the Justice Department and played a prominent role in the RED SCARE. In 1921 he became assistant director of the Bureau of Investigation, and in 1924, when it was reorganized as the FEDERAL BUREAU OF INVESTIGATION, he became its first director. During his 48-year tenure, he imbued it with exceptional professionalism and efficiency as a crime-fighting and anti-espionage force. He was an ardent anti-Communist. He failed to recognize the rise of national crime syndicates – whose networks could not be traced or controlled by local police – and also sanctioned violations of the FBI charter by illegal domestic surveillance and harassment of persons for political reasons.

Hoover Dam This dam on the Colorado River near Las Vegas was the largest single works project ever undertaken in the US. On 21 December 1928, Congress authorized it under the Boulder Canyon Project Act. Constructed by 4,000 workers from 1931 to 1935 at a cost of $108,000,000, it provided water for communities as far distant as Los Angeles. It is 726 feet high and 1,244 feet wide, and retains an artificial lake 115 miles long.

Hoover debt moratorium By mid-1931, a spiraling international financial panic made it impossible for European nations to repay US war debts from WORLD WAR I. On 20 June 1931, Herbert HOOVER proposed a year's moratorium on all Allied debt payments and a cessation of German war reparations. When Europeans again defaulted at the moratorium's end, the US passed the JOHNSON DEBT DEFAULT ACT.

hoovervilles This slang expression referred to shanty-towns where homeless persons or unemployed drifters congregated. Some of these camps had populations numbering several hundred. They became a nearly universal feature of the GREAT DEPRESSION and the term expressed widespread dissatisfaction with Herbert HOOVER's ineffective, laissez-faire policies.

Hopewell Culture This culture emerged about 300 BC, as the ADENA CULTURE was declining, and endured until AD 700; it was most highly developed in the eastern Ohio River valley. Hopewell society differed from its Adena predecessor in four ways: (1) its villages fed larger populations by more intensive agriculture; (2) its trading network extended over a far greater territory; (3) its earthworks were built on a larger scale and were more elaborate; (4) its artefacts show more craftsmanship. Hopewell Culture declined for unknown causes and was succeeded by the MOUND BUILDERS CULTURE.

Hopi Indians Speakers of one of the UTO-AZTECAN LANGUAGES, the Hopis lived in northeastern Ariz. when the Spanish first contacted them in 1540. They were pueblo-dwellers (*see* PUEBLO), and some of their towns may have originated as early as AD 1250. Their population in 1680 was about 2,800. They were in frequent conflict with NAVAHO INDIANS, but avoided war with Spaniards and Anglo-Americans. Due to their isolation, they avoided cultural disintegration and most rejected Christianity. In 1882 the US created a 3,860-square-mile reservation for them, but in 1962 Navahos won a court battle to share use of 75 percent of this grant. In 1987 they numbered 9,040 persons in 12 villages.

Hopkins, Esek (b. Scituate, R.I., 26 April 1718; d. Providence, R.I., 26 February 1802) He became a wealthy sea captain and profited greatly from privateering in the SEVEN YEARS' WAR. In 1775 Congress appointed him the first commander in chief of the Continental navy. On 4 March 1776, his fleet captured Fort Nassau, Bahamas, which yielded a large stock of military supplies. He thereafter ignored Congress's orders, kept his ships inactive for long periods, and allowed much of the US fleet to be blockaded in Narragansett Bay. Congress suspended him from command in March 1777 and revoked his commission in January 1778. The navy remained without a commander in chief for the rest of the Revolution.

Hopkins, Harry Lloyd (b. Sioux City, Iowa, 17 August 1890; d. New York, N.Y., 29 January 1946) Franklin ROOSEVELT appointed Hopkins a N.Y. relief administrator in 1931 and made him one of his chief aides when president. Hopkins was Roosevelt's major advisor on public relief and was the main architect of the NEW DEAL's strategy for combating the GREAT DEPRESSION with large work programs. Hopkins headed the CIVIL WORKS ADMINISTRATION to 1934, the WORKS PROGRESS ADMINISTRATION to 1938, and the Commerce Department to 1940. During WORLD WAR II, he was Roosevelt's special advisor on foreign affairs and his personal diplomatic envoy.

horizontal integration This was the situation when a company purchased or merged with its competitors to form a corporation large enough to dominate an industry. After 1870, it became a widespread business strategy. (*See also* VERTICAL INTEGRATION)

Horseshoe Bend, battle of (Ala.) On 27 March 1814, Major General Andrew JACKSON's 3,000 Tenn. militia, US regulars, and Cherokee-Chickasaw warriors captured the main CREEK INDIAN fort on the Tallapoosa River. US losses: 49 killed, 153 wounded. Creek losses: 557 warriors dead on battlefield, 250 drowned, 3 captured, 350 women captured, plus unknown children. Jackson's victory crushed Indian resistance in the CREEK WAR and convinced the FIVE CIVILIZED TRIBES – except the SEMINOLE INDIANS – that it was suicidal to wage war against Anglo-American frontier expansion.

House, Edward Mandell (b. Houston, Tex., 26 July 1858; d. New York, N.Y., 28 March 1938) He entered Democratic politics in Tex. during the 1890s. He helped elect Woodrow WILSON in 1912 and became his closest advisor. He served as Wilson's confidential envoy for difficult political negotiations in the US and on several secret missions to Europe during WORLD WAR I. He accompanied Wilson to France for negotiations for the treaty of VERSAILLES, although he opposed the journey, and differences over the treaty left their friendship strained when Wilson was disabled by a stroke.

House Committee on Un-American Activities On 26 May 1938, the House of Representatives created this committee to hold hearings on Fascist, Nazi, Communist, or other "un-American" organizations under Representative Martin Dies (Democrat, Tex.). It became a standing committee on 3 January 1945. The committee was most active after 1947 under J. Parnell Thomas (Republican, N.J.) in the COLD WAR, when it held highly publicized hearings on the influence of the COMMUNIST PARTY within government, academia, and Hollywood. It investigated Alger HISS, but was not part of Joseph MCCARTHY's inquisitions. It became discredited in the 1960s, was redesignated the Internal Security Committee in 1969, and was abolished in January 1975.

house divided speech As concluding speaker on 16 June 1858 at the Ill. Republican state convention, which had nominated him to run against Stephen DOUGLAS for the Senate Abraham LINCOLN said, "A house divided against itself cannot stand," and added that the US could not "endure permanently half *slave* and half *free*." Most of the speech suggested that Douglas, James BUCHANAN and Roger TANEY were conspiring to make SLAVERY a national institution. The speech was Lincoln's strongest denunciation of slavery before 1862, and was cited by Democrats in the election of 1860 to allege (wrongly) that he would not respect slavery's constitutional protections.

House of Burgesses This was the first elected legislature established in the THIRTEEN COLONIES. Its earliest session deliberated at Jamestown, Va., during 9–14 August 1619, and included two burgesses (townsmen) from any community or plantation that wished to join the governor and his council in drafting local ordinances. The burgesses did not conduct business separately from the council until the 1650s, and thereafter House of Burgesses referred only to the legislature's lower house. The 1776 Va. constitution renamed its lower chamber the House of Representatives.

Housing Act (July 1949) A measure forming part of the FAIR DEAL, this law marked the start of a major federal commitment to improve housing and the urban environment; it authorized construction of 810,000 low-rent units over six years, and federal rent subsidies of $308,000,000 per year. It spawned the Urban Renewal Administration. Between 1949 and 1966, the US Treasury provided over $5,000,000,000 to finance two-thirds of the planning, land, and clearing expenses of 1,700 urban renewal projects in over 800 cities. The GREAT SOCIETY greatly expanded the federal commitment to housing and slum clearance through the OMNIBUS HOUSING ACT, DEMONSTRATION CITIES AND METROPOLITAN DEVELOPMENT ACT, the HOUSING AND URBAN DEVELOPMENT ACT, and founding of the HOUSING AND URBAN DEVELOPMENT DEPARTMENT.

Housing and Urban Development, Department of On 9 September 1965, Congress created this department to oversee about 115 housing and urban development programs formerly supervised by the Housing and Home Finance Agency, Home Finance Agency, and Public Housing Administration.

Housing and Urban Development Act (1968) This measure, part of the GREAT SOCIETY, expanded upon the OMNIBUS HOUSING ACT (1965). It provided $5.3 billion for 1,700,000 new or rehabilitated housing units over a three-year period.

Houston, Samuel (b. near Lexington, Va., 2 March 1793; d. San Antonio, Tex., 26 July 1863) After being wounded at the battle of HORSESHOE BEND, Houston was given up for dead. Following a period as Tenn. governor (1827–9), he settled in Nacogdoches, Tex., in 1832. He won the TEXAS REVOLT with his victory at SAN JACINTO. He was Tex. president (1836–8 and 1841–4), and US senator (1846–59). After opposing SECESSION by Tex., he retired to private life.

Howe, Elias (b. Spencer, Mass., 9 July 1819; d. Brooklyn, N.Y., 3 October 1867) He began life as an apprentice in a factory making machinery for cloth manufacture, and invented the sewing machine, which was patented in 1846. After successfully defending his financial rights in several lawsuits over patent infringement, his design became standard in both the US and Europe. In 1865, he founded the Howe Machine Co. at Bridgeport, Conn., which won a gold medal for its most advanced machine at the 1867 Paris Exhibition.

Howe, Julia Ward (b. New York, N.Y., 27 May 1819; d. Newport, R.I., 17 October 1910) With her husband Samuel G. HOWE, she co-edited the abolitionist paper *The Commonwealth* and helped collect secret funds for John BROWN's raid on Harper's Ferry. In the spring of 1862, she composed "The Battle Hymn of the Republic."

Howe, Samuel Gridley (b. Boston, Mass., 10 November 1801; d. Boston, Mass., 9 January 1876) After serving as a volunteer in the Greek war for independence, Howe headed the first state school for the blind in Mass. during 1831–76. He became the foremost pioneer in developing techniques for teaching the sightless and educating the public on how they could be economically productive.

Howe, Sir William (b. London, England, 10 August 1729; d. Plymouth, England, 12 July 1814) In 1746 Howe entered the Royal Army. He commanded a regiment in North America during the SEVEN YEARS' WAR. Howe sympathized with American grievances against unconstitutional Parliamentary laws, yet in 1775 was ordered to the colonies as the British Army's commander in chief, a position he had not sought, and accepted with regret. He was defeated at BUNKER HILL, but captured New York City in 1776, and Philadelphia in 1777. During the REVOLUTIONARY WAR, Howe repeatedly tried to end hostilities peacefully by offering pardons to all rebels, even of the highest rank. Howe asked to be relieved of command on 22 October 1777 and was replaced in May 1778 by Henry CLINTON.

Howells, William Dean (b. Martin's Ferry, Ohio, 1 March 1837; d. New York, N.Y., 11 May 1920) He had little formal education, but expanded his horizons by working in his father's print shop from the age of 9. For composing a political biography of Abraham Lincoln (1860), he was appointed US consul at Venice (1861–5). He held senior editorial positions at the *Nation* and *Atlantic Monthly* until 1881, and then primarily supported himself by his short stories and novels. *The Rise of Silas Lapham* was his best book, but few others continued in print long after his death. Howells's primary contribution to literature was as a critic. In works such as *Criticism and Fiction* (1891) and *Literature and Life* (1902), he championed the emergence of a new realistic school of writing and praised authors like Frank NORRIS, Stephen CRANE, and Hamlin GARLAND.

Hudson, Henry (b. in England, ca. 1565; d. Hudson Bay, 1611) He sailed seeking the NORTHWEST PASSAGE for the English Muscovy Company, but was blocked by polar ice. In 1609, while on the same mission for the Dutch East India Company, he located Delaware Bay on 28 August, discovered Hudson River on 13 September, and ascended the river to modern Albany. Again under English hire, he began a final voyage in April 1610, discovered Hudson Bay on 3 August, and wintered on St James Bay. His crew mutinied the next spring and marooned him in the bay.

Hudson River school This group of artists was the first school of painting whose inspiration and subject matter came wholly from American experience. The school focused upon landscapes, and received its name because so much of its early work portrayed scenery in upstate N.Y.; its most prominent leaders were Thomas COLE, Asher Brown Durand, and Thomas Doughty. The school's technique emphasized magnificent, lush panoramas that exalted the wilderness as a symbol of national pride.

Hue, battle of (South Vietnam) On 31 January 1968, North Vietnamese troops captured Hue in the TET OFFENSIVE. Allied hesitancy to shell or bombard Hue's cultural, religious, and historical landmarks enabled the Nort Vietnamese to resist efforts by the Firs USMC Division, First Air Cavalry Divisio 101 Airborne Division, and South Vietnam ese forces to retake the city in house-to-hous fighting until 24 February. News coverag of Hue's lengthy recapture sowed doub among Americans that the VIETNAM WA could be won with acceptable US casualtie and strengthened the VIETNAM ANTIWA MOVEMENT.

Hughes, Charles Evans (b. Glens Fall N.Y., 11 April 1862; d. Osterville, Mass., 2 August 1948) In 1884 Hughes became Wall Street lawyer. A Republican reforme of the PROGRESSIVE ERA, he served a governor (1906–10), sat on the US Suprem Court (1910–16), lost the presidency in 191 by just 23 electoral votes, returned to Wa Street, and – as secretary of state (1921–6 – was primarily responsible for the WASH INGTON NAVAL CONFERENCE's succes He was made chief justice of the Suprem Court on 13 February 1930. He took middle position on the constitutionalit of Franklin D. ROOSEVELT's legislativ agenda. He dealt Roosevelt a severe blo by authoring *SCHECHTER POULTRY CORPO RATION* v. *UNITED STATES*, but wrote dec sions to uphold key NEW DEAL program in *ASHWANDER* v. *TENNESSEE VALLEY AU THORITY* and *NATIONAL LABOR RELATION BOARD* v. *JONES AND LAUGHLIN STEE CORPORATION*. Other important decision by Hughes include *NEAR* v. *MINNESOT* (*see GITLOW* v. *NEW YORK*), secon SCOTTSBORO CASE, *DE JONGE* v. *OR EGON*, *WEST COAST HOTEL COMPANY* v *PARRISH*, *MISSOURI EX REL. GAINES* v *CANADA*, *COLEMAN* v. *MILLER*, and *COX* v *NEW HAMPSHIRE*. He retired in 1941.

Huguenots These were Calvinists drive from France by religious persecution durin the 1600s. About 7 percent of immigrants NEW NETHERLAND were Huguenot Thousands fled to England and Holland be tween 1685 and 1705, and from there at lea 2,000 emigrated to Anglo-America – prim rily to N.Y., Pa., Va., and S.C. – by 170 Anglicized Huguenots continued to emigra in the 1700s, and by 1790 about 2 perce of US whites were of French descen (*See* FRENCH IMMIGRATION)

Hull, Cordell (b. Overton County, Tenn.,

October 1871; d. Washington, D.C., 23 July 1955) He served as Tenn. congressman (1907–30) and senator (1931–3). He was a reformer of the PROGRESSIVE ERA who drafted the legislation for the federal INCOME TAX of 1913 and 1916 and the 1916 federal inheritance tax law, favored tariff reduction, and supported the LEAGUE OF NATIONS treaty. As secretary of state (1933–44), he played a major role in developing the GOOD NEIGHBOR POLICY, promoted tariff reform, and helped found the UNITED NATIONS. He received the Nobel peace prize in 1945.

Hull House *see* ADDAMS, JANE

Humphrey, Hubert Horatio (b. Wallace, S. Dak., 27 May 1911; d. Washington, D.C., 13 January 1978) While mayor of Minneapolis, Humphrey led the successful fight for a strong civil rights plank in the 1948 Democratic platform. While Minn. senator (1948–64), he championed civil rights measures and the GREAT SOCIETY. He became Lyndon JOHNSON's vice-president in 1964, and won the Democratic nomination for president over Eugene MCCARTHY when Johnson withdrew in 1967. Humphrey's support for Johnson's policies on the VIETNAM WAR hurt him in the 1968 campaign, although he distanced himself from them late in the race by calling for a negotiated settlement. Humphrey carried only 11 states, but narrowly trailed Richard NIXON in popular votes by 43.4 percent to 42.7 percent. He returned to the Senate in 1970, sponsored the HUMPHREY–HAWKINS ACT, and died in office.

Humphrey–Hawkins Act (27 October 1977) This measure was the first US law that attempted to implement the EMPLOYMENT ACT's (1946) assumption of federal responsibility for achieving full employment and price stability. It established a national goal of reducing unemployment to 4 percent and keeping inflation under 3 percent by 1983. Under President Jimmy CARTER, who took responsibility for implementing it, unemployment rose to 10 percent and inflation to 13 percent by 1980. Although no other president has committed himself to the law's provisions, it remains in force, and by declaring that every American has a right to work, it implies a federal responsibility as the employer of last resort whenever joblessness exceeds 4 percent and inflation is low.

Hundred Days This term was coined to describe the 73rd Congress's session of 9 March to 16 June 1933, which passed these landmark laws in the FIRST NEW DEAL: EMERGENCY BANKING RELIEF ACT, ECONOMY ACT, BEER-WINE REVENUE ACT, CIVILIAN CONSERVATION CORPS, Federal Emergency Relief Act (*see* FEDERAL EMERGENCY RELIEF ADMINISTRATION), first AGRICULTURAL ADJUSTMENT ACT, TENNESSEE VALLEY AUTHORITY, FEDERAL SECURITIES ACT, abandonment of GOLD STANDARD, NATIONAL EMPLOYMENT SYSTEM ACT, HOME OWNERS REFINANCING ACT, BANKING ACT (1933), FARM CREDIT ACT, EMERGENCY RAILROAD TRANSPORTATION ACT, and NATIONAL INDUSTRIAL RECOVERY ACT.

hunkers These were a political faction that controlled the ALBANY REGENCY in the 1840s. They were so called by their rivals the BARNBURNERS because they opposed democratic reforms and seemed to "hunker" (hunger) after office for its own sake.

Huron Indians This nation which speaks one of the IROQUOIAN LANGUAGES was termed the Huron ("Troublemakers") by the French, but called themselves the Wendat. In 1600, they numbered about 18,000 in southeastern Ontario and were strategically situated to control the FUR TRADE between the French and western Indians. Smallpox carried off thousands in 1636. The FIVE NATIONS dispersed them during the BEAVER WARS and the refugees were absorbed by neighboring nations. One band survived, migrated to Ohio, and was thereafter known as WYANDOT INDIANS.

Hürtgen Forest, battle of (Germany) In September 1944, Lieutenant General Courtney Hodges's First US Army's 120,000 troops moved through the Hürtgen Forest (200 square miles) to cross the Roer River southwest of Aachen. Germany's Seventh Army chewed up six divisions before Hodges's men cleared most of the forest in mid-December. US losses were 33,000 (about equal to German casualties). Not until February 1945 did US troops capture the Roer dams and manage to cross the river.

Hutchinson, Anne Marbury (b. Alford, Lincolnshire, England, 1591; d. Eastchester, N.Y., ca. September 1643) With her husband, Hutchinson emigrated to Mass. in

1634. She was the principal leader of the ANTINOMIAN CONTROVERSY, for which she was banished to R.I. and settled at Portsmouth. She moved to Dutch jurisdiction on Long Island and was murdered by Indians in KIEFFT'S WAR.

Hutchinson, Thomas (b. Boston, Mass., 9 September 1711; d. Brompton, England, 3 June 1780) He was a Mass. assemblyman (1737–49, speaker 1746–8), governor's councillor (1749–66), deputy governor (1758–70), chief justice (1760–70), and governor (1770–4). He co-authored the ALBANY PLAN OF UNION and ruled against James OTIS in the case of the WRITS OF ASSISTANCE. Although personally opposed to Parliament taxing the colonies, he supported its authority, for which his mansion was looted in the STAMP ACT crisis. By insisting that customs regulations be carried out to enforce the TEA ACT (1773), he precipitated the BOSTON TEA PARTY. His position as governor became untenable after the HUTCHINSON LETTERS controversy and he was replaced by Thomas GAGE. He was America's most prominent Tory (*see* TORIES) and died in exile.

Hutchinson letters In late 1772, Benjamin FRANKLIN obtained letters written by Mass. Governor Thomas HUTCHINSON (1767–9), in which Hutchinson's statements could be interpreted as meaning that the traditional RIGHTS OF ENGLISHMEN must be curtaile in the THIRTEEN COLONIES to preserv British rule. Franklin sent them to Mass where-upon the legislature petitioned fo Hutchinson's removal in June 1773. The letters had three major results: (1) Franklin wa dismissed as the thirteen colonies' postmaster general and returned to Pa.; (2) the destroyed Hutchinson's credibility in Mass and forced Britain to replace him as governor with General Thomas GAGE; (3) the convinced many colonists that a ministeria conspiracy existed to extinguish representative democracy in the colonies.

Hyde amendment Representative Henr Hyde (Republican, Ill.) authored an amendment ending MEDICAID reimbursement fo ABORTIONS except when essential to sav the mother's life. Enacted on 30 Septembe 1976 over Gerald FORD's veto, the amendment came before the Supreme Court i *HARRIS* v. *MCRAE*. On 1 October 1993 Congress amended it to permit federal funding for abortions in cases of incest and rape

Hylton* v. *United States In 1796, the Suprem Court made its first judgment on the constitutionality of a federal statute, when it rule that Congress had the authority to pass tax on carriages in 1794. The Court woul first explicitly assert its right of JUDICIA REVIEW when deciding *MARBURY* v *MADISON*.

I

a Drang Valley, battle of (South Vietnam) On 14–18 November 1965, North Vietnamese Regulars attacked and pinned down two badly outnumbered battalions of the First Air Cavalry Division, but retreated after encountering heavy US resistance and being hit by B-52 aerial bombardment. US losses: 300 killed. Enemy losses: 1,770 killed. After Ia Drang, the Communists avoided committing large units to fight US troops and emphasized hit-and-run guerrilla tactics.

CC Interstate Commerce Commission (*see* INTERSTATE COMMERCE COMMISSION ACT)

celand, US occupation of On 7 July 1941, US forces landed on Iceland, at the government's request, to prevent its utilization as a base for Nazi military operations.

ckes, Harold LeClair (b. Frankstown, Pa., 15 March 1874; d. Washington, D.C., 3 February 1952) A Chicago lawyer and partner of Donald RICHBERG, Ickes became secretary of the interior and PUBLIC WORKS ADMINISTRATION (PWA) director in 1933. By methodically ensuring that every PWA project was economically sound and nonpartisan, he slowed his agency's ability to begin relief work and contributed to the creation of the CIVIL WORKS ADMINISTRATION (CWA) as an alternative public works agency. He primarily influenced the NEW DEAL by developing conservation programs. As a NATIONAL ASSOCIATION FOR THE ADVANCEMENT OF COLORED PEOPLE (NAACP) member, he fought to expand the number of blacks hired by public works agencies and federal contractors. He headed the Interior Department until 1946, the longest tenure of any US cabinet officer.

daho The US acquired Idaho by the LOUISIANA PURCHASE. In 1834 the Rocky Mountain Fur Co. built the first US outpost beyond the Continental Divide at Fort Hall (abandoned 1856). In 1860 Mormons began settling Idaho. A gold rush attracting up to 30,000 miners broke out in 1861 along the Snake River, and Idaho Territory was created out of Wash. on 4 March 1863. In 1870 it had 14,999 residents. The Northern PAIUTE, NEZ PERCE, and SHEEPEATER CAMPAIGNS took place in Idaho. Rapid development came after Idaho was entered by railroads in 1880 and the Coeur d'Alene silver boom began in 1884. It became the 43rd state on 3 July 1890. In 1900 Idaho had 161,772 residents (95 percent white, 3 percent Indian, 1 percent Chinese, 1 percent Japanese), of whom 94 percent were rural and 15 percent were foreign-born; it ranked 46th among the states in population, 43rd in the value of agricultural goods, and 49th in manufactures. The CAREY and NATIONAL RECLAMATION ACTS fostered large-scale agricultural development by irrigation. Food processing, tourism, and urban growth diversified the economy after 1945. In 1990 Idaho was the 42nd largest state and had 1,006,749 inhabitants (approx. 92 percent white, 5 percent Hispanic, 1 percent Indian, 1 percent Asian), of whom 20 percent were urban and 2.9 percent were foreign-born. Manufacturing employed 15 percent of the work force and mining 7 percent.

Illinois In December 1674, Fr Jacques Marquette founded a mission at modern Chicago, France's first outpost in Ill. In 1680 the Sieur de LA SALLE began building the first of several forts for the FUR TRADE in northern Ill. French settlers founded towns at Cahokia in 1698 and Kaskaskia in 1709. On 27 September 1717, Ill. was established as a district of LOUISIANA. The treaty of PARIS (1763) gave Ill. to Britain, and George Rogers CLARK conquered it for the US, but de facto control lapsed to the British from 1784 to Jay's Treaty. A trickle of Anglo-Americans began settling southern Ill. after 1800 and it was made a territory on 9 February 1809. It became the 21st state on 3 December 1818 and had 55,211 residents in 1820. Its only major Indian disturbance was the brief Black Hawk War.

Its population grew by 1,442 percent from 1820 to 1850, and then doubled in the 1850s. In 1860 it had 1,711,951 inhabitants, of whom over 99 percent were white and 19 percent were of foreign birth; it ranked fourth among the states in the value of its farmland and livestock and eighth in manufactures. In the Civil War, it furnished 259,092 USA troops (including 1,811 blacks), but it contained numerous Copperheads.

Rapid growth around Chicago attracted heavy in-migration from other states or Europe and 733,300 new residents moved to Ill. between 1880 and 1910. By 1900, it was 46 percent rural and had 4,821,550 inhabitants, of whom 98 percent were white and 20 percent were foreign-born; it ranked third among the states in population, second in the value of its agricultural goods, and third in manufactures. Moderate growth since 1930 has reduced its ranking among states to sixth largest by 1990, when it had 11,430,602 residents (75 percent white, 15 percent black, 8 percent Hispanic, 2 percent Asian), of whom 83 percent were urban and 8.3 percent were foreign-born. Manufacturing and mining employed 25 percent of all workers.

Illinois Indians The French originally called all Indians who traded furs with them in northern Ill. by this name. There may have been 10,500 Indians speaking Algonquian languages in Ill. in the 1660s, when contact was first made with French explorers. They welcomed French forts to carry on the fur trade, but were then attacked by the Iroquois Confederacy in the beaver wars during the period 1677–84. European epidemics and intertribal warfare steadily reduced the Illinois bands, until by 1768 observers of the Kaskaskias and Peorias and Mascoutens estimated just 1,100 warriors, indicating a total of about 5,000. These groups declined even further, leaving Ill. almost entirely vacant of Indians by 1810, and in the 1840s they agreed to accept a small reservation in Kans.

immigration Before 1700, over 90 percent of all immigrants to the present US were English or Welsh, of whom perhaps 10 percent had formerly resided in the West Indies. The first substantial wave of settlement was the Great Migration (1630–60), which brought nearly half that century's arrivals. An estimated 168,000 Europeans came during the 17th century: 120,000 to Va. and Md., 30,000 to New England, 10,000 to Pa. and N.J., 3,000 to S.C., 2,500 Dutch to N.Y., 2,000 Huguenots to N.Y., N.J., Va., and S.C., and 500 swedes to Del. This migration raised the English colonies' white population to 223,000 by 1700. The 17th century was the last period in which population growth resulted primarily from immigration rather than natural increase.

After 1700, only 20 percent of immigrants were English or Welsh, while Scotch Irish, Irish, and Pennsylvania Dutch predominated. Between 1700 and 1775 307,000 Europeans arrived: 73,000 English and Welsh, 84,400 Germans, 66,100 Ulster Scots, 42,500 Irish, 35,000 Scots, and 6,000 French or others. From 1780 to 1800 161,000 more came: 107,000 Irish, 22,000 English, Welsh, or Scots, 14,000 Haitian colonists, 2,000 French, 14,000 Germans, and 2,000 others. By 1800, these 636,000 immigrants had produced 4,306,000 descendants.

An estimated 184,000 immigrants entered the US between 1801 and 1819, primarily from the British Isles. In 1820 the US began documenting the arrival of foreigners, but it excluded no one (although the Naturalization acts denied citizenship to nonwhites). European emigration accelerated rapidly after 1846. From 1820 to 1860 5,060,000 Europeans settled in the US, and 90 percent of them settled in the northeast or midwest. In 1860 13 percent of the population were immigrants, whom the census described as predominantly English-speaking (59 percent) and western European: 39 percent Irish, 31 percent German, 14 percent British, 6 percent Canadian, 3 percent French and 2 percent Scandinavian.

State efforts to keep foreigners from becoming a public burden led to the immigration cases. Congress then passed the

Exclusion Act (18 August 1882), which ended unrestricted entry to the US by barring the insane, criminals, paupers, and (for ten years) CHINESE IMMIGRATION. Restriction of contract laborers followed with the CONTRACT LABOR ACT (1885). The CHINESE EXCLUSION RULING upheld Congress's right to bar nationalities from entrance. Gentlemen's Agreements later blocked JAPANESE IMMIGRATION.

Between 1866 and 1915, about 25,000,000 persons came to the US. The number of arrivals from northern and western Europe, so-called "old immigrants," steadily fell after 1883. After 1895, "new immigrants" from Mediterranean and Slavic nations predominated; they outnumbered "Nordic" migrants after 1895, and over 9,000,000 had entered the US by 1914. When immigration began averaging 1,000,000 annually (1910–14), fears rose that the US could not economically absorb those masses, and that eastern and southern Europeans posed special problems in being assimilated to American life.

The EMERGENCY QUOTA ACT (1921) instituted the first limitation on immigration by ethnic origins (designed to prefer northern and western Europeans) and also capped the number of annual entrants. The NATIONAL ORIGINS ACT (1924) set stricter quotas on Mediterranean and Slavic peoples. Admissions to the US dropped from 4,107,200 in the 1920s to 528,400 in the 1930s. Refugees from eastern and central Europe received preferential treatment after WORLD WAR II by the Displaced Persons acts (1948, 1950, and 1951). The MCCARRAN–WALTER ACT permitted Asian refugees to immigrate. These measures gave entry to 3,500,000 people from 1945 to 1960.

The IMMIGRATION REFORM ACT (1965) repealed the quotas system, but set the first limits on immigration from the western hemisphere; it authorized admission of up to 2,900,000 persons per decade. Because of this law, nonwhites have formed the bulk of immigrants since the the early 1970s. Preferential admission to anti-Communist refugees also allowed the admission of large numbers of BOAT PEOPLE and CUBANS. The greatest factor increasing the scale of non-European immigration was the rise in illegal MEXICAN and HAITIAN entries, which inspired passage of the futile SIMPSON–MAZZOLI ACT. Immigration consequently swelled to 4,493,000 in the 1970s and 7,338,000 in the 1980s. Between 1981 and 1990, legal and illegal immigrants accounted for 32.8 percent of total population growth. By 1991, the foreign-born numbered 14,020,000, 13.2 percent of the US population.

From 1820 to 1991, 58,821,181 foreigners entered the US, of which 32.5 percent entered during 1820–1900, 24.7 percent during 1901–20, 7.9 percent during 1921–40, 11.6 percent during 1945–70, and 23.3 percent during 1971–91. (One in six immigrants have returned home or gone to another country.) The greatest number of entrants have come from Germany (12.1 percent), Italy (9.2 percent), Great Britain (8.7 percent), Mexico (8.2 percent), Ireland (8.0 percent), Austria-Hungary (7.4 percent), Canada (7.3 percent), Russia (5.9 percent). It is estimated that had no immigration occurred after 1820, the US population in 1990 would have grown only to 121,710,000, just 49 percent of its actual level of 248,710,000.

Immigration and Naturalization Service* v. *Chadha On 23 June 1983, the Supreme Court held (7–2) that Article I of the CONSTITUTION is inconsistent with laws permitting the single-house LEGISLATIVE VETO, in which either chamber of Congress may vote to override a decision made by the executive department. Article I requires that legislative enactments must be passed by both houses and presented to the president.

immigration cases (*Chy Lung* v. *Freeman*, *Commissioners of Immigration* v. *The North German Lloyd*, *Henderson* v. *Wickham*) In 1876 the Supreme Court ruled that federal authority over interstate commerce precluded states from demanding that shipowners give bond attesting to the good character and healthfulness of any aliens they landed. The case left states unable to exclude undesirable foreigners from the US, and forced Congress to enact the first significant restrictions on IMMIGRATION in 1882. (*See also* CHINESE EXCLUSION RULING)

Immigration Reform Act (1965) This law repealed the NATIONAL ORIGINS ACT as of 30 June 1968. It set an annual limit of 170,000 immigrants from outside the western hemisphere and 120,000 from the western hemisphere. Preference for admitting immigrants was to be given to close relatives of US residents, professionals, artists, scientists, skilled or unskilled persons needed to fill labor shortages, and refugees from communism or national disasters. It dramatically changed the composition of IMMIGRATION. Entrants from Europe composed 50.2 percent of all immigrants from 1955 to 1964, but only 9.4 percent from 1985 to 1990, while entrants from Asia increased from 7.7 percent to 37.6 percent in the same period, and entrants from the West Indies increased from 7.1 percent to 13.7 percent.

Immigration Reform and Control Act (1986) *see* SIMPSON–MAZZOLI ACT

Immunity Act (1950) This act rescinded the FIFTH AMENDMENT's guarantee against self-incrimination for witnesses before congressional committees, when they had received immunity from prosecution for any crimes that might be revealed. It was upheld in *ULLMANN* v. *UNITED STATES*.

Impending Crisis of the South: How to Meet It In mid-1857, Hinton Rowan Helper, a middle-class, N.C. white, published this book, which argued that SLAVERY reduced economic opportunity for non-slaveowners and had kept the South from developing as rapidly as the North. Helper's work received widespread publicity, and stirred fears among southern planters that northern abolitionists and Republicans might build a significant political following among non-slaveholders. Such apprehensions contributed to the atmosphere of crisis that panicked southerners into SECESSION.

implied powers, doctrine of *see* LOOSE CONSTRUCTIONISM

impressment This was the forcible drafting of sailors to serve in the British navy. Because a large minority of men in the US merchant marine had been born in Britain, the Royal Navy insisted on the right to board US ships during the Napoleonic wars, and take any crewmen who were the King's subjects or military deserters. Impressment was a major cause of the WAR OF 1812.

In Re Debs In 1895 the Supreme Court denied a writ of HABEAS CORPUS to Eugene DEBS, American Railway Union president, then under contempt citation for ignoring an antistrike injunction issued under the SHERMAN ANTITRUST ACT in the PULLMAN STRIKE. The Court did not rule on the Sherman Act, but held that federal government could issue the injunction to protect interstate commerce and ensure the mail's delivery. The ruling validated injunctions as strike-breaking tools. From 1901 to 1928, federal injunctions halted 118 major strikes and were requested in another 116 labor disputes that ended before a final decree was issued. The NORRIS–LA GUARDIA ACT ended this practice.

In Re Gault On 15 May 1967, the Supreme Court extended (7–2) the DUE PROCESS protections of right to counsel and the privilege against self-incrimination to juvenile hearings. (*See IN RE WINSHIP* and *MCKIEVER* v. *PENNSYLVANIA*)

In Re Heff *see* BURKE ACT

In Re Winship On 31 March 1970, the Supreme Court held (5–3) that the FOURTEENTH AMENDMENT obliges juvenile courts to acquit defendants whose guilt is not proven "beyond a reasonable doubt." (*See IN RE GAULT and MCKIEVER* v. *PENNSYLVANIA*)

Inchon, battle of (South Korea) *see* KOREAN WAR

income tax The US levied its first income tax in August 1861 to finance the CIVIL WAR; it assessed 3 percent of all income above $800, and a surtax of 10 percent on income above $10,000 was later added. (The Confederacy also taxed incomes.) The Supreme Court upheld the constitutionality of the Civil War levy in *SPRINGER* v. *UNITED STATES* but reversed itself in *POLLOCK* v. *FARMERS' LOAN AND TRUST COMPANY*, which concerned income tax provisions of the 1894 tariff act. The 1908 Democratic platform supported a constitutional amendment to overrule *Pollock* and the SIXTEENTH AMENDMENT was ratified five years later.

The UNDERWOOD–SIMMONS TARIFF levied the first income tax, which exempted 95 percent of the population by assessing 1 percent of income over $3,000 for single persons and 1 percent over $ 4,000 for households (plus a graduated surtax on incomes above $20,000 that rose to 6 percent in excess of $500,000). The corporate income tax was 1 percent. During World War I, rates were 4 percent on individual income under $4,000 and 8 percent above that, and 10 percent on corporate income. Heads of household had a deduction of $2,000 and each dependant had a deduction of $200. Capital gains were untaxed until 1921. Rates declined steadily under the revenue acts of the 1920s, but began rising in the New Deal, especially with the Wealth Tax Act (1935), and in World War II. Tax withholding from paychecks was introduced in 1943.

Rates peaked in the 1950s with a range of 20–91 percent on individuals and a 52 percent corporate rate. Significant reduction began with the Tax Reduction Act (1964), which lowered individual rates to 14–70 percent and corporate taxes to 47 percent by 1965. The Economic Recovery Tax Act (1981) reversed a subsequent climb in rates, cut long-term capital gains taxes from 28 percent to 20 percent, and lowered the top marginal rate to 50 percent. The Tax Reform Act (1986) simplified the Internal Revenue code from 14 tax brackets to 3: 15, 28, and 33 percent.

Indentured convicts *see* convict servants

Indentured servants This term refers to Europeans or West Indians who were recruited as laborers in the thirteen colonies. In return for free passage to America, they signed contracts obliging them to work for up to seven years without pay. (The usual indenture lasted four years.) White servants may have comprised 15 percent of immigrants to the northern colonies before 1700. About 70 percent of immigrants to the Chesapeake came under indentures, of whom at least 84,000 arrived before 1700. Black slaves became the principal source of unfree field laborers after 1700, but the recruitment of indentured servants continued until the Revolution. From 1700 to 1775, about 25,000 servants arrived from England and 70,000 came from Ireland or Scotland. German servants were termed redemptioners.

Independent Offices Appropriations Act (28 March 1934) Enacted over a veto, it was Franklin D. Roosevelt's first legislative defeat. By adding $125,000,000 to the federal payroll and raising veterans' benefits by $228,000,000, Congress offset savings from the Economy Act (1933) and contradicted Roosevelt's pledge to cut unnecessary spending, but appeased two large voting blocs in an election year.

Independent Treasury Responding to the failure of pet banks in the panic of 1837, Martin Van Buren recommended on 5 September 1837 that the US do business only in specie and cease storing surplus funds in state banks. The Whig party preferred to retain the Distribution Act's provisions and kept the Independent Treasury (or Subtreasury) Bill from becoming law until 4 July 1840. The law gave exclusive care of US funds to the Treasury and required that all federal transactions be made in specie after 30 June 1843. Subtreasury depositories were built at the capital and six regional cities. A Whig Congress repealed the law on 13 August 1841, but a Democratic Congress revived it on 6 August 1846. It remained the foundation for US fiscal policy until the Federal Reserve system.

Indian Affairs, Bureau of This agency originated with the responsibility given the Department of War in 1789 over Indian affairs, and was created as a separate bureau in that department. In 1832 the commissioner of Indian affairs was established to advise the secretary of war, and in 1832 Congress outlined the internal structure of his bureau. In 1849 the bureau was transferred to the Department of the Interior. It did not recommend policy until 1933, when John Collier became its head; he instituted fundamental reforms, and drafted much of the Wheeler–Howard Act. The bureau was occupied by the radical American Indian Movement in November 1972.

Indian Claims Commission (13 August 1946) Congress created this independent federal agency to settle grievances against the US for treaty violations (previously handled by the Court of Claims). Upon its disbandment on 30 September 1978, it had heard 600 suits, settled 60 percent in the Indians' favor, and awarded $800,000,000 compensation. All pending claims were then transferred to the US Court of Claims.

Indian languages In 1500 modern US and Canada contained eight distinct Indian language groups – all unrelated to each other – which contained 53 separate linguistic families (or stocks) that included 200 to 300 individual languages. Of the 53 families, eight contained over two-thirds of all Indians: ALGONQUIAN (20 percent), SIOUAN (9 percent), ESKIMO-ALEUT (9 percent), IROQUOIAN (7 percent), MUSKOGEAN (7 percent), UTO-AZTECAN (6 percent), ATHAPASKAN (6 percent), and SALISH (6 percent) LANGUAGES.

Indian New Deal *see* COLLIER, JOHN

Indian Removal Act (28 May 1830) Congress acceded to executive plans for removing eastern Indians west of the Mississippi and authorized the creation of an Indian Territory as their RESERVATION. It appropriated $500,000 to finance their transportation.

Indian Reorganization Act *see* WHEELER–HOWARD ACT

Indian Springs, treaty of (Ga.) On 12 February 1825, Ga. bought 7,300 square miles (12.5 percent of the state) from CREEK INDIAN leaders whose power to sell the land was disputed by the entire nation. John Q. ADAMS renegotiated the transaction by the treaty of Washington (24 January 1826), but Ga. insisted that the 1825 treaty could not be abrogated and threatened to enforce it with state militia. When Adams backed down, Ga. was encouraged to begin dispossessing the CHEROKEE INDIANS.

Indian Territory *see* OKLAHOMA

Indian Trade Intercourse Act (22 July 1790) Congress forbade white settlement upon Indian lands, required traders to receive federal licenses, provided for punishing whites who committed crimes on Indian territory, and required congressional approval before any land purchase from Indians could be valid. Beginning in 1978, WAMPANOAG, NARRAGANSETT, and other Indians in Maine, Conn., N.Y., and S.C. began using the law to sue for recovery of lands bought by states that neglected to obtain congressional approval.

Indiana COUREURS DE BOIS pursued the FUR TRADE in Ind. as early as the 1680s. The first permanent French outpost was FORT OUIATONON in 1719. In 1735 the French founded Vincennes. The treaty of PARIS (1763) transferred the area to Britain, and George Rogers CLARK conquered it for the US, but de facto control lapsed to Britain from 1784 to JAY'S TREATY. Anglo-southerners began settling Ind. after the first treaty of GREENVILLE and it became a territory on 7 May 1800, when the present area of Ind. had 2,517 settlers, of whom most were French and 4 percent were black.

Indian resistance to settlement disappeared after TECUMSEH was killed in the WAR OF 1812, which engulfed the territory. Ind. became the 19th state on 11 December 1816. It grew by 817 percent from 1820 to 1860, when it had 1,350,428 inhabitants, of whom 1 percent were black and 9 percent were foreign-born; it ranked fifth among the states in population, sixth in the value of its farmland and livestock, and tenth in manufactures. In the CIVIL WAR, it furnished 196,363 USA troops (including 1,537 blacks), but had a large population of COPPERHEADS. Ind. was invaded by CSA cavalry in 1863 and was the site of ten military engagements.

It industrialized slowly and grew moderately until 1900, when it had 2,516,462 residents, of whom 66 percent were rural, 98 percent were white, and 6 percent were foreign-born; it ranked eighth among states in population, in the value of agricultural goods, and in manufactures. Urbanization and increasing economic diversification characterized its subsequent growth. In 1990 it was the 14th largest state and had 5,544,159 people (90 percent white, 8 percent black, 2 percent Hispanic), of whom 69 percent were urban and 1.7 percent were foreign-born. Manufacturing and mining employed 31 percent of workers.

industrial union This type of labor union organizes all workers in an industry regardless of skill or work specialization, as opposed to a CRAFT UNION. The CONGRESS OF INDUSTRIAL ORGANIZATIONS represented such bodies.

Industrial Workers of the World (IWW) Nicknamed the Wobblies, this union was founded at Chicago in June 1905 by William HAYWOOD, Eugene DEBS, Daniel DE LEON, and many radical members of the AMERICAN FEDERATION OF LABOR. It was a socialistic, pan-industrial union whose aggressive organizing tactics often brought brutal retaliation from the law and from vigilantes, including five Wobblies killed at Everett, Wash., one murdered at Butte, Mont., and one lynched at Centralia, Wash., in 1916–17. The US tried 105 IWW leaders for sedition (*see* SEDITION ACT, 1918) in WORLD WAR I and convicted 92. State prosecutors charged 5,000 IWW leaders under criminal syndicalist laws in the 1920s. After rising from a membership of 58,000 in 1919 to a peak of 100,000 in 1923, the IWW declined rapidly and was moribund by 1930.

Information Agency, US *see* US INFORMATION AGENCY

Ingle's Revolt After being arrested in 1644 for voicing support of Parliament's cause in the English Civil War, Captain Richard Ingle sowed sedition in Md. against Governor Leonard Calvert, whose loyalty lay with the King. In February 1645, Ingle captured St Mary's without a fight, drove Calvert to exile in Va., and looted the homes of Calvert's backers. Ingle controlled Md. until early 1647, when Calvert regained control with help from Governor William Berkeley of Va. Ingle's rule was so anarchic that the population, which had been about 500 in 1644, fell by more than half by 1646.

initiative This was a political reform of the PROGRESSIVE ERA pioneered on 2 June 1903 by Oreg., in which a successful petition drive by voters can force a bill or constitutional amendment to be placed on the ballot at the next election. As of 1993, constitutional initiatives are allowed in 17 states (of which 12 are west of the Mississippi).

Inner Light In the theology of the QUAKERS, the Inner Light was a source of moral insight prompted by divine assistance. The main purpose of Quaker meetings was to await and discuss inspirations provided by the Inner Light.

Inness, George (b. near Newburgh, N.Y., 1 May 1825; d. Bridge of Allan, Scotland, 3 August 1894) A largely self-taught painter, Inness made several trips to Italy and France to study art from 1847 to 1854. His early work reflected the HUDSON RIVER SCHOOL, but he developed a mature style that showed more subtlety of expression. He emerged as one of the leading US landscape painters, and his works included *Peace and Plenty* (1865), *Delaware Meadows* (1867), *Coming Storm* (1878), *Sunset in the Woods* (1883), *Niagara Falls* (1884), and *March Breezes* (1885).

insular cases *see DE LIMA* v. *BIDWELL*, *DOWNES* v. *BIDWELL*, *and DORR* v. *UNITED STATES*

Insull, Samuel (b. London, England, 11 November 1859; d. Paris, France, 16 July 1938) He built the largest US network of utility firms organized as a holding company. His empire supplied power to 4,500,000 people and had assets of $2.5 billion in 1929, when it collapsed in the GREAT CRASH. Subsequent investigations uncovered business practices that were recklessly irresponsible and probably criminal, although Insull was tried and acquitted on all counts of illegal behavior. The scandal produced calls for reform and influenced passage of the SECURITIES EXCHANGE ACT, the TVA Act, and the PUBLIC UTILITY HOLDING COMPANY ACT.

Inter-American Treaty of Reciprocal Assistance *see* RIO PACT

Interior, Department of the Created on 3 March 1849 as the the Home Department in a government reorganization, it assumed responsibility for the Bureau of INDIAN AFFAIRS, the Patent Office, the General Land Office, the Pensions Commission, and the Census Bureau. It later assumed responsibility for the Office of Education (1869), the Geological Survey (1879), the Reclamation Service (1902), the Bureau of Mines (1910), and the NATIONAL PARK SERVICE (1916). (The bureaus for Patents, Pensions, the Census, and Agriculture have since been shifted elsewhere in the cabinet.) Albert Fall, secretary of the Interior Department, was convicted of corruption in the TEAPOT DOME SCANDAL. During the NEW DEAL, it operated the CIVILIAN CONSERVATION CORPS and PUBLIC WORKS ADMINISTRATION. By tradition, its secretary is a westerner, and appointments have become watched as measuring an administration's commitment to conservationism.

Intermediate-Range Nuclear Forces Treaty This treaty covered land-based nuclear missiles, stationed in eastern and western Europe, with ranges from 310 to 3,415 miles. The US and USSR agreed to dismantle and destroy such weapons on 8 December 1987, and Senate ratification came on 27 May 1988.

internal improvements In the 19th century, this term referred to public works projects such as the building of roads, bridges, or canals.

Internal Security Act (1950) *see* MCCARRAN ACT

internal taxation During the Revolutionary era, internal taxes were defined as revenues levied directly on property (such as land or livestock), persons (such as POLL TAXES), or governmental functions (such as the STAMP ACT). After 1764, Parliament ceased trying to impose internal taxes and attempted to raise an American revenue by EXTERNAL TAXATION.

International Bureau of American Republics *see* PAN-AMERICAN UNION

International Church of the Four-square Gospel *see* MCPHERSON, AIMEE SEMPLE

International Communication Agency *see* US INFORMATION AGENCY

International Monetary Fund *see* BRETTON WOODS CONFERENCE

interposition The VIRGINIA RESOLUTIONS introduced this device (but did not define its scope) as a means by which states might protect their citizens from unconstitutional federal actions. The HARTFORD CONVENTION affirmed interposition as a means of redressing federal usurpations of STATES RIGHTS. NULLIFICATION emerged as the preferred method of interposing state authority against abuses of power by the federal government.

Interstate Commerce Commission Act (4 February 1887) After GRANGER LAWS had proved ineffective in regulating railways, this law was passed to prevent abuses by railroads operating across state lines. The law forbade charging discriminatory rates, demanding or taking kickbacks, and charging more for short trips than long hauls; it outlawed pooling arrangements between two or more railroads that eliminated competition. All rates had to be openly published and based on uniform accounting procedures; they could not be altered without 10-day public notice.

To enforce these provisions, Congress created the Interstate Commerce Commission (ICC), which was directed to ensure that all freight or passenger charges were fair and reasonable by reviewing rate schedules and annual financial reports. The ICC could not set rates, but could investigate complaints, issue cease-and-desist orders, and challenge questionable business practices in court. Because rate-setting involved complex factors, the ICC found it difficult to overturn rate schedules in court, and by 1900 it was stymied in regulating charges for freight and passengers. The HEPBURN ACT and later laws greatly strengthened it.

As a result of DEREGULATION, the ICC lost its power to set freight rates, except in rare situations where competition did not exist. The agency also lost virtually all authority to reject applications for new trucking or rail services. By 1994, the ICC had shrunk to 630 employees (from 2,000 in 1980); its primary duties entailed filing information on shipping rates provided by carriers. Deregulation made freight transportation so competitive that in the early 1980s the ICC stopped receiving public complaints alleging rate discrimination.

interstate highway system On 29 June 1955, the Federal Aid Highway Act was enacted to build the National System of Interstate and Defense Highways. Revenue raised by federal gasoline taxes would finance 90 percent of the costs borne by state highway departments in constructing the system, which was intended to link 90 percent of cities with populations over 50,000. By 1990, 42,400 miles of high-speed, multilane routes had been finished at a cost of $124.9 billion. Interstate highways amount to 1 percent of all road mileage, but they carry more than 20 percent of all traffic.

Intolerable Acts Following the BOSTON TEA PARTY, Parliament quickly passed four laws intended to strengthen British authority in America: the BOSTON PORT ACT, MASSACHUSETTS GOVERNMENT ACT, ADMINISTRATION OF JUSTICE ACT, and QUARTERING ACT (1774). All the laws had already been under consideration except the BOSTON PORT ACT. An unrelated measure, the QUEBEC ACT, was passed at the same time and was also considered an Intolerable Act. The CONTINENTAL CONGRESS convened in response to these laws, whose repeal became the primary demand of Americans from then until Independence.

Inuit This word means "the people" in the ESKIMO-ALEUT LANGUAGE and is the term they call themselves instead of ESKIMO, which is a derivation in the ALGONQUIAN LANGUAGES meaning "raw-meat eater."

Iowa The first white settlers were French who established lead mines near Dubuque in 1788. The US acquired Iowa by the LOUISIANA PURCHASE. Between 1824 and 1851, Indians sold their lands in the state, which was settled without major hostilities. Anglo-Americans began arriving in significant numbers in 1828, but the first auction of PUBLIC DOMAIN was not held until 1838. Having been under the jurisdiction of Mich. and Wis., Iowa was made a territory on 12 June 1838. It became the 29th state on 28 December 1846.

In 1860 it had 674,913 people, of whom 1,058 were black and 16 percent were foreign-born; it ranked 20th in population, 20th in the value of its farmland and livestock, and 24th in manufactures. During the CIVIL WAR, it furnished 76,242 USA troops, including 440 blacks.

From 1887 to 1898, when western Iowa often suffered from drought and low commodity prices hurt all farmers, POPULISM attracted strong political support. In 1900 Iowa had 2,231,853 residents, of whom 74 percent were rural, 99 percent white and 14 percent foreign-born; it ranked tenth among states in population, first in the value of its agricultural products, and 17th in manufactures. During the early 20th century, low commodity prices and drought crippled the Iowa economy. From 1920 to 1940, 240,600 out-migrants left the state. Another 178,800 left in the 1940s. Urbanization diversified the economy until the value of industrial products was over three times greater than that of agricultural goods by 1965. In 1990 Iowa was the 29th-largest state and had 2,776,755 inhabitants (96 percent white, 2 percent black, 1 percent Hispanic, 1 percent Asian), of whom 44 percent were urban and 1.6 percent were foreign-born. Manufacturing and mining employed 23 percent of workers.

Iran-Contra scandal From August 1985 to October 1986, NATIONAL SECURITY COUNCIL aides Lieutenant Colonel Oliver North and John Poindexter oversaw secret arms sales (via Israel) totaling $48,000,000 to Iran, hoping for good will to help free US hostages held by Islamic terrorists in Lebanon; they used the profits to supply anti-Communist guerrillas ("Contras") fighting the Sandinista regime in NICARAGUA, although the BOLAND AMENDMENTS made such aid illegal. Details of the arms diversion first became public on 6 November 1986, and led to televised hearings by a Senate-House committee, which reported, on 18 November 1987, no direct evidence proving that Ronald REAGAN ordered the operation. In 1989 Poindexter (7 April) and North (4 May) were found guilty of misleading Congress and destroying government documents, but an appeals court overturned both convictions on 20 July 1990 as impermissible under *MURPHY* v. *WATERFRONT COMMISSION* OF *NEW YORK*, and charges against them were dropped.

Iran hostage crisis On 22 October 1979, Mohammed Riza Pahlevi, a fugitive from Iran since being deposed as its Shah, was admitted to the US for medical treatment. On 4 November 1979, 500 militant Shiite Muslims ransacked the US embassy at Tehran, Iran, seized the staff, and declared them spies. When Jimmy CARTER failed to act decisively, the Ayatollah Khomeini threatened on 18 November to try the hostages as spies. A military rescue mission failed on 24 April 1980, when aircraft crashed with the loss of eight lives. On 28 April, Secretary of State Cyrus Vance resigned to protest the US attempt at using force. Imagination then failed the Carter administration and Iran exploited the opportunity to enhance its reputation through an extended humiliation of the US. Public outrage over the situation doomed Carter's chances for reelection in 1980. Citing concessions by the Carter administration to its demands, but apprehensive of armed retaliation by Ronald REAGAN, Iran freed 52 US personnel on 20 January 1981, the day Reagan was inaugurated.

Irish immigration From 1700 to 1775, about 109,000 Irish went to the THIRTEEN COLONIES, including 42,500 whose background was Catholic or Church of Ireland; the rest were SCOTCH-IRISH. Between 1780 and

1819, perhaps 167,000 Irish immigrated, most of whom were Catholic. By 1820, over 6 percent of all whites (about 500,000) were of Irish Catholic background, and their numbers were doubling every 30 years from natural increase. From 1820 to 1860, 1,956,557 Irish arrived, 75 percent after the potato famine struck; another 1,916,547 had come by 1900. The Irish comprised 35–45 percent of each decade's immigrants in 1820–60, but only 12.5 percent of arrivals in the 1880s and just 3.9 percent in 1901–10. Few Irish came after 1930, despite having a generous quota under the NATIONAL ORIGINS ACT. From 1820 to 1991, the US received 4,729,741 Irish, a number exceeded only by GERMAN, ITALIAN, BRITISH, and MEXICAN IMMIGRATION. The 1990 census counted 22,695,454 persons who reported their primary ethnic identity as Irish, or 11 percent of all whites.

Iron Act (12 April 1750) Parliament forbade the operation of steel mills or slitting mills in the colonies, but encouraged the production of bar and pig iron by allowing it to enter Britain duty-free under certain conditions. The law was amended in 1757 to grant duty-free status to all American bar and pig iron.

ironclads These were armored, steam-powered warships, with bows pointed for ramming wooden vessels of the Civil War. The USA commissioned 58 ironclads and the CSA commissioned 23. (*See* MONITOR)

Iroquoian languages The homeland of this family of INDIAN LANGUAGES was the St Lawrence–Hudson River region. Its major subdivisions are the languages of the MOHAWK, ONEIDA, SENECA-CAYUGA-ONONDAGA, TUSCARORA, HURON (WYANDOT), and CHEROKEE INDIANS. The Cherokee probably broke off and wandered south to the highlands of N.C., S.C., and Ga. about 3,500 years ago. The Tuscarora probably left the homeland for coastal N.C.-Va. 2,000 years ago. Separate dialects most likely began evolving among the IROQUOIS CONFEDERACY at least 1,200 years ago.

Iroquois Confederacy About 1520–40, the prophet Deganawida and his disciple HIAWATHA organized a non-aggression pact among five IROQUOIAN LANGUAGES nations: the MOHAWK, ONEIDA, ONONDAGA, CAYUGA, and SENECA INDIANS. The league established itself between the Hudson River and Niagara Falls, and may have included 25,000 members by 1610. The onset of European epidemics in the 1630s probably halved the total population by 1660. The Iroquois tried to replenish these losses by waging war to obtain captives for adoption, and by 1670 the number of foreign Indians among them ranged from a third to half. They also fought a series of BEAVER WARS to control the fur trade. Warfare and continuing epidemics reduced the Five Nations to 8,600 by 1691. By 1701 their participation as English allies in KING WILLIAM'S WAR cut their numbers to 7,000. They adopted a policy of neutrality between the English and French, and followed it until Sir William JOHNSON enlisted them on England's side in the latter part of the SEVEN YEARS' WAR. They incorporated the TUSCARORA INDIANS as a sixth nation in 1722, and by 1770 their population had grown to 9,000. Joseph BRANT led them as British allies during the REVOLUTIONARY WAR, but SULLIVAN'S CAMPAIGN despoiled their villages, drove most out of N.Y., and led to widespread starvation. Their numbers may have declined to under 5,000 by 1783. After surrendering extensive land claims in the second treaty of FORT STANWIX and later agreements, they ceased to be ranked as major powers.

Irving, Washington (b. New York, N.Y., 3 April 1783; d. Tarrytown, N.Y., 28 November 1859) Irving abandoned a short-lived New York law practice and began publishing satires and other light material in 1802. His burlesque *History of New York . . . by Diedrich Knickerbocker* (1809) solidified his reputation as a humorist. While living and writing in Europe from 1815 to 1832 (as US embassy attaché in Madrid and London, 1826–32), he authored *The Sketch Book of Geoffrey Crayon, Gent.* (1820), the first American literary book to win international renown (it included "Rip Van Winkle" and "The Legend of Sleepy Hollow"). Except for duty as ambassador to Spain (1842–6), he spent the rest of his life at Tarrytown, N.Y. Hailed as the foremost US man of letters in the early Romantic era, his works included *The Letters of Jonathan Oldstyle, Gent*

(1802), *The History of the Life and Voyages of Christopher Columbus* (1828), *A Tour of the Prairies* (1835), *Astoria* (1836), *The Adventures of Captain Bonneville, U.S.A.* (1837), *Life of George Washington* (5 vols, 1855–9).

sland hopping In WORLD WAR II's Pacific theater, Douglas MACARTHUR conceptualized this strategy of leapfrogging Japanese strongpoints to take critical positions that would cut enemy supply routes and isolate large bodies of imperial troops behind Allied lines without air or naval support.

sland Number 10, battle of *see* NEW MADRID, BATTLE OF

talian immigration Before 1861, 13,813 Italians arrived in the US. Large-scale immigration began in the 1880s, when 307,309 arrived, and a total of 1,040,479 had come by 1900. From 1901 to 1920, 3,155,401 immigrated. The NATIONAL ORIGINS ACT gave Italy a low quota, and it sent only 533,861 to the US from 1921 to 1991. Although more immigrants have come from Italy (5,403,424) than any country but Germany, it is estimated that half of all arrivals before World War I were temporary laborers who returned to Italy after accumulating several years' savings. The 1990 census reported 11,246,781 persons who described their primary ethnic identity as Italian, or 5.6 percent of all whites.

Ives, Charles Edward (b. Danbury, Conn., 20 October 1874; d. New York, N.Y., 19 May 1954) He received musical training from his father, graduated from Yale in 1898, and ran an insurance agency in New York until illness forced his retirement in 1930. From 1890 to 1921, he composed over 500 musical works, including four symphonies and more than 60 other scores for large ensembles. His New England background formed the largest source of inspiration for his works. He kept his compositions private until late in his life, and few of his pieces were performed before his death. His *Symphony No.3* received the Pulitzer prize in 1947. Ives has won widespread acclaim and is ranked among the leading US composers.

Iwo Jima, battle of On 17 February 1945, Major General Harry Schmidt's Third, Fourth, and Fifth Marine Divisions began landing on Iwo Jima, held by Lieutenant General Tadamichi Kuribayashi's 23,000 Japanese. Schmidt declared the island secure on 16 March, but minor resistance lasted until 26 March. US losses: 5,931 killed, 19,920 wounded. Japanese losses: 23,000 killed, 1,000 captured. Iwo Jima's capture brought Japan in range of the US fighters needed to escort B-29 bombers from Saipan.

J

Jackson, Andrew (b. Waxhaw, S.C., 15 March 1767; d. near Nashville, Tenn., 8 June 1845) He was wounded and captured in the REVOLUTIONARY WAR. In 1788 he moved to Tenn., where he opened a law practice and participated in the SPANISH CONSPIRACY. He was elected the first Tenn. congressman (1796) and was sent to the Senate (1797). He became a national military hero for his victories in the CREEK WAR, the first battle of NEW ORLEANS, and first SEMINOLE WAR. In the 1824 election, he ranked first among the four candidates (with 43.1 percent of the ballots and 99 electoral votes), but was denied the presidency by the "CORRUPT BARGAIN." Jackson beat Adams in 1828 with 56.0 percent of the popular vote, and defeated Clay in 1832 with 54.5 percent of the ballots. Jackson's enemies accused him of making appointments by the SPOILS SYSTEM and ridiculed his advisors as a KITCHEN CABINET. As president, Jackson gave the MAYSVILLE ROAD VETO, resolved the NULLIFICATION CRISIS, vetoed the second BANK OF THE UNITED STATES's charter, issued the SPECIE CIRCULAR, and implemented INDIAN REMOVAL.

Jackson, Rev. Jesse Louis (b. Greenville, S.C., 8 October 1941) He entered the CIVIL RIGHTS MOVEMENT in the SOUTHERN CHRISTIAN LEADERSHIP CONFERENCE and was at Martin Luther KING's side when he was assassinated. After directing OPERATION BREADBASKET in Chicago, he supervised that program nationwide (1967–71). He emerged as the most politically-influential black leader after forming People United to Save Humanity (PUSH) in 1971, a community self-help corporation for creating jobs, and the National Rainbow Coalition, a liberal Democratic splinter group. In 1984 Jackson became the first black to run a major national campaign for president and win sufficient votes (30 percent of delegates) to influence a party platform. In 1988 he again won the second largest number of delegates but failed to secure the liberal platform planks he wanted. He did not seek the nomination for president in 1992.

Jackson, Thomas Jonathan (Stonewall) (b. Clarksburg, W.Va., 21 January 1824; d. Guiney's Station, Va., 10 May 1863) Having graduated from West Point in 1846, Jackson was cited for gallantry in the MEXICAN WAR, and left the army to teach at Va. Military Institute in 1852. Appointed CSA brigadier general in the CIVIL WAR, he earned the nickname "Stonewall" at the first battle of BULL RUN, where he turned USA victory into defeat by holding firm long enough to allow CSA troops to counterattack the advancing Federals. Jackson's SHENANDOAH VALLEY CAMPAIGN was critical in forcing USA abandonment of the PENINSULAR CAMPAIGN. His brigade figured prominently in the CSA victory at the second battle of BULL RUN, and made the crucial attack that broke Union lines at CHANCELLORSVILLE, where Jackson was accidentally killed by one of his own sentries.

Jackson* v. *Georgia *see FURMAN* V. *GEORGIA*

Jacksonian democracy Also called Jacksonianism, this was a set of attitudes about representative democracy associated with Andrew JACKSON. It exalted egalitarianism and equal opportunity to an extreme degree, and made them the standard for measuring candidates and issues. By idealizing the common man as the republic's bedrock, it encouraged political reforms that widened the franchise, made more offices elective, and stimulated an increase in voter turnout.

James I (b. Edinburgh Castle, Scotland, 19 June 1566; d. Theobalds, Middlesex,

England, 27 March 1625) He chartered the VIRGINIA COMPANIES OF LONDON and PLYMOUTH to colonize VIRGINIA, where JAMESTOWN was named for him.

James II (b. St James's Palace, Middlesex, England, 14 October 1633; d. St Germain, France, 6 September 1701) As Duke of York, James had been the PROPRIETOR OF NEW YORK, which was named for him. His conversion to Catholicism (ca. 1671) turned most Englishmen and colonists against him well before he became king in 1685. He fled to France after the REVOLUTION OF 1688, which set off rebellions against his governors in the colonies.

James, Henry (b. New York, N.Y., 15 April 1843; d. London, England, 28 February 1916) Brother of William JAMES, he was educated in France and at Harvard Law School before becoming a professional writer. He established his permanent domicile at London in 1876. Despite taking British citizenship, he was generally considered the foremost American man of letters in the late 1800s because his subtle and sophisticated fiction often developed themes concerning Americans abroad and their reaction to European culture. His works included *The Americans* (1877), *Daisy Miller* (1878), *The Portrait of a Lady* (1881), *The Bostonians* (1886), *The Princess Casamassima* (1886), and *The Sacred Fount* (1901).

James, William (b. New York, N.Y., 11 January 1842; d. Chocoua, N.H., 26 August 1910) Brother of Henry JAMES, he earned a M.D. from Harvard (1869) and joined its medical faculty. James's *Principles of Psychology* (1890) was the first major piece of scholarship on that discipline by an American. His *Varieties of Religious Experience* (1902) was a pathbreaking essay demonstrating that the science of psychology did not conflict with religion. His most influential work was *Pragmatism* (1907), wherein he expounded the philosophy of PRAGMATISM, which would influence much of the PROGRESSIVE ERA's reform spirit.

Jamestown (Va.) On 20 December 1606, the VIRGINIA COMPANY OF LONDON dispatched 144 settlers under Captain Christopher Newport to settle Va. Newport chose a site on the lower James River and landed the voyage's 105 survivors on 24 May at Jamestown. Disease and malnutrition had cut the settlers' number to 38 by January 1608, when a relief expedition brought 120 new colonists. Unable to become self-sufficient in food (except under John SMITH's command, September 1608 to July 1609), the colony experienced an 80 percent death rate during the 1609–10 winter, and was on the verge of being abandoned in May 1610 when a relief expedition arrived with reinforcements and food. A system of military discipline then brought order to the settlement and prevented the occurrence of any more "starving times." Jamestown was the only settlement in Va. until 1611, when the present area of Richmond was occupied. It remained the capital to 1699.

Japanese immigration Japanese immigrants replaced Chinese workers barred by the CHINESE EXCLUSION ACT. Hawaii's Japanese population rose from 116 in 1884 to 61,111 in 1900, while on the west coast their numbers rose from 148 in 1880 to 24,326 in 1900. Japan agreed to limit emigration voluntarily by refusing to issue passports to laborers in the Gentlemen's Agreements of August 1900 and 1907–8. The NATIONAL ORIGINS ACT (1924) excluded all Japanese entrants because they would be ineligible for citizenship under the NATURALIZATION ACT (1790) until 1952. The Japanese became Hawaii's largest ethnic group, with about 30 percent of its population in 1960. By 1991, 467,844 Japanese had migrated to the US. The 1990 census counted 1,005,000 Japanese Americans, 0.4 percent of the population.

Japanese relocation When PEARL HARBOR was attacked, 112,000 Japanese lived on the Pacific coast, including 40,000 Issei (first or immigrant generation) and 72,000 Nissei (second or native-born generation). An executive order of 19 February 1942 authorized the secretary of war to evacuate them from the coast, where a Japanese attack seemed possible, to ten interior camps. No relocation of Japanese was undertaken in Hawaii. The Supreme Court upheld US actions in *HIRABAYASHI v. UNITED STATES* and *KOREMATSU v. UNITED STATES*. On 10 August 1988, the US created a $1,250,000,000 trust fund to compensate surviving internees for their financial losses.

Jay, John (b. New York, N.Y., 12 December 1745; Bedford, N.Y., 17 May 1829) He became N.Y. 's chief justice in 1777, president of the CONTINENTAL CONGRESS in 1778, envoy to Spain in 1780, and a US negotiator for the treaty of PARIS (1783). As secretary for foreign affairs, he negotiated the abortive JAY–GARDOQUI TREATY. He wrote five of the *FEDERALIST PAPERS*. He declined to be George WASHINGTON's first secretary of state, and instead was confirmed as the SUPREME COURT's first chief justice on 26 September 1789. He authored *CHISHOLM* v. *GEORGIA* and negotiated JAY'S TREATY with Britain, then left the Court in 1795 to be N.Y. governor. Renominated as chief justice on 18 December 1800 and confirmed the next day, Jay refused the appointment (made without his knowledge), and retired from politics at the age of 55.

Jay–Gardoqui Treaty On 20 July 1785, Congress directed John JAY to negotiate a treaty with Spain's minister to win trading rights at Spanish harbors, recognition of the 31st parallel as the US–Florida boundary, and reinstatement of the RIGHT OF DEPOSIT. Gardoqui resisted Jay for a year, then offered to grant export privileges if the US ceased demanding the right of deposit. On 29 August 1785, Congress voted 7–5 for such a compromise, two states less than was necessary for ratifying a treaty. Negotiations then ended, but the vote embittered the West and South at the North's readiness to win new markets for its exports by surrendering the right of deposit. The treaty of SAN LORENZO resolved US disputes with Spain.

Jay's Treaty Between 19 April and 19 November 1794, John JAY negotiated an agreement to resolve US–British foreign policy controversies. Britain refused to grant US shippers full neutral rights while trading with French ports or to pay restitution for US slaves it had freed in the Revolution, but agreed to: (1) withdraw all armed forces from US soil by 1 June 1796; (2) establish arbitration panels to assess damages for US shipping seized by its navy, and to obtain payment for British merchants who had been unable to collect debts from Americans during the Revolution; (3) to permit US ships under 70 tons full trading rights with its West Indian colonies, so long as they did not re-export sugar, molasses, cotton, coffee or cocoa.

The Senate expunged the article allowing US ships restricted access to West Indian ports, and ratified the treaty on 24 June 1795. Although widely unpopular in the US, Jay's Treaty defused the risk of war, resulted in Britain compensating US merchants $10,345,000 for seized cargoes (compared to $2,750,000 paid by the US to settle pre-Revolutionary debts to British merchants), and led Britain to countenance an unofficial opening of its West Indian trade for Yankee shippers. By creating better relations with Britain, the treaty indirectly led to a tripling of US exports to British ports from 1795 to 1800. It nevertheless alienated, and helped precipitate an undeclared naval war with, FRANCE.

jayhawker This term was used in BLEEDING KANSAS when referring to antislavery guerrillas, and was applied in the CIVIL WAR to Kans. Unionists who plundered Mo. communities indiscriminately.

Jefferson, Thomas (b. Albemarle County, Va., 13 April 1743; d. Monticello, Va., 4 July 1826) He was a planter and lawyer who became a firm opponent of unconstitutional Parliamentary taxes while sitting in the HOUSE OF BURGESSES (1769–75). He drafted the DECLARATION OF INDEPENDENCE. In his home state, he fought for the VIRGINIA STATUTE FOR RELIGIOUS FREEDOM, abolition of ENTAIL and PRIMOGENITURE, and state-funded universal education. He was Va. governor (1779–81), ambassador to France (1785–9), and US secretary of state (1789–93). As second vice-president (1797–1801), he authored the first KENTUCKY RESOLUTIONS. As third president, he made the LOUISIANA PURCHASE, dispatched the LEWIS AND CLARK EXPEDITION, stopped depredations by the BARBARY PIRATES, and imposed the embargo (*see* EMBARGO ACT). He was mainly responsible for founding the University of Virginia in 1819.

Jeffersonian democracy Also called Jeffersonianism, this is a set of assumptions about republican government associated with Thomas JEFFERSON and Albert GALLATIN. Jeffersonianism derived from ENLIGHTENMENT criticism of European states that centralized authority through large bureaucracies, wielded power by standing armies, rewarded political supporters with titles of nobility or profitable offices, and financed themselves by heavy taxation. Jeffersonianism espoused limited, frugal government that treated all citizens equally and allowed them maximum liberty to improve themselves. It affirmed that republics best upheld the public interest by setting strict limits on the use of political power, discountenancing special-interest legislation, and taxing nonessentials at modest rates.

Jenkins' Ear, war of Incensed by the testimony of Captain Robert Jenkins – who displayed one of his ears that Spain's Latin-American Coast Guard had once cut off – the House of Commons demanded revenge, and GEORGE II declared war on 23 October 1739. The THIRTEEN COLONIES provided 3,500 troops for Admiral Edward Vernon's (1684–1757) futile siege of Cartagena (Colombia) (March–April 1741), of whom 50–80 percent died of disease. In January–May 1740, Ga. governor James OGLETHORPE invaded Fla. and captured Forts San Francisco de Pupo, Picolata, San Diego, and Moosa; he besieged ST AUGUSTINE unsuccessfully in June–July. Oglethorpe repulsed a Spanish invasion of Ga. in 1742 at the battle of BLOODY SWAMP, and again attacked St Augustine in March 1743. Fighting on the Ga. frontier lapsed into small-scale raids after KING GEORGE'S WAR commenced. The treaty of AIX-LA-CHAPELLE restored peace.

jeremiad This was a genre of sermons developed by 17th-century New England PURITANISM. Named in reference to the lamentations of the prophet Jeremiah, it indicted society as a whole for spiritual languor and for permitting a variety of social evils, and then called for repentance. The jeremiad became the most common sermon type delivered at public occasions after 1660, and was the primary means by which the clergy preached the theme that New England had declined from the religious standards of its founding generation. The jeremiad has endured as the basic format for revivalistic preaching.

Jewish immigration The earliest known Jewish colonist, Elias Legardo, came to Va. in 1621. In September 1654, 23 Portuguese Sephardim founded the first Jewish community at New Amsterdam. Until 1775, most Jewish newcomers were Sephardic. An estimated 180,000 Jews, mostly German-speaking Ashkenazim, immigrated from 1800 to 1880, when there were 250,000 US Jews, and by 1900, there were 1,000,000. Between 1882 and 1924, about 2,300,000 Jews entered the country, primarily from Poland and Russia, and raised the group's population to 4,200,000. Because the Russian Revolution cut off a major source of immigration and the NATIONAL ORIGINS ACT allowed few eastern Europeans (of any religion) into the US, only 576,000 Jews entered the US from 1925 to 1975. In 1990 the 3,416 US synagogues included 5,944,000 practicing Jews (2.4 percent of the population).

Jim Crow laws These laws were the South's statutes imposing SEGREGATION. "Jim Crow" became a synonym for Negro after Thomas D. Rice wrote a minstrel dance tune by that name in 1832. The term "Jim Crow laws" first appeared in the 1890s when the South began legislating a formal code to ostracize blacks from white society.

Job Corps Established by the ECONOMIC OPPORTUNITY ACT and modeled after the CIVILIAN CONSERVATION CORPS this program of the GREAT SOCIETY operated 100 conservation camps (often at former military bases) where men or women aged 16–21 learned practical vocational skills and education for an 8th-grade literacy level in reading, writing, and mathematics. Trainees received living expenses, work clothes, and free medical care. By 1967, the program had grown to an annual enrollment of 42,000 trainees. The Job Corps shrank greatly under the Nixon administration, and was merged into the COMPREHENSIVE EMPLOYMENT AND TRAINING ACT in 1973. The US government spent $1.8 billion on the program through 1973.

John Birch Society In 1958 Robert Welch founded this public interest lobby to expose Communist influence in US politics. By the 1964 election, its Belmont, Mass., headquarters claimed 100,000 members. It demanded an end to US membership in the United Nations, Earl WARREN's impeachment, and the repeal of laws implementing the GREAT

SOCIETY; it also assailed the CIVIL RIGHTS MOVEMENT as Communist-inspired. From 1963 to 1967, the society was influential in the Republican Party, and in 1964 helped nominate Barry GOLDWATER (who was not a member).

Johnson, Andrew (b. Raleigh, N.C., 29 December 1808; d. Carter Station, Tenn., 31 July 1875) Born poor and a tailor's apprentice as a boy, Johnson moved to Greeneville, Tenn., and opened a modest tailor shop. He learned to read from his wife and used his skill as a natural orator to rise – as a Democrat – from alderman to US congressman by the age of 35. Johnson was the sole senator from a seceded state to support the Union during the CIVIL WAR. While serving as Tenn.'s military governor, he became Abraham LINCOLN's running mate on the ticket of the UNION-REPUBLICAN PARTY. He became president upon Lincoln's death in April 1865 and encountered bitter opposition from RADICAL REPUBLICANS for continuing Lincoln's lenient policies on RECONSTRUCTION. The radicals overrode his vetoes of their measures and the House impeached him on 24 February 1868, primarily for violating the TENURE OF OFFICE ACT. The Senate acquitted him on 16 May by a vote of 35–19, one vote less than the necessary two-thirds. He completed his term, but did not reenter government until 1875, when he sat in the Senate for a few months before his death.

Johnson, Hiram Warren (b. Sacramento, Calif., 2 September 1866; d. Bethesda, Md., 6 August 1945) A reformer of the PROGRESSIVE ERA, Johnson became Republican governor of Calif. in 1910 by campaigning for effective railroad regulation, unemployment insurance, RECALL, INITIATIVE, and REFERENDUM. He was Theodore ROOSEVELT's running mate in 1912. As US senator (1916–45), he opposed the LEAGUE OF NATIONS, declined to be Warren HARDING's running mate, lost the 1924 Republican presidential nomination to Calvin COOLIDGE, and opposed the NEW DEAL.

Johnson, Hugh Samuel (b. Fort Scott, Kans., 5 August 1882; d. Washington, D.C., 15 April 1942) After graduating from West Point in 1903, Johnson rose to brigadier general by 1918 and directed military purchasing under the WAR INDUSTRIES BOARD. He left the military and rose to head Moline Implement Co. by 1925. He became a member of the BRAINS TRUST in 1932 and was chosen to head the NATIONAL RECOVERY ADMINISTRATION (NRA) in 1933. After persuading most major industries to adopt NRA codes, Johnson was heavily criticized because many codes favored big corporations at the expense of labor and small business; he also alienated many interest groups in angry outbursts because he lacked political sophistication. He was asked to resign from the NRA on 15 October 1934 and emerged a major critic of the SECOND NEW DEAL by 1937.

Johnson, Lyndon Baines (b. near Stonewall, Tex., 27 August 1908; d. near Johnson City, Tex., 22 January 1973) He sat in Congress (1937–41), saw combat as a navy officer in WORLD WAR II, returned to the House in 1942, entered the Senate in 1948, and became majority leader in 1953. After losing the Democratic nomination for president in 1960, he became vice-presidential candidate. He succeeded John F. KENNEDY as president in 1963. A master of legislative influence, he galvanized Congress into passing his program for the GREAT SOCIETY. He won reelection in 1964 with 61.1 percent of the ballots (the greatest popular majority ever recorded) and carried all but six states. The VIETNAM WAR overshadowed his WAR ON POVERTY after 1964, and Johnson withdrew from the Democratic primary elections on 31 March 1968 to let Hubert HUMPHREY seek the presidency.

Johnson, Richard Mentor (b. Beargrass Creek, Ky., 17 October 1781; d. Frankfort, Ky., 19 November 1850) He entered Congress in 1806 and was a leading WAR HAWK. In the WAR OF 1812, he led a regiment of Ky. mounted riflemen and reputedly killed TECUMSEH at the battle of the THAMES RIVER. He was senator (1819–29), congressman (1829–37), and Martin VAN BUREN's vice-president (1837–41). Because so many tickets contested the 1836 election, Johnson did not win a majority of the ELECTORAL COLLEGE and became the only vice-president chosen by Senate vote.

Johnson, Tom Loftin (b. near Georgetown, Ky., 18 July 1854; d. Cleveland, Ohio, 10

April 1911) He was a streetcar entrepreneur who invented the first fare box for coins. He was elected twice to Congress as a Democrat in the 1890s, but lost a race for Ohio governor in 1903. As mayor of Cleveland (1901–9), he was influenced by the utopianism of Henry GEORGE and Edward BELLAMY. He introduced municipal planning, ended the practice of giving special tax breaks for railroads and utilities, lowered exorbitant streetcar rates, transferred control of the water system from private companies to the city, fought for HOME RULE, and won Cleveland a reputation as the best-governed US city. He was the very model of a reforming mayor of the PROGRESSIVE ERA.

Johnson, Sir William (b. Smithtown, County, Meath, Ireland, 1715; d. Johnstown, N.Y., 11 July 1774) Born William McShane, he came to N.Y. in 1738, changed his name, entered the FUR TRADE, and was adopted by the MOHAWK INDIANS. He became the foremost expert on northern Indian affairs in KING GEORGE'S WAR, and rapidly acquired high political offices and land grants. In the SEVEN YEARS' WAR, he was knighted and made baronet for winning the battle of LAKE GEORGE; he convinced the neutral IROQUOIS CONFEDERACY to fight the French, and took FORT NIAGARA. He negotiated the treaty of OSWEGO and the first treaty of FORT STANWIX.

Johnson Debt Default Act (13 April 1934) After the failure of European nations to honor their WORLD WAR I debts to the US after the HOOVER DEBT MORATORIUM, Congress forbade government loans to any foreign country delinquent in its war obligations. By 15 June 1934, when the US was owed over $22 billion (including future interest charges) all foreign countries had defaulted on their loans except Finland, which later paid in full. The Johnson Act was an expression of US isolationism, which failed to recognize that a major reason why Europeans could not honor their debts was the HAWLEY–SMOOT TARIFF's exclusion of their exports from US markets.

Johnson–Reed Act *see* NATIONAL ORIGINS ACT

Johnson* v. *De Grandy On 30 June 1994, the Supreme Court ruled (7–2) that states could GERRYMANDER election districts according to race without violating the VOTING RIGHTS ACT, if the purpose was to increase the chances of electing minority candidates to office (as earlier held in *Shaw* v. *Reno*, 1993). It denied the plaintiff's argument that the law compelled states to create the maximum number of minority-dominated districts possible, and held instead that states are only required to redistrict so that minorities have adequate opportunity to elect candidates of their own race roughly proportional to their share of population.

Johnson* v. *Zerbst On 23 May 1938, the Supreme Court held (6–2) that the SIXTH AMENDMENT guarantees assistance by a lawyer to defendants in federal courts facing criminal charges, unless that right is voluntarily waived.

Johnston, Albert Sidney (b. Washington, Ky., 2 February 1803; d. Pittsburg Landing, Tenn., 6 April 1862) In 1826 Johnston graduated from West Point with Jefferson DAVIS. He resigned from the army after duty in the BLACK HAWK WAR and joined the TEXAS REVOLT, as both brigadier general and secretary of war. He commanded Texans in the MEXICAN WAR, reentered the US Army in 1849, and led US forces in the UTAH WAR as brigadier general. He refused a Union command and held CSA lines in Ky.-Tenn. until 1862. When killed at SHILOH, he was considered the most experienced and promising CSA general.

Johnston, Joseph Eggleston (b. Prince Edward County, Va., 3 February 1807; d. Washington, D.C., 21 March 1891) In 1829 Johnston graduated 13th of 46 at West Point. He served in the BLACK HAWK, SEMINOLE, and MEXICAN WARS, before becoming CSA brigadier general in April 1861. He led the Army of NORTHERN VIRGINIA until the PENINSULAR CAMPAIGN, where severe wounds forced him to give up command. In November 1862, he took over all CSA armies in the west. He skillfully delayed William T. SHERMAN's advance on ATLANTA, but was relieved for avoiding direct battle with far superior USA forces, which soon took Atlanta from Johnston's successor, John B. Hood. Johnston again withdrew before Sherman's overwhelming strength through the Carolinas until surrendering his army on 26 April 1865. He died of pneumonia after standing bare-headed in chilly rain as a pallbearer at Sherman's funeral.

Joint Committee of Fifteen *see* JOINT COMMITTEE ON RECONSTRUCTION

Joint Committee on Reconstruction On 4 December 1865, Congress named a joint committee of nine congressmen and six senators to make proposals on safeguarding FREEDMEN's rights and readmiting ex-CSA states to congressional representation. Headed by Senator William Pitt Fessenden, a moderate, but dominated by Representative Thaddeus STEVENS, it adopted the RADICAL REPUBLICANS' most basic demands for southern RECONSTRUCTION. It drafted the FOURTEENTH AMENDMENT. On 20 June 1866, it declared the former CSA states ineligible for congressional representation and asserted that Congress – not the president – should determine the conditions for readmitting them.

Joliet, Louis *see* MARQUETTE AND JOLIET EXPLORATION

Jones, John Paul (b. Kirkbean, Kirkcudbrightshire, Scotland, 6 July 1747; d. Paris, France, 18 July 1792) Born John Paul, this ship captain took the name Jones after two incidents when crewmen died at his hands, and settled in Philadelphia about 1773. In 1776 he entered the US Navy. In the REVOLUTIONARY WAR, he took over 40 merchant vessels, defeated three warships, and fought the only battle on British soil by his capture of Whitehaven (23 April 1778). Jones was the sole naval officer voted a gold medal by Congress. He commanded a Russian fleet (1788–9), and then retired to Paris.

Jones, Thomas ap Catesby *See* MONTEREY INCIDENT

Jones Act (1916) *see* PHILIPPINES

Jones Act (1917) *see* PUERTO RICO

Jones Act (5 June 1920) This law repealed legislation creating wartime controls over the MERCHANT MARINE. It reorganized and continued the US Shipping Board, which was to regulate trade and mail routes. For the first time in US history, it excluded foreign flag ships from carrying cargoes between two US ports (a provision still in force). The MERCHANT MARINE ACT (1936) revised it.

Jones Act (2 March 1929) To halt the flagrant violations of the VOLSTEAD ACT by bootleggers, Congress imposed severe fines and jail sentences for persons dealing in illegal alcohol.

Jones–Connally Farm Relief Act (7 April 1934) This law defined beef, dairy cattle, rye, grain sorghum, flax, peanuts, and barley as basic commodities covered by the first AGRICULTURAL ADJUSTMENT ACT.

Jones–Costigan Sugar Act (9 May 1934) Having refused to define sugar cane and sugar beets as basic commodities in the JONES–CONNALLY FARM RELIEF ACT, Congress did so in this law, which also authorized the Agriculture Department to set quotas on sugar imports.

Jones* v. *Alfred H. Mayer Company On 17 June 1968, the Supreme Court interpreted (7–2) the CIVIL RIGHTS ACT (1866) as prohibiting racial discrimination in renting or selling homes by private persons. The Court held that the act's broad powers derived from Congress's authority under the THIRTEENTH AMENDMENT to eliminate all "badges of slavery," which would include segregated housing. The decision ended the immunity from federal prosecution enjoyed by private acts of discrimination since the 1883 CIVIL RIGHTS CASES, including restrictive housing covenants formed after *CORRIGAN* V. *BUCKLEY*.

Joseph, Chief *see* CHIEF JOSEPH

Judaism By 1750, JEWISH IMMIGRATION to the thirteen colonies had established five synagogues (New York, Philadelphia, Newport, R.I., Charles Town, S.C., and Savannah), all of which were of the Sephardic rite. In 1802 the first synagogue of the Ashkenazic rite was built in Philadelphia. In 1850, 50 synagogues (mostly Ashkenazic) existed in the US. In 1880 there were 270 synagogues and 250,000 Jews in the US, and in 1900 there were 1,000 synagogues and 1,000,000 Jews. American Jewry increasingly divided among an Orthodox body (largely from eastern Europe), Rabbi Isaac WISE's Reformed body (largely from central Europe), and Rabbi Sabato Morais's Conservative body. In 1957 there were 720 Orthodox, 600 Conservative, and 550 Reform synagogues.

US Jews increasingly secularized in the 20th century, and synagogue membership stagnated. The number of religiously-affiliated Jews was 5,600,000 (4.5 percent of all church members) in 1965, and 5,944,000 (4.0 percent of all church members) in 1990.

judicial review The principle that the federal courts have the right to determine the constitutionality of state and federal laws was first applied regarding a state statute in *WARE* v. *HYLTON* and first applied concerning federal legislation in *HYLTON* v. *UNITED STATES*. The Supreme Court first explicitly declared that judicial review was an integral part of its powers in *MARBURY* v. *MADISON*.

Judiciary Act (24 September 1789) This law, drafted by a committee under Senator Oliver ELLSWORTH, authorized an ATTORNEY GENERAL and established the initial structure and duties of the SUPREME COURT, three circuit courts, and 13 district courts. (Presiding over circuit courts were a district court judge and two Supreme Court justices.) In the first instance of the Supreme Court declaring a federal law unconstitutional, Section 13 of the act was struck down in *MARBURY* v. *MADISON*. The Court affirmed the constitutionality of Section 25 (allowing appeals from state courts to federal courts when a constitutional issue was involved) in *MARTIN* v. *HUNTER'S LESSEE* and in *COHENS* v. *VIRGINIA*.

Judiciary Act (27 February 1801) This law reduced the number of SUPREME COURT justices from six to five. It replaced the existing system of circuit courts (where two Supreme Court justices joined a district court judge) with 16 new circuit courts that were presided over by specially appointed judges (without any Supreme Court justices). To ensure the new courts would be staffed by FEDERALISTS, John ADAMS worked until 9 p.m. on 3 March by signing commissions for judges and court officials. To eliminate these "midnight appointments," Congress passed the JUDICIARY ACT (1802).

Judiciary Act (29 April 1802) This law repealed the JUDICIARY ACT (1801). It restored the SUPREME COURT's size to six justices. It again made circuit riding a duty of Supreme Court justices by replacing the 16 existing circuit courts with six courts, each headed by a Supreme Court justice.

Judiciary Reorganization Bill (1937) *see* COURT-PACKING BILL

Juilliard* v. *Greenman *see* LEGAL TENDER CASES

Jungle, The In 1906, Upton SINCLAIR published this novel about the exploitation of immigrant workers in Chicago. Its brief description of unsanitary conditions in the meat-packing factories caused a national uproar over life-threatening conditions in the food-processing industry. When independent investigations of meat-packers confirmed Sinclair's allegations, Theodore ROOSEVELT pressed Congress into passing the MEAT INSPECTION and PURE FOOD AND DRUG ACTS. Sinclair, who had dealt with the food problem only as a subplot in his novel, later quipped: "I aimed at the public's heart, and by accident I hit it in the stomach."

Justice, Department of On 22 June 1870, Congress created this department to assist the ATTORNEY GENERAL. The department oversees the duties of US attorneys, marshals, and the FBI.

K

Kahn, Alfred *see* DEREGULATION

Kaiser Aluminum* v. *Weber *see* *UNITED STEELWORKERS OF AMERICA ET AL.* v. *WEBER*

Kalmbach, Herbert Warren (b. Port Huron, Mich., 19 October 1921) He was assistant finance chairman for Richard NIXON's 1968 campaign, an unofficial CREEP fundraiser, and Nixon's personal attorney. He collected and disbursed cash for the burglars whose arrest triggered the WATERGATE SCANDAL. He implicated John EHRLICHMAN and other White House staffers in the conspiracy during testimony on 16–17 July 1973. In 1974 he served six months in prison for violating the Federal Corrupt Practices Act through illegal campaign contributions and selling an ambassadorship.

Kanagawa, treaty of On 31 March 1854, Japanese officials and Commodore Matthew PERRY signed this treaty (effective 22 June 1855) giving US ships their first access to Japanese ports at Shimoda and Hakodate. The agreement was soon supplemented by closer commercial and diplomatic ties negotiated by Townsend HARRIS.

Kansa Indians The Kansa (or Kaw) are a group speaking one of the SIOUAN LANGUAGES, that lived along the lower Missouri River. They may have numbered 3,000 in 1780. Although often in conflict with neighboring Indians, they avoided war with Anglo-Americans. In 1850 their 1,700 members accepted a 390 square-mile reservation on the Neosho River in Kans., but by 1873, when they relocated to the Arkansas River, they had been reduced to 533. In 1889 only 194 Kansa remained. They have a reservation in Osage County, Okla.

Kansas The US acquired Kans. by the LOUISIANA PURCHASE. The Indian Removal Act (1830) divided its eastern lands among Indians relocated from the midwest. The KANSAS–NEBRASKA ACT transferred these tribes to the Indian Territory (*see* OKLAHOMA) and opened the area to whites. BORDER RUFFIANS fought free-soil settlers during BLEEDING KANSAS. It was admitted as the 34th state on 29 January 1861.

In 1860 it had 107,204 residents, of whom 99 percent were white and 12 percent were foreign-born; it ranked 35th in population, 33rd in the value of its farmland and livestock, and 30th in manufactures. During the CIVIL WAR, it furnished 20,149 USA troops (including 2,080 blacks). Kans. JAYHAWKERS plundered Mo., and Mo. rebels terrorized Kans. in brutal guerrilla warfare that culminated in William QUANTRILL's sack of Lawrence. The RED RIVER WAR ended Indian raids on southern Kans.

The first HOMESTEAD ACT and the expansion of the railroads stimulated a mass exodus to Kans., whose population increased to 996,096 by 1880 and then grew by 43 percent in the next decade. Between 1887 and 1897, adequate rain for crops fell in only two years on the plains and commodity prices dropped sharply. Extreme economic hardship resulted in 149,800 persons leaving the state in the 1890s and strong political support for POPULISM. In 1900 Kans. had 1,470,495 residents (96 percent white, 4 percent black), of whom 78 percent were rural and 9 percent foreign-born; it ranked 22nd in population, 7th in the value of its agricultural products, and 16th in manufactures.

During the early 20th century, the problems of agriculture inhibited the growth of the Kans. economy. Farmers suffered from falling prices in the 1920s and DUST BOWL conditions in the 1930s. From 1920 to 1940, 246,900 persons left the state. The number of farms fell by half, from 177,000 in 1935 to 86,000 in 1970. Although the state's economy has greatly diversified, it has consistently ranked among the 10 largest agricultural producers. In 1990 Kans. was the 32nd largest state and had 2,477,574 inhabitants (88 percent white, 6 percent black, 4 percent Hispanic, 1 percent Asian, 1 percent Indian), of whom 54 percent were urban and 2.5 percent were foreign-born. Manufacturing and mining employed 23 percent of workers.

Kansas–Nebraska Act (30 May 1854) On 23 January 1854, Senator Stephen DOUGLAS introduced a bill organizing Kans. and Nebr. territories on the principle of POPULAR SOVEREIGNTY. He soon agreed to amend it with a repeal of the MISSOURI COMPROMISE. The Senate passed it by 23 votes and the House by 13. The act was the decisive event that led free-soil and antislavery northerners to coalesce as the REPUBLICAN PARTY. Its other legacy was BLEEDING KANSAS.

Kasserine Pass, battle of (Tunisia) Beginning on 14 February 1943, 150,000 forces of the AXIS under Field Marshal Erwin Rommel and General Jurgen von Arnim defeated US Army II Corps and French troops in a series of armored actions that drove the Allies 100 miles through Kasserine Pass. British counterattacks stopped the Germans on 22 February and retook Kasserine on 25 February. US casualties: 6,500. Other Allied casualties: 3,500. German casualties: 2,000

Katz* v. *United States On 18 December 1967, the Supreme Court reversed (7–1) *Olmstead* v. *United States* (4 June 1928), which ruled that wiretaps were not an unreasonable search; it held that unrestricted access to an individual's personal and business conversations violated the privacy that the FOURTH AMENDMENT was adopted to safeguard.

Katzenbach* v. *Morgan *see* *OREGON* v. *MITCHELL*

Kaw Indians *see* KANSA INDIANS

Keating–Owen Act *see* CHILD LABOR LAWS

Kefauver, (Carey) Estes (b. Madisonville, Tenn., 26 July 1903; d. Washington, D.C., 10 August 1963) He sat in Congress (Democrat, Tenn.) from 1939 to 1948, and in the Senate from 1948 to his death. He became nationally prominent for chairing the KEFAUVER HEARINGS, and was one of the few southern Democrats who openly supported Harry S. TRUMAN's position on civil rights. He lost the Democratic nomination for president to Adlai STEVENSON in 1952 and 1956, but served on Stevenson's ticket as vice-presidential candidate in 1956.

Kefauver hearings Senator Estes KEFAUVER's Senate Subcommittee to Investigate Interstate Crime held some of the earliest televised congressional hearings during 1951–2. The testimony revealed evidence of widespread corruption within the Internal Revenue Service and led to numerous resignations by high-ranking federal officials, including the Commissioner of Internal Revenue, George Schoeneman. The hearings catapulted Kefauver into national prominence as a contender for the Democratic nomination for president.

Kelley, Florence (b. Philadelphia, Pa., 12 September 1859; d. Philadelphia, Pa., 17 February 1932) She attended the University of Zurich, where she translated Friedrich Engels's *The Condition of the Working Class in England in 1844* into English (1877). Returning to the US as a socialist and crusading reformer, she worked with Jane ADDAMS. Her *Our Toiling Children* (1889) influenced Ill. to prohibit child labor and limit women's working hours in 1893. She campaigned for MINIMUM WAGE and maximum working hours reform, and collaborated in Louis BRANDEIS's brief for *MULLER* v. *OREGON*. She helped found the National Child Labor Committee in 1904, fought for the Keating–Owen CHILD LABOR LAW, helped organize the NATIONAL ASSOCIATION FOR THE ADVANCEMENT OF COLORED PEOPLE, and helped form the International Women's League for Peace and Freedom in 1919.

Kellogg–Briand Pact On 27 August 1928, at Paris, the US and 13 other nations signed this treaty, which pledged the signatories to renounce warfare, but relied solely on their good will. The pact ultimately was joined by 62 nations. The US reserved the right to use armed force in self-defense and to enforce the MONROE DOCTRINE.

Kelly, William (b. Pittsburgh, Pa., 11 August 1811; d. Louisville, Ky., 11 February

1888) He established an iron furnace at Eddyville, Ky., in 1846. Between 1847 and 1851, he developed the technique of refining pig iron into steel by directing air currents onto molten iron to produce heat from the reaction of oxygen with carbon. By drastically cutting fuel expenses, this process enabled steel output to expand enormously and revolutionized the industry. Kelly failed to patent the technique, however, and England's Henry Bessemer, who discovered it simultaneously, received the first US patent for the "Bessemer process" in 1856, a year before Kelly's own application. Both inventors compromised their claims in 1866.

Kelly Air Mail Act (1925) Congress relieved the POST OFFICE of operating its own air mail service, which had been flying since 1918, and directed that air mail would be carried by private companies on the basis of competitive bidding. Although certain abuses emerged that required passage of the AIR MAIL ACT (1934), this measure ultimately saved US taxpayers from the future expense of maintaining an enormous fleet of aircraft and paying a sizeable bureaucracy to operate them.

Kendall, Amos *see* KITCHEN CABINET

Kendall* v. *United States ex rel. Stokes In 1838 the Supreme Court held that US executive officials must comply with writs from federal courts ordering action to enforce the Court's authority, so long as they are empowered to do so by congressional statute. It did not violate the constitutional separation of powers, the Court said, for the judicial branch to compel the executive branch to take actions necessary to uphold the law, so long as the courts did not attempt to make political policies and impose them on a presidential administration.

Kennan, George F. *see* CONTAINMENT POLICY

Kennedy, John Fitzgerald (b. Brookline, Mass., 29 May 1917; d. Dallas, Tex., 22 November 1963) As a navy officer, Kennedy was decorated for heroism in the SOLOMON ISLANDS CAMPAIGN. He was Mass. congressman (1947–52) and US senator (1953–60). He lost a bid to be Democratic vice-presidential candidate in 1956, but won nomination for president in 1960 over Lyndon JOHNSON and Hubert HUMPHREY. Elected president in the closest race since 1884, he took 49.7 percent of the ballots and outpolled Richard NIXON by just 118,574 votes. He became the first Catholic and youngest man chosen as chief executive. He blundered into the BAY OF PIGS INVASION, but performed admirably in the BERLIN WALL and CUBAN MISSILE CRISES. He initiated US military involvement in the VIETNAM WAR, then approved a military coup that toppled Vietnam's civilian leaders and destabilized its politics. He initiated the KENNEDY ROUND OF GATT, and on 24 January 1963 proposed domestic cuts in INCOME TAX of $13.6 billion that were enacted as the TAX REDUCTION ACT (1964). Aside from the APOLLO PROJECT and the PEACE CORPS, Congress balked at enacting his other proposals before Communist sympathizer Lee Harvey Oswald shot him.

Kennedy, Joseph Patrick (b. Boston, Mass., 6 September 1888; d. Hyannis Port, Mass., 8 November 1969) He was a self-made millionaire whose ideas influenced legislation creating the SECURITIES AND EXCHANGE COMMISSION (SEC). As first chair of the SEC, he oversaw the writing of rules for stock trading and created a workable system of protecting investors based on self-regulation by the brokerage industry. After leaving the SEC in 1935, he became one of Franklin D. ROOSEVELT's most prominent business supporters, chaired the US Maritime Commission in 1937, and was ambassador to Britain in 1938. He was father of John and Robert KENNEDY.

Kennedy, Robert Francis (b. Brookline, Mass., 20 November 1925; d. Los Angeles, Calif., 6 June 1968) As attorney general for his brother John F. KENNEDY, Robert launched an ambitious program to attack organized crime, protect the civil rights of southern blacks, and prosecute corrupt labor leaders like Jimmy HOFFA. He resigned from the cabinet in 1964 and won a N.Y. Senate seat. He grew gradually alienated from Lyndon JOHNSON's VIETNAM WAR policy. After Eugene MCCARTHY revealed Johnson's vulnerability in Democratic primaries, Kennedy broke with the president, called for US withdrawal from Vietnam, and sought the Democratic nomination for president. While challenging Johnson's successor, Hubert HUMPHREY, he was assassinated by Sirhan Sirhan, a Marxist Palestinian refugee.

Kennedy round of GATT In 1962 John F. KENNEDY won congressional approval for US participation in the fourth round of GATT talks, known as the Kennedy round. On 30 June 1967, at Geneva, 53 nations agreed to cut tariffs by about 35 percent (totaling $40 billion) through 1972. Agricultural trade was liberalized, and provision was made for a program of grain aid totaling 4,500,000 tons for developing nations. The Kennedy negotiations were the most successful GATT round after 1951 and led to a significant expansion in world trade.

Kennesaw Mountain, battle of (Ga.) *see* ATLANTA, BATTLES FOR

Kent State University shootings (Ohio) After the 1970 CAMBODIA INVASION, when a re-energized VIETNAM ANTIWAR MOVEMENT swept colleges, Ohio national guardsmen were sent to keep order at Kent State University, where a campus building had been burned. On 4 May, after being stoned by protesters, guardsmen fired into a crowd and killed four students. A grand jury indicted 25 students or faculty associated with the protests for inciting a riot, but all were acquitted. An indictment for murder was made against eight guardsmen, but they were acquitted on 8 November 1974 in Cleveland for lack of evidence that they had acted with premeditation. A lawsuit asking for damages of $46,000,000 was filed against Governor James Rhodes, Kent State President Robert White, and 27 guardsmen, by 13 plaintiffs, but all defendants were acquitted on 27 August 1975 at Cleveland. A second civil-damage suit was filed against the state of Ohio, and was settled out of court on 4 January 1979 for $675,000 in damages.

Kentucky This state was relatively unknown to the English until the GIST EXPLORATION, but by the early 1770s, LONG HUNTERS had confirmed that it had no permanent Indian inhabitants. Indians gave up their claims by the treaties of CAMP CHARLOTTE and SYCAMORE SHOALS. In 1775 the first Anglo-American settlement beyond the Appalachians was made at Harrodsburg, just as Daniel BOONE blazed the WILDERNESS ROAD for the TRANSYLVANIA COLONY. In the REVOLUTIONARY WAR, the British directed Indian raids at Ky., which was the staging ground for George Rogers CLARK's campaigns. Population rose sharply after 1780. Dissatisfaction with US failure to pacify the Indians and secure the RIGHT OF DEPOSIT led its leaders to join the SPANISH CONSPIRACY. After the first treaty of GREENVILLE ended Indian warfare and the treaty of SAN LORENZO gained the right of deposit, its population doubled from 1795 to 1800. In 1800, it had 220,955 inhabitants, of whom 19 percent were slaves. Too far north to grow cotton, it was a major producer of tobacco, hemp, and livestock.

In 1860 it had 1,155,684 inhabitants, of whom 20 percent were slaves and 5 percent were foreign-born; it ranked ninth among the states in population, seventh in the value of its farmland and livestock, and 15th in manufactures. The CIVIL WAR badly divided Ky. The CONFEDERACY recognized it as its 13th state, although it never adopted a true act of SECESSION. It furnished perhaps 35,000 CSA regulars or "partisan rangers," 90,571 US regulars (66,868 white and 23,703 black), and 12,761 Federal militia. It was the site of 453 military engagements. Ky. became alienated from the Union due to the EMANCIPATION PROCLAMATION, recruitment of slaves as soldiers (whose families were freed by US law), the imposition of martial law from 5 July 1864 to 12 October 1865, and military intervention to ensure the election of pro-Union candidates.

In 1865 the legislature restored full civil liberties to CSA veterans and refused to ratify the THIRTEENTH AMENDMENT, which freed about 65,000 slaves in Ky. Ex-Confederates dominated the Democratic Party and state government, while the KU KLUX KLAN harassed Republicans and FREEDMEN. After the FIFTEENTH AMENDMENT's passage, blacks voted in Ky. and enjoyed most civil rights in court hearings.

The legislature never enacted "separate but equal" laws for secondary education or public facilities, but it segregated college campuses in 1904. Many localities established SEGREGATION. The legislature opened colleges to blacks in 1950, and the state appeals court opened public parks or other recreational areas to nonwhites in 1950. Ky.

desegregated with little resistance in the CIVIL RIGHTS MOVEMENT under progressive Democrats like Bert Combs, Edward Breathitt, and Henry Ward, and it was the only southern state to enact a civil rights act (27 January 1966).

Coal mining became its primary industry after 1890. In 1900 Ky. had 2,147,174 inhabitants, of whom 78 percent were rural, 13 percent were black, and 2 percent were foreign-born; it ranked 12th among the states in population, 15th in the value of its agricultural products, and 18th in manufactured goods. The state experienced net out-migration of 551,000 from 1900 to 1930. After diesel fuels began replacing coal and mines became increasingly mechanized, 909,000 persons left Ky. from 1940 to 1970. In 1990, it was the 23rd largest state and had 3,685,296 residents (92 percent white, 7 percent black, 1 percent other), of whom 52 percent were urban and 0.9 percent were foreign-born. Manufacturing employed 20 percent of workers and mining 9 percent.

Kentucky Derby This horse race is the oldest, continuously observed, American sporting event. Modeled on England's Epsom Derby, and first run in 1875, it was created to revive the moribund state of horse racing in Ky. The black jockey, Oliver Lewis, won the premier "run for the roses" on Aristides. The Ky. Derby, a 1.25-mile course, has become the first leg of the "Triple Crown," which also includes the Preakness (Md.) and Belmont (N.Y.) Stakes.

Kentucky Resolutions, first Authored by Thomas JEFFERSON, these resolutions were adopted by the Ky. legislature on 16 November 1798. They were essentially similar to the VIRGINIA RESOLUTIONS and asserted the right of states to judge when the federal government has acted unconstitutionally and to take any appropriate actions to protect their citizens' rights.

Kentucky Resolutions, second Written by John Breckinridge, speaker of the Ky. Assembly, and adopted by the legislature on 22 November 1799, this document responded to criticisms of the VIRGINIA and first KENTUCKY RESOLUTIONS by northern legislatures. The resolutions went beyond their predecessors by arguing that "nullification" by state action was the proper remedy for unconstitutional or tyrannical actions taken by federal authorities. The resolutions marked the first appearance in US politics of NULLIFICATION, although the manner of nullifying a US law was left unspecified.

Kentucky rifle Between 1725 and 1775, Pa. gunsmiths modified the *Jaeger*, a German gun for big game, into a weapon suited for American pioneers; they lightened its stock, lengthened its octagonal barrel from 30–40 inches to 40–45 inches, reduced its calibre from 0.60–0.70 to 0.38–0.45, and set a metal patchbox into its butt. The resulting firearm was exceptionally accurate, well balanced, functional, and economical of lead and powder. Although usually imagined as a white frontiersman's weapon, this rifle was widely possessed among Ohio valley Indians as early as 1755. Originally termed a Dutch or Pa. gun, it became known as the "Ky. long rifle" after that term was popularized in Samuel Woodworth's enormously popular song, "The Hunters of Kentucky" (1820).

Kentucky* v. *Dennison In 1861 the Supreme Court unanimously held that a state governor has discretion to refuse another state's request to turn over a fugitive from justice, because Article IV, Section 2 imposes only a moral obligation on states to cooperate in extradition proceedings and cannot be enforced by federal courts.

Kerouac, Jack (b. Lowell, Mass., 12 March 1922; d. St Petersburg, Fla., 21 October 1969) Born Jean Louis Kerouac, he briefly attended Columbia and then became the BEAT GENERATION's foremost novelist. He first gained fame with *On the Road* (1957), his best work, which was followed by *The Subterraneans* (1958), *The Dharma Bums* (1958), *Doctor Sax* (1959), *Lonesome Traveler* (1960), and *Big Sur* (1962). Kerouac's novels portrayed characters who rejected middle-class values, lived spontaneously, and tried to find meaning in life through a constant succession of new physical, mental, and emotional experiences. At his death, Kerouac was writing a book on Hindu mysticism and meditation.

Kerr–Smith Tobacco Control Act (28 June 1934) This law was enacted to ensure that the AGRICULTURAL ADJUSTMENT ADMINISTRATION's (AAA) voluntary covenants to reduce the national tobacco crop would not be undermined by another large surplus harvested by noncooperating farmers who refused to cut output. It taxed all tobacco auctioned in excess of individual quotas at 25–33 percent of its selling price. Any farmers who failed to enroll in an AAA crop-limitation agreement would be taxed on their entire output. Compulsory quotas kept total production at AAA levels, but became moot when the AAA was struck down in 1936.

Keyes* v. *Denver School District Number 1 On 21 June 1973, the Supreme Court gave its first decision on DE FACTO SEGREGATION in education. The justices ruled (7–1) that if racially imbalanced schools stemmed from deliberate policies of school officials, even if no law mandated segregating minority students, then their board must implement a plan to integrate them. In determining how a segregated system developed, the educational hierarchy bears the burden of proof to show that its policies were not responsible for racial separation. The Court ruled on unintentional de facto segregation in *MILLIKEN* V. *BRADLEY*.

Keynesian economics The English economist John Maynard Keynes was the most renowned expert on business cycles and monetary policy in the 1930s. His work changed the way US politicians understood the relationship between the federal budget and prosperity. By showing how budget deficits could replace private spending to stimulate economic growth during a depression, he freed politicians from the traditional wisdom that governments should retrench and cut their expenditures to a bare minimum during business contractions. As popularized by Walter LIPPMANN, his theories first influenced US policy during the SECOND NEW DEAL and the RECESSION OF 1937–8. Keynesianism fell from favor in the 1950s, but became fashionable again after 1960, when it was used (contrary to Keynes's actual theories) to justify failing to balance the budget in times of prosperity as well as during recessions.

Khe Sanh, siege of (Vietnam) On 21 January 1968, two North Vietnamese divisions began the siege of Khe Sanh airstrip, Quang Tri Province, later reinforced to 4,900 US marines and 1,000 South Vietnamese. US aircraft dropped 115,000 tons of bombs on the enemy, in addition to 150,000 shells fired by USMC artillery. The US Army's first Cavalry Division lifted the siege on 6 April 1968. US and South Vietnamese losses: 500 killed, 1,000 wounded. North Vietnamese losses: 10,000 killed, wounded. Because Khe Sanh was the only battle where Communist forces enjoyed artillery superiority, its allied casualty rate exceeded every other major battle in the VIETNAM WAR. US forces abandoned the airstrip in June.

Kickapoo Indians The French first met this group, which speaks one of the ALGONQUIAN LANGUAGES, in Wis. during the 1650s, when they may have numbered 2,000. They had appropriated lands of the ILLINOIS INDIANS by the 1760s. They fought as British allies from the REVOLUTIONARY WAR until the first treaty of GREENVILLE, and again in the WAR OF 1812. A band under Mecina tried to intimidate whites to prevent them from settling on the Ill. PUBLIC DOMAIN in 1819, but were forced into Mo. by US troops. The remaining Kickapoos left a few years later. Some raided whites in the BLACK HAWK WAR, but 100 enlisted as US Army scouts in the second SEMINOLE WAR in 1837. By the 1860s they had migrated to Kans., and from there many went to Mexico, from where they conducted raids on Tex. US troops invaded Mexico and attacked their village Remolino in May 1873. By 1875, 432 of the Mexican refugees had relocated in Okla. Kickapoo reservations are at Brown County, Kans., and a three-county area with headquarters at McLoud, Okla.

Kiefft's War On 26 February 1643, Governor William Kiefft's militia avenged a man killed in 1641 by massacring 100 Wesquaesgeek Indians and taking 30 captive. Fifteen hundred ALGONKIN warriors destroyed NEW NETHERLAND's outlying settlements and drove the refugees into NEW AMSTERDAM, defended by 60 soldiers and 250 militiamen. After forces under John La Montagne and John Underhill killed 600 Indians (February–March 1644), with few white casualties, fighting lapsed and by August peace had returned. The war resulted in Kiefft's replacement by Peter STUYVESANT, a decline of 900 in New Netherland's population (mostly from emigration), and perhaps 1,000 Indian deaths.

Kilbourn* v. *Thompson In 1881 the Supreme Court unanimously ruled that constitutional limitations exist on Congress's right to examine witnesses before its committees. Congress cannot cite witnesses for contempt for refusing to answer questions about their private affairs; nor can it force witnesses to testify at hearings unless the subject concerns anticipated legislation or another issue over which Congress has legal authority. *Kilbourn* was the first instance when the Court acted to protect citizens from abuses by congressional investigative committees. It served as precedent for *Watkins* v. *United States*.

King, Rev. Martin Luther (b. Atlanta, Ga., 15 January 1929; d. Memphis, Tenn., 4 April 1968) After becoming pastor of a Baptist church in Montgomery, Rev. King emerged as a leading advocate for the civil rights movement after winning the Montgomery bus boycott in 1955. He became the first president of the Southern Christian Leadership Conference in 1957. He was briefly jailed during the Birmingham desegregation violence in 1963 and led the 1965 Selma freedom march. He established himself as the principal black spokesman during the 1963 march on Washington, where he gave his "I have a dream" speech. He received the Nobel peace prize in 1964. After passage of the Civil Rights Act (1964) and the Voting Rights Act (1965), he planned civil disobedience drives in northern cities against de facto segregation and the Vietnam War. He was assassinated by James Earl Ray while in Memphis to support striking black sanitation workers. His death touched off racial violence in 125 cities in 29 states.

King, Rodney, incident On 3 March 1991, several white Los Angeles police were videotaped severely beating a black motorist stopped after a high-speed chase. The tape provoked international notoriety. When a Simi Valley jury acquitted the officers on state charges of using unlawful force, the most expensive, and second most violent, riots in US history erupted in central Los Angeles between 29 April and 1 May 1992. The rioting resulted in the deaths of 23 blacks, 18 Hispanics, 11 whites, and 2 Asians; it produced 2,383 injuries, 8,801 arrests (3,976 for felonies), 5,200 buildings burned or severely damaged, a billion dollars in property damage, and 20,000 jobs lost. The officers were retried for violating King's civil rights in Los Angeles federal court; two were found guilty on 17 April 1993 and received prison sentences of 30 months. King won compensatory damages of $3,800,000 on 19 April 1994, but was denied any punitive damages on 1 June 1994.

King, Rufus (b. Scarboro, Maine, 24 March 1755; d. Jamaica, N.Y., 29 April 1827) He served briefly in the Revolutionary War and opened a law office at Newburyport, Mass., in 1780. He sat in Congress (1784–6), where he introduced the clause to bar slavery by the Northwest Ordinance. He attended the Constitutional Convention and was influential in obtaining ratification by Mass. He relocated to New York City in 1788. While serving in the Senate (1789–96), he became a leader of the Federalist party and a director of the first Bank of the United States. He was ambassador to Great Britain (1796–1803). The Federalists nominated him for vice-president in 1804 and 1808, and for president in 1816, when he carried only Mass., Conn., and Del. He was senator again (1813–24), when he opposed the War of 1812, helped reestablish the second Bank of the United States, and opposed the Missouri Compromise. He proposed a scheme of abolitionism that compensated masters from sales of the public domain and then colonized freedmen overseas. His career ended with a second tour as ambassador to Great Britain (1825–6).

King, William Rufus Devane (b. Sampson County, N.C., 7 April 1786; d. Cahawba, Ala., 18 April 1853) A lawyer, King was a US congressman (Democrat, N.C., 1811–16), US senator (1819–44, 1848–52), and US vice-president (1853). Elected vice-president while in Cuba recovering from tuberculosis, he died 46 days after taking office.

King George's War On 25 October 1743 the Bourbon kings of France and Spain signed the second Family Compact, in which France pledged support for Spain's struggle against Britain in the War of Jenkins' Ear. On 15 March 1744, France declared war on

Britain, which then entered the War of the Austrian Succession (1740–8), or King George's [II] War as its Anglo-American phase was termed. Warfare along the Ga.–Fla. border lapsed into small-scale raids after 1743, and Canada became the main war theater.

From their fortress at LOUISBOURG, on Cape Breton Island, French troops raided Nova Scotia and French privateers preyed on Yankee ships. William PEPPERELL's New England militia won Britain's only significant victory (in America or Europe) by taking the citadel in 1745. In 1746, 4,000 Yankees volunteered for a projected siege of Quebec, and 8,000 colonials enlisted to attack Fort St Frederick (CROWN POINT, N.Y.) and then invade Canada, but both expeditions were canceled when Britain diverted the necessary ships and troops to European operations.

New England and N.Y. experienced numerous Indian raids after July 1745, but they suffered only two major defeats. On 29 November 1745, 520 French and Indians burned Saratoga, N.Y., killed 30, and took 109 prisoners. In August 1746, 700 French and Indians burned Fort Massachusetts, Mass., killed 11 militia, and took 19 prisoners. On 18 October 1748, the treaty of AIX-LA-CHAPELLE ended the war.

King Philip's War This war resulted from conflicts between Plymouth colonists and the WAMPANOAG INDIANS, headed by "King Philip" (Metacomet). By 1675 Philip had gained much influence among New England's 10,000 Indians, most of whom became his allies against the region's 50,000 whites. An armed confrontation began after Wampanoags looted and burned vacant buildings in Swansea on 20 June 1675. Philip attacked the town on 25 June. War engulfed New England when the Nipmuc, Pocumtuck, NARRAGANSETT, and ABNAKI INDIANS supported Philip. The Puritans enlisted support from the MOHICAN and Christian Indians; they starved Philip's followers into submission by burning their towns and destroying their winter food supplies. This scorched-earth strategy threw Philip's forces on the defensive by the spring of 1676. Indians surrendered in large numbers that summer and most fighting ended after Philip was shot on 12 August 1676, although Abnakis in Maine did not agree to make peace until 12 April 1678. Philip's men completely destroyed 12 of New England's 90 towns and badly damaged another 40; they left 1,200 homes in ashes, 8,000 cattle slaughtered, and 600 English dead. Four thousand Indians were killed, starved, or sold as slaves to the West Indies. The war left New England's Indians, except for the Abnakis, incapable of blocking further frontier expansion.

King William's War On 12 May 1689, King WILLIAM III joined England with the Netherlands and its allies against France in the War of the League of Augsburg, or King William's War as its Anglo-American phase was termed. In 1690 French and Indians destroyed SCHENECTADY, N.Y. (9 February), Salmon Falls, N.H. (18 March), Casco [Falmouth], Maine (20 May), and Fort Loyal [Portland], Maine (31 July). On 11 May 1690, William PHIPS captured the 72-man French garrison at Port Royal with 736 Mass. militia; he made a futile attack on Quebec, (5–11 October) (*see* QUEBEC, BATTLES OF (1)), in which he lost 10 percent of his 2,200 Yankees. Conn. and N.Y. militia mounted an abortive overland invasion of Canada, which failed for lack of supplies, but burned La Prairie, opposite Montreal (23 August 1690). In 1691, N.Y. militia and IROQUOIS CONFEDERACY warriors again raided La Prairie (1 August) and Mass. militia attacked ABNAKI INDIANS in Maine. In 1692 Abnakis and French destroyed York, Maine (25 January), burned much of Wells, Maine (21 June), and retook Port Royal. French raiders inflicted heavy losses at Oyster Bay [Durham], N.H. (23 June 1694), captured Fort William Henry [Pemaquid], Maine (15 July 1696), ravaged the Iroquois villages in winter 1693 and summer 1696, and fell on Haverhill, Mass. (15 March 1697). On 30 September 1697, the treaty of RYSWICK ended hostilities. The number killed probably equaled 850 Anglo-Americans, 700 Iroquois, 300 French-Canadians, and 100 Canadian Indians.

King's Mountain, battle of (S.C.) On 7 October 1780, Colonel William Campbell's 1,790 militia overran Major Patrick Ferguson's 1,000 TORIES and shot down about 100 attempting to surrender. US losses: 28

killed, 62 wounded. British losses: 157 killed, 861 captured (163 of whom wounded). The first US success following the fall of CHARLES TOWN, S.C., King's Mountain was the turning point in the southern campaigns; it encouraged southern WHIGS to suppress Tories and allowed Generals Morgan and Greene to mount offensive operations against forces under Cornwallis.

Kino, Fr Eusebio Francisco (b. near Trent, Italy, ca. 1645; d. Santa Magdalena, Ariz., 15 March 1711) He arrived in Mexico in 1681. From 1687 to 1711, he traveled 20,000 miles and built 24 missions in northern Mexico and Ariz., including San Xavier Del Bac, the earliest mission in Ariz. (1700). By discovering a land route to Calif. during November–December 1701, he proved Calif. was not an island.

Kiowa Indians Speakers of one of the UTO-AZTECAN LANGUAGES, the Kiowas began drifting south from Mont. in the 1500s, acquired horses, and established themselves in Okla. and northern Tex. They probably numbered 2,000 in 1780. They were successively decimated by cholera in 1849, smallpox in 1861–2, and measles in 1877. They frequently raided Tex., and to a lesser degree Kans., until defeated in the RED RIVER WAR. Their Andarko, Okla., reservation covers parts of seven counties.

Kip's Bay, battle of (N.Y.) On 15 September 1776, General William HOWE landed 13,000 redcoats and HESSIANS, and broke through Washington's defenses on Manhattan Island. US losses: 50 killed, 320 captured. British losses: minimal. The victory placed New York City under occupation, in which it remained until 25 November 1783, but failed to prevent Washington from withdrawing his army before Howe could cut off its avenues of escape.

Kirkland, (Joseph) Lane (b. Camden, S.C., 12 March 1922) He joined the AFL staff in 1948, became George MEANEY's chief assistant, and succeeded him as head of the AFL-CIO on 19 November 1979. His major accomplishments were to engineer readmission of the United Auto Workers in 1981 and the Teamsters Union in 1987. He has long been frustrated by a conservative drift in the Democratic party, and his opposition failed to stop the creation of NAFTA.

Kissinger, Henry Alfred (b. Fürth, Germany, 27 May 1923) A childhood refugee from Nazi Germany, Kissinger gained recognition as a leading academic expert of foreign affairs. In January 1969, he became Richard NIXON's special assistant for national security. Kissinger was a key architect of Nixon's strategy for ending US involvement in the VIETNAM WAR through a diplomatic settlement. Kissinger was the central negotiator and tactician for the PARIS PEACE ACCORDS of October 1972. He was the first foreign-born secretary of state (September 1973-January 1977). He and North Vietnam's Le Duc Tho shared the Nobel peace prize in 1973.

kitchen cabinet Andrew JACKSON was the first president to rely for political advice more heavily upon an informal circle of confidants (headed by Amos Kendall of Ky.) for political advice than upon his cabinet. Jackson's detractors called them by this name to imply that they lacked the credentials to merit being assembled in the White House's state rooms. This term now refers to any informal circle of presidential advisors.

Kleindienst, Richard Gordon (b. Winslow, Ariz., 5 August 1923) He opened a law practice in Phoenix and entered politics as a Republican. He lost a race for Ariz. governor in 1964. After serving as deputy to Attorney General John MITCHELL from January 1969, he took over that office on 12 June 1972. During his confirmation hearings, he lied when asked about any knowledge of improper contacts between International Telephone & Telegraph Co. (ITT) and Mitchell concerning a federal antitrust suit against the firm. (It was later revealed that ITT paid $400,000 for a favorable settlement of the case, and that some of the money was used as a "dirty-tricks" slush fund in the WATERGATE SCANDAL.) He became the first attorney general convicted of a criminal offense on 16 May 1974 when he pleaded guilty to misdemeanor charges of refusing to testify fully and accurately before a congressional committee. He was sentenced on 7 June to a suspended sentence of 30 days in jail and a $100 fine.

Klopfer* v. *North Carolina On 13 March 1967, the Supreme Court unanimously ruled that the FOURTEENTH AMENDMENT'S DUE

PROCESS clause obliged state courts to uphold the SIXTH AMENDMENT's guarantee of a speedy trial.

Knights of Labor Uriah Stephens founded this association in 1871 at Philadelphia and was its president until 1879. In January 1878, it was reorganized as the first national INDUSTRIAL UNION. It admitted unskilled laborers, farmers, and professionals; it did not require that local chapters be organized by industry, but did demand that 75 percent of each chapter's members be salaried workers. It grew rapidly in Terrence POWDERLY's presidency (1879–93), from 484 chapters to 5,892 in 1886. Despite Powderly's preference for settling labor disputes by arbitration, the Knights initiated several large-scale strikes or boycotts (1884–7) and lost much prestige after a failed strike against the Southwest Railroad Co. during March–May 1886. Because the HAYMARKET RIOT coincided with a national general strike called by the Knights for 1 May 1886 to win the eight-hour workday, the union became synonymous with anarchism and violence in the public mind. Membership fell from a peak of 700,000 in 1886 to 100,000 by 1890. It rapidly became extinct after 1893.

Knights of the Golden Circle *see* COPPERHEADS

Know-Nothing party The Order of the Star Spangled Banner was founded at New York in 1849 and evolved into a national organization, the American Party, after 1852. Members acquired the sobriquet Know-Nothing because they customarily answered questions about the group with: "I know nothing." The party's main goals were to delay naturalization until 21 years' residence and deny public office to aliens and Catholics. As the WHIG PARTY disintegrated, many ex-members joined the Know-Nothings. In 1854 it elected over 40 congressmen, took over the Mass. legislature, and won large minorities in the statehouses of N.Y., Pa., and Md. Its popularity peaked in 1856, when it nominated Millard FILLMORE for president and received 21.6 percent of the popular vote (but won only Md.). It almost immediately disintegrated and most supporters became Republicans.

Knox, Henry (b. Boston, Mass., 25 July 1750; d. Montpelier, Maine, 25 October 1806) As a Boston bookseller with a curiosity about artillery, Knox was one of the few Americans with any knowledge of gunnery when the REVOLUTIONARY WAR began, and was given charge of that branch of the Continental Army in November 1775. The siege of BOSTON was broken after he brought 60 tons of artillery over 300 miles from FORT TICONDEROGA in midwinter 1776. He ended the war as major general on George WASHINGTON's staff. He was army commander in chief (December 1783–June 1784), and first secretary of war (August 1789–December 1794).

Knox* v. *Lee *see* LEGAL TENDER CASES

Korean War Six months after Secretary of State Dean ACHESON singled out Japan as the only Asian country in whose defense the US would take immediate, unilateral military action, 95,000 North Koreans invaded South Korea on 25 June 1950. On the same day as the UNITED NATIONS asked members for troops to repel the aggressors, 27 June, Harry S. TRUMAN sent US air and naval forces to Korea; a day later, he ordered US Army units there from Japan. The US ultimately contributed 48 percent of all United Nations forces, and both UN commanders in chief: Douglas MACARTHUR and Matthew Ridgway.

By August, Communist forces had trapped UN troops within a 140-mile perimeter circling the Pusan Peninsula. On 15 September, MacArthur landed US troops behind enemy lines at Inchon harbor, and the next day UN forces at Pusan began breaking out of their encirclement to crush the Communists between themselves and MacArthur. By 30 September, the North Koreans had lost 100,000 men and fled from the south.

Two columns of UN troops pursued the Communists far into North Korea until 25 November, when 330,000 Chinese soldiers intervened at the Changjin and Chosin reservoirs. By 4 January 1951, the Chinese had inflicted heavy losses on the UN command and captured Seoul. UN forces resumed the initiative by 21 February with a counteroffensive that retook Seoul on 15 March and virtually cleared South Korea of Communist forces by 1 June. The war then stalemated along a 155-mile front on the border between the two Koreas. Truce negotiations began on 10 June 1951. An armistice ended the fighting on 27 July 1953 and separated the two Koreas with a demilitarized zone.

At the end of the war, US forces in Korea numbered 302,483 ground troops, supported by 261 US warships offshore. US losses included 33,629 battle deaths (27,704 army, 4,267 marines, 1,200 air force, 458 navy), 20,617 nonhostile deaths (9,429 army, 1,261 marines, 5,884 air force, 4,043 navy), 103,284 nonfatal wounds (77,596 army, 23,744 marines, 368 air force, 1,576 navy), and 7,140 captured (of whom 3,746 were repatriated), and 8,177 others missing in action. Aircraft losses totaled 1,466 for the air force and 1,248 for the navy and marines, of which half resulted from mechanical failure or accidents. Enemy fire hit 73 US warships and mines sank 5 others (4 minesweepers and 1 tugboat). Direct military expenses exceeded $54 billion. The war resulted in an estimated 415,000 Korean deaths in the South and 520,000 deaths in the North.

Korematsu* v. *United States On 18 December 1944, the Supreme Court held (6–3) that military necessity warranted a selective classification by race and forcible detention of US citizens during the Japanese relocation in World War II; it ruled that the president and Congress could take such action under their combined war powers.

Krock, Arthur (b. Glasgow, Ky., 16 November 1887; d. Washington, D.C., 12 April 1974) He rose from Louisville *Times* reporter to the New York *Times*' chief Washington correspondent. He and Walter Lippmann pioneered the syndicated editorial column. As one of the most powerful influences upon public opinion from the 1930s through 1960, he often received exclusive, executive-office interviews and was a regular vehicle by which presidents explained their policies to the public. He ranks as one of the giants of 20th-century journalism, and won three Pulitzer prizes.

Ku Klux Klan The Klan developed from a social club organized at Pulaski, Tenn., in May 1866. Under its first "imperial wizard," Nathan B. Forrest, southern Democrats rapidly adapted its secrecy, costumes, and ritual to intimidate Republicans from voting and reassert white supremacy. To curb the violence of Klansmen (and imitators like the Knights of the White Camelia, Pale Faces, White Brotherhood, Councils of Safety, etc.) directed at Reconstruction, Congress passed the Ku Klux Klan Act. The Klan contributed to restoring Democratic rule by undermining the morale of freedmen and white Republicans in the South. Acting as the Democratic Party's military arm, it exhausted northerners with the seemingly hopeless and endless task of suppressing white southerners by armed force until they gave up. The Klan withered away after Redemption.

William J. Simmons, an Atlanta self-promoter and entrepreneur, revived the Klan as of 16 October 1915, appointed himself imperial wizard, and went on to make a fortune selling its members uniforms and miscellaneous memorabilia – including CSA flags and symbols, which the original Klan had never used. Whereas the first Klan was primarily political, Simmons's group was nonpartisan. Although the first Klan had enlisted all whites, of whatever religion or birthplace, in defense of white supremacy, Simmons allowed in only native-born Protestants and preached a message that was not only racist, but also xenophobic, anti-Semitic and anti-Catholic. It grew rapidly after 1920 and became a national organization with more members in the North and West than the South. By 1925, perhaps 5,000,000 men (about every sixth adult male) were members, including a large minority of midwestern and western legislators.

Klan membership fell sharply in the late 1920s due to publicity about financial corruption and other scandals among Klan leaders. Having blundered into an ill-timed alliance with the pro-Nazi German Bund in 1940, the Klan again went into eclipse when the US entered World War II. The Klan reappeared during the late 1950s, but attracted few members and was largely confined to the South.

Ku Klux Klan Act (20 April 1871) This third Force Act outlawed secret paramilitary organizations like the Ku Klux Klan and empowered the president to suspend habeas corpus if necessary to suppress such groups.

Kusso War In 1671 S.C. ordered its militia to attack the Kusso tribe for conspiring with the Spanish; they were to enslave all captives. This glorified slaving raid cost few white lives, but took many prisoners and introduced large-scale use of Indian slaves to S.C.

Kwajalein, battle of *see* MARSHALL ISLANDS CAMPAIGN

L

La Follette, Robert Marion (b. Primrose, Wis., 14 June 1855; d. Washington, D.C., 18 June 1925) He opened a law office at Madison in 1880, and was a Republican congressman (1885–91). As governor (1901–5), he became the foremost exponent of reform during the PROGRESSIVE ERA by implementing his WISCONSIN IDEA. As senator (1906–25), he opposed the PAYNE–ALDRICH TARIFF, fought to give the INTERSTATE COMMERCE COMMISSION effective regulatory power over railroads, filibustered the ARMED SHIP BILL, voted against declaring war on Germany in 1917, and opposed the LEAGUE OF NATIONS. He lost the presidential nomination for the PROGRESSIVE PARTY to Theodore ROOSEVELT in 1912, but won Wis. and 16.6 percent of the popular vote as its candidate, in 1924.

La Follette Seamen's Act (4 March 1915) This law was enacted as part of the legislation for the NEW FREEDOM; it required the merchant marine to adopt stricter safety standards and better working conditions for sailors.

La Guardia, Fiorello Henry (b. New York, N.Y., 11 December 1882; d. New York, N.Y., 20 September 1947) He was a Republican congressman during the PROGRESSIVE ERA (1915–33, except while serving in WORLD WAR I), who opposed high tariffs, supported pro-labor legislation, and cosponsored the NORRIS–LA GUARDIA ACT. He beat TAMMANY HALL to become New York mayor (1933–45), and gave the city its most honest, efficient, and popular administration.

La Raza Unida *see* *RAZA UNIDA* party, *LA*

La Salle, Rene Robert Cavelier, Sieur de (b. Rouen, Normandy, France, November 1643; d. on the Brazos River, Tex., January 1687) He came to Canada in 1666 and received a royal patent in 1677 to explore the Mississippi valley. Starting at Lake Ontario in late 1679, he traversed the Great Lakes and Ill. to the Mississippi and became the first European to descend that river to its mouth. On 9 April 1682, he claimed the entire watershed for France and named the territory LOUISIANA. Between 1685 and 1687 he founded a French outpost in east Tex. but was murdered in a mutiny.

La Vérendrye expeditions Between 1731 and 1737, Canadian fur trader Pierre Gaultier de Varennes, Sieur de La Vérendrye, and his sons explored Lake Superior's northern shore, northern Minn., and Lake Winnipeg. During 1738–9, they traveled as far west as N.Dak. During 1742–3, his sons attempted to find a land route to the Pacific Ocean; they became the earliest Europeans to explore the western Dakotas, and may have entered Mont. and Wyo.

Labor, Department of On 14 February 1903 Congress created the Department of Commerce and Labor. On 4 March 1913, it was divided into separate departments for COMMERCE and Labor.

Labor Management Reporting and Disclosure Act (1959) *see* LANDRUM–GRIFFIN ACT

Lafayette, Marquis de (Marie Joseph Paul Yves Roch Gilbert du Motier) (b. Chavaniac, Auvergne, France, 6 September 1757; d. Paris, France, 20 May 1834) This nobleman entered the French army in 1771 offered his services to the Continental Army and was made a major general in July 1777 He was wounded at BRANDYWINE CREEK and rendered valuable liaison services with French forces, yet took no pay. He gave important aid to US diplomats in France during the 1780s. He spent five years in Prussian prisons during the Napoleonic wars and lost much of his fortune. He received the greatest personal acclaim ever accorded a foreign visitor during a triumphal US tour of August–September 1824, and is remembered as the most enduring symbol of Franco-American friendship.

Lafayette Escadrille Formed by seven US pilots on 17 April 1916 as a volunteer unit attached to the French air force in WORLD WAR I, this squadron attracted 267 US volunteers, of whom 224 qualified and 180 saw combat. Its members were often assigned to other French units as replacements. On 18 February 1918, the unit became the 103rd Pursuit Squadron of the US Army. The escadrille was credited with downing 199 German planes, at a cost of 51 killed in action, 11 noncombat deaths, 19 wounded, and 15 captured.

Laffer curve Economist Arthur Laffer proposed this relationship between marginal rates of INCOME TAX and revenues collected; he argued that cutting tax rates could increase government income. The correctness of Laffer's proposition depended on whether the tax code already acted to depress revenues by driving capital into unproductive tax shelters and stimulating the growth of an underground economy in which taxes went unreported. Laffer's curve was an article of faith for SUPPLY SIDE ECONOMICS.

Lake Champlain, battles of (1) *See* battle of VALCOUR ISLAND.

(2) On 11 September 1814, Captain Thomas MacDonough's force of 5 ships and 10 gunboats (45 long guns, 41 carronades, 850 seamen) defeated Captain George Downie's flotilla of 4 ships and 12 gunboats (60 long guns, 30 carronades, and 800 sailors). US losses: 52 dead, 58 wounded. British losses: 57 dead (including Downie), 72 wounded, 1 frigate, 1 brig, 2 sloops, 74 guns. McDonough's victory forced Lieutenant General George Prevost to end his invasion of N.Y., and abandon large stocks of military supplies.

Lake Erie, battle of On 10 September 1813, Captain Oliver H. PERRY's squadron of 9 ships (53 guns, 2 swivels, 530 seamen, 60 Ky. militia as marines) engaged Captain Robert Barclay's squadron of 6 ships (63 guns, 4 howitzers, 2 swivels, 440 sailors and marines). Perry's account of the battle reported: "We have met the enemy and they are ours – two ships, two brigs, one schooner, and a sloop." US losses: 21 killed, 63 wounded. British losses: 44 killed, 396 captured (including 103 wounded.) By establishing US naval supremacy on Lake Erie, Perry's victory forced British evacuation of FORT DETROIT (1813) and enabled US forces to pursue them into Canada, where the US won the decisive battle of the THAMES RIVER.

Lake George, battle of (N.Y.) On 8 September 1755, Colonel William JOHNSON's 3,500 colonials defeated Baron Dieskau's 1,600 French and Indians. Colonial losses: 189 killed or missing, 90 wounded (including Johnson), and 30 Mohawks killed. French losses: 147 killed (including Dieskau), 184 wounded. The battle left Johnson's army too disorganized to attack Fort St Frederic (CROWN POINT) as planned and it withdrew to Albany.

Lame Duck amendment *see* TWENTIETH AMENDMENT

Lancaster, treaty of (Pa.) On 4 July 1744, the IROQUOIS CONFEDERACY accepted £700 in gold to relinquish their claims in central Pa. and western Md. The treaty allowed the frontier to expand peacefully into the Juniata valley of Pa. and PIEDMONT west of Frederick, Md. It also strengthened the pro-British faction among the Confederacy, who helped dampen pro-French sympathies in KING GEORGE'S WAR.

Land Grant Act (1862) *see* MORRILL ACT

Land Ordinance of 1785 *see* ORDINANCE OF 1785

Landgraf* v. *USI Film Products *see* CIVIL RIGHTS ACT (1991)

Landon, Alfred Mossman (b. West Middlesex, Pa., 9 September 1887; d. Topeka, Kans., 12 October 1987) He opened a law practice at Independence, Kans., then entered the oil business, and was elected governor as a Republican in 1932. In 1934 he was the only Republican governor to defeat his Democratic opponent. He challenged Franklin D. ROOSEVELT for president in 1936, but won just 36.5 percent of the ballots and lost every state but Maine and Vt.

Landrum–Griffin Act (14 September 1959) Revelations of racketeering within the

Teamsters Union resulted in this Labor Management Reporting and Disclosure Act. It guaranteed union members fair elections free from coercion, set criminal penalties to punish gangsteristic actions by labor leaders, and required public reports to prevent embezzlement of union funds. It also strengthened the existing ban on the SECONDARY BOYCOTT.

Lanier, Sidney (b. Macon, Ga., 3 February 1842; d. Lynn, N.C., 7 September 1881) After graduating from Oglethorpe College, Lanier served in a Ga. unit in the Civil War, during which he began his only novel, *Tiger-Lilies* (1867). The Baltimore Symphony hired him as first flute in 1873, and the Johns Hopkins University gave him a teaching position in 1879. His poem "Corn," published in 1875, brought him critical acclaim. Lanier emerged as the late 19th century's foremost southern poet. His verse was most notable for attempting to imitate music in its melodies and rhythms. He died young of tuberculosis.

Lanier, Thomas *see* WILLIAMS, TENNESSEE

Laotian immigration *see* BOAT PEOPLE

Lassiter* v. *Northampton County Board of Elections On 8 June 1959, the Supreme Court unanimously upheld *WILLIAMS* v. *MISSISSIPPI* and affirmed a N.C. literacy test (*see* LITERACY TESTS) for voters. Such requirements did not violate the FOURTEENTH, FIFTEENTH, or SEVENTEENTH AMENDMENTS so long as they were enforced in a racially neutral manner.

Latrobe, Benjamin Henry (b. Fulneck, Yorkshire, England, 1 May 1764; d. New Orleans, La., 3 September 1820) Trained as an architect and civil engineer in England and Germany, Latrobe came to Va. in 1796. He influenced architectural design through his designs for prominent public buildings – such as the Va. Capitol's facade, the Bank of Pennsylvania, the Baltimore cathedral, the second BANK OF THE UNITED STATES, and Henry CLAY's mansion – which were widely imitated during the Greek Revival. While architect of the US Capitol (1803–17), he revised its design and began the process of rebuilding federal structures burnt by the British in 1814. He died while engineering a water supply system for New Orleans.

Latter-day Saints, Church of Jesus Christ of *see* MORMONS

Lavelle, Rita *see* ENVIRONMENTAL PROTECTION AGENCY

League of Nations The treaty of VERSAILLES created the league as an organization of world states to provide a forum for solving international problems peacefully. The US declined to join, because of Woodrow WILSON's refusal to accept Senate reservations limiting the treaty, especially ARTICLE X. The league began operating on 10 January 1920, held its last meeting on 14 December 1939, and was officially disbanded on 18 April 1946.

Lease, Mary Elizabeth Clyens (b. near Ridgway, Pa., 11 September 1853; d. Callicoon, N.Y., 29 October 1933) In 1870 Lease moved to Kans., where she taught and married. After she and her husband failed at farming, she became a self-educated lawyer. A superb orator, she joined the Populist movement (*see* POPULISM) and gave 160 speeches in its behalf during 1890. In 1891 a US senator blamed his defeat in the Kans. legislature on her. She is best remembered for telling audiences: "What you farmers need is to raise less corn and more hell!"

Lebanon, US intervention in On 9 May 1958, rioting erupted because Lebanon's pro-US president, Camille Chamoun, planned to run for office again (contrary to the constitution). Citing the danger of subversion from nearby Arab nations, on 15 July the US began landing marines under the EISENHOWER DOCTRINE. US troop numbers peaked at 6,000 marines and 8,500 soldiers. Under US pressure, Chamoun ended his candidacy. US troops stayed in Lebanon for 102 days. The intervention led to an anti-US backlash in Lebanon.

To help quell fighting among religious factions, Ronald REAGAN authorized 1,400 marines to join a multinational peacekeeping force in Beirut on 1 November 1982. On 18 April 1983, a bomb killed 16 Americans and 31 others at the US embassy. On 8 September, US involvement escalated into the use of naval gunnery and air strikes to protect the marines, who lost 6 dead from 29 August to 16 October. On 29 September, Congress approved the continued deployment of US troops in Lebanon. On 23 October, an Islamic terrorist drove a car carrying six tons of TNT into the US military's Beirut compound and killed 220 marines, 18 sailors, and 3 soldiers. On 4 December, hostile fire killed 8 marines and shot down 2 warplanes (leaving 1 airman dead and 1 captured). On 7 February 1984, the US ordered its troops evacuated to ships offshore, and on 30 March it formally withdrew from the peacekeeping force.

Lecompton constitution In 1857 the proslavery legislature for Kansas Territory (seated in 1855) arranged for elections to a convention that would draft a state constitution at Lecompton. Proslavery forces dominated the election and drew up a document authorizing slavery. Rather than permit a referendum on the document itself, the legislature only allowed a vote on whether slavery would be legally established, but qualified this choice by stipulating that any slaves already in the territory would be exempt from any future emancipation laws. Free-Soilers boycotted the election to protest this condition, and proslavery voters approved the document on 21 December 1857.

Because a Free-Soil majority had meanwhile been seated in the legislature, it called for a new election on terms acceptable to its own party. On 4 January 1858, antislavery voters turned out in force and defeated the Lecompton constitution. After Congress directed that the constitution be resubmitted to Kans. voters, it was again turned down overwhelmingly on 2 August 1858. An antislavery constitution drafted at Wyandotte was ratified on 4 October 1859, under which Kans. was admitted as a state.

Lee, Richard Henry (b. Westmoreland County, Va., 20 January 1732; d. Westmoreland County, Va., 19 June 1794) He was a consistent foe of Parliamentary taxation of the colonies after the stamp tax (*see* STAMP ACT). In 1774 he entered the CONTINENTAL CONGRESS, and on 7 June 1776 he was the first member to propose US independence. He was president of Congress (1784–5). He was chosen a delegate to the CONSTITUTIONAL CONVENTION, but did not attend. His opposition to consolidated government made him an Antifederalist (*see* ANTIFEDERALISTS) and he wrote 17 influential "Letters From the Federal Farmer" attacking the CONSTITUTION and demanding a BILL OF RIGHTS. He sat in the Senate (1789–92).

Lee, Robert Edward (b. Stratford, Va., 19 January 1807; d. Lexington, Va., 12 October 1870) Son of Revolutionary hero "Light Horse" Harry Lee, he graduated second at West Point in 1829 as an engineer officer. He was wounded and three times cited for gallantry in the MEXICAN WAR. He recaptured Harper's Ferry from John BROWN. Offered field command of USA forces in the CIVIL WAR, Lee became a CSA general instead. He took command of the Army of NORTHERN VIRGINIA on 1 June 1862, and repeatedly repulsed federal invasions of Va. until Ulysses S. GRANT's sledgehammer tactics forced his capitulation at APPOMATTOX COURT HOUSE. He was president of Washington College to his death, when his name was added to its title. On 22 July 1975, Congress restored his US citizenship.

Legal Tender acts The first Legal Tender Act (February 1862) authorized $150,000,000 in GREENBACKS, and required all creditors and vendors to accept them as payment for debts or goods sold. Under the second Legal Tender Act (1863), the US Treasury issued another $300,000,000.

legal tender cases In 1870 the Supreme Court ruled in *Hepburn* v. *Griswold* (4–3) on the LEGAL TENDER ACTS. The Court struck down the acts' provisions that forced creditors to accept paper money for debts contracted before their passage, as violations of Article I, Section 10 and the FIFTH AMENDMENT, by interfering with contracts and by diminishing the value of property without DUE PROCESS. In 1871, with two new justices on the bench, the Supreme Court heard two more cases about the Legal Tender acts (*Knox* v. *Lee* and *Parker* v. *Davis*); it overturned *Hepburn* (5–4) and declared that the government possessed the power to pass legal tender laws when confronted by emergencies in either war or peace time. In 1884, through *Juilliard* v. *Greenman*, the Court affirmed an 1878 law directing that GREENBACKS not be withdrawn from circulation, by ruling that Congress's power to make paper money a legal tender was not limited to wartime, but derived from its right to regulate the value of money under Article I, Section 8.

legislative veto This was a clause written into statutes that permitted the reversal of official actions taken by the president or executive agencies by majority vote of Congress or the Senate. About 200 laws included such provisions (including the WAR POWERS RESOLUTION, 1973) by 1983, when the legislative veto was ruled unconstitutional in *IMMIGRATION AND NATURALIZATION SERVICE* v. *CHADHA*.

Leisler's Rebellion After learning of England's REVOLUTION OF 1688 and an insurrection against the DOMINION OF NEW ENGLAND, towns in Westchester, Suffolk, and Queens counties replaced sheriffs and justices holding royal commissions with men of their own choosing in early May 1689. On 31 May 1689, Captain Jacob Leisler's militia took control of New York's fortifications to ensure the city's proper defense against a French attack. After Lieutenant Governor Francis Nicholson left for England on 11 June, administration of the colony fell to Leisler, who proclaimed WILLIAM III as king and organized defensive measures against the French.

Leisler not only made many powerful enemies in N.Y., but also refused to garrison royal troops in the colony's fortifications, for fear that their commander, Major Robert Ingoldesby, might be loyal to JAMES II. When Governor Henry Sloughter arrived on 29 March 1691, he arrested Leisler because his militia had skirmished with Ingoldesby's men on 27 March and left 2 killed and 7 wounded. Tried for treason with nine of his supporters in April, Leisler was hanged on 26 May, with his son-in-law Jacob Milborne. Parliament declared their convictions wrongful in 1695.

Lemke, William (b. Albany, Minn., 13 August 1878; d. Fargo, N.Dak., 30 May 1950) He grew up in N.Dak., opened a law office there in 1905, and became state Republican chairman in 1916. While sitting in Congress (1932–41), he championed farm interests and helped draft the FRAZIER–LEMKE FARM BANKRUPTCY ACT. He criticized the NEW DEAL as too concerned with fiscal responsibility and too unimaginative to restore prosperity. In 1936 he ran against Franklin D. ROOSEVELT as UNION PARTY nominee and received 1.9 percent of the vote. His political career ended in 1940 when he was defeated for the Senate.

Lemon* v. *Kurtzman On 28 June 1971, the Supreme Court ruled (8–10) that states might financially aid religious schools, but only if such aid satisfied three tests concerning the FIRST AMENDMENT's ban against state-established religions: such aid must advance a non-religious goal defined by law, it must neither promote nor injure a church, and it must not otherwise undermine the separation of church and state. *Lemon* became the definitive ruling for all subsequent cases testing state support for religious schools.

Lend Lease Act (11 March 1941) To circumvent the JOHNSON DEBT DEFAULT ACT's restrictions on federal financial loans to ex-Allies from WORLD WAR I, this law allowed the president to lend, lease, or otherwise transfer military equipment and other war-related goods to nations whose security was declared essential to US interests by the president. Congress voted for an initial exchange of $7 billion in war materiel. Lend lease began with the transfer of badly-needed escort ships to the British; when it was terminated on 21 August 1945, US aid to Britain and the USSR totaled $50.6 billion.

Let Us Now Praise Famous Men In 1936 author James Agee spent two months observing the lives of three Ala. sharecropper families for a national magazine, but when he presented his essays, with Walker Evans's photographs, his editor rejected their stark depiction of rural poverty as too disturbing for the magazine's middle-class readers. When Agee published his manuscript as the book *Let Us Now Praise Famous Men* in 1941, it was recognized as a classic social commentary whose uncompromising honesty validated Franklin D. ROOSEVELT's statement on 4 July 1938 "that the South presents right now the nation's No. 1 economic problem."

Letters from a Farmer in Pennsylvania John DICKINSON published these 14 essays in the Pennsylvania *Chronicle* between November 1767 and January 1768, after which almost every colonial paper reprinted them.

The *Letters* were the first major criticism of the TOWNSHEND REVENUE ACT and critical in mobilizing colonial opposition. Dickinson made the crucial distinction that EXTERNAL TAXATION was constitutional only if designed to regulate trade (such as by the MOLASSES ACT), but was illegitimate when intended to raise taxes, as the Townshend Act was.

Letters of Marque and Reprisal This term refers to a commission authorizing a ship captain to sail as a privateer against enemy commerce. The CONSTITUTION authorizes Congress to issue them under Article II, Section 8.

Levittowns In 1947 Abraham Levitt, with sons William and Alfred, began building a suburban community of prefabricated, one-plan, inexpensive homes (720 square feet) on eastern Long Island. In the early 1950s, two other Levittowns appeared near Philadelphia in Pa. and in N.J. The popularity and financial success of these ventures confirmed that a huge market existed for single-family housing and stimulated an enormous expansion of suburban building. Levittowns marked the beginning of the white middle-class exodus to suburbs that left minority groups as a majority in most large cities by 1980.

Lewis, John Llewellyn (b. Lucas, Iowa, 12 February 1880; d. Washington, D.C., 11 June 1969) He began working in coal mines at the age of 16. Long active in union politics, he was United Mine Workers president (1920–60). He successfully led major strikes by bituminous coal miners in 1919 and 1922. Elected AFL vice-president in 1934, he led his union out to found the CIO in 1935. Lewis campaigned hard for Franklin D. ROOSEVELT in 1936, but backed Wendell WILLKIE in 1940. He called the COAL STRIKE OF 1943 while the US was at war. By defying the government in the COAL STRIKE OF 1946, which threatened to cripple the postwar recovery, he brought on an economic crisis, triggered government seizure of the mines, and earned a contempt conviction. Arguably his century's most militant, single-minded, and successful labor leader, Lewis won substantial gains for miners by pitting their interests against the nation's general welfare.

Lewis, Meriwether (b. Albemarle County, Va., 18 August 1774; d. on Natchez Trace, Tenn., 11 October 1809) He was a captain in the First Infantry and private secretary to Thomas JEFFERSON, who named him to command the LEWIS AND CLARK EXPEDITION. In 1806 he was made governor of La. He probably committed suicide, but may have been murdered.

Lewis, (Harry) Sinclair (b. Sauk Center, Minn., 7 February 1885; d. Rome, Italy, 10 January 1951) He was a journalist turned author who wrote 23 novels and won the Nobel prize for literature in 1930. In *Main Street* (1920) and *Babbitt* (1922), he produced very popular books that expressed the scorn of his generation's intellectuals and academics for small-town life and the mainstream attitudes of middle-class businessmen. Lewis both reflected and shaped the tendency of Americans – especially those who were well-educated and urban – to accept rapid changes in values and behavior after 1920.

Lewis and Clark expedition On 18 January 1803, Thomas JEFFERSON asked Congress to appropriate $2,500 for exploring westward from LOUISIANA – then a French colony – to the Pacific. (The final cost was about $40,000.) Jefferson named Captain Meriwether LEWIS and Second Lieutenant William CLARK to command a "Corps of Discovery," which included 27 enlisted men, Lewis's slave, three interpreters, and six soldiers who would return after the first winter with scientific specimens.

On 14 May 1804, the party headed west for 1,600 miles from the Missouri's mouth in a 55-foot keelboat and two dugouts. After wintering near Bismarck, N.Dak., until 7 April 1805, the corps traveled by boat until 17 August, crossed the Rockies with horses, and reached the Pacific by the Columbia River on 18 November. The expedition started back on 23 March 1806 and reached St Louis on 23 September. The party covered 8,000 miles, experienced one death, and had one fight with Indians, who lost 2 killed. Lewis and Clark were the first whites to cross North America within the US; they greatly increased knowledge of the west, and gave the US a claim to the OREGON country.

Lexington, battle of (Mass.) At sunrise on 19 April 1774, en route to destroy American military supplies at Concord, Major John Pitcairn's six companies of redcoats ordered Captain John Parker's 70 MINUTEMEN to disperse from Lexington green. Hearing a gunshot of unknown origin, the British fired as Parker's men were walking away and charged with bayonets. Mass. losses: 8 killed, 10 wounded. British losses: 1 wounded. Lexington was the Revolution's first armed encounter.

Leyte Gulf, battle of On 23–5 October 1944, Vice Admiral Thomas Halsey's Third Fleet (6 battleships, 8 heavy carriers, 8 light carriers, 3 heavy cruisers, 9 light cruisers, 58 destroyers, 1,000 planes) and Rear Admiral Thomas Kinkaid's Seventh Fleet (6 battleships, 14 cruisers, 16 destroyers) defeated Japanese attack forces under Vice Admiral Takeo Kurita (2 battleships, 12 cruisers, 15 destroyers), Admiral Jisaburo Ozawa (4 carriers, 2 battleships, 4 cruisers, 8 destroyers), Vice Admiral Kiyohide Shima (2 heavy cruisers, 1 light cruiser, 4 destroyers), and Vice Admiral Shoji Nishimura (2 battleships, 1 heavy cruiser, 4 destroyers). Japanese losses: 4 carriers, 3 battleships, 6 heavy cruisers, 4 light cruisers, 11 destroyers, 1 submarine, 500 planes, 10,000 sailors. US losses: 1 heavy carrier, 2 light carriers, 3 destroyers. Leyte Gulf was the war's largest sea battle; it completed the virtual extinction of Japanese carrier aircraft begun at the battle of the PHILIPPINE SEA and left the enemy's navy too crippled to interfere with the US PHILIPPINE CAMPAIGNS.

Liberal Republican party By 1871, many Republicans were alienated from Ulysses S. GRANT's administration because of its scandals, opposition to CIVIL SERVICE REFORM, and reliance on military force for southern RECONSTRUCTION. As Liberal Republicans, they held a convention in 1872 at Cincinnati, adopted a platform of government reform and amnesty for ex-Confederates, and nominated Horace GREELEY (N.Y.) for president and B. Gratz Brown (Mo.) for vice-president. The Democrats' national convention also nominated Greeley and Brown, but the fusion ticket experienced utter defeat. The Liberal Republicans disappeared as an independent party and many became Democrats. In 1874 Liberal Republican votes helped Democrats carry the House of Representatives.

***Liberator*, the** On 1 January 1831, at Boston, William Lloyd GARRISON published the first issue of this weekly newspaper espousing ABOLITIONISM, and promised, "I am in earnest – I will not equivocate – I will not excuse – I will not retreat a single inch; and I will be heard!" The *Liberator* expressed the views of the radical wing of abolitionism, which advocated the disregarding of the rights of slaveowners under the US Constitution by giving immediate, uncompensated freedom to all slaves. Its paid subscribers never exceeded 3,000. It ceased publication on 29 December 1865, on the ratification of the THIRTEENTH AMENDMENT.

Liberty Party This party emerged on 13 November 1839 at a national convention at Warsaw, N.Y., as a moderate wing of ABOLITIONISM seeking a constitutional end to slavery. Its first candidate for president, James BIRNEY (Ohio), polled just 0.3 percent of votes in 1840, but by taking 2.3 percent of the ballots in 1844 he cost the WHIG PARTY that election by tipping N.Y. to the Democrats. It ran no ticket for president in 1848, when its members voted for FREE-SOIL PARTY candidates.

***Liberty* riot** On 9 May 1768, smuggled Madeira wine had been offloaded from John HANCOCK's ship *Liberty* at Boston. On 10 June, officials appointed under the AMERICAN BOARD OF CUSTOMS ACT ordered a British warship to seize the *Liberty* for smuggling. A large crowd soon gathered, attacked the customs officers, and beat several of them. The customs commissioners fled to a fortress in the harbor the next day and requested British troops to protect them. The riot led the British ministry to order Boston to be garrisoned with 2,000 redcoats, which landed on 2 October.

Libya, US intervention in On 5 April 1986, terrorists bombed a nightclub in Berlin popular with US soldiers, of whom one died and 60 were injured. After Ronald REAGAN said he possessed firm evidence that Libyan leader Muammar al-Qaddafi had ordered the attack, he ordered 32 US warplanes to bomb targets in Tripoli and Benghazi on 15 April. Libyan casualties were light, but the dead included Qaddafi's adopted daughter. A US Air Force jet was downed and its two crewmen killed. On 17 April, the bodies of an American and two Britons (who had been kidnapped earlier) were found in Beirut with a note saying they died as revenge for the Libya raid.

Lilienthal, David *see* ATOMIC ENERGY ACT (1946)

Limited Test Ban Treaty *see* NUCLEAR TEST BAN TREATY (1963)

Lincoln, Abraham (b. near Hodgenville, Ky., 12 February 1809; d. Washington, D.C., 15 April 1865) Raised in Ky. and Ind., he moved in 1830 to Ill., where he performed his first public service as a captain of volunteers in the BLACK HAWK WAR. Essentially self-educated, he opened a law office at Springfield in 1837. He sat in the legislature (1834–42), and then left politics after a term as a congressman for the WHIG PARTY (1846–8). The KANSAS–NEBRASKA ACT stirred him to reenter public life and he joined the REPUBLICAN PARTY in 1856. He lost a campaign for the Senate in 1858, but won national prominence by the LINCOLN–DOUGLAS DEBATES. As Republican presidential nominee in 1860, he took 39.8 percent of the popular vote and 180 electoral votes by carrying every free state to defeat John BRECKINRIDGE, Stephen DOUGLAS, and John BELL.

Lincoln dealt with the SECESSION crisis by waiting for the Confederacy to commit the first hostile act at FORT SUMTER. He built a fragile war coalition of Republicans, Democrats, abolitionists, and proslavery nationalists from the BORDER STATES, and then kept it together by extraordinary political sagacity. He pushed the Union military into waging offensive operations along an extended front to sap CSA resources and find weak spots to exploit. Although he defined the CIVIL WAR as a struggle to save the Union, he issued the EMANCIPATION PROCLAMATION. His direct and simple manner of speaking shone eloquently in the GETTYSBURG ADDRESS. Lincoln deserves primary credit for US victory, because he not only kept the North from succumbing to internal divisions and war weariness, but also defined overall strategy and identified the generals best qualified to crush the enemy. He won reelection in 1864 with 55 percent of the popular vote and took every state but three against George MCCLELLAN. Before he could implement his lenient RECONSTRUCTION policy, he was killed by John Wilkes BOOTH.

Lincoln–Douglas debates On 24 July 1858, Abraham LINCOLN challenged Stephen DOUGLAS to debate during their race for senator from Ill. They clashed at Ottawa (21 August), Freeport (27 August), Jonesboro (15 September), Charleston (18 September), Galesburg (7 October), Quincy (13 October), and Alton (15 October). The debates took place after *DRED SCOTT* v. *SANDFORD* and emphasized the issue of allowing slaves in unsettled territories. At Quincy, Lincoln strongly opposed slavery as "a moral, a social, and a political wrong," although he rejected interfering with it where it existed by law. Douglas countered with his FREEPORT DOCTRINE on excluding slavery from the territories. Lincoln lost the senate race in the legislature (54–41), but the debates catapulted him to national prominence and made him a major presidential contender in 1860.

Lindbergh, Charles Augustus, Jr (b. Detroit, Mich., 4 February 1902; d. Kipahulu, Hawaii, 26 August 1974) The son of a congressman, Lindbergh became an international hero – the "Lone Eagle" – by making the first nonstop, transatlantic flight from New York to Paris (3,610 miles) in 33.5 hours (20–1 May 1927) in the *Spirit of St Louis*. The flight stimulated rapid development of the US airline industry by generating mass enthusisam for aviation. Within a year, applications for pilot's licenses multiplied from 1,800 to 5,500, and the number of licensed planes increased from 1,100 to 4,700. Lindbergh later became a prominent isolationist who opposed US aid for Great Britain, but only until WORLD WAR II began.

linotype, invention of *see* MERGENTHALER OTTMAR

Lippmann, Walter (b. New York, N.Y., 23 September 1889; d. New York, N.Y., 14 December 1974) With Arthur KROCK, Lippmann shares the credit for developing the syndicated editorial column into a major feature of US journalism. Through his columns, Lippmann was the most influential writer to introduce the American public to KEYNESIAN ECONOMICS during the NEW DEAL. He was one of the most influential molders of public opinion from 1931 to the 1960s.

literacy tests After Reconstruction, southern states often required that voters be literate, in order to keep freedmen from the polls, since few of them had learned to read during slavery. Illiterate whites remained enfranchised either by fraud or various grandfather clauses. The Supreme Court affirmed literacy tests in *Williams* v. *Mississippi* and *Lassiter* v. *Northampton County Board of Elections*. The Voting Rights Act (1965) suspended them until 1970, when they were ruled unconstitutional in *Oregon* v. *Mitchell*.

Little Big Horn, battle of (Mont.) On 25 June 1876, during the third Sioux War, Sitting Bull and Crazy Horse's 2,500 Sioux and Cheyenne warriors annihilated four troops of the Seventh Cavalry under Colonel George Custer. US losses: 212 killed. Sioux losses: perhaps 300 dead.

Little New Deal This term was applied to state programs that supplemented the federal New Deal through relief agencies, business regulation, pro-labor legislation, unemployment benefits, and progressive taxation. Calif., Mich., N.Y., Pa., and Wis. enacted the most ambitious Little New Deal legislation.

Little NIRA When the National Industrial Recovery Act (NIRA) was declared unconstitutional in 1935, the Second New Deal enacted several laws that revived NIRA features or imposed industry-wide regulations resembling National Recovery Administration codes. These measures included the Connally Act, Guffey–Snyder Bituminous Coal Stabilization Act, Robinson–Patman Act, Walsh–Healey Government Contracts Act, and Miller–Tydings Act.

Little Rock desegregation violence (Ark.) The first major defiance by state governments of federal court orders ending school segregation occurred in September 1957. Governor Orval Faubus mobilized the National Guard, ostensibly to prevent violence, but really to block a federal court order integrating Little Rock Central High School. When an injunction barred Faubus from blocking admission of nine black students and he withdrew the guardsmen, rioting by whites erupted on 23 September. On 24 September, Dwight D. Eisenhower federalized the Guard and dispatched 1,000 US Army troops to enforce the desegregation injunction and keep order. Black students first entered the high school on 25 September and the crisis subsided.

Little Turtle *see* Miami Indians, Harmar's Defeat, *and* St Clair's Defeat

Lochner* v. *New York On 17 April 1905, the Supreme Court reversed *Holden* v. *Hardy* and struck down (5–4) a N.Y. law regulating the length of bakers' workdays. Because N.Y. failed to prove that the law protected health, it was held to be an impermissible extension of the state's police powers and improper interference with the right of parties to negotiate contracts. *Lochner* was reversed by *Muller* v. *Oregon*.

Loco-focos In 1834 this group emerged as a faction within the N.Y. Democratic Party to oppose legislative acts vesting special rights (especially monopolies granted by charters of incorporation) upon individuals or businesses. They also favored free trade, hard money, limited government, and democratic political reforms. Their name derived from a nominations meeting at Tammany Hall at which the reformers were left in the dark after the regular Democrats adjourned the meeting and extinguished the gaslights. They carried on by lighting candles with sulphurous matches called "loco-focos." Loco-focos were the most egalitarian of Jacksonian Democrats.

Lodge, Henry Cabot (b. Boston, Mass., 12 May 1850; d. Boston, Mass., 9 November 1924) He was a Republican congressman from Mass. (1887–92), and senator (1893–1924). He emerged as the Senate's foremost authority on foreign affairs and chaired its Foreign Relations Committee (1919–24). He authored the Lodge corollary. Lodge won Senate approval for 14 Reservations setting conditions on US ratification of the treaty of Versailles and membership in the League of Nations. These Reservations (especially on Article X) were anathema to Woodrow Wilson and became the major issue resulting in Senate defeat of the treaty.

Lodge, Henry Cabot, Jr (b. Nahant, Mass., July 1902; d. Beverly, Mass., 27 February

1985) After serving as Republican senator from Mass. (1937–44, 1947–53), Lodge was ambassador to the UN (1953–60), Richard NIXON's running mate in 1960, and ambassador to South Vietnam (1963–7) and West Germany (1968–9). He led the US team at the peace negotiations for the VIETNAM WAR from 1969 to August 1970.

Lodge corollary After a State Department protest led to cancelation of the sale of a strategic site on Mexico's western coast to a Japanese firm, Senator Henry Cabot LODGE authored a resolution expressing US disapproval for the sale of any militarily important position by a Latin-American government to another government or corporation from outside the western hemisphere. The resolution passed on 2 August 1912; it extended the MONROE DOCTRINE to Asian countries and all non-hemispheric businesses.

Lodge Force Bill *see* FORCE BILL (1890)

Loewe* v. *Lawler ("Danbury – Hatters case") On 3 February 1908, the Supreme Court unanimously ruled that unions were guilty of conspiring to restrain trade if they instituted SECONDARY BOYCOTTS. The ruling marked the first use of the SHERMAN ANTITRUST ACT against organized labor. Congress enacted provisions in the CLAYTON ANTITRUST ACT permitting this practice.

log cabin campaign The election of 1840 was so called because the WHIG PARTY used the log cabin as its campaign symbol and falsely claimed that aristocratic William Henry HARRISON was born in one.

Logan's Cross Roads, battle of (Ky.) *see* MILL SPRINGS, BATTLE OF

London, Jack (b. San Francisco, Calif., 12 January 1876; d. Glen Ellen, Calif., 22 November 1916) Born John Griffith London, he grew up in squalor around Oakland, ran away to sea at the age of 17, joined the Klondike gold rush, and was a hobo. He became a leading figure in the development of American writing that portrayed the struggle of life in realistic and honest terms; he was the most popular author of the decade 1900–10. His major works include *The Call of the Wild* (1903), *The People of the Abyss* (1903), *The Sea Wolf* (1904), *White Fang* (1906), *The Iron Heel* (1908), and the autobiographical *Martin Eden* (1909).

London naval conference After the WASHINGTON NAVAL CONFERENCE, a second disarmament conference met at Geneva from 20 June to 4 August 1927, but failed to agree on further reductions in naval forces. The US strongly backed a British initiative to conduct another round of arms reduction talks at London among the five largest naval powers. Between 21 January and 22 April 1930, France and Italy walked out, but the US, Britain, and Japan negotiated their own treaty. They modified the Washington conference's formula for dividing naval tonnage among themselves from 5 (US): 5 (Britain): 3 (Japan) to 10:10:7, so that Japan could add more destroyers, light cruisers, and submarines. They also extended the moratorium on warship construction through the treaty's expiration of 31 December 1936. The treaty called for scrapping 5 British, 3 US, and 1 Japanese capital ships (those displacing over 10,000 tons). The Senate confirmed the treaty on 21 July. Further attempts at arms reduction were made at Geneva in 1932 and 1933, but made no progress. Japan formally denounced naval disarmament on 29 December 1934 and in January 1936 announced its intention to build a fleet equal to those of Britain and the US. In 1938 Congress funded a major expansion of the US Navy.

Lone Wolf* v. *Hitchcock In 1903, the Supreme Court rejected claims by Okla. Indians that Congress had purchased Indian lands in violation of the Treaty of MEDICINE LODGE by not securing approval of land sales from 75 percent of all adult Indian males occupying the land, and so violated the FIFTH AMENDMENT. Citing *UNITED STATES* V. *KAGAMA*, the court ruled that federal courts lacked jurisdiction in such matters because Indian nations were wards of the United States. Congress had plenary (absolute) power concerning treaty relations with Indians, and its trusteeship over their RESERVATIONS was not subject to litigation.

Lone-Star State *see* TEXAS

Long, Huey Pierce (b. Winn Parish La., 30 August 1893; d. Baton Rouge, La., 10 September 1935) He entered the Senate in 1930. He criticized the NEW DEAL and proposed to end the GREAT DEPRESSION with his Share-Our-Wealth movement. Long would have taxed all income over $1,000,000

and confiscated all private fortunes over $5,000,000, which would be redistributed to guarantee every family at least $2,000 annually. Share-Our-Wealth clubs had 4,600,000 members by 1935. In November 1935, he declared he would run for president on a third party. Long's candidacy made a Republican victory likely by splitting the Democratic vote, until he was assassinated by Carl Weiss, a deranged physician. His followers rallied to Gerald K. Smith, a founder of the Union party in 1936, but rapidly dissolved as an organized movement.

long hunters From 1763 to 1775, Anglo-Americans who entered the Appalachians to trap, trade, or explore, and lived off the land for long periods were so called. Daniel Boone was the most famous. They played an important role in opening Ky. and Tenn. for settlement.

Long Island, battle of (N.Y.) On 27 August 1776, General William Howe's 22,000 British and Hessians routed Washington's 11,000 Continentals and militia. US losses: 200 killed, 1,097 captured (including two generals). British losses: 63 killed, 314 wounded. The Revolution's first pitched battle left Washington badly outnumbered and encircled at Brooklyn Heights. Washington prevented the annihilation of his 9,500 survivors by executing a night withdrawal across East River to Manhattan on 29–30 August.

long rifle *see* Kentucky rifle

Longfellow, Henry Wadsworth (b. Portland, Maine, 27 February 1807; d. Cambridge, Mass., 24 March 1882) A Bowdoin College graduate who traveled in Europe from 1826 to 1829, Longfellow was professor of modern languages and belles-lettres at Harvard (1836–54). He published his first book of poems, *Voices of the Night*, in 1839. Praised through most of his career as the most talented and popular US poet, he received honorary degrees from Oxford and Cambridge. Other major works include *Ballads and Other Poems* (1841), *Poems on Slavery* (1842), *Evangeline* (1847), *Hiawatha* (1855), *The Courtship of Miles Standish* (1858), *Tales of a Wayside Inn* (3 vols, 1863–74), *The Masque of Pandora* (1875), *Ultima Thule* (1880), and *In the Harbor* (1882).

Longhouse religion After a series of visions, Handsome Lake founded this religion among the Iroquois. Its beliefs were criti cal in enabling his followers to reverse pattern of cultural disintegration that followe defeat in the Revolutionary War. It teachings emphasized temperance, socia unity, peaceful relations with whites, the ac ceptance of white customs that helped Indi ans survive within a market economy, an an emphasis on upholding mutual obligation within nuclear families (rather than extende clans). The faith's rapid spread was the majo factor enabling the Seneca to regain a posi tive image of themselves, restrain the growt of social pathologies like alcoholism an intra-tribal violence, and revitalize their cul ture. It survives as Gaiwiio, or The Old Wa of Handsome Lake.

Looking Backward *see* Bellamy, Edwar

Lookout Mountain, battle of (Tenn.) *se* Chattanooga, battles for

loose constructionism This doctrine, princi pally based on the elastic clause, inter preted the Constitution as authorizin congressional laws for any activity or pur pose not explicitly forbidden to the federa government. Under this theory, Congres possessed a wide range of implied power under its broad authority to tax, coin money and regulate interstate commerce. *Mc Culloch* v. *Maryland* was the classi exposition of this argument. Loos constructionism was a key ideological ele ment of the Federalist and Whig par ties. (*See* strict constructionism)

Lord Baltimore *see* proprietors o Maryland

Lord Dunmore's War *see* Dunmore's Wa

lost generation Gertrude Stein coined thi expression to define the post-World Wa I intellectual milieu that was profoundl alienated from nationalistic idealism, enrap tured by thrills of personal experience, an cynical of the values held by the middle clas and business community. During the 1920s its most notable writers were F. Scot Fitzgerald, Ernest Hemingway, Sinclai Lewis, H. L. Mencken, John Do Passos, Archibald MacLeish, and Ezr Pound.

Louisbourg, sieges of (1) On 29 April 1745 General William Pepperrell's 3,600 Yan kee militia landed on Cape Breton t besiege Louisbourg, which Governor Loui

Du Chambon surrendered on 17 June. New England losses: 167 killed (30 dead of disease). French losses: 53 killed, 80 wounded, 600 regulars and 1,300 militia captured, 185 cannon, 18 mortars.

(2) On 7 June 1758, a British fleet of 41 ships (1,900 guns and 15,000 sailors) began landing Major General Jeffery AMHERST's 13,000 soldiers near Louisbourg, which Governor Captain Augustin de Drucour surrendered on 27 July 1758. British losses: 172 killed, 354 wounded. French losses: 1,790 killed and wounded (including those hospitalized as sick), 3,847 soldiers (including 2,990 regulars) and 1,790 sailors captured, 8 warships sunk and 3 captured, 221 cannon, 18 mortars, 7,500 muskets, 80,000 cartridges. Louisbourg's loss enabled Britain to besiege QUEBEC in 1759.

Louisiana In 1682 La. was named and claimed for France by the Sieur de LA SALLE. French colonists began arriving after 1700; they founded New Orleans in 1718 and Baton Rouge in 1719, and were joined by ACADIANS after 1760. Spain acquired La. by the treaty of PARIS (1763), but sent few colonists. French culture dominated southern La., where 40 percent of the 11,000 people were slaves in 1769. The treaty of SAN ILDEFONSO returned La. to France, which sold it to the US by the LOUISIANA PURCHASE. It entered the Union on 30 April 1812.

Anglo-Americans settled northern La. and large numbers of Europeans came to New Orleans. Cotton cultivation predominated in northern La. and sugar planting in the south of the state. In 1860 it had 708,002 people, of whom 47 percent were slaves and 11 percent were foreign-born; it ranked 17th among the states in population, 11th in the value of its agricultural goods, and 22nd in manufactures.

La. became the sixth CSA state on 26 January 1861. In the CIVIL WAR, it furnished 55,820 CSA troops and 29,276 USA soldiers (5,224 white and 24,052 black). La. was the site of 566 military engagements. USA forces occupied it after NEW ORLEANS was taken (1862).

By February 1864, a tenth of voters had sworn Union allegiance and elected a pro-US constitutional convention, which ended slavery. After white supremacists took over the legislature and passed a strict black code (*see* BLACK CODES), Washington imposed military rule on 2 March 1867, but restored self-government and congressional representation on 25 June 1868. Republican control ended eight-and-a-half years later on 2 January 1877. La. disfranchised most blacks in 1898 and enacted racial SEGREGATION after 1900.

In 1900 it had 1,381,625 people, of whom 74 percent were rural, 47 percent were black, and 4 percent were foreign-born; it ranked 23rd among the states in population, 23rd in the value of its agricultural goods, and 22nd in manufactures. From 1920 to 1970, it lost 343,500 out-migrants, mostly blacks moving to northern cities, and its racial composition shifted greatly. During the CIVIL RIGHTS MOVEMENT, its officials engaged in lengthy struggles with federal courts to frustrate school desegregation by token integration and other delaying tactics. The US Department of Justice spent 20 years of litigation (1974–94) before it certified that La. had fully complied with court orders to desegregate its college system. La. ranked as the 20th state by 1990, when its population was 4,219,973 (66 percent white, 31 percent black, 2 percent Hispanic, 1 percent Asian), of whom 69 percent were urban and 2.1 percent were foreign-born. Mining and manufacturing employed 23 percent of the work force.

Louisiana Purchase After learning that France had acquired La. by the treaty of SAN ILDEFONSO and that Americans had been denied the RIGHT OF DEPOSIT on 16 October 1802, Thomas JEFFERSON appointed James MONROE to negotiate the colony's purchase. Weary of colonialism because of the bloody Haitian revolution (1794–1804), France agreed on 30 April to sell the Louisiana Territory (827,990 square miles) for $11,250,000, plus US assumption of $3,750,000 in claims filed against France by American merchants for ship seizures. Senate ratification came on 20 October. Critics charged that territorial acquisition was not authorized by the Constitution, but in 1828 the Supreme Court upheld the government's power to do so in *American Insurance Company* v. *Canter.* The US took formal possession on 20 December 1804.

Louisville Joint Stock Land Bank* v. *Radford *see* FRAZIER – LEMKE FARM BANKRUPTCY ACT

Louisville Railroad Company* v. *Letson In 1844 the Supreme Court overturned, without dissent, *BANK OF THE UNITED STATES* v. *DEVEAUX* in regard to the "diversity" rule for determining which cases fell within federal rather than state jurisdiction. The Court ruled that corporations would be considered citizens of whatever state chartered them, and federal courts might accept any case in which the opposing party resided in another state. The decision extended the federal bench's influence over issues about business practices.

Lovejoy, Elijah Parish (b. Albion, Maine, 9 November 1802; d. Alton, Ill., 7 November 1837) In 1827 Lovejoy moved from Maine to St Louis, where in 1833 he began editing a paper espousing ABOLITIONISM, NATIVISM, and PROHIBITION. After moving to Alton, Ill., in 1836, he was elected to the legislature, organized a chapter of the AMERICAN ANTISLAVERY SOCIETY, and founded the Alton *Observer*, a paper favoring gradual, legal abolition. While trying to defend his press from a mob burning his office, he was shot dead.

Lovell* v. *Griffin On 28 March 1938, in a case involving Jehovah's Witnesses, the Supreme Court struck down (8–0) a city regulation forbidding distribution of any printed material on public streets without approval by a municipal official; it held that the FOURTEENTH AMENDMENT precluded states or localities from subjecting FIRST AMENDMENT rights to decisions made arbitrarily. The Court later held that although localities must permit free dissemination of printed matter, they could regulate its distribution.

Loving* v. *Virginia On 12 June 1967, the Supreme Court ruled unanimously that state laws forbidding interracial marriages violated the FOURTEENTH AMENDMENT's provisions for equal protection and DUE PROCESS. *Loving* marked the first instance when the Court unequivocally characterized legal classifications according to race as "inherently suspect" and required states to give a compelling reason for their use. After *Loving* ended state restrictions on interracial marriages, the number of mixed (white and black) couples doubled from 321,000 in 1970 to 719,000 in 1982, and then rose moderately to about 1,100,000 by 1990.

Lowell, James Russell (b. Cambridge, Mass., 22 February 1819; d. Cambridge, Mass., 12 August 1891) A Harvard graduate who joined that college's literature faculty in 1854, wrote abolitionist propaganda, and served as ambassador to both Spain and Britain from 1877 to 1885, Lowell emerged as a leading poet of the Romantic era. He did his best work in 1840–55, and then increasingly turned to literary and critical essays. His major works include *A Year's Life* (1841), *Poems* (1844), *Poems by James Russell Lowell, 2nd Series* (1848), *A Fable for Critics* (1848), *The Vision of Sir Launfal* (1848), *The Biglow Papers* (1848), *Fireside Travels* (1864), *Under the Willows* (1868), *The Cathedral* (1870), *Among My Books* (1870), *My Study Window* (1871), *Heartsease and Rue* (1888), and *Latest Literary Essays and Addresses* (1891).

Lower South This area includes the southeastern colonies or states where rice, cotton, and sugar were the primary staple crops: S.C., Ga., Ala., Miss., and La. Also included are those areas of N.C. and Tenn. within the cotton belt.

Loyalists *see* TORIES

Ludlow massacre (Colo.) In September 1913, 9,000 United Mine Workers struck at John ROCKEFELLER's Colorado Fuel and Iron Company and occupied tent cities outside the coal mines. State militia were brought in to protect the company property and keep order. On 20 April 1914, troops attacked a strikers' camp at Ludlow, fired into crowds, and burned the tents; they killed five strikers and caused the deaths of 13 women and children by smoke inhalation, at a cost of just one trooper. By the time the US Army stopped the bloodshed ten days later, 40 more persons were dead. The strikers went back to work when offered better working conditions, but did not win union recognition.

Ludlow Resolution In January 1938, Congress considered a constitutional amendment from Representative Louis Ludlow (Republican, Ind.) to require a national referendum before any declaration of war could become effective, except when an enemy invaded US territory. Public opinion strongly supported the idea, but Franklin D. ROOSEVELT opposed it as an encouragement to foreign aggression against the US. On 10 January, the House killed the measure by voting to return it to committee over the opposition of Republicans and western Democrats.

Lundy's Lane, battle of (Ontario) On 25 July 1814, by Niagara Falls, Major General Jacob Brown's 2,600 US troops fought a draw with Lieutenant General George Drummond's 2,900 British, although Brown left the battlefield that night after fighting ended. US losses: 171 killed, 572 wounded (including Brown), 112 missing. British losses: 84 killed, 559 wounded, 42 captured. Brown's heavy losses, combined with those earlier at CHIPPEWA RIVER forced him to withdraw to FORT ERIE.

***Lusitania*, HMS** On 7 May 1915, a German submarine torpedoed the unarmed ship *Lusitania* (1,198 passengers were drowned, including 128 US citizens). Strong US denunciations of this event – and of injuries to Americans aboard the *Arabic* (19 August 1915) – led Germany to issue the *Arabic* pledge (5 October 1915), which exempted passenger ships from surprise attacks. When US citizens were injured in a torpedo attack on the *Sussex* (24 March 1916), the US insisted that Germany halt unrestricted submarine warfare. Germany complied from 4 May 1916 to 1 February 1917. These events turned official policy and public opinion against Germany and helped draw the US into WORLD WAR I.

Luther* v. *Borden In 1849 the Supreme Court (5–1) declined to hear a case arising out of the DORR REBELLION, in which two rival governments challenged one another for control of R.I. The Court ruled that it lacked jurisdiction over issues that were fundamentally political; it then affirmed that Congress was the proper forum to settle this question, because the Constitution (Article IV, Section 4) vests it with the responsibility of guaranteeing each state a republican government. This decision's reasoning served as a precedent for *TEXAS* v. *WHITE*, which justified congressional statutes during RECONSTRUCTION.

Lutheran church The first Swedish Lutheran church was founded at Wilmington, Del., in 1638, and the first German Lutheran congregation was formed at New York in 1648. There were 4 Lutheran pulpits in 1660, 7 in 1700, 95 in 1740, and 228 in 1776, when their membership totaled 75,000 (3.75 percent of all whites). Largely due to German and Scandinavian immigration, the number of Lutherans rose from 100,000 in 1800 to about 1,500,000 in 1900, when 24 separate Lutheran organizations existed. The number of congregations grew from 800 in 1820 to 2,128 in 1860, and 10,787 in 1900. From 1900 to 1960, the number of Lutherans multiplied fivefold, to over 8,000,000. Most Lutherans consolidated into three main bodies: the Evangelical Lutheran Church in America (formed in 1987 by the American Lutheran Church, the Lutheran Church in America, and the Association of Evangelical Lutheran Churches), the Lutheran Church-Missouri Synod, and the Wisconsin Evangelical Lutheran Synod. Membership has stagnated since 1960. In 1990 there were 18,988 Lutheran congregations with 8,374,900 members (5.7 percent of all churchgoers), of whom 63 percent belonged to the Evangelical Lutheran Church in America, 31 percent to the Missouri Synod, 5 percent to the Wisconsin Evangelical Lutheran Synod, and 1 percent to 10 minor denominations.

lyceum movement Lyceums were community organizations that provided facilities for public lectures and other forms of adult education; many accumulated libraries and scientific apparatus. Josiah Holbrook founded the first lyceum at Millbury, Mass., in 1826. Within 15 years, lyceums existed in about 3,500 towns. They created a lecture circuit for speakers like Charles Dickens, Ralph EMERSON, Daniel WEBSTER, and William GARRISON.

lynching This term refers to the extra-legal public murder of persons by crowds that make no (or little) effort to hide their identities. Between 1882 and 1968, there were 4,743 lynchings, of which 60.4 percent took place before 1901 and 30.7 percent during 1901–20. Overall, 72.7 percent of the victims were black and 27.3 percent white. Only during 1882–90 were a majority of victims white (52.3 percent), and after 1900, they comprised just 9.9 percent of those killed by mobs. In 1921 pressure by the NATIONAL ASSOCIATION FOR THE ADVANCEMENT OF COLORED PEOPLE led Congress to debate a federal anti-lynching law, which passed the House but not the Senate. Unsuccessful attempts to enact this measure continued through the 1950s. Public lynching (as opposed to private conspiracies to commit murder) died out after 1920, with 389 occurrences during 1921–40 and 44 from then to 1968.

Lyon, Mary (b. Buckland, Mass., 28 February 1797; d. South Hadley, Mass., 5 March 1849) After attending seminaries in Mass., she taught (1821–34) in New England. After three years of fundraising and planning curriculum, she founded Mount Holyoke Female Seminary in 1837 at South Hadley, Mass., and was its principal until she died. This institution was the earliest permanent school established solely for advanced female education, and evolved into Mount Holyoke College.

Lyon, Matthew *see* SEDITION ACT (1798)

M

McAdoo, William Gibbs (b. near Marietta, Ga., 31 October 1863; d. Washington, D.C., 1 February 1941) He matured in Tenn., moved to New York, built the first tunnel under the Hudson River in 1904, and became active in Democratic politics. McAdoo became Woodrow WILSON's treasury secretary in 1913 and his son-in-law in 1914; he also chaired the Federal Reserve Board (*see* FEDERAL RESERVE SYSTEM), War Finance Corporation, and coordinated railroad traffic during WORLD WAR I. He withdrew from consideration as president in 1920 when Wilson declined to endorse him. The 1924 Democratic convention deadlocked between McAdoo, who favored PROHIBITION, and Al SMITH, who opposed it, for 102 ballots before turning to John DAVIS as a compromise. He moved to Los Angeles in 1922 and was in favor of the NEW DEAL as a Calif. senator (1932–8).

MacArthur, Douglas (b. Little Rock, Ark., 26 January 1880; d. Washington, D.C., 5 April 1964) After graduating first in his class from West Point in 1903, MacArthur saw duty under his own father in the PHILIPPINE INSURRECTION, was Theodore ROOSEVELT's aide de camp in 1906, and was twice wounded in WORLD WAR I, when he commanded a division. After serving in the Philippines (1922–30), he became army chief of staff (1930–5), during which time he dispersed the BONUS ARMY. He retired in 1937, but was recalled in July 1941 to organize the defense of the Philippines. In WORLD WAR II, he was supreme army commander in the Pacific theater and chief architect of Japan's defeat, especially through his innovative strategy of ISLAND HOPPING. He directed the occupation and democratization of Japan (1945–50). As commander of UN forces in the KOREAN WAR, he forced North Korean evacuation by his Inchon invasion, but was thrown on the defensive when Chinese forces crossed the Yalu River. His military career ended on 10 April 1951 when he was relieved of command for insubordination.

McCarran Act (23 September 1950) Overriding a veto, Congress created the Subversive Activities Control Board to register members of the COMMUNIST PARTY, forbid the hiring of Communists for national defense work, and bar anyone from the US who had joined a totalitarian group. In *Aptheker* v. *Secretary of State* (1964), the Supreme Court held that by withholding passports from Communists, it violated the FIFTH AMENDMENT right of freedom of travel. In *Albertson* v. *Subversive Activities Control Board* (1965), the Court struck down its compulsory registration of Communists as violating Fifth Amendment guarantees against self-incrimination. *Albertson* gutted the law's ability to monitor leftist groups, and Congress abolished its Control Board in 1973.

McCarran–Walter Act (30 June 1952) This law amended the NATIONAL ORIGINS ACT by permitting CHINESE, JAPANESE, and other Asian IMMIGRATION. It also established procedures to identify Communists and other subversives among foreign admittees, so that they could be denied entrance. The law permitted the deportation of subversives after they had gained residency, or even citizenship.

McCarthy, Eugene Joseph (b. Watkins, Minn., 29 March 1916) Originally a college professor, McCarthy was elected to Congress in 1948 and to the Senate in 1958. He became the leading Democratic critic of the policies on the VIETNAM WAR of Lyndon JOHNSON, whom he challenged for the 1968 Democratic presidential nomination. Johnson's narrow win in the N.H. primary was considered a moral victory for McCarthy and energized the VIETNAM ANTIWAR MOVEMENT. McCarthy's unexpected strength helped influence Johnson to withdraw in favor of Hubert HUMPHREY, but it also encouraged Robert KENNEDY to enter the race. Kennedy siphoned away many of McCarthy's supporters, and even after Kennedy was assassinated, McCarthy could not stop Humphrey's nomination. He retired from the Senate in 1970.

McCarthy, Joseph Raymond (b. Grand Chute, Wis., 14 November 1908; d. Bethesda, Md., 2 May 1957) As a Republican from Wis. and chair of the Senate Permanent Investigating Subcommittee, McCarthy held extensive hearings during 1953–4 into the influence of the COMMUNIST PARTY within government. The hearings were a thinly-veiled, partisan attack on the Democratic Party, and relied heavily upon political innuendo, demagoguery, guilt by association, and character assassination. As early as June 1953, Dwight D. EISENHOWER implicitly criticized his methods as un-American. McCarthy spawned a backlash against his crusade during protracted hearings on disloyalty within the army intelligence service (December 1953–January 1954), in which his abusive and bullying tactics were widely publicized. McCarthy was finally "condemned" by the Senate on 2 December 1954.

McCarthyism This term describes irresponsible and extreme tactics used to smear one's political opponents, that resemble Joseph MCCARTHY's investigation of Communist sympathizers.

McClellan, George B. (b. Philadelphia, Pa., 3 December 1826; d. Woodstock, Conn., 29 October 1885) McClellan graduated second at West Point in 1846. He was president of the Ohio and Mississippi Railroad when the CIVIL WAR began. Appointed USA major general, his victory at RICH MOUNTAIN, W.Va., made him a national hero and led to his being named commander in chief in November 1861. Out-generaled in the PENINSULAR CAMPAIGN, he was victorious at ANTIETAM, but failed to pursue and destroy the Army of NORTHERN VIRGINIA. His failure to launch another offensive against Richmond led to his relief on 7 November. He received 45 percent of the popular vote as Democratic nominee for president in 1864 but won just three states. He was governor of N.J. (1878–81).

McCleskey* v. *Kemp On 22 April 1987, the Supreme Court ruled (5–4) that to demonstrate that a death sentence was imposed in violation of the EIGHTH or FOURTEENTH AMENDMENTS, it is not sufficient to present statistical evidence indicating that racial bias results in more nonwhites being executed than whites for the same crime; it is necessary to prove that bias entered into a particular defendant's death sentence, or that the legal system itself is capricious or purposefully discriminatory.

McCord, James Walter, Jr *see* WATERGATE SCANDAL

McCormick, Cyrus Hall (b. Rockbridge County, Va., 15 February 1809; d. Chicago, Ill., 13 May 1884) In 1831 McCormick patented the first practical grain reaper, and successfully demonstrated its prototype in 1832. He began large-scale production at Rockbridge County in 1840, but relocated his manufacturing operations to Chicago in 1847 and remained the leading producer of reapers even after his patent expired the next year. McCormick's invention received international acclaim at the 1851 London Great Exhibition and at many European scientific exhibitions in the 1850s. His reaper enabled grain production to expand dramatically on the plains and was critical in maintaining US farm output during the CIVIL WAR.

McCulloch* v. *Maryland In 1819 the Supreme Court declared unanimously that Md. lacked authority to tax the BANK OF THE UNITED STATES, because "the power to tax involves the power to destroy." It also upheld the constitutionality of the bank's federal charter, as one of the "implied powers" possessed by Congress under Section 8's license to "make all laws which shall be necessary and proper." The decision countered the strict constructionist position that the federal government must not legislate beyond those activities expressly mentioned in the Constitution. By providing a strong argument for the loose constructionist position that Congress could take any action not specifically forbidden by the Constitution, the ruling furnished a theoretical justification for steadily expanding the scope of federal lawmaking.

McGillivray, Alexander (b. Little Tallassie, Ala., ca. 1759; d. Pensacola, Fla., 17 February 1793) The son of a Scottish Tory (*see* TORIES) and a mixed-race CREEK INDIAN mother, McGillivray rose to be the Creeks' leading diplomat and strategist. In 1786 he organized a lightning war that regained Creek lands unwillingly ceded in 1783 and 1785. By persuading both the US and Spain that his nation held the balance of power on the Ga.–Fla. border, he induced both countries to compete for his allegiance. He won concessions from the US in 1790 that protected Creek lands in the treaty of New York, and he made a secret treaty with Spain in 1792 to ensure continued access to military supplies. He died before achieving his goal of uniting the uncooperative Creek villages under a central authority capable of mobilizing all the nation's 5,500 warriors to halt white expansion.

McGovern, George Stanley (b. Avon, S.Dak. 19 July 1922) An army aviator in World War II and a history professor after the war, McGovern was elected to Congress (Democrat, S.Dak.) in 1956. After heading the FOOD FOR PEACE program (1961–3), he served in the Senate (1963–81). McGovern won the Democratic presidential nomination in 1972 on a platform of unilateral, immediate withdrawal of US troops from the VIETNAM WAR and an expansion of social welfare programs. He carried only Mass. and D.C., and won just 37.5 percent of the popular vote in the worst defeat ever suffered by a major party candidate. Republican attempts to spy on McGovern's campaign resulted in the WATERGATE SCANDAL that forced Richard NIXON's resignation.

McGuffey, William Holmes (b. near Claysville, Pa., 23 September 1800; d. Charlottesville, Va., 4 May 1873) After graduating from Washington College (Pa.) in 1826, McGuffey taught at Miami University (Ohio) before serving as president of Cincinnati College and Ohio University (1836–45). He became the most influential educator of his age by authoring a series of six elementary schoolbooks, the *Eclectic Readers* (1836–57), which sold over 120 million copies. These "McGuffey Readers" aimed to instill moral fiber and patriotism, and also exposed students to reading material and vocabulary equal to, if not above, the prevailing level in most late-20th-century American textbooks for equivalent grade levels.

McKeiver* v. *Pennsylvania (decided with *In Re Burrus*) On 21 June 1971, the Supreme Court ruled (5–4) that the SIXTH AMENDMENT did not require jury verdicts in juvenile trials.

McKinley, William (b. Niles, Ohio, 29 January 1843; d. Buffalo, N.Y., 14 September 1901) He reached the rank of USA major in the CIVIL WAR, and opened a law office at Canton, Ohio, in 1867. During 1876–90, he was a Republican congressman and sponsored the MCKINLEY TARIFF. He was elected Ohio governor in 1891 and 1893. In 1896, due in large part to Marcus HANNA's campaign strategy, he was elected president over William Jennings BRYAN, with 51.1 percent of the popular vote, on a platform advocating a strong currency and protectionism. McKinley presided over the DINGLEY TARIFF, the legal adoption of the GOLD STANDARD, HAWAII's annexation, and the SPANISH-AMERICAN WAR. He again defeated Bryan in 1900 with 51.7 percent of the vote. He was murdered by a radical socialist, Leon Czolgosz, a year later.

McKinley Tariff (1 October 1890) This measure was the first major tariff revision since 1883. It raised average import duties to the highest levels yet enacted by Congress: 49.5 percent. Passed shortly before mid-term elections, its unpopularity led to Republicans losing control of the House of Representatives (even sponsor William MCKINLEY lost) and sustaining large losses in the Senate. It helped elect a Democratic president in 1892, and was succeeded by the WILSON–GORMAN TARIFF.

McLaurin* v. *Oklahoma On 5 June 1950, in a SEPARATE BUT EQUAL case, the Supreme Court unanimously ruled that once black students gained admission to a formerly all-white college, they could not be segregated on campus by being excluded from facilities open to whites, such as classrooms, the library, or buildings for students' recreational use. (*See also* SWEATT V. PAINTER)

MacLeish, Archibald (b. Glencoe, Ill., 7 May 1892; d. Boston, Mass., 20 April 1982) After graduating from Yale and Harvard Law School and serving in World War I, MacLeish went to France as a poet in 1923, joined other American expatriates, and wrote *Streets of the Moon* (1926) and *Nobodaddy* (1926). He broke artistically and philosophically with the LOST GENERATION in 1928, returned to the US, and wrote *New Found Land* (1930), a poem resonant with rekindled patriotism. He won the Pulitzer prize for *Conquistador* (1932), an epic poem concerned metaphorically with the rise of European dictatorships. His verse increasingly addressed the problem of defending democratic values against fascism. *Collected Poems, 1917–1952* (1952) won him the Pulitzer prize, plus Bollinger and National Book awards, and *J.B.* (1957) received a third Pulitzer prize.

Macon's Bill Number 2 (1 May 1810) Drafted by Nathaniel Macon, this law replaced the NONINTERCOURSE ACT. It permitted the president to reopen trade with Britain and France, with the proviso that if either nation agreed to honor the US MERCHANT MARINE's neutrality by 3 March 1811, trade would cease with the other if it did not reciprocate within three months. Despite ordering US ships seized in French ports on 23 March 1810 and 1 November 1810, Napoleon deceived James MADISON into believing that France had complied with the law's conditions. Madison then permitted Franco-American trade to resume on 2 November 1810 and ordered commerce with Britain halted on 2 February 1811 unless it followed France's example. Britain did not accept US terms for resuming trade until 16 June 1812, two days before the US declaration of hostilities for the WAR OF 1812.

McMahon Act *see* ATOMIC ENERGY ACT (1946)

McNary–Haugen Bill During the 1920s, this measure was the most popular solution among farmers for reversing the sharp decline in crop prices. It would have created an Agricultural Credit Corporation to support prices by purchasing commodity surpluses (to raise demand) and then take them off the market (to lower supply) until prices rose so that they could be sold abroad. The Farm Board would buy crops at a fixed price (or parity), calculated as a fair exchange value representing their average level during 1905–14. It would sell the crops overseas at prevailing world prices, and would recoup any losses suffered by assessing an equalization fee on farmers (and in the bill's final version, also on food transporters, processors, and retailers). The bill was first introduced into Congress on 16 January 1924, but did not pass until 1927 (applicable to corn, wheat, rice, hogs, and cotton), and was then vetoed on 17 February; it was reenacted in 1928, but again vetoed in May. The next attempt at farm relief was the AGRICULTURAL MARKETING ACT of Herbert HOOVER.

McPherson, Aimee Semple (b. near Ingersoll, Ontario, 9 October 1890; d. Oakland, Calif., 27 September 1944) The wife of a Pentecostal missionary who died in China, Aimee Semple returned to the US and married Harold McPherson, whom she divorced when she became an itinerant evangelist in North America, Britain, and Australia. In 1918 she established the International Church of the Four-square Gospel in Los Angeles, where she constructed the Angelus Temple. Her religion emphasized fundamentalism, faith healing, and spectacular ceremonies that revolved around her weekly sermons. Through her use of radio broadcasts, charismatic preaching, and church services designed to serve as entertainment on an epic scale, she stands out as the most innovative, flamboyant, and eccentric of 20th-century evangelists. She died from an overdose of sleeping prescriptions.

Maddox, Lester *see* AMERICAN INDEPENDENT PARTY *and* GEORGIA

Madison, James (b. Port Conway, Va., 16 March 1751; d. Orange Country, Va., 28 June 1836) He helped draft the 1776 Virginia Constitution, strongly supported the VIRGINIA STATUTE FOR RELIGIOUS FREEDOM, and became a strong nationalist while serving in Congress. Having participated in the MOUNT VERNON CONFERENCE and ANNAPOLIS CONVENTION, he drafted the VIRGINIA PLAN at the CONSTITUTIONAL CONVENTION. He wrote 26 of the FEDERALIST PAPERS and co-authored another three. He drafted the BILL OF RIGHTS. He emerged as the most important Democratic leader in

Congress by 1793, abandoned his earlier nationalism, and wrote the VIRGINIA RESOLUTIONS. Elected president over Charles C. PINCKNEY in 1808 and De Witt CLINTON in 1812, his administration was dominated by the WAR OF 1812.

Madison Plan *see* VIRGINIA PLAN

Madrid, treaty of *see* SAN ILDEFONSO, TREATY OF

Mafia By 1900, in US cities with large Italian populations, secret criminal gangs had appeared that were modeled on Sicily's Mafia, or Cosa Nostra (Italian for "Our Affair"). During PROHIBITION, several such groups – whose members and leaders were not exclusively Italian – took control of bootlegging in the Northeast and Midwest. In the 1930s, they gained enormous influence over illegal gambling and prostitution; then in the 1940s they came to dominate loan-sharking, labor-racketeering, and heroin sales in major cities. By 1950, two dozen syndicates ("families") had divided the US into separate territories for the pursuit of criminal activities.

Although the Estes KEFAUVER HEARINGS had publicized the Mafia's involvement in interstate crime and political corruption as early as 1950, J. Edgar HOOVER failed to use the FBI's full resources against the Cosa Nostra. In 1961 Attorney General Robert KENNEDY launched a major offensive against the national syndicates, energized the FBI into mounting an anti-gangster campaign, and won hundreds of convictions on tax evasion, although few successful cases involved leading mafiosi. The Justice Department eventually won major convictions with the RICO section of the ORGANIZED CRIME CONTROL ACT (1970). During the 1980s, the heads of 22 Mafia families were indicted under RICO, and most were convicted (usually with evidence obtained from wiretaps authorized under Title II of the Omnibus Crime Control Act, (1968)). By the 1990s, the Mafia was increasingly vulnerable to FBI investigations and was losing a large share of its lucrative drug trade to a new criminal infrastructure organized by Hispanics, blacks, and Asians.

Magruder, Jeb Stuart (b. New York, N.Y., 5 November 1934) He was a deputy director for CREEP in 1972, when he became involved in the "dirty-tricks" program against George MCGOVERN's campaign that led to the WATERGATE SCANDAL, and in its cover-up. On 14 June 1973, in testimony before the Senate, he implicated John MITCHELL and H. R. HALDEMAN in the conspiracy. He served seven months' imprisonment in 1974 for conspiracy to obstruct justice.

Mahan, Alfred Thayer (b. West Point, N.Y., 27 September 1840; d. Quogue, N.Y., 1 December 1914) After graduating from Annapolis in 1859, Mahan fought in the CIVIL WAR, and became president of the Naval War College in 1886. During 1890–7, he published *The Influence of Sea Power upon History* and *The Interest of America in Sea Power*. Mahan argued that national destiny required the US to maintain a world-class navy that could protect the sea lanes for its overseas commerce. To supply and protect large fleets, he advocated building a canal in Central America and acquiring colonies to serve as military bases. Mahan's ideas influenced Congress to expand the navy significantly and helped convince the nation's elite that the US must pursue an imperialist and expansionist foreign policy.

Mahican Indians These speakers of one of the ALGONQUIAN LANGUAGES occupied both banks of the Hudson valley south of Lake Champlain and parts of western Mass. They were the parent stock of the PEQUOT and MOHICAN INDIANS of Conn. Blood feuds and competition over the FUR TRADE resulted in protracted warfare with the MOHAWK INDIANS in the 1600s. From a pre-contact population of 4,000, they declined to about 1,000 in the Hudson and Housatonic valleys by 1689, and a smallpox epidemic in 1690 cut their numbers to 500 by 1700. The only Mahicans to preserve their cultural identity were several bands that merged with DELAWARE INDIANS and the IROQUOIS CONFEDERACY during 1730–60; they gathered at the PRAYING TOWN of Stockbridge, Mass., where they were joined by remnants of other N.Y. Algonquians and numbered 227 in 1755. They were British allies in the SEVEN YEARS' WAR and American allies in the Revolution. By 1783–5, when about 420 Stockbridge Indians settled at Oneida Creek, N.Y., nearly all the group knew English and lived in white fashion as sedentary farmers. In 1828 they began a migration to Wis., where they eventually shared a federal reservation (*see* RESERVATIONS) with Delawares in Shawano County. In 1966 the Shawano reservation contained 380 of the members on the tribal roll.

Maine On 14 August 1607, the PLYMOUTH COMPANY put a settlement on the SAGADAHOC River, but the colonists abandoned it in September 1608. In 1622 the Council of New England (successor to the Plymouth Company) authorized grants to persons who would settle Maine. English fishing or trading outposts were built on the Saco River and Casco Bay during 1623–5, and the PILGRIMS built a trading post for the FUR TRADE on the Kennebec River. Sir Fernando Gorges assumed the Plymouth Company's claim to the area and obtained a royal charter as proprietor of the "Province of Maine," but was unable to prevent MASSACHUSETTS from annexing the settlements on 31 May 1652 and organizing them as York County. In 1677 Gorges's heir sold to Mass. his claims to Maine.

The Maine settlements suffered heavy losses in KING PHILIP'S WAR, KING WILLIAM'S WAR, and QUEEN ANNE'S WAR. DUMMER'S WAR removed the ABNAKI INDIANS, who were the principal barrier to settling the interior. The French and Indians also raided Maine in KING GEORGE'S WAR and the SEVEN YEARS' WAR. In the REVOLUTIONARY WAR, Maine was the site of 29 military actions on land and six at sea. Its frontier expanded sharply between 1770 and 1800, when population grew from 31,257 to 151,719. By 1800, 90 percent of its people were of English-Welsh stock.

From 1790 to 1820, much violence resulted from the uncertain state of real estate ownership, as rival speculators and land companies dispossessed farmers from their land. On 15 March 1820, Maine became the 23rd state as part of the MISSOURI COMPROMISE. It disestablished the CONGREGATIONAL CHURCH in 1820. The AROOSTOOK WAR flared up from disputes over its disputed boundary with Canada, which were resolved by the WEBSTER–ASHBURTON TREATY. Maine became the first state to enact PROHIBITION in 1851.

From 1800 to 1860, its population grew by 314 percent to 628,279, of which all but 1,327 were white and 6 percent were foreign-born; it ranked 22nd in population among the states, 26th in the value of its farmland and livestock, and 14th in manufactures. It furnished 70,107 USA troops in the CIVIL WAR (including 104 blacks).

Population growth stagnated after 1860, and from then to 1900 the number of residents rose just 11 percent. In 1900 it had 694,466 inhabitants, who were 56 percent rural, 99 percent white, and 13 percent foreign-born; it ranked 30th among states in population, 33rd in the value of its agricultural goods, and 21st in manufactures. Its textile industry declined after 1910, while food processing grew significantly. After 1950, tourism became important. To settle a lawsuit claiming title to 19,530 square miles (58 percent of Maine) bought in violation of the INDIAN TRADE INTERCOURSE ACT (1790), tribal groups extinguished their aboriginal title in return for 469 square miles (valued at $54,500,000) and a $27,000,000 trust fund. Maine suffered a net loss by out-migration in every decade after 1910 and ranked as the 38th largest state by 1990; it had 1,227,928 inhabitants (98 percent white, 1 percent Hispanic, 1 percent Asian or Indian), of whom 36 percent were urban and 3.0 percent were foreign-born. Manufacturing and mining employed 27 percent of workers.

***Maine* USS** On 15 February 1898, the battleship *Maine* blew up and sank at Havana, where it had served as a refuge for US civilians from Cuba's revolution; 266 of its 354 personnel died. On 21 March, without firm evidence, the navy reported that an underwater mine had caused the explosion. (The disaster's cause remains unknown.) Exhorting Americans to "Remember the *Maine*," YELLOW JOURNALISM inflamed war fever and helped push the McKinley government into the SPANISH-AMERICAN WAR.

Makin Atoll, battle of *see* GILBERT ISLANDS CAMPAIGN

Mallet explorations In 1739 Pierre and Paul Mallet, Frenchmen from Ill., explored the Arkansas River as far west as Colo. and in about June became the first white men to see the Rocky Mountains from the plains. They reached Santa Fe on 22 July and were placed under loose arrest as illegal traders. They were ordered deported and left Santa Fe on 1 May 1740.

Mallory* v. *United States On 24 June 1957, the Supreme Court unanimously held that police officers violated DUE PROCESS by interrogating a suspect without telling him of his constitutional rights and detaining him for an unjustifiably long period between his arrest and arraignment; it reversed the defendant's conviction. *Mallory* served as a precedent for expanding the rights of criminal suspects in *ESCOBEDO* V. *ILLINOIS*, *MIRANDA* V. *ARIZONA*, *HARRIS* V. *NEW YORK*, and *EDWARDS* V. *ARIZONA*.

Malloy* v. *Hogan On 15 June 1964, the Supreme Court unanimously extended the FIFTH AMENDMENT's guarantee against self-incrimination to state court proceedings.

Malvern Hill, battle of *see* PENINSULAR CAMPAIGN

Man Nobody Knows, The Advertising executive Bruce Barton published this book in 1925. He analyzed the career of Jesus Christ, whom he described as a super salesman and first-rate businessman able to identify outstanding middle-level managers (the apostles) to build his organization. Christianity consequently owed its success as much to superior marketing and advertising techniques as to its moral content. The book epitomized the crass business philosophy and commercialism of the 1920s.

Manassas, first battle of *see* BULL RUN, FIRST BATTLE OF

Manassas, second battle of *see* BULL RUN, SECOND BATTLE OF

Mandan Indians This group, speakers of one of the SIOUAN LANGUAGES, established itself along the upper Missouri River in the Dakotas about AD 1,200. In 1738 they inhabited nine villages along the Heart River in N.Dak. and numbered over 3,000. The LEWIS AND CLARK EXPEDITION wintered among them in 1804–5. They soon acquired guns, but lost half their population to smallpox and were driven northward by the SIOUX INDIANS. Smallpox struck the nation in late 1837 and by next spring only 145 Mandans were alive. The survivors merged with other groups and their descendants are now at Fort Berthold Reservation, N.Dak.

Mangum, Willie Person (b. Orange County, N.C., 10 May 1792; d. Durham County, N.C., 7 September 1861) He began practicing law in 1817. He was N.C. state senator (Democrat) (1823–6) and US senator (1830–6). For defending S.C. during the NULLIFICATION CRISIS and voting against the Force Act (1833) (*see* NULLIFICATION CRISIS), he received its 11 electoral votes for president in the 1836 election. In the late 1830s, he joined the WHIG PARTY, and declined its offer to run as vice-president in 1840. During 1841–52, he returned to the Senate, where he was president pro tempore from May 1842 to March 1845.

Manhattan Project On 2 October 1939, Albert EINSTEIN wrote a letter alerting Franklin D. ROOSEVELT to the possibility of Germany developing atomic weapons and stressing the need for US research to counter this threat. This warning led the US to award grants for atomic research at leading universities – the first major federal sponsorship of scientific work – and then to the founding in May 1943 of the Manhattan Project to build an atomic bomb. Under Robert Oppenheimer, who was assisted by Enrico Fermi, the project detonated its first atomic bomb at Alamogordo, N.Mex., on 16 July 1945. It produced just two other bombs before Japan surrendered, which were used at HIROSHIMA and NAGASAKI.

manifest destiny This term embodied an Anglo-American belief that the US had a special mission to establish its political values and support its growing population by expanding its jurisdiction over the unsettled (or sparsely populated) area west of the Mississippi. The words were first written about the annexation of TEXAS in the *Democratic Review* (July 1845) by John L. O'Sullivan, who championed "our manifest destiny to overspread the continent allotted by Providence for the free development of our yearly multiplying millions." The doctrine was expanded by filibusterers (*see* FILIBUSTERING) to include annexing Caribbean islands and Central American nations.

Manila Bay, battle of (Philippines) On 1 May 1898, Commodore George DEWEY's 5 US cruisers and 1 gunboat (53 heavy guns, 135 light guns, 1,611 crewmen) engaged Admiral Patricio Montojo's 2 Spanish cruisers and 5 gunboats (37 heavy guns, 110 light guns, 1,500 crewmen). Dewey destroyed every enemy ship, yet sustained minimal damage. US losses: 8 wounded. Spanish losses: 161 killed, 210 wounded. Dewey blockaded Manila, which surrendered on 13 August.

Mann, Horace (b. Franklin, Mass., 4 May 1796; d. Yellow Springs, Ohio, 2 August 1859) After serving (1827–37) in the Mass. legislature, in 1837 Mann secured passage of an educational reform bill and then devoted his next 11 years to improving schools as secretary of the state board of education. Mann became his age's foremost proponent of educational reform. Under his leadership, Mass. pioneered the basic reforms that created the modern American secondary school system: mandatory attendance of six months for school-age children, professional training for teachers at normal schools, centralizing local schools into larger districts, expanded access to high-school education, standardized curricula, and minimum standards for school budgets and teacher salaries.

Mann Act (1910) *see* White Slavery Act

Mann–Elkins Act (18 June 1913) This law strengthened the Hepburn Act by allowing the Interstate Commerce Commission (ICC) to suspend proposed rate changes for up to ten months pending investigation of their reasonableness, and to demand that the carriers prove them to be financially necessary. It revived the prohibition against charging higher rates for short hauls than for long hauls, which had been undermined by many court decisions. It extended ICC authority over telegraph, telephone, and cable communications systems. The law gave the ICC all the legal tools needed for effective railroad regulation except the authority to assess the value of railroad assets, which was provided by the Physical Valuation Act (1913).

manors *see* New York manors *and* Maryland

Manpower Act (1918) *see* Selective Service Act (1917).

Mapp* v. *Ohio On 19 June 1961, the Supreme Court ruled (5–4) that under the Fourteenth Amendment's due process clause, the Fourth Amendment forbade state courts from using evidence obtained by unreasonable searches or seizures. *Mapp* overruled *Wolf* v. *Colorado* (27 June 1949) which held that the Fourth Amendment forbade state officers from obtaining evidence through unreasonable means, but left state courts the option of admitting or excluding it.

Marais des Cygnes massacre (Kans.) On 19 May 1858, several dozen border ruffians under William Hambleton shot 11 unarmed, free-soil settlers execution-style in revenge for personal grudges felt by Hambleton. Five people survived by pretending to be dead.

Marbury* v. *Madison In 1803, after hearing William Marbury's demand that Secretary of State James Madison issue a magistrate's commission for the District of Columbia in his name signed by ex-President John Adams, the Supreme Court (without dissent) declared a federal law unconstitutional for the first time and invalidated Section 13 of the Judiciary Act (1789) on technical grounds. The Court explicitly claimed the right of judicial review by declaring "It is emphatically the province and duty of the judicial department to say what the law is. . . . This is of the very essence of judicial duty."

march from Selma (Ala.) *see* Selma freedom march

march on Washington (1941) In January 1941, A. Philip Randolph began organizing a march on Washington, D.C., by 100,000 blacks for 1 July to demand equal employment opportunity for blacks in defense work. To forestall the march, on 25 June 1941, Franklin D. Roosevelt issued Executive Order 8802, which prohibited job discrimination in defense industries and required a clause to that effect in all military-related contracts. It also established the Commission on Fair Hiring Practices as an enforcement agency. Although the order was often evaded, it was a major civil rights victory and encouraged the defection of black Republicans to the Roosevelt coalition.

march on Washington (1963) To press for passage of the Civil Rights Act (1964), the National Association for the Advancement of Colored People, Southern Christian Leadership

CONFERENCE, and National URBAN LEAGUE organized a march on the capital. On 28 August 1963, perhaps 250,000 people gathered at the Lincoln Memorial, where Martin Luther KING gave his "I have a dream" speech. John F. KENNEDY did not participate in the march, but met with its leaders at the White House. The march failed to achieve the act's passage that year, but it was instrumental in building a national consensus against racial discrimination that resulted in its passage a year later.

March to the Sea On 15 November 1864, having burned Atlanta's warehouses and railroad facilities, Major General William T. SHERMAN's 62,000 Federals began marching with 20 days' rations for Savannah, although such a campaign violated conventional military axioms by operating behind enemy lines without lines of communication or supply. Sherman brushed aside Major General Joseph Wheeler's 13,000 Confederates, systematically destroyed all railroads and other property of military value to the South, and commandeered large amounts of civilian foodstuffs. After despoiling a swath of land 60 miles wide and 250 miles long, he marched into Savannah on 21 December. USA losses: 2,200 killed, wounded. On 1 February 1865, Sherman began a similar march through the Carolinas to reach Va.

Mariana Islands *see* MICRONESIA, US TRUST TERRITORY OF

Mariana Islands campaign On 15 June 1944, Rear Admiral Richmond Turner's Fifth Amphibious Task Force (530 warships carrying 127,000 marines and soldiers under Lieutenant General Holland Smith) arrived off the Mariana Islands, held by 57,500 Japanese. By 10 August, Smith's men had eliminated organized enemy resistance on SAIPAN, TINIAN, and GUAM. US losses: 25,000 killed, wounded. Japanese losses: 45,000 killed or dead by suicide. The Marianas' capture outflanked enemy bases in the Caroline Islands, especially the Truk supply depot, and brought Japan within range of US heavy bombers.

Mariel boatlift On 21 April 1980, Communist Cuba began allowing large numbers of persons to flee by boat to Fla. Hoping for political gain among Cuban-American voters, President Jimmy CARTER approved unlimited entry to the US, whereupon 125,000 persons arrived through 26 September, when an outcry against the boatlift forced Carter to reverse the policy. About every sixth refugee, or Marielista, was a former criminal or mental patient. In 1984 Cuba agreed to repatriate 2,746 Marielistas sentenced to federal prisons for murder, various violent crimes, and drug trafficking. In 1993 Cuba agreed to repatriate another 1,567 Marielistas sentenced by federal courts for serious offenses.

Marine Corps Congress authorized the United States Marine Corps (USMC) on 10 November 1775. Marines first saw combat on 4 March 1776 when capturing Fort Nassau, Bahamas, in their first amphibious landing. Their primary mission was to fire from above decks as marksmen in battle. Disbanded in 1785 with the navy, the corps was reinstituted on 11 July 1798.

Starting with the wars with BARBARY PIRATES, the corps took responsibility for overseas amphibious operations. Although marine detachments served as infantry in the SEMINOLE, MEXICAN, and CIVIL WARS, their primary duty was to augment a ship's crew offshore. From 1800 to 1940, the corps made 180 landings in 31 countries.

The corps was gradually expanded from 1898 to 1917 into a major body of infantry, with supporting artillery. Two USMC regiments fought in France in WORLD WAR I. The corps's greatest military contribution came in WORLD WAR II, when its strength peaked at 485,113 and fielded six divisions (primarily to support Chester NIMITZ's central Pacific offensive). One USMC division fought in the KOREAN WAR and two in the VIETNAM WAR. The corps participated in post-World War II US interventions in LEBANON, the DOMINICAN REPUBLIC, GRENADA, and HAITI. In 1994 the regular USMC had an authorized strength of 174,000 (three divisions and three air wings) and received about 5 percent of the Defense Department budget.

Mariposa War This conflict was the only significant Indian disturbance during the CALIFORNIA GOLD RUSH. In 1850, after miners had invaded their lands, Tenaya led the Yokuts and Miwoks in attacking prospectors in the San Joaquin valley and Sierra

Nevada foothills. In 1851 James Savage's Mariposa Militia Battalion retaliated and dispersed the Indians after a few skirmishes.

Maritime Commission, United States *see* MERCHANT MARINE ACT (1936)

Marquette and Joliet exploration On 17 May 1673, Fr Jacques Marquette (1637–75), Louis Joliet (1648–1700), and five COUREURS DE BOIS left the Straits of Mackinac and became the first Europeans to find a water route to the Mississippi via Green Bay, Fox River, and Wisconsin River. They entered the Mississippi on 17 June and descended it to the Arkansas River by 17 July before returning north. Their voyage demonstrated that the Mississippi flowed to the Gulf of Mexico rather than to the Pacific Ocean.

Marshall, George Catlett (b. Uniontown, Pa., 31 December 1880; d. Washington, D.C., 17 October 1959) Marshall became an Army lieutenant in 1902. He served on the ALLIED EXPEDITIONARY FORCE staff under John PERSHING and was Pershing's aide (1919–24). He became army chief of staff in 1939 and was principally responsible for transforming the 170,000-man army of 1940 into a well-trained force of 7,200,000 by 1944. As chair of the combined chiefs of staff, with the rank of general of the armies in 1944, he was the chief architect of Allied victory in WORLD WAR II. He served as secretary of state (1947–9), and initiated the MARSHALL PLAN. He was recalled from private life to head the Department of DEFENSE (1950–1). He received the Nobel peace prize in 1953.

Marshall, John (b. Midland, Va., 24 September 1755; d. Philadelphia, Pa., 6 July 1835) During the Revolution, Marshall was a captain in the Va. Line. He attended one course of legal lectures at William and Mary, but was largely a self-taught lawyer. He was a delegate for the FEDERALISTS at the Virginia convention that ratified the CONSTITUTION. He was envoy to France during the XYZ AFFAIR, congressman for the FEDERALIST PARTY (1799–1800), and secretary of state (1800–1). After being confirmed as chief justice on 27 January 1801, Marshall took part in over 1,000 cases and wrote half their opinions. His major legacy was to force Congress and the presidency to respect the court as a coequal partner in government. He molded constitutional theory along lines that asserted federal supremacy at the states' expense, and also restricted the states' ability to interfere with property rights vested in government charters or private contracts. His landmark decisions included *MARBURY* v. *MADISON* and *COHENS* v. *VIRGINIA* on judicial review; *FLETCHER* v. *PECK*, *DARTMOUTH COLLEGE* v. *WOODWARD*, and *OGDEN* v. *SAUNDERS* on contracts; *GIBBONS* v. *OGDEN*, *BROWN* v. *MARYLAND*, and *WILLSON* v. *BLACKBIRD CREEK MARSH COMPANY* on interstate commerce; *MCCULLOCH* v. *MARYLAND*, *CHEROKEE NATION* v. *GEORGIA*, and *WORCESTER* v. *GEORGIA* on federal supremacy; and *BARRON* v. *BALTIMORE* on individual rights.

Marshall, Thomas Riley (b. North Manchester, Ind., 14 March 1854; d. Washington, D.C., 1 June 1925) Formerly Democratic governor of Ind. (1909–13), Marshall was US vice-president (1913–21). He was the first vice-president in nearly a century to serve two consecutive terms in that office. He took over Woodrow WILSON's ceremonial duties after his stroke, but refused to assume any executive powers. He is best known for his quip: "What this country needs is a good five-cent cigar."

Marshall, Thurgood (b. Baltimore, Md., 2 July 1908) From 1940 to 1961, Marshall headed the NAACP Legal Defense and Education Fund. He argued and won *BROWN* v. *BOARD OF EDUCATION OF TOPEKA* (1954). In 1962, he joined the US 2nd Court of Appeals. He was US solicitor general (1965–7), and won the government's case in *SOUTH CAROLINA* v. *KATZENBACH*. On 30 August 1967, he joined the Supreme Court as its first black justice. He resigned on 28 June 1991.

Marshall Islands *see* MICRONESIA, US TRUST TERRITORY OF

Marshall Islands Campaign During 1–4 February 1944, 41,000 troops of the Fourth USMC Division and Seventh US Army Division overran 8,000 Japanese on Kwajalein Atoll. US losses: 372 killed. Japanese losses: 7,970 killed. On 17–23 February, the 22nd USMC Regiment and 106th Infantry Regiment wiped out Eniwetok Atoll's 2,000 Japanese defenders. The Marshalls served as a base to destroy Japan's supply base at Truk and to launch the MARIANA ISLANDS CAMPAIGN.

Marshall Plan Faced with intractable economic stagnation in Europe, George C. MARSHALL proposed on 5 June 1947 that all European nations – including the USSR – cooperate with the US to stimulate a business and financial recovery. The USSR and eastern Europe declined to participate. Western European nations drafted programs for reconstructing their economies at Paris from 27 June to 2 July; on 22 September, they estimated that foreign aid of $16–22 billion would be needed to spark an economic expansion by 1951. On 19 December, Harry S. TRUMAN sent Congress a $17 billion European Recovery Program. Opposition to the Marshall Plan dissolved after Communists took over Czechoslovakia in February 1948. Congress appropriated $13 billion for aid to Europe, which was recovering strongly by 1951.

Martin* v. *Hunter's Lessee In 1816 the state court of appeals of Va. argued that its decisions were exempt from the appellate jurisdiction of the Supreme Court (specifically, that Section 25 of the JUDICIARY ACT [1789] was unconstitutional in giving the Court such jurisdiction). The Supreme Court ruled (without dissent) against Va. and affirmed its authority over state tribunals. The Court again dealt with this issue in *COHENS* v. *VIRGINIA*.

Martin* v. *Mott In 1827 the Supreme Court heard arguments that state authorities could set limitations on the manner in which their militias were taken into federal service during wartime. The Court ruled (without dissent) that when acting under a declaration of war, the president had full authority to call out any state's militia for duty under the regular army's officers, that state officers must enforce orders from the president as commander in chief, and that the courts had no jurisdiction to intervene.

Maryland In 1631 the first English settlement was made on Kent Island by William Claiborne and 100 men from Va. On 30 June 1632, JAMES I granted Md. as a PROPRIETARY COLONY to the second Lord Baltimore, Cecilius Calvert, for the refuge of English Catholics (*see* CATHOLIC CHURCH). On 25 March 1634, Governor Leonard Calvert landed with 200 colonists, who later founded St Mary's. The Calverts intended that the basic social institution of Md. be manors, from which Catholic landlords could hold their own baronial courts, have special political privileges, and support private chaplains who would function as the manors' de facto parish priests.

In 1644 INGLE'S REVOLT overthrew Calvert's administration. Proprietary authority was restored in 1646. To appease Protestants, then a majority, the TOLERATION ACT was passed in 1649. In 1654, Protestants ousted William Stone, the proprietor's governor. Stone led a revolt in 1655 against the new administration but was defeated on 25 March at the battle of the SEVERN RIVER. Parliament restored the colony's government to Lord Baltimore in January 1656. By 1660, Md. had 8,400 colonists.

Discontent with proprietary rule resulted in the abortive DAVYES' UPRISING in 1676 and the failed FENDALL'S REVOLT of 1681. In 1689 COODE'S REVOLT overthrew proprietary authority and resulted in Md. becoming a ROYAL COLONY on 27 June 1691. In May 1715, Md. was restored to the fourth Lord Baltimore, who was an Anglican.

The primary agricultural staple was tobacco grown on PLANTATIONS. Md. was mainly populated by INDENTURED SERVANTS imported under the HEADRIGHT system. It enacted the first statute defining SLAVERY in 1661, after which slaves gradually replaced white servants as the main form of unfree labor. In 1700, its population included 26,400 whites and 3,200 slaves. Its only Indian hostilities were a brief spate of raids by SUSQUEHANNOCK INDIANS from Pa. in 1675 and attacks by France's Indian allies in the SEVEN YEARS' WAR.

The settlement of its PIEDMONT followed the treaty of LANCASTER. The MASON–DIXON LINE surveyed its disputed boundary with Pa. By 1770, it was the fourth largest colony, but slaves made up 33 percent of its population. In the REVOLUTIONARY WAR, Md. provided eight of the 80 Continental regiments and outfitted 225 privateers; it was the site of 21 military actions on land and two on water. It was the seventh state to ratify the CONSTITUTION on 28 April 1788. By 1800, Baltimore was the third-largest US city.

In 1800 Md. was the sixth largest state and had 341,548 people, of whom 31 percent were slaves and 6 percent were free blacks; 57 percent of whites were of English-Welsh stock. The British invaded Md. in the WAR OF 1812. Its social development diverged from that of other southern states as it urbanized, industrialized, and attracted immigrants after 1810. In 1860 it had 687,049 people, of whom 13 percent were slaves, 12 percent were free blacks, and 11 percent were foreign-born; it ranked 19th among states in population, 18th in the value of its farmland and livestock, and 12th in manufactures. It was badly divided in the CIVIL WAR and initially kept under martial law to prevent its SECESSION. Md. provided 46,638 USA troops (including 8,718 blacks) and 25,000 CSA soldiers. It was invaded by CSA forces in 1862 and 1863, and was the site of 203 military engagements. After 1865, many localities mandated SEGREGATION, but the state dismantled the system with little resistance after 1954.

By 1900, Md. was the 26th state in size with 1,188,044 people, of whom 50 percent were rural, 20 percent were black, and 8 percent were foreign-born; it ranked 29th among states in the value of its agricultural goods and 14th in manufactures. Its growth rate accelerated from 1940 to 1970, when it received 976,000 new residents by in-migration, largely to the suburbs of Washington, D.C. By 1990, when it ranked as 19th in size, it had 4,781,468 residents (70 percent white, 25 percent black, 2 percent Hispanic, 3 percent Asian), of whom 93 percent were urban and 6.6 percent foreign-born. Manufacturing or mining employed 18 percent of its work force.

Maryland proprietors *see* PROPRIETORS OF MARYLAND

Mason, George (b. in Fairfax County, Va., 1725; d. Fairfax County, Va., 7 October 1792) He was a leading spokesman for the WHIGS in Va. after the STAMP ACT crisis. His bill of rights for the Va. Constitution was the first such document adopted in the US (29 June 1776), and served as a model for the federal BILL OF RIGHTS. A delegate to the CONSTITUTIONAL CONVENTION who joined the ANTIFEDERALISTS, he was the most vocal critic of the CONSTITUTION's lack of a bill of rights.

Mason–Dixon Line Between 1763 and 1768, Charles Mason and Jeremiah Dixon surveyed 233 miles of the boundary between Pa. and Md. along the parallel 39°42′23.6″ just beyond the Monongahela River. The line came to symbolize the cultural border between the free and slave states. The expression "Dixie," meaning the south, may have evolved as a contraction of Dixon.

Mason* v. *Haile In 1827 the Supreme Court ruled (6–1) that a legislature might eliminate imprisonment as a punishment for unpaid debts without violating the constitutional prohibition against state laws impairing contracts; it held that Article I, Section 10 does not prevent states from altering the legal consequences of defaulting on debts, so long as they leave creditors legal options for reclaiming all money owed to them.

Mass Transit Act (6 July 1964) This measure, part of the GREAT SOCIETY, appropriated $375,000,000 over three years for grants to subsidize bus, subway, and rail construction for commuters in urban areas. It extended indefinitely a $50,000,000 fund providing low-interest federal loans to metropolitan transportation agencies. It was the first major commitment of federal funds to mass transit expansion.

Massachusett Indians This nation, speaking one of the ALGONQUIAN LANGUAGES, occupied the eastern Mass. coast and numbered perhaps 3,000 in 1610, but had declined to 731 by 1631 because of European diseases. Under attack by more numerous northern Indians, it welcomed the PURITANS and sold large tracts of land to gain protection from its enemies. By 1644, the Massachusetts had become political dependants of Mass. Bay and in 1651 began gathering in PRAYING TOWNS. By 1675, they had become Christian and most fought with the English in KING PHILIP'S WAR.

Massachusetts In 1616 European sailors transmitted an unknown, but deadly plague that killed perhaps every third New England Indian, and depopulated much of the coast north of R.I. On 9 November 1620, the *MAYFLOWER* landed 101 English PILGRIMS at Cape Cod, which had been heavily hit by the epidemic. With the *MAYFLOWER* COMPACT, they founded the PLYMOUTH colony.

On 14 March 1629, Charles I granted the

MASSACHUSETTS BAY COMPANY all land between the Charles and Merrimack rivers as a CHARTER COLONY. The GREAT MIGRATION of PURITANS began on 12 June 1630, when Governor John WINTHROP landed with 700 colonists at Salem (settled the year before by an advance party), but concentrated the population around Boston. Mass. Bay chartered Harvard College in 1636, established North America's first press in 1639, and became the first civil society to mandate compulsory primary eduction in 1647 by its OLD DELUDER ACT. Its earliest religious dispute, the ANTINOMIAN CONTROVERSY, climaxed at Anne HUTCHINSON's trial. By 1650, about 16,000 English lived in the colonies of Mass. Bay and Plymouth.

Mass. Bay and Plymouth escaped serious Indian hostilities until 1675–6, when they fought KING PHILIP'S WAR. In 1680, England detached NEW HAMPSHIRE from Mass. Bay and made it a ROYAL COLONY. On 21 June 1684, Mass. Bay became a royal colony when England's Chancery Court vacated its charter. In May 1686, Mass. Bay and Plymouth were placed under the administration of the DOMINION OF NEW ENGLAND, which was overthrown (in the name of William III) by a bloodless uprising at Boston on 18 April 1689. On 17 October 1691, Mass. Bay received a new charter (as a royal colony) that gave it jurisdiction over MAINE and Plymouth. The SALEM WITCH TRIALS hysteria occurred during 1692–3.

In 1700 Mass. was the second largest colony, with 56,000 people, of whom almost 99 percent were English or Welsh. Its economy depended on subsistence farming, fishing, forestry products, and the MERCHANT MARINE. It played a major role in KING WILLIAM'S WAR, QUEEN ANNE'S WAR, KING GEORGE'S WAR, and the SEVEN YEARS' WAR. As the cynosure of the imperial crisis after 1763, it was the intended target for most of the INTOLERABLE ACTS, which provoked the calling of the first CONTINENTAL CONGRESS. In the REVOLUTIONARY WAR, Mass. outfitted 626 privateers (more than any other state) and usually mustered 15 of the 80 Continental regiments; it was the site of 101 military actions on land and 31 at sea. A postwar depression spawned SHAYS' REBELLION. Mass. was the sixth state to ratify the CONSTITUTION on 6 February 1788.

In 1800, Mass. was the fourth largest state and had 574,564 people (including 151,719 in Maine), of which 89 percent were of English-Welsh stock and 1 percent were black; 10 percent of the population lived in towns with over 5,000 people. In 1820, Maine became a separate state. Mass. was the first state to become predominantly urban (in the 1820s). It disestablished the CONGREGATIONAL CHURCH in 1833. Its industries attracted many Irish and British immigrants. It was the seventh largest state in 1860 and had 1,231,066 residents, of whom 99 percent were white and 21 percent foreign-born; it ranked 21st among states in the value of its farmland and livestock and third in manufactures. In the CIVIL WAR, it provided 146,730 USA troops (including 3,966 blacks).

By 1900, Mass. was only 9 percent rural and had 2,805,346 inhabitants, of whom 99 percent were white and 30 percent were foreign-born; it ranked seventh among the states in population, 31st in the value of agricultural goods, and fourth in manufactures. Its growth rate slowed after 1920, and by 1990 it ranked as 13th. In 1990 it was 90 percent urban and had 6,016,425 residents (88 percent white, 5 percent black, 5 percent Hispanic, 2 percent Asian), of whom 9.5 percent were foreign-born. Manufacturing or mining employed 24 percent of its work force.

Massachusetts Bay Company On 14 March 1629, CHARLES I chartered this company. Because Charles failed to specify a location for corporate meetings, the charter could be removed from England to increase the difficulty of its being annulled by legal proceedings and the company headquarters could be transferred to Mass., where it became the GENERAL COURT. (*See* CAMBRIDGE AGREEMENT) The company sponsored large-scale Puritan emigration to Mass. beginning with 700 colonists sent out with Governor John WINTHROP in 1630. In May 1635, The PRIVY COUNCIL voted to commence a judicial suit against the charter, but could not force Mass. to surrender it before the English Civil War began. Legal action against the charter was resumed in 1682, and resulted in the Court of Chancery annulling it on 21 June 1684.

Massachusetts Circular Letter Drafted by Samuel ADAMS, this letter was sent on 11 February 1768 by the Mass. assembly to the other colonial legislatures. The letter denounced the TOWNSHEND REVENUE ACT as unconstitutional and requested the other assemblies to take formal, but legal, actions in protest. The letter had little effect until the British ministry's HILLSBOROUGH CIRCULAR LETTER denounced it and demanded that Mass. rescind it. The Mass. Letter was then widely approved by other legislatures. On 30 June 1768, the Mass. assembly voted not to withdraw the letter (92–17) and was dissolved the next day. The controversy over the Mass. Letter was critical in uniting colonial leaders against the Townshend taxes.

Massachusetts Government Act (20 May 1774) This law, which amended the royal charter for Mass., had been under consideration by Parliament since the early 1770s, but was hurriedly passed after the BOSTON TEA PARTY. Parliament required that the legislature's upper house be appointed by the government instead of being elected by the lower house; it forbade towns to hold more than one meeting a year without permission of the governor; it allowed the governor to dispense with existing custom by appointing both judges and sheriffs without approval from the legislature's upper house; and it allowed sheriffs to pick jurors, instead of allowing them to be elected at large or chosen by town constables. Colonists saw the act as a blueprint for making their governments less democratic and termed it one of the INTOLERABLE ACTS.

Massachusetts* v. *Mellon On 4 June 1923, the Supreme Court unanimously dismissed challenges to grants-in-aid under the Sheppard–Towner Maternity Act. By dismissing arguments that such grants undermined federalism by enticing the states into financial dependence on the US Treasury, the Court left Congress free to expand the number of such grants until they formed a major federal subsidy for state and municipal budgets. The Court dismissed a companion suit, *Frothingham* v. *Mellon*, for like causes on 4 June.

Massachusetts* v. *Sheppard *see UNITED STATES* v. *LEON*

massive retaliation This was part of John DULLES's strategy of BRINKMANSHIP; it threatened that a Soviet ground invasion of western Europe, or a Communist first use of nuclear weapons, would trigger a counterattack by the full US arsenal of nuclear missiles and bombs. It was abandoned in John F. KENNEDY's administration for a "flexible response" policy, in which the US would respond to armed attacks or other crises with only as much force as was required to neutralize those threats.

Masters, Edgar Lee (b. Garnett, Kans., 23 August 1869; d. Melrose Park, Pa., 5 March 1950) A trained lawyer, Masters had literary ambitions and sought success as a poet, novelist, and biographer. He won critical acclaim for his *Spoon River Anthology* (1915), a series of free-verse monologues in which several hundred corpses speak from a small-town cemetery about their past. Masters's *Spoon River Anthology* was a pioneering literary work that foreshadowed a major theme in US literature, namely the "revolt from the village," or the alienation of urban 20th-century writers from the idyllic image of rural American life. Masters's poetry anticipated the fiction of Sherwood ANDERSON and *Main Street* by Sinclair LEWIS.

Matsu Island *see* QUEMOY-MATSU CONTROVERSY

Maury, Matthew Fontaine (b. near Fredericksburg, Va., 14 January 1806; d. Lexington, Va., 1 February 1873) He entered the navy in 1825, became its foremost expert on atmospheric conditions and oceanic currents, and published *Wind and Current Chart of the North Atlantic* (1847) and the first modern synopsis of oceanography, *The Physical Geography of the Sea* (1855). In 1853 at Brussels, an international conference on navigational aids declared his standardized method of registering oceanographic data to be the world's standard system. By the mid-1850s, it was estimated that Maury's improved charts had cut 47 days off the voyage from New York to San Francisco. He resigned his rank in 1861 to assume command of the CSA navy. Following a failed attempt to promote an exodus of former Confederates to Latin America, he served as professor of meteorology at Virginia Military Institute until his death.

***Mayaguez*, SS, incident** On 12 May 1975, a Communist gunboat claimed the SS *Mayaguez* had violated Cambodian territory and took the ship and its 39 crewmen into custody. When the Khmer Rouge failed to give up the *Mayaguez*, Gerald FORD ordered it retaken by force (despite information received from China by Henry KISSINGER that indicated further negotiations might win the ship's release). On 14 May, 200 US marines staged an abortive raid to free the crew (who were not at the location the marines attacked), and came under heavy fire, while the USS *Holt* seized the *Mayaguez* and air strikes bombed Cambodia. The Khmer Rouge then gave up the crew. The operation cost the US 15 killed and 50 wounded.

Mayflower The *Mayflower* was a ship of 180 tons, formerly in the wine trade, captained by Christopher Jones, that carried the PILGRIMS to PLYMOUTH. It began with 80 passengers, but took on another 22 when the pinnace *Speedwell* proved too leaky to continue.

***Mayflower* Compact** On 21 November 1620, the PILGRIMS adopted this document, which resembled a church covenant, to create a civil government for PLYMOUTH. All 41 men who signed it became FREEMEN, whatever their religious status, even those who were servants.

Maysville road veto (Ky.) On 27 May 1830, Andrew JACKSON vetoed a bill sponsored by Henry CLAY subscribing $150,000 in US funds for stock in a company building a turnpike from Lexington to Maysville, Ky., an inland port on the Ohio River. Pointing out that since the project lay within one state and connected to no existing system of federal INTERNAL IMPROVEMENTS, Jackson argued that it was an unconstitutional use of federal funds. Although partly motivated by Jackson's animosity toward Clay, the veto was in the spirit of STRICT CONSTRUCTIONISM and the tradition of the veto of the BONUS BILL of 1817. The veto strengthened the principle that federal funds should only be used for interstate transportation projects or harbors serving foreign trade, not intrastate public works.

Meade, George G. (b. Cadiz, Spain, 31 December 1815; d. Philadelphia, Pa., 6 November 1872) Born of US diplomats abroad, Meade graduated 19th of 56 cadets from West Point in 1835. Although his prior military career had been as an engineer, Meade performed well leading combat troops in the CIVIL WAR. He took command of the Army of the POTOMAC two days before the battle of GETTYSBURG, but failed to exploit his victory with a vigorous pursuit that might have destroyed the Army of NORTHERN VIRGINIA Meade remained the Army of the Potomac's commander to the end of the war, but operated under Ulysses S. GRANT's direct supervision after March 1864.

Meaney, George (b. New York, N.Y., 16 August 1894; d. Washington, D.C., 11 January 1980) He began his career as a plumber at 16 and became a full-time union organizer in 1922. He became AFL secretary-treasurer in 1939 and its president in 1952. He was a major leader in the movement to rid organized labor of racketeering, corruption, and Communist influence. His leadership was critical in engineering the AFL–CIO merger and he was that body's president until he resigned on 15 November 1979. Meaney insisted that labor be actively involved in shaping national politics and promoting anticommunism abroad. He supported the domestic agenda of the Democratic Party's liberal wing, but blocked AFL–CIO endorsement of George MCGOVERN, whom he viewed as soft on communism, and was highly critical of Jimmy CARTER.

Meat Inspection Act (30 June 1906) Public outcry caused by *The JUNGLE* led to passage of this law, which provided for enforcing sanitation regulations at stockyards and meatpacking factories. It required federal inspection of all facilities that prepared meat for interstate shipment.

Mechanicsville, battle of (Va.) *see* PENINSULAR CAMPAIGN

Medicaid (30 July 1965) A program of the GREAT SOCIETY, Medicaid funded medical benefits for welfare recipients or disabled persons who were not entitled to MEDICARE. Established by amendments to the Social Security Act (*see* SOCIAL SECURITY ADMINISTRATION), it is administered by the states subject to federal guidelines on eligibility and benefits. Combined outlays on Medicaid and Medicare rose from 5 percent of federal spending in 1970 to 17 percent in 1994, when they stood at $120 billion.

Medicare (30 July 1965) A program of the GREAT SOCIETY, Medicare was the greatest expansion of benefits in the history of social security (*see* SOCIAL SECURITY ADMINISTRATION). It reimbursed most medical expenses for 19,000,000 persons over 65 and others receiving long-term Social Security benefits. Hospital desegregation was also mandated. It became effective on 1 July 1966. Costs greatly exceeded initial projections, especially from 1980 to 1992, when spending rose from $35 billion to $132 billion.

Medicine Lodge, treaty of (Kans.) On 28 October 1867, peace terms were signed by the major nations of the southern plains: COMANCHE, KIOWA, Southern CHEYENNE, and ARAPAHO INDIANS. The treaty extended to the southern Plains Indians the policy introduced by the 1st Treaty of FORT LARAMIE, namely that the Great Plains would no longer be an all-inclusive reservation (*see* RESERVATIONS), over which its original peoples would have unrestricted freedom to roam. Each tribe was instead assigned a separate territory south of Kans. and required to stay within it. The US pledged to supply schools and agricultural instruction as a means of weaning the Indians from their own culture. The treaty marked the start of a US policy to confine Plains Indians within reservations and hasten their assimilation into white society.

Mellon, Andrew William (b. Pittsburgh, Pa., 24 March 1855; d. Southampton, N.Y., 26 August 1937) A founder of the Gulf Corporation, Union Trust Company, and Aluminum Company of America, Mellon was treasury secretary for Warren HARDING, Calvin COOLIDGE, and Herbert HOOVER. He advocated higher tariffs, lower tax rates, and reduced federal spending to balance the budget and retire the NATIONAL DEBT. He favored cutting taxes on the rich rather than the middle class, because the wealthy would invest their money to expand business while the middle class would spend excess cash. Congress enacted much of his reduction program in the REVENUE ACTS OF THE 1920S. He balanced the budget every year and reduced the national debt by 32 percent from 1921 to 1930. He was ambassador to Britain (1932–3).

Melville, Herman (b. New York, N.Y., 1 August 1819; d. New York, N.Y., 28 September 1891) His education ended at the age of 15 and he lived as a sailor from 1837 to 1844. He published his first book, *Typee* – a sea adventure – in 1846. Although little known during his own life, Melville was later ranked among the Romantic era's leading novelists, and many critics consider his *Moby Dick* (1851) to be the greatest of all American novels. Other major works include *Omoo* (1847), *Mardi* (1849), *Redburn* (1849), *White-Jacket* (1850), and *Billy Budd* (1851).

Memorial Day massacre On 30 May 1937, at Chicago, police fired on CIO demonstrators at the Republic Steel Mills, which were the object of a unionization drive, and then charged to disperse the crowd with nightsticks. The police killed 10 strikers and injured 84. The violence shocked the country, but the strike failed.

Memphis riot (Tenn.) On 1 May 1866, fighting erupted after two black army veterans escaped from an attempted arrest. Over the next two days, white mobs of civilians and Irish police violently invaded black neighborhoods. Before the US Army intervened on 3 May, the riots had produced 46 black deaths, 2 white deaths, 75 other casualties, 100 robberies, 5 black women raped, and the burning of 91 homes, 12 schools, and 4 churches. The riot shocked northern public opinion, and influenced the mid-term elections, which left the Republicans controlling two-thirds of each house of Congress and able to override Andrew JOHNSON's vetoes.

Mencken, H(enry) L(ouis) (b. Baltimore, Md., 12 September 1880; d. Baltimore, Md., 29 January 1956) In 1899 Mencken began his journalistic career as a police reporter for the Baltimore *Morning Herald*. In 1906 he joined the Baltimore *Sun*, through which he attracted a national following in the 1920s for his reporting on events such as the SCOPES TRIAL. He became one of the country's leading social critics while editing the *Smart Set* magazine. Although renowned and feared for his barbed criticisms of hypocrisy, mediocrity, and narrow-mindedness in American life, he was generous in bestowing praise when deserved, and instinctively sympathized with the underdog. His monumental study, *The American Language* (1919), remains a classic.

Menominee Indians Speakers of one of the ALGONQUIAN LANGUAGES, the Menominee were closely related to the FOX INDIANS and cultivated wild rice in southern Wis. When first contacted by Europeans, they probably numbered 3,000. They fought no major wars with the US. In 1854 they ceded virtually all their lands in Wis. except for a reserve on the Wolf River, where most remained rather than be resettled west of the Mississippi. Congress terminated their tribal status with the US government in the 1950s, but restored it in 1974 after the nation suffered serious economic setbacks when it tried to exploit its timber resources.

mercantilism This was an economic philosophy that dominated European attitudes on international trade after 1600. Its primary goal was to increase national wealth through a favorable balance of trade, which would increase a country's stock of SPECIE. To accomplish that goal, countries promoted industries that made them economically self-sufficient by excluding foreign merchants, shipping, and products from their domestic market to the maximum extent possible through devices such as monopolies and tariffs. The NAVIGATION LAWS promoted mercantilist goals.

merchant marine By excluding foreign ships from the THIRTEEN COLONIES' trade, the NAVIGATION LAWS encouraged expansion of the Anglo-American merchant marine, which totaled about 448 vessels in 1700 and 1,830 in 1740. Most colonial shipping operated out of New England. By 1775, North Americans owned perhaps 2,500 vessels (with average carrying capacity of 80–160 tons), which amounted to a third of all the British Empire's shipping. The REVOLUTIONARY WAR caused the merchant marine to contract until 1789, when just 54 percent of US foreign trade was carried in American hulls. The US merchant marine revived in the 1790s, and by 1800 it had largely displaced foreign shippers and carried 85 percent of the country's foreign commerce.

The merchant marine experienced great disruption due to the EMBARGO ACT and a British blockade in the WAR OF 1812. After 1815, it experienced steady growth, but most of this expansion came from vessels employed in the coastal trade between American ports, not foreign commerce. From 1845 to 1860, the merchant marine again grew rapidly due to the rise of shipyards specializing in clipper ships (sail vessels that could reach China from Boston in 110 days or less). Its carrying capacity more than doubled over these 15 years to 5,354,000 tons; it almost displaced the British as the world's largest national fleet, and was acknowledged to possess the world's swiftest vessels.

When steam power replaced sail for ocean-going vessels, US shipyards found themselves at a competitive disadvantage to those in Europe, and the merchant marine steadily declined. US tonnage registered in the overseas trade shrank by 30 percent from 1865 to 1914. An enormous expansion of the merchant fleet occurred in WORLD WAR I, when the government allowed American-owned ships of foreign origin to be entered in the US registry for the first time, to carry exports no longer serviced by European shippers. Tonnage in the foreign trade rose over 900 percent to 11,077,000 tons from 1914 to 1921, and the US merchant marine ranked as the world's largest.

Recognition of the merchant marine's military value led to passage of the Shipping Act (7 September 1916), which created the United States Shipping Board to regulate and promote the national fleet's growth. The JONES ACT (1920) gave US shippers a monopoly over all trade between US ports. The collapse of international trade in the 1920s led to a steady and dramatic reduction in US shipping, and the MERCHANT MARINE ACT (1936) was passed as a national defense measure to reverse this trend; it also replaced the Shipping Board with a United States Maritime Commission. At a cost of $13,000,000,000, the Maritime Commission built 5,777 vessels (39,000,000 gross tons) in WORLD WAR II, and increased the merchant marine from 1,100 to 5,550 ships, despite losses in the battle of the ATLANTIC. During the war, 5,662 merchant sailors were killed at sea.

The merchant marine declined greatly after 1945, largely because federal regulations and union pay scales increasingly made it uncompetitive with foreign carriers. Its main function was to service the monopoly it still enjoyed over the US coastal trade. By 1993, it included just 348 active, US-flag oceangoing vessels, which employed less than 10,000 citizens as sailors. Federal subsidies to coastal shippers cost $215,000,000 in 1992.

Merchant Marine Act (1920) *see* JONES ACT

Merchant Marine Act (26 June 1936) This law revised the JONES ACT (1920) by replacing the United States Shipping Board with the United States Maritime Commission. The Maritime Commission would help expand the MERCHANT MARINE for war by encouraging US ship construction by subsidies to US flag carriers in the export trade. It temporarily helped maintain the merchant marine in the 1930s, but its subsidies later fostered inefficiency that crippled the competitiveness of US shippers. (In 1950, the responsibilities of the commission were divided between a Federal Maritime Board and Federal Maritime Administration.)

Mercury Space Program *see* APOLLO PROGRAM

Meredith, James Howard (b. Kosciusko, Miss., 25 June 1933) In early 1961 Meredith applied for admission (with third year standing) to the University of Mississippi, but was blocked from admission because he was black by Governor Ross Barnett, who declared himself registrar. A federal court ordered his admission in 1962. Meredith's appearance on campus sparked riots on 30 September, that resulted in two deaths, but the National Guard enrolled him on 1 October. He completed his B.A. degree under federal guard and graduated in September 1963. To encourage voter registration among blacks, he embarked on a solitary, 220-mile "pilgrimage" from Memphis to Jackson, Miss., on 5 June 1966, but was shot the next day. The STUDENT NONVIOLENT COORDINATING COMMITTEE and SOUTHERN CHRISTIAN LEADERSHIP CONFERENCE then took over the march. The episode drew nationwide attention to racial problems in Miss. and resulted in renewed civil-rights activism there. Meredith earned a law degree from Columbia University in 1968.

Mergenthaler, Ottmar (b. Hachtel, Germany, 11 May 1854; d. Baltimore, Md., 2[illegible] October 1899) Shortly after emigrating in 1872, Mergenthaler moved to Baltimore and began experimenting to improve the laborious process of setting printer's type by hand. On 26 August 1884, he patented the linotype, which eliminated manual typesetting by using a keyboard to cast a full line of print in one bar or slug from molten metal. By sharply cutting production costs and the time needed to print large runs of papers, this invention enabled editors to increase circulation by reducing each paper's cost and to increase the length of issues by adding extra news and features.

Meritor Savings Bank* v. *Vinson On 19 June 1986, the Supreme Court ruled (9–0) that Title VII of the CIVIL RIGHTS ACT (1964) is violated by sexual discrimination whenever a business allows employees of one sex to engage in unwelcome conduct of a sexual nature, so as to create a work environment that is hostile or abusive to the other sex. The Court clarified *Meritor* in *Harris* v. *Forklift Systems, Incorporated* (9 September 1993), when it ruled unanimously that in determining when sexual harassment has created a hostile workplace, it is only necessary to prove that a "reasonable person" would perceive the workplace as threatening or demeaning, and not necessary to show that the victim suffered emotional harm.

Merrill's Marauders The 5307th Composite Unit (provisional reinforced regiment) under Brigadier General Frank Merrill was the only US Army ground force to fight in WORLD WAR II's Burma theater. After 2[illegible] March 1944, it supported joint operations of the British and Nationalist Chinese armies by infiltrating enemy lines in an exhausting campaign to take Myitkyina air base, where the disease-ridden regiment was repulsed on 17 May. Redesignated Mars Force, it fought south to Mandalay under Brigadier General Daniel Sultan in 1945.

Mesquakie Indians *see* FOX INDIANS

Metacomet *see* KING PHILIP'S WAR

Methodist Church American Methodism originated as a revival movement within the Church of England in the mid-1700s, led by John Wesley. Wesley briefly visited the THIRTEEN COLONIES in the 1730s, but had little mpact. The first Methodist church was founded at New York on John Street in 1766. The faith spread primarily by lay preachers, many dispatched from England by Wesley. The first American Methodist conference was held in 1773. In 1784 the Methodist Episcopal Church was established as a separate episcopate, with Francis Asbury as the first bishop.

The church experienced the highest growth rate of any denomination in the late 1700s. Its membership rose from 2,073 in 1774 to 65,980 in 1792, largely because its itinerant preachers won so many converts among the frontier's unchurched pioneers. After the church condemned SLAVERY in 1784, it gained a sizeable black contingent that would later found the AFRICAN METHODIST EPISCOPAL CHURCH and the AFRICAN METHODIST EPISCOPAL ZION CHURCH. Schism occurred in 1792 when James O'Kelly led 10,000 members in founding the Republican Methodist Church.

In the early 19th century, membership doubled every decade. The number of Methodist pulpits rose from 2,700 in 1820 to 19,883 in 1860, when the denomination was the nation's largest and had almost as many congregations as the Baptists and Presbyterians combined. Schism produced the Methodist Protestant Church in 1830. A pro-ABOLITIONISM wing withdrew in 1840 to form the Wesleyan Methodist Church. The slavery controversy led in 1844 to a sectional division with the formation of the Methodist Episcopal Church, South.

The combined total of Methodist congregations stabilized at about 54,000 after 1900, while membership rose from 5,500,000 to 10,500,000. In 1939 the fellowship was reunited when the Methodist Protestant Church merged with the Methodist Episcopal Church's northern and southern divisions as the Methodist Church. In 1968 it merged with the Evangelical United Brethren Church to form the United Methodist Church. Membership in the United Methodist Church declined from 10,304,200 in 1965 to 8,979,100 (6.1 percent of all churchgoers) in 1990, when there were 37,514 congregations. (Another 4,250,000 Methodists worshiped in separate denominations, primarily in the African-American churches.)

Meuse-Argonne offensive (France) From 26 September to 11 November 1918, the Allied Expeditionary Force's First Army (1,200,000 troops in 22 divisions) engaged 47 German divisions in heavily defended terrain. The campaign served no important strategic purpose, and its horrendous casualty toll almost led to John PERSHING's relief from command. German losses: 26,000 prisoners, 3,000 machine guns, 847 artillery pieces. US losses: 117,000 killed, wounded.

Mexican border, US campaigns on (1) During the CIVIL WAR, France violated the MONROE DOCTRINE by occupying Mexico and installing Archduke Maximilian as its ruler. After the last surrender of CSA troops, the US ordered Major General Philip SHERIDAN to the Rio Grande with 50,000 troops, and on 12 February 1866 gave an ultimatum to France to withdraw. In 1867 French forces returned to Europe and Mexican patriots executed Maximilian in June.

(2) Between May 1873 and July 1877, the US Army fought Indians in Coahuila, Mexico: on 18 May 1873 at Remolino against KICKAPOO INDIANS, and on both 30 July 1876 and September 1877 near Zaragosa against Lipan APACHE INDIANS. On 3 April, September 1877, 19 and 21 June 1878, nonviolent confrontations occurred between US and Mexican troops. On 29 July 1882, the US and Mexico signed a treaty allowing pursuit of Indians across their border.

Mexican border, US invasion of Following the raid on COLUMBUS, N. Mex., Brigadier General John PERSHING led 15,000 US troops across the Rio Grande on 15 March 1916 to pursue Francisco "Pancho" Villa. US forces reached Parral, 400 miles into Mexico, skirmished often with the insurgents, and engaged the Mexican Army at Carrixal on 21 June 1917. President Woodrow WILSON eventually federalized 150,000 national guardsmen for duty along the border. Villa eluded Pershing, who left Mexico on 5 February 1917. Clashes with Mexican guerrillas took place near Buena Vista, Mexico, on 1 December 1917, in San Bernardino Canyon, Mexico, on 26 December 1917, near La Grulla, Tex., on 8–9 January 1918, at Pilgares, Mexico, on 28 March 1918, at Nogales, Ariz., on 27 August 1918, and near El Paso, Tex., on 15–16 June 1919.

Mexican immigration Colonization from Mexico was modest to 1848. The Spanish-speaking population of all territory acquired by the treaty of Guadalupe Hidalgo was 80,000, of which 75 percent was in N.Mex. and Ariz. By 1900, there were 433,000 persons of Mexican background in the US (including 103,000 foreign-born), 0.6 percent of the entire population and 8.0 percent of the southwest (Tex., N.Mex., Ariz., Calif., and Colo.). The Mexican-born population doubled by 1910. The Mexican Revolution of that year stimulated the first major wave of immigration: up to 10 percent of all Mexicans relocated to the US and about 1,000,000 stayed. The National Origins Act placed no limits on Mexican entrants. The Great Depression produced a counter-migration out of the US, but labor shortages in World War II led immigration to resume after 1942. The Bracero Program drew 4,750,000 seasonal workers, and an equal number may have entered as undocumented migrants by 1964.

Although fewer than 800,000 Mexicans legally declared themselves permanent residents during 1930–69, at least 5,800,000 former Mexican nationals were US residents by 1970 (2.8 percent of the US and 14.4 percent of the southwest). The Immigration Reform Act (1965) placed an annual cap of 20,000 on Mexican entrants. Because Anglo-American and Chicano employers both sought Mexicans as inexpensive labor, undocumented workers flooded into the southwest (generally without their families until the early 1980s). The Simpson–Mazolli Act failed to end this situation. An estimated 4,836,652 Mexicans came to the US by 1991 (3,236,667 during 1971–91), and 52 percent of all immigrants were Mexican in 1991. On the 1990 census, 11,165,939 Americans (4.5 percent) gave their primary ethnic ancestry as Mexican.

Mexican War In December 1845, Mexico rebuffed US diplomatic efforts to negotiate its claim that the Nueces River, not the Rio Grande, was Tex.'s southern boundary. On 13 January 1846, James Polk ordered Brigadier General Zachary Taylor's 3,550 US regulars to the Rio Grande. On 25 April, Mexican forces in Tex. attacked 60 US troops, all captured or killed. Congress declared war on 13 May.

Taylor's army drove Mexican forces from Tex. at Palo Alto and Resaca de la Palma in May, and decisively defeated the enemy in September at Monterrey. In February 1847, Taylor's victory at Buena Vista ended fighting in northern Mexico. Colonel Alexander Doniphan had meanwhile crushed Mexican resistance in the upper Rio Grande valley at El Brazito, Tex., and Sacramento, Mexico. Colonel Stephen Kearney had entered Santa Fe unopposed on 25 September 1846 and led a small US force to Calif., where a peaceful revolt by US citizens under Captain John C. Frémont (supported by a US naval squadron) had overthrown Mexican authority. After being defeated at San Pasqual, Kearney joined forces with Commodore Robert Stockton and entered Los Angeles after their victory at San Gabriel. On 13 January 1847, the last pro-Mexican force in Calif. capitulated to Frémont.

Major General Winfield Scott captured the port of Vera Cruz in March 1847 as a base to assault Mexico. After victories at Cerro Gordo and Contreras-Churubusco, he stormed Chapultepec fortress in September and entered the capital; serious fighting then ceased. On 2 February 1848, Mexico signed the treaty of Guadalupe Hidalgo. The last US soldier left Mexico on 1 August 1848.

Wartime mobilization increased the army from 8,509 to 47,319 and the navy-marine corps from 12,217 to 12,989. Total enlistments included 31,024 in the regular army, 73,532 state volunteers, and 548 marines. The Mexican army's strength grew from 32,000 to about 50,000. War expenses cost about $73,000,000, excluding the peace treaty. Battle casualties killed 935 regulars, 607 volunteers, and 9 marines; disease or accidents killed 5,818 regulars, 6,408 volunteers, and 3 marines. The death rate in the war, 13.2 percent of land forces, exceeded that of all other US conflicts after 1783.

Mexico, US intervention in After Mexican officials seized US sailors at Tampico on 9 April 1914, and then refused to make a humiliating apology as demanded by Admiral Henry Mayo, the US Atlantic fleet concentrated off Vera Cruz. On 21 April, Mayo bombarded the city and landed 600 marines and sailors to intercept a shipment of German arms for the Mexican army, and the next day Congress approved the use of military force in the crisis. During 28–30 April, Brigadier General Frederick Funston brought the US occupation force at Vera Cruz to 4,000 soldiers and 3,300 marines. US forces remained until 23 November 1914.

Miami Indians This nation, speakers of one of the ALGONQUIAN LANGUAGES, called themselves Twightwees and by 1760 included splinter groups known as Weas and Piankeshaws. By 1768, all three groups had over 4,000 members, including an estimated 950 warriors. Their villages lay along the Miami, Maumee, and Wabash rivers. They were French allies in the SEVEN YEARS' WAR. In PONTIAC'S WAR, Miamis captured FORT MIAMIS and Weas took FORT OUIATONON. They raided Ky. as British allies in the REVOLUTIONARY WAR. Little Turtle, a Miami, led resistance to Anglo-American expansion in the Ohio valley from 1788 to the battle of FALLEN TIMBERS. They gave up large tracts in Ohio by the first Treaty of GREENVILLE. In the WAR OF 1812, they were British allies. Most went to Kans. by 1827 and to Okla. in the 1850s.

Miami riot (Fla.) Sparked by the acquittal of four Hispanic and white police tried for beating a black motorist to death, rioting erupted in black neighborhoods on 17 May 1980 and continued for two days. By 20 May, 3,600 national guardsmen had been mobilized, 18 persons lay dead, 300 were seriously injured, and 1,267 arrests had been made. The riot ranked as the most destructive US civil disturbance to that date, with property damage of $100,000,000.

Michigan In 1668 Fr Jacques Marquette founded a mission at Sault Ste Marie, France's first outpost in Mich. The French also built Fort St Joseph (1679), Fort Detroit (1701) and Fort Michilimackinac (1712). The treaty of PARIS (1763) transferred the area to Britain. Much of PONTIAC'S WAR occurred there. Britain used Fort Detroit as its main staging ground for Indian raids on the US frontier during 1776–95 and its troops occupied Mich. until JAY'S TREATY.

On 11 January 1805, the US created Michigan Territory, which British troops captured in the WAR OF 1812 and occupied until 1813. Anglo-American settlement proceeded slowly while the US bought out Indian claims from 1813 to 1831, during which time population rose from under 5,000 to 31,639. Heavy in-migration occurred in the 1830s, and Mich. had 212,267 residents by 1840. It became the 26th state on 26 January 1837.

In 1860 Mich. had 749,113 inhabitants, of whom 99 percent were white and 20 percent were foreign-born; it ranked 15th among states in population, 15th in the value of its farmland and livestock, and 17th in manufactures. In the CIVIL WAR, it furnished 87,364 USA troops (including 1,387 blacks).

Lumbering, mining, and manufacturing became important after 1870. By 1900, Mich. had 2,420,982 residents, of whom 61 percent were rural, 99 percent were white, 22 percent were foreign-born; it ranked ninth among the states in population, 13th in the value of agricultural goods, and tenth in manufactures. Its economy experienced rapid growth from expanding automobile production, which Henry FORD pioneered, and during 1910–30, 1,014,800 new residents moved to Mich. Military production for WORLD WAR II attracted another 251,400 in the 1940s. Its economy slumped badly when foreign competition and manpower reductions buffeted the auto industry after 1970. In 1990 it had 9,295,297 inhabitants (82 percent white, 14 percent black, 2 percent Hispanic, 1 percent Indian, and 1 percent Asian), of whom 80 percent were urban and 3.8 percent foreign-born; manufacturing or mining employed 30 percent of its workers.

Micronesia, US Trust Territory of In WORLD WAR I, Japan occupied the German protectorate of the Caroline, Marshall, and Northern Mariana Islands. The LEAGUE OF NATIONS mandated them to Japan in 1919. In WORLD WAR II, US forces seized them in the battle of PELELIU, in the Carolines, and the MARIANA and MARSHALL ISLANDS CAMPAIGNS. On 2 April 1947, the UN created a Strategic Trust Territory of these archipelagos (Micronesia), controlled by the US. Bikini and Eniwetok, in the Marshalls, were used for hydrogen bomb testing. The navy administered Micronesia until 1951, when the Department of the Interior took over. The Commonwealth of Northern Marianas became a self-governing US territory and its residents were made US citizens on 3 November 1986. The Carolines were divided into Palau (western islands) and the Federated States of Micronesia (eastern islands). On 21 October 1986, the Federated States and the Marshalls became sovereign republics in free association with the US, which provided their defense and some financial aid; the two republics joined the UN in 1991. Palau rejected free association with the US; on 22 December 1990, it came under UN control when the US trusteeship was dissolved.

middle passage Refers to the trans-Atlantic voyage of ships in the slave trade. The term is derived from the fact that the trans-Atlantic voyage came between the march of war captives or other prisoners in slave coffles from Africa's inland regions to the coast, and the distribution of slaves among farms and plantations of the American hinterland after being sold. Unsanitary and crowded shipboard conditions produced heavy loss of life, but mortality rates declined from the 1600s, when perhaps 15 to 25 percent of slave cargoes died, to the late 1700s, when loss of life averaged closer to 10 percent. A like percentage of European sailors also died of diseases contracted from slaves during the middle passage. The middle passage to the thirteen colonies and the United States probably claimed the lives of 50,000 to 65,000 Africans.

midnight judges *see* Judiciary Act (1801)

Midway, battle of On 3–6 June 1942, US task forces under Rear Admiral Jack Fletcher (1 carrier, 2 cruisers, 5 destroyers, 60 planes) and Rear Admiral Raymond Spruance (2 carriers, 9 destroyers, 6 cruisers, 120 planes) – supported by 109 aircraft on the Midway Islands – intercepted Vice Admiral Chuichi Nagumo's carrier task force (4 carriers, 2 battleships, 2 cruisers, 12 transports with 25,000 soldiers, 272 planes). US losses: 1 carrier, 1 destroyer, 150 planes, 307 sailors. Japanese losses: 3 carriers sunk, 1 carrier damaged and scuttled, 1 cruiser, 253 planes, 3,500 sailors dead and wounded. Midway was the turning point in the war against Japan, because the loss of four carriers crippled the Imperial Navy's offensive capability before it could destroy the US fleet.

Midway Islands On 5 July 1859, Captain N. C. Brooks of the *Gambia* discovered the two islands and claimed them for the US. On 28 August 1867, Captain William Reynolds of the USS *Lackawanna* occupied the atoll for the US. The navy established a way station there, which the Japanese failed to take at the battle of Midway. The navy administers the islands as a restricted Naval Defense Sea Area.

military-industrial complex Dwight D. Eisenhower's farewell address (18 January 1961) warned against "the acquisition of unwarranted influence, whether sought or unsought, by the military-industrial complex." Since then, the term has referred to the linkage between the military and the arms industry, especially regarding the appearance of cooperation to expand the defense budget.

militia This refers to an armed force of civilians organized and trained to fight as soldiers in an emergency. Every colony but Pa. established a militia, in which all males aged 16–45 were liable for duty. The militia fought all colonial conflicts until the Seven Years' War, when campaigning was done by specially raised regiments of provincial volunteers. In the Revolutionary War, militia served as reserves for the Continental army and as a police force to root out Tories. The Second Amendment guaranteed the states' right to maintain a militia and the Militia Act (8 May 1792) prescribed its organization. *Martin v. Mott* affirmed the president's authority over militia in wartime. The militia provided most US troops in the War of 1812, but not during the Mexican and Civil wars, when volunteer units were raised to reinforce the regulars (although militia performed significant services in the border states between 1861 and 1865). After 1870 militias were reorganized as the National Guard, and by 1896, only three states designated their state forces as militia. The Dick Act (21 January 1903) replaced the Militia Act (1792) and reconstituted all state forces as the National Guard, although the US Army's Militia Bureau was not renamed the National Guard Bureau until 1933.

Mill Springs, battle of (Ky.) On 19 January 1862, Brigadier General George THOMAS's 4,000 Federals defeated Major General George Crittenden's 4,000 Confederates. USA losses: 39 killed, 207 wounded. CSA losses: 125 killed, 309 wounded, 99 missing, 12 cannon, 150 wagons, 1,000 horses and mules. Defeat forced CSA forces to retreat into Tenn. and established USA military control over central Ky.

Millay, Edna St Vincent (b. Rockland, N.Y., 22 February 1892; d. Austerlitz, N.Y., 19 October 1950) She composed her first lengthy poem, "Renascence," when she was 19, and received much critical praise when it appeared in a prize anthology, *The Lyric Year* (1912). After an education at Barnard and Vassar, she joined Greenwich Village's bohemian culture and wrote verse in support of various political issues, such as the antiwar cause, the SACCO AND VANZETTI TRIAL, and equality for women. She received the Pulitzer prize for poetry in 1923. To encourage US support for Britain and France against nazism, she wrote *There Are No Islands Any More* (1940). Other works include *Buck in the Snow* (1928), *Fatal Interview* (1931), *Huntsman, What Quarry?* (1939), and *Collected Sonnets* (1941).

Miller, Arthur (b. New York, N.Y., 7 October 1917) A University of Michigan B.A. (1938), Miller had his first Broadway play, *The Man Who Had All the Luck*, produced in 1944, followed by *All My Sons* (1947). His *Death of a Salesman* (1949) won a Pulitzer prize and gained him international acclaim. He wrote *The Crucible* (1953) as an allegorical condemnation of MCCARTHYISM, and was himself convicted for contempt of Congress after refusing to name persons he knew to sympathize with the COMMUNIST PARTY (his sentence was overturned on appeal). He later wrote *A View from the Bridge* (1955), *The Fall* (1964), *Incident at Vichy* (1964), and *The Price* (1968). Miller was the late 20th century's greatest US playwright.

Miller–Tydings Act (18 August 1937) This statute, part of the LITTLE NIRA, restored certain exemptions from federal antitrust laws no longer applicable after the NATIONAL INDUSTRIAL RECOVERY ACT (NIRA) was ruled unconstitutional. It legalized "fair trade" laws that allowed producers to set minimum resale prices for their goods, so long as the resale agreements were not part of a conspiracy to fix prices with competitors. The law was intended to keep business profits of manufacturers and retailers at reasonable levels by reducing cut-throat competition.

Miller* v. *California On 21 June 1973, the Supreme Court (5–4) amended the definition of pornography prevailing since *ROTH* v. *UNITED STATES*. The Court ruled that the FIRST AMENDMENT did not prevent states from regulating obscenity, which was defined as material offensive to an average person according to his community's standards, that portrays sexual activity in a lewd manner devoid of any serious merit as literary, dramatic, artistic, or political expression. The decision marked the first time since *Roth* that the Court agreed how to define pornography, and it allowed states to enact more effective legislation to restrict offensive material.

Milliken* v. *Bradley On 25 July 1974, the Supreme Court ruled (5–4) that federal judges cannot order a school desegregation plan that requires busing between suburban and inner-city communities to end isolation of minority pupils, unless all districts bore actual responsibility for the problem of racial separation in education. (*See KEYES* v. *DENVER SCHOOL DISTRICT NUMBER 1*.)

Minersville School District* v. *Gobitis *see WEST VIRGINIA STATE BOARD OF EDUCATION* v. *BARNETTE*

Mingo Indians These were mainly SENECA INDIANS who migrated to the Ohio River after 1750. The murder of several Mingos precipitated Lord DUNMORE'S WAR. They did not establish a separate tribal identity.

minimum wage The minimum wage is the lowest hourly rate required by law for full-time, gainful employment. Mass. legislated the first US minimum wage in 1912. The Supreme Court struck down state minimum-wage laws as price-fixing schemes in *ADKINS* v. *CHILDREN'S HOSPITAL* (1923), but reversed itself in *WEST COAST HOTEL COMPANY* v. *PARRISH* (1937). Federal minimum-wage legislation began with the FAIR LABOR STANDARDS ACT, and subsequent increases have been legislated as amendments to that law. The minimum wage started at $0.25 an hour in 1938, rose to $0.75 in 1950, $2.00 in 1974, $2.30 in 1976, and $3.35 by 1981. In 1989 legislation prescribed raises to $3.80 in April 1990 and $4.25 in April 1991, and also broadened its coverage.

Minnesota In 1686 the French built the first white settlement in Minn. at Fort St Antoine, on Lake Pepin. The French only used the area as a source of furs and transferred possession of its eastern portion to Britain by the treaty of PARIS (1763). The US acquired the remainder by the LOUISIANA PURCHASE. In 1819 the US built Fort Snelling (near St Paul). Large-scale Anglo-American settlement began after the first major land cession by Indians in 1837. Minnesota Territory was created on 3 March 1849, and its population skyrocketed from 6,077 in 1850 to 172,023 a decade later. In 1860 it ranked 30th among states in poulation, 30th in the value of its farmland and livestock, and 31st in manufactures; 34 percent of its people were foreign-born.

Minn. became the 32nd state on 11 May 1858. During the CIVIL WAR, it sent 24,020 men (including 104 blacks) to the USA Army. In 1862, the first SIOUX WAR temporarily threw back the frontier. Wheat became the state's main export in the 1860s, lumbering flourished in north Minn. from 1870 to 1900, and iron mines became the main US source of that metal between 1884 and 1911. In 1900, Minn. had 1,751,394 residents, of whom 66 percent were rural, 99 percent were white, and 29 percent were foreign-born; it ranked 19th among the states in population, 11th in the value of its agricultural products and 13th in manufactures. By 1990, Minn. had 4,375,099 inhabitants (94 percent white, 2 percent black, 2 percent Asian, 1 percent Hispanic, 1 percent Indian), of whom 68 percent were urban and 2.6 percent were foreign-born. Manufacturing and mining employed 23 percent of workers.

Minor* v. *Happersett On 29 March 1875, the Supreme Court ruled unanimously that the FOURTEENTH AMENDMENT did not require states to let women vote and declared, "the Constitution does not confer the right of suffrage on anyone."

Minuit, Peter (b. Wessel on Rhine, Cleves, ca. 1580; d. while crossing the Atlantic, June 1638) On 4 May 1626, Minuit arrived at Manhattan Island, where he built a fort and founded NEW AMSTERDAM (later New York City). Named NEW NETHERLAND'S director-general (governor) in September 1626, Minuit served until 1631, when the DUTCH WEST INDIA COMPANY recalled him for having allowed the colonists to compete with the company in the FUR TRADE. Minuit went to Sweden, where he helped organize the company that founded NEW SWEDEN. He led the earliest Swedish colonizing expedition and founded Fort Christina at modern Wilmington in 1638. He died at sea returning to Sweden.

Minutemen Beginning in September 1774 certain regiments of Mass. militia began reorganizing themselves by forming a third of their best men into companies that could be assembled at a minute's notice. The Mass. provincial congress ordered all regiments to adopt the system on 26 October. It was Minutemen who fought at the battles of CONCORD and LEXINGTON. On 18 July 1775, the CONTINENTAL CONGRESS recommended that all states adopt the system and Conn., N.H., Md., and N.C. complied.

Miranda* v. *Arizona On 13 June 1966, the Supreme Court extended *ESCOBEDO* V. *ILLINOIS* by ruling that DUE PROCESS obliges police to tell suspects that they may remain silent, that any statements made can thereafter be used against them in court, and that they can consult an attorney, before any interrogation may begin. If police fail to apprise suspects fully of these privileges, then any confession obtained through questioning is inadmissible as evidence in court. Local police agencies experienced many problems incorporating a "Miranda rights" warning into their procedures for apprehending suspects, due to confusion over what constituted full notification, and the decision became extremely controversial regarding the question whether it protected the innocent or shielded the guilty. The Court clarified *Miranda* in other cases, particularly *EDWARDS* V. *ARIZONA*.

miscegenation This term refers to the production of racially-mixed offspring in or outside of marriage. (*See* SEGREGATION *and* *LOVING* V. *VIRGINIA*)

missile gap In the late 1950s, Democrats alleged that Dwight D. EISENHOWER'S tigh military budgets had allowed the USSR to exceed the US in missile production. The U-2 AFFAIR resulted from US attempts to establish Soviet offensive capability by reconnaissance flights over the USSR. After charging in the 1960 election that the Republican Party had endangered national security, John F. KENNEDY discovered as president that no such weapons gap existed.

Missionary Ridge, battle of (Tenn.) *see* CHATTANOOGA, BATTLES FOR

missions *see* CALIFORNIA MISSIONS, FLORIDA MISSIONS, PRAYING TOWNS

Mississippi In 1716, at modern Natchez, the French built Fort Rosalie, the first permanent white settlement in Miss. and the scene of the NATCHEZ WAR. Miss. was acquired by Britain in 1763 and by the US in 1783. On 7 April 1798, Congress created Mississippi Territory, which included Ala. When Miss. entered the Union on 10 December 1817, as the 20th state, the CHOCTAW and CHICKASAW INDIANS held about two-thirds of the state. After the Indians sold their last lands in 1832 and went to Okla., settlement accelerated rapidly.

By 1860, when Miss. grew 25 percent of all US cotton, it had 791,305 people, of whom 55 percent were slaves and 1 percent were foreign-born; it ranked 14th among states in population, 10th in the value of its farmland and livestock, and 28th in manufactures. Miss. became the third CSA state on 9 January 1861. In the CIVIL WAR, it furnished 78,000 CSA troops and 18,414 USA soldiers (545 white and 17,869 black). Miss. was the site of 772 military actions, more than all but three other states (Va., Tenn., and Mo.).

In July 1865, Andrew JOHNSON instituted a provisional civilian government, which abolished slavery, but refused to let FREEDMEN vote, enacted a severe black code (*see* BLACK CODES), and rejected the THIRTEENTH and FOURTEENTH AMENDMENTS. Washington imposed military rule in March 1867, but restored self-government and congressional representation on 23 February 1870. Republican control ended five-and-a-half years later on 3 November 1875. Miss. disfranchised most blacks in 1890 and later erected a strict system of SEGREGATION.

In 1900 it was the 20th largest state and had 1,551,270 people, of whom 92 percent were rural, 59 percent were black, and 1 percent were foreign-born; it ranked 18th among states in the value of its agricultural goods and 39th in manufactures. From 1920 to 1970, it lost 1,324,900 out-migrants, mostly blacks moving to northern cities, and the racial composition shifted greatly.

During the CIVIL RIGHTS MOVEMENT, Governor Ross Barnett's refusal to permit James MEREDITH to enroll at the University of Mississippi led to massive violence there in 1962. State and local officials long resisted federal court orders to implement provisions of the various CIVIL RIGHTS ACTS. Desegregation of state colleges proceeded slowly, and in 1992, while ruling upon *Ayers* v. *Fordice*, the Supreme Court held that Miss. had not yet eliminated the vestiges of racial separation in higher education, and ordered it to devise a workable plan to achieve integration.

Miss. ranked as the 31st largest state in 1990, when its population was 2,573,216 (63 percent white, 35 percent black, 1 percent Hispanic, 1 percent Asian), of whom 30 percent were urban and 0.8 percent were foreign-born. Manufacturing and mining employed 30 percent of the work force.

Mississippi flood of 1927 In the spring of 1927, heavy rains produced the most disruptive natural disaster of the 1920s. The Mississippi River flooded its entire length up to widths of 40 miles; it ruined spring planting and left 600,000 homeless. Herbert HOOVER directed federal–state relief efforts that found shelter, food, and medical care for 325,000 persons. Hoover's efforts received high praise for their effectiveness, capped his reputation as the nation's most capable administrator, and helped him win the presidency in 1928.

Mississippi Freedom Democratic Party This party was organized to demand full political representation for blacks within the state Democratic party. In 1964 it challenged the regular party's credentials at the Democratic national convention and received two seats as special delegates. At the 1968 convention, it allied with liberal whites under the title Loyal Democrats of Mississippi and denied that the regular delegation could fairly represent the state because of pervasive discrimination against black voters. The convention then denied the regular delegation its credentials and seated the Loyal Democrats. The episode forced the state Democratic Party to accept black participation.

Mississippi* v. *Johnson In 1867 the Supreme Court rebuffed a request from Miss. for an injunction barring President Andrew JOHNSON from enforcing the RECONSTRUCTION laws passed in 1867. The Court ruled unanimously that to ensure a proper balance of powers between departments of the US government, the federal courts must refrain from interfering with purely political issues or with routine executive actions to enforce congressional laws. The Court also dismissed *Georgia* v. *Stanton*, a companion suit attempting to block the secretary of war from implementing these same laws.

Mississippian Culture *see* MOUND BUILDERS CULTURE

Missouri In 1735 the French built the first white settlement at St Genevieve, where they mined lead and traded furs. In 1764 they founded St Louis. Anglo-Americans began settling in Mo. during the 1790s and the US acquired it by the LOUISIANA PURCHASE. Mo. became a territory on 4 June 1812 and the 24th state by virtue of the MISSOURI COMPROMISE on 10 August 1821. It was occupied without serious Indian hostilities. Its rural areas were settled from Ky., Tenn., and Va., while Germans and Irish predominated in St Louis.

In 1860 it had 1,182,012 inhabitants, of whom 11 percent were slaves and 14 percent foreign-born; it ranked eighth among states in population, ninth in the value of its farmland and livestock, and 11th in manufactures. Although it never voted a formal act of SECESSION, it was recognized by the CONFEDERACY as the 12th CSA state. It furnished 108,960 USA troops (100,616 white and 8,344 black) and 20,000 CSA soldiers. It was the site of 1,162 military actions, more than all but two other states (Va. and Tenn.).

The constitutional convention of 1864 ended slavery and barred ex-Confederates from office by strict oaths (*see* TEST OATH CASES), but disfranchised FREEDMEN until the FIFTEENTH AMENDMENT. Democrats again were the majority political party by 1870. They rewrote the constitution to their advantage in 1875 and dominated Mo. until long after 1900. Racial SEGREGATION was the norm until the 1950s.

By 1900, Mo. had 3,106,665 residents, of whom 64 percent were rural, 5 percent black, and 7 percent foreign-born; it ranked fifth among the states in population, sixth in the value of its agricultural products, and seventh in the value of its manufactured goods. Although its economy became increasingly diversified and urbanized, Mo. experienced a net out-migration of approximately 742,000 persons during 1900–50. In 1990 it was the 15th largest state and had 5,117,073 inhabitants (87 percent white, 11 percent black, 1 percent Hispanic, 1 percent Asian), of whom 66 percent were urban and 1.6 percent were foreign-born. Manufacturing and mining employed 25 percent of workers.

Missouri Compromise When Mo. requested admission as a slave state, the House voted in February 1819 that statehood be delayed until it voted to end SLAVERY by a definite date, but the Senate rejected this condition. The issue alarmed the South since representatives of slave states were a minority in the House, but composed half the Senate; if slave territories were denied statehood, then southern interests would be outvoted in both houses. Congress compromised on 2 March 1820 by (1) admitting Mo. as a slave state simultaneously with Maine as a free state, and (2) banning slavery in any territory organized north of a line drawn west from the Mo.–Ark. border. This measure began the practice of preserving the Senate's equal balance by admitting a slave and a free territory to statehood together. The KANSAS–NEBRASKA ACT repealed its ban on slavery north of 36°30′, and *DRED SCOTT* v. *SANDFORD* ruled it unconstitutional.

Missouri ex rel. Gaines* v. *Canada On 12 December 1938, the Supreme Court ruled (7–2) that states could not enforce SEGREGATION in schools unless each race enjoyed equal facilities; it ordered Mo. to enroll a black student at the state university's law school to remedy the lack of separate legal training for his race, and denied that the state's offer to pay the student's expenses at an out-of-state law program justified his exclusion from a segregated law school. On 5 June 1950, the Court clarified this issue further in *Sweatt* v. *Painter*, when it ruled unanimously that in states where separate law schools existed for whites and blacks, blacks could not be restricted to the segregated institution if its facilities were inferior to those provided for whites.

Missouri* v. *Holland On 19 April 1920, the Supreme Court ruled on whether the Migratory Bird Treaty (1918) violated the TENTH AMENDMENT by directing Congress to legislate in areas reserved for state governments. Extending its decision in *GEOFROY* V. *RIGGS*, the Court held (7–2) that because treaties are sanctioned by the collective authority of the US – and not merely the CONSTITUTION – they might confer powers on Congress beyond those expressly warranted in the Constitution – although presumably no treaty could allow any branch of government to transgress specific constitutional prohibitions or fundamental rights.

Mitchell, John Newton (b. Detroit, Mich., 5 September 1913; d. Washington, D.C., 9 November 1988) A finance lawyer in New York, Mitchell became Richard NIXON's law partner in 1967 and his campaign manager in 1968. He served as ATTORNEY GENERAL from 1969 until resigning in February 1972 to manage Nixon's reelection campaign, during which he became involved in the WATERGATE SCANDAL. He became the first US attorney general sentenced to prison on 21 February 1975, when he was given eight years for conspiracy to obstruct justice, obstruction of justice, and three counts of perjury.

Mitchell, William ("Billy") Lendrum (b. Nice, France, 29 December 1879; d. New York, N.Y., 19 February 1936) He enlisted in the SPANISH-AMERICAN WAR and remained in the army as a career officer. After directing air warfare operations in WORLD WAR I, he took command of army aviation forces in 1919. He became the military's foremost advocate of strategic air power and was the first person to expose the vulnerability of navy ships to air attack. Resenting his tactless aspersions on their competence, Mitchell's superiors had him court-martialed in 1925 for insubordination. He left the army in 1926, and died before WORLD WAR II proved his vision of air warfare to be entirely accurate.

Mobile Bay, battle of (Ala.) On 5 August 1864, Rear Admiral David Farragut's USA fleet (14 wooden ships and 4 ironclads) defeated Admiral Franklin Buchanan's CSA fleet (3 wooden ships and 1 ironclad). USA losses: 319 casualties, 1 ship. CSA losses: 312 casualties, 1 ironclad. The victory closed the bay to CSA blockade runners, but CSA forces held Mobile's forts until 12 April 1865.

Model Cities Act *see* DEMONSTRATION CITIES AND METROPOLITAN DEVELOPMENT ACT

Modoc Indians The Modocs are a Sahaptin-speaking group that lived along the Oreg.–Calif. border and were closely related to the Klamath nation. They acquired the horse and guns after 1835, and became increasingly aggressive toward other Indians. By a treaty of 1864, they agreed to join the Klamaths on a reservation in Oreg. When relations between the two groups grew strained, several Modoc bands returned to their former lands and precipitated the MODOC WAR. In 1961 federal supervision was ended over the Modoc-Klamath reservation and its 2,133 inhabitants.

Modoc War In 1869 the Modocs left their Oreg. reservation. When Brigadier General Edward Canby tried to return 30 families under Captain Jack on 29 November 1872, violence erupted and the Indians retreated to northern Calif.'s lava beds. On 11 April 1873 (Good Friday), Captain Jack murdered Canby and two civilians at a peace conference. Fighting ceased on 3 June when Modoc scouts captured Captain Jack, and subsequently 155 Modocs were sent to Okla. US losses: 37 soldiers killed and 50 wounded, 18 civilians killed and 2 wounded. Modoc losses: 11 killed, 4 hanged, and 2 wounded.

Mogollon Culture This culture developed in southwestern N.Mex. and southeastern Ariz.; it was the first Indian society to structure life around agriculture, permanent buildings, pottery-firing, basket-weaving, and fabric-making. Between 300 BC and AD 300, villages became fixed around farming sites, although a substantial portion of the food supply continued to come from hunting and gathering. The people lived in pit-houses and primarily grew corn, beans, and squash. This society merged into the ANASAZI CULTURE after 1200.

Mohawk Indians As the easternmost of the FIVE NATIONS, just west of the Hudson River, Mohawks were the most exposed to attacks by the French and their Algonquian allies during the colonial wars. By 1770, they numbered just 400 in two major villages west of Schenectady, N.Y. They had sold most of their former land claims, and were adopting white customs in agriculture and becoming Christians. Through the influence of Joseph BRANT and Sir William JOHNSON, they supported Britain in the REVOLUTIONARY WAR and moved to Canada.

Mohegan Indians *see* MOHICAN INDIANS

Mohican Indians This group, speakers of one of the ALGONQUIAN LANGUAGES, were a faction of the PEQUOT INDIANS who seceded in 1637 under Uncas, numbered 2,000, and resumed a variant of their ancestral name of MAHICAN INDIANS. They were English allies in the PEQUOT WAR and then absorbed many of their defeated kinsmen. Most Mohicans sold their Connecticut valley lands and moved to N.Y. They were English allies in KING PHILIP'S WAR. Disease and intertribal wars cut their numbers from 2,400 in 1643 to 750 by 1705, and 206 by 1774. A remnant has mixed with Pequots and keeps reservations at Ledyard and Trumbull, Conn.

Molasses Act (17 May 1733) After being lobbied by West Indian sugar planters, eager to monopolize the market for selling molasses to the THIRTEEN COLONIES' rum distillers, Parliament placed a six-pence duty per gallon of foreign molasses entering the British colonies. Since the tax was too high to be passed on to consumers, merchants normally bribed customs officers up to one penny not to enforce the law. The SUGAR ACT replaced this act in 1764.

Moley, Raymond (b. Berea, Ohio, 27 September 1886; d. Phoenix, Ariz., 18 February 1975) He was one of the original BRAINS TRUST trio. As assistant secretary of state, he was a major influence on the first NEW DEAL; he also was the main ghostwriter for Franklin D. ROOSEVELT until 1935, when he became alienated because the president failed to support his initiatives on international currency reform. He broke with Roosevelt over the COURT-PACKING BILL and opposed his reelection in 1940.

Molly Maguires This group was an Irish secret society of eastern Pa. railway workers who were prevented from unionizing and retaliated against the Philadelphia and Reading Railroad with property damage and assassinations. After the society was penetrated by a Pinkerton detective, 24 members were convicted of various crimes in the autumn of 1875, and ten of them were hanged for murder.

Mondale, Walter Frederick ("Fritz") (b. Ceylon, Minn., 5 January 1928) He entered Minn. politics in 1948 with the FARMER-LABOR PARTY, and became a protégé of Hubert HUMPHREY. He assumed Humphrey's Senate seat in 1964 and held it until 1976, then became Jimmy CARTER's running mate, and was vice-president (1977–81). He was Democratic candidate for president in 1984, but polled only 41.6 percent of the ballots and lost every state but his own. He was named ambassador to Japan in 1993.

money trust By 1912 charges emerged that a money trust (*see* TRUSTS) was evolving to monopolize credit, caused by the tendency for small banks to deposit surplus funds with larger banks, which in turn deposited their surpluses with a few large financial houses in New York City. Because capital flowed to Wall Street, its largest institutions allegedly exercised undue economic influence by consolidating smaller banks, trust companies, and insurance firms by purchase or by holding companies. The major financial houses were also buying large stock positions that enabled them to become directors on the boards of many industrial corporations, railways, and utilities. After the PUJO HEARINGS and Louis BRANDEIS's articles, "Other People's Money and How They Use It," concern over the money trust was a major factor in establishing the FEDERAL RESERVE SYSTEM.

monitor Designed by John ERICSSON for use in the CIVIL WAR by the US Navy, it was a shallow-draught, steam-powered, IRONCLAD ship firing one or two cannon from a circular, revolving turret.

***Monitor*, USS, v. CSS "*Merrimack*"** On 8 March 1862, at Hampton Roads, Va., Commodore Franklin Buchanan and 350 sailors of the 10-gun CSS *Virginia* (commonly termed the *Merrimack*, because it was formerly a USA ship by that name) engaged five USA warships (219 guns) and sank two and captured one (the US Navy's greatest single-day loss of ships before PEARL HARBOR). On 9 March, after a two-hour duel, Lieutenant Lorimer Worden and 58 sailors of the USS *Monitor* forced the *Merrimack* back to harbor. This fight was naval history's first battle of ironbuilt, steam-powered warships. The *Merrimack* remained in harbor until 9 May, when she was scuttled upon Norfolk's evacuation. The *Monitor* sank off Cape Hatteras on 31 December 1862.

Monmouth Courthouse, battle of (N.J.) On 28 June 1778, General George WASHINGTON's 13,000 troops fought General Henry CLINTON's 10,000 British to a standstill. That night, while the Americans slept on their arms expecting to renew hostilities the next day, Clinton retreated to New York. American casualties: 106 killed, 161 wounded, 58 missing. British losses: 251 killed, 170 wounded, 64 missing. (By 6 July, about 160 British and 440 HESSIAN deserters had entered American lines.) Monmouth was the first instance when Americans beat the British by virtue of battlefield proficiency rather than superiority of numbers. It was the last major battle fought in the northern states.

monopolies *see* TRUSTS

Monroe, James (b. Westmoreland County, Va., 28 April 1758; d. New York, N.Y., 4 July 1831) He fought in the REVOLUTIONARY WAR and was wounded at TRENTON. He read law under Thomas JEFFERSON, sat in the Va. legislature in 1782, served in Congress (1783–6), supported the ANTIFEDERALISTS at the Va. ratifying convention, served as US senator (1790–4), acted as ambassador to France (1794–6), held office as Va. governor (1799–1800 and 1811), assisted the LOUISIANA PURCHASE negotiations, served as minister to Britain (1803–6), and was secretary of state (1811–17, except while secretary of war in 1814–15). He triumphed in the 1816 election for president over Rufus KING and won reelection in 1820 without opposition. (A single elector cast a vote for John Q. ADAMS, however.) The ERA OF GOOD FEELINGS mainly reflected his personal popularity. His major accomplishment was the MONROE DOCTRINE.

Monroe Doctrine Acting on concern that Spain would reassert control over the republics of its former Latin-American colonies, James MONROE proclaimed on 2 December 1823 that the US would consider it a hostile act for any European power either to colonize any independent nation in the western hemisphere or to extend monarchy to the Americas, but that the US would respect existing European colonies. When promulgated, the policy was viewed as meaningless, since it was understood that the Royal Navy would prevent recolonization to protect British markets in South America. It was first termed the Monroe Doctrine in 1852. The doctrine served as a pretext for threatening war in the VENEZUELA BOUNDARY DISPUTE. It was amended by the ROOSEVELT COROLLARY and LODGE COROLLARY.

Montana The US acquired Mont. by the LOUISIANA PURCHASE. In 1829 the American Fur Co. built Fort Union (abandoned 1866) on the Missouri River and the first steamboat reached the post in 1833. When the FUR TRADE declined, nearly all whites abandoned Mont. Large-scale Anglo-American settlement began in 1862, when gold was discovered, and Mont. became a territory on 26 May 1864. By 1870, its population was 20,595. In the next decade, about $10,000,000 in gold flowed out of Mont. each year. The second SIOUX WAR was sparked by the BOZEMAN TRAIL's construction to the Virginia City, Mont., gold fields. Much of the third SIOUX WAR was fought in Mont., including the battle of the LITTLE BIG HORN. The NEZ PERCE CAMPAIGN ended in the territory.

Mont. was part of the CATTLE KINGDOM, but mining dominated its economy, and by 1887 it was the leading US copper producer. Rapid development came after two TRANSCONTINENTAL RAILROADS crossed the territory in the late 1880s. Mont. became the 41st state on 8 November 1889. In 1900 it had 243,329 residents (93 percent white, 5 percent Indian, 1 percent Japanese, 0.5 percent Chinese, and 0.5 percent black), of whom 65 percent were rural and 28 percent were foreign-born; it ranked 43rd in population, 37th in the value of its agricultural products, and 34th in manufactures. The CAREY and NATIONAL RECLAMATION ACTS promoted farming irrigation projects. Petroleum and coal extraction have diversified the state's economy, as have tourism and urbanization. By 1950, most residents were nonagricultural. In 1990 Mont. had 799,065 inhabitants (92 percent white, 6 percent Indian, 2 percent Hispanic), of whom 24 percent were urban and 1.7 percent were foreign-born. Manufacturing employed 8 percent of workers and mining 7 percent.

Monterey incident (Calif.) When Commodore Thomas ap Catesby Jones heard a rumor of war between the US and Mexico, he rushed his navy squadron from Callao, Peru, to Monterey. After a bloodless seizure of the town on 19–20 October 1842, Jones learned that his information was false and retired to sea. He was officially reprimanded with a transfer to another assignment, but was secretly praised by the secretary of the navy. He took command of the Pacific Squadron in 1847 during the MEXICAN WAR.

Monterey, battle of (Mexico) On 21 September 1846, Brigadier General Zachary TAYLOR's 6,000 US regulars and state volunteers attacked General Pedro de Ampudia's 9,000 Mexicans. On 24 September, trapped in the city center, Ampudia offered to surrender the city if allowed to leave under arms, protected by an eight-week armistice; and Taylor accepted this. US losses: 120 killed, 368 wounded. Mexican losses: 367 killed, wounded. The battle ended major fighting in northern Mexico for five months.

Montgomery bus boycott (Ala.) When a black woman, Rosa Parks, was arrested for sitting in the white section of a bus on 1 December 1955, Rev. Martin Luther KING mobilized the black community to boycott public transportation until segregated seating was ended. Influenced by a 65 percent drop in revenue over 381 days, the bus company integrated its seating on 21 December 1956. The boycott was the first major instance of black activism during the CIVIL RIGHTS MOVEMENT and marked the beginning of King's rise as a civil rights leader.

Montreal, battles of (1) On 8 September 1760, Governor Philippe de Vaudreuil surrendered Montreal's garrison (2,500 troops) to General Jeffery AMHERST's army of 15,000 men after a one-day siege, and ordered all French military resistance to cease in Canada.

(2) On 25 September 1775, Governor Guy Carleton's 235 British defeated an attack by Colonel Ethan ALLEN's 200 US troops and captured 40 men, including Allen. On 11 November 1775, Montreal's British garrison (150 men) evacuated the city to avoid capture by Major General Richard Montgomery's US forces. Montgomery occupied the city on 13 November and it remained in US hands until 9 June 1776.

Moody, Dwight Lyman (b. Northfield, Mass., 5 February 1837; d. Northfield, Mass., 22 December 1899) A Congregationalist (*see* CONGREGATIONAL CHURCH) with no formal theological training, Moody became the GILDED AGE's most influential evangelist. He began preaching as a non-denominational lay revivalist after 1865, and achieved international renown by drawing 2,500,000 listeners on his 1873–5 tour of the British Isles. With his chorister, Ira Sankey, he set the premier example of commitment to the spiritual needs of the urban poor, and inspired many Protestant churches to establish missions and settlement houses in the slums. He founded the Moody Bible Institute at Chicago in 1886 and retired from preaching in 1892.

Moore* v. *Dempsey On 19 February 1923, the Supreme Court held (6–2) that the SIXTH AMENDMENT demands that a defendant be tried by a court whose participants are not subjected to a pervasive mood of mob bias or crowd intimidation. The ruling reversed *Frank* v. *Mangum* (1915), when the Court affirmed a murder conviction from a jury constantly exposed to public hysteria and anti-Semitic prejudice, because review by the state supreme court served as an adequate guarantee for any denial of DUE PROCESS.

Moore's Creek Bridge, battle of (N.C.) On 27 February 1776, Colonel James Moore's 1,900 Continentals and N.C. militia defeated Donald McDonald's 1,700 Scottish TORIES. N.C. losses: 1 killed, 1 wounded. Scots Tory losses: 50 killed or wounded, 850 captured, 1,850 firearms. The victory crushed N.C.'s Tories, who remained quiescent until after the fall of CHARLES TOWN, S.C.

Moral Majority Rev. Jerry Falwell, a Lynchburg, Va., minister, founded this organization to express the religious community's dissatisfaction with the elimination of prayer in public schools, pornography, civil rights for homosexuals, legalized ABORTION, and a relaxation of opposition toward international communism. The organization reported that it registered 2,000,000 Christians to vote between 1980 and 1984. By giving strong and highly visible support to Ronald REAGAN, it made conservative, white, working-class Christians a major influence in the Republican Party for the first time since the 1920s. Falwell renamed his group the Liberty Federation in 1986 and then devoted himself increasingly to his ministry.

Morehead* v. *New York ex rel. Tipaldo *see* *ADKINS* V. *CHILDREN'S HOSPITAL*

Morfontaine, treaty of *see* CONVENTION OF 1800

Morgan, John Pierpont (b. Hartford, Conn., 17 April 1837; d. Rome, Italy, 31 March 1913) Educated in Europe (as befitted the son of an international financier), Morgan established himself at New York in 1860 and founded J. P. Morgan [&] Co., which grew into one of the world's greatest banking houses, with branches in Paris and London. The PANIC OF 1893 enabled him to acquire control over many bankrupt eastern railroads, so that his control eventually extended over the New York Central Railroad, the Erie Railroad, the New York, New Haven, and Hartford Railroad, the Southern Railroad, and the Atchison, Topeka, and Santa Fe Railroad. When a monetary crisis caused the US Treasury's gold reserve to plunge precipitously in 1895, Morgan prevented a financial panic by lending the government $65,000,000 in gold and earned a $7,000,000 commission. In 1901 he created the world's first billion-dollar business by purchasing US Steel from Andrew CARNEGIE. In the PROGRESSIVE ERA, J. P. Morgan & Co. came to symbolize the MONEY TRUST, fear of which stimulated the founding of the FEDERAL RESERVE SYSTEM.

Morgan* v. *Virginia On 3 June 1946, the Supreme Court denied (6–1) that states could legislate segregated seating on buses involved in interstate commerce, because such JIM CROW LAWS unduly burdened national passenger traffic with disruptive, confusing regulations. It was later expanded by *BOYNTON* V. *VIRGINIA*.

Morgenthau, Henry (b. New York, N.Y., 11 May 1891; d. Poughkeepsie, N.Y., 6 February 1967) Because he owned an estate near Franklin D. ROOSEVELT, Morgenthau developed a friendship with the future president and was named to head the Federal Farm Board in 1933. He became treasury secretary in 1934. He helped draft the LEND LEASE ACT, directed the greatest expansion in federal spending in US history, and organized the BRETTON WOODS CONFERENCE. After his Morgenthau Plan for deindustrializing post-WORLD WAR II Germany was rejected, he resigned from the Treasury in 1945.

Mormon War *see* UTAH WAR

Mormons Officially titled the Church of Jesus Christ of Latter-day Saints and based on the Book of Mormon's account of a Hebrew exodus to America, the Mormons were organized at Fayette, N.Y., on 6 April 1830 by Joseph SMITH. Neighbors were hostile to their tight-knit communitarianism and rejection of mainstream Protestantism, and drove them to seek refuge at Kirtland Mills, Ohio, and Independence, Mo. during 1831–2, then to find sanctuary at Nauvoo, Ill., in 1839. Reports of polygamy fanned anti-Mormon hysteria that resulted in Smith's murder in 1844 and the sack of Nauvoo in 1846. Brigham YOUNG led 15,000 survivors to winter quarters near Omaha, Nebr., and then overland to settle DESERET (Utah), by mid-1847.

Trouble with the US later flared in the bloodless UTAH WAR. The church undertook a vigorous colonization program that established over 360 settlements in Utah, Idaho, Wyo., Ariz., Nev., and Calif. by 1877. The church's missionary efforts won numerous converts who preserved Mormonism's majority status in Utah and made it dominant over large areas of neighboring states. Mormon polygamy resulted in protracted conflict with the US. After the Supreme Court upheld anti-polygamy laws in 1879, Congress passed the Edmunds-Tucker Act (1882), which disfranchised polygamists and placed Utah's elections under federal supervision.

The church capitulated to public opinion when the Supreme Court upheld the Edmunds-Tucker Act in 1890. It has since become the fastest-growing US denomination and by 1990 had 4,370,700 members (1.6 percent of the US population and 3.0 percent of all churchgoers).

Morrill Act (2 July 1862) This Land Grant Act applied to states not in rebellion and with significant amounts of PUBLIC DOMAIN. It gave qualified states 30,000 acres for each senator and representative to be used for endowing colleges providing agricultural and industrial education (so-called agricultural and mechanical schools). The law helped finance the founding of 69 land grant colleges. A second land grant act in 1890 provided annual cash payments of $25,000 to land grant colleges.

Morrill Tariff (2 March 1861) This law reversed the trend away from protectionism established since the WALKER TARIFF (1846). It replaced ad valorem duties with specific (fixed) rates that were assessed regardless of an item's actual worth; it also increased average rates from 5 percent to 10 percent. Duties were ratcheted upward in 1862, 1864, 1867, and 1869 until average rates reached 47 percent.

Morris, Robert (b. Liverpool, England, 31 January 1734; d. Philadelphia, Pa., 8 May 1806) In 1747 Morris was brought to Philadelphia and apprenticed to a merchant. In 1754 he become a partner in Willing & Morris, one of the city's largest trading firms. He emerged as an important Whig leader in 1775 (*see* WHIGS [REVOLUTIONARY]), when he was elected to the second CONTINENTAL CONGRESS. There he abstained from voting on independence, but signed the DECLARATION OF INDEPENDENCE. His privateering and business ventures prospered so well in the Revolution that he was considered the nation's wealthiest man by 1781. As superintendent of finance (1781–3), he dramatically improved the funding of the war effort – in part by tapping his own wealth – but resigned when Congress failed to support the public credit with a national revenue. He was the leading organizer of the Bank of North America (1781), the first national commercial bank in the US. He attended the CONSTITUTIONAL CONVENTION and declined an offer to be first secretary of the treasury in 1789, but sat as Pa. senator (1789–95). Unsound land speculations ruined him, and the first BANKRUPTCY ACT (1800) was enacted to permit his release from debtors' prison.

Morse, Samuel F. B. *see* TELEGRAPH

Morton, Levi Parsons (b. Shoreham, Vt., 16 May 1824; d. Rhinebeck, N.Y., 16 May 1920) A teacher and businessman, Morton was a congressman (Republican, N.Y., 1879–81), ambassador to France (1881–5), US vice-president (1889–93) – he was passed over for renomination with Benjamin HARRISON – and N.Y. governor (1895–7).

Motor Carrier Act (9 August 1935) This law was the first measure to subject the trucking industry to regulation by the INTERSTATE COMMERCE COMMISSION. It empowered the commission to set freight rates, maximum hours of operation, licensing standards for drivers, accounting procedures, and safety rules for equipment and driving.

Motor Carrier Act (1980) *see* DEREGULATION

Mott, Lucretia Coffin (b. Nantucket, Mass., 3 January 1793; d. Philadelphia, Pa., 11 November 1880) In 1818 Mott began preaching among QUAKERS, and later supported their Hicksite faction. She was present at the AMERICAN ANTISLAVERY SOCIETY's founding meeting. In 1837 she helped found the Antislavery Convention of American Women. After being denied admission to an international ABOLITIONISM convention in London in 1840 because of her sex, she gravitated to women's rights issues. She helped organize the SENECA FALLS CONVENTION and helped found the American Equal Rights Association in 1866.

Mound Builders Culture This culture flourished in the period 800–1400 in the Mississippi valley and the southeast. At certain ceremonial centers, they built large urban communities around huge earthworks, burial complexes, and temple mounds. They developed an extensive trade network ranging from the Great Plains to Fla. They supported a class of craftsmen who achieved a sophisticated level of artistry. Their Cahokia, Ill., center stretched for six miles and contained 85 burial and religious mounds, including one temple that rose 100 feet from a base of

16 acres. The Mound Builders abandoned their communities for reasons unknown.

Mount Vernon conference On 28 March 1785, at Mount Vernon, George WASHINGTON hosted delegates from Va. and Md. to discuss problems of navigation on Chesapeake Bay and the Potomac River. After reaching swift agreement on those issues, the delegates proposed further negotiations between the two states and Pa. over various financial and commercial issues. These proposals eventually led Va. and Md. to issue calls for the ANNAPOLIS CONVENTION.

muckraker Theodore ROOSEVELT coined this term to describe journalists in the PROGRESSIVE ERA who investigated corruption or abuses of power by politicians or the TRUSTS, because they reminded him of "the Man with the Muck-Rake" in *The Pilgrim's Progress*. The earliest major work of muckraking was Ida M. Tarbell's *History of the Standard Oil Company* (1903). Lincoln STEFFENS and Upton SINCLAIR were the greatest muckrakers.

mugwumps These were Republicans (most notably Carl SCHURZ) who deserted James BLAINE in the 1884 election for not supporting CIVIL SERVICE REFORM, and helped elect Grover CLEVELAND. They were single-issue reformers and most took orthodox Republican positions on the currency, business regulation, and tariff issues.

Muir, John (b. Dunbar, Scotland, 21 April 1838; d. Los Angeles, Calif., 24 December 1914) In 1849 Muir immigrated to Wis. with his parents. During 1867–8, he walked to Calif. His lobbying led Congress to establish Yosemite National Park in 1890. He founded the Sierra Club in 1892, and after 1897 dedicated himself to expanding reserves of wilderness land. He ranks as the first great US conservationist for his campaign to create the national park system

Mulford* v. *Smith *see* AGRICULTURAL ADJUSTMENT ACT, SECOND

Muller* v. *Oregon On 24 February 1908, the Supreme Court decided unanimously that because Oreg. could demonstrate that limiting work hours for certain female occupations promoted public health – based on the "Brandeis brief," in which Louis BRANDEIS emphasized quantitative evidence rather than legal precedent – it could set maximum hours for female laundry workers without infringing the employers' right to negotiate contracts. The ruling reversed *LOCHNER* v. *NEW YORK*, which had overturned *HOLDEN* v. *HARDY*. In 1917 the Court extended *Muller* by upholding another Oreg. statute that limited the maximum workday to 10 hours in *Bunting* v. *Oregon*.

Mulligan letters On 31 May 1876, Henry Mulligan, a Boston bookkeeper, told a congressional committee that James BLAINE promised political favors to railway executives in exchange for railroad stock and was hiding evidence of graft. On 5 June, Blaine attempted to squelch the controversy by reading excerpts from letters alluded to by Mulligan. The charges destroyed Blaine's chances of being nominated for president in 1876. When it was learned that he had selectively read from the letters to hide references dealing with Mulligan's charges, Blaine's reputation was badly damaged. The letters were a major factor in Blaine's narrow defeat in the election of 1884.

Municipal Bankruptcy Act (24 May 1934) This law allowed cities that had defaulted on their bond payments to reorganize their finances in federal bankruptcy courts once 51 percent of their bondholders consented to a refinancing plan. Bankruptcy judges could approve such plans if 75 percent of bondholders accepted their terms. By enabling cities to restructure their indebtedness and resume payments to their creditors, the law was instrumental in enabling the bond market to overcome its depressed financial state.

Munn* v. *Illinois *see* GRANGER CASES

Munsee Indians This people was a subgroup of DELAWARE INDIANS who migrated with the larger nation westward from Pa. in the 1760s. One Munsee band combined with MAHICAN INDIANS and a small remnant of Delawares; it now occupies a reservation in Shawano County, Wis., at Bowler. The other Munsees are in Okla.

Murchison letter Shortly before the 1888 election, British ambassador Lionel Sackville-West received a letter purporting to be from a naturalized US citizen from England named Charles Murchison (in reality from Calif. Representative George Osgoodby), who asked his opinion on how to vote for president. On 13 September, Sackville-West wrote back recommending Grover CLEVELAND, and on 24 October Republicans began denouncing his correspondence as foreign interference in US politics. The uproar helped defeat Cleveland by costing him part of the Irish vote in a very close election.

Murder Act *see* ADMINISTRATION OF JUSTICE ACT

Murfreesboro, battle of (Tenn.) *see* STONES RIVER, BATTLE OF

Murphy* v. *Waterfront Commission of New York On 15 June 1964, the Supreme Court unanimously ruled that the FIFTH AMENDMENT's protection against involuntary self-incrimination prevents any indictment (in either federal or state courts) from being based upon testimony given in exchange for immunity from prosecution.

Murray, John *see* UNIVERSALIST CHURCH OF AMERICA

Murray's Lessee* v. *Hoboken Land and Improvement Company In 1856 the Supreme Court unanimously held that the FIFTH AMENDMENT's guarantee of DUE PROCESS could not be diminished by Congress or legislatures to weaken the scope of legal protections existing when the BILL OF RIGHTS was ratified. This ruling marked the Court's first effort to define due process, which was held to comprehend English COMMON LAW and all specific legal rights embodied in the Constitution.

Muskie, Edmund Sixtus (b. Rumford, Maine, 28 March 1914) He was a Democrat who served as Maine governor (1955–9), US senator (1959–80), and Hubert HUMPHREY's candidate for vice-president in 1968. He ran unsuccessfully for the Democratic nomination for president in 1972 – partly due to political "dirty tricks" – and was secretary of state (1980–1).

Muskogean languages This family of INDIAN LANGUAGES occupied the area east of the Mississippi River, south of the Cumberland River, and west of the Savannah River. Its homeland evidently lay in this area. Its major subdivisions are the languages of the Muskogee (also called CREEK), SEMINOLE, CHOCTAW-CHICKASAW, Natchez, and the Alabama-Koasati Indians.

Muslims, Black *see* BLACK MUSLIMS

My Lai, massacre of (Vietnam) On 16 March 1968, Second Lieutenant William Calley's platoon of the 23rd Infantry Division shot 400–500 unresisting civilians. The only US casualty shot himself in the foot. The Army court-martialed 12 soldiers for assault or murder, but found all innocent except Calley. Sentenced to life imprisonment at hard labor on 29 March 1971, Calley had his punishment reduced to ten years in 1974 and was paroled on 8 November 1975.

Myrdal, Gunnar *see* *AMERICAN DILEMMA, AN*

Myers* v. *United States *see* TENURE OF OFFICE ACT

N

NAACP *see* NATIONAL ASSOCIATION FOR THE ADVANCEMENT OF COLORED PEOPLE

NAFTA *see* NORTH AMERICAN FREE TRADE AGREEMENT

Nagasaki, bombing of (Japan) On 9 August 1945, Major Charles Sweeney's B-29 bomber, *Bock's Car*, from Tinian Island, dropped a second atomic bomb on Japan and left 39,000 dead (23,753 known) and 23,300 known injured. Unaware that the US possessed no more atomic weapons, Japan offered surrender terms to the Allies the next day.

Nanking incident *see* CHINA, US INTERVENTION IN

Narragansett Indians This group, speakers of one of the ALGONQUIAN LANGUAGES, formed New England's largest Indian nation in 1620 (about 25 percent of that region's natives) and lived near Narragansett Bay. They largely escaped a European epidemic that ravaged the area north of Cape Cod in 1616–18 and numbered 4,000 (including their kinsmen, the Niantics of eastern Conn.), but 700 died from smallpox in 1633–34. As English allies, they played a crucial role in crushing Indian resistance in the PEQUOT WAR. They fought in KING PHILIP'S WAR, but suffered enormous losses when their largest stockade was overrun in December 1675 and were sold into overseas slavery in large numbers. Most Narragansetts merged with other tribes, but a remnant survived in R.I. In 1790 500 Narragansetts resided around Charlestown, R.I. In 1978, by a suit filed under the INDIAN TRADE INTERCOURSE ACT (1790), they received 2.8 square miles (worth $3,500,000) and agreed to extinguish their aboriginal title.

NASA *see* NATIONAL AERONAUTICS AND SPACE ADMINISTRATION

Nashville, battle of (Tenn.) On 15–16 December 1864, Major General George THOMAS's 49,770 Federals routed Brigadier General John Hood's 23,200 Confederates. USA losses: 387 killed, 2,562 wounded, 112 missing. CSA losses: no more than 1,500 killed and wounded, 4,462 captured (including 3 generals). Hood's army, the largest CSA command in the western theater, ceased to be an offensive threat.

Nashville convention (Tenn.) Meeting upon a recommendation made by the Miss. legislature on 6 March 1850, delegates from nine slave states debated a southern position on slavery in Calif. and N.Mex. They proposed on 10 June to extend the MISSOURI COMPROMISE line to the Pacific, but resisted appeals by extremists (especially Robert B. Rhett of S.C.) to declare secession justifiable if Congress would not maintain slavery's constitutional protections. A handful of the delegates reconvened at Nashville between 11 and 18 November to denounce the COMPROMISE OF 1850 and affirm the right of secession.

Nast, Thomas (b. Landau, Bavaria, 27 September 1840; d. Guayaquil, Ecuador, 7 December 1902) He came to New York in 1846, became a professional news illustrator at 15, and was the most talented American cartoonist by the late 1860s. His portrayals of William Tweed's misdeeds (*see* TWEED RING) captured the ominous nature of the corruption of the TAMMANY HALL system and played a major role in arousing public opinion to fight dishonest government. "My constituents don't know how to read," Tweed explained, "but they can't help seeing them damned pictures."

Nat Turner's Rebellion *see* TURNER'S REVOLT

Natchez Indians This nation, speakers of one

of the MUSKOGEAN LANGUAGES, occupied the east bank of the Mississippi around Natchez and along the Yazoo River. They numbered about 5,000 (including 1,200 warriors) in the early 18th century. They had only casual contact with the French before 1713, when a trading post was built among them. Although initially open to the French, the Natchez grew alienated after Fort Rosalie was built in 1716 and its garrison began using force against them and demanding land concessions. They retaliated in the NATCHEZ WAR, but were defeated, dispersed, and destroyed as a cultural entity.

Natchez Trace This road was the primary land route for trade and migration connecting the lower Mississippi with the Ohio valley. Largely built between 1802 and 1820, it extended 500 miles from Natchez, Miss., to Nashville, Tenn., where it connected with roads to Louisville and Maysville, Ky. It was heavily used by "Kaintucks" who took goods on flatboats to New Orleans and walked home via the trace – and also by murderous thieves who preyed on them.

Natchez War On 29 November 1729, NATCHEZ INDIANS captured Fort Rosalie (Natchez, Miss.), destroyed many outlying settlements, killed perhaps 250 French, and captured another 350. The French and CHOCTAW INDIANS destroyed the nine Natchez villages in 1730, killed about 1,000 warriors, and sent 450 captives as slaves to the West Indies.

Nation, Carry Amelia Moore (b. Garrard County, Ky., 25 November 1846; d. Leavenworth, Kans., 9 June 1911) She became attracted to PROHIBITION after marrying an alcoholic doctor in 1867. In 1900, while living at Medicine Lodge, Kans., she began a personal mission to close saloons that defied state laws against selling alcohol by destroying the premises with a hatchet. After extending her crusade across Kans. and into nearby states, she became a folk heroine who sold souvenir hatchets and edited a journal titled the *Smasher's Mail*. She influenced Kans. to enforce its alcohol laws strictly and won much support for prohibitionism.

Nation of Islam Rejecting new doctrines adopted by the BLACK MUSLIMS after Elijah Muhammad's death in 1975, Louis Farrakhan led a schism that appropriated the group's name for itself. Farrakhan and his disciples (about 10,000 in 1994) maintained the Muslims' traditional focus on black supremacy and separatism. Farrakhan's repeated use of anti-Semitic remarks produced enormous controversy.

National Advisory Commission for Aeronautics *see* NATIONAL AERONAUTICS AND SPACE ADMINISTRATION

National Aeronautics and Space Administration (NASA) In 1915 Congress funded the National Advisory Commission for Aeronautics to develop advanced technology and engineering for aircraft. In WORLD WAR II, it worked to improve military aircraft. After 1945, the agency pioneered jet propulsion for attaining faster speeds and higher altitudes. On 14 October 1947, Charles Yeager first broke the sound barrier in the agency's X-1 jet. After the launch of *SPUTNIK* it was reorganized on 29 July 1958 as NASA to oversee the Department of DEFENSE's aeronautical programs and conduct nonmilitary research for the SPACE RACE. During the APOLLO PROJECT, the number of its employees and outside contractors rose from less than 50,000 in 1961 to about 420,000 by 1966, when its budget peaked at $5.9 billion, and over 20 percent of all federal and private outlays for research went to NASA.

By 1975, US moon exploration had ended, NASA's budget had shrunk to $3.2 billion, and the manpower employed by the agency was half of its peak level. NASA's horizons expanded with the Viking Progam to reconnoiter Mars and the Voyager Progam to investigate the outer solar system. On 25 June 1973, NASA's Project Skylab launched the first US orbiting space station, manned by a three-man crew. To reduce the cost of using space for commercial or scientific purposes, NASA developed the space shuttle, a rocket that can be launched by a missile, serve as temporary skylab, and fly back to land on earth. NASA launched its first space shuttle, *Columbia*, on 12 April 1981, its second, *Challenger*, on 4 April 1983, its third, *Discovery*, on 30 August 1984, and its fourth, *Atlantis*, on 3 October 1985. These projects enabled NASA to increase its budget to $7.3 billion by 1985, when its prestige was crippled by the explosion of the *Challenger* and the death of its seven crew members (including a civilian school teacher) on 28 January at Cape Kennedy. This disaster, the world's worst space-flight catastrophe, forced NASA to suspend space shuttle flights until 29 September 1988. The loss of the *Challenger* and the end of the COLD WAR led Congress to curtail sharply the expansion of funding for NASA programs. From 1961 to 1994, NASA launched 94 manned missions into space.

National American Woman Suffrage Association The National Woman Suffrage Association and American Woman Suffrage Association merged in 1890 at New York to form this group under president Elizabeth Cady STANTON and vice-president Susan B. ANTHONY. It was later headed by Carrie Chapman CATT and Anna Howard SHAW. It had chapters in every state and worked for WOMEN'S SUFFRAGE primarily through state laws until 1916, when it joined the NATIONAL WOMAN'S PARTY's campaign for a constitutional amendment. It was the largest lobbying group to press for the NINETEENTH AMENDMENT, and disbanded in 1920.

National Association for the Advancement of Colored People (NAACP) This organization first met on 12 February 1909 at New York, in response to the Springfield, Ill., race riot of 1908 to fight discrimination. Its governing structure was organized under president Moorefield Storey in May 1910; its first officers were all white, except for W. E. B. DU BOIS. It lobbied for a national law to forbid LYNCHING, funded litigation to reestablish protection for civil rights under the FOURTEENTH and FIFTEENTH AMENDMENTS, and fought discrimination of all types; but it conceded the task of improving economic opportunity and providing social services to the National URBAN LEAGUE. Within a decade, the NAACP had over 400 branches and had displaced the NIAGARA MOVEMENT as the voice of civil rights progress. By the 1950s, its leadership was primarily black. It had 445,000 members by 1963, and ranked with the SOUTHERN CHRISTIAN LEADERSHIP CONFERENCE as the two most influential organizations of the CIVIL RIGHTS MOVEMENT. The NAACP officially rejected BLACK POWER at its Los Angeles convention of 4–9 July 1966. The NAACP gradually eclipsed other civil rights groups after 1975, and had an estimated 650,000 members and an annual budget of $15,000,000 in 1994. The organization faced increasing financial pressure in 1994 due to a $3,500,000 deficit, and attracted growing criticism for the efforts of President Benjamin CHAVIS to build alliances with spokesmen for extremist groups and black separatists, especially the NATION OF ISLAM.

National Association for the Advancement of Colored People* v. *Alabama ex rel. Patterson On 30 June 1958, the Supreme Court unanimously ruled that a state court's order for the NAACP to turn over its membership lists violated the right of association inherent in the FIRST AMENDMENT's guarantee of free assembly and speech. Unless a government showed a compelling interest in the disclosure of an organization's membership, it could not justify unduly restraining the participants' right to privacy, because privacy was often necessary to avoid harassment or retribution.

National Association of Manufacturers Founded in Cincinnati in 1895, it grew to represent 5,350 firms by 1922. It was the most influential lobbying group for large industrialists. In the 1920s, it was organized labor's most bitter opponent and launched the AMERICAN PLAN. It fought against greater government involvement in business regulation or in solving major economic problems. It lost three-quarters of its member businesses between 1929 and 1933, but the survivors vehemently denounced the NEW DEAL.

National Colored Farmers' Alliance *see* POPULISM

National Conservation Commission *see* PINCHOT, GIFFORD

National Credit Corporation To stem a wave of bank failures that spread across the US in late 1931, Treasury Secretary Andrew MELLON persuaded several prominent New York financiers to pool $500,000,000 of their private funds into a National Credit Corporation for loans to troubled banks. The corporation did nothing to halt the banking crisis, because it lent only to banks able to pledge large amounts of collateral, and not to the smaller banks that needed capital most desperately; it lent only $10,000,000 in October and November 1931. Its failure led to the founding of the RECONSTRUCTION FINANCE CORPORATION.

national debt After Alexander HAMILTON reorganized the national debt according to his REPORT ON THE PUBLIC CREDIT, it stood at $76,000,000 in 1790. It rose under the Federalists to $83,038,000 in 1800. Under Thomas JEFFERSON and Albert GALLATIN, it was cut to $45,210,000 by 1811. The WAR OF 1812 added $82,125,000, but sales of the PUBLIC DOMAIN essentially eliminated all federal debt by 1834. By 1866 the CIVIL WAR had created a $2,755,764,000 debt, which was reduced by 64 percent by 1890. The debt then stayed at about $1 billion until WORLD WAR I, which multiplied it to $25,484,506,000 by 1919. The last period of significant debt reduction was 1921–30, when Treasury Secretary Andrew MELLON cut it by 32 percent. The era of a large, permanent national debt began after WORLD WAR II, and its growth greatly accelerated after 1970, the last year in which the federal budget was balanced in the 20th century. The debt first reached $1 trillion in 1981 and had doubled by 1986. By 1993, interest on the debt amounted to about 15 percent of the federal budget, the second-largest component after Social Security (*see* SOCIAL SECURITY ADMINISTRATION).

National Defense Act (3 June 1916) This law established the modern structure of the army and state guards. In addition to the US Army, which was authorized to increase from 175,000 to 223,000 by 1921, the law created the first reserve force unconnected with state MILITIAS by establishing an Enlisted Reserve Corps of men who had served on active duty in the medical, ordnance, signal, or quartermaster branches (but this corps contained no units, only individuals who might be recalled to active duty). It also created the Reserve Officers' Training Corps (ROTC) to commission officers for an Officers' Reserve Corps by instruction at civilian colleges. The law furthermore gave the president authority to draft men from the NATIONAL GUARD (authorized at 450,000) into the regular army, and for the first time declared that governors retained no authority over any guard units that were federalized.

National Defense Education Act (2 September 1958) Passed in reaction to Soviet success in launching *SPUTNIK*, this law marked the first major effort to improve the quality of US education by federal subsidies to train teachers and scientists. It appropriated $280,000,000 to improve science and foreign language instruction in state schools, $295,000,000 for low-interest loans to college students (with substantial write-offs for those choosing to become secondary school teachers), and provided for 5,500 graduate student fellowships to encourage careers as college professors. Subsequent amendments to this law significantly increased federal support for financing higher education. Federal funding was a major reason for the steady rise in college enrollments from 2,600,000 in 1956 to 3,600,000 in 1960, 4,800,000 in 1963, and 6,000,000 in 1965, when the HIGHER EDUCATION ACT was passed.

National Democrats In 1896 "hard-money" Democrats repudiated William Jennings BRYAN and left the party. At a convention in Indianapolis, they denounced unlimited coinage of silver and nominated John M. PALMER (Ill.) as president and Simon BUCKNER (Ky.) as vice-president. The ticket won 1 percent of the popular vote (131,529).

national domain *see* PUBLIC DOMAIN

National Employment System Act (6 June 1933) Versions of this law had been introduced since 1930, but could not be enacted until the HUNDRED DAYS. It created the US Employment Service, the first national system for sharing information between the labor exchanges of public employment offices. The law provided federal subsidies for establishing a federal–state system of labor banks. It was supplemented by the SOCIAL SECURITY ADMINISTRATION's unemployment compensation system.

National Energy Act (15 October 1978) Recommended by Jimmy CARTER in early 1977 as his top priority, this law required 18 months for passage. Intended to reduce the threat of a second OIL EMBARGO by cutting imports through conservation, it imposed an energy tax on petroleum, encouraged production of natural gas by decontrolling that commodity's price, provided incentives for utilities to substitute coal or natural gas for oil, offered incentives for the development of alternative energy sources to fossil fuels, and encouraged energy conservation by a variety of regulations, loans, and grants. Considered by Carter his most important victory, its impact on reducing dependence upon foreign oil was marginal.

National Environmental Protection Act (1970) *see* ENVIRONMENTAL LEGISLATION

National Farmers' Alliance *see* POPULISM

National Grange *see* GRANGE

National Guard After the CIVIL WAR, most states reorganized their MILITIA as a National Guard, and by 1896, only three states still termed their state forces militia. The National Guard was called to keep peace 481 times from 1865 to 1906, of which 156 concerned labor disputes. The Dick Act (21 January 1903) established the National Guard in its modern capacity, and encouraged a closer relationship with the US Army by offering weapons and training assistance to guard units that agreed to drill more often and pass inspections based on regular-army standards. The NATIONAL DEFENSE ACT (1916) defined the National Guard's relationship to the army in peace and when federalized for war.

In WORLD WAR I, the guard provided 17 out of 43 army divisions and 20 percent of all enlistees. It furnished 18 out of 89 army divisions in WORLD WAR II. By 1950, the guard included 27 divisions, of which eight were activated in the KOREAN WAR. By the early 1970s, the guard had been cut to eight divisions, of which none did active duty in the VIETNAM WAR; of 410,000 guardsmen, only 12,234 were activated, and of these only of 7,000 served in Vietnam. At the height of the VIETNAM ANTIWAR MOVEMENT, the states mobilized 233,000 guardsmen on 201 instances for riot duty, including the KENT STATE UNIVERSITY SHOOTINGS. In August 1987, the Army National Guard totaled 453,854 troops (the world's 11th-largest army) and had a budget of $4.98 billion.

National Housing Act (28 June 1934) This law formulated a national housing program to provide financing for mortgages and home improvement loans, in order to stimulate construction activity during the GREAT DEPRESSION. It founded the Federal Housing Administration to insure banks, building and loan organizations, and mortgage firms against bad loans made to fund new housing or home repairs. It also founded the Federal Savings and Loan Insurance Corporation to insure deposits in savings and loan institutions regulated by the FEDERAL HOME LOAN BANK BOARD. It authorized the Federal Housing Association (FHA) to insure low-income housing projects and to sponsor national pools for buying mortgages from banks. (It was supplemented by the WAGNER–STEAGALL ACT). From June 1934 to December 1940, the FHA financed 494,500 new houses, gave home repair loans on 1,544,000 houses, and extended insured credit of $4.1 billion.

National Housing Act (1937) *see* WAGNER–STEAGALL ACT

National Industrial Recovery Act (NIRA) (16 June 1933) The BRAINS TRUST conceived the NIRA as an alternative to the BLACK–CONNERY BILL. It was the FIRST NEW DEAL's keystone law for business recovery and reform through a planned national economy. Title I created the NATIONAL RECOVERY ADMINISTRATION (NRA) to coordinate business and labor in drafting industry-wide codes (resembling the TRADE ASSOCIATIONS of the 1920s) to set wages, hours, fair competitive practices, standards of craftsmanship or manufacturing quality, and efficient levels of production. These codes for industrial self-regulation would be exempt from antitrust laws and have full legal force when approved by the president.

Section 7 of Title I defined fair labor practices, including a minimum wage of at least 30 cents an hour and abolition of child labor. Section 7(a) (termed "Labor's Bill of Rights") affirmed the right to organize unions and outlawed YELLOW-DOG CONTRACTS. Title II funded $3.3 billion for the PUBLIC WORKS ADMINISTRATION.

On 7 January 1935, Section 9 of Title I – enabling the president to prohibit from interstate commerce oil manufactured in violation of state quotas – was declared unconstitutional in *Panama Refining Company* v. *Ryan* (the first Court ruling to strike down a NEW DEAL law). The entire NIRA was struck down by *SCHECHTER POULTRY CORPORATION* v. *UNITED STATES*. The LITTLE NIRA revived several measures, but the trouble-ridden NRA was abandoned in the SECOND NEW DEAL that followed.

National Labor Reform Party *see* NATIONAL LABOR UNION

National Labor Relations Act (5 July 1935) This law restored labor's right to organize and bargain collectively under Section 7(a) of the NATIONAL INDUSTRIAL RECOVERY ACT (NIRA), which had been invalidated by the Supreme Court. It also defined specific unfair labor practices by management (such as YELLOW-DOG CONTRACTS) and outlawed them. It established a three-member NATIONAL LABOR RELATIONS BOARD (NLRB) to certify results of union elections, hear worker complaints against employers, issue cease-and-desist orders to end anti-union practices, and compel management to bargain with union representatives. Unlike the National Labor Board that functioned under the NIRA, the NLRB had statutory authority to prohibit unfair labor practices, and could enforce its decisions through the courts; it also was empowered to rule on whether new management tactics constituted unfair labor practices and could order them stopped. The Supreme Court upheld the law in *NATIONAL LABOR RELATIONS BOARD* v. *JONES AND LAUGHLIN STEEL CORPORATION*. It was the last major piece of labor legislation before the TAFT–HARTLEY ACT.

National Labor Relations Board (NLRB) After its establishment by the NATIONAL LABOR RELATIONS ACT, this agency was a critical factor in the dramatic rise in union membership (especially in the CIO) after 1935. By 1945 it had supervised 24,000 collective bargaining elections involving 6,000,000 workers and had ordered reinstatement of 300,000 fired workers with $9,000,000 in back pay. The board was strongly pro-labor, but even the most successful organizers, those from the CIO, won no more than 40 percent of elections. The board's readiness to halt unfair labor practices nevertheless enabled the CIO to organize most mass-production corporations by 1945.

National Labor Relations Board* v. *Jones and Laughlin Steel Corporation On 12 April 1937, the Supreme Court upheld (5–4) the NATIONAL LABOR RELATIONS ACT as constitutional. The Court ruled for the government by affirming the "stream of commerce" concept enunciated in *SWIFT AND COMPANY* v. *UNITED STATES*. The ruling ended the Court's attempts to restrict federal regulation of interstate commerce within a narrow sphere.

National Labor Union (NLU) On 20 August 1866, this organization was founded under the leadership of William H. Sylvis and Richard F. Trevellick. The NLU was the first federation uniting separate trade unions into a nationwide association. Its membership peaked at 640,000 before it founded the National Labor Reform party, which nominated Judge David Davis of Ill. for US president in 1872. The party disintegrated when Davis withdrew from the race, and the NLU collapsed during the PANIC OF 1873.

National Monetary Commission *see* FEDERAL RESERVE SYSTEM

National Municipal League Founded in May 1894 to promote good government, the league exemplified concepts current in the PROGRESSIVE ERA for reforming local politics and administration. It advocated replacing graft-ridden, patronage-oriented political machines by nonpartisan, businesslike administrations subject to firm control by voters rather than bosses. Its proposed reforms included a merit-based civil service, CITY COMMISSION GOVERNMENT (until 1915), CITY MANAGER GOVERNMENT (after 1915), HOME RULE, AUSTRALIAN BALLOT, at-large commission elections, nonpartisan elections, and municipal control over utilities and public transportation systems.

National Organization of Women Organized on 30 June 1966 at the third Conference of Commissions on the Status of Women in Washington, D.C., this group became the most prominent women's lobbying organization. Its influence derived from a willingness to take partisan positions and mobilize female voters to support specific legislation and Democratic candidates. It suffered a major defeat on the EQUAL RIGHTS AMENDMENT. By 1991, it had 250,000 members and was an important part of the Democratic Party coalition.

National Origins Act (26 May 1924) This law cut the number of immigrants annually admitted under the EMERGENCY QUOTA ACT (1921), from 357,000 to 164,000, and directed its reduction to 150,000 in 1927. It excluded all Asian immigrants under provisions of the NATURALIZATION ACT (1790). No limits were placed on migration from Canada or Latin America. It capped entrants from any country at 2 percent of all persons born there who were counted by the 1890 census. The most generous quotas went to northern and western Europe, from which relatively few immigrants came, at the expense of Slavic and Mediterranean nations, where there was great pressure to migrate. The law caused European immigration to drop from 2,477,853 in the 1920s to 348,289 in the 1930s; it decreased the US foreign-born population from 13.1 percent in 1920 to 4.7 percent by 1970.

National Park Service The first national park was Yellowstone, created in 1872. The Interior Department managed US parks and monuments until the National Park Service's creation on 25 August 1916. Stephen Mather, its first director, oversaw vigorous growth to 1929. By 1988, its responsibilities had expanded to cover 124,433 square miles, including 49 national parks, 77 national monuments, 112 historic parks or sites, and 104 other areas, including the White House. In 1993 the Park Service accommodated 59.8 million visitors, equal to about a quarter of the US population.

National Railroad Passenger Corporation *see* AMTRAK

National Reclamation (Newlands) Act (17 June 1902) This law created a Reclamation Fund from land sales in 16 western states to finance construction of dams and irrigation projects by its Bureau of Reclamation. In 1906 the bureau's reclamation projects supplied water to 22,300 acres that produced crops worth $244,900; by 1970 its projects irrigated 8,500,000 acres, on which 140,500 farms grew crops worth $2,000,000,000. The bureau assumed responsibility from the Corps of Engineers for building reservoirs and dams in the west in the Great Depression. The Newlands Act did more to stimulate farming and rural development in the west than any law since the first HOMESTEAD ACT.

National Recovery Administration (NRA) Created by the NATIONAL INDUSTRIAL RECOVERY ACT (NIRA), this agency supervised the drafting of industry-wide codes to regulate labor practices, price controls, and competitive practices in the economy's nonfarming sector. Under Hugh JOHNSON, it negotiated 541 industrial codes covering 2,000,000 workers, including most of the largest US employers. Despite Johnson's efforts to make labor and small business full partners in industrial self-regulation, big business dominated negotiations and drafted most codes to its own advantage. On 21 May 1934, the National Recovery Review Board cited numerous problems with the NRA codes: too many ignored the NIRA's pro-labor clauses, instituted subtle forms of price-fixing, and contained provisions that put small companies at a competitive disadvantage to big business. In September 1934, Johnson was replaced by a National Industrial Recovery Board directed to eliminate anti-competitive or anti-union practices in NRA codes. Frustrated by growing public criticism and big business's resistance to reforming the codes, the Roosevelt administration let the NRA codes die after *SCHECHTER POULTRY CORPORATION* v. *UNITED STATES* declared them unconstitutional.

National Republicans Following John Q. ADAMS's election, the DEMOCRATIC (or Democratic-Republican) PARTY split into two factions: followers of Andrew JACKSON, who retained the Democratic title, and partisans of Adams, Henry CLAY, and Daniel WEBSTER, who were termed National Republicans. The group favored LOOSE CONSTRUCTIONISM and programs like the AMERICAN SYSTEM; it never controlled the Senate, but had a majority in the House (1827–34). Its members were the preponderant part of the WHIG PARTY after 1834.

National Resources Committee On 30 June 1934, an executive order by Franklin D. ROOSEVELT established the National Resources Board to collect data and formulate long-range plans for developing the economic potential of water, soil, and other natural resources. It influenced federal policies for rural electrification and hydroelectric power plants. An executive order of 7 June 1935 reorganized it as the National Resources Committee.

National Road In 1802 and 1803, Congress set aside certain proceeds from selling public lands in Ohio to construct a road westward to and through that state. In 1806 these monies funded the survey of a route from Cumberland, Md., to the Ohio River at Wheeling. Construction began in 1811, and 130 miles to Wheeling were completed in 1818. This "Cumberland" Road was the first federally financed highway. On 4 May 1822, by vetoing a bill to let the US collect tolls for the road's upkeep, James MONROE helped set a precedent that federally funded highways would be maintained by the states. The Cumberland route was continued along Zane's Trace in Ohio and was known as the "National Road" when it reached Columbus in 1833. Federal financing pushed the road to Indianapolis by 1850.

National Security Act (26 July 1947) This law established the Department of DEFENSE, CENTRAL INTELLIGENCE AGENCY, and NATIONAL SECURITY COUNCIL.

National Security Council (NSC) This body was established on 26 July 1947 to advise the White House staff on foreign and domestic issues concerning national security. Formal meetings of the council include the president, vice-president, secretary of state, secretary of defense, and the assistant to the president for national security affairs, who directs the council's staff for research and analysis. By 1980 the NSC staff had grown to 1,600. The IRAN-CONTRA SCANDAL originated in illegal operations by its members.

National System of Interstate and Defense Highways *see* INTERSTATE HIGHWAY SYSTEM

National Union for Social Justice *see* COUGHLIN, CHARLES

National Urban League *see* URBAN LEAGUE, NATIONAL

National Woman's party In 1913 Lucy Burns and Alice PAUL formed the Congressional Union to work for WOMEN'S SUFFRAGE through a constitutional amendment, rather than by state laws as was the current strategy by mainstream suffrage advocates like the NATIONAL AMERICAN WOMAN SUFFRAGE ASSOCIATION. The Union campaigned by mobilizing women, in states where they could already vote, against candidates who did not support a national election. In June 1916, the Union merged with the Woman's party to form a National Woman's party to campaign against Woodrow WILSON. Paul's group sparked controversy because it publicized its views not only by parades and speaking rallies, but also by noisily picketing politicians, acting contemptuously toward Wilson and other national leaders, staging hunger strikes, and chaining themselves to public buildings. The National Woman's party reenergized the suffrage movement as it was reaching the practical limits of state action, and its leadership spurred more conservative women's groups to work for the NINETEENTH AMENDMENT, which was sent to the states in 1918. In 1923 it began a new campaign for Congress to approve an EQUAL RIGHTS AMENDMENT.

National Youth Administration (NYA) This agency was created by executive order on 26 June 1935 under the WORKS PROGRESS ADMINISTRATION to provide work for those aged 16–25 from jobless families and to help finance college by part-time work for students. In 1939–40, it paid benefits to 750,000 students attending 1,700 colleges and 28,000 high schools. During its life, it supplemented the incomes of 1,514,000 high school students, 620,000 college students, and 2,677,000 other young people in all large cities and 595 rural training centers. In 1942 the NYA became part of the War Manpower Commission to teach skills useful for military industries; it was disbanded in September 1943.

Native American Church After the demise of the GHOST DANCE RELIGION in the 1890s, an Indian prophet, Quannah Parker fused the hallucinatory use of peyote weed with religious ceremonies. This peyote cult incorporated Christianity's fundamental elements, but its distinguishing feature was the sacramental taking of peyote during all-night cermonies. Despite federal and state efforts to suppress it, the religion spread widely across the Great Plains RESERVATIONS and had evolved into an organized church by 1918, when it was incorporated in Okla. By 1930, about half of all the Plains Indians had become members. Federal attempts to discourage its growth ceased under BIA director John COLLIER.

Native Son *see* WRIGHT, RICHARD NATHANIEL

nativism This term refers to the prejudice or antagonism against groups of foreigners felt by native-born citizens. In the mid-19th century, it primarily expressed itself against Catholic immigrants through the KNOW-NOTHING PARTY. After 1880 nativism chiefly targeted Asians (*see* CHINESE EXCLUSION ACT *and* JAPANESE IMMIGRATION) and eastern Europeans. It culminated in the NATIONAL ORIGINS ACT.

NATO *see* NORTH ATLANTIC TREATY ORGANIZATION

Naturalization Act (26 March 1790) Congress extended citizenship to any (white) male immigrant, who had lived two years in the US and one year in the state where he renounced his native land, provided he was of "good character" and swore an oath to uphold the US Constitution. Foreign-born children under 21 would be naturalized upon their father becoming a citizen, and foreign-born children of US citizens received legal status as native-born.

Naturalization Act (29 January 1795) Congress amended the NATURALIZATION ACT (1790) by increasing the residency period to five years, and obliged aliens to declare their intention to seek citizenship three years before taking the necessary oath to renounce their homeland and any hereditary titles. It denied the states any authority over naturalization.

Naturalization Act (18 June 1798) Congress increased residency for citizenship to 14 years, and obliged aliens to spend the last five continuously resident in a single state. Enemy aliens could not receive citizenship while their homeland was at war with the US. On 14 April 1802, Congress repealed this measure – except for the provision concerning enemy aliens – and reinstated the 1795 act.

Naturalization Act (14 April 1802) Congress repealed the NATURALIZATION ACT (1798) – except for the provision on enemy aliens – and reinstated its 1795 act. This law was the last significant revision of citizenship requirements until the 20th century.

Navajo campaigns From 1846 to 1849, US troops engaged in five expeditions against NAVAJO INDIAN raiding parties. Clashes continued on a smaller scale in the 1850s. In September 1861, Navajo raids resumed to avenge several men killed by soldiers in a brawl. From 15 June 1863 to mid-1864, Colonel "Kit" CARSON's First N.Mex. Cavalry ravaged the Navajo country with allied HOPI, PUEBLO, and UTE INDIANS. Carson forced all Navajos to resettle 300 miles to the east at Fort Sumner, except for 4,000 who fled west into the desert. US losses: 41 killed, 45 wounded. Navajo losses: 664 killed, 227 wounded, 8,793 surrendered or captured, 49,722 cattle confiscated.

Navajo Indians Speakers of one of the ATHAPASKAN LANGUAGES, the Navajos migrated from the Great Plains to N.Mex. and Ariz. in the 16th century. They incorporated sheep and horses into their culture after 1630. By 1680 they numbered 8,000 and were frequent aggressors against the peaceful PUEBLO dwellers. Their persistent raiding provoked the US Army's NAVAJO CAMPAIGNS, which ended in their "long walk" of 300 miles to Fort Sumner, N.Mex., where two-thirds were confined during 1864–68. Upon returning to their homeland, they never again offered military resistance. In 1868 they received a reservation of 5,500 square miles in N.Mex., Ariz. and Utah. They now inhabit the largest US reservation: 23,640 square miles and 173,108 persons (1984).

Naval Expansion Act (17 May 1938) This law marked the start of US naval rearmament. For the previous decade, the navy had built new ships only on a replacement basis and had never reached the strength permitted by the WASHINGTON NAVAL CONFERENCE. This law appropriated funds to construct a full two-ocean navy.

Naval Stores Act (14 March 1705) Parliament attempted to lessen Britain's dependence on Baltic suppliers of masts, yardarms, bowsprits, pitch, turpentine, rosin, and hemp by offering bounties to colonists who produced these items in America. It also outlawed the cutting of pine trees on Crown lands in New England.

Navigation Act (3 October 1650) This law was England's first effort to exclude foreign nations (especially the Dutch) from its imperial commerce. It barred foreign merchant ships from trading in the colonies unless they obtained a license.

Navigation Act (9 October 1651) This act outlawed the importation of any Asian, African, or American cargoes into the British empire unless they came in "British" ships (those owned and captained by residents of Britain or its colonies, and manned by crews at least half British). European goods could be imported in ships of the same country from which they originated.

Navigation Act (13 September 1660) This law revised and strengthened the 1651 act. To qualify as an English ship, three-quarters of the crew must be residents of Britain or its colonies. (An amendment of 1662 required that ships be registered in Britain.) The law defined tobacco, sugar, indigo, dyewoods, ginger, and cotton as ENUMERATED COMMODITIES, which could only be shipped to England or to another colony. Captains clearing port were obliged to post bond that enumerated items would not be landed in foreign harbors, and could recover the money at their port of arrival. The bonding provisions were revised by the NAVIGATION ACT (1673).

Navigation Act (27 July 1663) This law required that all exports from Europe to the colonies had to be carried in English or colonial ships. All cargoes of European origin originally hauled in foreign ships had to be transshipped via England for sale to English merchants and reloaded on their vessels. The law excepted cargoes of Portuguese salt, wine from the Azores and Madeira, and horses, servants, and provisions from Scotland or Ireland.

Navigation Act (29 March 1673) This law ended a loophole in the 1660 act that enabled captains carrying ENUMERATED COMMODITIES to post bond at their port of departure that the items were destined for another colonial port, reclaim their money upon docking at that harbor, and then take the goods for sale at foreign harbors.

Navigation Act (10 April 1696) This law made no basic changes to earlier acts, but strengthened enforcement by imposing an oath on colonial governors (even of CHARTER and PROPRIETARY COLONIES), that they would uphold the NAVIGATION ACTS, reorganized the American customs service, gave customs offices broad powers of search and seizure, authorized the use of ADMIRALTY COURTS to try smuggling cases, nullified all provincial statutes contrary to the Navigation acts, and established penalties for governors and customs officers who failed to enforce the trade laws.

navigation laws These laws regulated British trade according to the principles of MERCANTILISM by excluding foreign merchants from the British empire's trade, stimulating certain colonial industries by bounties, and forbidding large-scale manufacturing in the colonies that would compete with British producers. The most important statutes were the NAVIGATION ACTS (1651, 1660, 1663, 1673, 1696), WOOLEN ACT, HAT ACT, NAVAL STORES ACT, MOLASSES ACT, and IRON ACT.

Navy, Department of the On 3 May 1798, Congress created the Department of the Navy, and on 11 July 1798, it reestablished the MARINE CORPS under the navy. In 1949 the Department of the Navy was placed under the Department of DEFENSE.

Navy, US On 13 October 1775, Congress authorized a Continental Navy for the REVOLUTIONARY WAR. After the navy was disbanded in 1783, its last warship was sold in 1785. On 10 May 1797, the navy was resurrected when the warship *United States* was commissioned. The Department of the NAVY held CABINET status from 1798 to 1949.

During its first century, the navy had insufficient ships and firepower to oppose world-class navies in fleet engagements. It nevertheless performed well in commerce raiding, coastal defense, and single-ship combat against FRANCE (an undeclared war), the BARBARY PIRATES, and in the WAR OF 1812. In the MEXICAN and CIVIL WARS, it imposed blockades, seized enemy ports, and landed the army in amphibious operations behind enemy lines. After 1865 it resumed its normal peacetime disposition, dispersed in small squadrons to protect American commerce and citizens overseas.

In 1880 the US Navy ranked 12th in size among the world's navies, and all its ships were wooden vessels from the Civil War. On 3 March 1883, Congress funded construction of three metal cruisers. It authorized additional steam-powered, armored warship in August 1886. As secretary of the Navy (1885–9), William C. Whitney largel eliminated wooden ships from the navy and modernized its operations. Whitney bequeathed the US a modern, steam-powered navy, which ranked third in the world by 1900.

Alfred MAHAN's doctrines influenced US leaders to see the navy as critical to protecting overseas economic interests. It was the navy that won the US its status as a world-class power in the SPANISH-AMERICAN WAR, the only conflict whose victory primarily stemmed from naval operations. By WORLD WAR I, the navy was reorganized into a battleship-dominated Atlantic fleet, which could easily undertake Pacific operations through the PANAMA CANAL.

The US emerged from World War I as a naval power equal to Britain. The WASHINGTON NAVAL CONFERENCE confirmed this status. Disarmament treaties pared the navy significantly until rearmament by Japan and Germany forced passage of the NAVAL EXPANSION ACT (1938), which began construction of a two-ocean navy. During WORLD WAR II, the US superseded Britain as the world's foremost naval power. Its tactics rested on aircraft carriers rather than highly vulnerable battleships.

The navy was transformed after 1945 by Hyman RICKOVER's nuclear revolution. Polaris (and later Poseidon) submarines became the US nuclear deterrent's most important element. Nuclear-powered "supercarriers" achieved operational independence from oil tankers, overseas bases, and oil embargoes. During most of the COLD WAR, the navy ranged between 450 and 600 ships, including 100 nuclear submarines and 12–15 aircraft carriers.

Near* v. *Minnesota *see* *GITLOW* v. *NEW YORK*

Nebbia* v. *New York On 5 March 1934, the Supreme Court, in affirming a N.Y. law setting milk prices, ruled (5–4) that a state could regulate any type of business activity in the public interest so long as no constitutional provision barred it from doing so and the state imposed no unreasonable burdens. The decision reversed *WOLFF PACKING COMPANY* v. *COURT OF INDUSTRIAL RELATIONS* by granting the states wide latitude in determining which sort of economic activity required legislative action for the public interest.

Nebraska The US acquired Nebr. by the LOUISIANA PURCHASE. The US Army occupied Fort Atkinson (near Omaha) from 1819 to 1827 and Fort Kearney from 1848 to 1871. The KANSAS–NEBRASKA ACT opened it for white settlement. In 1860 it had 28,826 residents, of whom all but 67 were white and 22 percent were foreign-born; it ranked 40th in population, 35th in the value of its farmland and livestock, and 38th in manufactures. In the CIVIL WAR, it provided 1,080 USA troops. It became the 37th state on 1 March 1867. Settlement proceeded peacefully, although Fort Robinson was built in 1874 to guard against raiders from the SIOUX and CHEYENNE INDIANS.

The first HOMESTEAD ACT and TRANSCONTINENTAL RAILROADS stimulated mass migration to Nebr., whose population grew almost tenfold from 1870 to 1890. Between 1887 and 1897, adequate rain for crops fell in just two years on the plains and commodity prices dropped sharply. Extreme economic hardship resulted in 153,900 persons leaving the state in the 1890s and strong political support for POPULISM. In 1900 Nebr. had 1,066,300 inhabitants, of whom 76 percent were rural, 99 percent white, and 17 percent foreign-born; it ranked 27th in population, 10th in agricultural products, and 19th in manufactures.

During the early 20th century, low commodity prices inhibited growth of the Nebr. economy. From 1920 to 1940, 217,600 persons left the state. Another 323,000 left from 1940 to 1970. Urbanization has since diversified the state economy. In 1990 Nebr. was the 36th largest state and had 1,578,385 residents (92 percent white, 4 percent black, 2 percent Hispanic, 1 percent Indian, 1 percent Asian), of whom 49 percent were urban and 1.8 percent were of foreign birth. Manufacturing and mining employed 19 percent of workers.

Neutrality Act (5 June 1794) This law was the first statute forbidding US citizens from enlisting in the military service of foreign nations, accepting foreign commissions as officers, or sailing as privateers under foreign LETTERS OF MARQUE AND REPRISAL. It was passed to halt Citizen GENÊT's recruitment of Americans to plunder British shipping and launch attacks on Spanish colonies for France.

Neutrality Act (31 August 1935) This law allowed the president to embargo arms exports (but not raw natural resources) to warring nations for six months and declare that travel on belligerent ships would be done at a citizen's risk.

Neutrality Act (29 February 1936) This law extended the NEUTRALITY ACT (1935) and prohibited loans or credits to warring nations.

Neutrality Act (1 May 1937) This law enabled the president to forbid warring nations from using loans or credit to buy US arms, munitions, or raw natural resources of military value (oil, steel, etc.); it also made travel on ships of warring nations illegal. After the torpedoing of the *REUBEN JAMES*, Congress amended this law on 13 November 1941 by permitting US merchant ships to be armed and to carry cargoes to warring nations approved by the president.

Neutrality Proclamation On 22 April 1793, George WASHINGTON advised Americans that France and Great Britain were at war, but cautioned citizens not to assist either nation since US policy was to continue peaceful relations with both. This declaration was supplemented by the NEUTRALITY ACT (1794).

Nevada The US acquired Nev. by the treaty of GUADALUPE HIDALGO. MORMONS founded the first permanent white settlement at Genoa in June 1850. After the COMSTOCK LODE was discovered in 1859, so many miners flocked to Nev. that it was made a territory on 2 March 1861 and the 36th state on 31 October 1864. In 1870 it had 6,857 inhabitants. Hostilities with Southern PAIUTE INDIANS erupted in 1860. Between 1859 and 1880, the Comstock lode and Washoe gold region yielded $300,000,000 in bullion. The mining boom had ended by 1800 and both the economy and population declined for about two decades. In 1900 Nev. had 42,335 residents (84 percent white, 12 percent Indian, 4 percent Chinese), of whom 83 percent were rural and 24 percent were foreign-born; it ranked last in population, 49th in agricultural goods, and last in manufactures. A copper mining boom ensued after 1900 and agriculture benefited by irrigation projects under the NATIONA RECLAMATION ACT. After 1945, touris and gambling promoted rapid growth. Be tween 1940 and 1970, 264,000 person moved to the state. In 1990 Nev. was th 41st largest state and had 1,201,833 residen (79 percent white, 6 percent black, 10 pe cent Hispanic, 2 percent Indian, and 3 pe cent Asian), of which 83 percent were urba and 8.7 percent were foreign-born. Minin employed 11 percent of workers and manu facturing 6 percent.

New Amsterdam The Dutch in NE NETHERLAND founded New Amsterdam i July 1625 when they transferred a settleme from Governor's Island to lower Manhatta Island. It grew from a village of 270 person in 1628 to a town of 120 houses and 1,0 residents in 1656. It came under English ru in 1664, was occupied during the thir ANGLO-DUTCH WAR, and was rename New York, after James, Duke of York, i 1674.

New Britain campaign By April 1942, th Japanese had established their main supp base at Rabaul, New Britain Islands. B February 1944, General Douglas MAC ARTHUR could move against Rabaul becaus his forces had secured the Huon Peninsu in the NEW GUINEA CAMPAIGNS and iso lated Japan's large garrison at Bougainvil in the SOLOMON ISLANDS CAMPAIGN MacArthur encircled Rabaul with air an naval bases on the Admiralty and St Matthi Islands, neutralized it with aerial bombar ment, and by June 1944 had reduced i 100,000-man garrison to strategic impotenc

New Deal On 2 July 1932, while acceptin the Democratic nomination for presiden Franklin D. ROOSEVELT promised "a ne deal for the American people." This expres sion came to represent Roosevelt's econom programs and political policies to end th GREAT DEPRESSION. The FIRST NE DEAL began during the HUNDRED DAY Several states had their own LITTLE NE DEALS. These measures cut unemployme from 24.9 percent in mid-1933 to 20.1 pe cent in mid-1935. A SECOND NEW DEA was conceived in 1935 with new program and higher budget deficits to accelera the recovery. Business spokesmen and th bipartisan AMERICAN LIBERTY LEAGU criticized the New Deal as strangling free enterprise and raising the NATIONAL DEBT, while others like Huey LONG, Charles COUGHLIN, and Francis TOWNSEND demanded more extreme measures. The Supreme Court struck down major New Deal laws until cowed by the COURT-PACKING BILL. After Republicans gained 75 congressional and seven Senate seats in the 1938 elections, they joined conservative Democrats to block further legislative initiatives. The New Deal failed to push unemployment below 14.9 percent (mid-1937) before 1941, when rearmament for WORLD WAR II ended the depression.

New Echota, treaty of (Ga.) In 1835 the US gave the CHEROKEE INDIANS an ultimatum demanding that they sell their land and move west. On 29 December 1835, under duress, the Cherokee sold their lands for $5,000,000 and title to a reservation (*see* RESERVATIONS) in Okla. Despite the protests of most Cherokee leaders, the Senate ratified it and the nation was sent west via the TRAIL OF TEARS.

New England Emigrant Aid Company Founded on 26 April 1854 by Eli Thayer as the Mass. Emigrant Aid Society, it was reincorporated as the New England Emigrant Aid Company on 21 February 1855. It encouraged and aided financially the migration of 2,000 antislavery settlers to BLEEDING KANSAS. It remained active until 1857.

new federalism This term was used by Richard NIXON and Ronald REAGAN to describe their intentions to slow the growth of the US bureaucracy and return control of important programs to localities. The central part of Nixon's program was REVENUE-SHARING. On 26 January 1982, while reviving the concept, Reagan proposed that in return for full federal assumption of MEDICAID and distribution of $28 billion in federal funds through 1991, the states should assume responsibility for over 40 transportation, health, education, and welfare programs. Congress never enacted the proposal.

New Freedom While campaigning for president in 1912, Woodrow WILSON developed this concept as an alternative to Theodore ROOSEVELT'S NEW NATIONALISM. Whereas Roosevelt accepted the emergence of large-business combinations so long as government regulation could restrain them from abusing the public, Wilson wanted to break up TRUSTS and reestablish an economic environment where small businesses could compete with large corporations. He also wished to eliminate protectionism entirely from the tariff, whereas Roosevelt merely called for downward revision.

New Frontier This term was the theme John F. KENNEDY chose for his presidential campaign and introduced on 15 July 1960. He wished to express a break with the Eisenhower administration's policies, which had sought few major legislative initiatives and focused primarily on foreign-policy issues, aside from balancing the federal budget. Although broad and ill-defined, the New Frontier came to be seen as a renewed effort to stimulate economic growth, which had stalled due to two recessions in the 1950s, and reduce poverty. When elected, Kennedy worked for this goal by cutting federal taxes and initiating the KENNEDY ROUND OF GATT, but was blocked by Congress from enacting federal programs to deal with social problems concerning poverty, health care, and education.

New Guinea campaigns Japanese forces had overrun New Guinea's northern coast by May 1942, when their attempt to take Port Moresby by sea failed at the battle of the CORAL SEA. An overland Japanese offensive, begun on 21 July, was within 30 miles of Port Moresby on 26 September before Australian forces stopped it. US–Australian troops under Lieutenant General Robert Eichelberger drove the enemy from Papua (southwestern New Guinea) by January 1943 at a loss of 2,850 Allied killed versus 12,000 Japanese dead. From 11 September 1943 to February 1944, General Sir Thomas Blamey's troops secured the Huon Peninsula, which placed the Allies in position to isolate Japan's main supply depot at Rabaul, in the NEW BRITAIN CAMPAIGN. Between 22 April and 30 July 1944, four Allied landings destroyed the enemy's airfields and reestablished control over New Guinea's northern coast. By August, the remaining Japanese forces had been isolated, deprived of their supply bases, and could no longer threaten the imminent PHILIPPINE CAMPAIGN.

New Hampshire In the spring of 1623, David Thompson founded the first European settlement at modern Rye on the Piscataqua River estuary. In 1629 the claims of the PLYMOUTH COMPANY within N.H. were acquired by John Mason, who wished to establish a PROPRIETARY COLONY, but was frustrated when Mass. annexed its towns in the 1640s. In 1650 N.H. contained 1,300 settlers. On 18 September 1680, it was separated from Mass. and made a ROYAL COLONY, and in September 1685 it was placed under the DOMINION OF NEW ENGLAND. In 1700, 5,000 whites lived in N.H.

The colony's frontier sustained major damage in KING PHILIP'S WAR, KING WILLIAM'S WAR, and QUEEN ANNE'S WAR, and experienced lesser damage in KING GEORGE'S WAR and the SEVEN YEARS' WAR. Its most important economic activity was lumbering. In the Revolution, it furnished three of the 80 Continental regiments and outfitted 43 privateers, but escaped major fighting. It was the ninth state to ratify the CONSTITUTION on 21 June 1788. It was the seventh state in size by 1800, when it had 183,858 inhabitants, of whom 84 percent were of English-Welsh stock and 860 were black. The state never formally abolished slavery, but the number of slaves dropped from eight in 1800 to none in 1810. It disestablished the CONGREGATIONAL CHURCH in 1819. The state increasingly industrialized after 1860.

From 1800 to 1860, its population grew by just 77 percent to 326,073, of whom only 494 were black and 6 percent were foreign-born; it ranked 26th among the states in population, 28th in the value of its farmland and livestock, and 16th in manufactures. It furnished 33,937 USA troops (including 125 blacks) in the CIVIL WAR. Its population grew slowly to 1900, when it had 410,791 residents, of whom nearly all were white, 45 percent were rural, and 6 percent were foreign-born; it ranked 36th among the states in population, 41st in the value of its agricultural products and 24th in manufactures. Population grew slowly until after 1950, when an influx of new inhabitants began relocating to the state. By 1990, it was the 40th-largest state and had 1,109,252 people (97 percent white, 1 percent black, 1 percent Hispanic, and 1 percent Asian), of whor 56 percent were urban and 3.7 percer were foreign-born. Manufacturing an mining employed 30 percent of the wor force.

New Harmony commune (Ind.) *se* OWEN, ROBERT D.

New Haven The colony of New Haven origi nated when Rev. John DAVENPORT founde Quinnipiac (New Haven, Conn.) in 1637. O 6 November 1643, it united with Stamfor Guilford, and Milford to establish an inde pendent government over the southwester section of modern Conn. New Haven re stricted voting to male church members based its legal system on the Mosaic law made no provision for jury trials, and al lowed each town to send two delegates to it General Court (legislature). New Have never acquired a royal charter, and becam extinct when it was annexed under the Con Charter of 1662.

New Jersey In the spring of 1643, the firs permanent European settlement was made a Fort Nye Elfborg on the Delaware River, a an outpost of NEW SWEDEN. The Dutc placed outposts opposite Manhattan as earl as 1641, but continuous occupation did no begin until the 1650s. England acquired N.J with NEW NETHERLAND on 7 Septembe 1664. On 28 October 1664, English settle ment began with purchase of the Elizabet area. CHARLES II made N.J. a PROPRI ETARY COLONY, from which EAST JER SEY and WEST JERSEY were formed. Whe East and West Jersey merged on 26 Apr 1702 as the ROYAL COLONY of N.J., th population numbered 14,000.

N.J. was settled without provoking India hostilities. The NEW JERSEY LAND DIS ORDERS resulted from confusion over prop erty titles issued by the PROPRIETORS O EAST JERSEY and of WEST JERSEY. At th peak of the REVOLUTIONARY WAR, N.J. provided four of the 80 Continental regi ments, but also provided four Tory regiment (*see* TORIES); it was the site of 238 militar engagements, more than any other state, an was the war's major theater from late 177 to early 1777. N.J. was the third state t ratify the CONSTITUTION on 18 Decembe 1787. In 1800 it was the seventh state i size and had 211,149 residents, of whom percent were black, over half were English or Welsh, and a fifth were Dutch.

N.J. abolished SLAVERY by a gradual emancipation law in 1804. By 1860 its population had grown by 218 percent and it had 672,035 people, of whom 4 percent were black and 18 percent were foreign-born; it ranked 20th among the states in population, 13th in the value of its farmland and livestock and 6th in manufactures. In the CIVIL WAR, it furnished 76,814 USA troops (including 1,185 blacks), but contained many COPPERHEADS and was one of only three states to vote against Abraham LINCOLN's reelection in 1864.

By 1900 it had 1,883,669 residents, of whom 29 percent were rural, 4 percent black, and 23 percent foreign-born; it ranked 16th in population, 30th in the value of its agricultural products, and 6th in manufactures. Thereafter, its population rose sharply. From 1900 to 1930, it gained 1,096,600 inmigrants, and another 1,360,000 from 1940 to 1970. By 1990 it was the ninth largest state and had 7,730,188 people (74 percent white, 13 percent black, 10 percent Hispanic, 3 percent Asian), of whom 89 percent were urban and 12.5 percent foreign-born. Manufacturing or mining employed 23 percent of workers.

New Jersey land disorders Between 1745 and 1754, at least 23 incidents of threatened or actual violence occurred in six counties of central N.J. where uncertain land titles left large numbers of residents threatened with losing their farms. Crowds resisted the serving of eviction orders, broke open jails, and assaulted militia and sheriffs assigned to guard prisoners. These events ranked as the third most dramatic outburst of rural violence in the 18th-century colonies, along with the 1766 uprising on the NEW YORK MANORS and the GREEN MOUNTAIN BOYS' mayhem.

New Jersey Plan On 15 June 1787, William Paterson offered an alternative to the VIRGINIA PLAN at the CONSTITUTIONAL CONVENTION. The N.J. Plan proposed a BICAMERAL LEGISLATURE in which each state had an equal vote in both houses, a plural executive elected by Congress, and a federal judiciary. Congress would possess power to levy taxes and to regulate foreign and domestic commerce. Foreign treaties and congressional statutes would be the supreme law of the land. The plan was rejected on 19 June, but its provision for equal representation in the upper house became part of the CONSTITUTION.

New Jersey proprietors *see* PROPRIETORS OF EAST JERSEY *and* OF WEST JERSEY

New Lights *see* GREAT AWAKENING, FIRST

New Madrid, battle of (Mo.) On 7 April 1862, Major General John Pope's 19,000 Federals captured Brigadier General William Mackall's fortifications at New Madrid and Island Number 10, including 3,500 CSA prisoners. Pope's victory opened the Mississippi to USA naval operations south to Memphis, which was taken on 6 June.

New Mexico In 1598, 500 Spaniards under Juan de Onate founded the first Spanish settlement at San Juan. In 1680, POPÉ'S REVOLT drove out the 2,800 Spanish living in the upper Rio Grande valley until Spanish authority was restored by 1692. The area remained sparsely settled when Anglo-Americans established overland trade via the SANTA FE TRAIL in 1821. When the US acquired N.Mex. by the treaty of GUADALUPE HIDALGO, almost 70,000 Spanish-speaking persons inhabited the territory. N.Mex. received the region east of the Rio Grande from Tex. by the COMPROMISE OF 1850.

In 1860 it had 93, 516 inhabitants (including modern Ariz.), of whom 95 percent were Hispanic; it ranked 35th in population, 35th in the value of its farmland and livestock, and 36th in manufactures. It was occupied by CSA forces from July 1861 to March 1862, and was the site of NAVAJO CAMPAIGNS. Hispanics outnumbered Anglo-Americans until after 1900 and played a leading role in politics. Economic development accelerated after 1881, when it was first linked to the Pacific by TRANSCONTINENTAL RAILROADS. Mining, cattle ranching, and sheep grazing were the 19th-century economy's mainstays. In 1900 N.Mex. was 87 percent rural; it had 195,310 residents (66 percent Hispanic, 26 percent Anglo-American, 1 percent black, and 7 percent Indian), of whom 87 percent were rural and 7 percent foreign-born; it ranked 44th in population, 46th in the value of its agricultural products, and 46th in manufactures. N.Mex. became the 47th state on 6 January 1912. Development of energy resources and rapid urbanization diversified the economy. In 1990 it was the 37th largest state and had 1,515,069 residents (50 percent Anglo-American, 38 percent Hispanic, 9 percent Indian, 2 percent black, and 1 percent Asian), of whom 48 percent were urban and 5.3 percent were foreign-born. Mining employed 10 percent of workers and manufacturing 8 percent.

New Nationalism On 1 September 1912, at Osawatomie, Kans., Theodore Roosevelt outlined a New Nationalism that would use federal powers to fight for social justice, through progressive inheritance and income taxes, improved working conditions for women and children, workmen's accident insurance, closer regulation of trusts (rather than their dissolution), and revising tariffs lower. This agenda epitomized the thesis of Herbert Croly's *The Promise of American Life*. As presidential candidate for the Progressive party, he ran on this program against the New Freedom of Woodrow Wilson.

New Netherland Dutch merchants had sponsored explorations of the mid-Atlantic region, such as Henry Hudson's voyage that located Hudson River, and had built a temporary trading post opposite modern Albany in 1614, but the first permanent settlement was not made until summer 1624, when the Dutch West India Company built outposts at New York Bay, Albany, and the Delaware River near Gloucester, N.J. On 4 May 1626, Peter Minuit founded New Amsterdam on Manhattan Island. The company claimed modern Del., Pa., N.J., and all land east of the Connecticut River. Because the company lacked the resources to exploit the Delaware valley, New Sweden's settlers trespassed on Dutch claims there until Peter Stuyvesant annexed them by force in 1655. The fur trade was New Netherland's economic mainstay, but the West India Company also tried to develop its economic resources by patroonships. The Dutch and Indians fought Kiefft's War, the Peach War, and the Esopus wars. Its population grew slowly, and by 1660 probably numbered just 5,500, of whom 600 lived along the Delaware River. On Sep. 1664, Stuyvesant surrendered New Netherland to an English task force under Colonel Richard Nicolls.

New Orleans, battles of (La.) (1) On 1 December 1814, Major General Edwar Pakenham began disembarking 11,000 British troops. On 23–4 December, Major General Andrew Jackson's 2,000 US troops killed 46, wounded 167, and captured 64 of Pakenham's advance guard of 1,800, at a loss of 24 dead, 115 wounded, and 74 missing. On 25–31 December, skirmishing left 1 British killed, 38 wounded, and 2 missing but cost 9 US dead and 8 wounded. On January 1815, British artillery bombardment and infantry raids left 11 US dead, 2 wounded, and 3 of Jackson's artillery damaged, while the British lost 32 killed, 4 wounded, and 2 missing. On 8 January 181 Jackson's 4,700 troops repulsed two frontal attacks by 5,300 regulars (with artillery and reserves of 3,200), who then retreated. US losses: 13 killed, 13 wounded, 19 missing. British losses: 192 killed (including Pakenham), 1,265 wounded, and 484 missing. New Orleans was the war's most lopsided US victory, but occurred 15 days after the treaty of Ghent. The battle offset public disillusionment over the US Army's poor war record and made Jackson a national hero.

(2) On 25 April 1862, Flag Officer David Farragut's USA fleet (9 sloops, 14 gunboats, 19 mortar schooners, transports carrying Major General Benjamin Butler's 15,000 troops) took the city from Mansfield Lovell's 3,000 CSA militia and 12 gunboats. USA losses: 37 killed, 147 wounded. CSA losses: 50 killed, wounded, 12 gunboats sunk.

New Orleans riot (La.) On 30 July 1866 whites attacked a Unionist meeting being held to advocate enfranchising La. freedmen and disqualifying prominent ex-Confederates from elections. The assailants killed 35 persons (mostly black) and wounded over 100, including former governor Michael Hahn. The massacre shocked public opinion in the North, and influenced the mid-term elections, which left Republicans controlling two-thirds of each house of Congress and able to override Andrew Johnson's vetoes.

New South movement This term refers to the values and program of post-Civil War southern intellectuals like Henry Grady (Atlanta *Constitution*), Edward De Leon (*De Bow's Review*), and Henry Watterson (Louisville *Courier-Journal*). They advocated reconciliation with the North, economic revitalization, and ending the race problem. *De Bow's Review* introduced the concept about 1870 and Edward De Leon coined the phrase itself. The New South creed advocated industrializing, diversifying agriculture, attracting immigrants, accumulating investment capital, and promoting a spirit of business enterprise. Booker WASHINGTON's program of industrial education for blacks complemented these goals.

New Sweden In 1637 a royal charter authorized the New Sweden Company, which was led by Willem Usselinx and Peter MINUIT, to colonize the Delaware River. Minuit landed with the earliest settlers near Lewes, Del., in March 1638 and then built Fort Christina near modern Wilmington. The Swedes built Fort Nye Elfborg in N.J. in 1642 and made the first settlement in Pa. at Tinicum, 9 miles south of modern Philadelphia, in 1643. The FUR TRADE was the colony's economic mainstay and the population never exceeded 500. NEW NETHERLAND claimed the Delaware valley and conflict between the colonies escalated after 1648. On 26 September 1655, Peter STUYVESANT completed a military conquest of New Sweden, which was then annexed.

New York In 1614 the first permanent European settlement was made at Fort Nassau, opposite modern Albany, as an outpost of NEW NETHERLAND. The DUTCH WEST INDIA COMPANY directed colonization after 1621 and founded NEW AMSTERDAM (modern New York) on 4 May 1626. The FUR TRADE was the most important economic activity and led to close ties between the IROQUOIS CONFEDERACY and Dutch. The Dutch and various ALGONQUIAN INDIANS fought KIEFFT'S WAR, the PEACH WAR, and the ESOPUS WARS. On 12 March 1664, CHARLES II gave his brother James, Duke of York, title to the PROPRIETARY COLONY of N.Y., which Colonel Richard Nicolls conquered on 7 September 1664 in the second ANGLO-DUTCH WAR. The Netherlands reoccupied the colony in 1673 during the third ANGLO-DUTCH WAR, but returned it to England in 1674. When the Duke of York was proclaimed JAMES II (6 February 1685), N.Y. became a ROYAL COLONY. When England overthrew James II, LEISLER'S REBELLION followed in N.Y.

In 1700 N.Y. had 19,000 colonists. It saw much fighting in KING WILLIAM'S WAR, QUEEN ANNE'S WAR, KING GEORGE'S WAR, and the SEVEN YEARS' WAR. As foodstuffs replaced furs as the most valuable export, it became the only colony where lifelong tenancy was widespread after 1715 on the NEW YORK MANORS. By 1775 settlement had spread through the Mohawk and Schoharie valleys, while 9,000 Iroquois occupied all of the colony's western half.

In the REVOLUTIONARY WAR, N.Y. mustered five of the Continental army's 80 regiments and had more TORIES than any other state; it was the site of 228 military engagements, second only to N.J., and was a major war theater in 1776 and 1777. The British occupied New York City from 1776 to 1783. SULLIVAN'S CAMPAIGN drove most of the Iroquois from western N.Y., but white settlers were reluctant to move there because British garrisons occupied the state at Forts Niagara, Ontario, and Oswegatchie until removed by JAY'S TREATY. N.Y. was the third state to ratify the CONSTITUTION on 18 December 1787. It abolished SLAVERY by gradual emancipation in 1799.

In 1800 it was the third state in size and had 598,051 residents, of whom slightly more than half were English or Welsh, a sixth were Dutch, and 5 percent were black. N.Y. was a major theater in the WAR OF 1812. It displaced Va. as the largest state in 1820, and continued to grow rapidly due to the ERIE CANAL and European immigration. Its politics were dominated by the ALBANY REGENCY and TAMMANY HALL. By 1860 it had 3,880,735 people, of whom 1 percent were black and 26 percent were foreign-born; it ranked first among the states in the value of both its manufactures and its farmland and livestock. N.Y. furnished 448,850 USA troops (including 4,125 blacks), but dissatisfaction with the war effort produced the Civil War DRAFT RIOTS in 1863.

By 1900 it stood first among states with 7,268,894 residents, of whom 1 percent were black, 26 percent foreign-born, and 27 percent rural; it ranked fourth in the value of its agricultural goods and first in manufactures. Between 1900 and 1930, 2,590,500 persons moved to the state. Growth moderated after 1930, and Calif. replaced it as the largest state in 1960. In 1990 it was 91 percent urban and had 17,990,455 people (approx. 69 percent white, 14 percent black, 12 percent Hispanic, 4 percent Asian), of whom 15.8 percent were foreign-born. Manufacturing or mining employed 30 percent of workers. In 1994, Tex. displaced it as the second-largest state.

New York draft riots *see* DRAFT RIOTS, CIVIL WAR

New York manors N.Y. was the only colony (besides Md.) to establish landed manors with special judicial and political privileges. PATROONSHIPS were precursors of the manors. From 1664 to 1697, N.Y. governors patented about 30 manorial grants totaling over 2,000,000 acres, but by 1750 all had disappeared through subdivision among the grantee's heirs, except Rennselaerswyck (850,000 acres), Livingston Manor (160,000 acres), Philipsburgh (92,000 acres), Cortlandt Manor (86,000 acres), Morris Manor (1,920 acres) and Gardiner's Island (3,300 acres). By 1760 these manors contained perhaps 6,000 tenants. The manors of Cortlandt, Livingston, and Rennselaerswyck could each elect a representative to the assembly. In 1766 major rioting erupted among tenants on the lower Hudson River, especially on Cortlandt and Livingston manors, that left four dead. In 1839–40, violence again flared among tenants in the ANTIRENT WAR, which resulted in laws that forbade leases of long duration and protected tenants' rights.

New York proprietor *see* PROPRIETORS OF NEW YORK

New York Suspending Act (2 July 1767) After the N.Y. assembly refused to obey the QUARTERING ACT (1765) in December 1766, Parliament declared that if the legislature did not comply by 1 October 1767, then none of its laws would have legal force. The law never went into effect because on 6 June, prior to its passage, N.Y. voted to furnish the military supplies stipulated by the act, but under protest that its appropriation was not done in recognition of the Quartering Act's constitutionality. To avoid future confrontations, Britain ceased trying to enforce the act after 1767.

New York* Times v. *Sullivan On 9 March 1964, the Supreme Court unanimously held that the FIRST AMENDMENT shielded the press from libel suits arising from journalistic reports that injured a public figure's reputation. There would be no protection if evidence proved that the press acted maliciously, either by publicizing statements known to be false or by an irresponsible failure to ascertain whether its charges were true. This ruling freed the press from the threat of meritless lawsuits when it had done its duty by investigating wrongdoing by public figures.

Newberry* v. *United States On 2 May 1921, the Supreme Court ruled (5–4) that Congress lacked jurisdiction to regulate how candidates campaigned in state primaries for federal elections, because a primary was "in no real sense part of the manner of holding the election." *UNITED STATES* v. *CLASSIC* reversed *Newberry*.

Newburgh conspiracy On 10 March 1783, an anonymous message (by Major John Armstrong) to Continental army officers circulated at their Newburgh, N.Y., camp. The message denounced Congress's failure to provide back pay or guarantee postwar pensions, and hinted that the army should take strong – but unspecified – measures to resolve these grievances. George WASHINGTON forbade a meeting scheduled for 11 March to draft an ultimatum to Congress; on 15 March, he deflated the conspiracy with a speech that expressed his confidence in Congress and counseled patience among the officers.

Newlands Act (1902) *see* NATIONAL RECLAMATION ACT

Newlands Act (15 July 1913) Congress replaced the ERDMAN ACT's provisions for resolving railroad labor disputes with a four-member Board of Mediation and Conciliation. Between 1913 and 1917, it settled 58 disputes between labor and management. Arbitration was made compulsory in WORLD WAR I, after which the Newlands Act was replaced by the ESCH–CUMMINS ACT.

Newton, Huey (b. Monroe, La., 17 November 1942; d. Oakland, Calif., 22 August 1989) He grew up in Oakland, Calif., where he and Bobby SEALE founded the BLACK PANTHER PARTY in 1966. In 1968 he was found guilty of voluntary manslaughter in the 1967 killing of a policeman, but his conviction was overturned on 29 May 1970. In 1974 charges for shooting a woman were dropped after two trials ended in hung juries. He fled to Cuba in 1974 after being charged with murder for a death in a street fight. Newton returned in July 1977 to face trial and announced that he had rejected violence and the Panthers for peaceful political behavior. Retried in 1978 and found guilty on murder charges, his conviction was overturned on appeal. He earned a Ph.D. in 1980. He was murdered by a street-gang member.

Nez Perce campaign In 1877 the US tried to force NEZ PERCE INDIANS in Oregon's Grand Ronde valley to sell their lands and join other Nez Perce in Idaho. On 13–16 June, resentful Indians murdered 19 whites; on 18 June, 135 warriors ambushed 111 US Cavalry and killed 34, at a loss of 3 Indians wounded. About 820 Nez Perce (including 300 fighting men) tried to reach Canada under hot pursuit by Brigadier General Oliver Howard's 735 soldiers and Indian scouts. After trekking 1,700 miles across the Continental Divide, CHIEF JOSEPH surrendered 400 people 50 miles from Canada on 5 October, while 300 others escaped the army. US losses: 35 settlers killed, 150 soldiers killed and 150 wounded. Nez Perce losses: 60 men and 60 women and children killed.

Nez Perce Indians This people, speakers of one of the SAHAPTIN LANGUAGES, originally occupied the Snake and Grande Ronde valleys of Wash., Oreg., and Idaho. They acquired horses about 1720 and bred herds for trading to other Indians, and later to pioneers on the OREGON TRAIL, and miners. When observed by the LEWIS AND CLARK EXPEDITION, they numbered about 3,000 in 60 villages. They split into factions during the 1860s over whether to sell land to the US; they eventually sold large quantities, and most accepted reservation status. They stayed at peace with the US until the 1870s, when the anti-reservation faction fought the NEZ PERCE CAMPAIGN. They are now settled on reservations at Nespelem, Wash., and Lapwai, Idaho.

Niagara movement This organization was founded at Niagara Falls, N.Y., in July 1905 by black leaders, including W. E. B. DU BOIS, to demand an end to racial discrimination. Its initial manifesto attacked SEGREGATION, BLACK DISFRANCHISEMENT, JIM CROW LAWS, lack of educational opportunity, and exclusion of blacks from labor unions. In contrast to Booker WASHINGTON's philosophy that blacks should avoid political confrontations until they had improved their economic status through industrial training, the Niagara activists advocated confronting lawmakers and the courts with demands for political and social equality. The movement never won broad support and was supplanted by the NATIONAL ASSOCIATION FOR THE ADVANCEMENT OF COLORED PEOPLE as the leading advocate for civil rights progress.

Nicaragua, US intervention in (1) In May 1910, a USMC battalion occupied Bluefields to protect US business interests during a civil war and encourage support for pro-US guerrillas, who took over the government. On 14 August 1912, 354 marines landed to aid a pro-US Diaz government toppled by a coup, and were joined on 4 September by two more battalions. At a loss of 5 killed and 16 wounded, the marines helped return the conservatives to power and largely withdrew in October. The US withdrew the USMC company guarding its embassy in 1921 after rioting marines destroyed a newspaper and killed 6 policemen. Between 1 January and 31 March 1926, 3,300 marines landed to support the pro-US Diaz government against General Augustino Sandino's rebels; marines sustained 47 killed and 66 wounded until the last were evacuated on 2 January 1933.

(2) From 1937 to 1979, the US provided significant support for the Somoza dictatorship, despite significant evidence of public discontent stemming from its political repression. The CIA financed and helped train a guerrilla army, the Contras, to topple Nicaragua's pro-Communist Sandinista government from 1982 until 1990, when elections forced the Sandinista regime of Daniel Ortega to share power in a rightist government headed by Violetta Barrios de Chamorro. US

anti-Sandinista activities culminated in the IRAN-CONTRA SCANDAL.

Nicollet explorations In the summer of 1634, Jean Nicollet de Belleborne left Quebec for Lake Huron, entered Lake Michigan via Michilimackinac, reached Green Bay, and descended the Fox River. He was the first European to explore the westernmost Great Lakes.

Niebuhr, Reinhold (b. Wright City, Mo., 21 June 1892; d. Stockbridge, Mass., 1 June 1971) After earning a B.D. (1914) and M.A. (1915) from the Yale Divinity School, Niebuhr was ordained an Evangelical minister and held a Detroit pastorate until 1928, when he joined the Union Theological Seminary faculty. He became professor of Christian Ethics in 1930. Although influenced by the SOCIAL GOSPEL and liberal in his inclinations (he was a founding member of AMERICANS FOR DEMOCRATIC ACTION), he explored questions of religious meaning and Christian duty in terms of a highly sophisticated and learned neoorthodoxy, which emphasized sinfulness, faith, and redemption. Niebuhr was the most profound and influential modern US theologian. His writings included *Does Civilization Need Religion?* (1927), *Moral Man and Immoral Society* (1932), *An Interpretation of Christian Ethics* (1935), *Beyond Tragedy* (1937), *The Nature and Destiny of Man* (1941–3), and *Faith and History* (1949).

Nimitz, Chester William (b. Fredericksburg, Tex., 23 February 1885; d. San Francisco, Calif., 20 February 1966) Nimitz graduated from Annapolis in 1905 and performed duty in the submarine service in WORLD WAR I. In WORLD WAR II, he assumed command of the Pacific after Admiral Husband Kimmel was relieved in December 1941. He directed the advance upon Japan via the central Pacific and by campaigns in the SOLOMON, GILBERT, MARSHALL, and MARIANA ISLANDS, PELELIU, and OKINAWA. At the end of the war, he commanded the largest naval force ever collected for warfare: 6,256 ships and 4,847 combat aircraft. He became special assistant for the Navy Department in 1947 and chief of the UN team mediating the Kashmir dispute in 1949.

Nineteenth Amendment Submitted to the states on 4 June 1919, last ratified on 18 August 1920, and officially proclaimed on 26 August 1920, it gave women the right to vote. At the time it was ratified, it gave women full voting rights in 19 states and partial rights in 14 others.

Ninth Amendment Submitted to the states on 25 September 1789, last ratified by Va. on 15 December 1791, and officially proclaimed on 30 December 1791, it obligated the federal government to respect not only all rights of citizenship specifically protected by the CONSTITUTION and BILL OF RIGHTS, but also the full range of other freedoms then enjoyed by the people. The Ninth Amendment encouraged the Supreme Court to presume that individuals enjoyed the widest scope of personal freedom consistent with maintaining public order, but has not been cited as the basis for any major court rulings.

NIRA *see* NATIONAL INDUSTRIAL RECOVERY ACT

Nix* v. *Williams On 11 June 1984, the Supreme Court allowed the "inevitable discovery" exception to the exclusionary rule (*see* *WEEKS* v. *UNITED STATES*) by holding that evidence improperly seized during a search can be admitted in court if ultimately or inevitably it would have been discovered by lawful means.

Nixon, Richard Milhous (b. Yorba Linda, Calif., 9 January 1913; d. New York, N.Y., 18 April 1994) After naval service in WORLD WAR II, Nixon entered politics as a Republican, sat in Congress from 1947 to 1950 from Calif., and became a senator in 1950. His dogged pursuit of Alger HISS's perjury led to nomination as vice-president in 1952. In 1960 he lost the closest race for president since 1884 with 49.5 percent of the vote, just 118,574 less than John F. KENNEDY, and in 1962 lost election as Calif. governor.

He exploited widespread dissatisfaction with the VIETNAM WAR to become president in the three-party contest of 1968, with 43.4 percent of the vote. He stated the NIXON DOCTRINE, began withdrawing troops from Vietnam, became the first US president to visit China, initiated DÉTENTE, and reversed the SUPREME COURT's liberal era under Earl WARREN by appointing four conservative justices. He took the US off the GOLD

STANDARD, initiated the Tokyo round of GATT, ended the DRAFT, established the ENVIRONMENTAL PROTECTION AGENCY and the Occupational Safety and Health Administration (OSHA), conceptualized the NEW FEDERALISM, introduced REVENUE-SHARING, and reduced the budget deficit to its lowest percentage of GDP since 1941. Congress did not act on his proposals to reform welfare or concentrate federal funding for health care on the indigent and an insurance against catastrophic illness.

He won a landslide victory in 1972 by polling 60.7 percent of the ballots and taking every state but Mass. He completed withdrawal of US forces from Vietnam in his second term and ended the war by the PARIS PEACE ACCORDS. The investigation of the WATERGATE SCANDAL implicated him in a conspiracy to obstruct justice, and he resigned on 9 August 1974 to avoid impeachment. He was spared further legal embarrassment by a pardon from Gerald FORD on 8 September.

Nixon Doctrine On 25 July 1969, President Richard NIXON announced that once the US had withdrawn from the VIETNAM WAR, it would continue to provide military security for Japan and other friendly Asian nations through its nuclear deterrent, but would not permit American troops to bear the main burden of waging ground combat to defend other nations. The doctrine represented a compromise between the CONTAINMENT POLICY and US disillusionment with Vietnam.

Nixon* v. *Herndon On 7 March 1927, the Supreme Court unanimously struck down a Tex. law barring blacks from voting in the Democratic primary. It held that the FOURTEENTH AMENDMENT's equal protection clause forbade states to legislate a WHITE PRIMARY. The Tex. legislature tried to circumvent the decision by empowering the Democratic party's state executive committee to set eligibility for voting. After the party excluded blacks, the Court invalidated its action (5–4) in *Nixon* v. *Condon* (2 May 1932); it reasoned that the party had merely acted as the state's agent, and that neither could disfranchise voters solely for reasons of race. The Court reversed itself in *GROVEY* v. *TOWNSEND*.

NLRB *see* NATIONAL LABOR RELATIONS BOARD

Nonimportation Act (18 April 1806) To retaliate for seizures of US ships trading with the French West Indies and IMPRESSMENT of US seamen, this law forbade the importation of British manufactures that could be provided by other countries or produced in the US, with effect from 15 November 1806. The US suspended its enforcement on 19 December as an incentive for Britain to negotiate an agreement settling these grievances. When Britain refused to compromise on the issue of American neutral rights, the law was put into effect on 14 December 1807, and then followed by the EMBARGO ACT.

Nonimportation Agreement, first This agreement was adopted on 31 October 1765 when New York City merchants agreed not to import British goods until the STAMP ACT was repealed. The boycott had been adopted almost universally by early 1766 and led to a sharp drop in trade, which led British merchants and manufacturers to lobby Parliament for the Stamp Act's repeal.

Nonimportation Agreement, second This agreement was formed to force repeal of the TOWNSHEND REVENUE ACT. An ineffective boycott of luxury goods was initiated by Boston in October 1767 and widely copied, but not until August 1768 did colonial merchants – beginning with New York City and Boston – resort to a total cutoff of British imports. The movement grew slowly and the last major city (Charles Town, S.C.) did not join until July 1769. The boycott eventually reduced British exports to America by 40 percent. On 12 April 1770, after intense lobbying by merchants eager for full resumption of trade, Parliament eliminated all the Townshend taxes except those on tea. Despite efforts to maintain the full boycott until the tax on tea was withdrawn, nonimportation collapsed between July and October 1770, when several major cities imposed a selective boycott on tea, but otherwise resumed importing British goods.

Nonimportation Agreement, third *see* CONTINENTAL ASSOCIATION

Nonintercourse Act (1 March 1809) This law repealed the EMBARGO ACT and allowed US ships to resume international trade with all countries but France and Britain. Commerce with these countries would only continue when either agreed to honor the American merchant marine's neutral rights. Trade was reopened with Britain on 19 April 1809 after the US received an assurance that the Royal Navy would not interfere with American shipping, but then closed on 9 August when Britain disavowed this promise. MACON'S BILL NUMBER 2 replaced this law.

nonseparating Puritans This group of adherents of PURITANISM wished to retain the structure of an established state church, but worked within the Church of England to set up autonomous congregations that could choose their ministers and administer the parish free of interference from bishops. Nonseparating Puritans established the ecclesiastical structures of Mass., Conn., and N.H.

Nootka Sound crisis In 1789 the Spanish navy arrested British fur traders occupying a post on Nootka Sound, British Columbia, which was claimed by Spain. When Britain hinted at war in an ultimatum, George WASHINGTON chaired the federal government's first cabinet debate on whether to resist British forces crossing the US to attack Spanish La. The crisis passed, but left Spanish officials worried that the US might allow British forces to march across its soil for an invasion. This apprehension motivated Spain to make generous concessions to the US in the treaty of SAN LORENZO, as a means of forestalling any Anglo-American military cooperation against La.

Noriega, Manuel *see* PANAMA, US INTERVENTION IN

Norman* v. *Baltimore and Ohio Railroad Company *see* GOLD STANDARD

Normandy, invasion of (France) On 6 June 1944 (D-DAY), in an operation directly commanded by British Field Marshal Bernard Montgomery, 23,000 paratroopers (one British and two US divisions) dropped behind German lines, while 702 warships (including 6 battleships, 23 cruisers, and 68 destroyers) and 4,781 supporting vessels (including 4,100 landing craft) landed 57,500 Americans and 75,000 British and Canadians to five beachheads defended by 30,000 German troops, 890 aircraft, and 130 tanks. The landing was supported by 12,000 Allied aircraft. Troops began landing at 0630 and met light resistance, except for the First US Division on Omaha Beach. Allied losses in the first 24 hours were 1,465 killed, 3,184 wounded, 1,928 missing, and 28 captured, of which half were US casualties. During the first 48 hours, the Allies landed 176,000 men and 1,500 tanks. By 1 July, almost 1,000,000 men, 500,000 tons of supplies, and 177,000 vehicles were put ashore; during that period, the Allies lost 122,000 men, versus German casualties of 156,000 (including 41,000 prisoners). Deaths among French civilians in Normandy totaled about 15,000.

Norris, Frank (b. Chicago, Ill., 5 March 1870; d. San Francisco, Calif., 25 October 1902) Born Benjamin Franklin Norris, he began his career as a novelist after completing his education at Berkeley and Harvard. He became a leading figure in the development of an American literature that portrayed the struggle of life in realistic and frank terms. His major works were *Moran of the Lady Letty* (1898), *Blix* (1899), *McTeague: A Story of San Francisco (1899), The Octopus* (1901), *A Man's Woman* (1901), *The Pit* (1903).

Norris, George William (b. Sandusky, Ohio, 11 July 1861; d. McCook, Nebr., 2 September 1944) After moving to Nebr. in 1885, Norris became active in politics as a Republican reformer during the PROGRESSIVE ERA. He served as a congressman (1903–12), and senator (1913–42). He played a major role in breaking House Speaker Joseph CANNON's stranglehold over congressional legislation. He opposed US involvement in WORLD WAR I and the LEAGUE OF NATIONS. He was one of the most influential senators during the NEW DEAL. He drafted the TWENTIETH AMENDMENT, whose passage came almost entirely from his own efforts. He was the leading advocate for farm relief laws and the TENNESSEE VALLEY AUTHORITY. He sponsored the RURAL ELECTRIFICATION ADMINISTRATION and farm-forestry acts. As one of Congress's leading liberals, he fought to outlaw YELLOW-DOG CONTRACTS and end the use of court injunctions against strikers by the NORRIS–LA GUARDIA ACT.

Norris–La Guardia Act (23 March 1932) This law forbade courts from issuing injunctions to end strikes, SECONDARY BOYCOTT's, or picketing; it also made YELLOW-DOG CONTRACTS unenforceable. It stopped federal judges from intervening on management's behalf during collective bargaining disputes, as had been common since IN RE DEBS.

Norris* v. *Alabama *see* SCOTTSBORO CASE, SECOND

Norris* v. *Boston *see* PASSENGER CASES

North, Lord Frederick (b. London, England, 13 April 1732; d. London, England, 5 August 1792) He entered Parliament in 1754, and succeeded Charles TOWNSHEND as chancellor of the exchequer in December 1767. He took over as prime minister from the Duke of GRAFTON in March 1770. North was primarily responsible for prolonging Britain's constitutional crisis with the colonies by blocking the repeal of the tea tax when the other Townshend duties were withdrawn in 1770. His ministry passed the TEA ACT (1773) and the INTOLERABLE ACTS. In February 1775, he persuaded Parliament to offer the colonies a conciliatory compromise, in which Britain would refrain from taxing the colonies directly, so long as their legislatures complied with requisitions from Parliament to enact taxes for subsidizing the cost of British troops and civil servants in the colonies. Since the offer amounted to a system of indirect taxation that the colonists had no option but to accept, it was rejected in America. He resigned as prime minister in March 1782 when it was clear that Britain must grant the US independence.

North American Free Trade Agreement (NAFTA) George BUSH's administration negotiated this treaty with Mexico and Canada, but William CLINTON won ratification on 20 November 1993 after overcoming stiff opposition by protectionists and organized labor. By phasing out tariffs and other barriers on the exchange of goods, services, and investments, over 15 years, the pact creates the world's largest free-trade zone and serves as a basis to integrate commerce within the western hemisphere as the Common Market does in Europe.

North Atlantic Treaty Organization (NATO) In September 1947, the Soviet Union and eight East European Communist nations united in a military alliance termed the Warsaw Pact. On 4 April 1949, the NATO Treaty was signed in Washington by the US, Canada, Britain, France, Italy, Netherlands, Belgium, Luxembourg, Norway, Denmark, and Iceland. Its signatories pledged that an attack on any member would trigger a unanimous counterattack by all. The US Senate ratified NATO on 21 July. (Greece and Turkey joined in 1952.) With Communism's collapse after 1989, several former Warsaw Pact nations inquired about NATO membership in 1993. At a NATO summit in January 1994, western leaders declined to offer full membership to any of its ex-adversaries, but began investigating a limited association that would involve joint training exercises and closer relations.

North Carolina At least as early as 1657, settlers had moved to Albemarle Sound in N.C. from Va. Modern N.C. was included within the PROPRIETARY COLONY of CAROLINA; it received its own legislature in 1665, experienced poor political relations with the proprietors (against whom CULPEPER'S REBELLION was directed), and became a ROYAL COLONY on 25 July 1729. Its settlers produced foodstuffs, tobacco, and forestry products. It was the scene of the TUSCARORA WAR and some fighting in the CHEROKEE WAR. After 1740, Anglo-Americans and Europeans occupied its PIEDMONT, where the REGULATOR movement erupted in 1771. By the Revolution, 35 percent of its 250,000 colonists were slaves.

Fighting as British allies, the CHEROKEE INDIANS attacked the frontier in 1776, but the militia drove them from the state and far into the mountains. N.C. had many TORIES, especially among its Scots, but they were decisively beaten at the battle of MOORE'S CREEK BRIDGE in 1776 and did not rise again until the British invaded in 1780. It was the site of 65 military actions and was the main theater of operations in 1780–1. Six of the 80 Continental regiments were usually from N.C. On 2 August 1788, N.C. rejected the CONSTITUTION, but ratified it later, on 21 November 1789 as the 12th state.

In 1800 N.C. was the fifth largest state and had 478,103 people, of whom 35 percent were slaves. Tobacco remained a leading staple, but cotton production grew rapidly after 1800. By 1860 it had 992,622 inhabitants, of whom 33 percent were slaves and less than 1 percent were foreign-born; it ranked 12th in population, 16th in the value of its farmland and livestock, and 21st in manufactures.

N.C. became the 11th CSA state on 20 May 1861. In the CIVIL WAR, it furnished 108,000 CSA soldiers and 8,191 USA troops (3,156 whites and 5,035 blacks). It was the site of 313 military engagements.

In May 1865 Andrew JOHNSON instituted a provisional civilian government, which ended slavery in October, but failed to enfranchise FREEDMEN. White supremacists took over the new legislature, and passed a black code (*see* BLACK CODES) denying freedmen full civil rights. Washington imposed military rule on 2 March 1867, but restored self-government and congressional representation on 25 June 1868. Republican control ended two years later on 3 November 1870. N.C. disfranchised most blacks in 1900 and then enacted racial SEGREGATION.

The cigarette industry's rise produced strong demand for tobacco and helped revive the state economy. In 1900 it was the 15th largest state and had 1,893,810 residents, of whom 90 percent were rural, 33 percent were black, and just 4,492 were foreign-born. From 1920 to 1970, it lost 773,300 out-migrants, mostly blacks leaving for northern cities, and its racial composition shifted significantly. During the CIVIL RIGHTS MOVEMENT, desegregation was implemented with a minimum of violence. Its economy became increasingly diversified with small industry after 1940 and Charlotte emerged as the largest city in the Carolinas by the 1980s. By 1990 N.C. ranked as the tenth largest state and had 6,628,637 people (75 percent white, 22 percent black, 1 percent Hispanic, 1 percent Asian, 1 percent Indian), of whom 57 percent were urban and 1.7 percent were foreign-born. Manufacturing and mining employed 34 percent of the work force.

North Carolina proprietors *see* PROPRIETORS OF CAROLINA

North Dakota The US acquired N.Dak. by the LOUISIANA PURCHASE. Anglo-American settlement began in 1856 as part of NEBRASKA. The US created Dakota Territory in 1861. In 1870 17 percent of Dakota's 14,181 settlers lived in N.Dak. The first HOMESTEAD ACT greatly stimulated in-migration after the third SIOUX WAR ended in 1878. When it became the 39th state on 2 November 1889, its population was 190,000.

Between 1887 and 1898, adequate rain for crops fell in just two years on the plains and commodity prices dropped sharply. During the 1890s, in-migration slowed greatly and strong political support arose for POPULISM. Growth resumed in 1898, and about 250,000 homesteaders came to N.Dak. from then to 1915. In 1900 N.Dak. had 319,146 inhabitants (98 percent white, 2 percent Indian), of whom 93 percent were rural and 35 percent foreign-born; it ranked 41st in population, 26th in agricultural products, and 44th in manufactures. Low commodity prices crushed farm values, which fell by $500 million from 1920 to 1925. Drought crippled output in the 1930s. From 1920 to 1940, 182,100 persons left the state. Another 109,400 left in the 1940s. The state's population had declined by 42,045 (6 percent) from 1930 to 1990. In 1990 it was the 46th-largest state and had 638,800 residents (94 percent white, 4 percent Indian, 1 percent Hispanic, 1 percent black or Asian), of whom 40 percent were urban and 1.5 percent foreign-born. Manufacturing and mining employed 23 percent of workers.

Northern Mariana Islands *see* MICRONESIA, US TRUST TERRITORY OF

Northern Securities Company* v. *United States On 14 March 1904, the Supreme Court (5–4) gave the US its first major victory under the SHERMAN ANTITRUST ACT by upholding the dissolution of James HILL's holding company formed between the Great Northern and Northern Pacific railroads; it affirmed the government's argument that, although exchanging stock to merge two corporations lay outside the realm of interstate commerce, such an action constituted a combination in restraint of trade if its purpose was to eliminate competition.

Northern Virginia, Army of The principal CSA land force defending Richmond, Va., against the Army of the POTOMAC, its commanders were Joseph E. JOHNSTON to 31 May 1862 and Robert E. LEE from 1 June 1862 to 9 April 1865.

Northwest Ordinance (13 July 1787) This law established the NORTHWEST TERRITORY and denied SLAVERY legal protection within its boundaries. It prescribed three stages for establishing states: (1) Congress would appoint a governor, executive secretary, and three judges to keep order; (2) once a territory contained 5,000 adult males (about 20,000 persons), its voters could elect a BICAMERAL LEGISLATURE (whose ordinances were subject to the governor's veto); (3) when the total population numbered 60,000, they could draft a constitution and be admitted to statehood (on an equal basis with the original thirteen) once Congress approved their constitution. This ordinance established the basic procedures for admitting all territories subsequently organized from the PUBLIC DOMAIN.

Northwest Passage This term referred to a water route linking the north Atlantic with Asia. Hopes of finding this shortcut to the spice trade motivated the earliest European explorers to map the North American coast and rivers. Hope of discovering a sea route to Asia was largely abandoned after Henry HUDSON's voyages. Roald Amundsen first succeeded in sailing around Canada to the Pacific in 1905. The first commercial ship to make this voyage was the tanker SS *Manhattan* in 1969.

Northwest Territory Also known as the "Old Northwest," this area lay north of the Ohio River and included the present states of Ohio, Ind., Ill., Wis., and Mich. In 1800 Congress dissolved the territory by dividing it into the separate jurisdictions of Ohio Territory and Indiana Territory. Arthur St Clair was its only governor. Its capitals were Marietta, Ohio (1788–90) and Cincinnati (1790–1800).

Nortz* v. *United States *see* GOLD STANDARD

Norumbega English geographers used this name to describe the region surrounding Cape Cod after 1600. The term was replaced by New England after 1616, when John SMITH published *A Description of New England*, which described his exploration of that area.

Norwegian immigration Norway began exporting significant numbers of people in the 1840s. The US received 474,684 Norwegians from 1820 to 1900, and a total of 801,778 arrived by 1991. The 1990 census counted 2,517,760 Americans who reported their primary ancestral background as Norwegian, 1.3 percent of all whites.

Noyes, John Humphrey *see* ONEIDA COMMUNE

NRA *see* NATIONAL RECOVERY ADMINISTRATION

NRC Nuclear Regulatory Commission (*see* ATOMIC ENERGY COMMISSION)

NSC *see* NATIONAL SECURITY COUNCIL

nuclear arms control International restrictions on nuclear weapons began with limits on testing through the NUCLEAR TEST BAN TREATY. The OUTER SPACE WEAPONS TREATY and NUCLEAR NON-PROLIFERATION TREATY forestalled potential problems. Progress in restraining the arms race between the US and USSR came in 1972 with the first accord of the Strategic Arms Limitation talks (*see* STRATEGIC ARMS LIMITATION TREATY (SALT)). The second SALT accord (1979) was never ratified by the Senate, although the US and USSR abided by its provisions. Proposals for a NUCLEAR FREEZE attracted broad support in 1982–3, but negotiations focused instead on the STRATEGIC ARMS REDUCTION TALKS and the INTERMEDIATE-RANGE NUCLEAR FORCES TREATY.

nuclear freeze During 1982, in reaction to lack of progress on NUCLEAR ARMS CONTROL, widespread support emerged for halting the testing, production, and deployment of nuclear weapons. The largest rally for disarmament in US history was held on 12 June 1982 by 800,000 pro-freeze supporters in New York City. Pro-freeze resolutions passed in nine states that November. On 3 May 1983, the National Conference of Catholic Bishops endorsed the freeze, as did the House of Representatives in a nonbinding resolution of 4 May. Ronald REAGAN preempted the freeze movement's support by proposing STRATIGIC ARMS REDUCTION TALKS and reviving negotiations on the INTERMEDIATE-RANGE NUCLEAR FORCES TREATY.

Nuclear Non-Proliferation Treaty (NPT) (1 July 1968) By this treaty, the US, USSR, and Britain agreed not to give nonnuclear nations the technology needed for nuclear weapons production. By June 1994, over 125 nonnuclear nations had promised not to become nuclear powers, but nonsigners included India, Pakistan, and Israel, all of which possessed the ability to build nuclear bombs. North Korea declared it would leave the treaty in March 1993, but later suspended its withdrawal; in August 1994, after diverting an unknown amount of weapons-grade plutonium from nuclear reactors, it began negotiations to ensure compliance with the NPT. The NPT set May 1995 as the date for renegotiating or renewing its terms among member nations.

Nuclear Regulatory Commission *see* ATOMIC ENERGY COMMISSION

Nuclear Test Ban Treaty (4 August 1963) The US, USSR, and Britain agreed not to conduct test explosions of nuclear weapons above ground, under water, or in outer space. Every major nation eventually signed the treaty, except China and France. It was amended by the THRESHOLD TEST BAN TREATY.

nullification The second KENTUCKY RESOLUTIONS introduced this term, but did not specify its scope or manner of operation, as a type of INTERPOSITION. The earliest understanding of nullification was evidently that state legislatures would pass laws blocking the enforcement of unconstitutional measures by US courts or marshals. In his SOUTH CAROLINA EXPOSITION AND PROTEST, John CALHOUN revived the concept and suggested how state conventions might employ it.

nullification crisis Dissatisfied with Congress's refusal to abandon protectionism in the TARIFF OF 1832, the S.C. legislature voted in October 1832 to call a nullification convention in the manner outlined by the SOUTH CAROLINA EXPOSITION AND PROTEST. On 24 November, the convention declared null and void the TARIFFS OF 1828 and 1832; it ordered federal officials to suspend customs in S.C. by 1 February 1833, denied the Supreme Court jurisdiction to judge its actions, and declared that S.C. would be justified in seceding from the Union if the US tried to collect the duties by force.

On 4 December, Andrew JACKSON repeated his earlier recommendations that tariff duties be lowered; on 10 December, he issued a proclamation to the people of S.C. denouncing nullification as unconstitutional and secession as treasonous; on 16 January 1833, he asked Congress to pass a Force Bill authorizing collection of the tariffs by military troops. Upon learning that Congress would debate lowering customs, the S.C. legislature suspended the nullification ordinance on 21 January. On 12 February 1833, Henry CLAY introduced the compromise TARIFF OF 1833, which reduced duties, but not as rapidly as S.C. would have wished. On 2 March, Jackson signed the Force Bill and Tariff. On 15 March, a newly-called S.C. convention repealed nullification, but passed an ordinance nullifying the Force Bill.

NYA *see* NATIONAL YOUTH ADMINISTRATION

Nye Committee On 23 April 1934, the Senate named Senator Gerald Nye (Republican, N.Dak.) to chair the special Senate Munitions Investigating Committee on the political role and profits of the US armaments industry before and during WORLD WAR I. The hearings, which lasted to 1936, tended to confirm Nye's preexisting belief that arms manufacturers helped manipulate the US into the war to increase their own profits. Although not strongly corroborated, the committee's indictment of the munitions industry was widely believed among the public, greatly increased isolationist sentiment and helped persuade Congress to pass the NEUTRALITY ACTS.

O

Oak Grove, battle of *see* PENINSULAR CAMPAIGN

OAS *see* ORGANIZATION OF AMERICAN STATES

Ochs, Adolph Simon (b. Cincinnati, Ohio, 12 March 1858; d. Chattanooga, Tenn., 8 April 1935) He began his career as a printer's apprentice in Knoxville, Tenn., and bought the Chattanooga *Times* in 1878. He acquired the New York *Times* in 1896 and edited it until 1935. Ochs demanded that the *Times* provide comprehensive and accurate news. His logo for it, "All the News That's Fit to Print," expressed his contempt for the cheap sensationalism of YELLOW JOURNALISM. Ochs set the standards for modern, responsible, and intelligent journalism.

O'Connor, Sandra Day (b. El Paso, Tex., 26 March 1930) A classmate of William REHNQUIST at Stanford University law school, in 1965 she was Ariz. assistant attorney general. She served in the US Senate (1969–75), was the first woman to serve as majority leader (Republican, 1972–5). She was appointed to the Ariz. Court of Appeals in 1979, then confirmed as the first female justice on the US Supreme Court in September 1981. She cast the deciding vote to uphold *ROE* v. *WADE* in *WEBSTER* v. *REPRODUCTIVE HEALTH SERVICE* and authored *Harris* v. *Forklift Systems, Incorporated* (*see MERITOR SAVINGS BANK* v. *VINSON*).

Office of Economic Opportunity *see* ECONOMIC OPPORTUNITY ACT

Office of Management and Budget *see* BUDGET AND ACCOUNTING ACT

Office of Strategic Services *see* CENTRAL INTELLIGENCE AGENCY

Ogden* v. *Saunders In 1827 the Supreme Court ruled (4–3) that a state might enact a bankruptcy law granting debtors protection from their creditors for debts assumed after the law took effect, although it added that no state bankruptcy law could offer relief to residents of another state. By distinguishing between contracts already negotiated and the conditions under which contracts might be entered into at future dates, the decision provided a significant exception to the Court's general insistence that contracts were inviolable and beyond the scope of state laws.

Oglethorpe, James Edward (b. London, England, 22 December 1696; d. Cranham Hall, Essex, England, 30 June 1785) Having entered Parliament in 1722, Oglethorpe was the principal sponsor of the establishment of GEORGIA, one of the 20 trustees appointed to oversee its development, and de facto governor (1732–43). He founded Savannah, on 12 February 1733, formed peaceful relations with the CREEK INDIANS, and fortified the frontier. In the war of JENKINS' EAR, he invaded Fla. and repulsed a Spanish invasion. He retired to England in 1743 after being court-martialed, and acquitted, of misadministering his military command. His relations with the Ga. trustees soured and he attended none of their meetings after 1749.

Ohio The treaty of PARIS (1763) ceded Ohio to Britain. It was the scene of DUNMORE'S WAR. As British allies, its Indians raided the frontier in the REVOLUTIONARY WAR. Britain exercised de facto control over the area after 1784 and encouraged Indian attacks from FORT MIAMIS. The first permanent white settlement was founded at Marietta on 7 April 1788 and in December Cincinnati was settled. Efforts to pacify the Indians failed at ST CLAIR'S DEFEAT but prevailed at FALLEN TIMBERS. The first treaty of GREENVILLE opened about two-thirds of Ohio to white settlement and JAY'S TREATY ended British military occupation. By 1800, it had 45,365 settlers (including 337 blacks) and became the 17th state on 1 March 1803. The Indians sold most of their lands by 1810 and the WAR OF 1812 was the last occasion when they threatened the Ohio frontier.

The NATIONAL ROAD and CANAL BOOM stimulated migration to Ohio, whose population increased by 302 percent from 1820 to 1860. In 1860 it had 2,339,511 inhabitants, of whom 98 percent were white and 14 percent were foreign-born; it ranked third among the states in population, second in the value of its farmland and livestock, and fourth in manufactures. It provided 313,180 USA troops (including 5,092 blacks) in the CIVIL WAR, but was also a major stronghold of COPPERHEADS. It was invaded by CSA cavalry in 1863 and was the site of 19 military engagements.

It experienced moderate growth after 1870 and was displaced as the most populous midwest state by Ill. in 1890. In 1900 it had 4,157,545 residents, of whom 52 percent were rural, 98 percent white, and 11 percent foreign-born; it ranked fourth in population among the states, third in the value of its agricultural products and fifth in manufactures. It became a major center of the petroleum, rubber, and machine-tool industries after 1900, but moderate growth led to its decline from the fourth-largest state in 1900 to sixth in 1990. In 1990 it was 79 percent urban and had 10,847,115 people (87 percent white, 11 percent black, 1 percent Hispanic, 1 percent Asian), of whom 2.4 percent were foreign-born. Manufacturing and mining employed 29 percent of its workers.

Ohio gang This term referred to associates, friends, and cronies of Warren HARDING who received high office during his administration. Harding was personally honest, although naive, and many of his scandal-ridden administration's problems orginated with this group's eagerness to enrich themselves through public office.

Ohio idea In 1867 Ohio Representative George Pendleton advocated using GREENBACKS to pay the principal of US bonds whose redemption was not required in gold or silver. The Democratic Party's 1868 platform endorsed this "Ohio idea" to inflate the money supply and ease the deflationary burden placed on debtors and small wage-earners by the contraction of the money supply.

oil embargo Following the outbreak of the Arab–Israeli War on 6 October 1973, Arab oil-producing states (which pumped 85 percent of global oil exports) scheduled monthly cuts of 5 percent in oil exports to the US and western nations until they stopped supporting Israel. The US was importing 35 percent of its petroleum (6,000,000 barrels daily), of which half came from Arab states. Richard NIXON signed the ALASKA PIPELINE Act on 16 November, and the Emergency Petroleum Allocation Act, to institute the rationing of oil within the US, on 27 November. An executive order (4 December) created a Federal Energy Office under William Simon. On 8 November, governors of 29 states reduced speed limits to 50 miles per hour as a conservation measure, and by 2 December, most gas stations were closing on Sundays due to lack of gasoline. On 15 December, the US was placed on DAYLIGHT SAVING TIME year round.

On 23 December, in the first of many such increases, Persian Gulf nations doubled oil prices. By early 1974, the US was about 17 percent short of its normal level of petroleum consumption, gasoline prices were skyrocketing, and lines stretching three miles to gas stations clogged roads. High oil prices and energy shortages contributed to a recession in 1974. On 18 March 1974, the Arab states lifted their oil embargo against the US. The NATIONAL ENERGY ACT (1978) was the most comprehensive effort to reduce dependence on imported oil by promoting energy conservation and alternate energy sources.

Ojibwa Indians This term is the proper name for a people who speak one of the ALGONQUIAN LANGUAGES, who inhabited the northern Great Lakes region. It is generally used in Canada, whereas in the US this group is commonly referred to as the CHIPPEWA INDIANS, a corrupt derivation of the name.

O'Kelly, James *see* METHODIST CHURCH

Okies This was a slang name for someone from the DUST BOWL who moved to Calif. as a migrant worker. About 300,000–400,000 left the southern plains for the Pacific coast of whom over half were from Okla., and the rest from Tex., Ark., Kans., and Colo. Their main highway west was Route 66. An attempt to restrict their entry was reversed by the Supreme Court in *Edwards v. California*.

Okinawa, battle of On 1 April 1945, Lieutenant General Simon Buckner's Tenth Army (183,000 men, including a USMC corps) began landing on Okinawa, held by General Mitsuru Ushijima's 130,000 Japanese; they overwhelmed final enemy resistance on 21 June. Rear Admiral Richmond Turner's task force took heavy losses from kamikaze attacks. US Army losses: 4,336 killed (including Buckner), 15,756 wounded. USMC losses: 3,277 killed, 16,044 wounded. US Navy losses: 4,900 killed, 4,800 wounded, 38 ships sunk, 763 aircraft destroyed. Japanese losses: 107,500 known dead, 7,400 captured, 16 ships, 4,000 planes, at least 70,000 civilians killed. Okinawa's conquest allowed the US to cut Japan's supply lines with Southeast Asia and China, and to reach Japan with medium bombers.

Oklahoma The US acquired Okla. by the Louisiana Purchase. It was settled by the five civilized tribes upon their removal west. Between 1818 and 1839, these Indians were allotted reservations in the eastern half of Okla. No territorial government was created because each tribe was self-governing. The rest of the Indian Territory was reserved for when the Indian population rose to the point at which it needed more land. The Kansas–Nebraska Act resettled many Indians from Kans., where they had been relocated from the midwest, to Okla. Because most of the five civilized tribes, who owned 7,369 slaves in 1860, supported the Confederacy in the Civil War, the US treated them as rebels who had forfeited their right to claim vacant lands in western Okla., and assigned these outlets as reserves for Indians from the southern plains. The plains nations raided Tex., Kans., and Mexico until subjugated in the Red River War.

The first railroad was built across Okla. in 1870–2. In 1889 the US authorized the sale of 9,375 square miles of public domain lands in western Okla. to whites. Following the Oklahoma land rush, Congress created Oklahoma Territory to govern the area sold to whites. In 1900 Okla. ranked 38th in population with 398,331 residents, of whom 91 percent were rural, 92 percent white (including 4 percent foreign-born), 5 percent black, and 3 percent Indian. The Indian Territory ranked 39th with 392,060 inhabitants, of whom 94 percent were rural, 77 percent were white (including 1 percent foreign-born), 9 percent black, and 13 percent Indian. The Indian Territory wanted statehood (as Sequoyah) separately from Oklahoma Territory, but on 16 November 1907, it was merged with Okla. to become the 46th state.

Okla. established a white primary in 1907 and disfranchised most blacks in 1910 by a literacy test (*see* literacy tests). The Ku Klux Klan grew rapidly in the 1920s and dominated the legislature. Numerous localities enacted segregation, and by 1964, just 28 percent of black pupils attended integrated schools.

It emerged as a leading producer of petroleum soon after 1900. Between 1920 and 1930, as farmers suffered from falling prices and conditions typical of the dust bowl, 269,400 Okies left the state in the Great Depression. Another 666,000 left from 1940 to 1970. By 1990, when urbanization and industrialization had greatly diversified the state economy, Okla. had 3,145,585 residents (81 percent white, 7 percent black, 8 percent Indian, 3 percent Hispanic, 1 percent Asian), of whom 59 percent were urban and 2.1 percent foreign-born. Manufacturing and mining employed 23 percent of all workers.

Oklahoma land rush After Congress voted to allow land claims by white settlers on the Cherokee Strip (3,000 square miles) of Oklahoma under the first Homestead Act, it set noon of 22 April 1889 as the opening day for staking claims, which were to be registered in order of filing. A mad stampede by 50,000 hopeful homesteaders staked out all the best land before nightfall. The day's land rush eliminated the last sizeable tract of open land suitable for non-irrigated farming. Smaller rushes were held until 1905, but that day has traditionally been viewed as marking the frontier's end.

Old Deluder Act (11 November 1647) This law replaced a 1642 statute that placed the burden of educating children on parents; it required every town with 50 or more householders to appoint a teacher and pay his wages, and required every town with 100 or more householders to set up a grammar school for college preparation. The law's nickname came from its preamble: "It being one cheife project of the ould deluder, Satan, to keepe men from the knowledge of the Scriptures." The statute marked the start of universal public education for Americans, and by 1671 all New England colonies but Rhode Island had adopted similar measures.

"Old Ironsides" The US NAVY's most famous ship, the USS *Constitution* was authorized on 27 March 1794 and launched on 21 October 1797. She served in the undeclared war with FRANCE, and in the wars with BARBARY PIRATES she made five attacks on Tripoli from 25 July to 4 September 1804. Her dramatic victories in the WAR OF 1812, especially over the HMS *Guerrière* (19 August 1812) and HMS *Java* (19 December 1812), gave major boosts to US morale. Her crew nicknamed her "Old Ironsides" after seeing several of the *Guerrière*'s cannon balls bounce off her hull. She became a training ship in 1833, and has been permanently docked at Boston Navy Yard since 1897.

Old Lights *see* GREAT AWAKENING, FIRST

Old Northwest *see* NORTHWEST TERRITORY

Older Americans Act (14 July 1965) This measure, part of the GREAT SOCIETY, appropriated grant money from the Department of HEALTH AND HUMAN SERVICES for state programs to fund public service jobs for retired persons and to organize volunteer programs benefiting the elderly. It also prohibited age discrimination in any programs that accept federal funds. The law established an Administration on Aging to supervise these activities and develop policies for the aged.

olive branch petition On 5 July 1775, the first CONTINENTAL CONGRESS made its last major effort at ending the political crisis in Anglo-American affairs and remaining in the British empire. This petition to GEORGE III, drafted by John DICKINSON, stated terms for reconciliation: a ceasefire in New England, the repeal of the INTOLERABLE ACTS, and negotiations to establish safeguards for the RIGHTS OF ENGLISHMEN in America. Since the petition and word of heavy British losses at the battle of BUNKER HILL reached England simultaneously, the British government refused to answer it favorably for fear of appearing weak after a defeat. George III instead declared New England in rebellion on 23 August.

Olmstead, Frederick Law (b. Hartford, Conn., 26 April 1822; d. Waverly, Mass., 28 August 1903) He attended Yale (1842–3), and wrote several popular books from 1856 to 1861 about his travels in the South. In 1858 he was named chief architect for New York's Central Park. He emerged as the foremost US landscape artist, and was the most influential voice in the movement to make the creation of public parks a priority in municipal planning during the late 19th century.

Omaha Indians This SIOUAN LANGUAGE group split off from the PONCA about 1650; they occupied the Missouri River basin of Nebr. and Iowa in the 1700s. Although often at war with the SIOUX, they avoided war with Anglo-Americans. They sold most of their lands in 1854, but then avoided mass-relocation to Okla. and have retained a RESERVATION in Thurston Co., Nebr. They numbered around 2,800 in 1780, suffered heavy losses during a smallpox epidemic in 1802, and were reduced to 900 persons by 1830, but by 1857 had risen to 1,200, about the same number as lived in 1906.

Olmstead* v. *United States *see KATZ v. UNITED STATES*

Omnibus Act (22 and 25 June 1868) On 22 June, Congress certified that Ark. had met its conditions for RECONSTRUCTION, and on the 25th it did so for N.C., SC., Ga., Fla., Ala., and La., all of which resumed their congressional representation. Ga.'s readmission was rescinded after the state expelled every black member from its legislature in September 1868, but was later restored in July 1870.

Omnibus Bill (1850) *see* COMPROMISE OF 1850

Omnibus Housing Act (1965) This measure, part of the GREAT SOCIETY, was the most far-reaching federal housing law since the HOUSING ACT (1949). It provided $8,000,000,000 to build housing for poor and middle-income families and established a rent-supplement program for them. The HOUSING AND URBAN DEVELOPMENT ACT (1968) expanded it.

Oneida Commune In 1837 John H. Noyes (3 September 1811–13 April 1886) and his "Bible communists" founded this commune at Oneida, N.Y., after fleeing indictment for adultery in Putney, Vt. Noyes had been expelled from Yale divinity school for affirming that sanctified individuals were incapable of sinning. Oneida was a complex, highly structured, and authoritarian society whose purpose was to imitate the communal living of early Christians. Aside from basic personal possessions, there was no private property and no individual incomes. Noyes proclaimed a doctrine of free love, but encouraged his male disciples to be continent, and employed a primitive system of eugenics to plan how pregnancies would occur. A splinter community existed at Wallingford, Conn. (1850–80). Oneida flourished economically, and was the 19th century's most successful utopian experiment. The community abandoned multiple marriage by 1879, when Noyes moved to Canada out of exasperation with internal dissent and the threat of legal indictments. Oneida reorganized itself as a corporation and was highly successful in producing silverware.

Oneida Indians As one of the FIVE NATIONS, the Oneidas lived on Lake Oneida's western shore between the MOHAWK and ONONDAGA INDIANS. New England Presbyterians made many conversions after 1767 and influenced the nation to break with the rest of the IROQUOIS CONFEDERACY in the REVOLUTIONARY WAR by fighting for US independence and joining SULLIVAN'S CAMPAIGN. The 900 Oneidas were confirmed in title to 9,000 square miles by the second treaty of FORT STANWIX, but sold off most of it over the next 25 years. Some moved to Wis. Oneidas now share a reservation with Onondagas at Nedrow, N.Y., and have others at Oneida, Wis., and Southwold, Ontario.

O'Neill, Eugene Gladstone (b. New York, N.Y., 16 October 1888; d. Boston, Mass., 27 November 1953) An actor's son, O'Neill studied at Princeton and Harvard. After a cycle of his one-act plays had been put on, he won a Pulitzer prize in 1920 for the Broadway production of *Beyond the Horizon* in 1920. He was the early 20th century's foremost playwright; he won additional Pulitzers for *Anna Christie* (1921), *Strange Interlude* (1928), and *Long Day's Journey into Night* (posthumously, 1956), and received the Nobel prize for literature in 1936. Other major plays included *The Emperor Jones* (1920), *Diff'rent* (1921), *The Hairy Ape* (1922), *All God's Chillun Got Wings* (1924), *Desire Under the Elms* (1924), *The Great God Brown* (1926), *Lazarus Laughed* (1927), *Marco Millions* (1928), *Dynamo (1929), Mourning Becomes Electra* (1931), *Ah, Wilderness* (1933), *Days Without End* (1934), *The Iceman Cometh* (1946), and *A Touch of the Poet* (posthumously produced 1957).

Onondaga Indians This group of Indians were the FIVE NATIONS' prime diplomats and maintained their council fire near modern Syracuse, N.Y. During the REVOLUTIONARY WAR, they were British allies, fled their villages in SULLIVAN'S CAMPAIGN, and suffered population losses of about 20 percent. About a third migrated to Canada and by 1790 only 400 lived in the US. Onondagas held 100 square miles in N.Y. in 1788, but by 1820 had sold virtually all of it off. They now occupy a reservation in Onondaga County, N.Y., with headquarters at Nedrow.

Opechancanough's first war On Good Friday, 22 March 1622, Opechancanough's POWHATAN CONFEDERACY launched surprise attacks on Virginia's settlements and killed 347 of the 1,200 colonists. Besieged at JAMESTOWN and unable to plant crops, another 500 died of epidemics and malnutrition that year. The English retaliated with a scorched-earth policy, and destroyed the enemy's villages and foodstocks during the next two winters. Opechancanough and Governor Francis Wyatt signed a peace agreement in April 1623. The war tipped the balance of military power from the Indians to whites.

Opechancanough's second war On 18 March 1644, Opechancanough's POWHATAN CONFEDERACY made surprise attacks on Virginia's outlying settlements and killed about 500 of the colony's 8,000 residents. After Governor William Berkeley burned their villages and winter food supplies, the Indians suffered heavy losses from starvation in the next two years. After Opechancanough was captured and killed in 1645, the Powhatans signed a peace treaty in October 1646 and gave up all land in the TIDEWATER south of York River. This war left the Indians too weak to resist English expansion and Va.'s frontier grew rapidly without Indian interference until BACON'S REBELLION.

open door policy On 6 September 1899, Secretary of State John HAY sent a circular letter to the British, Russian, Italian, German, French, and Japanese governments, in which he asked each nation to guarantee the other countries "equal and impartial trade" within their respective spheres of commercial influence in China, and also to respect Chinese territorial and political sovereignty. Because no nation rejected his proposal, although none committed themselves to observing it, Hay proclaimed on 20 March 1900 that the major powers had accepted an "open door policy" toward China. The policy nevertheless turned into a hollow expression of principle after the BOXER REBELLION, when outside powers toughened control over their own spheres of influence within China. The policy was undermined further by the ROOT–TAKAHIRA AGREEMENT.

open shop This term refers to a labor contract in which a worker has the freedom to refuse to join a union. Major efforts to establish open-shop contracts have included the AMERICAN PLAN and RIGHT-TO-WORK LAWS.

Operation Bootstrap By this program, Congress exempted 10 years' income tax upon the profits of factories built or expanded in PUERTO RICO. The island's economy lessened its dependence on agriculture; from 1947 to September 1959, Puerto Rico gained 581 new manufacturing plants, and over 1,600 had been built by 1988.

Operation Breadbasket Martin Luther KING initiated this project as a joint operation between the SOUTHERN CHRISTIAN LEADERSHIP CONFERENCE and STUDENT NONVIOLENT COORDINATING COMMITTEE to expand job opportunities for blacks in major cities. It used boycotts or other forms of selective purchasing against companies that resisted hiring blacks in numbers equal to their proportion of the local population. The program scored important successes under Jesse JACKSON in Chicago and Ralph ABERNATHY in Atlanta.

Operation Chaos On 10 June 1975, the Nelson ROCKEFELLER Commission revealed that the CIA had repeatedly violated its charter for over seven years in Operation Chaos, a domestic surveillance program on the VIETNAM ANTIWAR MOVEMENT that created dossiers on 13,000 individuals or organizations and indexed references on 300,000 persons. The commission report also described experiments in which federal employees were given mind-altering drugs without their knowledge over 10 years, during which a suicide resulted from the secret administration of LSD. The report led both houses of Congress to form permanent oversight committees for monitoring CIA policies and operations.

Operation Overlord This was the Allied codename for the invasion of NORMANDY.

Operation Vittles This was the Allied codename for the BERLIN AIRLIFT.

Oppenheimer, Robert *see* MANHATTAN PROJECT

Order of American Knights *see* COPPERHEADS

Ordinance of (20 May) 1785 This law established the land policy that would govern all future organization of the PUBLIC DOMAIN. It prescribed that land would be surveyed in uniform grids forming townships of 6 miles by 6 miles (23,040 acres). Townships would be subdivided into 36 sections of 1 square mile (640 acres), with each section divided into 4 quarter-sections of 160 acres each. Rent or sale of section no. 16 would be reserved for supporting schools. Sales were to be made at public auction in units of not less than 1 section, and at prices no less than $1 per acre.

Ordinance of 1787 *see* NORTHWEST ORDINANCE

Oregon Oreg. was claimed for Britain in 1778 by James Cook and for the US in 1791 by Robert GRAY. The ADAMS–ONIS TREATY settled the southern boundary with Calif. In 1818 the US and Britain agreed to a joint occupation, with the Columbia River serving as a buffer between them. US settlers began arriving along the OREGON TRAIL in 1843. The joint occupation fell apart in 1845 amid US calls of FIFTY-FOUR, FORTY OR FIGHT, but Britain recognized the US claim to Oreg. and modern Wash. in 1846. Oreg. was made a territory on 14 August 1848 and the 33rd state on 14 February 1859. A minor gold rush occurred along the southwestern coast in the 1850s. It was the scene of the ROGUE RIVER, and MODOC WARS, and NEZ PERCE CAMPAIGN.

In 1860 Oreg. had 52,465 residents, of whom all but 128 were white and 10 percent were foreign-born; it ranked 36th in population, 33rd in the value of its farmland and livestock, and 32nd in manufactures. In the CIVIL WAR, Oreg. furnished 1,810 men for the USA army. Rapid development came after Oreg. was linked to the system of TRANSCONTINENTAL RAILROADS in the 1880s. In 1900 Oreg. had 413,536 residents (95.4 percent white, 1.2 percent Indian, 2.5 percent Chinese, 0.6 percent Japanese, and 0.3 percent black), of whom 68 percent were rural and 16 percent were foreign-born; it ranked 35th among the states in population, 32nd in agricultural products, and 35th in manufactures. Large-scale lumbering began in 1900 under the Weyerhauser Co. and by 1938 Oreg. was the leading producer of forest products. Rapid urban growth further diversified the economy. In 1990, Oreg. was the 30th largest state and had 2,842,321 inhabitants (91 percent white, 2 percent black, 4 percent Hispanic, 1 percent Indian, and 2 percent Asian), of whom 69 percent were urban and 4.9 percent were foreign-born. Manufacturing and mining employed 24 percent of workers.

Oregon Trail This route began at Independence, Mo., followed the Platte River, proceeded along the Snake River west of Fort Hall, Idaho, crossed the Rockies by SOUTH PASS, and used the Columbia River to reach the Willamette valley. Its length was approximately 2,000 miles and required about five months to cross with livestock. It was discovered in stages by fur trappers. Robert Newell took the first wagons over it in 1840. The first substantial Anglo-American migration started in 1843, when Peter Burnett led a party of 1,000 persons, 100 wagons, and 5,000 stock over it. From 1845 to 1850, 3,000 to 5,000 Americans annually took the trail to Oreg., but generally in small parties of a dozen wagons and a hundred people. This migration gave teeth to the US claim to possess the Pacific northwest under the LOUISIANA PURCHASE.

Oregon* v. *Mitchell (decided with *Texas* v. *Mitchell, United States* v. *Mitchell, United States* v. *Arizona*) On 21 December 1970, the Supreme Court ruled unanimously that the VOTING RIGHTS ACT (1965) could suspend LITERACY TESTS nationwide. (In *Katzenbach* v. *Morgan* (1968), the Court had upheld Congress's power to forbid states from requiring voters to be literate in English.) It also upheld (8–1) a 1970 amendment to the act requiring a maximum of 30 days' residency for voting in presidential elections, but struck down (5–4) another 1970 clause imposing 18 as the minimum voting age for state elections. The TWENTY-SIXTH AMENDMENT reversed the decision.

Organization Man, The In 1956 William H. Whyte published this study of the corporate culture and attitudes of US business executives. Whyte condemned prevailing attitudes that prized conformity and loyalty to the organization above individuality; he also demonstrated that these values were exerting a negative influence on a broad range of popular attitudes and behavior. *The Organization Man* became one of the most influential books of the 1950s, and stimulated much critical thinking about how US society was being undermined by sameness and shallowness.

Organization of American States (OAS) This was an outgrowth of the PAN AMERICAN UNION and RIO PACT. On 30 April 1948, at Bogota, Colombia, motivated in large part by anti-Communist sentiments, 21 nations created the OAS as a regional security alliance. In 1954 the OAS condemned Communist activity in the western hemisphere. In 1962 it suspended Communist Cuba's membership and supported the US in the CUBAN MISSILE CRISIS; it imposed sanctions against Cuba for promoting Communist subversion from 1964 to 1975. The OAS endorsed US intervention in the

DOMINICAN REPUBLIC in 1965 and in HAITI in 1993, but declined to support US intervention in NICARAGUA during the 1980s or the US invasion of PANAMA in 1989.

organized crime *see* MAFIA

Organized Crime Control Act (1970) To provide greater law enforcement tools against organized crime, Congress strengthened the compulsory witness program, authorized greater use of witness immunity, and gave Justice Department task forces more financing for staff and investigations. Its RICO section permitted convictions on racketeering charges for someone who participated in or discussed any of several dozen crimes over a 10-year period. RICO was the key US statute that allowed leaders heading national crime syndicates to be successfully prosecuted for racketeering; it enabled the government to bring an entire criminal organization to trial, not just low-level perpetrators of crimes. It permitted the Justice Department to win numerous convictions of high-ranking officials of the MAFIA in the 1980s.

Oriskany, battle of (N.Y.) On 6 August 1777, Brigadier General Nicholas Herkimer's 600 militia fought off Joseph BRANT's 500 IROQUOIS CONFEDERACY and TORIES 10 miles from FORT STANWIX. N.Y. losses: 72 killed, 75 wounded. Indian losses: over 100 killed and wounded. The ambush kept Herkimer from reaching Fort Stanwix. Demoralized by their losses, the Indians deserted Lieutenant Colonel St Leger, who was left too weak to take Stanwix or prevent Burgoyne's surrender at SARATOGA.

Osage Indians The Osage were a group of speakers of one of the southern SIOUAN LANGUAGES, inhabiting Mo. and numbering 6,200 in 1780. They often fought with neighboring Indians, but avoided war with the US and provided the army with many scouts to hunt down the southern plains Indians. In 1830, 5,000 Osage left Mo. for a reservation in southern Kans. In part because many were pressured by Confederates into opposing the Union in the CIVIL WAR, they had to relocate in Osage County, Okla., in 1873. By combining agricultural resources with oil and gas royalties, they emerged as the wealthiest Indians below Alaska.

Osborn* v. *Bank of the United States In 1824 the Supreme Court decided whether Ohio's state auditor could be sued for damages stemming from his seizure, under the authority of a state law, of funds belonging to the second BANK OF THE UNITED STATES; it ruled (with one dissent) that the ELEVENTH AMENDMENT did not exempt states from being sued by US officials in federal court to obtain redress for a state officer's enforcement of an unconstitutional statute.

Osceola (b. on the Tallapoosa River, Ga., ca. 1800; d. Charleston, S.C., 31 January 1838) He was a SEMINOLE INDIAN (possibly half English) whose family moved from Ga. to the area below Tampa Bay, Fla., after the CREEK WAR. He fought in the first of the SEMINOLE WARS. In 1834 he emerged as the principal spokesman for Seminoles who refused to move west under the terms of the treaty of Payne's Landing (1832). By December 1836, his followers had begun killing pro-removal Indians and US officials in the initial stages of the second Seminole War. In October 1837, at negotiations arranged by a flag of truce, Fla. militia under General J. M. Hernandez seized Osceola and his leading subordinates. He died of an acute throat inflammation while imprisoned at Fort Moultrie, and was buried with full military honors by army officers embarrassed by the treachery used in apprehending him.

OSHA An abbreviation for Occupational Safety and Health Administration.

Ostend Manifesto In 1854, under pressure to acquire Cuba as a new slave state, the US offered Spain $130,000,000 to buy the island, but was refused. On 9 October 1854, at Ostend, Belgium, US ambassadors to Spain (Pierre Soule), France (John Mason), and Britain (James BUCHANAN) sent a private diplomatic message stating that if Spain insisted on retaining Cuba, the US would be justified in taking it by war. When the dispatch was discovered by the press and printed, it embarrassed the Franklin PIERCE administration and forced the US to disavow any further attempts to acquire Cuba.

Oswego, battles of (N.Y.) (1) On 11 August 1756, the Marquis de Montcalm's 3,000 French troops began besieging Colonel James Mercer's garrison, which surrendered on 14 August. British losses: 45 killed, 1,100 soldiers, 120 sailors, and 200 workmen captured, 55 cannon, 5 mortars, and 6 warships (26 cannon, 52 swivel guns). Indians massacred 40 British after the surrender. French losses: 30 killed.

(2) On 19 June 1813, Lieutenant Melancton Woolsey's US artillery drove off Captain James Yeo's squadron and prevented it from landing a British raiding party. On 6 May 1814, Captain James Yeo's 11 gunboats and 7 transports landed 900 British soldiers, who forced Lieutenant Colonel G. A. Mitchell's 300 US artillerymen to retreat. After seizing all US cannons and provisions, Yeo left Oswego. US losses: 6 killed, 38 wounded, 25 captured. British losses: 19 killed, 62 wounded.

Oswego, treaty of (N.Y.) On 25 July 1766, PONTIAC'S WAR formally ended when Pontiac signed a peace treaty with Sir William JOHNSON. (This agreement supplemented a truce negotiated by George Croghan in May 1765.) By treating Pontiac not as an enemy, but as an honored guest deserving lavish praise and valuable gifts, Johnson discredited him among his former Indian followers, who presumed that the Ottawa had sold out to the English. Although Pontiac had wished to continue hostilities as soon as he could revive Indian fears of white expansion into the Ohio valley, he fell into such disrepute that he was unable to rebuild his wartime alliance before another Indian murdered him in 1769.

Other America, The In 1962 Michael Harrington published this study of poverty in the US. Harrington documented the existence of widespread poverty in a direct, dramatic, and non-academic style that made the book accessible to a broad, popular audience. *The Other America* became a bestseller and was highly influential among politicians and molders of public opinion. It played a significant role in building national support for the WAR ON POVERTY.

"Other People's Money and How They Use It" *see* MONEY TRUST

Otis, James (b. West Barnstable, Mass., 5 February 1725; d. Andover, Mass., 23 May 1783) In 1750 Otis became a Boston lawyer. In 1761, while challenging the WRITS OF ASSISTANCE in court, he articulated the earliest colonial argument denying Parliament any power to alter the British constitution by infringing the RIGHTS OF ENGLISHMEN. It was Otis who placed the motion (adopted by the Mass. assembly) in June 1765 to call the STAMP ACT CONGRESS. He ranked second only to Samuel ADAMS as an opponent of unconstitutional British measures, until 1769, when he was savagely beaten by a customs officer. He drifted in and out of sanity after 1771, fought at BUNKER HILL, and was killed by a bolt of lightning.

Ottawa Indians This nation spoke one of the ALGONQUIAN LANGUAGES, and its homeland surrounded Lake Michigan. In 1600 they probably numbered about 3,500 south of Canada. By 1680 they reportedly supplied two-thirds of the furs exported from New France. Ottawas participated in BRADDOCK'S DEFEAT and were French allies in the SEVEN YEARS' WAR. They were the guiding spirit behind PONTIAC'S WAR, but never again played a prominent role in resisting Anglo-American expansion, although they fought as British allies in the REVOLUTIONARY WAR, the Ohio valley wars until the first treaty of GREENVILLE, and the WAR OF 1812. They relocated to Kans. after 1830 and to Okla. by 1860.

Outer Space Weapons Treaty (8 December 1966) At the United Nations, the US, USSR, and 26 other nations agreed to ban the use of nuclear weapons, and nuclear weapons testing, in outer space.

Owen, Robert Dale (b. Glasgow, Scotland, 8 November 1801; d. Lake George, N.Y., 24 June 1877) A utopian visionary, Owen emigrated in 1825 with his father, Robert Owen, a noted English reformer. In 1826 they founded the New Harmony, Ind., socialist commune, which failed economically. While in the Ind. legislature (1836–8), he was influential in requiring schools to be publicly financed. While in Congress (1843–7), he sponsored legislation establishing the Smithsonian Institution. As a private citizen and author, he helped to persuade Ind. to enlarge women's property rights and to liberalize divorce, and strongly espoused ABOLITIONISM.

Owen–Glass Act *see* FEDERAL RESERVE SYSTEM

Owens, "Jesse" (James Cleveland) (b. Danville, Ala., 12 September 1913; d.

Tucson, Ariz., 31 March 1980) While at Ohio State University (1934–7), Owens became the most prominent American track star, and broke many world records. As an African-American at the 1936 Berlin Olympics, Owens shattered Adolph Hitler's hopes of using the games as a propaganda platform for displaying German racial superiority. He not only won four gold medals, but set world records in two events and tied a world record in another. A furious Hitler left the stadium rather than acknowledge his triumphs. Owens ceased competing in sports after 1936.

P

Pacific Islands, US Trust Territory of *see* MICRONESIA, US TRUST TERRITORY OF

Pacific Telegraph Act (16 June 1860) Congress financed construction of telegraph lines from Mo. to San Francisco. The first message, from Washington, D.C., to San Francisco, was transmitted on 24 October 1861. The service put the PONY EXPRESS out of business.

Packers and Stockyards Act (15 August 1921) To ensure that farmers received fair prices for livestock, poultry, and dairy products, Congress forbade price manipulation and other unfair, monopolistic, or discriminatory practices in their purchase; it required stockyards and all marketing firms to register with the Department of AGRICULTURE and report their prices, fees, and charges.

Paine, Thomas (b. Thetford, Norfolk, England, 29 January 1737; d. New York, N.Y., 8 June 1809) In 1774 Paine emigrated to Philadelphia and became a newspaperman. In January 1776, he published *COMMON SENSE*, which made the most uncompromising argument for independence yet articulated in America. From 1776 to 1783, he was the unequaled propagandist of the Revolution and published his essays under the title of *The Crisis*. He served as a secretary for Congress and clerk of the Pa. assembly. Paine was imprisoned while trying to influence the French Revolution and in 1794 returned to the US, where he passed his life poor but honored on his Long Island farm.

Paiute campaigns (1) In 1860 Southern PAIUTE INDIANS burned a PONY EXPRESS station on the CALIFORNIA TRAIL and killed five whites near Pyramid Lake, Nev., while rescuing two girls being held there as concubines by miners. In an ambush at the Truckee Valley, Paiutes under Numaga killed 46 out of 105 miners sent to retaliate. In June Colonel Jack Hays led 800 Calif. and Nev. volunteers, dispersed his enemy at Pinnacle Mountain, and killed 25 Paiute warriors. Fighting ended late that summer when the army built Fort Churchill nearby.

(2) In early 1866, the northern Paiutes intensified raids against Idaho gold miners. In 40 skirmishes, the army and its SHOSHONI INDIAN scouts reported killing 329 Paiutes, wounding 20, and capturing 225. Colonel George Crook negotiated peace in July 1868. (For the hostilities of 1878, *see* BANNOCK–PAIUTE CAMPAIGN)

Paiute Indians This group, speakers of one of the UTO-AZTECAN LANGUAGES, occupied the Great Basin between the Rockies and Sierra Nevadas. The Northern Paiutes of Idaho and Southeastern Oreg. were known as Snakes. The Paiutes may have numbered 7,500 in 1845. Several PAIUTE CAMPAIGNS were fought. Paiutes now have a reservation in Utah, two in Oreg., and ten in Nev.

Palatines These were Protestant refugees from the lower Rhine Valley (the German-French Palatinate, or border region) to the THIRTEEN COLONIES. Substantial numbers first began arriving around 1710, when about 3,000 came to N.Y. and 600 settled in N.C. They comprised about two-thirds of the PENNSYLVANIA DUTCH, and a large minority came as REDEMPTIONERS.

Palau *see* MICRONESIA, US TRUST TERRITORY OF

Palko* v. *Connecticut *see* *BENTON* V. *MARYLAND*

Palmer, A. Mitchell *see* RED SCARE

Palmer, John McAuley (b. Scott County, Ky., 13 September 1817; d. Springfield, Ill., 25 September 1900) At the age of 14, Palmer moved to Ill.; he later became a lawyer in Springfield. Originally a Democrat, he helped to found the Ill. REPUBLICAN

PARTY in 1856. He rose from colonel of the 14th Illinois Infantry to major general during the CIVIL WAR. After being elected Ill. governor in 1868, he supported the LIBERAL REPUBLICAN PARTY in 1872, then rejoined the Democrats, and became US senator in 1891. The NATIONAL DEMOCRATS nominated him for president (with an ex-CSA general as running mate) in 1896 on a ticket that polled 1 percent of the popular vote.

Palmer raids *see* RED SCARE

Palo Alto, battle of (Tex.) On 8 May 1846, Brigadier General Zachary TAYLOR's 2,300 US regulars defeated General Mariano Arista's 6,000 Mexicans. US losses: 9 killed, 47 wounded. Mexican losses: 320 dead, 400 wounded. Fighting resumed on 9 May at RESACA DE LA PALMA.

Pan-American Union This organization evolved during ten meetings held to build economic, political, and cultural links within the western hemisphere. James BLAINE convened the first meeting at Washington from 2 October 1889 to 19 April 1890, when the US and 17 Latin-American nations founded the International Bureau of American Republics to facilitate communication between members. The US later worked through this agency to arrange reciprocal tariff agreements with various nations. In 1910 the bureau's name was changed to the Pan-American Union. The RIO PACT and charter of the ORGANIZATION OF AMERICAN STATES transformed the union into a mutual security alliance. The last Pan-American conference was held in 1954.

Panama, US intervention in (1) Between 3 and 15 April 1885, 700 US marines landed in Panama to protect Americans and reopen a railroad during a rebellion; they withdrew in May. (*See* PANAMA REVOLT *and* PANAMA CANAL) Marines landed every year from 1901 to 1904 and stayed at battalion strength in the US Canal Zone until 1914.

(2) In 1989 Fla. grand juries indicted President Manuel Noriega on evidence of using the Panamanian government to operate a massive drug-smuggling operation to the US. After the US imposed economic sanctions, Noriega's increasing hostility caused concern that US citizens in the former Panama Canal Zone might be at risk. After Panamanian police killed a US Navy officer on 16 December, 10,000 US soldiers invaded Panama on 20 December. Dissident Panamanians overthrew Noriega. The US lost 23 killed and 324 wounded, while about 350 Panamanians (half civilians) died. The US apprehended Noriega on 3 January 1990 and flew him to Miami, where he was found guilty of drug-smuggling on 9 April 1992 and later sentenced to 40 years.

Panama Canal On 2 November 1903, Theodore ROOSEVELT sent warships to prevent Colombia from quelling the PANAMA REVOLT. To ensure US protection against a Colombian reconquest, Panama signed the HAY–BUNAU–VARILLA TREATY to lease a US canal zone.

On 29 June 1906, Congress authorized funds to build the canal. Colonel William Gorgas enabled construction to proceed safely by his sanitation campaign that eliminated breeding grounds for mosquitoes carrying malaria and yellow fever. Under Colonel George Goethals, the Corps of Engineers built the 40.3-mile canal linking Cristobal and Balboa. The canal cost $365,000,000 and opened on 15 August 1914.

US occupation of the Canal Zone stirred Panamanian resentment, which expressed itself by massive rioting on 9 and 10 January 1964, and allowed Communists to portray the US as an imperialist power in the COLD WAR. After winning Panamanian assent to a treaty that guaranteed the zone's permanent neutrality (ratified on 16 March 1978 by the Senate), Jimmy CARTER won Senate approval on 18 April for a treaty transferring the canal in stages to Panama by 31 December 1999.

Panama Refining Company* v. *Ryan *see* CONNALLY ACT

Panama Revolt Following the HAY–HERRÁN CONVENTION's rejection by Colombia, Theodore ROOSEVELT sent US warships on 2 November 1903 to keep Colombia from suppressing a revolt in Panama, and on 5–6 November landed a USMC battalion. The US recognized Panama's independence on 6 November and signed the HAY–BUNAU–VARILLA TREATY on 18 November.

panic of 1819 A collapse in cotton prices, from 32 cents per pound in 1818 to 14 cents in 1819, triggered this recession, but a simultaneous contraction in credit made it exceptionally severe. When the second BANK OF THE UNITED STATES began demanding SPECIE from its debtors and requiring that state banks increase reserves of hard cash in 1819, it forced the financial system to raise hard cash by calling in loans while commodity prices were falling and gold or silver had become hard to acquire. A wave of farm foreclosures, business bankruptcies, and bank failures ensued. The recession was deepest in the South and West, where state banks had extended credit most recklessly and closed in great numbers. The panic was a political liability for the Bank of the United States, which was unjustifiably blamed as its cause, and was a factor in the bank's later failure to have its charter renewed. The panic lasted until 1821.

panic of 1837 A depression developed in mid-1837 as a result of a failed wheat crop in 1836, a 25 percent fall in cotton prices, a recession in Britain that dried up credit usually available to Americans carrying on international trade, and the impact of the SPECIE CIRCULAR, which caused land prices to fall and caused many state-chartered banks with inadequate reserves to fail. By mid-1837, banks had suspended payments in SPECIE in most major eastern cities. Several states later repudiated their debts. The recession caused the demise of most labor unions, which could not survive cut-throat competition for labor. The panic was the second longest US depression and lasted about six years, until 1843.

panic of 1857 On 24 August 1857, the Ohio Life Insurance and Trust Co.'s New York City office failed at a time when that city's financial institutions had given more credit than their reserves could support, for real estate and railroad loans. A financial panic ensued and many banks suspended payments in SPECIE. Compounding the recession were falling grain prices (due to rising world output after the end of the Crimean War) and a brief, modest decline in cotton prices. The panic influenced politics because northerners blamed a wave of bankruptcies on the TARIFF OF 1857, which set rates below protectionist levels. Business recovery began in early 1859.

panic of 1873 On 18 September 1873, the prominent banking firm of Jay Cooke & Co. went bankrupt due to collapse of its railroad securities. Cooke's demise precipitated a sharp drop in the stock markets and numerous business failures. The resulting depression created 3,000,000 unemployed at its peak; it also placed downward pressure on prices, especially of agricultural commodities, that reduced farm income and imposed great hardship in most rural areas. The deflationary cycle created much political pressure to increase the money supply and led to the emergence of the GREENBACK PARTY. The depression was the third longest on record, over five years, and lasted until mid-1878.

panic of 1893 This business contraction was the most severe US economic depression to that date (and its second greatest in history). On 5 May, the New York stock market fell because of unease over recent declines in the US Treasury gold reserve and several major business failures, and it crashed in panic selling on 27 June. Further declines in gold reserves produced a credit crisis that forced massive liquidation of business assets, and this crippled the economy. By the end of 1893, over 16,000 businesses had failed, including 491 banks and 156 railroads. The depression left every sixth man unemployed (2,500,000 jobless), placed in receivership 318 railroad firms with 67,000 miles of track (a third of all rail mileage), and inspired COXEY'S ARMY. It was the fourth-longest US depression, about four years, and did not end until mid-1897.

panic of 1907 On 13 March 1907, a stock market decline began when runs on the assets of several large New York finance firms meant that investors could not borrow money to cover investments made on credit. A severe credit contraction ensued that left many business failures. To stem the panic, in October the US Treasury deposited $38,000,000 in government funds with banks in New York so that commercial lending could resume at reasonable rates. To provide further liquidity to the money supply, on 30 May 1908 Congress passed the Aldrich–Vreeland Act, which authorized national banks to issue bank notes as currency that were not backed by US bonds. Although the recession lasted just one year, it identified serious flaws in the country's fragmented banking system and led to calls for reform. The Aldrich–Vreeland Act addressed these issues by its National Monetary Commission, whose report stimulated Congress to found the FEDERAL RESERVE SYSTEM.

Paoli, battle of (Pa.) On 21 September 1777, Major General Charles Grey's three British regiments, carrying unloaded muskets armed only with bayonets, routed Brigadier General Anthony WAYNE's 1,200 Continentals in a night attack. US losses: 200 killed, 100 wounded, 71 captured. British losses: 6 killed, 22 wounded. US propagandists branded the battle a "massacre" in which Americans were killed trying to surrender, but the evidence suggests otherwise.

Paris, treaty of (10 February 1763) This agreement ended the SEVEN YEARS' WAR. France transferred all its Canadian possessions to Britain, but retained the islands of St Pierre and Miquelon, plus fishing rights off Newfoundland. To Spain, France ceded LOUISIANA and the area from Mobile Bay to the Mississippi. Britain restored the Caribbean islands it seized from Spain and France, and took over EAST and WEST FLORIDA.

Paris, treaty of (3 September 1783) The REVOLUTIONARY WAR ended with this treaty. It recognized US independence, confirmed US possession of the NORTHWEST TERRITORY, set 31° latitude as the US southern boundary, recognized US fishing rights off Newfoundland, required each country's courts to honor debts claimed by the other's citizens, and pledged the CONGRESS OF THE CONFEDERATION to "earnestly recommend" to the states that they restore full political and property rights to TORIES. In a separate treaty, Britain transferred EAST and WEST FLORIDA to Spain, but without specifying the 31st parallel as its boundary.

Paris peace accords On 13 May 1968, the US began meeting with North Vietnamese representatives under Le Duc Tho in Paris to find a settlement for the VIETNAM WAR. US negotiators W. Averell Harriman (May 1968–January 1969) and Henry Cabot LODGE, JR. (May 1969–1970) failed to win concessions on the main US demand for a total, mutual withdrawal by both US and North Vietnamese forces, which would leave Vietnam permanently divided. By 1971, Richard NIXON had authorized Henry KISSINGER to undertake secret negotiations, and by 1972 Kissinger's "shuttle diplomacy" was bearing fruit. In October 1972, an agreement was reached whereby the North Vietnamese would give up all US prisoners and allow South Vietnam's president to stay in office; in return, the US agreed to stop bombing North Vietnam, accept Communist participation in South Vietnamese politics, withdraw all US troops, and drop its demand that North Vietnamese troops evacuate the South. Under pressure from renewed US bombing in December, North Vietnam gave its final assent to the October agreement. On 27 January 1973, North Vietnamese and US diplomats signed a ceasefire agreement that ended the fighting and permitted the complete withdrawal of US forces by the year's end.

Paris peace conference *see* VERSAILLES, TREATY OF

parity This term refers to a price for any farm commodity which is set to maintain its producer's purchasing power at a level sufficient for a decent standard of living. Farmers began demanding in the 1920s that parity be achieved through government intervention in the marketplace. The MCNARY–HAUGEN BILL and AGRICULTURAL MARKETING ACT were designed to raise agricultural prices back to the levels of 1919. Maintaining parity for farmers has been US policy since the NEW DEAL, which used the AGRICULTURAL ADJUSTMENT ADMINISTRATION to support agricultural income by restricting production, paying subsidies to farmers, and withholding surplus crops from the market by government storage programs.

Parker, Alton Brooks (b. near Cortland, N.Y., 14 May 1852; d. New York, N.Y., 10 May 1926) In 1873 Parker opened a law office at Kingston, N.Y., involved himself in Democratic politics, and became chief justice of the N.Y. Court of Appeals in 1897. In 1904 he handily defeated William R. HEARST on the first ballot for the Democratic presidential nomination. He won just 37.6 percent of the ballots in a huge defeat by Theodore ROOSEVELT, and retired from politics.

Parker, Quannah *see* NATIVE AMERICAN CHURCH

Parker, Ely Samuel (b. Pembroke, N.Y., 1828; d. Fairfield, Conn., 31 August 1895) He acquired a superior education and became a civil engineer after being rejected by the N.Y. bar as a lawyer because, being a SENECA INDIAN, he was not legally a US citizen. While a federal engineer at Galena, Ill., in 1857, he and Ulysses S. GRANT became friends. In September 1863, he joined Grant's staff as an engineer (captain). During the CIVIL WAR he earned promotions through brigadier general, served as Grant's military secretary, and wrote the CSA surrender terms at APPOMATTOX COURT HOUSE. He resigned from the army in 1869, served as Grant's commissioner of Indian Affairs from then to 1871, made and lost a fortune on Wall Street, and ended his career on the New York City police department.

Parker, Theodore (b. Lexington, Mass., 24 August 1810; d. Florence, Italy, 10 May 1860) A graduate of Harvard Divinity School (1836), Parker was ordained at the West Roxbury, Mass., church (1837). He opposed orthodox Unitarian theology, based on his reading of TRANSCENDENTALISM, and expressed his beliefs in *A Discourse on Matters Pertaining to Religion* (1842). In 1852 he resigned from his West Roxbury church and became a Congregational minister in Boston. A fervent supporter of ABOLITIONISM, he aided the NEW ENGLAND EMIGRANT AID COMPANY, the UNDERGROUND RAILROAD, and John BROWN's raid on Harper's Ferry.

Parker* v. *Davis *see* LEGAL TENDER CASES

Parkman, Francis (b. Boston, Mass., 16 September 1823; d. Jamaica Plain, Mass., 8 November 1893) Shortly after graduating from Harvard in 1844, Parkman traversed the OREGON TRAIL and lived among Indians to gain insight into their culture. The journey permanently crippled his frail physique and he slowly became a partially blind, semi-invalid. He devoted himself to researching the Anglo-French struggle for North America, and overcame his handicaps to become the late 19th century's foremost historian. Parkman based his conclusions on scrupulous research into archival sources and a keen insight into the brutal reality of frontier warfare. By virtue of his ability to evoke drama from ancient documents, create a sweeping narrative structure, and write compelling passages that enable readers to relive the past, Parkman ranks as the greatest composer of US historical literature. His major works are *The California and Oregon Trail* (1849), *History of the Conspiracy of Pontiac* (1851), *Pioneers of France in the New World* (1865), *The Jesuits in North America* (1867), *The Discovery of the Great West* (1869), *The Old Regime in Canada* (1874), *Count Frontenac and New France under Louis XIV* (1877), *Montcalm and Wolfe* (2 vols, 1884), and *A Half-century of Conflict* (2 vols, 1892).

Parsons' Cause In 1755 a drought drastically cut the tobacco crop in Va. and tripled the price of tobacco. Because salaries for the Church of England's clergy were paid in 17,280 pounds of tobacco per year, the legislature passed the Twopenny Act, a temporary measure permitting VESTRIES to pay their parsons in cash at the rate of two pence per pound (slightly higher than average prices in the past). The PRIVY COUNCIL disallowed the act on 10 August 1759, but did not state whether clergymen might claim compensation for the additional £180 they would have received in the Twopenny Act's absence. Rev. James Maury lost a well-publicized lawsuit for extra pay from his vestry, which was defended by Patrick HENRY. The controversy began Henry's rise to prominence and discredited the Anglican clergy, who appeared overly eager to profit by their parishioners' misfortunes.

Pasadena City Board of Education* v. *Spangler On 28 June 1976, the Supreme Court ruled (6–2) that, having instituted a court-approved plan for integrating an educational system, a school board is not required to make periodic adjustments to offset a shifting racial balance among students, if such a change was due to normal movements of population within that jurisdiction and was beyond the school board's control.

passenger cases (*Smith* v. *Turner*, *Norris* v. *Boston*) In 1849 the Supreme Court struck down (5–4) Mass. and N.Y. laws that taxed ship-borne passengers to finance care for indigent immigrants. The Court ruled that the federal government enjoyed sole authority to regulate foreign commerce, and that the states could not exercise any powers in this realm, even concerning policy matters over which Congress had taken no action.

patroonships On 7 June 1629, the Dutch West India Company offered to compensate anyone transporting 50 adults to New Netherland with an estate fronting 16 miles along a navigable river and including all unoccupied lands inland. The patroons (grantees) would be free from taxes for eight years and would have authority to hold courts on their estates. Of the three patroonships settled – Swaanendael in Del., Pavonia in N.J., and Rensselaerswyck near Albany – only the last was not abandoned and survived to be one of the New York manors.

Paul, Alice (b. Moorestown, N.J., 11 January 1885; d. Moorestown, N.J., 9 July 1977) During 1909–12, Paul worked with radical British suffragettes to win the right to vote. She returned to the US and in 1916 organized the National Woman's party to press for women's suffrage by a constitutional amendment. Her militant tactics stirred controversy and resulted in numerous arrests, often followed by her own hunger strikes, but they were critical in energizing the final push for the Nineteenth Amendment. Beginning in 1923, she began campaigning for an Equal Rights amendment. She also journeyed to Europe to support women's rights there and helped establish the World Woman's Party in 1938.

Pawnee Indians This group, speakers of one of the Caddoan languages, migrated from southeastern Tex. to the Platte River before 1600 and acquired horses from the Kiowa Indians. They may have numbered 10,000 in 1780, well after one of their bands separated to become the Arikaras. They fought with most Plains Indians, but had peaceful relations with the US Army, for whom they established a tradition of serving as scouts. Their Pawnee County, Okla., reservation had a population of 7,657 in 1984.

Paxton massacre (Pa.) On 14 December 1763, to avenge the deaths of whites in Pontiac's War, Lazarus Stewart led 57 "Paxton [Township.] Boys" in killing 7 men, 5 women, and 8 children of a Christian Conestoga Indian band (*see* Susquehannock Indians) in protective custody at the Lancaster County jail. None of the murderers were ever tried, but Stewart died at the raid on Wyoming Valley.

Payne–Aldrich Tariff (9 April 1909) This replaced the Dingley Tariff, which was unpopular among progressive Republicans who felt that more foreign competition would force trusts to reduce their charges on consumers. It cut average rates to about 38 percent, but not as far as many Republicans and nearly all Democrats wished. It became a major issue in the 1912 election, and was succeeded by the Underwood–Simmons Tariff.

Pea Ridge, battle of (Ark.) On 7–8 March 1862, Brigadier General Samuel Curtis's 11,250 Federals routed Major General Earl Van Dorn's 17,000 Confederates. Losses: 1,384 USA casualities, 800 CSA casualties. Van Dorn withdrew his forces to Miss. and allowed the Union to consolidate military control over Mo. and northern Ark.

Peace Corps An executive order of 1 March 1961 (statutory authority of 22 September) created the Peace Corps to send US volunteers to help underdeveloped countries improve their human resources or economic infrastructure by the demonstration of new farming techniques, health and sanitation projects, rural development, the fostering of entrepreneurship, and the spreading of literacy. Volunteers received 9–14 weeks' training, spent two years abroad in their host community, and earned a modest subsistence allowance (initially $50 a month). The corps was placed under ACTION in 1971, but became an independent agency by the International Security and Development Cooperation Act (1981). In 1991 it stationed 6,000 volunteers in 84 countries. Over 135,000 volunteers worked in over 100 countries between 1961 and 1993.

peace of Paris *see* Paris, treaty of (1763)

Peach War On 15 September 1655, 500 Algonquians landed at New Amsterdam, ransacked houses, threatened citizens, and wounded a man who had recently killed an Indian woman caught stealing peaches from his orchard. A skirmish resulted that left two or three losses on each side. The Indians then devastated settlements in Staten Island and N.J., killed 50 persons, and captured 100, burned 28 farms, slaughtered 600 cattle, and ruined 10,000 bushels of grain. About 70 prisoners were ransomed in October, and by September 1657, only four children remained with the Indians. The Dutch did not counterattack and Indian raids abated in 1656, although Indians killed three Dutch in 1657. In 1658 the Dutch reoccupied their burned settlements with Indian consent. On 6 March 1660, a peace treaty was signed with most of the hostile tribes, except those on the Hudson River soon to fight in the first ESOPUS WAR.

Peachtree Creek, battle of (Ga.) *see* ATLANTA, BATTLES FOR

Peale, Charles Willson (b. Queen Anne Co., Md., 15 April 1741; d. Philadelphia, Pa., 22 February 1827) He was a saddler who at the age of 20, acquired a consuming passion to paint. He studied with John S. COPLEY at Boston and joined the AMERICAN SCHOOL in 1767. He established a portrait studio in Philadelphia and was a militia officer in the Revolution. He executed some of the best likenesses of the founding fathers, and was the Revolutionary era's second greatest portraitist, after Gilbert STUART. He sired a dynasty of artists by his sons Rembrandt, Raphael, Titian, and Rubens.

Pearl Harbor, attack on (Hawaii) At 6:48 a.m. on 7 December 1941, Admiral Chiuchi Nagumo's task force (6 carriers, 2 battleships, 3 cruisers, 9 destroyers, 3 submarines, and 8 auxiliary ships) launched 184 planes against US Navy and Army forces under Admiral Husband Kimmel and Lieutenant General Walter Short. Of 94 US Navy vessels in port, 70 were combat vessels: 8 battleships, 2 heavy cruisers, 6 light cruisers, 29 destroyers, 5 submarines, 1 gunboat, 9 minelayers, 10 minesweepers. Japanese bombing commenced at 7:55 a.m., followed by a second wave of 169 planes at 8:50 a.m. All enemy planes withdrew by 9:50 a.m. Japanese losses: 64 dead, 1 combat submarine sunk, 5 midget submarines sunk, 29 planes downed. US losses: 2,403 killed (2,008 navy, 109 marines, 218 army, and 68 civilians), 1,178 wounded (710 navy, 69 marines, 364 army, and 35 civilians). The Japanese sunk, capsized, or rendered inoperable 8 battleships, 3 light cruisers, 3 destroyers, 4 auxiliary craft, 63 army aircraft (out of 231), and 87 navy aircraft. Japan's treachery blundered on three counts: (1) it failed to destroy Pearl Harbor itself, which restored all major ships sunk or disabled to combat duty except 2 battleships; (2) it attacked while all the Pacific Fleet's aircraft carriers were at sea; and (3) it discredited peace sentiment in the US and led to immediate US declarations of war against Japan and Germany.

Peary, Robert Edwin (b. Cresson, Pa., 6 May 1856; d. Washington, D.C., 20 February 1920) In 1881 Peary entered the navy engineer corps. Beginning with an expedition in 1886, he became the foremost expert on Greenland's geography and the first person to demonstrate that it was an island (1892). He led a team by dog sled to fix the exact position of the North Pole, which he reported locating on 6 April 1909, 15 days before Dr Frederick Cook claimed the same honor for Great Britain.

Pecora hearings In January 1933, Ferdinand Pecora, counsel to the Senate Banking and Currency Committee, began investigating unethical practices in the financial markets. Pecora's hearings were well publicized and revealed numerous examples of price fixing, insider trading, tax avoidance, conflicts of interest, and instances of criminal activity. Pecora's work continued into 1934 and resulted in the SECURITIES EXCHANGE ACT, which he helped write.

Peleliu, battle of On 15 September 1944, Major General William Rupertus's first USMC Division (later reinforced by the 81st Army Division) landed on Peleliu, held by 10,000 Japanese. Effective enemy resistance ended on 28 November. US losses: 6,336 casualties. Japanese losses: nearly 10,000 killed. Along with the army's seizure of Angaur Island (17 September–21 October), Peleliu's fall gave the US control of the Palau Islands (in the Caroline Archipelago), east of the Philippines.

Pendleton Act (16 January 1883) This law introduced CIVIL SERVICE REFORM to federal employment. It created a three-man Civil Service Commission to draft competitive examinations for hiring and promoting federal workers on the civil service list, which initially included a tenth of government civilian employees. It authorized presidents to expand the merit system unilaterally, which many did on leaving office to protect their own appointees from dismissal. It outlawed the practice of forcing civil servants to contribute to political campaigns or firing them for failing to give money.

Pendleton plan *see* OHIO IDEA

Peninsular campaign On 17 March 1862, Major General George MCCLELLAN'S 58,000 Federals began an amphibious operation to seize Richmond via the peninsula between the York and James rivers. An offensive diversion by Stonewall JACKSON prevented 18,000 Federals in the Shenandoah Valley (*see* SHENANDOAH VALLEY CAMPAIGNS) or 38,000 near Washington from reinforcing McClellan. By holding Yorktown from 5 April to 4 May, General Joseph JOHNSTON won time to prepare Richmond's defenses. On 31 May, Johnston's 48,800 troops checked 41,800 Federals at Fair Oaks-Seven Pines. USA losses: 790 killed, 4,384 wounded. CSA losses: 980 killed, 5,729 wounded. General Robert E. LEE took command from the wounded Johnston. Reinforced by Jackson's army, Lee fought the Seven Days' Battles: Oak Grove (25 June), Mechanicsville (26 June), Gaines's Mill (27–8 June), Garnett's and Golding's Farms (27–8 June), Savage's Station (29 June), White Oak Swamp (30 June), and Malvern Hill (1 July). Losses: 15,849 USA and 20,733 CSA casualties. On 3 July, Lee broke contact and returned to his lines at Richmond. On 3 August, McClellan was ordered from the peninsula for operations near the second battle of BULL RUN.

Penn, William (b. London, England, 14 October 1644; d. Ruscombe, Berkshire, England, 30 July 1718) Son of a rich and politically influential admiral, to whom CHARLES II owed a small fortune, Penn joined the QUAKERS about 1666, suffered imprisonment in 1668–9, and became a proprietor of WEST JERSEY in 1676 and EAST JERSEY in 1681. On 14 March 1681, Charles II canceled a £16,000 debt owed to Penn's father by granting him PENNSYLVANIA as a PROPRIETARY COLONY. The DELAWARE area was appended to the colony in 1682.

Penn's Frame of Government established an elective legislature in 1682. On 28 October 1682, he landed at New Castle, Del., to take possession of his lands and was governor for two years. He established amicable relations with the Indians that kept Pa. at peace until 1756 and laid out Philadelphia's distinctive design as a "greene Country Towne." Forced to return to England in 1684 on personal business, he was absent from Pa. until 1699. His close relationship with JAMES II led WILLIAM III to make Pa. a ROYAL COLONY from 1692 to 1694. Again in Pa. between 1699 and 1701, Penn issued the Charter of Privileges (1701), which made Pa. the only colony with a unicameral legislature. Ruined by the incompetent management and embezzlement of his estate, he was sent to debtors' prison from 1717 to 1718.

Pennsylvania In the spring of 1643, Swedes made the first permanent European settlement in Pa. at Tinicum Island, 9 miles below modern Philadelphia. Control of the area passed from NEW SWEDEN to NEW NETHERLAND in 1655 and to England in 1664. On 14 March 1681, CHARLES II awarded William PENN a charter for a PROPRIETARY COLONY, including Pa. and modern DELAWARE, to serve as a Quaker refuge (*see* QUAKERS). The first ship of English Quakers landed in December 1681 and Penn arrived in October 1682. On 23 June 1683, Penn and the DELAWARE INDIANS concluded a treaty of friendship that laid the basis for 70 years of peaceful frontier expansion. In 1704 Del. began governing itself as a separate colony, but with the governor of Pa. as its chief executive. By 1700, modern Pa. had 18,000 occupants, of whom 98 percent were white and 90 percent were English or Welsh.

Pa. expanded rapidly after 1720 due to PENNSYLVANIA DUTCH and SCOTCH-IRISH IMMIGRATION. It became the leading exporter of foodstuffs, and Philadelphia emerged as the largest colonial city by 1770. It was a major battleground in the SEVEN YEARS' WAR and PONTIAC'S WAR. In 1758 the first settlement was made in the Ohio valley at Pittsburgh. In the REVOLUTIONARY WAR, Pa. usually provided 10 of the Continental army's 80 regiments; it was the scene of 63 military actions. Philadelphia was the US capital for most years from 1776 to 1800. Pa. was the second state to ratify the CONSTITUTION on 12 December

1787. It was the site of the WHISKEY REBELLION in the 1790s.

In 1800, Pa. was the second largest state and had 602,365 residents, of whom 38 percent were German, 29 percent English or Welsh, 15 percent Scotch-Irish, 8 percent Scottish, and 7 percent Irish. Heavy immigration from Ireland, Britain, and Germany continued, and its population grew by 382 percent by 1860. It then had 2,906,215 inhabitants, of whom 2 percent were black and 15 percent were foreign-born; it ranked second among states in population, third in the value of farmland and livestock and second in manufactures. In the CIVIL WAR, it furnished 337,936 USA troops (including 8,612 blacks) and was the site of 32 military engagements, including GETTYSBURG.

As the Pa. economy increasingly industrialized, the population doubled between 1860 and 1900. By 1900, it had 6,302,115 people, of whom 45 percent were rural, 97 percent white, and 16 percent foreign-born; it ranked second among states in population, eighth in the value of its agricultural goods, and second in manufactures. The high point of its growth came during 1900–10, when 444,600 new residents moved to the state. From 1920 to 1970, it experienced a net out-migration of 1,761,900. By 1990, it had slipped from the second most populous state to fifth. It then was 85 percent urban and had 11,881,643 inhabitants (88 percent white, 9 percent black, 2 percent Hispanic, and 1 percent Asian), of whom 3.1 percent were foreign-born. Manufacturing employed 20 percent of its workforce and mining 7 percent.

Pennsylvania Dutch This term refers to Protestants from the European continent who settled PENNSYLVANIA before 1776. (Dutch was an anglicization of "Deutsch," the word Germans use for themselves.) Of the 67,000 continental Protestants who landed in Pa. during 1727–75, two-thirds were PALATINES, a quarter were from Switzerland, and the rest were HUGUENOTS or natives of the Netherlands who settled among Germans and adopted their language. About 17,700 German-speaking immigrants arrived at colonial ports outside of Pa. by 1775. A large minority came as REDEMPTIONERS.

Pennsylvania rifle *see* KENTUCKY RIFLE

Pennsylvania* v. *Wheeling and Belmont Bridge On 6 February 1852, the Supreme Court ruled (7–2) that a bridge over the Ohio River blocked interstate commerce and must be taken down or modified to permit passage by ships. This result led Congress to pass its first law overruling a Supreme Court decision and decree that ships, rather than the bridge, would have to be refitted. The Court affirmed in 1856 Congress's authority to overturn its rulings by statute.

Pentagon Proposed in 1941 to centralize military headquarters, the Pentagon was completed on 15 January 1943 and cost $83,000,000. It could hold over 50,000 workers. Its five stories contain 17.5 miles of corridors, including 10 that connect different wings surrounding a 5-acre court. It was designed so that no office would be farther than a 20-minute walk from its most distant point.

Pentagon papers Beginning on 13 June 1971, the New York *Times* printed classified documents stolen by Daniel Ellsberg and Anthony J. Russo from a 47-volume Department of DEFENSE study of the VIETNAM WAR's origins. Blocked by an injunction from further publication after 16 June, the *Times* won an appeal to the Supreme Court, which ruled (6–3) on 30 June that the FIRST AMENDMENT protected the secret documents. The selectively chosen Pentagon papers showed that the war's origins were convoluted and confused, but little more. On 11 May 1973, 15 counts of espionage, theft, and conspiracy against Russo and Ellsberg were dismissed in Los Angeles on a technicality, because government officials had conducted an illegal burglary and wiretaps to obtain evidence. The two men were never retried.

People's Party *see* POPULISM

Pepperrell, Sir William (b. Kittery, Maine, 27 June 1696; d. Kittery, Maine, 6 July 1759) When KING GEORGE'S WAR began, Pepperrell was a wealthy landowner and prominent politician in Maine. For commanding the Yankee forces that captured LOUISBOURG (1745), he was not only knighted, but also became the only native-born American to be given a baronetcy. In the SEVEN YEARS' WAR, he recruited a battalion of British regulars (the 50th, or "Pepperell's") in the colonies, and received rank as major general (1755) and lieutenant general (1759).

Pequot Indians In the late 16th century, about half the MAHICAN INDIANS left N.Y. for Conn., where the natives called them "Destroyers," or Pequots. They numbered 4,000 in 1636 as the PEQUOT WAR began, but half of them seceded to form the pro-English MOHICAN INDIANS. After their defeat in 1637, many were absorbed by the Mohicans. The surviving Pequots were English allies in KING PHILIP'S WAR. A remnant stayed in Conn. and have state reservations at Ledyard, Trumbull, and Kent.

Pequot War On 24 August 1636, the Puritans' (*see* PURITANISM) first major Indian conflict began when Mass. reacted to attacks on English ships by sending Captain John Endicott and 90 militia to demand that the PEQUOT INDIANS turn over the guilty parties. Rebuffed by the Pequots in September, Endicott destroyed two of their towns in Conn. Pequots raided the Conn. River settlements and had killed 30 whites by May 1637. On 26 May, Captain John Mason's 90 Conn. militia and 60 MOHICAN INDIANS burned an enemy palisade on the Mystic River and killed up to 400 inhabitants, while losing two English killed, 20 English wounded, and 20 Mohicans wounded. On 14 July, Mason surrounded several hundred Pequots in a swamp near New Haven, killed about 80 men, and captured several hundred women and children. Mohicans and other Indians killed or captured hundreds of Pequots in the following months. Of 2,000 Pequots, at least 800 died in the war, while less than 50 of Conn.'s 800 whites died. The war established Puritan military superiority over New England's Indians until KING PHILIP'S WAR.

Perkins, Frances (b. Boston, Mass., 10 April 1880; d. New York, N.Y., 14 May 1965) After working with Jane ADDAMS at Hull House, Perkins moved to N.Y., where she worked for improved working conditions and met Eleanor ROOSEVELT. In 1926 she became chair of the State Industrial Commission, which enforced labor statutes. She became the first woman to hold a US cabinet post in 1933 as secretary of labor. She was the leading advocate for the Social Security Act (*see* SOCIAL SECURITY ADMINISTRATION), which she influenced as chair of the President's Committee on Economic Security. She left the Labor Deptartment in 1945.

Perot, H(enry) Ross (b. Texarkana, Tex., 27 June 1930) In 1953 Perot graduated from Annapolis, and he left the navy in 1957. In 1962 he founded Electronic Data Systems, which he built into a firm worth $2 billion by 1984. On 18 March 1992, he became an independent candidate for US president, for UNITED WE STAND AMERICA, an organization heavily financed by himself. After dropping out of the race on 16 July – to foil a Republican plot against his daughter's wedding, as he later explained – he reentered on 1 October with James Stockdale (a hero of the VIETNAM WAR) as his running mate. Campaigning to eliminate the budget deficit and pay off the NATIONAL DEBT, Perot polled 19 percent of all votes, the highest showing by any third party candidate except Theodore ROOSEVELT and Millard FILLMORE. He launched an unsuccessful campaign to defeat the NORTH AMERICAN FREE TRADE AGREEMENT.

Perry, Matthew Calbraith (b. Newport, R.I., 10 April 1794; d. New York, N.Y., 4 March 1858) Brother of Oliver H. PERRY, he entered the navy in 1809 and later won favorable attention for his plans for officer education, improved gunnery training, and a naval engineer corps. He assisted the British in suppressing the slave trade in the mid-1840s and commanded the US amphibious force at the battle of VERA CRUZ, Mexico. In 1854 he received orders to take a naval squadron and act as envoy to Japan. Perry anchored off Yedo Bay on 8 July 1853 and over the next year negotiated the treaty of KANAGAWA, which established US commercial relations with Japan.

Perry, Oliver Hazard (b. South Kingston, R.I., 20 August 1785; d. on the Orinoco River, Venezuela, 23 August 1819) In 1799 Perry entered the navy, saw duty in the undeclared war with FRANCE, and fought in the wars with the BARBARY PIRATES. After winning the battle of LAKE ERIE, which enabled US forces to invade Canada, he composed the most modest and laconic victory message ever written: "We have met the enemy, and they are ours – two ships, two brigs, one schooner, and a sloop."

Perry* v. *United States *see* GOLD STANDARD

Perryville, battle of (Ky.) On 8 October 1862, Major General Don Buell's 36,940 Federals defeated General Braxton Bragg's 16,000 Confederates. USA losses: 845 killed, 2,851 wounded, 515 missing. CSA losses: 510 killed, 2,635 wounded, 251 missing. Defeat ended Bragg's hopes of establishing CSA control over Ky. and he retreated to Tenn.

Pershing, John Joseph (b. near Laclede, Mo., 13 September 1860; d. Washington, D.C., 15 July 1948) In 1886 Pershing graduated from West Point. He served in the cavalry during the APACHE CAMPAIGNS and was given the nickname "Black Jack" for commanding BUFFALO SOLDIERS. He fought at SAN JUAN HILL and in the PHILIPPINE INSURRECTION. It was 17 years before he rose from lieutenant to captain, but in 1906 he was promoted from captain to brigadier general over 862 senior officers. After leading the US invasion of the MEXICAN BORDER as major general, he commanded the ALLIED EXPEDITIONARY FORCE (AEF) as one of just five soldiers commissioned as general of the armies. He insisted that the AEF stay a single US command in WORLD WAR I and not be cannibalized as reserves for British and French forces. He was army chief of staff (1921–4).

Persian Gulf War On 1 August 1990, Saddam Hussein's army invaded Kuwait to annex its oil fields, possession of which would have given Iraq control over 25 percent of the world's oil reserves. George BUSH and the UN Security Council immediately condemned the aggression, which seemed likely to engulf Saudi Arabia after Iraq occupied all of Kuwait. Bush orchestrated an international coalition which would expel Iraq from Kuwait under UN auspices if its troops were not withdrawn by 15 January 1991; he won congressional approval to employ US forces on this mission in December 1990. Under the command of Lieutenant General Norman Schwarzkopf (US), the UN coalition assembled in Saudi Arabia with over 600,000 ground troops from 28 nations (350,000 US, 43,000 British, 40,000 Egyptian, 16,000 French, and 20,000 Syrian) to expel an estimated 500,000 Iraqi soldiers. On 17 January 1991, aerial bombing of Iraq commenced, and the UN ground offensive began on 24 Feb. Fighting lasted 5 days, until 28 Feb., when Kuwait was cleared of Iraqi troops. Coalition deaths included 146 US (35 by friendly fire), 24 British (9 by US friendly fire), 2 French, 1 Italian, and 39 from Arab states. Iraqi deaths were estimated at 8,000–25,000 soldiers and 5,000 civilians.

personal liberty laws Personal liberty laws were state statutes passed to make federal enforcement of fugitive slave laws more difficult. They typically forbade state officials to help arrest or detain accused runaways, and offered the accused a jury trial and DUE PROCESS in state courts. Although adopted by northern legislatures, they exemplified the STATES' RIGHTS tradition of interposing state authority to protect citizens from abuses of federal power. *PRIGG* v. *PENNSYLVANIA* held that such laws could not interfere with operation of the first FUGITIVE SLAVE ACT. Ten free states passed such laws after passage of the second FUGITIVE SLAVE ACT, but *ABELMAN* v. *BOOTH* again held them unconstitutional.

pet banks This term was applied to state banks chosen as depositories for US Treasury funds withdrawn from the second BANK OF THE UNITED STATES under Andrew JACKSON. By 1833, there were 23 pet banks, and the DISTRIBUTION ACT (1836) required there to be at least one in each state. During the PANIC OF 1837, the US lost $9,000,000 deposited in pet banks that failed.

Petersburg, battles of (Va.) On 9 June 1864, Major General Benjamin BUTLER's 4,500 Federals failed to dislodge Brigadier General Henry Wise's 2,500 CSA troops from Petersburg. On 15 June, Major General William Smith's 16,100 Federals failed to take the city from General Pierre Beauregard's 5,400 Confederates. By 18 June, 41,500 CSA troops under Gen. Robert E. LEE had repulsed all attacks by General Ulysses S. GRANT's 63,800 Federals. USA losses: 1,688 killed, 8,513 wounded, 1,185 captured. CSA losses: unknown. On 30 July, 20,700 Federals charged into a crater produced by exploding four tons of gunpowder under CSA trenches, but were driven back by 11,500 defenders. Losses: 3,798 USA and 1,500 CSA casualties. Petersburg was unsuccessfully besieged until April 1865, by which time there had been 42,000 USA and 28,000 CSA casualties. After Union victory at FIVE FORKS enabled Federals to cut off CSA supply lines, Grant's 63,300 men took the city from Lee's 18,600 Confederates on 2 April. Losses: 3,361 USA and 4,140 CSA casualties. Lee abandoned attempts to defend Richmond and began retreating to APPOMATTOX COURT HOUSE.

Peyote Cult *see* NATIVE AMERICAN CHURCH

Philippine campaigns (1) On 22 December 1941, Japan's Fourteenth Army (100,000 soldiers) invaded the Philippines, held by 23,600 US troops, 20,000 Philippine regulars, and 100,000 newly mobilized Philippine reservists. Allied forces held out for six months on BATAAN and CORREGIDOR.

(2) On 20 October 1944, General Douglas MACARTHUR landed the Sixth Army, later joined by the Eighth Army, on Leyte Island, which was held by just 16,000 of General Tomoyuki Yamashita's 270,000 troops. The US Navy defeated an attempt to destroy the invasion flotilla at the battle of LEYTE GULF. US forces sustained 15,584 casualties, and inflicted 70,000 on the Japanese, before enemy resistance ended in Leyte on 25 December.

(3) During 2 January–4 February 1945, the Sixth and Eighth Armies invaded Luzon Island; they took Manila in March and ended enemy resistance in May. US losses: 7,933 killed, 32,732 wounded. Japanese losses: 192,000 dead. Resistance by 102,000 Japanese in the southern Philippines (principally Mindanao) continued through the war's end.

Philippine Insurrection The US sent 12,000 troops under Major General Elwell Otis to occupy the Philippines when they were ceded in the SPANISH-AMERICAN WAR. Elwell's men dispersed rebels under Emilio Aguinaldo (leader of a failed revolt in 1896–7) on 4–6 February 1899 and prevented an uprising in Manila on 22 February. Aguinaldo's continued resistance led to the commitment of 47,500 US ground troops (including Philippino enlistees) by 31 December 1899, 75,000 by 31 December 1900, and 126,000 by the end of the conflict. Aguinaldo's capture on 23 March 1901 ended the rebel movement, which was declared suppressed on 4 July 1902. US forces fought in over 2,800 engagements. US losses: 4,234 killed, 2,818 wounded, at a cost of $600,000,000. Philippino insurgents' losses: 16,000 killed and wounded. Perhaps 200,000 civilians died from famine, diseases, or accidental deaths during the rebellion.

Philippine Sea, battle of the On 19–20 June 1944, in the MARIANA ISLANDS, Admiral Jisaburo Ozawa's task force (5 heavy carriers, 4 light carriers, 5 battleships, 11 heavy cruisers, 2 light cruisers, 28 destroyers) attacked Admiral Marc Mitscher's task force (7 heavy carriers, 8 light carriers, 7 battleships, 8 heavy cruisers, 13 light cruisers, 69 destroyers). On 19 June, Ozawa lost 243 of his 373 planes (compared to 29 US planes destroyed) in what was termed the "Great Marianas Turkey Shoot." US losses: 60 planes. Japanese losses: 2 carriers, 1 heavy carrier, 373 planes. The battle left Japan with just two operational carriers and destroyed two-thirds of its naval aircraft.

Philippines The US seized the Philippines in the SPANISH-AMERICAN WAR and they were ceded to the US by the treaty of Paris on 10 December 1898. The PHILIPPINE INSURRECTION erupted after the US failed to permit national independence. On 29 August 1916, the Jones Act (Organic Act of the Philippine Islands) reaffirmed the US intention to grant independence "as soon as a stable government can be established;" it was superseded by the Tydings–McDuffie Act (1934) providing for an interim commonwealth and independence by 1945. The PHILIPPINE CAMPAIGNS delayed nationhood until 4 July 1946.

Phips, Sir William (b. Maine, 2 February 1651; d. London, England, 18 February 1695) He was a self-made man who became rich recovering a sunken treasure off Haiti in 1686. For this accomplishment, he became the first American awarded a knighthood (1687). In 1690, during KING WILLIAM'S WAR, he was victorious at Port Royal, Nova Scotia, but his siege of QUEBEC was a failure. Named first royal governor of Mass. in 1691, he showed political courage by taking decisive action to stop the SALEM WITCH TRIALS.

Physical Valuation Act (1 March 1913) This law strengthened the INTERSTATE

COMMERCE COMMISSION's (ICC) authority under the HEPBURN and MANN–ELKINS ACTS. It allowed the ICC to assess its own valuation of railroad assets so that freight and passenger charges could be set according to a fair rate of return. This authority was the last power required by the ICC to exercise truly effective regulation of rail carriers in the public interest.

Piankeshaw Indians *see* MIAMI INDIANS

Pickett's Charge *see* GETTYSBURG, BATTLE OF

Piedmont This region includes the area of the US Atlantic seaboard lying west of the first line of waterfalls or riffles that block seagoing ships from further progress inland. Anglo-Americans had settled little of this area before QUEEN ANNE'S WAR ended (except for parts of New England), but its best lands were rapidly occupied after then as the GREAT WAGON ROAD was extended.

Piegan Indians *see* BLACKFOOT INDIANS

Pierce, Franklin (b. Hillsboro, N.H., 23 November 1804; d. Concord, N.H., 8 October 1869) He became speaker of N.H.'s assembly at 27, a Democratic congressman at 29, senator at 33, and brigadier general in the MEXICAN WAR at 42. In 1852 he defeated James BUCHANAN, Lewis CASS, and Stephen DOUGLAS for the Democratic presidential nomination on the 49th ballot. Pierce won the most sweeping electoral victory since 1820; he lost only four states and carried 50.9 percent of the popular vote against Winfield SCOTT and John HALE. His administration negotiated the GADSDEN PURCHASE, signed the first treaty with Japan, expanded the army, and recognized the FILIBUSTERING regime of William WALKER in NICARAGUA. Pierce failed to be renominated because he alienated free-soil Democrats by supporting the KANSAS–NEBRASKA ACT.

Pike's expeditions Between 9 August 1805 and 30 April 1807, Lieutenant Zebulon Pike led the army's first exploration of Minn., but failed to find the Mississippi River's source. On 15 July 1806, he led an army exploring party from St Louis to Pike's Peak, Colo. In early 1807, while probably engaged in an espionage mission to reconnoiter the Santa Fe area, he was arrested in the Rio Grande valley by Spanish troops, who returned him to Natchitoches, La., on 30 June 1807.

Pilgrims This term refers to PLYMOUTH's founding settlers. The group originated among English SEPARATING PURITANS at Leyden, Holland, led by William Brewster, who obtained financing from London merchants to plant a colony in Va. On 16 September 1620, the *MAYFLOWER* left Plymouth, England, with 102 Pilgrims, of whom 35 belonged to the Leyden exiles, and 67 had been recruited in London or Southampton (there were also 20 servants). One passenger died and a child was born en route. They sighted Cape Cod on 9 November, signed the *MAYFLOWER* COMPACT on 21 November, and disembarked at Plymouth on 26 December. By spring, half the group had died of disease or malnutrition. Systematically cheated by their London creditors, they did not pay off their debts and establish clear title to Plymouth until 1644.

Pinchot, Gifford (b. Simsbury, Conn., 11 October 1865; d. New York, N.Y., 4 October 1946) As chief of the US Forestry Division (1898–1901), he cooperated with his friend Theodore ROOSEVELT in launching a national "conservation" movement to reverse despoliation and waste of natural resources. He insisted on managing the environment to benefit all citizens, not just business interests. He headed the National Conservation Commission, founded in 1907, which began the first systematic inventory of US water, soil, mineral, and forest resources. He was fired as chief forester during the BALLINGER–PINCHOT CONTROVERSY. He was president of the National Conservation Association, and was elected Pa. governor in 1922 and 1930.

Pinckney, Charles Cotesworth (b. Charles Town, S.C., 25 February 1746; d. Charleston, S.C., 16 August 1825) Well-educated in England and France, Pinckney was a lawyer who fought in the REVOLUTIONARY WAR, was captured at the second battle of CHARLES TOWN, and rose to brigadier general. He was an important influence at the CONSTITUTIONAL CONVENTION. He declined offers from George WASHINGTON to become commander of the army, Supreme Court justice, secretary of war, and secretary of state, before serving as envoy extraordinary to France (1796–7), when he was involved in the XYZ AFFAIR. He was the candidate for the

FEDERALIST PARTY for vice-president in 1800. In two unsuccessful races for president against Thomas JEFFERSON, he took just two states in 1804 and five in 1808.

Pinckney, Eliza Lucas (b. Antigua, ca. 1722; d. Philadelphia, Pa., 26 May 1793) Having learned how to grow indigo on her father's Antigua plantation, she began experimenting with the plant in S.C. after moving there in 1738. She was influential in its development as a profitable export for S.C., which became the major source of indigo. She was the mother of CHARLES and THOMAS PINCKNEY.

Pinckney, Thomas (b. Charles Town, S.C., 23 October 1750; d. Charleston, S.C., 2 November 1828) Well-educated with his brother Charles in England, Pinckney was a lawyer who fought in the REVOLUTIONARY WAR, was captured at CAMDEN, and was S.C. governor (1787–9). While ambassador to Great Britain (1792–6), he negotiated the treaty of SAN LORENZO as envoy extraordinary to Spain. When the FEDERALIST PARTY nominated Pinckney for vice-president in 1796, Alexander HAMILTON attempted to manipulate the electoral college so that Pinckney would outpoll John ADAMS, but the scheme miscarried and Thomas JEFFERSON consequently became vice-president. Pinckney served as major general in the WAR OF 1812, but saw no action.

Pinckney's Treaty *see* SAN LORENZO, TREATY OF

piracy North African, Dutch, and French pirates threatened Anglo-American shipping from the 1640s. Piracy peaked from 1697 to 1725, a period when many buccaneers operated openly out of colonial harbors with the connivance of local merchants. In one of the most successful anti-crime campaigns ever waged, the Royal Navy systematically wiped out the freebooters by the late 1720s. Seizures of ships by the Barbary pirates began in the 1780s and led to the wars with BARBARY PIRATES. Piracy also revived in the Gulf of Mexico from 1814 to 1824, when US shippers suffered about 1,500 acts of piracy. By 1827 the US Navy had ended this menace by destroying the buccaneers' bases and stationing numerous warships along the southern trade lanes.

Pitt, William (b. London, England, 15 November 1708; d. Hayes, Middlesex, England, 11 May 1778) Having entered Parliament in 1735, Pitt became prime minister in June 1757 and achieved heroic status among Americans by leading Britain to victory in the SEVEN YEARS' WAR. GEORGE III pressured him to resign in October 1761. Pitt opposed his brother-in-law George GRENVILLE'S STAMP ACT and fought the DECLARATORY ACT. He became prime minister again in July 1766, but his health collapsed in March 1767 and leadership of his ministry fell to Charles TOWNSHEND, who pursued anti-American policies opposed by Pitt. Pitt resigned as prime minister in October 1768 because of poor health and was succeeded by the Duke of GRAFTON. He had entered the House of Lords as the Earl of Chatham in 1766, and there opposed Lord NORTH'S policies toward the colonies.

Plains of Abraham, battle of On 13 September 1759, Brigadier General James Wolfe's 4,686 British troops defeated the Marquis de Montcalm's 4,500 French. Wolfe and Montcalm both died of wounds. British losses: 65 killed, 546 wounded. French losses: 644 killed and wounded. British forces, which had been on the verge of withdrawing to Nova Scotia, entrenched themselves in the St Lawrence valley by taking Canada's capital and capturing France's largest army in the colony; they later repulsed the French in the battle of QUEBEC (1760).

Planned Parenthood Federation *see* SANGER, MARGARET

plantation The term *plantation* originally described a colony of English farmers, organized like a manor, established in Ireland during the Tudor-Stuart period. *Planters* were individuals who financed, organized, and supervised such operations. In the early Chesapeake, a planter was a man who paid his own passage to America, acquired land, and worked it with indentured servants. After 1700, in the colonies south of New England, *plantation* simply meant a family farm, as opposed to a tenancy, whether its owner possessed slaves or not. After 1800, *planter* acquired the more restricted meaning of a farmer owning more than 10 slaves.

Platt amendment On 2 March 1901, this rider was attached to the annual Army

Appropriation Bill. Its main provisions were that Cuba would never make a foreign treaty compromising its independence, that Cuba's national debt would never exceed the level that regular taxation could manage, that Cuba would concede the US a right to intervene militarily in cases of violent civil disorders, and that Cuba would lease the US a naval base. At strong US urging, Cuba's constitutional convention incorporated the Platt amendment into its constitution on 12 June. The amendment severely curtailed Cuban sovereignty, enabled the US Navy to lease Guantanamo Bay harbor, and allowed the landing of troops to protect US investments.

Plessy* v. *Ferguson On 18 May 1896, the Supreme Court affirmed a La. law segregating railway passengers. John M. HARLAN wrote the lone dissent. It established the principle that racially separate facilities were constitutional as long as they were equal, and did not violate the FOURTEENTH AMENDMENT's equal protection clause. The Court extended *Plessy* to school segregation in *CUMMING* v. *COUNTY BOARD OF EDUCATION* and ruled on what constituted equal facilities in *MISSOURI EX REL. GAINES* v. *CANADA*. The Court reversed *Plessy* in *BROWN* v. *BOARD OF EDUCATION OF TOPEKA* (1954).

Plyler* v. *Doe On 15 June 1982, the Supreme Court ruled (5–4) that a Tex. law allowing school districts to deny enrollment to children illegally brought into the US violates equal protection under the law. (*See precedent of YICK WO* v. *HOPKINS*)

Plymouth The colony of Plymouth was settled by the PILGRIMS in 1620. Although it reached agreements on its borders with the MASSACHUSETTS BAY COMPANY and the legatees of the PLYMOUTH COMPANY, it never received a charter from the Crown establishing its legal status. It was annexed by the royal charter given Mass. on 17 October 1691, when its population numbered about 7,400 living in the present area of Plymouth, Barnstable, and Bristol counties.

Plymouth Company On 20 April 1606, JAMES I awarded a patent authorizing the Virginia Company of Plymouth, England, to colonize the region north of Long Island. The company sponsored the failed outpost at SAGADAHOC, Maine, and then became inactive until revived on 3 March 1620, as the Council for New England, by a royal charter to Sir Fernando Gorges, Sir Francis Popham, and Raleigh Gilbert. In 1628 the council granted a patent, to colonize the territory between the Merrimack and Charles rivers, to the New England Company which was reorganized as the MASSACHUSETTS BAY COMPANY.

On 10 August 1622, the council granted the coastal districts of N.H. and Maine to Gorges and John Mason (in 1629 Mason took title to N.H. and Gorges to Maine). After Mason's death in 1635, his settlers in N.H. appropriated his lands. Gorges failed to prevent Mass. from annexing his lands in 1652, but his heirs won a ruling by the Lords of Trade in 1677 that Mass. had illegally taken Maine from them. Mass. then bought the Gorges claims for £1,250.

Pocahontas (b. Va., ca. 1595; d. Gravesend, England, 21 March 1617) Daughter of Powhatan, Pocahontas became an intermediary between English settlers and the POWHATAN CONFEDERACY in 1608, when she helped stage a reconciliation between her father and John SMITH. Seized as a hostage by the English in 1613, she became a Christian and married John ROLFE in 1614. As Lady Rebecca Rolfe, she became a celebrity during a tour of England, where she died of disease.

Poe, Edgar Allan (b. Boston, Mass., 19 January 1809; d. Baltimore, Md., 7 October 1849) An orphan since the age of 3 who studied briefly at the University of Virginia and West Point, Poe published his first book, *Tamerlane and Other Poems* in 1827. He emerged as one of the Romantic era's leading US literary figures. His writings explored macabre themes involving terror, madness, chaos, and psychological disintegration, and he was a major innovator of the detective genre of short stories. His major works include *Al Aaraaf, Tamerlane, and Minor Poems* (1829), *Poems by Edgar Allan Poe* (1831), *The Narrative of Arthur Gordon Pym* (1838), *Tales* (1845), and *The Raven and Other Poems* (1845). Alcoholism and opium abuse contributed to his early death.

Point Pleasant, battle of (W.Va.) On 10 October 1774, Colonel Andrew Lewis's 900 Va. militia defeated Cornplanter's 800

Shawnee Indians. Va. losses: about 225 killed and wounded. Indian losses: about 200 killed and wounded. The defeat demoralized the Shawnee, who accepted defeat in Dunmore's War by the treaty of Camp Charlotte.

Pointer* v. *Texas On 5 April 1965, the Supreme Court unanimously ruled that the Fourteenth Amendment's due process clause obliged state courts to uphold the Sixth Amendment's right of defendants to confront and cross-examine hostile witnesses.

Polish immigration This became significant after 1880. By 1900, 400,000 Poles had immigrated from jurisdictions in Austria, 384,000 from Prussia, and 170,000 from Russia. From then until 1914, another 400,000 came from Austria, 50,000 from Prussia, and 635,000 from Russia. An estimated 20 percent of these immigrants returned home to Europe before 1914. Poland was given a low quota under the National Origins Act, and its immigration dropped from 227,734 in the 1920s to 17,026 in the 1930s. Since 1945, 211,356 Poles have arrived in the US. The 1990 census reported 6,542,844 Americans who described their primary ethnic identity as Polish, 3.3 percent of whites.

Polish National Catholic Church *see* Catholic church

political action committees *see* Federal Elections Campaign Act

Polk, James Knox (b. Mecklenberg County, N.C., 2 November 1795; d. Nashville, Tenn., 15 June 1849) He came to Tenn. in 1806 and opened a law office at Columbia in 1820. He joined Andrew Jackson's wing of the Democratic Party and served as congressman (1825–39), speaker of the House (1835–9), and Tenn. governor (1839–41). As the first "dark horse" candidate for president, he became Democratic nominee over Martin Van Buren in 1844 and defeated Henry Clay with 49.6 percent of the ballots. His administration settled the question of the boundary of Oregon, established the Independent Treasury, ended protectionism by the Walker Tariff, and acquired the southwest by the Mexican War. He retired without seeking a second term.

poll tax The poll, or head, tax was the primary means of supporting local government in early America; it levied a fixed rate on each adult worker – both free and slave – as opposed to taxing income or land. After the Fifteenth Amendment prevented southern states from excluding blacks from elections, some states discouraged black political participation by requiring all voters to pay a poll tax. Grandfather clauses sometimes exempted whites. Poll taxes lowered turnout among blacks more than whites, because poverty discouraged most blacks from paying unnecessary taxes. The Supreme Court upheld poll taxes in *Breedlove* v. *Suttles*, but reversed itself in *Harper* v. *Virginia State Board of Elections*. The Twenty-fourth Amendment forbade states to apply them to federal elections. Federal courts struck down the last poll taxes for state elections in 1966 for Tex. (9 February), Ala. (3 March), Va. (25 March), and Miss. (8 April).

Pollock, Jackson (b. near Cody, Wyo., 28 January 1912; d. Southampton, Long Island, N.Y., 11 August 1956) After leaving high school in Los Angeles, Pollock studied painting in New York, where he was advised by Thomas H. Benton. In the mid-1940s, he experienced a strong reaction against mainline painting, and began exploring abstract art. He emerged as a prominent spokesman for American expressionists and gained international recognition by shows at Milan and Venice in 1950 and at Paris in 1952. He achieved great posthumous popularity after he died prematurely in a car crash.

Pollock* v. *Farmers' Loan and Trust Company In 1895 the Supreme Court overturned *Springer* v. *United States* and ruled (5–4) that the income tax violated Article I, Section 9 of the Constitution, since it levied a direct tax without apportionment according to population. The Sixteenth Amendment overcame the Court's objections.

Ponca Indians This Siouan language group split off from the Omaha Indians about 1650 and occupied S.Dak. and Nebr. in the 1700s. They often fought with the Sioux, but avoided conflict with Anglo-Americans. They declined from 600 in 1780 to perhaps 300 after a smallpox epidemic in

1802, and recovered to about 800 by 1842, about the same number living in 1906. They were forcibly removed to a reservation in Kay and Noble Counties, Okla., in 1877, but in the 1880s about a third were allowed to return to Nebr. and buy permanent homesteads.

Ponce de Leon, Juan (b. San Servos, Campos, Spain, ca. 1460; d. Cuba, ca. May 1521) On 2 April 1513, Ponce de Leon sighted land, claimed it for Spain, and named it FLORIDA. He was the first navigator to confirm that Fla. was a large land mass, by exploring its eastern and western coasts, but described it as an island upon returning to Puerto Rico in October. Lured in part by myths of a "fountain of youth," he landed at Fla. in February 1521, was driven offshore by Indian attacks, and later died of wounds.

Pontiac's War In 1763 the Ottawa leader Pontiac formed an alliance of Indians discontented with the establishment of British army garrisons south of the Great Lakes. On 16 May, Wyandots burned Fort Sandusky, Ohio. On 25 May, Potawatomis destroyed Fort St Joseph, Mich. On 27 May, Miamis captured Fort Miami, Ind. On 1 June, Weas captured Fort Ouiatonon, Ind. On 4 June, Chippewas and Sauks took Fort Mackinac, Mich. On 16 June, Senecas burned Fort Venango, Pa. On 18 June, Fort Presque'isle surrendered to 200 Senecas, Delawares, and Ottawas after a three-day siege. On 19 June, Senecas captured Fort Le Boeuf, Pa., but failed to prevent its 12 defenders from escaping under fire. On 21 June, the 18 defenders of Fort La Baye, Wis., handed the post over to Chippewas and were allowed to depart peacefully. On 28 May, Ottawas killed or captured 57 redcoats camped on Lake Detroit, and on 13 September, Senecas wiped out 72 troops escorting a supply train near Fort Niagara, N.Y.

Fighting largely ended in the eastern Ohio valley after Colonel Henry Bouquet won the battle of BUSHY RUN, Pa., and broke the siege of FORT PITT. When Pontiac failed to take FORT DETROIT (1763) after a five-month siege, most western Indians abandoned his cause. In 1764 Colonel John Bradstreet led 1,200 troops against the Great Lakes tribes, who signed a peace agreement on 12 August. In October 1764, Colonel Henry Bouquet led 1,170 troops against Shawnees, Delawares, and Mingos, who made peace and surrendered 200 prisoners on 14 November. In 1766 Pontiac renounced war in the treaty of OSWEGO.

Britain reacted to the war with the PROCLAMATION OF 1763. It also concluded that 10,000 British troops would be required to garrison territories conquered from France and Spain, to guard against another war. To offset these unexpected military costs, George GRENVILLE proposed the SUGAR and STAMP ACTS.

Pony Express On 3 April 1860, the Russell, Majors, and Waddell Freight Co. began transcontinental mail delivery from St Joseph, Mo., to Sacramento, Calif. (The Overland Mail Co. already carried transcontinental mail from Fort Smith, Ark., to Los Angeles via El Paso.) It operated 190 way stations, about 15 miles apart, and carried letters – at $5 each – from Mo. to Calif. in 10 days during the warm season and in 18 days during winter. The service lost money and needed government subsidies; it was ended in October 1861 when the transcontinental TELEGRAPH service opened.

pools *see* TRUSTS

Pope, John *see* VIRGINIA, ARMY OF, NEW MADRID, BATTLE OF, *and* SIOUX WAR, FIRST

Popé's Revolt On 10 August 1680, a Shaman of the PUEBLO INDIANS named Popé led an insurrection against Spanish authorities in N.Mex. and killed 400 whites, including 21 of the area's 33 priests. The Pueblos captured Santa Fe on 21 August and forced the 2,500 Spanish survivors of the massacre to fight their way to Mexico. Santa Fe was not reconquered by Spanish troops until 1692.

popular sovereignty Also known as squatter sovereignty, this was the policy by which Congress authorized a territory's settlers to vote on whether to permit or exclude SLAVERY prior to statehood. In his 1848 presidential campaign, Lewis CASS argued that this option be extended to settlers in the lands acquired in the MEXICAN WAR. The COMPROMISE OF 1850 and KANSAS–NEBRASKA ACT organized territories on this basis. *DRED SCOTT* V. *SANDFORD* made the issue moot.

populism This was an agrarian reform movement with a large following in the Great Plains, Rockies, and cotton-belt states during 1884–1900. Populists favored a SUBTREASURY PLAN, an INCOME TAX, regulation of railroad and warehouse rates, and free silver coinage (*see* SILVER COINAGE CONTROVERSY). Westerners organized the National Farmers' Alliance. Southerners formed the Farmers' Alliance and Industrial Union, which cooperated with the National Colored Farmers' Alliance.

In 1890 these groups entered state politics by endorsing Democrats or Republicans who supported their goals, and sometimes by running their own candidates; they sponsored four victorious governors, 44 congressmen, and two senators, plus winning majorities or substantial minorities in eight southern and four western legislatures. In 1892 they formed the People's (Populist) Party, ran James WEAVER for president (he polled 1,030,000 votes and carried six western states), and elected 5 senators, 10 congressmen, and 3 governors. In 1896 the Populists fused with Democrats by nominating William Jennings BRYAN, but had their own vice-presidential candidate (Thomas WATSON). Fusion candidates took 40 percent of the southern vote, and won by large majorities in Kans., Nebr., S.Dak., Mont., Idaho, and Wash., but the experiment undermined the Populists' credibility as a truly independent force in politics. The People's Party fared badly in the 1898 mid-term elections, and its presidential ticket under William Barker (Pa.) won just 50,232 votes in 1900; its last presidential candidate, Watson, polled 114,753 votes in 1904 and 28,131 in 1908.

Many "radical" programs advocated by Populists later became law, including the WAREHOUSE ACT (based on the Subtreasury), POSTAL DEPOSIT SAVINGS ACT, INCOME TAX, COMMODITY CREDIT CORPORATION (earlier the AGRICULTURAL CREDITS ACT's Federal Intermediate Credit Banks), and strict regulation of public carriers by the HEPBURN and MANN–ELKINS ACTS. Populism nevertheless was fatally flawed in failing to understand that US farm incomes were depressed because of international overproduction of grains and cotton. Populism transformed western politics by undermining the intense party loyalty felt in post-Civil War America.

Populist party *see* POPULISM

Port Hudson, battle of (La.) The garrison of Port Hudson, which was the key CSA strong point blocking the Mississippi north of Baton Rouge, repulsed US attacks on 14 March and 8–10 May 1863. The post fell to Major General Nathaniel Banks after a siege from 27 May to 9 July. USA losses: 3,000 killed, wounded. CSA losses: 1,700 killed and wounded, 5,500 captured, 60 cannon. Banks's victory eliminated the last CSA obstacle to US control over the Mississippi.

positive good defense of slavery Since the Revolutionary era, southerners had generally characterized SLAVERY as a necessary evil and had rarely censored antislavery views. This attitude changed in the 1830s because of anxiety created by TURNER'S REVOLT, the revival of ABOLITIONISM in the north, and reapportionment that cut southern representation in Congress. Certain that abolitionism would cause further slave violence and possibly a race war, southerners redefined slavery as a "positive good." Slavery made the South prosperous, and it afforded the only practical system of racial control to maintain white supremacy. The positive good defense also argued that slavery was good for blacks; it reasoned that, if emancipated, blacks could not compete with whites, would fail to be self-supporting, and degenerate into a lower standard of living than they had enjoyed as slaves. The positive good argument came to be almost universally believed in the South, where it created a reactionary backlash concerning race relations and stifled public debate about abolitionism.

Post Office On 26 July 1775, Congress created the Department of the Post Office (Benjamin FRANKIN, postmaster general), which became a federal bureau without CABINET status on 22 September 1789. Because it controlled more patronage than any other government agency, the Post Office was accorded cabinet status by Andrew JACKSON, and William Barry of Ky. was the first postmaster general with this rank. The Post Office inaugurated railway mail services in 1862, the money order system in 1864, and air mail in 1918 (*see* KELLY AIR

MAIL ACT). It gained authority to exclude materials injurious to public morals through *CHAMPION V. AMES*. Its only significant strike disrupted mail delivery throughout the country from 18 to 25 March 1970, except in rural areas and the South. The Postal Reorganization Act (12 August 1970) redesignated it as the US Postal Service, an independent agency (effective 1 July 1971) whose nine governors are appointed by the president and indirectly responsible to Congress for part of its budget. The postmaster general was then dropped from the order of succession to the presidency.

Postal Deposit Savings Act (25 June 1910) To provide the public with a sound alternative to depositing money in banks, which were often risky, Congress authorized the POST OFFICE to pay 2 percent interest on money placed in postal savings accounts. The FEDERAL DEPOSIT INSURANCE CORPORATION made postal banks unnecessary, but the service was not withdrawn until 1966.

Potawatomi Indians This nation, speakers of one of the ALGONQUIAN LANGUAGES, occupied the lower peninsula of Mich. when met by the French about 1640, and may have numbered 4,000. By 1760 they primarily occupied the southern shores of Lake Michigan and large parts of northern Ill. and Ind.; they numbered about 3,000. They were French allies in the SEVEN YEARS' WAR, fought in PONTIAC'S WAR, and were British allies from the REVOLUTIONARY WAR to the WAR OF 1812. Between 1820 and 1841, Potawatomis signed 47 treaties selling their NORTHWEST TERRITORY lands. Most relocated to Kans. by 1846 and then to Okla. They now have reservations in Forrest County, Wis., Menominee County, Mich., Jackson County, Kans., Potawatomi County, Okla., and Wallaceburg, Ontario.

Potomac, Army of the The principal land force defending Washington from the Army of NORTHERN VIRGINIA and threatening Richmond, Va., its commanders (major general) were George MCCLELLAN, 15 August, 1861–9 November 1862, Ambrose Burnside, to 26 January 1863, Joseph Hooker, to 28 June 1863, and George MEADE, to the end of the war. The Army of VIRGINIA was detached to John Pope from this force. As general in chief of the armies, Ulysses S. GRANT accompanied Meade's army after 12 March and exercised strategic direction.

Potsdam conference (Germany) Between 17 July and 2 August 1945, Harry S. TRUMAN, Winston Churchill, and Joseph Stalin discussed guidelines for occupying, demilitarizing, and democratizing the AXIS powers, and for trying war criminals. The Allies agreed to remove 6,500,000 ethnic Germans from Czechoslovakia, Poland, and Hungary to end German irredentism. On 26 July, the Allies sent Japan an ultimatum demanding unconditional surrender. To preserve the good will needed for ensuring Russian entry into the war against Japan, agreements on postwar governments in eastern Europe were left vague. (Russia would declare war on Japan six days before V-J DAY.)

Pound, Ezra Loomis (b. Hailey, Idaho, 30 October 1885; d. Venice, Italy, 1 November 1972) He taught briefly in the US before leaving in 1907 to travel widely in Europe. He settled permanently in Italy in 1924, and emerged as one of his generation's most praised poets. In WORLD WAR II, he became the most notorious American traitor by broadcasting fascist propaganda to the US from Rome. Arrested for treason and brought to Washington, he was never declared mentally competent to stand trial and was hospitalized for psychiatric evaluations until 1956, and then released and deported.

Powderly, Terrence (b. Carbondale, Pa., 22 January 1849; d. Washington, D.C., 22 June 1924) At the age of 13 Powderly became a railroad worker, and he was a machinist at 17. He was elected national president of the Machinist and Blacksmiths' Union in 1872 and head of the KNIGHTS OF LABOR in 1879. Powderly led the union until 1893 in its greatest period of expansion. He discouraged strikes over pay or working conditions, rejected the concept of irreconcilable class warfare, and tried to channel the union's energies into supporting CHILD LABOR LAWS, regulation of TRUSTS, and the CONTRACT LABOR ACT. He was mayor of Scranton, Pa. (1880–4), and director of the Immigration Bureau (1897–1902).

Powell, Colin Luther (b. New York, N.Y., 5 April 1937) Powell became an army second lieutenant in 1958 through the Reserve Officers' Training Corps. After serving in the

VIETNAM WAR (1962–3, 1968–9), he rose rapidly and became the first African-American appointed as the president's national security assistant (1987) and chairman of the joint chiefs of staff (1989). He commanded US forces during the PERSIAN GULF WAR. After his retirement in 1992, he became the first African-American about whom serious speculation circulated regarding a possible nomination for president by the Republican or Democratic Party.

Powell, John Wesley (b. Mt Morris, N.Y., 24 March 1834; d. Haven, Maine, 23 September 1902) Although his right arm was amputated at the battle of SHILOH, he led the first party to pass through the Grand Canyon and mapped 900 miles of uncharted waterways along the Green and Colorado rivers in 1869. He made further explorations in the 1870s and headed the US Geological Survey (1880–94).

Powell* v. *Alabama *see* first SCOTTSBORO CASE

Powhatan Confederacy Powhatan (also called Wahunsonacock) (ca. 1560–1618) united 200 villages of speakers of ALGONQUIAN LANGUAGES on Chesapeake Bay, containing 9,000 Indians, before the English settled VIRGINIA. His relations with John SMITH and other whites varied from friendly to hostile, but he let his daughter POCAHONTAS marry John ROLFE. After Powhatan died, his brother led the confederacy to its destruction in OPECHANCANOUGH'S FIRST and SECOND WARS.

pragmatism William JAMES, in *Pragmatism* (1907), propounded the philosophical arguments for the pragmatic method, which held that the validity of any idea, policy, belief, or institution depended on whether its consequences were useful to society. The logic of this position implied that periodic reform of human institutions was a necessary form of cultural evolution required to keep outdated conditions or attitudes from thwarting the common good. Pragmatism inspired much of the PROGRESSIVE ERA's spirit of change, by giving reformers a philosophical counterweight to argue against those defending the status quo with SOCIAL DARWINISM.

praying towns From 1651 to 1675, the Mass. GENERAL COURT created 14 "praying towns" for Indians to settle (under white supervision) while forming Congregational churches and learning white ways. Only in Natick and Punkapog did Indian congregations achieve full status as churches free of interference from whites appointed to oversee their affairs. By 1675, about 20 percent of New England's Indians lived in praying towns. Perhaps a third of the praying Indians fought the English in KING PHILIP'S WAR. In 1677 the General Court disbanded 10 of the towns and placed the rest under white supervision. No other praying towns were founded except Stockbridge, a refuge of the MAHICAN INDIANS, in 1736.

Preemption Act (4 September 1841) Congress broke with previous land policy, which favored speculators over small settlers, by allowing squatters not only to occupy public land before it was officially surveyed, but also to enter a claim and buy 160 acres at the minimum price of $1.25 an acre before it was put up for public auction. A provision to share proceeds from land sales with state treasuries was repealed in 1842. This act was repealed on 3 March 1891.

Presbyterian Church American Presbyterianism has roots in both PURITANISM and Scottish Presbyterianism. Puritans who left New England for N.Y. and N.J. organized Presbyterian congregations. The first Presbyterian church was founded by Puritans at Southampton, N.Y., in 1640. The first presbytery was formed in 1706. There were five congregations in 1660, 28 in 1700, and 160 in 1740. SCOTCH-IRISH IMMIGRATION influenced Presbyterianism along Scottish lines after 1730. The GREAT AWAKENING split the church badly, but the triumph of the pro-revivalist New Lights (*see* GREAT AWAKENING, FIRST) greatly increased its ability to win converts. In 1776 there were 532 Presbyterian churches with 410,000 members (20 percent of all whites).

It experienced schism in 1810 with the secession of the Cumberland Presbytery, which became the Cumberland Presbyterian Church. In 1858 the United Presbyterian Church of North America was founded in communion with the mother church in Scotland. Two rival general assemblies, the New Side and Old Side Presbyterians, competed for the fellowship's allegiance from 1838 until their reunion in 1869 as the Presbyterian

Church, USA. In 1864 the Presbyterian Church in the US was formed by two groups of southern synods that had separated in 1857 and 1861.

The number of all Presbyterian pulpits rose from 1,700 in 1820 to 6,406 in 1860, and 15,452 in 1900, while membership grew from about 500,000 in 1860 to 1,800,000 in 1900. In 1958 the United Presbyterian Church of North America merged with the Presbyterian Church, USA to form the United Presbyterian Church in the USA. Membership of the United Presbyterian Church fell from 3,292,200 in 1965 to 2,886,500 (2 percent of all churchgoers) in 1990, when there were 11,469 congregations. (Another 480,000 Presbyterians worshiped in the Presbyterian Church in the US [217,400] and eight minor denominations.)

Presidential Succession Act (21 February 1792) This law stipulated that in cases when neither president nor vice-president can fulfill the office of chief executive because of death, disability, resignation, or removal, then the Senate's president pro tempore would succeed the president, with the House of Representatives' speaker next in line.

Presidential Succession Act (19 January 1886) This statute amended the PRESIDENTIAL SUCCESSION ACT (1792) by adding the CABINET to the line of succession, starting with the senior officer and descending through the cabinet in order of each department's creation.

Presidential Succession Act (18 July 1947) This statute amended the PRESIDENTIAL SUCCESSION ACT (1886) by placing the speaker of the House first to succeed the president and vice-president, followed by the president pro tempore, and then the officers of the CABINET in order of each department's antiquity.

Prigg* v. *Pennsylvania In 1842 the Supreme Court struck down (9–0) an 1826 Pa. PERSONAL LIBERTY LAW that interfered with the first FUGITIVE SLAVE ACT by guaranteeing all suspected runaways the right to claim the BILL OF RIGHTS' protections in state courts. But, by holding (6–3) that authority over the return of escaped slaves belonged exclusively in federal hands, the decision made the Fugitive Slave Act's enforcement more problematical by relieving state officials of any legal obligation to cooperate with federal officials in sending runaways back south.

primary election *see* DIRECT PRIMARY

primogeniture This was a provision of Anglo-American inheritance law specifying that if a father died without a will, his eldest son would inherit all his estate. It existed in the colonies of R.I., N.Y., Md., Va., N.C., S.C., and Ga., but was abolished by them between 1776 (Va.) and 1798 (R.I.).

Princeton, battle of (N.J.) On 3 January 1777, Washington's 2,000 troops defeated Lieutenant Colonel Charles Mawhood's 1,200 British, but did not capture his supply train. US losses: 23 killed, 20 wounded, 1 captured. British losses: 28 killed, 58 wounded, 129 captured. Following his *coup de main* at the battle of TRENTON, Washington's victory revived Americans' willingness to oppose Britain. To avoid further losses, the British withdrew their exposed outposts in N.J. and left the state in rebel control.

privateers These were ships of the MERCHANT MARINE that received LETTERS OF MARQUE AND REPRISAL to attack enemy commerce in wartime. Privateering ceased to be countenanced after 1815.

Privy Council In Great Britain, this body was a select group of trusted or prominent political leaders who provided the monarch with confidential advice. The Privy Council and cabinet were separate, but some individuals sat on both. In the colonial era, the Crown based decisions to authorize or disallow provincial laws on advice from the Privy Council and BOARD OF TRADE.

prize cases In 1863 the Supreme Court (5–4) upheld seizures of neutral shipping made under President Abraham LINCOLN's proclamations of 19 and 27 April 1861, which placed southern ports under blockade prior to congressional authorization of hostilities. The Court ruled that the president was empowered to quell insurrections without waiting for congressional action or approval.

pro-slavery arguments *see* POSITIVE GOOD DEFENSE OF SLAVERY

Proclamation Line This was the western limit on Anglo-American frontier settlement specified by the PROCLAMATION OF 1763. As originally drawn, it was east of white settlements around Fort Pitt and the New River of Va., and west of the lands of the Mohawk Indians.

Proclamation of 1763 On 8 June 1763, the Board of Trade recommended that Anglo-American settlement be halted at the crest of the Appalachians and not resumed until policies were devised to found colonies in an orderly fashion without sparking violence with the Indians. Word of Pontiac's War led to George III signing a version of this plan on 7 October, that fixed the mountain crest as the dividing line between all whites and Indians, although many groups of each lived on both sides of the Proclamation Line. In 1768 the treaties of Hard Labor and Fort Stanwix (first) were the first of several agreements to push the Proclamation Line west for white expansion.

Proclamation to the People of South Carolina *see* nullification crisis

Progress and Poverty *see* George, Henry

Progressive Era This period stretched from the late 1890s to World War I; it was distinguished by efforts to reform politics and ameliorate the social problems created by industrialization and urbanization, which were publicized by muckrakers. Its social justice reformers were exemplified by Jane Addams, Gifford Pinchot, and Walter Rauschenbusch. Its political reforms were exemplified by the Wisconsin idea and proposals to control political bosses and democratize governing institutions like the Australian ballot, referendum, initiative, recall, direct election of senators, and women's suffrage. The Progressive agenda for reforming cities was exemplified by the National Municipal League's recommendations. The movement's outstanding political leaders were John Altgeld, Hiram Johnson, Tom Johnson, Robert La Follette, Theodore Roosevelt, and Woodrow Wilson, whose first term marked the high point of Progressive reform. Theodore Dreiser and Sinclair Lewis expressed many of the era's concerns in literature. Herbert D. Croly's *The Promise of American Life* best summarized the legacy of Progressivism.

Progressive Party In 1912 Theodore Roosevelt quit the Republican Party, ran as a Progressive, and threw the election to Woodrow Wilson by splitting the Republican vote. In 1919 a Committee of Forty-eight tried to revive the party by nominating Robert La Follette for president, but La Follette refused to run and the group put up no candidates in 1920. In 1924 this committee joined the Conference for Progressive Political Action and the AFL to run La Follette, a Republican, as president, and Burton Wheeler (Democrat, Mont.) as vice-president for the Progressive Party. The ticket won 16.6 percent of the vote, but took only Wis.'s 13 electoral votes. The party disintegrated after La Follette's death in 1925.

Prohibition In 1789, when the average American drank 40 gallons of distilled spirits or hard cider, the first temperance society was formed in Litchfield, Conn., to discourage drinking between planting and harvest time. What began as a movement to promote moderate consumption of alcohol evolved into a crusade to ban spirituous liquors entirely. Within a dozen years of its founding in 1826, the American Temperance Society had convinced 1,000,000 Americans to pledge absolute abstinence from alcohol. In 1846 Maine was the first state to outlaw alcohol, and 13 other states did so by 1855. The abstinence campaign then slowed until the Prohibition party's founding in 1869, followed by the Women's Christian Temperance Union in 1874. In the 1880s, Iowa, Kans., N.Dak., and S.Dak. went dry. The crusade intensified under the Anti-saloon League of America and charismatic leaders like Carry Nation. Congress supported state prohibition laws by the Webb–Kenyon Interstate Liquor Act. By 1917 26 states had banned liquor entirely, 19 states had local option laws, and only three states allowed unrestricted sales of liquor. In 1917, when the Eighteenth Amendment was proposed, 75 percent of Americans lived in dry counties.

After national Prohibition became law in 1919, a huge illegal industry – bootlegging – arose to fill demand for alcohol and spawned the rise of organized crime syndicates. The Democratic Party struggled at their 1924 convention between wets supporting Alfred Smith and drys backing William McAdoo, before turning to John Davis as a compromise. After Smith was nominated in 1928, he lost by a landslide in an election dominated by the Prohibition issue. Herbert HOOVER named a Commission on Law Observance and Enforcement to investigate problems caused by Prohibition. In January 1931, the commission reported that enforcement of the Eighteenth Amendment had failed, but did not recommend repeal. In the 1932 election, both parties' platforms recommended returning regulation of liquor back to the states, which was done by the TWENTY-FIRST AMENDMENT. After the forming of Alcoholics Anonymous in 1933, public policy shifted to treating alcoholism on an individual basis.

Prohibition Party This party held its first national convention at Chicago in 1869. Although mainly concerned with banning alcohol, it also supported currency inflation, antitrust legislation (*see* TRUSTS), and female suffrage. It nominated presidential tickets between 1872 and 1932, but never won more than 2.2 percent of all votes (1892) and failed to carry any states.

Project Apollo *see* APOLLO PROJECT

Project Skylab *see* NATIONAL AERONAUTICS AND SPACE ADMINISTRATION

Promise of American Life, The This book was published by Herbert D. Croly in 1914 and was the mature expression of the thinking of the PROGRESSIVE ERA about government's role in society. Croly argued that Thomas JEFFERSON's ideals of equality, self-improvement, and democracy could no longer be guaranteed by limited government. He asserted that social and economic change had created the need for a strong, central government, like that envisioned by Alexander HAMILTON. The modern world required government to prevent abuses of power by TRUSTS through regulation so that economic opportunity could be preserved. The government should also devise solutions for the social problems arising from urbanization and industrialization, because their causes were unlikely to be eradicated by laissez-faire approaches to reform. Croly's thesis expressed the philosophy underlying the NEW NATIONALISM and the NEW DEAL.

Prophet, the (Tenskwatawa) (b. near Springfield, Ohio, ca. 1778; d. Wyandotte County, Kans., ca. 1837) In 1805 Tenskwatawa, a drunkard and member of the SHAWNEE INDIANS, underwent a religious experience and proclaimed himself Prophet of a movement to reform morals and halt any further Anglo-American expansion. He won a large following by correctly predicting a total solar eclipse in 1806, but his brother TECUMSEH increasingly assumed the movement's leadership. His prestige was shattered in 1811, when he encouraged a rash attack on US troops that ended in a major defeat at the battle of TIPPECANOE CREEK.

Proposition 13 In November 1978, 65 percent of Calif. voters approved this referendum issue that slashed $7 billion in revenues by reducing the property tax rate from 3 percent to 1 percent. Less drastic curbs on state budgets were also passed in five other states in November 1978. The supreme courts of Calif. and the US rejected legal challenges to Proposition 13. This invigorated a national taxpayers' revolt over the high costs of government, and influenced Congress to pass a 25 percent cut in INCOME TAX proposed by Ronald REAGAN in 1981.

proprietary colonies These were colonies with charters that transferred full rights to establish a government, and absolute title to the soil, from the Crown to an individual or group. Since the proprietors hoped to profit from selling land and collecting quitrents, they established representative government and sold real estate on reasonable terms. The proprietary colonies were MARYLAND (except between 1691 and 1715), NEW YORK (to 1685), SOUTH CAROLINA (to 1721), NORTH CAROLINA (to 1729), PENNSYLVANIA (except between 1692 and 1694), DELAWARE, EAST JERSEY, and WEST JERSEY.

proprietors of Carolina On 3 April 1663, CHARLES II granted CAROLINA as a PROPRIETARY COLONY to Sir Anthony Ashley Cooper (Earl of Shaftesbury), Edward Hyde (Earl of Clarendon), Christopher Monck (Duke of Albermale), William Craven (Earl of Craven), Sir John Colleton, Sir George Carteret, John Lord Berkeley, and Governor Sir William Berkeley of Va. The proprietors' FUNDAMENTAL CONSTITUTIONS OF CAROLINA outlined their social and political plans, but were later rejected by the settlers. The S.C. and N.C. legislatures strongly opposed the proprietors and requested the status of ROYAL COLONIES. The eight proprietors surrendered their charter in 1729; seven of them received compensation of £2,500 each, while John Carteret (Earl of Granville) obtained title to all of N.C. lying 70 miles south of Va. The Granville proprietary colony proved highly lucrative after 1740, and was producing about £5,000 sterling in quitrents by the 1760s.

proprietors of East Jersey On 4 July 1664, CHARLES II granted N.J. to John Lord Berkeley and Sir George Carteret. EAST JERSEY passed to Carteret, whose heirs sold it for £3,400 on 2 February 1681 to 12 proprietors, who admitted 12 more partners by 1682. Most were Scots and 20 of the 24 were QUAKERS, including William PENN. Control gradually passed to non-Quakers, who wished to profit by land speculation, establishing estates, and commerce. Unable to overcome popular opposition to their rule, the proprietors gave up their power of government to the Crown on 15 April 1702, but kept all rights to ungranted lands. Confusion over land titles issued by them was the major cause of the NEW JERSEY LAND DISORDERS. In most of the years from 1722 to 1776, the N.J. assembly's speaker and a majority of the governor's council were East Jersey proprietors.

proprietors of Maryland In 1632 the first Baron Baltimore, George Calvert (1580–15 April 1632) persuaded CHARLES I to grant him Md. as a PROPRIETARY COLONY, but the charter was not issued until 30 June, after his death. The Calverts' Catholic faith aroused much opposition to their rule. Cecil Calvert, second Baron Baltimore (ca. 1605–30 November 1675) became the first proprietor, while his brother Leonard Calvert (1606–9 June 1647) served as governor of Md. until his own death. Charles Calvert (27 August 1637–21 February 1715) served as governor from 1661 to 1675, when he became third Baron Baltimore and the second proprietor. Charles remained in Md. until 1684; he was stripped of his political authority by WILLIAM III in 1689, but retained his property rights. Benedict Leonard Calvert (1679–16 April 1715) became fourth Baron Baltimore and converted to the Church of England, but did not regain the proprietorship. Charles Calvert (1699–24 April 1751), fifth Baron Baltimore, was restored as third proprietor in May 1715 because he was an Anglican. Frederick Calvert, sixth Baron Baltimore (1732–4 September 1771) was the fourth proprietor, and willed his estate to an illegitimate son, Henry Harford (1759–1834). By 1770, the proprietor was earning annual quitrents of £30,000 sterling from Md. The state confiscated the Calvert proprietorship in the Revolution and Parliament compensated Harford for his losses.

proprietors of New York On 22 March 1664, CHARLES II granted James, Duke of York, title to all of NEW NETHERLAND. James granted N.J. and Del. to other proprietors, but retained N.Y., which became a ROYAL COLONY when he was proclaimed king on 6 February 1685.

proprietors of Pennsylvania CHARLES II made William PENN (1644–1718) first proprietor on 14 March 1681. On 30 July 1718, Penn's sons inherited the proprietorship, with a half share to John (d. 1746) and quarter shares to Thomas (1702–75) and Richard (1706–71). Thomas Penn inherited John's share in 1746 and left three-quarters of the proprietorship to his four children on 21 March 1775. In 1771 John Penn left the remainder to his son John (1729–95), who was Pa. governor (1763–71), and Richard (1735–1811), who was Pa. governor (1771–6). By 1774, the Penns were earning about £10,000 (sterling) yearly in land sales, £10,000 in quitrents, and £6,000 from various royalties. The proprietorship ended after the Revolution when Pa. bought out the Penns' rights to quitrents and vacant lands for £130,000.

proprietors of West Jersey On 4 July 1664, CHARLES II granted N.J. to John Lord Berkeley and Sir George Carteret. Berkeley sold his rights in 1674 for £1,000 to a Quaker syndicate (*see* QUAKERS) that expanded to 120 investors (including William PENN) and founded WEST JERSEY. By 1688, half these proprietors had settled in West Jersey, where they dominated elections. In 1685 certain shares controlling the right to name the West Jersey governor passed out of Quaker hands, and political conflict increased between the assembly and the governor. On 15 April 1702, the proprietors surrendered their power of government to the Crown, but kept all rights to ungranted lands. They furnished numerous prominent leaders in the colonial legislature.

Prosser's Conspiracy In mid-1800, Gabriel Prosser, a slave in Henrico County, Va., organized several hundred slaves with a plan to seize Richmond and Governor James MONROE on 30 August. After heavy rains prevented a rendezvous on that day, black informers revealed the plan and many of the plotters were arrested, of whom 35 were hanged. Prosser evaded capture until 27 September (with a white ship captain's connivance), and was executed in October.

Protestant Episcopal Church The American Revolution (*see* REVOLUTIONARY WAR) generated enormous prejudice against the ANGLICAN CHURCH because most of its clergy were TORIES. Most Anglican clergy left the US and perhaps half the communicants joined other faiths. During the 1780s, the church was reconstituted as two rival episcopates, one under Bishop Samuel Seabury (ordained 1784) and the other under Bishops William White and Samuel Provoost (ordained 1787). In 1789 these bodies formally united as the Protestant Episcopal Church.

The Episcopal Church grew slowly and numbered about 30,000 in 1830, but its membership had risen to nearly 100,000 by 1853. It experienced schism when the Coadjutor Bishop of Ky. organized the Reformed Episcopal Church in 1873. The number of pulpits grew from 600 in 1820 to 2,145 in 1860, and 6,264 in 1900. Membership stood at 1,000,000 shortly before 1920. Due in large part to an energetic National Council (organized 1919), a revised Book of Common Prayer (1928), and an effective church press (founded 1952), the denomination's membership doubled from 1920 to 1945.

Schism resulted in 1976 from opening the priesthood to women, and the Anglican Church of North America was formed. The ordination of Bishop Barbara Harris in 1989 provoked the formation of the dissenting Episcopal Synod of America. Membership declined steadily from 3,250,000 in 1960 to 2,433,400 (1.6 percent of all churchgoers) in 1990, when there were 7,372 Episcopal churches and 14 seminaries.

public domain This term refers to lands owned by the US government. It included states outside the 13 original colonies, except Ky., Tenn., and Tex. By 1850, all acquisitions to the public domain totaled 1,778,615,000 acres (minus 35,000,000 acres granted by prior governments). Land division within the public domain was established by the ORDINANCE OF 1785 and states were formed according to the NORTHWEST ORDINANCE. Access to land was progressively liberalized by the PREEMPTION ACT, GRADUATION ACT, and HOMESTEAD ACTS. The public domain was closed for conservation purposes in 1935 to implement the TAYLOR GRAZING ACT. In 1949, 710,900 square miles, or 23.9 percent of the lower 48 states, remained under federal supervision as public domain. The WILDERNESS AREAS ACT led to 15 percent of the public domain being designated as protected areas.

Public Law 284 (11 April 1968) This statute, sponsored by Sam ERVIN, gave Indian defendants before RESERVATION courts all protections of the BILL OF RIGHTS (Indians already possessed these rights when appearing before federal or state courts). The law limited the FIRST AMENDMENT's scope to protecting free exercise of religion, rather than prohibiting any establishment of religion, to avoid judicial interference in the religious life of reservation Indians.

Public Utility Holding Company Act (28 August 1935) This law was intended to end abuses in the power industry resulting from the multiplication of interstate holding companies. (*See* INSULL, SAMUEL) By 1935, 140 holding companies controlled 1,500 utilities, which they often saddled with heavy fees or charges that had to be collected from consumers. By buying subsidiaries in several states, holding companies often evaded enforcement by regulatory agencies. The FEDERAL POWER COMMISSION received authority to regulate interstate electricity shipments and the FEDERAL TRADE COMMISSION gained power over interstate gas deliveries. The SEC oversaw the finances of holding companies and could recommend divestiture to halt the financial exploitation of subsidiaries. The SECURITIES AND EXCHANGE COMMISSION separated 753 utilities (valued at $10.3 billion) from abusive holding companies by 1952.

Public Works Administration (PWA) Title II of the NATIONAL INDUSTRIAL RECOVERY ACT (NIRA) allocated $3.3 billion for this agency, whose purpose was to create work for the jobless and to stimulate economic activity through federal expenditures on useful public construction projects. It funded 70 percent of building costs and local governments financed the rest. Since its director Harold ICKES required projects to meet high standards before releasing funds for them, the PWA did less to combat the GREAT DEPRESSION in 1933 and 1934 than had been anticipated. To compensate for PWA slowness in generating employment, the CIVIL WORKS ADMINISTRATION and WORKS PROGRESS ADMINISTRATION were established to provide emergency jobs. By funding the construction of most schools and urban sewer lines in the 1930s, plus massive projects like the Grand Coulee Dam, the PWA was responsible for hiring almost 140,000 workers in most years and indirectly creating jobs for 600,000 others. In 1939 it became part of the FEDERAL WORKS AGENCY, after spending $4.25 billion on 34,000 projects.

pueblo This Spanish word means "village" and was applied to Indian agricultural communities in Ariz. and N.Mex. built of stone or adobe. Spanish explorers discovered them in the 1540s. The oldest probably date from about AD 1250.

***Pueblo*, USS, incident** On 23 January 1968, the North Korean Navy attacked and seized the USS *Pueblo*, under Lloyd Bucher, an electronic surveillance ship. At the time, it was three miles outside that country's 12-mile territorial limit. The Koreans killed 1 crewman, wounded 4, and captured 78 others, whom it accused of spying. Due to its commitments to the VIETNAM WAR, the US could not retaliate and the crew was not released for 11 months.

Pueblo Indians This term includes groups of several different language stocks that evolved an urban culture of life in PUEBLOS. These societies are an outgrowth of early urbanization that flourished ca. 1000–1300 in the vicinity of Mesa Verde, Colo., but was abandoned due to severe drought. These Pueblos established new villages along the Rio Grande and in northeastern Ariz.; they evolved into the HOPI and ZUNI INDIANS, and other groups. The total number of all Pueblos was probably 35,000 at the time of POPÉ'S REVOLT. Suppression of that insurrection and epidemic diseases reduced their population to 12,000 by 1750 and 9,000 by 1821, but by 1987 there were about 42,000 persons living at 31 pueblos in N.Mex. and Ariz.

Puerto Rico On 25 July 1898, in the SPANISH-AMERICAN WAR, Major General Nelson Miles's US forces occupied Puerto Rico, which was transferred to the US by treaty on 10 December 1898. On 12 April 1900, the Foraker Act established a civil government for an unorganized territory, in which the president appointed a governor and council, which sat as the legislature's upper chamber, while the lower house was popularly elected. Its constitutional status was interpreted by *DE LIMA* v. *BIDWELL*, *DOWNES* v. *BIDWELL*, and *DORR* v. *UNITED STATES*. On 2 March 1917, the Jones (Organic) Act made the island a US territory and gave its people US citizenship, the right to elect both houses of the legislature, and extended the BILL OF RIGHTS.

On 1 November 1950, an assassination attempt by Puerto Rican nationalists on Harry S. TRUMAN failed. Rebels seized 10 towns on the island, but lost 31 dead and 12 wounded before being defeated by police and national guardsmen, who lost 14 dead. On 1 March 1954, five nationalists shot and wounded five congressmen in the House chamber. On 25 July 1953, Puerto Rico assumed commonwealth status and gained the right to demand independence. Significant progress in economic diversification came under OPERATION BOOTSTRAP, but the island has long experienced heavy out-migration to the mainland. On 14 November 1993, a non-binding plebiscite voted to retain commonwealth status rather than seek statehood or independence.

Pujo hearings On 27 April 1912, Representative Arsène Pujo's Banking Sub-Committee began hearings on the MONEY TRUST. The committee reported on 28 February 1913 that control over the national banking system had become highly concentrated through interlocking directorates and other forms of TRUSTS. The greatest concentration of power lay with the operations of J. Pierpont MORGAN's financial firms and John ROCKEFELLER's National City Bank, which together could name 341 directors on the boards of 112 corporations worth $22.2 billion (or about 10 percent of the US economy). Its findings strengthened arguments for establishing a publicly controlled FEDERAL RESERVE SYSTEM.

Pulitzer, Joseph (b. Mako, Hungary, 10 April 1847; d. Charleston, S.C., 29 October 1911) In 1864 Pulitzer came to the US and bought the St Louis *Post*. In 1883 he bought the New York *World*. Pulitzer was the most innovative journalist of his time, and pioneered techniques for reaching mass audiences that every major newspaper imitated to a degree. He increased the *World*'s circulation from 20,000 to 250,000 by 1886, and to 1,000,000 a dozen years later. Much of his popular appeal depended on emphasizing lurid and tawdry events. While competing with William R. HEARST's New York *Journal*, he shared the dubious honor of pioneering YELLOW JOURNALISM. His will left $2,000,000 to establish the Columbia University School of Journalism and another bequest to fund the Pulitzer prizes for achievement in journalism, literature, and the arts.

Pullman strike On 21 June 1894, Eugene DEBS led 150,000 members of the American Railway Union on strike against the Pullman Palace Car Co., to win back a wage cut of 25 percent. By boycotting all trains with Pullman cars, the union disrupted national rail services. When 3,400 special agents deputized by the US attorney general failed to ensure mail delivery, Grover CLEVELAND reinforced them on 4 July with 2,000 soldiers sent to Chicago, against the protests of the Ill. governor, John ALTGELD. Violence ensued, and by 20 July the trains had resumed running after a federal court injunction forbade the union from impeding mail delivery. The episode marked the first major use of a federal injunction to break a strike, a tactic sanctioned by the Supreme Court in *IN RE DEBS*.

Pure Food and Drug Act (30 June 1906) By creating a furor over unsafe food and medicinal products, *The JUNGLE* led to enactment of this law under pressure from Theodore ROOSEVELT. It prohibited the production for interstate shipment of any unsanitary, mislabled, or adulterated food, medicine, drug, or alcoholic beverage. The law resulted in rapid improvements in product safety by 1912. It was superseded by the FOOD, DRUG, AND COSMETIC ACT (1938).

Puritanism This was a movement to reform the Church of England along the model of Calvinist churches; it emerged in the 1570s. Puritans divided between those who favored organizing church authority along congregational or Presbyterian lines; they also split between the SEPARATING and NONSEPARATING PURITAN camps. All Puritans shared the common goal of eliminating vestiges of Roman Catholicism by giving laymen greater influence within their congregations, opposing the control of church affairs by bishops, eliminating all sacraments but baptism and communion, replacing the highly ceremonial Anglican liturgy with services centered around preaching, and using the ministry to guide the elect through their preparation for spiritual rebirth. Puritanism was suppressed in England after the Stuart monarchy's restoration in 1660. It gradually declined as the driving force in New England's religious life after the HALF-WAY COVENANT, and after 1700 its impulses dissolved into orthodox variants of Calvinism as practiced by Congregationalists and Presbyterians.

Purvis, Robert (b. Charleston, S.C., 4 November 1810; d. Philadelphia, Pa., 15 April 1898) Son of a cotton broker from England and a free mixed-race woman, Purvis was raised in Philadelphia and inherited a large fortune from his father. He first spoke in public for ABOLITIONISM at 17, contributed funds to found the *LIBERATOR*, sat on the AMERICAN ANTISLAVERY SOCIETY's first board of managers, and was elected the first president of the Pa. Antislavery Society. He long directed the UNDERGROUND RAILROAD's operation in southeastern Pa. and vigorously fought black DISFRANCHISEMENT by the Pa. legislature. He also supported temperance, women's rights, and penal reform. He declined appointment as the first director of the FREEDMEN'S BUREAU.

Pusan Perimeter, battle of (*see* KOREAN WAR)

PWA *see* PUBLIC WORKS ADMINISTRATION

Pyramid Lake War (Nev.) *see* PAIUTE CAMPAIGNS (1)

Q

Quakers George Fox founded the Society of Friends in England about 1647. Called Quakers because they trembled in the Lord's presence, they premised their beliefs on the INNER LIGHT, eliminated all formal sacraments, had no trained clergy, refused to show deference to any rank of society, insisted on absolute separation of church and state, and would neither swear oaths nor perform military service. They experienced frequent persecution before 1700, including the execution by Mass. of Mary DYER and four others between 1659 and 1661.

WEST JERSEY and PENNSYLVANIA were founded as Quaker refuges. Although N.J. and Pa. became predominantly non-Quaker after 1700, Quakers (or Friends) dominated the Pa. assembly to 1757 and were the largest voting bloc in the N.J. assembly to 1772. They were the only denomination to enforce ABOLITIONISM on members. Quakers made few converts after 1700 and lost many members because of their strict discipline. By 1800 they numbered only 50,000, about 1.2 percent of all whites, and were mainly concentrated in Pa. and N.J.

In 1827 schism split the Quakers into Orthodox and Hicksite factions over the doctrines of Elias Hicks, who exalted the Inner Light above scripture and revealed tradition. The Orthodox party again divided in 1845, when a similar dispute provoked a secession by John Wilbur's followers in a debate over Joseph J. Gurney's efforts to enhance scriptural authority over the Inner Light. The number of Quaker meetings rose from 350 in 1820 to 726 in 1860, and 1,031 in 1900, but membership has stagnated between 100,000 and 130,000 since 1840. Formed in 1917 to aid conscientious objectors, the American Friends Service Committee received the Nobel peace prize in 1947. In 1990 the five Quaker associations had 1,405 meetings and 118,070 members (0.1 percent of all churchgoers).

Quapaw Indians This SIOUAN LANGUAGE group occupied eastern Ark. when first contacted by Hernán de SOTO in 1541. They migrated northwest along the Arkansas River and eventually accepted reservation status in Ottawa Co., Okla. They engaged in no hostilities against the United States, but CSA officials drove many Quapaw from their lands because they would not give military assistance during the Civil War. The Quapaw declined from perhaps several thousand about 1750 to 476 in 1843 and 174 in 1885, before reviving to 305 (including mixed bloods) by 1909.

Quantrill, William Clarke (b. Canal Dover, Ohio, 31 July 1837; d. Louisville, Ky., 30 May 1865) A gambler and thief, Quantrill joined the BORDER RUFFIANS who plagued BLEEDING KANSAS. In the CIVIL WAR, he formed a CSA guerrilla band of 150 men, who included future outlaws Jesse James, Frank James, and Cole Younger. He was commissioned a captain after capturing Independence, Mo., on 11 August 1862, and later claimed to be a colonel. His men killed 150 men and boys – nearly all civilians – and destroyed property worth $500,000 at Lawrence, Kans., on 21 August 1863. At Baxter Springs, Kans., his men ambushed 100 USA troops, killed 65 (of whom many were murdered after being captured while already wounded), and mutilated the bodies. En route to Washington to assassinate Abraham LINCOLN, Quantrill was mortally wounded by Ky. militia near Wakefield.

Quartering Act (15 May 1765) Applicable only to five colonies where British troops resided in barracks within settled areas rather than frontier posts, this Parliamentary law mandated that the colonies' assemblies buy firewood, candles, vinegar, salt, bedding, eating utensils, and a liquor ration for the troops. Arguing that the law was an unconstitutional imposition of indirect taxation – i.e. Parliament forcing the colonies to tax themselves rather than imposing a tax directly – the N.Y. legislature refused to comply with it and was threatened by the NEW YORK SUSPENDING ACT. Britain ceased enforcing the act after 1767 and let it expire in 1768.

Quartering Act (2 June 1774) Parliament authorized colonial governors to shelter troops in unoccupied houses, barns, or other empty buildings in localities where no barracks existed, and where the local government had still refused to provide quarters more than 24 hours after the military commander had requested them. This law was one of the INTOLERABLE ACTS.

quasi-war with France *see* FRANCE, UNDECLARED WAR WITH

Quayle, J(ames) Danforth III (b. Indianapolis, Ind., 4 February 1947) He began practicing law in 1974 and entered Ind. politics as a Republican. He served as congressman (1977–80) and senator (1980–8). As George BUSH's choice for vice-president in 1988, he attracted widespread criticism for having avoided VIETNAM WAR service with the NATIONAL GUARD and not having sufficient experience to succeed Bush as president. As vice-president, he performed credibly, heading task forces on the space program's future and government interference with business competitiveness; he also traveled widely on foreign missions.

Quebec, battles of (1) On 21 August 1690, William PHIPS left Boston with 2,200 New England militia to attack Quebec, defended by 2,000 French under the Comte de Frontenac. On 7–8 October, Phips landed 1,200 men, but ran low on ammunition and gave up the siege on 11 October. Phips's losses: 30 killed and wounded, 200 dead from smallpox and shipwreck, 5 artillery pieces abandoned.

(2) On 28 April 1760, François de Levis's 6,910 French troops attacked Quebec (lost to the British on the PLAINS OF ABRAHAM), defeated Colonel James Murray's 3,900 British at Ste Foy, outside the city, and besieged the city. British losses: 259 killed, 823 wounded. French losses: 193 killed, 640 wounded. A British relief convoy broke the siege on 9 May. French failure to take Quebec ensured Britain's conquest of Canada.

(3) On 31 December 1775, General Guy Carleton's 1,800 redcoats and militia defeated Major General Richard Montgomery's 800 Continentals. US losses: 51 killed (including Montgomery), 36 wounded, 387 captured. British losses: 7 killed, 11 wounded. US forces besieged Quebec under Major General John Thomas until driven off by Carleton on 6 May 1776. Eleven thousand British reinforcements chased US troops up the St Lawrence and into New York by June.

Quebec Act (22 June 1774) Parliament created a permanent administrative system for governing the French-Canadian province of Quebec. It created a civil government that lacked a legislature, allowed civil cases and property disputes to be judged without juries according to French legal practice, guaranteed freedom of worship for Catholics, and extended Quebec's boundaries to the Ohio and Mississippi rivers in violation of land claims by the THIRTEEN COLONIES. The law was considered one of the INTOLERABLE ACTS.

Quebec Conference, first Between 11 and 24 August 1943, Winston Churchill and Franklin D. ROOSEVELT set Allied strategy for WORLD WAR II. They confirmed summer 1944 as the date for the invasion of NORMANDY, to be followed by an invasion of southern France; they also agreed to provide more resources for fighting the Japanese, especially in Burma.

Quebec Conference, second Between 11 and 16 September 1944, Winston Churchill and Franklin D. ROOSEVELT set Allied strategy for the period after WORLD WAR II. They planned Germany's occupation zones and considered the Morgenthau Plan (*see* MORGENTHAU, HENRY.)

Queen Anne's War When Louis XIV recognized a Catholic claimant to England's Crown rather than Protestant Queen ANNE, and schemed to upset Europe's balance of power by uniting France and Spain, he brought on the war of the Spanish Succession, known to Anglo-Americans as Queen

Anne's War. On 4 May 1702, England, the Netherlands, and Austria declared war on France and Spain. South Carolinians unsuccessfully besieged ST AUGUSTINE, Fla., in 1702. From December 1703 to January 1704, a S.C. expedition destroyed the FLORIDA MISSIONS. A French–Spanish attack on CHARLES TOWN, S.C., met disaster in 1706. After two futile sieges of Pensacola by S.C. militia in 1707, fighting lapsed on the Florida border.

French and Indians harassed New England with many raids, but captured no towns or forts except DEERFIELD, Mass., in 1704. The colonists launched invasions of Canada via Lake Champlain in 1708 and 1711, but both returned home without engaging the enemy. After unsuccessfully besieging the Canadian garrison at Port Royal in 1704 and 1707, Yankee militia captured the fort on 16 October 1710 and transformed Acadia into the British colony of Nova Scotia. In 1711 a task force with 12,000 troops under Admiral Hovenden Walker gave up an assault on Quebec without firing a shot after 1,000 British drowned in shipwrecks in the St Lawrence River. The treaty of UTRECHT ended the war on 11 April 1713.

Queenstown Heights, battle of (Canada) On 12–13 October 1812, Major General Isaac Brock's 1,000 British and Canadians defeated Major General Stephen Van Rensselaer's 2,300 N.Y. militia. Brock trapped 1,000 militia after the rest of Van Rensselaer's force refused to cross the Niagara River into Canada, and US Brigadier General Alexander Smyth, camped nearby at Buffalo, would not permit his 1,650 regulars to be commanded by Van Rensselaer, who was a militia officer. US losses: 90 killed, 925 captured. British losses: 14 killed (including Brock), 77 wounded, 21 missing. Brock's victory ended US hopes of occupying Canadian soil in 1812.

Quemoy-Matsu controversy When the Nationalist Chinese evacuated the mainland in 1949, they kept garrisons offshore on Quemoy and Matsu islands. The islands came under Communist artillery fire after 3 September 1954, but were not covered by the US–Taiwan mutual-defense treaty of 2 December 1954. On 29 January 1955, Dwight D. EISENHOWER signed a congressional resolution authorizing US military help in defending the islands, which had been subjected to increasingly heavy attack. Bombardment of the islands had been intermittent, but intensified greatly from 23 August 1958, and in September the US Navy began escorting Taiwanese resuppply vessels to them. Tensions eased on 25 October when the Beijing government announced that it would only shell the islands on alternate days. On 27 June 1962, John F. KENNEDY reaffirmed US support for the islands after 600,000 Communist troops were built up on the nearby mainland. Quemoy and Matsu then ceased to be a major flashpoint of the COLD WAR.

quids This was a small voting bloc of Democrats in Congress after 1805, led by John RANDOLPH of Roanoke. *Quid* was Latin for "something," and the group was sometimes called the tertium quids or third things (third party). The quids opposed the political pragmatism of Thomas JEFFERSON and James MADISON; they stood for unwavering adherence to STRICT CONSTRUCTIONISM and STATES' RIGHTS.

Quotas Act (1921) *see* EMERGENCY QUOTA ACT

Quotas Act (1924) *see* NATIONAL ORIGINS ACT

R

rack-renting This was the practice of raising the price of leases on tenancies to their maximum level when they came due for periodic renewal. Tenants who could not afford the new rate were thrown off the land. Ruthless use of rack-renting in Ulster after 1730 stimulated a large SCOTCH-IRISH IMMIGRATION to the thirteen colonies.

Radical Republicans The term *radical* was applied to those Republicans who advocated the most uncompromising policies to defeat the CONFEDERACY, end SLAVERY, achieve equal political rights for FREEDMEN, and keep ex-Confederates from regaining power in the South. The WADE–DAVIS BILL outlined their alternative to Abraham LINCOLN's plan for RECONSTRUCTION. By winning support from moderate Republicans, Radicals used the JOINT COMMITTEE ON RECONSTRUCTION to draft the FOURTEENTH AMENDMENT and draft a program of Congressional Reconstruction. Under Charles SUMNER, Thaddeus STEVENS, and Benjamin WADE, the radicals spearheaded the impeachment of Andrew JOHNSON, and swayed Congress to pass the RECONSTRUCTION ACTS, FIFTEENTH AMENDMENT, and the FORCE ACTS. The Radicals' influence declined greatly after Ulysses S. GRANT's first administration.

Radio Act (1927) *see* FEDERAL COMMUNICATIONS COMMISSION

railroad retirement acts On 27 June 1934, Congress created a comprehensive, compulsory retirement system for transportation workers subject to the INTERSTATE COMMERCE COMMISSION ACT. On 6 May 1935, in *Railroad Retirement Board et al.* v. *Alton Railroad Company et al.*, the Supreme Court (5–4) held that it violated the FIFTH AMENDMENT by improperly confiscating corporate property and it was not warranted under the Constitution's grant of federal authority over interstate commerce. Congress reenacted its provisions in the Wagner–Crosser Railroad Retirement Act (29 August 1935), but a district court struck down its financing measure, a tax on payrolls.

The Roosevelt administration solved the constitutional problem of financing railroad pensions by having the companies and unions draft a voluntary agreement to fund pensions by joint contributions from employees and railways. The Railroad Retirement Act (29 June 1937) enacted this formula, exempted railway workers from social security laws (*see* SOCIAL SECURITY ADMINISTRATION), and created the Railroad Retirement Board.

Because the number of railway workers shrank from 700,000 in 1980 to 400,000 in 1983, the system's 1,000,000 retirees faced pension reductions of 40 percent to prevent impending insolvency. The Railroad Retirement Act (12 August 1983) averted this prospect. It raised employee and employer payments by $0.5 billion over five years, contributed $1.7 billion in federal money (offset by higher taxes on retiree benefits), cut benefits for early retirement, and delayed cost-of-living increases by six months.

Railroad Revitalizaton and Regulatory Reform Act *see* DEREGULATION

railroad strike of 1877 After the largest eastern railroads announced a 10 percent pay cut, a general strike ensued, beginning on 17 July 1877 with walkouts at Baltimore and Ohio yards. Walkouts spread to other eastern lines and then west of the Mississippi, until two-thirds of US railway mileage was closed. Major riots occurred at Parkersburg, W.Va., Pittsburgh, Baltimore, Chicago, and St Louis. By the time federal troops and state militia restored order, almost 100 persons had died.

Railway Act (1920) *see* Esch–Cummins Act

Railway Labor Act (20 May 1926) This law was drafted to change the procedures for mediating labor disputes under the Esch–Cummins Act, which had failed to prevent or mediate a major strike in 1922. The law replaced the Railroad Labor Board with a Board of Mediation whose five members were presidential appointees. The new board could intervene in labor disputes, but could not impose compulsory arbitration. Although both labor and management were consulted during its preparation, labor was frustrated that the board continued to recognize the company union as the legitimate bargaining agent. The only significant labor legislation enacted in the 1920s, it was replaced by the Railway Labor Act (1934).

Railway Labor Act (27 June 1934) This law ensured that railway workers had the same rights to form unions and bargain collectively as industrial workers enjoyed under the National Industrial Recovery Act (NIRA). It replaced the Railroad Labor Board (*see* Railway Labor Act, 1926) by a National Railroad Adjustment Board. The board was empowered to disqualify a company union as a bargaining agent when it could be demonstrated that employees preferred representation by an independent union. The law enabled the railroads to be organized by the AFL.

Rainbow Coalition *see* Jackson, Jesse

Raleigh, Sir Walter (b. Hayes, Devon, England, ca. 1552; d. London, England, 29 October 1618) Sir Humphrey Gilbert's half-brother, Raleigh was a court favorite of Elizabeth I, who granted him a patent on 25 March 1584 to colonize North America. After sending out a reconnaissance party to Albemarle Sound, Raleigh founded the Roanoke Colony, which was his last venture at overseas settlement. He fell out of favor with James I and wrote a two-volume history of the world while imprisoned in the Tower of London (1603–16). After a brief release, he was arrested and executed for treason.

Randolph, A(sa) Philip (b. Crescent City, Fla., 15 April 1889; d. New York, N.Y., 16 May 1979) In 1925 Randolph founded the Brotherhood of Sleeping Car Porters, which became the first all-black union in the AFL. In 1941, to protest job discrimination by defense contractors, he organized the march on Washington that resulted in Executive Order 8802. In 1947 he founded the League for Nonviolent Civil Disobedience Against Military Segregation, which resulted in Executive Order 9981. He sat on the AFL-CIO executive council (1955–74).

Randolph, Edmund Jennings (b. James City County, Va., 10 August 1753; d. Clarke County, Va., 12 September 1813) He served as George Washington's aide in the Continental Army, as Va. attorney general, Va. governor, and delegate to the Annapolis convention. He introduced the Virginia Plan at the Constitutional Convention. Initially a supporter of the Antifederalists, he finally voted to ratify the Constitution. He became the first US attorney general on 26 September 1789 and secretary of state on 2 January 1794. After the British captured incriminating French documents suggesting that he had accepted bribes from France to influence US foreign policy, he was forced to resign from the cabinet. The allegations of misconduct later proved to be false.

Randolph, John (b. Prince Edward County, Va., 2 June 1773; d. Philadelphia, Pa., 24 May 1833) To avoid confusion with his cousin "Possum John," Randolph attached "of Roanoke" to his name. First sent to Congress in 1799, he directed the impeachment of Samuel Chase and was widely blamed for Chase's exoneration. He personally prevented the Yazoo land claims from being settled until 1814. When his cousin Thomas Jefferson sought $2,000,000 for questionable diplomatic purposes to negotiate US acquisition of East Florida in 1805, Randolph broke with him. He and his followers, the quids, thereafter espoused uncompromising strict constructionism and were the primary voice of opposition to every administration while in the House (1799–1813, 1815–24, 1827–9) and Senate (1825–7).

Ranger Space Program *see* Apollo Project

Rankin, Jeannette (b. Montana Territory, 11 June 1880; d. Carmel, Calif., 18 May 1973) She was a reformer of the Progressive

ERA in the WOMEN'S SUFFRAGE and peace movements. In 1916, as a Republican from Mont., she became the first woman to win election to Congress. After enraging her constituents by voting against US entry into WORLD WAR I, she became the first woman voted out of Congress in 1918. The isolationist mood of the 1930s seemed to vindicate her stand. She helped organize the National Council for the Prevention of War and again won election to Congress in 1940. She cast the sole vote against US entry into WORLD WAR II and left Congress in 1943. She was a persistent critic of the US CONTAINMENT POLICY.

Rappists About 1805 in Pa., George Rapp (1755–1847) founded a small communal sect of German-American mystics that practiced celibacy. In 1815 they founded New Harmony, Ind., which they sold to Robert OWEN in 1824, and then relocated to Economy, Pa. The group declined rapidly after Rapp's death, and became extinct in 1905.

Rauschenbusch, Walter (b. Rochester, N.Y., 4 October 1861; d. New York, N.Y., 25 July 1918) After graduating from the Rochester Theological Seminary in 1884, Rauschenbusch took over a Baptist congregation at New York. In 1907 he published *Christianity and the Social Crisis* – which outlined his theories on the SOCIAL GOSPEL, and was the most influential religious book of his time – and convinced many reformers of the PROGRESSIVE ERA that social, economic, and political change was a religious duty. His public esteem was badly tarnished after he criticized US entry into WORLD WAR I.

Rayburn, Samuel (b. Roane County, Tenn., 6 January 1882; d. Bonham, Tex., 16 November 1961) He matured in Fannin County, Tex., and was elected as a Democratic congressman in 1912. He played a major role in drafting the SECURITIES AND EXCHANGE COMMISSION and PUBLIC UTILITY HOLDING COMPANY ACT. In 1940 he became speaker of the House. During his tenure, he earned the title "Mr Speaker" because of his thorough domination of congressional legislation, arising from his mastery of intricate parliamentary procedure, his intimate knowledge of each member's political positions, and his shrewd ability to assess human character. Despite his "unreconstructed rebel" roots, Rayburn helped pass the CIVIL RIGHTS ACTS (1957, 1960).

Raza Unida* Party, *La On 17 January 1970, at Crystal City, Tex., 300 Chicanos founded *La Raza Unida* (The United People) Party. Affiliates were formed in 17 states, but *La Raza* attracted significant support only in Tex. The party polled 6 percent in the 1972 gubernatorial election. Its candidate for governor won just 2 percent of ballots in 1978, but siphoned enough votes from the Democratic Party to elect the Republican. *La Raza* never became a major third party, but by threatening to attract a sizeable Hispanic voting bloc, it stirred Democrats to court the Chicano constituency more seriously.

REA *see* RURAL ELECTRIFICATION ADMINISTRATION

Reagan, Ronald Wilson (b. Tampico, Ill., 6 February 1911) A movie actor with a talent for light comedy, Reagan served as an Army Air Force officer in World War II, and was Screen Actors Guild president (1947–52). He switched from the Democratic to the Republican Party in 1963, served as Calif. governor (1967–75), and challenged Gerald FORD for the 1976 nomination for president. He took 50.7 percent of the ballots (in a three-party race) and carried all but five states to become president in 1980, when his coat-tails gave Republicans control of the Senate. He was the oldest president ever elected, and survived an assassination attempt on 30 March 1981. He won reelection in 1984 in a landslide victory with 58.4 percent of the vote and 49 states.

Reagan won passage of the ECONOMIC RECOVERY TAX ACT (1981) and TAX REFORM ACT (1986), broke the AIR TRAFFIC CONTROLLERS' STRIKE, and directed US intervention in GRENADA, LEBANON, and LIBYA. His huge military build-up (especially the STRATEGIC DEFENSE INITIATIVE) placed the USSR under severe economic strain to maintain military parity with the US and contributed to the Soviet Union's later political collapse. His expectations for SUPPLY SIDE ECONOMICS failed to materialize and the budget deficit expanded enormously under him. The IRAN-CONTRA SCANDAL dominated his second term and tarnished his accomplishments. During the Reagan administration, INCOME TAXes were cut by 25 percent, inflation declined from 13 percent to 3 percent, a 33 percent growth in GDP created 18 million new jobs, and federal spending fell from 24.4 percent of GDP to 22.1 percent.

Reagan* v. *Farmers' Loan and Trust Company In 1894 the Supreme Court vindicated the jurisdiction of federal courts over rates set by state commissions regulating business prices and practices. Drawing upon the precedents of *San Mateo Company* v. *Southern Pacific Railroad* and *CHICAGO, MILWAUKEE and ST PAUL RAILROAD COMPANY* v. *MINNESOTA*, the Court held that adjudication of disputes over property seized without DUE PROCESS was an essential function of the federal bench.

Reaganomics *see* SUPPLY SIDE ECONOMICS

recall This was a reform of the PROGRESSIVE ERA pioneered by Ariz. in 1912, in which a successful petition campaign can force a special election to decide whether an elected officeholder should be removed from government.

recession of the 1920s The end of WORLD WAR I caused the federal budget to decline from $18.5 billion in 1919 to $6.4 billion in 1920. Although this decline in budgetary stimulus required an increase in investment and spending by the private sector, Congress raised taxes on individuals and corporations, while the Federal Reserve Bank restricted credit by raising its discount rate for member banks from 4.75 percent to 7 percent by 1920. Unemployment rose from 4.0 percent in 1919 to 11.9 percent in 1921, but subsided to 7.6 percent in 1922 and 3.2 percent in 1923. The recession contributed to the failure or merger of 2,024 banks (6.5 percent of the total) by 1925.

The economy's industrial and commercial sectors revived after 1921, but agriculture did not. Farm prices dropped sharply as world output rose after the war, and US farmers responded by overproduction, which created surpluses that drove commodity prices progressively downward through the 1920s. Farm income dropped from 15 percent of national output in 1920 to 9 percent in 1928; 454,866 owner-managed farms disappeared in the 1920s, and the farm population decreased by 3,000,000. The agricultural depression led to the closure of 5,400 rural banks during the decade.

recession of 1937–8 In 1937 the Roosevelt administration attempted to balance the federal budget by curtailing public works and cutting relief employment programs, while the Federal Reserve limited credit and reduced the money supply to prevent a resurgence of inflation. These actions weakened the economy, which already suffered from a lack of business confidence, and a severe recession ensued after the stock market plunged steeply on 7 September 1937. Over the following nine months, manufacturing employment fell by almost a quarter, industrial output by a third, the stock market by half, and profits by over three-quarters. By June, as the economy began to revive, 4,000,000 workers had become jobless. A major reason for the upturn in business activity was a greater willingness to use budget deficits for economic stimulus (*see* KEYNESIAN ECONOMICS).

Reciprocal Trade Agreements Act (1934) *see* TRADE AGREEMENTS ACT

Reconstruction This was the process by which the ex-Confederate states regained their full privileges within the Union after the CIVIL WAR. Reconstruction's first phase was dominated by presidential initiatives and began on 8 December 1863, with Abraham LINCOLN's Proclamation of Amnesty and Reconstruction. Believing that SECESSION was invalid and the Confederate states had never legally left the Union, Lincoln saw Reconstruction's primary purpose as convincing southerners to abandon rebellion and resume their loyalty to the Union, not to rewrite state constitutions. He offered to reestablish any state's government whenever 10 percent of the number who voted in 1860 swore allegiance to the Union (this was known as the Ten Percent Plan), obtained a presidential pardon, and agreed to accept the EMANCIPATION PROCLAMATION and other US laws about SLAVERY. (Temporarily barred from pardon were the Confederacy's highest ranking leaders, former US officials who violated their oaths by aiding the rebellion, and soldiers who mistreated black troops captured in battle.)

Under Lincoln's plan, provisional governments appeared in Tenn., Ark., and La. by 1864, but did not send delegations to Congress because so much of their territories were still in rebel hands. Congress attempted to set stricter standards for Reconstruction by the WADE–DAVIS BILL, but Lincoln pocket-vetoed it. Andrew JOHNSON agreed with Lincoln's policy of leniency, and on 29 May 1865 issued his Proclamation of Amnesty, which restored political rights to all rebels who took an oath of allegiance (except prominent CSA leaders and all owners of taxable property worth over $20,000). Johnson directed provisional governors to call constitutional conventions (even where less than 10 percent of voters had sworn allegiance). These would rescind the secession ordinances, end slavery, and repudiate the CSA war debt. He also insisted that the state legislatures ratify the THIRTEENTH AMENDMENT. Even after the MEMPHIS and NEW ORLEANS RIOTS, Johnson did not insist on protecting the FREEDMEN.

RADICAL REPUBLICANS broke with Johnson and formulated their own program on the JOINT COMMITTEE ON RECONSTRUCTION. Reconstruction began its second – or congressional – phase, on 9 April 1866, when Congress passed the CIVIL RIGHTS ACT (1866) over Johnson's veto. The Radical program also included strengthening the FREEDMEN'S BUREAU and proposing the FOURTEENTH and FIFTEENTH AMENDMENTS. Congress set strict criteria for readmitting the seceded states and placed the former Confederacy (except Tenn.) under military rule through its three RECONSTRUCTION ACTS (2 March 1867, 23 March 1867, and 19 July 1867). Congress established its supremacy over Reconstruction by impeaching Andrew JOHNSON, and the Supreme Court recognized that dominance in *EX PARTE MCCARDLE* and *TEXAS* V. *WHITE*.

Congressional Reconstruction placed southern governments under the control of Republicans, whom local Democrats scorned as CARPETBAGGERS, SCALAWAGS, or ex-slaves, and resisted them through the KU KLUX KLAN. By 1872 northern opinion was turning against the Radicals' program out of weariness and frustration with the problem of keeping the south under military occupation. The LIBERAL REPUBLICAN PARTY advocated leniency toward the south and Ulysses S. GRANT restored political rights to virtually all former rebels by the AMNESTY ACT. Republican governments steadily collapsed during the 1870s. The COMPROMISE OF 1877 effectively ended Reconstruction.

Reconstruction Act, first (2 March 1867) Congress invalidated the governments founded after the CIVIL WAR on presidential authority when this law passed over Andrew JOHNSON'S veto. It placed the ten unreconstructed states under five army generals, who could impose martial law if needed; it forced states to enfranchise the FREEDMEN and draft new constitutions that required approval by a majority of registered voters; and it denied congressional representation to any state that did not ratify the FOURTEENTH AMENDMENT. It provided for state elections to institute new governments (termed Reconstruction Governments), which would be Republican-dominated.

Reconstruction Act, second (23 March 1867) To implement the first RECONSTRUCTION ACT, which would be frustrated if county officials refused to cooperate in holding new elections, Congress empowered military commanders to register voters and outlined a schedule for adopting new state constitutions. Although passed over Andrew JOHNSON'S veto, this law's effectiveness was threatened when the attorney general issued an advisory opinion that cast doubt on the legal authority of military commanders to carry out its provisions.

Reconstruction Act, third (19 July 1867) To remedy legal problems with the second RECONSTRUCTION ACT identified by the attorney general, Congress empowered military commanders to remove state officials appointed or elected before the first RECONSTRUCTION ACT, and it gave election registrars discretion to disqualify from voting any persons who seemed to have falsely taken a loyalty oath. Passed over Johnson's veto, the law enabled military commanders to hold elections in every unreconstructed state but Tex. by December 1867.

Reconstruction Act, fourth (11 March 1868) After opponents of congressional RECONSTRUCTION in Ala. prevented ratification of a liberal state constitution, by boycotting the election to block its approval by a majority of voters, Congress amended the first RECONSTRUCTION ACT by permitting a simple majority of those voting to ratify state constitutions. It became law without Andrew JOHNSON's signature.

Reconstruction Finance Corporation (RFC) After the NATIONAL CREDIT CORPORATION proved incapable of stemming a BANK PANIC, Herbert HOOVER asked Congress to form a federal agency to extend credit of up to $2,500,000,000 to banks, insurance companies, and railroads. He signed legislation creating the RFC on 2 February 1932. The EMERGENCY RELIEF AND CONSTRUCTION ACT appropriated $2,000,000,000 more and expanded its functions in 1932. The RFC and its director, Charles Dawes, were widely criticized for extending relatively little credit to small banks and businesses. The RFC controlled the largest budget ever appropriated for any federal agency, but its resources proved inadequate to restore stability to the banking system or keep numerous railroads from defaulting on their bonds.

Under the EMERGENCY BANKING RELIEF ACT (1933), the RFC provided, by 1935, $1.3 billion to over 6,200 banks with purchases of preferred stock. The RFC was the main source of funds for most credit programs of the NEW DEAL, including the FEDERAL EMERGENCY RELIEF ADMINISTRATION, FARM CREDIT ADMINISTRATION, Federal Housing Association, Home Owners' Loan Corporation, and the RESETTLEMENT ADMINISTRATION. It financed the RURAL ELECTRIFICATION ADMINISTRATION and encouraged sales of household electrical products for the TENNESSEE VALLEY AUTHORITY by the Electric Home and Farm Authority. It established the Disaster Loan Corporation to aid victims of natural disasters. By 1940 the RFC had extended over $8 billion in credit. Its economic resources were used to finance military rearmament after 1940.

Red Bird's War *see* WINNEBAGO WAR

Red River War On 20 July 1874, Major General Philip SHERIDAN got orders to disarm 1,200 hostile COMANCHE, KIOWA, and CHEYENNE INDIANS raiding Tex. and Kans. By 23 April 1875, the army had fought over two dozen skirmishes in the Tex. panhandle, burned over 1,000 lodges, and captured over 1,500 horses, but killed barely 50 warriors. Exhausted by the army's relentless pursuit, the tribes returned to their RESERVATIONS in Indian Territory by May 1875 and had 26 war leaders imprisoned in Fla. The conflict broke the will of these tribes and ended Indian resistance on the southern plains.

red scare The STEEL STRIKE (1919) and other labor unrest created widespread unease about the influence of radical labor leaders. Reinforcing this anxiety were attempts by anarchists to murder John ROCKEFELLER, Oliver Wendell HOLMES, and Attorney General A. Mitchell Palmer. In this increasingly hysterical atmosphere, Palmer launched dragnet raids in November 1919 that arrested 650 suspected agitators, most of whom were immigrants or union leaders. (Few court cases were filed and just 43 were deported.) On 2 January 1920, federal marshals under J. Edgar HOOVER arrested 2,700 suspected Communists in 33 cities, and another 3,000 were taken into custody soon after, of whom 556 were deported as lawbreakers. The raids resulted in unnecessary violence and frequent abuses of civil liberties. The so-called Palmer raids ended in May 1920, after the public had grown skeptical that any Communist threat in fact existed.

Red Sticks *see* CREEK WAR

Redeemers This term referred to Democratic leaders who accomplished the South's REDEMPTION. Most Redeemers came from, or represented the interests of, the antebellum planter class, and many were influenced by the NEW SOUTH MOVEMENT. During the era of POPULISM, they became known as BOURBONS.

Redemption This term referred to the overthrow of Republican governments by southern Democrats after RECONSTRUCTION. The COMPROMISE OF 1877 ensured the Republicans' final defeat and enabled the REDEEMERS to establish a period of monolithic Democratic political dominance known as the SOLID SOUTH.

redemptioners These were Germans who obtained free passage to the THIRTEEN COLONIES by allowing themselves to be sold as INDENTURED SERVANTS at the best terms available in America. Their hope was to be redeemed from the prospect of lengthy service and hard labor by having relatives or former acquaintances from home who bought them at auction. Perhaps every third German immigrant, about 35,000 persons, arrived as a redemptioner before 1775.

Reed, Walter (b. Belroi, Va., 13 September 1851; d. Washington, D.C., 22 November 1902) In 1875 Reed joined the Army Medical Corps as a surgeon. In 1900 he chaired the Yellow Fever Commission to investigate the source of contagion for the disease, which had caused many US deaths in the SPANISH-AMERICAN WAR. Reed's experiments demonstrated that epidemics resulted from transmission by mosquitoes rather than humans; these findings enabled the disease to be eradicated by the elimination of areas of mosquito infestation. Reed's research had immediate practical application in the building of the PANAMA CANAL. By exterminating the breeding grounds for insects that carried infection, the US succeeded in preventing any major loss of life from yellow fever among construction workers, and also in virtually eliminating malaria.

referendum This was a reform of the PROGRESSIVE ERA pioneered on 2 June 1902 by Oreg. Under it, a successful petition campaign can allow a popular vote to either approve measures rejected by their legislature or repeal a law already enacted.

Reformed Episcopal Church see PROTESTANT EPISCOPAL CHURCH

Refreshings This term referred to an interdenominational revival in central N.J. stimulated by Rev. Theodore Freylinghausen (Dutch Reformed) and Rev. Gilbert TENNENT (Presbyterian) for six years after 1726. The revivalists anticipated the GREAT AWAKENING by emphasizing salvation as a universal experience – rather than preaching about theological distinctions – and by discarding formal, written sermons to preach in a more engaging style that was either extemporaneous or based on only a few notes.

Refuse Act (1899) *see* ENVIRONMENTAL LEGISLATION

Regents of University of California* v. *Bakke On 28 June 1978, the Supreme Court ruled (5–4) that it was illegal for a college admissions office to fix a set number of admissions for minorities and deny whites the chance to compete for those places on merit, because the CIVIL RIGHTS ACT (1964) forbade the denial to anyone of access to a federally funded program on the basis of race. The decision said that race can be one of several factors considered when choosing candidates for admission, and AFFIRMATIVE ACTION is an allowable factor, but strict racial quotas impermissibly violate equal protection.

regulator This was a colonial term, derived from the name of similar groups in England, meaning a member of a citizens' group that took the law into their own hands to end criminal problems that seemed beyond the ability of law officers and the courts to solve.

regulators of North Carolina During the mid-1760s, grievances multiplied in the N.C. backcountry against corruption by local officials. After the assembly ignored repeated petitions to end the problem, westerners began refusing to pay taxes. When the Orange County sheriff began seizing the property of tax resisters, Herman Husband organized an association of REGULATORS on 4 April 1768 to demand that local officials account for their use of public funds, and the movement spread to neighboring counties. Minor violence ensued when Husband's followers blocked law officers from serving legal writs. In September, Governor William Tryon took 1,400 militia to Orange County and confronted 800 armed regulators, who dispersed peacefully. Efforts to remove corrupt officials by court suits had failed by 1771, when the arrest of several regulator leaders led to violence against law officers by armed crowds. Tryon then suppressed the movement at the battle of ALAMANCE CREEK.

regulators of South Carolina In 1767 the S.C. backcountry experienced the peak of a crime wave by vicious gangs of thieves, which the legal system could not control. By October, posses of REGULATORS began to form in order to run down the outlaws. After suppressing or driving out the criminals, the regulators petitioned the assembly to establish circuit courts on the frontier, to enact a vagrancy statute and stiffer penalties for crime, to appoint more sheriffs and build more jails, and to increase the backcountry's legislative representation. The assembly enacted laws implementing all these requests, except increased representation, by June 1769.

Rehnquist, William Hubbs (b. Milwaukee, Wis., 1 October 1924) After service in the air force during World War II, Rehnquist was a law clerk on the Supreme Court (1952–3), became involved in Republican Party politics, and was US assistant attorney general (1969–71) before joining the Supreme Court in 1971. He was one of two dissenters against *ROE V. WADE*, and thereafter advocated giving states wide leeway to regulate ABORTIONS. He emerged as the Court's leading advocate for judicial restraint. On 17 September 1986, he was confirmed as chief justice.

Report on a National Bank *see* BANK OF THE UNITED STATES, FIRST

Report on Manufactures On 5 December 1791, Alexander HAMILTON proposed that Congress set tariffs on imports of manufactures to stimulate US industry, and promote INTERNAL IMPROVEMENTS to foster domestic markets for US industries. Congress took no major action to revise the TARIFF OF 1789, and the US did not enact significant tariff legislation until the TARIFF OF 1816.

Report on the Public Credit On 14 January 1790, Alexander HAMILTON reported his proposals for honoring the debts accumulated in the REVOLUTIONARY WAR. He itemized the federal debt (including unpaid interest) as $54,124,464, of which $11,710,378 was held in Europe, and proposed that it be reissued as interest-bearing bonds at face value. He also proposed that the US Treasury assume and reissue up to $21,500,000 of debts incurred by the states, for a total of $75,624,464 in federal obligations. Hamilton's proposal to fund the federal debt at par passed on 22 February, but his assumption of state debts failed in the House by two votes on 12 April, due to southern opposition. On 26 July, however, assumption passed after a few southerners switched their positions to win relocation of the national capital to the Potomac River. By 1793 the US had assumed or refunded state debts of $19,685,664. The funding established US creditworthiness in European financial markets on a solid basis.

Republican Party By tradition, the Republican party was founded on 28 February 1854 at Ripon, Wis. It gained members so rapidly among members of the WHIG, KNOW-NOTHING, and FREE-SOIL PARTIES opposing passage of the KANSAS–NEBRASKA ACT, that it elected 108 congressmen and 15 senators to Congress in 1854. The party insisted on barring SLAVERY from the territories, but did not advocate ABOLITIONISM. After winning the presidency and both houses of Congress in 1860, it solidified the allegiance of most northerners and FREEDMEN by Abraham LINCOLN's victory in the CIVIL WAR and its RECONSTRUCTION policies. It had little influence in the South after the COMPROMISE OF 1877, but by waving the BLOODY SHIRT, cultivating the GRAND ARMY OF THE REPUBLIC, and supporting high protective tariffs for industrialists, it dominated northern politics. After 1876 it was split by struggles between STALWARTS, HALF-BREEDS, and MUGWUMPS.

From 1860 to 1928, Republicans elected every president but Grover CLEVELAND and Woodrow WILSON; they controlled the Senate every year except during 1879–80, 1893–4, and 1913–20; they controlled the House every year except during 1875–80, 1883–8, 1891–4, and 1911–18. They became a minority party in the GREAT DEPRESSION, when blacks defected to join the ROOSEVELT COALITION. They lost the presidency and Senate in 1933, and the House in 1931. From then until 1953, they controlled the Senate and House only during 1947–8. Despite winning seven out of 11 presidential elections from 1952 to 1992 (all but John F. KENNEDY, Lyndon JOHNSON, Jimmy CARTER, and William CLINTON), they held the Senate only during 1953–4, 1981–6, and from 1995 onwards, and the House only during 1953–4, and from 1995 onwards. Their inability to recapture Congress from 1954 to 1994 stemmed from heavy losses occasioned by Barry GOLDWATER's 1964 defeat and the WATERGATE SCANDAL. In 1994 the Grand Old Party rebounded to capture both houses of Congress and half the governorships.

Resaca, battle of (Ga.) *see* ATLANTA, BATTLES FOR

Resaca de la Palma, battle of (Tex.) One day after the battle of PALO ALTO, on 9 May 1846, Brigadier General Zachary

TAYLOR's 1,700 US regulars routed General Mariano Arista's 5,000 Mexicans. US losses: 33 killed, 89 wounded. Mexican losses: 1,200 killed, wounded, 100 captured, 7 cannon. US forces then occupied Matomoros, Mexico.

reservations The first instance of whites isolating an Indian group within a defined area was the founding of Natick, Mass., as a PRAYING TOWN for remnants of the MASSACHUSETT INDIAN nation in 1651. A few such reservations developed behind the line of European settlement before 1820, but British and US policy was to treat the area beyond the frontier as a separate Indian country until it was purchased by treaty. After frontier migration left large Indian groups behind the line of settlement east of the Mississippi, reservations were created for them on the southern plains in KANSAS and OKLAHOMA. The northern plains were seen as a common reservation in which the native tribes had unrestricted freedom of movement until the treaties of MEDICINE LODGE and FORT LARAMIE began limiting individual nations within particular boundaries.

The largest number of reservations was established between 1867 and 1887. The DAWES SEVERALTY ACT attempted to break up reservations into private allotments, and resulted in large amounts of Indian land being sold to whites, before the WHEELER–HOWARD ACT reversed this policy. In 1984, 283 tribes and 200 Alaskan villages enjoyed official recognition by the Department of the Interior. Within the US, there are 261 federal reservations in 24 states, covering 81,277 square miles. Nine states have established 21 reservations, of which nine are in N.Y. Less than half of all Indians now live on reservations.

Reserve Officers' Training Corps *see* NATIONAL DEFENSE ACT (1916)

Reserves, US Army *see* ARMY RESERVES

Resettlement Administration This agency consolidated several programs for rural relief in 1935 under Rexford TUGWELL. It hoped to resettle 500,000 impoverished farm families on land that it purchased and subdivided among the dispossessed, but ultimately it relocated just 4,441 in its 164 resettlement projects. It operated 95 camps, with a capacity of 75,000, for migrant workers making long-distance moves between states.

Resolution Trust Corporation (RTC) This agency was formed on 9 August 1989 to save the Federal Savings and Loan Insurance Corporation from bankruptcy during the SAVINGS AND LOAN CRISIS. The RTC was headed by L. William Seidman up to his retirement in 1992, acting director Albert Casey to March 1993, acting director Roger Altman (whose involvement with the WHITEWATER SCANDAL at the RTC led to his forced resignation as deputy treasury secretary on 17 August 1994) to March 1994, and then deputy RTC director John E. Ryan. The RTC sold off its last trusts in 1994 and was disbanded in 1995.

***Reuben James*, USS** On 30 October 1941, a German submarine sank the *Reuben James* as it convoyed US merchant ships to Iceland, and killed about 100 sailors. The attack spurred Congress to amend the NEUTRALITY ACT (1937) by allowing US ships to land cargoes in Britain.

Reuther, Walter Philip (b. Wheeling, W.Va., 1 September 1907; d. near Pellston, Mich., 9 May 1970) He entered the factories at 16 and was active in United Auto Workers' (UAW) sit-down strikes to organize the automobile industry in the 1930s. He was UAW president from 1946 to his death. AS CIO president (1952–5), he led its merger with the AFL and was AFL-CIO vice-president until 1968, when he led the UAW out of the organization because of differences with George MEANEY over strategy. He affiliated his union to the Teamsters in 1969 (the alliance lasted to 1973). He pioneered such union benefits as the guaranteed annual wage, annual salary raises linked to productivity, cost-of-living increases, and numerous pension benefits. Reuther insisted that labor must take positions on leading political and foreign-policy issues, and exercised much influence within the Democratic Party.

Revels, Hiram R. (b. Fayetteville, N.C., 1 September 1827; d. Aberdeen, Miss., 16 January 1901) Born to free black parents, Revels was a college-educated minister of the African Methodist Episcopal Church before serving as a chaplain to black troops in the CIVIL WAR. In 1864 he settled in Miss., from where he was elected in 1870 to the

US Senate as the first black to hold that office. He retired in 1871 and was then president of Alcorn University, to 1882.

Revenue Act (1767) *see* TOWNSHEND REVENUE ACT

revenue acts of the 1920s These laws implemented Andrew MELLON's program of substantial reductions in INCOME TAX.

(1) The 1921 act ended an excess profits tax, cut the surtax on incomes, from 65 percent in excess of $1,000,000 to 50 percent in excess of $200,000, and raised deductions for household heads from $2,000 to $2,500 and for dependants from $200 to $500. It also increased the corporate tax rate from 10 percent to 12 percent and imposed the first US capital gains tax of 12.5 percent.

(2) The 1924 act rescheduled personal tax rates (formerly 4 percent under $4,000 and 8 percent above that) at 2 percent of the first $4,000, 4 percent of the next $4,000, and 6 percent above $8,000. It changed the surtax from 50 percent in excess of $200,000 to 40 percent in excess of $500,000.

(3) The 1926 act rescheduled personal tax rates at 1.5 percent of the first $4,000, 3 percent of the next $4,000, and 5 percent above $8,000. It increased deductions for households to $3,500 and for personal exemptions to $1,500. It repealed the gift tax and reduced maximum rates for the surtax and inheritance tax to 20 percent.

(4) The 1928 act decreased the corporate tax rate to 12 percent.

(5) The 1929 act set rates for one year at 0.5 percent on the first $4,000, 2 percent on the next $4,000, and 4 percent above $8,000.

Revenue Act (6 June 1932) This law began the process by which the REVENUE ACTS OF THE 1920S were reversed and federal income taxes were set at progressively higher rates. Congress failed to pass a projected manufacturers' sales tax of 2.5 percent, but increased the corporate tax rate to 13.75 percent, raised the maximum surtax rate from 20 percent to 55 percent, and imposed a 5 percent excess profits tax. Income was taxed at 4 percent on the first $4,000 and 8 percent above that.

Revenue Act (1935) *see* WEALTH TAX ACT

revenue-sharing This program of the NEW FEDERALISM gave cities and states a set percentage of federal revenues for use in financing any part of their budget. The State and Local Fiscal Assistance Act (20 October 1972) inaugurated this policy by awarding $9.67 billion. In 1981 Ronald REAGAN proposed to end revenue-sharing, since the states enjoyed a collective budget surplus while the US budget remained deeply unbalanced. By the time the program was finally halted on 30 September 1986, it had distributed $85 billion.

Revere, Paul (b. Boston Mass., 1 January 1735; d. Boston, Mass., 10 May 1818) A Boston silversmith, Revere became a courier for New England's Whig leadership (*see* WHIGS (REVOLUTIONARY)). On 18 April 1775, the Whigs sent Revere and William Dawes to warn John ADAMS and John HANCOCK that redcoats were marching to arrest them. Revere was captured en route, but Dawes succeeeded in spreading the alarm to CONCORD. Revere engraved the earliest Continental currency.

reverse discrimination *see* AFFIRMATIVE ACTION

revivalism *see* GREAT AWAKENING, FIRST; SECOND GREAT AWAKENING; BURNED-OVER DISTRICT; FINNEY, CHARLES; MOODY, DWIGHT; SUNDAY, BILLY; *and* GRAHAM, BILLY.

Revolution of 1688 Alarmed at the prospect of JAMES II establishing a Catholic dynasty and eliminating parliamentary government, leading English Whigs and Tories sought assistance from WILLIAM III, James's son-in-law. After William landed with troops at Devon on 5 November 1688, most of James's army deserted him and he fled to France in December. Parliament offered the throne to William and his wife Mary as joint sovereigns in January 1689. The revolution sparked LEISLER'S REBELLION, COODE'S REVOLT, the DOMINION OF NEW ENGLAND's overthrow, and KING WILLIAM'S WAR. Whigs later idealized William's accession as the "Glorious Revolution," because it established a constitutional monarchy subordinate to Parliament.

Revolutionary War On 19 April 1775, skirmishes at LEXINGTON and CONCORD, Mass., initiated hostilities. While under siege at BOSTON, the British suffered heavy losses at BUNKER HILL. American troops invaded

Canada in the fall of 1775 and took MONTREAL, but were defeated at QUEBEC. Having sustained disastrous casualties, they retreated under hot pursuit by superior British forces, which might have occupied the Hudson valley but for Benedict ARNOLD's resistance on Lake Champlain that culminated in the battle of VALCOUR ISLAND.

After artillery from FORT TICONDEROGA drove the British from Boston in March 1776, operations shifted to New York City. William HOWE's Royal Army solidified control of New York following battles at LONG ISLAND, HARLEM HEIGHTS, WHITE PLAINS, KIP'S BAY, and FORT WASHINGTON. George WASHINGTON's CONTINENTAL ARMY retreated across N.J. in late 1776, but threw Howe's forces on the defensive at TRENTON in December 1776 and PRINCETON in January 1777.

Britain's strategy in 1777 called for Philadelphia's capture by Howe and the Hudson valley's occupation by expeditions under Lieutenant Colonel St Leger and Major General Burgoyne. American victories at ORISKANY and FORT STANWIX repulsed St Leger's campaign. Burgoyne allowed FORT TICONDEROGA's garrison to escape capture, lost a tenth of his army at BENNINGTON, suffered defeat at FREEMAN'S FARM and BEMIS HEIGHTS, and then surrendered at SARATOGA to Major General Gates. Saratoga was the Revolution's turning point because it persuaded France to sign the FRANCO-AMERICAN ALLIANCE. (Spain declared war on Britain in 1779 and the Netherlands did so in 1780).

Howe's redcoats trounced Washington's army in Pa. at BRANDYWINE CREEK, GERMANTOWN, and PAOLI in the fall of 1777. While Howe occupied Philadelphia, Washington's inspector general, Baron von STEUBEN, drilled Americans in battlefield tactics at VALLEY FORGE until they equaled the British in fighting proficiency. When the British evacuated Philadelphia in June 1778, Washington drubbed them at MONMOUTH COURTHOUSE and bottled them up in New York.

Fighting in the North then shifted to the frontier. Colonel George Rogers CLARK established US control north of the Ohio River by capturing VINCENNES in 1779. Bloody raids on frontier communities like CHERRY VALLEY, N.Y., and WYOMING VALLEY, Pa., were avenged in 1779 by SULLIVAN'S and BRODHEAD'S CAMPAIGNS against the IROQUOIS CONFEDERACY.

The British meanwhile moved south. After taking SAVANNAH in December 1778, capturing CHARLES TOWN (third battle) in May 1780, and smashing an American army at CAMDEN, S.C., in August 1780, they gained control of Georgia and the Carolinas. American fortunes revived with small victories in S.C. at KING'S MOUNTAIN and COWPENS, which encouraged partisans like Francis Marion, Thomas Sumter, and Andrew Pickens to wage guerrilla warfare. Lieutenant General CORNWALLIS won Pyrrhic victories over Major General GREENE'S Americans at GUILFORD COURTHOUSE, HOBKIRK'S HILL and EUTAW SPRINGS. When Cornwallis's bloodied army limped into Va., Washington trapped him at YORKTOWN. Bereft of British naval support after the battle of CHESAPEAKE CAPES, Cornwallis endured a three-week siege before capitulating in October 1781. Serious hostilities then ended and negotiations began on the treaty of PARIS (1783).

Over half the free males aged 16 to 45 performed military duty: 220,000 as US troops and 21,000 as Tories. The US Navy commissioned 57 vessels (1,192 guns), but civilians outfitted 1,697 privateers (14,872 guns) carrying 58,400 crewmen. US ships captured 2,208 British merchant vessels (excluding 879 retaken by the Royal Navy) and 89 privateers. British sailors captured over half the US MERCHANT MARINE: 1,108 vessels (27 later regained by US ships) and 216 privateers. A total of 25,674 US troops died (6,090 in land combat, 1,084 in sea combat, 10,000 of disease, and 8,500 as enemy prisoners); 8,241 were wounded (7,783 on land, 458 on sea); and 18,572 were captured (15,542 on land, 3,030 on sea). The war cost $360,614,663 in CONTINENTALS, with gold value of $85,077,835.

Reynolds* v. *Sims On 15 June 1964, the Supreme Court, ruling in accordance with *BAKER* V. *CARR*, decided that the FOURTEENTH AMENDMENT'S equal protection clause requires both chambers of state legislatures to be apportioned according to "one person, one vote." A constitutional amendment to reverse this ruling narrowly failed to pass Congress. (*See* WESBERRY V. SANDERS)

Reynolds* v. *Smith *see* SHAPIRO V. THOMPSON

RFC *see* RECONSTRUCTION FINANCE CORPORATION

Rhode Island In June 1636, Roger WILLIAMS established the first European settlement at Providence. Portsmouth, Newport, and Warwick were founded by 1643. On 24 March 1644, Parliament (then in rebellion against the monarchy) created the four towns into a CHARTER COLONY. After the Stuart Restoration, Williams obtained a charter from CHARLES II on 18 July 1663 confirming the privileges given in 1644. R.I. was the only New England colony without an established church. Its only Indian hostilities came during KING PHILIP'S WAR. By 1700 it had 6,000 people, including 300 slaves.

The economy's most important activities were distilling, raising livestock, and overseas trade. In the Revolution, it provided two of the 80 Continental regiments and outfitted 15 privateers. The British occupied Newport, its largest city (1776–9). It was the site of 60 military actions on land and 11 on water. It abolished SLAVERY in 1784. It refused to ratify the CONSTITUTION in 1789 and did not become the 13th state until 29 May 1790. In 1800 it was the second smallest state and had 69,122 inhabitants, of whom 79 percent were rural, and 95 percent were white.

It became a major center of industry after December 1790, when Samuel SLATER began operating the first US water-powered textile factory. The charter of 1663, which continued in force after the Revolution, was replaced in 1843 following the DORR REBELLION. Its population grew by 153 percent from 1800 to 1860, when it had 174,620 residents, of whom 2 percent were black and 21 percent were foreign-born; it ranked 29th in population, 32nd in the value of its farmland and livestock, and 13th in manufactures. It furnished 23,236 USA troops (1,837 black) in the CIVIL WAR.

It became noted for its luxurious resorts for the wealthy after 1870. In 1900 it was the 34th state in size and was only 5 percent rural; it had 428,556 inhabitants, of whom 2 percent were black and 31 percent were foreign-born; it ranked 49th among the states in the value of its agricultural products and 15th in manufacturing. The immigration of numerous southern Europeans made R.I. the only state with a Roman Catholic majority. Growth has been moderate since 1900. In 1990 it was the 43rd largest state in size and had 1,003,464 people (approx. 89 percent white, 3 percent black, 5 percent Hispanic, and 2 percent Asian), of whom 93 percent were urban and 9.5 percent foreign-born. Manufacturing and mining employed 29 percent of workers.

Rhode Island* v. *Massachusetts In 1846, in its first case involving a boundary dispute between states, the Supreme Court affirmed (7–1) its own authority to decide the issue; it then unanimously upheld the claims of Mass., which ironically had argued that the Court lacked jurisdiction in this matter. (*See* FOSTER V. NEILSON, regarding the Court's jurisdiction over disputed international boundaries.)

Rich Mountain, battle of (W.Va.) On 11 July 1861, Brigadier General William Rosecrans's 4,000 Federals routed Lieutenant Colonel John Peagram's 1,300 Confederates near Beverley, and captured Peagram and 553 survivors on 12–13 July. Losses: 60 USA and 723 CSA casualties. Brigadier General Garnett's 3,700 Confederates retreated from northern W.Va. and Major General George MCCLELLAN'S 20,000 Federals established Union control over the area.

Richardson, Elliot Lee (b. Boston, Mass., 20 July 1920) He began practicing law in Boston in 1947 and entered politics as a Republican. He became secretary of health, education, and welfare in June 1970 and succeeded Richard KLEINDIENST as attorney general in April 1973. On 20 October 1973, he resigned rather than carry out Richard NIXON'S orders to fire Special Prosecutor Archibald COX to frustrate the investigation into the WATERGATE SCANDAL. His resignation was critical in leading Congress to begin hearings on whether Nixon should be impeached.

Richberg, Donald Randall (b. Knoxville, Tenn., 10 July 1881; d. Charlottesville, Va., 27 November 1960) A Chicago attorney and partner of Harold ICKES, Richberg was considered to be the foremost US expert on labor law when he joined the BRAINS TRUST in 1932. He had a major influence in drafting the NATIONAL INDUSTRIAL RECOVERY ACT (NIRA) and took over the NATIONAL RECOVERY ADMINISTRATION from Hugh JOHNSON in 1934.

Rickover, Hyman (b. Russia, 27 January 1900; d. Arlington, Va., 8 July 1986) He was raised in Chicago and graduated from Annapolis. He waged a lonely battle arguing the merits of building nuclear-powered naval ships, and in 1947 was made head of the navy's nuclear program and the naval reactor branch of the ATOMIC ENERGY COMMISSION. He supervised the design and construction of the world's first nuclear-driven submarine, the USS *Nautilus* (launched 1954). He is considered the father of the nuclear navy.

RICO *see* ORGANIZED CRIME CONTROL ACT

right of deposit Under the treaty of PARIS (1783), which Spain did not sign, the US claimed the right of sending goods down the Mississippi River and depositing them at Spanish New Orleans while they awaited overseas shipment. Spain closed the Mississippi to US commerce in 1784. This privilege was a major issue in the JAY–GARDOQUI TREATY, the treaty of SAN LORENZO, and LOUISIANA PURCHASE.

right-to-work laws Section 14(b) of the TAFT–HARTLY ACT allowed states to outlaw contracts requiring workers to join a union as a condition of employment. Nineteen states enacted such "right-to-work" laws by 1958, after which year no others were passed.

rights of Englishmen During the Revolutionary era, this term referred to longstanding civil rights enshrined in COMMON LAW and to political liberties protected by the Magna Carta and the 1689 English Bill of Rights. These legal protections formed the basis of the BILL OF RIGHTS ratified in 1791.

Riis, Jacob August (b. Ribe, Denmark. 3 May 1849; d. Barre, Mass., 26 May 1914) A journalist from Copenhagen, Riis came to New York in 1870. He shocked the PROGRESSIVE ERA's collective conscience with his lectures, articles, and photographs of the grim poverty prevailing in New York's tenement slums, especially through his classic *How the Other Half Lives* (1890). Riis worked to end child labor, create shelter for the homeless, and improve sanitation in the ghettos.

Rio de Janeiro conference from 15 to 28 January 1942, the US and 20 Latin-American republics consulted on adopting a common foreign policy during WORLD WAR II. The delegates voted to recommend that all nations in the western hemisphere cut off diplomatic relations with the AXIS. All countries did so, although Chile waited until January 1943 and Argentina delayed until January 1944.

Rio Pact On 2 September 1947, 20 Latin-American republics and the US signed the Inter-American Treaty of Reciprocal Assistance, which established a mutual defense pact among nations of the PAN-AMERICAN UNION. The Rio Pact was a preliminary step toward forming the ORGANIZATION OF AMERICAN STATES.

Ripley, George *see* BROOK FARM

River Raisin, battle of (Mich.) On 17 January 1813, Colonel William Lewis's 660 Ky. militia captured Frenchtown (Monroe), Mich., from 150 Canadians and Indians (US losses: 12 killed, 55 wounded), and were joined by Brigadier General James Winchester with 300 militia. On 22 January, Colonel Henry Proctor's 1,400 British and Indians attacked Winchester, who surrendered. Indians killed 30–100 Americans too badly wounded to join Proctor's withdrawal to Canada. US losses: 200 killed, 200 wounded, 500 captured. The defeat prevented Major General William H. HARRISON from retaking FORT DETROIT that winter.

Rivers* v. *Roadway Express, Incorporated *see* CIVIL RIGHTS ACT (1991).

Roanoke Colony Sir Walter RALEIGH financed the settlement of an advance party on Roanoke Island (N.C.), which was occupied from 27 July 1585 to June 1586. On 22 July 1587, Roanoke was reoccupied by 117 men, women, and children dispatched by Raleigh. Virginia Dare was the first English child born in America, at Roanoke on 18 August. The Spanish Armada crisis delayed the arrival of any relief parties from England until 17 August 1590, when Roanoke was found abandoned. The lost colonists were never found, and may have been lost at sea sailing to the Newfoundland fisheries in crude boats.

Robeson, Paul Bustill (b. Princeton, N.J., 9 April 1898; d. Philadelphia, Pa., 23 January 1976) After earning a law degree from Columbia, Robeson became an internationally acclaimed actor and one of the greatest bass-baritones of his time. For criticizing discrimination against his fellow African Americans, speaking favorably of the USSR (which awarded him the Stalin peace prize in 1952), and associating with Communists, his career was ruined in the McCarthy era, when he was blacklisted from performing in the US and denied a passport to work abroad. He was allowed to perform overseas after 1958, but had to retire in 1963 due to poor health.

Robinson, Edward Arlington (b. Head Tide, Maine, 22 December 1869; d. New York, N.Y., 6 April 1935) A descendant of Anne BRADSTREET, Robinson attended Harvard (1891–3), and paid to publish his first poetry collection, *The Torrent and the Night Before*, in 1896. After moving to New York's Greenwich Village in 1899, and struggling with poverty, he began receiving critical recognition and success with *The Man Against the Sky* (1916). His *Collected Poems* (1921), *The Man Who Died Twice* (1924), and *Tristram* (1927) won Pulitzer prizes. His work was known for its highly-crafted blank verse, natural rhythms, and economy of expression; his best remembered characters were the Yankee residents of mythical "Tillbury Town," such as Richard Cory and Miniver Cheevy. Other major works include *Captain Craig and Other Poems* (1902), *The Town Down the River* (1910), *Merlin* (1917), *Avon's Harvest* (1921), *Roman Bartholomew* (1923), *Cavender's House* (1929), *Matthias at the Door* (1931), *Talifer* (1933), *Amaranth* (1934), and *King Jasper* (1935).

Robinson, Jack (Jackie) Roosevelt (b. Cairo, Ga., 31 January 1919; d. Stamford, Conn., 24 October 1972) In 1945 Robinson signed to play in the minor leagues for the Brooklyn Dodgers; in 1947 he became the first African American to integrate major-league baseball when he joined the Dodgers and was named rookie of the year. His career, which lasted to 1956 (primarily as second baseman), pioneered the entry of blacks into professional sports, which had been exclusively white by custom. He was later active as a business executive and fund-raiser for civil rights causes. He was inducted into baseball's Hall of Fame in 1962.

Robinson–Patman Act (20 June 1936) This statute, part of the LITTLE NIRA, reimposed certain industry-wide, competitive regulations after the NATIONAL INDUSTRIAL RECOVERY ACT (NIRA) was declared unconstitutional. Directed primarily at chain-store retailers, it outlawed price discrimination that tended to eliminate competition, such as discounts or rebates given by manufacturers to high-volume purchasers.

Robinson* v. *California On 25 June 1962 the Supreme Court ruled (6–2) that state court proceedings were obliged to uphold guarantees under the EIGHTH AMENDMENT against cruel and unusual punishment. It then overturned a state law making narcotics addiction a crime.

Rockefeller, John Davison (b. Richford, N.Y., 8 July 1839; d. Ormond Beach, Fla., 23 May 1937) He matured in Cleveland, where he entered the oil refining business in 1862 and organized the Standard Oil Co. in 1867. He bought out or merged with competitors so rapidly that by 1879 he controlled 90 percent of US refining capacity, as well as a pipeline network and vast reserves of underground oil. In 1882 he consolidated his companies outside Ohio into the STANDARD OIL TRUST. By 1892 Rockefeller was worth $800,000,000 and had become to reformers of the PROGRESSIVE ERA a symbol of monopoly power built upon cut-throat competition. Following the trust's dissolution in 1911, Rockefeller retired and donated much of his billion-dollar fortune to philanthropy.

Rockefeller, Nelson Aldrich (b. Bar Harbor, Maine, 8 July 1908; d. New York, N.Y., 26 January 1979) Grandson of John ROCKEFELLER, he served the State Department (1940–51) and was special advisor to Dwight D. EISENHOWER (1954–5). In 1958 he broke the tradition that divorced politicians could not win high office by becoming N.Y. governor after a remarriage to "Happy" Murphy. He lost the 1964 Republican nomination for president to Barry GOLDWATER

After 15 years' service as N.Y. governor, he resigned on 18 December 1973 to devote himself full-time to chair commissions studying national problems and water conservation. On 19 December 1974, he became the second vice-president to take office under the TWENTY-FIFTH AMENDMENT.

Rockefeller Commission *see* OPERATION CHAOS

Rockingham, second Marquis of (b. Malton, Yorkshire, England, 13 May 1730; d. London, England, 1 July 1782) In 1750 Charles Watson-Wentworth entered the House of Lords as the second Marquis of Rockingham. GEORGE III named him prime minister in July 1765 to succeed George GRENVILLE. Well disposed toward American colonists, Rockingham reduced the SUGAR ACT's molasses duty from 3 to 1 pence and repealed the STAMP ACT, but was forced to accept passage of the DECLARATORY ACT. George III replaced him in August 1766 with William PITT. In March 1782, he succeeded Lord NORTH as prime minister, with directions to negotiate an end to the REVOLUTIONARY WAR.

Rodgers, Richard *see* RODGERS AND HAMMERSTEIN

Rodgers and Hammerstein The most successful partnership of the Broadway theater was between composer Richard Rodgers (b. 28 June 1902) and librettist Oscar Hammerstein (12 July 1895–23 August 1960) from 1943 to Hammerstein's death. Rodgers had earlier collaborated with Lorenz Hart on several musicals, and Hammerstein had adapted Jerome Kern's score for *Show Boat* (1927). Together, they won Pulitzer prizes for *Oklahoma* (1944) and *South Pacific* (1949). Their other successes included *Carousel* (1945), *The King and I* (1951), and *The Sound of Music* (1959).

Rodham Clinton, Hillary (b. Park Ridge, Ill., 26 October 1947) Married to William CLINTON in 1975, Hillary Rodham Clinton practiced law in Little Rock, Ark., and headed state committees on rural health services and educational standards. In 1993 she became chair of the US Task Force on National Health Reform, and supervised the drafting of the Clinton administration's legislation to reform medical insurance and provide universal health care. This legislation was defeated after a bitter congressional struggle in 1994.

Roe* v. *Wade On 22 January 1973, the Supreme Court ruled (7–2) that the option of choosing an ABORTION in the first trimester was a fundamental constitutional privilege stemming from the right to privacy encompassed by the FOURTEENTH AMENDMENT's guarantee of personal liberty as part of DUE PROCESS. *Roe*'s scope was modified by Congress through the HYDE AMENDMENT, and by the Court in *WEBSTER* v. *REPRODUCTIVE HEALTH SERVICES* and *HODGSON* v. *MINNESOTA*.

Roebling, John Augustus (b. Muhlhausen, Thuringia, 12 June 1806; d. Brooklyn, N.Y., 22 July 1869) He became a civil engineer in 1826 and came to the US in 1831. He manufactured the first wire rope made in the US in 1841 and built a factory at Trenton, N.J. to produce this essential material for suspension bridges. He emerged as the foremost US bridge engineer after building or designing suspension bridges at Pittsburgh (1846), Niagara Falls (1851), and Cincinnati (1857). He proposed and designed the Brooklyn Bridge, but died of tetanus in 1869 as ground was being broken. His son Washington completed the project.

Rogers's Rangers In 1757 Major Robert Rogers raised nine companies of Yankees to "range the woods" and raid the French. His most noted exploit was to destroy the ABNAKI INDIAN town of St Francois, Quebec, on 6 October 1759. During this raid, his 180 men suffered 30 percent casualties. Rogers left the Rangers in 1760. Major Joseph Gorham organized a corps of rangers as an official unit of the Royal Army in 1761, but his men were demobilized in 1763. In 1776 Rogers raised a Tory regiment (*see* TORIES), the Queen's Rangers, whose command passed to John Simcoe; they were then called Simcoe's Rangers.

Rogue River War Frustrated by random instances of thievery, whites murdered 23 Indians near Jacksonville, Oreg., on 8 October 1855. The next day, Indians retaliated by killing 27 settlers. Aggrieved by an influx of miners, about 300 warriors began attacking whites as far south as Calif. Oreg. volunteers drove the hostile Indians into the Rogue River valley, where the last renegades surrendered on 29 June 1856. The US then cleared southwestern Oreg. and northern Calif. of most Indians, whether they were hostile or not, by relocating 1,200 on a Pacific-coast reservation.

Rolfe, John (b. England, 1585; d. Bermuda Hundred, Va., 22 March 1622) Rolfe emigrated to Va. about 1610. In about 1612 he began experimenting with tobacco planting, and is credited with developing the successful techniques of cultivating and curing a marketable variety of that plant, which emerged as the colony's primary export after 1618. Rolfe married Pocahontas in 1614; he was killed by her uncle's warriors in Opechancanough's first war.

Roman Catholic church *see* Catholic church

Roosevelt, (Anna) Eleanor (b. New York, N.Y., 11 October 1884; d. New York, N.Y., 7 November 1962) Wife and fifth cousin of Franklin D. Roosevelt, she was the earliest first lady to involve herself with political issues during her husband's tenure. She visited and gave speeches at relief agencies, military bases, and workplaces. She broke with tradition by holding press conferences and authoring "My Day," a syndicated newspaper column, in which she supported civil rights and humanitarian issues. After 1945, she was a delegate to the United Nations, chaired its Commission for Human Rights, and helped found the Americans for Democratic Action.

Roosevelt, Franklin Delano (b. Hyde Park, N.Y., 30 January 1882; d. Warm Springs, Ga., 12 April 1934) He became assistant secretary of the navy in 1913 and was Democratic vice-presidential nominee in 1920 before being stricken with polio in 1921. As the only prominent Democrat to win a governorship in the Republican landslide of 1928, he was front runner for the Democratic presidential nomination in 1932 and won the general election with 57.4 percent of the vote and all but five states. As president, he fought the Great Depression with the New Deal, and used fireside chats to rebuild public confidence with his infectious optimism. His policies created the Roosevelt coalition, which ended the Republican party's domination of US politics. He redirected foreign affairs through his good neighbor policy, lend lease (*see* Lend Lease Act), and Atlantic Charter. He overcame opposition by isolationists to win funding for a large rearmament program that enabled the US to undertake a full-scale military mobilization immediately upon entering World War II. He molded wartime and postwar strategy with other Allied leaders during conferences at Casablanca, Quebec, Teheran, and Yalta. He was the only president to win reelection three times (by 60.8 percent in 1936, 54.8 percent in 1940, and 53.5 percent in 1944). He died five weeks into his fourth term.

Roosevelt, Theodore (b. New York, N.Y., 27 October 1858; d. Oyster Bay, N.Y., 6 January 1919) A reformer of the Progressive Era (Republican), Roosevelt held municipal offices in New York before becoming assistant secretary of the navy in 1897. He resigned in 1898 to organize the Rough Riders, became a national war hero, and was elected N.Y. governor. Chosen as William McKinley's running mate in 1900, he became president in 1901 and was reelected in 1904 with 57.4 percent of the vote over Alton Parker. He used the Sherman Antitrust Act to "bust up" trusts. He advocated legislation to preserve wilderness areas, pressured Congress into passing the National Reclamation Act, demanded the Hepburn Act for stricter railroad regulation, and supported the Meat Inspection and Pure Food and Drug acts. He was an overseas interventionist who announced the Roosevelt corollary and gained a US lease on the Panama Canal. He won the Nobel peace prize in 1905 for helping to end the Russo-Japanese War. He broke with William Taft and ran against him as Progressive party candidate in 1912, but won only 27.4 percent of the vote and six states. He remained active in public life primarily as a critic of Woodrow Wilson.

Roosevelt coalition This term refers to three constituencies whose votes enabled the Democratic Party to dominate national politics from the New Deal until the 1970s: the Solid South, organized labor, and blacks. The New Deal specifically tailored programs for southern economic development securing labor's right to organize, and promoting equal employment opportunities for blacks. Southern whites and labor had long been Democratic supporters, but blacks only became a Democratic voting bloc in the 1930s. The coalition began crumbling in the 1960s with the Solid South's defection, and was defunct by 1994 because southern whites and blacks could not coexist politically.

Roosevelt corollary On 6 December 1904, President Theodore ROOSEVELT asserted the US right to act as "an international police power" when countries covered by the MONROE DOCTRINE did not keep domestic order or honor international financial agreements. This corollary was used to justify armed US intervention in COLOMBIA, CUBA, DOMINICAN REPUBLIC, HONDURAS, HAITI, MEXICO, NICARAGUA, and PANAMA. This position (and other forms of "BIG-STICK" and DOLLAR DIPLOMACY) was abandoned by Franklin D. ROOSEVELT for the GOOD NEIGHBOR POLICY.

Root, Elihu (b. Clinton, N.Y., 15 February 1845; d. New York, N.Y., 7 February 1937) He was a lawyer who became active in Republican politics while US attorney in N.Y. While serving as secretary of war (1899–1904), he reformed army administration by establishing a general staff, drafted a military government for the PHILIPPINES, and devised the PLATT AMENDMENT. As secretary of state (1905–9), he finalized the ROOT–TAKAHIRA AGREEMENT. He received the Nobel peace prize in 1912 for his work as president of the Carnegie Endowment for World Peace.

Root–Takahira Agreement On 30 November 1908, the US and Japan clarified the TAFT–KATSURA MEMORANDUM with a bilateral exchange of policies that committed each nation to maintain the "existing status quo" in the Pacific, acknowledge each other's possessions in the Pacific, support the OPEN DOOR POLICY, and respect China's sovereignty and territorial integrity. The "status quo" clause legitimated the spheres of influence Japan had carved out in China and Korea, and also prevented the US from increasing its naval strength relative to Japan's.

Rosenberg trial Between 1944 and 1945, the USSR obtained top secret details of the MANHATTAN PROJECT. Convicted for atomic espionage as Soviet agents were Klaus Fuchs in Britain on 1 March 1950, and Harry Gold in the US on 9 December 1950. Gold implicated David and Ruth Greenglass, their in-laws Julius and Ethel Rosenberg, and Morton Sobell, all of whom had been associated with the COMMUNIST PARTY. Admitting their own guilt, Gold and the Greenglasses gave testimony against the Rosenbergs, who insisted that their naming as co-conspirators was part of a plot by Gold and the Greenglasses to win lighter sentences for themselves. On 29 March 1951, a jury found the Rosenbergs and Sobell guilty. All those convicted were given prison sentences except the Rosenbergs, the only defendants who refused to cooperate with prosecutors. After exhausting the appeal process, the Rosenbergs were executed on 19 June 1953 at Sing Sing, N.Y. Ethel Rosenberg's execution was controversial, given her incidental role in the conspiracy, because her indictment seemed part of an effort to pressure her husband into confessing.

Ross, John (b. Rossville, Ga., 3 October 1790; d. Washington, D.C., 1 August 1866) The son of a Scottish trader and a one-quarter Indian woman (his mother belonged to the CHEROKEE INDIANS) Ross served as the principal Cherokee leader (1819–26). In 1827 he induced the Cherokee to adopt a constitution written by himself, which he hoped would some day lead to statehood. Because of the superior education his father provided for him, he was the leading advocate for the redress of his nation's legal grievances and chief opponent of its involuntary removal west. After the TRAIL OF TEARS, he served as senior Cherokee leader and chief diplomatic representative to Washington until his death.

Rostker* v. *Goldberg *see* DRAFT, *and* CRAIG *v.* *BOREN*

ROTC Reserve Officers' Training Corps (*see* NATIONAL DEFENSE ACT, 1916)

Roth* v. *United States On 24 June 1957, the Supreme Court ruled (7–1) that the FIRST AMENDMENT did not protect pornography, and enunciated its first definition of obscenity: material that a typical person would consider as primarily concerned with lewdly exciting sexual desires. The Court revised this understanding of pornography in *MILLER V. CALIFORNIA*.

Rough Riders On 22 April 1898, Congress authorized enlistment of the First US Volunteer Cavalry Regiment for the SPANISH-AMERICAN WAR. Colonel Leonard WOOD and his subordinate, Lieutenant Colonel Theodore ROOSEVELT, recruited mostly westerners, whose horsemanship earned the nickname "Rough Riders." The regiment won widespread publicity for capturing Kettle Hill during the battle of SAN JUAN HILL, in which it lost 86 killed and wounded. The 568 Rough Riders who landed in Cuba sustained the army's highest casualty rate: 37 percent killed or wounded. The unit served 133 days before its demobilization at the end of the war.

royal colonies These were colonies governed directly by a governor appointed by the Crown, as opposed to CHARTER or PROPRIETARY COLONIES. Only West Florida and East Florida originated as royal colonies. Va. was proclaimed a royal colony in 1625, N.H. in 1680, N.Y. in 1685, N.J. in 1702, S.C. in 1721, N.C. in 1729, and Ga. in 1752. Pa. came under royal control temporarily from 1692 to 1694, as did Md. from 1691 to 1715.

RTC *see* RESOLUTION TRUST CORPORATION

Rubin, Jerry *see* CHICAGO EIGHT, *and* YIPPIES

Ruckelshaus, William Doyle (b. Indianapolis, Ind., 24 July 1932) Having entered politics as an Ind. Representative, Ruckelshaus lost a race for the Senate in 1968, was assistant US attorney general (1969–70), and ENVIRONMENTAL PROTECTION AGENCY (EPA) director (1970–2), before being appointed acting FBI director on 30 April 1972. He resigned during the SATURDAY NIGHT MASSACRE rather than fire Archibald COX. He again headed the EPA from March 1983 to January 1985.

Rule of 1756 This term referred to a legal principle regarding the rights of neutral shippers in wartime. It held that if a belligerent nation's commerce had been closed to another country's merchant marine in peacetime, that trade cannot then be opened in wartime. British courts held that neutral ships violating this principle were subject to seizure for aiding the enemy war effort. The ESSEX CASE applied this rule to BROKEN VOYAGES by US shippers in 1805.

Rural Electrification Administration (REA) On 11 May 1935, the REA was created by executive order to lend money to cooperatives and public utility companies for extending power lines to farms. By 1939, it had made low-interest, long-term electification loans to 417 cooperatives. Whereas just 4 percent of farms had access to power lines in 1925, 25 percent had in 1940, and by 1950 few rural homes lay beyond the reach of electricity.

Rural Rehabilitation Program As an agency of the FARM SECURITY ADMINISTRATION, it lent money to small farmers to buy equipment, livestock, or fertilizer for increasing their productivity. From 1937 to 1946, it made 893,000 rehabilitation loans, usually valued between $240 and $600. It also made grants to families who were victims of floods or other natural disasters.

Rush–Bagot Agreement On 16 April 1818, the Senate unanimously approved an agreement based on an exchange of notes by Richard Rush (acting US secretary of state) and Charles Bagot (British ambassador to the US) that ended the prospect of militarizing the Great Lakes. The arrangement limited the number of warships each side could station on the Canadian border, to one on Lake Champlain, one on Lake Ontario, and two on the upper Great Lakes; it also provided that no vessel could exceed 100 tons or carry more than one 18-pound gun. By scaling back naval forces sharply, it paved the way for full demilitarization later in the century.

Rusk, (David) Dean (b. Cherokee County, Ga., 9 February 1909; d. Athens, Ga., 20 December 1994) After holding a Rhodes Scholarship (1933–4) and army duty in World War II, Rusk served in the State Department's Far Eastern office (1946–52), headed the Rockefeller Foundation, and was secretary of state (1961–9). He consistently supported Lyndon JOHNSON's efforts to achieve victory in the VIETNAM WAR, and preferred a military solution to a negotiated settlement as the best guarantee of containing subversion from North Vietnam. He later taught international affairs at the University of Georgia.

Russo, Anthony J. *see* PENTAGON PAPERS

Ruth, "Babe" (George Herman) (b. Baltimore, Md., 6 February 1895; d. New York, N.Y., 16 August 1948) Beginning as a professional baseball player in 1914 with the Boston Red Sox, Ruth was sold to the New York Yankees in 1919. By emerging as a legend in his own time, the "Sultan of Swat," he was primarily responsible for revitalizing public interest in baseball, which had plummeted in 1919 after the scandal of the World Series being thrown. In 22 seasons with the Red Sox, Yankees, and Boston Braves, he hit 714 home runs (a record not broken until 1974, by Hank Aaron) and had a lifetime batting average of .342. The Hall of Fame named Ruth one of its first five members.

Ryan, John E. *see* RESOLUTION TRUST CORPORATION

Ryswick, treaty of (30 September 1697) This treaty ended KING WILLIAM'S WAR. It restored all conquered territories to their prewar status except for British claims on Hudson Bay, which were to be settled by an Anglo-French commission that would meet in 1699.

S

Sabotage Act (20 April 1918) This law forbade obstruction of the US war effort in WORLD WAR I by destroying property or interfering with the production or shipment of military supplies. It was largely aimed at radical labor unions, like the INDUSTRIAL WORKERS OF THE WORLD, who might strike to block war production. There were 10 arrests for anti-US sabotage.

Sac Indians *see* SAUK INDIANS

Sacagawea (b. Montana, ca. 1790; d. Fort Manuel, Mont., 1812) A SHOSHONI who was captured by Gros Ventres at the age of ten, Sacagawea was later bought by Toussaint Charbonneau, a COUREUR DE BOIS, as a wife. She, her husband, and their infant son, accompanied the LEWIS AND CLARK EXPEDITION as interpreters. Her most valuable service was winning friends among her relatives, the Shoshoni, who provided the horses needed to cross the Rockies.

Sacco and Vanzetti trial On 14 July 1921, Nicola Sacco and Bartolomeo Vanzetti received death sentences for the murder on 15 April of a paymaster and guard at a shoe factory in South Braintree, Mass. Because the evidence against them was circumstantial and the jury may have been prejudiced by frequent mention of their radical political beliefs, the verdict was widely condemned as a miscarriage of justice. Governor Alvan Fuller ordered the trial record examined by a special committee, which declared the verdict fair. When the two were executed on 23 August, the act received widespread denunciation in the US and overseas as a political lynching. Whether they were guilty or innocent has never been resolved.

Sackett's Harbor, battle of (N.Y.) On 29 May 1813, Brigadier General Jacob Brown's 650 US regulars and 500 N.Y. militia repulsed an amphibious raid by Sir George Prevost's 1,200 British. US losses: 160 killed, wounded. British losses: 260 killed, wounded.

Sacramento, battle of (Mexico) On 28 February 1847, Colonel Alexander W. Doniphan's First Missouri Regiment (940 men) defeated General Garcia Conde's 2,820 Mexican soldiers and 1,000 rancheros. US losses: 2 dead, 7 wounded. Mexican losses: 300 killed, 500 wounded. Having ended the chance of Mexican invasion from Chihuahua, Doniphan left Mexico.

Safe Drinking Water Act (1974) *see* ENVIRONMENTAL LEGISLATION

Sagadahoc (Maine) On 14 August 1607, Sir George Popham and Raleigh Gilbert led 120 men to the Sagadahoc (lower Kennebec) River and built Fort St George for the PLYMOUTH COMPANY. The colony suffered from lack of strong leadership. Popham died on 5 February 1608, and the settlers abandoned the fort in September 1608.

Sahaptin languages This family of INDIAN LANGUAGES was used by groups in southwestern Idaho, southeastern Wash., and northeastern Oreg. Its speakers included the NEZ PERCE INDIANS, the YAKIMA INDIANS, the Klikitat, Paloos, Tinino, Tyigh, Umatilla, Modoc, and the Wallawalla Indians.

St Augustine (Fla.) On 8 September 1565, Pedro Menendez de Aviles founded "San Augustin," the oldest continuously occupied European settlement in the US. In 1672 construction began on a moated, stone fortress, Castillo de San Marcos, which was still incomplete when Francis Drake ransacked the town on 7 June 1685. In October 1702, S.C. Governor James Moore looted St Augustine with 800 militia and Indians; he besieged the castle (held by Governor Joseph de Zuniga y Cerda's 400 troops) until withdrawing to S.C. on 26 December. On 9

March 1728, Colonel John Palmer's 200 S.C. militia and Indians burned a fortified village of the YAMASEE INDIANS within sight of the castle. Governor Manuel de Montiano's 1,100 Spanish troops withstood a siege by James OGLETHORPE's 1,300 British and 500 Indians (13 June–4 July 1740). In March 1743, Oglethorpe plundered St Augustine, but could not take the castle for lack of artillery.

St Clair's Defeat, battle of On 4 November 1791, Little Turtle's 2,000 Indians routed Major General Arthur St Clair's 2,300 regulars and militia at modern Fort Recovery, Ohio. US losses: 632 killed, 283 wounded. Indian losses: 61 killed. It was the US Army's worst defeat at Indian hands.

Saint-Gaudens, Augustus (b. Dublin, Ireland, 1 March 1848; d. Cornish, N.H., 3 August 1907) Taken to the US as a child, Saint-Gaudens studied sculpture abroad in Paris and Rome. He returned to the US, and became the foremost sculptor of monumental statues through his forceful characterizations and striking poses. He created *Abraham Lincoln* at Chicago's Lincoln Park, the *William Sherman* and *David Farragut memorials* in New York, the *Adams Memorial* (with its hooded *Grief*) at Washington's Rock Creek Cemetery, the *Shaw Memorial* at Boston, *The Puritan* in Springfield, Mass., and the *Charles Stewart Parnell Memorial* in Dublin.

St Lawrence Seaway The Wiley–Dondero Act (13 May 1954) provided funds to develop 400 miles of channels over a 2,000-mile route from Lake Superior to Montreal for ships with 27-foot draft. Upon completion on 25 April 1959, it had cost the US $130,000,000 and Canada $340,000,000; it was the largest waterway project cut since the PANAMA CANAL. In the first year after it opened, the seaway allowed an immediate increase of waterborne cargo from $13,000,000 to $21,000,000 along its route.

St Lô, battle of (France) On 25 July 1944, Allied aircraft laid down a massive carpet bombardment that allowed Lieutenant General George Patton's Third US Army to breach German lines at St Lô. On 1 August, Patton began maneuvers that forced the enemy to retreat east, but not before the Nazis lost 10,000 killed and 50,000 captured. The St Lô breakout enabled the Allies to advance to the Rhine.

St Mihiel offensive (France) On 12–16 September 1918, the ALLIED EXPEDITIONARY FORCE fought its first major independent operation in France. The First Army's 14 divisions (550,000 troops) and 110,000 French troops, overran German positions, captured 443 artillery pieces, and took 16,000 prisoners, but lost 7,000 US casualties.

Ste Foy, battle of *see* QUEBEC, BATTLES OF (2)

Saipan, battle of On 15–17 June 1944, General Holland Smith's Second USMC, Fourth USMC, and Twenty-seventh Army Divisions (71,000 men) landed on Saipan, held by Admiral Chuichi Nagumo's 32,000 Japanese; they ended organized Japanese resistance by 9 July. US losses: 12,000 USMC and 4,000 army casualties. Japanese losses: 30,000 killed or dead by suicide.

"Salary Grab" Act (3 March 1873) Congress raised its own pay from $5,000 to $7,500 (retroactive for two years), doubled the president's salary to $50,000, and increased compensation for the Supreme Court. Public outrage led Congress to repeal its own pay increases on 20 January 1874, although salaries for the president and Supreme Court were not reduced.

Salem witch trials (Mass.) On 29 February 1692, indictments named three women in Salem Village (now Danvers) as witches on the testimony of several young girls. Pretrial examinations were held that spring and the earliest cases were heard in June. By the time Governor William PHIPS suspended the trials on 29 October, 141 persons had been formally indicted, 200 others stood accused but not charged, 19 persons had been hanged, one man was pressed to death in an effort to make him enter a plea when charged, and five prisoners awaited execution. When the trials resumed on 3 January 1693, all the defendants were acquitted except for three, who were sentenced to hang. In May Phips discharged all remaining witchcraft cases and reprieved those awaiting execution. On 17 October 1711, the GENERAL COURT voided the convictions of those hanged and voted £578.12*s* to compensate their heirs. On 28 August 1957, the state legislature passed a resolution condemning the witch trials as tainted by hysteria.

Salerno, battle of (Italy) On 9 September 1943, Lieutenant General Mark Clark's Fifth US Army landed at Salerno, but was almost overwhelmed by AXIS forces until the British Eighth Army's advance relieved the pressure by 15 September. Salerno's success enabled the Allies to begin advancing north to Rome.

Salish languages This family of INDIAN LANGUAGES was originally spoken across British Columbia, northern Wash., northern Idaho, and northwestern Mont., with some branches on the Pacific coast south to Oreg. It is subdivided into 16 languages, including those of the FLATHEAD, Wenatchi, and Nisqualli Indians.

Salk, Jonas (b. New York, N.Y., 28 October 1914) A virologist with an M.D. from the New York University College of Medicine (1939), Salk developed (1951–3) a trial vaccine against poliomyelitis using monkey tissue. The Salk vaccine led to a precipitous decline in polio infections during the late 1950s, and was responsible for the disease's total eradication from the US by 1990. Congress made Salk the first recipient of its Medal for Distinguished Civilian Achievement in 1955.

Salomon, Haym (b. Lissa, Poland, ca. 1740; d. Philadelphia, Pa., 6 January 1785) After emigrating to New York City in 1772, Salomon pursued merchandising until the REVOLUTIONARY WAR. Upon moving to Philadelphia in 1777, he soon became the primary broker in US securities and other notes of indebtedness, and later served as paymaster to French forces in America. He emerged as the lender of last resort for the US Treasury, and by 1784 had used his own credit to furnish loans of about $660,000 in SPECIE. When he died, his estate was insolvent, because the government lacked the funds to honor its debts to him. His heirs were never fully compensated.

SALT *see* STRATEGIC ARMS LIMITATION TREATY, FIRST AND SECOND

Samoa On 17 January 1878, Samoan chieftains approved a treaty of friendship and commerce that allowed the US to build a naval station at Pago Pago. In 1879 the US, Britain, and Germany began treating Samoa like a three-party protectorate. German military intervention on the islands led to a military confrontation with the US and British navies that threatened armed conflict in 1888, until a hurricane on 15–16 March destroyed all warships but a British vessel. On 14 June 1889, at the Berlin conference, the three nations created a condominium and guaranteed the islands' independence. On 16 January 1900, the Senate ratified the treaty of Berlin, by which Britain renounced her claims and Samoa was partitioned between Germany (which gained the western islands) and the US (which gained the eastern islands, where Pago Pago lay). By 1904, Samoan chieftains had ceded their islands to the US. Samoa became a US territory on 4 March 1925, administered by the navy until 1 July 1951, when the Department of the INTERIOR took over. Its first constitution became effective on 17 October 1960 and was revised in 1967. It is a non-self-governing territory, but has been allowed to elect a non-voting delegate to Congress since 1981.

San Antonio Independent School District* v. *Rodriguez On 21 March 1973, the Supreme Court ruled (5–4) that equal protection does not entitle all children in a state to attend schools that receive roughly the same financing per pupil, because education is not a fundamental right guaranteed by the Constitution. Although great differences exist among school districts in the adequacy of their funding by property taxes, the Constitution provides no basis for federal intervention to reallocate tax resources among poor and rich districts. The ruling forced school-reform activists to use state courts for challenging financial disparities among school districts that arose from reliance on property taxes. Of 33 such suits filed through 1993, educational systems were found to violate state guarantees of equal protection under the law in Ala., Ky., Mass., Mont., N.J., N.Dak., Tenn., and Tex.

San Gabriel, battle of (Calif.) On 8–9 January 1847, Commander Robert F. Stockton's 565 US troops defeated Governor Jose Flores's 450 Calif. rancheros and four artillery crews. US losses: 1 dead, 13 wounded. Mexican losses: "considerable" (Stockton's words). The battle ended fighting in Calif.

by dispersing Mexican forces and allowing Stockton to occupy Los Angeles.

San Ildefonso, treaty of On 1 October 1800, Spain secretly transferred its La. colony to France, and confirmed possession by the treaty of Madrid (21 March 1801). Spanish officials continued to administer La. until 1804. The treaty spurred Thomas JEFFERSON to begin negotiations on the LOUISIANA PURCHASE.

San Jacinto, battle of (Tex.) On 21 April 1836, General Samuel Houston's 783 Texans routed President Antonio Lopez de Santa Anna's 1,400 Mexicans. The battle lasted 18 minutes. Texan losses: 9 dead, 30 wounded. Mexican losses: 630 killed, 200 wounded, 730 captured (including Santa Anna). The victory forced Santa Anna to recognize Texan independence.

San Juan Hill, battle of (Cuba) On 1 July 1898, Major General Jacob Kent's 10,000 troops drove General Arsenio Lenares Pomba's 1,200 Spaniards from the ridges above Santiago. Lieutenant Colonel Theodore ROOSEVELT became a national hero for leading his ROUGH RIDERS up Kettle Hill. US losses: 124 killed, 817 wounded. Spanish losses: 358 killed, wounded. Combined with the Spanish loss of EL CANEY, victory allowed US artillery to begin shelling the enemy fleet, which was then forced into the battle of SANTIAGO BAY.

San Lorenzo, treaty of On 27 October 1795, Thomas PINCKNEY signed this treaty at Madrid, by which Spain recognized the line set by the treaty of PARIS (1783) (31° latitude) as the southern US border and granted Americans the RIGHT OF DEPOSIT at New Orleans for three years. The Senate ratified it on 15 March 1796. The treaty stimulated settlement of the Ohio valley by providing an overseas outlet for western produce.

San Mateo Company* v. *Southern Pacific Railroad *see* *SANTA CLARA COUNTY* V. *SOUTHERN PACIFIC RAILROAD COMPANY*

San Pasqual, battle of (Calif.) On 6 December 1846, Captain Andres Pico's 160 California lancers defeated Colonel Stephen W. Kearney's 85 US regulars and then besieged the survivors. US losses: 18 killed, 13 wounded, 1 howitzer. Mexican losses: 27 dead, wounded. On 10 December, 180 US troops from San Diego drove off Pico's men. Kearney's men gave critical support that allowed US forces to win the battle of SAN GABRIEL and occupy Los Angeles.

Sand Creek massacre (Colo.) On 29 November 1864, Colonel John Chivington's 700 Colo. troops (with four howitzers) attacked 500 nonhostile CHEYENNE INDIANS who had sought US Army protection at Fort Lyon. Colo. losses: 9 killed, 38 wounded. Cheyenne losses: 200 killed.

Sandburg, Carl (b. Galesburg, Ill., 6 January 1878; d. Flatrock, N.C., 22 July 1967) After serving in the Spanish-American War, Sandburg attended Lombard College (Ill.) without graduating. While a Chicago newspaper reporter, he began publishing poems in journals. Verse in *Poetry* magazine (1914) won him critical acclaim, and *Chicago Poems* (1915) established his reputation. He received the Pulitzer prize for *Complete Poems* (1950). His poetry was characterized by bold expression and deep – if unsubtle – emotions. He authored a comprehensive, insightful, and gracefully composed biography of Abraham LINCOLN in six volumes, of which *The War Years* (1939) received the Pulitzer prize in history.

Sanger, Margaret Higgins (b. Corning, N.Y., 14 September 1879; d. Tucson, Ariz., 6 September 1966) She blamed the poverty of her youth on her parents' raising of 11 children. She joined the INDUSTRIAL WORKERS OF THE WORLD, and emerged as an early proponent of sexual education and family planning, for which she coined the term birth control. In 1914, she faced prosecution for violating postal regulations against mailing indecent materials (her publications on contraception), but in 1936 won a federal court ruling that legalized their shipment to doctors. In 1921 she founded the American Birth Control League (renamed the Planned Parenthood Federation of America in 1942). She founded hundreds of physician-supervised birth control clinics during her career.

Santa Clara County* v. *Southern Pacific Railroad Company In 1886 the Supreme Court held unanimously that the FOURTEENTH AMENDMENT intended that corporations be entitled to claim protection as legal persons from state violations of their civil rights. (That interpretation was first made in arguments presented during the adjudication of *San Mateo County* v. *Southern Pacific Railroad* in 1882.) The decision enabled businesses to challenge unfavorable decisions by state regulatory commissions with lawsuits claiming to have been deprived of their property (anticipated profits) without DUE PROCESS of law. The ruling reversed the Court's pro-regulatory position in the GRANGER CASES, and was later elaborated in *CHICAGO, MILWAUKEE AND SAINT PAUL RAILROAD COMPANY* v. *MINNESOTA* and *REAGAN* v. *FARMERS' LOAN AND TRUST COMPANY*, and *SMYTH* v. *AMES*. Because federal courts so often overruled decisions by state commissions under suit by corporations, the decision contributed to the growing ineffectiveness of state regulation and led to demands for federal laws to control public carriers and monopolies.

Santa Cruz Islands, battle of On 26 October 1942, Admiral Chiuchi Nagumo's carrier force (3 carriers, 2 battleships, 5 cruisers, 15 destroyers) defeated Admiral Thomas Kinkaid's task force (2 carriers, 1 battleship, 6 cruisers, 14 destroyers). US losses: 1 carrier sunk, 1 destroyer torpedoed, 50 planes destroyed. Japanese losses: over 100 planes destroyed.

Santa Fe Trail This trail connected N.Mex. with Mo. via the Arkansas River. When Mexico became independent in 1821, it ceased enforcing Spanish regulations that forbade trade with US merchants. In 1821–2, William Becknell of Mo. made a profitable business trip between Santa Fe and Franklin, Mo. The commerce over the trail grew so large by 1825, that Thomas H. BENTON persuaded Congress to fund an army survey of the route. The trail was 800 miles long and required about 10 weeks for loaded wagons. Half the US merchandise was resold by Mexican merchants in Chihuahua.

Santiago Bay, battle of (Cuba) On 3 July 1898, to avoid capture at Santiago following US victories at EL CANEY and SAN JUAN HILL, Admiral Pascual Cervera y Topete's squadron tried to escape the US blockade. Commodore Winfield Schley's five battleships and two cruisers (76 guns, 2,341 sailors) destroyed all of Cervera's four cruisers and two destroyers (42 guns, 2,261 sailors). US losses: 1 killed, 1 wounded, 3 ships hit by enemy fire. Spanish losses: 323 killed, 151 wounded, 1,720 captured. The victory left Spain no alternative but to accept US terms to end the SPANISH-AMERICAN WAR.

Santo Domingo, annexation of In 1869 Ulysses S. GRANT directed Orville Babcock, his secretary, to negotiate a treaty for US annexation of Santo Domingo, which seemed likely to be annexed by European powers and could serve as a refuge for US blacks to create their own society. The Senate rejected the treaty on 30 June 1870.

Saratoga, battle of (N.Y.) *see* BEMIS HEIGHTS *and* FREEMAN'S FARM, BATTLES OF

Saratoga, surrender at (N.Y.) On 17 October 1777, after defeats at FREEMAN'S FARM and BEMIS HEIGHTS, Major General John Burgoyne surrendered his army to Major General Horatio Gates at Saratoga (now Schuylerville), N.Y.: 300 officers (including 7 generals), 3,379 redcoats, and 2,412 HESSIANS. Saratoga was the turning-point of the REVOLUTIONARY WAR. By proving US military prowess against the British army, it won French recognition of US independence on 6 February 1778 and French entry into the war on 17 June 1778.

Sargent, John Singer (b. Florence, Italy, 12 January 1856; d. London, England, 15 April 1925) Born abroad of US parents, Sargent studied painting at Florence and Paris, and did not visit the US until the age of 20. During the 1870s, while working in Europe, he won international acclaim for his portraits and family groups. He returned to the US in 1887, and received major commissions to do murals for Boston's Public Library, its Art Museum, and Harvard's Widener Library. He ranked as his generation's leading portraitist for his mastery of technique and evocation of character. After returning to London, he was offered a knighthood in 1907, but declared himself ineligible as a US citizen.

Saturday night massacre On Saturday, 20 October 1973, Richard NIXON fired Attorney General Elliot RICHARDSON and Deputy Attorney General William RUCKELSHAUS for refusing to fire Special Prosecutor Archibald COX, who had subpoenaed several incriminating White House documents concerning the WATERGATE SCANDAL. Upon being named acting attorney general, Solicitor General Robert BORK carried out Nixon's order. The event galvanized the House Judiciary Committee into calling hearings to investigate impeachment charges against Nixon on 30 October.

Sauk Indians Speakers of one of the ALGONQUIAN LANGUAGES, the Sauks may have numbered 3,500 about 1650, when they lived around Lake Michigan. They cooperated closely with the FOX INDIANS, but never merged with them. In April 1712, both groups went to war with the French by attacking Fort Ponchartrain (Detroit), but were defeated and resettled in Iowa. By 1800, most of the 4,000 Sauks lived on the east bank of the Mississippi around Rock Island, Ill. In 1804 the Sauks ceded their Ill. lands by treaty to the US, but were allowed to remain there until the area was opened for settlement. Alienated by that treaty, many Sauks fought as British allies in the WAR OF 1812. Refusal to abandon their Ill. lands resulted in the BLACK HAWK WAR and forcible relocation to Iowa. They eventually sold all their Iowa lands and went to Kans. with the Foxes in 1845. They now have reservation headquarters at Horton, Kans., and Shawnee, Okla.

Savage's Station, battle of (Va.) *see* PENINSULAR CAMPAIGN

Savannah, battles of (Ga.) (1) On 29 December 1778, having learned from slaves where the town's defenses were weakest, Lieutenant Colonel Archibald Campbell's 3,500 British captured Savannah from Major General Robert Howe's 850 defenders. US losses: 83 killed, 11 wounded, 453 captured, 48 cannon, 23 mortars, and 6 warships. British losses: 7 killed, 19 wounded.

(2) From 22 September to 9 October 1779, Admiral General Count d'Estaing's 3,500 French and Major General Charles Lincoln's 1,500 Americans fruitlessly besieged Savannah. US losses: 125 killed, 332 wounded. French losses: 183 killed, 454 wounded. British losses: 40 killed, 62 wounded, 48 captured. Britain held Savannah until 11 July 1782. (*See* MARCH TO THE SEA)

savings and loan crisis As part of DEREGULATION in 1982, Congress passed the Thrift Institutions Restructuring Act, for which the home-mortgage industry had strongly lobbied. The law freed thrifts from restrictions that limited their activities to financing home loans with savings deposits, and gave them enormous latitude to invest their capital in commercial real estate, various financial instruments, and foreign loans. After a national real-estate boom collapsed due to overcapacity, and other loans became nonperforming, 748 thrifts (with deposits of $220 billion) went into federal receivership and their depositors had to be reimbursed by the Federal Savings and Loan Insurance Corporation. The savings and loan industry generated net losses until 1990. By February 1994, the savings and loan industry had contracted from 3,147 thrifts with assets of $1.35 trillion to 1,719 thrifts with assets of $785 billion. The RESOLUTION TRUST CORPORATION was formed to dispose of insolvent trusts, and by early 1994 it had spent $250 billion liquidating government liabilities (more than the cost of WORLD WAR II) and incurred losses of $136 billion.

Savo Island, battle of On 8–9 August 1942, en route to attack troop transports off GUADALCANAL, Vice Admiral Guichi Mikawa's 7 cruisers and 1 destroyer defeated Rear Admiral Richmond Turner's 6 cruisers and 4 destroyers, but withdrew without destroying USMC invasion transports. US losses: 3 US cruisers, 1 Australian destroyer, 1,000 casualties. Japanese losses: minimal.

scalawags During RECONSTRUCTION, southern Democrats referred to white southerners who ran for office as Republicans, as scalawags, a word meaning scoundrel or rascal. Most such individuals were moderates on racial issues who had been Whigs (*see* WHIG PARTY) before the CIVIL WAR, or who joined with the Republicans to prevent the government's complete domination by FREEDMEN and CARPETBAGGERS. Many voted Democratic after the COMPROMISE OF 1877.

Scales* v. *United States On 5 June 1961, the Supreme Court ruled (5–4) that the FIRST AMENDMENT does not forbid laws that impose restrictions and penalties upon members of an organization formed to promote the government's violent overthrow.

Schechter Poultry Corporation* v. *United States ("sick chicken case") On 27 May

1935, the Supreme Court unanimously struck down the NATIONAL INDUSTRIAL RECOVERY ACT for infringing the states' authority to regulate intrastate commerce and for violating the balance of power by improperly delegating legislative powers to the president for devising fair business competition codes.

Schenck* v. *United States On 3 March 1919, the Supreme Court unanimously held that the ESPIONAGE ACT did not violate the FIRST AMENDMENT, which offered no protection for speech that endangered the community, particularly in wartime. The Court upheld the sentence of a man convicted of publishing an anti-DRAFT pamphlet, because his words posed a "clear and present danger" of undermining the war effort.

Schenectady, raid on (N.Y.) On 9 February 1690, 114 Canadians and 96 Indians burned Schenectady, N.Y. N.Y. losses: 60 killed, 27 captured. French losses: 1 French and 1 Indian killed during attack, 17 French and 4 Indians killed by pursuing N.Y. militia. More lives were lost at Schenectady than at any other massacre in the French and Indian Wars.

Schmitz, John G. *see* AMERICAN INDEPENDENT PARTY

Schurz, Carl (b. Liblar, Germany, 2 March 1829; d. New York, N.Y., 14 May 1906) He emigrated to the US as a FORTY-EIGHTER. He helped found the REPUBLICAN PARTY, supported Abraham LINCOLN in 1860, and was made ambassador to Spain (1860–2) and Union general (1862–5). After editing a St Louis German-language paper, he served as senator (1869–75). He helped organize the LIBERAL REPUBLICAN PARTY and was a prominent MUGWUMP. He was secretary of the interior (1877–81), edited the New York *Evening Post* (1881–3), and headed the National Civil Service Reform League (1892–1900).

Schwarzkopf, Norman K. *see* PERSIAN GULF WAR

scientific management *see* TAYLORISM

SCLC *see* SOUTHERN CHRISTIAN LEADERSHIP CONFERENCE

Scopes trial After Tenn. enacted a law forbidding public school teachers to teach the theory of biological evolution, the AMERICAN CIVIL LIBERTIES UNION financed a test case involving John T. Scopes of Dayton (defended by Clarence DARROW). National coverage of the trial (10–21 July 1925), especially H. L. MENCKEN's reporting, portrayed it as a modern-day witchhunt that threatened both science and freedom of speech. Scopes was found guilty and fined $100, but the case was a watershed event that discredited Protestant fundamentalism as backward and intolerant. The trial's publicity hastened the gradual loss of the influence exerted by religious values on American life.

SCORE *see* SERVICE CORPS OF RETIRED EXECUTIVES

Scotch-Irish immigration Properly termed Scots-Irish, they were Protestant Irish whose families settled Ulster from Scotland in the Tudor–Stuart period. Driven from the land by RACK-RENTING, large numbers began coming to the colonies about 1718, and probably 66,000 had arrived by 1775. By 1790, perhaps 10.5 percent of all whites were Scotch-Irish in descent. The 1990 census counted 4,334,197 persons who described their primary ethnic identity as Scotch-Irish, 2.2 percent of all whites (not including those who simply gave their background as Scots or Irish).

Scott, Winfield (b. near Petersburg, Va., 13 June 1786; d. West Point, N.Y., 29 May 1866) In the WAR OF 1812, Scott rose to brigadier general and became a national hero after victories at CHIPPEWA RIVER and LUNDY'S LANE. He fought in the SEMINOLE and BLACK HAWK WARS, was given the army's command in June 1841, and led US forces to victory in the MEXICAN WAR. Scott ran for president for the WHIG PARTY in 1852, but lost. Nicknamed "Old Fuss and Feathers" for emphasizing details, he was too overweight to mount a horse by the CIVIL WAR; he drafted the ANACONDA PLAN, then gave up the army's command on 1 November 1861.

Scottish immigration An estimated 35,000 Scots came to the THIRTEEN COLONIES before 1775, and their descendants equaled about 5 percent of all whites in 1790. By 1820, the Scottish stock equaled about 390,000 persons and doubled every 30 years by natural increase. From 1820 to 1900, 368,280 Scots arrived in the US, and another 381,625 had come by 1950. The 1990 census counted 3,315,306 persons who reported their primary ethnic identity as Scottish, 1.7 percent of all whites.

Scottsboro case, first (*Powell* v. *Alabama*) On 7 November 1932, the Supreme Court ruled (7–2) that the FOURTEENTH AMENDMENT'S DUE PROCESS clause obliged state courts to uphold the SIXTH AMENDMENT'S guarantee that defendants in capital cases receive adequate legal counsel in preparing their defense. It overturned the conviction of several blacks charged with assaulting white women.

Scottsboro case, second (*Norris* v. *Alabama*) On 1 April 1935, the Supreme Court ruled (8–0) that the FOURTEENTH AMENDMENT'S DUE PROCESS clause obliged state courts to uphold the SIXTH AMENDMENT'S guarantee that defendants in capital cases be tried by an impartial jury. In a retrial of the first SCOTTSBORO CASE, it overturned the defendants' conviction because blacks were excluded from the jury deciding the case, and because extreme racial prejudice dominated the court atmosphere.

Seabury, Samuel *see* PROTESTANT EPISCOPAL CHURCH

Seale, Bobby (Robert G.) (b. Dallas, Tex., 22 October 1937) He grew up in Oakland, Calif., where he founded the BLACK PANTHER PARTY with Huey NEWTON. He was indicted for conspiracy to incite riot at the 1968 Democratic convention at Chicago, as part of the VIETNAM ANTIWAR MOVEMENT. On 5 November 1970, he was sentenced to four years in jail for contempt of court while on trial, but the sentence was later overturned on appeal. In 1971 his trial for murdering a fellow Black Panther in New Haven, Conn., ended in a hung verdict and charges were dismissed on 25 May. He ran unsuccessfully for mayor of Oakland in 1973.

SEATO *see* SOUTHEAST ASIAN TREATY ORGANIZATION

SEC *see* SECURITIES AND EXCHANGE COMMISSION

secession Following Abraham LINCOLN'S election, 11 slave states seceded from the Union. The "first secession" included seven states that left before Lincoln took office: beginning with S.C. (20 December 1860), then Miss. (9 January 1861), Fla. (10 January), Ala. (11 January), Ga. (19 January), La. (26 January), and Tex. (1 February). These seven formed the CONFEDERACY. After FORT SUMTER'S fall, a "second secession" added four states to the Confederacy: Va. (17 April), Ark. (6 May), Tenn. (7 May), and N.C. (20 May). Two BORDER STATES (whose legislatures refused to secede) were admitted as Confederate states after pro-southern citizens held conventions and voted to leave the Union: Mo. (31 October 1861) and Ky. (18 November 1861). The CSA constitution denied any state the right to secede. In *TEXAS* v. *WHITE*, the US Supreme Court ruled secession unconstitutional.

Second Amendment Submitted to the states on 25 September 1789, last ratified by Va. on 15 December 1791, and officially proclaimed on 30 December 1791, it guaranteed the right of citizens to keep and bear arms to ensure state militias could mobilize a force of men with weapons to counteract federal threats on their rights. No Supreme Court decision has ever definitively interpreted this amendment.

Second Great Awakening A great outburst of religious enthusiasm occurred simultaneously among New Englanders and westerners about 60 years after the First GREAT AWAKENING. Its New England phase developed gradually from efforts by college administrators like president Timothy DWIGHT of Yale to combat Deism with orthodox Calvinism. Revivals began among students about 1800 and spread to the general community. Its western phase erupted dramatically in August 1801 at the CANE RIDGE CAMP MEETING. Revivalism spread rapidly through the Ohio valley by means of camp meetings, which first assumed a key role in evangelization during the Second Great Awakening. Other innovations included nonstop "relay preaching" by teams of ministers and the incubation of conversions by isolating anxious penitents on "sinners' benches" while the crowd prayed for their salvation. The revivals' intensity peaked before 1810, but they influenced the next generation of evangelists to revive their techniques in the 1830s.

Second Hundred Days After his setback in *SCHECHTER POULTRY CORPORATION* v. *UNITED STATES*, Franklin D. ROOSEVELT initiated much of his SECOND NEW DEAL while keeping Congress in special session in the summer of 1935. He used executive orders to establish the NATIONAL RESOURCES COMMITTEE and NATIONAL YOUTH ADMINISTRATION. Congress passed the NATIONAL LABOR RELATIONS ACT, Social Security (*see* SOCIAL SECURITY ADMINISTRATION), MOTOR CARRIER ACT, BANKING ACT (1935), PUBLIC UTILITY HOLDING COMPANY ACT, FARM MORTGAGE MORATORIUM ACT, Wagner–Crosser Railroad Retirement Act (*see* RAILROAD RETIREMENT ACTS), GUFFEY–SNYDER BITUMINOUS COAL STABILIZATION ACT, and the WEALTH TAX ACT.

Second New Deal The NEW DEAL's final phase began with Franklin D. ROOSEVELT's 4 January 1935 message to Congress, in which he advocated a system of Social Security (*see* SOCIAL SECURITY ADMINISTRATION) and more federal hiring of the jobless. Its most productive period was the SECOND HUNDRED DAYS of mid-1935. Rather than try to manage the national economy by federal agencies and industry-wide business codes as in the FIRST NEW DEAL, the Second New Deal accepted a competitive marketplace based on free enterprise. It attempted to prevent concentrations of economic power and prevent monopolies by traditional solutions of the PROGRESSIVE ERA, like government regulation and antitrust laws. It nevertheless continued government overview of the farming sector by setting acreage allotments to restrict production, and assigning a federal responsibility to maintain PARITY for commodity prices. Also characterizing the Second New Deal was social reform legislation and expanded legal protections for labor. After the RECESSION OF 1937–8, which was blamed on a cutback in federal expenditures, the Roosevelt administration also accepted a greater willingness to stimulate the economy by deficit spending. The Second New Deal was over by 1940, when the government's focus shifted to foreign affairs and rearmament.

second party system This term refers to the partisan competition that resulted after the DEMOCRATIC PARTY split in the 1830s, and the WHIG PARTY fought the Jacksonian Democrats for the government's control. After the Whigs disintegrated during the 1850s, the REPUBLICANS quickly emerged to challenge the Democrats.

secondary boycott When engaged in a strike or other labor dispute, unions organized secondary boycotts by picketing companies that did business with their employer, to pressure management into concessions in order to avoid losing valuable customers whose own operations were then threatened by strikers. The Supreme Court held them to be unlawful conspiracies in restraint of trade in *LOEWE V. LAWLER*. Congress allowed secondary boycotts by the CLAYTON ANTITRUST ACT, but the Court again ruled against their use in *DUPLEX PRINTING PRESS COMPANY V. DEERING*. The NORRIS–LA GUARDIA ACT forbade the use of injunctions against them. The TAFT–HARTLEY ACT outlawed all secondary boycotts.

secret ballot *see* AUSTRALIAN BALLOT

Secret Service On 5 July 1865, Congress established the Secret Service to detect and arrest counterfeiters. Until the FBI was formed, it was responsible for investigating violations of federal laws and foreign espionage. The Secret Service received the task of protecting the life of the president in 1901, the life of the president-elect in 1913, the lives of the first family in 1917, the life of the vice-president in 1951, the lives of former presidents and first ladies in 1965, the lives of major candidates for president and vice-president in 1968, and the lives of visiting heads of state in 1971.

secretary of defense *see* NATIONAL SECURITY ACT

Securities Act (1933) *see* FEDERAL SECURITIES ACT

Securities and Exchange Commission (SEC) Established by the SECURITIES EXCHANGE ACT and later responsible for implementing the PUBLIC UTILITY HOLDING COMPANY ACT, it began operations under Joseph KENNEDY. He molded the SEC into an organization that tried to avoid undue interference in the stock market's operation by relying on self-enforcement by brokerage firms, but that impartially pursued charges of malfeasance.

Securities Exchange Act (6 June 1934) This law resulted from the PECORA

HEARINGS, which produced outrage over revelations of fraud in the financial markets. It amended the FEDERAL SECURITIES ACT (1933) and created the SECURITIES AND EXCHANGE COMMISSION (SEC) to enforce it. The law charged the SEC with preventing insider trading and stock manipulation, with protecting investors from dishonest practices, and with licensing dealers to trade in securities. However, the SEC lost the power to set margin requirements to the FEDERAL RESERVE SYSTEM.

Sedition Act (14 July 1798) This statute made sedition a high misdemeanor and defined the crime not only as efforts to incite rebellion or disobedience to federal laws, but also as a wide range of speech or writing concerned with political debate. Written broadly to forbid attempts to bring the US government into disrepute, its literal wording could be interpreted to prohibit any criticism of officials of the FEDERALIST PARTY, who then controlled the executive and legislative departments, even criticism made as part of the upcoming presidential election of 1800. Federalist prosecutors filed sedition charges against 17 persons, including editors of four of the five largest newspapers supporting the DEMOCRATIC PARTY, and won 10 convictions (among them Democratic congressman Matthew Lyon of Vt., who had to run for reelection from jail, but won). The law expired on 3 March 1801.

Sedition Act (16 May 1918) This measure amended the ESPIONAGE ACT by outlawing spoken or written efforts to subvert the US war effort in WORLD WAR I, but by encompassing several vague offenses, it permitted socialists and labor radicals to be prosecuted for expressing unpopular views. Forbidden were not only seditious attempts "to interfere with the operation or success of the [US] military or naval forces," but any activities which would "willfully utter, print, write, or publish any disloyal, profane, scurrilous, or abusive language about the form of government of the United States, or the Constitution of the United States, or the flag." Anyone who advocated, taught, defended, or suggested carrying out any such activities could be fined $10,000 and given five years in prison. By 1921, there had been 1,055 convictions out of 2,168 prosecutions for espionage or sedition, including Victor BERGER, Eugene DEBS, and William HAYWOOD. It was held constitutional in *ABRAMS* v. *UNITED STATES*.

segregation This is the official or unnofficial practice of limiting physical contact or personal interaction between the races. Before 1800, segregation laws were rare, except for bans on interracial marriage, which was outlawed in seven of the THIRTEEN COLONIES between 1664 (Md.) and 1798 (R.I.). Between 1780 and 1860, a haphazard pattern of DE FACTO SEGREGATION appeared in the North, where neighborhoods were usually exclusive by race, and in southern cities, where housing was mixed but blacks increasingly were excluded from some public places (hotels, restaurants, etc.) or set apart from whites in churches, hospitals, jails, etc.

In the South after 1865, segregation continued in churches, schools, military units, and government facilities, but blacks commonly had equal access to public accommodations and shared seats on transportation carriers with whites. Racial separation initially resulted from custom or local initiatives, but after 1890, southern legislatures instituted a system of DE JURE SEGREGATION to govern race relations according to consistent, inflexible rules. States first made separate seating mandatory on railroads, then streetcars and steamboats, and extended the principle to separate waiting rooms at depots and public places. The scope of these JIM CROW LAWS gradually spread, and after 1910, they began mandating residential segregation. By 1920, southern Jim Crow laws prohibited most interaction between whites and blacks outside the workplace. De facto segregation in housing and education hardened in the north.

PLESSY v. *FERGUSON* (1896) placed most segregation laws beyond legal challenge until its reversal by *BROWN* v. *BOARD OF EDUCATION OF TOPEKA* (1954). Responding to the CIVIL RIGHTS MOVEMENT, Congress passed the CIVIL RIGHTS ACTS (1964 and 1968). *LOVING* v. *VIRGINIA* outlawed anti-MISCEGENATION laws. De facto segregation nevertheless continued to shape patterns of housing and education, especially in the North and West. By the 1991–2 school year, 66 percent of black children attended predominantly nonwhite schools, and 34 percent of them went to schools that were 90–100 percent minority.

Seidman, L. William *see* RESOLUTION TRUST CORPORATION

Selective Service Act (18 May 1917) This law revived the DRAFT for WORLD WAR I, and created the modern system of selective service based primarily on age, marital status, and occupational criteria. It functioned by a decentralized system of over 4,000 local draft boards. The Manpower Act (31 August 1918) directed it to register all males aged 18–45. The law provided 45 percent of all military personnel; it was ruled constitutional in *ARVER V. UNITED STATES*.

Selective Service Act (1940) *see* SELECTIVE TRAINING AND SERVICE ACT

selective service system *see* DRAFT

Selective Training and Service Act (16 September 1940) This law established the first US peacetime DRAFT. It registered all men aged 21–35 and funded a 12-month training program for 1,200,000 regulars and 800,000 NATIONAL GUARD. Its first lottery was 29 October 1940. On 12 August 1941, by one vote, Congress extended it for 18 months to keep the army at full strength. The law and its amendments instituted the WORLD WAR II draft, which expired on 26 July 1947.

Selma freedom march (Ala.) To protest the use of intimidation and illegal stratagems to keep blacks from voting in Dallas County, Ala., Martin Luther KING tried to lead 500 followers in a protest march from Selma, the county seat, to Montgomery, on 7 March 1965, but the marchers were blocked by police who brutally beat and tear-gassed them. Widespread media publicity drew volunteers nationwide to join the march after it was approved by a federal judge. On 25 March, King and 25,000 supporters finished the five-day, 54-mile walk to Montgomery and called for a boycott of Ala. products until restrictions on black voting were ended. The march was influential in winning passage of the VOTING RIGHTS ACT (1965).

Seminole Indians These were CREEK INDIANS who established villages in Fla. in the 1700s and adapted to the local environment. By accepting runaway slaves as tribal members and raiding settlers in Ga. and Ala., they provoked the first SEMINOLE WAR. When most Seminoles followed OSCEOLA's lead in refusing to be moved to Okla. in the 1830s, a second war resulted that led to all but a few hundred being shipped across the Mississippi by force. Seminole reservations exist in Okla. at Wewoka and in Fla. in Hendry, Glades, and Broward counties.

Seminole wars (1) When US forces destroyed Fort Apalachicola (recently occupied by the British) in Spanish Fla., local SEMINOLE INDIANS and runaway slaves began raiding the US frontier. On 21 November 1817, Major General Andrew JACKSON invaded Fla. with 500 US regulars, 1,000 militia, and 2,000 CREEK INDIANS. Jackson burned Seminole towns, captured St Marks (7 April) and Pensacola (24 May), and executed two Britons for arming hostile Indians. The campaign ended on 31 October 1818, and influenced Spanish concessions in the ADAMS–ONIS TREATY.

(2) Repudiating the treaties of Payne's Landing (1832) and Fort Gibson (1833), OSCEOLA's followers refused to leave Fla. for Okla. Seminole resistance escalated into full-scale war by 28 December 1835, when Indians annihilated 110 regulars near Ocala. Pitched battles continued until Colonel Zachary TAYLOR defeated a large hostile force near Lake Okeechobee in December 1837. Using deceit, Major General Thomas Jessup apprehended Osceola in September 1837, and then threatened the Indians with starvation by destroying their crops. When the army officially terminated the war on 10 May 1842, only a few hundred renegades were still at large and 3,824 Seminoles had been sent to Okla. The campaign required 10,169 US regulars, of whom 328 were killed in combat and 1,138 died of disease. Thirty thousand militia were called out at various times, of whom 55 died in combat. The navy lost 69 dead.

(3) From December 1857 to May 1858, small roving parties of Seminoles skirmished with the Fourth Artillery around Fort Brooke, Fla.

Seneca Falls convention (N.Y.) On 19 July 1848, the first women's rights conference convened in the US to discuss "social, civil, and religious conditions and rights of women," under the leadership of Lucretia

MOTT and Elizabeth Cady STANTON. It issued a Declaration of Sentiments demanding the right to vote and an end to all discriminatory legislation against women.

Seneca Indians These were the westernmost and largest of the FIVE NATIONS. Of the IROQUOIS CONFEDERACY, they were the least attached to the English, and many fought with the French in the SEVEN YEARS' WAR and in PONTIAC'S WAR. By 1775, they numbered over 4,000, almost half the Iroquois. They inhabited all of N.Y. west of Elmira, but many also lived along the Allegheny River in Pa. and along the Ohio, where they were known as Mingos. Senecas fought for Britain in the REVOLUTIONARY WAR and lost their villages in SULLIVAN'S and BRODHEAD'S CAMPAIGNS; so many lost their lives or moved to Canada, that just 1,800 inhabited N.Y. by 1797 and their reservations covered only 310 square miles. They now possess four reservations in N.Y. and one in Okla., and share the Iroquois Confederacy tract at Oshweken, Ontario.

Senior Companion Program *see* ACTION

separate but equal This phrase summarized the legal philosophy behind DE JURE SEGREGATION in the US. The Supreme Court declared SEGREGATION laws constitutional so long as they met this test of *PLESSY v. FERGUSON*, but reversed itself in *BROWN v. BOARD OF EDUCATION OF TOPEKA* (1954).

separating Puritans This wing of PURITANISM rejected the concept of an established, state church, and insisted that each congregation enjoy complete autonomy to call and dismiss its minister. The ecclesiastical structure of PLYMOUTH and RHODE ISLAND was organized along the principle of separation.

Sequoyah (b. Tuskegee Town, Tenn., ca. 1770; d. Matamoros, Mexico, 1843) Also known as George Gist, Sequoyah was the son of a white explorer and a CHEROKEE INDIAN woman. He fought with the whites in the CREEK WAR. In 1818 he joined the first Cherokee migration west and moved to Pope County, Ark. In 1821 he perfected a written version of Cherokee, upon which he had been working since 1809, based on a new alphabet of 86 characters. In 1828 his system was used to publish the first Indian-language newspaper, the *Cherokee Phoenix*. In 1839 he described himself as president of the Western Cherokee.

Serra, Junipero (b. Majorca, Spain, 24 November 1713; d. Carmel, Calif., 28 August 1784) In 1730 Serra became a Franciscan priest. He gave up the life of a university professor in 1749 to become a missionary in Mexico. He accompanied the first Spanish expedition to settle Calif. and founded its first mission at San Diego on 16 July 1769. Serra was the father of Calif. missions, and established nine of the 21 founded by Franciscans.

Service Corps of Retired Executives (SCORE) This organization was formed in 1964 to allow small businessmen to obtain free advice and counseling from retired executives on financial problems or administrative difficulties. It became part of ACTION in 1971 and enrolled about 5,000 volunteer consultants, but was later discontinued

Seton, Elizabeth Ann Bayley (b. New York, N.Y., 28 August 1774; d. Emmitsburg, Md., 4 January 1821) In 1797 Seton founded the Society for the Relief of Poor Widows with Small Children in New York. While traveling in Italy with her husband, she was widowed and exposed to Catholicism (*see* CATHOLIC CHURCH). She became a Catholic in March 1805. In 1809, at Baltimore, she opened a Catholic elementary school, the first parochial school in the US. In 1810 she founded the first American order of nuns, the Sisters of Charity of St Joseph, and started St Joseph College for women, which she located at Emmitsburg, Md. She was pronounced venerable in 1959 and beatified in 1963.

seven days' battles (Va.) *see* PENINSULAR CAMPAIGN

Seven Pines, battle of (Va.) *see* PENINSULAR CAMPAIGN

Seven Years' War This war originated over disputed land claims to the Ohio valley. In 1753 French troops built Fort Presqu'Ile, Fort Le Boef, and Fort Machault within Pa.'s borders. In 1754 the French expelled an advance party of Va. troops sent by Colonel George WASHINGTON to fortify the forks of the Ohio, and then erected FORT DUQUESNE. Washington ambushed a French patrol 50 miles from Fort Duquesne on 28 May and the French retaliated by attacking his base at FORT NECESSITY, which the Virginians surrendered on 4 July.

Britain ordered a three-pronged offensive in 1755 to drive French troops from Fort Duquesne, CROWN POINT in N.Y., and Forts Beausejour and Gaspereau in Acadia. The French routed British forces eight miles from Fort Duquesne at BRADDOCK'S DEFEAT. Colonial militia defeated a French and Indian expedition at the battle of LAKE GEORGE, but then abandoned their advance on Crown Point. British forces took the French garrisons in Acadia, and then expelled 6,000 ACADIANS to the thirteen colonies.

GEORGE II formally declared war on France on 17 May 1756. The Marquis de Montcalm kept the British on the defensive by encouraging Indian raids on the frontier while he captured OSWEGO in 1756, took FORT WILLIAM HENRY in 1757, and inflicted massive British losses while defending FORT TICONDEROGA in 1758. Under Prime Minister William PITT and Major General Jeffery AMHERST, Britain resumed the offensive in 1758 by capturing the fortresses of LOUISBOURG, FORT FRONTENAC, and Fort Duquesne.

In 1759 Amherst directed the capture of FORT NIAGARA, Fort Ticonderoga, and crown point. Brigadier General James WOLFE occupied QUEBEC (1759) by his victory at the PLAINS OF ABRAHAM. After a French siege failed to regain Quebec in 1760, Amherst took MONTREAL and accepted Canada's formal surrender on 8 September.

Fighting then shifted to the frontier. Although French defeat ended Indian raids in the north, the CHEROKEE WAR erupted in early 1760 and continued until the summer of 1761. PONTIAC'S WAR was a later consequence of the Seven Years' War.

Britain declared war on Spain on 2 January 1762. Troops from North America helped take HAVANA, Cuba, in October. Britain capped its victory by acquiring Canada and Florida in the treaty of PARIS (1763).

The war produced America's first large-scale military mobilization. A minimum of 60,000 individuals served in colonial regiments and 11,000 enlisted in the Royal Army (a third of all redcoats). At least 30 percent of all free males aged 16 to 45 served in the army, and every fifth soldier evidently died in uniform.

Seventeenth Amendment Amendments on this topic were proposed as early as 1828. Andrew JOHSON issued a formal message calling for popular election of senators in 1868. The House adopted such amendments in 1893, 1894, 1898, 1900, and 1902, but the Senate refused to concur. Between 1875 and 1912, 29 states adopted senatorial primaries that effectively established direct election by voters. The Senate abandoned its opposition when a bribery scandal involving Senator William Lorimer's election by the Ill. legislature arose in 1911. The Seventeenth Amendment was sent to the states on 13 May 1912, last ratified on 8 April 1913, and officially proclaimed on 31 May 1913. It altered Article II, Section 3 by providing that US senators be elected in popular elections, rather than by state legislatures.

Seventh Amendment Submitted to the states on 25 September 1789, last ratified by Va. on 15 December 1791, and officially proclaimed on 30 December 1791, it guaranteed a jury trial in all civil suits disputing at least $20, and it required appeals to be decided according to accepted rules of COMMON LAW. In *Walker* v. *Sauvinet* (1876), the Supreme Court ruled (7–2) that the FOURTEENTH AMENDMENT'S DUE PROCESS clause did not mandate juries for civil trials in state courts; it has never applied the Seventh Amendment to the states.

Severn River, battle of (Md.) After having been ousted from office as governor of MARYLAND and replaced by William Fuller, William Stone raised a force to restore the authority of the second Lord Baltimore. On 25 March 1655, Stone's supporters were defeated. Stone was imprisoned and three of his lieutenants were executed.

Sevier, John (b. New Market, Va., 23 September 1745; d. Fort Decatur, Ala., 24 September 1815) He was the most important leader of the eastern Tenn. frontier, where he settled in 1773. He sat in the N.C. legislature (1777–80), was co-commander at the battle of KING'S MOUNTAIN, and led over a dozen expeditions (all victorious) against the Indians. He was elected president of FRANKLIN, for which he was outlawed by

N.C. and later pardoned. He served as first governor of Tenn. (1796–1801 and 1803–9) and in Congress (1811–15), where he supported the WAR HAWKS.

Seward, William H. (b. Florida, N.Y., 16 May 1801; d. Auburn, N.Y., 10 October 1872) Having entered politics in the ANTI-MASONIC PARTY, Seward joined the Whigs (*see* WHIG PARTY), and ran unsuccessfully for the REPUBLICAN presidential nomination in 1856 and 1860. As Abraham LINCOLN's secretary of state, he resolved serious diplomatic problems with Great Britain caused by the *TRENT* AFFAIR and the ALABAMA CLAIMS; under Andrew JOHNSON, he pressured France to withdraw its expeditionary force from Mexico, moved decisively to buy ALASKA from Russia in 1867, and persuaded Denmark to sell its West Indian colonies, but failed to win Senate approval for their acquisition.

Seward's folly ALASKA was ridiculed as William H. SEWARD's folly by journalists who assumed that it was a trackless, frozen wilderness not worth the $7,200,000 paid to buy it from Russia.

Seymour, Horatio (b. Pompey Hill, N.Y., 31 May 1810; d. Deerfield Hills, N.Y., 12 February 1886) Seymour entered N.Y. politics as a Democratic legislator. He lost the race for governor in 1850, held that office (1852–4), retired from politics until the CIVIL WAR, and was again elected governor in 1863. He favored conciliation toward the South as Democratic presidential candidate in 1868, and lost with 47.3 percent of the vote to Ulysses S. GRANT. He then left politics.

Shakers The United Society of Believers in Christ's Second Coming were termed Shaking Quakers or Shakers because their worship included vigorous and emotional dancing. They taught that Christ's second coming would be as a woman and would occur after humanity was gathered into their communities, which held property in common. Insisting that sex was the root of all evil, they required absolute chastity. Mother Anne Lee left England to found the church in America in 1774. At their zenith in the 1850s, they numbered over 5,000, scattered in 20 communities, mostly in N.Y. and New England, but declined steadily and were virtually extinct in 1988.

"Shame of the Cities, The" *see* STEFFENS, LINCOLN

Shapiro* v. *Thompson (decided with *Washington* v. *Legrant* and *Reynolds* v. *Smith*) On 21 April 1969, the Supreme Court extended *EDWARDS* V. *CALIFORNIA*; it ruled that when states denied welfare to persons living less than a year within their borders, they violated a citizen's rights to travel freely and to enjoy both DUE PROCESS and equal protection of the laws. The Court ruled on this issue concerning aliens in *GRAHAM* V. *RICHARDSON*.

Share-Our-Wealth movement *see* LONG, HUEY

Sharpsburg, battle of (Md.) This was once a common name for the battle of ANTIETAM.

Shaw, Anna Howard (b. Newcastle, England, 14 February 1847; d. Moylan, Pa., 2 July 1919) Having matured in Mich., Shaw earned college degrees in divinity and medicine, was the first woman ordained by the METHODIST CHURCH, and was a temperance lecturer. She became a full-time speaker and organizer for WOMEN'S SUFFRAGE about 1885. From 1904 to 1915, she was president of the NATIONAL AMERICAN WOMAN SUFFRAGE ASSOCIATION. In WORLD WAR I, she headed the Woman's Committee of the Council of National Defense.

Shaw* v. *Reno *see JOHNSON* V. *DE GRANDY*

Shawnee Indians Bands of this nation, speaking one of the ALGONQUIAN LANGUAGES, had become widely dispersed by the late 1600s, when they may have numbered 3,000 persons. Most occupied Ohio and western Pa., but a large group lived along the Savannah River (by which name they were known) and ultimately migrated back to the Ohio valley via Pa. Despite numbering just 1,800 about 1770 – including 300 warriors – they were among the most determined opponents of Anglo-American expansion into the Ohio valley; they fought in the SEVEN YEARS' WAR, PONTIAC'S WAR, DUNMORE'S WAR, the REVOLUTIONARY WAR, and the campaigns in the NORTHWEST TERRITORY through 1794. They ceded large areas of land in central and southern Ohio by the first treaty of GREENVILLE. Under TECUMSEH and the PROPHET, they led a pan-Indian confederacy against further white expansion, but were defeated at TIPPECANOE CREEK, and then fought as British allies in the WAR OF 1812. They had relocated to Kans. by 1845 and to Okla. in the 1850s. In 1984, they numbered 7,263 on reservations in Okla.

Shays' Rebellion When postwar depression and high taxes multiplied the number of New Englanders facing foreclosure for nonpayment of debts, Mass. crowds began preventing courts from convening on 31 August 1786. On 26 September, 500 armed men under Daniel Shays forced adjournment of the Mass. supreme court at Springfield. In January 1787, Governor James Bowdoin ordered 4,000 militia under General Benjamin Lincoln to protect the US arsenal at Springfield from a threatened attack by 1,200 men under Shays. On 25 January, militia held off an attack on the arsenal by supporters of Shays. Shays retreated to Petersham, where he was defeated and captured by Lincoln's forces on 4 February. Tried and sentenced to hang, Shays was pardoned on 13 June 1788. His supporters won relief for their grievances after winning the 1788 legislative elections. By spreading alarm that civil unrest threatened the US, Shays' Rebellion increased public support for a stronger central government to replace the enfeebled ARTICLES OF CONFEDERATION with a new constitution.

Sheepeater campaign In mid-February 1879, renegades of the BANNOCK–PAIUTE CAMPAIGN murdered five Chinese prospectors in northern Idaho. The army blamed the Sheepeaters (outcasts of the Bannocks and SHOSHONI inhabiting marginal mountain ranges, who numbered only 30 warriors) and sent 125 cavalry after them in May. By 2 October, the army had taken 51 Sheepeaters, who were placed on the Fort Hall, Idaho, Reservation.

Shelley* v. *Kraemer *see* *CORRIGAN* V. *BUCKLEY*

Shelterbelt Program To combat severe wind erosion and prevent recurrences of the DUST BOWL, in July 1934 Franklin D. ROOSEVELT proposed expanding an Agriculture Department program that since 1913 had encouraged farmers to plant "shelterbelts" of trees west of their fields. The Forest Service drew up plans for creating a shelterbelt of 3,000,000,000 trees, planted 100 miles wide, from Canada to Tex. The WORKS PROGRESS ADMINISTRATION took responsibility for the project in 1937, and by 1942 it had protected 30,000 farms with 217,000,000 trees on 362 square miles.

Shenandoah Valley campaigns (1) Between 23 March and 9 June 1862, Major General Stonewall JACKSON, with no more than 17,000 Confederates, diverted perhaps 36,000 Federals from reinforcing George MCCLELLAN in the PENINSULAR CAMPAIGN by defeat at Kernstown (23 March) and victories at McDowell (13 May), Front Royal (23 May), Winchester (25 May), Cross Keys (8 June), and Port Republic (9 June). Losses: 6,221 USA and 2,736 CSA casualties. Jackson's campaign enabled CSA forces to prevent McClellan from taking Richmond.

(2) Between 19 September 1864 and 2 March 1865, Major General Philip SHERIDAN's 48,000 Federals destroyed Major General Jubal Early's CSA army (23,000 in September 1864) at the battles of Winchester (19 September), Fishers Hill (20 September), Toms Brook (9 October), Cedar Creek (19 October), and Waynesboro (2 March). Losses: 11,268 USA and 10,066 CSA casualties. The Federals also methodically destroyed the valley's ability to provision the CSA army by seizing or destroying its livestock, foodstuffs, mills, granaries, and railroad facilities.

Shepherd, Alan *see* SPACE RACE

Sheppard–Towner Act (23 November 1921) To combat unacceptably high rates of infant mortality, this law authorized the first federal appropriation for social welfare. It authorized eligible states to share $1,470,000 in matching funds for use by public health personnel to teach elementary prenatal and maternal hygiene to new mothers. Before the program ceased in 1929, 45 states had qualified for grants. The law was criticized by many doctors as socialistic.

Sheridan, Philip Henry (b. Albany, N.Y., 6 March 1831; d. Nonquitt, Mass., 5 August 1885) Raised in Ohio, Sheridan graduated 34th of 52 cadets from West Point in 1853. During the CIVIL WAR, he rose from captain to major general by the age of 32. In April 1864, he took over the Army of the POTOMAC's cavalry and in August he launched his devastating SHENANDOAH VALLEY CAMPAIGN, which made him a national hero. His victory at FIVE FORKS forced the fall of PETERSBURG and Richmond. At the war's end, only Ulysses S. GRANT and William SHERMAN had contributed more to Union victory than Sheridan. He led 50,000 troops in the first MEXICAN BORDER CAMPAIGN. After duty as military governor of La. and Tex., he directed the RED RIVER WAR and other operations on the southern plains, where he coined the expression: "the only good Indian is a dead Indian."

Sherman, James Schoolcraft (b. Utica, N.Y., 24 October 1855; d. Utica, N.Y., 30 October 1912) A lawyer and banker, Sherman was US congressman (Republican, N.Y., 1887–91, 1893–1909) and US vice-president (1909–12). He was a hearty, popular man known as "Sunny Jim," who was renominated for vice-president, but died before the election.

Sherman, William Tecumseh (b. Lancaster, Ohio, 8 February 1820; d. New York, N.Y., 14 February 1891) In 1840 Sherman graduated sixth of 42 cadets from West Point as an artilleryman. After the MEXICAN WAR, he resigned from the army, became president of Louisiana State University, and reentered the military in the CIVIL WAR. He became major general after being cited for gallantry at SHILOH, where he was wounded; he took a major role in the VICKSBURG and CHATTANOOGA campaigns. Sherman became principal US military commander in the west in March 1864, and then drove on ATLANTA. His MARCH TO THE SEA and his Carolinas campaign forced the surviving CSA armies there into surrendering to him on 26 April 1865. By the war's end, only Ulysses S. GRANT had contributed more to Union victory than Sherman. He served as commander of the army (lieutenant general) 1869–83.

Sherman Antitrust Act (2 July 1890) Congress passed this law to prevent interstate TRUSTS from becoming anti-competitive monopolies. It outlawed all combinations or conspiracies to restrain marketplace forces concerning interstate commerce or trade (such as conspiracies to rig freight rates, fix prices, or blacklist competitors). The Supreme Court seriously undercut its scope in *UNITED STATES* v. *E. C. KNIGHT COMPANY*, which ruled that manufacturing was not part of commerce; and in *IN RE DEBS*, it declared labor unions subject to its provisions. The Sherman Act had little impact from 1890 to 1901, when the US used it to file just 18 suits (including four against unions), although its broad powers were upheld in *UNITED STATES* v. *TRANS-MISSOURI FREIGHT ASSOCIATION* and in *ADDYSTON PIPE AND STEEL COMPANY* v. *UNITED STATES*. The law became an effective weapon against monopolies under Theodore ROOSEVELT, and won major victories in *NORTHERN SECURITIES COMPANY* v. *UNITED STATES*, *SWIFT AND COMPANY* v. *UNITED STATES*, *STANDARD OIL COMPANY OF NEW JERSEY ET AL.* v. *UNITED STATES* and *UNITED STATES* v. *AMERICAN TOBACCO COMPANY*.

Sherman Silver Purchase Act (14 July 1890) Congress rejected demands to replace the BLAND–ALLISON ACT with unlimited coinage of silver, but passed this compromise law. The Sherman Act required the Treasury to make monthly purchases of 4,500,000 ounces in silver, which approximated the output of US mines, and issue an equal amount of paper money redeemable at face value in silver or gold (as the Treasury chose to pay). The act increased the supply of paper money, but not in the amount necessary to expand the money supply, because the Treasury could buy silver at depressed market quotes of 20 ounces per ounce of gold (rather than 16 to 1 as in 1876). The act stirred anxiety about inflation among the business community, and undermined confidence in the US gold reserve. Grover CLEVELAND wrongly blamed the PANIC OF 1893 on the act and won its repeal on 1 November 1893. The repeal led Democrats to repudiate Cleveland's position in favor of William Jennings BRYAN in 1896.

Sherman's March to the Sea *see* MARCH TO THE SEA

Shiloh, battle of (Tenn.) On 6 April 1862, General Albert JOHNSTON's 40,300 Confederates attacked Major General Ulysses S. GRANT's 42,700 Federals, but retreated on 7 April when 20,000 reinforcements joined Grant, and the expected CSA reinforcements failed to arrive. USA losses: 1,754 killed, 8,408 wounded, 2,885 missing. CSA losses: 1,723 killed (including Johnston), 8,012 wounded, 959 missing. Shiloh was the bloodiest battle fought in America to that date. CSA forces withdrew to Corinth, Miss., and left western Tenn. in Union hands.

Shipping Act (1916) *see* MERCHANT MARINE

Shoshoni Indians This group, speakers of one of the UTO-AZTECAN LANGUAGES, occupied southern Idaho and central Wyo. They acquired horses about 1690. Smallpox destroyed most of their Canadian bands in 1781 and the US bands were raided by BLACKFOOT INDIANS until 1837. The Shoshoni may have numbered 3,000 in 1845. The Idaho bands were forced to cease raiding the OREGON TRAIL by the SHOSHONI WAR, and in 1868 they agreed to live on lands around Fort Hall, Idaho. The Wyo. bands under Washakie kept peace with the US, accepted a reservation at Wind River (which they later had to share with ARAPAHO INDIANS), and fought for the US Army in the third SIOUX WAR. To accommodate white settlers, the Shoshoni lost parts of their reservation, on which oil deposits were later found, but won a court suit for $30,000,000 in 1935 as compensation.

Shoshoni War After a prolonged period when Idaho SHOSHONI INDIANS harassed travelers and overland stages on the OREGON TRAIL, an expedition marched against them from Fort Douglas, Idaho. On 27 January 1863, Colonel Patrick Connor's 250 Calif. volunteers attacked their Bear River valley, Idaho, camp; by killing 224 Shoshoni and capturing 164, at a loss of 21 dead and 46 wounded, they brought the raids to an end.

Shreveport rate cases (*Houston, East and West Texas Railway Company* v. *United States, Texas and Pacific Railway Company* v. *United States*) On 8 June 1914, the Supreme Court extended the "stream of commerce" doctrine enunciated in *SWIFT AND COMPANY* v. *UNITED STATES* to intrastate transportation systems through its "Shreveport Doctrine." The Court ruled (7–2) that Congress can regulate intrastate rail rates if they form such an integral part of interstate rates, that setting rules for the former necessarily requires modifications in the latter.

Shriver, (Robert) Sargent, Jr (b. Westminster, Md., 9 November 1915) Brother-in-law to John F. KENNEDY, Shriver was the first director of the PEACE CORPS (1961–6), head of the Office of Economic Opportunity (1966–8), and ambassador to France (1968–70). On 5 August 1972, he replaced Thomas EAGLETON as George MCGOVERN's vice-presidential nominee. He ran unsuccessfully for the Democratic nomination for president in 1976.

Siberian intervention In August 1918, two US Army regiments (10,000 men) landed at Vladivostok, Siberia, with international forces to block Japanese intervention in the area and secure the Trans-Siberian Railroad from the Bolsheviks. The troops skirmished with Bolsheviks until they withdrew in April 1920.

Sicily campaign On 10 July 1943, 160,000 troops of General Bernard Montgomery's British Eighth Army and George Patton's US Seventh Army began invading Sicily, held by 275,000 Italians and 70,000 Germans. A hundred thousand AXIS troops evacuated Sicily from 11 to 17 August, when the campaign ended. Allied casualties: 31,158 killed and wounded. Axis casualties: 167,000 killed and captured, including 10,000 German casualties.

sick chicken case *see SCHECHTER POULTRY CORPORATION* v. *UNITED STATES*

silent majority While dismissing widespread press coverage of the VIETNAM ANTIWAR MOVEMENT's opposition to their VIETNAM WAR policies, Richard NIXON and Spiro AGNEW argued in 1968 that the media failed to have due regard for the "silent majority" with conservative views because it did not engage in public demonstrations. The term became a synonym for the core of Nixon's support, which largely came from white, middle-class voters – including many Democrats – alienated by the rapid social change and violence of the 1960s.

Silent Spring In 1963 Rachel Carson published this study of how DDT and other persistent agricultural pesticides moved up the food chain and threatened a wide range of species, including those widely consumed by humans. The title alluded to declining numbers of certain bird species, which Carson attributed to DDT's effect in producing eggshells too thick to permit the birth of chicks. The book influenced public policy, and in June 1972 ENVIRONMENTAL PROTECTION AGENCY Director William RUCKELSHAUS banned the use of DDT on crops after 1 January 1973. Carson was the first person to sensitize public opinion to the broader problems of environmental degradation facing the US.

silver coinage controversy Between 1873 and 1900, controversy erupted over whether the US currency should be based on both silver and gold. As GREENBACKS steadily contracted, circulating cash fell from $31.18 per capita in 1865 to just $19.00 by 1875. When the CRIME OF '73 dropped the silver dollar from the currency, debtors and farmers denounced the measure as a "gold conspiracy" to shrink the money supply, which would make debts harder to pay by causing a decline in both wages and prices for agricultural goods. Westerners favored bimetallism because their economy would benefit if increased demand for silver revived the mining industry.

The BLAND–ALLISON ACT resumed silver coinage on a small scale, but failed to satisfy critics. The SHERMAN SILVER PURCHASE ACT committed the Treasury to buy nearly the entire output of western mines, but at half the price its owners desired. Banking and business interests opposed large Treasury purchases of silver for fear that a ruinous inflation would result. Grover CLEVELAND shared the hard-money view and persuaded Congress to repeal the Sherman Act in 1893, but in the process split Democrats over the issue. In 1896 Democrats and Populists (*see* POPULISM) both endorsed unlimited coinage of silver, to be bought at a ratio of 16 ounces of silver to 1 ounce of gold (twice the market price); they both nominated William Jennings BRYAN, a free-silver man, while the Gold Democrats, (*see* NATIONAL DEMOCRATS) ran their own ticket. Bryan lost badly and free silver never recovered. The US officially adopted the GOLD STANDARD in 1900. The issue reemerged in the GREAT DEPRESSION and led to the SILVER PURCHASE ACT (1934).

Silver Purchase Act (19 June 1934) By 1934, western miners were suffering from low silver prices and falling employment, while a deflationary spiral led many to conclude that the money supply needed to be expanded sharply to revive the economy. These concerns led Congress to direct that the Treasury buy silver until either its silver stocks equaled a third of gold reserves or silver's price reached $1.29 an ounce. The law increased the profits of silver firms, but did little to improve the US economy, and was curtailed in 1935.

Simmons, William J. *see* KU KLUX KLAN

Simms, William Gilmore (b. Charleston, S.C., 17 April 1806; d. Charleston, S.C., 11 June 1870) He abandoned a Charleston law practice for journalism and a writing career. He had published five volumes of poetry by 1832, and his first novel, *Martin Faber*, appeared in 1833. The antebellum era's most prominent southern author and man of letters, Simms produced verse, novels, plays, biographies, proslavery tracts, and both a geography and history of S.C. Most of his works were historical romances set in colonial or Revolutionary S.C. His output included *The Yemassee* (1835), *Border Beagles* (1840), *The Kinsman* (1841), *Beauchampe* (1842), *The Forayers* (1855), *Eutaw* (1856), and *The Cub of the Panther* (1869).

Simpson, Jerry (b. Westmoreland County, Nova Scotia, 31 March 1842; d. Wichita, Kans., 23 October 1905) In 1878 Simpson settled in Kans. A Union veteran (12th Ill. Infantry), he left the Republican Party to advocate Henry GEORGE's ideas through the GREENBACK PARTY and then joined the Populist party (*see* POPULISM). He was a shrewd campaigner who became known as "Sockless Jerry" or the "Sockless Socrates" after his enemies falsely rumored that he did not use stockings. He ran for Congress five times from 1890 to 1898, and won in 1890, 1892, and 1896. He left politics after his last defeat and became a rancher in N.Mex.

Simpson–Mazzoli Act (17 October 1986) Congress revised the law on IMMIGRATION to extend amnesty to illegal aliens living continuously in the US since before 1 January 1982, and to give them until 4 May 1988 to apply for legal residence. To keep large-scale illegal immigration from resuming, it subjected employers who knowingly hired illegal aliens to fines of up to $10,000 per worker. The law proved a failure because of government unwillingness to undertake a broad-based campaign against employers who violated its provisions. By May 1994, the number of illegal aliens in the US had risen to 3,800,000 and was increasing at an annual rate of 400,000 arrivals.

Sinclair, Upton (Beall) (b. Baltimore, Md., 20 September 1878; d. Bound Brook, N.J., 25 November 1968) With the publication of *The JUNGLE*, the first of many novels advocating social justice and reform, Sinclair emerged as one of the leading MUCKRAKERS. Other such novels include *Damaged Goods* (1913), *King Coal* (1917), *The Profits of Religion* (1918), *The Brass Check* (1919), *They Call Me Carpenter* (1922), *The Goose Step* (1923), *The Goslings* (1924), *The Wet Parade* (1931), and *Upton Sinclair Presents William Fox* (1933). He narrowly lost election to be governor of Calif. in 1934 while running an EPIC (End Poverty in Calif.) campaign. He won the Pulitzer prize in 1943 for *Dragon's Teeth*, which dealt with Adolph Hitler's rise to power.

single tax *see* GEORGE, HENRY

Siouan languages This family of INDIAN LANGUAGES was the largest linguistic stock on the Great Plains and Missouri River valley, but had splinter groups established in Wis., S.C., and southern Miss. Its major subdivisions are the languages of the Dakota (SIOUX), CROW, MANDAN, Iowa, HIDATSA, OMAHA-OSAGE-PONCA-QUAPAW-KANSA, WINNEBAGO, YUCHI, and CATAWBA INDIANS.

Sioux Indians These Indians call themselves the Dakota, but are best known as Sioux, a term the French corrupted from an Ojibwa word meaning "enemy." They occupied the upper Mississippi valley in 1780 and may have numbered 25,000. They included three main divisions: Santee (Sisseton, Mdewakanton, Wahpekute, and Wahpeton bands), Yankton (Yankton and Yanktonai bands), and Teton (Brule, Blackfoot, Hunkpapa, Miniconjou, Oglala, Sans-Arc, and Two-Kettle). The Santee fought the first SIOUX WAR and were then restricted to RESERVATIONS in Minn., S.Dak., N.Dak., and Nebr. Most Yankton peacefully accepted reservation status in S.Dak. after 1865. The Tetons were aggressive BUFFALO followers and warred with neighboring Indians over hunting territories; after the the second and third SIOUX WARS, they were settled on reservations in N.Dak., S.Dak., and Mont. The Tetons' last engagement with the army was the WOUNDED KNEE massacre.

Sioux War, first On 17 August 1862, an argument between settlers and Sioux escalated into the murder of five whites near Acton, Minn. Little Crow's Sioux (never more than 1,000 warriors) killed about 400 civilians and soldiers in a week, besides capturing about 370 whites and mixed-race people. After several attacks on forts, towns, and military camps failed, 2,000 Indians had surrendered to make peace by 1 November. Several thousand fugitives fled to N.Dak., where US forces under Major General John Pope pursued, harassed, and defeated them in 1863–4.

Sioux War, second In August 1866, up to 2,000 of Red Cloud's Sioux (and many CHEYENNE INDIANS) began harassing US soldiers building three forts on Wyo.'s BOZEMAN TRAIL. In August 1868, the army abandoned the forts by the treaty of FORT LARAMIE. US losses: 306 cattle, 304 mules, 161 horses, 58 civilians killed and 20 wounded, and 105 soldiers killed, including 79 at the FETTERMAN MASSACRE. Sioux losses: 60–100 killed.

Sioux War, third In the summer of 1876, Major General George Crook's 2,425 US soldiers entered Mont. to force 1,500–3,000 Sioux and Cheyenne warriors under SITTING BULL and Crazy Horse on to reservations. Crook's men retreated after the battle of the Rosebud on 17 June and the battle of the LITTLE BIG HORN. The Indians dispersed into small bands to escape retaliation, but were then harassed and run down by Crook through the winter. By summer, most Indians had surrendered, except Sitting Bull's Hunkpapa Sioux, who escaped to Canada and returned peacefully to the US in July 1881.

Sirica, John Joseph (b. Waterbury, Conn., 19 March 1904; d. Washington, D.C., 14 August 1992) Sirica was appointed to the US district court for Washington, D.C. in 1957 and became senior judge in 1971. He presided over the WATERGATE SCANDAL burglary trial from 8 to 30 January 1973, during which James McCord revealed criminal involvement by the White House staff. He heard the suits against Richard NIXON during 1973–4 to compel release of tapes and documents relating to the break-in and its cover-up, and he presided over the trials of John MITCHELL, H. R. HALDEMAN, and John EHRLICHMAN.

sit-in movement The first sit-in was staged in 1943 at Jack Spratt's restaurant in Chicago, but the tactic was rarely used before the 1960s. The sit-in campaign against southern SEGREGATION began on 1 February 1960, when four black college students asked to be served at Woolworth's lunch counter in Greensboro, N.C.; they were turned down, and refused to leave. Sit-ins spread to six other cities in a week and to seven other southern states within a month. Woolworth's opened its counters to all races on 25 July 1960 after the controversy had cost it $200,000 in lost business. FREEDOM RIDERS extended the tactic to other public accommodations. In *Garner et al.* v. *Louisiana* (11 December 1961), the Supreme Court affirmed the legality of sit-in tactics, and reversed the convictions of 16 black students convicted of breaking the peace for seeking service at a whites-only food counter in Baton Rouge.

Sitting Bull (b. near the Grand River, S.Dak., ca. 1831; d. Standing Rock, S.Dak., 15 December 1890) A member of the Hunkpapa band of the Teton division of the SIOUX INDIANS, Sitting Bull (Tatanka Iyotake) became a renowned war leader fighting the CROW INDIANS in his youth, and did not come into conflict with whites until the first SIOUX WAR, after which he harassed the US Army for two years. Following the second SIOUX WAR, in which he did not participate, he became principal leader of all Teton bands, a position never before held by one individual. He led the Teton in the third SIOUX WAR and orchestrated their victory at LITTLE BIG HORN, but relocated his Hunkpapa band into Canada to avoid retaliation by superior US forces. When the depletion of the BUFFALO threatened his people with starvation, he surrendered to the US authorities on 19 July 1881. He was imprisoned, and then assigned to Standing Rock Agency, S.Dak. He toured as a celebrity with William CODY's Wild West Show in 1885. During the revival called the GHOST DANCE RELIGION, he was ordered under arrest on suspicion of inciting unrest and was killed by Indian police sent to apprehend him.

Sixteenth Amendment Drafted after the Supreme Court declared federal INCOME TAXES unconstitutional in *POLLOCK* v. *FARMERS' LOAN AND TRUST COMPANY* (1895), submitted to the states on 12 July 1909, last ratified on 3 February 1913, and officially proclaimed on 25 February 1913, it empowered Congress to collect income taxes that were not levied among the states according to population. The Supreme Court (7–2) upheld the first income tax (1913) levied under this amendment in *Brushaber* v. *Union Pacific Railroad Company* (24 January 1916).

Sixth Amendment Submitted to the states on 25 September 1789, last ratified by Va. on 15 December 1791, and officially proclaimed on 30 December 1791, it guaranteed defendants in criminal cases the right to be tried quickly and publicly by an impartial jury in the judicial district where the alleged crime occurred; it afforded the further rights to be told of pending charges, to confront one's accusers, to compel witnesses in one's behalf, and to enjoy legal counsel. Its protections were extended to state court proceedings by the first SCOTTSBORO CASE (adequate legal counsel), second SCOTTSBORO CASE (impartial juries), *GIDEON* v. *WAINWRIGHT* (mandatory counsel for felony defendants), *POINTER* v. *TEXAS* (confrontation of hostile witnesses), *WASHINGTON* v. *TEXAS* (power to subpoena witnesses), *KLOPFER* v. *NORTH CAROLINA* (speedy trial), and *DUNCAN* v. *LOUISIANA* (jury trial for felony defendants). Among other significant rulings on the Sixth were *BURCH* v. *LOUISIANA*, *EX PARTE QUIRIN*, *MCKEIVER* v. *PENNSYLVANIA*, *ESCOBEDO* v. *ILLINOIS*, *EDWARDS* v. *ARIZONA*, *JOHNSON* v. *ZERBST*, *STRICKLAND* v. *WASHINGTON*, and *MOORE* v. *DEMPSEY*.

Skinner* v. *Oklahoma On 1 June 1942, the Supreme Court struck down unanimously a state law ordering involuntary sterilization of certain convicted criminals, as violating the FOURTEENTH AMENDMENT's equal protection provisions. As the Court's earliest recognition that the area of procreation entailed basic rights beyond the government's jurisdiction without a compelling need for public safety, this ruling anticipated the espousal of a constitutional right to privacy in *Griswold* v. *Connecticut* and *Roe* v. *Wade*.

Skylab Project *see* NATIONAL AERONAUTICS AND SPACE ADMINISTRATION

Slater, Samuel (b. Belper, Derbyshire, England, 9 June 1768; d. Webster, Mass., 21 April 1835) At the age of 15 Slater was apprenticed as a millwright for textile machinery. He emigrated to the US in 1789 and built, from memory, advanced spinning frames of types Parliament had forbidden to be exported. In 1791, at Pawtucket, R.I., Slater opened the first US cotton factory harnessing water power to drive spinning frames according to the Arkwright patent. The opening of Slater's mill marked the earliest instance of the US textile industry closing the technological gap between itself and England's most sophisticated mills, and began a process by which the pace of industrialization steadily accelerated in New England. Slater expanded his operations and died a wealthy man.

slaughterhouse cases (*Butcher's Benevolent Association of New Orleans* v. *Crescent City Livestock Landing and Slaughterhouse Company, Esteban* v. *Louisiana*) On 14 April 1873, the Supreme Court ruled on an appeal by butchers against a La. law allowing a company to monopolize the slaughterhouse business in New Orleans; it denied (5–4) the butchers' claim to have had property taken contrary to the FOURTEENTH AMENDMENT's guarantee of DUE PROCESS. The Court ruled that the Fourteenth only concerned state violations of civil rights associated solely with national citizenship, and did not extend to rights derived from state citizenship, such as those concerning property, participation in state elections, and eligibility for jury duty. The case created a distinction between national and state citizenship, wherein most political and economic rights derived from state constitutions through state laws, and lay beyond the protection of US authority. The ruling severely limited the Fourteenth Amendment's authority to keep states from denying blacks full legal protection or excluding them from politics.

slave code This term referred to the statutes passed by a colony, state, or territory setting rules for all aspects of slave life. Va. and Md. developed their codes haphazardly and incrementally, while S.C. largely reenacted the slave laws of Barbados. All codes barred slaves from bringing court suits in their own behalf, severely limited their rights as defendants in criminal cases, and subjected them to heavier punishments than whites. The codes authorized masters to use force against slaves in ways that would have constituted assault, battery, and manslaughter (but not willful murder) if used against a free person. To neutralize the FREEPORT DOCTRINE, the DAVIS RESOLUTIONS demanded a territorial slave code be enacted by Congress.

slave revolts Only seven slave revolts or conspiracies occurred within the US involving over 30 rebels. An intended insurrection was discovered at New York City in April 1712 and 21 blacks were executed. Another plot was foiled at New York in February 1741 that resulted in the conviction of 101 slaves, of whom 31 were hanged or burned. The colonial era's only insurrection to result in violence was the STONO CREEK REBELLION in 1739. PROSSER'S CONSPIRACY was suppressed in Va. in 1800, and VESEY'S CONSPIRACY was betrayed by a Charleston informer in 1822. In 1811 perhaps 400 slaves rose against their masters in La.; the insurrectionists took few white lives before being put down by militia and US regulars, but about 75 of their number died fighting or were executed. TURNER'S REVOLT was the antebellum era's only significant insurrection, although John BROWN tried to inspire slaves to rebel in 1859.

slave trade The first slaves brought to work in the British colonies were 20 Africans sold at JAMESTOWN, Va., in August 1619. Large-scale importations did not begin until the 1680s, then rose gradually, and peaked in the pre-Revolutionary decades. A rough estimate of the number of slaves imported to the present United States would include 28,000 arriving through 1700, 171,000 in 1701–60, 75,000 in 1761–75, and 53,000 in 1781–1810. By 1 January 1808, when the overseas slave trade became illegal, Anglo-Americans had probably imported 327,000 Africans, and another 28,000 had come to

La. while under French or Spanish rule. Perhaps 50,000 slaves were smuggled to the US between 1808 and 1861. Total slave imports from overseas were most likely about 405,000 from 1619 to 1861.

slavery In August 1619, at Jamestown, Va., a Dutch privateer landed the first blacks known to arrive in the US, who were sold as unfree laborers. No laws governed the status of Anglo-America's earliest blacks, but by 1640 a system of de facto slavery had evolved in the Chesapeake that permitted some blacks to be held in lifetime servitude and for their children to inherit that status. Beginning in the 1660s, legislation began codifying these extralegal arrangements into the earliest SLAVE CODES.

Slavery existed in all THIRTEEN COLONIES, but was strongest in the South, NEW YORK, and NEW JERSEY. Large-scale SLAVE REVOLTS or conspiracies remained relatively infrequent. ABOLITIONISM led to the virtual extinction of slavery in the North from 1776 to 1810, and to the SLAVE TRADE's outlawing in 1808. By increasing the demand for unfree labor, the invention of the COTTON GIN resulted in the rapid redistribution of most slaves from the UPPER SOUTH to the LOWER SOUTH. By 1860 about every fourth southern family possessed at least one slave, but most of the 4,000,000 US bondsmen belonged to "planters," who possessed twenty or more.

Antislavery activists created both the UNDERGROUND RAILROAD and the AMERICAN COLONIZATION SOCIETY. Slavery first became a politically divisive issue in the MISSOURI COMPROMISE debate. It eventually dominated national politics through the controversies concerning the POSITIVE GOOD DEFENSE OF SLAVERY, the WILMOT PROVISO, the COMPROMISE OF 1850, the *DRED SCOTT* V. *SANDFORD* decision, *UNCLE TOM'S CABIN*, POPULAR SOVEREIGNTY, BLEEDING KANSAS, and John BROWN's raid.

During the CIVIL WAR, the US government steadily undermined slavery to weaken the CONFEDERACY. The EMANCIPATION PROCLAMATION freed all slaves behind CSA lines. The THIRTEENTH AMENDMENT ended the institution throughout the US. Congress established the FREEDMEN'S BUREAU to assist ex-slaves in bettering themselves.

Slidell, John *see* *TRENT* AFFAIR

Smith, Al(fred) Emmanuel (b. New York, N.Y., 30 October 1873; d. New York, N.Y., 4 October 1944) Smith was the son of a Union veteran and matured on the east side of lower Manhattan. As a PROGRESSIVE ERA governor of N.Y. (1918–28), he won the Democratic nomination for president in 1928. As the first Roman Catholic candidate for president, and an opponent of PROHIBITION, Smith lost in a massive landslide; he received only 40.9 percent of the ballots and carried only six states. He criticized the NEW DEAL as an AMERICAN LIBERTY LEAGUE founder.

Smith, Gerald K. *see* LONG, HUEY

Smith, Green Clay (b. Richmond, Ky., 4 July 1832; d. Washington, D.C., 28 February 1895) He rose from colonel of the Fourth Kentucky Cavalry to US major general in the CIVIL WAR, during which he was wounded and cited for gallantry. He was Ky. Republican congressman (1863–5), Mont. governor (1866–9), and then became a Baptist minister. As PROHIBITION PARTY nominee for president in 1876, he won 1 percent of the vote.

Smith, Jedidiah Strong (b. Bainbridge, N.Y., 6 January 1799; d. on the Cimarron River, Kans., 27 May 1831) In 1822 Smith became a fur trapper under William ASHLEY. He located the SOUTH PASS and was the first to recognize its importance as a route to the west. In 1826–7, while hunting new beaver grounds, he led the first Anglo-Americans to reach Calif. (at San Gabriel) by the Mojave Desert, scaled the Sierra Nevada Mountains eastward, and crossed the Great Basin of Nev. From then to 1830, he explored Calif., Oreg., British Columbia, Mont., and Wyo., and saw 24 companions die in Indian ambushes. He was finally killed by Comanches while on a trading expedition to Santa Fe. Smith was the West's most important explorer, for his discoveries demonstrated that Anglo-Americans could reach Oreg. and Calif. with pack trains and wagons.

Smith, John (b. Willoughby, Lincolnshire, England, ca. 1579; d. London, England, 21 June 1631) After fighting the Turks as a mercenary, Smith joined the JAMESTOWN expedition as a soldier. Denied his seat on the Va. council for brawling, he spent 1607–8 mapping Chesapeake Bay and establishing relations with the POWHATAN CONFEDERACY after he had been captured by them. Elected president of the council in September 1608, he imposed military discipline, acquired sufficient food for the winter from the Indians, and kept mortality during that winter down to 5 percent – the lowest rate in the colony's early history. Although Smith had brought order to the colony, a relief convoy brought news in July 1609 that changes in the VIRGINIA COMPANY OF LONDON's charter left him without legal authority to govern the colony. He returned to England that September after being badly injured in an explosion, while Va. – bereft of his leadership – suffered its greatest starving time over the next winter. Smith's *A Description of New England* (1616) described his experiences on a voyage of discovery in 1614, and was largely responsible for popularizing the name "New England" for the area around Cape Cod. Smith ranks as the first heroic figure in US history.

Smith, Joseph, Jr (b. Sharon, Vt., 23 December 1805; d. Carthage, Ill., 27 June 1844) Smith reported that during 1823–7, near Manchester, N.Y., an angel showed him golden plates recording an ancient Hebrew migration to America. He published this *Book of Mormon* in March 1830, and in April founded the Church of Jesus Christ of Latter-day Saints, or MORMONS. His challenge to mainstream Protestantism aroused enormous hostility that drove the Mormons westward. In 1831 he took his followers to Kirtland Mills, Ohio, then to Jackson County, Mo., and in 1839 to Nauvoo, Ill., where local hysteria over Mormon polygyny led to Smith's murder in 1844. Before he died, Smith had attracted 35,000 converts to Mormonism.

Smith Act (28 June 1940) Congress required aliens to register annually and strengthened deportation procedures. It also outlawed teaching or advocating the violent overthrow of the US government, and organizing groups for that purpose. Its constitutionality was affirmed in *DENNIS ET AL.* v. *UNITED STATES*, but severely restricted by *YATES* v. *UNITED STATES*. Yates set such strict standards for winning convictions for sedition that the government virtually stopped seeking prosecutions under the law after 1957.

Smith–Connally Anti-strike Act (25 June 1943) Congress gave the president authority to seize factories if strikes threatened to disrupt essential war production, and outlawed labor stoppages in any plant seized for this reason. Under the law, the army operated the railroads to preempt a strike from 27 December 1943 to 28 December 1944.

Smith* v. *Allwright On 3 April 1944, the Supreme Court reversed (8–1) *GROVEY* v. *TOWNSEND* and held that the FOURTEENTH and FIFTEENTH AMENDMENTS forbid political parties to ban blacks from voting in primaries that choose candidates for federal and state elections.

Smith* v. *Turner *see* PASSENGER CASES

Smyth* v. *Ames In 1898 the Supreme Court struck down an 1893 Nebr. law setting railway rates, as a seizure of property without the FOURTEENTH AMENDMENT's guarantee of DUE PROCESS. The Court ruled that a state's rate structure must meet the test of allowing a reasonable rate of profit on the value of a company. The decision left the question of what constituted a fair rate of return to be adjudicated separately on every occasion when a public carrier challenged decisions by state regulatory commissions. The ruling made it easier for big business to challenge state regulations in federal courts, which often ruled against the states.

Snake Indians *see* PAIUTE INDIANS

Snake War *see* PAIUTE CAMPAIGNS

SNCC *see* STUDENT NONVIOLENT COORDINATING COMMITTEE

social darwinism This was a philosophical approach to society and government derived from theories of natural selection, as popularized in Britain by Charles Darwin's *The Origin of Species* (1859) and extended to modern civilization by Herbert Spencer's writings. It elevated the struggle for survival to the level of a natural law, which produced long-term good for the human race and progress. As applied to political issues, it exerted a profoundly conservative disinclination to curb abuses of economic power by

TRUSTS or to alleviate rising levels of poverty by either government programs or private efforts. During the PROGRESSIVE ERA, social darwinism became increasingly discredited by competing viewpoints, especially the pragmatism of William JAMES and the SOCIAL GOSPEL.

Social Gospel This was a reevaluation of Christian duty in light of the widespread poverty, moral decay, and inequality that characterized the PROGRESSIVE ERA's urban, immigrant ghettos. The Social Gospel insisted that it was not enough for Christians to preach against sin, but that a religious obligation existed to improve society by eliminating poverty's causes. Perhaps the most influential Social Gospel theologian was Walter RAUSCHENBUSCH. It added a significant religious dimension to the motivation of Progressive reformers; it also challenged many to question SOCIAL DARWINISM and the ethics of laissez-faire industrial development.

Social Security Administration Congress established Social Security on 14 August 1935. It created an insurance program for old age pensions, an unemployment compensation system, and programs for financial support of dependent children, the handicapped, and blind. (Pensions for railway workers were funded under the RAILROAD RETIREMENT ACTS.) All programs operated as a state–federal partnership except retirement insurance, which was administered solely by Washington. Because it excluded agricultural laborers, household servants, anyone hired by a business with less than 10 employees, state employees, and persons working for charitable or religious organizations, the initial law covered only half the work force. On 24 May 1937, Social Security's constitutionality was upheld in *Steward Machine Company* v. *Davis* and *Helvering* v. *Davis*,

On 10 August 1939, benefits and eligibility requirements were liberalized significantly. The pension fund was financed by payroll taxes paid by both employee and employer. The tax rate rose from 1 percent each to 2.5 percent each by 1960, and by 1990 had reached 7.65 percent for employees and 6.2 percent for employers. MEDICARE and MEDICAID were added as Social Security programs during the GREAT SOCIETY. On 15 August 1994, Social Security was removed from the Department of HEALTH AND HUMAN SERVICES and made an independent federal agency. By 1994, it was the federal budget's largest component.

Socialist Labor party *see* DE LEON, DANIEL

Socialist Party of America This party was founded in July 1901 at Indianapolis by Victor BERGER, Eugene DEBS, and others seeking a broad-based, non-ideological, socialist alternative to Daniel DE LEON's Socialist Labor party. Its influence peaked in 1912, when it had 118,000 members, won 6 percent of the presidential election vote, had elected 79 mayors in 24 states, and held over 1,100 other offices in 340 cities. Its appeal quickly declined, especially after its leaders loudly criticized US entry into WORLD WAR I. By 1919, a third of its executive committee was in jail and its 1920 presidential candidate ran for office from prison. Its most radical factions left in 1919 to found the Communist Labor and COMMUNIST PARTIES. It still had 80,000 members in 1922, but had few political successes after then, and last attracted a significant following when Norman THOMAS received 2.2 percent of the vote for president in 1932.

Society of the Cincinnati *see* CINCINNATI, SOCIETY OF THE

Society of Friends *see* QUAKERS

Soil Conservation Act (27 April 1935) To combat erosion from floods, wind, and poor farming techniques, Congress elevated the Soil Conservation Service to permanent status and transferred it from the Interior to the Agriculture Department. Under Hugh Bennett, it launched numerous programs to educate farmers and ranchers on preventing unnecessary loss of topsoil and restoring fertility.

Soil Conservation and Domestic Allotment Act (29 February 1936) Although labeled a conservation measure, this law reinstituted the procedures for limiting farm acreage of the AGRICULTURAL ADJUSTMENT ADMINISTRATION, which had been ruled unconstitutional the previous month. It paid farmers for both cutting back their acreage of crops it defined as exhausting the soil – wheat, corn, cotton, tobacco, and other major commodities – and planting grass in their place to preserve fertility. Participation was entirely voluntary, however, and without compulsory quotas enforced by marketing, the act was a failure and overproduction resulted. It was replaced by the AGRICULTURAL ADJUSTMENT ACT (1938).

Sojourner Truth *see* TRUTH, SOJOURNER

Solid South This term referred to the consistency with which Democratic presidential candidates carried the ex-CONFEDERACY – including Ky. and Mo. – after REDEMPTION was completed in 1877. From 1880 to 1924, these 13 states supported the Democratic national ticket in every election but 1896 (Ky.), 1904 (Mo.), 1908 (Mo.), 1920 (Mo., Tenn.), and 1924 (Mo., Ky.). In 1928, only S.C., Ga., Ala., Miss., La., and Ark. supported Al SMITH, who was Catholic and anti-PROHIBITION. In 1948, the STATES' RIGHTS PARTY carried S.C., Ala., Miss., La., and a Tenn. electoral vote.

Dwight D. EISENHOWER broke the Solid South for Republicans in 1952 – by taking Fla., Tenn., Tex., Va., and Mo. – and in 1956 – by taking Fla., La., Tenn., Tex., Va., and Ky. In 1960, Republicans took Fla., Tenn., Va., and Ky. The CIVIL RIGHTS MOVEMENT alienated white southerners from the national Democratic Party leadership so badly, that in 1964, S.C., Ga., Ala., Miss., and La. voted Republican. The AMERICAN INDEPENDENT PARTY played a major role in undermining the loyalties of southern white Democrats, by allowing them to vote for it rather than for Republicans. From 1964 to 1992, the Democratic Party carried the South only in 1976 and 1992, when southern governors headed its ticket. In 1994, the Grand Old Party made major gains in southern congressional races.

Solomon Islands campaign US marines invaded GUADALCANAL to keep the Japanese from basing aircraft there in August 1942; they secured the island, and the nearby Russell Islands by February 1943. On 20 June 1943, USMC and army forces began attacking Japanese bases on and near New Georgia Island, and these were taken by 25 August. On 26–7 October, New Zealanders seized the Treasury Islands. On 1 November USMC and army units established a beachhead on Bougainville Island (which the Japanese resisted until March 1944), while Allied aircraft destroyed its Japanese airfields. By March 1944, US capture of the Admiralty and St Matthias Islands isolated Japanese garrisons in the Solomons by cutting their supply lines to Rabaul, against which the Allies next advanced in the NEW BRITAIN CAMPAIGN.

Somalia, US intervention in On 4 December 1992, George BUSH ordered 28,000 US troops to ensure delivery of international food supplies within Somalia, where civil war had produced 300,000 deaths by starvation. On 4 May 1993, control of the mission passed to the UN, but 4,700 US troops remained as part of a 28-nation peacekeeping force of 25,000. The first US military death occurred on 12 January. Violence escalated with Mohamed Farah Aidid's followers, and climaxed on 3 October in a skirmish that left 18 US dead, 78 wounded, and a helicopter shot down. On 7 October 1993, William CLINTON announced that US troops would be withdrawn. US forces lost 30 killed in combat, 14 dead in accidents, and 175 wounded prior to their withdrawal on 25 March 1994. On 15 March 1994, all US embassy personnel left Somalia because of the continuing strife.

Sons of Liberty This group was a secret Whig society (*see* WHIGS (REVOLUTIONARY)) that emerged in 1765. They took their name from a parliamentary speech by Isaac Barré, who characterized Americans "these sons of Liberty." Their primary contribution was to nullify the STAMP ACT by pressuring most stamp distributors to resign before the law took effect. They disbanded in 1766.

Soto, Hernán de (b. Estremadura Province, Spain, ca. 1500; d. Concordia Parish, La., 21 May 1542) A CONQUISTADOR from Peru, Soto landed at Tampa Bay, Fla., on 28 May 1539 with 600 Spaniards for the first major land exploration in the southeast. Marching to S.C., he turned west and crossed the Mississippi about 25 miles below Memphis, then discovered the Arkansas River and returned to the Mississippi. After his death, Luis de Moscoso de Alvarado pushed on into Tex., perhaps to the Trinity River, and then reached Mexico in crude boats in September 1543 with 311 survivors.

South Carolina In April 1670, English settlers made the first permanent settlement at Charles Town, as part of the PROPRIETARY COLONY of CAROLINA, to be governed by the FUNDAMENTAL CONSTITUTIONS OF CAROLINA. The area of S.C. obtained its own legislature in 1670. Political conflicts with the proprietors resulted in S.C. becoming a ROYAL COLONY on 29 May 1721.

Grazing cattle and cutting lumber were the main activities of the early colonists, but rice production dominated their economy after 1690. Slaves became a majority of the population by 1710 and rose up in the STONO CREEK REBELLION of 1739. S.C. was a battleground in the WESTO and YAMASEE WARS, QUEEN ANNE'S WAR, and the CHEROKEE WAR. After 1740, settlers from northern colonies and Europe settled its PIEDMONT, where the REGULATOR movement occurred in the 1760s.

In 1775, S.C. had 170,000 colonists, of whom 59 percent were slaves. In the REVOLUTIONARY WAR, Cherokees attacked the frontier in 1776, but were then driven out of the state entirely. TORIES were numerous, but remained suppressed after a British invasion was repulsed at CHARLES TOWN in 1776. S.C. furnished six of the 80 Continental regiments at the war's height. The British captured Charles Town in 1780 and occupied the state, but were harassed by guerrillas under Francis Marion, Andrew Pickens, and Thomas Sumter; they held Charles Town until 1782. S.C. was the site of 149 military actions, the third highest number of all states.

S.C. was the eighth state to ratify the CONSTITUTION on 23 May 1788. It was the seventh largest state by 1800, with 345,591 people, and the population had become predominantly white (57 percent). The COTTON GIN revolutionized S.C. agriculture. Cotton displaced foodstuffs and tobacco as the leading crop of the PIEDMONT and surpassed rice as the leading staple by 1800; it created a huge demand for slaves, which were again a majority (51 percent) of residents by 1820. The NULLIFICATION CRISIS threatened armed conflict with the US in 1832. Heavy out-migration occurred after 1810 until it was the 17th largest state in 1860. It then had 703,708 people, of whom 57 percent were slaves and 1 percent were foreign-born; it ranked 17th in population, 17th in the value of its farmland and livestock, and 27th in manufactures.

S.C. became the first CSA state on 20 December 1860. In the CIVIL WAR, it furnished 44,000 CSA soldiers and 5,462 USA troops (all black). It witnessed 239 military engagements and a campaign by General William T. SHERMAN that devastated its interior in early 1865.

In June 1865, Andrew JOHNSON instituted a provisional civilian government, which abolished slavery, but refused to enfranchise FREEDMEN or repudiate its CSA war debt. White supremacists took over the legislature and enacted a strict black code (*see* BLACK CODES). Washington imposed military rule in March 1867, but restored self-government and congressional representation on 25 June 1868. Republican control ended eight years later on 12 November 1876. S.C. disfranchised most blacks in 1895, and then enacted SEGREGATION.

In 1900 it was the 24th state in size and had 1,340,316 inhabitants, of whom 87 percent were rural, 58 percent black, and just 5,528 were foreign-born; it ranked 24th in the value of its agricultural goods and 32nd in manufactures. From 1920 to 1970, it lost 960,400 out-migrants, mostly blacks moving to northern cities, and its racial composition shifted significantly. During the CIVIL RIGHTS MOVEMENT, it was the last state to admit blacks to state colleges (not until 28 January 1963). It resisted secondary school desegregation until 1968, when only 15 percent of black pupils attended integrated classes, but by 1971, all school districts were technically in compliance with federal desegregation orders and 93 percent of black students attended integrated schools. In 1990, S.C. ranked as the 24th largest state and had 3,486,703 residents (69 percent white, 30 percent black, 1 percent Hispanic), of whom 61 percent were urban and 1.4 percent were foreign-born. Manufacturing and mining employed 34 percent of all workers.

South Carolina Exposition and Protest Written anonymously by John CALHOUN, this pamphlet explained how NULLIFICATION could be used to repeal the TARIFF OF ABOMINATIONS by individual states. It postulated that state conventions, specially elected to embody the people's sovereignty, could declare null and void a federal law that violated the Constitution. The law would then cease to be operational within that state until three-fourths of the states passed a constitutional amendment overriding the nullification.

South Carolina* v. *Katzenbach On 7 March 1966, the Supreme Court affirmed (8–1) the VOTING RIGHTS ACT (1965) as a constitutional means of protecting suffrage under the FIFTEENTH AMENDMENT.

South Dakota The US acquired S.Dak. by the LOUISIANA PURCHASE. Whites first settled it in 1817 at Fort Pierre, a fur trading post. Anglo-American settlement began in 1856 as part of NEBRASKA. The US created Dakota Territory in 1861. In 1860, Dakota Territory had 4,837 residents, of whom all were white and 37 percent were of foreign birth; it ranked last in population, value of farmland, and manufactures. The territory sent the USA army 206 troops in the CIVIL WAR. In 1870, 83 percent of Dakota's 14,181 settlers lived in S.Dak. A gold mining rush into the Black Hills sparked the third SIOUX WAR, which ended Indian hostilities by 1878. In the 1880s, population skyrocketed by 254 percent and S.Dak. became an important extension of the CATTLE KINGDOM. It became the 40th state on 2 November 1889.

During 1887–97, adequate rain for crops fell in just two years on the plains and commodity prices also dropped sharply. During the 1890s, in-migration virtually ceased and strong political support arose for POPULISM. In 1900, S.Dak. had 401,570 inhabitants (95 percent white, 5 percent Indian), of whom 90 percent were rural and 22 percent were foreign-born; it ranked 37th among states in population, 25th in agricultural products, and 43rd in manufactures. During the early 1900s, low commodity prices inhibited growth of the S.Dak. economy. Real estate values sank 58 percent in the 1920s, and 53 percent of all farmers were tenants by 1940. From 1920 to 1940, 146,400 persons left the state. Another 71,200 left in the 1940s. The economy steadily diversified and the value of manufactured products increased by 400 percent from 1940 to 1965. In 1990, S.Dak. was the 45th largest state and had 696,004 residents (91 percent white, 7 percent Indian, 1 percent Hispanic, 1 percent black), of whom 30 percent were urban and 1.1 percent were foreign-born. Mining and manufacturing employed 17 percent of workers.

South Pass (Wyo.) This pass was first entered in 1812 by John ASTOR's fur trappers but was neither publicized nor utilized until its rediscovery by Jedidiah SMITH in the spring of 1824. The pass became the central artery for MANIFEST DESTINY, because it allowed easy passage along the Platte and Sweetwater rivers through the Rockies, rather than following the Missouri and crossing the difficult Bitterroot Mountains. South Pass enabled settlers to take wagons to the Pacific coast, and so it became the CUMBERLAND GAP of the OREGON and CALIFORNIA TRAILS.

Southeast Asian Treaty Organization (SEATO) On 8 September 1954, the SEATO Treaty was signed at Manila by the US, Philippines, Thailand, Pakistan, Australia, New Zealand, Britain, and France. (Taiwan, which was under threat by the People's Republic of China, was excluded on the pretext of not being in southeast Asia.) SEATO's treaty was based on NATO and required the parties to regard an attack on one as an attack on all. Since most of the area's nations remained neutral, SEATO remained a weak organization that did little more than maintain channels of mutual consultation. Pakistan withdrew in 1972 and France in 1973. The alliance was disbanded by mutual consent on 30 June 1977.

Southern Christian Leadership Conference (SCLC) Martin Luther KING and Ralph ABERNATHY founded the SCLC in January 1957 at Montgomery, Ala. Its goal was to eliminate racial discrimination by peaceful tactics ranging from lawful demonstrations to nonviolent civil disobedience. The SCLC was instrumental in building a national consensus for the CIVIL RIGHTS ACT (1964) and the VOTING RIGHTS ACT (1965) by the publicity it attracted in the BIRMINGHAM DESEGREGATION VIOLENCE, the SELMA FREEDOM MARCH, and the 1963 MARCH ON WASHINGTON. Its last major project was OPERATION BREADBASKET. By 1963, The SCLC ranked equal to the NATIONAL ASSOCIATION FOR THE ADVANCEMENT OF COLORED PEOPLE as a force in the CIVIL RIGHTS MOVEMENT, but its influence declined significantly after Rev. King's death in 1968. In the late 1980s, the SCLC had 350 chapters.

Southern Homestead Act *see* HOMESTEAD ACT, SECOND

Southern Manifesto Following a series of federal desegregation orders after *BROWN v. BOARD OF EDUCATION OF TOPEKA*, 19 US senators and 81 congressmen from southern states issued a declaration on 11 March 1956 that they would use "all lawful means" to overturn the Supreme Court decision.

Southern Tenant Farmers' Union On 26 July 1934, Henry East and Harry Mitchell founded this interracial, pro-socialist union to press for better wages and contracts for cotton tenants. Because it revealed violations of AGRICULTURAL ADJUSTMENT ADMINISTRATION subsidy programs, the union earned the hatred of many landlords who bitterly fought its organizing drives, but its links with COMMUNISTS also engendered widespread hatred. By the summer of 1935, its 30,000 members had won a major strike that almost doubled the wages of cotton pickers. Harassment of the union led to the appointment of a federal commission to investigate southern tenancy, and finally to passage of the BANKHEAD–JONES FARM TENANCY ACT and the creation of other programs to assist tenants. The union declined rapidly after 1941 and was defunct by 1943.

sovereign immunity This legal concept exempts a sovereign government from being a defendant in its own courts if it wishes to exercise that option.

space race The US–USSR space race began with *SPUTNIK*'s orbit in 1957. The US effort was directed by NASA, and it launched the first successful satellite, Explorer I, on 31 January 1958. On 12 April 1961, USSR cosmonaut Yuri Gagarin became the first man in space and orbited the earth once, followed by the first manned (nonorbital) US rocket flight with Alan Shepherd on 5 May 1961. The US then initiated the APOLLO PROJECT to land US astronauts on the moon. The first US astronaut to orbit the earth was John Glenn on 20 February 1962. The USSR made the first unmanned, nondestructive moon landing on 3 February 1966, but by then the US had pulled ahead in manned flight technology. On 27 December 1968, a US rocket returned from the first manned orbit of the moon. On 20 July 1969, the US won the space race by landing Neil Armstrong and Edwin Aldrin on the moon.

space shuttle *see* NATIONAL AERONAUTICS AND SPACE ADMINISTRATION

Spanish-American War Americans became increasingly hostile to Spain because of the inhumane measures it used to fight Cuban rebels after 1895. When the USS *MAINE* exploded at Havana in March 1898, public opinion held Spain responsible and demanded US aid for the rebels. On 20 April, Congress threatened hostilities unless Cuba received independence, which Spain refused, and on 22 April the US put Cuban ports under blockade. On 24 April, Spain declared war on the US, which reciprocated the next day.

Spain, with 18,000,000 people, had 155,302 regular troops in Cuba, plus 41,518 Cuban loyalists, while the organized Cuban rebels numbered just 15,000. The US, with a population of 70,000,000, expanded its regular army from 30,000 to 209,714 by June, including many NATIONAL GUARD units. The US Navy had 69 warships, and bought 67 additional ships within 90 days, compared to Spain's 49.

Commodore George DEWEY's squadron fought the war's first battle on 1 May, when he destroyed Spain's Philippine squadron at MANILA BAY. Blockaded by Dewey and besieged by Philippine rebels, Manila's garrison surrendered on 13 August. US occupation produced the PHILIPPINE INSURRECTION.

US forces under Major General William Shafter landed unopposed in Cuba on 22 June. Shafter's victories at EL CANEY and SAN JUAN HILL trapped Spanish forces in Santiago, where Spain's Cuban squadron lay bottled up by the US Navy until it was annihilated in the battle of SANTIAGO BAY on 3 July. On 17 July, 24,000 enemy troops at Santiago surrendered to Shafter. On 25 July, Major General Nelson Miles invaded PUERTO RICO, which fell with little resistance.

From 21 April to 13 August 1898, the war effort mobilized 306,760 persons, including 280,564 soldiers, 22,875 sailors, and 3,321 marines. The military sustained 4,108 casualties from 1 May to 31 August: 385 battle deaths (369 soldiers, 10 sailors, 6 marines), 2,061 non-combat deaths (soldiers only), 1,662 battle wounds (1,594 soldiers, 47 sailors, 21 marines). The war cost about $400,000,000.

Soon after the fall of Santiago, Spain requested an armistice, which was signed on 12 August. By a peace treaty signed at Paris on 10 December (ratified by Congress on 6 February 1899), Spain granted Cuban independence, ceded Puerto Rico and GUAM to the US, and gave the US title to the Philippines for $20,000,000. The war reduced Spain to a second-class power; it created an overseas US empire, but otherwise marked the end of major US territorial expansion.

Spanish Conspiracy After Spain denied US citizens the RIGHT OF DEPOSIT in 1784, and the US government indicated its willingness to accept the Mississippi's closure to American commerce by the JAY–GARDOQUI TREATY, many western politicians doubted whether the ARTICLES OF CONFEDERATION could protect their interests. Several leading Tenn. and Ky. politicians (most notably Andrew JACKSON) held secret negotiations about accepting Spanish citizenship if Spain would restore the right of deposit and restrain Indians from raiding the frontier. The intrigue died out in the early 1790s.

Spanish Succession, war of the *see* QUEEN ANNE'S WAR

specie This was a term in common use before Federal Reserve banknotes became the primary US currency; it denoted hard money, i.e. minted dollars of silver or gold, rather than paper money.

Specie Circular On 11 July 1836, Andrew JACKSON proclaimed that after 15 August, US land offices would only accept SPECIE as payment for public lands. (Until 15 December, however, paper money would be accepted as payment for tracts up to 320 acres so long as the purchaser lived in the state or territory where the land was located.) The Circular was intended to depress a wave of land speculation which had been fed by an outpouring of promissory notes printed by WILDCAT BANKS, and thus to benefit pioneers by lowering land prices. But it created a greater demand for specie that produced a shortage of hard money. Actual settlers found it more difficult to pay for farms, while speculators nevertheless managed to acquire specie through their superior financial resources. Congress passed a bill overriding the Circular, but Jackson pocket-vetoed it in March 1837. The Circular contributed to the PANIC OF 1837. Congress ended the policy by a joint resolution of 21 May 1838.

Specie Resumption Act *see* GREENBACKS

Spirit of St Louis *see* LINDBERGH, CHARLES

Spock, Benjamin McLane (b. New Haven, Conn., 2 May 1903) Spock earned an M.D. from Columbia (1929). In 1946 he published *The Common Sense Book of Baby and Child Care* (later *Baby and Child Care*), which sold about 750,000 copies annually, or about one for every two US couples, during most of the BABY BOOM. Whereas previous medical advice had emphasized setting firm boundaries for children and maintaining discipline, Spock viewed human development positively and advised treating infants with flexibility and understanding. His ideas revolutionized childrearing practices and were widely blamed for social problems affecting the Woodstock generation (*see* WOODSTOCK ROCK FESTIVAL), such as rising sexual permissiveness and drug use. In *A Better World for Our Children* (1994), Spock leveled his own criticisms at the middle-aged adults once raised on his ideas, whom he described as self-centered, materialistic, and lacking the commitment needed to raise emotionally healthy children.

spoils system This term refers to the practice of hiring and firing government workers for reasons that are primarily political and secondarily based on merit. It was popularized by an 1831 speech by N.Y. senator William Marcy, who said "to the victor belongs the spoils." Partisan considerations had always influenced patronage appointments but were increasingly dominant after the administration of Andrew JACKSON, who removed every fifth federal employee for political reasons during his two terms. The ALBANY REGENCY became a model for state machines whose influence derived heavily from patronage. CIVIL SERVICE REFORM ended the spoils system.

Spooner Act *see* HAY–HERRÁN CONVENTION

Spotsylvania Court House, battle of (Va.) On 9–12 and 18 May 1864, General Robert E. LEE's Confederates repulsed attacks by Lieutenant General Ulysses S. GRANT's 65,800 Federals. USA losses: 10,119 killed and wounded, 800 missing. CSA losses: 9,500 killed and wounded, 4,000 captured. Unable to break Lee's lines, Grant maneuvered to turn his flank at COLD HARBOR.

Springer* v. *United States In 1881 the Supreme Court ruled that the 1861 INCOME TAX was constitutional, because it was not a direct tax and did not have to be divided among the states according to their respective populations. The Court later overturned *Springer* by *POLLOCK* v. *FARMERS' LOAN AND TRUST COMPANY*.

Springfield race riot (Ill.) *see* NATIONAL ASSOCIATION FOR THE ADVANCEMENT OF COLORED PEOPLE

Sputnik On 4 October 1957, the Soviet Union placed the first manmade satellite, *Sputnik I*, into orbit. On 3 November it orbited a dog on *Sputnik II*. When the US attempted to launch its own satellite on 6 December, the booster rocket exploded. *Sputnik* began the SPACE RACE between the US and the USSR by sparking a rapid expansion of funding for missile research and creation of the NATIONAL AERONAUTICS AND SPACE ADMINISTRATION. The US also increased funding for college education by the NATIONAL DEFENSE EDUCATION ACT.

Squanto *see* WAMPANOAG INDIANS

Square Deal Theodore ROOSEVELT coined this phrase in the 1904 election to convey the essence of his domestic policies for the economy and antitrust (*see* TRUSTS) actions: a "square deal" for laborers and consumers as well as big business. High points of the Square Deal included the HEPBURN ACT, MEAT INSPECTION ACT, PURE FOOD AND DRUG ACT, and Roosevelt's settlement of the COAL STRIKE OF 1902.

squatter sovereignty *see* POPULAR SOVEREIGNTY

Staggers Rail Act *see* DEREGULATION

stalwarts This was the faction of GILDED AGE Republicans representing the state machines controlled by party bosses, whose leading spokesman was Roscoe Conkling of N.Y. Their main rivals were the HALF-BREEDS. Since stalwart success depended on government contracts, political appointments, and other forms of patronage, they opposed MUGWUMP demands for CIVIL SERVICE REFORM. The name was a slander fixed on them by reformers, based on a statement reputedly made by Charles Guiteau when he assassinated James GARFIELD: "I am a stalwart [i.e. party loyalist] and [Chester] ARTHUR is president now."

Stamp Act (22 March 1765) This law was the first direct tax levied on the colonies by Parliament and was intended to offset by up to £100,000 the expenses of garrisoning the frontier with redcoats. As of 1 November, it required the colonists to buy specially stamped (watermarked) paper for printing newspapers, pamphlets, all legal documents, property titles, customs papers, commissions to public office, licenses, college degrees, and cards. The STAMP ACT CONGRESS protested the measure. Americans began a NONIMPORTATION AGREEMENT, and nullified the law by forcing the resignation of all officials commissioned to exchange the stamped paper for taxes by December. Pressured by merchants and manufacturers to end the tax so that the Nonimportation Agreement would be lifted, Parliament repealed the Stamp Act on 18 March 1766, but also passed the DECLARATORY ACT. Total revenues collected under the law were just £3,292.

Stamp Act Congress During 7–25 October 1765, representatives from nine provinces met at New York City to seek repeal of the STAMP ACT. The congress denounced the tax in a "Declaration of Rights and Grievances," which was sent to Parliament and GEORGE III. No further intercolonial conferences would be held until the CONTINENTAL CONGRESS convened in 1774.

Standard Oil Company of New Jersey et al.* v. *United States On 15 May 1911, the Supreme Court ordered (8–1) the STANDARD OIL TRUST dissolved. It nevertheless reversed its earlier ruling that the SHERMAN ANTITRUST ACT forbade any combination in restraint of trade, and substituted the "rule of reason," which permitted TRUSTS or other businesses to cooperate among themselves if they did not unduly interfere with competition.

Standard Oil Trust Organized in 1879 by John ROCKEFELLER, this industrial combination was the first TRUST organized to control the interstate market for a product; it did so by both HORIZONTAL and VERTICAL INTEGRATION. The trust was created secretly by naming nine trustees to coordinate all operations by Rockefeller oil companies in the US with his Ohio-based Standard Oil Co.; it controlled 75 percent of global kerosine production. The trust brought much-needed efficiency to the domestic oil industry, and permitted a 70 percent decline in the cost of kerosine but at the cost of unconscionable business ethics. The monopolistic aspects of Rockefeller's empire avoided public scrutiny because the trust was not registered or chartered. It was savagely denounced by PROGRESSIVE ERA reformers, most notably in Ida M. Tarbell's *History of the Standard Oil Company* (1903) and Henry D. Lloyd's *Wealth Against Commonwealth*, which alleged that in his efforts to influence the Pa. legislature, Rockefeller did everything but refine the members. It was dissolved by *STANDARD OIL COMPANY OF NEW JERSEY ET AL.* V. *UNITED STATES*.

Stans, Maurice Hubert (b. Shakopee, Minn., 22 March 1908) A N.Y. investment banker, Stans was secretary of commerce under Richard NIXON and chief fundraiser for Nixon's 1968 and 1972 campaigns. On 14 June 1973, he was implicated by Jeb MAGRUDER in the cover-up of the WATERGATE SCANDAL, which he denied knowledge of in testimony before the Senate. On 12 March 1975, he pleaded guilty to five misdemeanor counts of violating federal election laws as a member of CREEP, for which he was fined $5,000 on 14 May.

Stanton, Edwin M. (b. Steubenville, Ohio, 19 December 1814; d. Washington, D.C., 24 December 1869) An antislavery Democrat from Ohio, Stanton's first major office was US attorney general in 1860. He succeeded Simon Cameron as secretary of war in 1862, and served Abraham LINCOLN ably, but opposed Andrew JOHNSON'S RECONSTRUCTION policies. Stanton's dismissal from office, contrary to the TENURE OF OFFICE ACT, was the main offense cited in impeaching Johnson. He died awaiting confirmation to be a Supreme Court justice.

Stanton, Elizabeth Cady (b. Johnstown, N.Y., 12 November 1815; d. New York, N.Y., 26 October 1902) After her career as a reformer had begun in ABOLITIONISM and temperance, Stanton shifted to women's rights after 1840. In 1848 she joined with Lucretia MOTT and others to organize the SENECA FALLS CONVENTION. She enlisted Susan B. ANTHONY into the movement in 1851. Stanton headed the National Woman Suffrage Association (1869–90), and was the first president of the National American Woman Suffrage Association (1890–2).

Staple Act *see* NAVIGATION ACT (1663)

Star Wars *see* STRATEGIC DEFENSE INITIATIVE

***Stark*, USS** On 17 May 1987, while protecting oil tankers from attacks by the Iranian navy during the Iran–Iraq War, the US frigate *Stark* was hit by two missiles from an Iraqi warplane that mistook it for an Iranian ship. The attack killed 37 sailors. Fear that another such attack was under way led the missile cruiser *Vincennes* to shoot down on 3 July 1988 an Iranian passenger plane mistaken for a hostile jet fighter. The Iranian plane had not filed a flight path with international authorities. The US paid compensation to the survivors among the 290 victims.

START *see* STRATEGIC ARMS REDUCTION TALKS

State, Department of On 29 November 1775, Congress assigned foreign communications to a Committee of Secret Correspondence, which was redesignated on 17 April 1777 as the Department for Foreign Affairs. On 27 July 1789, Congress established the Department of Foreign Affairs as a CABINET office (renamed the Department of State on 15 September) and named Thomas JEFFERSON its first secretary on 26 September.

State and Local Fiscal Assistance Act *see* REVENUE-SHARING

states' rights The concept of states' rights originated as a means of protecting constitutional freedoms threatened by federal abuses of power under the ALIEN AND SEDITION ACTS. The essence of states' rights is INTERPOSITION, which was initially propounded by the VIRGINIA RESOLUTIONS. The classic example of states' rights legislation enacted to preserve individual freedoms from unconstitutional federal laws was the PERSONAL LIBERTY LAWS, which attempted to guarantee the BILL OF RIGHTS' protections to free black citizens.

Interposition also served as an expedient theory rationalizing opposition to federal policies by regional minorities that could not block unwanted congressional laws. States' rights thus was used to justify the HARTFORD CONVENTION's demands for a local veto over trade embargoes, to vindicate S.C. in the NULLIFICATION CRISIS, and to validate the south's SECESSION. After 1945, states' rights was perverted from its origins – a means of enabling states to protect individual rights from federal interference – and became a pretext for many states to deny civil rights to racial minorities.

States' Rights Party This organization met in July 1948 at Birmingham, Ala., to nominate a southern Democratic alternative to Harry S. TRUMAN, whose pro-civil rights stance had alienated many white southerners. It nominated Strom THURMOND (S.C.) for president and Fielding Wright (Miss.) for vice-president. The ticket won just 2.4 percent of the popular vote, but carried four states with 39 electoral votes.

steel strike (1892) *see* HOMESTEAD STRIKE

steel strike (1919) In August 1919, labor leaders (including Samuel GOMPERS) formed a National Committee for Organizing Iron and Steel Workers, who had largely remained nonunionized since the HOMESTEAD STRIKE. On 22 September, the committee ordered a strike that soon was backed by 400,000 workers. By October, attempts to man the mills with strikebreakers led to violence and the NATIONAL GUARD's mobilization in many states. The committee admitted defeat and ended the walkout on 8 January 1920. The strike resulted in 20 deaths. Because William Foster, a leading Communist, was prominent in the episode, the strike reinforced public anxiety that radicals were fomenting labor violence, and contributed to the RED SCARE raids.

steel strike (1952) In March 1952, major steel firms rejected a government-mediated settlement awarding higher wages without a corresponding rise in steel prices, and a strike ensued. To prevent a halt in armaments production during wartime, Harry S. TRUMAN seized the steel mills on 8 April, but was overruled by *YOUNGSTOWN SHEET AND TUBE COMPANY V. SAWYER*. The steelworkers called another strike, which was resolved on 24 July by Truman's intervention, in which labor received a 16 cent raise and a modified UNION SHOP, while the firms were permitted to raise steel prices.

Steffens, Lincoln (b. San Francisco, Calif., 6 April 1866; d. Carmel, Calif., 9 August 1936) In 1892 Steffens entered journalism at New York and was an associate of Jacob RIIS; he became a freelance journalist in 1906. A true MUCKRAKER, Steffens produced the PROGRESSIVE ERA's classic exposé of urban political corruption in his magazine series "The Shame of the Cities" (1903–5), which indicted boss rule and graft. Steffens became more radical as he aged, visited the Soviet Union, and praised the Russian Revolution.

Stein, Gertrude (b. Allegheny, Pa., 3 February 1874; d. Neuilly-sur-Seine, France, 27 July 1946) After studying under William JAMES at Radcliffe, Stein spent four years at the Johns Hopkins Medical School, but declined to take her final exams. In 1903 she established herself in Paris, where she headed a circle of writers and authors that became a magnet for many fellow expatriate Americans. She coined the term LOST GENERATION to describe the post-World War I literary scene, to which she contributed both fiction and criticism. Her works include *Three Lives* (1909), *Tender Buttons* (1914), *The Making of Americans* (1924), *How to Write* (1931), *The Autobiography of Alice B. Toklas* (1933), *Lectures in America* (1935), *The Geographical History of America* (1936), *Picasso* (1939), *What Are Masterpieces* (1940), and *Wars I Have Seen* (1944).

Steinbeck, John (b. Salinas, Calif., 27 February 1902; d. New York, N.Y., 20 December 1968) After attending Stanford, without taking a degree, Steinbeck worked at a variety of low-paying jobs while writing fiction. He published his first book, *Cup of Gold*, in 1929, but did not achieve critical and commercial success until *Tortilla Flat* (1935). His best work sketched empathetic, yet realistic, portrayals of dispossessed, lonely, and hard-pressed people who were victimized by social injustice or intolerance. He won the Pulitzer prize for *The Grapes of Wrath* (1939) and received the Nobel prize for literature in 1962. Other major works included *In Dubious Battle* (1936), *Of Mice and Men* (1937), *The Moon is Down* (1942), *Cannery Row* (1945), *The Pearl* (1947), *The Wayward Bus* (1947), and *East of Eden* (1952).

Stephens, Alexander Hamilton (b. Taliaferro County, Ga., 11 February 1812; d. Atlanta, Ga., 4 March 1883) A University of Georgia graduate (1832), Stephens opened a law office at Crawfordville. He entered Congress as a Whig in 1843, but became a Democrat in 1852. Although opposed to the MEXICAN WAR, he fought efforts to bar SLAVERY from territories acquired by it until he left Congress in 1858. Elected CSA vice-president on 9 February 1861, he had a stormy relationship with Jefferson DAVIS. Ga. elected him to the Senate in 1866, but he was disqualified from taking his seat. He edited the Atlanta *Southern Sun* (1871–3), sat in Congress (1873–82), and won election as Ga. governor in 1882.

Stephens, Uriah *see* KNIGHTS OF LABOR

Steuben, Friedrich Wilhelm Augustus von (b. Magdeburg, Prussia, 17 September 1730; d. Utica, N.Y., 28 November 1794) After he had been a captain under Frederick the Great in the Seven Years' War, Steuben became a volunteer in Washington's army in 1777. Named drillmaster at VALLEY FORGE, he was responsible for raising the army's skills in battlefield maneuvers to a level roughly equal to the British army's by mid-1778. He was made inspector general, with rank of major general, in May 1778, and served to March 1784.

Stevens, Thaddeus (b. Danville, Vt., 4 April 1792; d. Washington, D.C., 11 August 1868) In 1814 Stevens moved to Pa., which elected him to Congress in 1848 as an anti-slavery Whig. He helped found the REPUBLICAN PARTY. At the end of the CIVIL WAR, he emerged as the House's leading RADICAL REPUBLICAN and foremost opponent of Andrew JOHNSON's plan to readmit ex-CSA states on lenient terms that failed to protect the FREEDMEN's political rights. He had enormous influence over the JOINT COMMITTEE ON RECONSTRUCTION. He chaired the House members appointed to manage Andrew Johnson's impeachment in the Senate, but was little involved because he was near death.

Stevenson, Adlai Ewing, Sr (b. Christian County, Ky., 23 October 1835; d. Chicago, Ill., 14 June 1914) A lawyer who was Democratic governor of both Ky. and Ill., Stevenson was US congressman (Democrat, Ill., 1875–7, 1879–81), assistant postmaster general (1885–9), and US vice-president (1893–7). As vice-president, he presided fairly over a Senate that had recently rejected him for a US judgeship; although a "soft-money" man, he never embarrassed President Grover CLEVELAND, a "hard-money" advocate, with open disagreement. He was the father of Adlai E. STEVENSON, Jr.

Stevenson, Adlai Ewing, Jr (b. Los Angeles, Calif., 5 February 1900; d. London, England, 14 July 1965) He was an Ill. lawyer who served with the AGRICULTURAL ADJUSTMENT ADMINISTRATION, Navy Department, and State Department. He became Ill. governor in 1948 by a landslide victory. An intellectual, liberal, and witty Democrat, he was nominated for president in 1952 (with running mate John Sparkman of Ala.), but carried only nine southern or BORDER STATES and took 44 percent of the ballots. Renominated in 1956 (with Estes KEFAUVER of Tenn.), he won 42 percent of the popular vote and seven states. He was US ambassador to the UN from 23 January 1961 to his death.

Steward Machine Company* v. *Davis *see* SOCIAL SECURITY ADMINISTRATION

Still, William Grant (b. Woodville, Miss., 11 May 1895; d. Los Angeles, Calif., 3 December 1978) He began his career performing with violin, cello, and oboe for theater orchestras and dance bands. He turned to composing symphonic music after 1925. His *Afro-American Symphony* (1931) was acclaimed as the first work of its kind to combine the black spiritual tradition with European classical music. He completed *A Bayou Legend* in 1940. Still's work earned him the title of dean of black classical composers.

Stimson Doctrine In September 1931, Japan invaded Manchuria with the intention of exploiting its natural resources through a puppet state. On 7 January 1932, Secretary of State Henry Stimson declared that the US would not recognize any territories or diplomatic agreements resulting from armed aggression. On 11 March, the LEAGUE OF NATIONS adopted the doctrine to protest Japanese aggression. The Stimson Doctrine laid the basis for the later US policy of denying Japan access to materials needed for its war against China.

stock market crash *see* BLACK THURSDAY

Stockbridge Indians *see* MAHICAN INDIANS

Stockdale, James *see* PEROT, H. ROSS

Stone, Barton *see* DISCIPLES OF CHRIST

Stone, Harlan Fiske (b. Chesterfield, N.H., 11 October 1872; d. Washington, D.C., 22 April 1946) From 1899 to 1924, Stone divided his time between his Wall Street law practice and teaching law at Columbia University. He served as attorney general in 1924 and joined the Supreme Court in 1925. Because Stone voted to uphold NEW DEAL programs and progressive state laws – despite his Republican background – Franklin D. ROOSEVELT nominated him as 11th chief justice in 1941 (confirmed 27 June). Major decisions by Stone included *GRAVES* v. *NEW YORK EX REL. O'KEEFE*, *UNITED STATES* v. *DARBY LUMBER COMPANY*, *UNITED STATES* v. *CLASSIC*, and *HIRABAYASHI* v. *UNITED STATES*. He was chief justice less than five years.

Stones River, battle of (Tenn.) On 31 December 1862, General Braxton Bragg's 34,700 Confederates drove Major General William Rosecrans's 41,400 Federals from their lines, but withdrew after losing 1,700 men in an assault on 2 January 1863. USA losses: 1,677 killed, 7,543 wounded, 3,686 missing. CSA losses: 1,294 killed, 7,945 wounded, 2,500 missing. Bragg placed his army to block an assault on Chattanooga by Rosecrans, whose advance to the battle of CHICKAMAUGA did not start until June.

Stono Creek Rebellion (S.C.) On 9 September 1739, about 100 slaves robbed plantations, stole weapons, and killed about 20 whites. All but perhaps 30 rebels were killed or captured by about 60 militia that day at Stono Creek, about 20 miles from Charles Town. The survivors were overtaken on 15 September while trying to escape to Fla. Over the next month, at least 20 of the prisoners were executed. This event was the only one of the SLAVE REVOLTS to claim a large number of white lives in the colonial era. The next significant insurrection was TURNER'S REVOLT, almost a century later.

Stony Creek, battle of (Canada) On 6 June 1813, Lieutenant Colonel John Harvey's 700 British troops surprised and routed 1,300 sleeping US militia under Brigadier Generals William Winder and John Chandler. US. losses: 17 killed, 38 wounded, 99 captured (including Chandler and Winder). British losses: 23 killed, 136 wounded, 55 missing. The battle threw US troops on the defensive and forced their retreat to FORT GEORGE.

Stony Point, battle of (N.Y.) On 16 July 1779, Brigadier General Anthony WAYNE's 1,200 Continentals (carrying unloaded muskets armed only with bayonets) stormed Lieutenant Colonel Henry Johnson's fortifications. US losses: 15 killed, 85 wounded. British losses: 20 killed, 74 wounded, 472 captured, 12 cannon. As the most skillful assault ever executed by the Continental Army, the battle avenged Wayne's defeat at PAOLI and exemplified the Continental Army's fighting abilities.

Stowe, Harriet Beecher *see* *UNCLE TOM'S CABIN*

Strader* v. *Graham In December 1850, the Supreme Court was asked to rule whether slaves owned in Ky. had become free by virtue of being taken to live in a non-slave state, and could not be returned to bondage. The justices voted that federal courts lacked jurisdiction over the case, and declared that a slave's legal status was rightly judged by the laws of his master's state. *Strader* was reaffirmed in *DRED SCOTT* v. *SANDFORD*.

Strategic Arms Limitation Treaty, first (SALT I) (26 March 1972) The product of negotiations begun on 17 November 1969 by the US and USSR, this agreement halted testing and deployment of offensive intercontinental ballistic missiles (ICBMs) and submarine-launched missiles. It limited the US to 1,054 ICBMs and 656 submarine missiles, and the USSR to 1,400 ICBMs and 950 submarine missiles. SALT I was observed past its expiration of 3 October 1977 by mutual agreement while SALT II negotiations continued. The ANTIBALLISTIC MISSILE TREATY was part of SALT I.

Strategic Arms Limitation Treaty, second (SALT II) (18 June 1979) This agreement placed a ceiling of 2,400 intercontinental ballistic missiles (ICBMs), submarine-launched missiles, and nuclear bombers on both the US and USSR; it also capped the number of missiles with multiple warheads to 1,320 on each side. The number of nuclear delivery systems was to drop to 2,250 after 1981. It was to last through 1 January 1985. After it passed the Senate Foreign Relations Committee, Jimmy CARTER suspended the ratification process to protest the USSR invasion of Afghanistan. The Carter and Reagan administrations nevertheless abided by its provisions past its expiration. The START discussions succeeded the SALT negotiations.

Strategic Arms Reduction Talks (START) Proposed by Ronald REAGAN on 9 May 1982, these talks supplanted SALT and were conducted in "umbrella discussions" that included the INTERMEDIATE-RANGE NUCLEAR FORCES TREATY and US curtailment of STRATEGIC DEFENSE INITIATIVE research. The talks differed from previous efforts in the field of NUCLEAR ARMS CONTROL in attempting to reduce stockpiles of missiles rather than place a ceiling on the deployment of future warheads. US negotiator Kenneth Adelman began the talks on 29 June 1982 at Geneva in hopes of eliminating over half of all nuclear weapons. Progress was complicated by Soviet demands that disarmament be accompanied by US discontinuance of the Strategic Defense Initiative. Agreement was finally reached on reducing each side's long-range nuclear weapons by 50 percent. A START accord was signed by George BUSH in July 1991, but made impractical by the Soviet Union's dissolution, which left Russia, Ukraine, and Kazakhstan each possessing nuclear weapons. Bush signed a revised agreement with Russia in June 1992, and the Senate ratified it on 2 October 1992, but Kazakhstan and Ukraine withheld approval pending further negotiations aimed at having them surrender their nuclear arsenals to Russia.

Strategic Defense Initiative (SDI) On 23 March 1983, Ronald REAGAN recommended intensive research on a space-based antiballistic missile system (popularly known as "Star Wars") against Soviet intercontinental ballistic missiles. The proposal was a fundamental shift from long-standing US reliance on MASSIVE RETALIATION to deter nuclear war; it provoked enormous controversy regarding its feasibility, cost, and likelihood of upsetting the STRATEGIC ARMS REDUCTION TALKS negotiations. The SDI was a significant part of the Reagan military build-up that induced the Soviets to raise their armaments spending to unsustainable levels, which in turn precipitated an economic-political crisis for the USSR by the late 1980s. On 13 May 1993, after spending $30 billion on SDI development, the Pentagon announced that further research would be discontinued.

Strickland* v. *Washington On 14 May 1984, the Supreme Court ruled (7–2) that the SIXTH AMENDMENT did not require a conviction's reversal on the grounds that counsel was ineffective, unless it were demonstrated that an attorney's errors were so egregious that they denied the defendant a reasonable probability of being acquitted.

strict constructionism This doctrine held that the CONSTITUTION should be interpreted as limiting the federal government to those activities and powers specifically delegated to Congress. The TENTH AMENDMENT strongly supported such a view, which was opposed by LOOSE CONSTRUCTIONISM. Strict constructionism was a key element in the ideology of early leaders of the DEMOCRATIC PARTY, especially Thomas JEFFERSON, James MADISON, and John RANDOLPH.

Stuart, Gilbert (b. North Kingston, R.I., 3 December 1755; d. Boston, Mass., 9 July 1828) He studied painting at Edinburgh (1769–72) and at London with the AMERICAN SCHOOL (1775–81). He won critical acclaim for his *Portrait of a Gentleman Skating* (1782), which resulted in numerous commissions and exhibitions at the Royal Academy [of Art]. In 1793 he returned to the US, where he opened a studio at Philadelphia. Stuart painted the most accurate and lifelike portraits of the early republic's political leaders, including Washington, Adams, Jefferson, Madison, and Monroe. He moved to Boston in 1805.

Stuart, James Ewell Brown (Jeb) (b. Patrick County, Va., 6 February 1833; d. Richmond, Va., 12 May 1864) In 1854

Stuart graduated 13th of 46 cadets from West Point. He was wounded fighting Indians, served in BLEEDING KANSAS, and joined Robert E. LEE's capture of John BROWN at Harper's Ferry. He joined the CSA army, although his wife's father was a Union general, and became brigadier general after fighting well at the first battle of BULL RUN. He was the war's premier cavalryman as commander of the Army of NORTHERN VIRGINIA's mounted forces, and was known as the "eyes of the army." On only one instance did he fail Lee, in the GETTYSBURG campaign, when he allowed himself to be cut off by the Union army for three days and could not provide the timely intelligence Lee needed for victory. He was mortally wounded engaging Philip SHERIDAN's forces at the battle of YELLOW TAVERN.

Student Nonviolent Coordinating Committee (SNCC) Southern black college students organized the SNCC in 1960 as part of the CIVIL RIGHTS MOVEMENT. It immediately demonstrated more militance than the NATIONAL ASSOCIATION FOR THE ADVANCEMENT OF COLORED PEOPLE, SOUTHERN CHRISTIAN LEADERSHIP CONFERENCE, or National URBAN LEAGUE. Its members were active in the SIT-IN MOVEMENT, as FREEDOM RIDERS, and in voter registration drives. When Stokely CARMICHAEL succeeded John Lewis as president in 1966, he placed the SNCC in the forefront of disavowing integration and nonviolence in favor of the BLACK POWER MOVEMENT. As the attraction of black power faded, and the cutting edge of civil rights progress shifted from direct action against segregation to court challenges, the SNCC lost its prominence and had broken up by the early 1970s.

Stuyvesant, Peter (b. Scherpenzeel, Friesland, Holland, ca. 1610; d. New York, N.Y., February 1672) A professional soldier, Stuyvesant was hired by the DUTCH WEST INDIA COMPANY in 1635. He became governor of Curaçao in 1644 and lost his right leg in battle that year. In 1647 he was named director general (governor) of NEW NETHERLAND. He negotiated a mutually acceptable boundary with Conn. in 1650 by the treaty of Hartford and forcibly annexed NEW SWEDEN in 1655. His administration was vigorous and efficient, but also marked by extreme intolerance toward religious minorities, for which his superiors rebuked him. After surrendering the colony to the English in 1664, he retired to a farm by New York City.

Subtreasury Act (1840) *see* INDEPENDENT TREASURY

Subtreasury Plan Supporters of POPULISM first proposed a Subtreasury Plan in 1889. It would have allowed farmers to store their harvest at federal warehouses during periods of low prices, and to obtain federal loans worth 80 percent of the crops' market value. The plan's intention was to enable farmers to keep commodities off the market when prices were low, and support themselves with loans until they rebounded. It was well suited to cotton, which did not spoil in storage, and was most popular among southern Populists. Its main features became law in the WAREHOUSE ACT.

Subversive Activities Control act *see* McCARRAN ACT

Suffolk Resolves (Mass.) To protest the INTOLERABLE ACTS, a convention of delegates from Mass. towns met in Suffolk County on 9 September 1774 and adopted resolutions drafted by Joseph Warren. The resolves declared that the Intolerable Acts were unconstitutional and should not be obeyed, that a provincial congress be formed to receive taxes until the MASSACHUSETTS GOVERNMENT ACT was repealed, that preparations for military defense be made, and that the arrest of any patriot leaders would result in seizures of royal officials.

Sugar Act (5 April 1764) Parliament amended the MOLASSES ACT (1733) by reducing import duties on non-British molasses from the West Indies from sixpence to threepence per gallon. By halving the duty, Britain believed it had set the amount at a rate that could be passed on to consumers by rum distillers and expected the law to produce up to £100,000, which would offset the expenses of garrisoning redcoats on the frontier. The Sugar Act was the first Parliamentary law passed for the purpose of raising revenue for the British treasury.

The law also burdened New England's trade by defining potash, pearl ash, hides, iron, whale fins, and lumber as ENUMERATED GOODS and taxing wine imported from

Portugal's Atlantic islands, which had been duty-free. By establishing a maze of regulations to verify compliance with the NAVIGATION ACTS, that were neither well designed for American conditions nor properly publicized, it subjected many cargoes to the threat of seizure for smuggling violations, which in fact were nothing more than innocent, technical violations of customs rules. The law finally gave jurisdiction over all colonial smuggling cases from the THIRTEEN COLONIES to a new ADMIRALTY COURT at Halifax, Nova Scotia. Besides facing criminal charges without juries, which were not used in Admiralty trails, a defendant was required to prove his own innocence, rather than making the state establish guilt.

Widespread smuggling resulted from the threepence duty on molasses until 1 November 1763, when it was reduced to one penny, but also applied to imports from the British Caribbean. The Sugar Act was the only British tax that ever produced a significant colonial revenue; it collected £306,399 from 1765 to 1774. Its complex regulations for validating legal trade encouraged customs officers to abuse their authority and file smuggling charges for innocent mistakes made in loading cargoes or certifying their legal status.

Sullivan, John Lawrence (b. Roxbury, Mass., 15 October 1858; d. Abingdon, Mass., 2 February 1918) In 1878 Sullivan became a professional boxer. For the next eleven years, he toured the US, Europe, and Australia as bare-knuckle champion and was undefeated upon retiring in 1889. After a dismal interlude as a traveling actor, he risked his heavyweight champion status by accepting a challenge from the younger James J. Corbett, who knocked him out (using gloves) in 21 rounds at New Orleans on 7 September 1892. The Sullivan–Corbett fight was the GILDED AGE's greatest sporting event, and ended the career of Sullivan, who ranks as America's first major sports hero.

Sullivan, Louis Henri (b. Boston, Mass., 3 September 1856; d. Chicago, Ill., 14 April 1924) Educated at the Mass. Institute of Technology and the École des Beaux Arts in Paris, Sullivan became an architect in Chicago. Following his dictum "form follows function," he was the foremost originator of the Chicago school of architecture, which would prove far better suited for designing skyscrapers than contemporary styles like Romanesque Revival and Victorian Gothic. Sullivan created the first architectural style that was distinctively American, and not inspired by a foreign tradition. His notable structures, with their vertical lines and subtle ornamentation, included the Chicago Auditorium (1889), Wainwright Building at St Louis (1890), the Schiller (1892), Stock Exchange (1894), and Gage (1898) buildings at Chicago, and the Prudential Building (1895) at Buffalo.

Sullivan's campaign To prevent further depredations like CHERRY VALLEY, N.Y., and WYOMING VALLEY, Pa., Washington ordered all SENECA, CAYUGA, and ONONDAGA INDIAN villages destroyed. Major General John Sullivan's 2,500 Continentals undertook that mission from May to November 1779. Sullivan routed Joseph BRANT's Iroquois near modern Elmira, N.Y., on 29 August 1779 (40 US killed and wounded, 12 Iroquois killed) and destroyed 40 Seneca and Cayuga villages. Colonel Goose Van Schaick burned the Onondaga towns, killed 20 warriors, and captured 37. BRODHEAD'S CAMPAIGN ravaged the Seneca towns on the Allegheny River in Pa. and N.Y. The Iroquois fled to Canada, where hundreds died of starvation and exposure to the elements that winter when 5 feet of snow fell on the refugees. Sullivan's campaign eviscerated the Iroquois and left them too weak to resist postwar pressure to permit white settlement on their lands by the treaties of FORT STANWIX.

Sumner, Charles (b. Boston, Mass., 6 January 1811; d. Washington, D.C., 11 March 1874) He helped found the FREE-SOIL PARTY in 1848 and the REPUBLICAN PARTY in 1854. He entered the Senate in 1851 and became an ABOLITIONIST martyr after giving his "CRIME AGAINST KANSAS" SPEECH. After resuming his seat in 1860, he was a prominent RADICAL REPUBLICAN, an influential member of the JOINT COMMITTEE ON RECONSTRUCTION, and a leader in Andrew JOHNSON's impeachment.

Sunday, Billy (William Ashley) (b. Ames, Iowa, 19 November 1862; d. Chicago, Ill., 6 November 1935) He played professional baseball for the Chicago White Stockings

(1883–91). After being ordained as a minister in the PRESBYTERIAN CHURCH in 1895, he used a theatrical and emotional preaching style to succeed Dwight MOODY as the country's premier evangelist. He claimed to have led 300,000 souls to salvation. His popularity peaked after 1910, when his support for PROHIBITION was a major factor in passing the EIGHTEENTH AMENDMENT.

superfund *see* COMPREHENSIVE ENVIRONMENTAL RESPONSE, COMPENSATION AND LIABILITY ACT

supply side economics This was a program for stimulating business investment by reducing taxes and other federal burdens on private enterprise. Ronald REAGAN adopted it as the theoretical centerpiece of his fiscal policies. Its fundamental proposition was that heavy government borrowing crowded out capital needed for business expansion, and should be reduced by spending cuts. Supply-siders also accepted the LAFFER CURVE's validity.

Supreme Court The JUDICIARY ACT (1789) established a Supreme Court of one chief and five associate justices, nominated by the president and confirmed by the Senate. The Court's size changed to five in 1801, seven in 1807, nine in 1833, ten in 1863, eight in 1866, and nine in 1869. The justices served as appellate judges "riding circuit" until 1891.

Under Chief Justice John MARSHALL, the Court asserted federal supremacy over the states. Under Chief Justice Roger TANEY, it consolidated its position – won under Marshall – as equal partner of the president and Congress. The Court resisted corporate attempts to use the FOURTEENTH AMENDMENT against government regulation in the 1870s, but by 1886 it was hostile to Progressive efforts to restrain anticompetitive practices and to improve conditions for workers; it also endorsed SEGREGATION and other JIM CROW LAWS.

The Court's conservatism intensified under Chief Justice William TAFT, but faced with Court-packing (*see* COURT-PACKING BILL) for opposing the NEW DEAL, it gradually liberalized after 1937. Under Chief Justice Earl WARREN, it issued landmark decisions on segregation, civil rights, DUE PROCESS, and individual rights. Since 1970, a Republican majority has modified many Warren Court rulings, but left most as precedent.

The Court first struck down a state law in *WARE* V. *HYLTON* (1796), first overturned a federal statute in *MARBURY* V. *MADISON* (1803), and first declared part of a state constitution (Ohio's) void in *Dodge* v. *Woolsey* (1856). Its earliest ruling reversed by congressional law was *PENNSYLVANIA* V. *WHEELING AND BELMONT BRIDGE*. The Court struck down 106 US statutes through 1980: 2 in 1803–57, 21 in 1858–99, 14 in 1900–19, 14 in 1920–32, 16 in 1933–49, and 39 in 1950–80.

Cases filed with the Court rose from 51 in 1803 to 253 in 1850 and 1,816 in 1890, before Congress passed the Court of Appeals Act (1891), which cut the caseload to 275 by 1892. The Court's docket increased to 723 in 1900, 1,039 in 1930, 2,296 in 1960, 4,212 in 1970, 4,781 in 1980, and 6,316 in 1990. The actual number of cases accepted by the Court (including summary decisions) has risen from 2 in 1791 to 286 in 1987.

Susquehannock Indians This group, speakers of one of the IROQUOIAN LANGUAGES, occupied the Susquehanna valley of Pa. They may have numbered 5,000 in 1600, but declined sharply after smallpox first hit them about 1660. They entered the FUR TRADE in the 1630s and soon acquired guns, which made them formidable foes. They were raiding IROQUOIS INDIAN beaver convoys as early as 1661 and repulsed a SENECA INDIAN invasion in 1663, but fell on the defensive during the BEAVER WARS and were decisively defeated in 1675. Some survivors dispersed to the Chesapeake, where they were attacked and enslaved by whites, many were adopted by Senecas, and a few bands remained in Pa., where they merged with DELAWARE INDIANS or were known as Conestogas. One of the last remnants were victims of the PAXTON MASSACRE.

***Sussex*, sinking of the** *see LUSITANIA*, HMS

Sutter, John Augustus (b. Berne, Switzerland, 15 February 1803; d. Washington, D.C., 18 June 1880) In 1834 Sutter emigrated to N.Y. In 1839 he settled in Calif., where he was granted 50,000 acres, built Sutter's Fort (near Sacramento), and planned to build a colony called New Switzerland. The

CALIFORNIA GOLD RUSH began when his carpenter discovered the metal in 1848. Sutter failed to capitalize on the gold rush's opportunities and went bankrupt.

Swann* v. *Charlotte-Mecklenberg County Board of Education On 20 April 1971, the Supreme Court unanimously affirmed the use of busing, assigning pupils to schools by racial quotas, and merging school districts as temporary ways to end state-imposed SEGREGATION in education. These remedies became the primary tools employed to dismantle racially separate school systems by federal judges, but they provoked a conservative backlash among white southern voters.

Sweatt* v. *Painter On 5 June 1950, in a SEPARATE BUT EQUAL case, the Supreme Court unanimously ruled that a qualified black applicant could not be denied admission to a segregated white law school if the facilities provided for black legal education were so inferior to those for whites that they could not provide equal schooling. (*See also* *MCLAURIN* V. *OKLAHOMA*)

Swedish immigration The colony of NEW SWEDEN left a significant Swedish population in Del., N.J., and Pa. Large-scale immigration began in the 1840s, and massive out-migration occurred after 1868, when western Europe's last great famine drove out 103,000 by 1873. From 1820 to 1900, 771,631 Swedes came to the US. Total immigration reached 1,285,717 by 1991. The 1990 census counted 2,881,950 Americans who described their primary ethnic identity as Swedish, 1.4 percent of whites.

Swift and Company* v. *United States On 30 January 1905, the Supreme Court unanimously upheld the company's conviction for anticompetitive practices under the SHERMAN ANTITRUST ACT. The Court ruled for the government according to the "stream of commerce" concept, which held that meatpacking and other intrastate businesses were subject to federal regulation if they formed an essential part of a marketing arrangement involved in interstate commerce. The decision ended much of the exemption from federal antitrust legislation enjoyed by manufacturing corporations since *UNITED STATES* V. *E. C. KNIGHT COMPANY*; it was a precedent for *NATIONAL LABOR RELATIONS BOARD* V. *JONES AND LAUGHLIN STEEL CORPORATION*. The Court extended its "stream of commerce" doctrine to intrastate transportation systems in the SHREVEPORT RATE CASES.

Sycamore Shoals, treaty of (Tenn.) On 17 March 1775, Richard Henderson's TRANSYLVANIA COLONY paid the CHEROKEE INDIANS £10,000 for 26,563 square miles of Ky. and Tenn. between the Ohio and Cumberland rivers. The sale enabled Henderson to dispatch Daniel BOONE to blaze the WILDERNESS ROAD and found Boonesborough.

Sylvis, William H. *see* NATIONAL LABOR UNION

T

Taft, Robert Alphonso (b. Cincinnati, Ohio, 8 September 1889; d. Washington, D.C., 31 July 1953) The son of William H. TAFT, he graduated first in his Harvard law school class. He served in the Ohio legislature (1921–36), was nominated to be Republican candidate for president in 1936, and entered the US Senate. He became the leading Republican isolationist and strongly opposed lend lease (*see* LEND LEASE ACT) and other US prewar assistance to Britain. After 1945, he co-sponsored the TAFT–HARTLEY ACT and vigorously attacked the Truman administration as an ineffective foe of communism. Although senate majority leader and known as "Mr Republican," he was passed over for president in 1952 in favor of Dwight D. EISENHOWER. He died of cancer soon after.

Taft, William Howard (b. Cincinnati, Ohio, 15 September 1857; d. Washington, D.C., 8 March 1930) In 1883 Taft opened a legal practice at Cincinnati, and was appointed to the Ohio supreme court at 30. He was governor of the PHILIPPINES (1901–4), secretary of war (1904–8), and elected president in 1908 with 51.6 percent of the popular vote. He carried on Theodore ROOSEVELT's antitrust policies, but broke with him over the PAYNE–ALDRICH TARIFF. He failed reelection in 1912 (taking just 23.2 percent of the popular vote), when Roosevelt's candidacy split the Republicans. He chaired the National War Labor Board (1918–19) and enthusiastically endorsed US membership in the LEAGUE OF NATIONS. On 30 June 1921, he was confirmed as ninth chief Justice. He led the Court to be more pro-business and conservative.

Taft Commission *see* COMMISSION ON EFFICIENCY AND ECONOMY

Taft–Hartley Act (23 June 1947) Passed over Harry S. TRUMAN's veto, this law regulated union administration and defined unfair practices by labor. It required unions to register and file financial reports to the Labor Department, and forbade Communists from serving as their officers. It forbade strikes without a majority vote by workers. It allowed a president to halt strikes prejudicial to the national interest by obtaining an injunction for an 80-day "cooling-off" period, so that an executive commission could investigate grievances and make recommendations, and after that Congress might enact a legislative solution.

The law outlawed CLOSED SHOPS, but not UNION SHOPS. It defined as illegal union practices: SECONDARY BOYCOTTS, jurisdictional strikes, demanding kickbacks to perform work, and union payments to political campaigns. It protected management's right to explain its position during organizational campaigns, to petition the NATIONAL LABOR RELATIONS BOARD for elections to decertify unions or change union representation, and sue unions for breach of contract or strike-related damages. The LANDRUM–GRIFFIN ACT strengthened several of its provisions.

On 8 May 1950, the Supreme Court upheld (5–1) its requirement that union officials not be affiliated with the COMMUNIST PARTY as a proper precaution to prevent political strikes from blocking interstate commerce in *American Communications Association, CIO et al.* v. *Douds.*

Taft–Katsura Memorandum On 29 July 1905, Secretary of War William TAFT and Japan's foreign minister finalized a secret agreement that the US would not criticize Japanese infringements of Korean sovereignty if Japan accepted US control over the PHILIPPINES. On 21 December, Japan declared Korea to be a protectorate of itself. (*See* ROOT–TAKAHIRA AGREEMENT)

Tammany Hall The Society of St Tammany was founded as a fraternal and benevolent organization in 1786, and chartered on 12 May 1789. In the 1790s, Aaron BURR transformed it into a partisan vehicle for mobilizing Democratic voters. Tammany's votes ensured Thomas JEFFERSON's winning margin in the 1800 election. It emerged as New York's most powerful political club and built an imposing hall that became its symbol. Tammany's success rested on machine-like efficiency in turning out its voters, whose loyalty it earned by providing jobs and social-welfare services to incoming waves of immigrants. By 1860 Tammany was the most powerful city machine in the US and a major kingpin in the national Democratic Party. Increasingly dependent on voter fraud and graft to stay in power, it became synonymous with corruption and HONEST GRAFT, especially after Boss William Tweed's administration (*see* TWEED RING). After attaining near unassailable power under Mayor Charles Murphy (1902–24), its control was broken by the reform administration of Republican Fiorello LA GUARDIA (1933–45). Tammany's influence also withered because NEW DEAL programs made its social-welfare services less important to the poor. Carmine De Sapio revived the Tammany system in the 1950s, but the organization became moribund after another decade.

Taney, Roger Brooke (b. Calvert County, Md., 17 March 1777; d. Washington, D.C., 12 October 1864) He entered public life in the FEDERALIST PARTY, but became a Jacksonian Democrat. He was Md. attorney general (1827–31), US attorney general (1831–3), acting secretary of war (1831), and acting secretary of the Treasury (1833–4) before being confirmed as fourth chief justice on 15 March 1836. Taney was the first Catholic on the SUPREME COURT. His most important and enduring decision was *CHARLES RIVER BRIDGE* v. *WARREN BRIDGE*. In *DRED SCOTT* v. *SANDFORD* and *ABELMAN* v. *BOOTH*, he led the Court in affirming that SLAVERY enjoyed constitutional protections beyond the power of either Congress or the states to violate. Taney's other major decisions included *BANK OF AUGUSTA* v. *EARLE*, *LUTHER* v. *BORDEN*, *KENDALL* v. *UNITED STATES EX REL. STOKES*, *HOLMES* v. *JENNISON*, *KENTUCKY* v. *DENNISON*, and *EX PARTE MERRYMAN*.

Tarawa Atoll, battle of On 20 November 1943, General Holland Smith's 12,000 marines began landing against Rear Admiral Keiji Shibasaki's 4,836 Japanese soldiers. Japanese resistance ended on 23 November. US losses: 1,056 killed, 2,292 wounded. Japanese losses: 4,819 killed, 17 captured. Tarawa's capture ended the threat from its Japanese airfield and gained a base for the MARSHALL ISLANDS CAMPAIGN.

Tarbell, Ida M. *see* MUCKRAKERS, *and* STANDARD OIL TRUST

Tariff of Abominations (19 May 1828) Passed after intense lobbying by northeastern manufacturers, this law set import duties at their highest levels until the MORRILL TARIFF. Rates rose on most clothing from 33.3 percent to 45 percent and on wool from 15 percent to 50 percent. Charges also rose sharply on foreign iron and hemp, to near 50 percent. The tariff was designed to raise about $20,000,000 in revenue until 1830, when Congress modified duties to cut taxes by $4,500,000, but left rates on clothing, wool, hemp, and iron untouched.

Tariff of (4 July) 1789 The first US tariff was written to ensure a regular income from customs duties to finance the federal budget and not to create an economic advantage for US industries (except that a 10 percent discount was given to items imported by the US MERCHANT MARINE rather than foreign ships). The REPORT ON MANUFACTURES's recommendation for protectionism was rejected. General rates were set at 5 percent (raised to 7.5 percent in 1792), and ad valorem rates averaged 8.5 percent (raised to 12.5 percent by 1812 and 25 percent by 1814) with a high of 15 percent.

Tariff of (27 April) 1816 This law was enacted largely to shield domestic industries that developed during the WAR OF 1812 from competition by British manufacturers, which had far lower operating costs. Duties were fixed on most imported clothing and iron at 25 percent, but were set to decline to

20 percent in 1891. Ad valorem rates averaged 15 percent, with a high of 30 percent on leather, hats, paper, and various goods.

Tariff of (20 April) 1818 Passed to relieve complaints that British manufacturers were driving their US counterparts out of business by dumping goods at below-market prices, this tariff increased duties on iron imports and postponed a scheduled 20 percent reduction in the rates on clothing until 1826.

Tariff of (22 May) 1824 This law increased rates on imported clothing from 25 percent to 33.3 percent. Rates were set on raw wool at 15 percent to benefit domestic producers, and duties were increased on iron products, glass, lead, hemp, and cotton bagging.

Tariff of (19 May) 1828 *see* TARIFF OF ABOMINATIONS

Tariff of (14 July) 1832 This measure cut import duties by a total of $5,000,000 by reductions in general items and goods for which no protectionist lobby existed. Because it left rates on clothing and iron at about 50 percent, it was viewed as special-interest legislation passed to benefit the northeast at southern expense. It was the immediate spark of the NULLIFICATION CRISIS.

Tariff of (2 March) 1833 Henry CLAY introduced this measure as part of a compromise to end the NULLIFICATION CRISIS. It expanded the number of duty-free goods, and reduced imposts at two-year intervals until 1842, when no rates would exceed 20 percent.

Tariff of (30 March) 1842 This tariff phased in higher duties that would restore rates to the TARIFF OF 1832's approximate level. By reinstituting protectionism, it cut customs revenues and forced an end to sharing the US Treasury surplus by the DISTRIBUTION ACT.

Tariff of (30 July) 1846 *see* WALKER TARIFF

Tariff of (3 March) 1857 This law set rates at an average level of about 20 percent, the lowest level since 1816. By ending protectionism, this Democratic measure sparked claims by northern businessmen that it had prevented recovery from the PANIC OF 1857, and consequently it increased the popularity of Republicans in the 1860 election.

Tariff of (2 March) 1861 *see* MORRILL TARIFF

Tariff of (14 July) 1870 This law retreated from the MORRILL TARIFF's protectionism by removing all duties from 130 items (mainly raw materials) and making small cuts in many rates.

Tariff of (6 June) 1872 This law lowered duties on all manufactured products by 10 percent.

Tariff of (3 March) 1875 This law returned duties to their approximate levels in the TARIFF OF 1870.

Tariff of (3 March) 1883 This law reduced imposts by 5 percent, but left rates at levels that were protectionist.

Tariff of (1 October) 1890 *see* MCKINLEY TARIFF

Tariff of (28 October) 1894 *see* WILSON–GORMAN TARIFF

Tariff of (7 July) 1897 *see* DINGLEY TARIFF

Tariff of (9 April) 1909 *see* PAYNE–ALDRICH TARIFF

Tariff of (3 October) 1913 *see* UNDERWOOD–SIMMONS TARIFF

Tariff of (27 May) 1921 *see* EMERGENCY TARIFF ACT (1921)

Tariff of (21 September) 1922 *see* FORDNEY–MCCUMBER TARIFF

Tariff of (17 June) 1930 *see* HAWLEY–SMOOT TARIFF

Tassafaronga, battle of On 30 November–1 December 1942, while bringing supplies to GUADALCANAL, Admiral Raizo Tanaka's 8 Japanese destroyers defeated Rear Admiral Carlton Wright's 5 US cruisers and 7 destroyers. US losses: 1 cruiser sunk, 3 cruisers disabled, 400 casualties. Japanese losses: 1 destroyer sunk.

Tax Reduction Act (26 February 1964) Proposed by John F. KENNEDY, but enacted under Lyndon JOHNSON, this law cut taxes by $11.5 billion over two years. It reduced individual INCOME TAX rates from a range of 20–91 percent to 16–77 percent in 1964 and to 14–70 percent in 1965. Corporate rates were cut to 50 percent in 1964 and 48 percent in 1965.

Tax Reform Act (27 September 1986) Following two years of pressure from Ronald REAGAN, Congress passed tax reductions and made major changes to the Internal

Revenue code. Top marginal rates fell to 34 percent for individuals (from a former high of 50 percent) and 26 percent for businesses (from a former high of 46 percent). Tax brackets were compressed from 14 into 3, which set effective rates at 15, 28, and 33 percent. Offsetting the rate cuts were the elimination of many tax shelters, business expenses, and deductions from personal income.

Taylor, Edward (b. Coventry, England, 1642; d. Westfield, Mass., 24 June 1729) A Harvard graduate (1671) who was a lifelong minister at Westfield, Mass., Taylor authored colonial Anglo-America's best poetry. He wrote 200 "Preparatory Meditations" (1682–1725) and several longer poems. His compositions remained unappreciated and unpublished until 1939.

Taylor, Frederick W. *see* TAYLORISM

Taylor, Zachary (b. Orange County, Va., 24 November 1784; d. Washington, D.C., 9 July 1850) After growing up on a Ky. plantation, Taylor entered the army in 1808. He fought in the WAR OF 1812 – when he won acclaim for repulsing an Indian attack on Fort Harrison, Ind. – the BLACK HAWK WAR, and the second SEMINOLE WAR, when he scored a major victory at Lake Okeechobee in 1837. As a MEXICAN WAR hero and La. planter, he was elected WHIG PARTY president with 47.4 percent of the ballots over Lewis CASS and Martin VAN BUREN. After 15 months in office, he died suddenly during the conflict over the COMPROMISE OF 1850.

Taylor Grazing Act (28 June 1934) This law was intended to prevent damage to open ranges from overgrazing. It directed the Interior Department to set aside 12,500 square miles as livestock ranges, which would be leased to cattlemen through 10-year permits. (The land reserved for grazing was increased to 22,000 square miles in 1936.) The law resulted in closing the PUBLIC DOMAIN to occupation because in 1935 the president declared an end to entering land under the first HOMESTEAD ACT so that the grazing districts could be delineated.

Taylorism From 1880 to 1910, Frederick W. Taylor devised this system for scientific management of industrial output, which was publicized and widely imitated after 1910. Taylor was the first major efficiency expert to explain how productivity could be raised significantly by establishing a research department to identify ways of improving technology, monitoring performance with time-and-motion studies, suggesting how to eliminate unnecessary steps in the work process, and motivating workers by bonus incentive plans. His ideas inaugurated the modern study of business management, contributed to significant increases in manufacturing productivity by 1929, and stimulated PROGRESSIVE ERA reformers to apply his analytical tools to finding solutions to social and economic problems.

Tea Act (10 May 1773) Confronted with the prospect of the bankruptcy of the East India Company, whose administrators and military forces performed valuable services for Britain in India, Parliament passed this law to revive sales of the company's tea in the THIRTEEN COLONIES. Because the colonies were boycotting legally imported British tea to protest the TOWNSHEND REVENUE ACT's taxes – but consuming less expensive smuggled varieties – increasing the volume of East India tea sold not only benefited the company, but also accomplished Parliament's long-standing goal of establishing an INTERNAL TAX by the Townshend Revenue Act.

The Tea Act reduced the cost of East India tea by cutting the duties previously collected when it entered Britain; the law also allowed the company to lower costs by selling tea directly to colonial consumers, rather than being forced to auction teas for overseas markets to merchants who added their own charges as middlemen when they retailed the tea. East India tea could consequently undersell any smuggled competitor, even when the Townshend tax of three pence per pound was added. Americans succeeded in preventing any East India tea from being landed at all colonial ports except Charles Town, S.C., where it was kept in customs warehouses and not released for sale, and Boston, where the BOSTON TEA PARTY resulted.

teach-ins Concerned over rising US military involvement in the VIETNAM WAR, University of Michigan faculty held a "teach-in" on 24 March 1965 that attracted 2,500 students. Similar meetings became a major means of enlisting students in the VIETNAM ANTIWAR MOVEMENT. A "national teach-in" involved 122 colleges on 15 May 1965.

Teacher Corps *see* HIGHER EDUCATION ACTS (1965 and 1967)

Teapot Dome scandal In 1921 Secretary of the Interior Albert Fall persuaded Warren HARDING to give his department responsibility for managing navy oil reserves at Teapot Dome, Wyo., and Elk Hills, Calif. In 1922 Fall secretly leased the petroleum fields to oil businessmen upon taking interest-free loans of $125,000. When the scandal broke in 1923, Fall was forced to resign. He was the first cabinet officer convicted of high crimes committed while in office, and went to prison for a year in 1931. Teapot Dome was the Harding administration's worst scandal.

Tecumseh (b. near Springfield, Ohio, ca. 1768; d. near Moraviantown, Ontario, 5 October 1813) In 1805 Tecumseh, the main SHAWNEE INDIAN leader, and his brother, the PROPHET (Tenskwatawa), began organizing a pan-Indian alliance to halt Anglo-American expansion. Just as Tecumseh seemed likely to unite northern Indians and the FIVE CIVILIZED TRIBES, the Prophet suffered a demoralizing loss in a rash attack on US forces at TIPPECANOE CREEK, Ind. When the WAR OF 1812 erupted soon after, Tecumseh lent Britain enough Indian support to keep US forces on the defensive until mid-1813. After he was killed at the battle of the THAMES RIVER, his followers abandoned Britain and signed the second treaty of GREENVILLE. Tecumseh was the last Indian leader who seriously challenged US control of the NORTHWEST TERRITORY.

Teheran conference (Iran) Between 28 November and 1 December 1943, Winston Churchill and Franklin D. ROOSEVELT met with Joseph Stalin for the first time to discuss military strategy and arrangements for peace after WORLD WAR II. Stalin promised to enter the war against Japan as soon as possible. (Russia entered six days before V-J DAY.) The US and Britain acquiesced in Russia's keeping territory in eastern Poland that it had seized while Germany's ally. The Allies laid plans for convening the DUMBARTON OAKS CONFERENCE.

telegraph Samuel F. B. Morse (1791–1872) filed a patent for the telegraph in 1837 (granted 1844) and developed Morse code to send messages. Congress spent $30,000 for an experimental wire from Baltimore to Washington, over which Morse transmitted the first long-distance message ("What hath God wrought!") on 24 May 1844. The PACIFIC TELEGRAPH ACT created a transcontinental wire service. The TRANSATLANTIC CABLE linked the US to Europe.

Teller, Edward (b. Budapest, Hungary, 15 January 1908) In 1930 Teller earned a Ph.D. in theoretical physics at the University of Leipzig, and was a research assistant in Germany until he came to the US in 1935 as a refugee from the Nazis. In 1941 he became a US citizen, went to Columbia to work with Enrico Fermi on nuclear fission, and joined the MANHATTAN PROJECT to build an atomic bomb. During WORLD WAR II, he did pathbreaking theoretical work on nuclear fusion, needed for a hydrogen bomb. After the USSR acquired the atomic bomb, Teller emerged as the leading spokesman for a priority program to build a US thermonuclear weapon; he was assistant director of the Los Alamos, N.Mex., research facility (1949–51), during which period the major hurdles to H-bomb production were overcome. He emerged as the scientific community's most vigorous advocate of nuclear weapons development, and strongly criticized proposals for bans or moratoriums on testing. After 1953 he divided his energies between the Berkeley physics department and the ATOMIC ENERGY COMMISSION'S (AEC) laboratory at Livermore, Calif. He received the AEC's Fermi award in 1962.

temperance movement *see* PROHIBITION

Ten Percent Plan *see* RECONSTRUCTION

Tennent, Rev. Gilbert (b. County Armagh, Ireland, 5 February 1703; d. Philadelphia, Pa., 23 July 1764) He was a minister in the PRESBYTERIAN CHURCH whose preaching helped stimulate the REFRESHINGS. He led the "New Light" faction within his denomination during the first GREAT AWAKENING. By suggesting that most Presbyterian ministers were spiritually unfit to lead their congregations to salvation, his sermon, "The Danger of an Unconverted Ministry" (1740), sparked a struggle between pro-revivalist and anti-revivalist parties that ended in schism. Tennent became pastor of Philadelphia's Second Presbyterian Church in 1743 and was instrumental in reuniting his denomination on terms favorable to the New Lights in 1758.

Tennessee In January 1769, when the first whites settled on the Watauga River, Tenn. had no permanent Indian occupants outside of its southeastern mountains. In 1779 the earliest settlements outside the mountain barrier were made at Nashville. In the REVOLUTIONARY WAR, Tenn. was engulfed by raids by CHEROKEE INDIANS and Britain's other Indian allies. Population rose sharply in the 1780s. Dissatisfaction with eastern failure to pacify the Indians or gain the RIGHT OF DEPOSIT led Tenn. leaders to organize the state of FRANKLIN and join in the SPANISH CONSPIRACY. Tenn. came under US control as the Southwest Territory on 7 August 1789. When it entered the Union on 1 June 1796, 14 percent of its 77,000 inhabitants were slaves. By 1800 it contained 105,602 settlers.

Cotton and tobacco dominated the Tenn. economy, except in the mountains, where there were few slaves and production of foodstuffs predominated. In 1860 it had 1,109,801 residents, of whom 25 percent were slaves and 2 percent were foreign-born; it ranked 10th among states in population, 8th in the value of its farmland and livestock, and 19th in manufactures. On 7 May 1861, it became the 10th CSA state. In the CIVIL WAR, it furnished 115,000 CSA troops and 51,255 USA soldiers (31,092 white and 20,133 black). Tenn. was the site of 1,462 military engagements, more than any state but Va.

In March 1862, Andrew JOHNSON organized a military government, and Tenn. regained full status as a state on 24 July 1866, before congressional RECONSTRUCTION began. By denying ex-Confederates the right to vote, Republicans controlled the state until 4 October 1869. Tenn. disfranchised most blacks by POLL TAX and imposed SEGREGATION.

In 1900 it had 2,020,616 people, of whom 84 percent were rural, 24 percent were black, and 1 percent were foreign-born; it ranked 14th among states in population, 16th in the value of its agricultural goods, and 25th in manufactures. From 1920 to 1940, it lost 590,700 out-migrants, mostly blacks moving to northern cities, and the racial composition shifted significantly. The TENNESSEE VALLEY AUTHORITY greatly stimulated economic development. Tenn. ranked as the 16th largest state in 1990, when its population was 4,877,185 (83 percent white, 16 percent black, 1 percent Hispanic), of whom 68 percent were urban and 1.2 percent were foreign-born. Manufacturing employed 23 percent of the work force and mining 7 percent.

Tennessee, CSA Army of the This army was the principal CSA battle force in the west. Formed on 20 November 1862 by uniting the armies of Ky. and Miss., it fought from STONES RIVER to its virtual destruction at NASHVILLE. Its commanders were Braxton Bragg to December 1863, Joseph E. JOHNSTON to July 1864, John B. Hood to January 1865, Richard Taylor to February 1865, and Johnston again to its surrender on 26 April 1865.

Tennessee, USA Army of the This army was the principal USA battle force in the west. Formed on 16 October 1862 from troops west of the Tennessee River in Ky., Tenn., and northern Miss., it fought from SHILOH through the MARCH TO THE SEA. Its commanders were Ulysses S. GRANT to October 1863, William T. SHERMAN to March 1864, James McPherson to July 1864, Otis Howard to May 1865, and John Logan to August 1865.

Tennessee Valley Authority (TVA) On 18 May 1933, the TVA was created to develop the economy of the Tennessee River drainage basin with dams, hydroelectric plants, and transmission lines, and also to sell inexpensive electricity and fertilizers in the region; it would also prevent recurrent flooding, improve river navigation, and sponsor environmental conservation programs. The TVA was an independent public corporation governed by a board of three and initially headed by Arthur Morgan. By improving five dams and building 20 new ones, the TVA transformed a river subject to violent, uncontrolled deluges into a 652-mile inland-transportation system with a nine-foot channel. By 1942 the TVA generated more energy than any

US utility and had cut the region's cost of electricity by 33 percent from 1933. The Supreme Court ruled it constitutional in *ASHWANDER* v. *TENNESSEE VALLEY AUTHORITY*.

Tenth Amendment Submitted to the states on 25 September 1789, last ratified by Va. on 15 December 1791, and officially proclaimed on 30 December 1791, it was designed to prevent a consolidated central government from increasing its power at the states' expense; it reserved for the states and their citizens all powers neither denied explicitly to them nor delegated to the US. The amendment's goal of narrowly limiting the scope of federal authority was frustrated by the SUPREME COURT's nationalistic interpretation of the Constitution in *MCCULLOCH* v. *MARYLAND* and *COHENS* v. *VIRGINIA*.

Tenure of Office Act (2 March 1867) Passed over Andrew JOHNSON's veto, this act required the president to seek the Senate's approval before dismissing any federal officials who required senatorial confirmation. Eight of the eleven charges in Johnson's impeachment trial alleged that he violated this law by dismissing Secretary of War Edwin STANTON on 21 February 1868 and naming Lorenzo Thomas in his place. The law was repealed at Grover CLEVELAND's request on 5 March 1887. The Supreme Court declared the law to have been unconstitutional in *Myers* v. *United States* (1926).

term limits The most significant grassroots political phenomenon of the 1990s was a movement by voters to enact term limits that would restrict the number of times an officeholder could seek reelection. Beginning with Colo. in 1990, referendums on term limits were approved in Ariz., Ark., Calif., Colo., Fla., Mich., Mo., Mont., Nebr., N.Dak., Ohio, Oreg., S.Dak., Utah, Wash., and Wyo. by 1992. In 1994 term-limit proposals were approved in Alaska, Idaho, Mass., Maine, Nev., and Okla. In 1994 the Supreme Court agreed to decide, in a case from Ark., whether state referendums could impose term limits on candidates for Congress and the Senate.

termination Indian policy To hasten the acculturation of Native Americans into mainstream US society, Congress and the BIA devised policies aimed at the eventual termination of the federal government's trusteeship over reservation Indians. It created the Voluntary Relocation Program in 1952 to encourage migration from economically depressed RESERVATIONS to urban job markets, and in 1956 the BIA introduced off-reservation educational activities like the Adult Vocational Training Program. In 1953, Congress made tribal Indians subject to the same PROHIBITION laws as whites and authorized Calif., Minn., Nebr., Oreg., and Wis. to extend unilaterally their legal codes onto reservations. During 1954 to 1962, Congress ended federal trusteeship over 61 Indian groups. The United States abandoned its termination policy because too many tribes suffered serious economic setbacks when thrown upon their own resources. By 1978, Congress had renewed the US trust relationship with MENOMINEE, MODOC, OTTAWA, Peoria, and WYANDOT nations.

Terry* v. *Adams On 4 May 1953, the Supreme Court affirmed *SMITH* v. *ALLWRIGHT* and ruled that the Tex. Democratic WHITE PRIMARY was unconstitutional; it held that participation in the primary was an essential aspect of voting rights, because since the Democratic primary's victors invariably won the next general election, excluding blacks violated the FIFTEENTH AMENDMENT.

test oath cases (*Cummings* v. *Missouri*, *Ex Parte Garland*) In 1867 the Supreme Court heard challenges to the 1865 Mo. constitution and an 1865 federal law because both forced various persons to swear that they had been loyal Unionists in the CIVIL WAR. The Court ruled (5–4) that it violated the Constitution's ban on BILLS OF ATTAINDER and EX POST FACTO LAWS to bar persons from professions or government offices if they could not take such oaths because of past disloyalty or misconduct.

Tet offensive On 30 January 1968, 80,000 North Vietnamese and Vietcong attacked the garrisons of 105 cities and the US embassy. They failed to hold any major objective except HUE more than a week and sustained perhaps 45,000 deaths, compared to just 1,100 US and 2,300 South Vietnamese. The Vietcong never recovered from their staggering losses, and North Vietnamese regulars thereafter formed that side's military backbone. News coverage nevertheless emphasized the enemy's initial success, the prolonged battle for Hue, and the sharp rise in US casualties. As American public opinion became more confused, demoralized, and sympathetic to the VIETNAM ANTIWAR MOVEMENT, Tet emerged as the war's turning point for having decisively undermined US resolve to achieve full military victory.

Texas On 20 June 1716, Spain founded the first permanent white settlement, the mission San Francisco de los Tejas. By 1810 Tex. contained just 4,000 Christians (of all races). To develop the province, Mexico invited Stephen AUSTIN and other Anglo-Americans to establish colonies as a barrier against COMANCHE INDIAN raids. By 1835 there were 32,500 Anglo-Americans and 3,500 Spanish Texans. It was independent from the TEXAS REVOLT until the 1845 annexation of TEXAS. (The one-star flag from that period gave Tex. its nickname as the "Lone-Star State.") It became a major cotton producer. In 1860 it had 604,215 residents, of whom 30 percent were slaves and 7 percent were foreign-born; it ranked 25th among states in population, 22nd in the value of its farmland and livestock, and 29th in manufactures.

Tex. became the 7th CSA state on 1 February 1861. In the CIVIL WAR, it furnished 65,000 CSA troops and 2,012 USA soldiers (1,965 white and 47 black). Tex. was the site of 90 military engagements.

In June 1865, Andrew JOHNSON instituted a provisional civilian government, which ended slavery in February 1866, but refused to let FREEDMEN vote. White supremacists took over the legislature, passed a black code (*see* BLACK CODES), and rejected the FOURTEENTH AMENDMENT. Washington imposed military rule on 2 March 1867, but restored self-government and congressional representation on 30 March 1870. Republican control ended three years later on 14 January 1873.

Tex. disfranchised most blacks by POLL TAX, enacted a WHITE PRIMARY in 1903, and imposed racial SEGREGATION after 1900. Influenced by progressive leaders like Lyndon JOHNSON and John Connally, its government largely acquiesced in federal desegregation efforts after 1954.

After the southern herds of BUFFALO were thinned and the Indians were pacified by the RED RIVER WAR, settlement greatly expanded north and west. Tex. was the center of the CATTLE KINGDOM and became the largest US producer of cotton. In 1900 it had 3,048,710 residents, of whom 83 percent were rural, 20 percent black, and 6 percent were foreign-born; it ranked sixth among states in population, fifth in the value of agricultural products, and 23rd in manufactures. Oil rose to be a major industry after the first large field was discovered in 1901. DUST BOWL conditions badly damaged agriculture in the 1930s. In WORLD WAR II, the aerospace industry and expansion of military bases emerged as significant parts of the state economy. During the 1940s, the shift to a primarily urban population led to even greater economic diversification. Population grew rapidly from domestic inmigration and MEXICAN IMMIGRATION. In 1990 Tex. was the third-largest state and had 6,986,510 people (61 percent white, 12 percent black, 25 percent Hispanic, 2 percent Asian), of whom 82 percent were urban and 9.0 percent were foreign-born. Mining and manufacturing employed 23 percent of workers. In 1994 Tex. surpassed N.Y. in population and became the second-largest state.

Texas, annexation of The US first formally offered to buy Tex. from Mexico under John Q. ADAMS, and all presidents did so until the TEXAS REVOLT. The rise of ABOLITIONISM led many northerners to oppose the admission of another slave state, but in 1844, John CALHOUN spurred John TYLER to negotiate an annexation treaty, which was defeated by WHIG PARTY senators eager to embarrass a Democratic president. The 1844 election pitted James POLK, who favored annexation, against Henry CLAY, who opposed it. Polk saw his victory as a mandate to make Tex. a state, but before he took office, Tyler won congressional approval for annexation on 1 March 1845. Mexico vehemently protested the act, which led to the MEXICAN WAR.

Texas and Pacific Railway Company* v. *United States *see* SHREVEPORT RATE CASES

Texas Revolt Alienated by Mexico's refusal to restore political privileges enjoyed since 1822 (including SLAVERY), Anglo-Americans under William Travis took over the Anahuac garrison on 30 June 1835. After Mexican President Antonio Lopez de Santa Anna's army entered the province, Texans declared independence on 1 March 1836. By early April, Santa Anna had massacred the garrisons of the ALAMO and GOLIAD and driven rebel commander in chief Samuel HOUSTON's forces into retreat. Houston's counterattack at SAN JACINTO decisively defeated the Mexicans and forced Santa Anna to sign a treaty on 14 May 1836 recognizing Texan independence.

Texas* v. *Mitchell *see* *OREGON* V. *MITCHELL*

Texas* v. *White In 1869, in a case over the legality of the Confederate government's financial obligations, the Supreme Court ruled on the constitutionality of Congress's RECONSTRUCTION policies. The Court held (6–3) that although SECESSION was illegal and the southern states had never legally left the Union, Congress might pass laws concerning their political organization to fulfill its constitutional duty of guaranteeing every state a republican government in the aftermath of a rebellion (as already decided in *LUTHER* V. *BORDEN*).

Thames River, battle of (Ontario) On 5 October 1813, Major General William H. HARRISON's 3,300 Ky. militia and 140 US regulars overran Brigadier General Henry Proctor's 830 British and TECUMSEH's 600 Indians near Moraviantown. US losses: 15 killed, 30 wounded. British losses: 12 killed, 36 wounded, 477 captured. Indian losses were unknown, but included Tecumseh's death. The victory destroyed British military power west of Lake Ontario, crushed Indian resistance, and compelled Indian submission to the second treaty of GREENVILLE.

Thanksgiving Va. celebrated the earliest such holiday in 1614 by the governor's edict, but the modern holiday evolved from the first such feast held by the PILGRIMS in October 1621. They celebrated Thanksgiving on a sporadic rather than a regular basis. The second CONTINENTAL CONGRESS proclaimed the first national Thanksgiving for 18 December 1777, in gratitude for the surrender at SARATOGA. George WASHINGTON proclaimed two Thanksgiving celebrations (1789 and 1795), and James MADISON announced another at the end of the WAR OF 1812. The holiday remained a local custom for New Englanders until Abraham LINCOLN made it a national observance during the CIVIL WAR, beginning in 1862.

Third Amendment Submitted to the states on 25 September 1789, last ratified by Va. on 15 December 1791, and officially proclaimed on 30 December 1791, it forbade soldiers from being quartered in homes during peacetime without the owner's consent, and it prohibited quartering during wartime unless authorized by law.

thirteen colonies Nineteen colonies were founded within the modern US, but PLYMOUTH, NEW HAVEN, EAST JERSEY, and WEST JERSEY had become defunct by 1776. Only 13 provinces became independent in 1776: N.H., Mass., R.I., Conn., N.Y., N.J., Pa., Del., Md., Va., N.C., S.C., and Ga. The ROYAL COLONIES of EAST and WEST FLORIDA remained in the British empire, but were ceded to Spain in 1783.

Thirteenth Amendment Submitted to the states on 1 February 1865, last ratified on 6 December 1865, and officially proclaimed on 18 December 1865, it abolished SLAVERY, which had already been outlawed in all but two states; it freed 65,000 slaves in Ky. and 1,000 in Del. *ARVER* V. *UNITED STATES* ruled that its meaning of involuntary servitude did not apply to a military DRAFT. Miss. is the only state then in the Union that has never ratified this amendment.

Thomas, George Henry (b. Southampton County, Va., 31 July 1816; d. San Francisco, Calif., 28 March 1870) In 1840 Thomas graduated 12th of 42 cadets from West Point. He served in the SEMINOLE WAR, was twice cited for gallantry in the MEXICAN WAR, and was badly wounded while fighting Indians in 1860. Promoted to USA brigadier general in 1861, he won an important victory at MILL SPRINGS, Ky. As major general, he earned the nickname "Rock of CHICKAMAUGA," when his corps beat off furious CSA attacks long enough to protect the Army of the TENNESSEE from annihilation. He held CHATTANOOGA against a CSA siege and captured Missionary Ridge. His troops formed half the USA forces that captured ATLANTA. He crushed the last major CSA army in the western theater at NASHVILLE. Only Ulysses S. GRANT, William T.

SHERMAN, and Philip SHERIDAN contributed more to Union victory than Thomas.

Thomas, Isaiah (b. Boston, Mass., 30 January 1750; d. Worcester, Mass., 4 April 1831) He was the primary printer for materials publicizing the views of Samuel ADAMS and founded the Massachusetts *Spy*, the WHIGS' principal newspaper in Revolutionary New England. He became the most respected and prolific printer of his day, and wrote the earliest history of his profession (2 vols, 1810). He was the first president of the American Antiquarian Society, which was founded largely at his initiative in 1812.

Thomas, Norman Mattoon (b. Marion, Ohio, 20 November 1884; d. Huntington, N.Y., 19 December 1968) He worked in settlement houses in New York slums and was ordained a Presbyterian minister in 1911. He joined the SOCIALIST PARTY OF AMERICA, opposed US entry into WORLD WAR I, and helped found the AMERICAN CIVIL LIBERTIES UNION. He ran for president on the Socialist ticket every year from 1928 to 1944, but never polled more than 1 percent except in 1932 (2.2 percent). He opposed the US CONTAINMENT POLICY for communism and aided the VIETNAM ANTIWAR MOVEMENT.

Thomas, Theodore (b. Essen, Germany, 11 October 1835; d. Chicago, Ill., 4 January 1905) Trained as a violinist by his father, he emigrated with his parents to New York in 1845. After a short career as a solo violinist, he organized his own touring orchestra in 1862. Thomas was the first great American symphonic conductor, and a key figure in expanding the popularity of classical music in the US. He became conductor of the Brooklyn Philharmonic Society in 1866, director of Cincinnati's College of Music in 1878, conductor of the N.Y. Philharmonic Society in 1880, and director of the American Opera Company in 1885. When asked in 1891 – while he was temporarily without a position – whether he would go to Chicago to head his own orchestra, he replied that he would go to Hell for his own orchestra, and became conductor of the Chicago Symphony. During a stewardship lasting until 1905, he began the building of this orchestra into a world-class organization.

Thoreau, Henry David (b. Concord, Mass., 12 July 1817; d. Concord, Mass., 6 May 1862) He was a philosopher, essayist, and social critic who belonged to Ralph W. EMERSON's intellectual circle. His best known works were *Walden, or Life in the Woods* (1854), in which he upheld self-reliance and simplicity over materialism and commercialism, and his essay "Civil Disobedience," (1849) in which he outlined how unconscionable laws might be discredited by passive resistance that creates martyrs whose unjust punishment will shame the public conscience.

Three Mile Island accident On 28 March 1989, a malfunction at Metropolitan Edison Company's Three Mile Island nuclear reactor near Harrisburg, Pa., pushed internal temperatures up to 5,200° F. (nearly hot enough to melt the uranium core). Radioactive gases escaped through the plant's venting system, and small amounts of radiation seeped from the plant for 13 days. By 2 April, 40 percent of the population living within 10 miles had evacuated their homes. The Nuclear Regulatory Commission declared the emergency over on 9 April. Although no injuries were sustained, it was the worst nuclear accident in US history and led to a strong backlash against nuclear power among the public.

Threshold Test Ban Treaty (3 July 1974) This agreement between the US and USSR strengthened the NUCLEAR TEST BAN TREATY by setting limits on the megatonnage permitted in underground nuclear tests.

Thrift Institutions Restructuring Act *see* SAVINGS AND LOAN CRISIS

Thurmond, J(ames) Strom (b. Edgeville, S.C., 5 December 1902) After service with the army in WORLD WAR II, Thurmond was elected S.C. governor (Democrat) in 1946. As STATES' RIGHTS PARTY nominee for president in 1948, he polled 2.4 percent of ballots and carried four states. During 28–9 August 1957, he gave the US Senate's longest filibuster (24 hours, 18 minutes). He became a Republican on 16 September 1964, but learned to court the black vote. Thurmond chaired the Senate Judiciary Committee (1981–7), and won his last Senate campaign at the age of 87 in 1990.

tidewater This term refers to the coastal plain of the Atlantic US seaboard east of the first line of riffles that would block seagoing ships from further inland travel. Before the end of QUEEN ANNE'S WAR, few Anglo-Americans had settled beyond this region outside of New England, where it was most narrow.

Tilden, Samuel Jones (b. New Lebanon, N.Y., 9 February 1814; d. Yonkers, N.Y., 4 August 1886) In 1834 Tilden opened a law office in New York City. He became a rich and well-connected corporate lawyer who principally represented railroads. He emerged as a major Democratic leader in ending the TWEED RING's corruption and reforming New York government, and was elected N.Y. governor in 1874. As Democratic presidential nominee in 1876, he received 51 percent of the votes (outpolling Rutherford HAYES by 247,448 ballots), clearly won 184 electoral votes (just one short of a majority), and claimed a disputed vote from Oreg. The Republicans claimed 19 disputed votes from the South, however, and Congress created an ad hoc election committee to award the questionable votes. Influenced by the COMPROMISE OF 1877, the committee made Hayes president by awarding every contested vote to him. To prevent partisan politics from again deciding a presidential election, Congress enacted the ELECTORAL COUNT ACT.

Timber and Stone Act (3 June 1878) Congress authorized public lands in Wash., Oreg., Calif., and Nev. to be sold in plots of 160 acres at $2.50 an acre, provided the land was wooded and "unfit for civilization." The law was widely abused, and by 1902 lumber companies had fraudulently obtained 2,891,000 acres in Oreg. and Calif. It was repealed on 3 March 1891.

Timber Culture Act (3 March 1873) Congress permitted settlers to claim 160 acres of public land on the Great Plains if they planted trees on 40 acres within a decade. In 1873 the tree requirement was reduced to 10 acres because of the difficulty of raising trees in the arid west. Of 245,000 applications made under this law, only about 60,000 complied with its provisions and got title to their land.

Timucua Indians This group of Indians spoke a language isolate of undetermined origin and occupied both coasts of Fla. The FLORIDA MISSIONS converted large numbers to Catholicism, especially on the east coast near ST AUGUSTINE. In QUEEN ANNE'S WAR, their missions were destroyed and large numbers were taken to S.C. as slaves. The Timucuan population dwindled further after 1720 due to warfare with other Indians and diseases contracted from Europeans. By 1821 few Timucua survived except a handful of non-Christians in southern Fla.

Tinian, battle of On 24 July 1944, the Second and Fourth USMC Divisions landed on Tinian Island, held by 9,000 Japanese, and eliminated organized Japanese resistance by 1 August. US losses: less than 2,000 casualties. Japanese losses: almost 9,000 casualties.

Tippecanoe Creek, battle of (Ind.) On 7 November 1811, Governor William H. HARRISON's 350 US regulars and 620 Ind.-Ky. militia repulsed an attack by the PROPHET's 700 Shawnees and other Indians. On 8 November, Harrison burned the Indians' town. US losses: 62 killed, 126 wounded. Indian losses: 200 killed, wounded. The battle ended the first treaty of GREENVILLE's peace between Indians and whites.

Tison and Tison* v. *Arizona On 21 April 1987, the Supreme Court extended *GREGG* v. *GEORGIA* by ruling (5–4) that the EIGHTH AMENDMENT allows execution for persons whose behavior contributes importantly to a murder and shows reckless indifference to human life, but who do not themselves kill or intend to kill the victims.

Tlingit Indians This group of Indians occupied the ALASKA coast south of Yakutat Bay. Their speech was closely related to the family of ATHAPASCAN LANGUAGES and their culture was based on a maritime economy and trapping rather than agriculture. They acquired firearms from British and US fur traders in the late 1700s. In 1799 Russian fur traders encroached on their territory and founded Sitka, which the Tlingit destroyed in 1802, and the Russians recaptured with much bloodshed in 1804. Tlingits launched major assaults on Russian outposts in 1805, 1809, 1813, and 1818. By frustrating Russia's attempts to establish firm control over the Alaska coast – despite many deaths from smallpox in 1836–40 – their resistance was a major factor in the Czar's decision to sell Alaska to the US in 1867.

Toleration Act (21 April 1649) After Protestants became numerous in MARYLAND and rebelled against its Catholic governor in 1645, the colony's Catholic leaders promulgated the Toleration Act, which offered freedom of worship to all orthodox Christians believing in the Trinity, except blasphemers. This measure was the earliest American ordinance offering religious freedom to the broad majority of citizens, but it inspired no imitators among other colonies. It was itself repealed in November 1654 following a successful insurrection by Protestants, and had long been forgotten by the mid-18th century.

Tompkins, Daniel D. (b. Scarsdale, N.Y., 21 June 1774; d. at Tompkinsville, N.Y., 11 June 1825) A lawyer and N.Y. governor (Democrat 1807–17), Tompkins was US vice-president (1817–25) under James MONROE. He spent much of his career as vice-president litigating court cases over expenditures made as governor in the WAR OF 1812.

Tonnage Act (20 July 1789) This law attempted to protect the US MERCHANT MARINE and ship-building industry from foreign (mainly British) competition through discriminatory port fees of six cents per ton on US-owned ships, 30 cents on foreign-owned ships, and 50 cents on vessels both owned and built in Europe. Along with customs discounts given to goods carried in US bottoms in the TARIFF OF 1789, it contributed to cutting the tonnage of US foreign trade carried in European vessels from 46 percent in 1789 to 15 percent in 1800.

Topeka Constitution Following an election marked by widespread fraud that returned a pro-slavery majority to the first legislature of Kansas Territory, free-soil settlers convened their own convention from 12 October to 2 November 1855 at Topeka and drafted a constitution forbidding slavery. Franklin PIERCE rejected it as unlawful.

Tories During the REVOLUTIONARY WAR, the WHIGS termed their enemies Tories, a term associated with Jacobites who favored the Catholic Stuart dynasty's claim to the British throne over the Protestant Hanovers. (Britain's Tories were widely viewed as deeply loyal to the crown and lukewarm about defending Parliament from royal encroachments upon representative government.) Organized groups of Tories did not appear until after early 1775, and they preferred to call themselves Loyalists. There were few Tories in New England and Va. (5 percent or less), but elsewhere they often numbered a quarter of all whites. Overall, perhaps one in six adult, white males were Tories when the Revolutionary War began, but most had become WHIGS by its conclusion. Over 60,000 may have left the US for Canada or Britain by 1783. Indian nations and most slaves were pro-British for reasons of self-interest rather than politics.

Townsend, Francis Everett (b. near Fairbury, Ill., 13 January 1867; d. Los Angeles, Calif., 1 September 1960) In 1934 Townsend, a Calif. doctor, proposed to end the GREAT DEPRESSION by an Old-Age Revolving Pension Plan, in which every person over 60 would receive a monthly pension of $200 and be required to spend it all in 30 days. (It would have added $24 billion to federal outlays, then at $6.5 billion.) By 1935, 3,000 Townsend Clubs existed, with over 500,000 members, and his *Townsend National Weekly* had 200,000 subscribers. Congress voted down the plan as impractical, despite receiving pro-Townsend petitions with 20,000,000 signatures. After helping form the UNION PARTY in 1936, Townsend's popularity faded due to Social Security's passage (*see* SOCIAL SECURITY ADMINISTRATION).

Townshend, Charles (b. Raynham, Norfolk, England, 29 August 1725; d. London, England, 4 September 1767) In 1747 Townshend entered Parliament. He became president of the BOARD OF TRADE in March 1763. He worked actively for the repeal of the STAMP ACT, and was mistakenly viewed by many colonists as pro-American. He joined William PITT's ministry as chancellor of the exchequer in August 1766. After Pitt's health collapsed in March 1767, Townshend emerged as the ministry's de facto leader and won passage of the TOWNSHEND REVENUE ACT, NEW YORK SUSPENDING ACT, and AMERICAN BOARD OF CUSTOMS ACT. Having created a crisis in British-colonial relations, he died unexpectedly (probably of typhus).

Townshend acts (*see* AMERICAN BOARD OF CUSTOMS ACT, NEW YORK SUSPENDING ACT, *and* TOWNSHEND REVENUE ACT

Townshend Revenue Act (29 June 1767) To offset the reduction of taxes by £500,000 on rents of British landlords, Charles TOWNSHEND wrote this law to raise EXTERNAL TAXATION of £37,000 a year in the colonies. He hoped the revenues would eventually be appropriated for paying the salaries of governors and other royal officials to reduce their dependence on provincial assemblies for their income. The law placed import duties on tea, glass, red and white lead, paper, and paint, of which the tea tax was projected to collect £20,000. To keep British tea competitive and deter smuggling, however, the law released the East India Company from paying £60,000 in import duties on tea landed in Britain that was subsequently shipped to America. The measure thus actually lost revenue for Britain's Treasury.

Colonial opposition to the law grew after publication of *LETTERS FROM A FARMER IN PENNSYLVANIA* and the MASSACHUSETTS CIRCULAR LETTER controversy. The second NONIMPORTATION AGREEMENT led Parliament to repeal all the Townshend duties on 12 April 1770, except the tea tax. Total taxes collected under the Revenue Act (1767) amounted to just £33,155 by 1774, of which £13,202 was raised in 1768.

Toxic Substances Control Act (1976) *see* ENVIRONMENTAL LEGISLATION

Trade Agreements Act (12 June 1934) This law reversed the high-tariff policies that led to a one-third decline in US trade between 1929 and 1932. It authorized the president, on his own authority, to negotiate bilateral agreements revising customs duties by as much as 50 percent from the HAWLEY–SMOOT TARIFF on a most-favored nation basis. Congress renewed the act every three years between 1937 and 1951, and after then for various intervals. Tariff reduction continued under rounds of the GENERAL AGREEMENT ON TARIFFS AND TRADE and NORTH AMERICAN FREE TRADE AGREEMENT.

trade associations In WORLD WAR I, the WAR INDUSTRIES BOARD promoted cooperation among all firms competing within their respective industries to maximize military production. By 1921, 2,000 voluntary trade associations had been formed to implement guidelines for production, quality standards, and pricing. Upon Secretary of Commerce Herbert HOOVER's strong recommendation, US anti-TRUST laws were waived for these organizations during the 1920s. Despite their potential for crippling competition by price-fixing and other restraints on trade, Hoover argued that the associations promoted economic efficiency by allowing businessmen to solve industry-wide problems before they threatened to trigger a recession. Trade associations were a precedent for the industry-wide codes of the NATIONAL INDUSTRIAL RECOVERY ACT.

Trading with the Enemy Act (6 October 1917) Congress outlawed commerce with enemy nations and established censorship over the foreign-language press and international communications. To manage enemy-owned business property, it created the office that produced the ALIEN PROPERTY CUSTODIAN SCANDAL.

Trail of Broken Treaties caravan In 1972, the AMERICAN INDIAN MOVEMENT organized a caravan that would converge on Washington from various parts of the United States and demand that US–Indian relations return to their pre-1871 status by renegotiating all treaties and restoring a 110 million acre land base. After arriving at Washington on 1 November, armed Indians occupied the BIA building until 8 November, during which time they did much damage to the building and stole official files. Native-American leaders divided over the event's lawlessness, which produced a backlash among many white Americans formerly sympathetic with their grievances.

Trail of Tears As required by the treaty of NEW ECHOTA, small groups of CHEROKEE INDIANS began migrating to Okla. in 1836, but most felt that the treaty was invalid and refused to go. In 1838 the army forced 15,000 Cherokee west. Poor administration, inadequate rations, and lack of proper winter quarters resulted in 3,000 Indian deaths.

transatlantic cable In 1854 New York businessman Cyrus West Field organized a company (capitalized at $1,500,000) to lay a transatlantic telegraph cable. When finished on 5 August 1858, the cable connected Trinity Bay, Newfoundland, with Valentia, Ireland. Queen Victoria sent the first message to James BUCHANAN on 16 August.

transcendentalism This was an early 19th-century philosophical movement influenced by Immanuel Kant's skepticism about the limitations of pure reason; it sought to supplement logic and traditional knowledge by seeking truth through spiritual intuition. In 1836 its leading advocates formed the Transcendental Club, which held informal discussions at Boston and Concord, Mass. Ralph W. EMERSON was its principal theoretician and publicist. Transcendentalism provided intellectuals with a secular philosophy that affirmed the need to scrutinize and then follow one's conscience.

transcontinental railroads On 1 July 1862, to encourage the completion of a rail line across the Rockies, Congress passed the first Pacific Railroad Act, which chartered the Central Pacific Co. to build east from Sacramento, and the Union Pacific Railroad to build west from Omaha, until they met. The law offered land grants of 20 square miles staggered alternately on both sides of the track and gave the companies government loans as financing. The construction crews drove the last spike on 10 May 1869 at Promontory Point, Utah.

The next transcontinental railroad was completed in 1881, when the Southern Pacific Railroad met the Atlantic and Pacific Railroad at Deming, N.Mex. to link Los Angeles with Albuquerque. In 1883 the Northern Pacific Railroad linked St Paul with Seattle. In 1885 the Southern Pacific Railroad joined New Orleans with Los Angeles. In 1887 the Santa Fe Railroad connected Chicago and Kansas City with Los Angeles. In 1889 James HILL pushed the Great Northern Railroad from Duluth to Seattle. In 1909 the Chicago, Milwaukee, St Paul, and Pacific Railroad connected Chicago and Seattle via Iowa, S. Dak., and Mont.

Transportation, Department of This department was created on 15 October 1966 (effective 1 April 1967) to promote highway safety, develop national transportation policy, and write guidelines for the use of federal funds in transportation projects.

Transportation Act (1920) *see* ESCH-CUMMINS ACT

Transylvania Colony On 27 August 1774, Richard Henderson formed the Louisa Company to lease or buy KENTUCKY from the CHEROKEE INDIANS and plant a colony; he reorganized it as the Transylvania Company on 6 January 1775. In March 1775, he bought 26,563 square miles (including part of TENNESSEE) by the treaty of SYCAMORE SHOALS. He then financed the blazing of the WILDERNESS ROAD and the building of Boonesborough, Ky., by Daniel BOONE. Henderson won support among many in Ky. for organizing a Transylvania government, but could not get his title confirmed by either VIRGINIA, which had jurisdiction over Ky., or the CONTINENTAL CONGRESS. When Va. established Kentucky County in 1776, Transylvania collapsed. In 1797–8, the company claims were settled by awarding its owners, or their heirs, title to about 625 square miles in Ky. and Tenn.

Treasury, Department of the Congressional committees supervised national finances during the Revolution. On 30 July 1779, Congress organized the Board of Treasury, which it replaced with a Department of Finance on 7 February 1781 and a Board of Treasury on 28 May 1784. On 2 September 1789, Congress created the Department of the Treasury and named Alexander HAMILTON its first secretary on 11 September. Its principal agencies are the Internal Revenue Service, Customs Service, SECRET SERVICE, US Mint, and Bureau of Engraving and Printing.

***Trent* affair** On 8 November 1861, Captain Charles Wilkes, commanding the US warship *San Jacinto*, halted the British mail steamer *Trent*. Wilkes apprehended John Slidell and James Mason, Confederate envoys sailing for Britain, and had them detained at Boston. The seizure aroused militant anti-US sentiment in Britain, whose press called for armed retaliation. To prevent the Confederacy from reaping any further diplomatic or military advantages from the controversy, on 26 December, William SEWARD ordered Mason and Slidell released. US relations with Britain thereafter improved.

Trenton, battle of (N.J.) On 26 December 1776, Washington's 2,400 troops captured the HESSIAN outpost at Trenton. US losses: 4

killed, 8 wounded. Hessian losses: 23 killed, 918 captured (including 84 wounded). The first significant US victory since Boston's capture, Trenton boosted flagging American morale.

Trevellick, Richard F. *see* NATIONAL LABOR UNION

Triangle Shirtwaist factory fire On 25 March 1911, in New York City, fire broke out at the Triangle Shirtwaist Co. Due to locked or inadequate escape routes, 146 workers were trapped and died. The owners were tried on criminal charges, but were acquitted on 7 December 1911. One of the worst US industrial accidents, the tragedy led the N.Y. legislature to pass a model safety code for businesses and to revise its labor laws.

Trist, Nicholas *see* GUADALUPE HIDALGO, TREATY OF

Truax* v. *Corrigan In 1921 the Supreme Court struck down a state law that exempted strikers and union picketers from injunctions issued by state courts during labor disputes, as the law violated DUE PROCESS under the FOURTEENTH AMENDMENT. The ruling let business circumvent the CLAYTON ANTITRUST ACT's prohibition on federal injunctions against strikers by using state judges to order picketing workers back to work.

Truman, Harry S. (b. Lamar, Mo., 8 May 1884; d. Kansas City, Mo., 26 December 1972) After serving with the Allied Expeditionary Force in WORLD WAR I, Truman became active in Democratic politics at Kansas City with the Pendergast Machine, which sponsored his successful race for the Senate in 1934. His strong support for NEW DEAL measures led to his selection as vice-president by Franklin D. ROOSEVELT, whom he succeeded as president in April 1945. Truman ended WORLD WAR II by bombing HIROSHIMA and NAGASAKI.

He proposed the FAIR DEAL to promote full employment, improve the quality of life, and further civil rights, but accomplished few of these goals after the Republican Party regained control of Congress in 1946. He was expected to lose the 1948 election, because his pro-civil rights actions (such as integrating the military by EXECUTIVE ORDER 9981) led many southern Democrats to desert him for a STATES' RIGHTS PARTY candidate, while northern liberals seemed likely to vote for Henry WALLACE's third-party bid. He waged an aggressive campaign and won with 49.6 percent of the vote.

In 1952 he seized the nation's steel mills to avert a strike in wartime, but was overruled in *YOUNGSTOWN SHEET AND TUBE COMPANY* v. *SAWYER*. The COLD WAR dominated his presidency. Resisting the public impulse to withdraw from world affairs – despite the emerging challenge of communism – Truman initiated the MARSHALL PLAN and TRUMAN DOCTRINE, directed the BERLIN AIRLIFT, and fought the KOREAN WAR. He retired in 1952.

Truman Doctrine On 12 March 1947, Harry S. TRUMAN declared as national policy a commitment to lend defensive assistance to pro-US governments facing external aggression or internal subversion by Communist forces. To implement this doctrine, $400,000,000 was appropriated on 22 May for military and economic aid to Greece and Turkey, then under attack by pro-Soviet guerrillas.

Trumbull, John (b. Lebanon, Conn., 6 June 1756; d. New York, N.Y., 10 November 1843) After serving as a Continental Army officer, Trumbull went to study painting with the AMERICAN SCHOOL in London, where he was briefly held in the Tower of London for treason. He became the dean of US historical painting through such masterpieces as *The Battle of Bunker's Hill* (1785), *Death of General Montgomery at Quebec* (1787), and *The Declaration of Independence* (1794). He painted the historical murals for the US Capitol Building.

Trust Territory of the Pacific Islands *see* MICRONESIA, US TRUST TERRITORY OF

trusts In the PROGRESSIVE ERA, combinations of big business that influenced large segments of the economy were termed trusts. Trusts included: pools, in which several companies ensured higher profits by agreeing to cease price competition; holding companies, in which one firm's corporate board took over rival enterprises by purchasing a dominant share of their stock; and monopolies, in which a single company gained nearly exclusive control over the marketing of a good or service. Between 1897 and 1904, 4,227 companies merged into 257 corporations, as a result of which 318 trusts may have owned 40 percent of US manufacturing assets. The Supreme Court's interpretation of DUE PROCESS under the FOURTEENTH AMENDMENT blocked state efforts to regulate trusts through the GRANGER LAWS. The main federal laws governing trusts were the INTERSTATE COMMERCE COMMISSION ACT and SHERMAN ANTITRUST ACT. During the NEW DEAL, the Supreme Court gave states broad regulatory powers over business in *NEBBIA* V. *NEW YORK*, and affirmed extensive federal authority over business practices in *NATIONAL LABOR RELATIONS BOARD* V. *JONES AND LAUGHLIN STEEL CORPORATION*.

Truth, Sojourner (b. Hurley, N.Y., ca. 1797; d. Battle Creek, Mich., 26 November 1883) Born into slavery as Isabel Baumfree, she ran away in 1827 when her master refused to abide by the N.Y. emancipation law. As the result of a religious experience in 1843, she left her home in New York City, took the name Sojourner Truth, became a traveling ABOLITIONIST speaker, and won renown for her 1852 address, "Ain't I A Woman." She was the earliest black woman to play a notable role in any debate on American public policy. After slavery ended, she led a nationwide petition drive for Congress to reserve part of the PUBLIC DOMAIN for FREEDMEN.

Tubman, Harriet (b. Dorchester County, Md., ca. 1821; d. Auburn, N.Y., 10 March 1913) Born Araminta Ross, she escaped from slavery and earned the sobriquet "Moses," as the UNDERGROUND RAILROAD's most renowned conductor, with a reward of $40,000 on her head. She made 19 trips to Md. and conveyed over 300 slaves north, including her parents, two children, and a sister. After the second FUGITIVE SLAVE ACT (1850), she guided escapees all the way to Canada. After 1865, she founded the Harriet Tubman Home for Indigent and Aged Negroes.

Tugwell, Rexford Guy (b. Sinclairville, N.Y., 10 July 1891; d. Santa Barbara, Calif., 21 July 1979) He was one of the original BRAINS TRUST trio. He influenced the FIRST NEW DEAL by advocating a planned national economy managed through federal and business oversight. He helped draft the AGRICULTURAL ADJUSTMENT ADMINISTRATION as under secretary of agriculture (1934–5), headed the RESETTLEMENT ADMINISTRATION (1934–7), and then left Washington. He was governor of Puerto Rico (1941–6).

Turner, Frederick Jackson (b. Portage, Wis., 14 November 1861; d. Pasadena, Calif., 14 March 1932) After receiving his Ph.D. from Johns Hopkins in 1890, just as the frontier was closing with the OKLAHOMA LAND RUSH, Turner established his reputation as an original synthesist by reading "The Significance of the Frontier in American History" to the American Historical Association in 1893. Turner pioneered the sub-discipline of social history within his profession, and was the first great conceptual genius in US history. His *The Significance of Sections in American History* won the Pulitzer prize in 1932.

Turner's Revolt Nat Turner, a slave in Southampton County, Va., organized an insurrection to begin on 21 August 1831, a date when most local white men had gone to attend a revival nearby in N.C. Turner's men killed 55 whites, of whom 24 were children and 18 women. The militia killed perhaps 100 slaves in restoring order, and 16 captured rebels were later hanged. Since this uprising was the first slave revolt since the STONO CREEK REBELLION to kill a significant number of masters, southern whites were emotionally unprepared for its violence and exaggerated the danger of its recurrence. Southerners thereafter assumed that any discussion of slavery would spark future insurrections and saw ABOLITIONISM as a direct threat to their lives. The revolt was a major factor contributing to the POSITIVE GOOD DEFENSE OF SLAVERY and to southern efforts to censor abolitionist writings and speech.

turnpikes Privately-capitalized turnpike corporations began the first large-scale expansion of US highways. The first major toll road, the 62-mile Lancaster, Pa., Turnpike was built in 1790–4. The average turnpike cost $100,000 per 25 miles to build. The turnpike boom built 5,000 miles of road by 1825, then was eclipsed by a CANAL BOOM.

Tuscarora Indians These Indians were an alliance of three groups of speakers of IROQUOIAN LANGUAGES numbering about

5,000 in northeastern N.C. As frontier expansion reached their territory, they accumulated a series of grievances against unscrupulous fur traders and slave dealers, for which they could obtain no satisfaction from the N.C. government. They retaliated in the TUSCARORA WAR, but were badly beaten. Most of the survivors joined the IROQUOIS CONFEDERACY in N.Y., and settled along the Susquehanna River. During the American Revolution (*see* REVOLUTIONARY WAR), a large minority fought for the Continental Congress, but another faction were British allies. Perhaps half the nation perished in the war and a fifth of the survivors resettled in Canada. By 1789 just 340 lived in N.Y., with another 130 in Canada. The Tuscaroras eventually sold all their common land except a small reservation near Niagara Falls.

Tuscarora War On 22 September 1711, TUSCARORA INDIANS destroyed the Swiss community of New Bern, N.C. In January–April 1712, Colonel John Barnwell's 30 S.C. militia and 500 allied Indians stormed several fortified towns and established a truce, which the Tuscaroras soon violated. On 20 March 1713, Colonel James Moore's N.C. militia and 800 allied Indians destroyed the main enemy fort at Nooherooka; they killed 192 Tuscaroras and captured 392, who were enslaved, at a loss of 22 whites killed and 24 wounded, plus 35 allied Indians killed and 58 wounded. A peace treaty ended hostilities on 8 June 1713. About 20 percent of the 5,000 Tuscaroras were killed or enslaved. Most of the survivors migrated to New York and joined the IROQUOIS CONFEDERACY. The war ended resistance to white expansion in N.C. and brought peace to the N.C. frontier until 1760.

Tuskegee syphilis scandal From 1932 to 1972, US Public Health Service doctors diagnosed over 500 blacks living near Tuskegee, Ala., as having contracted syphilis, but purposefully kept the patients ignorant of their condition for the sake of conducting a secret, clinical study of the long-term effects of leaving the disease untreated by antibiotics. The experiment ended abruptly when the *Washington Star* exposed it on 25 July 1972, but by then over 100 of the subjects had died of the disease or related complications. In December 1974, an out-of-court settlement paid $10 million to the study's 120 survivors, to persons who contracted syphilis from them, and to heirs of the deceased.

TVA *see* TENNESSEE VALLEY AUTHORITY

Twain, Mark (b. Florida, Mo., 30 November 1835; d. Redding, Conn., 21 April 1910) Born Samuel Langhorne Clemens, he adopted Mark Twain (a riverboat term signifying two fathoms of water) for his pen name after having been a journeyman printer, boat pilot, CSA volunteer, and prospector. He published his first story, "The Celebrated Jumping Frog of Calaveras County," in 1865. Twain became a traveling lecturer and satirized the GILDED AGE (a term he coined) in numerous stories and books. He now ranks as not only the greatest of all US humorists, but also one of its finest authors. Twain's *Huckleberry Finn* (1885) is considered by many critics to be the best American novel. His writings influenced fictional style by popularizing the use of regional dialects in dialogue and by pioneering the technique of narrating a story from one point of reference. Other major works include *Roughing It* (1872), *The Gilded Age* (1873), *The Adventures of Tom Sawyer* (1876), *Life on the Mississippi* (1883), *A Connecticut Yankee in King Arthur's Court* (1889), *The Tragedy of Pudd'nhead Wilson* (1894), *What is Man?* (1906), and *The Mysterious Stranger* (1916).

Tweed Ring On 8 July 1871, evidence of corruption in Mayor William M. Tweed's administration began appearing in the New York *Times*, along with riveting cartoons by Thomas NAST. Through false receipts, kickbacks, exorbitant bills, nonexistent leases, and fake repairs, Tweed and others stole $75–200 million in public funds. Samuel TILDEN took a leading role in ensuring Tweed's prosecution and sponsoring legislation to curb TAMMANY HALL's corruption. Tweed was convicted on 27 October 1872 and died in prison.

Twelfth Amendment Submitted to the states on 12 December 1803, last ratified on 15 June 1804, and officially proclaimed on 25 September 1804, it altered Article II, Section 1 of the Constitution to have the electoral college elect the president and vice-president on separate ballots, to prevent another instance like the election of 1800, when a tied vote between Thomas Jefferson and his running mate, Aaron Burr, almost denied Jefferson the presidency. The Twentieth Amendment modified it.

Twentieth ("Lame Duck") Amendment Submitted to the states on 2 March 1932, last ratified on 23 January 1933, and officially proclaimed on 6 February 1933, it changed Article I, Section 4 of the Constitution by providing that Congress would begin its annual session on 3 January instead of the first Monday in December; and it altered the Twelfth Amendment by moving the president's inauguration to 20 January instead of 4 March. This measure is the only amendment that resulted from the efforts of a single man, George Norris, who drafted and proposed it.

Twenty-first Amendment Submitted to the states on 20 February 1933, last ratified on 5 December 1933, and officially proclaimed that day, it repealed the Eighteenth (Prohibition) Amendment. It was implemented by the Beer-Wine Revenue Act (1933).

Twenty-second Amendment Submitted to the states on 21 March 1947, last ratified on 27 February 1951, and officially proclaimed on 1 March 1951, it disqualified anyone from being elected president more than twice, or from being reelected more than once if he had served over two years of another president's term, but exempted Harry S. Truman.

Twenty-third Amendment Submitted to the states on 17 June 1960, last ratified on 29 March 1961, and officially proclaimed on 3 April 1961, it authorized the District of Columbia to participate in presidential elections by appointing as many electors as its population would merit if it were a state, but no more than those appointed by the smallest state.

Twenty-fourth Amendment Submitted to the states on 27 August 1962, last ratified on 23 January 1964, and officially proclaimed on 4 February 1964, it prohibited states from requiring payment of a poll tax to vote in any federal election. The Supreme Court forbade the use of poll taxes to exclude voters from state elections in *Harper v. Virginia State Board of Elections*.

Twenty-fifth Amendment Submitted to the states on 6 July 1965, last ratified by Nev on 10 February 1967, and officially proclaimed on 23 February 1967, it altered Article II, Section 1 of the Constitution, and the Twentieth Amendment's Section 3. It set provisions for Congress to fill a vacant vice-president's office by approving a presidential nominee (used for Gerald Ford and Nelson Rockefeller). It also set procedures for a vice-president to become acting president if the president were unable to discharge his duties, and for the president to resume his responsibilities once he recovered his abilities.

Twenty-sixth Amendment This amendment overturned *Oregon v. Mitchell*, which ruled that an amendment to the Voting Rights Act (1965) could not impose 18 as the voting age in state elections. Sent to the states on 23 March 1971, last ratified by Ohio on 30 June 1971, and officially proclaimed on 5 July 1971, it extends the privilege of voting in state and federal elections to all citizens on their eighteenth birthday. The amendment allowed 25,000,000 new voters to participate in the 1972 presidential election.

Twenty-seventh Amendment After being submitted to the states on 25 September 1789, this amendment won six states' approval by 1800, one in 1873, and 32 from 1978 to 7 May 1992, when Mich. completed its ratification; it was officially proclaimed on 19 May 1992. It forbids any law raising congressional or Senate salaries to take effect until after a new House of Representatives has been elected.

Twightwee Indians *see* Miami Indians

Tydings–McDuffie Act *see* Philippines

Tyler, John (b. Charles City County, Va., 29 March 1790; d. Richmond, Va., 18 January 1862) In 1809 Tyler opened a law office in his home county. He was a Democratic congressman (1817–20), Va. governor (1825–7), and US senator (1827–36). He was Hugh White's running mate in 1836. He resigned as senator when instructed by his legislature to support Andrew Jackson on the second Bank of the United States. The Whig party nominated him as vice-president under William H. HARRISON, and he became the first vice-president to take over the White House in 1841. He broke with the Whigs by vetoing an effort to establish a third federal bank in 1841 and supporting the annexation of TEXAS. He left public life until 1861, when he was elected to the CSA Congress.

Tyson and Brothers* v. *Banton *see* WOLFF PACKING COMPANY V. COURT OF INDUSTRIAL RELATIONS

U

U-2 affair On 1 May 1960, an unarmed US reconnaissance plane, a U-2, was shot down during a spy mission over the USSR and pilot Gary Powers was captured. USSR Premier Khrushchev denounced the US and canceled a summit meeting scheduled for that month with Dwight D. EISENHOWER. The incident escalated tensions in the COLD WAR and damaged US prestige among nonaligned nations. On 19 August 1960, Powers was convicted of espionage and sentenced to 10 years in prison, but was exchanged for a Communist spy on 10 February 1962.

Ullmann* v. *United States On 26 March 1956, the Supreme Court held (7–2) the IMMUNITY ACT to be constitutional in accordance with *COUNSELMAN* v. *HITCHCOCK*. The Court ruled on similar issues in *WATKINS* v. *UNITED STATES* and *BARENBLATT* v. *UNITED STATES*.

UN *see* UNITED NATIONS

Uncle Tom's Cabin During 1851–2, Harriet Beecher Stowe published this novel serially in the Washington *National Era*. In its first year, the book sold 300,000 copies in the US and 1,500,000 in Britain; its stage adaptation proved enormously popular. This melodramatic account of a Christ-like slave crushed by a sadistic master swayed northern public opinion to be more favorable toward ABOLITIONISM and hastened the process by which northerners became alienated from, and hostile toward, white southerners. In the CIVIL WAR, Abraham LINCOLN reportedly greeted Stowe by saying, "So you're the little woman who started this great war!"

underground railroad This term referred to a haphazard, semisecret network of routes and hiding-stations used by free blacks and white abolitionists to help slaves escape to free states or Canada. After Pa. abolished slavery, the Philadelphia area gained a reputation as a relatively safe haven for runaways, and drew many slaves from the South. Cincinnati, Indianapolis, and Chicago were important destinations for renegade bondsmen in the West. By 1820 a system had developed by which conductors guided slaves at night to stations, where they stayed hidden until the next leg of their journey. Virtually all stations were in the free states, where they served to protect escapees from arrest by law officers enforcing the FUGITIVE SLAVE ACTS. At least 3,200 northerners aided the railroad, which probably assisted 500 slaves per year.

Underwood–Simmons Tariff (3 October 1913) This measure replaced the PAYNE–ALDRICH TARIFF because the 1912 elections put Congress under Democratic control. To enable European manufacturers to compete with US industry, it lowered average rates to 29 percent and ended duties on iron, steel, wool, and sugar. To compensate for lost revenues, Congress enacted the first income tax under the SIXTEENTH AMENDMENT. It was supplemented by the EMERGENCY TARIFF ACT (1921).

Uniform Time Act (1966) *see* DAYLIGHT SAVING TIME

Union party In 1936 this party was formed by followers of Fr Charles COUGHLIN, Francis TOWNSEND, and Huey LONG, to oppose Franklin D. ROOSEVELT. It nominated William LEMKE (Republican, N.Dak.) as president and Thomas O'Brien (Democrat, Mass.) as vice-president. It advocated federal assistance to refinance all home and farm mortgages, generous federal stipends to the elderly, protective tariffs, higher taxes on the wealthy, more federal employment programs, and stricter business regulation.

Lemke won just 1.9 percent of votes and the party was disbanded in 1939.

Union Republican party In 1864 the REPUBLICAN PARTY chose to run its candidates as Union Republicans to lessen its image as a partisan organization. The party attempted to build a broad-based coalition by appealing to Democrats; it dropped Abraham LINCOLN's first vice-president, Hannibal Hamlin, a Maine Republican, in favor of Andrew JOHNSON, a Tenn. Democrat. The ticket won all but three states.

union shop This term refers to a labor contract that obligates all workers to join the union that negotiated it, but does not require that a person already belong to that union in order to be hired (as in closed shops). The AMERICAN PLAN fought against such contracts during 1919–29. The TAFT–HARTLEY ACT permitted union shops.

Unitarianism American Unitarianism emerged as a reaction to the lingering influence of orthodox Calvinism in the CONGREGATIONAL CHURCH; it rejected predestination in favor of a doctrine of universal salvation, and denied the doctrine of God's tripartite identity. William E. CHANNING was its most important theologian, and TRANSCENDENTALISM greatly influenced its early development. The American Unitarian Association was formed in 1825. The number of Unitarian pulpits rose from 150 in 1820 to 264 in 1860, 455 in 1900, but fell to 357 in 1950. In 1961 the Unitarians merged with the UNIVERSALIST CHURCH OF AMERICA into the Unitarian Universalist Association. The association's membership stagnated from 167,900 in 1965 to 182,200 in 1990, when there were 1,010 congregations.

United Church of Christ In 1957 the Congregational Christian Churches (*see* CONGREGATIONAL CHURCH) merged with the Evangelical and Reformed Church to form this denomination, which had 2,250,000 members. In 1985 it had 1,701,500 members (0.7 percent of the US population) and 6,427 churches.

United Colonies of New England On 19 May 1643, MASSACHUSETTS, CONNECTICUT, NEW HAVEN, and PLYMOUTH organized the Confederation of the United Colonies of New England. (When RHODE ISLAND later asked for membership, it was rejected for its refusal to sanction an established church based on orthodox PURITANISM.) Each colony appointed two commissioners who met annually to manage disputes between their respective governments, relations with non-English colonies, religious matters, and Indian affairs. All the confederation's actions required six of the eight commissioners' votes. Because Mass. would not abide by policies infringing its own interests, when outvoted by the three smaller colonies, the confederation created a facade of cooperation that masked New England's underlying lack of unity. Yearly meetings ceased after 1664 until KING PHILIP'S WAR reinvigorated the confederation, but the union was dissolved in 1684.

United Jewish Organizations of Williamsburgh v. Carey On 1 March 1977, the Supreme Court ruled (7–1) that the VOTING RIGHTS ACT (1965) authorized N.Y. to redistrict its legislature by creating districts with a majority of nonwhite voters, even if a white religious minority's political representation suffered in the process.

United Nations The DUMBARTON OAKS CONFERENCE drafted a general plan for creating an international organization to promote world peace and security. Between 25 April and 26 June 1945, delegates from 50 countries drafted the UN charter. Governing the UN was a general assembly, in which each country had one vote, and an 11-nation security council, of which six seats rotated among all UN members and five were permanently held by the US, USSR, Britain, France, and China. A secretariat, headed by a secretary general, served as the UN bureaucracy. An international court of justice was to adjudicate controversies between countries. A trusteeship council supervised dependencies or protectorates established under member nations, such as the Trust Territory of MICRONESIA (US).

Largely through the efforts of Ralph BUNCHE, the UN developed expertise in operations to keep peace or repel aggression, of which the US was deeply involved with the KOREAN and PERSIAN GULF WARS. By 1994 the UN had 184 members. The US consistently paid the largest share of the UN budget, 25 percent to 1987, when the other five Security Council members collectively contributed just 17 percent.

United Public Workers* v. *Mitchell *see* HATCH ACT

United States Information Agency This agency was established on 1 August 1953 as a means of combating Soviet propaganda in the COLD WAR. Its best known program was the Voice of America, which broadcast popular entertainment and news for wireless listeners behind the Iron Curtain. It maintained libraries and reading rooms overseas, and produced documentaries for foreign viewing. It was replaced on 3 April 1978 by the International Communications Agency, but its original name was restored in 1982.

United States* v. *American Tobacco Company In 1911 the Supreme Court ruled that a federal suit under the SHERMAN ANTITRUST ACT should be settled by reorganizing the company rather than entirely dissolving it. At that time, the company was capitalized at $502,000,000 and controlled nearly all domestic cigarette production at its 150 factories.

United States* v. *Arizona *see OREGON* V. *MITCHELL*

United States* v. *Bankers Trust Company *see* GOLD STANDARD

United States* v. *Butler On 6 January 1936, the Supreme Court (6–3) struck down the first AGRICULTURAL ADJUSTMENT ACT (1933) and ruled that the US had no constitutional power to regulate intrastate farm production through a program whose controls were coercive and not voluntary. The tax on food processing companies, which financed subsidies to farmers, was consequently not within the taxing power of Article I, Section 8.

United States* v. *Classic On 26 May 1941, the Supreme Court reversed *NEWBERRY* V. *UNITED STATES* and ruled (5–3) that the federal government could regulate state political primaries when they served as the main instrument for choosing congressional and presidential candidates.

United States* v. *Cruikshank In 1876 the Supreme Court unanimously invalidated the indictment of whites charged with murdering blacks in the COLFAX MASSACRE at New Orleans. The Court ruled that the FOURTEENTH AMENDMENT could only be used to prosecute states for civil rights violations, and could not serve as a basis for trying individuals who violated other citizens' rights. The ruling took the responsibility for protecting ex-slaves' civil rights away from the jurisdiction of federal courts, and gave it to the states, which had little sympathy for the cause of equal rights for blacks.

United States* v. *Curtiss-Wright Export Company On 21 December 1936, the Supreme Court affirmed (7–1) a congressional law empowering the president to embargo weapons from reaching warring nations in Latin America at his own discretion. The law did not wrongly delegate legislative authority, because, given the president's sole responsibility for conducting foreign relations, Congress can grant him wider powers over international affairs than he could hold for internal matters.

United States* v. *Darby Lumber Company On 3 February 1941, the Supreme Court unanimously reversed *HAMMER* V. *DAGENHART* and upheld the FAIR LABOR STANDARDS ACT (1938). Using as precedent the "constant stream of commerce" concept (*SWIFT AND COMPANY* V. *UNITED STATES*), it ruled that Congress could legislate on any aspect of commerce and that there was no exclusive area of intrastate commerce reserved solely for state regulation.

United States* v. *E. C. Knight Company In 1895 the Supreme Court (8–1) heard the government's case that a near monopoly of sugar refining violated the SHERMAN ANTITRUST ACT. The Court declared the Sherman Act's anti-monopoly clauses unconstitutional as they regarded manufacturing; it ruled that the government's authority to regulate interstate commerce did not extend to manufacturing. The ruling crippled enforcement of the Sherman Act. *SWIFT AND COMPANY* V. *UNITED STATES* ended much of the exemption from federal antitrust regulation conferred on manufacturing corporations by this ruling.

United States* v. *Grimaud In 1911 the Supreme Court reaffirmed and elaborated on *WAYMAN* V. *SOUTHARD* by declaring that Congress might vest the president with very wide administrative discretion (in this case over the PUBLIC DOMAIN) without necessarily violating the balance of government powers. By broadening the scope of the "administrative discretion" considered constitutionally permissible as presidential authority, the ruling provided a legal basis for the mushrooming of federal regulatory agencies, whose effectiveness required wide latitude to interpret congressional statutes through their decisions and regulations.

United States* v. *Harris In 1883 the Supreme Court crippled the second FORCE ACT's effectiveness by declaring that the FOURTEENTH AMENDMENT did not authorize federal prosecutions against private citizens who conspired to deprive persons of their civil rights. It held that Congress only had power to forbid state officials from denying all persons equal protection under the law. (*See also* *UNITED STATES* V. *CRUIKSHANK and* *UNITED STATES* V. *REESE*)

United States* v. *Hudson In 1816 the Supreme Court ruled that because the US possessed no criminal COMMON LAW, federal courts had no jurisdiction over criminal activity – except to enforce criminal statutes passed by Congress. The ruling left each state free to evolve its own approach to defining felonies and misdemeanors.

United States* v. *Kagama In 1886, the Supreme Court reversed *Ex Parte Crow Dog* (1883), which denied US courts jurisdiction over crimes committed by and against members of RESERVATIONS unless a particular tribe had specifically abrogated its exclusive rights over internal legal affairs. The court affirmed a subsequent Congressional statute allowing federal courts to return indictments for certain crimes committed on reservations. They ruled that Indian nations are "the wards of the nation" and dependent on the United States, "but had no constitutional relationship to the states."

United States* v. *Lanza On 11 December 1922, the Supreme Court ruled (8–0) that the FIFTH AMENDMENT's protection against DOUBLE JEOPARDY does not exempt the defendant from being prosecuted in both federal and state courts for the same offense. *Lanza* was reaffirmed in 1959 by *Abbate* v. *United States* and *Bartkis* v. *Illinois*.

United States* v. *Leon (decided with *Massachusetts* v. *Sheppard*) On 5 July 1984, the Supreme Court allowed an exception to its exclusionary rule (*see* *WEEKS* V. *UNITED STATES*) by holding that evidence obtained improperly by a defective search warrant can be admitted as evidence if law officers acted "in good faith" and were honestly mistaken.

United States* v. *Mitchell *see* *OREGON* V. *MITCHELL*

United States* v. *Mosley On 21 June 1915, the Supreme Court reaffirmed EX PARTE YARBROUGH by declaring (7–1) the first FORCE ACT to be a legitimate exercise of powers under the FIFTEENTH AMENDMENT in order to prevent corruption and fraud in federal elections.

United States* v. *Nixon *see* EXECUTIVE PRIVILEGE, *and* WATERGATE SCANDAL

United States* v. *Reese In 1876 the Supreme Court struck down the first FORCE ACT's clauses that made it illegal to interfere with any citizen's voting rights. The Court ruled (8–1) that the act improperly interfered with the states' rights to set eligibility for voting, and exceeded the FIFTEENTH AMENDMENT's authority. It held that the Fifteenth forbade states to disfranchise blacks for reasons of race, but left the states discretion to exclude certain classes of people from voting for reasons unrelated to race. The decision enabled southern legislatures to reduce the number of black voters through LITERACY TESTS, the WHITE PRIMARY, POLL TAX, and GRANDFATHER CLAUSE.

United States* v. *Texas On 29 February 1892, the Supreme Court held (7–2) that a state could not assert the right to be sued only with its own consent in federal court if the US had brought suit against it. The Court ruled that upon ratifying the Constitution, states accepted the extension of federal jurisdiction over all cases to which the US was a party, including any filed by the US against states.

United States* v. *Trans-Missouri Freight Association In 1897 the Supreme Court upheld (5–4) use of the SHERMAN ANTITRUST ACT to break up an agreement by 18 railroads to manipulate freight rates.

United States* v. *Wade *see* *ESCOBEDO* V. *ILLINOIS*

United States* v. *Weber *see* *UNITED STEELWORKERS OF AMERICA ET AL.* V. *WEBER*

United States* v. *Wong Kim Ark On 28 March 1898, the Supreme Court ruled (6–2) that the FOURTEENTH AMENDMENT confers citizenship on all children born in the US who remain under its jurisdiction, even if their parents are resident foreigners ineligible to be citizens.

United Steelworkers of America et al.* v. *Weber (decided with *Kaiser Aluminum* v. *Weber* and *United States* v. *Weber*) On 27 June 1979, the Supreme Court ruled (5–2) that the CIVIL RIGHTS ACT (1964) does not outlaw voluntary plans for AFFIRMATIVE ACTION that set numerical goals for rectifying the underrepresentation of minorities in certain work environments, even if promotions are not awarded to white workers as their seniority and job performance would have normally merited.

United We Stand America H. Ross PEROT founded and financed this tax-exempt, "educational" organization to support his campaign for president in 1992. Due to Perot's indecisiveness and unwillingness to decentralize authority, it failed to evolve into a true political party or play any role in the 1994 mid-term elections. It fell from 1,300,000 members in 1992 to about 300,000 in late 1994.

Universalist Church of America This denomination originated in the preaching of John Murray, an Englishman who emigrated in 1770 after being excommunicated from Methodism for affirming that Christ's death had atoned for all humanity's sins, not merely an elect predestined by God. Murray founded the first Universalist congregation at Gloucester, Mass., in 1779. Universalists divided over the soul's status after death, with "Restorationists" arguing that all individual sins required punishment after death, while "Ultra-Universalists" insisted that divine reconciliation awaited every soul at death. A church convention defined Restorationism as dogma in 1803. Universalism attracted few converts, and was largely restricted to New England and the upper-midwestern states. It merged with UNITARIANISM to form the Unitarian Universalist association in 1961.

Upper South This term refers to the colonies or states where tobacco, hemp, or foodstuffs were the primary staple crops: Md., Va., Ky., and Mo. The tobacco and mountainous districts of N.C. and Tenn. are commonly considered part of this area.

Urban League, National In 1910 the Committee on Urban Conditions of Negroes was founded to assist rural blacks migrating to northern cities. In 1911 it formed the National League on Urban Conditions Among Negroes (now National Urban League) by merging with the Committee for Improving the Industrial Conditions of Negroes in New York (1906) and the National League for the Protection of Colored Women. The Urban League emphasized economic and social problems of urban blacks and left issues concerning civil rights and social discrimination to the NATIONAL ASSOCIATION FOR THE ADVANCEMENT OF COLORED PEOPLE'S agenda.

Executive-director Whitney M. Young, Jr. (1961–71) revitalized the league, which had long been handicapped by inadequate finances, and won millions of dollars in corporate contributions. Young also lobbied hard for government job-training programs to assist minority employment opportunities. A consistent foe of the BLACK POWER MOVEMENT, Young's Urban League won increasing respect and influence by advocating interracial cooperation and conciliation. After Young's death, the league lost much corporate funding and public influence. Under John E. Jacob (1982–94), it increasingly operated at a deficit, which reached $3,600,000 by 1989. In 1994, under President Hugh Price, it had 113 affiliated chapters.

Uruguay round of GATT Between September 1986 and December 1993, the US and 110 other members of GATT cut worldwide tariffs totaling $740 billion and adopted greater protection for copyrighted materials. The Uruguay round cut US tariffs by $10 to $14 billion during its first five years, and $26 billion during its second five years. The treaty also replaced GATT with the World Trade Organization to settle trade disputes. Senate ratification occurred on 1 December 1994.

USHA United States Housing Authority.

Utah Mountain men built private stockades, starting with Kit CARSON's fort in 1834, but permanent Anglo-American settlement did not begin until Brigham YOUNG arrived with the MORMONS' advance party in the Salt Lake Valley on 24 July 1847. The US acquired Utah by the treaty of GUADALUPE

HIDALGO. Congress rejected Mormon plans to create an expansive state called DESERET and organized Utah Territory in 1851 by the terms of the COMPROMISE OF 1850. Relations with the US deteriorated and resulted in the bloodless UTAH WAR. Relations with Indians were amicable, except for minor outbreaks of violence with UTE INDIANS in 1853 and 1865. By 1860, the territory had 40,244 inhabitants, of whom 32 percent were foreign-born; it ranked 37th in population, 38th in the value of farmland and livestock, and 37th in manufactures.

Farming flourished with large-scale irrigation projects. Mining expanded rapidly after 1869, when the TRANSCONTINENAL RAILROAD was completed in Utah. On 4 January 1896, it became the 45th state. In 1900, Utah had 276,749 residents (99 percent white, 1 percent Indian), of whom 62 percent were rural and 19.4 percent were foreign-born; it ranked 42nd among states in population, 44th in agricultural products, and 42nd in manufactures. Due to severe problems in mining and agriculture, Utah lost 60,000 out-migrants from 1920 to 1940. The economy revived with the discovery of major uranium deposits in 1952 and the federal government's rise as the state's biggest employer (10 percent of all workers). In 1990 Utah was the 35th-largest state and had 1,722,850 inhabitants (91 percent white, 5 percent Hispanic, 1 percent black, 1 percent Indian, 2 percent Asian), of whom 76 percent were urban and 3.4 percent were foreign-born. Mining employed 7 percent of workers and manufacturing 15 percent.

Utah War In 1857 James BUCHANAN removed Brigham YOUNG as governor of UTAH upon complaints of not enforcing US laws and ordered Colonel Albert S. JOHNSTON's Second Cavalry to occupy Utah. In August 1857, Mormon hysteria over the invasion resulted in the massacre of 120 emigrants by Mormons under John D. Lee at Mountain Meadows. Tensions ebbed after Buchanan was persuaded to pardon Young on 12 June 1858 and the army agreed to establish its quarters 40 miles from Salt Lake City, which Young had ordered abandoned as they approached. All US occupying forces were withdrawn during the CIVIL WAR.

Ute campaigns (1) Facing Coloradans' demands to surrender much of their 12,000,000-acre reservation, and exasperated by pressure from the Bureau of INDIAN AFFAIRS to abandon their traditional ways, 100 UTE INDIANS blundered into exchanging fire with 120 US cavalry, and then murdered 10 civilians on the White River Indian Agency on 29 September 1879. By November 1880, 1,500 US troops forced most Utes into Utah.

(2) In 1906 many Utes left their reservation and terrorized Wyo. until the Sixth and Tenth Cavalry returned some to their reservation and placed others temporarily on a Cheyenne River reservation.

Ute Indians Speakers of one of the UTO-AZTECAN LANGUAGES, the Utes farmed in western Colo. and northern Utah until the late 17th century, when they acquired horses and became seminomadic. They established trading connections with Santa Fe during the 18th century. When MORMONS occupied the Great Salt Lake in 1847, the Utes numbered about 4,000; they relocated across mountain ranges to avoid contact with whites. Pressured by the Colo. gold rush, they signed a treaty in 1863 giving up the gold fields, but retaining rights to 25,000 square miles in western Colo. The first UTE CAMPAIGN resulted in their losing the Colo. lands and being put on a small reservation in Utah. A bloodless campaign also occurred in 1906. In 1950, the INDIAN CLAIMS COMMISSION compensated them with $31,700,000 for the loss of their Colo. land in 1880. The group's headquarters is on the Uintah and Ouray Reservation at Fort Duchesne, Utah.

Uto-Aztecan languages This family of INDIAN LANGUAGES evidently originated from a common tongue in Mexico 5,000 years ago and spread north of the Rio Grande. More Indians probably spoke these languages, on both sides of the Rio Grande, than any other language stock about 1500. From a heartland in southern Calif. and western Ariz., groups migrated to southern Idaho and northern Tex. Its major subdivisions are the languages of the HOPI, Pima-Papago, Yaqui-Mayo, PAIUTE-UTE, BANNOCK-Snake, and SHOSHONI-COMANCHE INDIANS.

Utrecht, treaty of (11 April 1713) This treaty ended the war of the Spanish

Succession (*see* QUEEN ANNE'S WAR). Britain won title to Newfoundland, Nova Scotia (then Acadia), and an undefined area around Hudson Bay. Both sides agreed not to interfere with the freedom of Indians to trade furs with whomever they wished. France retained Cape Breton Island, on which it would build LOUISBOURG.

V

V-E Day (8 May 1945) This abbreviation stands for Victory in Europe Day, the date when German authorities signed preliminary, unconditional terms of surrender to the Allies at Reims. The Berlin government formally ratified the surrender the next day. On 5 June, Germany was divided into US, British, French, and Soviet occupation zones.

V-J Day (15 August 1945) This abbreviation stands for Victory over Japan Day, the date when Japan unconditionally surrendered and WORLD WAR II ended. On 2 September, Japan's government signed the formal document of surrender on the USS *Missouri* in front of Douglas MACARTHUR.

Valcour Island, battle of On 11 October 1776, Brigadier General Benedict Arnold's 15 gunboats (750 crewmen) held their own against Lieutenant Colonel Thomas Carleton's more heavily armed 20 gunships (900 crewmen) on Lake Champlain. Carleton then pursued Arnold for two days, during which almost every US vessel was lost. US losses: 87 killed and wounded, 110 captured, 11 vessels sunk or scuttled to avoid capture. British losses: minor. Although defeated, Arnold's fleet had blocked Carleton from invading N.Y. with 13,000 troops until it was too late for him to capture FORT TICONDEROGA and Albany as intended. Had Carleton taken Albany, Burgoyne's campaign of 1777 might have reestablished royal control over N.Y.

Valley Forge (Pa.) After defeat at GERMANTOWN, 10,000 Continental soldiers entered winter quarters at Valley Forge, Pa., on 19 December 1777. Perhaps 25 percent died of disease or malnutrition that winter. On 18 June 1778, the Continentals – augmented with new recruits – left the encampment highly skilled in battle drill due to Baron von STEUBEN's training; the army emerged roughly equal in fighting ability to the British Army, which it fought to a draw at their next major encounter at MONMOUTH COURTHOUSE, N.J.

Van Buren, Martin (b. Kinderhook, N.Y., 5 December 1782; d. Kinderhook, N.Y., 24 July 1862) In 1803 Van Buren opened a law office. After rising through N.Y. government, he assumed leadership of the ALBANY REGENCY. While US senator (1821–8), he supported William CRAWFORD for president in 1824 and Andrew JACKSON in 1828. Named secretary of state in 1829, he replaced John CALHOUN as Jackson's heir-apparent, in some part due to the Peggy EATON AFFAIR and Calhoun's vindictive blocking of his appointment as ambassador to Britain. He was vice-president (1833–7). Running as Democratic candidate for president in 1836 with Richard M. JOHNSON, he won with 50.9 percent of the ballots. The PANIC OF 1837 cost him reelection in 1840, when he polled 46.9 percent of the ballots. He lost the 1844 Democratic nomination for president to James POLK. He led the BARNBURNERS' revolt against the Albany Regency's anti-reform leaders, vigorously opposed extending slavery to the territories, and was the FREE-SOIL PARTY's nominee for president in 1848, when he received 10.1 percent of the votes, but carried no states.

Vanderbilt, Cornelius (b. Staten Island, N.Y., 27 May 1794; d. New York, N.Y., 4 January 1877) He was born to a family of modest means and ceased attending school at the age of 11. When just 16, he acquired a small boat as a ferry service from Staten Island to New York, and by the age of 21 he had won military contracts to provision island forts around New York. As New York City grew, so did his shipping business, and by the time he was 40 Vanderbilt was worth

$500,000. He operated a toll route across Nicaragua for the CALIFORNIA GOLD RUSH, and considered building an Atlantic–Pacific canal until the traffic fell. He entered the railway business in his sixties, and consolidated the major lines around New York City. He died his age's greatest transportation magnate, and left an estate of $100,000,000.

Varick, James *see* AFRICAN METHODIST EPISCOPAL ZION CHURCH

Veblen, Thorstein Bunde (b. near Cato, Wis., 30 July 1857; d. Palo Alto, Calif., 3 August 1929) He matured in Minn. and studied economics at Yale (Ph.D., 1894). In 1899, Veblen published his most influential book, *The Theory of the Leisure Class*, which argued that the upper classes wasted economic resources by trying to establish their social superiority with ostentatious displays of wealth. He later held up engineers and social scientists as the best qualified professionals to organize the economy and build an equitable society. His theories reinforced the antipathy of PROGRESSIVE ERA and NEW DEAL intellectuals toward the business community, and encouraged them to use the government for ending social inequities and redistributing income.

Venezuela boundary dispute When gold was discovered along the ill-defined boundary between Venezuela and Britain's Guiana colony, each country rejected the other's territorial claims. The US accepted a Venezuelan plea to arbitrate the dispute in 1887, but Britain rejected the offer. In 1894 Grover CLEVELAND declared that British pressure upon Venezuela to surrender territory would violate the MONROE DOCTRINE and – after Britain declined a US proposal to mediate a solution – hinted on 17 December that the US would assist Venezuela militarily if Britain did not submit the controversy to arbitration under US supervision. To avoid an armed confrontation, in January 1895 Britain agreed to let a US commission establish the true boundary. When the arbitration board issued its report on 3 October 1899, it upheld Britain's claim to most of the disputed lands. The controversy raised US diplomatic prestige and reinforced its pretensions as the dominant power in Latin-American affairs.

Vera Cruz, battle of (Mexico) On 9 March 1847, Commodore Matthew C. PERRY's fleet landed Major General Winfield SCOTT's 13,600 soldiers (without opposition) in the US Army's first major amphibious operation. Scott besieged Vera Cruz (22–7 March), then occupied the city. US losses: 19 killed, 63 wounded. Mexican losses: 80 troops killed, wounded, 200 civilians killed, wounded. On 8 April, Scott began his advance upon Mexico City.

Vermont In February 1724, the first Anglo-American settlement was founded at Fort Dummer, near modern Brattleboro. In 1749 N.H. began issuing land grants west of the Connecticut River, an area that was NEW YORK's legal jurisdiction. In 1767, after the PRIVY COUNCIL ordered N.H. to cease this practice, almost half the modern state – 4,500 square miles – had been patented to speculators. By then, 727 families (mostly from Conn.) had founded 97 towns in Vt.

After 1764, N.Y. issued its own land grants to speculators, who were expected to evict trespassers with N.H. titles in court. Ethan ALLEN's GREEN MOUNTAIN BOYS countered this threat with intimidation and violence. In the Revolution, Green Mountain Boys took FORT TICONDEROGA (1775), Vt. militia fought the battle of BENNINGTON, and the state was the site of ten other military actions. In 1777 a convention at Windsor declared Vt. an independent state and wrote a constitution, which was the first to abolish SLAVERY and allow universal manhood suffrage. Congress refused to admit Vt. without approval from N.Y., and N.Y. did not agree to do so until 1789, subject to payment of a $30,000 claims settlement by Vt. It became the 14th state on 4 March 1791.

In 1800 Vt. was the fourth smallest state and had 154,465 residents, of whom less than 1 percent were black and 85 percent were of English-Welsh stock. The second Battle of LAKE CHAMPLAIN saved the state from British invasion in the WAR OF 1812. Its limited potential for agriculture inhibited population growth and the number of residents only doubled between 1800 and 1860. In 1860 it had 315,098 inhabitants, of whom just 709 were black and 10 percent were foreign-born; it ranked 29th among states in population, 23rd in the value of its farmland and livestock, and 23rd in manufactures. In the CIVIL WAR, it furnished 33,288 USA troops (including 120 blacks) and was raided from Canada by CSA guerrillas who robbed the St Albans bank. Its population stagnated after 1865.

In 1900 Vt. was 73 percent rural and had 343,641 residents, of whom nearly all were white and 13 percent were foreign-born; it ranked 40th among the states in population, 35th in the value of its agricultural products and 33rd in manufactures. It experienced a net out-migration of population every decade from 1900 through the 1950s and ranked as the 3rd smallest state in 1990. In 1990 Vt. had 562,758 inhabitants (98 percent white, 1 percent Hispanic, 1 percent Asian), of whom 23 percent were urban and 3.1 percent foreign-born. Manufacturing and mining employed 24 percent of workers.

Verrazano, Giovanni de (b. near Florence, Italy, ca. 1480; d. France, ca. 1527) Commissioned by Francis I of France to find a westward route to Asia, Verrazano left Dieppe in December 1523 and sighted the Carolina coast about 19 March 1524. He explored the mainland northward and made the first verified sighting of New York harbor about 17 April and then sailed as far as Nova Scotia. French territorial claims in North America derived from this voyage.

Versailles, treaty of Negotiated during the the Paris peace conference of 18 January to 28 June 1919, this agreement concluded WORLD WAR I. Woodrow WILSON represented the US and was frustrated that his FOURTEEN POINTS had little influence on the settlement. The BIG FOUR included many provisions implementing "secret treaties," which themselves violated Wilson's call for a peace based on open covenants openly conceived; they also ignored his calls to protect freedom of the seas and free trade. The treaty branded Germany as the war's aggressor, forced it to surrender territories and pay reparations to the victors, broke the Hapsburg empire up into nation states, arranged to reduce all armed forces, founded a Permanent Court of International Justice, and created the LEAGUE OF NATIONS.

The treaty failed Senate ratification because of opposition to US membership in the League, which was seen as infringing national sovereignty, especially by ARTICLE X. When Wilson refused to compromise with Henry Cabot LODGE on terms for US participation in the League, Lodge threw his influence toward those senators most opposed to it: Robert LA FOLLETTE, William BORAH, and Hiram JOHNSON. While trying to rally public support for the treaty's unconditional acceptance during a 9,500-mile stumping campaign, Wilson was incapacitated by a stroke on 25 September 1919. His continued refusal to accommodate Lodge's objections left the treaty with insufficient support for ratification, and the last significant attempt to find common ground failed on 19 March 1920. With the Versailles treaty dead, the US made peace with Germany by the treaty of BERLIN.

vertical integration This was the situation when a single corporation controlled every function required to do business, to include obtaining raw materials, manufacturing, and operating its own retail network. It became a widespread business strategy after 1870. (*See also* HORIZONTAL INTEGRATION)

Vesey's Conspiracy On 30 May 1822, a black informer revealed a conspiracy headed by Denmark Vesey, an ex-slave who had bought his freedom after winning a lottery in 1800, to incite a SLAVE REVOLT at Charleston, S.C. The authorities arrested 139 blacks and 4 whites. From 18 June to 9 August, judges condemned 47 blacks to death, of whom 37 were executed.

vestry In the Church of England, the vestry is a group of laymen who manage their parish's financial affairs. Unlike English vestries, their colonial counterparts did not formally induct ministers to their parishes, and so parsons enjoyed no independent right to their salary and were reliant on the vestry's good will. The vestry filled its own vacancies and invariably chose members of the gentry. In the South, poor relief (welfare) was provided by vestries rather than the county court.

Veterans Administration *see* VETERANS AFFAIRS, DEPARTMENT OF

Veterans Affairs, Department of (VA) This department originated as the Veterans Administration, an independent agency created on 21 July 1930 to consolidate all federal programs for veterans in a single agency. Congress renamed and elevated it to cabinet status on 15 March 1989. The VA's largest program is the Veterans Health Administration, which was the largest US health care system in 1993; it operated 172 medical centers with 80,000 beds, 362 outpatient and community clinics averaging 23,000,000 patient visits annually, 128 nursing homes with 71,000 patients, and 35 domiciliaries caring for 26,000 persons; it had 243,038 employees, and a $16 billion budget.

Veterans Compensation Act *see* BONUS BILL (1924)

Vice-Admiralty Courts *see* ADMIRALTY COURTS

Vicksburg, siege of (Miss.) On 19 and 22 May 1863, Major General Ulysses S. GRANT's 35,000 Federals lost 3,200 casualties assaulting John Pemberton's 30,000 Confederates. Grant besieged the city and his army grew to 71,000 by 4 July, when the garrison of 29,396 surrendered. The victory freed Grant's troops for the CHICKAMAUGA campaign and gave USA warships control of the Mississippi River south to PORT HUDSON, whose fall five days later split the Confederacy and allowed midwesterners to export goods through New Orleans.

Vietnam antiwar movement Soon after the first bombing of North Vietnam on 2 March 1965, college TEACH-INS began denouncing the VIETNAM WAR. Most antiwar protests were nonviolent, but draft board files were vandalized, college Reserve Officers' Training Corps buildings burned, and a bomb killed a University of Wisconsin graduate student at a computer lab on 24 August 1971. In March 1968, Lyndon JOHNSON withdrew from the Democratic primary after public dismay over the TET OFFENSIVE's casualties led to unexpected support for his antiwar opponent, Eugene MCCARTHY. The CHICAGO DEMOCRATIC CONVENTION RIOT occurred as Democrats nominated Johnson's choice for president, Hubert HUMPHREY, over McCarthy. In November 1969, 300,000 war protesters marched in Washington, D.C. In April 1970, the invasion of CAMBODIA sparked militant campus demonstrations nationwide that climaxed in the KENT STATE UNIVERSITY SHOOTINGS on 4 May and the death of two Mississippi State University students on 15 May. Classes closed on over 400 campuses as students boycotted lectures to protest the invasion and killings. The PENTAGON PAPERS appeared in 1971, but by mid-year, antiwar activism had waned due to the DRAFT's suspension and US troop withdrawals.

Vietnam War US civilian and military advisors had served in South Vietnam since 1954 and they numbered 900 when John F. KENNEDY's presidency began. On 1 October 1960, South Vietnamese Communists (Vietcong) formed the National Liberation Front to reunite the South with Ho Chi Minh's North Vietnam by political unrest and guerrilla warfare, which Ho Chi Minh actively supported. Kennedy approved a counterinsurgency program on 28 January 1961. South Vietnam's President Ngo Dinh Diem requested more advisors on 9 June and a bilateral defense treaty on 1 October. Kennedy reaffirmed the US commitment to South Vietnamese independence on 15 December 1961.

The Vietcong made rapid gains in rural areas and exploited widespread, often violent, protests against Diem in the cities. A military coup (planned with Kennedy's knowledge) assassinated Diem on 2 November 1963. South Vietnam's political instability, corruption, and growing war-weariness frustrated US efforts to build effective local resistance to the Vietcong, who showed remarkable discipline, self-sacrifice, and single-mindedness.

US involvement deepened after Congress passed the GULF OF TONKIN RESOLUTION (1964). On 2 March 1965, the US began bombing North Vietnam; on 7 May, the first major US combat unit (173rd Airborne Brigade) landed in South Vietnam; on 6 April, Lyndon JOHNSON directed US troops to conduct offensive operations. During 1965, US forces in Vietnam rose from 23,300 to 184,000 (reaching a peak strength of 543,400 by April 1969). The VIETNAM ANTIWAR MOVEMENT began expanding significantly in 1965.

Ho Chi Minh poured North Vietnamese regulars south via Laos. Except for the IA DRANG VALLEY and KHE SANH, the Communists avoided major battles until the TET OFFENSIVE of January 1968. Tet was a major military defeat for Ho Chi Minh, but became the conflict's turning point because Americans were shocked by a sharp rise in US deaths and the ferocity of enemy attacks. Anticipating endless streams of US casualties sustained to prop up a corrupt, incompetent military government, US opinion steadily shifted against the war. When faced with skyrocketing demands to increase US troops in Vietnam, Clark CLIFFORD and other senior officials advised Johnson on 25 March to cease escalating the war and seek a negotiated peace.

Formal peace talks began in Paris on 12 May 1968. The bombing of North Vietnam stopped on 31 October. On 14 May 1970, shortly after massive US protests against his invasion of CAMBODIA, Richard NIXON proposed mutual force withdrawals by North Vietnam and the US. Nixon pursued a "Vietnamization" policy designed to withdraw US troops as quickly as the poorly trained, poorly armed, and poorly led South Vietnamese forces could be strengthened to face the highly professional North Vietnamese regulars. Bombing of North Vietnam resumed on 26 December 1971, when US strength in the south was 156,800 troops. The PARIS PEACE ACCORDS ended hostilities on 27 January 1973, when just 24,000 Americans remained in South Vietnam. Except for US embassy personnel, all US forces were withdrawn in 1973. North Vietnamese forces invaded South Vietnam in 1975 and took Saigon. The last 50 Americans were evacuated on 30 April.

In all, 8,762,000 Americans performed Vietnam-era military service: 4,386,000 army, 794,000 marines, 1,740,000 air force, 1,842,000 navy. About 2,000,000 servicemen served in or offshore Vietnam. US losses: 47,244 battle deaths (30,868 army, 13,065 marines, 1,737 air force, 1,574 navy); 10,751 noncombat deaths (7,270 army, 1,750 marines, 815 air force, 916 navy); 153,329 hospitalized wounded (96,811 army, 51,399 marines, 939 air force, 4,180 navy); 150,375 lightly wounded (104,725 army, 37,234 marines, 2,518 air force, 5,898 navy); 2,483 missing (767 army, 941 air force, 733 navy, 42 civilians). South Vietnamese forces lost 223,748 killed and 570,600 wounded. Communist forces lost up to 660,000 killed. About 300,000 civilians died in South Vietnam and 65,000 in North Vietnam.

The war's direct expenses amounted to about $106,800,000,000. The US Navy and Air Force flew about 527,000 bombing missions carrying 6,162,000 tons of explosives (three times the tonnage dropped by US bombers in World War II).

Vietnamese immigration *see* BOAT PEOPLE

Viking Program *see* NATIONAL AERONAUTICS AND SPACE ADMINISTRATION

Vincennes, battle of (Ind.) On 17 December 1778, Lieutenant Colonel Henry Hamilton's 35 redcoats, 140 TORIES, and 500 Indians captured a small garrison placed at Vincennes on 20 July by Colonel George Rogers CLARK. On 23 February 1778, Clark and 175 Ky. militia besieged Fort Sackville, which Hamilton surrendered on 24 February. US losses: 1 wounded. British losses: 5 Indians killed, 79 redcoats captured (7 wounded). Clark's victory ended British military power south of Fort Detroit and enabled the US to keep possession of all lands below the Great Lakes by the treaty of PARIS (1783).

***Vincennes*, USS, incident** *see* *STARK*, USS

Vinland This region was named "Land of Vines" by its discoverer, Leif ERICSON, about 1000. Norse Vikings planted brief settlements there about 1004–05, 1009–10, and 1014, but abandoned them after conflict with native peoples. One of these sites has been excavated at L'Anse-aux-Meadows in Newfoundland.

Vinson, Frederick Moore (b. Louisa, Ky., 22 January 1890; d. Washington, D.C., 8 September 1953) At the age of 21 Vinson passed the Ky. bar exam. He entered Congress at 33 and became influential in passing NEW DEAL legislation. He served as judge of the US Court of Appeals for Washington, D.C. (1938–43), held several high administrative posts, and was secretary of the Treasury (1945–6) before being confirmed as chief justice on 20 June 1946. The Vinson Court issued several important decisions undermining racial SEGREGATION, of which Vinson wrote *Shelley* v. *Kraemer* (*see* *CORRIGAN* v. *BUCKLEY*), *MCLAURIN* v. *OKLAHOMA*, and *SWEATT* v. *PAINTER*. Many opinions about subversive activities were given in Vinson's tenure, of which Vinson authored *AMERICAN*

Communications Association, CIO et al. v. Douds, Dennis et al. v. United States, and the case of Julius and Ethel Rosenberg.

Virgin Islands On 24 October 1867, Denmark agreed to sell the US its West Indian islands for $7,500,000, but the Senate failed to ratify the treaty. To keep Germany from acquiring the islands for a naval base, on 4 August 1916 the US signed a treaty to purchase them from Denmark for $25,000,000 and take formal possession on 31 March 1917. The navy administered the Virgin Islands until the Department of the Interior took over in 1931. In 1927 US citizenship was extended to the islanders, who were allowed to vote in 1936 providing they were literate in English. The president appointed the islands' governor until 1970, when the office became elective. The Virgin Islands are now a non-self-governing territory with a nonvoting delegate in Congress.

Virginia In 1607 the Virginia Company of London planted the first permanent English colony at Jamestown. The company's charter was revoked by James I on 24 May 1624 and it was formally declared a royal colony on 13 May 1625. The Powhatan Confederacy ceased to be a major threat after the two Opechancanough wars. The headright system encouraged the importation of large numbers of indentured servants to work on plantations. Tobacco dominated the economy after 1619, but falling prices (due to overproduction) resulted in a long agricultural depression from 1660 to 1715. Civil war briefly erupted in Bacon's Rebellion in 1676.

The number of slaves expanded greatly after 1680 and by 1720 they accounted for most unfree field workers. Settlement rapidly spread over the Piedmont after 1720. Always the most numerous colony, Va. contained 504,000 persons, or a fifth of the thirteen colonies' population about 1775. Va. produced few Tories, but furnished 15 of the 80 Continental regiments at the height of the war; it was the site of 69 military actions on land and 11 at sea, including the decisive victory of Yorktown. It was the 10th state to ratify the Constitution, on 25 June 1788.

By 1792, having ceded its claims to the Northwest Territory and Kentucky, Va. had been reduced to its modern boundaries plus West Virginia. In 1800 it had 886,149 residents, still more than any other state, of whom 39 percent were slaves and 2 percent were free blacks. It lay too far north to grow cotton and its main staple remained tobacco. Va. was replaced as the most populous state by N.Y. in 1820, and by 1840 it was only the fourth-largest; in 1860 it ranked fifth in population among states, fifth in the value of farmland and livestock, and ninth in manufactures. By 1860 slaves made up 39 percent of the 1,219,630 persons within modern Va., but just 5 percent of the 376,688 in modern W.Va., while 2 percent of all inhabitants were foreign-born.

Va. became the eighth CSA state on 17 April 1861. In the Civil War, W.Va. seceded and became a separate state. Va. sent the CSA army 160,000 troops, more than any other state. Since the CSA capital was at Richmond, it witnessed 2,154 military engagements, more than any other state. In May 1862, the Union established a provisional civilian government for areas within US lines. By 1866, this government had ended slavery, but refused to let freedmen vote, passed a black code (*see* black codes), and rejected the Fourteenth Amendment. Washington imposed military rule in March 1867, but restored self-government and congressional representation on 26 January 1870, three months after Republican control ended on 5 October 1869. Va. disfranchised most blacks in 1902 and then enacted segregation.

From 1870 to 1900, 223,500 out-migrants left Va. In 1900 it was the 17th state in size and had 1,854,184 inhabitants, of whom 82 percent were rural, 36 percent were black, and 6 percent were foreign-born: it ranked 21st among states in the value of its agricultural goods and 20th in manufactures (including cigarettes). Since the 1940s, a major factor in its growth has been the expansion of Washington's suburbs and of military bases. During the civil rights movement, its government resisted school integration for almost 20 years before Republican Governor Linwood Holton took office with a promise to make Va. "a model of race relations." Va. ranked as the 12th state in size in 1990, when its population was 6,187,358 (76 percent white, 19 percent black, 3 percent Hispanic, 2 percent Asian), of whom 73 percent were urban and 5 percent were foreign-born. Manufacturing and mining employed 23 percent of workers.

Virginia, Army of On 26 June 1862, the USA detached units from its Army of the POTOMAC to form this force under Major General John Pope, who was to coordinate operations with Major General George MCCLELLAN against the Army of NORTHERN VIRGINIA. After its defeat at the second battle of BULL RUN, Pope was reassigned to command of the first SIOUX WAR and his army was reconsolidated with the Army of the Potomac.

Virginia Capes, battle of *see* CHESAPEAKE CAPES, BATTLE OF

Virginia Company of London On 20 April 1606, JAMES I granted a patent to the Virginia Company (headquartered in London) to colonize North America's southern mainland. After founding JAMESTOWN, Va., it obtained a new charter extending its borders 200 miles north and south of Point Comfort (Chesapeake Bay), and west to the Pacific. On 22 March 1612, its third charter gave it jurisdiction over Bermuda. Despite the development of tobacco as a profitable export, the company consistently lost money on the colony because of mismanagement and corruption by its officers, and had to resort to lotteries after 1612 to raise investment capital. OPECHANCANOUGH'S FIRST WAR and the suspension of its lottery privileges forced the company into bankruptcy in 1622. The PRIVY COUNCIL assumed control of company affairs in July 1623 and James I revoked its charter on 24 May 1624.

Virginia Company of Plymouth, England *see* PLYMOUTH COMPANY

Virginia dynasty This term refers to election of Virginians as four of the five first presidents (WASHINGTON, JEFFERSON, MADISON, and MONROE). No resident of Va. has been elected president since 1820, but William H. HARRISON was elected from Ohio in 1840, vice-president John TYLER assumed the office in 1841, Zachary TAYLOR was elected from La. in 1848, and Woodrow WILSON was elected from N.J. in 1912.

Virginia Plan On 29 May 1787, at the CONSTITUTIONAL CONVENTION, Edmund RANDOLPH proposed 15 resolutions (drafted by James MADISON) as the basis for a national government. The Virginia Plan called for a bicameral legislature – in which representation would be based on population in both houses – a chief executive, and judiciary. The legislature's lower house would elect both the upper house (from nominees submitted by the states) and the chief executive. Congress would have authority to veto state laws. The plan served as the main basis for discussion at the convention, but was modified after discussion of the NEW JERSEY PLAN and CONNECTICUT COMPROMISE.

Virginia Resolutions James MADISON framed this document, which was adopted by the Va. legislature on 24 December 1798. The resolutions declared that states reserved the right to judge federal laws when they ratified the CONSTITUTION – which was characterized as a compact among the states – denounced the ALIEN AND SEDITION ACTS as unconstitutional, and declared that states may use INTERPOSITION to stop the federal government from violating their citizens' rights. It was supported by both KENTUCKY RESOLUTIONS.

Virginia Statute for Religious Freedom (16 January 1786) Although the Anglican Church had already been disestablished in 1776, this measure provided additional protection for freedom of religion by vigorously denouncing and outlawing any form of state interference with private religious opinions. This statute, largely the product of Thomas JEFFERSON's efforts, was the Revolutionary era's most liberal expression of religious freedom.

virtual representation In 18th-century Britain, the lack of direct representation by many communities was justified according to this political theory. Virtual representation maintained that whatever his constituency, a member of Parliament represented all British subjects because he considered their interests in deciding how to vote on issues. The theory also held that American colonists were represented in Parliament, although the colonies elected no representatives. It was the major British argument for imposing taxes on the colonists, until refuted by Daniel DULANY.

VISTA *see* VOLUNTEERS IN SERVICE TO AMERICA

Voice of America *see* US INFORMATION AGENCY

Volstead Act (28 October 1919) Congress passed this law to enforce the EIGHTEENTH AMENDMENT, and enacted it by overriding Woodrow WILSON's veto. Effective as of 16 January 1920, it defined spirituous liquor as any drink with over 0.5 percent alcoholic content. It was amended by the BEER-WINE REVENUE ACT (1933).

Volunteers in Service to America (VISTA) The ECONOMIC OPPORTUNITY ACT (1964) created this GREAT SOCIETY program. It recruited volunteers to live among and perform community service work for economically disadvantaged neighborhoods in the urban or rural US. Its personnel donated a year's work in return for minimum wages and insurance benefits. In 1971 it was placed under ACTION.

von Steuben, Baron *see* STEUBEN, FRIEDRICH VON

Voting Rights Act (6 August 1965) Proposed by Lyndon JOHNSON, this law suspended, for five years, LITERACY TESTS and other discriminatory devices for registering voters in all states or election districts where under 50 percent of adults voted in 1964; it empowered federal examiners to register voters in such areas; and it enacted criminal penalties for obstructing, discouraging, or intimidating anyone from voting. After five years, Washington's federal district court must approve any changes in election laws passed in states or counties where less than half of adults had voted in August 1965. The law was held constitutional in *SOUTH CAROLINA* V. *KATZENBACH*. From 1965 to 1969, registered black voters tripled from one to three million in ex-CSA states. Congress amended and extended the act by the CIVIL RIGHTS ACT (1970). The Court ruled on redistricting under the law in *UNITED JEWISH ORGANIZATIONS OF WILLIAMSBURGH* V. *CAREY* and *JOHNSON* V. *DE GRANDY*.

Voyager Program *see* NATIONAL AERONAUTICS AND SPACE ADMINISTRATION

voyageurs These were French Canadians hired to paddle large canoes for COUREURS DE BOIS. They lived Indian-style, sired many mixed-race children, and often entered the FUR TRADE.

W

Wabash, St Louis and Pacific Railroad Company* v. *Illinois In 1886 the Supreme Court invalidated an Ill. law forbidding higher rates for railroad freight hauled for short distances than for long trips; it held (6–3) that Ill. had infringed Congress's exclusive power to regulate rates charged in interstate commerce. The decision reversed the Court's interpretation in the GRANGER CASES; in combination with *CHICAGO, MILWAUKEE AND ST PAUL RAILROAD COMPANY* v. *MINNESOTA* and *REAGAN* v. *FARMERS' LOAN AND TRUST COMPANY*, it enabled railroad and warehouse corporations to challenge unfavorable decisions by state regulatory commissions in federal courts, which often ruled that state regulation violated their property rights.

WAC Abbreviation for the Women's Army Corps.

Wade, Benjamin F. (b. Feeding Hills, Mass., 27 October 1800; d. Jefferson, Ohio, 2 March 1878) At the age of 21, Wade settled in Ohio, which sent him to the Senate in 1851 as a free-soil Whig. He helped found the Republican Party. During the CIVIL WAR, Wade emerged as a leading Radical Republican (*see* RADICAL REPUBLICANS) and co-sponsored the WADE–DAVIS BILL. He bitterly opposed Andrew JOHNSON's moderation on RECONSTRUCTION, and upon becoming the Senate's president pro tempore in 1867, he stood next in line to the presidency during Johnson's impeachment. Apprehension over the extreme measures Wade might pursue as chief executive possibly won Johnson enough votes to avoid removal from office. Wade resigned from Congress in March 1869.

Wade–Davis Bill In 1864 Representative Henry Davis and Senator Benjamin WADE co-sponsored a plan to replace Abraham LINCOLN's program for the RECONSTRUCTION of Confederate states. The Wade–Davis Bill would have: (1) delayed any state's reconstruction until Confederate resistance had ended and a majority of white citizens had sworn unequivocal allegiance to the US; (2) required Senate confirmation for provisional governors appointed over such states; and (3) insisted that southern states ratify new state constitutions that disavowed SECESSION, ended SLAVERY, disfranchised CSA leaders, and repudiated the CSA war debt. The bill disqualified few ex-rebels from political activity and did not demand suffrage for FREEDMEN. After Lincoln pocket-vetoed the bill on 4 July, its outraged sponsors issued the WADE–DAVIS MANIFESTO.

Wade–Davis Manifesto On 5 August 1864, Horace GREELEY's New York *Tribune* printed a denunciation of Abraham LINCOLN for having vetoed the WADE–DAVIS BILL. The manifesto condemned the president for usurping Congress's legislative powers by attempting to reconstruct the South by executive orders. RADICAL REPUBLICANS also circulated anonymous calls that Lincoln be replaced with another nominee for president. The manifesto's strident language offended most moderate Republicans and produced a backlash that enhanced Lincoln's image while discrediting Radical Republican leaders.

wages and hours law *see* FAIR LABOR STANDARDS ACT

Wagner, Robert Ferdinand (b. Hesse-Nassau, Germany, 8 June 1877; d. New York, N.Y., 4 May 1953) He was brought to New York in 1885, and matured into a reform-minded, PROGRESSIVE ERA Democrat. In 1926 he won election to the Senate. He made important contributions to the EMERGENCY RELIEF AND RECONSTRUCTION ACT, the NIRA (especially concerning labor's collective bargaining rights), and Social Security (*see* SOCIAL SECURITY ADMINISTRATION). He sponsored the federal Emergency Relief Act (*see* FEDERAL EMERGENCY RELIEF ADMINISTRATION) the NATIONAL EMPLOYMENT SYSTEM ACT, the Wagner–Crosser Act (*see* RAILROAD RETIREMENT ACTS), the NATIONAL LABOR RELATIONS ACT, and the WAGNER–STEAGALL ACT.

Wagner–Connery Act *see* NATIONAL LABOR RELATIONS ACT

Wagner–Crosser Railroad Retirement Act *see* RAILROAD RETIREMENT ACTS

Wagner–Peyser Act *see* NATIONAL EMPLOYMENT SYSTEM ACT

Wagner–Steagall Act (1 September 1937) Because the NATIONAL HOUSING ACT (1934) had failed to fund any substantial public housing projects, Congress created the US Housing Authority (USHA); it provided $500,000,000 for use as loans to fund up to 90 percent of expenses in building homes for low-income families. The law marked the start of the federal government's commitment to eliminate substandard housing. By January 1941, the USHA had approved loans for 511 low-rent apartment complexes with 161,162 units. During WORLD WAR II, the agency planned and financed new housing around military bases.

Waite, Morrison Remick (b. Lyme, Conn., 29 November 1816; d. Washington, D.C., 23 March 1888) Waite opened a law office in Ohio in 1839 and later specialized in railroad cases. A former Whig (*see* WHIG PARTY) who joined the Republicans, his first federal appointment came as a commissioner for the *ALABAMA* CLAIMS, which brought him national renown. While chairing Ohio's 1873 constitutional convention, he was nominated as sixth chief justice. Despite having no judicial experience, he was a forceful, learned chief justice who led the Court in restricting the scope of the FOURTEENTH and FIFTEENTH AMENDMENTS in *UNITED STATES* v. *REESE*, *UNITED STATES* v. *CRUIKSHANK*, *MINOR* v. *HAPPERSETT*, and *Walker* v. *Sauvinet* (*see* SEVENTH AMENDMENT). He also wrote *Munn* v. *Illinois* (*see* GRANGER CASES).

Wake Island On 4 July 1898, in the SPANISH-AMERICAN WAR, US troops en route to the Philippines seized Wake. Th US annexed the uninhabited island of thre square miles in 1899 and formally occupie it in 1900. It became a refueling and repai station for the navy and commercial airline The Japanese captured it in the battle c WAKE ISLAND and surrendered it on 4 Sep tember 1945. The navy administered Wak until 1962, the Departments of INTERIO and TRANSPORTATION from then to Jun 1972, and the air force after that.

Wake Island, battle of On 11 Decembe 1941, Major James Devereux's 388 U marines repulsed Rear Admiral Sadamich Kajioka's Japanese task force (9 cruisers an destroyers, 4 transports) by sinking 2 destroy ers and damaging 7 other ships. After 1 days of heavy bombardment, 800 Japanes overran the defenders on 23 December.

Walker, Dr Thomas *see* CUMBERLAN GAP

Walker, William (b. Nashville, Tenn., 1 Ma 1824; d. Honduras, 12 September 1860 After joining the CALIFORNIA GOLD RUSH Walker launched an abortive FILIBUSTERING effort to seize Baja California an Sonora in 1853. Intending to create a centra American empire, reestablish SLAVERY, an build an Atlantic–Pacific canal, Walker an 60 US mercenaries became embroiled i Nicaragua's civil war during June 1855 Walker emerged as dictator in July 1856 After being ousted in May 1857, he attempte reconquests in November 1857 (only to b restrained by the US Navy), and in Augus 1860 (when he was captured by the Honduran authorities, who then executed him).

Walker Tariff (30 July 1846) A Democratic measure advocated by James K. POLK this law abandoned protectionism and se duties according to the government's nee for revenue. It replaced specific (fixed) rate on goods with ad valorem duties based o the declared worth of goods, and cut average rates to 26.5 percent, their lowest level since 1816.

Walker* v. *Sauvinet *see* SEVENTH AMENDMENT

Walking Purchase *see* DELAWARE INDIAN

Wallace, George Corley (b. Clio, Ala., 2 August 1919) Having lost a race for Ala governor by running as a moderate in 1958 Wallace ran as an extreme segregationist i

1962 and won. He defied court-ordered integration of the University of Alabama until 11 June 1963, when he personally blocked entry of two black students, but was forced to yield by the assistant attorney general, who was backed by federal troops. Ineligible to serve two consecutive terms as governor, Wallace had his wife Lurleen elected in his stead in 1966. Running as the AMERICAN INDEPENDENT PARTY's 1968 nominee for president, he carried five states and 13.5 percent of all ballots. On 15 May 1972, while seeking the Democratic nomination for president, he was shot and paralyzed at Bel Air, Md., by Arthur Bremer. After serving as Ala. governor (1970–8), he won a fourth term in 1982 as a racial moderate and received a significant share of the black vote.

Wallace, Henry Agard (b. Adair County, Iowa, 7 October 1888; d. Danbury, Conn., 18 November 1965) He was the editor of an Iowa farmers' journal when he became secretary of agriculture in 1933. He developed the AGRICULTURAL ADJUSTMENT ADMINISTRATION and other NEW DEAL programs for farmers. He became vice-president in 1941, but was replaced by Harry S. TRUMAN and became secretary of commerce in 1945. He broke with Truman and resigned in 1946. As Progressive candidate for president in 1948, he was much criticized for favoring better relations with the Soviet Union and being endorsed by US Communists (*see* COMMUNIST PARTY); he won 2.4 percent of ballots. He then left politics.

Walsh–Healey Government Contracts Act (30 June 1936) This statute, part of the LITTLE NIRA, reimposed certain industry-wide wage and workplace standards after the NATIONAL INDUSTRIAL RECOVERY ACT (NIRA) was ruled unconstitutional. Influenced heavily by Frances PERKINS, it authorized the Department of LABOR to set wages, hours, and benefits for all employees of any company doing over $10,000 in business with the US government. It set maximum working time at eight hours daily and 40 hours weekly, forbade child and convict labor, and required contractors to pay a MINIMUM WAGE set by the Labor Department based on an area's prevailing pay scales.

Wampanoag Indians Speakers of one of the ALGONQUIAN LANGUAGES, this group occupied eastern R.I. and PLYMOUTH colony. They lost perhaps half their population to European diseases (1616–18), and numbered about 1,200 in 1620. Under Squanto, they welcomed the PILGRIMS as military allies to counter their NARRAGANSETT INDIAN enemies. Their population steadily declined from disease and their relations with whites deteriorated as Plymouth tried to extend its authority over them. KING PHILIP'S WAR arose from Wampanoag grievances and was led by its sachem Metacomet. Most Wampanoags were killed or sold into overseas slavery. A remnant remained in Cape Cod and Martha's Vineyard; they numbered about 680 in 1790, but fewer than 50 were pure-blooded Indians. In 1978 a federal court denied a Wampanoag claim for 25 square miles on Cape Cod under the INDIAN TRADE INTERCOURSE ACT (1790); it ruled that the Wampanoags were tax-paying citizens in 1790, not tribal members.

wampum This term referred to a string of beads, ground from clamshells, and sewn together in various lengths and designs. It was used by ALGONQUIAN and IROQUOIAN INDIANS as money, records of treaties or land sales, and ceremonial belts.

War Department On 14 June 1775, Congress established the Continental Army, which was disbanded to less than a thousand men in 1783. On 7 August 1789, Congress created the War Department and named Henry KNOX its first secretary on 12 September. Responsibility for Indian affairs lay with this department until 1849. In 1949 it was eliminated and the army was placed under the Department of DEFENSE.

war hawks These were highly nationalistic, young Democratic congressmen from the West and South who pressed for war with Britain in 1811–12. The most prominent were John CALHOUN (S.C.), Richard M. JOHNSON (Ky.), Felix Grundy (Tenn.), and Henry CLAY (Ky.), who became speaker of the House of Representatives in 1811.

War Industries Board On 28 July 1917, this agency was formed to supervise production of military materials for WORLD WAR I by civilian manufacturers. The board accomplished little until Bernard BARUCH took it over on 4 March 1918. Baruch formed corporations into industrial committees to ration scarce raw materials, coordinate production, and set prices for civilian and military customers. The board in effect created industry-wide cartels that dominated their sectors of the economy, yet enjoyed legal exemption from anti-TRUST laws. Its industrial committees were the precedent for the TRADE ASSOCIATIONS of the 1920s and the NATIONAL INDUSTRIAL RECOVERY ACT's industry-wide codes in the NEW DEAL.

War Labor Disputes Act *see* SMITH–CONNALLY ANTI-STRIKE ACT

War of 1812 Citing Britain's IMPRESSMENT of US sailors and its failure to comply with MACON'S BILL NUMBER 2, James MADISON asked for a declaration of war on 1 June 1812 and Congress complied on 18 June. Madison proclaimed hostilities to commence on 19 June. Britain announced blockades of Delaware and Chesapeake bays on 26 December, and of Charleston, New Orleans and Savannah on 26 May 1813, but allowed neutral trade through New England until 25 April 1814. Before US commerce was entirely cut off, the British captured 500 US merchant ships. The US Navy seized 165 enemy merchant vessels, and 526 privateers took 1,334 British prizes.

Led by TECUMSEH, the Great Lakes Indians assisted the British in taking FORT DETROIT and FORT DEARBORN in 1812. After destroying a US force at the RIVER RAISIN in 1813, the British held all territory northwest of the Maumee and Wabash rivers. William H. HARRISON blunted the British offensive at FORT STEPHENSON and FORT MEIGS in mid-1813. Oliver H. PERRY's victory at the battle of LAKE ERIE forced British evacuation of Detroit and enabled Harrison to invade Canada. Harrison's victory at the battle of the THAMES RIVER in October 1813 established US military superiority in the northwest and forced peace on the Indians by the second treaty of GREENVILLE.

In late 1812, the British repulsed US incursions into Canada from Fort Niagara at FORT GEORGE and QUEENSTOWN HEIGHTS. They also frustrated US forces from crossing Niagara River near Buffalo at FORT ERIE (November 1812). An expedition to capture Montreal via Lake Champlain retreated on 19 November when state militia refused to enter Canada.

US forces captured FORT TORONTO in 1813 in the hope of occupying Lake Ontario's northern shore, but abandoned the post and shifted operations to the Niagara River. US troops took Fort George and Fort Erie, but defeats at STONY CREEK and BEAVER DAM forced withdrawal from Canada. US forces abandoned expeditions to attack Montreal after defeats at CHATEAUGAY RIVER and CHRYSLER'S FARM. The British raided along Lake Ontario, but were repulsed at OSWEGO and badly defeated at SACKETT'S HARBOR. In December, the British captured FORT NIAGARA, burned Buffalo, and unleashed Indian raids on western N.Y.

Napoleon's defeat in 1814 permitted Britain to reassign 14,000 veterans to North America. To prevent US reinforcements from being sent to the Canadian front, a British expedition to Chesapeake Bay scattered militia at BLADENSBURG, Md., and then burned Washington (*see* DISTRICT OF COLUMBIA). After US defense of FORT MCHENRY saved Baltimore from capture, the British left to attack New Orleans. The British invaded N.Y. from Montreal, but withdrew when beaten at LAKE CHAMPLAIN. US forces crossed Niagara River, captured Forts Erie and George, bested the enemy at CHIPPEWA RIVER, and fought a drawn battle at LUNDY'S LANE. This campaign's heavy losses dictated a withdrawal to Forts George and Erie, from which US troops finally retreated under siege to N.Y.

US defeats encouraged southern Indians to initiate the CREEK WAR in 1813 with the FORT MIMS massacre. Major General Andrew JACKSON crushed the Creeks in 1814 at HORSESHOE BEND. Jackson took command at NEW ORLEANS, where he repulsed a British invasion two weeks after a truce was declared by the treaty of GHENT on 24 December 1814. The war's main consequences were to annex WEST FLORIDA, establish US military dominance over the frontier tribes, and leave them unable to resist Indian removal west of the Mississippi.

An estimated 286,730 troops served in the war, most of whom were militia doing short tours. Military expenses were $93,000,000.

The NATIONAL DEBT rose from $45,210,000 to $99,834,000.

War of Jenkins' Ear *see* JENKINS' EAR, WAR OF

War of the League of Augsburg *see* KING WILLIAM'S WAR

War of the Spanish Succession *see* QUEEN ANNE'S WAR

War on Poverty To achieve his GREAT SOCIETY, Lyndon JOHNSON declared "war on poverty" on 8 January 1964. On 16 March 1964, he outlined an anti-poverty offensive budgeted at 1 percent of the US budget ($962,500,000) under the ECONOMIC OPPORTUNITY ACT. He also proposed the APPALACHIAN REGIONAL DEVELOPMENT ACT, the OLDER AMERICANS ACT, and FOOD STAMPS. An estimated 39,851,000 Americans (22 percent) had incomes below the poverty line in 1960, and the War on Poverty helped cut that number to 25,420,000 (13 percent) by 1970.

War Powers Resolution (7 November 1973) To establish guidelines for the use of military force overseas, Congress voted to require that presidents inform Congress within 48 hours if they either sent troops to engage in a foreign conflict or significantly increased US combat forces overseas. If Congress failed to endorse any such actions within 60 days, then the president would be obliged to cease military operations, unless he certified that an additional 30 days were needed to complete a safe withdrawal of American forces. If Congress believed that an immediate evacuation was necessary before the 60- or 90-day deadlines expired, then it could order a withdrawal through a concurrent resolution, which would be exempt from a presidential veto. The resolution was enacted over Richard NIXON's veto.

Ware* v. *Hylton In 1796 the Supreme Court first demonstrated its authority to judge the legality of state laws by striking down (4–0) a 1777 Va. statute that violated the terms of the treaty of PARIS (1783) concerning the recovery of debts owed to British creditors.

Warehouse Act (11 August 1916) This law enacted the main features of the populist SUBTREASURY PLAN. To enable farmers to withhold commodities from sale when prices fell, it allowed the Department of Agriculture to designate warehouses where they could store their crops and be issued receipts legally valid as collateral for loans. The law covered cotton, tobacco, grains, flaxseed, and wool.

Warhol, Andrew ("Andy") (b. Cleveland, Ohio, 6 August 1928; d. New York, N.Y., 22 February 1987) Warhol began as a commercial artist in New York during the 1950s, and began creating new styles and images for popular art in 1960 with enlarged comic strip figures. He became well known for his silk-screen inkings of photographs, including Marilyn Monroe, Mao Tse-dung, and a can of Campbell's soup. Much of his work can be seen as a wry commentary on aspects of US culture like consumerism and personality cults. His New York studio, "The Factory," was a major avant-garde social center. Until the late 1970s, when his prominence diminished, Warhol was the most influential and successful pop artist in the world.

Warren, Earl (b. Los Angeles, Calif., 19 March 1891; d. Washington, D.C., 9 July 1974) Warren served as Calif. attorney general (1939–43) and Calif. governor (1945–53). He was Republican candidate for vice-president in 1948, and sought the presidential nomination in 1952 before backing Dwight D. EISENHOWER. Eisenhower made him chief justice in 1953, but later termed the appointment his worst mistake as president. Confirmed on 1 March 1954, Warren led the Court to declare racial SEGREGATION unconstitutional, to establish "one man, one vote" as the criterion for legislative apportionment, and to extend most BILL OF RIGHTS protections to state courts. Warren wrote the landmark opinions *BROWN* v. *BOARD OF EDUCATION OF TOPEKA* (1954), *COOPER* v. *AARON*, *SOUTH CAROLINA* v. *KATZENBACH*, *REYNOLDS* v. *SIMS*, *MIRANDA* v. *ARIZONA*, and *LOVING* v. *VIRGINIA*. He headed the Warren Commission to investigate John F. KENNEDY's assassination. He resigned in 1969.

Warren, Mercy Otis (b. Barnstable, Mass., 25 September 1728; d. Plymouth, Mass., 19 October 1814) Sister of James OTIS and wife of James Warren, she educated herself in public affairs and supported the Revolutionary WHIGS by lampooning British politicians and soldiers in anonymous plays such as *The Adulateur* (1772), *The Defeat* (1773),

The Group (1775), and *The Blockheads* (1776). Her other works included *Poems Dramatic and Miscellaneous* (1790) and *History of the Rise, Progress, and Termination of the American Revolution* (3 vols, 1805). Her writings give her a claim to the honor of being considered the Revolution's de facto poet laureate.

Warren, Robert Penn (b. Guthrie, Ky., 24 April 1905; d. Stratton, Vt., 15 September 1989) After his Rhodes scholarship at Oxford (1928–30), Warren taught on several faculties, including Louisiana State University, where he wrote his Pulitzer prize-winning roman à clef about Huey LONG, *All the King's Men* (1946). He was a leading figure in the "southern renaissance" of literature. He won two Pulitzer prizes in poetry, for *Promises* (1957) and *Now and Then* (1979). He was appointed the first official poet laureate of the US in 1986.

Warren Potato Control Act (24 August 1935) This law was enacted to ensure that the AGRICULTURAL ADJUSTMENT ADMINISTRATION'S (AAA) voluntary covenants to reduce the national potato crop would not be undermined by a large surplus harvested by noncooperating farmers who refused to cut output. By imposing a heavy tax on farmers who failed to enroll in AAA crop-limitation agreements, it effectively made production quotas mandatory.

Washington Britain's claims to Wash. produced the NOOTKA SOUND CRISIS with Spain. In 1824 Hudson's Bay Company built Fort Vancouver on the Columbia as its headquarters for the local fur trade. The first Anglo-American settlement was Marcus Whitman's mission near Walla Walla in 1836. In October 1845, the first US settlement was made on Puget Sound by eight Americans near Olympia. A British-American joint occupation of the northwest ended with the FIFTY-FOUR, FORTY, OR FIGHT controversy, which resulted in British recognition of the US claim over Wash. in 1846. Wash. remained part of OREGON until it became a territory on 2 May 1853. In 1860 it had 11,594 residents, of whom 27 percent were foreign-born and just 30 were black; it ranked 40th in population, 37th in the value of its farmland and livestock, and 35th in manufactures.

Wash. was the scene of the CAYUSE and YAKIMA WARS. Development accelerated rapidly after the first TRANSCONTINENTAL RAILROAD entered the territory in 1883. On 11 November 1889, it became the 42nd state. In 1900 it had 518,103 residents (96 percent white, 1 percent Indian, 1 percent Japanese, 1 percent Chinese, 1 percent black), of whom 59 percent were rural and 22 percent were foreign-born; it ranked 33rd in population, 34th in the value of agricultural products, and 29th in manufactures. The economy diversified away from agriculture and lumbering through shipbuilding, placement of military bases, the aircraft industry's rise after 1916, and inexpensive electricity from Columbia River dams in the 1930s. In 1990 it was the 19th largest state and had 4,866,692 residents (87 percent white, 3 percent black, 4 percent Hispanic, 4 percent Asian, 2 percent Indian), of whom 82 percent were urban and 6.6 percent were of foreign birth. Manufacturing and mining employed 25 percent of workers.

Washington, Booker Taliaferro (b. Franklin County, Va., 5 April 1856; d. Tuskegee, Ala., 14 November 1915) Born a slave, Washington grew up in W. Va. and attended Hampton Institute (1872–5). In 1881 he was named to head and organize the Normal and Industrial Institute for Negroes at Tuskegee, Ala. Working from scratch, he overcame enormous difficulties to build a nationally-recognized vocational school. He skyrocketed to national prominence at the 1895 Atlanta Exposition, when he proposed a compromise to improve race relations, in which blacks accepted white political supremacy and whites left blacks free to improve themselves economically by vocational education. NEW SOUTH MOVEMENT intellectuals applauded this vision of black progress through industrial training, but his accommodationism sparked a backlash among those blacks who founded the NIAGARA MOVEMENT and the NATIONAL ASSOCIATION FOR THE ADVANCEMENT OF COLORED PEOPLE. Washington was nevertheless far from servile; he exercised enormous influence over Republican patronage in the south and tried to end second-class citizenship for blacks by secretly financing legal challenges to JIM CROW LAWS.

Washington, D.C. *see* DISTRICT OF COLUMBIA

Washington, D.C., treaty of (1826) *see* INDIAN SPRINGS, TREATY OF

Washington, D.C., treaty of (1871) *see* *ALABAMA* CLAIMS

Washington, George (b. Westmoreland County, Va., 22 February 1732; d. Mount Vernon, Va., 13 December 1799) Hoping to gain officer's rank in the British army, Washington won a reputation for bravery in the SEVEN YEARS' WAR, but in 1761 settled on a plantation inherited from his brother. In 1759 he entered the HOUSE OF BURGESSES, where he was a consistent opponent of unconstitutional Parliamentary taxes. He sat in the first CONTINENTAL CONGRESS and became the Continental Army's commander on 15 June 1775. In the REVOLUTIONARY WAR, he won the siege of BOSTON, threw British forces on the defensive at TRENTON and PRINCETON, kept the Continental Army from disintegrating at VALLEY FORGE, frustrated the CONWAY CABAL, sealed victory at YORKTOWN, and scotched the NEWBURGH CONSPIRACY. He became a prominent postwar nationalist, who sponsored the MOUNT VERNON CONFERENCE and chaired the CONSTITUTIONAL CONVENTION. As president (1789–97), he resolved the nation's outstanding military and diplomatic problems by JAY'S TREATY and the treaties of GREENVILLE and SAN LORENZO. He retired from public life in 1797.

Washington, treaty of (Ga.) *see* INDIAN SPRINGS, TREATY OF

Washington, treaty of (1871) *see* *ALABAMA* CLAIMS

Washington naval conference Acting on a resolution of 14 December 1920 by Senator William BORAH, Warren HARDING invited the major nations to discuss reducing their naval forces and resolving international problems. On 12 November 1921, Charles Evans HUGHES, chair of the conference, presented a bold plan that formed the basis for history's most sweeping voluntary disarmament program. As finally adopted, the US, Britain, and Japan scrapped 1,908,000 tons of capital ships (those displacing over 10,000 tons) and agreed to a ten-year moratorium on ship construction. To forestall future arms races, the conferees established the relative size of their own navies according to fixed ratios of 5 for the US, 5 for Britain, 3 for Japan, 1.67 for France, and 1.67 for Italy. Poison gas and unrestricted submarine warfare were outlawed. The FOUR POWER TREATY was signed separately on 13 December. The conference closed on 6 February 1922. (*See also* LONDON NAVAL CONFERENCE)

Washington* v. *Davis On 7 June 1976, the Supreme Court clarified *GRIGGS* v. *DUKE POWER COMPANY* by ruling (7–2) that employers may use aptitude or qualification tests in their hiring decisions, even if whites score higher than minorities. Charges of job discrimination cannot be based solely on "disparate impact" (i.e. statistical evidence that certain personnel standards have a disproportionate impact upon minorities); rather there must be reasonable grounds for concluding that an employer deliberately intended to discriminate against nonwhite applicants. The CIVIL RIGHTS ACT (1991) included ambiguous provisions designed to overturn *Washington* by allowing disparate impact as a test of job discrimination, while rejecting racial quotas.

Washington* v. *Legrant *see* *SHAPIRO* v. *THOMPSON*

Washington* v. *Texas On 12 June 1967, the Supreme Court ruled unanimously that the FOURTEENTH AMENDMENT'S DUE PROCESS clause obliged state courts to uphold the SIXTH AMENDMENT's guarantee that defendants be able to subpoena witnesses to testify in their behalf.

Washington's farewell address With advice from Alexander HAMILTON, George WASHINGTON wrote this address of 17 September 1796 to announce his withdrawal from public life, warn citizens of the dangers of allowing political factions to dominate government, and recommend that the US avoid permanent foreign alliances in order to escape involvement in other nations' wars.

Washita Creek, massacre at (Okla.) *see* CHEYENNE CAMPAIGNS

Water Pollution Control Act *see* ENVIRONMENTAL LEGISLATION

Water Power Act *see* FEDERAL POWER COMMISSION

Water Quality Act (2 October 1965) This law obliged states to set standards for depolluting water by 1 July 1967, and obtain federal approval for them, or be subject to US guidelines. It established the Federal Water Pollution Control Administration, increased federal grants offered for sewage-treatment plants, and appropriated matching funds annually to assist local antipollution projects during 1966–9.

Water Quality Improvement Act *see* ENVIRONMENTAL LEGISLATION

Watergate scandal On 17 June 1972, police arrested five burglars at the Democratic National Headquarters in Washington's Watergate Building. On 29 August, Richard NIXON categorically denied that any of his White House staff had prior knowledge of the crime, and the episode had no impact on his reelection campaign. On 7 February 1973, the Senate appointed a seven-member committee under Sam J. ERVIN to investigate the Watergate affair and any violations of election law in the 1972 campaign. On 23 March, federal judge John SIRICA announced that one of the accused burglars, James McCord, revealed that White House staff had approved the Watergate break-in as part of an effort to disrupt George MCGOVERN's campaign for president; on 28 March, McCord named John MITCHELL as the "overall boss" of this dirty-tricks operation before Ervin's committee.

Subsequent testimony produced evidence of a criminal conspiracy to plan – and then cover up – the burglary, involving H. R. HALDEMAN, John EHRLICHMAN, L. Patrick GRAY, Jeb MAGRUDER, John DEAN, Charles COLSON, Dwight CHAPIN, Maurice STANS, and Herbert KALMBACH. On 18 May, Archibald COX was appointed special prosecutor to investigate possible criminal activity. On 25 June, Dean named Nixon as helping to plan the burglary's cover-up.

After it was revealed on 16 July that Nixon had systematically taped his conversations and phone calls since 1970, Cox and the Ervin committee both subpoenaed them. Nixon claimed EXECUTIVE PRIVILEGE in refusing to surrender the tapes to Ervin and tried to quash Cox's subpoena by the SATURDAY NIGHT MASSACRE. On 23 October, Nixon gave Judge Sirica certain tapes, which were later found to have several gaps at key places. On 30 October, the House Judiciary Committee started hearings on whether to impeach Nixon; between 27 and 30 July 1974, it voted to recommend three counts of impeachment: obstruction of justice concerning the Watergate burglary, abusing presidential powers, and refusing to obey congressional subpoenas. Under order from the Supreme Court (*United States* v. *Nixon*) since 24 July to release all tapes of White House conversations, which contained proof of the impeachment charges, Nixon resigned effective 9 August 1974.

Watkins* v. *United States On 17 June 1957, using *KILBOURN* V. *THOMPSON* as precedent, the Supreme Court reversed (6–1) the contempt citation of a union official who refused a congressional committee's order to indicate whether fellow labor leaders had Communist connections. Declaring "there is no congressional power to expose for the sake of exposure," the Court ruled that House or Senate investigations were only proper when conducted as part of their lawmaking duties. It further held that Congress must clearly stipulate the purpose and jurisdiction of its hearings, and that witnesses could refuse to answer questions not relevant for those stated goals. *Watkins* was modified by *BARENBLATT* V. *UNITED STATES*.

Watson, Thomas ("Tom") Edward (b. near Thomson, Ga., 5 September 1856; d. Washington, D.C., 26 September 1922) He was a Ga. lawyer who quit the Democratic Party and supported POPULISM. He lost three races for Congress and was Populist Party vice-presidential nominee in 1896. As Populist presidential nominee, he won 114,753 votes in 1904 and 28,131 in 1908. Watson abandoned his early willingness to build an interracial Populist coalition and became a virulent racist and anti-Semite. He returned to the Democratic Party and was elected US senator in 1920.

Waves This acronym designated the women's corps of the US NAVY in WORLD WAR II: Women Accepted for Voluntary Emergency Service.

Wayman* v. *Southard In 1825 the Supreme Court first ruled that it was constitutional for Congress to empower Executive Department officials to write regulations or rules for implementing the goals of a US statute. The Court held that if Congress granted the president administrative discretion to make certain decisions under the terms of a specific law, it did not surrender any of its lawmaking authority in a way that unbalanced the Constitution's separation of powers between legislative and executive branches.

Wayne, Anthony (b. Waynesboro, Pa., 1 January 1745; d. Erie, Pa., 15 December 1796) In 1776 Wayne became colonel of the Fourth Pennsylvania Regiment, and rose to brigadier general in February 1777. He avenged a major defeat suffered at PAOLI, Pa., by a superbly executed victory at STONY POINT, N.Y., where he won the nickname "Mad Anthony" for his daring. After a decade as a civilian, he returned to the army in 1792, won the battle of FALLEN TIMBERS, and negotiated the treaty of GREENVILLE (1795).

Wea Indians *see* MIAMI INDIANS

Wealth Against Commonwealth *see* STANDARD OIL TRUST

Wealth Tax Act (30 August 1935) Congress sharply raised tax rates on personal income over $75,000, up to 75 percent on amounts exceeding $5,000,000. (The highest marginal tax rate had been 59 percent.) It revised the existing corporate rate – then a uniform 13 percent – by lowering taxes on small business to 12.5 percent, increasing the rate on income above $50,000 to 15 percent, and setting a 6 percent surtax when profits exceeded 10 percent and a 12 percent surtax on profits over 15 percent. The law omitted Franklin D. ROOSEVELT's request for a tax increase on inheritances above $40,000, but raised rates on estates and gifts. Revenue acts in subsequent years continued this trend toward a more progressive code by raising rates and closing income-tax loopholes.

Weathermen This was a radical wing of Students for a Democratic Society that used sabotage and violence against the US government and local police forces as part of the VIETNAM ANTIWAR MOVEMENT. It began disintegrating after seven of its top leaders died on 6 March 1970 when a dynamite cache accidentally exploded in a New York City apartment. From 1969 to 1972, over 400 acts of violence were attributed to the group, including bombings of the US Capitol (1 March 1971) and the PENTAGON (19 May 1972).

Weaver, James Baird (b. Dayton, Ohio, 12 June 1833; d. Colfax, Iowa, 6 February 1912) He rose from lieutenant, Second Iowa Infantry, to US brigadier general in the CIVIL WAR. He left the Republicans to represent the GREENBACK PARTY in Congress. He was Greenback nominee for president in 1880; he carried no states, but received 3.4 percent of the ballots. As Populist Party (*see* POPULISM) presidential candidate in 1892, he received 8.5 percent of ballots cast and took six western states with 22 electoral votes.

Weaver, Robert Clifton (b. Washington, D.C., 29 December 1907) In 1933 Weaver entered public service as an aide to Harold ICKES. He was a member of the BLACK CABINET in the NEW DEAL. He left government to teach college and then held several posts concerning housing for N.Y. In 1965 he was named head of the federal Housing and Home Finance Agency, and then became the first black cabinet officer when named secretary of the Department of HOUSING AND URBAN DEVELOPMENT on 12 January 1966. In 1969 he became president of Baruch College.

web press, invention of *see* HOE, RICHARD M.

Webb–Kenyon Interstate Liquor Act (1 March 1913) This law was the first major federal PROHIBITION statute. Enacted over a veto, it banned interstate delivery of liquor to dry states.

Webster, Daniel (b. Salisbury, N.H., 18 January 1782; d. Marshfield, Mass., 24 October 1852) He entered Congress from N.H. as an opponent of the WAR OF 1812. In 1816 he opened a law office at Boston. He appeared often before the Supreme Court, where he argued *DARTMOUTH COLLEGE* v. *WOODWARD*, *MCCULLOCH* v. *MARYLAND*, *GIBBONS* v. *OGDEN*, and *OGDEN* v. *SAUNDERS*. He returned to Congress (1825–6) and was sent to the Senate in 1827. Having begun his career promoting regional interests and free trade, he became a nationalist and protectionist by 1828. Webster was second only to Henry CLAY as an orator, and gave his supreme performance in the

WEBSTER–HAYNE DEBATE. Shifting from the NATIONAL REPUBLICAN to the WHIG PARTY, he was a strong supporter of the second BANK OF THE UNITED STATES – which retained him as a lawyer. As one of three regional Whig nominees for president in 1840, he took just 2.7 percent of the popular vote and carried only Mass. He became secretary of state in 1841, and negotiated the WEBSTER–ASHBURTON TREATY. As senator (1845–50), he supported the WILMOT PROVISO and was critical in winning northern support for the COMPROMISE OF 1850.

Webster, Noah (b. West Hartford, Conn., 16 October 1758; d. New Haven, Conn., 28 May 1843) In 1783 Webster published his first textbook, *A Grammatical Institute of the English Language*, a speller that was reprinted in over 15,000,000 copies by 1840. In 1828 he published *An American Dictionary of the English Language* (2 vols). By standardizing the spelling and pronunciation of words according to the customs of the THIRTEEN COLONIES, rather than English practice, he freed American speech patterns to evolve their own national idiom.

Webster–Ashburton Treaty The treaty of PARIS (1783) had left the exact demarcation of Maine's northern boundary to a later date. After the Senate rejected a border arbitrated by the Netherlands in 1831, as too generous to Canada, the AROOSTOOK WAR forced negotiations to resume in 1841. With Secretary of State Daniel WEBSTER and President John TYLER eager to end the controversy, Lord Ashburton won US agreement to give up 893 square miles it would have received by the 1831 decision – to which the US was certainly entitled – but let the US keep 7,000 of Maine's disputed 12,000 square miles and made concessions on the border line west of Lake Superior. The treaty fixed the current Canadian–US border as far west as Oreg. The Senate ratified it on 20 August 1842.

Webster–Hayne debate Between 19 and 27 January 1830, Senator Daniel WEBSTER (Mass.) and Senator Robert Hayne (S.C.) debated the nature of the Union and CONSTITUTION. The exchange was a defining moment in the sectional conflict between the North, which saw its economic development benefiting from a strong federal government, and the South, which looked to STATES' RIGHTS for its protection as its congressional representation declined relative to the North.

Webster* v. *Reproductive Health Services On 3 July 1989, the Supreme Court modified *ROE* v. *WADE* by upholding (5–4) a Mo. law that forbade ABORTIONS to be performed by public employees or in tax-supported hospitals or other government facilities.

Weeks* v. *United States On 24 February 1914, the Supreme Court unanimously declared that federal court hearings must honor the exclusionary rule, which requires that evidence obtained in violation of the FOURTH AMENDMENT cannot be presented in court. This rule was extended to state courts in *MAPP* v. *OHIO*. The Court modified its application in *NIX* v. *WILLIAMS* and *UNITED STATES* v. *LEON*.

welfare capitalism *see* AMERICAN PLAN

Welsh immigration A significant Welsh population moved to the US in the colonial period and equaled about 4 percent of all whites in 1790. By 1820, the Welsh stock numbered about 330,000. From 1820 to 1900, 42,976 Welsh arrived, and from then to 1950, another 46,627 came. The 1990 census counted 1,038,603 persons who reported their primary ethnic identity as Welsh, 0.5 percent of whites.

Wesberry* v. *Sanders On 17 February 1964, the Supreme Court, ruling in accordance with *BAKER* v. *CARR*, declared (6–3) that significant differences in population between a state's congressional districts violated Article I of the Constitution; it required state legislatures to apportion districts as evenly as possible (*see* *REYNOLDS* v. *SIMS*).

West, Benjamin (b. near Swarthmore, Pa., 10 October 1738; d. London, England, 11 March 1820) A Pa. Quaker, West traveled to Italy to study painting, and then set up a studio at London in 1763. His *The Death of General Wolfe* (1771) – a huge, panoramic masterpiece of heroic romanticism – won him lasting renown as the greatest artist of the historical genre before Jacques Louis David. He became court painter to GEORGE III in 1772, and succeeded Joshua Reynolds as president of the Royal Academy (of Art) in 1792. His studio was the AMERICAN SCHOOL's social center.

West Coast Hotel Company* v. *Parrish In 1937 the Supreme Court reversed *ADKINS* v.

Children's Hospital and upheld (5–4) the right of Wash. state to enact minimum-wage legislation for women.

West Florida After Britain acquired Fla. by the Seven Years' War, it established West Florida as a royal colony in 1763. It was bounded on the west by the Mississippi from Lake Ponchartrain to the Yazoo River, on the north by a line drawn due east from the Yazoo's mouth, and on the east by the Chattahoochee and Apalachicola rivers. There were too few settlers to merit establishing an assembly, although about 200 Conn. families settled near the mouth of the Big Black River. The area south of 31° reverted to Spain by the treaty of Paris (1783). The US claimed that the Louisiana Purchase included Fla. west of the Predido River, and on 27 October 1810, James Madison proclaimed the US justified in establishing a military occupation of the area. On 14 May 1812, Congress incorporated West Florida into Mississippi Territory. The US occupied West Florida in the War of 1812 and refused to return it to Spain after 1815.

West Jersey On 4 July 1664, anticipating the conquest of New Netherland, Charles II granted modern N.J. to John Lord Berkeley and Sir George Carteret. Berkeley sold his proprietary rights in 1674 to the proprietors of West Jersey, who formed a colony on the Delaware River. The proprietors founded the first English settlement at Salem in November 1675, and they stimulated the emigration of 2,000 Quakers by 1682. Factional divisions within the proprietors' ranks frustrated the formation of a workable government, and the Crown assumed control of West Jersey on 15 April 1702.

West Virginia About 1726, Morgan ap Morgan became the first white settler of W.Va., in Berkeley County. When Wheeling became its first transmontane settlement in 1772, no Indians occupied W.Va. It was the scene of Dunmore's War. British-directed Indian raids lasted from the American Revolution (*see* Revolutionary War) to the first treaty of Greenville. In 1800 modern W.Va. had 78,592 inhabitants, 9 percent of Va. residents.

In 1860 it had 376,688 inhabitants, of whom 5 percent were slaves. The Civil War created W.Va. After Va.'s secession from the Union, a convention established, on 11 June 1861, a provisional Union government at Wheeling for the northwestern counties. Union victory at Rich Mountain gave federal forces control over 75 western counties, including 25 that had voted for secession. W.Va. was admitted as the 35th state on 20 June 1863, and abolished slavery in February 1865. It furnished 32,068 USA troops (including 196 blacks) and about 10,000 CSA soldiers. Democrats won control of the state in 1870.

Railroads and coal mining diversified the economy in the late 19th century. In 1900 W.Va. had 958,800 residents, of whom 87 percent were rural, 4 percent were black, and 2 percent were foreign-born; it ranked 28th among states in population, 28th in the value of its agricultural products, and 31st in manufactures. As its agricultural base declined, it lost 127,400 out-migrants from 1920 to 1940. After diesel fuels began replacing coal and mines became increasingly mechanized, 1,347,600 persons left the state from 1940 to 1970. Its population declined by 212,075 from 1950 to 1990. In 1990 W.Va. was the 34th largest state and had 1,793,477 residents (96 percent white, 3 percent black, 1 percent Hispanic), of whom 36 percent were urban and 0.9 percent were foreign-born. Mining employed 12 percent of workers and manufacturing 15 percent.

West Virginia State Board of Education* v. *Barnette On 14 June 1943, in a case concerning Jehovah's Witnesses, the Supreme Court reversed *Minersville School District* v. *Gobitis* (1940) and ruled (6–3) that the First Amendment protected the right of school children to abstain from saluting the US flag if such behavior compromised their religious beliefs.

Western Reserve When Conn. ceded its trans-Appalachian lands to the US in 1786, it reserved about 4,700 square miles around modern Cleveland, Ohio, as compensation for Revolutionary War services and the claims of the Conn. Land Company. Jurisdiction of the Western Reserve passed to Ohio Territory (as Trumbull County) on 10 July 1800.

Westinghouse, George (b. Central Bridge, N.Y., 6 October 1846; d. New York, N.Y., 12 March 1914) He served in the Civil

WAR, and then began designing railroad equipment. In 1869 he patented the first compressed air-brake, which radically altered rail travel by enabling locomotives to stop quickly and safely after reaching maximum speeds. He also improved techniques for signaling right-of-way on tracks, so that trains could travel in both directions on single-track lines without danger of collision. An interest in electrical power resulted in his founding the Westinghouse Electric Co. in the 1880s. Westinghouse patented over 400 inventions.

Westmoreland, William Childs (b. Spartanburg County, S.C., 26 March 1914) After graduating from West Point in 1936, Westmoreland saw combat in both WORLD WAR II and the KOREAN WAR. As commander of US forces in the VIETNAM WAR from June 1964 to July 1968, he directed the escalation of US involvement from 20,000 advisors and logistics personnel into a frontline combat force of 500,000. Hampered by poor intelligence, Westmoreland underestimated enemy strength prior to the TET OFFENSIVE, and then threw Lyndon JOHNSON's advisors – plus much of the American public – into shock by requesting 206,000 reinforcements on 27 February 1968. He was promoted to army chief of staff and retired in 1972.

Westo Indians These Indians were an interior nation who occupied both banks of the Savannah River and totaled 1,600 about 1670; their precise ethnic identity is unknown. They began trading skins with S.C. merchants in 1674, but disrupted the flow of furs from other sources by raiding villages of coastal Indians. They were dispersed in the WESTO WAR and lost their tribal identity after consolidating with the CREEK INDIANS.

Westo War In summer 1680, S.C. declared war on the WESTO INDIANS for attacking Indians friendly to S.C. Most Westo casualties resulted from raids by S.C.'s Indian allies, who sold them into slavery for trade goods. By 1683, S.C. officials estimated that all but 50 Westos had been captured, killed, or had fled west out of reach.

Wheeler, William Almon (b. Malone, N.Y., 30 June 1819; d. Malone, N.Y., 4 June 1887) A lawyer, banker, and businessman, Wheeler was a N.Y. legislator (1850–9), US congressman (Republican, N.Y. 1861–3, 1869–77), and US vice-president (1877–81) under Rutherford HAYES. He had little national reputation when elected vice-president. He presided well over the Senate, but ill-health thereafter ended his public career.

Wheeler–Howard Act (18 June 1934) Also termed the Indian Reorganization Act, it halted land allotments under the DAWES SEVERALTY ACT, authorized tribes to buy additional lands, made available loans for tribal businesses, gave Indians hiring preference for civil service jobs, and permitted tribes to write constitutions for their own self-government. Only 99 of 172 tribes immediately exercised their option to accept its provisions instead of those of the Dawes Act.

Wheeler–Lea Act *see* FOOD, DRUG, AND COSMETIC ACT

Wheeler–Rayburn Act *see* PUBLIC UTILITY HOLDING COMPANY ACT

Whig Party This party originated as a congressional faction opposed to Andrew JACKSON's policies. The name became popular after Henry CLAY used it in a Senate speech on 14 April 1834. (The name's Revolutionary pedigree implied that Jackson was usurping dangerous powers more appropriate for a king than a president.) The party's support came from NATIONAL REPUBLICANS, westerners hoping for federal expenditures to develop their region's economy, southern Democrats with LOOSE CONSTRUCTIONIST principles, and the ANTI-MASONIC PARTY's remnants. John CALHOUN and other STATES' RIGHTS partisans allied with Whigs against Jackson, but remained Democrats. The party's leaders were Henry CLAY, John Q. ADAMS, and Daniel WEBSTER, who supported the AMERICAN SYSTEM and the DISTRIBUTION ACT. It elected presidents in 1840 and 1848, held Senate majorities (1841–4), and controlled the House (1841–2 and 1847–8). The party disintegrated after running its last candidate for president in 1852.

Whigs (Revolutionary) American opponents of Parliamentary taxes imposed on the colonies termed themselves Whigs, which was the name of the English political party given primary credit for preserving representative government by the REVOLUTION OF 1688, framing England's Bill of Rights (1689), and opposing those who favored a Jacobite, Catholic monarchy. The term carried over into the REVOLUTIONARY WAR for supporters of the CONTINENTAL CONGRESS.

Whiskey Rebellion The 1791 federal excise tax heavily burdened pioneers in western Pa., where distilling was barely profitable before the tax. Small-scale violence flared in 1791–3, until July 1794 when law officers tried to summon 60 tax evaders for trial at Philadelphia's federal court. Rioters burned the chief tax collector's home, killed a US soldier, and openly discussed leaving the Union. On 7 August 1794, George WASHINGTON called out militia from Pa., N.J., Md., and Va.; when he led 12,900 troops across the mountains that fall, resistance collapsed. One hundred and fifty suspected rebels were arrested, 20 were sent east for trial, and 2 were sentenced to death for treason in May 1795, but Washington pardoned both.

Whiskey Ring On 1 May 1875, St Louis papers reported that the city's supervisor of US revenues, John McDonald, had conspired with distillers to defraud the Treasury of over $2,000,000 in excise taxes. McDonald was a friend and appointee of Ulysses S. GRANT. The government indicted 238 persons for corruption, including Grant's private secretary Orville Babcock (who was acquitted). The scandal left Grant's administration badly discredited in public opinion.

Whistler, James Abbott McNeill (b. Lowell, Mass., 10 July 1834; d. London, England, 17 July 1903) After spending part of his youth abroad in Europe, Whistler attended West Point without being commissioned (1851–4), and worked as a coast guard draftsman. He lived in Paris as a painter (1855–70), and then moved his studio to London. He was one of the first occidental painters to seek inspiration from oriental art. Whistler was fully versatile with oil, watercolor, and etching. His etchings revealed a brilliant impressionist technique, while his "symphonies" and "nocturnes" arranged color and mass with special inventiveness. He was his generation's best known US painter, and perhaps second in greatness only to Thomas EAKINS. Whistler's most famous work is *Portrait of My Mother*.

White, Edward Douglass (b. Lafourche Parish, La., 3 November 1845; d. Washington, D.C., 19 May 1921) After fighting in the CSA Army during the Civil War, White opened a law office at New Orleans in 1868, joined the La. supreme court at the age of 33, and entered the Senate in 1888. He became US Supreme Court justice in 1894 and was confirmed as chief justice on 12 December 1910. He was the Court's second Catholic chief justice. His important opinions include *STANDARD OIL COMPANY OF NEW JERSEY ET AL.* v. *UNITED STATES*, *GUINN* v. *UNITED STATES* and *ARVER* v. *UNITED STATES*.

White, Hugh Lawson (b. Iredell County, N.C., 30 October 1773; d. Knoxville, Tenn., 10 April 1840) In 1793 White moved to Tenn. He fought in the Indian campaigns, became a lawyer in 1796, sat on the Superior Court, and served in the US Senate (1825–40). He helped formulate the INDIAN REMOVAL ACT and became president pro tempore in December 1832. He opposed the choice of Martin VAN BUREN as Andrew JACKSON's successor in 1836, joined the WHIG PARTY, and ran against him on a ticket with John TYLER; he polled 9.7 percent of the vote, and carried Tenn. and Ga. He resigned from the Senate when his legislature instructed him to vote for the SUBTREASURY ACT.

white citizens councils Following *BROWN* v. *BOARD OF EDUCATION OF TOPEKA* (1954), white citizens councils acted as the principal means of resisting desegregation. The first council was formed in June 1954 at Indianola, Miss. They rapidly spread through the south, but were absent from the BORDER STATES. Headed by leading businessmen and politicians, they held public protests against integration and conspired to threaten the jobs or financial credit of black civil rights activists. The councils were a major factor in embittering race relations and frustrating US efforts to end SEGREGATION through the early 1970s.

White Oak Road, battle of (Va.) *see* FIVE FORKS-WHITE OAK ROAD, BATTLE OF

White Oak Swamp, battle of (Va.) *see* PENINSULAR CAMPAIGN

White Plains, battle of (N.Y.) On 28 October 1776, General William HOWE's 13,000 redcoats and HESSIANS routed the main body of Washington's army, but failed to cut off their avenues of retreat. US losses: 25 killed, 125 wounded. British losses: 214 redcoats and 99 Hessians killed and wounded.

white primary After RECONSTRUCTION, the Democratic Party in many southern states excluded blacks from voting in primary elections. Because winning the Democratic nomination was usually tantamount to winning the general election, white primaries left blacks little influence over southern politics. The Supreme Court sanctioned them in *GROVEY* v. *TOWNSEND*, which was reversed in *SMITH* v. *ALLWRIGHT* and *TERRY* v. *ADAMS*.

White Slavery Act (25 June 1910) Officially the Mann Act, it outlawed interstate transportation of women (including nonwhites) for immoral purposes, which was punishable by five years' imprisonment and a $5,000 fine (double if the female was under 18). Although intended to break up prostitution rings, it was abused to harass interracial romances, minor offenses, and even harmless behavior. In 1940 the Justice Department ordered the FBI to limit white slave investigations to cases of commercial prostitution.

Whitefield, George (b. Gloucester, England, 16 December 1715; d. Newburyport, Mass., 30 September 1770) A priest in the ANGLICAN CHURCH, Whitefield adopted METHODIST CHURCH techniques of outdoor evangelization and emerged as the 18th century's greatest revivalist. His first visit to the colonies was in Ga. during May–September 1738. His second trip in 1739 sparked the first GREAT AWAKENING. He made five other tours of the colonies in 1744–8, 1751, 1754–5, 1763–4, and 1769–70.

Whitewater scandal In 1993 allegations emerged that Morgan Guaranty Savings & Loan, a bankrupt Arkansas thrift taken over by the RESOLUTION TRUST CORPORATION (RTC) in the SAVINGS AND LOAN CRISIS, illegally diverted funds to the Whitewater Land Development Corporation, a failed real-estate investment partly owned by William J. CLINTON and Hillary RODHAM CLINTON, or to Clinton's 1984 gubernatorial campaign. A special federal prosecutor was appointed to investigate these matters, and whether RTC administrators showed favoritism to the Clintons. The controversy seriously undermined Clinton's leadership, especially after the related resignations of White House counsel Bernard Nussbaum (for delaying transfer of evidence about the case to law officials) and acting RTC supervisor Roger Altman, a friend of the Clintons (for withholding full disclosure from Congress that he permitted Treasury personnel to brief White House personnel on the investigation's progress).

Whitman, Walt (b. Huntington, Long Island, N.Y., 31 May 1819; d. Camden, N.J., 26 March 1892) He grew up in Brooklyn, left school at the age of 11, worked at several odd jobs until becoming a journalist in 1841, and was a hospital nurse in the Civil War. In 1855 he published *Leaves of Grass*, of which nine editions were updated and printed in his lifetime. This book marked Whitman as the Romantic era's most original and daring US poet, and profoundly influenced later authors by its rejection of traditional stylistic conventions, its exuberant embrace of distinctively American subjects, and its frank handling of sexual topics and terms. Other major works include *Drum Taps* (1865), *Passage to India* (1871), *Democratic Vistas* (1871), and *Good-bye, My Fancy* (1891).

Whitman massacre *see* CAYUSE WAR

Whitney, Eli (b. Westboro, Mass., 8 December 1765; d. New Haven, Conn., 8 January 1825) While residing on a Ga. plantation, Whitney designed the COTTON GIN in 1793. Since the gin's basic principle was simple, it was easily pirated and he could not establish copyright protection for exclusive rights. He returned north and won a contract in 1798 to produce military muskets at New Haven, where he revolutionized the manufacture of firearms – which were previously made by highly skilled craftsmen according to a buyer's individual specifications – by introducing standardized assembly of interchangeable parts by unskilled workers.

Whitney, William C. *see* NAVY, US

Whittier, John Greenleaf (b. Haverhill, Mass., 17 December 1807; d. Hampton Falls, N.H., 7 September 1892) A largely self-educated journalist, abolitionist, and member of the Mass. legislature (1835), Whittier was 14 when he composed his first verses, some of which were soon published by William Lloyd GARRISON, who became his friend. He examined subjects concerning the lives of common people and emerged as a leading US poet of the Romantic period. His major works include *Legends of New England* (1831), *Voices of Freedom* (1846), *Poems* (1848), *Songs of Labor and Other Poems* (1850), *Snow-Bound* (1866), *Ballads of New England* (1870), and *At Sundown* (1890).

Whyte, William H. *see* ORGANIZATION MAN, THE

Wichita Indians This CADDOAN LANGUAGE group lived in Kans. and Okla. when first contacted by Francisco de CORONADO in 1541. Under pressure from hostile Indians, they migrated south-west to the Red River basin and raided Spanish Tex. from 1758 to 1772. They avoided serious conflicts with Anglo-Americans, but often fought with hostile neighboring Indians. They took refuge in Kans. during the Civil War, and then accepted a RESERVATION in Caddo Co., Okla. They numbered perhaps 3,200 in 1778, but European epidemics reduced them to about 700 in 1868 and to 340 in 1900.

Wigglesworth, Michael (b. Yorkshire, England, 16 October 1631; d. Malden, Mass., 10 June 1705) At the age of 7, Wigglesworth was brought to Mass. He attended Harvard, became a minister, and spent most of his life as a clergyman in Malden, Mass. His jog-trot epic of the Last Judgment, *The Day of Doom* (1662), was both the first book of original poetry and the earliest American-authored volume of poetry printed in the thirteen colonies. *The Day of Doom* was reprinted regularly until 1800 and became early America's first best-seller. No copies of the first three editions survive, probably because the poem was so popular that it was read and reviewed until the books inevitably wore out.

Wilbur, John *see* QUAKERS

Wild West Show *see* CODY, WILLIAM

wildcat banks This term originated in the 1830s to describe state-chartered banks that printed large numbers of banknotes without adequate SPECIE as backing. Virtually all such institutions failed in the PANIC OF 1837 and left many innocent creditors holding worthless script that had been used as collateral or had circulated as money in cash-short areas. The word "wildcat" became a synonym for irresponsible finance after Mich. was flooded by valueless banknotes illustrated with a panther.

Wilderness, battle of the On 5–6 May 1864, General Robert E. LEE's 61,025 Confederates outmaneuvered and badly mauled Lieutenant General Ulysses S. GRANT's 101,895 Federals. USA losses: 2,246 killed, 12,037 wounded, 3,383 missing. CSA losses: 7,750 killed, wounded. Grant then advanced on SPOTSYLVANIA COURT HOUSE to turn Lee's flank.

Wilderness Areas Act (3 September 1964) Passed after three years of opposition from miners and loggers, this law created the National Wilderness Preservation System by permanently banning development on 9,100,000 acres of PUBLIC DOMAIN, including 54 national forests. By 1994, there were 602 wilderness areas totaling 95,800,000 acres, of which about 60 percent are in Alaska. Wilderness areas make up 15 percent of public domain and 4 percent of the US.

Wilderness Road Immediately after helping negotiate the treaty of SYCAMORE SHOALS, Daniel BOONE and eight axmen blazed this road from the Holston River in Tenn., via CUMBERLAND GAP, to the Kentucky River in spring 1775. Forking off from the GREAT WAGON ROAD at Roanoke, Va., it was the southern route westward for pioneers who could not make the easy trip via the Ohio River. It was not improved to carry wagon traffic until 1795.

Wilkins, Roy (b. St Louis, Mo., 18 February 1903; d. New York, N.Y., 8 September 1981) A University of Minnesota graduate, Wilkins became a journalist. He became assistant secretary for the NATIONAL ASSOCIATION FOR THE ADVANCEMENT OF COLORED PEOPLE (NAACP) in 1931 and edited its journal, the *Crisis* after 1934. In 1955, he became NAACP executive director; he was second only to Martin Luther KING in influence upon the CIVIL RIGHTS MOVEMENT. He pursued mainstream political goals and opposed the BLACK POWER MOVEMENT.

William III (b. The Hague, Netherlands, 4 November 1650; d. Kensington Palace, Middlesex, 8 March 1702) The REVOLUTION OF 1688 placed William III on the British throne as joint-sovereign with his wife Mary. They were crowned on 11 April 1689. His

European wars against France sparked KING WILLIAM'S WAR in the colonies.

Williams, Roger (b. London, England, ca. 1603; d. Providence, R.I., 25 March 1683) A devout follower of SEPARATING PURITANISM, Williams was ordained a minister about 1628 and went to Mass. in 1631. In 1635 he was banished for denying the legislature's right to enact laws interfering with private religious beliefs and for questioning the Mass. charter's legality. He founded Providence, the first settlement in R.I., and secured a charter from Parliament recognizing R.I. as a colony in 1644. Under his leadership, R.I. was the only New England colony that did not establish a state church. He served as the colony's governor (1654–1657), and was responsible for persuading CHARLES II to make R.I. a CHARTER COLONY in 1663.

Williams, Tennessee (b. Columbus, Miss., 26 March 1914; d. New York, N.Y., 25 February 1983) Born Thomas Lanier, he grew up in St Louis, attended both the University of Missouri and Washington University, Mo., and finally received a degree from the University of Iowa. He achieved critical acclaim as a playwright with *Battle of Angles* (1940) and *The Glass Menagerie* (1945). He won Pulitzer prizes for *A Streetcar Named Desire* (1947) and *Cat on a Hot Tin Roof* (1955). Among US dramatists writing from 1945 to 1990, he ranks second only to Arthur MILLER.

Williams* v. *Mississippi On 25 April 1898, the Supreme Court ruled unanimously that the FOURTEENTH AMENDMENT did not prohibit a state from denying the vote to persons who failed a literacy test (*see* LITERACY TESTS). *LASSITER* v. *NORTHAMPTON COUNTY BOARD OF ELECTIONS* reaffirmed *Williams*.

Willkie, Wendell Lewis (b. Elwood, Ind., 18 February 1892; d. New York, N.Y., 8 October 1944) The president of a N.Y. utility company, Willkie was a lifelong Democrat who had never run for public office when he emerged as a prominent critic of the NEW DEAL in the late 1930s. He registered as a Republican in 1939 and was that party's nominee for president in 1940 against Franklin D. ROOSEVELT. He won 44.8 percent of the ballots but took only 10 states, eight more than Alfred LANDON in 1936.

Willson* v. *Blackbird Creek Marsh Company In 1829 the Supreme Court ruled, without dissent, that states could enact regulations that extend over some aspects of interstate commerce if they do not conflict with federal laws. The decision was later reaffirmed in *COOLEY* v. *BOARD OF WARDENS*.

Wilmington Ten (N.C.) *see* CHAVIS, BENJAMIN F.

Wilmot Proviso On 8 August 1846, Congressman David Wilmot (Democrat, Pa.) proposed an amendment to a bill funding negotiations to end the MEXICAN WAR. Wilmot's Proviso would have banned SLAVERY from any territory acquired from Mexico. The CALHOUN RESOLUTIONS stated southern opposition. Every northern legislature but one went on record to support the proviso. After passing the House twice in 1846–7, it died in the Senate. Because Democrats and Whigs both ignored this issue in the 1848 election, the FREE-SOIL PARTY was founded. Wilmot reintroduced the issue of slavery in the territories – dormant since the MISSOURI COMPROMISE, aside from TEXAS annexation – as the central problem of US politics. This controversy thereafter dominated public affairs through POPULAR SOVEREIGNTY, the COMPROMISE OF 1850, the KANSAS–NEBRASKA ACT, BLEEDING KANSAS, the FREEPORT DOCTRINE, and the DAVIS RESOLUTIONS.

Wilson, Henry (b. Farmington, N.H., 16 February 1812; d. Washington, D.C., 22 November 1875) Born Jeremiah Jones Colbath, he changed his name after reading a story with that title by Edgar Allan POE. A self-made man who was a cobbler, teacher, businessman, and journalist, Wilson served as Mass. legislator (1844–6, 1850–2), US senator (Republican, Mass., 1855–73), and US vice-president (1873–5). His ill-health prevented him from regularly presiding over the Senate as vice-president.

Wilson, (Thomas) Woodrow (b. Staunton, Va., 28 December 1856; d. Washington, D.C., 3 February 1924) He was the first president to earn a Ph.D. (Johns Hopkins, 1885), became a nationally renowned educational leader, and was Princeton University president (1902–10). A PROGRESSIVE ERA reformer, he served as N.J. governor (1910–11). In 1912, after a come-from-behind victory over Champ CLARK for the Democratic nomination for president, he promised a NEW FREEDOM and took 41 states, but just 41.9 percent of the vote. He actively involved himself in passing the UNDERWOOD–SIMMONS TARIFF, FEDERAL RESERVE SYSTEM, FEDERAL TRADE COMMISSION, and CLAYTON ANTITRUST ACT. He won reelection narrowly by just 12 electoral votes and with 49.4 percent of the ballots on the campaign slogan "he kept us out of war."

The peaceful president twice ordered US intervention in MEXICO, including a major invasion of the MEXICAN BORDER. Unrestricted submarine warfare led him to bring the US into WORLD WAR I in 1917. He attempted to influence a just peace by his FOURTEEN POINTS and attended the Versailles peace negotiations, but was disappointed by their final outcome. He waged a futile struggle to win US ratification of the treaty of VERSAILLES and American entry to the LEAGUE OF NATIONS until he was incapacitated by a stroke at Pueblo, Colo., on 25 September 1919. He refused to resign, but was unable to function adequately for the rest of his term.

Wilson–Gorman Tariff (28 August 1894) This tariff replaced the MCKINLEY TARIFF and was enacted because Democrats controlled both houses of Congress, but became law without Grover CLEVELAND's signature. It reduced average rates from 49.5 percent to 39.9 percent. It was succeeded by the DINGLEY TARIFF.

Wilson* v. *New In 1917 the Supreme Court (5–4) declared the ADAMSON [EIGHT-HOUR] ACT constitutional, by ruling that, although it fixed wages for railroad workers engaged in interstate commerce, Congress had the power to set a temporary standard in emergencies.

Wilson's Creek, battle of (Mo.) On 10 August 1861, Brigadier General Nathaniel Lyon's 5,400 Federals retreated after attacking Brigadier General Sterling Price's 11,600 Confederates. USA losses: 223 killed (including Lyon), 721 wounded, 291 missing. CSA losses: 257 killed, 900 wounded, 27 missing. Lyon's loss left the Confederates dominant in southwest Mo. until after the battle of PEA RIDGE.

Winnebago Indians When first contacted by the French in 1634, these speakers of one of the SIOUAN LANGUAGES occupied east-central Wis. and numbered 3,800. They were neutral during PONTIAC'S WAR, but supported TECUMSEH's confederacy against Anglo-American expansion, fought as British allies in the WAR OF 1812, drew back from the edge of a major conflict during the WINNEBAGO WAR, and played a minor role in the BLACK HAWK WAR. Smallpox killed at least 500 in 1836, and they declined from 4,500 in 1843 to 2,500 by 1852 and 1,200 by 1865. They moved to Minn. in 1846, to S.Dak. in 1862, and Nebr. in 1865. Winnebago reservations are now located at 10 counties in Wis. (headquartered at the Dells) and Thurston County, Nebr.

Winnebago War An influx of lead miners into southeastern Wis. strained relations with Red Bird's WINNEBAGO INDIANS in the 1820s. When false rumors circulated that two Winnebagos had been executed by the US Army, Red Bird and three others killed two men and scalped an infant girl on 28 June 1827. On 30 June, Winnebagos killed two boatmen on the Mississippi. The murders resulted in a massive mobilization of Wis. and Ill. militia, who began advancing on the Winnebagos. Red Bird prevented an attack on his people by surrendering himself, and died in prison at Prairie du Chien.

Winthrop, John (b. Edwardstone, Suffolk, England, 22 January 1588; d. Boston, Mass., 26 March 1649) Possessor of a prosperous manor and devout adherent of NONSEPARATING PURITANISM, Winthrop was recruited by the Massachusetts Bay Company as first governor of Mass. in August 1629. He led the GREAT MIGRATION's vanguard when he brought 700 colonists to Mass. and founded Boston in 1630. He served as governor every year from 1629 to his death, except 1635–6, 1641, and 1645.

Wirt, William *see* ANTI-MASONIC PARTY

Wisconsin In 1670 French priests established three missions in Wis. When the treaty of PARIS (1763) transferred the area to Britain, permanent French trading posts existed at Green Bay and Prairie du Chien. The British exercised de facto control of Wis. until JAY'S TREATY. Large-scale Anglo-American settlement began in 1825, and by 1829 the population had risen from 200 to 10,000. It escaped serious Indian hostilities, except for the WINNEBAGO WAR and some fighting in the BLACK HAWK WAR. Between 1833 and 1854, Indians sold most of their Wis. lands and the population rose rapidly. Wis. became a territory in 1836 and the 30th state on 29 May 1848.

In 1860 it had 775,881 inhabitants, of whom 99 percent were white and 36 percent were foreign-born; it ranked 15th among states in population, 19th in the value of its farmland and livestock, and 18th in manufactures. In the CIVIL WAR, it furnished 91,327 USA troops (including 165 blacks).

Lumbering and manufacturing became major industries after 1860. Wis. attracted large numbers of European immigrants, especially Germans, Irish, and Norwegians. In 1900 it had 2,069,042 people, of whom 62 percent were rural, 99 percent white, and 32 percent foreign-born; it ranked 13th among states in population, 12th in the value of its agricultural goods, and 9th in manufactures. It was highly influential in pioneering PROGRESSIVE ERA reforms by its WISCONSIN IDEA. It experienced modest growth in the 20th century as it grew more urban and industrial. In 1990 it had 4,891,769 inhabitants (91 percent white, 5 percent black, 2 percent Hispanic, 1 percent Indian, 1 percent Asian), of whom 67 percent were urban and 2.5 percent were foreign-born. Mining and manufacturing employed 30 percent of workers.

Wisconsin idea This term referred to Robert LA FOLLETTE's program to make state government more efficient and more responsive to voters than to special interests. It was the most influential model for political reform in the PROGRESSIVE ERA. To reform government, La Follette advocated placing greater legal constraints on political bosses, giving voters more power to circumvent bosses through direct primaries (*see* DIRECT PRIMARY) and other opportunities for public opinion to express itself (such as the RECALL and INITIATIVE), and bringing disinterested technical experts from outside politics to staff regulatory commissions or highly specialized agencies.

Wise, Isaac Mayer (b. Steingrub, Bohemia, 29 March 1819; d. Cincinnati, Ohio, 26 March 1900) A rabbi who had attended the universities of Prague and Vienna, Wise emigrated in 1846 and headed a Cincinnati synagogue from 1854 to his death. In 1875 he founded Hebrew Union College, the first US institution for training rabbis; in 1889 he established the Central Conference of American Rabbis, and headed it until he died. Wise was the founding father of Reform JUDAISM, and his weekly paper, the *Israelite*, was its guiding spirit. He challenged Jews not only to revitalize their faith by modifying its practices to suit modern conditions, but also to integrate themselves fully in American life and to act collectively as a force for social justice.

witchcraft *see* SALEM WITCH TRIALS

Wobblies *see* INDUSTRIAL WORKERS OF THE WORLD

Wolf* v. *Colorado *see* *MAPP* V. *OHIO*

Wolff Packing Company* v. *Court of Industrial Relations In 1923 the Supreme Court held that states could not regulate business activities unless they concerned a vital public interest, like anticompetitive practices. The ruling, which was reaffirmed in *Tyson and Brothers* v. *Banton* (1927), greatly limited the scope of state business regulation, until its reversal by *NEBBIA* V. *NEW YORK*.

women's suffrage The first instance of female participation in elections occurred in N.J. (1776–1807), where women property owners were allowed to vote on the same basis as men. The movement to win female voting rights began at the SENECA FALLS CONVENTION in 1848. The leading suffragettes were Susan B. ANTHONY, Elizabeth Stanton, and Lucy Stone. In 1854 Washington's territorial assembly considered making women voters. Women first gained the right to vote in 1869 in Wyoming Territory, then Utah Territory (1870), Washington Territory (1883), Colo. (1893), and Idaho (1896). An attempt to win female suffrage through the courts failed in *MINOR* V. *HAPPERSETT*. By 1917, women enjoyed full suffrage in 15 states and partial rights in another 13. The NINETEENTH AMENDMENT made this right universal.

Wood, Leonard (b. Winchester, N.H., 9 October 1860; d. Washington, D.C., 7 August 1927) He earned an M.D. from Harvard (1884) and entered the army. He won the

Medal of Honor in the APACHE CAMPAIGNS. He commanded the ROUGH RIDERS. As the military governor of Cuba after the SPANISH-AMERICAN WAR, he eradicated yellow fever by 1901 through a mosquito-extermination campaign. After serving in the Philippines (1903–5), he became army chief of staff in 1910. His poor relations with Woodrow WILSON led to his being passed over to command the Allied Expeditionary Force in favor of John PERSHING. He lost the 1920 Republican presidential nomination to Warren HARDING and spent the rest of the decade on special missions in the Philippines.

Woodruff* v. *Parham *see* *BROWN* V. *MARYLAND*

Woodstock rock festival (N.Y.) Between 15 and 17 August 1969, 400,000 college students and other adolescents from the eastern US gathered at Max Yasgur's farm in Bethel, N.Y., for a three-day festival of rock music by leading performers. Exuding an atmosphere of playful spontaneity, widespread experimentation with drugs, and behavior calculated to offend adult sensibilities, Woodstock defined the HIPPIE values and attitudes of a self-conscious youth culture impatient with traditional social restraints on personal behavior.

Woolen Act (4 May 1699) Intended primarily to protect English woolen manufacturers from Irish competition, this law restricted the clothing industry in Ireland. It also attempted to curtail the production of clothing in the colonies by limiting its sale to the province in which it was made, so that British manufacturers would enjoy the greatest possible market for their goods.

Woolman, John (b. Rancocas, N.J., 19 October 1720; d. York, England, 7 October 1772) Shopkeeper, schoolmaster, and tailor, Woolman traveled through the thirteen colonies as an itinerant QUAKER preacher. He was the leading spirit in Quaker ABOLITIONISM, and published *Some Considerations on the Keeping of Negroes* (1754), and *Considerations on the True Harmony of Mankind* (1770). His autobiographical writings, begun as a journal in 1736, rank among the most direct and eloquent personal revelations composed in colonial America, and were termed "a classic of the inner life" by their editor, John Greenleaf WHITTIER.

Worcester* v. *Georgia On 3 March 1832, in a case related to *CHEROKEE NATION* V. *GEORGIA*, the Supreme Court overturned the conviction of two missionaries who defied a state law requiring all whites living among CHEROKEE INDIANS to obtain state licenses. The Court held that since the federal government had exclusive power over Indian affairs, Georgia could not regulate behavior on reservations and its law was void. Georgia ignored the decision, however, and no effort was made to enforce the Court's ruling by Andrew JACKSON, who allegedly remarked, "John MARSHALL has made his decision, now let him enforce it!"

Works Progress Administration (WPA) The WPA was established by executive order on 6 May 1935, received its initial funding from the EMERGENCY RELIEF APPROPRIATION ACT, and was the successor to the FEDERAL EMERGENCY RELIEF ADMINISTRATION. Under director Harry HOPKINS, it became the most important federal employment program. It spent 85 percent of its budget on wages, at about $50 per month, and its monthly employment averaged 2,300,000. Its programs predominantly involved manual laborers, but it also sponsored work for 40,000 authors and artists in the Federal Music Project, Federal Writers' Project, Federal Theatre Project, and Federal Art Project. The WPA gave work to 8,500,000 different persons (about a third of all jobless) on 1,410,000 projects, at a cost of $11.4 billion. It built, repaired, or improved 124,000 bridges, 651,100 streets or highways, 125,100 public buildings (including 5,900 schools and 2,500 hospitals), 8,200 parks, and 853 airfields. Political manipulation of WPA workers in the 1938 elections led to the HATCH ACT. The Reorganization Act (1939) redesignated it as the Works Projects Administration and placed it under the FEDERAL WORKS AGENCY. Colonel Francis Harrington assumed control in 1938. The agency was disbanded on 30 June 1943.

Works Projects Administration *see* WORKS PROGRESS ADMINISTRATION

World Trade Organization *see* URUGUAY ROUND OF GATT

World War I After August 1914, when war erupted between the Central Powers (Germany, Austro-Hungary, Turkey) and the

Allies (Britain, France, Belgium, Italy, Serbia, Russia), the US remained neutral. Skillful Allied propaganda and German submarine attacks on civilian ships swung US public opinion against the Central Powers. Protests over US lives lost on the HMS *LUSITANIA* and other torpedoed ships led Germany to halt such attacks on 4 May 1916. When Germany resumed unrestricted submarine warfare on 1 February 1917, Woodrow WILSON ordered the arming of merchant ships on 12 March. The ZIMMERMANN NOTE's release on 1 March indicated German intentions to encourage armed conflict with Mexico. Wilson asked Congress on 2 April to declare war, which was done on 6 April.

The US military on 6 April included 127,000 army regulars, 80,000 national guardsmen, 87,000 sailors, and 13,700 marines. The SELECTIVE SERVICE ACT (1917) registered 24,200,000 men, of whom 2,149,000 were drafted, 1,600,400 enlisted for the army (including 302,000 national guardsmen), and 338,000 either did not report for duty or deserted immediately. The COMMITTEE ON PUBLIC INFORMATION directed propaganda efforts. War hysteria produced serious violations of FIRST AMENDMENT rights. Censorship or abridgments of free speech were enacted by the ESPIONAGE, SEDITION, SABOTAGE, and TRADING WITH THE ENEMY ACTS. Vigilantes also harassed socialists, pacifists, and others with unpopular views.

The first US troops landed in France on 26 June 1917. By the end of the war, 2,084,000 US troops had reached Europe. The Allied Expeditionary Force (AEF) under General John PERSHING trained and saw no significant combat until the third battle of the Aisne, when the First Army Division captured Cantigny on 28–31 May 1918, the Third Army Division repulsed enemy attacks at Château-Thierry on 1–4 June, and the Second Army Division (with the Fourth Marine Brigade) took Belleau Wood on 6 June. A total of 85,000 US troops took part in the second battle of the Marne (18 July–6 August), 54,000 took part in the Somme offensive (8 August–11 November), 85,000 took part in the Oisne-Aisne offensive (18 August–15 September), and 108,000 took part in the Ypres-Lys offensive (19 August–11 November). The AEF conducted only two major independent operations, the ST MIHIEL and MEUSE-ARGONNE campaigns. Outside of France, 1,200 US troops fought at the battle of Vittorio Veneto between 24 October and 4 November, and another 14,000 served in the SIBERIAN INTERVENTION.

The ARMISTICE ended fighting at 11 a.m., 11 November 1918. The treaty of VERSAILLES restored peace on 28 June 1919. World War I mobilized 4,057,101 Americans in the army, 599,051 in the navy, and 78,839 in the marines, of whom 1,390,000 went into battle. A total of 53,407 died in combat (50,510 soldiers, 436 sailors, 2,461 marines), 204,002 were wounded (193,663 soldiers, 819 sailors, and 9,520 marines), and 63,156 died of nonhostile causes (55,868 soldiers, 6,898 sailors, and 390 marines).

Direct military expenses were $26,000,000,000, and raised the NATIONAL DEBT from $2.975 billion to $25.5 billion. The war effort absorbed about half of US production. From April 1917 to January 1921, prices increased by 169 percent. In the war's last year, US agricultural exports supported 44 percent of Britain's population, 14 percent of all French, and 11 percent of all Italians. The last Americans returned from occupation duty in Germany on 24 January 1923.

World War II Congress declared war with Japan on 8 December 1941, the day after its attack on PEARL HARBOR. Germany and Italy declared war with the US on 11 December. Japan quickly overran GUAM and WAKE ISLAND, invaded the PHILIPPINES, established bases south to New Guinea, and occupied two of the ALEUTIAN ISLANDS. The US Navy checked the enemy in the CORAL SEA, and by June 1942 had blunted Japan's naval offensive at MIDWAY, which the Japanese attacked to forestall recurrences of the DOOLITTLE RAID. By April 1943, British, US, and Canadian naval forces had won the battle of the ATLANTIC.

General Douglas MACARTHUR planned the drive from the south Pacific to the Philippines, while Admiral Chester NIMITZ directed operations in the central Pacific aimed at bringing Japan within range of army air force bombers. Chief of Staff George

MARSHALL developed overall strategy and appointed General Dwight D. EISENHOWER as commander of the European-Mediterranean theater. Lieutenant General Albert Wedemeyer's US Fourteenth Air Force (including the FLYING TIGERS) transported over 70 percent of supplies used by British forces in Burma and nearly all arms sent to Chinese troops, but the only US ground unit in the China-Burma theater was MERRILL'S MARAUDERS.

The first major US offensive hit the Japanese on GUADALCANAL in August 1943. By February 1944, Allied ISLAND HOPPING campaigns in NEW GUINEA, the SOLOMON ISLANDS, and NEW BRITAIN had isolated Japan's primary logistical base at Rabaul, and left several large enemy armies trapped behind Allied lines. In October 1944, MacArthur began his second PHILIPPINE CAMPAIGN, during which the US Navy smashed enemy sea power at the battle of LEYTE GULF.

Nimitz meanwhile defeated the Japanese in the GILBERT ISLANDS, MARSHALL ISLANDS, MARIANA ISLANDS, and PELELIU. By June 1944, long-range bombers could hit Japan from SAIPAN. By March 1945, fighter-escorts could fly from IWO JIMA. By June 1945, medium-range bombers could reach Japan from OKINAWA. US submarines had sunk two-thirds of Japan's tankers and half of her merchant ships by January 1945.

Americans landed in November 1942 to assist Britain in clearing AXIS forces from North Africa, but saw little action except at KASSERINE PASS. By May 1943, Axis forces had retreated to Italy, but left behind 275,000 German and Italian prisoners. Allied leaders at the CASABLANCA CONFERENCE ordered an invasion of Italy, so the US Army landed at SICILY, SALERNO, and ANZIO in 1943. Rome fell on 4 June 1944. The last German army in Italy surrendered on 2 May 1945.

The Eighth US Army Air Force began operations against Germany from England in August 1942; from May 1944 to the end of the war, it deployed 1,000 heavy bombers in daytime raids (despite the loss of 2,400 bombers and 120,000 casualties), while Britain's 1,000 bombers flew night missions. By June 1944, the Allies had 3,000,000 men in Britain for the invasion of NORMANDY, in France. After breaking through Nazi lines at ST LÔ in July, allied forces drove toward Germany, which they entered near Trier on 12 September. After being set back in the HÜRTGEN FOREST and the battle of the BULGE, US forces breached the Rhine, Germany's last natural defense, on 7 March 1945 at Remagen by taking the last bridge still spanning the river.

Germany surrendered on 8 May 1945. The use of atomic bombs (not perfected in time for use on Germany) on HIROSHIMA and NAGASAKI led Japan to surrender on 14 August.

During the war, the army expanded from 1,643,000 to 8,293,766. Military mobilization enrolled 11,260,000 soldiers, 4,183,466 sailors, 669,100 marines, and 241,093 coast guardsmen. There were 41,322 combat deaths in the Pacific and 280,677 in Europe (264,742 army, 36,950 navy, 19,733 marines, 574 coast guard), 115,187 deaths from nonhostile causes (83,400 army, 25,664 navy, 4,778 marines, and 1,345 coast guard), and 671,801 nonfatal wounds (565,861 army, 37,778 navy, 67,207 marines, 955 coast guard). The Germans captured 95,000 US prisoners, of whom 1,140 died, and the Japanese took 25,600 US POWs, of whom 10,650 died. The MERCHANT MARINE lost another 5,662 men killed at sea. US industry built 296,000 planes, 102,000 tanks, and 88,000 ships or landing craft. Direct war expenses totaled $288 billion and the NATIONAL DEBT rose from $56.3 billion in December 1941 to $252.7 billion in December 1945

Wounded Knee, battle of (S.Dak.) On 29 December 1890, as 500 troops of the Seventh Cavalry and First Artillery were disarming 450 Teton-SIOUX INDIANS of the GHOST DANCE RELIGION (including 230 women and children), firing ensued after an Indian shot a soldier. US losses: 25 killed, 39 wounded. Teton losses: 150 killed, 50 wounded.

Wounded Knee reservation seizure (S.Dak.) On 7 Feb. 1973, 200 armed AMERICAN INDIAN MOVEMENT members took control of Wounded Knee, S.Dak, from its Oglala SIOUX tribal leaders, who were accused by a local faction of corruption. During a

70-day siege by federal marshalls sent to restore order, two Indians were killed and a US marshall was paralyzed. A negotiated settlement ended the siege peacefully. Criminal indictments were returned against Dennis Banks, Russell Means, and Clyde Bellecourt, but charges against them were dropped because of misconduct by prosecutors.

WPA *see* WORKS PROGRESS ADMINISTRATION

Wright, Frank Lloyd (b. Richland Center, Wis., 8 June 1869; d. Phoenix, Ariz., 10 April 1959) A civil engineer from the University of Wisconsin (1888), Wright became a draftsman for Louis H. SULLIVAN, and established his own architectural office in 1894. Wright became the 20th century's most original architect with a style that designed buildings so that their structure and materials blended naturally into the surrounding environment. Wright's architecture influenced builders and urban planners in much of the world, particularly western Europe, but ironically his ideas were largely ignored in the US.

Wright, James C., Jr (b. Fort Worth, Tex., 22 December 1922) In 1963 Wright (Democrat, Tex.) entered Congress and became House majority leader in 1976. On 17 April 1989, the House Ethics Committee reported 69 charges of unethical conduct, involving acceptance of improper gifts or evasion of House rules on outside income, that merited further investigation. To avoid further hearings, Wright resigned on 31 May. The House majority whip, Representative Anthony Coelho (Democrat, Calif.) also resigned from the House at this time to avoid investigation of similar charges.

Wright, Patience Lovell (b. Bordentown, N.J., 1725; d. London, England, 23 March 1786) She was the first major American sculptor. A widowed N.J. Quaker, she had exhibited waxworks in Philadelphia, New York, and Charles Town before relocating to London in 1772. She was immediately recognized as London's most accurate sculptor (working from wax impressions) and received numerous commissions from the British aristocracy and royal family.

Wright, Richard Nathaniel (b. near Natchez, Miss., 4 September 1908; d. Paris, France, 28 November 1960) He had lived in several Deep-South states before moving in 1932 to Chicago, where he worked as a writer, and then to New York in 1937. He became a Communist and wrote for that party's publications, but quit in 1944. In 1940 he published *Native Son*, a critically acclaimed novel about the racism, despair, and rage pervading black northern ghettoes. *Native Son*, a Book-of-the-Month Club selection, was the first major work of black fiction to reach a significant white audience, educate them on the pervasive racism in US society, and help sway public opinion toward greater progress on civil rights. His novel *Black Boy* (1945), which examined life in the segregated South, also attained widespread white readership as another Book Club offering. Wright entered a self-imposed exile in 1947 and moved to Paris, where he spent the rest of his life.

Wright brothers Orville (19 August 1871–30 January 1948) and Wilbur (16 April 1867–30 May 1912) Wright made the world's first successful airplane flight at Kitty Hawk, N.C., on 17 December 1903. In 1905 they made a record flight of 24.5 miles.

Wright* v. *Vinton Branch *see* FARM MORTGAGE MORATORIUM ACT

writs of assistance These writs were general search warrants allowing customs officers to enter homes, warehouses, or ships to hunt for smuggled goods. They came into large-scale use in Boston during 1760 and their legality was challenged in court by James OTIS. In 1761 Mass. Chief Justice Thomas HUTCHINSON ruled against Otis, in part because such warrants were legal in Britain.

Wyandot Indians These were HURON INDIAN refugees from the BEAVER WARS that wandered through the upper Great Lakes before settling in northern Ohio in the early 18th century. They raided Anglo-Americans during the SEVEN YEARS' WAR, PONTIAC'S WAR, the REVOLUTIONARY WAR, and the post-Revolutionary fighting in the Ohio valley, and WAR OF 1812. Having sold most of their land in Ohio and Mich., they moved to Kans. by 1842 and Okla. by 1867. They declined from about 1,000 in 1768 to 423 in 1959.

Wyandotte Constitution (Kans.) *see* LECOMPTON CONSTITUTION

Wygant* v. *Jackson Board of Education On 19 May 1985, the Supreme Court ruled (5–4) that it violated FOURTEENTH AMENDMENT guarantees of equal protection under the law for an employer to fire white workers protected by seniority in order to preserve the jobs of minority workers hired later as part of a plan for AFFIRMATIVE ACTION. It held that innocent workers could not be victimized by racially-based layoffs unless a "narrowly tailored" court settlement justified such an action to remedy the effects of past discrimination.

Wyoming The US acquired Wyo. by the LOUISIANA PURCHASE and treaty of GUADALUPE HIDALGO. In August 1832, Benjamin Bonneville built a fort by the Green River (abandoned 1835). In 1834, fur traders built Fort Laramie, which became an army post in 1849. Large-scale white settlement began when the TRANSCONTINENTAL RAILROAD entered Wyo. in 1867. It became a US territory on 25 July 1868 and had 9,118 settlers by 1870. Wyo. was the main locale of the second SIOUX WAR. A major part of the CATTLE KINGDOM, its herds increased from 300,000 head in 1880 to 1,500,000 during the great cattle freeze of 1886–7. Sheep grazing competed with ranching until sheep outnumbered cattle by 6,000,000 to 1,000,000 about 1905. Wyo. became the 44th state on 10 July 1890. In 1900 it had 92,531 residents (96 percent white, 2 percent Indian, 1 percent Chinese or Japanese, 1 percent black), of whom 71 percent were rural and 19 percent were foreign-born; it ranked 49th among states in population, 45th in the value of its agricultural goods, and 47th in manufactures. Economic development has been dominated by industries extracting coal, oil, aluminum, and iron. In 1990 Wyo. was the smallest state in population and had 453,588 inhabitants (91 percent white, 6 percent Hispanic, 2 percent Indian, 1 percent black), of which 30 percent were urban and 1.7 percent foreign-born. Mining employed 15 percent of workers and manufacturing 6 percent.

Wyoming Valley, raid on (Pa.) On 3 July 1778, having marched 200 miles from Fort Niagara, N.Y., Major John Butler's 400 TORIES and 500 of the IROQUOIS CONFEDERACY routed Colonel Zebulon Butler's 360 militia at Forty Fort; they then burned 1,000 buildings and drove off 1,000 cattle. US losses: 227 killed, 61 captured. British losses: 3 killed, 8 wounded. The enormous loss of life and ensuing panic, coupled with a Tory-Iroquois raid on CHERRY VALLEY, N.Y., led Washington to order SULLIVAN'S and BRODHEAD'S CAMPAIGNS against the Iroquois.

X

X, Malcolm (b. Omaha, Nebr., 19 May 1925; d. New York, N.Y., 21 February 1965) Born Malcolm Little, he experienced a religious conversion while in prison, joined the BLACK MUSLIMS, and changed his name to Malcolm X. Besides instilling pride in African heritage and setting high moral standards for blacks, he preached that all whites were irredeemably evil; he also taught that African-American society and culture could only be saved through black separatism. He was the first major black leader to reject integration after Marcus GARVEY. He became an orthodox Muslim, broke with the Black Muslims in March 1964, and revised his beliefs to accept cooperation with liberal whites who supported civil rights. He was assassinated for his apostasy by three Black Muslims, who were convicted for his murder on 10 March 1966.

X-1 aircraft *see* NATIONAL AERONAUTICS AND SPACE ADMINISTRATION

XYZ affair On 31 May 1797, John MARSHALL, Charles C. PINCKNEY, and Elbridge GERRY were named commissioners to negotiate a treaty to improve relations with France. They arrived at Paris on 4 October, but the Duc de Talleyrand, French foreign minister, delayed talks until 18 October, when three of his anonymous agents (known as messeigneurs X,Y, and Z) intimated that talks would not start until Talleyrand received a bribe of $250,000 and France obtained a loan of $12,000,000. The delegation refused, and John ADAMS sent Congress proof of Talleyrand's bribe effort on 3 April 1798. The XYY affair inflamed US public opinion against France and badly discredited Democratic party candidates in the election of 1798.

Y

Yakima Indians This group, speakers of one of the SAHAPTIN LANGUAGES, was closely related to the NEZ PERCE INDIANS and was the largest Indian nation in the upper Columbia River valley. They incorporated the horse into their culture after 1735, and experienced regular contact with Anglo-Americans after 1845. In 1855 leading Yakimas conceded possession of land outside certain bounds to the US and agreed to let whites cross their territory, but this agreement stirred great discontent among many villages and led to the YAKIMA WARS. They now have a reservation in Yakima and Klickitat counties, Wash., at Toppenish.

Yakima wars In September 1855, angry over recent treaty concessions to whites, YAKIMA INDIANS killed six miners, murdered their US agent, and forbade whites to enter their lands. On 6–9 October, 500 Yakimas defeated 100 soldiers from Fort Dalles, Wash., killed 5 and wounded 17, and captured their howitzer. Indians on Puget Sound then began hostilities; they attacked Seattle on 26 January 1856 with Yakima help. By 11 July, fighting had ended east of the Cascades. On 17 July, Oreg. volunteers defeated 300 Indians in the Grand Ronde Valley. The presence of 500 US regulars in Yakima territory caused fighting to peter out by autumn 1856, but without a formal Yakima capitulation. Fighting resumed on 17 May 1858, when 1,000 Yakimas and other Indians defeated 164 US soldiers. Colonel William Wright's 600 US troops defeated Kamiakin's 4,000 warriors on 1 September at the battle of Four Lakes (killing 60 Indians without a single loss) and ended the war on 5 September by defeating 700 warriors at the battle of Spokane Plain. By hanging 16 hostiles as examples and forcing all Indians on to reservations, Wright ended large-scale resistance to white settlement in the Columbia basin.

Yalta conference (Ukraine) Between 4 and 11 February 1945, Winston Churchill, Joseph Stalin, and Franklin D. ROOSEVELT discussed the war against Japan and the political status of eastern Europe after WORLD WAR II. In return for a Russian promise to declare war on Japan, it was agreed that Russia would gain control of the Kurile Islands, the lower half of Sakhalin Island, the right to occupy northern Korea, a military lease for the harbor at Port Arthur in Manchuria, and recognition of Outer Mongolia as a Soviet satellite. The Allies also agreed that Ukraine and Byelorussia would be seated as independent nations in the future UNITED NATIONS. The Allies declared that postwar governments in eastern Europe would be organized by free and secret elections that excluded only non-democratic (i.e. Fascist) elements. By not establishing exact guidelines for restoring elective democracy in liberated areas, the conference enabled Russia to interpret the Yalta agreements on its own terms and establish totalitarian regimes in eastern Europe.

Yamasee Indians This nation, speakers of one of the MUSKOGEAN LANGUAGES, occupied southeastern Ga. and northern Fla. in the 1590s, when Spanish missions were founded among them. In 1684–5 – when they numbered about 1,200 – the Yamasee destroyed the missions, resettled along the Savannah River, began trading deerskins with S.C. merchants, and later were English allies in the TUSCARORA WAR. By 1715, having been alienated from the English by degrading mistreatment from fur traders, they orchestrated a general assault on S.C. in the YAMASEE WAR, but were badly defeated the next year. They fled to Fla., where the

Spanish welcomed them and let them launch attacks on the English. S.C. militia suppressed the Yamasee raids in the ANGLO-SPANISH WAR of 1727–8. Within a century, the survivors had lost their cultural identity by merging with CREEK or SEMINOLE INDIANS.

Yamasee War On 15 April 1715, YAMASEE INDIANS, CREEK INDIANS, and nearby tribes killed and plundered 160 fur traders and then attacked S.C. settlements within 12 miles of Charles Town. The English managed to harvest winter food supplies while a counteroffensive by 600 S.C. whites, 100 Va. volunteers, and 500 slaves drove back the enemy. In 1716 the Yamasees were deserted by their Indian allies and attacked by CHEROKEE INDIANS. Having lost many enslaved and killed, the tribe resettled in Fla. Serious fighting ended in mid-1716. Minor raiding continued, but subsided after the Creeks made peace on 15 November 1717. The Yamasee War established white dominance on the S.C. frontier, which stayed at peace until the CHEROKEE WAR.

Yankee This term was Dutch slang for an Englishman, and may have derived from *Jan Kees* (John Cheese). From 1700 to 1860, it was used exclusively when speaking of New Englanders. Only in the CIVIL WAR did it come to refer to all northerners. During WORLD WAR I, it entered common European usage as a synonym for all Anglo-Americans – to the mortification of southerners.

Yates* v. *United States On 17 June 1957, the Supreme Court restricted the scope of the SMITH ACT by modifying *DENNIS ET AL* v. *UNITED STATES*. The Court held that in order to convict a person of advocating violent overthrow of the government, the government must prove that the defendant committed overt subversive acts, and neither acted as a passive follower nor espoused abstract principles. The ruling's strict standards for convicting Communists and others with seditious ideologies discouraged the US from actively using the Smith Act to prosecute sedition.

Yazoo land claims On 7 January 1795, the Ga. legislature sold four land companies 35,000,000 acres of the Yazoo River watershed (in Ga. and Ala.) for $400,000. In 1796 a newly elected legislature repudiated the sale, which had been influenced by bribery and corruption, but not before the land companies had sold shares to innocent parties. When Ga. ceded its western lands to the US in 1802, the land companies and third-party purchasers demanded compensation for their losses and their claims blocked settlement of the Yazoo region. Thomas JEFFERSON and James MADISON wanted the federal government to honor the various parties' claims, but their efforts were denounced by John RANDOLPH as a scheme to enrich corrupt speculators sitting in Congress. The Supreme Court ruled on the case in *FLETCHER* v. *PECK*. In 1814, with Randolph temporarily in private life, the US resolved the controversy by awarding $4,200,000 to the speculators and other claimants.

Yeager, Charles *see* NATIONAL AERONAUTICS AND SPACE ADMINISTRATION

yellow-dog contract This was a labor contract that enabled employers to fire a worker who joined a labor union. The ERDMAN ACT, NATIONAL INDUSTRIAL RECOVERY ACT and NATIONAL LABOR RELATIONS ACT either banned them or provided other guarantees for union organization.

yellow journalism This was a style of reporting events that pandered to a vulgar taste for lurid, sensational news as a means of outselling a competitor's newspapers. It emphasized emotional, simplistic arguments over reasoned, objective analysis. Its pioneers were Joseph PULITZER's New York *World* and William Randolph HEARST's New York *Journal*. (Its name derived from a *Journal* cartoon figure called the "Yellow Kid.") Its most notorious abuse was the deliberate inflaming of war fever after the USS *MAINE*'s sinking, which helped spark the SPANISH-AMERICAN WAR.

Yellow Peril From 1880 to 1910, hysteria developed in the western US over unrestricted CHINESE and JAPANESE IMMIGRATION. Newspapers warned of a "yellow peril" that would lower living standards, spawn crime, and leave Anglo-Americans a minority on the Pacific coast. This anxiety coincided with apprehension over Japan's victory in the Russo-Japanese War (1905). These concerns resulted in riots against Asian laborers, the CHINESE EXCLUSION ACT, the Gentlemen's Agreements (*see* JAPANESE IMMIGRATION) and the GREAT WHITE FLEET's voyage.

Yellow Tavern, battle of (Va.) On 11 May 1864, Major General Philip SHERIDAN's 10,000 USA cavalry defeated Major General J. E. B. STUART's 4,500 CSA cavalry and killed Stuart, whose death cost the Confederacy its best cavalry leader.

Yick Wo* v. *Hopkins In 1886 the Supreme Court unanimously extended the FOURTEENTH AMENDMENT's protections to all persons in the country, including noncitizens. The ruling followed logically from *SANTA CLARA COUNTY* v. *SOUTHERN PACIFIC RAILROAD COMPANY*, given on the same day, which declared corporations to be legal persons.

Yippies An acronym for Youth International Party (YIP), this group was founded in February 1968 by Jerry Rubin, Abbie Hoffman, Paul Krassner, and Ed Sanders. Its members followed the HIPPIE lifestyle and staged public protests, demonstrations, and other media events as part of the VIETNAM ANTIWAR MOVEMENT. Yippies were prominent at the CHICAGO DEMOCRATIC CONVENTION RIOT of 1968, when they nominated a hog named "Pigasus" for president. Abbie Hoffman summarized their ideology in *Steal This Book* (1971), which held up the pay toilet as the ultimate symbol of how miserably Americans were exploited by their capitalist ruling class; he advocated radical action to transform the US into a utopia where everything would be free, including his own book. (Hoffman and Rubin were later expelled as leaders for failing to share speakers' fees they earned with the YIP.)

York, battle of (Canada) *see* FORT TORONTO, BATTLE OF

Yorktown, battle of (Va.) On 6 October 1781, George WASHINGTON commenced besieging Lieutenant General Charles CORNWALLIS's army at Yorktown with 7,980 Continentals, 3,150 militia, 7,800 French soldiers, and a French naval force with 1,000 sailors offshore. Trapped without hope of naval evacuation since the battle of CHESAPEAKE CAPES, Cornwallis surrendered at 2:00 p.m. on 17 October. US losses: 24 killed, 65 wounded. French losses: 60 killed, 192 wounded. British losses: 156 killed, 8,081 captured (including 326 wounded), 214 artillery pieces, and 24 naval transports. Yorktown was the war's last major battle; it led Lord NORTH's government to resign and forced Britain to concede US independence.

Young, Brigham (b. Whitingham, Vt., 1 June 1801; d. Salt Lake City, Utah, 29 August 1877) Young matured in N.Y., lived near Joseph SMITH, and became a MORMON convert in 1832. He quickly rose to a position of influence in the church and became its chief leader upon Smith's murder in 1844. He led the first wagon train to reach the Salt Lake valley in July 1847. In December 1847, he was named president and prophet of the church. His skills were crucial in organizing and financing the migration of 20,000 Mormons to Utah in the next five years. He served as governor and Indian superintendent of Utah Territory from 1851 to the UTAH WAR. Young was acquitted of bigamy in 1871, despite having married over 20 wives and fathered 57 children. He started four temples during his stewardship, helped found three colleges, and directed the founding of 360 Mormon settlements in the west.

Young, Whitney M., Jr *see* URBAN LEAGUE, NATIONAL

Young America movement This was an intellectualized celebration of US patriotism, enlisting journalists and politicians in extravagant praise of the country's institutions in the 1840s. Its spokesmen embraced MANIFEST DESTINY as a positive force in the west's civilization and economic development. The movement's proponents viewed the CONSTITUTION as inspiring revolts against despotism (such as the revolutions of 1848 in Europe) and becoming the model for an enlightened democratization of the world.

Youngstown Sheet and Tube Company* v. *Sawyer On 2 June 1952, the Supreme Court ruled (6–3) that President Harry S. TRUMAN had exceeded his authority in seizing the country's steel mills to preclude a strike during the KOREAN WAR. The justices held that the president's power as commander in chief did not justify the action, which required legislative approval from Congress.

Youth International Party *see* YIPPIES

Yuchi Indians This SIOUAN LANGUAGE group lived in east Tenn. when first contacted by Hernán de SOTO in 1540. Yuchi bands later dispersed; some integrated with the SHAWNEE and CHEROKEE, but most relocated to Ga. and Ala., where they allied with the CREEK. Some joined the SEMINOLE in Fla. by 1810. They never received recognition as an independent nation by the United States, and after 1830 they were removed with their affiliated tribes to Okla. where their descendants live on the reservations of other tribes. The Yuchi declined from about 2,500 in 1650, to 1,100 in 1830, and 216 in 1930.

Z

Zenger trial In 1732 N.Y. Governor William Cosby claimed that part of his own salary was wrongly appropriated by his predecessor, Acting Governor Rip Van Dam. Cosby appointed a special chancery court, which rendered verdicts without a jury, in which he sued Van Dam; he also dismissed Van Dam's supporters from political office and threatened their land titles. Cosby's enemies hired John Peter Zenger to edit the New York *Weekly Journal*, which began publication on 5 November 1733 and denounced Cosby as a danger to civil liberties and property rights. Cosby prosecuted Zenger for seditious libel, but Zenger was acquitted on 4 August 1735. The case blocked further abuse of seditious libel prosecutions in N.Y., but was not interpreted as a major precedent for freedom of the press until after 1820.

Zimmermann note On 19 January 1917, Alfred Zimmermann, German foreign secretary, sent his ambassador in Mexico a coded message promising an alliance between the two nations if the US declared war on Germany. In that event, Germany would help finance a Mexican effort to reconquer territories lost by the treaty of GUADALUPE HIDALGO. British intelligence decoded the telegram and gave the US a copy on 24 February. When revealed to the press on 1 March, it inflamed US public opinion against Germany in WORLD WAR I.

Zuni Indians This group of PUEBLO INDIANS occupied the Zuni River valley in western N.Mex. and first met Spaniards in 1540. They did not take part in POPÉ'S REVOLT and avoided war with both Spaniards and Anglo-Americans, although they suffered from raids by APACHE INDIANS. They probably numbered 2,500 in 1680. The US recognized their homeland in McKinley and Valencia counties, N.Mex., as a reservation, which contained 8,135 Zunis in 1984.